What people are saying about the *Key Word Study*:

Inductive Bible Study students know that understanding the author's intended meaning is vital to proper interpretation of the Word of God. *The Bible Knowledge Key Word Study* is a welcome addition to the library of those who seek to understand the use and meanings of words as the biblical authors used them, in context, book by book. We look forward to using this valuable new tool in the years ahead.

—Kay Arthur
Co-founder/CEO,
Precept Ministries International

The Bible Knowledge Key Word Study has the potential of becoming one of the most useful quick reference tools for students and teachers of the Bible in the church. The principles of sound word study are explained and followed, including close attention to the fact that meaning is found not in the isolated words but in the way they are used with other words in clauses, sentences, and paragraphs. Moreover, the authors clarify the connections between passages and the testaments that are so important to theological understanding, reflection, and application of the Bible in the lives of people today.

—Richard E. Averbeck
Professor of Old Testament and Semitic Languages,
Trinity Evangelical Divinity School

I wish this tool had been available for my ministry over the last 25 years. This *Bible Knowledge Key Word Study* series will save the serious student or communicator of God's Word much time and protect from many errors of interpretation. The introductory prefaces alone are worth special attention, as they teach the method of term analysis practiced throughout the volumes. I highly commend this new tool for the accurate interpretation and proclamation of the Scriptures.

—Dr. Mark L. Bailey
President,
Dallas Theological Seminary

The Bible Knowledge Key Word Study belongs on one's desktop—open, next to an open Bible and an open volume of *The Bible Knowledge Commentary*. Arranged by book, chapter, and verse, it is convenient and practical. Its selective analysis of key words within their contexts keeps the focus where it belongs: on the biblical propositions themselves. For the serious student and expositor, this resource series bridges the gap between linguistic/exegetical keys and theological dictionaries.

—Dr. William D. Barrick
Professor of Old Testament,
Director of Doctoral Studies,
The Master's Seminary

The study of biblical words is both a science and an art. The editors are masters of both. For ministers and Bible teachers who want quick access to responsible but concise word studies, this volume fits the bill.

——Dr. Daniel I. Block
Associate Dean
John R. Sampey Professor of Old Testament Interpretation
The Southern Baptist Theological Seminary

While comments tied merely to individual words do not replace a full-fledged commentary on a biblical book, if one is looking for concise, accurate insights on biblical words in the specific contexts in which they appear, the method and contents of this work can hardly be bettered.

—Dr. Craig Blomberg
Professor of New Testament Studies,
Denver Seminary

Drs. Eugene Merrill and Darrell Bock (KWS NT editor) have opened the windows, and a fresh breeze has blown across my Bible study. This morning I learned the fascinating history behind the word translated "idle tales," which were attributed to the women running from the empty tomb. I'm reading through my Bible with this easy-to-use tool.

—Dee Brestin,
Author, *A Woman's Journey* series, and
The Friendships of Women

Effective communication requires careful definition, clear illustration, and convincing application. The communication of the ancient Scriptures to modern audiences necessitates great skill in all these areas. The *Key Word Study* will help immeasurably.

—Stuart and Jill Briscoe
Authors and ministers at large,
Elmbrook Church (Brookfield, WI)

This volume is a gold mine of valuable information that will wonderfully illuminate the biblical text. It is written in a clear style, which makes the lexical and background material easily accessible and useful for a wide audience. What is more, the editor prefaces this book with a concise introduction on how to do word studies. Take out your Bible, open *The Bible Knowledge Key Word Study*, and let the journey into a deeper knowledge of God's truth begin!

—Dr. M. Daniel Carroll R.
Professor of Old Testament,
Denver Seminary

I predict that *The Bible Knowledge Key Word Study*, aside from the Bible itself, will become the single most helpful tool for anyone whose serious desire is to be "rightly dividing the word of truth." It holds a prominent place on my study desk. Read it and reap.

—Dr. O. S. Hawkins
President,
Southern Baptist Convention Annuity Board

If a student of the Scriptures wants the most accurate and scholarly word study available, here it is. My colleagues, Drs. Merrill and Bock, have teamed up to produce a truly reliable reference that is a treasure chest full of usable insights from the living Word, ready for searching minds. I recommend it without reservation.

—Howard G. Hendricks
Distinguished Professor and Chairman,
Center for Christian Leadership,
Dallas Theological Seminary

For busy people, discovering *The Bible Knowledge Key Word Studies* is like a carpenter discovering the complete tool kit. It's all there—lexical analysis, original language transliterations, translation comparisons, pointed commentary, biblical references, and best of all, each entry explains the best contextual meaning of the word. With the Key Word Studies, teaching God's Word with accuracy and authority just got a lot easier.

—Woodrow Kroll
President,
Back to the Bible

What Drs. Merrill and Bock have given us wonderfully captures the sense and meaning verse by verse in an elegantly simple fashion. What a useful tool to help gain a greater relationship with the Word, whether from the pulpit or the pew!

—J. Otis Ledbetter
Pastor, Author, and
Co-founder of the Heritage Builders Association

What a great tool for the Christian worker on the fast track! Because it addresses the vocabulary of the text, the *Key Word Study* will go a long way towards getting at the text's meaning. It's like hearing a good teacher in staccato fashion bringing insight upon insight. The cross-referencing is especially valuable, as is the statistical information. A very handy tool for teachers and pastors, and a decidedly helpful resource to nourish any Bible reader's curiosity.

—Elmer A. Martens
Professor Emeritus of Old Testament,
Mennonite Brethren Biblical Seminary

The Bible Knowledge Key Word Study volumes will seriously enhance the ministry of the layperson and pastor in personal Bible study, and in teaching and preaching. Its accurate and clear presentations of meaning, based on sound and learned judgment by esteemed scholars, assures that the series will take a prized place among Bible study resources. At last top-rate scholarship has provided the Church a clear and certain path through the maze of Hebrew and Greek words that have been an obstacle to a richer understanding of God's Word.

—Kenneth Mathews
Professor of Divinity,
Beeson Divinity School,
Samford University

Serious students of the New Testament have found everything Merrill and Bock write to be worth reading. This reference work is no exception. It is a full and empty book: amazingly full of helpful data and insight and surprisingly free of the tangential, idiosyncratic and insignificant material that fills too many commentaries.

—Dr. Al Mawhinney
Professor of NT/Academic Dean,
Reformed Theological Seminary–Orlando

What a wealth of knowledge at one's fingertips! The *Key Word Study* is a powerful resource that I not only intend to use, but I'll recommend that any serious Bible students use it.

—Josh McDowell
Author and Speaker

I'm very excited and grateful to have this tremendous resource available to augment the use of my favorite commentary, *The Bible Knowledge Commentary*. I love to learn the meaning behind words, and these volumes will give me greater understanding for my speaking, teaching, and writing. I appreciate the way the words are explained with simple yet powerful ideas that make the biblical text come alive.

—Kathy Collard Miller
Author of the *Daughters of the King* Bible study series,
Princess to Princess, and a popular women's conference speaker

These *Key Word Study* volumes will be in my library! What a great tool!

—Beth Moore
Author and popular speaker,
Living Proof Ministries

The Bible Knowledge Key Word Study is a tool useful to any who read, study, or reflect on God's Word. Hats off to editors Eugene Merrill and Darrell Bock (KWS, NT) for these companion volumes, which will add to the excitement that always accompanies Scripture intake. Knowing the significant meanings of key words in each passage will add real biblical meat to one's daily or weekly diet of the Word, all to the ultimate improvement and strengthening of faith and practice.

—Tom Phillips
Vice President,
Billy Graham Evangelistic Association

The Bible Knowledge Key Word Study is another fine resource from Victor Books, known for its commitment to providing books that bring insight and depth to Bible study for young and mature Christians alike.

—Dr. Larry Richards,
Author of the *Home Bible Study Library* series

Preachers need all the help they can muster to understand the Bible themselves and then communicate its message to others. *The Bible Knowledge Key Word Study* is a good investment in your budget for books.

—Dr. Haddon W. Robinson
Harold John Ockenga Professor of Preaching,
Gordon-Conwell Theological Seminary

This is a well-conceived work occupying a special place between a full commentary and a traditional Bible word study. By providing the meaning of key words in their contextual setting, often with helpful background, this unusual work provides a ready tool for the understanding of Scripture. Written for the lay person as well as the pastor, the reading of Scripture will be greatly enriched with this work open alongside.

—Robert L. Saucy
Distinguished Professor of Systematic Theology,
Talbot School of Theology

Some of my best friends are books, especially when they take me to deeper levels of understanding God's Word. I'm adding the *Key Word Study* to my 'best friends' list.

—Dr. Joseph M. Stowell
President,
Moody Bible Institute

Any tool that helps us dig more effectively into God's infallible Truth is worth owning. This series—*The Bible Knowledge Key Word Study*—is just such a tool. It helps people like you and me find hidden treasures in God's Word.

—Luci Swindoll
Author and Speaker,
Women of Faith

A great tool to open the student of Scripture to its vocabulary, through mentors who are steeped in the language of Scripture. The contributions of these editors are good examples of outstanding commentators who guide the serious student through the biblical texts.

—Dr. Willem A. VanGemeren
Professor of Old Testament,
Director of the Ph.D. in Theological Studies,
Trinity Evangelical Divinity School

A valuable tool for all serious students of the Bible. The newest believer and most seasoned veteran teacher will be helped by using these volumes. The studies are marked by clarity, brevity, orthodoxy, and practicality. How fortunate we are to have this new tool available to us!

—Dr. Warren W. Wiersbe,
Author and conference speaker

The verbal inspiration of the Bible means that God the Holy Spirit inspired not just the concepts of Scripture but their very words. Thus to understand what God has communicated to us in the Bible, we need to comprehend its very words—their origins, uses, and meanings. *The Bible Knowledge Key Word Study* is an excellent resource for Bible students who want to know the backgrounds of important Bible words and the meanings of those words in their contexts. Here is a helpful tool for all who seek to understand and communicate the Bible accurately.

—Dr. Roy B. Zuck
Senior Professor Emeritus of Bible Exposition,
Dallas Theological Seminary
Author, and Editor, *Bibliotheca Sacra*

THE
BIBLE
KNOWLEDGE
KEY WORD
STUDY

GENESIS—DEUTERONOMY

THE
BIBLE
KNOWLEDGE
KEY WORD
STUDY

GENESIS—DEUTERONOMY

EDITOR

Eugene H. Merrill

Run So That You May Win
ivictor.com

Victor is an imprint of
Cook Communications Ministries, Colorado Springs, Colorado 80918
Cook Communications, Paris, Ontario
Kingsway Communications, Eastbourne, England

THE BIBLE KNOWLEDGE KEY WORD STUDY: GENESIS–DEUTERONOMY
© 2003 by Cook Communications Ministries

First Printing, 2003
Printed in the United States of America

1 2 3 4 5 6 7 8 9 10 11 12 Printing/Year 13 12 11 10 09 08 07 06 05 04 03

Editor: Eugene H. Merrill, General Editor; Craig A. Bubeck, Sr. Editor
Interior Design: Pat Miller

Library of Congress Cataloging-in-Publication Data

The Bible knowledge key word study : Genesis-Deuteronomy / editor,
Eugene H. Merrill.
    p. cm.
Includes indexes.
  ISBN 0-7814-3446-7 (hardcover)
  1. Bible. O.T. Pentateuch--Language, style. 2. Bible. O.T.
Pentateuch--Commentaries. I. Merrill, Eugene H.
  BS1225.53 .B53 2003
  222'.10447--dc21
                                        2002151903

CONTENTS

PREFACE

Darrell L. Bock and Eugene H. Merrill

I. INTRODUCTION TO THE *BIBLE KNOWLEDGE KEY WORD STUDY*

Watching a building under construction fascinates people. After the edifice has been constructed piece by piece, it eventually reveals a master plan. Similarly, words—the building blocks of Scripture—reveal mind-changing concepts about God and his world. The construction of words determines not only the meaning of the parts but also shapes the concepts of the whole. Studying the words of the Bible involves investigating the most basic components that lead to exegetical and theological discovery. When one examines these words, one is looking at the units that form the starting point for exegetical and theological meaning. There is something exciting about understanding not only what is before the student of Scripture but in determining how that understanding is present.

The *Bible Knowledge Key Word Study (KWS)* volumes are designed for lay people and pastors who want a ready reference to the basic meaning of certain key words in their individual context. They also seek in spots to give some relevant information on the background to the word's use that may inform its particular use in a specific context. As such this tool is not a "word study book" or lexicon because a given entry is not intended to give an exhaustive look at a given term. Other tools, such as lexicons or word dictionaries, give a comprehensive look at a term. Rather, the individual entries in KWS highlight the use of the word in a specific passage and help to explain why it has that meaning in that given locale. Thus, the KWS is designed as a tool that can be kept to one side and used for reference as one reads through Scripture. This is also why the work proceeds in the order of Scripture itself. This essay serves also to introduce the reader to the common abbreviations found in the series.

The relationship of these volumes to *The Bible Knowledge Commentary (BKC)* is also important for the reader to appreciate. The contributors were selected because they have taught the books and written about them with expertise in the original languages. Each contributor to the *Key Word Study* volumes was allowed to treat the book and its terms as he saw fit. This means that in some locations there will be differences in how the text is read between these volumes and the BKC. These differences reflect the range of possibilities that often are a part of interpretation. Thus there has been no effort to "match" interpretations between the volumes. In the case of a few individual biblical books, this difference would influence how the book as a whole is being read. In some cases these differences, as they touch on lexical questions specifically, are noted in terms of a discussion of interpretive options.

Each contributor to the series was asked to focus on a few key concerns, establishing why a given term was discussed:

1. Contributors might discuss those words where debate exists about how the term should be translated in a given context. In such cases the possibilities for meaning are noted in the entry by the notation of how various English translations have handled the term in question in that passage. Among the translations consulted are the *King James Version (KJV)*, the *New King James Version (NKJV)*, the *Revised Standard Version (RSV)*, the *New Revised Standard Version (NRSV)*, the *NET Bible* (NET), the *New American Standard Bible (NASB)*, the *New International Version (NIV)*, and the *New Living Translation (NLT)*, the *New English Bible (NEB)*, the *Revised English Bible (REB)*, and the *Contemporary English Version (CEV)*. Then there is an attempt to explain why a particular rendering is a better one or where the decision is uncertain.

2. Certain words possess a significance specific to the meaning of a passage, making discussion of their meaning important for an understanding of the larger passage. This is precisely what makes that particular term a "key" one to discuss.

3. Other texts have a particularly significant background to their meaning in Hebrew and Greek and so the entry makes explicit what that background is for those who do not know or work with the languages or for those whose language skills are not polished.

4. Some entries possess all of these qualities. All discussions of foreign language are transliterated, so the student not knowing the biblical languages can recognize how the form of the term is pronounced. At the end of each discussion entry, the basic lexical form of the term appears so it can be easily looked up in a more detailed lexical source. Those who know the languages will have to convert the transliterated form into the proper script.

The contributors were asked to discuss the key information about a term concisely, noting key supportive resources (like lexical tools) briefly so that if readers wished to look up more information about a term they would be directed to additional discussion. The significance of the choice is also often developed in a sentence or two. The goal was to be explanatory and concise with a view to showing how a given term contributes to the larger passage.

Each entry was to be concise and describe the term using everyday language. The goal of this tool is to make the linguistic background and the theological-interpretive point of the term clear in its context. Additional descriptions of the term's use in the Bible might be supplied but was not a requirement for a given discussion of a term. Since the work is not a commentary, not every term possible was discussed. Choices were made either because the term has a key role in the verse or the background enhances understanding. In general, only one or two words in a verse receive treatment. A few verses are not discussed and a few verses treat more than one word. If the same word is used several times significantly in one book with the same basic force, the contributor has selected where to discuss that word in detail and then referred back or forward to that full discussion. This helped us to avoid needless repetition.

The entries possess the following form:

1:33 The one who <u>baptizes</u> (*baptizōn*)—Like the Synoptic Gospels, John presents Jesus as the one who would "baptize" people with the Holy Spirit (Matt. 3:11; Mark 1:8; Luke 3:16). See also 1:25. [*baptizō*].

The verse is indicated first, unless the entry is a second or subsequent entry in that verse, then it begins with the phrase in bold. The bold is the contributor's translation of the word or phrase under discussion. If a word in a phrase is the point of the discussion, then the English term focused on is underlined. Then the term is transliterated in the form it has in the verse. This allows the English-only student to know the pronunciation of the word in context. Sometimes a slight difference between the student's English translation and that of the entry may mean the student will need to figure out which term in his translation is referred to in the bold. Since people use a wide variety of translations, it was thought best to let the contributor select his translation and explain it. For several entries, translation alternatives have been noted for the student. The discussion of the term follows. At the end of the entry the term in brackets is the transliterated lexical form of the term, in case the student with some knowledge of the language wishes to find out more information on the word in a lexicon. This form will allow the student to know the base form listed in a lexicon and how the base term is pronounced. In some cases more than one word is listed in these brackets. This indicates that the discussion covers more than one lexical term.

Our prayer is that this tool proves useful to many as they engage in quiet times, Bible study, or preparation for teaching.

II. ABOUT METHOD IN WORD STUDIES

Anyone who studies the Bible for very long knows that interpretation is often not a straightforward matter of immediate agreement about what the Bible teaches. Like any other deep and complex work, disagreement can emerge about what a text exactly teaches. Obviously, the terms of Scripture are an important part of such discussions. What can get in the way of agreement? How is the interpreter to hurdle the obstacles that lead to such disagreement? How do we proceed with the possibilities of what the biblical text might and does mean? How sensitive should we be to the types of disagreements that arise? Are some differences more important than others? The rest of this introductory essay will attempt to explain what hinders our understanding of the meaning of words and how words should be handled interpretively. In thinking through word analysis, one should first consider several fundamental questions: What are the basic rules of word study? What obstacles impede an understanding of the meaning of words? These two questions form the next two sub-sections of this essay.

In a third sub-section we will overview the two important approaches to word study, the diachronic approach (or "through time," comprehensive word study) and the synchronic (or "at a given time," more focused word study) approach. The fourth and final sub-section will detail the stages of word analysis, including a list of common errors that often accompany the study of words. A proper method may not remove all the ambiguity and debate—after all, humans are finite creatures—but it should allow exegetes to understand why a passage speaks as it does and to articulate clearly one's own understanding to others so that together they can discuss and benefit from each other's insights and observations on the Scriptures.

A. Fundamental Rules of Word Study

In thinking about words and interpretation, there are three fundamental rules that should have general assent:

1. *The exegete must initially pursue the meaning intended by the author for his original audience.*[1] Communication fundamentally involves the transfer of an idea from one mind to another. In biblical study the interpreter's goal is to understand what the original author said through the terms he used. One needs to recognize that words do not automatically have meaning. They receive their meaning from the author who produced the words. Most of the entries in the KWS deal with meaning at this level, because it is the starting point for all reflection about what a passage teaches.

   Another point emerges from this consideration. To communicate, the message must be potentially sharable with the audience. It must relate to a category of meaning that the writer's audience can perceive—or else the message is incomprehensible. This observation does not deny that an author can communicate new sense in the words that he uses. It does suggest, however, that when the author intends new meaning, he will signal it so that the audience can grasp the new force of the term.[2]

2. *To establish the precise meaning of a word, one must recognize its possible range of meanings.* Often an interpreter simply assumes that a word has a certain meaning. However, the meaning of terms can change—from situation to situation, from person to person, most importantly, from context to context. Therefore, the exegete must exercise care in studying the words that compose the message of Scripture to be most sensitive to the context of a given usage. This is why the KWS works with words in a given context as it discusses their meaning. Words do not have an "automatic" general meaning. They have a range of meanings, which yields a specific sense in a specific context.

3. *Words operate in a context and receive meaning from that context.* This point is crucial. Words as separate, isolated entities do not provide the key to the meaning of Scripture. Instead, words *in relationship* to other words form the basis of the concepts that represent the message of a text. Thus the major concern of the interpreter in determining the meaning of a word is the setting of the word in its verse, paragraph, and book. In other words, words are like chess pieces on a chess board. Their importance and force is determined by their relationship to other pieces in the sentence and paragraph.

These three fundamentals provide a solid foundation for lexical analysis—a crucial discipline that the interpreter must appreciate in order to interpret the Word of God correctly.

B. The Complexities of Meaning
i. The Meanings of Meaning

Part of what makes meaning so difficult to ascertain is its very complexity. Most of us do not think about how many levels of meaning we interact with in dealing with words and trying to interpret them. Formally speaking, meaning and the study of words are bound together with the formal and broader academic discipline called semantics.[3]

Semantics is the study of "signification" or "meaning." It can offer to the interpreter many insights regarding the issue of method in studying words. The goal of this discipline at the lexical level is to examine how meaning is communicated through words.

In semantics one of the problems of lexical meaning is, in fact, determining what one means by speaking about a word's meaning![4] Semanticists have produced as many as 25 possible senses for meaning, but a few distinctions are extremely significant for exegesis and indicate the need for careful analysis. A list of these distinctions follows.

1. *Entailment meaning* pertains to a word or idea that implies some type of conclusion or implication not explicit in the term or context. For example, a passage that shows Jesus engaged in an activity that only God can perform entails the idea that Jesus is divine, even though the specific theological assertion that Jesus is God is not explicitly made in the text (e.g., Mark 2:1-12).

2. *Emotive meaning* applies to the use of a term that carries emotional force. So when James calls his readers adulterous people for their poor behavior (4:4), he is picking a term with emotive meaning to purposely shame them. A sensitive interpreter will note this emotive force to the term.

3. *Significance meaning* refers to a term or concept that takes on new meaning when brought into a context different from the original one (e.g., the NT use of the OT may bring additional force to an earlier text). So when Jews are seen as enemies of Messiah in Acts 4:25-27, using an appeal to Psalm 2, the category of enemy has expanded from the general expectation of a Psalm that used to be read by the nation of Israel about those who opposed God's chosen ruler. The switch in who is referred to shows how much things have changed with Jesus' coming and the rejection of him by many Jews. A text that used to express Jewish hope now surfaces their position as currently opposed to the Gospel.

4. *Encyclopedic meaning* denotes all the possible meaning that a term may have. One generates such a full list from a dictionary, lexicon, or exhaustive word study tool.[5] This range of possible meanings allows for a variety of possible interpretations, as well as misinterpretation. The goal of an interpreter is to take these possibilities for meaning and determine which particular meaning fits in a given context.

5. *Grammatical meaning* refers to the grammatical role of a term, such as the categories that one learns in an intermediate grammar course. Some interpreters use this limited area of meaning to secure meaning, when in fact often all it does is limit the possible meaning. Just as words have possible meanings, so grammatical categories often have a variety of possible forces or uses, with the exact force being determined by contextual factors.

6. *Figurative meaning* indicates the use of a term because of the association it makes, not because the term's sense and referent are directly applied to what the term describes. For example, when Jesus speaks of faith that can "move mountains," he is not referring to the use of earth-moving equipment but to faith that can do marvelous things. Many exegetical debates turn on whether a term is literal or figurative, which is always an appropriate question to consider. Usually an understanding of genre, idiom, and authorial style can help in interpreting figures.

These senses of meaning can be significant in assessing the force of a given term, and must receive attention in thinking through the study of a term. However, they are not as central to the study of a term as the three basic elements of a word.

ii. The Three Elements of a Word

Considered most abstractly, words are made up of three basic elements that contribute most directly to their intended meaning: sign, sense, and referent. In reality a word is a symbol that communicates meaning within a given culture or subculture.[6] A word does not have meaning; it is assigned meaning through cultural convention and usage.

The first element of a word is the *sign*, the collection of symbols that comprise a word. For example, the English word "p-a-r-a-c-l-e-t-e" is made up of nine alphabetic symbols. These symbols allow us to identify and pronounce the word. If we know the symbols and the coding patterns of the language, then we can understand the meaning. Sometimes a word is obscure because we do not know the symbols that comprise it. If one went to Israel and tried to read Hebrew without having studied the language, that person could not even get started in working with meaning because he or she would not even be able to read the symbols that make up the words. Without translation or explanation, the reader would be unable to work with the text. The contributors to the KWS are rendering a service to readers by applying their knowledge of Hebrew and Greek and experience with the language in interacting with the text of the original languages. This kind of interpretation of a document in its original language is technically known as exegesis.

The second element of a word is *sense*, which is the content associated with the symbol.[7] The sense of a word is closely related to the lexical "definition" of the word. However, the concept referred to by the sense of the term need not precisely identify what a text is actually referring to with a given term. For example, the Greek term for paraclete means "comforter," which by itself is ambiguous in English, since it could refer specifically either to an object similar to a quilt or to a sympathetic encourager. The ambiguity results in part from an ambiguity the "receptor" language (in this case English) possesses. In addition, one must identify what exactly is referred to as a comforter. In this case, the sense of the term is really a description of an attribute as opposed to making an identification of what exactly is being described. So the sense often gets one closer to the meaning of a text, but it does not always specify or identify clearly what exactly is being referred to by the sense meaning. Interpretation requires that we inquire into what exactly is being described. The context in which the word appears will help us not only to determine the term's sense, but also, hopefully, its referent (what it actually refers to). Nonetheless, once the general content of the term is clear, one begins to know the general direction of the passage in terms of its meaning.

The third element of a word is the *referent*. The referent is the actual thing denoted by a term in a specific context. In John 14–16, for example, the referent of "paraclete" is clearly neither a human sympathetic figure nor a blanket; rather the term refers to the one Jesus will send after his resurrection to be with believers. This is specifically a reference to the Holy Spirit. It is the identification of the referent, where that is possible, that produces specificity and clarity in interpretation.

The complex nature of a word's meaning and its various elements requires that the interpreter exercise great care in approaching the study of words. Once the student of the Bible has grasped the fundamentals of word study, the meaning of meaning, and the basic elements of a word, then he or she can proceed with care and precision in the actual procedure of word analysis.

III. Diachronic and Synchronic Word Analysis

Word meanings can be examined in two ways. First, words can be studied historically by examining how they have been used in the past and how they have changed in meaning through time. This is called *diachronic word analysis*, the approach of the technical word study tools like *TDOT, TDNT, NIDOTTE,* and NIDNTT.[8] These reference tools examine a word's use beginning with the OT period and continuing through the NT or even the patristic period (that is, the time of the church "fathers"). Examining words in this way indicates the possible senses that a term may have.

Second, words can also be studied within a given period (e.g., the intertestamental period, or pre-A.D. 70), or within the writings of a specific author (e.g., Paul, John, Matthew, Philo, or Josephus). This is called *synchronic word analysis*. This is perhaps the most crucial phase of lexical analysis since the meaning of a word in its specific context, either temporal or literary, is the major concern of the interpreter.

The following sections present an example of both the diachronic and synchronic processes used for word analysis. Assumed in the work of the contributors are various levels of such a process of word study. The KWS is merely the result of a process like the method described here. The following section will be of value to anyone who has worked in Hebrew and Greek and has access to a wide range of tools in these languages. Those who do not have facility in those languages should proceed to the discussion of word study method in the Bible itself and to the discussion of common errors made in word studies.

A. Basic Procedure for Biblical Word Analysis: Getting Ready

Getting ready to examine words and their usage on our own requires various tools. These tools come in two forms, book resources and computer tools. Basic book resources include major lexicons, like *Brown, Driver and Briggs (BDB)* and *Koehler, Baumgartner, and Stamm* (HALOT) for Hebrew and *Liddell-Scott-Jones* (LSJ) for general Greek usage, or *Moulton and Milligan* (MM) for Koine Greek usage, and *Bauer-Arndt-Gingrich-Danker* (BAGD) or its recent update, *Bauer-Danker-Arndt-Gingrich* (BDAG). They might include concordances like *Even-Shoshan* for the Hebrew Bible and *Hatch-Redpath* for the Greek Old Testament (LXX) or a solid concordance of the Greek NT or secondarily of a solid NT translation. Computer programs can help accomplish the same thing as a concordance. In fact, for the LXX and other tools, a computer concordance may be the most effective tool to use, if the text the computer tool uses is an up-to-date edition of the text in question. Here for the PC, we have found the *Logos Library* computer system to be most helpful for such study, while the search program *Accordance* has proven most helpful for the Macintosh platform. Both come with individual modules of selected key ancient works in their "scholarly" collections that allow you to search a range of ancient materials for information. For computer help with classical Greek, there is the *Thesarus Linguae Graecae* (TLG) and online there is the *Perseus* project (www.perseus.tufts.edu). These last two tools require a detailed acquaintance with Greek. Other tools that can be used for reference by advanced students include the eleven-volume *Theological Dictionary of the Old Testament* (TDOT), The five-volume *New International Dictionary of Old Testament Theology and Exegesis*, the ten-volume *Theological Dictionary of the New Testament* (TDNT), the four-volume *The New International Dictionary of New Testament Theology* (NIDNTT), and the three-volume *Exegetical Dictionary of the New Testament* (EDNT).[9] Unfortunately there are no solid one-volume lexical tools that are up-to-date and readily accessible to the English based student. This is another reason we have produced the KWS volumes. For personal diachronic word study, the above noted tools are part of a basic resource library.

Several options exist as to which terms to select for closer analysis. First, one could choose to study any words whose English definitions are unclear. Second, words that have apparent synonyms and antonyms in the context make good candidates. Third, words that are used rarely or only once (*hapax legomenon* [used only once]) are also good candidates, especially if they appear to carry conceptual weight in a passage. Fourth, figures make a good choice, since their precise meaning is often not transparent. The most crucial words, however, are those terms that are either repeated or that appear to bear the conceptual weight of a passage. One must understand these to ascertain the meaning of a passage.

An expositor should learn how to spot the key terms in a given passage. If a personal reading of the text does not reveal these key terms, then the use of lexically sensitive commentaries on the Hebrew and Greek text or solid commentaries working from an interaction with the languages behind an English translation can often help to locate them. Another way to discover these key terms is by comparing different English translations. If the translations render the original text with clearly distinct English terms, then perhaps the term behind the differences merits closer examination.

B. Word Study Method: Four Stages of Diachronic Word Study and Two Stages of Synchronic Usage as Illustrated by a NT example. The same methods apply to OT Word Study.

i. Diachronic 1: Examining for Classical Uses

A diachronic word study includes four distinct stages, each of which utilizes a certain tool or set of tools.[10] The examination of terms used during the classical Greek period (900 B.C.–330 B.C.) requires the use of the Liddell-Scott-Jones lexicon.[11] Next, one enters the Hellenistic or Koine period (330 B.C.–A.D. 330). Here one will consider three groups of material: the LXX, popular non-biblical sources, and the NT. A study of the Septuagint (LXX) will involve the use of the concordance of Hatch and Redpath.[12] An examination of terms in non-biblical sources of the Koine period involves using both LSJ and the volume of Moulton and Milligan.[13] The study of terms in the NT will involve the use of a NT concordance, the most up-to-date being the work produced by Bachmann and Slaby or computer programs tied to the Nestle-Aland 27th edition or the UBS 4th edition of the Greek New Testament.[14]

Practically speaking, the best way to proceed is to use some sheets of paper and record the results of the study in these four periods, which will ultimately help to organize one's thoughts and formulate one's conclusions about the data. Such study can also be recorded in a computer word processing format. For exegesis, the most significant results will emerge as one moves closer to the text in question, with primary consideration being given to context and authorial intention.[15]

The following sections illustrate the four stages of a word study, using the Greek noun ajrrabwvn (transliterated and pronounced *arrabōn*), the possible definitions based upon usage are: (1) earnest-money, caution-money; (2) pledge, earnest; and (3) present, bribe.[16] The examples in the writings of Isaeus[17] and Aristotle show that ajrrabwvn is a commercial term that refers to the initial payment in a series of payments. Classical sources to which LSJ refers may be checked in *The Loeb Classical Library* (LCL).[18]

The study of a word's usage in the classical period yields a base from which to draw possible meanings. Only in the case of rarely used words, however, does it have significant importance, though the examples may illustrate the force of the term.

ii. Diachronic 2: Examining for Hellenistic Biblical Uses. (LXX)

In this particular step, one studies the use of Greek terms in the LXX, the Greek translation of the Hebrew Old Testament.[19] Here the study becomes more interesting and complicated: more interesting, because one of the objectives of this step is to determine possible religious or theological meaning for terms in the LXX; more complicated, because this step involves a knowledge of Hebrew.

This particular step, however, is not free from potential errors. One common error is simply to discover the Hebrew word behind the Greek translation in the LXX, and then determine the translation of the Hebrew word to get the Greek idea. This procedure ignores three important facts. First, words in languages do not overlap exactly in meaning.[20] Second, the LXX is often a paraphrase and not a word-for-word rendering of the Hebrew.[21] In fact, in some places the exact wording behind the LXX is very uncertain. Third, often a particular Greek term was chosen not because the translator was attempting to render a specific Hebrew term but because of the way the passage had been traditionally read and translated. These facts should warn the exegete against hastily concluding that a term has picked up its Greek sense from the Hebrew or that a term indicates technical Hebraic usage. The words may be used in a similar manner, but that does not mean they carry exactly the same sense.

Once the exegete has generated a list of Hebrew words that the Greek LXX terms translate, then he should study the meanings of those Hebrew terms in a Hebrew lexicon and, if possible, a theological dictionary for biblical Hebrew words.[22]

Looking up ajrrabwvn in the LXX reveals that this term occurs only in Genesis 38:17, 18 and 20,[23] the passage about Tamar and Judah. In these verses the meaning of ajrrabwvn clearly is "pledge," since an object was given to Tamar as a guarantee. The term as used here indicates a "business" deal; though no money was exchanged, a family seal, cord, and staff were. A glance at the Hebrew term °wúbr;[e (which is translated "pledge," NIV), shows that the LXX term is merely a transliteration of the Hebrew term. It is a "loanword," that is, a borrowed word.

iii. Diachronic 3 and Synchronic 1: Examining for Hellenistic Non-biblical (or Koine) Uses

When we move to this period, we begin to cross from diachronic analysis to synchronic analysis. The objective in this phase of study is to trace the variety of meanings a given term has within the time period of 330 B.C. to A.D. 100. Actually, the Koine period extends beyond this later date, but when studying NT usage the student need not move beyond the period of the NT writings.

A significant resource for the study of Hellenistic Greek words in non-biblical sources is the volume by Moulton and Milligan.[24] This tool illustrates the use of Koine Greek words as found in papyri and epigraphical remains. Some examples are left untranslated, but fortunately, most examples are translated or summarized, as well as dated. Some examples postdate the NT period and should be excluded. However, many excellent examples occur that vividly illustrate the everyday usage of many terms.[25]

A quick look at ajrrabwvn in Moulton and Milligan discloses several important items.[26] First, the entry notes that the term is a Semitic loanword, an observation we made earlier after comparing the LXX term with the Hebrew term that it translated. Second, the entry gives alternate spellings of the term. Third, according to several helpful examples, ajrrabwvn is used for a deposit of 1,000 drachmae for the purchase of a cow, a deposit of 160 drachmae for a land purchase, and a downpayment of eight drachmae for the services of a mouse catcher. These examples clearly indicate the use of ajrrabwvn as a commercial term. A note to the entry says, "The above vernacular usage amply confirms the NT sense of an 'earnest,' or a part given in advance of what will be bestowed fully afterwards, in 2 Cor. 1:22, 5:5, Eph. 1:14."[27] In this entry, they have not only defined the NT term with "earnest" but have also paraphrased it with "a part given in advance of what will be bestowed fully afterwards."[28]

In some cases, the study of terms in the Koine period will surface new meanings. Usually, however, the Koine sources will supply information about the common understanding of terms in the period contemporary to the NT writings.

iv. Diachronic 4 and Synchronic 2: Examining for Biblical Uses (NT)

The objective of this phase of word study is to determine the meaning of a term in the NT. There are a variety of ways to do this. First, one can study the use of a term author by author, creating lists for each writer of the NT material. This approach allows the student to make valuable biblical-theological observations by observing each author's distinctive treatment of terms. Second, the use of a term can be studied within a specific genre (i.e., within the Gospels, Pauline Epistles, Apocalypse, etc.). The value of this division is that one can examine how genre may affect the use of certain terms and images. Third, one can also study the use of a term by proceeding through the text in chronological order. This process is perhaps less helpful in the Gospels, since these documents in their final written form portray events that occurred considerably earlier. But in Paul or in the general Epistles this third approach can help trace the development of a writer's theology or the theology of the early church. (Here, "development" may simply mean the introduction of a new topic that naturally produced new associations.)

Now what does one find about ajrrabwvn?[29] It occurs only 3x in the NT, all in Pauline letters. Its use in 2 Corinthians 1:22; 5:5; and Ephesians 1:14 shows that it is related both to the Holy Spirit and to the idea of sealing. According to 2 Corinthians 1:22, God "put his Spirit in our hearts as a deposit [ajrrabwvn], guaranteeing what is to come." In 2 Corinthians 5:5 Paul states that God "has given us the Spirit as a deposit [ajrrabwvn], guaranteeing what is to come." Ephesians 1:13–14 says that believers "were marked in him with a seal, the promised Holy Spirit, who is a deposit [ajrrabwvn] guaranteeing our inheritance until the redemption of those who are God's possession. . . ." Thus the gift of God's Spirit to believers not only indicates God's ownership (seal) of them, but also a pledge of his future inheritance for them. Clearly, for Paul the Spirit is a pledge, a promise of more to come.

This concludes the basic four-step process. A question that the exegete might now ask, however, is "Which tools should I own?" Ideally, all the tools that have been mentioned should be owned. But at a minimum, one should own the Bauer lexicon, a Greek NT concordance, and either TDNT or NIDNTT. The advantages of TDNT are that its articles offer a full array of ancient references, often cite portions of the pertinent ancient texts, and frequently include notes about the exegetical possibilities in a given passage. NIDNTT has the advantage of examining concepts, of being more up-to-date in its discussion and method, and of being more succinct. Also, the one-volume abridgement of TDNT (often referred to as "little Kittel") is helpful as a quick reference guide and gateway to the larger TDNT.[30] Another helpful tool that presents compact discussion of key data is the Exegetical Dictionary of the New Testament (EDNT).[31] All such tools also need to be evaluated for their own method and approach, especially as they relate to certain historical judgments about the date and authorship of NT books or the relevance of issues tied to debates about relevant historical background to certain key terms. Thus such tools are for advanced students who understand how they work and are aware of the limitations and suppositions.

IV. Avoiding Errors: Common Fallacies Made in Word Analysis

Before turning to the final step of the procedure, one additional issue needs attention: to note the common fallacies made in the word-study process.[32] Several of the most common fallacies are listed in the following paragraphs.

1. The *etymological fallacy*, also known as the "root fallacy," assumes that the meaning of a word is governed by the meaning of its root or roots.[33] Also, it may assume that what a word originally meant is what a later author meant by the term. Though the sense may be related, it is not certain that an author cites a term with a knowledge of the meaning of its component parts. Thus it is best not to appeal to etymology unless contextual factors make it clear the author is aware of this meaning.

2. *Illegitimate totality transfer* assumes that a word carries all of its senses in any one passage. It could be called "meaning overload." However, linguists agree that the "correct meaning of any term is that which contributes the least to the total context."[34] One of the implications of this error is that technical meaning or unusual meaning for terms need to be determined contextually rather than imported from other contexts. It is best not to give a term added nuance in a given context unless double entendre or some type of technical meaning is clearly signaled by context, authorial style, or genre.

3. Another error is the problem of *semantic anachronism*, in which a late meaning of a word is read back into an earlier term. What often contributes to this error is the way the church today uses biblical terminology. Often a meaning develops that differs from ancient usage. A simple example of this is "salvation," which in the popular modern church almost always means justification-sanctification-glorification. Today the term refers broadly to the whole package, rather than to any one of these

specific elements, as was possible in earlier usage. In other words, later meaning should not be read back into earlier usage. Another example of this problem is when appeal is made to later Jewish or Greek materials to support a first-century meaning for a term that lacks attestation for that sense in earlier sources. Obviously keeping a careful eye on the dates of sources guards against this error.

4. *Semantic obsolescence* is when one assigns to a term an early meaning that is no longer used. In NT word study this would be the same as giving a classical Greek meaning to a first-century Koine Greek term. An English illustration can suffice. One reason why the KJV is difficult to read in places is because some meanings of its terms have fallen out of use since A.D. 1611. A term may exist but it no longer carries the meaning it once had.

5. The *prescriptive fallacy* argues that a word has only one meaning and means the same thing in every passage. For example, if a word has the meaning "X" in 13 out of 14 occurrences, then it must mean "X" in the disputed case. But word meanings are determined by context, not word counts.[35]

6. The *word-idea fallacy* assumes that the study of a term is the study of an idea. But the study of a concept is broader than word study, and many terms can be related to a single concept. For example, if one studies the concept of Jesus as King, one is not limited to those texts where the term "king" (*basileus*) appears. Other relevant terms for study might include "rule," "reign," "kingdom," etc.

7. The *referential fallacy* limits meaning only to a specific referent. However, in contexts where principles are given, where commands are offered, where figures are used, or where abstractions are expressed, it is faulty to limit the meaning to a single referent. In such cases, the specific referent of a term is not the only object to which the passage can be related.[36]

   When the OT prophets, for example, characterized the return from exile as a "new exodus," they applied an earlier image of the OT to their own experience. When the NT authors cited OT passages that originally referred to *Yahweh* and applied them to Jesus, they interpreted the OT in light of activities that Jesus performed that matched the text. They were not confined to relegating their understanding of such passages only to God in heaven. It should be noted, however, that as one moves beyond the author's original referents, the interpreter is moving beyond the technical realm of exegesis—whose goal is to recover the original intention of the author—and into application.

8. *Verbal parallelomania* refers to the practice of some biblical exegetes who claim that the presence of the same term in several different contexts automatically indicates conceptual parallelism, borrowing of terms, or literary dependency. Admittedly, many ancient cultures used similar terms in vaguely similar contexts, and the Ancient Near Eastern and Greek religious world used terms that also appear in the Bible. However, Philo's use of the term *logos* does not mean that it has the same sense for him as it does for the apostle John. Only careful, comparative study of all relevant texts will establish the veracity of possible parallels, borrowings, or literary dependencies.

9. Perhaps the most serious error is the *selective evidence fallacy* wherein one cites only the evidence that favors the interpretation one wants to defend. Certainly, unintentional errors in judgment do occur sometimes. However, the intentional avoidance

of certain facts will always result in inaccurate and biased conclusions.

These nine fallacies present a cross section of some of the obstacles that can hinder the exegete in determining the meaning of words. At one time or another every exegete trips over one or more of these obstacles while engaged in the enterprise of interpretation. This is why dialogue with other reference works is an essential part of the process. Thus we include one final step in the analysis of words: comparing the results of our study with the results obtained by other biblical scholars.

V. Checking other Authorities: BAGD,[37] BDAG, TDNT, NIDNTT

A check of these sources shows that our analysis of ajrrabwvn agrees with that of others. For example, the *TDNT* article says the word "always implies an act which engages to something bigger."[38] Thus the Spirit is "the guarantee of their full future possession of salvation,"[39] an excellent description of the contextual force of the term ajrrabwvn. *NIDNTT* agrees with this description but also notes that since the Spirit is a gracious gift from God, one should not speak of God as our debtor.[40] This is one instance in which the image differs from its daily use. *BAGD* defines ajrrabwvn as a "first installment," "deposit," "down payment," and "pledge." It is a commercial or legal term that denotes "pay[ing] part of the purchase price in advance, and so secur[ing] a legal claim to the article in question, or mak[ing] a contract valid."[41]

This concludes the final step of the process of word analysis. Thus the use of a term has been traced through various periods (diachronic word analysis), as well as the NT period (synchronic word analysis).

Lexical analysis is demanding but necessary. Through lexical study the barriers that hinder one's understanding of the meaning of terms are often overcome or significantly lowered. The exegete who strives to understand the basic rules of word study, who grasps the complexities of meaning, who appropriates and implements sound methodology, and who avoids the common fallacies made in word study will be able to achieve a high level of accuracy in interpreting words, the building blocks of Scripture.

Conclusion: Welcome to the Key Word Study Volumes

The contributors to the KWS volumes offer their study with the hope that the meaning and key lexical details of the Bible are made accessible to a larger public. This essay, though technical in spots, presents the underlying method that informs proper, careful lexical study for those who have some background in the study of Hebrew and Greek. A parallel essay as it applies to the OT will introduce those volumes. It is our prayer that the user of the *KWS* will find instruction and personal edification through the use of these volumes.

Darrell L. Bock

(supplemented for the OT by Eugene H. Merrill)

---

1 This is the *initial* goal of the exegete. The exegete is preoccupied with the message of the human author. Initially the goal is to understand the message as set forth in the

setting in which the author operated. The process of correlating that message with other biblical texts, either earlier or later ones, is the task of a subsequent theological process. In this latter phase one wrestles with concepts like the "progress of revelation," the "fuller sense" that God intended, the use and application of the OT in the NT, and the personal application of the text. All of these involve subsequent reflection beyond the initial exegetical concern with the message of a given document in a given setting. E. D. Hirsch presents a fine discussion and defense of authorial intention in *Validity in Interpretation* (New Haven: Yale University Press, 1967). For a fine caveat in regard to authorial intention, see J. P. Louw, *Semantics of New Testament Greek* (Philadelphia/Chico: Fortress/Scholars, 1982), 48. The complex issue of *sensus plenior* is handled nicely by D. J. Moo, "The Problem of Sensus Plenior," in *Hermeneutics, Authority, and Canon*, ed. D. A. Carson and J. Woodbridge (Grand Rapids: Zondervan, 1986), 179-211, 397-405. For an overview of OT interpretation see Tremper Longman III, *Literary Approaches to Biblical Interpretation* (Grand Rapids: Eerdmans, 1987).

In speaking of authorial intention, one does not try to reproduce what the author must have been thinking at a given point or why he wrote. Rather, the interpreter's goal is to ascertain what the writer wanted to communicate through the terms he chose for his message. Speaking about an author's intention is more appropriate than speaking about the meaning of the text, since words do not carry meaning autonomously and their meaning can be variously construed when detached from their original setting. The concern of the exegete is the meaning that emerged from the author's choice of expression, the sense he gave to the words in presenting them.

2 This means that in historically sensitive interpretation one will not use later NT passages to determine the referents of OT passages. Since meaning can emerge in a variety of ways when one introduces the factor of the passage of time, going to later revelation at this stage of the exegetical-interpretive process would possibly cloud the force of the original message, if not obscure it altogether. For this complex area see D. L. Bock, "Evangelicals and the Use of the Old Testament in the New," Bibliotheca Sacra 142 (1985): 209-23, 306-18, which surveys and evaluates four models offered by evangelicals to deal with this particularly difficult issue and more recently Bock's "The Use of the Old Testament in the New," in Foundation for Biblical Interpretation. David S. Dockery, Kenneth A. Mathews and Robert B. Sloan, eds. (Nashville: Broadman & Holman, 1994), 97-114.

3 See J. Barr, *The Semantics of Biblical Language* (Oxford: Oxford University Press, 1961), 1; Ellen Van Wolde, "A Text-Semantic study of the Hebrew Bible, Illustrated with Noah and Job," *Journal of Biblical Literature* 1131, (1994): 19-35; A. Thiselton, "Semantics and New Testament Interpretation," in *New Testament Interpretation*, ed. I. H. Marshall (Grand Rapids: Eerdmans, 1977), 75-104, esp. 75; M. Silva, *Biblical Words and Their Meaning: An Introduction to Lexical Semantics* (Grand Rapids: Zondervan, 1983). For an excellent study of all aspects of semantics as it applies to NT Word Studies, see J. P. Louw, *Semantics of New Testament Greek*. This study addresses meaning as it is related to words, sentences, and paragraphs. For the broader discipline of semantics, see S. Ullmann, *The Principles of Semantics*, 2d ed. (Oxford: Blackwells, 1957), 1-137, 197-258; idem, *Semantics: An Introduction to the Science of Meaning* (Oxford: Blackwells, 1962).

4 G. B. Caird, *The Language and Imagery of the Bible* (Philadelphia: Westminster, 1980), 37-61.

5 In a normal lexicon the meanings of a word are simply listed along with passages that reflect a particular meaning. They can also be charted semantically in relation to the term's "field of meaning," where the senses are charted as categories of meaning that a word may have and are placed alongside other terms that can be associated with that category of meaning (see Thiselton, "Semantics," 91, where he charts out the word *pneuma*; see also Louw, *Semantics*, 60–66). Words that address the same conceptual area are said to share the same semantic domain. A semantic domain lexicon examines words according to conceptual groupings. See J. P. Louw and E. A. Nida, eds., *Greek-English Lexicon of the New Testament Based on Semantic Domains* (New York: United Bible Societies, 1988). The abbreviation for this work in these volumes is LN. For another excellent treatment of the various relationships among words, see Silva, *Biblical Words*, 118–35.

6 This point is illustrated by the existence of different languages and alphabets, which are simply different symbolic systems for representing concepts in words.

7 Silva, *Biblical Words*, 101–3.

8 *Theological Dictionary of the Old Testament,* ed. G. Johannes Botterweck and Helmer Ringgren, trans. John T. Willis, Geoffrey W. Bromiley, and David E. Green, 11 vols.(Grand Rapids: Eerdmans, 1974-2001); *New International Dictionary of Old Testament Theology and Exegesis,* ed. Willem A. Van Gemeren, 5 vols. (Grand Rapids: Zondervan, 1997); *Theological Dictionary of the New Testament,* ed. E. Kittel and G. Friedrich, trans. G. W. Bromiley, 10 vols. (Grand Rapids: Eerdmans, 1964–76); and *The New International Dictionary of New Testament Theology,* ed. E. Brown, 4 vols. (Grand Rapids: Zondervan, 1975–85). The difference in these tools is that TDOT and TDNT list individual lexical terms tied to a specific root form, while NIDOTTE and NIDNTT organize words according to concepts, groups of similar lexical terms, or synonyms that may not necessarily share the same root form.

9 These tools are for advanced students because sometimes these tools make critical assumptions about date and the authorship of biblical works or about issues tied to historical background that require significant historical knowledge by the student who uses these tools. Key bibliographic information for these tools follows in the discussion of the individual sub-sections to which the tool applies

10 A fifth step could be added that studies the use of NT terms in Christian patristic literature. For this latter step, use G. W. H. Lampe, *A Patristic Greek Lexicon* (Oxford: Clarendon, 1961–68), which gives one access to the use of terms in the writings of the church fathers. The most complete collection of Greek patristic texts is J.P. Migne, *Patrologia Graeca,* 161 vols. (New York: Adlers, 1965–1971). Many of these texts have been translated and can be located in other series. A possible sixth step could examine the use of related terms in Jewish or rabbinic literature (e.g., Hebrew or Aramaic equivalents). For this step, judiciously use H. L. Strack and P. Billerbeck, *Kommentar zum Neuen Testament aus Talmud und Midrasch,* 6 vols. (München: Beck, 1921–61). See also M. Jastrow, *A Dictionary of the Targumim, the Talmud Babli and Yerushalmi, and the Midrashic Literature* (London: Judaica, 1971).

11 H. G. Liddell and R. Scott, *A Greek-English Lexicon: A New Edition Revised and Augmented Throughout with Supplement*, rev. H. S. Jones and R. McKenzie, 9th ed. (Oxford: Oxford University Press, 1924–40; Supplement, 1968). Hereafter abbreviated as LSJ. The intermediate lexicon by Liddell-Scott is abbreviated as LS.

12 E. Hatch and H. A. Redpath, *A Concordance to the Septuagint and the Other Greek Versions of the Old Testament (Including the Apocryphal Books)*, 2 vols. (1897; reprint, Graz: Akademische Drucкü. Verlagsanstalt, 1975; reprint Grand Rapids: Baker, 1983).

13 J. H. Moulton and G. Milligan, *The Vocabulary of the Greek New Testament* (Grand Rapids: Eerdmans, 1974).

14 H. Bachmann and H. Slaby, eds., *Computer-Konkordanz zum Novum Testamentum Graece* (New York: W. de Gruyter, 1980). Another concordance that could be used is that by W. F. Moulton and A. S. Geden, *Concordance to the Greek Testament*, 5th ed. (Edinburgh: T. & T. Clark, 1897; supplement, 1977), a work based on the 1881 text of Westcott and Hort. Major advantages of the *Computer-Konkordanz* include not only its use of the most recent Greek text but also the larger context it provides for each word it cites. Advanced students will profit by using the *Vollständige Konkordanz zum griechischen Neuen Testament*, ed. K. Aland, 2 vols. (Berlin: Walter de Gruyter, 1978, 1983), a multi-volume tool that offers complete word statistics. Most popularly circulating concordances on the NT, such as Strong's and Young's, work with the King James. Other concordances are specific to a given English translation. Though these concordances are adequate for the pursuit of the basic meanings of terms, the best concordances are those grounded in Greek and tied to more recent editions of the text. Some argue that the best form of the NT text is that which underlies the *King James Version*. However, this claim ignores the fact that our manuscript base for the Greek NT has improved since the time of the production of the *King James Version* in the seventeenth century.

15 It should be stressed that in lexical matters evidence for usage is weighed, not counted. Thus a word whose meaning is uncertain will not necessarily reflect the most popular sense; and the context will always be the most important factor.

16 LSJ, 246.

17 LSJ cites Isaeus 8.20; however, the term of the entry is not found in this section but in 8.23. This example illustrates the value of looking up references, for then errors and typos can be discovered and removed.

18 *The Loeb Classical Library* (Cambridge, Mass.: Harvard University Press) is an extensive collection (approx. 450 vols.) of both Greek and Latin texts with English translations.

19 For a helpful presentation on the value of the LXX for biblical studies, see F. W. Danker, "The Use of the Septuagint," in his *Multipurpose Tools for Bible Study*, 3d ed. (St. Louis: Concordia, 1970), 81–95 and Karen H. Jobes and Moises Silva, *Invitation to the Septuagint* (Grand Rapids: Baker, 2000).

20 For example, English has one word for "history," while German has two, Geschichte and Historie. To equate either of the German words with the English is to lose some

of the precision in the German terminology. The problems in this area are detailed by Silva, *Biblical Words*, 52–73.

21 In fact, the translation quality of the LXX varies from book to book. For details, see J. Roberts, *The Old Testament Text and the History of the Ancient Versions* (Cardiff: University of Wales Press, 1951), 172–87. For a recent overview of Septuagintal studies, see E. Tov, "Jewish Greek Scriptures," in *Early Judaism and its Modern Interpreters*, ed. R. Kraft and G. W. E. Nickelsburg (Philadelphia: Fortress, 1986), 223–37.

22 F. Brown, S. R. Driver, and C. A. Briggs, eds., *A Hebrew and English Lexicon of the Old Testament* (Oxford: Clarendon Press, 1907); L. Koehler and W. Baumgartner, eds., *Lexicon in Veteris Testamenti Libros*, 2d ed. (Leiden: Brill, 1958). The latter volume is undergoing a complete revision under a new name (*Hebräisches und aramäisches Lexikon zum Alten Testament*, 3 vols. [Leiden: Brill, 1967, 1974, 1983]). The student should also consult the ongoing work of G. J. Botterweck and H. Ringgren, eds., *Theological Dictionary of the Old Testament*, (Grand Rapids: Eerdmans, 1974–), of which several volumes have been published (12 volumes are projected).

23 Hatch and Redpath, *Concordance to the Septuagint*, 160.

24 See n. 13. This work is somewhat dated (1932); however, it is in the process of being updated by a working group of the Society of Biblical Literature (SBL), but it is uncertain when the update will be produced. For very advanced students, there is a series of papyri collections that can be referred to that updates information available in Mouton and Milligan.

25 Moulton and Milligan contains only a small sampling of all of the occurrences of a given word, so it should not be regarded as providing an exhaustive treatment of terms in this period. Exhaustive treatments of this material do not exist in a single collected form. However, some papyri updates are available online on the Perseus project site at www.perseus.tufts.edu.

26 Moulton and Milligan, *Vocabulary*, 79.

27 Ibid.

28 The entry includes several intriguing later examples. One example relates ajrrabwvn to "purchasing a wife." A second example speaks of the engagement ring as an ajrrabwvn. Again, the picture of an object as a pledge is very clear here.

29 Bachmann and Slaby, *Computer-Konkordanz*, 222.

30 "Little Kittel" (Grand Rapids: Eerdmans, 1985), prepared by G. Bromiley, is the one-volume abridged edition of *TDNT*.

31 Horst Balz and Gerhard Schneider, eds. *Exegetical Dictionary of the New Testament*. 3 vols. (Grand Rapids: Wm. B. Eerdmans, 1990-93). Another word tool, C. Spicq, *Theological Lexicon of the New Testament*. 3 vols. (Peabody, Mass: Hendrickson Publishers, 1994), is helpful but very selective in the words it covers. When this work is cited it is abbreviated as Spicq.

32 For a more comprehensive discussion of fallacies, see D. A. Carson, *Exegetical Fallacies* (Grand Rapids: Baker, 1984), 25-66. He notes 16 such fallacies. This essay shall note only the more common errors.

33 See Louw, *Semantics*, 23–31; Silva, *Biblical Words*, 35–51; Barr, *Semantics*, 107–60.

34 E. A. Nida, "The Implications of Contemporary Linguistics for Biblical Scholarship," *Journal of Biblical Literature* 91 (1972): 86; Louw, Semantics, 51–52.

35 This raises a key issue that often complicates exegesis, especially for the beginning student. One does not establish a meaning merely by showing that a term's sense is contextually possible. Often commentators think their work is done when they have shown that a context could support the defended sense. However, the sense that should be chosen is the one that is the most likely among the options. Often a context can support a variety of senses, but the meaning is the one that fits the context the most naturally and with the least amount of contextual strain.

36 This fallacy is the most abstract of the ones mentioned and is difficult to explain briefly. For a more detailed discussion, see Silva, *Biblical Words*, 103–8.

37 *BAGD* is the abbreviation for W. Bauer, *A Greek-English Lexicon of the New Testament and Other Christian Literature*, trans. W. F. Arndt and F. W. Gingrich, rev. Ed. F. W. Gingrich and F. W. Danker (Chicago: University of Chicago Press, 1979). The revised third edition of this lexicon was released in 2000 and is abbreviated as BDAG as Danker's role warranted an elevation in the noting of his contribution to the lexicon. The earlier version of the lexicon is cited for the example here.

38 TDNT, 1:475.

39 Ibid.

40 *NIDNNT*, 2:39–40.

41 *BAGD*, 109.

Carl R. Anderson, Jr., B.A., Th.M., Ph.D., Dallas Theological
   Seminary
   Pastor, Trinity Fellowship Church
   Genesis 37–50

Stephen J. Bramer, B.A., Th.M., Ph.D., Dallas Theological Seminary
   Associate Professor of Bible Exposition,
   Dallas Theological Seminary
   Leviticus

David L. Brooks, B.A., Th.M., Ph.D., Dallas Theological Seminary
   Associate Professor of Hebrew and Old Testament,
   The Criswell College
   Numbers

Robert B. Chisholm, Jr., B.A., Th.M., Ph.D., Dallas Theological
   Seminary
   Professor of Old Testament Studies, Dallas Theological
   Seminary
   Genesis 25–36

David M. Fouts, B.A., Th.M., Ph.D., Dallas Theological Seminary
   Professor of Bible and Hebrew, Bryan College
   Genesis 1–11

Harold R. Holmyard, III, B.A., Th.M., Th.D., Dallas Theological
   Seminary
   Researcher in Biblical Studies, Dallas, Texas
   Genesis 12–24

Gordon H. Johnston, B.A., Th.M., Ph.D., Dallas Theological
   Seminary
   Associate Professor of Old Testament Studies
   Dallas Theological Seminary
   Exodus

Eugene H. Merrill, B.A., M.Phil., Ph.D., Columbia University
   Distinguished Professor of Old Testament Studies, Dallas
   Theological Seminary
   General Editor, *Preface, Deuteronomy*

ABBREVIATIONS
AND
ANCIENT SOURCES

For extra-biblical sources, standard abbreviations are used. They can be found in a comprehensive list in *The SBL Handbook of Style: For Ancient Near Eastern, Biblical and Early Christian Studies*. Edited by Patrick H. Alexander, John F. Kutsko, James D. Ernest, Shirley A. Decker-Lucke, and for the Society of Biblical Literature David L. Petersen. Peabody, Mass: Hendrickson, 1999. Only a few of the more prevalent, but less well-known abbreviations appear in the list below.

AB   Anchor Bible

ABD   *Anchor Bible Dictionary*

AHw   *Akkadisches Handwörterbuch.* W. von Soden. 3 vols. Wiesbaden, 1965–1981.

ANET   *Ancient Near Eastern Texts Relating to the Old Testament.* Edited by J. B. Pritchard, 3rd ed. Princeton, 1969.

ASV   *American Standard Version*

BDB   Brown, F., S. R. Driver, and C. A. Briggs. *A Hebrew and English Lexicon of the Old Testament.* Oxford, 1907.

BHS   Biblia Hebraica Stuttgartensia

CBQ   *Catholic Biblical Quarterly*

CEV > CDA   *A Concise Dictionary of Akkadian,* Contemporary English Version

DCH   *Dictionary of Classical Hebrew.* Edited by D. J. A. Clines. Sheffield, 1993–

Enc Jud   *Encyclopedia Judaica.* 16 vols. Jerusalem, 1972

Abbreviations and Ancient Sources

Eng.   This indicates a differing versification in English versions from the Greek or Hebrew texts, with chapter and verse noted.

ESV   *English Standard Version*

GKC   *Gesenius' Hebrew Grammar*. Edited by E. Kautzsch. Translated by A. E. Cowley. 2nd ed., Oxford, 1910.

HALOT   Koehler, L., W. Baumgartner, and J. S. Stamm, *The Hebrew and Aramaic Lexicon of the Old Testament*. Translated and edited under the supervision of M. E. J. Richardson. 4 vols. Leiden, 1994–1999.

IBHS   *An Introduction to Biblical Hebrew Syntax*. B. K. Waltke and M. O'Connor. Winona Lake, Indiana, 1990.

ISBE   *International Standard Bible Encyclopedia*. Edited by G. W. Bromiley. 4 vols. Grand Rapids, 1979–1988.

JB   *Jerusalem Bible*

JETS   *Journal of the Evangelical Theological Society*

JNES   *Journal of Near Eastern Studies*

JPSTC   The JPS Torah Commentary

KBL   Koehler, L., and W. Baumgartner, *Lexicon in Veteris Testamenti libros*. 2nd ed., Leiden, 1958.

KJV   *King James Version*

LXX   Septuagint (The Greek OT)

MT   Masoretic Text

NAC   New American Commentary

NASB   *New American Standard Bible*

NCV   *New Century Version*

NEB   *New English Bible*

NET   *New English Translation*

Abbreviations and Ancient Sources

NIDNTT	*New International Dictionary of New Testament Theology.* 4 vols., 1975–85.
NIDOTTE	*New International Dictionary of Old Testament Theology and Exegesis.* Edited by W. A. VanGemeren. 5 vols. Grand Rapids, 1997.
NIV`	*New International Version*
NJPS	*Tanakh: The Holy Scriptures: The New JPS Translation According to the Traditional Hebrew Text.*
NKJV	*New King James Version*
NLT	*New Living Translation*
NRSV	*New Revised Standard Version*
NT	New Testament
OT	Old Testament
Q	Part of an abbreviation that usually includes a number before it. It specifies a document from Qumran. The number tells in which cave at Qumran the document was found. These documents are part of the Dead Sea Scrolls.
Rab.	*Rabbah.* This abbreviation is preceded by the biblical book (with its normal abbreviation) covered as part of a larger work of Jewish exposition known as the *Midrash Rabbah,* a work of around the fourth century A.D. The ten biblical books covered are Genesis through Deuteronomy, Lamentations, Ruth, Ecclesiastes, Song of Songs, and Esther.
REB	*Revised English Bible*
RSV	*Revised Standard Version*
Syr.	Syriac
TDNT	*Theological Dictionary of the New Testament*, edited by Gerhard Kittel and Gerhard Friedrich, 10 vols., 1964 English edition.
TDOT	*Theological Dictionary of the Old Testament.* Edited by G. J. Botterweck and H. Ringgren. Translated by J. T. Willis, G. W. Bromiley, and D. E. Green. 11 vols. Grand Rapids, 1974–
TEV	*Today's English Version*

TLOT   *Theological Lexicon of the Old Testament.* Edited by E. Jenni, with assistance from C. Westermann. Translated by M. E. Biddle. 3 vols. Peabody, Mass., 1997.

TWAT   *Theologisches Wörterbuch zum Alten Testament.* Edited by G. J. Botterweck and H. Ringgren. Stuttgart, 1970–

TWOT   *Theological Wordbook of the Old Testament.* Edited by R. L. Harris, G. L. Archer Jr., B. K. Waltke. 2 vols. Chicago, 1980.

Vulg.   Vulgate

WBC   Word Biblical Commentary

x   Abbreviation for the number of times a word or phrase is used or appears (e.g., 3x = 3 times).

ZPEB   *Zondervan Pictorial Encyclopedia of the Bible.* Edited by M. C. Tenney. 5 vols. Grand Rapids, 1975.

TRANSLITERATIONS

Hebrew Transliterations

The *Bible Knowledge Key Word Study* uses the standard transliteration system for Hebrew. Below is a chart of how the letters correspond. This chart can help the reader with Hebrew pronunciation.

Consonant Pronunciation

The letters and diacritical marks on the left side of the column are articulated according to the matching elements on the right side. For the most part, they are identical in Hebrew and English but the exceptions should be carefully noted.

ʾ	—	*silent*	l	—	l
b	—	b	m	—	m
g	—	g	n	—	n
d	—	d	s	—	s
h	—	h	ʿ	—	*silent*
w	—	w	p	—	p
z	—	z	ṣ	—	ts
ḥ	—	ch *(as in Bach)*	q	—	q
ṭ	—	t	r	—	r
y	—	y	ś	—	s
k	—	k	š	—	sh
			t	—	t

Vowel Pronunciation

The vowel letters on the left side of the column, with their various diacritical marks, are pronounced according to the matching elements on the right side. The words in parentheses indicate how the vowels sound in each case.

It should also be noted that, since the Hebrew language in Old Testament times had no written vowels, it became necessary at a later time when Hebrew was less commonly used to improvise a vowel system using diacritical marks rather then letters. These are more technically called vowel points. When we render Hebrew into modern languages we must supply vowels to indicate the presence of these vowel points. The divine name Yahweh occasionally appears without vowels as Yhwh (or YHWH) since the name was considered by some too holy to pronounce and thus its pronunciation is not certain even today. Therefore, we make no attempt to pronounce it but instead, with longstanding tradition, read it Adonai (LORD). The verb forms that appeaer at the end of some KWS articles have been left unpointed (without vowels) so they can be more easily looked up in the lexicons. As they are, they remain unpronouncible.

a	—	a *(bat)*	ê	—	e *(they)*
e	—	e *(better)*	ê	—	e *(better)*
i	—	i *(bitter)*	î	—	i *(machine)*
o	—	o *(bottle)*	ô	—	o *(role)*
u	—	u *(ruler)*	û	—	u *(ruler)*
ā	—	a *(father)*	ă	—	a *(amuse)*
ē	—	e *(they)*	ĕ	—	e *(remote)*
ō	—	o *(role)*	ŏ	—	o *(collide)*

In the index on transliteration we follow the alphabetization of English in rendering the order of words.

GENESIS

David M. Fouts (1-11) / Harold R. Holmyard (12-24)
Robert B. Chisholm (25-36) / Carl R. Anderson (37-50)

1:1 In the beginning (*bĕrē'šît*)—The presence of this term without the article present (anarthrously) has led many to suspect that "created" (*bārā'*) must have originally been vocalized as an infinitive construct (*bĕrō'*). This would then support a rendering of a temporal construction in the protasis: "When God began to create . . ." or "When God was creating . . ." followed by the apodosis in v. 2. Either of these renderings supports Gen. 1 as being a re-creation account rather than an account of original creation. However, one often finds temporal adverbs in the OT being used anarthrously yet with definiteness (*rē'šît* in Isa. 46:10; *rō'š* in Prov. 8:23, Eccl. 3:11, Isa. 40:21, 41:4, 26, 48:16; *qedem* in Neh. 12:46, Isa. 45:21, 46:10; *'ôlām* in Gen. 3:22). For this reason, the article was not necessary in this case to establish the absolute beginning of the creative process that Genesis one describes. [*rē'šît*]

God (*'ĕlōhîm*)—The term is unique to the OT, with other Ancient Near Eastern nations often utilizing instead the noun El (as the Ugar. *'ēl*) or one of its cognates (Akkad. *ilu*) for the chief of the gods in their pantheons. In Ugaritic mythology, El is the wise ancient creator of the other gods. In the Babylonian creation account, the Enuma Elish, the process of creation was accomplished by the sometimes violent interactions within the pantheon, leaving Marduk in command at the end of the process (later named Ashur by the Assyrians). In perhaps what was meant as a polemic against the myths of the other nations, Genesis names *'ĕlōhîm* (plural of *'ĕlôah*) as the sole Creator of all there is, not from a process of violence, but simply by the power of the spoken word (cf. 1:3, 6, 9, 11, 14, 20, 26). Another option would be to see the Genesis account as primary, with Ancient Near Eastern mythologies deriving from it.

Oftentimes juxtaposed with YHWH, the personal name for God (see 2:4 below), *'ĕlōhîm* is also often used interchangeably with another OT designation for God, El (Gen. 33:20) and may be so with the derivatives of El as El Elyon, El Olam, El Shaddai, El Roi. Perhaps it is because of the number of differing names for God (especially as seen in Genesis) that the people of God adopted this exclusive plural form to express the totality of his individual manifestations.

The divine *'ĕlōhîm* is seen in the OT as righteous (Ps. 7:9), as holy (Josh. 24:19), as living (Jer. 10:10), as everlasting (Isa. 40:28), as true (2 Chron. 15:3). He is the God of Abraham, Isaac, and Jacob (Gen. 26:24; Exod. 3:6; Ps. 47:9), and called the God of Israel (Gen. 33:20) and the God of the Hebrews (Exod. 5:3). He is the God of all flesh (Jer. 32:27). For the believer, he is a rock of protection (2 Sam. 22:3; cf. Ps. 43:2), he is the source of righteousness (Ps. 4:1), he is the God of salvation (Ps. 18:46; Isa. 17:10; Mic. 7:7; Hab. 3:18), and he is our praise (Ps. 109:1). [*'ĕlōhîm*]

Created (*bārā'*)—In the Qal stem, as here, the verb occurs 38x, always with God as the subject, or with reference to God as the Creator. In the Niphal stem (the passive voice), it occurs 10x, always with God as the agent. Creation in the OT then is seen as the act of God alone. In many cases, as in the context of Gen. 1 and 2, it can act as a synonym for *'āsâ* (to make). Its presence in a given context neither requires nor precludes *creatio ex nihilo*. Context must be determinative. [*br'*]

The heavens and the earth (*'ēt haššāmayim wĕ'ēt hā'āreṣ*)—While many point out that the two terms can refer to skies and land, and that the latter is far the more frequent understanding of *'ereṣ* in the Pentateuch, the Scriptures as a whole are consistent in their understanding that God is the God of the entire world, not just of a given land (cf. Jer. 32:27; Num. 16:22; 27:16). As such, the phrase should be understood as merism for everything, rather than restricted to only the land of Palestine. Had the passage been intended solely to depict the preparation of Palestine, it is likely that YHWH would have been named (see below at 2:4). [*šāmayim, 'ereṣ*]

1:2 Now the earth was (*hayĕtâ*)—The verb is best understood as a simple past tense, but has been understood by others as a past perfect (the earth had become). The latter is an attempt to better understand the *tōhû wābōhû* (see below). In order to render the verb with this nuance (had become), one would normally expect a

lāmed preposition prefixed to both the *tōhû* and the *bōhû*, which is not present here. Too, the past perfect use of the verb normally has an antecedent text to provide a basis for the past perfect. This is also not present here. Similar constructions (verb *hyh* following a disjunctive *waw*) in other contexts are normally rendered "was" (Gen. 3:1, Judg. 8:11, Jonah 3:3, Zech. 3:3). [*hyh*]

Formless and empty (*tōhû wābōhû*)—Most often treated together, the juxtaposed terms could actually be seen as an hendiadys, translated "a formless void." The first term occurs far more frequently than the second, which occurs a total of 3x. The use of the two terms together in Jer. 4:23 is probably an allusion to the Genesis account applied by the prophet to the destruction of Jerusalem and Judah at the time of Nebuchadnezzar's third invasion in 586 B.C. Isa. 34:11 employs both terms and predicts a similar wasting of Edom. Alone, *tōhû* can refer to a wasteland (Deut. 32:10; Job 6:18), empty arguments (Isa. 29:21), and idols that have no substance (1 Sam. 12:21; Isa. 41:29). Even idol-makers accomplish nothing (Isa. 44:9). The emphasis in this passage then seems to be that the earth then existed with no purpose, it had no value, it was not yet ready to sustain the life that God was about to bring about. [*tōhû, bōhû*]

Darkness (*ḥāšek*)—Darkness is most often seen as the absence of light, yet Isaiah affirms that it, too, was created by God (Isa. 45:7). It often is used metaphorically as times of distress and difficulty, and may include an aspect of judgment (Exod. 10:21-22; Job 19:8; Ps. 35:6; Eccl. 11:8; Isa. 5:30; cf. the feminine noun from the same root in Isa. 8:22 and Isa. 50:10). The presence of the term in Gen. 1:2 has led some to posit (with *tōhû wābōhû*) that the earth's condition was a result of judgment by God, but this is not mandated. [ḥōšek]

The surface of the <u>deep</u> (těhōm)—The basic meaning appears to be that of oceanic depths (BDB, 1062), though it can refer to subterranean sources of water (Deut. 8:7, Amos 7:4) or even rivers (Ezek. 31:4; Ps. 42:7). The term occurs 36x in the Hebrew Bible, 14 of which occur in near proximity to mayim, "water." In poetic passages, the two terms are often synonymously parallel (Ezek. 26:19, Ps. 33:7). At other times, the term is used in parallel with the term yām, "sea" (Exod. 15:8; Isa. 51:10). There have been attempts to link this term etymologically with the goddess Ti'amat of other Ancient Near Eastern cosmogonies. If there is a connection to be seen here with the other Ancient Near Eastern cosmologies, its presence here could be seen as a polemic, expressing the precreative state of chaotic waters. [těhōm]

And the <u>spirit of God</u> (werûaḥ 'ělōhîm)—It is unlikely that this phrase should be translated "a mighty wind" due to the presence of the verb rḥp (Ross, Creation and Blessing, 107), which indicates a hovering or brooding over in the sense of the care of a mother eagle (Deut. 32:11). The presence of God's spirit ensures the care of God in the creative process. [rûaḥ]

1:3 And God <u>said</u> (wayyō'mer)—Creation is always viewed in Scripture as the result of the spoken word of God (cf. Ps. 33:7-8; John 1:1-3; Heb. 11:3; 2 Peter 3:5) and with good justification. The phrase is repeated in the passage ten times (1:3, 6, 9, 11, 14, 20, 24, 26, 28, 29), nine of which utterances result in immediate response in the created order. The power of the divine word is a repeated theme in the Bible (cf. Isa. 55:11). ['mr]

<u>Let there be</u> light (yehî)—The verb

expressing the phrase is in the jussive form. Only two types of jussives are commonly recognized; the jussive of request, from an inferior to a superior; and the jussive of command, from a superior to an inferior. It is doubtful that almighty God is making a request of anyone, particularly since the actions were carried out very quickly. Scriptural evidence seems to indicate that the greater the king's power, the faster his commands are completed. As a case in point, Ahasuerus' orders to execute Haman are quickly carried out (Esth. 7:8-9). Conversely, the diminishing power of a king could yield, not quick obedience, but rather outright disobedience, as in the case of Saul nearing his death (1 Sam. 31:4). The other verbs used in sequence following "and God said" are likewise jussives of command. [hyh]

1:4 The light was <u>good</u> (kî ṭôb)—Literally, that (it was) good. Ross (Creation and Blessing, 108) states: "that which is good is conducive for and enhances life," whereas BDB (374) assigns "excellent" to its meaning here. Certainly, completeness also may be indicated in this term as well since in the near context of Gen. 2, the aloneness of Adam was "not good," and it was only after the entire creation was completed that things were "very good." [ṭôb]

1:5 There was <u>evening</u> and there was <u>morning</u> (wayěhî 'ereb wayěhî bōqer)—The phrase offered repeatedly in chapter 1 is "and there was evening and there was morning day x." This syntax is unique. The expression "morning and evening" is more prevalent, and normally indicates daily activities, such as the sacrifices offered morning and evening (cf. 1 Chron. 16:40; 2 Chron. 2:4; Exod. 18:13). When evening precedes morning outside of Gen. 1, such as in Exodus 27:21 and Lev.

24:3, it refers to a daily task with emphasis on overnight activity (keeping the lamps burning in the tabernacle). In Num. 9:21, it refers to the fiery cloud of God's presence overshadowing the tabernacle overnight. Paired together in either order, the terms are most frequently used as collectives, and are rarely found in the plural. In Dan. 8:14, these singular terms are qualified by the numerical modifier 2,300 (the KJV renders this as 2,300 days). ['ereb, bōqer]

The first <u>day</u> (yôm 'eḥād)—Careful observation reveals that there are only four ways that yôm is used in Gen. 1:1–2:4:

As daylight: 1:5, 14, 16, 18

As a measurement of time: 1:15

With numbers (ordinal and cardinal): 1:5, 8, 13, 19, 23, 31; 2:2, 3

As the object of preposition bě (temporal adverb "when"): 2:4

In none of these cases can yôm be understood as an indefinite and lengthy period of time, from a syntactical standpoint (nor from a lexicographical standpoint either). To do so would require a genitival relationship, used in construct with other nouns. There are two uses of this type of syntactical relationship: one, a specific day in time (Lev. 23:27-8; Judg. 13:7; Eccl. 7:1; numerous others); and two: what could be understood as an undefined period of time: day of battle (1 Sam. 13:22; Job 38:23), day of calamity (Deut. 32:35; Prov. 27:10), day of vengeance (Prov. 6:34; Isa. 34:8), day of prosperity (Eccl. 7:14), day of gladness of heart (S. of S. 3:11 = wedding day), day of the Lord (Joel 1:15, 2:1), day of salvation (Isa. 49:8), others (but see 2 Kings 7:9 and 19:3). As in the singular, the plural of yôm (yāmîm) offers further development as in the days of the Philistines, the days of Noah, the days of Uzziah, the days of Ahasuerus, the days of Josiah, etc. The "days" of one's life are normally also expressed in years

(Gen. 35:28, 47:9; Ps. 90:10).

The point is that at no place in Gen. 1:1–2:4 does this type of construct relationship exist involving the use of yôm. In fact, "day" and "days" are never used elsewhere in the Hebrew Bible in any syntactical construction with the sense of multiple thousands or millions of years, i.e, the time required for evolution to take place. [yôm]

1:7 And it was so (wayhî-kēn)—This phrase (also 1:9, 11, 15, 24) is found outside of Genesis only in Judges 6:38 and 2 Kings 15:12. In the latter two examples, the statement is offered to suggest completeness. In the first, the fleece of Gideon was found exactly as he had proposed. In the second, an earlier stated prophecy is said to have been completed. A similar idea of completion is found throughout Gen. 1 in the repetitive cycle of God's decree, fulfillment, the assessment of being good, and expression of limited time passage. That the expression wayhî-kēn indicates completion in the context of Gen. 1 is also supported by Ps. 33:8-9. [kēn]

1:11 According to their various <u>kinds</u> (lě mînô)—The singular form is used collectively for this term that seems to indicate certain similarities that set one group off from another as distinct. The recently coined term baraminology, in vogue among creation scientists, is a hybridization of the Hebrew bārā' with the present term mîn, and is the study of "created kinds" as distinct from the older taxonomy of "genus, species," etc. (cf. Pete J. Williams, "What Does min Mean? CENTech Journal 11:3 [1997]:344-52). [mîn]

1:14 Let them be <u>for signs</u> (le'ōtōt)—Though the word is seen in the near context of Gen. 4:15 referring to the mark of Cain, its normal use and its connection here with the term *mō'ēd* ("season") seem to lean toward the meaning of "signs, miracles, as pledges or attestations of divine presence and interposition" as part of the purpose of the sun, moon, and stars (*BDB*, 16; cf. Exod. 4:8; Ps. 65:8 etc.). One immediately thinks of this use in the long day of Josh. 10, the shadow of Hezekiah's steps in 2 Kings 20, and the star of Balaam's prophecy fulfilled at Bethlehem (Num. 24:17 with Matt. 2:2), as well as the apocalyptic prophecies of the book of Revelation. [*'ōt*]

1:20 Living creatures (*nepeš ḥayyâ*)—The first term by itself often indicates the life of individual men and animals, as contrasted with death or the loss of *nepeš* (Exod. 21:23, Deut. 19:21; 2 Sam. 23:17). It can also refer alone to the total individual person (Gen. 49:6; Lam. 3:24; Ps. 25:13). Distinct in the mind of the Hebrews from the vegetation created on day three (Ross, *Creation and Blessing*, 111), the two terms juxtaposed together refer almost always to animal life (so *BDB*, 312). Man, called by these two terms together only in Gen. 2:7, is also distinct from the rest of the animal world by his possession of the *nĕšāmâ* breathed into him by God and by his designation as the representative of God who has dominion over the creation (see discussions below). [*nepeš, ḥayyâ*]

1:26 Let us make (*na'ăśeh*)—Much should not be made over the use of *'śh* in this passage as exegetically differing from *br'*. One must notice the statement in 1:27 that includes *br'* and the similar use of *'śh* in 1:31 and in 2:2-3 to describe the creative work of God *in toto*. Another question arises for many in the use of the first person plural cohortative. It is easy to understand a cohortative of resolve rather than request (à la the jussives of command

throughout the passage), but the plural seems intrusive. Ross refers to it as "either a plural of majesty or a potential plural, expressing the wealth of potentials in the divine being" (Ross, *Creation and Blessing*, 112). [*'śh*]

Man (*'ādām*)—This term, etymologically related to *'ădāmâ*, "ground" is the term used in this case to refer to mankind collectively (also in Gen. 6:1-7; 9:5-6). It is also the term for individual men in numerous places; at various times man is depicted as subject to death (Num. 16:29), as sinful (1 Kings 8:46), and as warriors (Isa. 22:6). It is of course the name given to the first male, the representative of all of humanity. [*'ādām*]

In our image (*bĕṣalmēnû*)—This term normally refers to the physical representations of idols worshipped in the Ancient Near Eastern world (Num. 33:52; 2 Kings 11:18; Amos 5:26), with especial significance in Dan. 2:31-35 and 3:1-18, the latter of which represents the image of Nabu, the god of King Nebuchadnezzar. Its sense in Gen. 1 seems to be emphasizing that man is to be God's representatives on earth exercising dominion over the creation. The major difference between man as the *ṣelem* of God and the idols as the *ṣelem* of false gods is that living man reflects living God, whereas lifeless idols represent lifeless nonentities. [*ṣelem*]

According to our likeness (*kidmûtēnû*)—The difference appears to be that *ṣelem* serves as the indicator of a representative, whereas *dĕmût* refers more to a comparative likeness (*BDB*). Many Ancient Near Eastern deities were easily distinguishable by their images that depicted physical characteristics particular to their alleged activities. The intention here was that mankind was to reflect certain of the activities of the living God. [*dĕmût*]

Let them rule (*wĕyirdû*)—The word *rule* is found in other contexts to indicate a rule over enemies (Lev. 26:17; Ezek. 34:4), or an improperly established rule (Jer. 5:31), but it can also mean a dominion rightly established by God (Ps. 49:14; 110:2; 1 Kings 4:24; Isa. 41:2). The divinely established purpose of mankind then as the image and likeness of God was to exercise authority over the created order as God's representatives. [*rdh*]

1:28 God blessed them (*waybārek*)—Appearing first in 1:22 with reference to the animal fecundity in order to increase their numbers, 1:28 repeats that same blessing for man, adding to it the command to subdue the earth in keeping with his divine purposes that mankind have dominion over the created order. God's blessing makes possible the accomplishment of that purpose. "That which is blessed functions and produces at the optimum level, fulfilling its divinely designated purpose" (M. Brown, *NIDOTTE*, 1:759). [*brk*]

2:1 In all their vast array (*wĕkol-ṣebā'ām*)—The term *ṣābā'* normally refers to armies in the OT (Gen. 26:26; Exod. 6:26; Num. 1:3; Josh. 5:14; Judg. 4:7), most notably in the phrase "Lord of Hosts," which is probably a reference to God's sovereignty over all armies, earthly and heavenly (1 Sam. 1:11; 2 Sam. 7:26-7; Ps. 24:10; Isa. 44:6). In the context of Gen. 1 the term probably refers to the constituent parts of the universe, expressed by the merism "heavens and earth," although one cannot rule out the possibility that this also includes the hosts of the unseen world as well. [*ṣābā'*]

2:2 On the seventh day he rested (*wayyišbōt*)—The verbal root forms the basis for the noun "Sabbath" (*šabbāt*),

which for Israel extends from Friday evening at sundown until sundown Saturday. This fact is based on the pattern established in Gen. 1 for a day in the phrase "and there was evening and there was morning, the *x*th day." The term "to rest" in the basic stem may be understood as "to cease" as in a finality to an action or event (Isa. 24:8; Josh. 5:12; Ezek. 12:23; Ps. 46:9). It does not intimate a stoppage of all activity as it can in the causative stem (*BDB*, 992). The point of this passage is that on the seventh day God stopped doing creative activity as revealed in chapter 1 It does not mean that he ceased other divine activities, nor does it mean that the seventh day lasted any longer than the other six days. [*šbt*]

2:3 Made it holy (*wayqaddēš*)—The verb indicates a setting apart for God's purposes, a sanctificat ion as it were. It is a denominative use of the Piel stem based on the adjective that means "holy." Places, persons, angels, times, altars and sacrifices could all be consecrated or dedicated as holy (*BDB*, 871). It was because of the specialness of the seventh day that Israel was likewise to sanctify the day unto God (Exod. 20:8). [*qdš*]

2:4 This is the account (*tôlĕdôt*)—From the verbal root that means to beget, to bring forth or to give birth (*BDB*, 410) comes this noun that is translated "generations" in many versions. It is normally the accounting of what happened over time to the descendancy or progeny of given persons. The phrase serves as the major marker of division within the book, occurring in this form some 10 times (2:4; 5:1; 6:9; 10:1; 11:10; 11:27; 25:12; 25:19; 36:1,9; 37:20). This verse differs only in that it indicates that what follows in chapters 2–4 is an account of what happened to people who were made from the dust of the ground (i.e., what the earth "brought forth" as it were; cf. 2:7). [*tôledôt*]

The LORD God (*yhwh*)—The first mention of the personal name for God in the Bible identifies him as the God who created all things in 1:1–2:4a (cf. Isa. 45:7, 8, 18; Ps. 33:6-9; 148:5). The name itself is thought by many to be etymologically related to the verb "to be" (cf. Exod. 3:14-15). Some have seen in this either his self-existence, or the aspect that he is the author of being (life).

It is most appropriate, since the personal name YHWH carries with it the connotation of relationship of God with his people, that the name appear in this chapter that offers specifics on the creation of man and woman (Umberto Cassuto, *The Documentary Hypothesis*, 31-33). He is revealed as the maker of covenant with Abraham, Isaac, and Jacob (Gen. 15:18; Deut. 4:31), with Israel (Exod. 24:7-8; Lev. 26:9; Deut. 29:1), with David (2 Sam. 23:2, 5; cf. 7:1-17), as well as the New Covenant with the reunited Israel (Jer. 31:31-33).

Relationship with people is also seen in terms that combine the Tetragrammaton with some aspect of his care for his people. He provided a sacrificial ram in place of Isaac, so Abraham called that site *yhwh yir'eh*, the LORD will provide (Gen. 22:14). Moses built an altar, naming it *yhwh nissî* ("The Lord is my banner") in Exod. 17:15 to commemorate the promise God made to blot out the enemy Amalekites. For Gideon, he is *yhwh šālôm*, the LORD of Peace who offered him peace (Judg. 6:24). For Jerusalem, he will someday be *yhwh ṣidqēnû*, the LORD our righteousness (Jer. 33:16) and *yhwh šāmmâ*, the LORD who is there (Ezek. 48:35). For Israel as a nation, he is *yhwh mĕqaddiškem*, the LORD who sanctifies you (Exod. 31:13).

It is probably appropriate to note here that the LXX translates *yhwh* normally as *kyrios*, giving OT significance to the NT statement that Jesus is Lord (John 13:13; Rom. 10:9; Phil. 2:11) as well as to the self-affirmation of Jesus in John 8:58: "Before Abraham was, I AM," understood by the Pharisees as his claim to deity (by way of Exod. 3:14). [*yhwh*]

2:5 No plant of the field (*'ēśeb haśśādeh*)—Over the centuries, this verse has caused numerous individuals to stumble, since 1:11 seems to indicate that vegetation was created on day three and this verse seems to indicate that they did not appear until man's appearance, affirmed in 1:26ff terms as having occurred on day six. However, one must note the terms employed in both contexts. In chapter 1, the plants were perennial (bearing seed within them). In chapter 2, these plants are annual, in need both of rain and the cultivation efforts of man in order to produce. [*'ēśeb, śādeh*]

Had not yet sent rain (*lō' himṭîr*)—The causative verb is related to a common noun for rain and may foreshadow the Flood of Noah in chapters 6–8. In other contexts, appropriate rain is symbolic of God's blessing (Deut. 11:14; 28:12; Ps. 147:8), but its untimeliness, overabundance, or absence may be indicators of God's judgment (1 Sam. 12:17; Isa. 5:6; Ezek. 38:22). [*mṭr*]

To work (*la'ăbōd*)—The term is full of significance in other Pentateuch contexts inasmuch as it is often used to express service to God (Exod. 23:25; Num. 4:23; 18:23; Deut. 11:13) and thus may foreshadow that activity later to be emphasized. It was the express purpose of God for Adam that he "work" the Garden (cf. 2:15), thus in the process serving God in the capacity of worker and keeper. Without this intervention of man, cultivated crops would not have been. [*'bd*]

The ground (*ha'ădāmâ*)—The ground, from which Adam was to be created (2:7), and etymologically related to the word Adam (*BDB; TWOT,* 1:10), was that which was to be worked by man in his service to God (2:5; 2:15). As such, this may also foreshadow the covenant relationship between God and Israel in that part of the Mosaic Covenant involved both the gift of the ground by God to Israel and the working of that ground to produce offerings to God (M. Grisanti, *NIDOTTE,* 1:272-73). [*'ădāmâ*]

2:6 But streams came up (*wĕ'ēd ya'ăleh*)— The problem created by the mention of no rain in 2:5 is resolved by the watering system then present. The earth was then watered by "streams" (and by rivers in 2:10). The term is unusual, and translated as "springs" by the LXX. Its only other biblical occurrence is in Job 36:27 in synonymous parallelism with clouds, suggesting a meaning of "mist" or "vapor" in that context and perhaps here as well. [*'ēd*]

2:7 The Lord God formed the man (*wayyîṣer*)—The word suggests the masterful purpose of a potter skillfully designing a vessel with specific purposes. The active participle is often used substantively as "potter" (Jer. 18:2, 6; Zech. 11:13). Israel was formed to be the people of God (Isa. 43:21). The earth was formed to be inhabited (Isa. 45:18). God remains involved in the forming of the individual in the womb (Isa. 44:2; 49:5). It is highly significant that the verb appears in the passive stem (Pual) in Ps. 139:16 where David affirms that even the days of his life were formed for him before they took place. In this passage, God is intimately and personally involved with making man with specific purpose and design. [*yṣr*]

From the dust from the ground (*'āpār*)—Appearing independently, the noun serves as an adverbial accusative of material. Dust is never associated with great value in Scripture. It is often associated with death (Gen. 3:19; Ps. 22:15; 30:9; 104:29; Dan. 12:2). God is ever mindful that we are but dust (Ps. 103:14). Without the intervening activity of God, man has little value and no life. Dust is just the medium of the Master Sculptor, molded according to his purposes. [*'āpār*]

The breath of life (*nišmat*)—That which separates man from the rest of the animal kingdom is both the image of God and the "breath" of life (*nĕšāmâ*—the form in the text is in construct) imparted by God (Ross, *Creation and Blessing,* 123). It is this same "breath" from God that gives man understanding (Job 32:8), and enables a conscience within him that is open to the scrutiny of God (Prov. 20:27). [*nĕšāmâ*]

2:9 The tree of life (*wĕ'ēṣ haḥayyîm*)—The tree of life is that which ostensibly provided sustenance for continued existence. It was this tree that was to be guarded after the Fall to keep man from taking its fruit and living "forever" (3:22). One does not know if one bite of its fruit would have yielded continued physical existence forever, or if it would have been necessary to continually eat from it to produce those same results.

Either way, it was to be no longer accessible after the Fall. Metaphorically, the phrase is used in Prov. 3:18 and 11:30 referring to obtaining wisdom and living righteously respectively, but it is not used in the same sense as Gen. 2–3 again until the end times when the tree is found in the heavenly New Jerusalem (Rev. 2:7; 22:2, 14, 19). [*ḥayyîm*]

The tree of <u>the knowledge</u> (*hadda'at*)— The tree of life brings life to those who eat from it, but this is the tree that is forbidden (2:17). The noun comes from a verbal root that in Genesis often suggests intimate experiential knowledge (Gen. 4:1; 19:8; 22:12), and is a synonymously parallel term for wisdom in the book of Proverbs (i.e., that gained by experience: Prov. 2:6, 10; 3:19-20; cf. Exod. 35:31). It was this complete experiential knowledge, particularly of evil, that was to be avoided. [*da'at*]

Good and evil (*ṭôb wārā'*)—The contrasting extremes should be regarded as merism here, meaning the knowledge of all things. Since the knowledge of all things is a prerogative held only by God (3:5, 22), it was forbidden for man to eat from this tree (2:17). That which is good "indicates a state or function appropriate to genre, purpose or situation" (Robert P. Gordon, *NIDOTTE*, 2:353). Evil is likewise context sensitive, ranging from a saddened countenance (Neh. 2:2) to the wildness of animals (Lev. 26:6; Ezek. 5:17) to things of low quality (bad figs in Jer. 24:2; bad water in 2 Kings 2:19) to doing that which violates covenant with God (Deut. 4:25). The juxtaposed terms here probably focus on the moral aspects and consequences of goodness and evil as they appear to be also in Deut. 30:15 (good is connected with life while contrasting evil and death). Only by man's abstaining from the fruit of this tree could the creation continue as "very good" (1:31), reflecting the character of the Creator. By disobediently eating the fruit of this tree, man would experience evil personally, introducing death into the created order, rendering that order no longer good, and rendering evil the thoughts, heart, and practices of mankind (Gen. 6:5; 8:21; Jer. 7:24; 17:9; Prov. 8:13). [*ṭôb, ra'*]

2:15 To work it and <u>take care of it</u> (*ûlěšomrāh*)—This term, meaning "to watch" or "to keep" (*BDB*, 1036), is now joined with the verb "to work" (see 2:5 above). It too is frequently used in the Pentateuch with reference to observing and keeping God's law (Exod. 19:5; Lev. 22:31; Deut. 5:1). Perhaps foreshadowing the Law in the sense of preserving it, the thought in this passage is that man's service to God in the Garden was to preserve the Garden, best accomplished by obedience to the commands of God. Certainly, however, the basic tasks of husbandry would have been in view as well. One would do well to note that work was part of the responsibility of man before the Fall. [*šmr*]

2:16 Lord God <u>commanded</u> (*wayṣaw*)— Technically the only command employing the root *ṣwh* before the Fall (there are other roots used as imperative verbs in the blessing of God in Gen. 1:28), this term governs both a freedom and a prohibition. Though man may eat freely of any other tree of the Garden, man must not eat the fruit of the tree of the knowledge of good and evil (2:17). The verb serves as the basis for the common noun *miṣwâ*, commandment (hence the later term Bar Mitzvah, "son of the commandment"), and therefore foreshadows ubiquitous usage in the remainder of the Pentateuch regarding the commandments of God (Lev. 26:3; Num. 36:13; Deut. 6:25). [*ṣwh*]

2:17 <u>When you eat from it</u> (*běyôm 'ăkolkā mimmenû*)—Literally "in the day of your eating from it." The NIV has correctly rendered the nuance of the prepositional phrase "in the day" as the temporal adverb "when" governing the infinitive construct "of your eating" (D. Fouts, "How Short an

Evening and Morning: Response Two" *CENTech Journal* 11:3 [1997]:303). [*běyôm*]

You will surely die (*môt tāmût*)— Traditionally, the infinitive absolute *môt* has been understood as adding sureness to the event of death: "you will certainly die." It is true that this is a normal usage of the infinitive absolute. However, it may be that in this case, "dying you will die" would be a better understanding. That which occurs in Gen. 3 offers the paradigm inasmuch as separation from God would occur instantly (spiritual death) and decay would begin in the human body, eventually resulting in physical death as well. The root is seen often in other Ancient Near Eastern literature, especially in the nominal form representing the pagan deity Môt. [*mwt*]

2:18 It is <u>not good</u> (*lō'-ṭôb*)—Before the creation could be declared "very good" by God in 1:31, man needed woman to complete the concept of the image of God. Both are needed as representatives of God exercising dominion over the created order. Alone and by himself, man is incomplete, and thus unable to fulfill the task that God had given him. [*ṭôb*]

Helper (*'ēzer*)—One must be careful not to think in terms of a servant here, because God is also named a helper of man (Ps. 33:20; 46:1; 63:7). The verbal term seems to lean toward the idea of assisting someone who has a significant need (help in the conquest in Josh. 1:14; David's mighty men offered him help in 1 Chron. 12:21), often involving someone in danger (Josh. 10:6; Ps. 79:8-9). Man is not in significant danger in Gen. 1, and he has no need for a helper to name the animals (1:19-20). But he does have the more significant task of working and keeping the Garden. A woman is to assist the man in accomplishing that

which God has given him to do. Together, man and woman are able to serve God by keeping the Garden, representing him as his image to the created order. Together, and complete, the created order is "very good" (1:31). [*'ēzer*]

Suitable for him (*kěnegdô*)—The term involves a preposition (*neged*) normally indicating that which is in front of, or opposite. Here, the idea seems to be that a correspondence to the man is needed. Of all the animals observed and named by the man, none was found to be corresponding to him (2:20). Another human opposite to Adam was needed. One who could make up what he lacked, one who could find supply in what he could offer, was needed. Like him in humanness, this one was needed to make him complete, needed to rectify the "not good" existence of being alone in attempting to meet his responsibilities before God. [*neged*]

2:21 One <u>of the man's ribs</u> (*miṣṣal'ōtāyw*)— The term *ṣēlā'* normally involves the side of an object, as in the sides of the ark of the covenant (Exod. 25:12, 14) or the inside chambers of the temple of Solomon (1 Kings 6:5) or the framework of the eschatological temple of Ezek. 41. Certainly the term involves some of the supporting side structures of Adam's body, so perhaps more tissue than just a rib was taken, a suggestion supported by the man's statement in 2:23. [*ṣēlā'*]

2:22 The LORD God <u>made</u> a woman (*wayyiben*)—The root (*bnh*) finds cognates in several Semitic languages. In Assyrian, *banû* means to build or create, as does *bny* in Ugaritic, so perhaps it functions here as a simple synonym of *br'*. Yet, the term is often used in other contexts for building from existing materials (Gen. 11:4; 1 Kings 9:17; Neh. 2:17), similar to the idea in this passage. "The process involves a purposeful master craftsman constructing a helper suitable for the man he had carefully formed (*yṣr*), using material from that man" (D. Fouts, *NIDOTTE*, 1:679). Woman therefore was crafted with architectural precision, design, and purpose. [*bnh*]

2:23 This is now (*happa'am*)—The Hebrew word is derived from a word that involved repetition, such as a hoof beat or the repetitive striking of an anvil with a hammer. Hence, the meaning of an occurrence of regular intervals marking the passage of time arose. It can be used of a final attempt in a series of appeals (Gen. 18:32; Judg. 6:39), or of a one-time occurrence (Exod. 10:17). Its most frequent use seems to convey the idea of something finally occurring after a period of waiting (Gen. 29:34-35, 30:20b, 46:30; Judg. 16:18, 28), although it can also be used of a sudden discovery (Exod. 9:27; Judg. 15:3). The sense in this passage seems to combine nuances from these latter two ideas. [*pa'am*]

Woman (*'iššâ*)—Derived from a distinct root (*'nš*) rather than from the normal term for man (*'îš*), its presence here offers a paronomasia in the Hebrew text due to assonance. The root suggests that which is soft or delicate (*BDB*, 61), and the noun is often translated as "wife." She is therefore assigned the task by God to be a helper corresponding to the man, his wife, perhaps exhibiting those gentler qualities. She is to assist him in the responsibilities given by God, and to make up that which he lacks in accomplishing those tasks. [*'iššâ*]

2:24 A man will leave (*ya'ăzāb*)—The term means to leave or to forsake (*BDB*, 736). The point is that the man is to leave his parents solely for the purpose of becoming one flesh with his wife. It probably does not mean that he is to forsake them completely (cf. Exod. 20:12; 1 Tim. 5:8). He leaves the authority of their home to establish his own home. Other uses of the term include abandoning the Mosaic Covenant (Deut. 29:25; Dan. 11:30), specifically at times in the sense of breaking it (Deut. 31:16-17). Too, we can have confidence in a covenant-keeping God never to abandon or forsake those in covenant with him (Josh. 1:5; cf. Heb. 13:5). Ross offers that since the narrator is probably speaking rather than God, the imperfect verb should be translated as a characteristic present tense, explaining why a man leaves and cleaves (Ross, *Creation and Blessing*, 127). [*'zb*]

And be united (*wědābaq*)—The old term "cleave" though outdated, still conveys the very close physical contact that this word conveys. It is used of Ruth staying with Naomi (Ruth 1:14), of a tongue sticking to the roof of a mouth (Job 29:10; Ps. 22:15; Lam. 4:4), of staying close to an enemy in battle (1 Sam. 14:22; 31:2), and even staying close to the Lord (Josh. 23:8; 2 Kings 18:6). A nominal form (*debeq*) can refer to soldering (Isa. 41:7). The point of this joining together of man and woman is to achieve the oneness of flesh. [*dbq*]

One flesh (*lebāśār 'eḥād*)—An Assyrian cognate for flesh is the term *bišrû*, which means a blood relation (*BDB*, 142). The idea of oneness of flesh then seems to be that the man and the woman, though from differing families, become as close as blood relatives, thus making separation more difficult for both of them. It involves the physical love making ("the cleaving") which binds two people from differing backgrounds closely together. [*bāśār*]

2:25 Were both naked (*'ărûmmîm*)—The term clearly means to be without clothing. In post-Fall contexts, the root is often employed as a humiliating consequence of judgment (Deut. 28:48; Hos. 2:3; Amos 2:16), but in this context probably is metaphorical for pure innocence of the couple (they felt no shame). This is supported by the events of chapter 3 where after violating the command of God, the couple attempted to cover their nakedness. [*ărûmmîm*]

They felt no shame (*wĕlō' yitbōšāšû*)—On the very likely chance that the Ugaritic root *bṯṯ* is cognate to the Hebrew *bōš*, it has been suggested that the verb "denotes the feeling of rebuke when behavior exceeds the expected norms of conduct" (Philip J. Nel, *NIDOTTE*, 1:621). This aspect is well illustrated by Ezra 9:6, wherein Ezra confesses the sins and shame of Israel before God. The Hithpolel stem expresses a reciprocal nuance: the man and woman had no shame with one another. Concerning their state of innocence, Cassuto has written: "since they did not yet know good or evil, nor had they yet learned that sexual desire could also be directed towards *evil ends*, they had no cause to feel ashamed at the fact that they were naked; the feeling of shame in regard to anything is born only of the consciousness of the evil that may exist in that thing" (Umberto Cassuto, *Genesis 1*, 137). [*bwš*]

3:1 Now the serpent (*wĕhannāḥāš*)—Without introduction and without explanation, the serpent immediately appears in the text in antithesis to the LORD God. The serpent was well known to the hearers/readers of the account as he often represented the epitome of evil in the Ancient Near Eastern world. Other cultures viewed a serpent as present during primeval events, usually in a negative role. It is clear from the verse, however, that even the serpent that opposes the

Creator is himself a creature of that same God. [*nāḥāš*]

Was more crafty (*'ārûm*)—In the very short space between Gen. 2:24 and 3:1 is a word play contrasting the nakedness/innocence of the couple with the shrewdness/craftiness of the serpent. They are together both *'ărûmmîm* (naked) and the serpent is *'ārûm* (differing roots). The root used here can elsewhere be used in a positive sense (Prov. 14:8; 15:5; 22:3). Obviously, in context, its presence here is negative as it is in Job 15:5 and Ps. 83:3. [*'ārûm*]

3:2 You must not eat from any tree (*lō' tō'kĕlû mikkōl 'ēṣ*)—Instead of focusing on the freedom given in the commandment of God in 2:16-17 to eat freely from all of the trees save one in the garden, the serpent concentrates on the one tree forbidden. In the questioning of God's specific word on the subject, he thereby has questioned the goodness of God. [*kōl*]

3:3 God has said (*'āmar 'ĕlōhîm*)—The fact is that the initial prohibition was offered by the LORD God (*yhwh 'ĕlōhîm*) in 2:16-17. The woman in innocence apparently forgot the personal relationship with him in employing *'ĕlōhîm* alone in her response (as had the serpent in his questioning of God's word). [*'ĕlōhîm*]

Or you will die (*pen-tĕmutûn*)—Whereas God has said in 2:17, "you will surely die (*môt tāmût*)," the woman now introduces a modal nuance with the imperfect form of the verb *mût*: "lest you die" (the change in number from singular to plural is expected given the context). On the woman's paraphrasing of God's original words, Ross has written: "There is no violation in free paraphrasing of the words of the Lord. However, if the precise wording of the original commandment is weakened the appeal to sin grows stronger"

(Ross, *Creation and Blessing*, 135). [*pen*]

3:4 You will not surely die (*lō'-môt těmutûn*)—What began for the serpent as a questioning of God's command has now become an outright denial and with greater precise knowledge of that prohibition than had the woman. This is indicated by the serpent's employ of the exact phrasing used by God (infinitive absolute with specific future imperfect form) negated by "not." [*lô'*]

3:6 Pleasing to the eye (*ta'ăwâ*)—The phrase "connotes a physical beauty that evokes a desire that is less superficial" (William C. Williams, *NIDOTTE*, 1:305). The noun can mean a longing or desire that can have positive or negative nuances, depending on the context (Ps. 21:2; 106:14). The verbal form in the intensive stem (Piel) can reflect a lustful or covetous desire (Num. 11:4; Prov. 13:4). Many commentators offer that the temptation passage in Genesis forms the foundation for the comments of the Apostle John in 1 John 2:16: "lust of the flesh, *lust of the eyes*, and the boastful pride of life." However, one is also quick to point out that the woman existed in the state of innocence, and desires later understood to be sinful were not for her. This one command in the Garden she would break, but she had not done so yet. [*ta'ăwâ*]

Desirable (*wěnehmād*)—Like "pleasing" above, this verb in the passive stem can be understood as positive or negative depending on context. In the verbal stems, the nuance is most often negative (Prov. 1:22, Isa. 1:29; 44:9). In the nominal uses, the nuance is most often positively reflecting the value or costliness (hence, desirability) of something (2 Chron. 32:27; 36:10; Ezra 8:27; Jer. 3:19). In the immediate context, in view of God's command not to eat

from it, and in view of the serpent's temptation to the contrary, its desirability certainly generated negative results. [*nehmād*]

Gaining wisdom (*lěhaśkîl*)—The term is not the normally expected word translated "wisdom" (*hokmâ*), but is rather *śkl*, "be prudent" (*BDB*, 968), although it is found at times synonymously parallel with the former term (Ps. 111:10). It is a word that is often associated with the learning process. At times it is used synonymously paralleled or paired with the term for knowledge (as in the tree of knowledge) or its synonyms (*da'at* Job 34:35; cf. *dē'â* in Jer. 3:15; *maddā'* in Dan. 1:17). Obtaining this prudence is quite often seen as having positive results (Prov. 1:3; 16:23; 1 Sam. 18:5). Too, it is later seen as a gracious gift of God (2 Chron. 30:22; Dan. 9:22; Neh. 9:20). One may think therefore that the woman interpreted the tree of knowledge of good and evil as that which would benefit her in the learning process, with positive results. Unfortunately, though that benefit may have come eventually by God's grace, she short-circuited the process by taking the fruit for herself and giving it to her husband. [*śkl*]

Who was with her (*'immāh*)—The lexicon by *BDB* (768x) offers a definition of the preposition as "close to, beside" when dealing with the locality of a person (cf. Deut. 5:31; 1 Sam. 1:26), though at least at times it can refer to near proximity (Gen. 25:11; 35:4). Since they had not yet left the Garden, Adam was not far away when the woman partook of the fruit. He was with her. [*'im*]

3:7 Coverings (*hăgōrōt*)—The nominal form probably is limited in this context to coverings of the privates. It is used elsewhere in nominal and adjectival forms to refer to a part of a woman's dress (Isa.

3:24), to a belt of a warrior (1 Kings 2:5), and to a waist cloth (Ezek. 23:15). Likewise, the verbal form is used in the common expressions "to gird up one's loins" (2 Kings 4:29) and "to gird on sackcloth" (Isa. 15:3; Ezek. 27:31; Joel 1:8). The point of the passage is that now that they know their nakedness they are ashamed. They seek to remedy the situation with materials at hand, rather than seeking a remedy from the One to whom they were accountable. [ḥăgōrâ]

3:12 The woman you put here with me (nātattâ)—The verbal term Adam employs indicates his awareness that the woman was a gift (ntn—to give; cf. Gen. 1:29) from God, but the second person singular form may indicate that he was shifting the blame for his disobedience to both the woman and to God. [ntn]

3:13 The serpent deceived me (hiššî'anî)—The vocalization of this term seems to be onomatopoeic, reflecting the hissing of the serpent. As the man had passed blame to the woman and implicated God in the process, so also the woman passes blame to the serpent. One might add that since God created the serpent, she also was implicating the Maker in her failure. The verbal root always indicates a beguiling or a deceiving (BDB, 674). In Jer. 4:10, the prophet accuses God of deceiving his people and later (Jer. 29:8) records God's warning against the deceptions of false prophets. Judah is challenged to fall neither to the (alleged) deceptions of King Hezekiah nor to those of God (2 Kings 18:29; 19:10). One's heart can also be deceiving (Obad. 3; cf. with 'āqōb in Jer. 17:9). [nš']

3:14 Cursed are you ('ārûr 'attâ)—Whereas formerly the serpent had been more crafty

('arûm) than all the beasts of the field, now he would be more cursed ('ārûr: passive participle from 'rr) than that same group. The irony displayed by the play on words cannot be missed. Whereas the blessing of God is a pronouncement that results in good and life, the curse of God is a pronouncement that results in evil and death. The root of the verb "to curse" is often used in tandem with the root of the verb "to bless" and always displays the contrastive idea (Gen. 12:3; 27:29; Num. 22:6; Mal. 2:2; cf. the listing of the blessings and curses in Deut. 27–28). One could note also the strong contrast between these words and the common Jewish expression bārûk 'attâ yhwh 'ĕlōhēnû (Blessed are you, LORD our God). ['rr]

3:15 I will put enmity (wĕ'êbâ)—The root of this term also serves as the basis for the common Hebrew word for enemy ('ōyēb: Exodus 15:6; Lev. 26:7; Josh. 10:13) and may, as thought by some, also serve as the basis for the name of Job ('iyyōb: an object of enmity—BDB). In this form, the noun occurs only four other times in the OT. In three of these, physical violence is part of the strife (Num. 35:21; Ezek. 25:15; 35:5). The fourth expresses a case where violence is present, but enmity is not (Num. 35:22). This phrase could explain mankind's general revulsion of reptiles and may foreshadow the hostility of the Jewish religious leaders against Jesus the Messiah (cf. John 8:42-47). ['êbâ]

   Between your offspring and hers (ûbēn zar'ăkā ûbēn zar'āh)—The noun is common in the OT as representing descendancy (Gen. 9:9; 12:7; 16:10; 1 Sam. 1:11; Ps. 37:25). Of great significance as applied to the seed of Abraham by the Apostle Paul in Gal. 3:16, the term here has been taken as the progeny of the serpent and the ultimate descendant of the woman; i.e., Christ.

Hence this verse has been called the *proto evangelium*, the first gospel. [*zera'*]

He will crush your head (*hû' yĕšûpĕkā rō'š*)—The verb *šwp* indicates a darkening of some kind. In Job 9:17, the verb is paralleled synonymously with the phrase "multiply bruises" (*peṣa'*), suggesting that this is the darkening of the flesh after being wounded. In Ps. 139:11, darkness is said to hide (*šûp*) the psalmist (i.e., making him dark as well by covering him). The significance for the serpent is that the ultimate seed of the woman (emphatic *hû'*) will with his heel bruise the head of the serpent, in all likelihood a fatal blow. In the process, though, the serpent will succeed at inflicting a fatal wound on that man (NIV: and you will strike his heel). [*šwp*]

3:16 Your pains in childbearing (*'iṣṣĕbônēk wĕhērōnēk*)—Literally "your labor and your conception" but understood to be a hendiadys as the NIV has translated it. The first noun is from a verbal root that means "to pain" or "to grieve" (*BDB*, 781), and the derivative nouns deal with sorrow and labor (Ps. 127:2; Prov. 10:22). This specific form *'iṣṣābôn* is seen also in 3:17 and only once again in 5:29 where it refers both times to the labor of work. Perhaps the labor of childbirth was to be increased to the point of pain as a result of the woman's participation in disobedience. More painful labor will be involved for both of those who willingly chose to disobey God's command (cf. 3:17). The second noun, *hērāyôn*, is derived from the verb "to become pregnant" (*BDB*, 248). It is thought that the noun functions in the abstract sense of conception, as it is used that way also in Hos. 9:11 and Ruth 4:13. As such, it should be understood in this verse as a metonymy of cause ("the conception") put for the effect (both child-birth and childrearing). [*'iṣṣĕbôn, hērāyôn*]

Your desire (*tĕšûqātēk*)—This noun is found only in three places in the OT. In Song of Songs 7:10 it seems to indicate physical desire, and that may be nuanced in this passage. However, the nearer context of Gen. 4:7 seems to be the most illustrative. In that context, God tells Cain that sin is crouching (*rōbēṣ*: like a lion Gen. 49:9; Ps. 104:22) at the door, and its desire is for Cain, but Cain is to master it (*mšl*) instead. This suggests that there is a desire for mastery on the part of the woman over the man, perhaps by means of sexuality. This view is supported by the antithetical concept of the next line, wherein the man will instead rule (*mšl*) over her. [*tĕšûqâ*]

He will rule over you (*wĕhû' yimšol-bāk*)—The verb is a verb of mastery. It is used in Gen. 24:2 in reference to the chief steward of Abraham's household. Sometimes the rule is harsh (Judg. 14:4; Neh. 9:37; Prov. 22:7; Isa. 19:4), at other times the rule is inappropriate or the result of judgment (Isa. 3:4, 12; Lam. 5:8). It is clear that God is the ruler over all of his creation (Ps. 22:28; 66:7; 89:9), and that man is appropriately the ruler of that over which God intended him to exercise dominion (Ps. 8:6). Now, as a result of the woman's participation in the disobedience to God, she must labor harder with children and be in subjection to her husband. [*mšl*]

3:17 Because you listened to your wife (*kî šāma'tā lĕqôl 'ištĕkâ*)—Though commonly "listen to the voice" is understood idiomatically in the OT for obedience (Gen. 22:18; Deut. 4:30; 30:8; 1 Sam. 12:14), this prepositional phrase is best thought of as circumstance attendant to the main verb of eating from the forbidden tree. In other words, the man is judged for disobediently eating the fruit, not for listening to the voice of his wife. The contrast is striking though: by obeying his wife, the man had disobeyed his Creator. [*šmʿ*]

3:19 To dust you shall return (*wĕʾel-ʾāpār*)—The material from which man was formed in 2:7 will be that which receives him as a tomb (cf. Ps. 104:29; Eccl. 3:20). One will also note that dust was to be the food of the serpent (3:14), perhaps metaphorically foreshadowing the deleterious effects the tempter would have on mankind (although many would see simply an expression of abject humility of the defeated; cf. Ps. 72:9; Mic. 7:17). [*ʾāpār*]

3:20 Adam named his wife (*wayyiqrāʾ hāʾādām šēm ʾištô*)—Adam had named the animals brought to him by God in 2:19-20, an event that Cassuto says showed his lordship and dominion over them (Cassuto, *Genesis 1*, 130). Now in turn and only after the Fall into sin, Adam names his wife Eve (related to the word for life), demonstrating (along with the verb *mšl* in 3:16) his dominion over her. Such naming indicating dominion is seen also in Num. 32:38 and 2 Kings 23:34, as well as Gen. 1:5, 8, 10 wherein God names day and night, heaven and earth. [*qrʾ*]

3:22 And live forever (*wāḥay lĕʾōlām*)—Assuming that the initial form is a perfect tense (double geminate root: *ḥyy*), it must be understood with the *waw* consecutive after the jussive phrase *pen-yišlaḥ yādô* "lest he send forth his hand" (NIV: "he must not be allowed to reach out his hand") and translated with a potential nuance: "and be able to live." The noun *ʿōlām* can refer to people, objects, and events of the ancient past (Gen. 49:26; Ps. 24:7; Isa. 44:7; 63:9). It can also refer to the continual existence, or perpetuity, of people, places, and events (Eccl. 1:4; Isa. 25:2;

Ps. 148:6) and of God, his attributes, or his covenants (Isa. 40:28; Deut. 32:40; Ps. 136:1ff; Gen. 9:16; Isa. 55:3). The first appearance of the term commonly translated "forever" in Scripture occurs joined with the potential of life. Normally to express eternity the noun would appear in an intensified plural. However, there are places where the singular suffices (Ps. 90:2; Isa. 9:6; Mic. 4:7). Since such extreme safeguards were made to keep man from eating the fruit of the tree of life, one may think that the ideas of perpetuity or eternity are in view. [*ḥyy, ʿōlām*]

3:24 The cherubim (*hakkĕrubîm*)—Most often associated with the decorations of the ark of the covenant in the tabernacle (Exod. 25:18-22; 2 Sam. 6:2) or the first temple (1 Kings 6:23-35), these creatures obviously both represent God's presence and serve him by blocking the way to the tree of life (at least until the Flood). They are described in Ezek. 10 as having four faces (man, cherub, eagle, lion), having four wings (as distinct from the seraphim of Isa. 6), and having many eyes. Together with the flaming sword that was in continual motion, they would have been quite successful at keeping people away from the Garden. [*kĕrûb*]

4:1 Adam lay with his wife (*wĕhāʾādām yādaʿ ʾet-ḥawwâ ʾištô*)—As it was in the case in the discussion above on knowledge in Gen. 2:9, the verbal root *ydʿ* suggests a completeness of knowledge in a given area, with emphasis on experience. In this case, Adam's knowing of Eve resulted in her conceiving a child. It is used in this sense of sexual intimacy elsewhere in Scripture (Gen. 19:8; 24:16; Num. 31:18, 35; Judg. 11:39). As such, one may understand the term in such contexts as a euphemism. [*ydʿ*]

4:3 As an offering to the LORD (*minḥâ layhwh*)—The basic idea of the term seems to be that of a gift (Gen. 32:13, 20), at times involving political tribute (Judg. 3:15; 1 Kings 4:21; 2 Kings 17:3). This first occurrence of this word in Scripture seems to imply that the LORD God had imparted some revelation concerning fellowship with him after the Fall. Perhaps founded on his actions in 3:21 of sacrificing animals in order to cover the nakedness/shame of the man and woman, an offering (*minḥâ*) was now necessary to approach God. Certainly this is consistent with later Mosaic Law where the term serves as the main term for grain (or meal) offering (Lev. 2:1-14; Num. 4:16; Josh. 22:23, etc.), though at least in this case both the offerings of the brothers are named *minḥâ* (cf. 4:4). [*minḥâ*]

4:4 Abel brought fat portions (*ûmēḥelbēhen*)—Commonly seen in Lev. 3 with reference to peace offerings, the fat of those offerings represented the best of the meat (cf. Deut. 32:14; Ps. 63:5). This superlative idea is supported inasmuch as the term is often juxtaposed with the terms *šemen* (oil), *yayin* (wine), *dāgān* (corn), and *ḥiṭṭâ* (wheat) always representing the best of those crops (Num. 18:12, 29-30; Ps. 81:16). The fat portions of the meat sacrifices were reserved for God and were not to be eaten by man (Lev. 3:16-17). [*ḥēleb*]

Firstborn of his flock (*mibbĕkōrôt*)—Abel presented the best part from among the best animals he had: the first born of the flock that season. The term is seen elsewhere with the same sense in Deut. 12:6, 17 and 14:23. Though the form is a feminine plural, *BDB* (114) reads an irregular plural of *bĕkôr* rather than the expected *bĕkôrâ*, which means "birthright" (Gen. 25:31-34). The contrast between Cain and Abel was not that the offerings themselves were not expected; Abel's was the best he had to offer, Cain's was out of his surplus (4:3: "some of the fruits of the soil"). [*bekôrâ*]

4:7 Will you not be accepted? (*hălô' im-têṭîb śĕ'ēt*)—Literally: "Is it not that if you do well, a lifting up." God had not looked at Cain's offering (*šā'â* in 4:5). Unable to establish fellowship with his maker by haphazardly offering an unacceptable sacrifice, Cain's countenance had fallen with anger. God affirms that a chance remains for that fellowship if he will do well (*'im-têṭîb*); this chance is expressed by the noun *śĕ'ēt*. The root means "to lift up" and is common Semitic. This rarely occurring noun is used of the excellency of God (Job 13:11; 31:23), the honor given to Jacob's firstborn Reuben (Gen. 49:3), and even to the rising of a boil on the flesh (Lev. 13:2, 10). It may be illustrated in part by the use of the verbal root in the great priestly blessing of Num. 6:24-26. [*śe'ēt*]

Sin (*ḥaṭṭā't*)—The alternative to Cain's doing well with resulting fellowship and honor is that sin is waiting to attack. The noun, first appearing here in the Scripture, is common. Its root meaning is well illustrated by the verbal form in Judges 20:16 where the 700 left-handed men of Benjamin could sling a stone at a hair and not miss (*lō' yaḥăṭi'*). Sin is therefore an act that misses the target God has established. Though men are told to repent from sin (1 Kings 8:35), and turn aside from it (2 Kings 10:31), there is none who is able to avoid sin completely (1 Kings 8:46; Prov. 20:9; Eccl. 7:20). Though God will punish sin (Exod. 32:34; cf. Hosea 13:12), he will forgive, pardon, and remove it when confessed and atoned for (Ps. 32:5; 1 Kings 8:36; Isa. 27:9). He is able to blot it out (Isa. 44:22) and to remember it no more (Isa. 43:25). [*ḥaṭṭā't*]

Is crouching at the door (*rōbēṣ*)—The warning for Cain is that an honorable lifting up may occur if he does well, but the alternative is that sin is lying at the door. The term almost always deals with some type of animal in a reclined position, either at rest or preparatory to attack (Gen. 49:9; Isa. 13:21; Ezek. 29:3). Either way, by a lowered position, sin will keep Cain from the honor (the lifting up) and fellowship with God. This is the desire (*tĕšûqâ*) of sin personified appropriately as the member of the animal kingdom, most recently represented by the serpent. Cain is warned to master it; that is, exercise dominion over it (*mšl*). [*rbṣ*]

4:8 And killed him (*wayyahargēhû*)—There are a number of terms throughout the Semitic languages that describe killing. This particular root almost always involves violence and often with bloodshed in the process. At times a sword is used as in battle (Num. 31:8; 2 Sam. 12:9; Ezek. 26:8). At times it involves the improper killing of animals (Isa. 22:13) or the violent destruction of plants (Ps. 78:47). The nominal forms suggest slaughter (*hereg* in Isa. 30:25; *hārēgâ* in Jer. 19:6). That Cain's murder of Abel was violent is also revealed in that his blood was shed (4:10). [*hrg*]

4:10 Your brother's blood (*dĕmê 'āḥîkā*)—The normal term for blood in the OT is *dām* in the singular (1 Kings 22:35; Prov. 30:33; Ezek. 16:38). Scripture is clear on the point that the life is in the blood (Gen. 9:4; Lev. 17:14; Deut. 12:23), and is not to be eaten (Lev. 3:17; 19:26). The intensive plural form (as here) is often used to express violence (2 Sam. 3:28; Isa. 9:5; 33:15; Hos. 1:4). In this case, the blood is personified ("the voice of the blood of your brother") as a witness to this crime of premeditated murder. [*dām*]

4:12 A restless wanderer (*nā' wānād*)—Both are participles (translated as a hendiadys in the NIV), perhaps to express continual motion. The first term indicates a state of instability. It is used of the shaking of the leaves (Judg. 9:9), of quivering lips (1 Sam. 1:13), of staggering drunkards (Isa. 29:9), the trembling of an earthquake (Isa. 6:4; 24:20). The second term conveys an idea of wandering aimlessly (Jer. 4:1), but it can have the nuance of fleeing quickly (Jer. 49:30). Cain would discover the truth Isaiah would later affirm: there is no peace for the wicked (Isa. 48:22). [*nā', nād*]

4:13 My punishment (*'ăwōnî*)—Normally the noun refers to an iniquity, often paralleling *ḥaṭṭā't* or other terms for sin (1 Sam. 20:1; Job 13:23; Ps. 32:5; 107:17; Isa. 53:5; Dan. 9:16). It can also mean the guilt of iniquity (Isa. 59:3; Ezek. 16:49) or the consequences or punishment for that iniquity (Exod. 28:38; 1 Sam. 28:10; Isa. 5:18). It is the latter in view here. [*'ăwōn*]

5:1 This is the written account (*zeh sēper tôlĕdōt*)—Similar to the expression found in 2:4 (see discussion at that point), the phrase only here includes the term "this is the book." The noun *sēper* is from a verbal root that means to count, to recount, or to relate (*BDB*, 707). Biblical use of the noun indicates a scroll rather than our understanding of a bound book. The purpose of such a scroll was to record an enduring written account for future use (Exod. 24:7; Deut. 31:26; 1 Sam. 10:25; Job 19:23; Dan. 12:4). This book specifically included the family history of Adam from this point to the next occurrence of the phrase in 6:9. [*sēper*]

5:5 And he died (*wayyāmōt*)—The process that began for Adam who died spiritually the moment he disobeyed God now culminates in physical death as well. After 930 years of toilsome labor, Adam returned to the dust from which he was taken (3:19) and his spirit returned to God (Eccl. 12:7). The phrase continues repeatedly with each successive generation, completing the book of Genesis with the death of Joseph, and each time driving home the message that the wages of sin is death (Rom. 6:23). [*mwt*]

5:24 Enoch walked with God (*wayyithallēk ḥănôk*)—The verb *hlk* appears in the reflexive stem (Hithpael), here with the sense of a continual process. Enoch, as a way of life, walked with God. One may compare this usage of the stem/verb with Gen. 24:40; 48:15; 1 Sam. 12:2; 2 Kings 20:3; Ps. 35:14; 116:9; Isa. 38:3. [*hlk*]

    Then he was no more (*wĕ'ênennû*)—This phrase involves the use of *'ayin*, the particle of nonexistence, with the third person masculine suffix. Of all other individuals mentioned in the genealogy of chapter 5, Enoch alone did not die. His earthly existence nonetheless ended, and that at a premature age, "because God took him away" (NIV). [*'ayin*]

5:29 He named him Noah (*wayyiqrā' 'et-šĕmô nōaḥ*)—The etiological statement offered with the naming of Noah (*nōaḥ*) was that he was to give rest to mankind from their toilsome labor with the cursed ground (anticipating *mĕnûḥa* from *nwḥ*, but finding instead *yĕnaḥămēnû* from *nḥm*, lit. "he will give us comfort"). It is not properly an etymology, since there is no etymological connection known to have existed between *nōaḥ* (root: *nwḥ*) and *nḥm*. [*nōaḥ*]

6:2, 4 The sons of God (*bĕnê-hā'ĕlōhîm*)—The term can mean either people or angels. The specific interpretation as to their identity exceeds this present work. The phrase refers to angels (both fallen and unfallen?) in Job 1:6 and 2:1, and this meaning is probably to be indicated as well in Job 38:7. This view is supported as well by the synonymous term *bĕnê 'ēlîm* also referring to angels (Ps. 29:1; 89:6). Though the exact phrase is not used elsewhere, some have appealed to similar phrases as depicting human children of God (Deut. 14:1; 32:5; Ps. 82:6). With this alternative in mind and with contextual considerations from comparative Semitic literature, some see here either sons of Seth or harem-building despots. [*bēn*]

6:3 Will not contend (*lō' yādôn*)—The root of the verb appears to be *dyn*, "to judge," (*BDB*, 192) but the normally expected imperfect form would be *yādîn*. Because of this, and because of the difficulty of this verb in the context, Cassuto has suggested instead a root *dnn* supported by Talmudic Aramaic, meaning: "*to remain* or *exist perpetually in a given place*" (Cassuto, *Genesis 1*, 296). If true, this could produce the form in the MT, but it would be a *hapax legomenon*. [*dyn*]

6:4 The Nephilim (*hannĕpilîm*)—Based on the root *npl*, "to fall," this is a much debated term. In this verse, they are called heroes of old (*haggibbōrîm 'ăšer mē'ôlām*) and men of renown (*'anšê haššēm*), the offspring of the union between the sons of God and the daughters of men. Despite their reputation among men, the existence of these "fallen ones" seems to be the precipitating factor in God's decision to blot out man from the earth. The postdiluvian giants by the same name (Num. 13:33) were ostensibly from another provenance. [*nĕpîlîm*]

6:5 Every inclination of the thoughts of his heart was only evil all the time (*wĕkol-yēṣer maḥšĕbôt libbô raq ra' kol-hayyôm*)—

Several of the roots employed in this condemnation of man's evil have been seen before (*yṣr* in 2:7; *ra'* in 2:11, 17; and *yôm* repeatedly in chapter 1). Two of these need further illumination. The first (*yēṣer*) is used in the sense of the purposeful formation of the thoughts (*BDB*, 428: "what is framed in the mind"). The second (*kol-hayyôm*) is an illustration of the idiomatic usage of *yôm* used with an article and with the adjective *kol* with the meaning of "continually" (lit.: "all the day"). The word translated by the NIV as "thoughts" (*maḥšĕbôt*) reflects the plans of the innermost being. God uses the term of himself in claiming superiority of the quality of his thoughts over those of man (Isa. 55:8-9), whose thoughts may at times be righteous (Prov. 12:5) or evil (Prov. 6:18; Ezek. 38:10). The combination of all of the terms means "one's frame of thinking or planning that directs the heart or the mind, is used with 'evil' for the carnal thinking that motivates humans to pursue the most corrupt behavior requiring God's heaviest judgment (Gen. 6:5; cf. 8:21)" (John E. Hartley, *NIDOTTE*, 2:308). [*maḥăṣābâ, yēṣer*]

6:6 The Lord was grieved (*wayyinnāḥem*)—The term can be used in the sense of being moved to compassion for someone (Jer. 15:6; Ps. 90:13; Judg. 21:6), but due to the neighboring expression "his heart was filled with pain" (*wayyit'aṣṣēb 'el-libbô*) and the impending judgment, it should probably be understood as "to rue," or "to suffer grief" for one's own doings (*BDB*, 637). This is the most usual usage of the Niphal stem (Exod. 13:17; Judg. 21:15; 1 Sam. 15:11, 35; Jer. 42:10; Zech. 8:14). [*nḥm*]

6:7 I will wipe mankind (*'emḥeh 'et-hā'ādām*)—The verb *mḥh* can mean to remove a name from a scroll by blotting the ink (Exod. 17:14; Num. 5:23; Ps. 69:28).

It is used in the sense of wiping clean a dish or face (2 Kings 21:13; Prov. 30:20; Isa. 25:8). It was used in the expression "to blot out the memory" (Judg. 21:17; Deut. 9:14; Ps. 109:13) and is the common expression indicating the blotting out of sins (Ps. 51:1, 9; 109:14; Isa. 44:22; Jer. 18:23). The common trait in these various usages may be that a complete removal (often by means of water) is involved in the use of the verb, with little evidence remaining from that removal. Ink stains may remain in a book after the word is blotted out; temporal consequences may remain from cleansed sin; the memory of a people may be removed, but literary/archaeological evidence remains. Mankind was to be wiped out in the Flood, but Noah and his family remained. [*mḥh*]

6:8 Noah found favor (*wĕnōaḥ māṣā' ḥēn*)—The first occurrence of what becomes a common Hebrew idiom (Gen. 18:3; 19:19; Exod. 33:13; Judg. 6:17; 1 Sam. 20:29; etc.), the term NIV translates as "favor" is actually the word for grace (*ḥēn*). It is a term used of the elegance of women (Prov. 11:16; 31:30), of a precious gemstone (Prov. 17:8), and of pleasant speech (Ps. 45:2; Eccl. 10:12). It is used of acceptance by men and by God (Prov. 13:15; Zech. 4:7). It probably does not here have the later connotation of the Gk. *charis*, meaning unmerited favor, since in this context it is the constant and blameless righteousness of Noah in contrast to the wickedness of mankind that gains the notice of God (cf. v. 9). Compared to all others, Noah looked really good to God. [*ḥēn*]

6:9 Noah was a righteous man (*nōaḥ 'îš ṣaddîq*)—The adjective provides the first occurrence of a most significant root (*ṣdq*) in the OT. Reimer says of this polyvalent word: "semantic nuance is better derived from context than morphology" (David J. Reimer, *NIDOTTE*, 3:746), so only a few observations might be helpful. Righteousness may be either human righteousness that is based on some standard (as the Mosaic Law) or divine righteousness, which is perfect. The concept involves justice, fairness, and proper ethical behavior. Its reference point can be the community, the tabernacle/temple, the Law, or God himself. In this context, the behavior of Noah was such that he stood in sharp contrast with those around him. Whereas their thoughts were only evil continually (v. 5), his ways were blameless (*tāmîm*) as he continually walked with God (*hithallek*), as Enoch had done. Whatever standard God or society had set, Noah had striven to meet it. [*ṣaddîq*]

Blameless among his generation (*tāmîm hāyâ bĕdōrōtāyw*)—When applied to sacrificial animals, the term *tāmîm* means to be without blemish (Exod. 12:5; Lev. 1:3; Ezek. 43:22). When applied to God, his ways and works are perfect (Deut. 32:4; 2 Sam. 22:31), as is his Law (Ps. 19:7). Regarding man, the term is at times paralleled with the term *yāšār*, "upright" (Job 1:1 [singular *tām*]; Prov. 2:21, 11:5, 28:10). Noah met the standards of a life above reproach. The generation that surrounded him (*bĕdōrōtāyw*) had not even come close. [*tāmîm, dōr*]

6:11 The earth was corrupt (*wattiššāḥēt hā'āreṣ*)—In this passive (Niphal) stem, the verb means to be marred, spoiled, injured, or ruined (*BDB*, 1007). In Jer. 13:7, it refers to a ruined linen waistcloth. In Jer. 18:4, it is a ruined pot. In Exod. 8:24, the land of Egypt was ruined by infestation of flies. In Ezek. 20:44, Israel's idol worship is considered "corrupt practices" that once having been judged by God, now await his restorative work of grace.

The idea is that the earth was rendered useless by the evil pervasive in man. [*šḥt*]

And full of violence (*wattimmālē' hā'āreṣ ḥāmās*)—God's purposes had been for man to fill the earth (*ml'*) and subdue it (1:28), but man had filled it with violence instead. The term for violence (*ḥāmās*) is cognate to the Arabic form of *ḥāmās*, a terrorist organization that has been operating in Israel. The biblical term seems to always involve violence that is born out of wicked unrighteous behavior (Exod. 23:1; Ps. 72:14; Ezek. 7:11; Amos 3:10). On the other hand, Isaiah's suffering servant of the Lord was not to have done any violence (Isa. 53:9), a truth in keeping with his righteous character (Isa. 53:11). [*ḥāmās*]

6:14 Make yourself an ark (*'ăśēh lĕkā tēbat*)—This ark (*tēbâ*) is to be distinguished from the ark of the covenant (*'ărôn habbĕrît*) seen often in the Pentateuch and Former Prophets (cf. Josh. 3:6). Specifically, Noah's type of ark, being perhaps an Egyptian loan word for a coffin (*BDB*, 1061), was used to carry people safely in a watery environment (cf. Exod. 2:3). It thus became the vehicle of deliverance for God's chosen family (cf. 1 Peter 3:20). It differs from a normal boat in that it is meant only to float, not to navigate currents. [*tēbâ*]

6:17 I am going to bring floodwaters (*wa'ănî hinnî mēbî' 'et-hammabbûl mayim*)—The dubious idea of the Creator destroying his Creation is reflected in the emphatic *wa'ănî hinnî* (and I, behold I). These are not normal local floodwaters (Heb *šeṭep*), these are the waters of the *mabbûl*, a great storm. The term is found 11x in Gen. 6–11 and once again only in Ps. 29:10, where God is said to have ruled supreme over the Flood. *BDB* (550x) suggests an origin in the Old

Assyrian verb *nabâlu*, to destroy. The stated purpose is that this Flood should blot out life on the earth by destroying everything by means of water. [*mabbûl*]

Everything on earth will perish (*kōl 'ăšer-bā'āreṣ yigwā'*)—The verb basically means to die (Eugene H. Merrill, *NIDOTTE*, 1:835) and may be seen paralleled or juxtaposed with "to die" (*mût*) in Job 3:11 and 14:10. There is, however, at least the possibility that the term can be nuanced in the sense of the escaping breath of the dying. When Abraham died, we are told that he both expired and died (*wayyigwa' wayyāmot*: Gen. 25:8, 17). The same was said of Isaac (Gen. 35:29), and of Jacob it is said that he expired and was gathered to his people (euphemism for death and burial; Gen. 49:33). If this nuance is accepted, it becomes an entirely appropriate expression for death by drowning in the impending Flood. [*gw'*]

6:18 I will establish my covenant with you (*wahăqimōtî 'et-bĕrîtî 'ittāk*)—This is the first mention of the term covenant in the OT. Significant theologically throughout God's dealings with man, other covenants include the Abrahamic (Gen. 15:18), the Mosaic/Palestinian (Exod. 24:7; Deut. 29:1), the Davidic (2 Sam. 23:5), and the New Covenant (Jer. 31:31ff). Here, the covenant promised to Noah in Gen. 6, and serving for him as a point of hope, is established in Gen. 9 after God's faithful deliverance of Noah through the Flood. [*bĕrît*]

7:2 Every kind of clean animal (*mikkōl habbĕhēmâ haṭṭĕhôrâ*)—Looking forward to the issues of ceremonial cleanness, uncleanness, and holiness found in Leviticus, Noah is told to bring into the ark numerous types of clean animals, intended for post-Flood sacrifice (cf. 8:20). [*ṭāhôr*]

8:1 But God remembered Noah (*wayyizkōr'ĕlōhîm'et-nōaḥ*)—This common verb occurs here for the first time in the OT. The term often means to call to mind a past circumstance (Gen. 42:9; Num. 11:5; Ps. 77:11), but it can mean to call to mind a then present circumstance as well (Gen. 19:29; 30:22; Neh. 5:19; 6:14; 13:14, 22, 31). Often, this remembrance is based in a covenant relationship between God and man (Exod. 2:24, 6:5, 32:13; Lev. 26:42; Ps. 111:5). This could be the implication here. Because of the covenant relationship to be established by God with Noah (6:18), God did not abandon him to destruction. [*zkr*]

8:20 An altar to the Lord (*mizbēaḥ layhwh*)—Occurring here for the first time in the OT, Noah builds an altar to offer some of the clean animals for sacrifice to the Lord. The term is frequently used to refer to the altar of the tabernacle/temple (Exod. 27:1ff; 1 Kings 8:22), but also refers to altars built elsewhere (to YHWH: 1 Kings 18:30; to idols: 1 Kings 12:32-33; 2 Chron. 33:3, 5). Based on the root "to slaughter for sacrifice" (*zbḥ*), its basic meaning is "place of sacrifice." [*mizbēaḥ*]

He sacrificed burnt offerings (*wayya'al 'ōlōt*)—The phrase employs the cognate accusative (*'ōlâ*) to nuance the verb "to go up" (*'lh*) in the causative stem and translates "to offer up." These are the common terms used in Leviticus in describing the process of offering up a whole burnt offering to God (Lev. 1:3ff). It is also the demand placed on Abraham by God to sacrifice Isaac as a whole burnt offering (Gen. 22:2-13). With so few clean (and thus edible) animals available, such an offering was a significant sacrifice for Noah and his family to make immediately post-Flood. [*'lh, 'ōlâ*]

8:21 The pleasing aroma (*'et-rēaḥ hannîḥōaḥ*)—Thus God regards appropriate sacrifices made to him (Exod. 29:25; Lev. 3:5; Num. 15:3ff). [*nîḥōaḥ*]

9:6 Sheds the blood (*šōpēk dam*)—Using a verb that often indicates the proper pouring out of blood when making proper animal sacrifice (Lev. 4:7, 18, 25, 30, 34), God now legislates against the mortal shedding of innocent human blood (cf. Lev. 17:4; 1 Kings 2:31; Ps. 79:10). He requires the death of the one who causes death, protecting humanity from extinction, while at the same time foreshadowing the *lex talionis* of Exod. 21:23-25. [*špk*]

9:13 I have set my rainbow (*'et-qaštî nātattî*)—Normally associated with warfare, the bow was used in battle (Gen. 27:3; 48:22; 1 Chron. 5:18; Lam. 2:4). Here, that which resembled a bow fit for God (both enormous and brilliantly colored), serves as a frequently appearing sign of the covenant God makes with mankind never again to destroy the earth by means of the waters of the Flood (*mabbûl*). The battle imagery suggested by the bow may imply that the most recent battle fought and won against evil was now over (cf. Gen. 8:21). [*qešet*]

9:22 His father's nakedness (*'ēt 'erwat 'ābîw*)—The noun is associated with the external genitalia of the female (Lam. 1:8 [metaphor]; Ezek. 16:8, 36-37; cf. Exod. 28:42) and is often used as a euphemism for cohabitation (Lev. 18:6ff). Thus, some have thought that Ham slept with his mother (i.e., by "uncovering his father's nakedness"). Arguing against this is Noah's intoxicated uncovering of himself (9:21), the modest covering of Noah's nakedness by the other brothers (9:23), and Noah's words affirming his knowl-edge of what Ham had done to him. Ham's focus was probably on his father's privates. [*'erwâ*]

9:25 Cursed be Canaan (*'ārûr kĕnā'an*)—Ham's son was named Canaan, the root of which means "to be humbled" (*BDB*, 488). Following the indiscretion of his son Ham, Noah pronounces a curse on Ham's son, which continues through his progeny. The Canaanite people would be a constant thorn in the flesh of God's people, who were destined to inherit the land of promise. The curse is that the "humbled people" would be servants to the descendants of Japheth and the descendants of Shem, the latter best represented in the OT by the Israelites. The Canaanites are mentioned as being in possession of the land promised to Abram (Gen. 13:7), and are allowed continuance there until the proper time of judgment (cf. Amorites in Gen. 15:16). They are in possession of the land just before the Conquest by Israel (Deut. 7:1). When Joshua failed to consult with God, he was deceived by a group of Canaanites from Gibeon, which led to their becoming bond-servants to Israel, specifically in the service of the tabernacle (Josh. 9:22-27). The most important point to note here is that the color of skin is not at issue. A specific people descended from Ham were ultimately to become servants of Israel, and this is borne out in the pages of the OT. Their pigmentation is never mentioned. [*kĕnā'an*]

10:24 Eber (*'et-'ēber*)—In the genealogical lineage from Noah (through Shem) to Terah, father of Abram, this one's name serves as the eponym for the term Hebrews (*'ibrîm*), though this is debated. Gentiles normally used the term Hebrew about God's OT people, as did God's people when they referred to themselves to the Gentiles (Gen. 14:13). [*'ēber*]

10:25 Peleg (*peleg*)—The noun means a "canal," whereas the verbal root is best translated "to divide" (by means of water in Job 38:25). Peleg's name is explained by the etiological phrase: "in his days the earth was divided." Traditionally, this has been understood as a literary foreshadowing of the main event in chapter 11, the Tower of Babel. Recent attempts have been made to suggest instead the process of continental drift, but these seem tenuous at best. Another possibility demanding further study is that Peleg was named such because he was instrumental somehow in the extensive canalization of the land of Mesopotamia (cf. D. Fouts, "Peleg in Gen. 10:25," *JETS* 41 [1998]:17-21). [*peleg*]

11:1 A common speech (*ûdĕbārîm 'ăḥādîm*)—A phrase foreign to Western ears but not unexpected in Hebrew grammar (i.e., the plural of the numeral one modifying "words") is used (joined with "one lip" in the same verse) to convey the common speech present at that time. [*dābār*]

A plain in **Shinar** (*biq'â be'ereṣ šin'ār*)—Shinar is thought to have been an ancient name for a region in Mesopotamia (cf. Gen. 14:1; Dan. 1:2; Zech. 5:11 [LXX]). [*šin'ār*]

11:4 So that we may make a name for ourselves (*wĕna'ăšeh-lānû šēm*)—The term name (*šēm*) often refers to the character or reputation of an individual or group (cf. Gen. 6:4; Ps. 9:2; 44:8; Eccl. 7:1). It appears therefore that the post-Flood world wanted self-glory rather than glorifying God; they desired to reach God by

self-effort as well, implicit in the tower with a top reaching to heaven. Too, they desired not to be scattered over the earth, when God had commanded them to do just that (Gen. 9:1). [*šēm*]

11:6 Then nothing they plan to do (*kōl 'ăšer yāzmû la'ăšôt*)—When used of God, the verb normally indicates his plans for punishment (Jer. 4:28; 51:12; Lam. 2:17) or for blessing (Zech. 8:15). When used of man, it conveys the devising of evil plans (Deut. 19:19; Ps. 31:13). This meaning is supported by the related noun *zimmâ*, which in all but one case refers to the evil devices of evil men (Lev. 18:17; Hos. 6:9; Prov. 10:23); and supported as well by another related noun *mezimmâ*, which while dealing with humans conveys the idea of wicked thoughts (Ps. 10:4; Job 21:27). [*zmm*]

Will be impossible for them (*lō'-yibbāṣēr mēhem*)—The verb when used in the Qal stem means "cutting off" as of clusters of grapes (Lev. 25:5; Judg. 9:27); or in the sense of making something inaccessible, as a fortified city (Num. 13:28; 2 Kings 19:25). In the Niphal stem as here and in Job 42:2, the idea is that nothing would be inaccessible for them. [*bṣr*]

11:7 Let us go down and confuse their **language** (*nērĕdâ wĕnābĕlâ*)—Speaking as if in counsel with himself (cf. Gen. 1:26), God proposes to confuse the language of the people conspiring against his purposes. The verb "to confuse" (*bālal*) is offered as the etiological reason for the name Babel (v. 9), although some have suggested instead the Assyrian "gate of god" (*bāb-ili*). This then becomes the reason for the scattering of the nations: not as the result of the blessing of God (9:1; cf. 1:28), but as the result of the judgment of God (v. 9). [*yrd, bll*]

11:9 That is why it was called <u>Babel</u> (*bābel*)—Perennially in Scripture the city of opposition to God and God's people, Babel served as the site for the later capital city Babylon (cf. 2 Kings 17:24; Ps. 137:1; Isa. 14:4, 22; cf. Rev. 17–18). [*bābel*]

11:26 <u>Abram</u> (*'abrām*)—A combination of two words, *'āb* and *rām*, this initial name of the patriarch renamed Abraham in Gen. 17 meant "exalted father" (P.A. Verhoef, *NIDOTTE*, 4:351). It is at this point that there is a major break in Genesis. Chapters 1–11 focus on the four events of Creation, Fall, Flood, and Babel. Chapters 12–50 concentrate primarily on the patriarchs Abraham, Isaac, Jacob, and Joseph. Prior to being renamed Abraham by God, heirless Abram was called from Ur in Mesopotamia to move to the land of Canaan, a possession promised to him by God (Gen. 12:1, 7). After sojourning there for a while, a famine drove him into Egypt, where he endangered the future matriarch Sarai (Gen. 12:10-20). Returning to the land of promise, Abram was forced into battle to recover his captured nephew Lot, who had earlier moved to the regions of Sodom and Gomorrah (Gen. 13–14). Returning from that battle, Abram was encountered by Melchizedek, the king of Salem (early Jerusalem?), who also functioned as a priest to God most high (Gen. 14:17-20). Despite the fact that God ratifies his covenant with Abram in Gen. 15, Abram nonetheless maneuvers around the promise of God for a legitimate heir when Ishmael is born (Gen. 16). Reconfirming the covenant relationship in Gen. 17, Abram is both circumcised and renamed Abraham. [*'abrām*]

12:1 And from your relatives (*ûmimmôladtĕkā*)—This is the rendering of most translations, although a couple try to join the word with land (JPS translates the word in Gen. 12:1 as "native" in the phrase "native land"; cf. TEV at 24:4). When the word clearly modifies "land," most translations understand it of "birth"; however, SB at Gen. 11:28 has "land of his kindred" and NAB (cf. TEV) has "land of my kin" at 24:7. The word is related to the verb "give birth." Context indicates the correct nuance, and translations may differ from one another in interpretation from text to text. The term's nine occurrences in Genesis indicate the importance of the family, those connected by birth. [*môledet*]

And from the house of your father (*ûmibbêt 'ābîkā*)—This first occurrence of a phrase used 149x in the OT shows its function of indicating descent from a father or forefather. Because extended families often lived together, Abraham, though married, may not have moved far from his father until God's call, and his brother Nahor may have lived nearby. So "house" could indicate household members and include more than two generations. Although the phrase in Genesis refers to a literal father, it later could denote a patrilineal subdivision of an Israelite tribe (Num. 1:18; 2:2; Exod. 6:14), or even an entire tribe (Num. 17:2). [*bêt 'āb*]

12:2 And I will bless you (*wa'ăbārekkā*)—The word's general sense may be to endow someone with special power (Gen. 1:28) or to declare him thus endowed (Gen. 12:2) (*HALOT*, 160). Its force here may build on God's will to bless at creation (Gen. 1:28). Receiving the deity's blessing was a central aim of the ancient world, as it could convey fertility, prosperity, protection, deliverance, healing, empowerment, and favor (M. L. Brown, *NIDOTTE*, 1:758). People can bless others in the sense of wishing or praying God's blessing on them (Gen. 24:60), and they can bless God by praising him or invoking praise for him (Gen. 24:27, 48). There is debate about the force of the verbs for *bless* in Gen. 12:2-3. An imperative at the end of v. 2, "be a blessing," probably expresses God's intended result: "Leave . . . go . . . and be a blessing." Most translations say that all nations would be blessed through Abraham (Gen. 12:3), but NJB and JPS say that the nations "will bless themselves" by him. The issue concerns the Hebrew verb conjugations in five similar passages, three of which are apparently passive (Gen. 12:3; 18:18; 28:14) and two perhaps reflexive (Gen. 22:18; 26:4) (*DCH*, 2:268, 271). The passive verb in Hebrew can be reflexive, so some treat all the verbs as reflexive. However, reflexive verbs can often be passive, so all the verbs may be passive. The LXX and Vulg. take them as passives; so does the NT in reference to Gen. 12:3 (Acts 3:25; Gal. 3:8, 14). The LXX and Vulg. also treat similar words at Ps. 72:17 as passive (V. P. Hamilton, 375). [*brk*]

Your name (*šĕmekā*)—God's intent to make Abraham's name great should be understood as part of God's witness to the world through a chosen people. One's "name" could be his standing, reputation, or fame (*HALOT*, 1549). A literal translation for the "men of renown" in Gen. 6:4 is "the men of name," and Solomon considered a good name more valuable than wealth (Prov. 22:1). Ultimately, glory belongs to God and his name (1 Chron. 22:7; Zech. 14:9; Ezek. 36:23), but he has manifested himself through his servants by giving them a great name; that is, fame based on a divinely guided life (cf. 2 Sam. 7:9; 1 Kings 1:47; Ps. 72:17). To that end God sometimes named or renamed an individual (Gen. 17:5, 15, 19), since names themselves were meaningful in the

ancient Near East and consisted of words; he changed the patriarch's name from "Abram" ("exalted father") to "Abraham" ("father of many") (NIV note at Gen. 17:5). There can be a contrast between this man whose name God made great and the sinners at the Tower of Babel who intended to make a name for themselves (Gen. 11:4) (V. P. Hamilton, 372). [*šēm*]

12:3 And those cursing you (*ûmĕqallelkā*)—The verse uses two different words for cursing, one for man's action, and the other for God's response. P. J. Nel takes the former as involving a low opinion or contemptuous treatment (*NIDOTTE*, 3:922). Sarah had little worth in Hagar's eyes once Hagar became pregnant by Abraham (Gen. 16:4). The treatment in Gen. 12:3 might involve pronouncing a curse formula on Abraham and his descendants (L. J. Coppes, *TWOT*, 800). At this time of widespread dependence on the supernatural realm, curses and blessings were an important part of life, utilized in international (1 Sam. 17:43; Deut. 23:5) and personal relations (Exod. 21:17; 2 Sam. 16:7). [*qll*]

I will curse (*'ā'ōr*)—Abraham's adversary might mouth a curse, but God could, in turn, put the foe in the state of the curse (Coppes, ibid.). God is the ultimate focus of the curse in much of the OT, as the source of the threat and execution of punishment (V. P. Hamilton, *TWOT*, 1:76). By his obedience Abraham became God's representative. Just as God could supply power for abundant life in a blessing, so he could withhold that power or even turn it against a person. The first use of this word was in pronouncing punishment at the Fall (Gen. 3:14, 17). Perhaps God allowed Sarah's poor treatment of Hagar and Ishmael (Gen. 16:6, 9; 21:12) because of their bad attitudes towards

Abraham's family members. The promise of God's protective curse was part of the heritage of the patriarchs and Israel (Gen. 27:29; Num. 24:9). [*'rr*]

Families (*mišpĕḥōt*)—While "families" is a dominant translation here (NASB, NKJV, JPS, NRSV), "peoples" (NIV, REB), "clans" (NJB, SB), and "communities" (NAB) also occur. The word could refer to the species in the ark (Gen. 8:19), or the tribal groupings among the nations (Gen. 10:5). It points to the extended family or clan, with some recognition of blood relationship (*HALOT*, 651). The word had a metaphorical use as a type or part into which something was divided (Jer. 15:3), and it could refer to various levels of family up through a national unit (*BDB*, 1046-47). In Gen. 24:38 it indicates Abraham's relatives, including but not limited to those of his father's household. [*mišpāḥâ*]

12:5 Their possessions (*rĕkûšām*)—The noun derives from a verb meaning "to collect, acquire" that follows the noun in this verse (*HALOT*, 1236). Eleven of the noun's twenty-eight OT appearances are in Genesis, where it generally signifies the personal property of the patriarchs. The word indicated movable property (Gen. 12:5), regularly consisted of domesticated animals (Gen. 13:6; 36:7), and sometimes broadened to include household furnishings or tools (Gen. 12:5; 14:11) (C. L. Rogers and W. T. Koopmans, *NIDOTTE*, 3:1121). It could connote wealth. [*rĕkûš*]

12:7 To your offspring (*lĕzar'ăkā*)—A broader translation of this word might be "seed," which can refer to plants (Gen. 1:12) or animals (Gen. 7:2-3), but here to Abraham's heirs. It is first used of people in Gen. 3:15 and designates an individual son in 4:25 (cf. Gen. 15:3). God characteristically established his covenant not only with the individual but also with his descendants (Gen. 9:9; 12:7; 26:3; 2 Sam. 7:12). God's promises to Abraham in Gen. 12 were the beginning of the chosen people of Israel, and the greatest number of metaphorical references to seed as descendants occur in God's promises to the patriarchs in Genesis (e.g., Gen. 15:18; 22:17-18; 24:7; 28:13-14; 32:13; 48:19; V. P. Hamilton, *NIDOTTE*, 1:1151-52). God made promises about Hagar's offspring (Gen. 16:10; 21:13), but it was through Sarah's that he established an everlasting covenant. The OT often stresses this divine concern for the special seed (Exod. 33:1; Deut. 1:8), since the promise was never forgotten (Neh. 9:8). The same "seed" language became part of the Davidic covenant (2 Sam. 7:12; 1 Kings 2:33; Ps. 89:29), where it joined the Abrahamic promises in texts like Jer. 33:26. When national judgment overtook Israel, the prophets reiterated these promises (Isa. 43:5; 54:3; 61:9; 66:22; Jer. 30:10). The NT maintains this same hope in the promises to Abraham's seed (Luke 1:55; Acts 3:25; 7:5; Rom. 4:13), but it expands that seed to include all believers in Christ, even if they are Gentiles (Rom. 4:16-17; 9:8, cf. 4:12, 24; 9:24). Because Jesus Christ is the seed about whom the promises were spoken to Abraham (Gal. 3:16, 19), those who are in Christ are part of that seed (Gal. 3:29). [*zera'*]

Altar (*mizbēaḥ*)—Noah built the first altar mentioned in the Bible (Gen. 8:20), and Abraham the second. The noun, related to a verb meaning "slaughter for sacrifice" (*BDB*, 256), signifies a place of sacrifice, and sacrifice to God is as old as Adam's son Abel (Gen. 4:4). An altar could be made of plain dirt (Exod. 20:24), but the gift of an animal to God was usually costly; God required "clean" animals and birds for sacrifice (Gen. 8:20). Altars were also made of stone or of wood with bronze or gold overlay (Josh. 8:31; Exod. 38:1; 30:1-6). Sometimes built to commemorate an event, an altar might receive a name (Gen. 33:20; Exod. 17:15; Judg. 6:24). The sacrificial altar became central to the religion of Israel, where God considered any altar illegitimate that was not for him and according to his specifications. The altar in Gen. 12:7 was a sign of reverence and gratitude to God for his appearance and promises to Abraham. In Gen. 22 Abraham's altar became a picture of substitutionary sacrifice (H. Wolf, *TWOT*, 1:233). The OT altars and sacrifices pointed to realities beyond themselves because there is an altar in heaven (Rev. 6:9; 9:13), so Israel's altars were copies of the heavenly reality (Heb. 8:5; 9:23). And the Law's sacrifices were a foreshadowing of what Christ accomplished in his death (Heb. 10:1-18), for his sacrifice was effective at the heavenly altar (Heb. 9:11-14). [*mizbēaḥ*]

12:10 to sojourn (*lāgûr*)—This verb (82x) means to "dwell" or "reside" in a somewhat temporary way, and had a specialized use for those of foreign extraction who lived somewhere. In the latter case, the people might take up a lengthy residence but normally did not have inheritance rights (*BDB*, 157). Abraham would reside as a dependent alien (*HALOT*, 184) in Egypt, and later in Philistine Gerar (Gen. 20:1; 21:34). Abraham's nephew Lot, who came to Canaan with Abraham, is described as a sojourner there (Gen. 19:9), as were all the patriarchs (Exod. 6:4; Gen. 35:27). Israel later grew into a nation while living as aliens in Egypt (Gen. 47:4). The relief, or lack of it, that Israel found as sojourners in Egypt became the grounds for their obligation to show the same love to aliens that they had for themselves (Lev. 19:34). A sojourner in Israel was under many of the same laws as a native

citizen (Num. 15:15-16), and had the religious rights of a native if he underwent circumcision (Exod. 12:48). [*gwr*]

The famine (*hārā'āb*)—This is the first biblical mention of famine, a condition that could afflict Canaan if winds from the Mediterranean did not bring in rain. Plant diseases, insects, war, or excessive rain were other causes of famine. The Hebrew word basically means "hunger" but could include lack of water (Amos 8:11; 1 Kings 18:1-2). The majority of people in biblical times were subsistence farmers and herdsmen, quite vulnerable to instabilities of climate or politics. Since Egypt collected water from a large area through the Nile, it offered a place of escape for people in Canaan when the rains failed there (R. J. Way, *NIDOTTE*, 3:1133-35). Scripture describes God as caring for the land of Canaan even before the Israelites returned there from Egypt (Deut. 11:12). So if it lacked the rain he provided (Jer. 5:24; 14:22), his judgment on it may have been the reason. [*rā'āb*]

12:17 And He inflicted (*wayĕnagga'*)—While the basic meaning of this word is "touch," it often implies striking blows, whether those of a person (Prov. 6:33), ram (Dan. 8:7), destructive wind (Job 1:19), or army (Josh. 8:15). Metaphorically, God's hand may strike (1 Sam. 6:9; Isa. 53:4), or men's hands (2 Sam. 7:14; Ps. 89:32). The result is harm (Gen. 32:25; 1 Chron. 16:22). The related noun appears in Gen. 12:17 as "diseases"; these are "blows" or "plagues" as divine judgments on Pharaoh for appropriating Abraham's wife. Evidently there was sin in the process, despite Pharaoh's ignorance of Sarah's marital status. [*ng'*]

13:2 Wealthy (*kābēd*)—The verbal root of this adjective means to "be heavy, weighty," but only rarely has its literal sense. More often the weight is metaphorical, whether of sin, work, or honor; so there are numerous derived ideas such as painful, difficult, honorable, and rich. The adjective appeared earlier of a famine being "heavy" or "severe" in the land (Gen. 12:10). Here what is heavy is the mass of Abraham's cattle and precious metals. The adjective seems to lack the meaning "honorable" in the OT, but can carry the connotation of number or volume (J. N. Oswalt, *TWOT*, 1:426-27). In Gen. 13:2 the idea may be a combination of number, volume, and richness. [*kābēd*]

In cattle (*bammiqneh*)—Jabal was regarded as the father of those, of whom Abraham was one, who live among tents and "herds" (Gen. 4:20; cf. Heb. 11:9). Although the noun derives from a verb meaning to acquire, the noun virtually always indicates livestock. In Genesis the livestock of the patriarchs serve as a visible sign of God's blessing on them (Gen. 13:6; 26:14; 31:9; 36:7; 46:6). [*miqneh*]

13:3 His tent (*'ohŏlō*)—The significance of tent living for Israel is suggested by the 349 OT instances of this word for tent. A. Tomasino describes the tent as goatskin curtains extended over a wooden framework and bound together with ropes that tied to pegs in the ground (*NIDOTTE*, 1:300). It was basically in the shape of a bell around a central upright that held up the roof. That this was the patriarchs' home suggests that they were strangers and aliens on the earth without an abiding home (Heb. 11:9, 13). [*'ōhel*]

13:6 Support (*nāśā'*)—The fundamental meaning of this verb is "carry." Here the land is not able to carry the livestock of Abraham and Lot by providing sufficient food and water for them. The very bless-

ing of God compelled these men to live apart. God had told Abraham to leave his family (Gen. 12:1), so this separation may have been inevitable. But Gen. 12:1 could speak in general terms about Abraham's sacrifice in moving to Canaan from Haran, and Lot was a righteous man (2 Peter 2:7). Elsewhere the verb can signify to "lift" eyes (Gen. 13:10) or "lift" a face in gladness by granting a favor (Gen. 19:21). In Gen. 18:24, where the direct object is a city, most translations have "spare" or "forgive." The prayer seems to be that God "lift" the burden of sin from the city. [*nś'*]

13:7 Dispute (*rîb*)—While this word appears to have a primary sense of physical combat (W. White, *TWOT*, 2:845), the controversy in Gen. 13:7 may have been verbal sparring over limited pasture and water. Not only were Abraham and Lot related, but a similar contention in Gen. 26:20 involves a verbal claim to ownership of a well. The word often has legal implications, which here would be the right to use land resources. God chose the occasion to bless Abraham by reconfirming his ultimate possession of all the land (Gen. 13:14-17) (J. M. Bracke, *NIDOTTE*, 3:1105). It also led to Abraham's lengthy settlement at Hebron (Gen. 13:18). This word is related to the word "discord," or "strife," of 13:8, which occurs only twice in the OT (cf. Num. 27:14). [*rîb*]

13:9 Separate (*hippāred*)—The separation of Lot from Abraham shows how nations were formed. Lot's descendants became Moab and Ammon, countries that bordered Israel. Used of rivers dividing from a source in Gen. 2:10, the word first describes the division of peoples into nations at 10:5, 32. In 25:23 God speaks of Esau and Jacob separating into nations, and in Deut. 32:8 the word describes

God's sovereign dispersion of all nations. Esth. 3:8 applies it to Israel's separate status among the peoples. [*prd*]

13:13 Wicked (*rā'îm*)—Many translations characterize the people of Sodom as "wicked." NJB translates "vicious" here. The adjective has a wide range of usage, often signifying "bad" or "evil." The word indicates the polar opposite of "good," as in the phrase "knowledge of good and evil" (Gen. 2:9). It is appropriate for those who have fallen far from what God created them to be (Gen. 1:31). When Er was "evil" in God's sight, God killed him (Gen. 38:7). On the other hand, Laban had the power to do Jacob evil, and God commanded him not to do it (Gen. 31:29). God is sovereign of the world, so he stands behind whatever happens, whether good or evil (Isa. 45:7). But the word does not always have a moral overtone. In Gen. 19:19, where the bad thing is a shower of burning sulfur, most translate the word as "disaster" (e.g., NIV, REB, NRSV, NLT, NASB, TEV). God does not want people to do evil, but he allows it and its consequences for the accomplishment of his ultimately good purposes. [*ra'*]

And sinners (*wĕḥaṭṭā'îm*)—This Hebrew adjective ("sinful") derives from a verb meaning to miss the mark or to sin. The verse shows that God is ultimately the object of sin's hostility. These people defied God's standards to a great degree, as the narrative confirms. The two highlighted adjectives (wicked, sinners) joined by "and" may function together to form a single idea (hendiadys), as the English words "down and dirty" can. Ps. 1:5 contrasts "sinners" with the "righteous." [*ḥaṭṭā'*]

13:15 Forever (*'ad-'ôlām*)—The etymology of this common word, which has about 460 occurrences in the OT (440x in Hebrew and 20 in Aramaic), is uncertain, but it has a range of meaning from "long time" to "eternity." The long time could be a lifetime ("slave for life"; Deut. 15:17), or an enduring condition ("continual enmity"; Ezek. 25:15). It could stretch forward to the future (Gen. 3:22), look back to remote antiquity (Gen. 6:4), or describe the ongoing present (Ps. 73:12) (*HALOT*, 798-99). The plural forms generally are not numerical but intensify meaning; the singular does not function independently as a subject or object but only modifies or combines with other terms. Often the word gives the highest possible intensification of a word in a future-oriented sense: "permanent possession" or "endless joy." There are cognate words in several ancient languages, with Moabite showing the two ideas of "for always, perpetual" and "since time immemorial" (H. D. Preuss, *TDOT*, 10:531-36). Since God's existence is without end in the past and future, both meanings of this word suit him. The word in Genesis, and through Scripture, can usually be taken as "always" or "forever" when the idea is not "ancient." That is, even when it refers to temporally limited ideas, there may be an element of hyperbole in the expression. The translations widely agree that "forever" is proper here at Gen. 13:15. If they are correct, God promised that Israel would always be the true owners of the land of Canaan. [*'ôlām*]

14:1 King (*melek*)—Gen. 14:1-2 suggests that much of the ancient world was governed by kings. The king's status was closely connected to belief in divine beings. In Egypt the king was a god and son of a god in view of his office. Predestined by the gods to reign, he represented them. Mesopotamia, too, thought that kingship came down from heaven and that the king was predestined to rule. Even though not personally divine, he represented the divine world to his subjects. Areas closer to Israel also held that the gods installed the king (H. Ringgren, *TDOT*, 8:349-52). [*melek*]

14:13 Dwelling (*šōkēn*)—Abraham had made Hebron his home, for this participle speaks of settling down. This is where his wife died (Gen. 23:2), and where the couple was buried (Gen. 23:19, 25:9). But Abraham would leave Hebron for a lengthy time period (Gen. 20:1-22:19). The verb *škn* (129: "settle, reside") has a more common synonym (*yšb*) (1088: "live, sit, inhabit") with which it sometimes appears in parallelism (e.g., Isa. 13:20; 18:3). The difference between the two may be that *škn* emphasizes nearness and closeness, providing a word for "neighbor" (Ps. 79:4, 12) (V. P. Hamilton, TWOT, 2:925), or that it is less tied to being in a particular locality than *yšb* (*HALOT*, 1497). Noah wished that Japheth could "dwell" in the tents of Shem (Gen. 9:27). Isaac was to "settle" in Gerar, Israel "settled" in the land beyond Migdal Eder, and Zebulon would "live" by the seashore (resp., Gen. 26:2; 35:21-22; 49:13). The emphasis of the verb on the act of dwelling may slightly favor the geographical interpretation of Gen. 16:12 and 25:18. Ishmael "dwelt" either to the east of his brothers or in hostility to them. [*škn*]

14:14 His relative (*'āḥîw*)—The NKJV has "brother" here, for that is the word's fundamental meaning (Gen. 4:2; 9:22), but NAB has the more specific "nephew" because the term is broad enough to cover numerous relations. It could designate a fellow tribesman (Num. 16:10), or a fellow Israelite (Lev. 25:46). In Gen. 9:5 it indi-cates a fellow human being. Perhaps that is why "brother" can be such a flexibly broad term in the NT, referring to fellow Christians (Rom. 15:30), fellow Israelites (Acts 2:29), or a fellow human being (Matt. 7:3, 5; Luke 17:3). [*'āḥ*]

14:18 Priest (*kōhēn*)—Ugaritic documents of the mid-second millennium B.C. use this word with the same meaning, as do later Phoenician, Punic, and Aramaic texts. In both Egypt and Mesopotamia the king was in theory the highest cultic offi-cial (H. Ringgren, *TWOT*, 7:62-5). So it is only Melchizedek's ministry to the true God that is surprising, but it has an anal-ogy later in Jethro's priesthood (Exod. 18:1). J. B. Payne saw a transition from individuals serving as their own priests to Noah the patriarch serving as priest for his family (Gen. 4:3; 8:20) (*TWOT*, 431); the king as priest was a further enlarge-ment of the priestly role. [*kōhēn*]

14:19 Most High (*'elyôn*)—This is the first of 53 OT uses of this word. It occurs as a divine name in the Aramaic Sefire inscrip-tions (8th c. B.C.), and there are related terms with this meaning in Old South Arabic and Phoenician. H.–J. Zobel asserts that this divine epithet appears only in poetic OT texts; he regards the four occurrences in Gen. 14 as stereotypi-cal language. The concept of what is high-est resides in the word, and when the word occurs in parallelism with El, another divine name (Num. 24:16; Ps. 73:11), it is a name for God (*TDOT*, 11:123-26). [*'elyôn*]

14:20 Delivered (*miggēn*)—God "handed over" or "surrendered" Abraham's ene-mies into his power (*HALOT*, 545). The idea of "give, grant" is common to this root in six other Semitic languages (D. N.

Freedman and M. P. O'Connor, *TDOT*, 8:85); so in Gen. 14:20 the word probably emphasizes the divine grace to Abraham. [*mgn*]

A tenth (*ma'ăśēr*)—Tithes were due to a god in ancient Egypt, Sumer, Babylon, and South Arabia, but most take Abraham's tenth, and later Jacob's (Gen. 28:22), as freewill offerings rather than tribute. God would incorporate the tithe into Israel's laws (Lev. 27:30). R. North supposes that Abraham gave a tenth of his personal booty to Melchizedek. When invited to keep all the property, Abraham refused to keep anything belonging to the five kings. He kept only what his men needed, which may have comprised Abraham's other nine tenths (*TDOT*, 11:406). [*ma'ăśēr*]

14:22 I have raised my hand (*hărîmōtî yādî*)—In order to convey the oath implication of the action, the NIV translates two Hebrew words as "I have raised my hand . . . and have taken an oath." JPS, NJB, TEV, SB, and REB take the action as occurring the moment Abraham spoke: "I swear. . . ." Abraham raised his hand to heaven calling on God to witness his words. [*rwm*]

Creator (*qōnēh*)—God might be invoked as either the Creator or the owner of everything (*BDB*, 888-89). That the issue is ownership of battle spoils may influence NASB and NKJV to consider God the "possessor" (NKJV: "Possessor") of heaven and earth, but most translations and lexicons choose something like "Creator." The word has this latter notion in Ugaritic, Phoenician, and Aramaic texts; within the OT this may be the sense in Gen. 4:1; Exod. 15:16; Deut. 32:6; Ps. 139:13, and Prov. 8:22 (V. P. Hamilton, 411-12). [*qnh*]

14:23 A single thread or sandal thong (*miḥûṭ wĕʿad śĕrôk-na'al*)—This is courtly, stereotypical language. Likewise, the Hittite king Suppiluliuma would not take anything, even a straw or splinter, from his ally. A similar Akkadian formula concerns a blade of straw or sliver of wood, while an Aramaic one mentions a blade of straw or piece of string (V. P. Hamilton, 413-14). This emphatic speech to a pagan king was part of Abraham's testimony that he relied entirely on his God, the Creator, for whatever he had. Since he addressed the head of a wicked city, which God would soon destroy (Gen. 18:20-19:29), Abraham may have been separating himself from possible corruption (cf. 2 Cor. 6:17). [*ḥûṭ*] [*śĕrôk-na'al*]

15:1 In a vision (*bammaḥăzeh*)—This word, also occurring in Num. 24:4, 16 and Ezek. 13:7, derives from a verb meaning "see" or "behold" that often indicates supernatural communication (Exod. 24:11; Hab. 1:1; Amos 1:1). The word of God evidently came to Abraham with visual aspects, but it was probably an internal seeing, perhaps like a dream without being asleep. [*maḥăzeh*]

Shield (*māgēn*)—Scripture characterizes God as a "shield" in about 19 other places (e.g., Deut. 33:29; 2 Sam. 22:3, 31; Pss. 3:3; 18:30; 84:11; Prov. 2:7; 30:5). Usually the word occurs with similar terms such as sword, rock, savior, refuge, and horn of salvation. In an oracle the goddess Ishtar called herself the shield of the Assyrian king Esarhaddon (H. Ringgren, *TDOT*, 8:85). Several scholars, supposing that "shield" is actually a form of the verb translated as "delivered" above at Gen. 14:20, render Gen. 15:1: "I am going to give" (or "I am he who gives") "you your very great reward" (D. N. Freedman and M. P. O'Connor, *TDOT*, 8:65-86). But if the noun "reward" in Gen. 15:1 is a parallel word, matching nouns that appear with this word elsewhere in the OT, then this word may be a noun here. [*māgēn*]

Your reward (*śĕkārĕkā*)—Most translations supply a linking ("to be") verb and treat the last words in Gen. 15:1 as a separate clause: "your reward will be very great." A simpler structure (e.g., NIV, NKJV) takes the noun as parallel to "shield": "your shield, your very great reward." The NET Bible notes that the words "very great" often modify the noun they follow, which here is "reward" (e.g., Gen. 41:49; Deut. 3:5; Josh. 22:8; 2 Sam. 8:8; 12:2). While this word can mean wages, maintenance, or payment, some interpret the reward here as Abraham's "booty" for leaving his homeland (*HALOT*, 1331). God had already proved himself a shield against Chedorlaomer, and although Abraham had taken no booty, God promised to be his reward. [*śākār*]

15:2 Lord (*yhwh*)—The writer of Genesis has Abraham speak the name Yahweh, rendered here conventionally as "Lord" (cf. Gen. 14:22). It was a name by which God did not make himself known to Abraham according to Exodus 6:3. Perhaps God did not reveal the power or meaning of the name earlier (cf. Exod. 3:13-15). To Moses God revealed that he was the "I AM," the self-existent One. The words in Exodus also emphasize God's sovereign freedom to be what he chooses. Abraham may have used Yahweh as a proper name without grasping its import; it is probably a third person form of the verb to "be" or "become": "He is" or "He will be." [*yhyh*]

Childless (*ʿărîrî*)—A more literal rendering of the word (cf. Lev. 20:20-21; Jer. 22:30) would be "stripped" or "destitute" (R. B. Allen, *TWOT*, 2:700). Abraham had

such a sense of deprivation concerning his lack of a child that it interfered with his enjoyment of God as his "great reward." Abraham seems to have felt that other gifts would not be meaningful without the gift of a child. This background clarifies just how glad he was when God promised him one (Gen. 15:4), and how sorely the subsequent delay would test his trust in the Lord. [*ʿărîrî*]

15:3 Heir (*yôrēš*)—This is a participle of a verb (232x) meaning to "take possession of" (*HALOT*, 441-42). When the one who takes possession is in the second generation, the word gains the sense of being an heir of someone or inheriting (Gen. 15:4; 21:10). In some verses, like Gen. 15:7-8, the word could mean either *possess* (most translations) or *inherit* (NKJV, SB). Even in the patriarchal narratives with their theme of a divine heritage, the meaning "take possession" is prominent (Gen. 22:17; 24:60; 28:4). In Gen. 45:11 the danger was being dispossessed or impoverished. [*yrš*]

15:4 From your body (*mimmēʿêkā*)—The word indicate either the belly, the seat of emotions, or the reproductive organs (resp., Ezek. 3:3; Isa. 63:15; Ruth 1:11) (V. P. Hamilton, *TWOT*, 2:518-19). Here, of course, the reference is to the latter, as in Gen. 25:23. [*mēʿeh*]

15:6 And he trusted (*wĕheʿĕmin*)—Once or twice the word means "stand firm" or "allow," but its normal sense is "believe" or "believe in," often with reference to God (e.g., Exod. 14:31; Deut. 1:32) (*BDB*, 53). Abraham took God at his word, as God expects people to do (cf. Num. 14:11; 20:12; Isa. 7:9). A noun from this verb is regularly translated as "faithfulness" (Ps. 88:11). [*ʿmn*]

And he credited it (*wayyaḥšĕbehā*)—The word has to do with thinking, whether it is to count, calculate, esteem, regard, plan, or invent. Here God ascribes a moral and spiritual worth to Abraham's faith, with which he is pleased (cf. Ps. 106:30-31). There is debate as to whether God or Abraham is the verb's subject; the context and the NT (Rom. 4:3) favor God (J. E. Hartley, *NIDOTTE*, 2:303, 305-06; V. P. Hamilton, 425). [*ḥšb*]

As righteousness (*ṣĕdāqâ*)—Two Jewish translations (JPS and SB) take this word as "merit," with Abraham's belief regarded as meritorious. But Christian translations have "righteousness," based on the Pauline citation of Gen. 15:6 (Gal. 3:6; Rom. 4:3) in the sense that God credits believers with a righteousness that they do not actually possess, except by virtue of the Savior Jesus Christ. This important biblical word appears only 3x in Genesis. The Lord used it in 18:19 in its basic sense of adherence to an ethical or moral norm, the norm there being the "way of the Lord." Abraham conformed to the expectation of trusting God (Gen. 15:6). Jacob's relationship with Laban was in accord with the agreement that they had made, thus honest (Gen. 30:33). This is a feminine word in Hebrew (156x); and there is also a masculine one (118x), but a difference in meaning between them may be unprovable. With respect to God, the norm of "righteousness" is his character and will. His standards govern human conduct. With respect to humanity, the word pertains to interpersonal relationships, one's standing before the law, and responsibilities in covenant with God (H. G. Stigers, *TWOT*, 2:752). [*ṣĕdāqâ*]

15:10 And he cut in two (*wayĕbatēr*)—The phrase "cut a covenant" occurs repeatedly in the OT, and this episode shows what the cutting involved (cf. Jer. 34:18). The verb for "cut" in Gen. 15:10 is different from the normal one as it stresses the pieces into which the object is cut. This is the sole OT use of the verb, but the related noun stands in this verse and elsewhere. [*btr*]

15:13 Stranger (*gēr*)—This is the nominal form (93x) of the verb "sojourn" of Gen. 12:10. Such a person had left his home for reasons such as war, disease, starvation, or legal difficulties, in order to find safety and a place to stay elsewhere. He no longer lived among blood relatives as a native citizen but was dependent on the hospitality of his hosts (H. G. Stigers, *TWOT*, 1:155). The "stranger" enjoyed an intermediate status between a native and a foreigner (D. Kellerman, *TDOT*, 2:443), having abridged rights concerning land ownership, marriage, suing at law, worship, and warfare (*HALOT*, 201). In Israel many laws apply to both the native and the "stranger" (e.g., Exod. 12:19; Lev. 16:29, 17:12) but there were also laws to guarantee the stranger's protection (Exod. 22:21; Lev. 19:33-34). Since he could become circumcised and participate in Israelite religious life (Exod. 12:48), he could have a more permanent status than a temporary resident (*tôšāb*). Abraham later described his own status in Canaan with this term *gēr* (Gen. 23:4), which passed into NT characterization of Christians (Heb. 11:13; 1 Peter 2:11). Moses' naming of his son in Exod. 2:22 shows the fulfillment of the prophecy in Gen. 15:13. [*gēr*]

And they will enslave them (*wa'ăbādûm*)—This common verb for work and service here entails the Egyptians forcing the Israelites to do work. The book of Exodus shows the betrayal and cruelty involved. The idea of slavery was part of ancient culture, and

God permitted it in the Mosaic Law (Lev. 25:46). But since God had promised to bless Abraham (Gen. 12:2-3), his offspring probably underwent such suffering in part due to their sin. The sons of Jacob displayed evil toward Joseph, married Canaanites, and practiced Canaanite ways (Gen. 37:1–38:26). The Israelites continued to worship other gods (Ezek. 20:7-8; 23:3; Josh. 24:14). [*'bd*]

And mistreat (*wĕ'innû*)—The Egyptians would "afflict" and "humble" the Israelites (*BDB*, 776). The same word is used of Sarah's harshness toward Hagar (Gen. 16:6) and Shechem's rape of Dinah (Gen. 34:2). In Gen. 16:9 Hagar was to "submit" to Sarah, or allow herself to be afflicted; the verb there has a reflexive or passive sense. This is one of the more frequent words for oppression and subjugation in the OT (about 80) (P. Wegner, *NIDOTTE*, 3:449-51). God was sovereign in this affliction of Abraham's seed (Ps. 105:25). But since mistreatment is also the lot of the righteous in a fallen world (John 15:18; 2 Tim. 3:12), it is difficult to make sweeping generalizations about the reasons for Israel's long affliction in Egypt. [*'nh*]

15:14 Am going to execute judgment (*dān*)—God was going to punish Egypt according to his standard of justice. The word pertains to governing, whether executive, legislative, or judicial. Of the two main Hebrew verbs for judging, this less used one may be older and more poetic (R. D Culver, *TWOT*, 1:188). In Genesis it also occurs at 30:6 and 49:16, and forms a wordplay with the name Dan in 49:16. [*dyn*]

15:15 Your fathers (*'ăbōtêkā*)—The phrase "go to your fathers" functions as a euphemism for death. The Hebrew term for "father" served also for "grandfather" and "forefather" (*BDB*, 3). Here the latter idea seems clear because of the plurality. Since Abraham was not buried with his forefathers, God may speak idiomatically of burial or may refer to a spiritual reunion. Other verses in Genesis that speaking of joining the dead in death are 37:35 and 49:29. [*'āb*]

In peace (*bĕšālôm*)—The LXX translates with a word for peace. The Hebrew verb behind the noun means to remain whole and enjoy fine health, so the noun can mean wholeness or healthiness. This wide-ranging word has associated ideas such as prosperity, success, welfare, friendliness, or salvation, and can even be a greeting (Judg. 19:20) (*HALOT*, 1506-07). Some other uses in Genesis are at 26:29; 28:21; 29:6; 37:4; 41:16; 43:27, and 44:17. Abraham would come to a good end, perhaps dying in his sleep. [*šālôm*]

In old age (*bĕśêbâ*)—The noun and its related verb specifically indicate being white or gray due to advanced age, but the words can simply signify advanced age (cf. Gen. 42:38; 44:29). Gen. 25:8 shows the fulfillment of the prophecy in 15:15. [*śêbâ*]

15:16 And the fourth generation (*wĕdôr rĕbî'î*)—The word can refer to a cycle of time, particularly a lifetime. This verse has led some to view a generation as 100 years long in the ancient mind, since Israel lived in Egypt 430 years (Exod. 12:40; Gal. 3:17). The idea would be four lifetimes, since people were living longer then (V. P. Hamilton, 436). The word can also refer to one's contemporaries, his generation (Gen. 6:9; 7:1); in the plural it often points to the indefinite future as a series of generations (Gen. 9:12; 17:7). [*dôr*]

The sin (*'āwōn*)—The noun relates to a verb meaning bend or twist that can imply distortion, crookedness, or perversion. To distort the law is to "sin" or "do something perverted." The noun has only this secondary sense of sin, perversion, or crookedness (C. Schultz, *TWOT*, 2:650). Although there was no formal law, the Canaanites were perverting divine standards for righteous behavior that they knew in their hearts (Rom. 1:32; 2:14-15). The word can also indicate the guilt (Gen. 44:16) or punishment of sin (Gen. 4:13; 19:15). [*ăwōn*]

15:18 Covenant (*bĕrît*)—The etymology of this word is uncertain, but some evidence suggests a link with an Akkadian word meaning "fetter," which is related to a word meaning "between" (M. Weinfeld, *TDOT*, 2:255). Covenants were widely used in the ancient Near East between individuals or nations as agreements, treaties, contracts, and obligations. They were often formal, involving a ceremony, stipulations, blessings and curses, divine witnesses, and written documents. Genesis records covenants between men (Gen. 21:27-32; 26:28; 31:44); Abraham had help against Chedorlaomer because of a covenant with his neighbors, perhaps a mutual defense pact (Gen. 14:13). Weinfeld notes that covenants in the ancient world reflect familial relationships, often using the same language. One between equals was between "brothers," but one between unequal partners could be between a "father" and a "son," that is, a suzerain and a vassal. Of the latter kind there were two types, a treaty covenant stressing the vassal's obligation and a covenant of grant stressing the master's. There is debate whether a covenant could be entirely one-sided, as a promise, or whether it always implied obedience on the part of the promise's recipient (E. B. Smick, *TWOT*, 1:131). Actually the

covenant of grant was a reward for loyal service; however, it was an inalienable gift of land or dominion (Weinfeld, 188-89). This seems to be the kind of covenant between God and Abraham. For this reason God would never forsake Israel (Lev. 26:44-45), disobedience to the Law could not overthrow the Abrahamic promises (Gal. 3:16-17), and the gifts and calling of God are irrevocable (Rom. 11:28-29).

God made a covenant with Noah (Gen. 6:18; 9:9-17), and this one with Abraham is central to the history of Israel, because it was also for his descendants (cf. Gen. 17:2-21). God delivered Israel from Egypt on the basis of this Covenant (Exod. 2:24; 6:5). The Mosaic (Exod. 19:5), Davidic (2 Sam. 23:5), and New covenants (Jer. 31:31; Luke 22:20) developed from it so that Israel possessed several covenants (Rom. 9:4). Since Christians are under the New Covenant, they, too, depend on the Abrahamic Covenant (2 Cor. 3:6). [*bĕrît*]

16:5 The wrong done to me (*ḥāmāsî*)—Sarah may have taken an oath putting the blame for her mistreatment on Abraham (cf. Jer. 51:35) (*HALOT*, 329), or she may simply have told Abraham that he was responsible (V. P. Hamilton, 443, G. Wenham, 2). The word can signify "wrong" (Isa. 53:9), but is almost hyperbolic here, since its basic meaning is "violence" (cf. Gen. 6:11, 13; 49:5-6). Sarah felt abused by the loss of honor she had suffered as a result of what she may have regarded as selfless generosity in giving Hagar to Abraham. She felt it amounted to psychological violence and was caused in one way or another by her husband. [*ḥāmās*]

Into your arms (*bĕḥêqekā*)—The word is literally "bosom," and is understood as the "lower, outer front of the body where loved ones (infants and animals) are pressed closely" (*HALOT*, 312). The NLT translates: "I myself gave her the privilege of sleeping with you." It was the place where a man's woman lay (Micah 7:5), and in ancient Hebrew literature some variation of the words "wife/husband of your bosom" is a common phrase (e.g., Deut. 13:6; 28:54, 56) (*DCH*, 3:216). [*ḥêq*]

16:7 The Angel of the Lord (*mal'ak*)—The word "angel" is more literally "messenger." A "messenger" could be human or superhuman and could be sent by men or God. It could be a personal envoy or a political one (resp., Prov. 13:17; 2 Kings 9:18). If sent by God it could be a prophet (Hag. 1:13), a priest (Mal. 2:7), or an angel (Gen. 19:1). The biblical phrase "angel of the Lord" can refer to an ordinary angel (Matt. 2:19; Acts 5:19), but in the OT (58x) the phrase can refer to a theophanic angel, that is, an angel who manifests God himself (*BDB*, 521). It is often not possible to differentiate between God and his angel in human confrontations (D. N. Freedman and B. E. Willoughby, *TDOT*, 8:311-20). People usually take him to be a man at first, but eventually realize that he is God (Gen. 18:2, 22; Judg. 6:11-22; 13:3-22). When the text mentions a single angel of the Lord, it is probably God himself appearing in human form. Generally he brings good news or deliverance, and in Genesis does so in times of personal crisis. The angel of the Lord appears much more in Genesis and Judges than in books describing later times. The early church fathers identified the angel of the Lord with the preincarnate second Person of the Trinity (G. Wenham, 9). [*mal'ak*]

16:10 Multiply (*'arbeh*)—Context clarifies that the verb has the idea of making numerous here, rather than its other sense of making great (*HALOT*, 1177). The promise to Hagar reflects Abraham's own desire (Gen. 17:20). God used an intensive form to guarantee the promise; he first did so at Gen. 3:16, where the promise was great pains in childbirth. He does so next at Gen. 22:17, in a promise to multiply Abraham's offspring, and then at Josh. 24:3 when noting the fulfillment of Abraham's promise. God's emphatic words in Gen. 22:17 confirm earlier promises (e.g., Gen. 17:2) and precede restatements to Abraham's heirs (Gen. 26:4, 24; 28:3; 35:11; 48:4). So the promises became part of the family's heritage (Gen. 28:3). Events proved God's word true (Gen. 47:27; Exod. 1:7). The promises to Hagar and Abraham recall God's blessed mandate for the human race, like that for the birds and sea creatures (Gen. 1:22), to "multiply" on the earth (Gen. 1:28), a purpose reinstated after the Flood (Gen. 8:17; 9:1, 7). [*rbh*]

16:13 God of Seeing (*'ēl ro'î*)—Some, with the LXX and Vulg., want to adjust the punctuation to read this noun as a suffixed participle "seeing me" (G. Wenham, 2). Others want to change the suffixed participle at the end of the verse from "seeing me" to the noun "seeing" (C. F. Keil, 222). A couple of versions at the end of the verse have "seeing him" (NASB, NRSV), perhaps due to a variant reading in the SP. Hagar saw the Angel of the Lord, whom she identified with God. One reason for Hagar's amazement at seeing God may have been a notion that face-to-face confrontation with God would bring death (Deut. 5:26; Exod. 33:20). God saw her especially in the sense of caring for her in time of need. When Abraham found a ram to sacrifice instead of his son, he named the place "the Lord will see," meaning that God would provide (Gen. 22:14). [*ro'î*]

17:1 Almighty (*šadday*)—The translation of this word is based on the Vulg. and on some renderings of the LXX. The LXX also sometimes translates it as "God," either with or without a pronominal suffix like "my." Rabbinic scholars took it to be a compound signifying "the one who is sufficient." Scholars agree that the meaning of the Hebrew term is still uncertain, although it functions as a divine name or title. The term is commonly associated with an Akkadian word for mountain, and this is probably correct (*HALOT*, 1421-22). The word could mean "the one of the mountain" (V. P. Hamilton, *TWOT*, 2:907). Gods were regularly connected with mountains in the ancient Near East (cf. Isa. 14:13), and the God of Israel would have a close link with both Mount Sinai (Judg. 5:5) and Mount Zion (Zech. 14:5; Isa. 52:7). The name "El," which means "God" in Gen. 17:1, was also a name for the high God in the Ugaritic pantheon, who had his home in a mountain (J. C. L. Gibson, 73, 75). [*šadday*]

Walk (*hithallēk*)—Walking as a metaphor for life conduct is common to both testaments (cf. Rom. 6:4; 8:4; 2 Cor. 5:7). The verb in Gen. 17:1 emphasizes moving "about," "to and fro," "in this direction and that" (*BDB*, 235). So one's walk is his life movement, his behavior. Abraham claimed to have done what God asked here (Gen. 24:40). The OT speaks elsewhere of walking before God (e.g., 1 Kings 8:23; Ps. 116:9), or in wisdom (Prov. 28:26), or truth (Ps. 86:11; 3 John 1:3). His people are to walk in his ways (Deut. 10:12; Josh. 22:5; Zech. 3:7) and his statutes (1 Kings 6:12; Neh. 10:29; cf. 2 John 1:6). They could walk in the name of God (Mic. 4:5). God even speaks of favorable relations as his walking among the Israelites (Lev. 26:12). [*hlk*]

Blameless (*tāmîm*)—Related to a verb meaning "to be perfect" or "completed" (*HALOT*, 1753), the adjective mostly indicates animals fit for sacrifice because they are without blemish (Exod. 12:5). Since the word can designate what is whole or intact (Ezek. 15:5), it can be used to say that a day or a year is complete (Josh. 10:13; Lev. 25:30). Morally, such a person is free of blame, avoiding ungodly practices (Deut. 32:4) and sin (2 Sam. 22:26). It can be a word for "integrity" when paired with "faithfulness" (Josh. 24:14; Judg. 9:16, 19), and can be descriptive of one's speech or walk (Amos 5:10; Ps. 15:2). The first person so described in Scripture is Noah (Gen. 6:9), and in the Psalms it is almost a synonym for "righteous" (Ps. 37:18). God guides such people and reveals himself to them correspondingly (2 Sam. 22:33, 26). The word summarizes God's character (2 Sam. 22:31), work (Deut. 32:4), Law (Ps. 19:7), and knowledge (Job 37:16). In such cases "perfect" is a good translation. The standard set for Abraham here seems similar to Jesus Christ's call for disciples to be "perfect as your Father in heaven in perfect" (Matt. 5:48). [*tāmîm*]

17:5 Multitude (*hămôn*)—This key word in explaining Abraham's name change can imply an abundance or company of nations (C. P. Weber, *TWOT*, 1:219). The word can refer to troops (Judg. 4:7; 1 Sam. 14:16) or to the whole population of Israel (2 Sam. 6:19). It also designates the "uproar" a multitude creates (Isa. 13:4). The sound can be a "tumult" of war (2 Sam. 18:29) or of rain (1 Kings 18:41). Abraham was father not only to Israel, but to the nations descended from Ishmael (Gen. 17:20; 25:12-16), Esau (Gen. 36:1-29), and the sons of Keturah (Gen. 25:1-4; 1 Chron. 1:32-33). [*hāmôn*]

Nations (*gôyim*)—While the word means "people," it is people with particular reference to political or geographical ties, and so resembles the modern word "nation" (R. E. Clements, *TDOT*, 2:427). After occurring 6x in the "Table of Nations" (Gen. 10), 18 of the word's other 19 appearances in Genesis are in connection with prophetic promises to Abraham's family (e.g., Gen. 12:2; 15:14; 18:18; 25:23; 35:11; 46:3). [*gôy*]

17:6 And I will make you fruitful (*wĕhiprētî 'ōtĕkā*)—This word was used of plants or animals bearing fruit or offspring (Isa. 32:12; Gen. 1:22). It could be applied to humans in vivid metaphors (Gen. 49:22; Jer. 23:3) and similes (Ps. 128:3; Ezek 19:10), but often was just the appropriate verb to indicate human production of offspring (*HALOT*, 963-64). God promised to make Abraham fruitful as he intended man to be in creation (Gen. 1:28; 8:17; 9:1, 7). Isaac may have recalled the promise when using the word to connote a flourishing condition (Gen. 26:22), but certainly did so in blessing Jacob (Gen. 28:3). God almost repeated Isaac's blessing to Jacob (Gen. 35:11; cf. 48:4). Joseph found it true as he named his son with a word that sounds like "doubly fruitful" (Gen. 41:52 and NIV note), a fact his father echoed (Gen. 49:22). For the promise was fulfilled in Egypt (Gen. 47:27). [*prh*]

17:8 As a possession (*la'ăḥuzzat*)—Related to a verb meaning to "hold" or "seize," the Hebrew could be translated "holding" (JPS, NRSV, SB), with reference to landed property as here and regularly, or to property in general (Lev. 25:45-46) (*HALOT*, 32). Although mostly referring to a larger tract of land, the word when modified by "grave" can designate a "burial site" (Gen. 23:4, 9, 20). The phrase

"permanent possession" in Gen. 17:8 recurs in Gen. 48:4 (cf. Lev. 25:34). A connotation of the word is "inheritance," perhaps because land holdings were so central to ancient inheritance. God is the "possession" of the Levites, as opposed to land (Ezek. 44:28). [*'ăḥuzzâ*]

17:9 You will keep (*tišmōr*)—This common verb has a broad range of usage, including "guard, watch, keep, protect, tend, preserve" (*BDB*, 1036-37). Cain asked if he was his brother's "keeper" (Gen. 4:9). God "protects" Jacob wherever he goes, Jacob "retains" thoughts, and Egypt "preserves" food (resp., Gen. 28:15; 37:11; 41:35). One can "celebrate" a festival (Exod. 23:15), "discharge" an office (Num. 3:10), or "maintain" justice (Hosea 17:7), but in a covenant context the word implies obedience to stipulated provisions such as circumcision here (Gen. 17:10-14). The opposite action would be to break the covenant by not being circumcised (Gen. 17:14). Likewise, one can "keep" a charge, a law, or a commandment by faithfully doing what God has required (Gen. 26:5). In Gen. 18:19 the word means to "adhere to" the way of the Lord by doing righteousness and justice. In 24:6 and 31:29 it is almost "beware," as one must "take care" or "be on one's guard" lest he do something wrong (*HALOT*, 1584). [*šmr*]

17:10 Must be circumcised (*himmôl*)—Jer. 9:25-26 indicates that in the seventh century B.C. circumcision was practiced not only in Israel but in Egypt, Edom, Ammon, Moab, and probably the Arabian desert. Ezek. 28:10 implies that it was done in Phoenicia. No evidence proves that it occurred in Mesopotamia, but Egyptian records of circumcision go back to the twenty-third century B.C. (G. Mayer,

TDOT, 8:159-60). God evidently appropriated an existing cultural practice and made it the sign of his covenant with Abraham's family (Gen. 17:11). Circumcision involved cutting off the foreskin of the male sex organ, and while usually performed on the eighth day of life in Israel (Gen. 17:12; 21:4; Luke 2:21), could be an adult activity (Gen. 17:24; 34:24). As a sign of the Abrahamic Covenant and a qualification for sharing in the Passover (Exod. 12:48), circumcision seemed necessary, in the eyes of many early Christians, for sharing in Christ (Acts 15:1, 5). The apostle Paul clarified that circumcision was not necessary for a Christian (Rom. 2:28-29; 1 Cor. 7:18-19; Gal. 5:6). [*mwl*]

17:11 As a sign (*lĕʾôt*)—A "sign" is something that conveys information, and the content of the information depends on the situation. The word probably has a non-theological origin, since it is used for such things as fire signals and family emblems (P. A. Kruger, *NIDOTTE*, 1:331-32). A "sign" could distinguish (Gen. 4:15; Exod. 8:23; 12:13) or commemorate (Exod. 13:9; Num. 16:38). A sign could be something as basic as an event (Exod. 3:12); in the OT God often gave signs as proofs of his reality and activity. The first sign of a divine covenant was the rainbow (Gen. 9:17). The covenant sign in Gen. 17:11 served as a reminder of duty (*HALOT*, 26), but it also had distinguishing and commemorative functions with regard to the entire covenant. As the sign of the Sabbath recalled God's work in creation (Exod. 31:13), so circumcision recalled God's choice of the Abrahamic seed. [*ʾôt*]

17:12 Foreigner (*ben-nēkār*)—This phrase is literally "son of a foreigner," but because "son" in Hebrew often designated a category of people, a "son of a foreigner" is equivalent to a "foreigner." In Israel this was a term for Gentiles. The word "stranger" of Gen. 15:13, while also generally indicating a foreigner, has less emphasis on "foreignness" than this word. In post-biblical literature the "stranger" came to be associated with the proselyte, perhaps because the Mosaic Law so regularly puts the "stranger" under the same legal obligations as the native. But "foreigners" were unfit to participate in the Passover (Exod. 12:43); neither could they enter the sanctuary, for they were uncircumcised (Ezek. 44:7, 9). In Neh. 9:2 separation from foreigners implies divorcing Gentile wives (B. Lang, *TDOT*, 9:429). [*nēkār*]

17:14 And he must be cut off (*wĕnikrĕtâ*)—This general word for "cut" can speak of cutting poles or garments (Exod. 34:13; 2 Sam. 10:4), but in Genesis is used two ways, of cutting a covenant (e.g., Gen. 15:18; 21:27; 31:44) and of cutting off life. The connection of cutting with covenant is discussed above at Gen. 15:10 and apparently relates to the cutting of sacrificial animals used in a covenant-making ritual, but Gen. 17:14 threatens the cutting off of a person. One ongoing question is whether this metaphorical cutting off can only refer to death. The NRSV in Gen. 41:36 translates the word as "perish" in connection with a famine. If "cutting off" can be something less than death, like banishment, the text is never explicit to that effect. Another question is whether the agent is always divine (E. B. Smick, *TWOT*, 1:457). The agent in Gen. 9:11 is God through the Flood, and God occasionally declares himself the agent (Lev. 17:10; 20:3). The offence that merited being cut off could easily escape human detection, such as making incense like that of the altar or eating sacred meat while ceremonially unclean (Exod. 30:38;

Lev. 7:21). So God may have had to be the Agent in some cases, but the nation was probably to execute judgment when it possessed evidence to convict a criminal. For example, Exodus 31:14 announces the penalty for Sabbath violation as the cutting off of the guilty party, and Num. 15:36 shows God instructing human government to execute the Sabbath breaker. Likewise, Lev. 20:17 seems to indicate public execution of judgment when stating that certain guilty parties were to be cut off "in the sight of their people." [*krt*]

From his people (*mē'ammêhā*)—This very common OT word (2954x) apparently first meant "paternal uncle." It expanded to cover paternal relationships, or one's clan, and widened to signify "people" as an ethnic or national group (Gen. 11:6; 26:10), but with an emphasis on kinship, religious, and geographical ties (e.g., Gen. 23:13). It can indicate people in general as a collection of individuals (Gen. 32:7), such as in a city (Gen. 19:4). As a plural word it may refer to national or racial groups (Gen. 27:29), but several times, as here in Gen. 17:14, the plural indicates "relatives," perhaps particularly on the father's side (cf. Gen. 25:8; Lev. 19:16; Num. 9:13) (*HALOT*, 837-39). ['*am*]

He has broken (*hēpar*)—To break a covenant is to "violate" its terms, "frustrate" its purpose, or "annul" its effect. These concepts in the verb apply to other areas, as one can "violate" the fear of God by not maintaining it (Job 15:4), "frustrate" good counsel by making it appear unwise (2 Sam. 15:34; 17:14), or "annul" a vow by canceling it (Num. 30:8). One can "break" God's commandments or Law (Num. 15:31; Ps. 119:126). But the most common use of the word is with respect to breaking a covenant (cf. Judg. 2:1; Jer. 11:10; Isa. 33:8) (*BDB*, 830). [*prr*]

17:17 And he laughed (*wayyiṣḥāq*)—This flexible word regularly raises interpretative questions regarding its sense and nuance. Since Abraham receives no correction about his laughter here as Sarah does for hers in 18:12, could Abraham have smiled (V. P. Hamilton, 125, n. 10)? However, the name Isaac, or "He-Laughs," derives from the occasion of Abraham's act. If Sarah's initial laughter at the news of a child expresses an element of doubt, in Gen. 21:6 she says that God has brought her the laughter of joy over Isaac. In Gen. 19:14 the word means "joke," but in 21:9 "make fun of" and in 39:14-17 "make sport of." In Gen. 26:8 it refers to love play, but in Exodus 32:6 to wild entertainment (cf. Judg. 16:25). [*ṣḥq*]

17:20 He will father (*yôlîd*)—This is the most common word for giving birth (588x) and can cover either maternal or paternal parental involvement; it can even describe laying eggs (Jer. 17:11). It sums up the woman's part of pain and pregnancy in Gen. 3:16, but also the father's role as the one through whom descent was tracked (cf. Gen. 4:18). The act of fathering could concern more than two generations because a man was regarded as fathering all those descended from him. An important biblical concept is that God empowers one to give birth (Gen. 4:1; 16:2; 18:13-14) (P. R. Gilchrist, *TWOT*, 1:378-80). Metaphorically, one can give birth to evil (Job 15:35), and a day gives birth to its events (Isa. 26:18; Prov. 27:1). God gave birth to Israel and to Israel's king (Deut. 32:18; Ps. 2:7). [*yld*]

17:21 I will establish (*'āqîm*)—God had to keep Noah alive through the Flood in order to establish his covenant with him (Gen. 6:18; 9:9). God promised that he would ratify or confirm his covenant with the unborn Isaac, and he did so in Gen. 26:3-5. God's covenant with Abraham was passed down to Isaac. Exod. 2:24 seems to speak of a single covenant with Abraham, Isaac, and Jacob, and 1 Chron. 16:16-18 shows this to be the case. However, Lev. 26:42 reveals that each of the patriarchs had his own covenant; God personally renewed his covenant with each of them. The word means to "arise" or "stand up," and also to "cause to stand." The idea in many cases can be to "carry out" or "give effect to" a covenant (Lev. 26:9), vow, word, or plan (*BDB*, 879). This frequent OT word (663x) has many specialized meanings. A similar usage occurs in Gen. 23:17, 20, where property is "deeded" to someone by payment of its price to the former owner in the presence of witnesses; it is confirmed as belonging to him. [*qwm*]

18:1 And He appeared (*wayyērā'*)—This passive form of the verb "to see" can also mean "be seen" or "be visible" (*BDB*, 908), and first occurs in Gen. 1:9, where God commanded the dry land to "appear." In Gen. 8:5 the mountaintops appeared after the Flood. God caused the rainbow to appear after the rain as a sign (Gen. 9:14). In Gen. 12:7 God appeared to Abraham, so that he built an altar. He appeared to him twice more (Gen. 17:1; 18:1), and appeared at least twice to Isaac (Gen. 26:2; 26:24) and Jacob (Gen. 35:1; 35:9). The appearance in Gen. 18 was visible and bodily. The Lord fostered especially close ties with these men because his plans for human salvation by a Messiah sent to a chosen nation began to unfold with Abraham. When God appeared to Moses, he recalled appearing to the patriarchs (Exod. 6:3). His appearances would continue through Israel's history (Lev. 9:4; Deut. 31:15; 1 Sam. 3:21; Ps. 84:7), but often through the

Angel of the Lord (Judg. 13:21-22), or in a glorious cloud (Exod. 16:10; Num. 14:10), or in a dream (1 Kings 3:5; 9:2). His normal place of appearance was within the Holy of Holies at Israel's shrine (Lev. 16:2). He will appear to Israel at the end of the age (Zech. 9:14; Mal. 3:2; Ps. 102:16), an appearance that Christians understand to be by the Lord Jesus Christ (1 Tim. 6:14). [*r'h*]

18:3 My lord (*'ădōnāy*)—This is the rendering of most translations, which suppose Abraham did not yet realize that he addressed God (JPS, SB, REB, and TEV have "my lords" or "sirs"). But the NKJV translates "my Lord" here, concluding that Abraham knew that he addressed God. The Hebrew form is a special one that the Jewish copyists of the Bible may have used to designate God. Scholars have taken part of it as a suffix meaning "my," but the LXX just translated the whole term as "Lord." Some scholars feel that the special form involved no suffix but rather was an indication of emphasis and noun status (O. Eissfeldt, *TDOT*, 1:70; B. Waltke and M. O'Connor, 124), so that the meaning is "Lord of all." The only places where this special form might refer to human beings are Gen. 18:3; 19:18; Isa. 21:8, and Ezra 10:3. The same issue arises in Ezra, where some interpreters think that "lord" refers to God, while most translations do not. At Isa. 21:8 most translations have "Lord," but some do not (NIV, NLT, TEV). If the translation should be "my Lord" in Gen. 19:18, then Lot would have been addressing God. Since the special form is part of the system of vowel indication added to the original letters by post-biblical Jewish scholars, it may be that their decision about the sense of the word at Gen. 18:3 could be mistaken.

When not referring to God in Genesis,

"lord" can signify one's husband, a title of respect to strangers, or a master of a servant (resp., Gen. 18:12; 19:2; 24:9). It can be an appropriate title for a king or a vizier (Gen. 40:1; 42:30). [*'ādôn*]

Favor (*ḥēn*)—Every place this word stands in Genesis it is accompanied by the phrase "in the eyes of." If a person finds favor in someone's eyes, he is pleasing to that one. The noun at base indicates aesthetic "grace" or beauty in a person or object (cf. the related verb in Prov. 26:25), and secondarily the "favor" that this pleasing quality produces in another person. The ancients felt that favor registered on the face, particularly in the eyes. The word next most often translated as "favor" is literally "face" (D. N. Freedman and J. R. Lundbom, *TDOT*, 5:24-25). But favor in the OT often results from moral and spiritual qualities, such as when Noah found favor in God's eyes (Gen. 6:8); Lot also found favor so as to be spared destruction (Gen. 19:19). Laban found favor with God because of Jacob's presence (Gen. 30:27), and Jacob sent Esau gifts to procure favor (Gen. 32:5). God can give a person favor in the eyes of those around him (Gen. 39:21). [*ḥēn*]

18:11 Were old (*zĕqēnîm*)—This is the most general word for old age (Gen. 19:4: "young and old") and can refer to a woman (Zech. 8:4) despite deriving from a word meaning "beard." After the book of Genesis, this adjective when functioning nominally most often takes on the technical sense of a leader in a community, whether a city, tribe, or nation. That usage occurs in Genesis only at 50:7 of the "elders of Israel." In Gen. 24:2 the NRSV translates "the oldest," but the NIV has "chief"; some translations (JPS, NAB, NJB) may combine age and rule with the translation "senior." The aged (*yāšîš*) were

regarded as full of wisdom due to their experience (Job 12:12), and they were also often family patriarchs. So older men were natural sources of leadership and advice (J. Conrad, *TDOT*, 4:122-24). Nonetheless, in Genesis the word "old" generally connotes loss of powers and nearness to death. [*zāqēn*]

18:14 Is it too hard (*hăyippālē'*)—This is the first OT use of this word whose root meaning is "to be wonderful." Most often it refers to what God does, for the word points to what is beyond human ability or expectation. Such acts stir up wonder, but their central purpose is evidentiary, attesting to the presence and power of God. (V. P. Hamilton, *TWOT*, 1:723). One epithet for God is that he is the One who does wonders (Judg. 13:19). The 10 plagues of Egypt were "My wonders," since divine judgments can astound with wonder (Deut. 28:59; Isa. 29:14), and the term is quite frequent in the Psalms and Job (e.g., Pss. 40:5; 78:4; Job 37:14). The word can be used of the human sphere about wonderful love (2 Sam. 1:26), excessively difficult judicial decisions (Deut. 17:8), impossible acts (2 Sam. 13:2), or outrageous words (Dan. 11:36). Statements quite like Gen. 18:14 come again in Jer. 32:17, 27, while God contrasts himself with man in Zech. 8:6. [*pl'*]

18:15 But she denied (*wattĕkaḥēš*)—This is the translation of the NRSV, NLT, and TEV, but several other translations have something like "lied" (JPS, NJB, REB, NIV). The word implies deceptive behavior, such as lying (Lev. 6:2), fawning before an enemy (Deut. 33:29), or even an olive tree's failure to produce olives (Hab. 3:17). Often the deception can be an apparent acknowledgement that is not genuine (*BDB*, 471). So one may be false in his profession of God (Isa. 59:13; Josh. 24:27) or deny him outright (Job 31:28; Prov. 30:9). In Job 8:18 the word has the meaning "deny," which also seems suitable here as Sarah denied that she laughed. [*kḥš*]

18:17 Should I hide (*hamkasseh 'ănî*)— This verb essentially means "cover," as in a cloud covering the ground or shame covering a face (Ezek. 38:16; Obad. 10), but it often takes a different nuance from the context. One may cover sins in order to hide them (Prov. 28:13) or to forgive them (Ps. 32:1). Concealing is a frequent sense of the verb (Lev. 16:13; Isa. 51:16; Ps. 40:10; Mal. 2:16). God had the authority to keep secret (*str*) the reality of Sodom's judgment (Deut. 29:29), but felt that by not disclosing it to Abraham he would have been concealing it. This attitude of revealing truth to his servants is characteristic of God (Amos 3:7; Prov. 3:32; Ps. 25:14). [*ksh*]

18:19 I have chosen him (*yĕda'tîw*)—The verb (1,003x) is the basic one for "know," a word that pertains to some internalization of experience with life, including the relationship resulting from the experience. The word has a wide range of nuances that only particular contexts can clarify (T. E. Fretheim, *NIDOTTE*, 2:410); up to this point in Genesis the word has signified intellectual (Gen. 3:5) and sexual (Gen. 4:1) knowledge. In Gen. 18:19 it seems to function as in Amos 3:2, where the knowing is selective. God knew Abraham in a way that he did not know others; NJB, REB, NLT, and NAB at Gen. 18:19 have, "I have singled him out." Similar passages regarding God's special knowledge of a person include Exod. 33:12, 17; Deut. 34:10; and 2 Sam. 7:20. A number of scholars find this to be a technical word in covenant-making that

implies mutual recognition by the suzerain and vassal; God acknowledges Abraham as a genuine servant in a covenant relationship with him (V. P. Hamilton, *Genesis 18–50*, 18).

In Gen. 19:5 the Sodomites use this word in a brutal wordplay. They ask Lot to bring out the strangers so that they might "know" them. The aim is not to make acquaintance, or investigate identity, but to have forced, homosexual sex. The same word means to have sex in v. 7 when speaking of daughters having not "known" a man. It is by such Sodomite actions that the Lord sees and "knows" (Gen. 18:21) that the outcry of the city is as bad as reported. [*yd'*]

He will direct (*yĕṣawweh*)—The root idea of this verb is to "order" or "command," and from it derives the common OT word for "commandment." In much of Genesis the verb means to command (e.g., Gen. 2:16; 6:22) or give orders (Gen. 12:20; 42:25), but here the tone might be softened to "instruct" (JPS; *HALOT*, 1011), "charge" (NRSV, REB), or "direct" (NIV, NAB, NLT). As head of his family Abraham is to do everything in his power to ensure that his offspring relate to the Lord in obedience as he does (cf. Gen. 26:5). Other passages that suggest this authority based on parental love include Gen. 27:8; 28:1; 49:29. [*ṣwh*]

Way (*derek*)—The noun (775x) denotes a way, road, path, or journey (resp., Gen. 3:24; 16:7; 49:17; 42:25). Metaphorically it may refer to a kind of behavior, such as sexual intercourse or menstruation (Gen. 19:31; 31:35). More generally it can designate the whole course of life. According to Gen. 6:12 humanity corrupted its "way" on the earth; among the many ways to live, it is the way of the Lord that is the right one. "Way of the Lord" in this sense occurs five other places in the OT (Judg.

2:22; 2 Kings 21:22; Jer. 5:4-5; Prov. 10:29), and "ways of the Lord" 5x (2 Sam. 22:22; 2 Chron. 17:6; Pss. 18:21; 138:5; Hosea 14:10). A similar phrase with another word for Lord occurs in Ezek. 18:25, 29; 33:17, 20. The NT repeats this idea of a spiritual way of the Lord in Acts 18:25. The metaphorical use of the word is about as common as its nonmetaphorical use (BDB, 202-04). [derek]

And justice (ûmišpāṭ)—This important word (425x) occurs as a common noun only 3x in Genesis. It derives from a verb broader in scope than "judge," since the activity could involve ruling a nation. So while the noun is especially frequent in judicial settings with denotations such as verdict, law, case, court, and justice, it has such other possible meanings as custom (Gen. 40:13), right, manner, decision, and even plan (BDB, 1048-49). Abraham expects God as Earth's sovereign to conform to an absolute standard of "justice" in his punishment of people (Gen. 18:25). The pairing of justice with righteousness happens 26 times in the OT. A righteous person does these two things and lives on account of them (Ezek. 18:5, 27), for God does these things (Ps. 33:5; Jer. 9:24; Isa. 33:5). These are what a human king should do (1 Kings 10:9; 2 Sam. 8:15), and what the Messiah will do (Jer. 23:5; 33:15). [mišpāṭ]

18:20 The outcry (za'ăqat)—This is a "plaintive cry" or "cry for help" (HALOT, 277). Such a cry could rise to God (Isa. 30:19; Neh. 9:9). The related verb in Gen. 4:10 speaks of Abel's blood crying for vengeance, so the outcry of Sodom and Gomorrah could be that of their victims. It was an outcry or "outrage" (JPS) because of Sodom, one to which God could not be unresponsive. A quite similar word for "outcry" in 18:21 and 19:13 (ṣĕ'āqâ) may just involve a different spelling of the word, but since the two terms appear together at least 3x (V. P. Hamilton, Genesis 18–50, 20), there may be a slight difference in nuance. The language describes God in human terms, since he knows all things and did not have to investigate to see whether the reality matched the report. [zĕ'āqâ]

And their sin (wĕḥaṭṭā't ām)—This is the second time this word (298x) has appeared (Gen. 4:7), and it will occur twice more in Genesis of sins against people (Gen. 31:36; 50:17). It derives from a verb meaning to "miss the mark," "go wrong," or "sin." The noun additionally came to apply to items related to sin, such as guilt, punishment, or a sin offering (BDB, 306, 308-9). The word "sin" in Gen. 18:20 clarifies that the "outcry of Sodom and Gomorrah" was because of their sin against their inhabitants and probably against their neighbors. A person could sin against God directly (Lev. 4:14), but also any sin against a person involved sinning (ḥṭ') against God (Ps. 51:4). [ḥaṭṭā't]

18:23 Will You sweep away (tispeh)—The action is a sweeping or snatching away, as a beard by a razor (Isa. 7:20), a captive by the enemy (Isa. 13:15), or the good of the land by injustice (Prov. 13:23). Men can sweep away the lives of others (1 Sam. 27:1; Ps. 40:14), but the predominant use of the word is for divine judgment as in Gen. 18:23-24; 19:15, 17 (cf. Num. 16:26; 1 Sam. 12:25; Amos 3:15). Even if men sweep away lives, the Lord may be behind it (1 Chron. 21:12). The verb implies a swift change and powerful removal (P. J. J. S. Els, NIDOTTE, 277-78). [sph]

The wicked (rāšā')—Abraham contrasts such people with "the righteous," as he does in the only other use of the word in Genesis at 18:25. The contrast exists 80 times in Scripture, half of them in Proverbs, and it helps to define this sort of person. He is one disobedient to God's standards and a threat to his community (G. H. Livingston, *TWOT*, 863-64). The related verb means to be wicked or guilty (*BDB*, 957), and the adjective implies a guilty or wicked person, often a criminal. [*rāšā'*]

19:1 And he bowed (*wayyištaḥû*)— Bowing was an external action that expressed some other intention such as greetings, respect, homage, submission, or worship (resp., Gen. 19:1; 23:7; 43:26; 27:29; 22:5). In God's presence bowing, due to its other meanings, naturally expressed worship. In this context, "worship" often stands in conjunction with the word "serve" (e.g., Deut. 8:19). The word means "bow" 18x and "worship" 5x in Genesis, with several passages indicating that the worship included bowing (Gen. 24:26, 48, 52; 47:31; cf. Heb. 11:21). Lot's bowing with his face to the ground when greeting strangers shows the high value put on hospitality and the commonness of bowing, which could involve prostration. Such bowing evidently occurred throughout the ancient Near East according to surviving texts and artwork (H. D. Preuss, *TDOT*, 4:250). Lot's response to these strangers, in contrast with that of the other Sodomites, is like Abraham's (Gen. 18:2). [*ḥwh*]

19:2 Your servant (*'abdĕkem*)—This noun, derived from the verb translated "enslave" at 15:13, can also mean "slave." But Lot is voluntarily extending hospitality to strangers, so his language is a self-deprecating form of polite address. The common word (803x) had a wide range of meaning including ambassador, vassal,

king, king's officer, army officer, or army soldier (resp., 2 Sam. 10:2, 19; 1 Sam. 19:1; 29:3; 17:8). In Gen. 24:10 it is the chief servant of Abraham, who was in charge of all he had. The term described God's worshipers as servants (Isa. 54:17), sometimes in the formal sense of Levites (Ps. 134:1), and implied high honor when applied to individuals (Hag. 2:23) (*BDB*, 713-14). For this reason "My Servant" can be an honorific title for the Messiah in Isaiah (e.g., Isa. 42:1). The NT continues this tradition when Mary, Paul, James, and Jude identify themselves as God's servants (Luke 1:38; Titus 1:1; James 1:1; Jude 1:1), and when Moses is given this title (Rev. 15:3). [*'ebed*]

19:9 And he would be the judge (*wayyišpōṭ*)—This is the verb mentioned at 18:19 as related to "justice." Since it has broad application to government, all three branches of it (R. D. Culver, *TWOT*, 947), some translations emphasize the executive branch here: "he acts the ruler" (JPS) or "he dares to give orders" (NAB). The Sodomites probably applied both nuances. Lot had judged them by calling what they attempted to do "evil" and had tried to rule them by telling them not to do it (Gen. 19:7). This is the word used of God as the "One who judges/rules" the whole earth (Gen. 18:25). Sarah called on God to judge between her and Abraham, and Laban asked him to judge between himself and Jacob (Gen. 16:5; 31:53). The Sodomites show no concern for justice, mocking someone trying to uphold it. [*špṭ*]

19:19 Your kindness (*ḥasdĕkā*)—This is an important word (251x) that like the previous one embraces both emotion and action. A relational term linked with covenant loyalty (Exod. 20:6; Deut. 7:9; 2 Sam. 22:51), it describes God's caring action on behalf of his people, such as delivering them from Egypt (Exod. 15:13). God's kindness to Israel is an expression of his everlasting love (Jer. 31:3). At Exodus 15:13 some translations stress "mercy" (NKJV, NAB), or "faithfulness" (SB, TEV), but "love" (JPS) is the predominant translation, which is often modified: "steadfast" (ESV, NRSV), "unfailing" (NLT, NIV), "faithful" (NJB), or "constant" (REB). The basic meaning of the word may be "kindness"; there is often an element of reciprocity, because kind treatment sparks kind treatment in return (Judg. 1:24; 1 Sam. 15:6). It is a fundamental quality that God expects from his people (Mic. 6:8), and that he abundantly possesses (Exod. 34:7) (H.-J. Zobel, *TDOT*, 5:45-64). This is the first of 11 occurrences of the word in Genesis. Sarah showed loyal love to Abraham by a ruse on his behalf, and Joseph showed Jacob this love by a proper burial (Gen. 20:13; 47:29). Abimelech expected Abraham to return him the kindness Abraham had received from him (Gen. 21:23). Abraham's servant viewed success in his mission as God's kindness to Abraham (Gen. 24:12, 14, 27, 49). Jacob and Joseph were also recipients of God's kindness (Gen. 32:10; 39:21). [*ḥesed*]

19:25 And He overthrew (*wayyahăpōk*)— This verb can simply mean "turn," as a wind turns (Exod. 10:19), or a sword turns this way and that (Gen. 3:24). It can also mean "turn" in the sense of "change," as when water turned to blood (Exod. 7:20), but the word has a special use regarding destruction where it means "overturn." Besides at Gen. 19:21, 25, 29, the word occurs in a recollection of Sodom's destruction (Deut. 29:22; cf. a related noun at Isa. 13:19; Jer. 49:18; Amos 4:11). Sodom and Gomorrah became a model of the judgment that God would pour out on sinful people (2 Peter 2:6). So when God promised to "overthrow" Jerusalem, Nineveh, or the world's kingdoms (resp., 2 Kings 21:13; Jonah 3:4; Hag. 2:22), he was likely to mean a complete destruction turning everything upside down. Yet the word could also describe the human overthrow of a country (1 Chron. 19:3) (V. P. Hamilton, *TWOT*, 1:221). [*hpk*]

19:29 And He remembered (*wayyizkōr*)— The context suggests that God's remembering consisted of taking actions on Abraham's, and so Lot's, behalf. The word (235x) can also mean "consider," "mention," or "be mindful of" (*DCH*, 3:105), indicating mental activity (Gen. 40:23; 42:9), verbal expressions (Gen. 40:14; 41:9), or thoughts accompanied by appropriate actions (Gen. 8:1). When God "remembered" people in Genesis, his activity always included actions to benefit them, whether removing the Flood, preventing its reoccurrence, rescuing Lot, or giving Rachel a baby (resp., Gen. 8:1; 9:15-16; 19:29; 30:22). God behaved this way throughout the OT (Judg. 16:28; 1 Sam. 1:11; 2 Kings 20:3). He remembered his covenant with Israel by delivering them from Egypt (Exod. 2:24; 6:5). If he sent Israel into exile, he would remember his covenant so as to restore them if they repented (Lev. 26:42, 45). His people had a corresponding responsibility to remember the Lord and his activity that they might follow him (Exod. 13:3; Zech. 10:9). Of course, God can also remember in order to punish sin (Hos. 9:9; Jer. 31:34). [*zkr*]

20:3 In a dream (*baḥălôm*)—Egyptian, Hittite, and Mesopotamian accounts of their gods revealing themselves to people in dreams show that the concept was a familiar one. And symbolic dreams might not involve direct divine appearance in the dream (Gen. 37; Dan. 2). People believed that dreams were God's business and communicated the future (Gen. 40–41). In both Egypt and Mesopotamia people would spend the night in a temple in hopes of receiving a dream oracle (M. Ottosson, *TDOT*, 4:421-32). God appeared to Solomon in a dream at a worship center (1 Kings 3:5-15), but there is no evidence that he sought a dream oracle. God came unsought to Jacob at Bethel and Beersheba (Gen. 46:1-4; 28:10-22). It was customary for God to speak to prophets in dreams (Num. 12:6), but he spoke this way to many other individuals in the Bible in order to accomplish his will. His visit to Abimelech, like that to Laban (Gen. 31:24), served to prevent someone from hurting his chosen people. His appearance to Abimelech, who evidently intended to take Sarah as a wife, was quite important. God had promised to give Sarah and Abraham a child who would become a mighty nation (Gen. 18:10, 18-19), but Abimelech could have interfered with the fulfillment of this promise. [*ḥălôm*]

Husband (*bāʿal*)—This fairly common word (161x) at base means "lord" but often has the sense of "owner." It also frequently signifies "husband," for a man was the lord and owner of his wife in a real sense because men regularly purchased their wives (Exod. 22:16-17; 1 Sam. 18:25) (W. T. Koopmans, *NIDOTTE*, 1:682). One was lord of a wife to such an extent that he could nullify a vow she had made even before the marriage (Num. 30:6-8). The other three uses of the word in Genesis concern Abraham's allies as "owners" of a covenant with Abraham, Joseph as a "possessor" of dreams, and archers as "lords" of arrows (resp., Gen. 14:13; 37:19; 49:23). The noun appears here with a related verb (*bʿl*) that means to be lord or to be married. [*baʿal*]

20:4 Innocent (*ṣaddîq*)—This adjective (206x) also means "righteous" and is related to the noun "righteousness" (*ṣĕdāqâ*) of Gen. 15:6. Noah was the only man with this status in his generation (Gen. 6:9; 7:1). It is the opposite of being "wicked" (Gen. 18:23-26, 28). Abimelech describes his nation as "innocent" because he as its head had not committed adultery with Sarah. His taking her had not yet culminated in sex, so he retained a certain righteousness or innocence regarding that sin. The word can signify to be in the right (Exod. 9:27; 1 Sam. 24:17). Several translations have "just" (NRSV, NLT, NAB) at Deut. 32:4 where the word describes God. It also describes the Messianic Servant in Isa. 53:11. Habakkuk 2:4 says that the "righteous" man will live by his faith, or faithfulness, and the NT cites this verse to describe the Christian (Rom. 1:17; Gal. 3:11). [*ṣaddîq*]

20:5 In the integrity (*bĕtom*)—The basic sense of the word is "perfection" but here the idea is "guilelessness" in the phrase "integrity of my heart." This phrase also occurs in Ps. 101:2, where the whole psalm more or less shows what it means. It is the quality by which King David led the nation (Ps. 78:72) and in 1 Kings 9:4 is paired with the word "uprightness." The word "integrity" often implies "purity" or "innocence" (Pss. 7:9; 26:11; 41:13; Prov. 19:1) (*HALOT*, 1744). Another translation might be "blamelessness." [*tōm*]

My heart (*lĕbābî*)—This word appears 265x, and a more common spelling of the same word (*lēb*) occurs another 602x. The term could denote the internal, physical organ (1 Sam. 25:37) but most often indicated the core or central part of a person, applying variously to the mind, will, conscience, understanding, or heart. It could refer to one's overall strength, inmost affections, courage, or mental state (resp., Gen. 18:5; 34:3 and 50:21; 42:28; 45:26). It is the part of man by which he thinks evil (Gen. 6:5-6; 8:21) or thinks to himself (Gen. 17:17; 24:45; 27:41). The heart related to practically every non-physical aspect of a person (A. Bowling, *TWOT*, 1:466). Laban accused Jacob of stealing his heart by running off with Laban's daughters (Gen. 31:26). The two occurrences of this word in Gen. 20:5-6 indicate the conscience; Abimelech felt no guilt about what he had done because Abraham and Sarah had not given him the whole truth. [*lēbāb*]

And in the cleanness (*ûbĕniqyōn*)—Rather than the literal "in the cleanness of my hands," one might say "with clean hands." The root verb may relate to the idea of emptiness but generally means to be exempt from punishment or to acquit. The related adjective (*nāqî*) also means free of obligation or punishment, as well as innocent, guiltless, or clean (G. Warmuth, *TDOT*, 553-63). It is the person with clean (*nāqî*) hands and a pure heart who can stand in God's holy place (Ps. 24:3). The noun occurs in four other verses besides Gen. 20:5, in Pss. 26:6 and 73:13 linked with "hands" as here. The psalmist spoke metaphorically of purifying his heart and washing his hands in "innocence." In Amos 4:6 the "cleanness of teeth" is due to lack of food. The idolatrous people of Samaria were incapable of "purity" (Hosea 8:5). [*niqqāyôn*]

20:6 So I kept (*wā'ehśōk*)—The fundamental idea of the verb is holding back a person or thing, the subject having power over the object (L. J. Coppes, *TWOT*, 1:329). God held Abimelech back from sinning, restraining him (cf. 2 Sam. 18:16) either inwardly or by circumstance. God held David back from evil by a visit from

the wife of a man David intended to kill (1 Sam. 25:39), and David prayed that God would "keep" him from presumptuous sin (Ps. 19:13). The word can also mean "spare" (2 Kings 5:20), and God's action was positive for Abimelech in Gen. 20:6. In its three other uses in Genesis, the verb means to "withhold." Abraham did not withhold his son from God but was ready to sacrifice him; Potiphar did not withhold anything from Joseph except his wife (Gen. 22:12, 16; 39:9). To "not withhold" is essentially to give (Prov. 21:26). [*hśk*]

20:7 Prophet (*nābî'*)—This is the only occurrence of the word (325) in Genesis. It has a Semitic background from a verb meaning to "name, call," and a noun meaning "one who has been called." In Hebrew and other West Semitic languages the word denotes an intermediary called by God to speak on his behalf. The word "prophet," derived from the Greek and reflecting biblical usage, is the best translation of the Hebrew word. Ancient societies in Syria (Mari), Canaan, Assyria, and Arabia were familiar with the idea of one mediating a god's words (H.-P. Müller, *TDOT*, 9:130-37). Since Abraham was a prophet, Abimelech could expect Abraham's prayers to be effective for Abimelech and his nation Gerar. Psalm 105:14-15 refers in part to this incident. [*nābî'*]

And he will pray (*wĕyitpallēl*)—The derivation of the word (80x) is obscure, but the broad meaning of the verb in this form is "pray" (E. Gerstenberger, *TDOT*, 11:568-69), with perhaps 25 cases when it means to "intercede" for another (V. P. Hamilton, *Genesis 18–50*, 64). In another form its idea is "expect" (Gen. 48:11). God did answer Abraham's prayer (Gen. 20:17), and he generally responded favorably when this verb appears. The two times prayer would clearly go unanswered were when it addressed a false god (Isa. 16:12; 44:17; 45:20) or when God had already decided not to grant a specific request (Jer. 7:16; 11:14; 14:11). Intercession for others is a mark of God's man (Job 42:8; Dan. 9:20; Ezra 10:1; Neh. 1:4, 6), and the most frequent use of this verb is in Solomon's prayer on behalf of his nation (9x in 1 Kings 8). [*pll*]

20:9 And how have I sinned (*ûmeh-ḥāṭā'tî*)—Many translate the word here with something like "wronged" (NIV, JPS, NAB, NJB, TEV; cf. Gen. 44:32). This verb is related to the adjective "sinful" of 13:13 and the noun "sin" of 18:20. The word family is represented about 580x in the OT and provides the main words for sin. The concept of sin derives from the verb's more prosaic sense of missing a mark or way (Judg. 20:16; Prov. 8:36; 19:2) (G. H. Livingston, *TWOT*, 1:277). Joseph felt that adultery was sinning against God (Gen. 39:9), perhaps guided by knowledge of Abimelech's nearly sinning with Sarah (Gen. 20:6). Here Abimelech incredulously asked what sin he had committed against Abraham such that Abraham would bring this liability for sin on him. Elsewhere in Genesis the word means to accept the blame at 43:9 and 44:32, and possibly also 31:39, where most translate with the idea of accepting the loss. The cupbearer and baker "offended" Pharaoh (Gen. 40:1). [*ḥṭ'*]

20:11 Fear (*yir'at*)—Fear of God is a key concept of OT religion, and perhaps was the earliest term for religion in Hebrew and related languages (H. F. Fuhs, *TDOT*, 6:297). Many feel that "reverence" can be a good translation of the word (Ps. 2:11; Job 15:4). Fear can be an appropriate emotion when it warns of danger, and for sinful human beings fear of a holy God is proper (Ps. 90:11). Abraham's thought was that lack of it would lead to harmful, criminal behavior. The noun occurs in Genesis only here, but this high esteem for fear of God characterizes Scripture (Isa. 33:6; Ps. 19:9). God wanted the Israelites to have it (Exod. 20:20; Jer. 32:40); it causes rulers to rule well (2 Sam. 23:3; Isa. 11:2-3). Fear of the Lord is the beginning of wisdom (Ps. 111:10; Prov. 9:10), and Proverbs tries to inculcate it (Prov. 2:5). [*yir'â*]

20:16 Also you are vindicated (*wěnōkāḥat*)—This word, which occurs 6x in Genesis, has primarily a judicial force (P. R. Gilchrist, *TWOT*, 1:376-77), but it includes a range of ideas such as decide, judge, convict, convince, and reprove. The sense at this verse is probably "shown to be right" or "vindicated" (*BDB*, 407). In Gen. 21:25 Abraham "rebuked" (cf. Gen. 31:42) or "complained to" Abimelech because his servants seized a well that Abraham had dug. Abraham's servant sought the woman God had "appointed" (NRSV, NLT, NKJV, NASB) or "decided upon/on" (NAB, SB) as a wife for Isaac (Gen. 24:14, 44). People would "judge" from the evidence whether Laban or Jacob was right (Gen. 31:37). [*ykḥ*]

20:17 And He healed (*wayyirpā'*)—This West Semitic word's root meaning may have been to put something or someone back together, to restore. God is the One who had shut up these wombs (Gen. 20:18) that he now healed, so he had inflicted the physical condition on the women. His action conforms to the covenant language that associated health with blessing (Exod. 23:25-26; Deut. 7:12-15) and disease with curses (Deut. 28:27,

35) (A. K. Chan, T. B. Song, and M. L. Brown, *NIDOTTE*, 3:1162-63). The Abrahamic Covenant promised curses for those who cursed Abraham (Gen. 12:3), and Abimelech had more or less done this. The participial form of the verb (69x) is translated as "physicians" in Gen. 50:2. The word often indicates healing from disease or trauma (e.g., Lev. 13:37; Exod. 21:19). God later imposed sicknesses on the Egyptians and identified himself as Israel's Healer (Exod. 15:26). Both judicial affliction and merciful healing are what God claimed to do, stating that he wounds and he will heal (Deut. 32:39). [*rp'*]

21:1 Took note (*pāqad*)—This is the first of seven places where this word (304x) stands in Genesis. This translation (NAB, JPS, NASB) is in line with what some take to be the root idea of the verb, a taking note or an attending to with care. The sense in Gen. 50:24-25 is much the same. But translations vary widely at Gen. 21:1, probably due to uncertainty about the word itself (V. P. Hamilton, *TWOT*, 2:731). A neutral idea like "treated" (NJB) or "dealt with" (NRSV) may be suitable, for the word can have implications of divine blessing or judgment depending on the context. A standard lexicon gives five main meanings for the word's basic form: inspect, see to something, muster, command, and avenge (*HALOT*, 955-58). In Gen. 39:4-5 the meaning is "put in charge," while in 40:4 and 41:34 it is "assign" or "appoint." [*pqd*]

21:10 Drive out (*gārēš*)—This is the same word used for God's driving Adam and Eve out of the Garden of Eden, and Cain out of his presence (Gen. 3:24; 4:14). God drove the Canaanites out of Canaan (Exod. 23:28) and described himself as One who drove out the enemy ahead of Israel (Deut. 33:27). Pharaoh "drove out" Moses and Aaron from his palace (Exod. 10:11). Sarah manifested great hostility towards Hagar by choosing this word. Jephthah interpreted an experience not too different from Hagar's as hate (Judg. 11:2, 7). The word is used in biblical (Lev. 21:7) and post-biblical Hebrew of casting out or divorcing a wife (P. J. J. S. Els, *NIDOTTE*, 1:898). [*grš*]

21:22 His army (*ṣĕbā'ô*)—There is a related verb meaning "go to war," which has some use concerning service in Israel's religion (Num. 4:23; 8:24-25). The noun generally refers to the army or to army service, but sometimes to service in worship of God (Num. 4:23), or hard service of whatever kind (Job 7:1; 14:14; Isa. 40:2) (T. Longman III, *NIDOTTE*, 3:733-35). It can militarily depict the nation of Israel (Exod. 6:26) or the heavenly bodies (Dan. 8:10-11; cf. Judg. 5:20), both armies seen as under God's control. In Genesis the word 3x designates Abimelech's troops, and once all that is in heaven and earth (Gen. 2:1). The latter usage seems metaphorical, as may often be the case with the heavenly bodies. [*ṣābā'*]

21:23 Swear (*hiššābĕ'â*)—The etymology of this word (183x) is uncertain. It is similar in form to the number seven, an important symbolic number in the Bible, but "seven" is only rarely associated with swearing in the OT. Other Semitic languages do not use this verbal root for swearing (*HALOT*, 1396-97). This first occurrence in Genesis does include "seven" in part of what was sworn (Gen. 21:28-31); the NIV notes that Beersheba in v. 31 can mean either "well of seven" or "well of the oath." Perhaps Abraham was making a wordplay. Oaths taken before God were an important means of making agreements in the ancient Near East (Gen.

25:33; 26:28-31; 50:25), and oaths were highly respected (Gen. 47:31; 50:5-6). They would probably include calling down judgment on oneself for breaking one's word (V. P. Hamilton, *Genesis 18–50*, 90). Making an oath in a god's name was a standard procedure (Gen. 24:3; 31:53). God himself took an oath in his own name (Gen. 22:16; cf. 24:7; 26:3). [*šbʿ*]

That you will not deal falsely (*'im-tišqōr*)—Though the verb can mean "deal falsely," and the related noun "deception" or "falsehood" (*BDB*, 1055), the word here may have a technical meaning of acting against contractual terms. Old Aramaic shows the same idea of breaching a trust and breaking an agreement (*HALOT*, 1647). The verb appears five other places in the Bible. It is paralleled with lying in Lev. 19:11 and is something that God does not do (1 Sam. 15:29). God expected that his people would not act this way either (Isa. 63:8). [*šqr*]

21:30 As a witness (*lěʿēdâ*)—This word for witness or attestation, used 4x in the OT, appears to be the grammatically feminine form of a more common masculine word (69x). Other translations here are "legal proof" (NET), "evidence" (NJB), and "public confirmation" (NLT). In Gen. 31:52 the masculine word describes a masculine noun, and the feminine form a feminine one. The feminine word always concerns objects as witnesses in legal situations (H. Simeon-Yofre, *TDOT*, 10:506). By accepting the seven lambs, Abimelech accepted Abraham's oath that the well was his. In Gen. 31:52 the pillar is a witness to a boundary between Laban and Jacob. In Josh. 24:27 the witness stone, having heard the words of God and Israel, would testify to Israelite unfaithfulness. In each case there is a covenantal arrangement before God, and the object is

a somewhat symbolic witness, since God was the true witness before whom the oath was taken (Gen. 31:50). [*'ēdâ*]

22:1 Tested (*nissâ*)—God put Abraham to the test. When men do this to God, the testing is generally equivalent to tempting (*HALOT*, 702), but God acts with Abraham's ultimate benefit in view. The verb involves the idea that something previously hidden becomes revealed and known, and here God acts to expose what Abraham has within himself (F. J. Helfmeyer, *TDOT*, 9:443-44). This is the only occurrence of the verb in Genesis, but God often tested his people after the Exodus (Exod. 15:25; 16:4; 20:20; Deut. 8:2; 13:3; Judg. 2:22), and they tested him (Exod. 17:2, 7; Num. 14:22). [*nsh*]

22:2 You love (*'āhabtā*)—This word (217x) appears 14x in Genesis, showing the strength of the patriarchal family relationships. Abraham loved his son, Isaac his wife and mother, Isaac and Rebekah their sons, and Jacob his wife and son (resp. Gen. 22:2; 24:67; 25:28; 29:18; 37:3). The word is like the English word in referring to different kinds of love, such as love for food (Gen. 27:4, 9, 14), bribes (Isa. 1:23), sleep (Isa. 56:10), or sex (Isa. 57:8). But in the OT it predominantly describes love between persons. In Genesis the word does not relate directly to God, but elsewhere it often does, one source claiming 32x for God's love and 24x for man's love of God (P. J. J. S. Els, *NIDOTTE*, 1:278-79). [*'hb*]

And sacrifice him (*wěha'ǎlêhû*)—This is the causative form of a common verb (890x) meaning "go up." The verb has many uses, and its basic form describes Abraham going up from Egypt to Canaan, the sun going up, a bud blossoming, and Reuben climbing into bed (resp., Gen. 13:1; 19:15; 40:10; 49:4). The causative form occurs 27x for offering sacrifice. Since the verb appears so often with a cognate noun meaning "whole burnt offering" (61x), the likely explanation of this causative is that the offerer made the sacrifice go up in flames or smoke (*BDB*, 749). A sacrificial offering was not complete until it was burned. But another explanation is that the offerer brought the sacrifice up onto the altar (H. F. Fuhs, *TDOT*, 11:80, 90). In Gen. 8:20-21 the same phrase as here in 22:2, 13 describes Noah sacrificing offerings of pleasing aroma to God. Abraham prepared wood for the sacrificial fire (Gen. 22:7), as Noah doubtless did. ['lh]

As a burnt offering (*lĕʻōlâ*)—This is the kind of sacrifice most often mentioned in the OT (286x), whose distinctive is that the whole animal was burned, leaving nothing for the offerer or priest. Some think it was the original kind of sacrifice, with other types developing from it. The description of it in the Law (Lev. 1:1-17) involved cutting a ceremonially clean animal into pieces and burning all the pieces on an altar; a bird was handled slightly differently. Since the offerer laid his hand on the head of the animal before burning it (Lev. 1:4; 8:18), there is a good possibility that he viewed the animal as a substitute for himself; at least he identified with it (G. L. Carr, *TWOT*, 667). The sacrifice could indicate the offerer's entire consecration to the Lord. It could also serve to make him acceptable to the Lord, evidently removing sin and any divine wrath associated with it (Lev. 1:3-4, 9, 13, 17) (E. E. Carpenter, *ISBE*, 4[1988]:268). Abraham ultimately offered a ram as a burnt offering (Gen. 22:13). [ʻōlâ]

22:3 His servants (*nĕʻārāyw*)—This word (244x) is one of a family of terms concerned with youth and has two well-established meanings. More than half the time it signifies "boy" or "youth," including even infants (Exod. 2:6), about 100x indicating a son within the family circle (H. F. Fuhs, *TDOT*, 9:479). It can also identify a servant. A less frequent word for servant than the one treated at Gen. 19:2, it usually implies a personal assistant or household servant (*BDB*, 654-55). Young men were suitable for such service. A "servant" could be a man in Abraham's household who fought against Chedorlaomer or who prepared a calf for Abraham's dinner guests (Gen. 14:24; 18:7). In 19:4 and 21:12 the word has its other meaning of youth, and in 22:5 it means "servants" once and "boy" once. It has the range of ideas of a NT term (*pais*) rendered "servant" of Jesus in Acts 4:27, 30; the KJV translated the NT word "child." [naʻar]

22:9 And he bound (*wayyaʻăqōd*)—From this verb comes the Jewish name for the incident, the Akedah, or binding, of Isaac. Each step required more dedication on Abraham's part; more difficult than the binding would be raising the knife to strike his son. This verb occurs only here in the Bible. In cognate languages the verbal root means to tie in a knot or put in fetters (*HALOT*, 873). [ʻqd]

22:10 To slay (*lišḥōṭ*)—This is a vivid term for killing since its normal sense is "slaughter," a word usually found in connection with animals sacrificed on the altar (e.g., Exod. 12:21, but cf. Gen. 37:31). Yet the word describes nonsacrificial killing of people 9x (e.g., Num. 14:16; Judg. 12:6). A similar sacrificial killing of people receives mention in Isa. 57:5; Ezek. 16:21; 23:39. One interpretation of Heb. 11:17-19 is that the slaying of Isaac was a type of the violent death and the resurrection of Jesus Christ (*BAGD*, 612). Hebrews notes that Abraham, whom the Bible elsewhere calls a father of many nations (Gen. 17:4-5; Rom. 4:17-18), offered his only son, who had received the promises. Likewise God the Father offered his unique Son, who had received the promises, to be slain on our behalf. [*šḥṭ*]

22:24 And his concubine (*ûpîlagšô*)—Since dictionary definitions may put a concubine below the status of a wife, it is necessary to see that the Hebrew word implies a genuine marriage, but on a secondary level. This was polygamy, but not fornication (V. P. Hamilton, *TWOT*, 2:724). Several women called "concubines" were also called wives. For instance, Keturah and Bilhah were "concubines" (1 Chron. 1:32; Gen. 35:22) but they were also called wives (Gen. 25:1; 30:4). The father of a concubine was the father-in-law to her partner, who was his son-in-law (Judg. 19:4-5). In the days of the kings their concubines would provide not only companionship but care for the palace (2 Sam. 15:16; 20:3). A concubine might have been under the authority of the wife, but she was not a slave. This word is attested in no Semitic languages apart from Hebrew. (V. P. Hamilton, *NIDOTTE*, 3:618-19). [*pilegeš*]

23:2 To lament (*lispōd*)—In many languages the verbal root here involved lamenting. Isa. 32:12 and the LXX translations of this word suggest that beating the breast may have been a fundamental part of the action. 1 Kings 13:30 and Jer. 22:18 indicate that verbal expression could also be present, as does Mic. 1:8 when speaking of "lamenting like the jackals." This word so often occurs alongside a report of someone's death or a burial that it seems

to signify ritualistic practices accompanying lament for the dead. It regularly occurs in the presence of the dead before burial. Secondarily, it can encompass bodily motions and sounds accompanying grief in other situations (Mic. 1:8; Joel 1:13) (J. Scharbert, *TDOT*, 10:299-303). Sometimes it is one item in a list of lament actions (Jer. 16:6; 25:33; Joel 1:13; Ezek. 24:16). As here, weeping is a parallel action in Eccl. 3:4. [*spd*]

And to weep for her (*wĕlibkōtâh*)—The Hebrew word implies an action that comes from the mouth and voice, but tears could accompany it. The Bible describes people who were quite demonstrative in this regard, and today people in the Near East tend to weep loudly, not quietly. One could weep in any number of circumstances, whether complaining over food (Num. 11:4), rejoicing about romance (Gen. 29:11), fearing loss of a blessing (Gen. 27:38), or meeting someone long lost (Gen. 33:4; 46:29) (V. Hamp, *TDOT*, 2:116-20). Weeping can be an important activity in one's relationship to God, but in Genesis the weeping concerns feelings about another human being. [*bkh*]

23:4 An alien (*wĕtôšāb*)—This verse shows that one could be a "stranger" (see at Gen. 15:13) as well as an "alien." The translations vary in their handling of these two terms here, some of them combining the terms into a single concept (NJB: "stranger resident"; JPS: "resident alien"). The word, occurring 14x in the OT, comes from a verb meaning to sit or live, and another translation might be "temporary resident." In Israel it referred to a temporary wage earner who did not own land and it could be a synonym for "hired servant" (Lev. 22:10). Such a person was not as integrated into the national life of Israel as the "stranger," and did not have as many rights, since he could not share in the Passover, and his children could be sold as slaves (Exod. 12:45; Lev. 25:45) (*HALOT*, 1713). But he could flee to a city of refuge if need be (Num. 35:15) (W. C. Kaiser, *TWOT*, 412). Since the entire land ultimately belonged to God, he characterized all Israelites the way that Abraham described himself here (Lev. 25:23). So pious Jews adopted this self-identification (Ps. 39:12; 1 Chron. 29:15), which became a Christian self-identification in the phrase "strangers and aliens" at 1 Peter 2:11. [*tôšāb*]

23:19 Buried (*qābar*)—The Romans cremated dead bodies, but the Jews buried them. It was a great indignity for a corpse to have no burial and so suffer the ravages of wild beasts and decomposition (1 Kings 14:11). Abraham's request had urgency to it because decomposition set in quickly, and Canaan does not seem to have had the embalming techniques of Egypt (Gen. 50:2, 26). Burial methods in Canaan changed over time, and the cave burial characterizes the Early Bronze Age (3000–2000 B.C.). This was the period during which Abraham lived (c. B.C. 2166–1991) (E. H. Merrill, *Kingdom of Priests*, 31). The biblical practice of burial probably stems from belief in an afterlife. Jacob expected to go down to his son when he died, but this could not be reunion in the grave, since Joseph had supposedly been eaten by wild beasts (J. B. Payne, *ISBE*, 1[1979]:556-61). [*qbr*]

24:2 His household (*bêtô*)—The NRSV has "house," and that is the basic meaning of the word (Lev. 14:37, 39). But it may miscommunicate, since Heb. 11:9 states that Abraham, Isaac, and Jacob lived in tents. The word has a wide range of meaning. Egypt is a "house of slaves," a place where they live (Exod. 13:3). The word can describe God's temple, a king's palace, or a prison (resp., 1 Kings 6:5; Jer. 39:8; Gen. 39:20). Num. 16:27 describes Korah, Dathan, and Abiram as living in tents, but v. 32 says that the earth swallowed them, their "houses," and the property. Here "house" probably means the household, including family members and servants (T. R. Ashley, *Numbers*, 320). That is the idea in nearly 600 of its over 2,000 occurrences (*BDB*, 109). It first has this sense in Gen. 7:1, when Noah and his "house" are commanded to enter the ark. But servants are not included in Gen. 7:1, nor later when the nation of Israel was divided into patriarchal "houses," groups of families descended from a single heir. [*bayit*]

My thigh (*yĕrēkî*)—This was the fleshy part of the upper thighs, from the hips to the thighs (*HALOT*, 439). In Gen. 32:25 it denotes Jacob's hip, and in Song of Songs 7:1 the curves of the thighs and hip. Passages like Genesis 46:26 and Exodus 1:5, where a father's children come from his "thigh," can suggest that the word is a euphemism for the sexual organ, and there may be a custom of touching sexual organs in an Akkadian oath (V. P. Hamilton, *Genesis 18–50*, 139). Perhaps this whole area of the body was associated with procreation. The same kind of oath with a hand under the thigh in Gen. 47:29 has to do with a burial request. So the elderly men may request this gesture as a reminder to the person taking the oath of the issues at stake. Abraham's line could be corrupted if a good wife for his son was not found. Joseph's responsibility to bury his father was that of a son from his father's loins. [*yārēk*]

24:5 Is not willing (*lō'-tō'beh*)—The basic sense that suits all OT uses of the word, and also the root's use in Egyptian and Aramaic, is "to show intention in a certain direction," with the thrust being behavioral rather than psychological implications of the intention (B. Johnson, *TDOT*, 1:24-25). Only two of the fifty-four references to this verb lack a negative qualifier, so it mostly indicates what people are not willing to do. The verb can mean "yield" (Deut. 13:8), since the issue is often willingness to do something requested or obligatory (J. B. Payne, *TWOT*, 1:4-5). The unwillingness is many times a refusal to do God's will, and sometimes a divine unwillingness to punish. [*'bh*]

24:8 Then you are free (*wĕniqqîtā*)—This verb, related to the noun "cleanness" treated at 20:5, basically involves freedom or exemption from punishment. The root may originally have pertained to pouring out, and thus to being empty or clean, but every OT use of the verb concerns ethical or judicial topics. Num. 5:31 shows that guilt is the opposite state from that implied by this verb. The word can denote either freedom from guilt (Judg. 15:3) or from guilt's punishment (Exod. 21:19). Often the judge is the Lord, whether mentioned (Jer. 30:11) or implied (Prov. 16:5). Here and at Gen. 24:41 the servant will be free from the obligations of the oath should the woman refuse to accompany him. Similarly, the spies will be "free" (the related adjective *nāqî*) from their oath to Rahab if she fails to keep all the stipulations of their agreement (Josh. 2:17, 20). On the other hand, the woman who has not committed adultery will be free of the curse that otherwise would assault her (Num. 5:19) (M. C. Fisher and B. K. Waltke, *TWOT*, 2:596-97). [*nqh*]

From my oath (*miššĕbu'ātî*)—This noun, derived from the verb "swear" of 21:23, occurs 30x, and its other appearance in Genesis at 26:3 refers to God's oath to Abraham that he would give him Canaan. Oaths and swearing in the OT do not involve foulmouthed words but rather assurances that one will keep his word. They were legally binding (Exod. 22:11). There would be a promise along with a curse that appealed to a god for its enactment if the promise was not kept, something like: "May God do such and such should I/you fail to do this." One who broke an oath could expect to experience divine wrath (Josh. 9:20). The story of Saul's oath in 1 Sam. 14:24-45 shows the great force an oath could have before men and God. What seemed to be divine promises could be things God swore to do (2 Sam. 7 with Ps. 89:3-4), and God acted to fulfill his oaths (Jer. 11:5) (T. W. Cartledge, *NIDOTTE*, 4:32-33). In Gen. 24:8 "my oath" is the oath that Abraham asked the servant to take, the oath to Abraham. [*šĕbû'â*]

24:12 Give success (*haqrê*)—Many translations have something like "give success/good fortune" here. The simple form of the verb means to "meet, encounter, happen to," and a literal translation of the phrase could be: "please cause (it) to happen before me" (V. P. Hamilton, *Genesis 18–50*, 145). The servant is asking God to bring to pass what he wants to happen. God should ordain it. The same phrase occurs in Gen. 27:20 when Jacob deceptively claims to have obtained meat so fast because God made it happen. The word's other uses in Genesis at 42:29 and 44:29, and the majority of them in the OT, also concern what "happens" to a person. [*qrh*]

24:16 Beautiful (*ṭōbat mar'eh*)—A literal translation would be "good of appearance" (cf. Gen. 26:7). The word "good"

(530x) has broad application, like its English counterpart, and the root appears in many Semitic languages. The term's fundamental reference is to what caused something to be desirable. The original focus was utilitarian, good in the sense of "useful" or "advantageous," so "good for something." Good counsel achieved a desired result (2 Sam. 17:14). What was "good" in the sight of a person seemed beneficial to him (Gen. 16:6; 19:8; 20:15). Good cows were suitable for eating, providing plenty of food (Gen. 18:7; 27:9; 41:2, 26). What God created was "good" for his intended purpose (Gen. 1:4, 10). Canaan was the "good" land (Exod. 3:8) both in itself and as a gift of God. Since God was "good" (2 Chron. 30:18) and the source of goodness (Ps. 16:2), he defined good. So "good" could be a moral term (Gen. 2:9; 31:24), since God was moral and made us in his image. When "good" applied to beauty, it did not occur alone but with a word like "appearance" or "sight" that designated what was visual (I. Höver-Johag, *TDOT*, 5:297-316). [*ṭôb*]

Virgin (*bĕtûlâ*)—The traditional understanding of this word as always denoting virgin is under assault. There is now a widespread view that a common Semitic word signified a young girl at or just after puberty but developed a narrower meaning of virgin in Aramaic and Hebrew. The Hebrew word may have meant a girl of marriageable age, and in many biblical verses (e.g., Isa. 23:4; Jer. 31:13; Ezek. 9:6) the word is contrasted with "young men" to designate a stage of life. Good evidence in other Semitic languages indicates that related words did not imply "virgin" in the technical sense. In Israel an unmarried teenager was expected to be a virgin, since the penalty for premarital sex could be death (Deut. 22:14-21). In three

of the 51x the word occurs, it must denote a virgin (Lev. 21:13-14, Deut. 22:19; Ezek. 44:22); in 2 Sam. 13:2 virginity is strongly implied. But in Joel 1:8 it cannot mean "virgin" unless the woman mourned a "husband" who was only a fiancé. Esther 2:17 called members of a harem "virgins" even after they had spent a night with the king. In Genesis 24:16 and Judges 21:12 the word occurs alongside phrases explaining that the person had not had sexual relations (B. K. Waltke, *TWOT*, 1:137-39; M. Tsevat, *TDOT*, 2:338-43). [*bĕtûlâ*]

24:21 Made successful (*hahiṣlîaḥ*)—This verb in cognate languages also means to succeed, prosper, or thrive (*HALOT*, 1025-27; Alex Luc, *NIDOTTE*, 3:804-5). The verb is causative in Genesis 24:21, but otherwise there are several parallels with Judges 18:5, where men inquire of God to learn whether their journey will be successful. The verb appears three more times in this episode (Gen. 24:40, 42, 56), showing that the servant's pensiveness was due to a prior promise from Abraham that God would make his journey successful. God also would make Joseph successful (Gen. 39:2-3, 23). A project involving disobedience to God might temporarily succeed (Dan. 11:36), but not ultimately (Num. 14:41; 2 Chron. 13:12), because it is God who gives success (2 Chron. 26:5; Ps. 118:25). God cursed the disobedient with lack of success (Deut. 28:29), but adherence to his word brought success (Josh. 1:8). The Spirit sometimes "rushed" on a person so that he had supernatural power (Judg. 14:6, 1 Sam. 11:6; cf. 2 Sam. 19:17). [*ṣlḥ*]

24:26 And he bowed (*wayyiqqōd*)—This verb (15x) never occurs without an accompanying verb that was translated "bowed" at Gen. 19:1. The new verb (*qdd*) always stands first in the pair. Another meaning for it is "kneel down," and it is the preparatory action for the second verb (*HALOT*, 1065). Sometimes the action is to the ground (Exod. 34:8), including putting the face there (1 Sam. 24:8; 28:14; 1 Kings 1:31; 2 Chron. 20:18). In all 15 cases this verb may describe the physical action, while the accompanying verb carries the idea of homage or worship.

Since the entire action emphasizes deep respect and devotion, it appears in the OT at critical times (L. J. Coppes, *TWOT*, 784-85). [*qdd*]

24:27 Abandoned (*'āzab*)—Other translations here could be "forsaken" (NASB, NKJV, NRSV) or "withheld" (JPS, cf. NJB). The elementary meaning of the verb is "leave." Someone separates himself from a person or thing, discontinuing relations with the object. The one leaving frees himself from whom or what is left. People in the ancient Near East had strong family and tribal bonds, so there were obligations to make oneself available for others (Prov. 27:10), even enemies and strangers in Israel (Exod. 23:5; Lev. 19:10) (E. Gerstenberger, *TDOT*, 10:584-87). Of course there can be healthy leaving (Gen. 2:24; 39:6), but often the leaving of one person from another could be stressful (Gen. 44:22; Ruth 1:16). Being forsaken by God was even more distressing (Isa. 49:14; Lam. 5:20); God later promised Jacob never to do this (Gen. 28:15). Sometimes God would abandon those who abandoned him (2 Chron. 12:5; 24:20), but his love and mercy prevented him from abandoning his own (Neh. 9:17, 19, 31). Like Abraham's servant, other saints spoke of God not forsaking but extending his kindness to them (Ruth 2:20; Ezra 9:9). [*'zb*]

Or His faithfulness (*wa'ămitô*)—Another basic translation of this word is "truth," which NASB and NKJV have here; SB has "trustworthiness." A further idea in the word may be "constancy" (*HALOT*, 68-69). Most translate this word as "right" in 24:48, where it modifies "way." In 24:49 the servant uses the same pair of words as here: "kindness and faithfulness." The word pair occurs so frequently in Scripture (e.g., Gen. 47:29; Josh. 2:14) that some translations render it with a single phrase like "constant kindness" (NAB) or "steadfast faithfulness" (JPS). But in Gen. 32:10 the first word occurs in the plural and the second in the singular, showing that they kept their separate meanings. Among the attributes that God declares to be his are this pair of kindness and faithfulness/ truth (Exod. 34:6). Israel in turn was to treat God with faithfulness (Josh. 24:14). Sometimes the word can be understood either as faithfulness or truth (Exod. 18:21; Josh. 2:12), but other times the word clearly meant truth (Gen. 42:16; Judg. 9:15; Deut. 13:14). This is the most common noun related to the verb translated as "trusted" above at Gen. 15:6 (R. W. L. Moberly, *NIDOTTE*, 1:428). [*'ĕmet*]

Led me (*nāḥanî*)—This verb (39x) stands only here and at v. 48 in Genesis. It can mean lead, guide, bring, and possibly offer (*DCH*, 5:653). The leading can be by anyone or anything (1 Sam. 22:4; Prov. 11:3), but here as so often in the OT, especially the Psalms, the leading is by God. God led Israel and leads all nations (Pss. 77:21; 67:4). Abraham's servant concluded that the favorable circumstances of his trip could only be explained as divine supervision of events. God characteristically guides believers (Isa. 58:11), so they expected God to lead them and prayed for him to do so (Pss. 139:10; 27:11). God defines his sons as those who are led by his Spirit (Rom. 8:14). [*nḥh*]

24:43 The young woman (*hā'almâ*)—The evidence from cognate languages and from related Hebrew words suggests that this word pertains to the idea of youth (*BDB*, 761; H. Ringgren, *TDOT*, 11:159). As with "virgin" at 24:16, the age range seems to be that of marriageability (*HALOT*, 836). While "young woman" may have had a less specific meaning than "virgin," it too could imply virginity, since the LXX translated it twice with a word that generally referred to a virgin, at Gen. 24:43 and Isa. 7:14. Matt. 1:22-23, perhaps the angel's word, cites Isa. 7:14 as fulfilled in Christ. If there was prophecy of a virgin birth in Isa. 7:14, Joseph could believe his wife's account of her pregnancy (A. A. MacRae, *TWOT*, 672). In Exod. 2:8 the word indicates a "young girl," in Ps. 68:25 young girls playing tambourines, in Prov. 30:19 a "young woman," and in S.of S. 1:3 and 6:8 unmarried girls. There may be singing instructions related to young women at 1 Chron. 15:20 and the heading to Psalm 46:1. Again, the nation of Israel would have expected unmarried young girls to be virgins. [*'alma*]

24:60 Their enemies (*śōně'āyw*)—The basic sense of the verb is "hate," but the participle is often used as another way to designate enemies (Exod. 1:10) (*HALOT*, 1339). These can be personal enemies (Prov. 26:24), national enemies (Ps. 106:10), or enemies of God (2 Chron. 19:2). But another way to translate would be "ones hating them," and the verb can function as the polar opposite of the Hebrew word translated "love" (2 Sam. 19:6). Isaac thought the Philistines hated him because they filled up his wells and asked him to move away from them (Gen.

26:27). God saw that Leah as a wife was "hated," or "unloved" (Gen. 29:31). Joseph's brothers "hated" him because Jacob loved Joseph more than them (Gen. 37:4). [*śn'*]

24:67 And he was comforted (*wayyinnāḥēm*)—This is the rendering of NIV, NKJV, NASB, TEV, and NET. It would be easy to suppose, since God was active in the servant's mission, that Isaac was comforted by God. This is true in one sense, but the verb in this form normally has a reflexive idea like comfort/console oneself, and the idea here may be "found consolation" (*HALOT*, 688). It has that sense in Gen. 38:12, where Judah consoled himself over the loss of his wife. The form can also mean "be sorry" (Gen. 6:6-7) or "change one's mind" (Exod. 13:17). [*nḥm*]

25:8 Good old age (*śêbâ ṭôbâ*)—"The presence of this phrase in Abraham's obituary is significant for it provides another reminder of God's faithfulness to his promises. At least 89 years before Abraham's death (compare Gen. 16:16 with 25:7), the Lord promised the patriarch he would live a long life and "be buried at a good old age" (Gen. 15:15). [*śêbâ*]

25:21 Prayed (*wayye'tar*)—This word normally refers to a petition to God for relief from distress (Exod. 8:30; 10:18; 2 Sam. 21:14; 24:25; Job 33:26). In this passage, where Isaac prays for his barren wife, it carries the nuance "to intercede on behalf of another," just as it does in Exod. 8:30 and 10:18, where Moses intercedes on behalf of Pharaoh, asking the Lord to bring relief from the plagues. [*'tr*]

Barren (*'ăqārâ*)—The Hebrew term usually refers to a woman who is unable to conceive a child. Rebekah was the second in a line of barren women whom the Lord enabled to give birth. The list includes Sarah (Gen. 11:30), Rebekah, Rachel (Gen. 29:31), Samson's unnamed mother (Judg. 13:2-3), and Hannah (1 Sam. 2:5). In at least three of these cases (Rebekah, Rachel [Gen. 30:22], and Hannah) God granted the ability to conceive in response to prayer. In a cultural context in which the native Canaanite population worshiped the fertility deities Baal and Asherah in order to have children, these stories of the Lord enabling barren women to conceive should have had a powerful impact on the Israelites, for they demonstrated that he, not the Canaanite gods, possessed the power to give and take life. Hannah emphasized this theme in her thanksgiving song on the occasion of Samuel's birth (1 Sam. 2:1-10). She praised the Lord for giving the barren woman children (v. 5b), thereby demonstrating his incomparability to all other gods (v. 2). [*ăqārâ*]

Answered his prayer (*wayyēʿāter*)—The verb is the same one translated "prayed" earlier in the verse, though here it appears in a different Hebrew verbal stem (Niphal) and carries the idea of "submitting to" (or "answering") a petitionary prayer. The expression sometimes refers to God answering a plea for relief from distress caused by sin (2 Sam. 21:14; 24:25; 2 Chron. 33:13-19; Isa. 19:22), but on other occasions, as here, it describes his response to those who ask him in faith to intercede and grant them success (1 Chron. 5:10; Ezra 8:23). [*ʿtr*]

25:23 The older will serve the younger (*rab yaʿăbōd ṣāʿîr*)—The Hebrew word translated "older" (meaning literally "great") is not the usual term for "firstborn" (*bĕkōr*). The word translated

"younger" can refer to something that is small or insignificant, but often it is used of one's age. In Gen. 43:33 and 48:14 it is an antonym for "firstborn" (*bĕkōr*). The terminology appears to reflect the idiom of northern Mesopotamian family law. (See E. A. Speiser, *Genesis*, AB [New York: Doubleday, 1964], 194-95.) The first half of the verse, which speaks of nations and people groups, rather than individuals, suggests that the prophecy transcends the immediate future. Subsequent developments indicate that this is a prophecy of Israel's eventual dominance over the Edomites (Esau's descendants). The prophecy does not pertain directly to the individual brothers, for Esau never did submit to Jacob. In fact Jacob later called himself Esau's servant and bowed down before his older brother (Gen. 32:3-5, 19-20; 33:1-3). However, Isaac's paternal blessing anticipated a time when the recipient would rule over his brothers (Gen. 27:29) and Isaac subsequently told Esau that he would someday serve his brother (Gen. 27:40). The fulfillment of these various prophecies came during the period of the Davidic empire when the Israelites (Jacob's descendants) subjugated the Edomites (2 Sam. 8:11-14). [*rab, ṣāʿîr*]

25:26 Jacob (*yaʿăqōb*)—The precise etymology of the name is uncertain, though it may derive from a verbal root meaning "protect, guard" (*HALOT*, 422, 872). According to v. 26, the name was given as a pun on the word heel, *ʿāqēb*), for Jacob was holding his brother's heel as he came out of the birth canal. [*yaʿăqōb*]

25:27 A quiet man (*ʿîš tām*)—This expression appears to contrast with the description of Esau as "a skillful hunter, a man of the open country." Elsewhere *tām* has an ethical connotation, meaning "honest, blameless" (Job 1:1, 8; 2:3), but this sense seems unlikely here, for the phrase is qualified by "staying among the tents," and the story that follows characterizes Jacob as deceitful. Perhaps the narrator sets the reader up for the irony that follows. Esau was an aggressive hunter who used deception to trap his prey, while Jacob was a more domestic type who did not seem to possess the natural inclination toward deception that a good hunter must have. But ironically, in the story to follow Jacob is more like the cunning hunter, Esau more like the unsuspecting victim. [*tmm* > *tām*]

25:28 Loved (*wayye'ĕhab*)—This word, which is used twice in this verse, carries the meaning "preferred, favored" in this context. This is typically the case when the word is used of parental love for a child. (P. J. J. S. Els, *NIDOTTE*, 1:293-94.) ['*hb*]

25:31 Your birthright (*bĕkōrātĕkā*)—The word is related to the term "firstborn" (*bĕkōr*) and refers to the special right(s) of the firstborn. It is not entirely clear what this entailed in patriarchal times. If the Mosaic Law is a guide to earlier patriarchal practice, the possessor of the birthright may have received a double share of the family inheritance (Deut. 21:17). Apparently the birthright did not involve surrendering the paternal blessing, which Jacob later had to steal from his brother through deceit (Gen. 27), nor is it to be equated with the Abrahamic promise, for Isaac later prayed that Jacob would receive this (Gen. 28:4). [*bĕkōrâ*]

25:33 Swear (*hiššābĕ'â*)—The verb refers to making an oath that would legally secure the transaction. An oath was binding, superseding a mere statement of good intentions (Gen. 47:29-31; 50:5-6). [*šb'*]

25:34 Despised (*wayyibez*)—The verb, which refers to treating someone or something with contempt, reflects the narrator's assessment of Esau's action. It indicates that Esau did not place the proper value on his birthright. He placed a higher priority on his immediate physical needs and exhibited appalling lack of foresight. His devaluing of the birthright shows that he was unworthy of it in the first place. (See Robert Alter, *The Art of Biblical Narrative* [New York: Basic Books, 1981], 45.) The author of Hebrews goes so far as to view Esau's action as proof that he was a godless (or profane) man who had no regard for the things valued by God (Heb. 12:16-17) [*bzh*]

26:2 Appeared (*wayyērā'*)—In Genesis this word describes divine appearances to the patriarchs (called theophanies), whether literally or in a dream. Apparently the Lord took visible, human form when revealing himself in this way (Gen. 18:1-2; 28:13). In each instance he affirmed his promise to bless Abraham and his descendants. (See Gen. 12:7; 17:1; 18:1 [cf. v. 10]; 26:24; 35:1 [cf. 28:13; 48:3], 9-12.) [*r'h*]

26:3 I will be with you (*'ehyeh 'immĕkā*)—This statement, which includes the verb "I will be," is a promise of the divine presence that anticipates God's enablement. (On other occasions the verb is omitted; in these cases the focus is on the present reality of God's presence. See, for example, Gen. 26:24; 28:15.) The Lord made this same promise to Jacob just before his return home (Gen. 31:3), to Moses prior to his trip to Egypt (Exod. 3:12), and to Joshua before he led the people across the

Jordan River (Josh. 1:5). In each instance the recipient of the promise faced a major crisis and was very much aware of his need for supernatural enablement and provision. The same is true in Isaac's case, for a famine had devastated the land of Canaan and the patriarch was tempted to travel to Egypt. [hyh]

I will bless you *(wa'ăbārĕkekā)*—Here the Lord extends to Isaac the promise made to Abraham (Gen. 12:2; 22:17). The blessing included possession of the land of Canaan, numerous descendants, compared here to the stars in the sky (Gen. 15:5), and widespread fame (Gen. 22:17). [brk]

Will confirm *(wahăqimōtî)*—The Lord had already ratified his promise to Abraham in response to the patriarch's obedience in offering up his son Isaac (Gen. 22:15-18). So the verb here means "bring to pass, fulfill." It anticipates the actual realization of the promise. For other examples of the verb used with this shade of meaning, see Lev. 26:9; Num. 23:19; Deut. 8:18; 9:5; 1 Sam. 1:23; 1 Kings 6:12; Jer. 11:5 (used with "oath" as in Gen. 26:3). [qwm]

The oath I, *haššĕbu'â 'ăšer nišba'tî)*—This refers to God's promises to Abraham, which were ratified by divine oath as part of God's unconditional covenant with the patriarch (see Gen. 22:16). This oath/covenant included possession of the land (Gen. 15:17-21; Gen. 24:7; Exod. 6:4, 8; Ps. 105:8-11; Jer. 11:5), numerous descendants (Gen. 22:17), and worldwide fame (Gen. 22:18). [šb'> šĕbu'â]

26:4 I will make your descendants . . . numerous *(hirbêtî 'et-zar'ăkā)*—This aspect of the promise echoes Gen. 22:17, where God told Abraham he would give him descendants as numerous as the stars in the sky. The promise is reiterated here

(without the comparison to stars). Prior to Jacob's departure for Paddan Aram, Isaac prayed that the promise might be realized through Jacob's descendants (Gen. 28:3). When Jacob returned to Bethel, the Lord instructed him to "increase in number" (Gen. 35:11; cf. 48:4). [rbh]

Will be blessed *(hitbārăkû)*—Scholars debate whether the the verb should be understood as passive, "all nations on earth will be blessed" (perhaps making Isaac's offspring a channel or instrument of blessing) or as reflexive/reciprocal, "and all the nations of the earth will bless themselves/one another" (that is, by using the name of Isaac's offspring in their blessing formulas). The situation is complicated by the fact that this promise occurs in four other passages: Gen. 12:3 (the blessing is through/by Abraham here); 18:18 (through/by Abraham); 22:18 (through/by Abraham's offspring); 28:14 (through/by Jacob and his offspring). The Niphal form of the Hebrew verb is used in 12:3; 18:18 and 28:14, while the Hithpael form appears in 22:18 and 26:4. The forms appear to be interchangeable, as is often the case with verbs appearing in these two stems. The Niphal of *brk* occurs in only these three passages, so one cannot appeal to usage for clarification. However, the Hithpael form of the verb occurs in four other texts (Deut. 29:18; Ps. 72:17; Isa. 65:16; Jer. 4:2) and is quite instructive for our understanding of the Abrahamic promise.

(a) In Deut. 29:19 the Hithpael of *brk* is reflexive, as indicated by the accompanying prepositional phrase "on himself" (literally, "in his heart") and the following statement, "I will be safe, even though I persist in going my own way." Here the idea of pronouncing a blessing on oneself carries the idea "consider oneself to be blessed."

(b) In Ps. 72:17 the Hithpael of *brk* could be understood as passive or middle, referring to the actual bestowing of blessing through the ideal king depicted here, but it is more likely that a formulaic blessing is in view. The following line uses the Piel of *'šr* in the sense, "regard/declare to be happy, fortunate" (Gen. 30:13; Job 29:11; Prov. 31:28; S. of S. 6:9; Mal. 3:12, 15). If the nations regard the king as a prime example of one who is fortunate and blessed, it is understandable that they would use his name in their blessing formulas. The form is most likely reflexive/reciprocal, "all nations will pronounce blessings among themselves by him" (i.e., using his name as an example of blessing in the formula, see Ruth 4:11), though a passive rendering is possible, "all nations will be formally blessed (i.e., have blessings pronounced over them) by him" (i.e., with his name being used in the formula as an example). In either case the idiom *bārak bĕ* means "pronounce a blessing by" with a paradigmatic name following the preposition (see Gen. 48:20).

(c) In Isa. 65:16 the Hithpael of *brk* also refers to a formulaic pronouncement of blessing, for the parallel line refers to swearing an oath in the name of the God of truth. The Hithpael could be reflexive (see Deut. 29:18, though no phrase like "in his heart" occurs here) or passive, "whoever has a blessing pronounced over him in the land will have that blessing pronounced over him in the name of the God of truth." In this case the idiom *bārak bĕ* means "pronounce a blessing by," with God's name following the preposition as the agent of blessing (see Deut.10:8; 21:5; 2 Sam. 6:18; 1 Chron. 16:2; 23:13; Ps. 129:8).

(d) In Jer. 4:2 the Hithpael of *brk* is used of a formulaic blessing, for the preceding line refers to the formulation of an oath in the Lord's name and the following line

mentions verbal praise of the Lord. The Hithpael could be understood as reflexive/reciprocal (see Ps. 72:17), or as passive, in the same sense as proposed above for Isa. 65:16: "the nations will have blessings pronounced over them in the name of the Lord." In either case the Lord is mentioned in the formula as the agent of blessing (see Isa. 65:16).

In each of the four cases cited above a formal pronouncement or invocation of blessing is in view. Once this is recognized it is really not that important whether one sees the Hithpael as passive or as reflexive-reciprocal. If the verb is passive, then one may translate in Gen. 26:4: "by your offspring all nations on earth will have blessings pronounced over them" (that is, with the name of your offspring being used in the formula of blessing). If the verb is reflexive-reciprocal, then one may translate: "by your offspring all nations on earth will pronounce blessings among themselves" (that is, using the name of your offspring in the blessing formula). In other words, Abraham's/Isaac's offspring will gain such widespread fame that other nations will hold them up as a paradigm of divine blessing when they formulate blessings. The promise anticipates Isaac's offspring becoming at least a prime example of divine blessing. Though it does not specifically say they will be a channel or instrument of blessing, it leaves the door open for their having a more significant impact on the nations. [brk]

26:5 Obeyed me (*šāma'* . . . *bĕqōlî*)—This rather common Hebrew expression, which literally means "hear my voice," carries the nuance, "obey me." Abraham's obedient response to God's commandments, culminating in his willingness to offer up his son, provided the evidence

God needed to ratify his covenantal promise to the patriarch (Gen. 22:12-18). [*šm'*]

Kept my requirements *(wayyišmōr mišmartî)*—The expression carries the primary meaning of faithfully discharging an obligation (see, for example, Lev. 8:35; Num. 1:53). Here it pictures Abraham obediently carrying out the charge or obligations that the Lord placed upon him (note the following qualifying terms). These included the commands to leave his homeland (Gen. 12:1 [cf. v. 4]); to serve the Lord blamelessly (Gen. 17:1 [cf. 24:40]), to circumcise the males in his household (Gen. 17:9-14 [cf. v. 23; 21:4]), and to offer up his son (Gen. 22:2 [cf. vv. 3-12]). [*šmr*]

My commands, my decrees and my laws *(miṣwōtay ḥuqqōtay wĕtôrōtāy)*—These terms summarize what was included in God's charge to Abraham. For specific examples of what these requirements entailed, see the preceding note. Elsewhere the terms refer to the commands of the Mosaic Law (see, for example, Deut. 6:2; 11:1; 28:15, 45; 30:10, 16; 1 Kings 2:3; Neh. 9:14). By anachronistically using this terminology here, the narrator depicts Abraham as the law keeper par excellence and as a model for Israel to follow (cf. Gen. 18:18-19). (See Allen P. Ross, *Creation and Blessing* [Grand Rapids, Mich.: Baker, 1988], 458-59.) [*miṣwâ, ḥōq, tôrâ*]

26:14 Envied *(wayyĕqannĕ'û)*—The verb refers here to jealousy prompted by Isaac's success and prosperity (see Gen. 30:1; 37:11). In each case in Genesis where the term appears jealousy prompts conflict. Here God's protective blessing is evident as he eventually guides Isaac to a well he can call his own (v. 22). [*qn'*]

26:16 You have become . . . powerful *('āṣamtā)*—The word echoes the promise of Gen. 18:18, where the Lord anticipates the descendants of Abraham becoming "a great and powerful *('āṣûm)* nation." It also foreshadows Exodus 1, which tells how the Israelites "became . . . numerous" (vv. 7, 20; *wayya'aṣmû*), prompting the Egyptians to take drastic measures against them (vv. 9-10). In both Gen. 26 and Exodus 1 enemies threaten God's chosen people as he begins to fulfill his promise to Abraham. This is a reminder that God's program does not go unopposed. As he works out his purposes for his people, they can expect conflict. [*'ṣm*]

26:22 We will flourish *(pārînû)*—Isaac's statement of faith in God's ability to bless him echoes the Lord's promise to Abraham in Gen. 17:6: "I will make you very fruitful" *(hiprētî)*. The term also appears in Isaac's blessing upon Jacob as he prepared to leave for Paddan Aram (Gen. 28:3) and in the Lord's instructions to Jacob when he returned to Bethel (Gen. 35:11; cf. Gen. 48:4). [*prh*]

26:24 Do not be <u>afraid</u> *('al tîrā')*—The Lord's assuring word to Isaac takes the form of a so-called salvation oracle, a literary form attested elsewhere in ancient Near Eastern literature. In this type of oracle the deity typically assures the worshiper with the words "fear not," a promise of the divine presence, and an expanded statement of how the deity will intervene on behalf of the worshiper. For examples see *ANET*, 501-02, 605. [*yr'*]

I am with you *('ittĕkā 'ānōkî)*—In this promise of the divine presence the verb is omitted (contrast v. 3). In this case the focus is on the present reality of God's protective presence. This precise form of the statement (with the preposition *'et*) occurs only here in Genesis. Elsewhere the preposition *'im* is used (Gen. 28:15; 31:38). [*'et, 'ănōkî*]

My servant (*'abdî*)—This title reflects Abraham's special relationship to God and his role as one who carries out God's will (see Ps. 105:6, 42). It may allude to Gen. 17:1, where the Lord instructs Abraham: "Walk before me and be blameless." The expression "walk before" (Hithpael form of the verb *hlk*, "walk," collocated with *lipnê*, "before") sometimes means "walk in front of" (Esth. 2:11) or "live in one's presence" (Pss. 56:13; 116:9), but it can also carry the metaphorical nuance "serve" (1 Sam. 2:30, 35; 12:2; 2 Kings 20:3 = Isa. 38:3). In Genesis (see 24:40; 48:15) it probably has this figurative shade of meaning. In combination with "be blameless" it means "serve me faithfully." Sarna compares the expression "walk before" to an Akkadian phrase that refers to loyalty and appears in Assyrian land grants rewarding faithful subjects. (See Nahum M. Sarna, *Genesis*, JPSTC [Philadelphia: Jewish Publication Society, 1989], 123). Weinfeld understands the phrase "be perfect" as a reference to perfect or loyal service and compares it to a semantically equivalent expression in Assyrian royal grants. (See Moshe Weinfeld, "The Covenant of Grant in the Old Testament and in the Ancient Near East," JAOS 90 [1970]), 186). [*'bd > 'ebed*]

26:25 Called on the name of the LORD (*wayyiqrā' běšēm yhwh*)—In Genesis the phrase appears to refer to formal worship through sacrifice and prayer (see Gen. 4:26; 12:8; 13:4; 21:33). In 12:8 and 13:4 it is associated with an altar. [*qr'*]

27:12 A curse (*qělālâ*)—In this context, where the term stands in contrast to a blessing (see the next note), the word refers to a formal appeal to God to bring calamity down upon another. A prime example of such a curse can be found in Judg. 9, where Jotham appeals to God for justice in the form of judgment upon Abimelech and the Shechemites for their evil deeds against his family. Once the judgment falls, the narrator informs us: "The curse (*qělālâ*) of Jotham son of Jerub-Baal came on them." (See as well 2 Sam. 16:5-14; Ps. 109:17-18; Jer. 29:22). [*qll > qělālâ*]

A blessing (*běrākâ*)—The word refers here to the formal paternal blessing on the firstborn (see as well vv. 35-36). In this blessing Isaac asked God to grant his son agricultural abundance, superiority to other nations (including the descendants of his brother), and special protection (see vv. 27-29). The effective and binding nature of this blessing becomes apparent in v. 37, where Isaac understands the formalized blessing as having already given Jacob lordship and prosperity. He uses the perfect form of the Hebrew verb (see *śamtîw*, "I have made him," and *nātattî*, "I have sustained"), indicating that the action is as good as done from the speaker's standpoint. [*brk > běrākâ*]

27:28 Heaven's dew (*ṭal haššāmayim*)—The term translated "dew" may refer here to a mist or light drizzle (see Mark D. Futato, NIDOTTE, 2:363). By metonymy it refers here to the crops that benefit from it (note v. 28b). The Canaanites believed that the fertility deity Baal provided the dew. An Ugaritic legend attributes the disappearance of rain and dew to Baal's weakness. (See J. C. L. Gibson, *Canaanite Myths and Legends* [2nd ed., Edinburgh: T & T Clark, 1978], 115). One of Baal's daughters is even named Dew (Tallaya) (see Gibson, 46, 48). In his blessing of the Israelite tribes Moses polemicized against this

Baal- theology by depicting Israel's God as the incomparable deity who "rides on the heavens" and provides his people with "grain and new wine" (Deut. 33:26-28), the very staples mentioned by Isaac in Gen. 27:28b. (See Robert B. Chisholm, Jr., "The Polemic Against Baalism in Israel's Early History and Literature," *BSac* 150 [1994], 275). [*ṭal*]

27:29 Those who curse you *('ōrĕreykā)*—The term "curse" refers here to a formalized prayer in which the petitioners call down calamity upon an enemy. (See the note on 27:12 above, though a synonym is used there.) The language is reminiscent of Gen. 12:3, but there the synonym *(qll)* appears and the enemy is seen as an individual (the participle is singular in 12:3), not a group. [*'rr*]

Be cursed *('ārûr)*—The term here carries the nuance "be judged with calamity." Appropriate punishment is envisioned; those who sought to harm Isaac's son by calling judgment down upon him would find that the anticipated calamity would come upon them instead. Isaac is here asking God to protect his son in a special way, insulating him from the verbal attacks of his enemies. [*'rr*]

27:35 Deceitfully *(bĕmirmâ)*—With this word Esau characterizes Jacob's action as one of deceit. Jacob's treachery comes back to haunt him when Laban tricks him into marrying Leah before Rachel. In Gen. 29:25 Jacob accuses Laban of deceiving him, using the verbal root *(rmh)* of *mirmâ*, the term used in Gen. 27:35. Later his sons use deceit *(mirmâ)* in dealing with the Shechemites (Gen. 34:13), threatening the well-being of the family. [*rmh* > *mirmâ*]

27:36 He has deceived me *(wayya'qĕbēnî)*— Using a different word

for deceit here, Esau puns on Jacob's name. The name Jacob *(ya'ăqōb)* sounds like the verb employed here *('qb)*, which appears to be derived from the noun *'āqēb*, "heel." The verb apparently means "grab the heel" and depicts Jacob as one who comes up behind his brother and betrays him (see HALOT, 872). [*'qb*]

27:40 Throw his yoke *(pāraqtā 'ullô)*—The metaphor anticipates the liberation of Esau's descendants, the Edomites, from political subjugation to Israel. During the time of David, Israel subdued Edom (2 Sam. 8:11-14), but Edom freed itself from Israelite domination during the reign of Jehoram of Judah (848–841 B.C.) (2 Kings 8:20-22). [*prq*]

27:41 I will kill my brother *('ahargâ 'āḥî)*—Esau's statement contributes to the theme of fratricide that mars the pages of Genesis. Cain ruthlessly murdered his brother Abel (Gen. 4:8, 14-15, 25) and Joseph's brothers later plotted to murder him (Gen. 37:20). [*hrg*]

28:3 God Almighty *('ēl šadday)*—This divine title (El Shaddai) depicts God as the sovereign king and judge of the world who both gives and takes away life. The derivation and meaning of Shaddai are uncertain. The most likely proposal is that it means "the one of the mountain" and originally depicted God as a royal judge who in Canaanite style (see Isa. 14:13; Ezek. 28:14, 16) dispenses justice from his sacred mountain. The patriarchs knew God primarily as El Shaddai (Exod. 6:3). When the title is used in Genesis, God appears as the source of fertility and life (see Gen. 17:1-8; 28:3; 35:11; 48:3). When blessing Joseph, Jacob referred to Shaddai (we should probably read El Shaddai here, along with several ancient textual witnesses) as the one who bestows abundant blessings, including children, alluded to in the expression "blessings of the breast and womb" (Gen. 49:25). [*'ēl, šadday*]

A community of peoples (*qĕhal 'ammîm*)—The noun *qhl* usually refers to an assembly or congregation. Here it is associated with God's promise to give numerous descendants and seems to refer to a large organized community or nation. At Bethel God uses a similar phrase as he promised Jacob that a "community of nations" (*qĕhal gôyim*) would descend from him (Gen. 35:11). Jacob later recalls this promise at Bethel, though he employs the phrase utilized by Isaac in Gen. 28:3 (Gen. 48:4). [*qāhāl, 'am*]

28:4 The blessing given to Abraham (*birkat 'abrāhām*)—This phrase refers collectively to the divine promises to Abraham, including numerous offspring and possession of the land of Canaan. Isaac's request that this promise be given to Jacob shows that it is not to be equated with the birthright or the paternal blessing of Gen. 27:27-29. The Lord answered Isaac's prayer at Bethel by offering the Abrahamic blessing to Jacob (Gen. 28:13-15). [*brk > bĕrākâ*]

The land where you now live as an alien (*'ereṣ mĕgureykā*)—This phrase also echoes God's promise to Abraham (Gen. 17:8). Isaac prayed that Jacob might actually take possession of the land, the divine title deed to which God had already granted Abraham (v. 4b; cf. Gen. 15:18). [*'ereṣ, gēr*]

28:8 The Canaanite women (*bĕnôt kĕnā'an*)—The repetition of this phrase (literally, "daughters of Canaan") drives home the contrast between Jacob, who, like Isaac before him (Gen. 24:3, 37), was

not allowed to marry a Canaanite woman, and Esau, who disgusted his parents by intermarrying with the native Canaanites (see Gen. 27:46; 36:2). This is an important theme (see Gen. 34:9 as well) for it reminds a later generation of Israelites that they were not to intermarry with the morally corrupt Canaanites, who were destined for destruction by divine decree. [*bat*]

28:11 Under his head (*mĕra'ăšōtāyw*)—This phrase (see v. 18 as well) probably does not mean "under his head," but "near his head" (see usage in 1 Sam. 19:13, 16; 26:7, 11, 16 [qere]; 1 Kings 19:6). The purpose of this action is not clear, but stones are often viewed in a superstitious way in primitive cultures and sometimes considered to be protective charms. (See J. G. Frazer, *Folklore in the Old Testament* (reprinted; New York: Hart Publishing Company, 1975) 231-37. Jacob's theological perspective appears to be undeveloped at this point (see the note on "God's house," v. 22); he may very well have placed a stone near his head to ward off evil. [*rō'š*]

28:12 He had a dream (*wayyaḥălōm*)—In Genesis dreams have a revelatory or quasi-prophetic function. Through dreams God previewed the future (Gen. 37:5-9; 40:5-19; 41:1-36) and gave warnings and instructions (Gen. 20:3-6; 31:10-13, 24). Here he extended the Abrahamic promise to Jacob and assured him of protection on his journey. [*ḥlm*]

A stairway (*sullām*)—This word, which occurs only here in the Hebrew Bible, is traditionally understood as a ladder, but the term is cognate with Akkadian *simmiltu*, "stairway," and probably refers to a stepped ramp such as one would see on a ziggurat. (See Harold R. "Chaim") Cohen, *Biblical Hapax Legomena in the Light of Akkadian and Ugaritic*

[Missoula, Mont.: Scholars Press, 1978], 34.) In the Akkadian literature various deities, who are specifically called messengers, are depicted ascending and descending such a ramp, called the stairway of heaven, as they move back and forth between the heavens and the netherworld. [*sullam*]

28:13 I am the LORD (*'ănî yhwh*)—This statement of self-identification echoes Gen. 15:7, where the Lord appeared to Abram and reminded him that he had called him out of Ur in order to give him the land of Canaan. Here he employs this same statement as he extends the promise of the land to Jacob. The Lord utilized the statement again when he announced to Moses that he intended to deliver his people from Egypt and lead them to the land he promised to give to Abraham, Isaac, and Jacob (Exod. 6:2-8). [*yhwh*]

The God of your father Abraham and the God of Isaac (*'ĕlōhê 'abrāhām 'ābîkā wē'lōhê yiṣḥāq*)—This precise compound title occurs only here in the Hebrew Bible, but the link with God's promise to Isaac (Gen. 26:24) is unmistakable. There God identified himself as the God of your father Abraham and reiterated the promises of the Abrahamic Covenant, which he had earlier extended to Isaac (Gen. 26:3-5). By here identifying himself as the God of both Abraham and Isaac, the Lord made it clear that Jacob was the recipient of the promised blessings. In 31:53, Laban, a polytheist, may refer to two distinct deities, the God of Abraham and the God of Nahor. It is possible that multiple deities are in view for the term God could be taken as a numerical plural in one or both expressions. That plural deities are in view is indicated by the plural verb form *yišpĕṭû*, "may they judge," which follows. The appositional phrase (ren-

dered "the God of their father" in NIV) is best translated as "the gods of their father," referring to the deities worshiped by Terah, the father of both Abraham and Nahor (Gen. 11:26-27). [*'ĕlōhîm*]

28:14 The dust of the earth (*ka 'ăpar hā'āreṣ*)—This phrase is yet another echo of the Abrahamic promise. After Lot departed from Abram, the Lord promised to give the patriarch all the land he could see in every direction and to make his descendants as numerous as the dust of the earth (Gen. 13:15-16). [*'āpār*]

You will spread out (*pārạṣtā*)—The verb form is singular, reflecting the concept of corporate solidarity between a progenitor and his descendants. Jacob is personally addressed for rhetorical reasons. Jacob would "spread out" through his offspring. [*prṣ*]

To the west and to the east, to the north and to the south (*yāmmâ wāqēdĕmâ wĕṣāpōnâ wānegbâ*)—The terminology echoes the promise in Gen. 13:14-15, where God told Abram to look in all directions and promised to give him every place he could see. As in that text, this promise of land is joined with the promise of numerous descendants. [*yām, qedem, ṣāpôn, negeb*]

28:15 I am with you (*'ānōkî 'immāk*)—The statement is structurally different from the one made to Isaac in Gen. 26:24. Here the pronoun comes first and the preposition *'im* is used, rather than *'et*. However, the thrust of the promise is the same. As in Gen. 26:24 the verb *hyh* "to be," is omitted (contrast Gen. 26:3), placing the focus on the present reality of God's protective presence. This precise form of the statement occurs only here in Genesis. [*'im*]

Will watch over you (*ûšĕmartîkā*)—Jacob later uses this same verb to describe his responsibility as a shepherd who watches over flocks (Gen. 30:31). Perhaps it was God's shepherd-like watchcare that later prompted the shepherd Jacob to refer to the Lord as his Shepherd (Gen. 48:15; 49:24). [*šmr*]

28:17 The house of God *(bêt 'ĕlōhîm)*—Jacob was convinced that God resided in this place, for it was here that heaven and earth met and "the gate of heaven" opened to allow God's messengers to go back and forth between the two realms (see v. 12). Recognizing the special nature of the site, he named it Bethel, meaning "house of God" (v. 19). In 28:22 he applies the phrase to the stone pillar he erected and anointed. Unless the phrase is simply idiomatic (perhaps originally reflecting primitive notions of deity), one gets the impression that Jacob expects God to reside in it and accept his offerings at this shrine. The phrase "house of God," as used in v. 22, has a parallel in the Aramaic Sefire treaty where the phrase "houses of the gods" refers to the monuments upon which the words of the treaty are inscribed. (See Joseph A. Fitzmyer, *The Aramaic Inscriptions of Sefire* [Rome: Pontifical Biblical Institute, 1967], 82-83, 90.) Perhaps Jacob's statement reflects a primitive, as yet undeveloped view of God. [*bayit*]

28:18 A pillar *(maṣṣēbâ)*—In later texts this term is used of idolatrous standing stones, but in Genesis the word seems to refer to monuments set up for various reasons (see Gen. 31:45; 35:14, 20). Here Jacob pours oil on the pillar (cf. Gen. 35:14) apparently setting it apart as holy and for divine use. For further discussion see the note on "God's house" (v. 22). [*nṣb > maṣṣēbâ*]

28:20 If God will be *('im yihyeh 'ĕlōhîm)*—The vow in vv. 20-22 is conditional. The construction (*'im* + the imperfect) should be translated "if [not "since"] God will be with me" (see Gen. 18:26, 28, 30; 30:31; 31:50; 32:8; 34:15). The second part of the conditional sentence (v. 21b) is best translated, "then Yahweh will become [this is the force of the Hebrew construction *hāya . . . lĕ*] my God." In a remarkable and ironic twist of events, Jacob holds God at arm's length and makes what appears to be an unconditional promise into a conditional one. Though God's commitment to Jacob is clear, Jacob's commitment to God is conditional. He will become a follower of God only if God protects him and brings him back safely to the land. [*'im, hyh*]

28:22 I will give you a tenth *('aśśēr 'a 'ăśśᵉrennû)*—Jacob's propensity to bargain is apparent here. He vowed that if God kept his promise to protect, he would make it worth the effort by giving back to God one-tenth of all that God gave him. He even made the statement emphatic (note the infinitive absolute prior to the finite verbal form). Apparently the practice of giving God a tithe was already known in this early, pre-Mosaic period (see Gen. 14:20). [*'sr*]

29:14 My own flesh and blood *('aṣmî ûbᵉśārî)*—This phrase (literally, "my bone and my flesh") indicates kinship (Judg. 9:2; 2 Sam 5:1; 19:12-13; cf. Gen. 2:23). It is significant to the plot structure of the story for it suggests that Laban, because he is a relative of Jacob, is trustworthy. But that proves to not be the case, just as Jacob's kinship with Esau did not prevent him from deceiving his brother. [*'eṣem, bāśār*]

29:25 You deceived me *(rimmîtānî)*—The verb used here is the root of the noun *mirmâ*, "deception," which Isaac uses earlier to describe Jacob's deceit in stealing the paternal blessing (Gen. 27:35). The repetition of the root focuses our attention on the theme of poetic justice. Jacob used deceit to victimize Esau; now he himself is the victim of deceit. In the providence of God what goes around, comes around. [*rmh*]

29:26 The younger daughter . . . before the older one *(haṣṣĕ'îrâ lipnê habbĕkîrâ)*— The term translated "younger daughter" is the feminine form of *ṣā'ir*, a word used to refer to Jacob as the younger brother in Gen. 25:23. Laban drew Jacob's attention to the priority of the firstborn, an important principle in this culture. Jacob should have known this principle, but he showed disregard for it in his dealings with Esau. His disregard for a principle he obviously devalued made him vulnerable to Laban's deceit. [*ṣā'îr, bĕkōr*]

29:31 Not loved *(śĕnû'â)*—The Hebrew word literally means "hated" (see v. 33 as well). The language is hyperbolic and idiomatic. Favoritism, not hatred, is in view. Verse 30 makes it clear that Leah was not literally hated. Jacob simply loved Rachel more than Leah (note the comparative *min* in the Hebrew text). In Hebrew idiom "love" sometimes means "treat in a special way," while "hate" means "to withhold special favor." Deut. 21:15-17 refers to two wives, one of whom is "loved," while the other is "hated" (i.e., unloved). [*śn'*]

He opened her womb *(wayyiptaḥ 'et raḥmāh)*—Genesis consistently portrays God as directly responsible for human fertility (Gen. 18:10; 21:1-2; 25:21; 49:25). He closed and opened the womb as he saw fit (Gen. 20:18; 30:22). Here it appears to be his mercy and sense of justice that prompt him to enable Leah to have children. After the birth of Reuben, Leah triumphantly proclaimed: "the Lord has seen my misery" (v. 32). She understood her misery as prompting God's intervention. [*ptḥ*]

29:32 Has seen *(rā'â)*—The Lord saw her affliction in the sense that he looked on her favorably and responded in a positive way to her need. The precise expression "look upon misery" is found in two texts. Hannah prayed that the Lord might look on her barren condition and give her a son (1 Sam. 1:11) and David, when cursed by Shimei, hoped that God might look on his misery and repay him blessing for the unjust curse (2 Sam. 16:12). A similar expression is often used of God's sympathy for the needy which prompts him to intervene on their behalf (Gen. 31:42; Exod. 3:7; 4:31; Deut. 26:7; 2 Kings 14:26; Neh. 9:9; Pss. 9:13; 25:18; 31:7; 119:153; Lam. 1:9). [*r'h*]

My misery *(bĕ'onyî)*—The word refers to misery or pain, whether physical or emotional. Often the one so described is the victim of oppression or mistreatment (Exod. 3:7; 1 Sam. 1:11). As used by Leah the term may refer to Jacob's favoritism toward Rachel, for she anticipated that Jacob would now love her. The word is later used for the hardship Jacob experienced at the hands of Laban (Gen. 31:42). As in Leah's case, Jacob's misery prompted God to intervene. [*'ŏnî*]

29:33 Heard *(šāma')*—In naming Reuben, Leah ascribed sight to God, using the verb "see" in the sense of "look upon with favor." Here she ascribes to him the sense of hearing. It was as if God heard about the reality of Leah's unfavored (literally "hated") status and then responded to the news by bestowing his favor on Leah. Whether God is depicted as actually seeing or merely hearing about her misery, the point is clear—he responds favorably to those who are suffering, especially when they are the victims of unfair or unjust actions. [*šm'*]

29:35 I will praise *('ôdeh)*—This term, which is especially prominent in the Psalms and Chronicles, carries the idea of giving thanks to God for his intervention and help. For Leah the birth of another son would lessen the pain of being the unfavored wife. She felt it was appropriate to thank God for this expression of his compassion. [*ydh*]

30:1 Became jealous *(wattĕqannē')*—Jealousy inevitably leads to conflict. The Philistines' jealousy of Isaac prompted them to drive him from their land, but God overcame their hostility and blessed Isaac (Gen. 26:14-22). Here Rachel's jealousy of Leah results in the sisters competing for Jacob's affections and attempting to draw God into their dispute. But despite this conflict, God blessed the family by giving children to all the participants in the struggle. Later the jealousy of Joseph's brothers (Gen. 37:11) caused them to seek his life and seemingly threaten the future of the family. But God actually used their jealousy and its sinful expression to further his purposes (see Gen. 45:5-7). [*qn'*]

30:2 Am I in the place of God *(hătahat 'ĕlōhîm 'ānōkî)*—Rachel demanded that Jacob give her children (v. 1), but Jacob argued that God alone gives or withholds *(māna')* the capacity to bear children, a view that the narrator shares (see Gen. 29:31; 30:22). Joseph used this same question to make the point that God alone pos-

sesses the right to judge individuals for their deeds (Gen. 50:19). [*tahat*]

30:6 Has vindicated me *(dānannî)*—The verb here has the nuance "give a favorable judgment." Rachel, who was in competition with her sister Leah, believed that God had vindicated her. While the narrator believes that God does give the capacity to bear children (see the preceding note), he does not indicate if Rachel's perspective was correct. Did God really give Bilhah a child so jealous Rachel (vv. 1, 8) could be vindicated in her struggle with her sister? We must be careful, when interpreting narrative literature, not to assume that statements made by characters necessarily reflect the divine perspective. The narrator tells us that God (1x) took sides with Leah initially (Gen. 29:31), (2x) allowed Leah to have a fifth son (Gen. 30:17), and (3) mercifully removed Rachel's disgrace by giving her her very own son (Gen. 30:22-23), but he never attributes the birth of the surrogate mothers' sons to God. The narrator would certainly agree that God gave Bilhah and Zilpah the capacity to have children, but not necessarily for the reasons perceived by the feuding Leah and Rachel. God's intention in giving these sons may have been simply to fulfill his promise to make Jacob fruitful, rather than to fuel the conflict between the two wives. Scholars are divided in their opinions on the matter. Wenham doubts that the narrator agrees with Rachel's assessment. (See Gordon Wenham, *Genesis 16–50*, WBC [Dallas: Word Books, 1994]), 245.) Humphreys, however, sees God being "drawn into matters of family politics as he insures the generation of seed to fulfill his promise made first to Abraham." Behind the words of Rachel and Leah, he states, "we might imagine a Yahweh struggling to keep some balance and neutralize the tensions that lace Jacob's marriage to rival sisters." (See W. Lee Humphreys, *The Character of God in the Book of Genesis: A Narrative Appraisal* [Louisville: Westminster John Knox, 2001], 177.) [*dyn*]

He has listened to my plea *(šama' bĕqōlî)*—The expression (literally, "hear my voice") usually means "to obey" (Gen. 22:18; 26:5; 27:8, 13, 43). Occasionally, when used of a superior party's hearing a subordinate (such as in prayer) it carries the nuance "accede to one's request" (Gen. 21:12; Num. 21:3; Deut. 1:45; Josh. 10:14; Judg. 13:9; 1 Sam. 19:6; 25:35; 2 Sam. 12:18). Rachel apparently prayed that God would vindicate her and interpreted the birth of Dan as his positive response to her request. Was she correct? See the preceding note. In 30:17 the narrator makes it clear that God listened to Leah, meaning that he answered her prayer for another child. We are not told why he did so. Initially God enabled Leah to bear children because of her disadvantage as the unloved wife (Gen. 29:31). Perhaps from God's perspective, Rachel's manipulative actions (Gen. 30:1-16) once more placed Leah at a disadvantage (v. 20 may suggest this), prompting him to intervene on behalf of Leah. However, Leah's interpretation of why God gave her this son is different from this. (See the following note.) Leah's pregnancy, despite the fact that she surrendered the mandrakes (apparently viewed as an aphrodisiac by the women), makes it clear that ultimately God alone, apart from human device or superstition, gives and withholds children. [*šm'*]

30:18 Has rewarded me *(nātan . . . šĕkārî)*—Elsewhere the Hebrew expression (literally, "pay a wage/fee") is used of financial transactions (Gen. 30:28; Exod. 2:9; Deut. 24:15; 1 Kings 5:6; Jonah

1:3). Leah apparently felt that God was under some type of obligation to repay her because of her willingness to give her maidservant Zilpah to Jacob (see vv. 9-12). Though the narrator makes it clear that God responded to Leah's prayer, he stops short of agreeing with Leah's reason for why he did so. See the earlier discussion of v. 6. [*ntn, śākār*]

30:22 Remembered *(wayyizkōr)*—The verb does not refer here to recalling information; it is idiomatic, meaning "to respond or treat favorably" (Gen. 8:1; 19:29). The narrator draws attention to God's intervention, emphasizing God's capacity to bring life from even a barren womb. [*zkr*]

Listened to her and opened her womb *(wayyišma' 'ēleyhā . . . wayyiptaḥ 'et-raḥmāh)*—The repetition of these expressions testifies to God's fairness and mercy. According to v. 17, he listened to Leah and gave her a fifth son. Now he listens to tormented Rachel. According to Gen. 29:31, he opened Leah's womb; here he finally opens Rachel's womb and gives her the ability to bear her very own son. [*ptḥ*]

30:23 My disgrace *(ḥerpātî)*—In this culture it was humiliating for a woman to be unmarried and childless (Isa. 4:1) or for a wife to be barren and unable to provide her husband with children. Rachel's use of this term expresses her deep-seated feelings and suggests why God finally intervened on her behalf. [*ḥrp > ḥerpâ*]

30:28 I have learned by divination *(niḥaštî)*—Divination, or omen reading, was used in the ancient Near Eastern world to acquire secret information from the gods about present realities or future events. Various means were utilized, including correlating the juxtaposition of casual phenomena and observing the inner organs of sacrificial animals. (See Malcolm J. A. Horsnell, *NIDOTTE*, 3:945-51, as well as Frederick H. Cryer, *Divination in Ancient Israel and its Near Eastern Environment*, JSOTSup, 142 [Sheffield: JSOT, 1994], and Robert R. Wilson, *Prophecy and Society in Ancient Israel* [Philadelphia: Fortress, 1980], 90-98.) The Hebrew Bible condemns such practices as pagan (2 Kings 17:17; 21:6). Because Laban received a truthful message through divination does not mean that God approved of such a practice, but it does show that his providence sometimes works outside approved boundaries when he is bringing his purposes to pass. (See Gen. 44:5, 15, as well as Bruce K. Waltke with Cathi J. Fredricks, *Genesis: A Commentary* [Grand Rapids: Zondervan, 2001], 418.) Later God communicated to Laban through a dream (Gen. 31:24). [*nḥš*]

31:9 Has taken away *(wayyaṣṣēl)*—Laban's sons accused Jacob of taking their father's wealth (in the form of flocks) by dishonest means (v. 1). But from Jacob's perspective his prosperity was the work of God himself, whom he pictures as snatching away Laban's sheep and giving them to him. Jacob explained that God revealed to him through a dream that he had intentionally blessed Jacob at Laban's expense because of Laban's dishonest mistreatment of Jacob (vv. 10-12). Shortly after this Rachel and Leah agree with Jacob's assessment (vv 14-16) as they complain of how their father had spent their dowry. In their opinion Jacob's prosperity was God's way of restoring to them what their father had taken. As when he intervened on behalf of unloved Leah, God again took the side of those who were in a position of disadvantage (see v.

12). In 32:11 Jacob requested that God deliver him from his brother Esau, who, as far as Jacob knew, still wanted to kill him. [*nṣl*]

31:19 Household gods *(tĕrāpîm)*—This term probably refers to images of the family's protective "gods" (see vv. 30, 32). Perhaps these idols were associated with ancestral worship and/or were used for divination. (See Patrick D. Miller, *The Religion of Ancient Israel* [Louisville: Westminster/John Knox, 2000], 71-72.) Rachel's obsession with them testifies to the fact that Jacob's family was at this point corrupted by pagan influences. These would need to be discarded before the family returned to Bethel and formalized its commitment to God (see Gen. 35:2-4). Some suggest that possession of the household gods would have guaranteed Jacob's right to inherit Laban's wealth, but this proposal seems highly unlikely. (See Moshe Greenberg, "Another Look at Rachel's Theft of the Teraphim," *JBL* 81 [1962], 239-48.) [*tĕrāpîm*]

31:42 The fear of Isaac *(paḥad yiṣḥāq)*—This divine title, which occurs only in this context (see v. 53 as well), depicts God as the one whom Isaac fears. This particular term for fear occurs only here in Genesis. Elsewhere the word and its related verb usually refer to sheer terror or trembling. If the word does indeed refer to Isaac's response to God, it probably carries the nuance of "treat with awe/respect," though this nuance of the noun is rarely if ever attested elsewhere (though see Ps. 36:1 and the use of a feminine form of the noun in Jer. 2:19). [*pḥd*]

He rebuked *(wayyôkaḥ)*—The verb can sometimes refer to a verbal rebuke. Since it refers to God's warning to Laban not to harm Jacob (see vv. 24, 29), the verb may carry this shade of meaning here. However, the verb has no object in the Hebrew text (NIV adds "you"). Consequently the word may here mean "decided, rendered judgment" (see *HALOT*, 410; *BDB*, 406). His word of warning to Laban was tantamount to a legal decision in Jacob's favor. [*ykḥ*]

31:49 Keep watch (*yiṣep*)—This verb is used elsewhere of watching a situation carefully, such as a watchman on the city wall would do. By using it here, Laban cast God in the role of the guarantor of his agreement with Jacob. Laban would be unable to ensure his daughters' well-being (v. 50), so he appealed to God to guarantee their fair treatment by Jacob. [*ṣph*]

31:50 A witness (*'ēd*)—The heap of stones set up by Jacob would serve as a witness in the sense that it would be a tangible reminder of the agreement, but ultimately God would be the guarantor of the covenant. In this role he would observe the behavior of the parties involved and testify (like a witness in a legal setting), as it were, to any wrongdoing he observed. In his capacity as witness, he would also punish the wrongdoer (see v. 53). (See Robert B. Chisholm, *NIDOTTE*, 3:337.) [*'ûd > 'ēd*]

32:1 Met him (*wayyipgĕ'û-bô*)—The appearance of angels signals God's presence, just as it did at Bethel, and suggests that Jacob may soon encounter God, as he did at Bethel (see Gen. 28:12-13). Angels appeared to Jacob on the eve of his leaving the land (Gen. 28); now they appear again as he prepared to enter it. The expression *pāga' bĕ-* can carry a neutral meaning ("meet," Gen. 28:11; Josh. 16:7), but more often it has a negative connotation and is used of hostile encounters or

actions (Num. 35:19, 21; Josh. 2:16; Judg. 8:21; 15:12; 18:25; 1 Sam. 22:17-18; 2 Sam. 1:15; 1 Kings 2:25, 29, 31-32, 34, 46; Ruth 2:22). It may have a neutral sense in Gen. 32:1, but since God wrestles with Jacob shortly after this, this ambiguous expression may have a double meaning and signal that struggle. (See Thomas W. Mann, *The Book of the Torah: The Narrative Integrity of the Pentateuch* [Atlanta: John Knox, 1988], 59.) [*pg'*]

32:2 Camp of God (*maḥănēh 'ĕlōhîm*)—In light of the divine promise of protection in Gen. 31:3, the appearance of the angels should have been encouraging to Jacob. In fact Jacob's reference to the camp of God may suggest he believed God was traveling with him. [*maḥăneh*]

32:4 My master . . . your servant (*la'dōnî . . . 'abdĕkā*)—Ever the manipulator, Jacob instructed his messengers to identify him as Esau's servant. In introducing the instructions to the messengers, Jacob even referred to Esau as his master, as if to signal to the messengers how Esau was to be approached and treated. The actual message (v. 5) also refers to Esau as Jacob's lord (*'ādōn*). See also vv. 18, 20. [*'ādōn*, *'ebed*]

32:10 I am unworthy (*qāṭōntî*)—This statement of humility marks a key turning point in Jacob's relationship with God. Mann explains: "Jacob finally confesses what we have known all along: 'I am not worthy of the least of all the loyalty and all the faithfulness which thou hast shown thy servant' (v. 10). If there is a moment of righteousness in Jacob's life, it is surely here, where he acknowledges that the blessing he enjoys is not one he has earned, but the gift of a gracious God." (See *The Book of the Torah*, 60.) [*qṭn*]

Kindness (haḥăsādîm)—The plural form of the noun ḥesed, rather than generalizing about God's kindness, points to God's many individual acts of kindness toward Jacob since he left his home and encountered the Lord at Bethel. According to Clark, the noun ḥesed "is not merely an attitude or an emotion; it is an emotion that leads to an activity beneficial to the recipient." He explains that an act of ḥesed is "a benificent action performed, in the context of a deep and enduring commitment between two persons or parties, by one who is able to render assistance to the needy party who in the circumstances is unable to help him or herself." (See Gordon R. Clark, *The Word* Hesed *in the Hebrew Bible* [Sheffield: Sheffield Academic Press, 1993], 267.) *HALOT* (336-37) defines the word as "loyalty," or "faithfulness." Other appropriate glosses might be "commitment" and "devotion." In Genesis the term is used of human loyalty (Gen. 20:13; 21:23; 24:49; 40:14; 47:29) and of God's devotion to Lot (Gen. 19:19), Abraham (Gen. 24:12, 14, 27), and Joseph (Gen. 39:21). [ḥesed]

Faithfulness (hā'ĕmet)—This term, which is often paired with its synonym ḥesed (see the previous note), has the primary meaning "sure, reliable, constant." In Gen. 24:40 it is used of the "right" road upon which God led Abraham's servant in his quest to find a bride for Isaac. On the human plane it is used of the truthfulness of one's words (Gen. 42:16) and of loyalty within a family sphere (Gen. 24:49; 47:29). Here Jacob emphasizes (note the use of "all" before the word in the Hebrew text) God's continual commitment to him while he was in a foreign land, as evidenced by the way the Lord blessed him with a large family. ['mn > 'ĕmet]

You have shown ('āśîtâ)—The use of this verb, which literally means "to do,

act," indicates that the divine qualities mentioned prior to this (kindness and faithfulness) are not mere abstract attributes. God revealed these qualities through tangible actions on behalf of Jacob. Commenting on this and similar passages, Sakenfeld observes that "loyalty is never something purely abstract or intangible. If loyalty does not issue in appropriate action, then it has faded away or ceased to exist." (See Katherine Doob Sakenfeld, *Faithfulness in Action: Loyalty in Biblical Perspective* [Philadelphia: Fortress, 1985], 87.) ['śh]

32:11 I am afraid (yārē' 'ānōkî)—Like his father Isaac before him, Jacob was subject to fear when circumstances threatened his well-being (Gen. 26:7; 28:17; 31:31; 32:7). In typical fashion he concocted a scheme in an attempt to pacify his brother, but he also confessed his fear before God, acknowledged his unworthiness, and asked God to deliver him. For an excellent discussion of how this account reveals two sides of Jacob's character, see Mann, *The Book of the Torah*, 59-60. He observes: "Jacob's preparations for his reunion with Esau reveal two sides to his character that approach contradiction. . . . We do not have two Jacobs here; we have only the one man, at once calculating and contrite, an inextricable combination expressed by the position of Jacob's prayer in between his two precautionary maneuvers. First he plans, then he prays, then he plans again." [yr']

32:12 Like the sand of the sea, which cannot be counted (kĕḥôl hayyām 'ăšer lō'-yissāpēr mērōb)—Nowhere prior to this are these words spoken to Jacob. In the earlier narratives of Genesis these words are spoken only to Abraham (cf. Gen. 16:10; 22:17). We should not assume, however, that the earlier narratives contain everything God said to Jacob; God may very well have made this statement at Bethel (Gen. 28) or on some subsequent occasion. Nevertheless, from a literary point of view, Jacob appears to identify with Abraham and to appropriate the ancient promise to his illustrious ancestor. The statement actually combines the language of two separate formulations of the promise of numerous offspring. The phrase "sand of the sea" is reminiscent of the promise made in Gen. 22:17, which anticipates Abraham's offspring becoming as numerous "as the sand which is on the shore of the sea" (literal translation). The statement "which cannot be counted" comes from Gen. 16:10, where God promises that Abram's descendants would be "too numerous to count." [*spr*]

32:24 A man (*'îš*)—As we find out by the end of the episode, Jacob's opponent was no man; he was God himself, or at least an angel, in physical form. For dramatic effect the narrator assumes Jacob's perspective here. We, like Jacob, must wait to discover the truth. [*'îš*]

32:25 He could not <u>overpower</u> him (*lō' yākōl lô*)—The expression means "to overcome, defeat, overpower" (*BDB*, 408). If the adversary was actually God, by taking human form he placed some obvious limitations upon himself. The passage reminds us that God will sometimes exercise self-restraint when relating to human beings in order to give the relationship a genuine "give-and-take" dimension. What was the significance of the wrestling match and the adversary's words? The reference to Jacob wrestling "with God and with men" was a commentary on his life up to this point. Just as Jacob had literally wrestled with the adversary during the night, so he had

wrestled with men and ultimately with God throughout his life. He prevailed in the wrestling match and received a blessing, despite being severely injured in the process. In the same way, after receiving several injuries, he prevailed in his struggle with God when he prayed for deliverance (see vv. 9-12). He had finally come to the point where he was willing to trust God with his future. The wrestling match is a microcosm of Jacob's experience. Rather than being the culminating act in his development, it illustrates his life's struggles and brings out the significance of his prayer. The blessing reminds us once more of God's intention to fulfill his promises through Jacob (see Gen. 28:13-15; 31:3). [*ykl*]

32:26 For it is daybreak (*kî 'ālâ haššāḥar*)— Why did Jacob's adversary feel compelled to leave before the light of dawn? If this was indeed God, then this may indicate that it would have been inappropriate and perhaps even deadly for Jacob to have seen God face-to-face in the full light of day. See Exod. 33:20. [*šaḥar*]

Unless you <u>bless</u> me (*kî 'im bēraktānî*)— Many assume that Jacob discovered early on in the struggle that the adversary was God and therefore demanded a blessing. The request for a blessing, then, was the culminating point in Jacob's developing relationship with God. He finally grabbed hold of the promised blessing.

However, is there another way to read the episode? Perhaps Jacob did not suspect the adversary was God until the adversary renamed him (v. 28). Jacob's request for a blessing may suggest he suspected the adversary was God, but this does not necessarily follow. Having wrestled with the adversary all night, Jacob may have been concerned that his opponent would seek to harm him again or perhaps curse him. The best way to circumvent such a development was to make the adversary pronounce a blessing on him, ensuring protection for Jacob in the future. When the adversary asked for Jacob's name, it appeared that he was simply looking for the information with which to formulate an individualized blessing. But then he gave Jacob a new name, explaining that Jacob had wrestled with God. This clue as to the adversary's identity prompted Jacob to seek verification, but the adversary refused to comply, though he did grant the blessing. At this point Jacob was convinced that the adversary was none other than God himself. [*brk*]

32:27 What is your name? *(mah šĕmekā)*—The question is apparently rhetorical. The adversary may have been reminding Jacob of his deceptive character before giving him a new name (see Wenham, *Genesis 16–50*, 296). If nothing else, the question served to keep the adversary's identity disguised until just the right moment. [*šēm*]

32:28 Israel *(yiśrā'ēl)*—The name apparently means "God fights," suggesting that Jacob has engaged God in conflict. The verb *śārâ* (translated "struggled" by NIV) apparently means "to fight." It appears elsewhere only in Hosea 12:3-4, which alludes to this incident. This change in name marked a transition in the patriarch's life. From birth Jacob was a deceiver who tried to gain security and prosperity by tricking others. (On the name Jacob, see Gen. 25:26 and 27:36.) After the incident at Peniel he would be Israel, the one who wrestled with God and came to the place where he realized that security and prosperity are divine gifts. The incident in 35:10 seems to duplicate this naming

episode. In vv. 11-15 other earlier incidents are repeated as well—God makes Jacob the recipient of the Abrahamic promise (cf. vv. 11-12 with 28:13-15) and Jacob once again sanctifies the site and names it Bethel (cf. vv. 14-15 with 28:18-19). This series of so-called doublets has prompted some to conclude that we have competing versions of these events deriving from different sources. A more likely explanation is that earlier declarations were formalized (made official) and earlier events reactualized in chapter 35. When Jacob returned to Bethel his spiritual journey was complete. The Lord had fulfilled Jacob's condition for establishing a relationship (cf. Gen. 35:3 with 28:20) and Jacob was more than ready to serve him. God again gave him a new name and reiterated the promise, linking it with Jacob's new name as if to remind him that dependence on the God who promises was the key to the divine blessing being realized. On his initial visit to Bethel, Jacob was not ready to accept the God who promises on God's terms. After the wrestling match at Peniel, he was prepared to do so. The renaming at Peniel was reactualized as the promise was reiterated and Jacob reactualized his worship, this time without making a bargain with God. [*yiśrā'ēl*]

32:29 Why do you ask my name? *(lāmmâ zeh tiš'al lišmî)*—Jacob asked for the adversary's name, apparently to verify that this really was God. The adversary refused to comply with that request, but he did give Jacob the blessing for which he asked. Some suggest that the adversary, if God, refused to give his name for fear that Jacob might use it improperly or try to employ it in some magical way. However, since Jacob already knew God's name (see v. 30), this explanation seems improbable.

It is more likely that the question is rhetorical and implies that he should already have known this information. One could paraphrase: "Why are you asking my name? You should know who I am by now!" Elsewhere the construction *lāmmâ zeh* consistently introduces a rhetorical question and/or carries a critical connotation (see Gen. 18:13; 25:22, 32; 33:15; Exod. 2:20; 5:22; 17:3; Num. 11:20; 14:41; Josh. 7:10; Judg. 13:18; 1 Sam. 17:28; 20:8; 26:18; 2 Sam. 3:24; 12:23; 18:22; 19:42; 1 Kings 14:6; Jer. 6:20; 20:18; Amos 5:18; Job 9:29; 27:12; Prov. 17:16). [*lāmmâ zeh*]

32:30 I saw God face to face *(rā'îtî 'ĕlōhîm pānîm 'el panim)*—Jacob was certain that he had seen God face-to-face and that he had actually wrestled with God in the flesh. Was his perception of his experience correct? The narrator never specifically identifies the adversary as God, though the adversary himself seemed to suggest as much when he said to Jacob, "You have struggled with God and with men." However, it is possible that he identified himself with God in a representative sense. Hosea 12:3-4 identifies Jacob's adversary as both God and an angel, suggesting that the adversary was a messenger sent by God, undoubtedly with full divine authority. The prophet appears to be following the lead of Jacob himself, who later referred to God as "the Angel who has delivered me from all harm" (see Gen. 48:15-16). [*r'h*]

My life was spared *(wattinnāṣēl napšî)*—The statement is usually translated "and yet my life is rescued," as if it refers to the fact that his life had been spared despite his seeing God face-to-face. (In this regard see Exod. 33:20.) It is more likely that the statement refers to the fact that he had been granted deliverance from Esau through the blessing (whether

explicitly or implicitly). In v. 12 Jacob prayed that God would rescue him. Here he acknowledges that God had answered his prayer. It may seem odd that the Hebrew verbal construction (a *wayyiqtol* form) would refer to a still future act, but from Jacob's perspective he had already experienced deliverance through the blessing. (In the traditional view the *wayyiqtol* has an antithetical force.) [*nṣl*]

33:3 Bowed down *(wayyištaḥû)*—The passage is dripping with irony. The paternal blessing stolen by Jacob envisioned a time when the recipient's brothers would bow down before him (Gen. 27:29). But Jacob, despite having pilfered the paternal blessing through deceit, bowed down before Esau in humility and fear. While divine providence allowed Jacob to steal the blessing, the superiority envisioned in the blessing was not experienced by Jacob during his lifetime. As far as we know, Esau never bowed down before Jacob. On the contrary, God turned the tables on Jacob, forcing him to bow before the brother whom he had wronged. The paternal blessing was eventually realized when Jacob's descendants, the Israelites, subjugated Esau's offspring, the Edomites. [*ḥwh*]

33:5 Has graciously given *(ḥānan)*—The verb carries the basic meaning of "show favor, have compassion" (see *HALOT*, 334-35). The verb is rare in Genesis (see v. 11; Gen. 43:29). The related noun *ḥēn* is used frequently in Genesis of human favor or compassion (see, for example, v. 10), but is only rarely used of God (Gen. 6:8; 18:3). In this context Jacob refers to the divine blessings of fertility and prosperity (v. 11). [*ḥnn*]

34:7 Disgraceful thing *(nĕbālâ)*—When combined with the verb *'sh*, "to do," the word usually refers, as here, to heinous sexual crimes (adultery or rape) that violate God's moral standard (see Deut. 22:21; Judg. 19:23-24; 20:6, 10; 2 Sam. 13:12; Jer. 29:23). Here the action is said to be against Israel in the sense that Dinah belonged to her father Israel. (Elsewhere when the phrase *běyiśrā'ēl* is used with "do a disgraceful thing," it means "in Israel," but here the preposition is better taken in an adversative sense, "against." The name Israel almost always refers to the individual patriarch in Genesis, not the family.) [*něbālâ*]

34:9 Intermarry *(hithattěnû)*—The request posed a grave danger to the family for intermarriage with the Canaanites would jeopardize the family's identity and distinctiveness and with it God's promise to Abraham. See the note on Gen. 28:8. Later generations of Israelites reading the story would find it extremely relevant for the Lord made it clear that his people were not to intermarry with the Canaanites (Deut. 7:3; Josh. 23:12; Ezra 9:14). [*htn*]

35:2 Foreign gods *('ĕlōhê hannēkār)*—Rachel's theft of her father's household gods (Gen. 31:19) indicated that paganism was present in Jacob's family. Here we discover that members of Jacob's household possessed foreign gods. Before returning to Bethel and soldifying his covenantal relationship with God, Jacob wisely commanded his family to discard these idols. In so doing he became an example for later generations of Israelites who were to reject foreign gods (Josh. 24:20, 23; 1 Sam. 7:3; 2 Chron. 33:15). [*nēkār*]

Purify yourselves *(hittahărû)*—This refers to physical cleansing that consecrated one for worship or service. The term is used frequently of ritual purifica-

tion in cultic contexts (Lev. 14:4, 7-8, 11, 14, 17-19, 25, 28-29, 31; Num. 8:7; Ezra 6:20; Neh. 12:30; 13:22; 2 Chron. 30:18). In Josh. 22:17 the point is made that Israel had not ritually cleansed themselves following their idolatry at Peor (cf. Num. 25:1-9). This indicates that idolatry had a defiling effect, necessitating ritual cleansing before one approached the presence of God. This explains why Jacob told his idolatrous household to purify themselves before entering Bethel, the "house of God." [*thr*]

35:3 Answered *(hā'ōneh)*—Jacob here testified to the fact that God answered his prayer when he cried out for help. This probably refers to the prayer he offered on the eve of his confrontation with Esau (Gen. 32:9-12). God responded to this prayer by blessing and protecting Jacob (see Gen. 32:29-30). Jacob had learned that God responds to the pleas of his needy people. [*'nh*]

35:5 Terror of God *(hittat 'ĕlōhîm)*—The phrase apparently refers to a supernaturally induced terror sent by God on the inhabitants of the area. Despite Jacob's fear that the residents of the region would retaliate against his family because of the incident at Shechem (Gen. 34:30), God once again proved true to his promise by intervening in Jacob's experience and protecting him from potential danger (Gen. 28:15; 31:3). [*hittâ*]

37:1 Father had stayed *(měgûrê)*—The story of Joseph begins in chapter 37 with Jacob residing in the land of his fathers, the land promised to Abraham, Isaac, and Jacob (Israel). The term translated as "stayed" in the NIV is the noun *māgôr* derived from the common Hebrew verb *gwr* meaning "to sojourn" (*BDB*, 157; *HALOT*, 1:184 "to dwell as alien and dependent"). The term *māgôr* occurs 11x in the OT, 5x in Genesis (17:8, 28:4, 36:7, 37, 47:9). Here in chapter 37:1 it refers to the place of one's sojourning, the most common use of the term (*BDB*, 158; "sojourning place"; *HALOT*, 1:544; "temporary abode, land of domicile"). Some translations attempt to emphasize this aspect of the patriarchal sojourning. For example, the Tanakh (JPS) translates the phrase as "the land where his father had sojourned." The term reminds the reader that the patriarchs never owned the land promised them by God (with the notable exception of the cave of Machpelah), but were only sojourners in the land (cf. Heb. 11:9-10). [*māgôr*]

37:3 Now Israel <u>loved</u> Joseph (*'āhab*)—In Hebrew, as in English, the verb "to love" (*'hb*), is used in a surprisingly wide range of contexts. Here in Genesis the same verb (13x in Genesis) can refer to romantic love, as with Jacob's love for Rachel (Gen. 29:18, 20), to Isaac's love of wild game (Gen. 27:4), and to familial love of a parent for a child, as for example in Genesis 22:2 where Abraham is told to sacrifice the child he loves (*'hb*). However, love for children is seldom stated in the OT (E. Jenni, *TLOT*, 1:48) but where it is mentioned, as in this passage, it draws attention to its special significance in the narrative (Gen. 22:2; 25:28; 37:3). Here in Gen. 37:3, Jacob's love for Joseph is tied to Jacob's love for Rachel, Joseph's mother (Gen. 29:30). Because she was the beloved wife, her sons became the beloved sons. (P. J. J. S. Els, *NIDOTTE*, 1:277-99). [*'hb*]

37:5 Joseph had a <u>dream</u> (*wayyaḥălôm*)—Throughout the ancient Near East people believed dreams were a means by which the gods revealed their will to mankind. The discovery of the Ugaritic texts at Ras Shamra provided several texts where dreams were regarded as a means of divine revelation. In the epic of Keret, the god El used a dream (Ug. *ḥlm*) to reveal to Keret information regarding the birth of a son (*CTA*, 14[1K], I, 26f]. In the OT, the verb *ḥlm* occurs 26x (24x in qal, 2x in hiphil). In 20 of these 26 occurrences the verb is followed by its cognate noun *ḥălōm* (dream), as it is here in Gen. 37:5: "And Joseph dreamed (*wayyaḥălôm*) a dream (*ḥălōm*)." The occurrences of this verb are clustered in two books: Genesis, particularly the Joseph narrative, and Daniel. It is significant that both of these texts involved foreign kings. In the OT, dreams are often regarded as divine revelation (Num. 12:6-8, Job 33:16), as they prove to be in the dream Joseph dreamed here in Gen. 37. Yet there are also warnings that dreams can deceive and mislead (Deut. 13:1-6; Jer. 23:25-32) [M. Ottosson/G .J. Botterweck, 4:421-32; G. Smith, *NIDOTTE*, 2:153-55) [*ḥlm*]

37:9 Were <u>bowing down</u> (*mištaḥăwîm*)—Joseph's second dream sounded even more grandiose and egotistical than the first. In this dream he saw the heavenly bodies (including 11 stars) bowing down to him. The term "bowing down" was formerly regarded as the hithpael of the verb *šḥh* (*BDB*, 1005). Later, when the Ugaritic material was available, a NW-Semitic verb (*ḥwy*), "to be prostrate before," was discovered. Modern lexicons now recognize the term as the sole use of the hištaphel stem in the Hebrew Bible, a hištaphel of the verb *ḥwh* meaning "to bow down" (*ḥwh* II, *HALOT*, 1:295-6). The verb is used 170x in the MT. The most common usage of the verb is bowing before God/gods in worship (T. Fretheim, *NIDOTTE*, 2:43). When the verb is used in reference to people it is an action that shows honor or recognition of someone's higher status. For example, it is used of bowing before a king (2 Sam. 14:4, 16:4). Here in Genesis 37:9, the use of the term provides a foreshadowing of what actually would occur when the brothers would later meet Joseph (Gen. 42:6). [*ḥwh*]

37:11 Were jealous (*wayĕqannᵉû*)—The verb *qn'* is used in this verse to describe the brothers' reaction to Joseph's dream and it is used in a surprisingly broad range of meanings. The same verb (*qn'*) can refer to God's holy zeal for his name (Ezek. 39:25), or Rachel's jealousy of her sister Leah (Gen. 30:1). The verb reflects strong passions that can be positive or negative. When used in reference to people, it can be used positively to describe the zeal of Phineas (Num. 25:13) and Elijah (1 Kings 19:14). It can also be used negatively to describe the Philistines' envy of Isaac's flocks (Gen. 26:14). In Genesis 37, *qn'* describes the passionate envy of Joseph's brothers. *HALOT* cites this verse under the definition of "to be envious of" (*HALOT*, 2:1100, 1.i) and "to get heated, become excited about" (*HALOT*, 2:1100, 1.ii.). This reflects both the simple envy and the intensity of the emotion that goes with it. The Tanakh (JPS) translation of the verse attempts to capture this nuance with, "So his brothers were wrought up with him." (H. G. L. Peels, *NIDOTTE*, 3:938-40). [*qn'*]

37:19 That dreamer (*ba'al hahălōmôt*)—As Joseph approached, his brothers derisively referred to him as "that dreamer." The term "dreamer" is an adjectival phrase in which a noun in the construct *ba'al* ("owner, husband, lord"; *BDB*, 127) is followed by a noun in the genitive, *hălōmôt* ("dreams") that expresses the character or nature of the person

described (*IBHS*, 9.5.3). In this verse, the phrase would literally mean "owner of dreams." Most English Bibles translate the phrase as "that dreamer." Joseph, the "owner/lord of the dreams," would indeed find his skill with dreams as the means by which he would be exalted from prison to Pharaoh's palace. [*ba'al hahălōmôt*]

37:22 Don't shed any blood ('al-tišpĕkû)—The verb translated "shed [blood]" is the verb *špk*, which does not describe the gradual pouring of a liquid, but "sudden, massive spillage" (*HALOT*, 2:1629). Its most common object is blood (*dām*), as in this verse (v. 37). The verb is immediately followed by this object ("blood") 16x in the OT. This shedding of blood can be used positively in the sense of shedding the blood of a sacrificial animal (Exod. 29:12; Lev. 4:7, 11, 25). However, its more common usage is to refer to the wanton, criminal shedding of blood. The first use of the term in the OT occurs in Gen. 9:6 where God commanded that those who shed blood "will by man have their blood shed." The phrase "shedding of blood" is used by the prophets to describe Israel's sin as well as her punishment. The prophet Ezekiel often utilized this phrase, employing it 4x in a single chapter (Ezek. 22:3, 6, 12, 27). Here in Gen. 37:22, Reuben uses the phrase to urge his brothers not to murder their brother Joseph. [*špk*]

37:27 Our flesh and blood (*beśārēnû*)—The noun *bāśār* is used 266x in the OT (*HALOT*, 1:164; 270x , G. Gerleman, *TLOT*, 1:283) with a wide range of meaning. It can refer to skin, meat, sacrificial meat (with Leviticus having the most occurrences, 61x), part of the body, or a whole body (*HALOT*, 1:164). Although the LXX commonly translates the term with *sarx*, the term in Hebrew does not carry the distinctive Pauline nuance. *Bāśār* is also used to designate close family relationships. In Gen. 2:23 Adam responds to the creation of Eve with the famous words, "This is now bone of my bone and flesh of my flesh." The idiom "bone [*'eṣem*] and flesh [*bāśār*]" is used on several occasions to describe family relations (Gen. 29:14; Judg. 9:2; 2 Sam. 19:12). Sometimes *bāśār* ("flesh") is used alone (often with a first person suffix) to designate these same family connections (Gen. 2:24; Neh. 5:5; Isa. 58:7) as it is here in Gen. 37:27. Several translations, such as NIV and TEV, employ the English idiom "flesh and blood" to approximate the meaning of *bāśār* in this passage. (R. Chisholm, *NIDOTTE*, 1:777-9). [*bāśār*]

37:35 To the grave *(šĕ'ōlāh)*—The term *šĕ'ôl* (or *šĕ'ōl*), appearing for the first time in the OT in this verse, occurs a total of 66x in the OT. It is not found in any other Semitic languages prior to Hebrew (G. Gerleman, *TLOT*, 3:1279). In spite of extensive scholarly investigation, there is no consensus regarding its etymology. The term commonly occurs with the locative *hā* (or directive *hā*) suffix, as in this passage. The fact that *šĕ'ôl* never occurs with the article suggests that the term is a proper name. Its common usage with the verb *yrd* ("to go down"), often in the hiphil ("brought down"), suggests that *šĕ'ôl* is viewed as the underworld, the abode of the dead (*HALOT*, 2:1369). Like the Babylonian underworld (Akk. *erṣetu*; *CDA*, 74), the "land of no return" (Akk. *lā tarû*), Sheol was the place where one lives an attenuated existence, cut off from the praise and worship of God (Isa. 38:18). (E. Merrill, *NIDOTTE*, 4:6-7) [*šĕ'ôl*]

38:7 Wicked in the LORD'S eyes *(ra')*—The Hebrew word *ra'* (or *rā* ') is used both as an adjective and as a noun, and at times it is difficult to distinguish one from the other (*HALOT*, 1250). In this verse, the term is used as an adjective. As an adjective, there are numerous meanings that do not have a negative moral connotation, including "poor, damaged, heavy, of little worth" (*HALOT*, A.1, 2, 3, 9). Its most common meaning, however, is "bad, evil, wicked" (*BDB*, 948). In this passage Er has the distinction as the first person in the OT to be described by a common OT idiom: one who was "evil in the eyes of the Lord." This phrase, common in the deuteronomistic material, became a stock phrase to describe the kings of Israel and Judah, occurring 30x in 1 and 2 Kings. [*ra'*]

Lord put him to death *(wayĕmitēhû)*—The term *mwt* ("to die") is broadly attested throughout the Semitic languages. For example, it is used in the east with the Akkadian term *mâtum* (*CDA*, 205), and in the west with the Ugaritic *mt*. In Canaanite mythology, Mot (Ug. *mt*) is the god of death who slays Lord Baal (H. Ringgren, *Religions of the Ancient Near Eastern*, 134). The Hebrew verb *mwt* is a common verb, occurring approximately 600x in the Qal in reference to the death of any living creature, including humans. In the hiphil, the causative stem, *mwt* means to kill, to cause to die (*HALOT*, 1:562). Here in this passage (Gen. 38:7), the term used is in the hiphil, which occurs about 130x in the OT. While there are numerous passages where God is the subject of the verb, most of these occurrences are used to describe God's sovereignty over death and life, as in Deut. 32:39: "There is no god beside me. I put to death (*'āmît*) and I bring to life." There are few passages that directly describe God killing an individual (using the hiphil of *mwt*; different

Hebrew terms are used to describe this, as with Uzzah in 2 Sam. 6:7). In Exod. 4:24 *mwt* (hiphil) is used in the perplexing example of Yahweh seeking to kill Moses (*wayĕbaqqēš hămîtô*). The closest parallel to the use of *mwt* in Gen. 38:7 is 1 Chron. 10:14. The Chronicler looked back on King Saul's rejection and death due to his unfaithfulness to Yahweh: "So the Lord put him to death (*wayĕmîthû*; *mwt*, hiphil) and turned the kingdom over to David." Although Saul may have fallen on his sword (1 Sam. 31:4) the Chronicler sees his demise as Yahweh's divine judgment. [*mwt*]

38:21 The shrine prostitute (*qĕdēšâ*)—In v. 15 Judah saw his disguised daughter-in-law and assumed she was just a common prostitute (Heb. *zōnâ* or *zônâ*). Later in v. 21, he described her as a "shrine prostitute," using the term *qĕdēšâ*. This term is the feminine form of the masculine noun *qādēš* meaning a "cult prostitute" (*HALOT*, 2:1074). Both terms are derived from the verb *qdš* meaning "to set apart, to be holy, to dedicate, to consecrate." In Babylonia and Assyria, the cognate term *qadištum* was used for a female cult official (*CAD*, Q:147). In the Canaanite religion, these women (Ug. *qdšm*) were "consecrated" (*qdš*), that is, "set apart," for cultic service. Most scholars believe this included religious prostitution. In the OT, the term *qĕdēšâ* occurs only in two other passages. In Deut. 23:18 Moses commanded that there were to be no male or female cult prostitutes among the Israelites. Hosea condemns the men of Israel (Hosea 4:14) for consorting with prostitutes and sacrificing with cult prostitutes (*haqqĕdēšôt*). [*qĕdēšâ*]

38:26 She is more righteous (*sādĕqâ*)— The verb *sdq* and its related terms (*sedeq*, *sĕdāqâ*, *saddîq*) have been the subject of extensive critical study, not only because of the importance of these terms in the OT, but also because of the distinctive Pauline emphasis on forensic righteousness in the NT. While there is significant difference of opinion among scholars, many suggest the basic idea of the *sdq* word group to be that which is in accord or harmony with accepted or expected norms and standards. This is illustrated by non-theological usage of the terms, such as "just weights" (Deut. 25:15), and by the extensive use of these terms in the Wisdom literature, particularly the book of Proverbs. Here, for example, the term *saddîq* ("the just, upright") occurs more often than in any other OT book (66x; K. Koch, *TLOT*, 2:1048-1049). These non-theological uses have brought extensive comparison with the Egyptian concept of Ma'at, the world order in which there were proper norms for correct behavior and living (K. Koch, *TLOT*, 2:1048). The OT usage of the term in the context of personal relationships suggests acting in conformity to the accepted expectations of faithfulness and loyalty engendered by that relationship. Koch reflects his emphasis on the importance of this relational loyalty by his primary definition of *sdq* as, "to be communally faithful" (*TLOT*, 2:1046). The meaning of the phrase, "she is more righteous than I" (*sādĕqâ mimmenî*) in this passage (Gen. 38:26) is debated. Generally, this is understood in a relative sense, with Tamar being less guilty and thus more righteous than Judah. However, two of the primary grammars (GKC, IBHS) understand this as a "comparison of exclusion" (*IBHS*, 14.4e) in which only the subject (Tamar) is in the right. In other words, Tamar is the one who has acted within the expected norms of family relationship. Judah, on the other hand, failed to provide Tamar with the husband who would protect and provide for her (cf. D. J. Reimer, *NIDOTTE*, 3:744-69). [*ṣdq*]

39:2 The Lord was <u>with</u> Joseph (*'et*)—The preposition *'ēt* is not a particularly significant term theologically. However, its usage in this context is important, both contextually and theologically. This preposition (not to be confused with the more common particle *'et* which is used to mark the direct object) occurred widely among the Semitic languages (e.g. Akk. *itti* "with"). The term can mean simply "with," but it often bears the connotation of "with the help of" (*HALOT*, 1:101). When used in reference to God it speaks of God's presence and provision. This expression of the Lord "with" someone also occurs frequently using the synonymous preposition *'im* (Gen. 26:3, 28; 48:21). In this context (Gen. 39:2) the phrase "the Lord was with Joseph," is particularly significant since the circumstances in his life would certainly have called into question God's saving presence. Two more times in this chapter (39:21, 23), the phrase is repeated, even though Joseph's situation goes from bad to worse. His faithfulness to God and to Potiphar leads not to reward but to prison. Yet in the confines of prison a sovereign God was accomplishing his purposes for his people (Gen. 50:20; Rom. 8:28). [*'ēt*]

Gave him <u>success</u> (*maṣlîaḥ*)—The Lord was with Joseph; thus he found success while still in prison. The term translated "success" in this passage is the Hebrew verb *ṣlḥ* (hiphil participle). There is some variation in the lexicons regarding this verb. *BDB* lists two distinct verbs: I *ṣlḥ*, "to rush, advance," and II *ṣlḥ*, "to succeed" (*BDB*, 852). On the other hand,

HALOT lists only a single verb, yet admits that it may be necessary to recognize a separate Hebrew verb for the group of passages that speak of the Spirit (*rûaḥ*) "rushing" upon someone (Judg. 14:6, 19; 15:14) as *BDB* does with I *l* (*HALOT*, 2:1026). In the qal (25x in OT), the primary meaning is "to be successful, to be prosperous." In the hiphil (40x), the causative stem, it means "make successful." Success is defined not by modern notions of success, but as fulfilling a purpose (A. Luc, *NIDOTTE*, 3:804-5). The verb can be used in reference to a weapon that "succeeds" (Isa. 54:17), a tree that thrives (Ps. 1:3), or a journey completed (Gen. 24:6). God's Word "succeeds" (Isa. 55:11) and does not return to him empty (*rêkām*). In Gen. 39:2, the verb appears as a hiphil participle following the term "man" (*'îš*), an adjectival clause where the second term (*ṣlḥ*) modifies or describes the character or nature of the person (*IBHS*, 9.5.3). Because God was indeed with him, Joseph was a "successful man" (*'îš maṣlêaḥ*). [*ṣlḥ*]

39:5 The Lord <u>blessed</u> (*wayĕbārek*)—One of the key themes in the book of Genesis is God's blessing of the patriarchs as part of his gracious covenant with them (Gen. 12:2-3; 14:19-20; 17:16; 22:17-18; 24:1; 25:11). However, in this passage (Gen. 39:5), it is not a patriarch or member of his family who gets blessed but a foreigner (Potiphar). Yet the text makes it clear why Potiphar's house was blessed. It was blessed on account of (*biglal*) Joseph, who bore the blessing. Older lexicons such as *BDB* listed all occurrences of *brk* under the same root, meaning both "to kneel" and "to bless." Here it was assumed there was a connection between kneeling and the bestowal of a blessing. Modern lexicons list two separate roots: I *brk* "to kneel down" and II *brk* "to bless" (*HALOT*,

1:159). The verb *brk* is found in the NW Semitic languages (Ugaritic, Phoenician-Punic, Aramaic). Joseph Scharbert (*TDOT*, 2:283) points out that in these texts the most common subject is deity. When man is the subject of *brk*, the term commonly means, "to wish or desire that the deity would bless someone." Less frequently *brk* is used just as a greeting formula. In Hebrew, *brk* appears most commonly in the Piel (235x), as it does here in Gen. 39:5. *HALOT* defines *brk* in the Piel as "to bless: to endue someone with special power" (1:160). This "special power" is not magic, but is God's power at work to bring good to those who are recipients of his favor. Here in Genesis the good that Yahweh brings is evidenced by "giving vitality, prosperity, abundance, or fertility" (J. Scharbert, *TDOT*, 1:294). Here in Gen. 39:5, the text describes the extent of this blessing given to Potiphar by stating that the blessing (*birkat*) of Yahweh was both within his home and in his fields. Joseph may have been far from the land promised to his fathers but his fathers' God continued to bestow his blessing upon him. (M. L. Brown, *NIDOTTE*, 1:757-67) [*brk*]

39:14 This Hebrew (*'ibrî*)—The term "Hebrew" (*'ibrî*), so well known today, occurs only 34x in the OT, where it designates a people and not their language. There has been intense and heated debate regarding the etymology of this term (for bibliography, see D. N. Freedman/B. E. Willoughby, *TDOT*, 10:430-32; for major theories, *HALOT*, 1:783). The languages of the peoples surrounding Israel mention a group or social unit called the *habiru* (or *hapiru*). The term has been found in Akkadian texts from Sumer, Alalakh, Nuzi, and El Amarna. The Ugaritic texts likewise mention a group named *'pr(m)*. Egyptian texts tell of *'pr(w)* of Palestinian origin, who are regarded as plunderers and bandits (*TDOT*, 10:436). Numerous scholars have linked the *'ibrîm* (Hebrews) with the *habiru*, a connection not without difficulties. These difficulties include both phonological problems (b/p shift and an a/i shift), as well as the fact that the *hapiru* are not regarded as an ethnic or geographical unit. Their setting appeared to have been more urban, very different from the pastoral, agrarian lifestyle of the patriarchs. It is probably best to not link the term *'ibrî* (Hebrew) with the *hapiru*, unless further evidence should warrant such a connection (*TDOT*, 10:444). More likely, the term is related to the personal name Eber (*'ēber*), the great-grandson of Shem (Gen. 10:24-25). Probably *'ibrî* is also related to the noun *'ēber* (identical in spelling to the proper name Eber) meaning, "beyond," especially used to designate the land beyond the river (Euphrates) from where the patriarchs originated (Josh. 24:2, 15). In the OT, the term Hebrew (*'ibrî*) is the name often used by foreigners in referring to the Israelites (or "Proto-Israelites"; Freedman, *TDOT*, 10:431), as well as the way the Israelites distinguished themselves from other ethnic groups (Exod. 3:18). It appears that during the course of Israelite history the name Hebrew was supplanted by the term "sons of Israel" or just "Israel," although in Jonah 1:9, the wayward prophet tells his shipmates, "I am a Hebrew." [*'ibrî*]

To make sport of us (*lĕṣaḥeq*)—The Hebrew verb *ṣḥq*, "to laugh," occurs 13x in the OT (6x qal, 7x Piel). Only two of these 13 occurrences are found outside of the book of Genesis (Exod. 32:6, Judg. 16:25). Within the book of Genesis this verb (ṣḥq) has been used at key points in the narrative. It described the laughing unbelief of Abraham and Sarah (Gen. 17:17; 18:12, 13, 15, 15), and thus the naming of their son Isaac (yiṣḥāq). Hagar's son (Ishmael) was laughing at/mocking (meṣāḥēq) Isaac (Gen. 21:9). Abimelek, the Philistine king, realized that Rebecca was probably not Isaac's sister when he saw Isaac caressing (meṣāḥēq) her (Gen. 26:8). Here in chapter 39, the last two occurrences of the verb in Genesis (vv. 14, 17) are used by Potiphar's wife in her accusation against Joseph. The nuance of the term (lĕṣaḥeq, Piel) here is probably closest to Ishmael's mocking (Gen. 21:9), which neither the archaic translation "make sport of" (NIV, NASB) or "insult" (NRSV, TEV, NLT [v. 14]) seems to capture. The NLT translation in v. 17 tries to reflect the laughing/mocking nuance of the verb with the phrase "to make a fool of me." [ṣḥq]

40:1 Offended their master (ḥāṭĕʾû)— Even though Joseph was falsely accused and sent to prison, nevertheless "God was with Joseph" (Gen. 39:23). God providentially placed in the same prison two men close to the throne of Pharaoh: the royal cupbearer and baker (Gen. 40:1). They were imprisoned because they "offended" (ḥṭʾ) their master. This verb (ḥṭʾ) is one of the three key terms in the OT for "sin" (along with pšʾ "to rebel" and ʿāwōn "guilt/iniquity"). Most often, the offence is directed against God (designated with the particle lĕ 52x). However, the verb is employed to describe offences against people as well (with lĕ 14x; K. Koch, TDOT, 4:311). Some lexicographers point to a basic meaning of the verb as "to miss the mark," based upon a few passages such as Judg. 20:16 where soldiers are described as able to

"sling a stone . . . and not miss (yaḥăṭiʾ)" (cf. K. Koch, TDOT, 4:311). In Gen. 40, the cupbearer and baker have "missed the mark" in maintaining the norms of expected behavior in regard to the king and thus, providentially, end up in prison with Joseph. [ḥṭʾ]

40:14 Remember me (zĕkartānî)—God enabled Joseph to interpret the cupbearer's dream and assured him that he would be restored to his position of serving Pharaoh. Then he implored him to "remember me" (zĕkartānî) and show me kindness." The Hebrew verb zkr "to remember" is a crucial theological term in the OT. Consequently, it has received substantial scholarly attention and study (bibliography: W. Schottroff, TDOT, 4:64). Earlier in the book of Genesis, this verb was used significantly with God as the subject: God remembered Noah (Gen. 8:1), he promised to remember his covenant (Gen. 9:15-16), God remembered Abraham when his judgment came upon Sodom and he rescued Lot (Gen. 19:29), and he remembered Rachel in her barrenness and gave her a son (Gen. 30:22). Here in Gen. 40:14, it is not God, but man, who is called to remember. The verb zkr occurs 222x in the OT, primarily in the qal (TLOT, 1:382). It is often paired with its antonym škḥ, "to forget" (Deut. 9:7; 1 Sam. 1:11; Isa. 7:10, 54:4). The term zkr usually suggests more than just casual remembrance. W. Schottroff writes, "zkr connotes an active relationship to the object of its memory that exceeds a simple thought process" (TLOT, 1:383). Memory is to be purposeful and focused. God provided "reminders" to his people to help them maintain a focused and active memory of his past mercy. These include tassels (Num. 15:39), unleavened bread (Deut. 16:1-3), Passover (using the cognate noun *zikkārôn*, Exod. 12:14, 13:19), and a pile of stones in the Jordan (Josh. 4:6-7). Memory is particularly to be retained when one has been the recipient of acts of kindness and help. In Judg. 8, it is reported after the death of Gideon that the people turned away from God. They "forgot" the Lord who had delivered them and they did not "show kindness" ("do *hesed*") to Gideon's family (Judg. 8:34-35). They were indebted to the Lord and to Gideon but they failed to actively "remember" with their deeds. In Gen. 40:14, the cupbearer should not only purposely remember Joseph, but should "show kindness" to him as well. (*HALOT*, 1:269-71; Leslie C. Allen, *NIDOTTE*, 1:1100-06) [*zkr*]

Show me kindness (*hāsed*)—Few words in the Hebrew Bible have received as much focus and attention as the term *hesed*. It is a key term used to describe God's kindness and mercy to mankind, as well as what is desired and expected in human relationships. Although it is most often used in reference to God's *hesed*, it is the person-to-person use of *hesed* that has garnered the most attention. In particular, the focus has been upon defining the nature of the relationship between those who show *hesed* to another, especially in terms of the expected obligations within the context of their relationship. The term (*hesed*) is used 246x in the OT. God is the one showing *hesed* three times as often as people show *hesed*. When God is the subject of the term (*hesed*) it points to God's "faithfulness, goodness, and graciousness" (*HALOT*, 1:337). When used in human relationships it often reflects the "joint obligation" (*HALOT*, 1:337) that one has to another within a relationship. It is used to describe the loyal faithfulness expected within families (Gen. 20:13), within friendships (1 Sam. 20:8), and between a king

and his subjects (2 Sam. 3:8). This connotation of loyal behavior to one another is strengthened by the common joining of *hesed* with the term *'emet* ("faithfulness, truth"). Moreover, the word *hesed* is often used in the idiomatic phrase "to do *hesed*" (Gen. 19:19; 20:13; 21:23; 40:14; 47:29), an act of loyalty and kindness based upon the expected obligations within the relationship. This idea of mutuality and obligation is not as clearly seen in Gen. 40:14. H. J. Stoebe writes, "no duty exists in Gen. 40:14 for the cupbearer to mention Joseph, for Joseph did him no actual service by interpreting his dream" (*TLOT*, 2:455). However, this conclusion is contradicted by the cupbearer's own words. He stated, "I remember my faults today" (Gen. 41:9; NRSV), with the word "fault" (*hēṭ'ě*) the most common Hebrew term for sin, or error. Joseph had "done *hesed*" to the cupbearer and asked him to remember him. It would be two years and another dream before the cupbearer finally remembered Joseph. [*hesed*]

41:8 Magicians (*harṭumê*)—Pharaoh's dream left him troubled and he sent for his professional "magicians" (*harṭumê*; *HALOT*, 1:353, "soothsayer-priests") to explain this unusual dream. The title "magician" (*harṭom*) is not a Semitic word, but is a loan word from Egyptian (*hr[y]-tp*; *HALOT*, 1:353), which was brought into Hebrew, biblical Aramaic (*harṭom*), and Akkadian (Neo-Assyrian; *harṭibi*; *CDA*, 109, "Egyptian diviner"). In the OT, the term is clustered in three passages, all of which are dealing with foreign kings: Pharaoh and Joseph (Gen. 41:8, 24), Moses and the Egyptian magicians (Exod. 7:11-22; 8:3-14; 9:11), and Daniel and the Babylonian magicians (Dan. 1:20; 2:2). In all three cases there is a strong polemical and theological emphasis. In spite of their powers, which were significant at least initially with the magicians Moses dealt with (Ex.7:11-12; 7:22; 8:7), ultimately they were powerless before Yahweh the true Sovereign of the world. [ḥarṭōm]

41:25 God has <u>revealed</u> (*higgîd*)—This common verb (*ngd*), occurring over 330x in the OT, is most often used in common-place communication meaning "to tell, declare, inform" (*BDB*, 616-7). The verb is not used in the qal, appearing most often in the hiphil, and as well as the hophal, its passive counterpart. When God is the subject of the verb, the term often has a more significant, theological connotation, "indicating some form of divine revela-tion to humans of something previously unknown" (R. O'Connell, *NIDOTTE*, 3:17). In the book of Isaiah this nuance is common (Isa. 41:23-26; 42:9), as Yahweh declares himself the only true God who can predict that which is to occur. Within the Joseph narrative there are 14 occur-rences of this term, often with this sense of "revelation" as Joseph deals with reve-latory dreams of the cupbearer, baker, and Pharaoh. Several translations, including NIV and NRSV, translate this usage of *ngd* as "to reveal." [*ngd*]

41:32 <u>Firmly decided</u> (*nākôn*)—When Joseph finished interpreting Pharaoh's dream, he explained the reason why there were not one, but two similar dreams: because this matter (*haddābār*) "had been firmly decided (*nākôn*) by God" (NIV). The form *nākôn* is a Niphal participle (m.s.) from the verb *kwn*. This term is attested broadly among the Semitic lan-guages (Akk. *knu*; Ug. *kn*, *knn*; *HALOT*, 1:464). In the MT the verb has an active sense using the hiphil ("to equip, care for, prepare"; 110x) and the polal ("to estab-lish, found"; 29x) and a stative usage with

the Niphal ("to be firm, true, certain"; 66x) (E. Gerstenberger, *TLOT*, 2:603). The Niphal participle *nākôn* is used to describe that which is certain or firm, such as the pillars of the temple (Judg. 16:29). It can refer to the certainty of God's interven-tion, using the simile "as surely as the sun rises (*kĕšaḥar nākôn*)" in Hos. 6:3. In Deut. 13:15[14] *nākôn* also is used with the term *haddābār* ("word, thing, matter" (cf. Gen. 41:32). In this context the issue involves Israelites who have been accused of turn-ing to other gods. The charge was to be thoroughly investigated and the guilty killed "if it is true, the fact is established" (*'emet nākônhaddābār*). In Gen. 41:32, the nuance of the use of *nākôn* in regard to the dream is that God has established, made firm, or made certain the fulfillment of the dream. (E. Gerstenberger, *TLOT*, 2:602-6; E. Martens, *NIDOTTE*, 2:615-17) [*kwn*]

41:33 A discerning (*nābôn*) and wise (*ḥākām*) man—In light of the coming "feast and famine," Joseph recommended the appointment of a "discerning and wise man." The two terms Joseph used to describe this person, *nābôn* (Niphal par-ticiple, of *byn* "to be wise," used adjecti-vally) and *ḥākām* (adj., "skillful, clever, wise") appear to be broadly synonymous. They appear together repeatedly as a word pair (Gen. 41:33, 39; Deut. 4:6; 1 Kings 3:12). By itself, the term *ḥākām* has a narrower meaning. It can mean "skillful" and is used in reference to those skilled in woodwork (Isa. 40:20), in sailing (Ezek. 27:9), or mourning (Jer. 9:17). When it occurs together with *nābôn*, the connota-tion is "the more mental/intellectual trait of wisdom" (G. H. Wilson, NIDOTTE, 2:133). In Gen. 41, Pharaoh did not have to look far to a find a discerning and wise man. (*HALOT*, 1:122; 1:314). [*byn*, *ḥākām*]

41:38 The spirit of God (*rûaḥ*)—Pharaoh was amazed by Joseph's ability to interpret his dream and impressed by his sage advice. There was but one logical conclusion: this was a man enabled and empowered by the spirit (*rûaḥ*) of God. Here in this verse (41:38) it is Pharaoh speaking of the spirit of God, and it is interesting to think of what this statement would have meant to him in the context of Egyptian religion. The Hebrew word for "God" in this verse is Elohim, which would allow a translation of "a spirit of a god/gods" (NEB; "a spirit of a god"). Whatever it meant to Pharaoh, it is clear that the Israelite author understood this *rûaḥ* as the same spirit/Spirit of God active in Creation (Gen. 1:2), who equiped Bezalel to build the tabernacle (Exod. 31:3; 35:31), and the *rûaḥ 'elôhîm* who inspired a pagan seer named Balaam (Num. 24:2), as well as an Israelite king (1 Sam. 10:10; 11:6). The phrase "spirit of God" (*rûaḥ 'elôhîm*) occurs 16x in the OT (contra *NIDOTTE*, 11x in OT; 3:1075). The phrase "spirit of the Lord [YHWH]" (27x) is generally synonymous with the "spirit of God," except that "Spirit of the Lord" seems to be the preferred idiom to describe divine empowerment for service. Seven times in the book of Judges it is the *rûaḥ YHWH* who designates and calls a man to lead the nation (Judg. 3:10; 6:34; 11:29; 13:25; 14:6, 19; 15;14). In Gen. 41:38, the ability of Joseph to do what the trained dream interpreters could not do, and to offer a plan of action, gave Pharaoh sufficient evidence that the power of God was indeed present in Joseph's life. [*rûaḥ*]

41:51 His firstborn (*habbĕkôr*)—The story of Esau selling his birthright to Jacob earlier in the book of Genesis (Gen. 25:29-35) highlighted the significance of the firstborn (*bĕkôr*). The firstborn son had a place of special honor and received a double portion of the family inheritance (Deut. 21:15-17). For the parents, the birth of the firstborn was a time of great joy. For the father it was an evidence of his procreative ability, as in Gen. 49:3, where Jacob describes Reuben, his firstborn, as "the first-fruits of my vigor" (NRSV, JPS) (*rē'šît 'ônî*). Here in Gen. 41:51, the birth of Joseph's firstborn is another sign of the reversal of fortunes he is experiencing, another evidence of God's blessing upon his life. [*bĕkôr*]

Manasseh (*mĕnaššeh*)—The name of Joseph's firstborn is based on the rare verb *nšh*, "to forget," a poetic synonym of the verb *škḥ*. The frequency of its occurrence is not clear because of its similarity to *nšh* || *nš'* ("to lend") and *nś'* ("to lift up"). The verb is unquestionably used with the meaning "to forget" in Isa. 44:21, Lam. 3:17 and Job 39:17. In Gen. 41:51, the name Manasseh is derived from the Piel participle of *nšh* with the nuance of "causing me to forget." Joseph saw the gift of a son as God's means of helping him forget his past suffering. [*mĕnaššeh*]

41:52 Ephraim (*'eprāyim*)—Again a son is born to Joseph, and once again his name is significant. Joseph named him *'eprāyim* (Ephraim), a name derived from the verb *prh*, "to be fruitful." This is used in an effective wordplay, as the text reads, "the name of the second he called *'eprāyim* because *hipranî* (hiphil perfect; "he made me fruitful"). The use of the verb *prh*, "be fruitful," draws the reader back to the promises Yahweh made to the patriarchs, that he would indeed make them fruitful (Gen. 17:6, 20; 28:3; 35:11). It may be that the name looks forward as well, as the name serves as a wish/blessing for the fecundity of the tribe that would bear the name Ephraim. [*'eprayim*]

My suffering (*'onyî*)—Joseph rejoiced in God's blessing received in the land he aptly called "the land of my suffering (*'onyî*)." The noun *'ŏnî* is derived from the Hebrew verb *'nh*, "to be wretched, afflicted" (*HALOT*, II *'nh*; 1:853-4; *BDB*, III *'nh*, 776). The term has been used 3x previously in Genesis. In Gen. 16:11, the Angel of the Lord assured Hagar that God had "heard of your misery (*'onyēk*)." Likewise, Leah believed God had seen "her misery," in this case her lack of love from her husband (Gen. 29:32). Jacob told his father-in-law of the "hardship (*'onî*)" he had experienced (Gen. 31:42). Gen. 41:51 mentions Joseph's "troubles" using the generally synonymous term *'āmāl*, a word, however, with a broader semantic field ("trouble, acquisition, care, anxiety, need, harm," *HALOT*, 1:845). Both terms (*'nî*, *'ml*) are used in parallel in Deut. 26:7 and in Ps. 25:18 ("See my affliction [*'onyî*] and my distress [*wa'ămālî*]"). [*'ŏnî*]

42:5 The sons of Israel (*benê yiśrā'ēl*)—Previously, Jacob's sons had been referred to as the *běnê ya'ăqōb*, "sons of Jacob" (Gen. 34:7, 13, 25; 35:22). Now for the first time as they enter Egypt they come as the "sons of Israel" (*běnê yiśrā'ēl*) [The phrase itself occurs as well in Gen. 32:32 and 36:31, referring to the later national/ethnic entity and not to the literal sons of Israel]. The phrase becomes the standard means of designating the brothers (Gen. 45:21; 46:5, 8; 50:25). The appearance of this phrase (*běnê yiśrā'ēl*) in this verse may suggest that they are now regarded not just as a collection of brothers but as a nation, one of many nations coming to buy food. It may also be used to suggest to the reader that this is the people going into Egypt whom God would later take out from Egypt (Exod. 1:7; 3:10; 6:6) (N. Sarna, *Genesis*, 292; G. Wenham, *Genesis 16–50*, 406) [*běnê yiśrā'ēl*]

42:7 He <u>recognized</u> them, but he <u>pretended</u> to be a stranger (*wayyakkirēm wayyitnakkēr*)—Joseph found himself in a unique position when his brothers appeared before him. The revelatory dreams of his youth were coming to pass before his eyes: now he had power over his brothers. Joseph recognized them, yet they had no idea they stood before the brother they had sold into slavery. In the Hebrew text this is skillfully presented by the repetition of the verb *nkr* 4x within two verses, twice in v. 7 and twice in v. 8 (*wayyakkēr . . . lō' hikkiruhû*). Here in v. 7, the two verbs translated "recognized" and "pretended" are from the same Hebrew verb, the verb *nkr*. The meaning and etymology of *nkr* is debated. *HALOT* lists a single bipolar root (*nkr*) which includes antithetical meanings even within the same root, as for example in the hithpael, "to make oneself known" (Prov. 20:11) and, "to make oneself unrecognizable" (1 Kings 14:5) (*HALOT*, 1:699-700). This is explained in reference to a phenomenon in Arabic grammar where a verbal root can have both its normal meaning and its opposite (B. Lang, *TDOT*, 9:424) Other grammarians and lexicons distinguish two different roots: one root with the basic idea of "to recognize" and a second root, possibly derived from the term *nokrî* ("foreigner"), which yields the meaning of "to disguise, to act as a stranger" (*TDOT*, 9:424-25; *BDB*, 647-48). Here in Gen. 42:7-8, the repetition of the verb subtly reinforces the "reversal of fortune" motif common in the Joseph narrative as well as reminding the reader that God was indeed "with" Joseph. [*nkr*]

42:15 You will be <u>tested</u> (*tibbāḥēnû*)—Joseph's brothers are told they will be tested to prove their contention that they are indeed *kēnîm* ("honest men") and not spies. The verb in question (*bḥn*, "to test, to put to the test") occurs about 28x in the OT, usually in the qal and 3x in the Niphal (Gen. 42:15, 16; Job 34:36) (E. Jenni, *TLOT*, 1:207). It occurs most often in poetic texts, in contrast to its close synonym *nsh* that more commonly is found in prose. The term most often appears with God as the subject of the testing (M. Tsevat, *TDOT*, 2:70). In Gen. 42, Joseph is the one testing the veracity of the claims of his brothers, testing them even though he already knows they are telling the truth. M. Tsevat maintains that "*bḥn* almost always has a religious connotation in the OT" (*TDOT*, 2:71). In reality, the testing of the brothers is more than testing their claims. It is the testing of the character and faith of the brothers. Have the brothers who betrayed him changed? Are they walking with God as Joseph has been despite his struggles? [*bḥn*]

42:18 I <u>fear</u> God (*yārē'*)—After briefly imprisoning his brothers, Joseph makes a promise backed up by the phrase "as the Lord lives" and the assurance that he fears God (*yārē'*). The term *yārē'* is a verbal adjective from the common verb *yr'*, used 284x in the OT meaning, "to fear, to cause to fear" (H. P. Stähli, *TLOT*, 2:569-70). The term (*yārē'*) is used 45x in the OT, most often in reference to fearing God. The fear of the Lord is a major theme in the OT, a concept that includes awe, terror, respect, obedience, and worship (Deut. 10:12-13; discussion in *NIDOTTE*, 2:527-33). This concept is expressed in various ways. In Deuteronomy, the common expression uses the qal infinitive of the verb *yr'*, "to fear the Lord" (Deut. 4:10; 5:29; 6:24; 8:6;

10:10). The noun *yir'â* ("fear") is used 5x in the book of Isaiah to describe the fear of the Lord. The phrase *yir'â YHWH* most often occurs (14x) in the book of Proverbs, serving almost as the motto or main theme of the book (Prov. 1:7, 29; 2:5, 8:13; 9:10). The third major idiom for referring to the fear of the Lord is used here in Gen. 42:18, using the verbal adjective *yārē'*. The term was used earlier in Gen. 22:12, in the offering of Isaac. The angel of the Lord told Abraham, "Now I know that you fear (*yārē'*) God." This adjective also occurs 27x in the Psalms (using the plural construct [*yārē' YHWH*]), serving almost as a title for the righteous, the pious who are seeking to serve God (H.-P. Stähli, *TLOT*, 2:575-76). The specific nuance of the use of this verbal adjective in Gen. 42:18 is not certain. Some commentators suggest the usage of the term here as a more generalized statement of piety, reflecting "a certain international religious morality" (H. Gunkel, *Genesis*, 425). But the picture presented in Genesis does not suggest a weakening of the term at all; rather it presents a man of faith who truly did fear the Lord through worship, reverence, and obedience. [*yr'*]

42:21 Punished (*'ăšēmîm*)—Joseph's brothers recognized through their troubles that they were reaping the consequences of their sins, namely, that they were being "punished" (*'ăšēmîm*) for what they did to Joseph. This word (*'āšēm*) is a verbal adjective from the verb *'šm*, which means, "to be guilty, to pay for one's guilt" (*HALOT*, 1:94). The verb and its cognate terms occur 103x in the OT, with most of the occurrences, understandably, found in Leviticus and Numbers (R. Knierim, *TLOT*, 1:191). R. Knierim maintains that the basic meaning of the verb *'šm* and its cognates is the idea of "guilt-obligatedness," the liability that one incurs because of a sin or trespass (TLOT, 1:193). The verbal adjective ('āšēm; pl. 'ăšēmîm) used here in Gen. 42:21 occurs in two other passages. In 2 Sam. 14:13, it is used in reference to the guilt of David due to his political and familial failures. In Ezra 10:10, it refers to the guilt of the priests who had married foreign wives. But here in Gen. 42:21, most English translations render the term "punished" (NIV, NRSV, JPS). This is a possible interpretation since the verbal root contains both the idea of guilt as well as the punishment that is incurred because of the guilt. However, it may be better to render the term in reference to the guilt of the brothers, as for example, "truly we are guilty concerning our brother" (NASV, also KJV; E. Carpenter/M. Grisanti, NIDOTTE, 1:554). ['āšēm]

42:22 An accounting for his blood (nidrāš)—Joseph's brothers recognized their guilt in their treatment of Joseph. In this verse, Reuben reminded them of how he warned them not to sin ('al-teḥeṭ'û) against Joseph, but they refused to listen. Now they would give "an accounting for his blood" (dāmô hinnē nidrāš). The verb drš is used 165x in the OT with a range of meaning, including "to seek, to inquire, to care for, to investigate" (HALOT, 1:233). When the verb is used in legal contexts, it carries a specific connotation (D. Denninger, NIDOTTE, 1:995). When humans are the subject the meaning is "to investigate, to inquire," to determine the facts or the truth in a matter (Deut. 13:14; 17:4, 9; 19:18). When God is the subject of the verb, it means "to require," as in Ezek. 34:10, where God states his opposition against Israel's leaders ("shepherds"), and states that he will "require" (drš) his flock from them. In Mic. 6:8, God requires (drš) from his people that they will "act

justly, love mercy and walk humbly with your God." In Gen. 42:22, God requires someone's life for the life ("blood") that was taken. In Gen. 9:5, the verb is used 3x when God commanded Noah: "Surely I will require (drš) your lifeblood; from every beast I will require it. And from every man, from every man's brother I will require the life of man"(NASB). In Gen. 42:22, Reuben reminds his brothers of what is required for their deed, not realizing that they stand before the brother against whom they sinned. [drš]

For his blood (dāmô)—The word dām ("blood") is a common Semitic term, appearing in both East Semitic (Akk. dāmu) and West Semitic languages (Ug. dm). In the OT it occurs 360x and is the only Hebrew term for blood (G. Gerleman, TLOT, 1:337). It is not surprising that its most frequent occurrence is in Leviticus (88x). The term can be used for either animal or human blood. Lev. 17:11 states the significance of the blood: "For the life of a creature is in the blood (kî nepeš habāśār bĕdām)." Thus, blood must not be eaten (Lev. 3:17). It has special significance in finding atonement for sin. In Lev. 17:11, the verse continues: "I have given it to you ("blood") to make atonement for yourselves on the altar ('al-hammizbēaḥ lĕkappēr 'al-napšētêkem). Thus blood was not something one could be casual about. In Lev. 17, the opening verses prohibit the slaughter of animals, unless their blood is presented as an offering (Lev. 17:1-3). To fail to do so meant that "bloodguilt shall be imputed to that man"(dām yēḥāšēb; Tanakh). Thus the taking of life, especially human life (Gen. 9:5-6), was a serious affair. The taking of human life wantonly or violently made one even more culpable (Gen. 9:5). Here in Gen. 42:22, Reuben's words regarding God "requiring blood" points out the heinous nature of their sin and the sure retribution it would bring from God. [*dām*]

42:28 Their hearts sank . . . trembling (*wayyēṣē' libbām wayyeherdû*)—When Joseph's brothers encamped that evening on their trip home, they found to their dismay their money in the mouth of their bags. Their emotional response is described by two phrases, one unique, another common. "Their hearts sank" (*wayyēṣē ' libbām*) is literally "their hearts went out," using the common verb *yṣ'* "to go out." This particular idiom does not occur elsewhere in the OT, although similar phrases meaning to lose courage do occur: hearts "sink" (*npl* "fall"; 1 Sam. 17:32), hearts shake (*nw'* "shake, quiver"; Isa. 7:2), and hearts melt (*mss* "melt"; Josh. 2:11; 5:1; 7:5; Ezek. 21:12). The second descriptive term (*wayyeherdû*) uses the verb *hrd* "to tremble" (*HALOT*, 1:350-51). This verb occurs 39x in the OT (23x Qal, 16 Hiphil). Hebrew has a surprisingly large repertoire of words meaning "to shake, tremble, quiver," with NIDOTTE listing 22 verbs within this semantic field (M. van Pelt/W. C. Kaiser, *NIDOTTE*, 2:265). The verb *hrd* often appears in the context of theophany in order to describe the terror of being present before the numinous. For example, it is used when God appears on Mt. Sinai (Exod. 19:16, 18). In Gen. 42:28, the verb is used in the context of receiving bad news, just as it is used in 1 Kings 1:49 when Adonijah's guests hear that David had just made Solomon king and not Adonijah. In this verse (Gen. 42:28), the two phrases effectively convey the utter loss and despair of the brothers as they find their money returned, and ask, "What is this that God has done to us?" [*yṣ'*, *lēb*, *hrd*]

43:6 You have brought this trouble (*harē'ōtem*)—In Gen. 43:2, Jacob told his sons to return to Egypt to buy more grain. Judah reiterated the warning given by Joseph not to return without Benjamin. In his angry reply, Jacob (v. 6) accused his son of bringing "this trouble on me" (*harē'ōtem lî*). This verb (I *r''*, *BDB*, 949; *HALOT*, 2:1269-70) is possibly derived from the adjective *ra'* ("evil, bad") and noun *ra'* ("evil, harm"). It appears in the qal (25x) and the hiphil (68x; D. Baker, *NIDOTTE*, 3:1156). In the qal, it means "to be evil, displeasing," while in the hiphil it means "to do evil, treat badly" (*HALOT*, 2:1269-70). When the hiphil is used with the preposition *lî*, it has the connotation "to do something bad to someone" (*HALOT*, 2:1270), indicating an action or emotion from outside the subject (D. Baker, *NIDOTTE*, 3:1157). Jacob believed his sons had unnecessarily told Joseph about another brother and thus bitterly exclaimed, "Why did you treat me so badly . . . " (NRSV, NASB). [*r''*]

43:9 Will guarantee (*'ē'erbennû*)—The verb *'rb* (*HALOT* "I *'rb*," listing four other homonymous roots, 1:876-77), meaning, "to take on pledge, give on pledge" (*BDB*, 786), is most familiar in its usage in the book of Proverbs. Here the wisdom writers repeatedly warn of the danger of "putting up security" for others who may end up defaulting on their debt (Prov. 6:1; 11:15; 17:18; 22:26), and of instructions when taking something in pledge (Prov. 20:16 | | Prov. 27:13). This same verb (*'rb*) can be used in a broader sense of "coming to one's aid, showing care" (Isa. 38:14; Jer. 30:21; Ps. 199:22). But here in Gen. 43:9, as well as in Gen. 44:32, the verb is used in a specialized technical sense of "being responsible for someone" (*HALOT*, 1:876) with the connotation of guaranteeing a person's safety (R. Wakely, *NIDOTTE*, 3, 514-15). This technical usage may be comparable to a similar phrase in Akkadian, *ana qatāti erēbu*, "stand surety for" (*CDA*, 287), literally "enter into the hands"; also *ana qatāti leqû*, "to stand surety for" (*CDA*, 180). In Genesis, this usage of the term in this technical sense would suggest a remarkable transformation in Judah, whose actions (ch. 38) brought shame upon himself and his family. Now Judah offers to take the blame and to take Benjamin's place as a slave if he should fail to bring him back to Jacob (R. Wakely, *NIDOTTE*, 3:514-15). ['*rb*]

43:14 God Almighty (*'ēl šadday*)—This important (and debated) name of God appears several times in the patriarchal narratives (Gen. 17:1; 28:3; 35:11; 43:14; 48:3). Like the divine name YHWH, the term *šadday* has engendered a tremendous amount of scholarly attention (for suggested etymologies and evaluation, see M. Weippert, *TLOT*, 3:1306-09). Not only is the etymology of the name obscure, but so is its original meaning. M. Weippert writes, "As the varied and somewhat even capricious translation of *'ēl šadday* in the OT versions show, antiquity no longer understood the meaning of the name" (*TLOT*, 3:1305). The Septuagint used a variety of terms to translate the Hebrew word *šadday*, most often with the Greek word *pantokratōr* ("The Almighty"). Likewise, Jerome's Vulgate translation followed the lead of the LXX with its use of *omnipotens*. However, "The Three" (Aquila, Symmachus, and Theodotion) consistently rendered *'ēl šadday* with *hikanos*, "sufficient, the Sufficient One," reflecting an ancient Jewish exegetical tradition of dividing *šadday* into *še-* and *dēy* ("Who suffices") (*Genesis Rabbah* 5:8). While this etymology may not find mod-

ern support, it may be that the meaning of *'ēl šadday* as it is used in the patriarchal narratives does suggest the concepts of power, strength, or ability. While *'ēl šadday*, like the other compound 'El names (*'ēl 'ôlām*, *'ēl bēt'el*, *'ēl 'elyôn*) may reflect Israel's pre-Mosaic Canaanite heritage, it is important to remember that in the OT, these terms are always identified with Yahweh (cf. Exod. 6:2-3; also G. Wenham, "The Religion of the Patriarchs," in *Essays on the Patriarchal Narratives*, A. R. Millard and D. J. Wiseman). In Gen. 43:14, Jacob invokes *'ēl šadday's* blessing and protection upon his sons as they once again return to Egypt to buy grain. [*'ēl šadday*]

Grant you mercy (*raḥămîm*)—The plural noun *raḥămîm* is derived from the word *reḥem*. The verb *rḥm*, the adjective *raḥûm*, and the plural noun *raḥāmîm* are derived from *reḥem* and at their most basic meaning describe the love, the compassion, the pity that a mother has for the child she carried in her womb. The plural noun *raḥămîm* often is used in emotionally charged contexts, expressing deep emotions (1 Kings 3:26; Isa. 63:15; Jer. 16:5; M. Butterworth, *NIDOTTE*, 3:1094). God who himself is "compassionate (*raḥûm*) and gracious" (11x in OT), can give someone *raḥămîm* when he stands before another person. When Daniel was in Babylon and asked not to defile himself by eating the unclean foods, "God disposed the chief officer to be kind and compassionate (*raḥămîm*) toward Daniel" (Dan. 1:9, Tanakh). When Nehemiah decided to approach the king regarding the sad state of the city of Jerusalem, he prayed, "Give success to your servant today, and grant him mercy (*raḥămîm*) in the sight of this man!" (Neh. 1:11, NRSV). In Gen. 43:14, Jacob invokes *'ēl šadday's* blessing and protection of his sons as they return to Egypt and asks that he might give them *raḥămîm* "before the man," a request that he would indeed grant. [*raḥămîm*]

43:23 Your God, the God of your father (*'ĕlōhêkem wē'lōhê 'ăbîkem*)—The steward explained the phenomenon of the silver in their bags as the work of "your God, the God of your father" (*'ĕlōhêkem wē'lōhê 'ăbîkem*). The phrase, "God of my father/your father," has occurred repeatedly in the Jacob narrative, especially in Jacob's discussion with Laban in Gen. 31 (Gen. 31:5, 29, 42, 53; 32:9; 46:1). When God appeared to Jacob in his dream at Bethel, God identified himself as "I am the LORD, the God of your father Abraham and the God of Isaac." Twenty years later, in his heated argument with Laban, he told him how bad his situation would have been except that the "God of my father, the God of Abraham and the Fear of Isaac" had been with him (Gen. 31:42). This phrase "God of your/my father" points to the continuity of God's faithfulness to the patriarchs, even though they were often not faithful to Yahweh. Here in Gen. 43:1, the phrase reminds the brothers, and the reader, of God's faithfulness in spite of the faithlessness of Joseph's brothers. The NRSV translation of this phrase as "your God *and* the God of your father" seems to add an unnecessary ambiguity to the expression. The *waw* in the expression *'ĕlōhêkem wē'lōhê 'ăbîkem* must certainly be explicative in this context: "your God, that is, the God of your father." (*HALOT*, 1258; C. Westermann, *Genesis 37-50*, 124). [*'ĕlōhêkem wē'lōhê 'ăbîkem*]

43:29 God be gracious (*yoḥnĕkā*)—When Joseph saw his brother Benjamin, he responded "God be gracious (*'ĕlōhîm yoḥnĕkā*) to you, my son." The Hebrew verb *ḥnn* appears most commonly in the OT in the qal (57x) and usually (41x of 57x) with God as the subject (T. Fretheim, *NIDOTTE*, 2:203). Joseph's greeting to his beloved brother asks that God's favor would be upon his brother (cf. Num. 6:25). H. J. Stoebe (*TLOT*, 1:446) argues that in this passage the verb *ḥnn* is "diminished to a greeting corresponding to the English 'God be with you'." Yet this hardly seems to do justice to the term in its context. Verse 29 emphasizes Joseph's gaze upon his brother and the special significance this boy had to him personally ("he lifted up his eyes and saw his brother, the son of his mother . . ."). Moreover, only Benjamin receives this "greeting," not the other brothers. Claus Westermann observes, "This is not a common, formal greeting; it is a wish that has in mind God's personal attention" (C. Westermann, *Genesis 37–50*, 126. [*ḥnn*]

43:30 Deeply moved (*nikmĕrû*)—The Hebrew verb *kmr*, used here to describe the emotional state of Joseph as he meets Benjamin, occurs only 4x in the OT. Its usage in the cognate languages and in the OT suggests a basic meaning of "to be hot" (*HALOT*, 1:481). The verb is used in this concrete sense only in Lam. 5:10, where the people complain that their skin is "as hot as an oven." The other three uses of *kmr* have a metaphorical sense of being excited or agitated (Gen. 43:30; 1 Kings 3:26; Hos. 11:8). In all three passages, that which becomes "excited" is one's compassion (*raḥămîm*) for another (assuming in Hos. 11:8 the emendation of *niḥûmây* to *raḥămây*, as with *BHS*, *HALOT*, many commentators). The nuance of the Niphal in this passage (Gen. 43:40) may be that of an ingressive stative. IBHS defines this as "the subject coming to be in a particular state." They use this passage as an example of this type of Niphal and translate the phrase as "And his compassion grew hot . . ." (*IBHS*, 23.3.c.5, 386) (note G. Wenham, "his affection for his brother boiled up," *Genesis 16–50*, WBC, 414). Joseph was so overcome with emotion that he "sought (a place) to weep" (*wayĕbaqqēš libkôt*). [*kmr*]

44:4 Repaid good with evil (*šillamtem*)— When Joseph's brothers left Egypt with the grain they had purchased, they were unaware that Joseph had once again returned their money to them. But on this occasion, Joseph had his steward put his own personal silver cup in the sack of Benjamin. Here in v. 4 Joseph instructed his steward to catch up with the brothers and "discover" the stolen cup. Then the steward would rebuke them, by rhetorically asking, "Why have you repaid good with evil?" The verb translated "repaid" (*šillamtem*) is the Piel perfect of *šlm*. The cognate noun *šālôm*, related to this verb, is one of most well known words in Hebrew, often translated as "peace, wholeness." Yet the basic meaning of the verb is disputed. G. Gerleman, in his TLOT article on *šlm*, asserts that the primary meaning of the verb is "to have enough," and, in its most common usage (Piel, 89x), the meaning is "to pay, repay." He writes, "the concept of requital underlies all forms of the root *šlm*, and this semasiologically fertile term facilitated a great multitude of possible usages esp. for the much-utilized noun *šālôm*" (*TLOT*, 3:1340). HALOT notes Gerleman's thesis (*HALOT*, 2:1506-07) and rejects it, noting that the concept of sufficiency and repayment is semantically too far afield from the well-attested meaning of the term in Akkadian, where *šalāmu* means "to be healthy, intact" (*CDA*, 350). Moreover, the consistent translation of *šālôm* in the LXX with *eirēnē* ("peace") argues against Gerleman's position (*HALOT*, 2:1507). It

is better to maintain a basic meaning of the verb as "to be whole, healthy, complete." In the Piel, as used in Gen. 44:4, the meaning is that of making complete, namely, "restitution." This meaning of "repay" is not the core meanng of *šlm* (*contra* Gerleman), but an extension of the meaning, "to be whole, complete." Here in this verse, the steward asks the brothers if this is how they should repay, or recompense, Joseph's kindness to them. [*šlm*]

44:5 Uses for divination (*yĕnahēš*)—The steward chided the brothers for "stealing" the silver cup by informing them that, not only was this expensive cup Joseph's personal drinking cup, but that it served an important purpose for the practice of divination (*nahēš yĕnahēš*). The verb *nhš*, "to give omens, foretell" (*HALOT*, 1:690) occurs 11x in the OT, always in the Piel. Most of the other OT terms related to divination occur with *nhš* in 2 Chron. 33:6, where the sins of King Manasseh are listed. It tells how he not only passed his own son through the fire, but that he "practiced sorcery (*'nn*), divination (*nhš*) and witchcraft (*kšp*), and consulted mediums (*'ôb*) and spiritists (*yiddĕ'ōnî*)." The type of divination ("cup divination") used here in Gen. 44:5 (also 44:15) is known from ancient times. Divination was strictly forbidden according to OT law (Lev. 19:26; Deut. 18:10). Joseph's claim that his brothers should have known he would discover them through divination (v. 15) caused some consternation for ancient rabbis who viewed Joseph as a paragon of virtue and piety. Their conclusion was that Joseph only *claimed* to practice divination, and is never described as actually practicing it (N. Sarna, *Genesis*, 304). [*nhš*]

44:10 Free from blame (*nĕqiyyim*)—

Joseph's brothers vigorously denied the accusation of stealing Joseph's divining cup (vv. 7-8). In fact, they offered to have the guilty party executed, and the rest of them would then become slaves to Joseph (v. 9). The steward altered the punishment (v. 10) to impact only the guilty party: the thief would become a slave, the others would be "free from blame" (*nĕqiyyim*). This term is the plural form of the adjective *nāqî*, occurring 44x in the OT (G. Warmuth, *TDOT*, 9:554). The meaning of the adjective reflects the semantic range of its cognate verb *nqh*, "be unmarried (with the prep. *min*), to be without blame, to declare to be free from punisment" (*HALOT*, 1:720). When the adjective (*nāqî*) and the verb *nqh* are used in legal settings they are "technical terms of exoneration" (*TDOT*, 9:557). Here in Gen. 43:10, it means the guilt of the thief will not be upon the other brothers, but only upon the one who stole the cup. [*nāqî*]

44:16 Prove our innocence (*niṣṭaddāq*)—The verb *ṣdq* ("to be just, righteous," *BDB*, 842), an important theological term in the OT, is found only twice in the book of Genesis. Its first occurrence is in Gen. 38:26, in Judah's famous statement regarding Tamar: "She is more righteous (*ṣādĕqâ*) than I." Here in Gen. 44:16, the use of the verb is unusual on several counts. First, the form of the verb is unusual morphologically because of the peculiar charactertistics of the hithpael stem (*IBHS*, 26.1.1, 424). Second, it is the only occurrence of *ṣdq* in the hithpael in the OT. The meaning of the verb in hithpael would be "to prove oneself innocent" (*HALOT*, 2:1004), possibly with the nuance of the hithpael as a "benefactive reflexive, a reflective action 'done on one's own behalf'" (*IBHS*, 26.2.e, 430). Here in Gen. 44:16 the brothers ask rhetorically, with such overwhelming evidence how could they possibly prove themselves innocent? [*ṣdq*]

44:18 Do not be angry (*'al-yiḥar*)—As Judah began his impassioned speech before Joseph, he asked in good court style for permission to speak without angering him. The verb *ḥrh* occurs 93x in the OT and usually in the qal (82x). Its basic meaning is "to be/become hot" (*HALOT*, 1:351). However, as G. Sauer points out, the verb, as well as its substantives (*ḥārōn*, *ḥŏrî*), are used only figuratively in the OT to describe anger, whether human or divine (*TLOT*, 473). In the OT, two-thirds of the occurrences of *ḥrh* in the qal have "nose" (*'ap*) as its subject, just as Gen. 44:18 does here: "Do not let your nose be hot." The nose was seen to be reflective of the emotion, possibly because of the flaring of the nostrils when angry (J. Creach, *NIDOTTE*, 2:266). In HALOT this idiom (*ḥārāh 'appô*) is translated as "his wrath was kindled" (*HALOT*, 1:351). In his TLOT article, G. Sauer captures the nuance of the term with his translation of Gen. 44:18 as "Do not let your wrath become inflamed . . ." (*TLOT*, 2:473). [*ḥrh*]

44:33 In place of the boy (*taḥat hanna'ar*)—The preposition *taḥat* is not a major theological term, but it does have theological significance in the context of this passage. As Judah completes his soliloquy before Joseph his plea is heartfelt: "please let your servant remain here as my lord's slave in place (*taḥat*) of the boy." This preposition (*taḥat*) often means "below" (Gen. 1:7, 9), as well as "in place of." For example, this is illustrated in Gen. 4:25 when Eve told Adam that God had given her Seth in place of (*taḥat*) Abel. More significant is the usage in Gen.

22:13, where Abraham looked up and saw the ram caught in the thicket and sacrificed it "in place of (*taḥat*) his son." This concept of substitution is important in the context of the sacrificial system, with the role of the Levites (Num. 3:41-45), as well as with the Servant of the Lord (Isa. 53:11). Here in Gen. 44:33, the theme highlights the profound change that has occurred in Judah and the brothers, a change now evidenced by Judah's self-sacrificing love for his brother Benjamin. [*taḥat*]

45:1 Made himself known (*běhit-wadda'*)—The long awaited *dénouement* of the narrative finally occurs in this verse, as Joseph "made himself known" (*běhit-wadda'*) to his brothers. The verb used in this phrase, "made himself known," is *yd'* ("to know"), one of the most commonly attested verbs among the Semitic languages, as well as one of the most common verbs in the OT, used over 1000x in the Hebrew Bible (J. G. Botterweck, *TDOT*, 5:449). It appears most commonly in the qal (about 800x), in a broad range of nuances, including, "to know, to notice, to take care of, to understand, to copulate" (*HALOT*, 1:390-391). Here in Gen. 45:1, the form of *yd'* (*hitwadda'*) is unusual. It is one of only two occurrences of *yd'* in the hithpael in the Hebrew Bible (Num. 12:6), with the meaning "to make oneself known." Normally this meaning of self-revelation is expressed by the Niphal of *yd'* (Ezek. 20:5, 9: 35:11; 36:32; 38:23). In this passage (Gen. 45:1) Joseph "made himself known," bringing to his brothers the greatest surprise of their lives. [*yd'*]

45:3 They were terrified (*nibhălû*)—When Joseph broke the news to his brothers that he, who held their lives in his hands, was none other than the brother they nearly murdered and then sold into slavery, the response was predictable: they were terrified (*nibhălû*). How would Joseph get his revenge for their crimes? The term used here is the verb *bhl*, used 50x in the OT and most commonly in the Niphal (24x/50x), as in this verse. This verb is part of a rich depository of Hebrew terms that depict fear, terror, trembling, or shaking. Exod. 15, the Song of the Sea, provides a good example of the various terms that are generally parallel with the verb *bhl*. In Exod. 15:11, Yahweh is described as, "majestic in holiness, awesome (vb. *yr'*, "to fear") in praise." Verses 14-15 describe the impact that Yahweh will have on the other rulers of the nations who will oppose him, as Pharaoh had just done. The NIV translates as, "The nations will hear and tremble (*ḥîl*); anguish (*rā'ad*) will grip the people of Philistia. The chiefs of Edom will be terrified (vb. *bhl*), the leaders of Moab will be seized with trembling (vb. *rgz*), the people of Canaan will melt away (vb. *mwg*); terror (*'êmâ*) and dread (*paḥad*) will fall upon them." Often, as in Exod. 15, it is God and his judgments that brings terror upon people (Job 22:10; Isa. 13:8; Ezek. 26:18). Here in Gen. 45:3 it is not directly divine judgment that brings terror to them, but human judgment. It is unclear if people in Joseph's era would have made a clear distinction between divine and human judgment. HALOT captures the powerful emotional connotation of *bhl* in the Niphal with their suggested translation, "to be horrified, to be out of one's senses" (*HALOT*, 1:111) [*bhl*]

45:5 It was to save lives (*lěmiḥyâ*) God sent me—Joseph's response to his brothers' horror was not to deny their sin; he clearly told them that he was Joseph, "the one you sold into slavery (v. 4)." But, in spite of their sin, God was sovereignly at work, accomplishing his good purpose and keeping his covenant. That greater purpose was "to save lives" (*lĕmiḥyâ*; preposition *lĕ* denoting purpose and the noun *miḥyâ*). This noun, a verbal abstract from the verb *ḥyh* ("to live"), occurs only 8x in the OT. The meaning of this noun (*miḥyâ*) reflects the nuances of the verb from which it is derived (G. Gerleman, *TLOT*, 2:415). It can mean "becoming alive," as in the growth of new flesh (Lev. 13:10, 24). It can also refer to the recovery of life (Ezra 9:8), or of provisions themselves (Judg. 6:4; 17:10; Prov. 27:27; *HALOT*, 1:568). The verb *ḥyh* in the hiphil can mean "to keep alive" (*HALOT*, 1:309) and this is the nuance of *miḥyâ* here in Gen. 45:5. This concept of "keeping alive" is used in the Joseph narrative with the hiphil of *ḥyh* in the very next verse (v. 6), as well as in 47:25 and 50:20, all in reference to God's sovereign plan of sending (*šlḥ*) Joseph on ahead to Egypt to preserve the family. [*miḥyâ*]

45:7 To preserve a <u>remnant</u> (*šĕ'ērît*)—The word "remnant" (*šĕ'ērît*) is an important theological term and concept in the OT. Here in Gen. 45:7, *šĕ'ērît* appears for the first time in the OT and is not used again in the Pentateuch. This fact, along with the difficult syntax of the verse, has led some critical scholars to question the originality of the verse in its context (C. Westermann, *Genesis 37–50*, 143-44). *šĕ'ērît* is used 66x in the OT to describe that which remains (Isa. 44:17) or those that are left remaining. It can refer to those who survived the assaults of the Assyrians and Babylonians, as well as to those who returned from exile in Babylonia, especially in the books

of Haggai and Zechariah (Hag. 1:12, 14; 2:2; Zech. 8:6, 11, 12). The remnant theme is particularly prominent in the writing of the eighth-century prophets such as Amos, Micah, and Isaiah. The term appears in contexts of salvation (9:12), as well as overwhelming judgment (Isa. 10:19ff), or possibly both salvation and judgment (Isa. 7:3). In the midst of the Syro-Ephraimite conflict, Isaiah is commanded by God to name his son *šĕ'ērît yāšûb*, "a remnant will return." The first use of *šĕ'ērît*, here in Gen. 45:7, is highly significant in that it shows that even before "Israel was Israel," God was at work preserving his people. The prophet Amos possibly looked back upon this passage in Amos 5:15: "Hate evil, love good; maintain justice in the courts. Perhaps the Lord God Almighty (*YHWH 'ĕlōhê ṣĕbā'ôt*) will have mercy on the remnant of Joseph (*šĕ'ērît yôsēp*)." There in the turmoil and unbelief of the eighth century, there was hope that God, who had acted so decisively and sovereignly in the life of Israel and his children, would once again act on behalf of Israel's descendants, if he found true repentance in his people. (S. H. Park, *NIDOTTE*, 4:15). [*šĕ'ērît*]

By a great <u>deliverance</u> (*liplêṭâ*)—In this verse, Joseph explained to his brothers why God sent him ahead to Egypt. The Hebrew text uses the preposition *lĕ* to introduce two parallel purpose clauses: to "preserve a remnant" and to "save your lives (NIV)" (*lĕhayôt lākem*). The syntax of the final clause (*liplêṭâ gĕdōlâ*), also introduced by *lĕ*, is difficult and impacts the lexical nuance of the term *pĕlêṭâ*. This word (*pĕlêṭâ*), related to the verb *plṭ* ("to escape, to save"), occurs 20x in the OT. It can mean, "escapees, survivors" (Exod. 10:5; Joel 2:3) or the process of one's escaping, that is, "deliverance" (E. Ruprecht, *TLOT*, 2:989). Some translations, such as NIV and NASB, translate this second half of v. 7 as "to keep you alive by a great deliverance," understanding the final *lĕ* clause as expressing the agent or means of the saving of life. Other translations, such as NRSV and NEB, along with some commentators, regard the final *lĕ* clause as expressing the object of the verb (*WOC*, 11.2.10.g), yielding a translation of "to keep alive for you many survivors." Probably this translation is to be prefered, as it best fits the parallelism of the verse and reflects the LXX understanding of the passage. [*pĕlêṭâ*]

45:18 Eat the fat of the land (*'et-ḥēleb*)—The news that Joseph had been reunited with his brothers pleased Pharaoh and his promise was magnanimous: "I will give you the best (*ṭûb*) of the land of Egypt and you can enjoy the fat (*'et-ḥēleb*) of the land." Obviously the ancient idiom, "the fat of the land," communicated something different then than it would today. The term *ḥēleb* ("fat") occurs most often in Leviticus and Numbers (54x/90x), because of the importance of fat in the sacrificial system. The laws concerning what portions of the fat were to be offered to Yahweh and whether fat was available for human consumption are difficult and debated. G. Münderlein (*TDOT*, 4:391-97) argues for a diachronic development in the laws regarding fat. He suggests that early in Israel's history, fat was a delicacy that was eaten, but that only later in their history the law restricted their consumption, because of the belief that "All of the fat is the Lord's" (Lev. 3:16; for discussion and analysis: J. Milgrom, *Leviticus 1–16*, 203-05; R. Way, *NIDOTTE*, 2:137-40). In spite of the uncertainty, it is clear that in the OT the fat was Yahweh's portion and, as such, it had a special significance. Thus, because the fat was the Lord's, the

term *ḥēleb* could be used metaphorically to mean, "the best," as in Deut. 32:14, where Yahweh provided for his people not only rams and goats, but "fat- kidneys of wheat," that is, the "finest kernels of wheat (NIV)." Here in Gen. 45:18, Pharaoh offers Joseph's family the best Egypt had to offer. [*ḥēleb*]

45:26 Jacob was stunned (*wayyāpŏg libbô*)—The news that Joseph was alive had a powerful impact upon the elderly patriarch. The phrase "he was stunned"(*wayyāpŏg libbô*) uses the rare Hebrew verb *pwg*. This verb appears only three other times in the OT (Hab. 1:4; Pss. 38:9; 77:3). The verb does not appear in the earlier Semitic languages (Akkadian, Ugaritic, Amorite), but does appear in Jewish Aramaic ("grow weary, grow cold"), Syriac ("to grow cold"), and Arabic (*faja* "to go cold"; *HALOT*, 2:916). These meanings are reflected in the use of *pwg* in the OT. In the Psalms passages (38:9; 77:3), the meaning of growing weary or faint fits their context. In Hab. 1:4, the prophet laments that the violence and injustice endemic in the society has gone unchallenged and unpunished by God, with the result that, "Therefore, the law is paralyzed (*tāpûg tôrâ*)." Here in Gen. 45:26, the term is used in reference to Jacob's heart (*lēb*), that "his heart went cold." Many translations render the phrase as "he was stunned" (*NIV, NRSV, NASB, NLT, TEV*). The *Tanakh* (JPS) translation as "his heart went numb," may capture the nuance of the Hebrew text more accurately. [*pwg*]

45:27 Jacob's spirit revived (*wattĕḥi*)—After Jacob heard his sons' account of how they met Joseph and he saw the carts Joseph had sent, his spirit (*rûaḥ*) revived (*wattĕḥi*). This common verb (*ḥyh*) occurs often in Genesis (59x), usually with its common meaning in the qal of "to be alive, to stay alive" (*HALOT*, 1:309). However, the qal can also have the connotation of "to revive, recover." This can refer to actual resuscitation of the dead, as, for example, the corpse who was thrown into the grave of Elijah (2 Kings 13:21). It can also refer to the revival of life, as for example for Abimelech who unwittingly took Sarah into his harem (Gen. 20:7), or to the recovery of Hezekiah who had a fatal illness (Isa. 38:1, 6, 16, 21). Here it refers to Jacob's spirit being revived after it "went cold" when he heard the news about Joseph. (G. Gerleman, *TLOT*, 1:411-417) [*ḥyh*]

46:2 In <u>visions</u> (*běmar'ōt*)—At Beersheba God communicated his promise to Jacob "in visions (*běmar'ōt*)." The noun *mar'â* is derived from the common Hebrew verb *r'h*, "to see." While the verb occurs over 1,300x in the OT, this noun appears only 12x (D. Vetter, *TLOT*, 3:1177). In Exod. 38:8 the term refers to the bronze mirrors the women brought out of Egypt. In the 11 other occurrences of *mar'â*, it refers to visions through which God communicated to his people. Typically these visions came to prophets (Ezek. 1:1; 8:3; 40:20; Dan. 10:7, 8, 16). When Yahweh spoke to Moses and Aaron at the entrance of the tent of meeting in the wilderness (Num. 12:6), he told them: "When a prophet of the Lord is among you, I reveal myself to him in visions (*bamar'â*), I speak to him in dreams (*baḥălôm*)." Although these experiences are called visions, there are times when the experience does not appear to be visual, but only auditory, as when God called Samuel three times (1 Sam. 3:4, 6, 8). Yet this experience is described in v. 15 as a *mar'â*. Likewise, here in Gen. 46:2, there is no mention of

Jacob seeing anything. Rather, God only spoke to him, reiterating and reconfirming the promise of the patriarchs to Jacob, adding the promise that he would bring Jacob back, and that Joseph would "close his eyes" (Gen. 46:4). [*mar'â*]

46:3 I am God (*'ānōkî hā'ēl*)—When God appeared to Jacob in his night vision at Beersheba, he identified himself with the phrase, "I am God, the God of your father (*'ānōkî hā'ēl 'ĕlōhê 'ābîkā*)." The term *'ēl* is one of the most ancient and well attested words among the Semitic languages, occurring in all but Ethiopic. The etymology of the term is debated and unclear (W. H. Schmidt, *TLOT*, 1:101). The term in the Semitic languages (*'ēl*; Akk. *ilu*) can designate the noun "god" or the proper name 'El. This is particularly true in the Canaanite literature discovered at Ugarit. Here El (*'il*) served as the head of the pantheon, the father of the gods (*'ilm*). In the OT the term occurs 238x, appearing most often in the Psalms (77x), Job (55x) and Isaiah (39x). It is rarely found in the historical books of Samuel, Kings, or Chronicles. In Genesis it is found 18x, mostly in the patriarchal narratives. Often the term *'ēl* is found in compound names, as in Gen. 14 when Abraham met Melchizedek, who is identified as a priest of El-Elyon, to whom Abraham paid his tithe (Gen. 14:18-20). In Gen. 33:20 Jacob, after his successful meeting with Esau, moved to Shechem and built an altar, naming it El Elohe Israel (*'ēl 'ĕlōhê yiśrā'ēl*). In this important (and debated) phrase there seems to be the deliberate identification of Jacob's God with El, the god of the people of the land. Here in Gen. 46:3, this phrase, "I am God, the God of your father," reminds Jacob of God's relationship to his grandfather and his father. It also serves to remind him of the promises given to each of them, promises that are summarized again in this passage (vv. 3-4). (T. Fretheim, *NIDOTTE*, 1:400-01) [*'ēl*]

A great nation (*lĕgôy*)—At the heart of the promise to the patriarchs was the statement that their descendants would become a *gôy gādôl*, a "great nation" (Gen. 12:1; 17:20; 18:8: 21:18; 46:3). The term *gôy*, along with the related term *'am* ("people"), is used often in theologically important contexts and has been the subject of extensive investigation (bibliography: A. R. Hulst, *TLOT*, 2:899-900; R. H. O'Connell, *NIDOTTE*, 3:431-32). The semantic field of the two terms bears the general meaning of "people, peoples." The terms often appear together in parallel (Deut. 32:21; Josh. 3:14, 16; Jer. 6:2; 50:41). How the two terms differ has been variously described. It appears that *'am* (1,868x in OT) has a more relational aspect, suggesting a connectedness to the family, tribe, or clan. On the other hand, *gôy* (561x in OT), is a people not so much linked by familial or ethnic ties, but by territorial and political considerations (A. R. Hulst, *TLOT*, 896-98). Later in OT history, the term *gôy* took on more specialized meaning, referring to foreign, pagan nations (Lam. 1:3; 2:9; Ps. 44:3; Ezra 6:21). Clearly here in the promise to the patriarchs it is not used in this sense. It is an interesting and debated question concerning why these verses promise to make them a great *gôy* instead of a great *'am*, the term that would more significantly emphasize the familial link between the members. This is most likely explained by the fact that the promise to the patriarchs to become a great nation is so significantly tied to the promise of the land that territorial concerns impacted the choice of the term used to describe what the patriarch's descendants would one day become. [*gôy*]

47:4 We have come to live (*lāgûr*)—When Joseph introduced Pharaoh to five of his brothers (Gen. 47:1-2), Pharaoh asked them their occupation. The brothers replied that they were shepherds and that, "we have come to live here awhile (*lāgûr bā'āreṣ bā'nû*)" (v. 4). The verb *gwr* in this phrase is found only in the NW Semitic languages. In the OT it occurs about 80x, always in the qal, except for one possible occurrence of the hithpoel (Hos. 7:14) (*HALOT*, 1:184; *BDB*, 158). The verb means "to sojourn" or, in a weaker sense, "to dwell." At times it is difficult to be sure which nuance is most appropriate in a given context. For example, in Gen. 20:1, the NIV states that Abraham "stayed (Heb. *wayyāgār*) in Gerar." Both the NASB and JPS refer to his "sojourning" in Gerar, while NRSV uses the phrase "While residing in Gerar as an alien." In the patriarchal narratives the concept of sojourning, that is, living as a resident alien, is typically in view. Although the patriarchs had been promised the land they did not yet own it, a situation which was of critical importance for Abraham when he needed a burial plot for Sarah (Gen. 23). Here in Gen. 47:4, the nuance is clearly on their status as resident aliens (Note *HALOT*'s definition of *gwr* as "to dwell as an alien and dependent," 1:184). Jacob and his family were not Egyptians, they did not speak the language, and they owned no land. And they were shepherds, a detestable occupation in the eyes of the Egyptians (Gen. 46:44). Moreover, God had told Jacob in the vision at Beersheba that he would bring him back again to the land (Gen. 46:4). Thus, the nuance of "sojourn, live as a resident alien," fits well in this context of Gen. 47:4. [*gwr*]

47:27 They were fruitful (*wayyipĕrû*) **and increased greatly in number** (*wayyirĕbû*)

—God blessed Jacob and his family during their sojourn in Egypt. The descriptive phrase "they were fruitful and increased greatly" uses two Hebrew verbs often conjoined as a word pair. The verb *prh* (29x), "to bear fruit, be fruitful" (*BDB*, 826), together with the verb *rbh* (>200x) "to make numerous, to make great" (*HALOT*, 2:1177), appear together in theologically important contexts in the book of Genesis. In the Creation account, this word pair is used in the divine command to the fish and birds on day five: *pĕrû ûrbû* ("be fruitful and multiply"; Gen. 1:22, 28). After the Flood, the same command was repeated to Noah in Gen. 9:1, 7. The word pair is used again in Genesis, in the blessing upon Ishmael (Gen. 17:20). When Jacob was leaving for Haran, to escape the wrath of his brother, his father blessed him with the blessing, "May El Shaddai bless you and make your fruitful (*wĕyaprĕkā*) and increase your numbers (*wĕyarbekā*)" (Gen. 28:3). Moreover, God himself spoke the same blessing to Jacob after he returned from Haran. God changed his name from Jacob to Israel (Gen. 35:10) and declared in v. 11, "I am El Shaddai: be fruitful (*pĕrē*) and increase in number (*ûrbē*)." Now, as Israel and his family sojourned in Egypt, the power of the blessing was being actualized in their experience. In the midst of devastating famine they were thriving. [*prh*, *rbh*]

47:29 Put your hand under my thigh (*yĕrēkî*)—As the time of his death drew near, Jacob asked his son Joseph: "If I have found favor in your eyes, put your hand under my thigh (*yĕrēkî*) . . ." The exact meaning of this gesture as part of an oath formula is not clear. The word translated as "thigh" is *yārēk*, which occurrs 34x in the OT. In nine passages (Exod. 25:31; 37:14; 40:22, 24; Lev. 1:11; Num.

3:29, 35; 8:4; 2 Kings 16:14) it refers to the side or base of an object, such as the altar or lampstand (*HALOT*, 1:439). The other occurrences all refer to "the fleshy part of the upper thigh" (*HALOT*, 1:439). This term appears earlier in the narrative about Jacob, when he wrestled the mysterious man until dawn, who then touched his *yārēk* and knocked it out of joint (Gen. 32:26[25]). But the term *yārēk* has another connotation as well. The NIV translation of Exod. 1:5a reads, "The total number of people born to Jacob . . ." Literally this phrase is, "All the souls who came out of the *yārēk* of Jacob." (also Judg. 8:30). Here the term *yārēk* refers to the procreative powers of Jacob. Thus, it is possible that in the oath formula used here (cf. Gen. 24:2), there was the custom of swearing while placing a hand under the genitals. Possibly this was a form of self-imprecation, suggesting sterility or loss of descendants (*TLOT*, 2:500). [*yārēk*]

47:31 Swear to me (*hiššābĕ'â*)—The verb *šb'*, "to swear," is an important term in the OT, not only because the swearing of oaths was so common in OT times, but because it goes to the heart of God's faithfulness to keep the oaths he swears to his people. While the verb is important, its origin and etymology are obscure. There is not a single Semitic verb that means "to swear" common among the Semitic languages, and the verb is not attested in any of the Semitic languages that preceded Hebrew (*HALOT*, 2:1396). Attempts to derive the verb from Arabic roots or from the Hebrew word for "seven" (*šeba'*) have not been generally accepted (C. A. Keller, *TLOT*, 3:1292). In the OT, the term occurs 154x, primarily in the Niphal (154x) but also in the hiphil (31x). Central to the idea of the biblical oath was the idea of making a solemn pledge, usually concerning a future circumstance, in which God was invoked as witness and as one who stood behind this oath. It was implicitly understood that God was in some way invoked or involved, even when he was not specifically mentioned (*HALOT*, 2:1397; cf. C. A. Keller, *TLOT*, 3:1294). Often a formal oath formula was used, in which one who swore would say, "thus may Yahweh do to me/you if . . ." (e.g. 1 Sam. 3:17; 2 Kings 6:31). Sometimes only a shortened form of the formula was used, with the phrase, "As Yahweh lives . . ." (2 Kings 2:2; 3:14). Here in Gen. 47:31, Jacob's impassioned request is that Joseph swear to him that when he died his body would rest with his fathers in the cave of Machpelah. [*šb'*]

48:4 A community of peoples (*liqhal 'ammîm*)—When the time of Jacob's death drew near, Joseph was summoned to his father's side. Jacob reminded his beloved son how El Shaddai had appeared to him at Luz (Bethel), promising to make him fruitful (cf. Gen. 47:27) and a "community of nations" (*liqhal 'ammîm*). It is interesting that Jacob referred back to the divine promise given at Bethel (Gen. 35:11-12), even though the terms he uses here ("fruitful, community of peoples"), are nearly identical to the blessing of Isaac which Jacob received before leaving for Haran (Gen. 28:3-4). The term *qāhāl* has as its basic meaning the idea of "assembly," the gathering of people for various purposes. In its 124 appearances in the OT, it can refer to the gathering of men for war ("contingent," *HALOT*, 2:1079), the people gathered for worship (Pss. 22:23, 26; 35:18; 40:10), or even designate an entire people, as with the phrase, "the *qāhāl Yahweh*" (Num. 16:3; 20:4). However, there are times when "*qāhāl* is a quantitative term, with no notion of an actual assembly" (H.-P. Müller, *TLOT*, 3:1122), as

with *qāhāl gōyîm* ("a community of nations," Gen. 35:11) and *qāhāl 'ammîm* (Gen. 28:3; 48:4). These are defined by HALOT as "a crowd" (*HALOT*, 2:1080; 3a). Jacob reminded his son (Gen. 48:4) how God would multiply their descendants, whose number would one day be like the stars in the sky (Gen. 15:5; 22:17; 26:4) or like the sand on the seashore (Gen. 22:17; 32:12). [*qāhāl*]

An everlasting possession (*'ôlām*)—Jacob reminded Joseph not only of the multiplication of their descendants, but of another crucial part of the promise to the patriarchs—the gift of the land (*'ereṣ*, cf. Gen. 48:21). Here the land, that is, the land of Canaan, is referred to as "an everlasting possession" (*'ăḥuzzat 'ôlām*). The term *'ăḥuzzâ*, "property" (*HALOT*, 1:32) is used earlier in Genesis. It occurs in Gen. 23, when Abraham negotiated the purchase of a property where he could bury Sarah (Gen. 23:4, 9, 20) and in the previous chapter, where Pharaoh gave Jacob and his sons *'ăḥuzzâ* in the land of Goshen (Gen. 47:11). Now the dying Jacob is looking back at the promise made to his grandfather Abraham in Gen. 17:8, where when Abraham was 99, God appeared to him, changed his name to Abraham and said, "The land of Canaan . . . I will give as an *'ăḥuzzat 'ôlām* to you and your descendants" (NIV). This term *'ôlām* occurs 440x in the OT, most often appearing in Psalms (143x). The term does not mean "eternity" in the philosophical sense of the term. E. Jenni writes, "We might therefore best state the 'basic meaning' as a kind of range between 'remotest time' and 'perpetuity'" (*TLOT*, 2:853). That the term *'ôlām* does not mean "eternal, eternity," is evidenced in passages in which *'ôlām* refers to an individual lifetime (A. Tomasino, *NIDOTTE*, 3:347). For example, in Exod. 21:6, a Hebrew slave who wanted to remain a slave could appear before the judges and declare his desire to remain a slave to his master. An awl was then used to pierce his ear and he would thus be that master's slave *lĕ'ôlām*, that is, "for life" (NIV). The term *'ôlām* can refer to past time ("ancient gates," Gen. 24:7, 9) or future time. Here in Gen. 48:4, the term is used in a construct phrase, a common way to express the idea of distant time, such as with the phrase *bĕrît 'ôlām* ("everlasting covenant"; Gen. 9:12, 16; Ps. 105:8; 111:5, 9). The land of Canaan would be an "everlasting possession" for Jacob's offspring. [*'ôlām*]

48:12 From Israel's knees (*birkâw*)—The moving scene of the dying patriarch meeting his grandsons and blessing them brings the Joseph narrative to an emotional resolution. As Jacob himself declared, "I never expected to see your face again, and now God has allowed me to see your children too" (Gen. 48:11). Here in v. 12 Joseph removed his sons from Israel's knees (*birkâw*). The preceding text had not stated that the boys were on his knees, or as Westermann maintains, leaning on his knees (C. Westermann, *Genesis 37–50*, 187). The word *berek* ("knee") was often regarded in the past as the probable source for the important Hebrew verb *brk*, "to bless" (*BDB*, 138-39). It was thought that one received a blessing while kneeling. This derivation is no longer common among scholars (C. A. Keller, *TLOT*, 1:266; J. Scharbert, *TDOT*, 2:281; *HALOT*, 1:159-61). Possibly in popular etymology the connection of blessing and the knees related to what transpired in this passage, the practice of a child sitting on the knees of the adult to receive a blessing. This practice, observed here and in Gen. 50:23, along with the related examples from other ancient Near Eastern sources, has pointed to the possibility of this practice as the source of the verb *brk*, "to bless" (M. J. Selman, *TynBul.*, 27(1976):114-36; William C. Williams, *NIDOTTE*, 1:755). Here in Gen. 48:12, it is unclear if Jacob blessed his grandsons first, while they were on his knees, and then blessed them again by placing his hand upon their heads. Whatever the actual practice, it is clear he passed on the blessing, which his grandfather, his father, and he had received from God. [*berek*]

48:14 Israel reached out his right hand (*yĕmînô*)—Verse 13 describes how Joseph positioned his sons Manasseh and Ephraim before his father, so that Jacob's right hand would rest upon Manasseh, the firstborn. But here in v. 14, Jacob crosses his arms, placing his right hand (*yāmîn*), the hand of blessing, not upon Manasseh, the firstborn, but upon Ephraim. The term *yāmîn* is commonly found among the Semitic languages and occurs in Egyptian as well (*'imn*). In the OT it occurs about 140x, with a basic meaning of "right," used as an adjective in reference to the "right thigh," the "right eye," or the "right side" (*HALOT*, 1:415). In Gen. 48:17 it refers to the "right hand" (*yad-yĕmînô*). But often the term appears alone, functioning not as an adjective but as a noun, meaning the "right hand." This usage of *yāmîn* to designate the "right hand" occurs about 50x in the OT, most often in reference to Yahweh's powerful, saving *yāmîn*. But it can also denote the right hand of people, as here in Gen. 48:14 (F. C. Putnam, *NIDOTTE*, 2:467). The right side was seen in biblical times as a place of honor and respect. David seated his favorite wife, Bathsheba, at his right side (1 Kings 2:19), and Yahweh called upon David's "Lord" to sit at his right side (Ps. 110:1). Yahweh swears by his right hand (*bîmînô*) in Isa. 62:8. Thus, it was important for Joseph that Jacob's right hand rest upon Manasseh, the first-born. But, as Jacob knew so well, the sovereign plan of God may differ from the plans of men. [*yāmîn*]

48:15 God before whom my fathers . . . walked (*hithallěkû*)—When Jacob began his blessing of Ephraim and Manasseh, he referred to God as "The God before whom my fathers Abraham and Isaac walked (*hithallěkû*)." The verb *hlk* is one of the most common verbs in Hebrew (>1,500x), meaning "to walk." It is most common in the qal (1,412x), where it is used prosaically, as well as metaphorically, with religious significance (G. Sauer, *TLOT*, 2:369), such as to "walk right-eously" (Isa. 33:15), or "walk blamelessly" (Ps. 15:2). Often *hlk* is used metaphorically with the meaning of "to follow," sometimes in reference to following Yahweh (Jer. 2:2), but more often nega-tively in following other gods. The verb often appears with the term *'aḥěrê* ("after") to designate "following after [other gods]" (Deut. 4:3; 6:14; 8:19; 11:28; 13:3; 28:14). When *hlk* is used in the hith-pael (64x) this verb has the important the-ological significance of walking before or walking with Yahweh, namely, living in fellowship and obedience to him. In the book of Genesis, *hlk* in the hithpael occurs on six occasions before its appearance here in Gen. 48:15 (Gen. 5:22, 24: 6:9; 17:1; 24:20). It is this same God—before and in fellowship with whom Abraham and Isaac lived their lives—that Jacob now invokes to bring blessing upon his grand-sons. [*hlk*]

God who has been my shepherd (*hārō'eh 'ōtî*)—Jacob's description of the God whom he had followed continues

with the phrase, "who has been my shep-herd (*hārō'eh 'ōtî*)." Twenty-three times in the book of Genesis the verb *r'h* occurs (always qal), both as a transitive verb meaning "to feed, graze, shepherd, pas-ture" (*HALOT*, 2:1259-60), as well as a substantival participle designating one as a "shepherd" (*r'ōeh, rō'îm* [pl.]), as here in Gen. 48:15. Here for the first time in the OT, God is metaphorically viewed as the shepherd of his people. As J. A. Soggin points out, it is understandable how in the rural agrarian society of ancient Israel, where caring for livestock was so common, that the title "shepherd" could be applied to rulers, kings, and even God. Moreover, in the Babylonian and Assyrian cultures, long before Abraham, both the king and the gods were referred to as shepherd (Akk. *rē'ûm, CDA*, 303), or as shepherding humanity (Akk. *re'ûm*). Both Hammurapi and Ashurbanipal bore the title of "Shepherd" (J. A. Soggin, *TLOT*, 3:1248). In the OT, the theme of Yahweh as shepherd is most commonly associated with "the Shepherd Psalm," Ps. 23. But the theme of God as shepherd occurs in the blessing of Jacob in Gen. 49:24 (see below), as well as in Isa. 40:11, Hos. 4:16, Mic. 7:14 and Pss. 28:9 and 80:2. In the Psalms, God's people are often referred to as his "flock" (*'ēder*), or as the "sheep" (*ṣō'n*), whom he shepherds (Pss 74:1; 77:21[20]; 78:52; 79:13; 95:7; 100:3). Jacob's hope, here in Gen. 48:15, is that the God who had shepherded him all his life would care for his grandsons as well. [*r'h*]

48:16 The Angel who has delivered me (*hammal'āk*)—Jacob continued in his description of his God as the "*mal'āk* who delivered me." This term for "messenger, angel" (*mal'āk*) is found 213x in the OT, often describing human messengers sent as representatives of the community or of an individual to other people, to communicate their needs, concerns, or demands. Of particular interest is the common usage of the "*mal'āk YHWH*" (58x) and the "*mal'āk 'ĕlōhîm*" (11x) in the OT. These divine messengers come to announce deliverance or to bring deliverance (see below). While these messengers appear in human form they, or one of them, "speaks in God's name and occasionally appears as Yahweh himself" (S. Noll, *NIDOTTE*, 2:942). This has prompted a significant amount of scholarly attention, with a number of theories offered to explain this phenomenon (cf. R. Ficker, *TLOT*, 2:671). Here in Gen. 48:16, it is God whom Jacob describes as "the angel/messenger" who had delivered him. Nahum Sarna writes, "Admittedly, 'Angel' as an epithet for God is extraordinary, but since angels are often simply extensions of the divine personality, the distinction between God and angel in biblical texts is frequently blurred" (*Genesis*, 328). [*mal'āk*]

The Angel who has delivered me (*haggō'ēl*)—Jacob described the *mal'āk*, the divine messenger, as the one who "has delivered me" (*gō'ēl*). This uniquely Hebrew term here makes its only appearance in the book of Genesis. The root *g'l* occurs 118x in the OT with the basic meaning "to redeem" (*HALOT*, 1:169). The verb is used 59x, usually in the qal (51), as well as in the Niphal (8x). Moreover, the qal participle (*gō'ēl*) is often used substantivally (46x) (J. J. Stamm, *TLOT*, 1:288-89). The usage of this root is clustered within the OT, as for example, in Lev. 25 and 27 (31x), which deal with the redemption of property during the sabbatical and Jubilee years, and with the redemption of an Israelite whose poverty has forced him to sell some of his property. The other passage in which *g'l* and its related terms

(*gō'ēl*, *gĕ'ullâ*) appear is in the book of Ruth (23x). In the book of Ruth, it appears the role of the *gō'ēl* included not only redemption of Naomi's property, but a levirate marriage to Ruth as well (Ruth 4:5, 10). But the root *g'l* is also frequently used in a nontechnical sense to describe God's redemption of an individual or of his people. Both Isaiah (24x) and the Psalms(11x) witness this use of *g'l* to describe God's saving power to redeem and deliver. Often when *g'l* is used in this sense it is found in parallel with the other great "saving" terms of the OT, such as *pdh* ("to free, redeem"), *nṣl* ("to deliver, save") and especially *yš'* ("to save"; Isa. 49:26; 60:16; 63:9; Ps. 72:13; 106:10). Here in Gen. 48:16, *haggō'ēl* (qal participle with a verbal nuance) is used to designate God's saving power. God, who is Jacob's Shepherd, his Angel, had redeemed him from all harm (*rā'*). God had indeed rescued Jacob, both from his brother when he fled, and later when he returned (Gen. 28; 32), as well as from his uncle (Gen. 31). [*g'l*]

49:1 What will happen to you in days to come (*bĕ'aḥărît hayyāmîm*)—Jacob's words spoke to the future destiny of each of the tribes. The phrase used here, *bĕ'aḥărît hayyāmîm* ("in days to come"), appears 13x in the OT, 9x in prophetic books (Isa. 2:2; Jer. 23:20, 30:24, 48:47, 49:39; Ezek. 38:16; Hos. 3:5; Mic. 4:1; Dan. 10:14). In the NIV this phrase is rendered with different nuances, such as a simple future ("in days to come," Ezek. 38:16), indefinite future ("a time yet to come," Dan. 10:14) and the eschatological future ("in the last days," Isa. 2:2 || Mic. 4:1). In Gen. 49:1, the use of the phrase is most similar to Deut. 31:29 where Moses also speaks of the days to come for Israel. The contexts are also parallel, where in each the elderly leader is about to pass away and thus gives his prophetic words of God's future work among his people (V. Hamilton, *Genesis 18–50*, 646). [*'aḥărît, yôm*]

49:3 Reuben . . . first sign of my <u>strength</u> (*'ônî*)—While each of Jacob's sons is mentioned in his testament, they are not all given equal attention. The brothers who are mentioned significantly in the Joseph narrative are the same brothers who receive most of the attention in the prophetic oracle from their father. For example, Judah and Joseph are the focus in 10 of the 25 verses of this chapter, while Zebulon, Issachar, Dan, Gad, Asher, and Naphtali together share only eight verses (G. Wenham, *Genesis 16–50*, 468-69). Jacob's testament naturally begins with Reuben, "you are my first-born (*běkōrî*), my might, the first sign (*wěrē'šît*) of my strength (*'ônî*)" (Gen. 49:1). The term "strength" is the Hebrew term *'ôn* which is used 10x in the OT. It can refer to physical strength, as for example in Job 40:26, which speaks of the strength of behemoth (*běhēmôt*). It can also mean financial strength, that is, "wealth" (Hos. 12:9; Job 20:10). In four other passages, including here in Gen. 49:3, the term *'ôn* refers to a man's procreative strength (*HALOT*, 1:22). In each of these four passages (Gen. 49:3, Deut. 21:17; Pss. 78:51, 105:36) the word *'ôn* follows the word *rē'šît* ("first, beginning, first fruit"). Tanakh (JPS) translates the phrase in these four passages as "the firstfruits of my/his/their vigor." [*'ôn*]

Gen. 49:4 And <u>defiled</u> it (*ḥillaltā*)—Jacob's word to his firstborn moved quickly from privilege (v. 3) to punishment for an earlier crime (v. 4). Jacob reminded Reuben how he once "went up onto your father's bed"

and "defiled it (*ḥillaltā*)." Jacob confronted him with the sordid incident in Gen. 35:22 when Reuben slept with Bilhah, Jacob's concubine. The word "defiled" is the Hebrew verb *ḥll*, "to defile, pollute, profane" (*BDB* and *HALOT* both recognize three separate homonymous *ḥll* roots, I *ḥll* "to profane"; II *ḥll* "to pierce," III *ḥll* "to play the flute.") In the OT era, life was lived in the constant tension of the holy versus the profane (*ḥōl*). Any action done contrary to God's will as revealed in the law could profane that which was holy. Thus, there are many things that are profaned or defiled in the OT. Most commonly that which was profaned was Yahweh's name, a concept often found in the prophets (Lev. 18:21; 19:12; Amos 2:7; Ezek. 20:39; 36:21). Not only his name, but Yahweh's priests could be defiled (Lev. 21:4, 9, 21), the temple could be profaned (Ezek. 23:39), his land could be profaned (Jer. 16:18), his covenant defiled (Mal. 2:10), and his altar profaned (Exod. 20:25). The defilement here, perpetrated by Reuben, is unique in that it is the only reference to the defilement of a couch, and by metonymy, his father's marriage relationship with Bilhah. Because of that sin, he (and his tribe) will "no longer excel" (v. 4). He and his descendants should have expected to have the preeminent position among the tribes. Yet because of his crime, his tribe did not excel; in time the Reubenites, living on the east side of the Jordan, were slowly absorbed into the tribe of Gad (V. Hamilton, *Genesis 18–50*), 647). [*ḥll*]

49:7 <u>Cursed</u> be their anger (*'ārûr*)—Jacob turned from addressing Reuben to speak to Simeon and Levi. Here again there is not much blessing in "The Blessing of Jacob"! The two brothers are reproved for their wanton violence in the massacre at Shechem (Gen. 34). Here in v. 7, Jacob uses the common (38x) "curse formula" in the OT, the "'ārûr-formula" (C. A. Keller, *TLOT*, 1:180). In this formula the verb '*rr* appears as a qal passive participle followed by the subject: "Cursed be X" (J. Scharbert, *TDOT*, 1:408-09). J. Scharbert maintains that at the core of this curse formula is the idea of the exclusion of the cursed from his clan, tribe, or family (*TDOT*, 1:409). Already in Genesis this has occurred in the reference to the serpent (Gen. 3:14) as well as to Cain (Gen. 4:11). Here in Gen. 49:7, the use of the 'ārûr—formula is unique: the subject cursed is not a person but their anger. The significance of this is not entirely clear. C. Westermann (*Genesis 37–50*, 226) and C. A. Keller (*TLOT*, 1:180) suggest this is a softening of the curse, a judgment upon their anger but not upon them personally. J. Scharbert (*TDOT*, 1:411) maintains that both brothers are indeed placed under the curse and the author spoke of their "anger" to avoid naming the two brothers. Because of their violence Jacob would scatter and disperse them in Israel. In time the Levites would be assigned to their 48 Levitical cities throughout the land. The tribe of Simeon seems to have been weakened, and in time, absorbed by the tribe of Judah (V. Hamilton, *Genesis 18–50*, 652). ['*rr*]

49:8 Judah, your brothers will <u>praise</u> you (*yôdûkā*)—"The blessing on Judah has provoked more discussion than the whole rest of the chapter" (G. Wenham, *Genesis 16–50*, 475). In these five verses (vv. 8-12) occur some of the most difficult exegetical and hermeneutical challenges within the book of Genesis. Clearly the opening phrase, "Judah (*yĕhûdâ*), your brothers will praise you (*yôdûkā*)," summarizes the dominant theme of these verses: the unqualified praise of Judah. Here the verbal root *ydh*,

"to praise," is used. It is one of the most common verbs for "praise" in the OT (II *ydh* HALOT; BDB has one root meaning both "to shoot" and "to praise," while HALOT and other modern lexicons separate these into two homonymous roots). When Judah was born, his mother Leah rejoiced with the birth of her fourth son and exclaimed, "This time I will praise (*'ôdeh*) the Lord" and she named him Judah (*yĕhûdâ*; Gen. 29:35). The exact meaning of *yĕhûdâ* is not certain; it may be a shortened form of the name Jehudael (*yĕhûdā' ēl*, "May 'El be praised") or it may be a noun meaning "praise" (G. Wenhem, *Genesis 16–50*, 244). Jacob uses this wordplay on Judah's name to describe his son as the heroic leader of the family who would triumph over his enemies (v. 8). [*ydh*]

49:10 The <u>scepter</u> will not depart (*šēbeṭ*)— The first occurrence of the term *šēbeṭ* in the OT occurs here in v. 10, in Jacob's prophecy about Judah and the tribe who will bear his name. This noun is common among the Semitic languages and in Egyptian (*šbd*) as well (*HALOT*, 2:1388). Its primary meaning is "stick, rod" as well as "scepter," the rod which was the sign of authority of a leader. By extension the term came to designate the people who were under the authority of the leader, thus resulting in the meaning "tribe" (*HALOT*, 2:1388; cf. D. Fouts, *NIDOTTE*, 4:24). Ps. 45, a royal psalm, illustrates this use of *šēbeṭ* with the meaning of "scepter," the symbol of royal authority. It describes the king's throne as an eternal throne, in which, "a scepter of justice (*šēbeṭ mîšōr*) will be the scepter of your kingdom (*šēbeṭ malkûtekā*)" (Ps. 45:7). Here in Gen. 45:10, the meaning of *šēbeṭ* as "scepter" is not in doubt, since the following parallel line speaks of the "*mĕḥōqēq* between his feet." This term *mĕḥōqēq* is the polel participle of the verb *ḥqq*, "to inscribe, enact, decide" (*HALOT*, 1:347). This participle is often used substantivally to designate "a commander, ruler" (Judg. 5:14; Isa. 33:22), as well as the ruler's scepter (Num. 21:18; Ps. 60:9). Judah and the tribe that descends from him is promised authority among the tribes, a situation that came to pass when the Davidic monarchy came about. [*šēbeṭ*]

Until Shiloh comes (*'ad kî-yābō šîlōh*)—A famous OT scholar once declared this phrase the most famous *crux interpretum* in the OT (W. Moran, *Biblica*, 39 (1958):405-25). Even a casual look at the English translations reveals that this phrase has been translated and understood in very different ways. The KJV, followed by the ASV and NASB, translates the phrase "until Shiloh come(s)," which is faithful to the MT but baffling in term of its meaning. The understanding of "Shiloh" as an ancient title or name for the Messiah did not appear in Christian interpretation until the sixteenth century, although this was suggested in the Jewish Talmud much earlier (*b. Sanh. 98b*; R. Youngblood, *NIDOTTE*, 4:1222). A variant of this translation that is also possible is "until he (Judah) comes to Shiloh," which at least provides a possible understanding of the expansion of Judah unto the city of Shiloh in the the northern kingdom. The NIV, along with the RSV, REB, and NLT, translate the phrase as something like "until he comes to whom it belongs" (NIV). This interpretation's strength is that is follows the ancient versions' understanding of the passage. The versions, primarily the LXX, seemed to have read the consonantal MT text as not *šîlōh* but as *še lôh*, "which is to him." Thus, Judah would have preeminence until the coming of the one owning the scepter.

The third major option, followed by the NRSV, NAB, NEB, Tanakh (JPS), and TEV, is to emend the vowels of the consonantal MT text to *šay lô*, "tribute to him." Thus NRSV reads, "until tribute comes to him." Each of these three interpretations is respectful and judicious with the MT. Possibly the second interpretation, "until it comes to whom it belongs," is to be preferred because of the early versional evidence (LXX, Old Latin, Syriac). All three major interpretations of this perplexing phrase are suggestive of messianic expectation. Both the Aramaic Targum (*Targum Onkelos*) and Qumran (*4Q Patr. 3*) clearly understood this phrase messianically. (*HALOT*, 2:1478; V. Hamilton, *Genesis 18–50*, 654-61; G. Wenham, *Genesis 16–50*, 476-78; R. Youngblood, *NIDOTTE*, 4:1220-23). [*šîlōh*]

The obedience of the nations (*yiqhat*)—A difficult verse ends with a difficult term. The term translated "obedience" is the Hebrew term *yĕqāhâ*. It appears in the OT only here and possibly in Prov. 30:17. While *BDB* lists Prov. 30:17 as the second occurrence of *yĕqāhâ* in the OT, HALOT does not (*HALOT*, 1:430). This is because HALOT is following numerous scholars who propose that *lîqăhat* ("obedience") in Prov. 30:17 be read as *lihăqat* ("old age). This not only provides better parallelism in the verse (Prov. 30:17) but also seems to reflect the LXX translation of the term as *gēros* "old age" (E. Merrill, *NIDOTTE*, 2:518-19). Thus, the only certain occurrence of the term *yĕqāhâ* is here in Gen. 49:10. The meaning of the term is based upon the Arabic *wqh* meaning "to obey" (V. Hamilton, *Genesis 18–50*, 655). This translation as "obedience" fits well in the context of the verse. The one "who is to come" will accept the obedience of the nations, as David did as king, and as David's "greater son" will one day do as well. [*yĕqāhâ*]

49:16 Dan will judge (*yādîn*)—Just as Jacob began his blessing of Judah with a wordplay on his son's name (v. 10), so he does again in his blessing of Dan: "Dan (*dān*) will judge (*yādîn*)." The verb *dyn*, common among the Semitic languages, has a basic meaning of "to judge" (*BDB*, 192). The verb is used 24x in the OT (23x Hebrew; 1x Aramaic), often with the connotation of pleading the cause of another, as for example, the poor or the orphan (Isa. 3:13; Ps. 72:2). The exact nuance of the verb here in Gen. 49:16 is not clear. The English translations suggest various connotations. The Tanakh (JPS) and NLT both translate the phrase as "Dan will govern." This is certainly possible (Zech .3:7) but seems awkward in this context and difficult in terms of the history of the tribe of Dan. The NIV translation of "Dan will provide justice for his people" not only reflects the concept of vindication but also better captures the naming of Dan when the boy was born. In Gen. 30:6, Rachel rejoiced after enduring the scorn of her fertile sister and exclaimed, "God has vindicated me (*dānannî*)." Thus she named her son "Dan." It is not clear how the tribe of Dan functioned in the way predicted here in Gen. 49:16. Gordon Wenham sees this fulfillment historically in a manner suggested long ago in the Aramaic Targum on Genesis (*Targum Neofiti*) which looked to Samson and his victories over the Philistines (Judg. 17-18) as the tribe of Dan's contribution to the nation (G. Wenham, *Genesis 16–50*, 481). [*dyn*]

49:22 Joseph is a wild ass (*bēn pōrāt*)— Jacob's blessing of his beloved Joseph is five verses long (vv. 22-26), in stark contrast to that of Gad, Asher, and Naphtali, whose blessing is expressed in a single verse for each (vv. 19-21). Joseph's blessing begins with a metaphor, the meaning of which is disputed. Most of the English translations understand *bēn pōrāt* as a plant metaphor, as in the NIV translation, "Joseph is a fruitful vine." This translation regards *pōrāt* as a qal feminine participle from the verb *prh* "to bear fruit" (so *HALOT*, 2:963; 1a). The term *bēn* "son" in this phrase is used in a periphrastic two-word construction common in Hebrew, in which the second noun (*pōrāt*) follows the first noun (*bn*), and thus, "represents a person as possessing some object or quality" (*GKC*, 128.s). Here this would suggest "son of fruitfulness," in this case referring to plants, "a vine of fruitfulness," or a "a fruitful vine." This is the traditional interpretation, reflected as far back as the Aramaic Targums. But as Speiser points out, this interpretation has problems (E. A. Speiser, *Genesis*, 367-68). Throughout this blessing, the metaphors have been primarily animal metaphors, not plants. The identification with Joseph as a vine makes v. 23 seem odd as he is "attacked by archers." Plus, the term "son" (*bēn*) is never used in reference to plants but is used in reference to animals (Speiser, 367-68). Speiser understands *pōrāt* not as the participle of *prh*, but the feminine form of the noun *pere'* meaning "wild ass." This interpretation, along with his understanding of the parallel phrase *bānôt ṣā'ădâ* in v. 22 as "wild asses" based upon Arabic cognates, has been embraced by conservative exegetes such as V. Hamilton and G. Wenham, and with a slight variation, by J. Walton as well. The Tanakh (JPS) translates v. 22 as such: "Joseph is a wild ass, a wild ass by a spring—wild colts on a hillside." [*prh*/*pōrāt*]

49:24 <u>Mighty one</u> of Jacob, (*'ăbîr ya'ăqōb*)—In spite of the archers' attack against him, Joseph remained resolute and strong (vv. 24a) because the hands of *'ăbîr ya'ăqōb*, "the Mighty one of Jacob," sustained him. The term *'ābîr* ("mighty") is used 6x in the OT, always as part of a divine name (H. Schmidt, *TLOT*, 1:20). In Akkadian, the cognate term is also used as an epithet of god, in the phrase *bēl abāru*, "Mighty Lord" (*CDA*, 2). Besides this passage in Gen. 49, *'ābîr* occurs 3x in Isaiah (Isa. 1:24; 49:26; 60:16) and twice in Psalms (Ps. 132:2, 5). The connection of *'ābîr* with the nearly identical term *'abbîr* ("strong, powerful") is not certain. HALOT regards *'ābîr* as "artificially differentiated" from *'abbîr* (HALOT, 1:6; cf. M. Meyer, *Hebräische Grammatik*, 2:30). Kapelrud follows the general explanation of the difference between the two forms as a differentiation on the part of the Masoretes to protect the name of God from associations common with the term *'abbîr*, which often describes horses and particularly bulls (Pss. 22:13[12]; 50:13) (A. Kapelrud, *TDOT*, 1:42). This is certainly understandable in light of the failure of God's people. The golden calf incident in the wilderness (Exod. 32), and the northern kingdom of Israel's use of golden calves at their temples in Bethel and Dan (1 Kings 12:28-30), would be enough to make the Masoretes squeamish about any association of God with calves and bulls. In Gen. 49:24, Jacob acknowledges that *'ăbîr ya'ăqōb* (the Mighty One of Jacob) had sustained his beloved son and would indeed sustain him and his people in the days to come. [*'ābîr*]

The Shepherd, the <u>Stone</u> of Israel (*rō'eh 'eben yiśrā'ēl*)—In his blessing of Joseph, Jacob described his God with a lengthy collection of divine titles and names that begins in v. 22 and continues to v. 26. These various names and titles have been the source of extensive study and discussion regarding the nature of patriarchal religion (bibliography: C. Westermann, "Excursus on the Designations for God in 49:22-28," *Genesis 37–50*, 239). Here in the second part of Gen. 49:24, Jacob describes God not just as the "Mighty One of Jacob," but as "shepherd" (*rō'eh*) and "Stone of Israel" (*'eben yiśrā'ēl*). Separating the phrase "Mighty One of Israel" from "Shepherd, the Stone of Israel" is the term *miššam*, "from there." The insertion of this term between the two titles of God is odd. Tanahk (JPS) translates the last half of 24 as "by the hands of the Mighty One of Israel—*There*, the Shepherd, the Rock of Israel–." This translation seems to reflect the ancient rabbinic interpretation of the verse, that Jacob pointed heavenward as he spoke of the Shepherd, the Stone of Israel (N. Sarna, *Genesis*, 343). The Syriac translation seems to have read the Hebrew term not as *miššam* ("from there") but as *miššem* ("by the name of"). This understanding of the term has been followed by numerous commentators and is reflected in the NRSV translation of v. 24b: "by the hands of the Mighty One of Israel, by the name of the Shepherd, the Rock of Israel." This is now the second time Jacob referred to God as his shepherd. In the last chapter (48:15), when Jacob blessed Ephraim and Manasseh, he described God as "the God who has been my Shepherd (*hārō'eh 'ōtî*) all my life to this day." This was the first time in the OT that the metaphor of God as Shepherd appeared, a metaphor that appears again here in Gen. 49:24. But here in this verse the next metaphorical title of God, as the "Stone (*'eben*) of Israel," is unique. The term "rock" (*ṣûr*) is often used as a metaphorical title for God in the OT. In 32, Moses refers to Yahweh 5x as the Rock (Deut. 32:4, 15, 18, 30, 31). In the Psalms, the designation of God as Rock (ṣûr) is used over 40x to express the confidence and hope in God as protector and savior (Pss. 18:2, 31, 46; 19:14; 27:5). Yahweh is the "Rock (ṣûr) of Israel" (2 Sam. 23:3; Isa. 30:29). However, only here (49:24) is ʾeben used as an epithet of God in the OT. It is not clear why the word "stone" (ʾeben) is not more often used in reference to God. Since the term ʾeben is the normal word for common fieldstones lying on the ground, it is understandable that ṣûr, which often describes larger, more imposing rocks of the mountains, would better convey the image of power and protection (A. S. van der Woude, TLOT, 2:1068). Possibly the significance of stones as part of the Canaanite cult, which the prophets denounced (Jer. 2:27, 3:9; Ezek. 20:32), made the word "stone" (ʾeben) undesirable for use as a metaphor for Yahweh (A. Kapelrud, TDOT, 1:51). Maybe Jacob's use of the unique phrase "The Stone of Israel" reflects his own experience. In Gen. 28, while near Bethel on his journey to Haran, Jacob used an ʾeben as his pillow (v. 11) and lay down to sleep. That night God graciously confirmed to Jacob his care and gave him his promises that he would bring Jacob back to the land. In the morning, Jacob used that same ʾeben as a pillar upon which he poured a libation of oil (v. 28). For Jacob (Israel), Yahweh was indeed the Stone of Israel. [ʾeben]

49:25 Your father's God who helps you (wĕyaʿzĕrekā)—Jacob's blessing of Joseph continued in v. 25 with additional descriptions of the God of Jacob and Joseph. Jacob seems to take one of his favorite names of God, ʾEl Shaddai (cf. Gen. 43:14), and splits it to form two descriptive phrases. Jacob refers to "ʾEl of your father who helps . . ."

and "Shaddai who blesses . . ." This phenomenon also occurs in Num. 24:4, 16 and in Job 8:3, 5. The phrase "who helps you" employs the verb ʿzr, "to help." Although this verb occurs 80x in the OT, its use here in this verse is the only appearance of the verb in the book of Genesis. HALOT suggests that the term is usually found in the later books of the OT (HALOT, 1:810), appearing 10x in 1 Chronicles, 12x in 2 Chronicles, and 16x in the Psalms. God is the subject of the verb ʿzr in about 30 different passages, including 7x in Isa. 41:10–50:9 (U. Bergmann, TLOT, 2, 873). The Joseph narrative is indeed a record of God's help in the life of Joseph and his family. [ʿzr]

Blesses you with the blessings of the heavens (birkōt šāmayim)—Jacob speaks of the help that God (ʾēl) brings, and then, in a parallel phrase, speaks of Shaddai who "blesses with the blessings of heaven." Blessing is an important theme in the book of Genesis, especially as an essential element of God's promises to the patriarchs (Gen. 12:2-3; 14:19-20; 17:16; 22:17-18; 24:1; 25:11). In Gen. 47:7, the aged patriarch Jacob, who had received the blessing from God, met Pharaoh and blessed him. In this last section of the Testament of Jacob (vv. 24-28), the final occurrences of the verb brk, "to bless," and the noun bĕrākâ, "blessing," are found. Here in vv. 25 and 26 the noun bĕrākâ appears 5x in just two verses (16x in Genesis; C. A. Keller, TLOT, 1:267). The very first blessing mentioned is the "blessings of heaven" (birkōt šāmayim), a phrase unique in the OT. Jacob then uses the phrase "blessings of the deep below" (birkōt tĕhôm) as a merism, in which the two opposing terms together designate the totality of the blessing. All of these blessings are meant for Joseph: "Let them rest on the head of Joseph . . ." (v. 26).

Gordon Wenham writes, "Here in two verses, like the finale of a fireworks display, the root occurs 6x (*brk*) . . . making a brilliant climax to the last words of Jacob. The God-given blessings of the future will far outshine those already experienced" (G. Wenham, *Genesis 16–50*, 486). [*běrākâ*]

50:15 Hold a grudge (*yiśṭĕmēnû*)—Joseph and his brothers kept their promise to their father: they buried him in the family tomb in the cave of Machpelah. But Jacob's absence also evoked fear among the brothers that Joseph would now seek his revenge against them. They were afraid he would still "hold a grudge (*yiśṭĕmēnû*) against them." The verb used in this passage is the verb *śṭm*, which is a by-form of the verb *śṭn* (*HALOT*, 2:1316). Both verbs have as their basic meaning "to be hostile to, have animosity toward" (G. Wanke, *TLOT*, 1268). Both verbs (*śṭm*, *śṭn*) occur only in the qal and each is used 6x in the OT. Half of the occurrences (3x/6x) of *śṭm* are found in the book of Genesis (Bruce Baloian, *NIDOTTE*, 1230-31). In the aftermath of Jacob's deception of his father (Gen. 27:41), the passage reads, "Esau held a grudge (*wayyiśṭōm*) against Jacob because of the blessing." In the Testament of Jacob (Gen. 49:23), *śṭm* is used poetically to describe the hostility and harassment of the archers who were attacking Joseph. Here in chapter 50, the brothers are still concerned that Joseph harbored lingering hostility against them for their previous crimes. [*śṭm*]

50:17 Forgive your brothers (*śā'*)—The brothers' unwarranted fear of reprisal from Joseph leads to their concocting a story about Jacob asking Joseph to forgive his brothers. This fictitious request for forgiveness in Hebrew is the alliterative phrase *'ānā śā' nā' peš'a* ("Please! Forgive now! the sin . . ."). The term "forgive" (*śā'*) is the imperative of the verb *nś'*. The verb *nś'* is common among the Semitic languages and in Hebrew, occurring 654x in the OT (F. Stolz, *TLOT*, 2:769). Its primary meaning is "to lift, to bear" and it is used in a wide range of contexts. The verb is used in relation to sin to express two diametrically opposed concepts. In the law, the meaning "to bear sin" is to bear the consequences or guilt of one's actions (Lev. 5:1, 17: 7:18; 17:16; 19:8, 17; 20:17). Yet the same verb, also in legal contexts, can bear the opposite meaning: "to lift (away) sin, to carry (away) sin," that is, "to forgive" (Lev. 10:17; Num. 14:18; Josh. 24:19). In the book of Genesis this use of *nś'* to designate forgiveness has occurred in Gen. 18:24 and 26, where Abraham bargained with the divine messenger for Sodom, asking if he would not spare or forgive (*nś'*) the city on account of just 50 righteous people. Here in Gen. 50:17, the brothers ask Joseph, through the ruse of their father's request, to "lift away" their transgression (*peš'a*) against him. This figurative meaning of *nś'* is expressed elsewhere in the OT with other terms, such as *slḥ*, "to forgive," *kpr*, "to atone," *ksh*, "to cover, forgive," and *nqh*, "to declare innocent" (F. Stolz, *TLOT*, 2:772). [*nś'*]

50:20 You intended to harm me (*ḥăšabtem*)—Joseph responded to his brothers with words of comfort: "Don't be afraid" (v. 19). Yet he did not deny the reality of their sins. He stated, "You intended (*ḥăšabtem*) to harm me." The verb used in this phrase is *ḥšb*, "to think, devise, reckon" (*BDB*, 362-63). Seybold suggests two basic semantic elements in this verb: the "element of calculation" and "the element of planning" (*TDOT*, 5:230). Here in this passage (Gen. 50:20), Joseph emphasizes that their acts were not acci-

dental or unintentional; they were deliberate and intended to bring harm (*rā'â*,
"evil, harm"). But, as Joseph went on to
explain, God also had his plans. He
"intended it for good" (*ḥăšabtem lĕṭōbâ*), to
preserve their lives. [*ḥšb*]

50:21 He reassured them (*wayĕnaḥēm*)—
Joseph "reassured (*wayĕnaḥēm*) his
brothers" by emphasizing that God's
intention was opposite of theirs and, that
he would not only forgive them, but also
provide for them. The verb translated as
"reassured" is the verb *nḥm*, occurring
most often in the Niphal and Piel. Its
basic meanings are well illustrated in the
book of Genesis. In the Niphal (48x in
OT), the verb can mean "to regret, be
sorry" (*HALOT*, 1:688), as in Gen. 6 when
God "regretted" creating man (Gen. 6:6,
7). The Niphal of *nḥm* can also mean "to
console oneself," as for example, when
Isaac was consoled after his mother's
death by his marriage to Rebekah (Gen.
24:67). In the Piel (51x in OT) the verb
means, "to console," and this is the form
in which the verb appears here. In Gen.
37:35, when the brothers reported to
Jacob that Joseph was dead, his sons and
daughters "sought to comfort (*lĕnaḥămô*)
him" but to no avail. Now Joseph "com-
forts" his brothers, not because of their
sadness but because of their fear. He
reassured them and "spoke kindly to
them" (NIV). This phrase "spoke kindly"
(*'al-libbm*) literally means to speak "to the
heart," and, when used with the verb
nḥm, "means a comfort that penetrates to
the heart and thus becomes a reality"
(H. J. Stoebe, *TLOT*, 2:735) [*nḥm*]

50:24 Surely come to your aid (*pāqōd
yipqōd*)—As Joseph drew near to death,
he spoke his final words to his brothers.
Joseph knew that his death would bring

not only sadness to them but fear as well.
Joseph had been their patron and
provider. Their status would now be
much more precarious in his absence.
Thus, his first words were words of
assurance: "God will surely come to
your aid (*pāqōd yipqōd*)." The verb used
here is the verb *pqd*, one of the most perplexing verbs in the OT. There is no consensus regarding its basic meaning. In its
303 occurrences in the OT, it demonstrates a broad range of meaning (T.
Williams, *NIDOTTE*, 3:658). This broad
range of meaning is found as well in the
Akkadian term *paqādu*. It can mean "to
entrust, handover," "to care for," "to
review," and "to appoint" a person to an
office (*CDA*, 264). These same nuances
are found in the Hebrew Bible as well.
Earlier in the Joseph narrative, Joseph
was "entrusted, put in charge
(*wayyipqidēhû*)" of Potiphar's estate
(Gen. 39:4, 5). When he was in prison he
was "assigned" (*wayyipqōd*) oversight
and care for the cupbearer and the baker
(Gen. 40:4). But here in Gen. 50:24 the
verb has an important theological meaning (cf. Gen. 21:1), used "as a term for
Yahweh's beneficial attention to individuals or to the people Israel in the sense of
'to see attentively, regard or look upon,
see after someone'"(W. Schottroff, *TLOT*,
2:1024). This care that Joseph promises to
his brothers is expressed in the double
use of the verb (*pāqōd yipqōd*). Here the
infinitive absolute (*pāqōd*) is followed by
the same verb in a finite form (*yipqōd*; qal
imperfect), a construction in which "the
verbal idea is intensified" (*IBHS*,
35.3.1.b). This is reflected in the NIV
translation as "*surely* come to your aid."
Joseph would no longer care for his
brothers, but Joseph's God would indeed
care for his people in the dark days that
lay ahead. [*pqd*]

EXODUS

Gordon H. Johnston

1:7 They were exceedingly _fruitful_
(_pārû_). From an inauspicious beginning
came a great nation. The verb _pārâ_, "bear
fruit" refers to propagation (Gen. 1:22, 28;
8:17; 9:1, 7; 28:2-3) (_BDB_, 826.1; _HALOT,_
3:964.2a), just as the related noun _perî_
"fruit" often describes one's offspring
(Gen. 30:2; Deut. 7:13) (_BDB_, 826.2). The
use of this term creates a striking
metaphor, comparing the dramatic population growth of the Hebrews to the
growth of a fertile vine (cf. Gen. 49:22; Ps.
128:3; Isa. 17:6; 32:12; Ezek. 19:10). The
narrator mirrors this dramatic growth by
multiplying terms: "They _were fruitful_
(_pārû_), _teemed_ (_wayyišreṣû_), _multiplied_ (_way-
yirbû_) and _became strong_ (_wayya'aṣemû_)
exceedingly (_bim'ōd me'ōd_)" (Bullinger,
Figures of Speech in the Bible, 211). In addition, the terminology in v. 7 (lit. "they
were _fruitful_ and _multiplied_") alludes to
God's blessing of humanity at creation
("Be _fruitful_ and _multiply_!" Gen. 1:28; 9:1;
cf. 8:17; 9:7), and his promise to multiply
the patriarchs' descendants ("Be _fruitful_
and _multiply_—a nation will descend from
you!" Gen. 35:11). Just as Genesis opened
with God's blessing on humanity at creation, Exodus begins with his blessing of
the Hebrews in Egypt. So the report that
the Hebrews became "fruitful" shows
that the patriarchal clan was fulfilling its

commission and prospering under God's
blessing (Gen. 47:27). Although they were
no longer in the Promised Land, this allusion shows that God was blessing the
Hebrews nonetheless, and fulfilling his
promise to multiply the descendants of
Abraham, Isaac, and Jacob (Gen. 12:2;
13:16; 15:5). (_NIDOTTE_, 3:676-80; _TWOT_,
2:733-34) [_prh_]

The land _was filled_ with them (_wat-
timālē'_). The verb _mālē'_ "to fill [the land]"
is hyperbolic for the dramatic spike in the
population growth of the Hebrews (_BDB_,
570.2). The expression _wattimālē' hā'āreṣ_
"the land was filled [with them]" is a theologically pregnant allusion to the repetition of this well-known phrase in Genesis.
At the climactic moment of God's creation
and blessing of humanity we read, "God
blessed them, saying, 'Be exceedingly
fruitful so that you may _fill the earth_'"
(_ûmil'û 'et hā'āreṣ_) (Gen. 1:28). Although
humanity became exceedingly fruitful
(Gen. 6:1), man's rebellion abounded all
the more: "_the earth was filled_ (_wattimālē'
hā'āreṣ_) with violence" (Gen. 6:11). After
starting anew with Noah, we again read,
"God blessed [them], saying, 'Be exceedingly fruitful so that you may _fill the
earth_'" (_ûmil'û 'et hā'āreṣ_) (Gen. 9:1). Just as
God blessed humanity with fertility to fill
(_mālē'_) the earth (_hā'āreṣ_) in Gen. 1, we see

that God was blessing the Hebrews with fertility to fill (*mālē'*) the land (*hā'āreṣ*) in Exod. 1. In the land of Egypt, the Creator was blessing the patriarchal clan as a microcosm of the new creation. In fulfillment of God's promise to bless the descendants of Abraham (Gen. 12:2; 13:16; 15:5), the Hebrews were becoming the showcase of God's blessings. (*NIDOTTE*, 2:939-41; *TWOT*, 1:505-06) [*ml'*]

1:9 Much too numerous for us (*rab we'āṣūm mimmenû*). This expression can be understood in two ways depending on the function of the preposition *min*: (1) comparative sense (*BDB*, 582.6a): "much more numerous than us" (KJV, NAB, ASV, NASB, NIV, CEV), meaning the Hebrews outnumbered the Egyptians; or (2) elative sense, referring to what is "too much" for someone to bear (*BDB*, 582.6d): "much too numerous for us" (NJPS, TEV, NLT), meaning the number of Hebrews was becoming a threat to the Egyptian majority (e.g., Gen. 4:3; 18:14; 30:7; Exod. 18:18; Deut. 17:8; Ruth 1:12; 1 Kings 19:7; Pss. 38:5; 131:1; 139:6; Isa. 61:3; esp. Josh. 19:9; 1 Kings 19:7). Syntactically, either option is viable; however, the latter might be preferable. Historical records from this period indicate that native the Egyptian population was about two million, while the population of Semitic slaves was much less (Hoffmeier, *Israel in Egypt*, 123). Archaeological evidence has revealed the presence of Semites in the area of Goshen. Their numbers may have exceeded those of the Egyptians in the area but not the total native population in Egypt as a whole. (*NIDOTTE*, 3:487-99; *TWOT*, 2:690) [*ṣm*]

1:10 Lest they gain ascendancy over the land (*we'ālâ min*). The construction *'ālâ* +

min may be taken in two different ways: (1) It may refer to departure from a location: "to go up from" [a place] (*BDB*, 748.1; *TLOT*, 2:887). In fact, this expression often refers to Israel's departure from Egypt (Exod. 3:8; 17:3; 32:1, 4, 7, 8, 23; 33:1; Num. 16:13; 20:5; 21:5; 32:11; Deut. 20:1; Judg. 11:13, 16; 1 Sam. 15:2, 6; 1 Kings 12:28; Isa. 11:16; Hos. 2:15[17]; Amos 3:1; 9:7; Mic. 6:4). However, one wonders whether Pharaoh would have been afraid of the Hebrews departing Egypt because the Egyptians had not yet enslaved them. Throughout their history, the Egyptians were intent on keeping free Semites out of—not keeping them within—Egypt. (2) It may have military connotations: "to march out" [from a place] to attack an enemy (Josh. 10:7, 9; Ezek. 39:2; cf. Jer. 4:7; 49:19; 50:44) and "to gain ascendancy over" [a land] by conquering it and taking possession (Hos. 2:2) (*HALOT*, 2:829.3e). The latter may be preferable in light of Pharaoh's expressed fear that in the event of war, the Hebrews might join in an attack against Egypt and so "rise up and take possession of the land" (NET, NJPS margin, TEV margin). Ironically, his worst fears would be realized: the Hebrews would not only gain ascendancy over Egypt through the plagues but also escape from the land. (*NIDOTTE*, 3:402-04; *TLOT*, 2:883-96; *TWAT*, 6:84-105; *TWOT*, 2:666-67) [*'lh*]

1:17 They feared God (*wattîre'nā*). The verb *yr'* has a three-fold range of meanings: (1) "to fear, be afraid," (2) "to revere, be in awe," and (3) "to honor" (*BDB*, 431; *HALOT*, 2:432). When the fear of the LORD refers to the foundation of worship, it means to stand in awe of God (Lev. 19:14; 25:17; Ps. 33:8; Eccl. 3:14; 8:12-13). Here it refers to the foundation of moral ethics (Prov. 1:7; 9:10). Knowing that God punishes sin, the one who fears God avoids what offends him (Exod. 20:20; Job 28:28; Prov. 3:7; 8:13; 16:6; Eccl. 12:13) and does what pleases him (Deut. 5:29; 6:2; 8:6; 10:12, 20; 13:4; 1 Sam. 12:14, 24; 2 Chron. 6:31; 19:7; Pss. 112:1; 128:1; Eccl. 12:13). Their fear of God (cause) motivated them to protect the Hebrew male babies (effect). Their fear of God was greater than their dread of any reprisal from Pharaoh (cf. Acts 4:19). (*NIDOTTE*, 2:527-33; *TDOT*, 6:290-315; *TLOT*, 2:586-78; *TWOT*, 1:339-401) [*yr'*]

He gave them houses (*bātîm*). The term *bayit* "house" is figurative (synecdoche of container for what it contains), referring not to a physical dwelling but to the family that dwells within it (Gen. 12:1, 17; Exod. 1:21; Deut. 25:9) (*HALOT*, 1:125.4; *BDB*, 109.5; *NIDOTTE*, 1:656.5). For example, Joshua and his "house" (= family) would serve the LORD (Josh. 22:15). Elsewhere the term "house" is associated with the clan (Num. 4:18; Josh. 7:14-18; Judg. 20:12; 2 Sam. 3:6). Because the midwives protected the patriarchal family ("the *house* of Joseph," 1:1), God rewarded them by giving them families ("houses") of their own—a nice display of poetic justice. Just as God's punishment fits the crime, his rewards are *apropos*. (*NIDOTTE*, 1:655-57; *TDOT*, 2:107-16; *TLOT*, 2:232-36; *TWOT*, 1:105-07) [*bayit*]

2:10 Son (*bēn*). The term *bēn* here refers to an adopted child (Ruth 4:17; Es. 2:7, 15; Ps. 2:7) (*HALOT*, 1:137.1; 1:672). During the New Kingdom, the princes of subject kings of western Asia were brought into Egypt to be trained to later serve as Egyptian vassals in their homelands (Hoffmeier, *Israel in Egypt*, 140-43). The picture of Moses being taken to the court by a princess where he was reared and educated is consistent with this royal edu-cational institution. Before becoming Israel's deliverer, Moses was a foster son of the princess or a child of this institution sponsored by the daughter of Pharaoh. (*NIDOTTE*, 1:671-77; *TDOT*, 2:145-65; *TLOT*, 1:238-45; *TWOT*, 1:113-16) [*bēn*]

She named him Moses (*mōšeh*) **for she said, "Out of the water I drew him"** (*mešîtihû*). Because it was the Egyptian princess, not his Hebrew mother, who named him, the name *mōšeh* is probably from the Egyptian noun *msi* "child, son" (*BDB*, 602; *HALOT*, 2:642-43; *TLOT*, 1:242.4) (Hoffmeier, *Israel in Egypt*, 140-42). However, in an ironic twist the narra-tor relates *mōšeh* instead to the similar sounding Hebrew verb *māšâ* "to draw out [of water]" (2 Sam. 22:17; Ps. 18:16) (*BDB*, 602; *HALOT*, 2:642). The narrator associ-ates his name with his deliverance from the waters of the Nile which foreshad-owed his role as Israel's deliverer through the waters at the Reed (Red) Sea. Through this wordplay the narrator emphasizes that the sovereign hand of God was on Moses from his infancy to his future role as Israel's deliverer. (*NIDOTTE*, 2:1120-21; *TDOT*, 7:28-43; *TWOT*, 1:529-30) [*mšh*]

2:23 The Israelites wailed (*wayyē'ānehû*). The verb *'ānah* has a two-fold range of meanings: (1) "to sigh" as an inaudible expression of emotional grief (Prov. 29:2; Isa. 24:7; Lam. 1:4, 8; Ezek. 9:4; 21:11, 12); and (2) "to groan, wail" as an audible expression of physical distress (Exod. 2:23; Lam. 1:11) (*BDB*, 58.1, 2; *HALOT*, 1:70-71). The related noun *'ānahah* "sigh, groan, wail" refers to crying out in physi-cal pain or emotional despair (Job 3:24; 23:2; Pss. 6:6[7]; 31:10[11]; 102:5[6]; Isa. 21:2; 35:10; 51:11; Jer. 45:3; Lam. 1:22) (*BDB*, 58; *HALOT*, 1:71). It is an intense lament uttered in response to emotional distress and physical pain (*NIDOTTE*,

1:455). Because '*ānaḥ* appears with *na'aqâ* "moaning, groaning" (v. 24), the nuance "sighed" (KJV, ASV, NASB) is too weak, while "complained" (CEV) misses the point; "groaned" is better (NKJV, NAB, RSV, NRSV, NIV, TEV). God heard their "groaning" and responded in deliverance (vv. 24-25). The omniscient God hears the groans of his people and treats them as petitions: "Lord, all my desire is known to you; my sighing (*we'ānḥātī*) is not hidden from you" (Ps. 38:9). Likewise, Paul said, "We do not know how to pray as we should, but the Spirit himself intercedes for us alongside our groanings that are too deep for words" (Rom. 8:26). (*NIDOTTE*, 1:455-56; *TWOT*, 1:57) ['*nḥ*]

Their cry for help rose up to God (*watta'al*). The verb '*ālâ* "to rise up" personifies their prayers ascending heavenward (1 Sam. 5:12; Jer. 14:2) (*BDB*, 749.8; *HALOT*, 2:828.1). Just as incense ascends upward in the temple, the prayers of God's people "ascend" to God (Ps. 141:2). This personification of prayer creates a dramatic anthropomorphic picture of God: their prayers arose heavenward and came into his presence, grabbing his attention, so to speak (Gen. 6:13; 2 Kings 19:28; Ps. 74:23; Isa. 37:29; 65:6; Jer. 2:22; Lam. 1:22; Jonah 1:2). The point is that their cries for help came to God's attention (He heard their cries) and captured his full attention. (He took special note of their plight.) (*NIDOTTE*, 3:402-04; *TLOT*, 2:883-96; *TWAT*, 6:84-105; *TWOT*, 2:666). ['*lh*]

God remembered his covenant (*wayyizkōr*). When humans are the subject, *zākar* "to remember" (*BDB*, 269) often refers not simply to the mental process of recalling something forgotten but to the resultant action prompted by this (*BDB*, 269.I.1; *NIDOTTE*, 1:1102-03). When the omniscient God is the subject, it is anthropomorphic and functions in a cause/effect

sense for action taken by God (*TLOT*, 1:385.4). God "remembering" his people means that he blesses, shows kindness, grants requests, protects, delivers, and rewards (Gen. 8:1; 19:29; 30:22; Exod. 32:13; Num. 10:9; Deut. 9:27; Judg. 16:28; 1 Sam. 1:11, 19; Neh. 5:19; 13:14, 22, 31; Job 14:13; Pss. 8:5; 9:13; 25:7; 74:2; 88:6; 106:4; 115:12; Jer. 15:15; 31:20).

The expression "God *remembered* his covenant" casts him in the role of a covenant-keeping Suzerain about to come to the aid of his vassal. In ancient Near Eastern treaty texts, the ruler (suzerain) often promised to "remember" (*zkr*) [= fulfill] his oath to protect his servant (vassal) (*TLOT*, 1:384). When humans "remember" a covenant, the expression is figurative (cause for effect) for fulfilling covenant promises and obligations (Jer. 14:21; Amos 1:9). Likewise, God "remembering" his covenant is figurative (cause for effect) for fulfilling his covenant promises (Gen. 9:15, 16; Exod. 2:24; 6:5; Lev. 26:42, 45; 1 Chron. 16:15; Ezek. 16:60; Pss. 105:8; 106:45; 111:5; Jer. 14:21; cf. Neh. 1:8; Pss. 105:42; 119:49) (*NIDOTTE*, 1:1101). God had promised Abraham that he would rescue his descendants from slavery in Egypt (Gen. 15:13-16)—now hundreds of years later, God "remembered" this promise, that is, he was about to fulfill it (*NIDOTTE*, 1:1100-06; *TDOT*, 4:64-82; *TLOT*, 1:381-88; *TWOT*, 1:241-43). [*zkr*]

2:25 God took notice (*wayyēda'*). The verb *yāda'* "to know" here means "to take notice of [something], show regard for [someone]" (*BDB*, 394.2; *HALOT*, 2:390.1) (Pss. 1:6; 31:7[8]; 37:18; Hos. 13:5). It functions figuratively (metonymy of cause for effect) for responding to the needs of someone: "to take care of" [someone] (*HALOT*, 2:391.4) (Gen. 39:6; Job 9:21). When God sees his people in need, he responds (2 Sam. 7:20; Ps. 37:18; 144:3; Nah. 1:7) (*HALOT*, 2:391.7; *TLOT*, 2:515.IV.1). For example, "I cared (*yd'*) for you in the wilderness, in the land of drought" (Hos. 13:5, NASB). Here the sequence is God "seeing" and "taking notice" (= responding in care), as in, "You saw all my suffering, and You cared (*yd'*) for me" (Ps. 31:7[8], CEV). Some translations render Exod. 2:25 in a woodenly literal manner: "God knew" (KJV, NAB, RSV, NASB, NRSV, NJPS, NKJV); however, others bring out the cause/effect dimension more explicitly: "God was concerned about them" (NIV), "He was concerned for them" (TEV), "He felt deep concern for their welfare" (NLT) and "He felt sorry for them" (CEV). One ancient version captured the sense quite well: "He decided to save them" (Targum Onkelos). The omniscient God is neither impassible nor dispassionate; he responds in compassion to those whom he sees suffering unjustly. (*NIDOTTE*, 2:409-14; *TDOT*, 5:448-81; *TLOT*, 2:508-21; *TWOT*, 1:366-68) [*yd'*]

3:1 The <u>mountain</u> of God (*har*). This designation does not imply that Moses had a prior revelation at the site or that the mountain was well-known by others. It is an anachronistic designation of this previously unheralded and unnamed mountain now so named after God's revelation to Moses and later to all Israel (Exod. 4:27; 18:5; 24:13; Num. 10:33). The theme of the divine mountain as the locus of absolute holiness and divine revelation was widespread throughout the ancient world. Many ancient Near Eastern mythological texts depict the gods of Egypt, Canaan, and Mesopotamia as dwelling on the cosmic mountain from which they would reveal themselves. The ideology of the divine mountain is also a frequent theme

in Scripture. The first land that appeared from the waters at creation was pictured as a primordial mountain (Gen. 1:9-10), and Mount Zion is portrayed as the "navel" of the earth. In the ancient Near East, the universe was conceived in spatial terms in which the mountains formed a natural meeting point between heaven and earth. So in the ancient Near East, the gods were frequently associated with dwelling on the mountains. For example, the Canaanite gods El and Baal were thought to live on individual mountains where their thrones were located and from whence they theophanized (e.g., Baal's home was reputed to be Mount Zaphon). Even Mot, the god of death, was thought to inhabit a subterranean mountain. As Selman notes, while the OT frequently associates Yahweh with mountains, it diverges from ancient Near Eastern mythological conceptions of the sacred mountain in several ways: (1) Yahweh's mountain theophanies are related to real historical events—what the other gods only did in mythology, Yahweh actually did in history, revealing himself on this "mountain of God" in real space-time-history. He is no mere god of mythology but the only true living God of history. (2) Yahweh was not confined to one mountain, but revealed himself at a variety of mountains: Moriah (Gen. 22:2; 2 Chron. 3:1), Sinai (Exod. 3:1; 19:2-3), Ebal and Gerizim (Deut. 27:4, 12; Josh. 8:30-33), Tabor (Judg. 4:4; 5:5), Carmel (1 Kings 18:19-39; 2 Kings 4:25-27), Horeb (19:10-19), Perazim (2 Sam. 5:20; Isa. 28:21), and Mount Zion in Jerusalem (e.g., Ps. 68:16; Isa. 2:1-4; 4:5; Mic. 4:1-4). (3) Yahweh was not limited to the mountains, as were mythological pagan "mountain gods" (1 Kings 20:23, 28), but could reveal himself wherever he chose (M. Selman, *NIDOTTE*, 1:1052-53). So God's theophany at a mountain both fit within ancient Near Eastern expectations, but also radically exceeded them, dramatically showing that Yahweh is the true living God, far superior to all rivals! (*NIDOTTE*, 1:1051-55; *TDOT*, 3:427-47; *TLOT*, 2:1072-73; *TWOT*, 1:224-25) [*har*]

3:2 **Angel** of the LORD (*mal'ak 'adōnāy*). The term *mal'ak* "messenger" is derived from the verb *lā'ak* "to send [a messenger]," and refers to a representative sent on a mission (*BDB*, 521; *HALOT*, 2:585). The term may refer to (1) human messengers of a human king (1 Sam. 23:27; 2 Sam. 11:19; Neh. 6:3; Ezek. 23:40) or (2) various messengers of God: (a) prophets (2 Chron. 36:15; Isa. 44:26; Hag. 1:13); (b) priests (Eccl. 5:5; Mal. 2:7); (c) the wind as the vehicle of God's cosmic "message" (Ps. 104:4); and (d) angels as the heavenly mouthpiece of God (Exod. 33:2; Num. 20:16; 2 Sam. 24:16; etc.) (*HALOT*, 2:585). The traditional English "angel" is simply a transliteration of the Greek translation *angellos* "messenger." In the ancient Near East the messenger of a king was commissioned to deliver a royal message, speaking as the mouthpiece of the king—often in the first person. Likewise, the angelic representative of the LORD delivers an oracle from God in the first person. He is the heavenly representative of Yahweh and the vehicle of revelation of God. There is often a fluid interchange between the "the angel of Yahweh" and God himself (Gen. 16:13; 21:17-19; 22:12, 16-18; 48:16; Exod. 23:20-23; Judg. 6:14, 16; 13:20-21; Mal. 3:1). For example, Jacob equates "the God who has shepherded me" with "the angel who has protected me" (Gen. 48:16). While the angel of the LORD spoke to Hagar (Gen. 16:11), she proclaimed that the LORD spoke to her (Gen. 16:13). Similarly, the narrator says

that the angel of the LORD appeared to Moses (Exod. 3:2), while Moses understood this as the LORD himself (Exod. 4:1, 5). This does not mean that Moses viewed God as a mere angel, but it does suggest that he was aware of an angelic presence sent by God to represent him. Here the narrator so closely associates the two that they become virtually indistinguishable. Isaiah refers to "the angel of his face" (Isa. 63:9) who may be identical to the divine "presence" (literally "face") referred to in Exod. 33:14-15 and Deut. 4:37. Although the angel of the LORD is in some way identified with but distinct from God, this is neither a clear revelation of the Trinity nor an explicit preincarnate appearance of Christ. Indeed, the NT affirms that the Son of God is far superior to any angel and that it is unfitting to put him in the same class as angels (Heb. 1:4-14). The angel of the LORD is probably a member of the heavenly counsel, specially commissioned by God to function as the vehicle of divine revelation. And it is not even clear from Scripture whether or not the title "the angel of the LORD" always refers to the same heavenly being in each and every usage. (*NIDOTTE*, 2:941-43; *TDOT*, 8:308-25; *TLOT*, 2:666-72; *TWOT*, 1:464-65) [*mal'ak*]

Appeared (*wayyērā'*). When used with human subjects, the middle (Niphal) sense of *r'h* "to see" means "appear, show oneself [to someone]" (*BDB*, 908) (Gen. 46:29; Exod. 23:17; 34:20, 23, 24; Lev. 13:7; Deut. 16:16; 31:11; 1 Sam. 1:22; 1 Kings 18:1, 2; Pss. 42:2; 84:7; Isa. 1:12). When God or the angel of Yahweh is the subject of this form (Niphal) (Exod. 3:2; Judg. 6:12; 13:3, 21), the verb means "to appear, become visible" (*BDB*, 908.1a) or perhaps better, "let himself be seen" (*HALOT*, 3:1160.3). So this term emphasizes the sovereign choice of God in determining when he allowed himself to be seen and to whom he revealed himself. (*NIDOTTE*, 3:1007-15; *TLOT*, 3:1176-83; *TWAT*, 7:225-66; *TWOT*, 2:823-25) [*r'h*]

As a flame of fire (*belabbat*). The preposition *be* is traditionally taken in a locative sense: "*in* a flame" (KJV, NKJV, NAB, ASV, NASB, RSV, NRSV, NIV) but it may function as *beth essentiae* (*BDB*, 88.7; *GKC* §119.i): "*as* a flame" (NLT, TEV, NET note). Theophanic fire is a recurring symbol of divine theophanies (Exod. 19:18; Ps. 18:8 [9], 12-13[13-14]). This is why the bush was ablaze and not consumed. Attempts to explain the source of the first as volcanic gases or St. Elmo's fire miss the point. [*be*]

3:5 Holy ground (*'admat qōdeš*). The root *qdš* "holy" primarily describes the status of something with a numinous quality, and secondarily what is set apart, unique, distinct, consecrated or marked by ethical purity (*BDB*, 871; *HALOT*, 3:1072). What made this mountain holy was the presence of the Holy One in its midst. It was not inherently nor permanently holy; it became sacred space only when Yahweh theophanized to Moses and remained holy ground only as long as his presence remained there. Moses was forbidden from drawing near because sacred space is set apart from the profane to protect it from desecration lest divine judgment break out for violating its sanctity. Hence the demand that Moses remove his sandals was a sign of humility and reverence (identifying Moses with the dust and dirt) or a sign of consecration to avoid bringing the dust and dirt of the profane earth into the presence of the Holy One. (*NIDOTTE*, 3:877-87; *TLOT*, 3:1103-18; *TWAT*, 6:1179-1204; *TWOT*, 2: 786-89) [*qdš*]

3:8 Land overflowing with milk and honey (*ḥālāb ūdebāš*). The Promised Land is described for the first of many times in this manner (Exod. 3:8, 17; 13:5; 33:3; Lev. 20:24; Num. 13:27; 14:8; 16:13-14; Deut. 6:3; 11:9; 26:9, 15; 27:3; 31:20; Josh. 5:6; Jer. 11:5; 32:22; Ezek. 20:6, 15; Sir. 46:8). The expression is hyperbolic, as if the land were streaming with milk and honey (cf. Amos 9:13). The description of Canaan as a "land flowing with milk and honey" matches the description of the land found in several ancient Near Eastern texts (*ANET3* 18–23, 237-38). The term *ḥālāb* "milk" refers to the milk of sheep and goats (Prov. 27:27), rarely from cows (Deut. 32:14) (*HALOT*, 1:315; *BDB*, 316.a.1), one of the main products of pastoralists in the ancient Near East. The abundance of milk was stereotypical of God's choicest blessings (Isa. 55:1; 60:16; Joel 3:18 [4:18]). The term *debāš* "honey" refers occasionally to the product of bees (Judg. 14:8,9, 18) but most often to the sweet syrup boiled down from honey grapes, dates, figs, and fruit of the carob tree (Deut. 8:8; 2 Kings 18:32; Ezek. 16:13) (*HALOT*, 1:212-13; *BDB*, 185; *NIDOTTE*, 1:916-7). Honey was a sought-after delicacy (Gen. 43:11; 2 Sam. 17:29; 1 Kings 14:3; Prov. 24:13; 25:16; Jer. 41:8; Ezek. 27:17), so an abundance of honey represented a fertile land. There are three major views about the meaning of the idiom "a land flowing with milk and honey": (1) the natural fertility and productiveness of the land of Canaan (*NIDOTTE*, 1:917); (2) a merism for the whole land of Canaan: milk from goats and sheep herded in the Negev (south), and honey from fruits cultivated in Galilee (north)—the entire land of Canaan offered fertile fields for husbandry and abundant lands for herding; or (3) two different modes of existence in ancient Israel: "honey" refers to the best product of the settled farmers, and "milk" designates the main product of pastoralists' herds; they allude to the interdependence and symbiosis between the two major ways of life in the land (*NIDOTTE*, 1:916-17; 2:135-37; *TDOT*, 4:386-91). [*ḥālāb*]

3:12 "I will be with you" (*'ehyeh 'immāk*). Although these two terms in and of themselves are routine words, this expression has profound theological significance (*NIDOTTE*, 1:1023-24; *TLOT*, 2:920.4). The construction *hāyâ* "to be" plus the preposition *'im* "with" denotes accompaniment, most often to protect, empower, bless, secure success, and bring victory over enemies (*BDB*, 227.III.4.d; *TLOT*, 2:920.4). In response to Moses' protest that he was not qualified to demand of Pharaoh the release of Israel—"Who am *I* (to do this)?"—God responded, as it were, "The question is not who *you* are, but who *I* am, and *I* will be *with* you!" It was not a question of Moses' fitness for the task but of who God is—he would be "with" him to empower and protect him. This formula of divine reassurance is an inducement to secure trust and covenant loyalty from humans (Gen. 26:3; 28:15; 31:3; 48:21; Josh. 1:5; 6:27; Judg. 1:19; 2:18; 1 Sam. 3:19; 18:12; 20:13; 1 Kings 1:37; 1 Chron. 11:13; 2 Chron. 17:3). Just as God promised to be "with" the patriarchs (Gen. 26:3; 28:15; 31:3; 48:21), he now promised the same to Moses, so there is continuity between the Abrahamic and Mosaic covenants. Note: The promise—*'ehyeh 'immāk*, "I will be with you"—is the basis for the subsequent wordplays on the divine name: *'ehyeh 'ašer 'ehyeh*, "I am [who] I-Am" (3:14a), *'ehyeh*, "I-Am" (3:14b) and *yahwēh*, "He-Is" (3:15). [*'im*]

3:14 "I-Am Who I-Am" (*'ehyeh 'ašer 'ehyeh*). This is one of the most perplexing yet fascinating sayings in Scripture, therefore it merits extensive discussion. The ancient versions translated it in four different ways: (1) "I am the One who is"

(*LXX*), (2) "I Am Who I Am" (Jerome), (3) "I am I-AM" (*Targum Onkelos, Targum Neofiti, Samaritan Targum, Syriac Peshitta*), and (4) "I will be who I will be" (Aquila, Theodotion). It has been interpreted in nearly a dozen different ways by contemporary scholars:

Eternality of God: "I am [the eternal] I AM." God declares he is eternal, above time and living in the eternal present-tense, experiencing no past or future. In alluding to Exod. 3:14, Jesus asserted his eternal pre-existence: "Before Abraham was born, I Am" (John 8:58). Evaluation: Exod. 3:12-16 does not deal with eternality or ontology but with God's promise to be "with" Moses and Israel.

Self-Existence of God: "I am the One who is." he asserts that he is the only true living God. Proponents point to the LXX: "the One who is." Evaluation: This is not the normal Hebrew idiom to assert absolute monotheistic existence, e.g., "I am he, and there is no other" (Isa. 41:4; 52:6).

Creator-Redeemer: "I create what I create." Some scholars revocalize the MT as causative (Hiphil) forms *'ahyeh 'ašer 'ahyeh*, "I create [= cause to be] what I create [= cause to be]." The God who created can surely redeem Israel. Evaluation: This view depends entirely on questionable revocalization. The verb *hyh* "to be" occurs over 3,500x in the OT but never in the causative stem (Hiphil). And vv. 12-15 focus on Yahweh's role as Redeemer, not Creator.

New Revelation of God's Character: "I am who I will be," "I will be who I am," or

"I will be who I will be." Although he had revealed himself as El Shaddai in the past, he would now act as Yahweh and fulfill his redemptive promises to Israel. Evaluation: This does not take *'ehyeh* as a divine name, which vv. 14b-15 seem to demand ("This is My name"). It assumes that the name Yahweh had been revealed to the patriarchs but that God acted only as El Shaddai up to now (see 6:3).

Assurance of Divine Presence: "I am the One who will be [with you]" or "I am the One Who Is At Hand." This reiterates the promise "I will be with you" (v. 12). It may be compared to the Amorite divine name *'ehwi-malik* "the King is at hand." The divine names *'Ehyeh* (v. 14) and *Yahwēh* (v. 15) play on the promise of v. 12. Evaluation: Why did he not call himself, "I will be the one who will be *with you ('immāk)*" to make the connection with the promise more explicit? While the repetition of *'ehyeh* creates a wordplay between vv. 12 and 14, this does not seem to fully explain the meaning of *'Ehyeh* in v. 14 nor *Yahwēh* in v. 15.

Incomprehensibility of God and His Name: "I am who I am." This reflects the ineffable NAME and mystery of *deus absconditus* (the hidden God). The divine name is incomprehensible because the infinite transcendent God is beyond the limits of any self-identifying name (Judg. 13:18). Evaluation: God does in fact declare that Yahweh ("He-Is") is the name by which he is to be known (v. 15).

Evasive Obfuscation: "I am who I am." This is not the revelation of the Divine Name but a refusal to reveal it. In the

ancient Near East knowledge of the name gave the worshiper the ability to manipulate the deity, similar to the name Rumpelstiltskin in the fairy tale. Evaluation: There is no contextual evidence that Moses was seeking to control or manipulate God. God does in fact reveal his name as Yahweh: "This is My name" (v. 15). It is difficult to believe that the 6800+ uses of Yahweh in OT are only testimony to God's refusal to reveal his name. This view is at odds with the fact that God regularly reveals a name when appearing to Israel's ancestors (Gen. 15:7; 35:11)—including the name Yahweh that he revealed when he appeared to Moses (Exod. 3:6).

Debate Terminating Device: "I am who I am." This is an example of an *idem per idem* formula, in which two identical verbs are connected by a relative pronoun to create a redundantly indefinite expression when the speaker does not desire to be more explicit, e.g., "I will have mercy on whom I will have mercy" (Exod. 33:19) (cf. Gen. 43:14; Exod. 16:23; 1 Sam. 23:13; 2 Sam. 15:20; 2 Kings 8:1; Esth. 4:16; Ezek. 12:25). The main function of *idem per idem* is to end a debate by eliminating opportunity for response. This is a terse rebuff of Moses' latest objection. In response to his first objection, "Who am I?" God said, in effect, "It is not a matter of who *you* are but who *I* am!" Then Moses objected, "Then who are *you*? What is your *name*?" To which, in effect, Deity retorted, "It does not matter *what* My *name* is: I *am* who I *am!*" Evaluation: The construction *'ehyeh 'ašer 'ehyeh* fits the *idem per idem* form. But it is questionable whether its function fits this formula, for God announces that

Yahweh is his eternal memorial-name (v. 15). Would a debate terminating device function as the name by which God is known for all generations?

Ehyeh is Popular Etymology of Yahweh: "I am *Ehyeh* [= I-Am]." The second *'Ehyeh* puns on the preceding promise *'ehyeh 'immāk* "I will be with you" (v. 12) and subsequent name *Yahwēh* "He-Is" (v. 14). This popular etymology does not provide a linguistic explanation of the meaning of the divine name *Yahwēh* but merely sounds like it, creating a link with the promise in v. 12. So Yahweh is the God who will be with Moses and the Israelites. Evaluation: This view fits the context of vv. 12-15. It assumes that Yahweh alone is the name of God; however, the reverse seems to be the case: God refers to himself as *Ehyeh*, "I-Am," but man must naturally refer to him as *Yahweh*, "He-Is."

The Second Ehyeh is the Divine Name: "I am *Ehyeh* [I-Am]." Two names are revealed in vv. 14-15: "Tell them, *Ehyeh* [I-Am] has sent me to you'" and "Tell them *'Yahweh* [He-Is] has sent me to you.'" God refers to himself by the first person name, *Ehyeh*, "I-Am," but Moses and all others must naturally refer to him by the third person name, *Yahweh*, "He-Is." On the one hand, *Ehyeh*, "I-Am," puns on the promise *'ehyeh 'immāk* "I will be with you" (v. 12). On the other hand, *Ehyeh* and *Yahweh* function as personal pronouns—"I-Am" and "He-Is"—which substitute for a more descriptive name, maintaining the ineffable incomprehensibility of the essence of God. Since he cannot be adequately defined by any limiting name, he is known simply

as "He-Is." Evaluation: This fits the context of vv. 12-15. It explains the shift from 1cs *'Ehyeh*, "I-Am," to third-person masculine *Yahweh*, "He-Is." God refers to himself elsewhere in the OT by the name *'Ehyeh* (Hos. 1:9). The divine name *'Ehyeh* appears in the common Nabatean name *bdẕhyw*, "servant of *Ehyeh*," which is the name of a worshiper of *'Ehyeh* (= Yahweh?).

The First Ehyeh is the Divine Name: A variation of the preceding view, the first *'ehyeh* is the divine name and *'ašer 'ehyeh* explains its meaning: "*Ehyeh* [I-Am] because I am." In response to Moses' question, "What is your name?" God answers, "Ehyeh! Because I am!" The structure is typical of etiological statements: name + explanation introduced by *'ašer* "because." For example, "It was called *'Mizpah* [= *Watchtower*]'* because (*'ašer*) he said, 'May the LORD *keep watch* between you and me'" (Gen. 31:49) (cf. Gen. 22:14). So our expression may be paraphrased: "My name is I-Am (*'ehyeh*) because that is who I am (*'ašer 'ehyeh*)." The second *'ehyeh* is an allusion to *'ehyeh 'immāk*, "I will be with you" (Exod. 3:12). God promised to be with the Hebrews just as he promised to be with Moses. Evaluation: This view enjoys the same basic support as the preceding view.

3:15 YHWH = Yahweh = LORD (*yhwh*). The declaration, "I am Yahweh," is the most frequent self-predication in the OT. The pronunciation and meaning of the NAME (traditionally translated "LORD") is a fascinating as well as complicated topic so the discussion that follows is more technical than normal.

During the Second Temple Period, orthodox Judaism viewed the NAME as unspeakably holy, so it ceased to be pronounced in public reading of Scripture. When vowel signs were added to biblical Hebrew manuscripts in the Middle Ages, Jewish scribes devised a technique to prevent the pronunciation of the NAME by those reading Scripture. They replaced the original vowels for *yhwh* with those of *'ădōnāy*, "my Lord," which was pronounced in its place. In the compound name *'ădōnāy yhwh*, its vowels were placed with those of *'elōhîm*, "God," which was pronounced in its place. As a result, the original pronunciation of *yhwh* (the so-called Tetragrammaton) was eventually lost.

The popular pronunciation "Jehovah" is a conflation of the consonants *yhwh* and vowels of the surrogate *'ădōnāy*. This pronunciation is traced to Petrus Galatinus, confessor to Pope Leo X, who in A.D. 1518 transliterated the consonants *yhwh* with the Latin letters *yhvh* along with the vowels of *'ădōnāy*, producing the hybrid "Jehovah." Although this form was contested by scholars as an ungrammatical aberration (Le Mercier, Drusius, Capellus), "Jehovah" eventually passed from Latin into English and other European languages and has been hallowed in hymns and several translations (KJV, ASV).

Scholars generally agree that the original pronunciation of the NAME was probably *yahwē(h)* = Yahweh. Four lines of evidence suggest this. (1) The consonants are firmly established as *yhwh*. (2) The evidence suggests that the first vowel was *ā* thus *yāhwh*. This is seen in *yāh*, "Yah," the short form of the NAME (BDB, 219) which appears 44x in poetic texts: *yāh* appears 27x in the formulaic *halelû-yāh*, "Praise the LORD!" (e.g., Ps. 106:1) and 17x in other poetic texts (Exod. 15:2; 17:2; Pss. 68:18[19]; 77:11[12]; 89:8[9]; 94:7, 12;

115:18; 118:5, 17, 18, 19; 122:4; 130:3; 135:4; Isa. 12:2; 26:4). The short NAME *yāh* occurs in many Hebrew personal names: (a) at the end of names the form is *-yāhû* (e.g., *'uzziyāhû* Uzziah, *'eliyāhû* Elijah) or *-yāh* (e.g., *'obadyāh* Obadiah, *gedalyāh* Gedaliah); and (b) at the beginning of names it is *yehô-* which is the reduced form of *yāhô* (e.g., *yehônatan* Jonathan, *yehôakin* Jehoakin) or the contracted form *yô-* (e.g., *yônatan* Jonathan, *yôyakin* Jehoakin). (3) If *yhwh* is from the root *hwh*, "to be" (see below), Hebrew phonology suggests that the final vowel is *ē*; hence, *yhwh* would be pronounced *yahwē(h)* (TDOT, 5:512). However, it is spelled *yhw* in Aramaic letters from Elephantine (ca. 400 B.C.) which suggests the alternate vocalization *yāhû* (TDOT, 5:505). (4) The pronunciation *yahwē(h)* is reflected in the transliteration of the NAME in Greek inscriptions of the third and fourth centuries A.D., as *Iabe* and *Iabai*, and also *Iaoue* and *Iaouai*, while *Iao* reflects the alternate pronunciation *yāhû*.

Scholars generally agree that *yhwh* is from the root *hwh* (later spelled *hyh*) "to be, to come to pass, to be at hand" (BDB, 217-19). (Note: The fact that *yhwh* in vv. 15-16 reflects the early form *hwh* rather than the later *hyh* attests to the antiquity of the NAME, and lends support for the antiquity of the Mosaic narratives). The repetition of *hwh ' hyh* "to be" in Exod. 3:12-16 suggests that the names *Yahwēh* "He-Is" (v. 15-16) and *'Ehyeh* "I-Am" (v. 14) are indeed related to this root.

The form *yhwh* features the consonant *y-* prefixed to the root *hwh*, suggesting that it is a third person form of the prefixed conjugation. The prefixed conjugation can denote present and future actions hence *yhwh* is often nuanced "He-Is" (present) or "He-Will-Be" (future). However, West Semitic languages can form divine names by prefixing *y-* to the root. For example, the Ugaritic divine name *ygrš*, "Smiter = He-Who-Smites," is from the root *grš*, "to smite." If *yhwh* follows this pattern, it carries a gnomic characteristic meaning from *hwh* "to be, to be at hand," meaning "He-Is" or "He-Is-At-Hand," rather than a future nuance "He-Will-Be."

The third person form, *Yahwēh*, "He-Is" (v. 15) not only plays on the first person form *'Ehyeh*, "I-Am" (v. 14) but also corresponds in basic meaning as the following parallelism indicates: "Thus you shall say to the Israelites, "*Ehyeh* [I-Am] has sent me to you'" (v. 14) and "Thus you shall say to the Israelites, *'Yahweh* [He-Is] has sent me to you'" (v. 15). So God refers to himself in first person as *'Ehyeh*, "I-Am," but others must refer to him in third person as *Yahwēh*, "He Is." (*NIDOTTE*, 4:1295-1300; *TDOT*, 5:500-21; *TLOT*, 2:522-26; *TWOT*, 1:210-212) [*yhwh*]

3:15 This is my memorial name (*zikrî*). Its frequent parallelism with *šēm* "name" suggests that the term *zeker* refers to the name of God (Pss. 6:5[6]; 30:4[5]; 97:12; 102:13; 135:13; 145:7; Isa. 26:8; Hos. 12:6). This noun is traditionally rendered "memorial-name" on the reasoning that it is related to the verb *zākar*, "to remember" (e.g., Exod. 2:24) (*BDB*, 269-71). However, the verb *zākar* sometimes means "to call upon, invoke, praise" (*NIDOTTE*, 1:1104), parallel to the Akkadian *zakārtu* "to utter, call upon, invoke, praise" and *zikru* "name, mention, utterance, fame" (*HALOT*, 1:271). So Hebrew *zeker* can refer to the reputation by which a person is remembered (Prov. 10:7; Eccl. 9:5), the fame by which he is praised (Hos. 14:8) or the name invoked in worship (Ps. 6:5[6]; 30:4[5]; 97:12) or called upon in prayer (Jonah 2:8) (*BDB*, 270-71). The Exodus

made the name Yahweh famous (Exod. 9:16; 10:1-2) and demonstrated that Yahweh delivers those who call upon him (Exod. 2:23-25; 3:7-9). Israel was not simply to remember the name Yahweh but to make it the object of their praise and proclamation and the name they invoked in time of trouble. (*NIDOTTE*, 1:1100-06; *TDOT*, 4:64-82; *TLOT*, 1:381-88; *TWOT*, 1:241-43) [*zeker*]

3:16 I have paid close attention (*pāqōd pāqadtî*). The basic meaning of *pāqad* is "to observe, take note of, pay close attention to" (*BDB*, 823; *HALOT*, 3:955-57; *NIDOTTE*, 3:658). It often appears with verbs of visual perception and mental cognition: *r'h* "to see" (Exod. 4:31; Ps. 80:14[15]), *byn* "to discern" (Job 7:18; Ps. 80:15) and *zkr* "to remember" (Pss. 8:4[5]; 106:4; Jer. 14:10; 15:15; Hos. 8:13; 9:9). It often functions figuratively (metonymy of cause for effect) to describe God's response to what he sees (*NIDOTTE*, 3:659.5). God takes note of those in need, then comes to their aid (Gen. 21:1; 1 Sam. 2:21). So *pqd* can also mean "to be concerned about, care for, help" (Gen. 50:24-25; Exod. 3:16; 4:31; Ruth 1:6; Zech. 10:3) (*BDB*, 823; *HALOT*, 3:955-57; *NIDOTTE*, 3:657). When God saw the plight of the Israelites, he was concerned for them, and intervened to deliver (Exod. 3:16-17; 4:31). Translations equivocate between the cause and effect nuances of *pqd*: "I have observed, watched over, seen" (KJV, NKJV, NIV, RSV, NRSV, NLT, TEV, CEV) and "I am concerned about you" (NAB, NASB). The expression *pāqōd pāqadtî* (infinitive absolute + finite verb of the same root) emphasizes the intensity ("I have paid *close* attention" or "I am *very* concerned") or certainty ("I have *surely* paid attention" or "I am *certainly* concerned") of God's concern for Israel. God does not exercise his omniscience in a dispassionate manner. Seeing the plight of his people causes him concern and moves him to intervene on their behalf. (*NIDOTTE*, 3:657-63; *TLOT*, 2:1018-31; *TWAT*, 6:708-23; *TWOT*, 2:731-32) [*pqd*]

3:17 I will bring you up out of the affliction of Egypt (*'a'ălê*). Scripture repeatedly states that Yahweh rescued Israel from slavery by "bringing" them "up" from Egypt (Exod. 17:3; 32:1; Lev. 11:45; Deut. 20:1; Josh. 24:17; Judg. 6:13; Jer. 16:14=23:7) (*BDB*, 749.1.a; *HALOT*, 2:830.2). God's later deliverance of Israel from exile is depicted similarly: "The LORD *brought up* the Israelites from the land of the north and from all the countries where he had banished them" (Jer. 16:15=23:8). The causative (Hiphil) of *'lh* "to go up" followed by preposition *min*, means "to bring up [persons] from [a place]" (*BDB*, 749; *HALOT*, 2:829-30). It often refers to God rescuing individuals from affliction or a life-threatening situation which is figuratively depicted as some kind of lower region, often associated with chaos or the netherworld in the ancient Near East. For example, Hebrew poets often describe God's deliverance of individuals from life-threatening situations by picturing him raising them up and out of a cistern-prison (Ps. 40:3), the bowels of Sheol (Ps. 30:4), the pit (Jonah 2:7) or the grave (Ezek. 37:12) (*BDB*, 749.1.b). So the use of this term casts Yahweh in the role of the Deliverer, rescuing his people from the life-threatening locale of Egypt, which is pictured hyperbolically as the place of death, the very personification of Sheol or the grave (*NIDOTTE*, 3:402-04; *TLOT*, 2:883-96; *TWAT*, 6:84-105; *TWOT*, 2:666-70) [*'lh*]

3:20 I will stretch out my hand . . . then he will release you (*wešālahtî . . . yešallah*). The verb *šlh* "send forth" is repeated in v. 20 in two different meanings, creating a dramatic wordplay. In v. 20a *šlh* means "to stretch out" one's hand to hit someone (Gen. 37:22; 1 Sam. 22:17; 24:7; 26:9; 2 Sam. 1:14) (*BDB*, 1018.3b; *HALOT*, 4:1513.1c). This bold anthropomorphism pictures God as a mighty warrior engaged in hand-to-hand battle with his enemy (Exod. 9:15). Ironically, Pharaoh is often depicted in Egyptian art as stretching out his powerful hand to strike his victims— here the Divine Warrior is about to stretch out his hand to strike Pharaoh! However, in v. 20b, *šlh* means "to send away, let go, set free" (Exod. 4:21, 23; 5:1, 2) (*BDB*, 1019.3). So this wordplay pictures the correlation between divine intervention and human response: God will "stretch out" (*šlh*) his hand against the Egyptians (v. 20a), causing them to "release" (*šlh*) the Hebrews (v. 20b). (*NIDOTTE*, 4:119-23; *TLOT*, 3:1330-34; *TWAT*, 8:46-70; *TWOT*, 2:927-28) [*šlh*]

I will smite the Egyptians (*wehikkētî*). The use of this term casts God in the role of a mighty warrior. The intensive (Hiphil) stem of *nkh* "to smite, strike" (*BDB*, 645-46; *HALOT*, 2:697-98; *NIDOTTE*, 3:102-04) often refers to hitting someone with a fist (Exod. 21:11, 13, 15). Here the Divine Warrior is portrayed anthropomorphically hitting corporate Egypt: "I will stretch out my hand and strike the Egyptians." While human assailants strike with fists or weapons, the Divine Warrior "smites" (*nkh*) his enemies with agricultural infertility (Deut. 28:22; Amos 4:9; Hag. 2:17), blindness (Gen. 19:11; Deut. 28:28; 2 Kings 6:18), incurable disease (Deut. 28:22, 27, 35; 1 Sam. 5:9), epidemics (Num. 11:33; 14:12; 2 Sam. 24:15-17), and the miraculous plagues on

Egypt (Exod. 3:20; 7:25; 9:15; 12:12, 13, 29; 1 Sam. 4:8) (*BDB*, 646.4; *HALOT*, 2:698.3). This term can refer to physical assault (1 Sam. 17:49; 2 Sam. 10:18; 1 Kings 22:34; 2 Kings 3:25; 9:24, 27), murder (Gen. 4:15; 37:21; Exod. 2:12; Lev. 24:18; Deut. 19:6; 27:24; 1 Sam. 17:36; 2 Sam. 2:23), or military destruction (Josh. 11:10; 1 Kings 22:34; 2 Kings 9:24), so it often refers to God destroying his enemies (Amos 3:15; 6:11; Zech. 9:4). This verb frequently refers to corporeal punishment (Deut. 25:2; 2 Sam. 24:17; Prov. 17:10; 19:25; 23:13-14) and may refer to chastisement or judgment (Lev. 26:24; 1 Kings 14:15; 1 Chron. 21:7; Isa. 5:25; 9:12; 27:7; 30:31; 57:17; 60:10; Jer. 2:30; 5:3; 14:9; Ezek. 32:15). God's plagues on Egypt are indeed viewed as mighty acts of judgment (Exod. 12:12). God's declaration that he would "strike" (*nkh*) Egypt is just retribution because the Egyptian taskmasters had brutally "struck" (*nkh*) the Hebrew slaves (Exod. 2:11). The punishment would fit the crime. (*NIDOTTE*, 3:102-05; *TDOT*, 9:415-23; *TWOT*, 2:577-79) [*nkh*]

My extraordinary deeds (*niple'ôtay*). The term *pl'* designates what is beyond the pale of the ordinary: the "unusual, extraordinary, miraculous" (*BDB*, 810; *HALOT*, 3:928). The plural *niple'ôt* always describes the mighty deeds of God intervening in history to miraculously deliver his people and judge their enemies (*BDB*, 810.4; *HALOT*, 3:928.3) (Exod. 15:11; 34:10; Josh. 3:5; Judg. 6:13; 1 Chron. 16:9, 24; Job 5:8; 9:10; Pss. 9:2; 26:7; 77:15; 78:12[11]; 88:11, 13; 89:6; Isa. 25:1; Jer. 21:2; Mic. 7:15; Sir 11:4; 43:25). Because divine interventions go beyond customary experience (Deut. 4:32-34) they evoke reactions of astonishment, fear, wonder, and praise from their beholders (*NIDOTTE*, 3:616) hence the passive (Niphal) form *niple'ôt*

literally means "what is feared, what is held in wonder." God's mighty act of delivering the Hebrews from Egypt was the supreme act of divine intervention in the OT, so it is no surprise that in the historical books *niple'ôt* always describes or recalls the Exodus events (Exod. 3:20; 34:10; Josh. 3:5; Judg. 6:13). These extraordinary deeds formed the basis of the faith, hope, and worship of subsequent generations (1 Chron. 16:9, 12, 24; Neh 9:17; Pss. 71:17; 78:4, 11, 32; 105:2, 5; 106:7, 22; 111:4; 145:5; Jer. 21:2; Mic. 7:15). Yahweh's ability to perform such marvels demonstrates that he alone is God (Ps. 86:10). His ultimate goal for his miraculous deeds in Egypt was to demonstrate unequivocally to the whole world that he alone is the only true living God (Exod. 6:7; 7:5; 9:16; 10:1-2; 11:9; 14:4, 17-18). (*NIDOTTE*, 3:615-17; *TWAT*, 6:569-83; *TLOT*, 2:981-86; *TWOT*, 2:723) [*niple'ôt*]

3:22 You will plunder the Egyptians (*weniṣṣaltem*). The use of this term pictures Israel as a victorious army, despoiling a conquered enemy. The intensive (Piel) meaning of *nṣl* has military connotations: "to plunder, take spoil, pick bare, strip off [possessions from a corpse]" (*BDB*, 664.1; *HALOT*, 2:717.1). This term often describes a conquering army looting the property of a defeated enemy to claim the spoils of war. Occasionally the term refers to bystanders who stumble on the aftermath of a battle that wiped out both warring parties, allowing the bystanders to loot the corpses of fallen warriors on both sides—without ever having to lift a finger in the actual battle. For example, Jehoshaphat's army plundered the spoil from the corpses of three armies which had killed each other off (2 Chron. 20:25). Likewise, the Hebrews would plunder the Egyptians without ever having to lift a hand against them! In an ironic reversal of the normal convention, the Egyptians would cooperate with this plunder of their valuables—offering their valuables to the Israelites as inducement to leave Egypt before Yahweh destroyed it! This prediction was fulfilled after the Divine Warrior "defeated" Pharaoh and the gods of Egypt in an act of holy war (Exod. 12:36). It is also ironic that *nṣl* was used in v. 8 of God "delivering" the Hebrews from Egypt, enabling the Hebrews to "plunder" (Hiphil of *nṣl*) the Egyptians (v. 22). The Hebrews merely had to trust in Yahweh and see his mighty deliverance—a sequence repeated at the Reed (Red) Sea: "Stand firm and you will see the deliverance the LORD will bring you today . . . The LORD will fight for you; you need only to be still!" (Exod. 14:13-14). (*NIDOTTE*, 3:141-47; *TDOT*, 9:533-40; *TLOT*, 2:760.3a; *TWOT*, 2:594) [*nṣl*]

4:3 The staff became a snake (*wayehî lenāḥāš*). Although this syntactical construction is mundane, the content of this expression is theologically profound. The construction *hyh* "to become" + preposition *lĕ* "into" may refer to one object becoming something else (*BDB*, 226.II.2e; *HALOT*, 1:244.7c). For example, when God breathed his breath into the clay, it "became a living being" (*wayehî lenepeš ḥayyâ*) (Gen. 2:7). Just as the Creator turned lifeless clay into a living being (Gen. 2:7), he now turned a wooden staff into a living snake (Exod. 4:3), then back into a wooden staff (v. 4). While some of the later plagues might have naturalistic explanations, there is no naturalistic explanation for this event. No other force in heaven or earth could have accomplished this. The same God who brought life out of this lifeless rod in the wilderness would centuries later bring life out of the dead at Calvary. [*hyh*]

4:5 So that they might believe (*lĕma'an ya'amînû*). Theological debates about the relationship of divine influence and human response in saving faith would do well to consider this statement. Expressions of purpose/result in Hebrew are not always readily distinguishable; the precise sense of most constructions must be determined from the context. However *lĕma'an* "in order that" is used almost exclusively to denote intended purpose but not actual result (*BDB*, 775.2). Out of its 270+ usages it almost always introduces an intended purpose clause and only rarely a result clause (Lev. 20:3; 2 Kings 22:17; Amos 2:7). In this construction the imperfect verb *ya'amînû* denotes a contingency: intended purpose not guaranteed result. So each of the scenarios being discussed had an intended purpose but not a guaranteed result. Because of human freedom there would be no guarantee that the Hebrews would believe the first miracle. It was in fact necessary for Moses to perform all the miracles not just the first to convince the people that Yahweh had appeared to him (vv. 29-31). God had previously announced that he would so work that Israel would eventually believe (Exod. 3:18) but it was not certain at this point—at the very least from the perspective of Moses—when and even if Israel would believe. [*lĕma'an*]

4:8-9 But if they do not believe (*wehāyâ 'im lō' ya'amînû*). This construction depicts a real condition, that is, a genuine contingent situation (the protasis is introduced by *'im lō'* "If . . . not" + imperfect functioning as a modal of possibility: "they might believe"). This construction is repeated twice in vv. 8-9. In preparing Moses to address the Israelites, the omniscient God presents three scenarios: (1) If the Israelites do not initially believe Moses, he should perform the first miracle: "that they may believe that Yahweh … has appeared to you" (vv. 4-5); (2) If they are not convinced, he should perform the second miracle: "If they do not believe (*wehāyâ 'im lō' ya' amīnû*) you or heed the first miraculous sign, they might believe the second" (v. 8); and (3) If they still do not believe, Moses should perform a third miracle: "But if they do not believe (*wehāyâ 'im lō' ya' amīnû*) even these two signs or heed what you say, then take some water from the Nile and pour it on the ground, and it will become blood on the ground" (v. 9). While God was certain that the Israelites would eventually believe (Exod. 3:18), here he raises the question of when they would believe—after the first, second or third miracle. Theologians have interpreted these conditional statements in three ways: (1) Determinists posit that God has foreordained every human act in history including the free decisions of man therefore God has absolute foreknowledge of all future events because all future events are certain. While the response of Israel was certain from God's viewpoint, it was not certain from the viewpoint of Moses. So God adopted the perspective of Moses to seemingly prepare him for every contingency in his mind, so as to encourage his faith and embolden him for the task. (2) Molinists, named after L. Molina, a sixteenth century Pelagian, suggest that the relation between divine sovereignty and human freedom means that God does not have absolute foreknowledge but middle knowledge. God allows for free will but also knows every possible scenario of what might happen. God knew that the

Israelites would eventually believe and that any one of the three scenarios was possible, but only these three scenarios were possible. (3) Open theists suggest that Israel's response had not been foreordained by God because God created man with genuine libertarian freedom. Since the free will decision of Israel whether to believe or not had not been foreordained, it could not be foreknown which of the three signs would eventually convince them. So God prepared Moses for every contingency, except for the unthinkable—that they might not be convinced by any of the signs! Against this last option, however, is the fact that God does indeed state that he knew in advance that Israel would eventually believe (Exod. 3:18). ['im lō]

4:14 The anger of the LORD flared up ('*ap*). The term traditionally rendered "anger" is literally "nose" ('*ap*). Because anger is expressed physically through flared or blood-flushed nostrils, '*ap* "nose" often functions figuratively (metonymy of association) for anger (Gen. 27:45; 49:6, 7) (*BDB*, 60.3; *HALOT*, 1:76.3). The development of meaning from "nose" to the gesture of "snorting" in anger is self-evident (*TLOT*, 1:168). Divine anger is often depicted anthropomorphically as God's nose becoming red hot (Exod. 32:12; 2 Kings 24:20; Ps. 115:6) or his nostrils breathing out fire or smoke (Deut. 33:10; Job 41:10-13; Ps. 18:8, 15 = 2 Sam. 22:8, 15; Ezek. 8:17). This bold anthropomorphic imagery dramatically depicts the terrifying anger of God in much more emphatic terms than had the narrator simply stated, "Then the LORD became angry." (*NIDOTTE*, 1:462-65; *TDOT*, 1:351; *TLOT*, 1:166-69; *TWOT*, 1:58) ['*ap*]

The anger of the LORD flared up (*wayyiḥar*). This term portrays the anger of

God in a dramatic sense. The verb *ḥrh* "to burn, kindled" is used literally of fire and figuratively of anger (*BDB*, 354; *HALOT*, 1:351.1). Anger is often compared to fire because it can be "kindled" in an ingressive sense (Gen. 44:18; Job 19:11), "burn" in a progressive sense, and "consume" its objects in a terminative sense (Ps. 89:47; Isa. 7:4; Ezek. 21:31; Lam. 2:4). The verb *ḥrh* is used 32x of divine anger with the majority of uses in the Exodus and wilderness narratives of God's response to Israel's rebellion (Exod. 4:14; 22:23[24]; 32:10-11, 19, 22; Num. 11:1, 10, 33; 12:9; 22:22; 32:10; Deut. 6:15; 7:4; 11:17; 29:26; 31:17). When God's anger was "kindled," he *became* angry. Classical theologians such as Augustine and Aquinas argued that God is impassible: because he is independent in his being, he does not experience emotions in response to the actions of created beings. They interpreted expressions such as "the anger of the LORD was kindled" as anthropopathic imagery. However, many evangelical theologians now acknowledge that God not only has genuine emotions but experiences ingressive fluctuations in emotion as he responds appropriately to his creation. God genuinely *becomes* angry at human rebellion; his anger can be *aroused*. This does not diminish the immutability of God but it challenges theologians to refine what immutability means. Although God is ontologically and morally immutable, he is relationally mutable. (He *responds* to human moral acts in keeping with his morally immutable attributes.) Because God is morally immutable it is only natural that he *becomes* angry at rebellion. The wise submit to the LORD because his anger can "flare up in a moment" (Ps. 2:12). (*NIDOTTE*, 2:265-68; *TDOT*, 5:171; *TLOT*, 2:472-74; *TWOT*, 1:324-25) [*ḥrh*]

4:21 I will harden his heart (*'ăḥazzēq*). This is the first of eight references to God hardening Pharaoh's heart using the intensive (Piel) of *ḥzq* "to be firm, strong" (Exod. 4:21; 9:12; 10:20, 27; 11:10; 14:4, 8, 17). The basic (Qal) stem of *ḥzq* means "to be firm, strong" (*BDB*, 304; *HALOT*, 1:302). When it refers to volition—as in the expression "his heart was hard"—it describes positive resolve (2 Chron. 16:9; 31:4) or sinful obstinance (Exod. 7:13, 22; 8:19[15]; 9:35). The intensive (Piel) stem, which is used here, means "to strengthen," and when referring to volition it means "to make rigid, harden, make obstinate" (Josh. 11:20; Jer. 5:3) (*BDB*, 304.5; *HALOT*, 1:303.1.f). The adjective *ḥzq* refers to volitional obstinance: "hard heart" (Ezek. 2:4) and "hard face" (Ezek. 3:8). The basic (Qal) stem of *ḥzq* "to be resolute" (Hag. 2:4) is used 4x in Exodus, attributing hardness to Pharaoh's heart: he was unrelentingly obstinate in his refusal to release Israel even in the face of the plagues (Exod. 7:13, 22; 8:19; 9:35). The intensive (Piel) stem is used 8x of God hardening Pharaoh's heart: after Pharaoh's resolve was weakened by the plagues, God strengthened his resolve so that he was once again unwilling to release the slaves (Exod. 4:21; 9:12; 10:20, 27; 11:10; 14:4, 8, 17). (*NIDOTTE*, 2:63; *TDOT*, 4:301-08; *TWOT*, 1:276) [*ḥzq*]

His heart (*libbô*). While the English term "heart" is often associated with emotions, the Hebrew term *lēb* "heart" has a broad range of associations embracing intellect, emotion, and will (*BDB*, 523-26; *HALOT*, 2:513-15). Here it refers to the volition: the inclination, resolution and determination of the will (*BDB*, 525.4; *HALOT*, 2:514.4) (Exod. 25:2; 35:5, 22, 29; Judg. 5:15; 9:3; 2 Sam. 15:13; 1 Kings 11:3; 2 Chron. 12:14; Ezra 7:27; Neh. 2:12; 7:5; Job 11:13; Pss. 10:17; 57:8; 78:8, 37; 112:7;

119:112; Eccl. 1:13, 17; 7:21; 8:9, 16). According to ancient Egyptian religion, when one stood before the divine inquest after death, the Egyptian was advised to harden his heart before the gods to prevent his conscience from giving himself away as a sinner. In a dramatic reversal of the Egyptian protocol, Pharaoh's hard heart would spell his doom. And God would further harden his heart as an act of judgment, warranting further judgment on Egypt. (*NIDOTTE*, 2:749; *TDOT*, 7:399-437; *TLOT*, 2:638-42; *TWOT*, 1:466). [*lēb*]

4:22 My son (*běnî*). While father/son imagery often reflects a familial relationship (Deut. 8:5; Ps. 103:13), here it draws on covenant terminology. In ancient Near Eastern suzerain-vassal treaties the subordinate was identified as "son" to express the vassal's submission to his suzerain (2 Kings 8:9) (*HALOT*, 1:137.3; *BDB*, 120.1c). For example, Ahaz became the servant and "son" of the Assyrian Tiglath-pileser when he submitted to him (2 Kings 16:7). Because Israel would enter into a conditional suzerain-vassal form of covenant with Yahweh at Sinai, the term "son" might cast Israel in the role of the vassal (servant) of God. In addition, father/son imagery also occurs in unconditional royal grant covenants in which a ruler would reward a faithful servant with a grant of land, adopting him as his son as the legal basis for bestowing his inheritance. The Abrahamic and Davidic Covenants are modelled after unconditional ancient Near Eastern royal grant covenants, while the Mosaic Covenant follows the pattern of the conditional suzerain-vassal covenants. Israel's status as the "son" of Yahweh follows these two covenant models (Deut. 14:1; 32:5, 20; Pss. 80:16; 82:6; Isa. 1:2, 4; 30:1,9; Jer. 3:14, 22; 4:22; 31:20; Hos. 2:1; 11:1) (*TDOT*, 1:17-19;

2:155-57). However, since Israel is described as Yahweh's "son" before the inauguration of the Mosaic Covenant (Exod. 19–24), the imagery here probably reflects the unconditional royal grant covenant rather than the conditional suzerain-vassal covenant. Reflecting typical royal grant imagery, Exod. 3–4 highlights the twin themes of the gift of land (Exod. 3:8, 17) and Yahweh's adoption of Israel as "son," making him the legal heir of the land (Exod. 4:22). While royal grant sonship was originally transferred from one individual to another in the patriarchal period (from Abraham to Isaac to Jacob), it was now democratized to include the entire nation as the corporate covenant "son" of God. This provides the segue between the Abrahamic Covenant with the patriarchs and the Mosaic Covenant with the nation.

Israel was the "son" of God in a much different sense than Pharaoh who, according to Egyptian religion, was the seminally begotten "son" of Amon-Re, making Pharaoh god incarnate (*NIDOTTE*, 1:671). Yahweh's declaration that he would deliver his "son" was poignant. Pharaoh, the mythological son of Amon-Re, had oppressed Israel, the adopted son of Yahweh. And when Pharaoh would refuse to release Yahweh's son, Yahweh would retaliate against Pharaoh's son in the tenth plague—an ironic display of poetic justice for Pharaoh's oppression of Israel, God's son. (*NIDOTTE*, 1:671-77; *TDOT*, 2:145-59; *TLOT*, 1:238-45; *TWOT*, 1:113-16) [*bēn*]

My firstborn (*běkorî*). The term *běkorî* "My firstborn" is appositional to *běnî* "My son," further clarifying Israel's role as God's son: "My *firstborn* son." In Semitic society the firstborn son was generally given preferential status, and allotted two-thirds of the inheritance ("a double portion") (Deut. 21:15-17). However, the father was not bound by the law of primogeniture if the firstborn was unworthy of this privileged position; so he had the right to make all his heirs share alike or to elevate a chosen son to the position of "firstborn" (as reflected in Abraham's designation of Isaac, Isaac's designation of Jacob, and Jacob's designation of Joseph). Although all the nations were God's "sons," Israel was God's "firstborn" (Exod. 4:22; Jer. 31:9) and designated heir (Deut. 32:8-9)—even though Israel was not first in order nor greatest in number (Deut. 7:7-8) (NIDOTTE, 1:659). As God's chosen firstborn Israel enjoyed a privileged position among the nations: (1) a unique covenant relationship with God (Exod. 19:5-6; Deut. 4:32-34); (2) a double portion among the nations (Isa. 61:5-7); (3) future possession of the other nations as its inheritance (Amos 9:11-12); and (4) the destiny of becoming head of all nations (Deut. 32:18; Jer. 31:7). (NIDOTTE, 1:658-59; TDOT, 2:121-27; TWOT, 1:108-10; TDNT 6:872-76) [bākōr]

4:23 That they may _worship_ Me (weya'abdēnî). The verb 'bd has a three-fold range of meanings: "to serve, honor, worship" (BDB, 713.4; HALOT, 2:773.7-8). This verb usually has cultic connotations: (1) to worship God by performing service in the cult (Exod. 13:5; Num. 3:7; 4:23; 8:11, 25; 16:9; Josh. 22:27), (2) to serve Yahweh by sacrificing to him (Exod. 10:26; Isa. 19:21), and (3) to honor God through cultic ritual (Exod. 3:12; 4:23; Deut. 6:13; Judg. 2:7; 1 Sam. 7:3; 1 Chron. 28:9; Ps. 100:2; Jer. 2:20; Mal. 3:14, 18). Carpenter notes: "The verb refers to the performance of the cult in the sense of worship, honor, serve in a purely religious sense, in addition to caring for its physical upkeep and maintenance . . . The

verb is often used theologically with respect to the cult of Israel in its service and care for the tabernacle, temple, its appurtenances, and its personnel" (NIDOTTE, 3:305-6). The goal of the Exodus was the worship of Yahweh at Sinai, as the prefixed waw of purpose indicates, "_so that_ they may worship me." The appropriate response of deliverance is to worship, honor, and serve God (1 Chron. 28:9; Mal. 3:18). (NIDOTTE, 3:304-09; TLOT, 2:819-32; TWAT, 5:981-1012; TWOT, 2:639-41) ['bd]

4:31 They bowed down (wayyiqqedû). The verb qdd, "to bow down" (BDB, 869; HALOT, 3:1065), describes the physical gesture of prostrating oneself to the ground to express homage to an individual of higher social or political status, such as a king (Gen. 43:28; 1 Sam. 24:9; 28:14; 1 Kings 1:16, 31; 1 Chron. 29:20); and submissive worship of YHWH (Gen. 24:26, 48; Exod. 4:31; 12:27; 34:8; Num. 22:31; 2 Chron. 20:18; 29:30; Neh. 8:6). It is derived from the noun qodqōd, "crown of the head" (BDB, 869; HALOT, 3:1071) because it involved bowing one's head to the ground. It often occurs with 'arṣâ "[bowed down] to the ground" (Exod. 34:8; 1 Sam. 24:9; 28:14; 1 Kings 1:31; 28:14 1 Kings 1:31; 2 Chron. 20:18; Neh. 8:6), indicating that the worshiper would prostrate himself on the ground before God. Although external acts can become empty ritual, genuine worship expresses itself in heartfelt external demonstrations of obeisance. The Hebrew concept of worship centered not around emotional expressions as much as the volitional decision to submit oneself to God. (NIDOTTE, 3:868; TWAT, 6:1157-59; TWOT, 2:785) [qdd]

5:1 _Release_ my people (šallaḥ). The verb šlḥ refers to freeing slaves (Gen. 30:25;

Exod. 21:26; Deut. 15:12; Jer. 34:9, 11, 14, 16), prisoners (Zech. 9:11), and subjugated peoples (Ps. 44:2[3]; Isa. 58:6) (*BDB*, 1019-20.1; *HALOT*, 4:1515.2-3). This oft repeated demand (Exod. 3:20; 4:21, 23; 5:1; 6:1; 7:16, 26; 8:16; 9:1, 13; 10:3; 11:1) is best nuanced, "Free/Release my people!" (traditionally, "Let my people go!"). Moses was not merely seeking release time from their labor but the total abolition of Hebrew slavery to Egypt so that the people might become a new nation dedicated to the worship of God in the land of Canaan. (*NIDOTTE*, 4:119-23; *TWAT*, 8:46-70; *TLOT*, 3:1330-34; *TWOT*, 2:927-28) [*šlḥ*]

5:2 "I do not know Yahweh!" (*yāda'tî*). The verb *yāda'* "to know" is used as a technical term for a vassal's legal obligation to recognize and submit to his superior. For example, the Hittite king Suppiluliumas demanded that Huqqanas submit to him and him alone: "O Huqqanas, you must *know* only the Sun [= Suppiluliumas] regarding lordship . . . Any other you must not *know!*" In an Assyrian text, a vassal says to Ashurbanipal, "You are the king whom the gods *know*," that is, he is the king whom the gods recognize as legitimate ruler. Similarly, Israel was to recognize Yahweh as the sole legitimate God: "I am Yahweh your God from the land of Egypt, therefore gods other than me you shall not *know*" (Hos. 13:4). When Pharaoh retorted, "I do not know Yahweh that I should obey him and let Israel go," this was a blatant refusal to recognize him as God with sovereign authority over him. Ironically enough, Pharaoh's defiant response set the agenda for things to come. For the plagues were designed that Pharaoh and all Egypt might "know" that Yahweh alone is the true living God (Exod. 7:5, 17; 8:10, 22; 9:14, 29; 10:2; 11:7;

14:4, 18). (*NIDOTTE*, 2:409-14; *TDOT*, 5:448-81; *TLOT*, 2:508-21; *TWOT*, 1:366-68) [*yd'*]

5:3 The God of the Hebrews <u>has manifested himself</u> to us (*niqrā'*). The middle (Niphal) of *qr'* II means "to encounter, meet" without pre-arrangement (*BDB*, 899.1) or "to allow oneself to be met" (*HALOT*, 3:1131.1) (Num. 23:3,4, 15, 16). We could nuance it "to manifest oneself" (*NIDOTTE*, 3:984). In describing divine-human encounters it often describes a theophany or appearance of God (Num. 23:3-4, 15-16) (*NIDOTTE*, 3:985). It also emphasizes the lack of human predetermination and stresses the element of chance from a human viewpoint (Ruth 2:3; 2 Sam. 1:6) (*NIDOTTE*, 3:984). A divine encounter was never planned nor orchestrated by man. Even when a prophet sought a meeting with God it was not an assured thing (Num. 23:3). Moses did not seek this encounter—God manifested himself by his independent will. (*NIDOTTE*, 3:976-78; *TLOT*, 3:1164-69; *TWAT*, 7:147-61; *TWOT*, 2:811-13) [*qr'*]

6:1 Because of my mighty <u>hand</u> (*beyād ḥazāqâ*). The term *yad* "hand" is an anthropomorphism for God's power (*BDB*, 389.1.e.2; *HALOT*, 2:387.4). The expression "mighty hand" pictures God as a mighty warrior in hand-to-hand combat (Exod. 6:1; 13:3,9, 14, 16; Deut. 6:21; 7:8; Josh. 4:24), stretching out his arm to strike Egypt with full strength (Exod. 9:15). God's mighty hand provided deliverance for his people (Exod. 14:31) and destruction of his enemies (Exod. 7:5). The biblical narrator repeatedly reports that Yahweh redeemed Israel from Egypt with a mighty hand and outstretched arm (Exod. 3:20; 4:17; 6:1; 7:19; 13:3,9, 14, 16). The literature and art of Egypt during the

New Kingdom period repeatedly pictures Pharaoh with a mighty hand and outstretched arm, wielding a weapon over the head of his conquered enemies. The biblical narrator probably used the expressions "mighty hand" and "outstretched arm" as a conscious polemic against the Egyptian picture of Pharaoh as the mighty warrior *par excellence*— Yahweh, not Pharaoh, was the ultimate mighty warrior (*NIDOTTE*, 2:403). (*NIDOTTE*, 2:402-05; *TDOT*, 5:393-426; *TLOT*, 2:497-502; *TWOT*, 1:362-64) [*yād*]

6:3 El Shaddai (*'ēl šadday*). Although this divine name was used of God from antiquity (Gen. 17:1; 28:3; 35:11; 43:14; 48:3; 49:25; Exod. 6:3; Num. 24:4, 16; Ruth 1:20, 21; Pss. 68:15; 91:1; Ezek. 1:24; 10:5; Joel 1:15), its precise meaning eludes contemporary scholars. For centuries, rabbinic Judaism explained *šadday* as the short pronoun *ša-* "the one who" plus the noun *day* "sufficiency," meaning "The One Who is Sufficient" or "The Self-Sufficient One." However, most contemporary scholars suggest that *šadday* (a) features an intensive (plural) form with a first person singular ending similar to *'adōnay* (lit. "my LORD," but later meaning simply "Lord"), and (b) is derived from the root *šdd* or *šd*, of which there are five candidates (*BDB*, 994-95; *HALOT*, 4:1420-22; *NIDOTTE*, 1:410): (1) Arabic *šdd* "to be strong," so Hebrew *'ēl šadday* might mean "The Strong One" or "The All-Powerful One." (2) Ugaritic *šdd* "to devastate" which is related to Hebrew *šōd* I "devastation," so *'ēl šadday* might mean "The Devastator," which may be reflected in *šōd miššadday* "devastation from the Devastator" (Isa. 13:6; Joel 1:15). (3) Akkadian *šadû(m)* "mountain," so *'ēl šadday* might mean "God of the mountains," picturing God as the one who

revealed himself in mountain theophanies. (4) Akkadian *šēdu* "beneficial, protecting spirit (singular); malevolent demons (plural)," which is paralleled in Hebrew (Deut. 32:17; Ps. 106:37); so *'ēl šadday* might mean "My Divine Protector." (5) Less likely is Hebrew *šōd* II "breast," picturing *'ēl šadday* as the source of human fertility.

It was *'ēl šadday* who established the covenant with Abraham (Gen. 17:1) and Jacob (Gen. 35:11). When Yahweh identified himself to Moses as *'ēl šadday*, the God of the patriarchs, he not only linked Mosaic Yahwism with the patriarchal religion, but also indicated that the patriarchal promises now would be passed on to Israel through Moses (*NIDOTTE*, 1:401). The patriarchs invoked *'ēl šadday* as the source of blessing (Gen. 28:3; 43:14; 49:25), but he is also the source of prophetic judgment (Isa. 13:6; Joel 1:15; cf. Ruth 1:20, 21). He blesses those who keep the covenant but curses those who breach covenant.

The worship of *šadday* in the ancient world is attested from ancient Near Eastern inscriptions, not only lending credibility to Israel's ancient worship of God by this name but also helping us understand the significance of the divine name: (1) Egyptian *šadê-'ammi* "Shadday is my patron," is the title of a patron god, similar to the notion that *'ēl šadday* was the patron God of Abraham, Isaac, and Jacob. The first person ending -*āy* of *'ēl šadday* pictures him as a personal patron God, as also suggested by the parallelism between *'ēl šadday* as *'ēl 'abika* "the God of your father" (Gen. 49:25). (2) The divine name *šdy* "Shadday" appears in several ancient Arabic inscriptions. (3) Northwest Semitic religions refer to *šdym* (plural of "Shadday") as a group of deities subordinate to El, the Northwest Semitic high god, so Hebrew *'ēl šadday* may designate the Most High God over all other heavenly beings. (*NIDOTTE*, 1:401; *TLOT*, 3:1304-10; *TWAT*, 7:1078-1104; *TWOT*, 2:907) [*šadday*]

7:3 I will harden Pharaoh's heart (*'aqšê*). The verb *qšh* "to be hard" appears here in the causative (Hiphil) sense "to make hard, stubborn, obstinate" (Deut. 2:30; 10:16; 2 Kings 17:14; 2 Chron. 30:8; 36:13; Neh. 9:16, 17, 29; Job 9:4; Ps. 95:8; Prov. 28:14; 29:1; Jer. 7:26; 17:23; 19:15), here of God hardening Pharaoh's heart (Exod. 7:3) (*BDB*, 904.3; *HALOT*, 3:1152.1.b). The root *qšh* also appears in expressions that refer to stubbornness (Exod. 32:9; 33:3, 5; 34:9; Deut. 9:6, 13; 31:27; Isa. 48:4). Pharaoh's refusal to release Israel offered God just cause to unleash his plagues displaying his mighty power. Later, when Pharaoh would eventually become willing to relent, God would harden his heart so he would refuse to release Israel, giving God just reason to continue to smite Egypt in judgment. Once Yahweh gained glory and all Egypt recognized who he is, he would then effect the release of Israel. So Yahweh's ultimate goal was more than simply the release of the Hebrews—it was to display his power. (*NIDOTTE*, 3:997; *TLOT*, 3:1175-76; *TWAT*, 7:205-11; *TWOT*, 2:818) [*qšh*]

So that I may multiply my signs (*wehirbêtî*). The intensive (Hiphil) sense of *rbh* "to be many, be great" may refer to (1) numerical increase: "to multiply, increase, make many" (*BDB*, 915.1) or (2) increase in social esteem: "to make great, increase in intensity" (*BDB*, 915.2). Pharaoh's obstinance would give God legitimate cause to increase the number of plagues and their intensity. his ultimate goal in his attacks on Egypt was not simply to win the release of the Hebrew slaves, but to magnify his own reputation in the eyes of the Hebrews, the Egyptians and the whole world who would hear what he had done in Egypt (Exod. 7:5, 17; 8:10, 22; 9:14, 16, 29; 10:2; 14:4, 18; cf. Deut. 4:32-40; Josh. 2:10-11). Here, God tells Moses that if he had not hardened Pharaoh's heart, the initial miracle would have convinced Pharaoh to release Israel. But this would be "too easy, too fast," so to speak, and it would not leave the kind of lasting impression that he had in mind. Instead he would harden Pharaoh to give him legitimate reason to unleash all of his mighty acts on Egypt, thereby providing undeniable proof to all that he indeed was the only true living God. So we see that God's chief goal is not merely the deliverance of his people, but his glory (*NIDOTTE*, 3:1037-41; *TLOT*, 3:1194-1201; *TWAT*, 7:294-320; *TWOT*, 2:826-27) [*rbh*]

7:9 Wonder (*môpēt*). In Egyptian religion, the validity of one's claim to be the mouthpiece of a god was demonstrated by performing a miracle. As evidence that Moses was the genuine prophet of God, Yahweh graciously accommodated Pharaoh's demand that Moses perform a *môpēt* "wonder." Although its etymology is uncertain, *môpēt* "wonder, sign, portent" might be derived from the noun *'pt* "calamity, wonder, portent" and its related verb "to suffer calamity" (*BDB*, 68; *TWOT*, 152). The term *môpēt* "wonder" refers to a special display of God's power, whether through celestial phenomena (2 Chron. 32:31; Joel 2:30[3:3]) or miraculous display for the verification of a divinely announced act of future judgment (1 Kings 13:3, 5), but most often of the plagues in Egypt as the display *par excellence* of the mighty power of God in judgment of Egypt (Exod. 4:21; 7:3,9; 11:9, 10; Deut. 4:34; 6:22; 7:19; 26:8; 29:2; 34:11;1

Chron. 16:12; Pss. 78:43; 105:27; 135:9; Jer. 32:20, 21) (*BDB*, 68-69.1; *HALOT*, 2:559). This term is often used with *'ôt* "sign" as the portent of even more ominous things to come (Exod. 7:3; Deut. 4:34; 6:22; 7:19; Pss. 78:43; 105:27; 135:9), *massâ* "testing" to emphasize its role in calling for a human response (Deut. 4:34; 7:19; 29:2), *niplā'â* "wonder" to describe its miraculous nature (1 Chron. 16:12; Ps. 105:15), and *mišpatîm* "judgment" as an act of divine retribution against sin (1 Chron. 16:12; Ps. 105:5). (*NIDOTTE*, 2:879-81; *TWAT*, 4:750-59; *TWOT*, 1:67) [*môpēt*]

7:10 His rod became a serpent (*tannîn*). While the term used in 4:3 to describe the staff of Moses turning into a snake was *nāḥāš*, the term used here is *tannîn*, which can refer to a "snake" (Deut. 32:33; Ps. 91:13) or "crocodile" (Ezek. 29:3; 32:2) (*BDB*, 1072.1; *NIDOTTE*, 4:314; *HALOT*, 4:1764.B.2). One wonders why the narrator shifted from the precise term *nāḥāš* "snake" in 4:3 to this more ambiguous term. Perhaps it was to create a literary allusion to a well-known ancient Egyptian myth that claimed that a magician during the reign of Cheops (= Khufu) made a wax model of a crocodile, then cast it into the Nile where it became alive, then took hold of it with his hand and it became a wax model again. The miracle of Moses demonstrated his superiority, not only over the Egyptian magicians in his own day, but also over the most illustrious legendary magicians in Egyptian history. The irony of Moses turning his rod into a cobra and back into a rod would not have been lost on Pharaoh: the cobra (*uraeus*) was the symbol of the Egyptian monarchy. The patron cobra-goddess of Lower Egypt, worn over the forehead on the headdress of the pharaohs, was emblematic of divinely

protected sovereignty, and it served as a menacing symbol of death to the enemies of the crown. So this miracle demonstrated the power of Moses, and especially Yahweh, over the very symbol of Egyptian might and power. (*NIDOTTE*, 4:313-14) [*tannîn*]

7:11 Occultic skills (*bĕlahăṭêhem*). The noun *lahaṭ* III "occult skills, magic arts" (always plural), which is related to *lāṭ* "secret, secret arts, magic," is from the verb *lhṭ > lwṭ* "to cover, wrap up" (1 Sam. 21:10; 1 Kings 19:13; Isa. 25:7). It refers to "things kept under wraps," that is, the closely guarded secrets practiced by Pharaoh's magicians and kept from non-initiates (Exod. 7:22; 8:3, 14) (*BDB*, 532; *HALOT*, 2:521). In non-occultic contexts, it means "surreptitiously, secretly, stealthily" (Judg. 4:21; Ruth 3:7; 1 Sam. 18:22; 24:5). The Egyptian sorcerers, probably devotees to the Egyptian moon god Thoth (god of magic and divination), were summoned by Pharaoh to counter the miraculous signs of Moses and Aaron (Exod. 7:11). The counterfeit miracles of the Egyptian sorcerers are not to be dismissed simply as magic tricks or sleight of hand (*ISBE* 4:377-78). These magicians were part of a religious guild steeped in mysterious learning and secret lore. According to Scripture, idolatrous religious systems were energized by demonic power (Deut. 32:16-17; Ps. 106:36-37; 1 Cor. 10:20). In addition to certain counterfeit signs and wonders, this demonic power may even enable human beings to predict the future on a limited basis (Deut. 13:1-3; Acts 16:16-18). Occultic magic was common in the ancient Near East and inseparable from the practice of religion, involving spells, incantations, charms/amulets, and special rituals to manipulate natural powers and to influence situations, people, and gods. Occultic magicians often served in the courts of pagan kings (Exod. 7:22; Dan. 2:2). The line between occultic magic and mantic divination was not absolute for they were often interrelated (Exod. 7:11; Lev. 19:26; Deut. 18:10-14; 2 Kings 21:6 = 2 Chron. 33:6; Isa. 47:9, 12; Dan. 2:2) (ISBE 3:213-19; ABD 4:464-71). Their use of spells contrasts with the simplicity of Aaron's action, which was unaccompanied by any incantation or praxis, because it was the revelation of the power of Almighty God (Exod. 7:11, 22; 8:3, 14). (NIDOTTE, 2:771-72; TDOT, 7:473-74; TWOT, 1:473) [lāṭ]

7:12 They threw down their staffs and they turned into serpents (wayyihyû lĕtannînim). The phrase hyh "to become" + preposition lĕ "into" may refer to one object turning into something else (BDB, 226.II.2e; HALOT, 1:244.7c). Did the Egyptian magicians duplicate the miracle of Yahweh? The records of ancient Egypt describe snake charmers who made snakes rigid as rods (Erman, The Ancient Egyptians, 36-38). Modern Egyptian snake charmers can induce a catatonic rigidity in cobras by exerting pressure on a nerve below their heads, creating a rod-like appearance. When they throw the snake to the ground, the jolt relieves the pressure on this nerve and restores its mobility. So it is possible that the Egyptian magicians merely executed a mountebank's trick from their conventional repertoire. On the other hand, Scripture acknowledges that pagan occultic magic was empowered by demonic forces, and was able to manifest displays of power (Deut. 13:1-3). In any case, Yahweh demonstrated his superiority over the Egyptian magicians and their gods: rather than turning a living snake into a lifeless rod (as the Egyptian magicians did), he turned a lifeless rod into a living snake, then back into a lifeless rod. [hyh]

7:13 Pharaoh's heart was hard (wayyeḥezaq). This is the first of four uses of the basic (Qal) stem of ḥzq "to be strong, hard" in Exodus to describe Pharaoh's heart (Exod. 7:13, 22; 8:19[15]; 9:35). The verb ḥzq refers to Pharaoh's will: "to remain resolute" (Deut. 12:23; Josh. 23:6; 1 Chron. 28:7), "to act determinedly" (Deut. 31:6; Josh. 10:25; 2 Sam. 13:28; Isa. 35:4; Ps. 31:25; 1 Chron. 28:10; 2 Chron. 15:7; 19:11; 25:8; 32:7; Ezra 10:4). Used with lēb "heart," it means "to be rigid, obstinate" (Exod. 7:13, 22; 8:15; 9:35; Hag. 2:4) (BDB, 304; HALOT, 1:302). The related adjective ḥazaq, "strong, hard," is used literally of a rock (Ezek. 3:9) and figuratively of an obstinate will (heart) that refuses to repent (Ezek. 2:4). The adjective ḥazaq, "strong, mighty," is also used in Exodus in reference to Yahweh's arm that performed the miracles in Egypt (Exod. 3:19; 13:9; 32:11) which were actually intended to harden Pharaoh's heart (Exod. 9:12). The use of this term in Exod. 4–14 depicts a battle between Pharaoh's "hard" (ḥzq) heart and Yahweh's "strong" (ḥzq) arm. Ironically, when Yahweh revealed his "strong" arm, the heart of Pharaoh became "hard," as God had predicted (Exod. 4:12). When Aaron's snake swallowed the snakes of the magicians, Pharaoh should have realized that the power of Yahweh was greater than the power of his magicians, but instead he was obstinate. Although the use of the basic (Qal) form of ḥzq here recalls the causative (Piel) form of ḥzq in 4:21 ("I will harden his heart"), this passage does not explicitly state that the hardness of Pharaoh's heart was due to Yahweh hardening it. Although God would eventually harden Pharaoh's heart, this was not yet necessary for Pharaoh's heart was already hard in and of itself. Only when the mighty acts of God's judgments on Egypt weakened his resolve would Yahweh harden his heart to ensure that divine judgment would be prolonged on Egypt. However, at this point Pharaoh's resolve was still firm and would not be in "need" of self-hardening until the second and fourth plagues, and of divine hardening until the sixth plague. It is important to note that Yahweh did not initiate the hardening of Pharaoh's heart. Pharaoh had already shown himself obstinate in all of his initial encounters with Moses (7:13, 14, 22; 8:19[15]; 9:7), long before the first explicitly reported act of divine hardening (9:12). Before God hardened his heart the first time (9:12), Pharaoh had already twice hardened his own heart (8:15[11], 32[28]). When Yahweh first hardened Pharaoh's heart, he was not dealing with an innocent or neutral individual. Hard-heartedness was an inherent sinful characteristic of Pharaoh, as Yahweh had foreknown (3:19). Ironically, in Egyptian religion the ideal response from Pharaoh before the gods was to harden one's heart in order to successfully pass the test of divine examination of the human heart for sin. This Egyptian approach to divine testing was the worst thing Pharaoh could have done before the one true God! (*NIDOTTE,* 2:62-63; *TDOT,* 4:301-08; *TLOT,* 1:403-06; *TWOT,* 1:276-77) [*hzq*]

7:14 The heart of Pharaoh was hard (*kābēd*). This is the first of two uses of the basic (Qal) form of the verb *kābēd* "to be heavy" to describe Pharaoh's heart (Exod. 7:14; 9:7) (*HALOT,* 2:455.2). When the verb *kābēd* "heavy, burdensome" (*BDB,* 457) is used of body parts associated with volition (ear, heart), the idea is

unresponsiveness (*NIDOTTE,* 2:577-78) (*BDB,* 457.2 wrongly suggests "insensible"). So "his heart was *kābēd* (heavy)" (Exod. 7:14; 9:7) is equivalent to "his heart was *hzq* (strong)" (Exod. 7:13, 22; 8:19[15]; 9:35), both depicting Pharaoh's obstinance. Just as "hard" ears refuse to listen to God (Isa. 59:1), a "hard" heart refuses to obey or submit to him (Exod. 4:21). Because Pharaoh's heart was "hard" (*kābēd*) God afflicted him with "severe" (*kābēd*) plagues (Exod. 8:24[20]; 9:3, 18, 24; 10:14) as a form of poetic justice: the punishment fit the crime. (*NIDOTTE,* 2:577-87; *TDOT,* 7:13-22; *TLOT,* 2:590-602; *TWOT,* 1:426-28) [*kbd*]

7:20 The water turned blood-red (*dām*). The expression *hāpak* + *ledām* (traditionally translated "[the water] turned into blood") occurs 4x in reference to this plague on the Nile (Exod. 7:17, 20; Pss. 78:44; 105:29). One's view of the nature of this divine miracle is revealed by answering this question: Does this mean the chemical composition of the water (H_2O) was ontologically changed into hemoglobin ($C_{738}H_{1166}FeN_{203}O_{208}S_2$) or merely that the hue of the water became blood-red? Careful attention to detail in word study can help inform our decision. First, *dam* "blood" (*BDB,* 196) is related to the noun *'dm* "to be red" (*BDB,* 10) so it easy to see why it refers to "blood" (Gen. 9:6; Lev. 17:11; Prov. 30:33) or other objects that are red (2 Kings 3:22; Joel 2:31) such as red wine (Gen. 49:11; Deut. 32:14) (*HALOT,* 1:224-25; *TLOT,* 1:337.1). Second, the construction *hāpak* + *lĕ* "to turn into" (*BDB,* 245) can refer to: (1) ontological transformation: sea turned into dry land (Pss. 66:6; 114:8); (2) transformation of the color of an object (Lev. 13:16, 55; Ps. 41:4; Jer. 13:33; 30:6; Dan. 10:8); (3) phenomenological transformation so one object looks like something else: sun turned into darkness and moon into blood (Joel 2:31); and (4) metaphorical transformations: justice turned into wormwood (Amos 6:12). Third, *hāpak + ledām* "turn into blood" is used in a phenomenological sense (language of appearance) elsewhere (*BDB*, 245.1.c): "the sun will turn into darkness and the moon will into blood" (Joel 2:31), the color of the sun will become dark and the moon blood-red in phenomenological terms. Fourth, *dām* is used elsewhere of water which takes on a blood-red appearance due to natural phenomenon. For example, when the sun shone on the surface of a body of water, its appearance became so red that the Moabites mistook it for the shed blood of the Israelite army in the water: "The sun was shining over the water, and from the distance the water *appeared as red as blood* to the Moabites. 'That's blood!' they said. 'The kings must have fought among themselves and killed each other!'" (2 Kings 3:22-23, NJPS).

Some scholars attempt to explain the Nile turning blood-red in the light of natural phenomena that occur periodically in the Nile valley: unusually heavy rainfall washed an unusual amount of red sediment into the Nile, giving the water a red hue. To view this in light of natural phenomenon does not diminish divine involvement in the plagues (*NIDOTTE*, 4:1057). From a theological perspective, this would be a matter of God harnessing the forces of nature to accomplish his purpose. This was an act of poetic justice: the Egyptians killed Hebrew infants by casting them into the Nile, so Yahweh would figuratively strike the Nile in return, turning it blood-red as a ominous object lesson of coming judgment.

This would have been an ominous sign of judgment to the Egyptians. In ancient Near Eastern literature water turning into the color of blood was stereotypical of the worst kind of calamity. In an ancient Sumerian text the goddess Inanna plagued the land by turning all its waters into blood. Likewise, an ancient Egyptian text, Ipuwer, describes judgment by the gods of Egypt thus: "the River [= Nile] is blood" and "people thirst for water" (*ANET3*, 441). Another Egyptian text states that if Rameses II would be defeated in battle, the water of Egypt would take on the color of blood. Since the plagues on Egypt were judgments against the gods of Egypt (Exod. 12:12) the contamination of the Nile also might have discredited the Egyptian god Hapi, the personified Nile god. Turning the Nile to blood would symbolize Yahweh slaying him. (*NIDOTTE*, 1:963-66; *TDOT*, 3:234-50; *TLOT*, 1:337-39; *TWOT*, 1:190-91) [*dām*]

8:2 I will <u>smite</u> your country (*nōgēp*). The use of this term vividly portrays Yahweh as the Divine Warrior. The verb *ngp* "to strike" is used literally of a person striking another person in a fight, producing a fatal or non-fatal injury (Exod. 21:22, 35) (*HALOT*, 2:669.1) and figuratively of God smiting his enemies as the Divine Warrior (*BDB*, 619; *HALOT*, 2:669.2a). The Divine Warrior smites his enemies with illness (2 Sam. 12:15; 2 Chron. 21:18), death (1 Sam. 25:38; 26:10; 2 Chron. 13:20; Ps. 89:24), military defeat in battle (Judg. 20:35; 1 Sam. 4:3; 2 Chron. 13:15; 14:11; 21:14), or with plagues (Exod. 8:2[7:27]; 12:23, 27; Josh. 24:5; Isa. 19:22; Zech. 14:12 , 18). It is related to the noun *negep* "striking, fatal injury" (*BDB*, 620.1), used of the climactic plague of the death of the firstborn of Egypt (Exod. 12:13; 30:12) and more generally of pestilence (Num. 17:11, 12; Josh. 22:17). It refers to a divine blow executed by God with disastrous consequences for the victims (*NIDOTTE*, 3:25-26; *TDOT*, 9:210-13; *TWOT*, 2:551-52). [*ngp*]

8:8 Plead to Yahweh (*ha'tîrû*). This is the first of four occasions when Pharaoh pleaded to Moses to pray to Yahweh to withdraw plagues (Exod. 8:8[4], 28[24]; 9:28; 10:17). The basic (Qal) sense of *'ātar* "to plead, supplicate, entreat" is used of prayer to God (Gen. 25:21; Exod. 8:26; 10:18; Judg. 13:8; Job 33:26), while the passive (Niphal) "to be supplicated, be entreated, be pleaded with" is used of God granting the entreaty (Gen. 25:21; 2 Sam. 21:14; 24:25; 1 Chron. 5:20; 2 Chron. 33:13, 19; Esth. 8:23; Isa. 19:22). Here the intensive/causative (Hiphil) form is used: "to plead earnestly" (*HALOT*, 2:905) or "to make supplication" (*BDB*, 801) (Job 22:27; Sir 37:15; 38:14). This term describes the powerful, appeasing effect of a man on God (*TLOT*, 2:962). Elsewhere cultic offerings normally accompany this petitionary prayer (2 Sam. 24:25; Job 33:26; Zech. 3:10). However, this would not have been the case here because Moses was reluctant to sacrifice in Egypt (Exod. 8:26). Nevertheless, the use of this term reveals the intensity of Pharaoh's plea that Moses intercede on his behalf. Scripture highlights the petitionary power of the prophets of God (Gen. 20:7; Exod. 32:11-14; 1 Sam. 7:7-11; 1 Kings 18:16-46) as a model for petitionary prayer (James 5:16-18). (*TLOT*, 2:961-62; *TWAT*, 6:489-91; *TWOT*, 2:708-09) [*'tr*]

8:15 When Pharaoh saw there was relief, he hardened his heart (*wehakbēd*). This is the first of 3x in Exodus in which the causative (Hiphil) of *kābēd* "to be hard, heavy" describes Pharaoh hardening his heart (Exod. 8:15, 32; 9:34). The verb *kābēd* "to be hard, heavy" is used with *lēb*

"heart" of a willful obstinate, unresponsive disposition (*BDB*, 457.2). The causative (Hiphil) form "to make heavy, to harden" emphasizes Pharaoh's personal culpability (8:32[28]; 9:34) (*BDB*, 458.2). A similar image of "hardened ears" occurs elsewhere, "They refused to pay attention; they stubbornly turned their backs and stopped up (Hiphil of *kābēd*) their ears" (Zech. 7:11). Most translations render this literally, "he hardened his heart" (KJV, NKJV, ASV, RSV, NRSV, NASB, NIV, NLT); some nuance it: "he became stubborn" or "obstinate" (NAB, TEV, CEV). While Yahweh eventually hardened Pharaoh's heart (Exod. 9:12; 10:1, 20, 27; 11:10; 14:4, 8, 17), here the narrator stresses Pharaoh's culpability (e.g., 7:13, 14; 9:7, 35). Pharaoh's heart was originally hard (as indicated by the basic Qal forms in 7:13, 14, 22; 8:19[15]; 9:7, 35); however some plagues made him willing to negotiate with Moses—but as soon as those plagues were removed, Pharaoh hardened his heart, reverting to his original defiant disposition (Exod. 8:15[11], 32[28]; 9:34). Even when grace is shown to the wicked, they do not learn righteousness (Isa. 26:10).

According to the narrator, Pharaoh hardened his own heart during the second (8:8-15), fourth (8:25-32) and seventh (9:27-35) plagues. The second plague weakened his resolve and he was willing to negotiate temporary release of Israel on the condition that Yahweh remove the plague (8:8-11). But once Pharaoh experienced relief, he "hardened his heart" and resumed his original posture (8:12-15). He remained obstinate despite the third plague; his "heart was hard" (8:19). The fourth plague made Pharaoh compliant once again and he was willing to negotiate the release of Israel on the condition that God stop the plague (8:25-29). But once again as soon as there was relief, he "hardened his heart" and reverted to his previous position (8:30-32). At the onslaught of the seventh plague Pharaoh once again became willing to negotiate the release of Israel on the condition that the plague cease (9:27-32). But once there was relief, "he sinned again" and "hardened [his] heart" (9:34). (*NIDOTTE*, 2:577-87; *TDOT*, 7:13-22; *TLOT*, 2:590-602; *TWOT*, 1:426-28) [*kbd*]

8:22 I will set apart the region of Goshen (*wehiplêtî*). While the basic (Qal) meaning of *plh* is "be separate, distinct" (*BDB*, 811), "be treated specially, excellently" (*HALOT*, 3:930) or "be treated differently, be distinguished" (*NIDOTTE*, 3:620) (Exod. 33:16; Ps. 139:14), the causative (Hiphil) sense is "to make separate, set apart" (*BDB*, 811), "to treat specially, treat excellently" (*HALOT*, 3:930) or "to treat with distinction" (*NIDOTTE*, 3:620). The verb *plh* refers to making a person/group distinct due to the revelation of God to that person/group. This is the first of three occasions when God explicitly announced that he would make a distinction in his treatment of the land of Goshen (Exod. 8:22[18]; 9:4; 11:7). The exclusion of Goshen from the biting swarms was divinely designed that Pharaoh might recognize that Yahweh was sovereign over Goshen and Egypt: "that you will know that I, Yahweh, am in the midst of the land." It was one thing for Pharaoh to acknowledge the Hebrews had their own god—it was something else to admit that he was also sovereign over Egypt! (*NIDOTTE*, 3:620; *TWOT*, 2:724) [*plh*]

8:29 Stop dealing deceptively (*hatēl*). The verb *tālal* II has a three-fold range of meanings: (1) "to deceive, cheat" (Gen. 31:7; Job 13:9; Jer. 9:4); (2) "to play a cruel joke [on someone], make a fool of [someone]" (Judg. 16:10, 13, 15); and (3) "to mock, trifle with [someone]" (Exod. 8:29) (*BDB*, 1068; *HALOT*, 4:1739-40). Here it indicates the pretense of promising to do something but not following through (*NIDOTTE*, 4:298-99). It is intentional deception that makes a mockery out of its object. Laban acted deceptively with Jacob, promising one thing but doing something else (Gen. 31:7). Samson made a mockery out of Delilah by making a pretense of telling the truth (Judg. 16:10, 13, 15). Pharaoh dealt deceptively with Moses, repeatedly promising to release the slaves if Yahweh withdrew the plagues, but never fulfilling his promise. The sovereign God is not one with whom to trifle! (*NIDOTTE*, 4:298-99; *TWAT*, 8:662-71; *TWOT*, 2:971) [*tll*]

9:3 The hand of the LORD (*yad*). The term *yad* "hand" is an anthropomorphism, representing the mighty and irresistible power of God and the acts of God (Deut. 32:39) (*BDB*, 389.1e.2; *HALOT*, 2:387.4). It depicts poetic justice: Moses warned Pharaoh not to "tighten his grip" on the Hebrews, lest YHWH strike back with his "hand." The ancient Egyptian art of this period often portrayed Pharaoh with a strong hand, gripping his enemy in one hand and raising a club to strike him with the other. In an ironic reversal of this imagery, it is the mighty hand of Yahweh—not Pharaoh—that prevails. And Pharaoh is presented as the victim, not the victor. (*NIDOTTE*, 2:402-05; *TDOT*, 5:393-426; *TLOT*, 2:497-502; *TWOT*, 1:362-64) [*yād*]

9:3 Severe pestilence (*deber*). The noun *deber* II "plague, pestilence" (*BDB*, 184) or "bubonic plague" (*HALOT*, 1:212) refers to a deadly epidemic disease, plague or pestilence (2 Chron. 6:28; 20:9; Ps. 91:3, 6; Hos. 13:14; Hab. 3:5) that can wipe out a population (Exod. 9:15; 2 Sam. 24:15; Ezek. 5:12). It is often an act of God's judgment (Exod. 5:3; Lev. 26:25; Num. 14:12; Deut. 28:31; 2 Chron. 7:13; Jer. 14:12; Amos 4:10) (*TDOT*, 3:126-27). Its victims here are cattle (Exod. 9:3; Ps. 78:50), so it has been diagnosed as anthrax, foot-and-mouth disease, or Rift Valley fever (*NIDOTTE*, 1:915-16; *TDOT*, 3:125-27). [*deber*]

9:12 The LORD hardened the heart of Pharaoh (*wayeḥazzeq*). In previous episodes Pharaoh hardened his own heart (Exod. 7:13, 22; 8:15[11], 19[15], 32[28]; 9:34-35). However, now for the first time the narrator explicitly states that Yahweh hardened Pharaoh's heart (as he had previously declared in Exod. 4:21; 7:3). Yahweh will again harden Pharaoh's heart in the last three plagues (Exod. 10:1, 20, 27; 11:10) as well as at the Reed (Red) Sea (Exod. 14:4, 8, 17). Only once more—in the midst of the seventh plague—is Pharaoh viewed as autonomously responsible for his own obstinacy (Exod. 9:34-35). In the first sets of plagues the narrator used the basic (Qal) stem of *ḥazaq*, as in "Pharaoh's heart was hard" (Exod. 7:13, 22; 8:19), to emphasize Pharaoh's autonomous responsibility for his own obstinacy. However, now the intensive (Piel) stem "to make rigid, harden, make obstinate" (Jer. 5:3) appears with Yahweh as the subject (*BDB*, 304.5). Previously Pharaoh hardened his own heart when his magicians were able to reproduce or reverse the miracles of Yahweh. When his magicians were impotent against Yahweh in this plague (Exod. 9:11), Pharaoh's resolve began to weaken, so God strengthened his resolve so that he was once again obstinate. Why? God wanted a just reason to

make his power all the more known, so that his mighty name might be proclaimed throughout the entire earth (Exod. 9:15-16).

We may draw several observations about God's role in hardening Pharaoh's heart. First, when God hardened his heart, he did not violate his moral freedom nor cause him to act contrary to his own natural impulse. It was Pharaoh's natural, sinful nature to refuse to release the slaves (Exod. 7:13, 22; 8:19). When he was willing to release Israel, he was acting contrary his nature—under compulsion by God's acts of judgment (4:20-21). When God withdrew the plagues, he reverted to his original obstinacy.

Second, God's repeated hardening of Pharaoh's heart (9:12; 10:1, 20, 27; 11:10; 14:4, 8, 17), which he had announced in advance (4:21; 7:3), was not contrary to his stated goal to force Pharaoh to release the people (3:19-20). The LORD's agenda was larger than just saving his people from slavery—He wanted to gain glory from the Egyptians and display his power to the watching world so that all observers might recognize that he is indeed Yahweh (Exod. 6:7; 7:5; 9:16; 10:1-2; 11:9; 14:4, 17-18). And when the Israelites saw the great power of the LORD displayed against the Egyptians at the Reed (Red) Sea—an event that never would have happened unless God had continually hardened Pharaoh's heart to build up to this climactic moment—they worshiped Yahweh and placed their faith in him (Exod. 14:31). The ultimate goal was theocentric (the glory of God) not anthropocentric (deliverance of Israel). So prolonging judgment on Egypt—by repeatedly hardening Pharaoh's heart—allowed Yahweh to accomplish this greater purpose. Although Israel's deliverance was slightly delayed, it was eventually made all the more miraculous, and Yahweh's reputation was greatly enhanced. Indeed the report of his mighty deeds reached all the way into Canaan, causing the hearts of the Canaanites to melt because they realized that "Yahweh your God is God in heaven above and on earth below" (Josh. 2:10-11).

Finally, divine hardening of Pharaoh's heart was an act of divine retribution for his mistreatment of the Hebrew slaves. By refusing to allow Pharaoh to capitulate earlier, he ensured that Egypt's destruction would be complete. (NIDOTTE, 2:63-87; TDOT, 4:301-08; TLOT, 1:403-06; TWOT, 1:276-77) [ḥzq]

9:16 I have spared you (he'ĕmadtîkā). This form (Hiphil) of 'āmad "to stand" has a wide range of meanings: (1) causative: "to raise up, appoint" (1 Chron. 15:17; 2 Chron. 8:14; Neh. 7:3); (2) intensive: "to maintain" the opposite of overthrow (Prov. 29:4); and (3) permissive: "to spare" instead of destroy (1 Kings 15:4) (BDB, 764.2; HALOT, 2:841.3). The LXX takes the permissive sense, "For this purpose you have been preserved"—God could have destroyed the Egyptians had he wished (v. 15) but he spared them to reveal his power through a series of prolonged plagues (v. 16). Aquila adopts the causative sense: "For this purpose I raised you up"—God appointed Pharaoh through whom to display his power. Although Paul seems to develop the causative sense in his use of this passage in Rom. 9:17, he is probably making a midrashic use of this passage rather than reflecting the original historical contextual meaning. The context here clearly does not deal with predestination but the providential preservation of Pharaoh in history. God could have wiped out Pharaoh and the Egyptians, but he spared them to prolong the display of his mighty power. (NIDOTTE, 3:432-34;

TLOT, 2:921-24; TWAT, 6:194-204; TWOT, 2:675) ['md]

I have spared you to display my power to you (har'ōtekā). The causative (Hiphil) of r' h "to see" means "to exhibit, cause [someone] to see [something]" (BDB, 908.1.a; HALOT, 3:1161). While creation is a witness to the existence of God (Ps. 19:1-6; Rom. 1:19-23), the plagues on Egypt revealed God's power. Although God is normally hidden from man (Ps. 89:46 [47]; Isa. 45:15), at rare moments in human history, such as at the Exodus, the hidden God revealed his power. Its memory is still a resounding witness to the fact of his existence and that he alone is the true, living God. (NIDOTTE, 3:1007-15; TLOT, 3:1176-83; TWAT, 7:225-66; TWOT, 2:823-25) [r' h]

So that My fame may resound throughout the world (šemî). The term šēm "name" may refer to God's personal name or his representative reputation (BDB, 1027-28). The ancient Semitic conception of the name was often more than mere identification; it embodied an individual's character. In fact, the act of naming someone was often viewed as determinative of one's destiny. When God brought the creation into existence, he gave everything a name programmatic to its function, so the name was equivalent to its existence. Conversely, to not have a name or to have it cut off was tantamount to non-existence.

The term šēm often represents the nature or attributes of the person/deity so named. For example, the name of the moon god, Sin, in Akkadian is literally "Thirty," standing for the thirty days of the moon cycle, while the name of his daughter is literally "Fifteen," because she is portrayed as only half as powerful. In Scripture, the "name" of Yahweh represents his moral character. For example, we read that "His name is 'Jealous'" (Exod. 34:14) and "His name is 'Holiness'" (Isa. 57:15). Similarly, the proclamation of the LORD's name to Moses on Sinai is a recitation of his moral attributes: "He passed in front of Moses, proclaiming [the name] Yahweh: 'Yahweh, the compassionate and gracious God, slow to anger, abounding in love and faithfulness, maintaining love to thousands . . ." (Exod. 34:5-7).

Its frequent parallelism with *zeker* "fame" (Exod. 6:3) (*BDB*, 270-71) suggests that *šēm* often connotes "fame" or "glory" (Gen. 6:4; Num. 16:2; 1 Chron. 5:24; 12:31; Zeph. 3:19, 20; Ezek. 39:13) (*BDB*, 1028.2.b), particularly the fame of God as embodying his character (Exod. 3:15; Jer. 33:2; Amos 5:8; 9:6) (*BDB*, 1028.3). The "name" often connotes one's reputation, e.g., God promised to make the names of Abraham and David famous (Gen. 12:2; 2 Sam. 7:9). So "men of renown" (lit. "men of name") were famous people (Gen. 6:4). The display of his might during the Exodus made Yahweh famous, so to speak (Exod. 10:1-2; Josh. 2:8-11; 1 Sam. 6:6). Indeed, the ultimate purpose of the plagues was not simply to deliver the Hebrews—God could have done that quickly if he had wished (vv. 14-15)—but to create an unparalleled witness by prolonging the display of his power (Deut. 4:32-35). A momentary "flash in the pan" display would not have produced such a profound impression that transformed the Hebrews into a community of believers forever committed to the only true, living God (Exod. 4:31; 14:31). (*NIDOTTE*, 4:147-51; *TLOT*, 3:1348-67; *TWAT*, 8:122-76; *TWOT*, 2:934-35) [*šēm*]

9:17 Yet you still exalt yourself against my people (*mistôlēl*). The basic (Qal) meaning of *sll* is "to pile up, lift up" some-

thing (Jer. 50:26) or "to exalt" someone (Ps. 68:5), while the reflexive (Hithpolel) meaning here is "to exalt oneself, behave high-handedly, act insolently" (*BDB*, 699; *HALOT*, 2:757). Used with the preposition *be* it means "to act insolently against" someone. The hostile connotations of the term are reflected in the related Hebrew noun *sōlelâ* "assault ramp," an object that is raised up. Pharaoh acted in presumptuous, arrogant pride and hostility when he refused to release the Hebrews to worship Yahweh. His was the sin of arrogance and *hubris*.(*NIDOTTE*, 3:264-67; *TWAT*, 5:867-72; *TWOT*, 2:626-27) [*sll*]

10:1 I will harden his heart (*hikbadtî*). The narrator highlights the dynamic relationship between divine sovereignty and human freedom by the interplay of the basic (Qal) and intensive (Hiphil) meanings of *kābēd* (*NIDOTTE*, 2:750). Twice "Pharaoh's heart was hard (*kābēd*)" (Exod. 7:14; 9:7), 3x Pharaoh "hardened (Hiphil) his heart" (Exod. 8:15[11], 32[28]; 9:34), and here Yahweh "hardened (Hiphil) his heart" (Exod. 10:1). The causative (Hiphil) *kābēd* "make heavy, harden" emphasizes God's role in making Pharaoh obstinate and willfully unresponsive to his command (Exod. 8:11, 28; 9:34; 10:1) (*BDB*, 458.2; *HALOT*, 2:456.2). Elsewhere Pharaoh's heart is viewed as hard in and of itself: *ḥzq* (Qal) "to be hard" (Exod. 7:13, 22; 8:19[15]; 9:35) and *kbd* (Qal) "to be hard" (Exod. 7:14; 9:7). On other occasions, the plagues softened Pharaoh's obstinacy, making him willing to release the Hebrews; however, once God withdrew the plague, Pharaoh returned to his old self: "he hardened [causative Hiphil of *kbd*] his heart" (Exod. 8:15[11], 32[28]; 9:34). Here God announced that he would "harden" his heart (10:1) so that he would be justified in sending more plagues, and so magnify his fame (10:2). When God hardened the heart of the Egyptian (10:20), he reverted to his original posture of obstinacy (10:27-28). Pharaoh's refusal to comply with Moses was by divine design so God might have justification for devastating Egypt.

There are two basic views to explain the relation between Pharaoh hardening his heart and God hardening his heart: (1) Some scholars suggest that the narrator provides two different perspectives: from a human perspective Pharaoh hardened his own heart, but from the divine perspective God was hardening his heart all along. One set of texts deal with the language of appearance (Pharaoh's heart was initially hard, then he later hardened his own heart), while the other set of texts are more theologically precise (ultimately it was God who hardened Pharaoh's heart all along). (2) Others suggest that Pharaoh's hardening developed in three stages: (a) Pharaoh's heart was initially hard in and of itself during the first plagues (Exod. 7:13, 14, 22). (b) When God increased the severity of the plagues, he became willing to relent on the condition that the plagues be withdrawn; however, once there was relief, Pharaoh hardened his own heart, returning to his original position of obstinacy (Exod. 8:15[11], 32[28]). (c) When the ever intensifying plagues eventually made Pharaoh willing to release the slaves unconditionally, God hardened Pharaoh's heart to restore his original obstinance—to prolong the display of his mighty power so that all might be fully convinced that Yahweh alone is the only living God (Exod. 9:12; 10:1, 20, 27; 11:10; 14:4, 8, 17). (*NIDOTTE*, 2:577-87; *TDOT*, 7:13-22; *TLOT*, 2:590-602; *TWOT*, 1:4226-28) [*kbd*]

10:2 So you may recount (*tesappēr*). Derived from the root *spr* "to count," the verb *spr* (Piel) describes repeated action: "to report, tell, recount, narrate" a memorable event (Gen. 24:66; Num. 13:27; Ps. 59:13; Isa. 43:26; Joel 1:3) (*BDB*, 708.1; *HALOT*, 2:766.4). This verb usually has theological content, most often the mighty deeds of the LORD (Pss. 9:2; 26:7; 40:6; 44:2; 73:28; 75:2; 78:4; 79:13). The expression here is unusual: "recount in the ears of" (cf. Ps. 44:1, "we have heard with our ears") places the emphasis on the oral retelling from one generation to another. This communication of his past intervention in the history of Israel primarily took place in the family from fathers to children and grandchildren (Exod. 10:2; Judg. 6:13; Pss. 22:31; 44:2; 48:14; 78:3, 6; Joel 1:3). The main pedagogical strategy to bring the new generation to faith was to dramatically retell how Yahweh had miraculously rescued their forefathers from the clutches of the Egyptians (Deut. 6:20-25). This narration of the acts of God was an essential element in the transmission of OT tradition. (*NIDOTTE,* 4:1291-92; *TLOT,* 2:810.4; *TWAT,* 5:929-44; *TWOT,* 2:632-34) [*spr*]

I have dealt harshly with the Egyptians (*hit'allaltî*). The basic (Qal) meaning of *'ll* is "to be busy" and its intensive (Polel) meaning is "to deal with someone severely" by inflicting injury and pain (Lam. 3:51) and "to treat violently, injure someone" (Isa. 3:12). Here the reflexive-iterative (Hithpael) has a broad range of meanings: (1) "to deal with someone wantonly or ruthlessly," (2) "to play a dirty trick on someone, to make a toy of someone," and (3) "to busy oneself, divert oneself" (*BDB*, 759; *HALOT*, 2:834) (Exod. 10:2; Num. 22:29; Judg. 19:25; 1 Sam. 6:6; 31:4; Jer. 38:19; 1 Chron. 10:4; Ps. 141:4). It may depict someone amusing himself by toying with someone else as in Balaam's donkey making a fool of the prophet (Num. 22:29); or dealing ruthlessly with someone as in the violent rape of a woman (Judg. 19:25). It is related to the nouns *'ălîlâ* "wantonness, caprice, ruthlessness," *ma'ălal* "ruthless deed, severe treatment, youthful wantonness," and *ta'ălûlîm* "wantonness, caprice" (*BDB*, 760). Did the LORD make sport of the Egyptians or deal ruthlessly with them? Several suggest the first approach: "I have made a toy of the Egyptians" (*BDB*, 759.1), "to play a dirty trick on" (*HALOT*, 2:834), and "the Egyptians/Pharaoh are made sport of/dallied with by the LORD" (*NIDOTTE*, 3:423). This would be a bold anthropomorphism. The point would be that God was shaming and disgracing Egypt, making them look foolish in their arrogance and stubbornness. Others adopt the second approach: "God treated the Egyptians severely because . . . they hardened their hearts. It is clearly within God's power and prerogative to punish and discipline but he never acts in jest" (*TWOT*, 2:671). The translators are also split: (1) "I have made sport of the Egyptians" (RSV), "I have made fools of the Egyptians" (TEV, NRSV), "I have made a mockery of the Egyptians" (NASB); (2) "I have dealt harshly with the Egyptians" (NIV), "I have dealt ruthlessly with the Egyptians" (NAB), "My harsh treatment of the Egyptians" (CEV). The use of this term in 1 Sam. 6:6 may be decisive. The Philistines, recalling Yahweh's judgments on Egypt, sought to avoid a similar fate: "Why are you hardening your hearts as the Egyptians and Pharaoh did? When he treated them harshly (Hithpael of *'ll*), did they not send the Israelites out so they could go on their way?" The Philistines, who were already suffering from the hand of God, wanted to avoid not being made sport of, but the kind of harsh treatment the Egyptians suffered. While the omnipotent God was merely toying with the Egyptians in one sense (He could have totally destroyed them if he had chosen to unleash his full power against them, Exod. 9:15-16), the emphasis here is on the harsh treatment Yahweh inflicted on Egypt. This was re-tributive justice for the harsh treatment the Egyptians had inflicted on the Hebrew slaves (1:11-14). (*NIDOTTE*, 3:423-25; *TWAT*, 6:151-60; *TWOT*, 2:670-71) [*'ll*]

10:7 Snare (*môqēš*). This colorful figure of speech casts God in the role of the hunter who cleverly sets out bait to lure Pharaoh into a trap. Used literally to refer to a "wooden snare" for catching birds or a lure in a fowler's net (Hos. 9:8), it is figurative of what lures or ensnares someone into a destructive situation (Exod. 23:33; 34:12; Deut. 7:16; Judg. 2:3; 8:27; 1 Sam. 18:21; Josh. 23:13; Pss. 64:6; 69:23; 106:36; 140:6; 141:9; Prov. 18:7; 20:25; 22:25; 29:25; Isa. 8:14; Jer. 50:24; Amos 3:5) (*BDB*, 430; *HALOT*, 2:560). Moses repeatedly baited Pharaoh into a destructive confrontation with Almighty God. (*NIDOTTE*, 2:525-27; *TDOT*, 6:288-90; *TWOT*, 1:399) [*môqēš*]

12:8 Unleavened bread (*ûmaṣṣôt*). The term *maṣṣâ* "unleavened bread" (*BDB*, 595) is from a root that means "to be tasteless" (*HALOT*, 2:621). It is a flat bread made from barley meal and water, baked with unleavened dough so it could be prepared quickly in contrast to leavened dough that required time to rise (Gen. 19:3; Judg. 6:20; 1 Sam. 28:24). On the eve of the Passover deliverance from Egypt, the Hebrews were to prepare themselves to depart at a moment's notice: "You are to eat dressed to travel . . . You are to eat in haste" (v. 11). Once the tenth plague struck Egypt, Pharaoh would give the Hebrews a small window of opportunity to flee in a hurry before he would change his mind. The eating of the bread also might have had a sacral significance because it was consumed in association with the eating of a ritually slaughtered lamb. This hastily eaten meal formed the basis for the Feast of Unleavened Bread to be celebrated for fourteen days from the fifteenth to the twenty-eighth day of the first month of the Jewish religious calendar (Exod. 12:14-20). Details of the celebration of this feast appear elsewhere (Exod. 23:10-19; 29:23; 34:18-26; Lev. 8:2, 26; 23:6; Num. 6:15, 17; Deut. 16:16; Josh. 5:11; 2 Kings 23:9; 2 Chron. 8:13; 30:13, 21; 35:7; Ezra 6:22; Ezek. 45:21). During the two-week celebration only "unleavened bread" (*maṣṣâ*) was eaten; leaven must not be "found" (*māṣā'*) in one's home—the wordplay reinforcing the concept (Exod. 12:19). In later Judaism unleavened bread came to be viewed as a symbol of purity, reflected in Paul's allusion: "Let us celebrate the festival, not with the old yeast, the yeast of vice and evil, but with the bread without yeast, the bread of sincerity and truth" (1 Cor. 5:6-8). As the feast celebrated the departure from Egypt, the name *maṣṣâ* "unleavened bread" also forms a wordplay on the similarly pronounced root *māṣaṣ* "to suck out, squeeze out" as a metaphor for departure (A. Ross, *NIDOTTE*, 4:448-53). [*maṣṣâ*]

12:11 Passover (*pesaḥ*). The noun *pesaḥ* "Passover" always refers to the festival established on the eve of the tenth plague that effected the release of the Hebrews from Egypt (Exod. 12:11, 21, 27, 43, 48). The term *pesaḥ* is probably related to the verb *pāsaḥ* which has a two-fold range of meanings: (1) "to limp" and (2) "to leap,

hop over, pass by, spare, protect" (*BDB*, 820; *HALOT*, 3:947). The physical action of limping (2 Sam. 4:4; cf. 2 Sam. 9:13; 19:27; Job 29:15; Prov. 26:7; Isa. 35:6; Jer. 31:8) and leaping over something (1 Kings 18:21, 26) lends itself to the idea of skipping over or passing over/by something. Used figuratively, this pictures God sparing (= skipping over) his people when he sent destruction upon Egypt (Exod. 12:13, 23, 27). The only other use of the verb *pāsaḥ* in this sense in the OT also describes God protecting his people in a passage filled with terms of divine deliverance: "The LORD of hosts will *protect* Jerusalem; he will *shield* and *deliver* it, he will *spare* (*pāsaḥ*) and *rescue* (*nāṣal*) it" (Isa. 31:5). In the narrative of the tenth plague the verb *pāsaḥ* "to pass by, spare" occurs 3x with the preposition *'al* "over" to connote "to pass over" in the sense of sparing the Hebrews: "The blood shall be a sign for you, upon the houses where you are; and when I see the blood, I will *pass over* (*pāsaḥ* + *'al*) you, and no plague shall fall upon you to destroy you, when I smite the land of Egypt" (Exod. 12:13); "For the LORD will *pass through* (*'ābar*) to slay the Egyptians; and when he sees the blood on the lintel and on the two doorposts, the LORD will *pass over* (*pāsaḥ* + *'al*) the door, and will not allow destruction to enter your houses to slay you" (Exod. 12:23); "It is the sacrifice of the LORD's *Passover* (*pesaḥ*), for he *passed over* (*pāsaḥ* + *'al*) the houses of the people of Israel in Egypt, when he slew the Egyptians but *spared* (*nṣl*) our houses" (Exod. 12:27). The close association between the verb *pāsaḥ* "to pass [over]" and the noun *pesaḥ* "Passover" (v. 27a) creates a tight wordplay (popular etymology) as the basis of the name of this national religious festival. (*NIDOTTE*, 3:642-44; *TWAT*, 6:659-82; *TWOT*, 2:728-29) [*pesaḥ*]

12:12 I will execute judgment on all the gods of Egypt (*šōpeṭîm*). Here and elsewhere the ten plagues are described as "judgment" on the gods of Egypt (Num. 33:4; Jer. 46:25). From the perspective of Egyptian religion, the plagues made a mockery of Egyptian paganism (Exod. 10:2; 12:23-27; 16:1-14; cf. Jubilees 48:5). The Nile, the so-called life-blood of the land of Egypt, was personified as the god Hapi, and its annual inundation was regarded as a manifestation of Osiris. So the first two plagues nullified the powers of these two deities. The plague of frogs seems to mock the frog goddess Heqt, who was believed to assist women in labor and who was the consort of Khnum, the god who fashioned human beings out of clay. The plague of darkness represented the defeat of the sun god Re, symbol of cosmic order. The plague of darkness would have evoked the Egyptian myth in which the monster Apophis, symbolic of darkness and the embodiment of all that is evil, daily vied for victory over Re. So by exercising sovereignty over every realm of power in Egyptian mythology, Yahweh demonstrated that he alone is the one true, living God. (*NIDOTTE*, 2:1142-44; *TLOT*, 3:1395d; *TWAT*, 8:408-28; *TWOT*, 2:947-49) [*šōpēṭ*]

12:16 Holy convocation (*miqrā'*). The noun *miqrā'* is from the verb *qārā'* "to call out, proclaim; to summon, invite; to assemble, gather [by summoning]" (*BDB*, 894-96; *HALOT*, 3:1128-31). It refers to a corporate group publicly gathered together as a formal "assembly, convocation" (*BDB*, 896.1; *HALOT*, 2:629.1b), usually to celebrate a sacred day or festival (Lev. 23:2, 4, 7, 27, 37; Num. 28:18, 25; 29:1, 7, 12; Isa. 1:13). This term emphasizes the corporate aspect of the festivals, an important feature of the national religious holiday that celebrated the redemption of "all Israel." The Hebrew emphasis on corporate worship and annual religious festivals may offer a much-needed balance to contemporary western evangelicalism—too often characterized by rugged individualism. While members of the New Covenant community are not under the religious calendar of Old Covenant Judaism (Rom. 14:5-6; Gal. 4:10; Col. 2:16-17), the underlying concept of the sacred corporate gathering for worship remains: "Let us not forsake our assembling together as is the habit of some" (Heb. 10:25). (*NIDOTTE*, 3:971-74; *TLOT*, 3:1158-64; *TWAT*, 7:117-47; *TWOT*, 2:810-11) [*miqrā'*]

12:23 The Destroyer (*hammašḥît*). The noun *mašḥît* is derived from the root *šḥt* which refers to physical or moral "corruption, destruction" (*BDB*, 1007-8). It is related to the noun *šaḥat* "pit" which often refers to the grave or Sheol (*BDB*, 1001; *HALOT*, 4:1472-73). The noun *mašḥît* itself often refers to physical or military "destruction" (Exod. 12:13; 2 Chron. 20:23; 22:4; Prov. 18:9; 28:24; Ezek. 5:16; 21:31[36]; 25:15; Dan. 10:8). This destruction is often wrought by a human army (1 Sam. 13:17; 14:15; Isa. 54:16; Jer. 51:4) or demonic angel as the agent of destruction: "the destroyer" (2 Sam. 24:16) (*BDB*, 1008; *HALOT*, 2:644). While there is some debate whether the term here refers to abstract physical "destruction," the LXX and most contemporary scholars view this as a personal angelic agent of divine destruction: "the destroyer" or "the destroying angel." In v. 13 *mašḥît* clearly refers to physical destruction. However, the article on *hammašḥît* in v. 23 might suggest a personal agent ("*the* destroyer") as in *hammal'āk hammašḥît* ("*the* angel of destruction") in 2 Sam. 24:16. Both the LXX and NT often picture a destroying angel as the personal agent of God's judgment which is otherwise pictured as a plague. For example, Num. 16:45-50 states that a "plague" sent by God slew 14,700 Israelites, while 1 Cor. 10:10 attributes this divine judgment to the agency of an angel: "the destroyer." In other biblical narratives, Yahweh brings the slayer against Israel (2 Sam. 24:16; 1 Chron. 21:15) or Judah (Jer. 4:7; 22:7; Ezek. 9:1-6). The conception of the angelic slayer might go back to the function of the army unit with the same designation (1 Sam. 13:17; 14:15; Isa. 54:16; Jer. 51:4). (NIDOTTE, 4:92-93; TLOT, 3:1317-19; TWAT, 7:1214-18; TWOT, 2:917-18) [mašḥît]

13:21 Pillar of <u>cloud</u> ('ānâ). When Israel departed from Succoth, the divine presence began to guide them as a pillar of cloud by day and a pillar of fire by night, enabling them to travel uninterrupted (Exod. 13:21-22; Num. 14:14; Neh. 9:12, 19; Ps. 99:7). The cloud shaded Israel from the scorching sun which would have made travel by day difficult, while the fire gave them light so they could travel at night, enabling Israel to put as much distance as possible between themselves and Pharaoh (v. 21). The pillar of cloud and fire also protected Israel when the Egyptians approached, moving between the two camps at night (14:19-20) then throwing the Egyptians into a panic in the morning when they began to pursue the Hebrews (14:24). The cloud also represented the divine presence when Moses entered the tent of meeting and conversed with God, allowing him to speak to God "face-to-face," so to speak (33:7-11). When the tabernacle was completed, the cloud settled upon it and the glory of God filled

it, representing the divine presence at day by cloud and at night by fire (40:34-35, 38). When the cloud lifted up, Israel set out on its journeys following the divine guidance (Exod. 40:36-37; Num. 10:11-12; 14:14). At momentous points the cloud descended and stood at the entrance of the tent of meeting from whence God addressed select audiences (Num. 12:5-10; Deut. 31:15-23). It is important to note that this numinous cloud both revealed and concealed the divine presence. While it was the vehicle of the glory of God, it also limited that revelation by obscuring a clear view of the "face" of God—a vision forbidden mortal man (Exod. 33:18-20; Lev. 16:2). Some have proposed the cloud and fire were embers of an active volcano in the area, but this is difficult to prove geologically and does not square with the text: the pillar was limited in location to Israel's camp, guided Israel through the terrain, entered and exited the tabernacle, and served as the vehicle of divine revelation to Moses and the people. When all the biblical data is considered, any natural explanation of the phenomena of the pillar of cloud and fire in Exod. 13:21 seems strained. ['ānâ]

14:4 "I will <u>get glory</u> from Pharaoh" (we'ikkābedâ). The use of this term is highly ironic. The verb kbd "to honor" functions here not in the passive sense "be honored," but in the middle/reflexive (Niphal) sense: "get glory for oneself" (Exod. 14:4.17, 18; Lev. 10;3; Isa. 26:15; Ezek. 28:22; 39:13; Hag. 1:8) (BDB, 457.2; HALOT, 2:455.4). Because neither Pharaoh nor the Egyptians would willingly glorify God, Yahweh would muster glory for himself by what he would do to them at the Reed (Red) Sea. Up to this point, he had not been given appropriate honor from Pharaoh. Now he would receive his just due by magnifying himself by destroying the Egyptian army (*TLOT*, 2:595). As a result, the Israelites would see his "glory" (*kābôd*) and "glorify" him by their response of praise and worship. (*NIDOTTE*, 2:577-78; *TDOT*, 7:13-22; *TLOT*, 2:590-602; *TWOT*, 1:426-28) [*kbd*]

14:13 "Do not fear!" (*'al tîrā'û*). In the ancient Near East, before an army went into battle, the king often sought a pre-battle divine oracle of assurance of victory: "Do not fear! Victory will be yours!" For example, the Assyrian king Esarhaddon claimed that Ishtar the goddess of war gave him an oracle of victory: "Fear not, O king. I will not abandon you . . . I will crush your foes with my own hands!" (*TLOT*, 2:574). Using this standard formula of comfort, the only true living God often gave absolute assurance to his people before battle against their enemies in a prophetic war oracle, "Do not fear!" (Num. 21:34; Deut. 1:21, 29; 3:2, 22; 20:1, 3; 31:6, 8; Josh. 8:1; 10:8, 25; 11:6; 2 Kings 6:16; 2 Chron. 20:15, 17; 32:7; Neh. 4:8; Isa. 7:4) (*HALOT*, 2:433.3b; cf. *BDB*, 431.1a). The appearance in v. 13 of this oracle-like assurance of victory to the seemingly defenseless Hebrews is startling. For Yahweh would not simply empower them to defeat their enemies (in keeping with typical ancient Near Eastern protocol), he himself would intervene to fight on their behalf! They would need only to "Stand still and see the triumph of the Lord!" (*NIDOTTE*, 2:527-33; *TDOT*, 6:290-315; *TLOT*, 2:568-78; *TWOT*, 1:399-401) [*yr'*]

Stand still and witness the Lord's triumph (*yešû'at*). When used in contexts of military battle, the term *yešû'â* has a basic two-fold range of meanings: (1) "help, rescue, deliverance" and (2) "victory, tri-

umph" (*BDB*, 447; *HALOT*, 2:446). It is often used of God rescuing his people in battle from mortal danger or helping them achieve victory over their enemies in battle (Gen. 14:18; Exod. 15:2; Deut. 32:15; 1 Sam. 2:1; 1 Chron. 16:23; 2 Chron. 20:17; Job 30:15; Pss. 3:3, 9; 9:15; 13:6; 14:7; 20:6; 21:2, 6; 35:3, 9; 62:2, 7; 67:3; 68:20; 69:30; 70:5; 78:22; 80:3; 89:27; 91:16; 96:2; 98:2; 106:4; 118:14, 21; 119:123, 155, 166, 174; 140:8; 149:4; Isa. 12:2; 25:9; 33:2; 59:11, 17) (*HALOT*, 2:446.A.1a). The alternately spelled *tešû'â* also refers to (1) "deliverance" from defeat in battle (Judg. 15:18; 2 Kings 5:1; 1 Sam. 11:13; 19:5; 2 Sam. 19:3; 23:10, 12; 1 Chron. 11:14; Prov. 21:31; Pss. 33:17; 144:10) and (2) "victory" in battle (Exod. 15:2; 2 Sam. 22:51; 2 Chron. 20:17; Pss. 20:6; 21:2, 6; 28:8; 44:5; 68:20; 74:20; 118:14, 15, 21; 149:4; Isa. 12:2; 33:6; 59:17; Hab. 3:8) (*BDB*, 447.4). In many cases, God would give "help" to his people in battle by empowering their swords or weapons to conquer their enemies (1 Sam. 17:47; Pss. 18:29; 60:12; 108:13). Here, however, the Lord himself would intervene dramatically, bypassing human agency in a wondrous display of the Divine Warrior fighting directly against their enemies (e.g., Judg. 7:9-23; 2 Kings 6:24-7:16; 19:35; 2 Chron. 20:1-25). So in the miracle at the Sea, the Lord not only rescued the Hebrews from the Egyptian army but also routed them to win a resounding victory: "He triumphed gloriously" (Exod. 15:1). (*NIDOTTE*, 2:556-62; *TDOT*, 6:441-63; *TLOT*, 2:584-87; *TWOT*, 1:414-16) [*yešû'â*]

14:24 The Lord looked down upon the Egyptian army (*wayyašeqēp*). The verb *šqp* "to look down from above" (from the standpoint of the one observed) is derived from the related noun "ceiling, roof, sky" (*BDB*, 1054; *HALOT*, 4:1645).

Elsewhere it refers to a person looking down from a mountaintop over a plain or valley below (Num. 21:20; 23:28; 1 Sam. 13:18) or looking down from an upper window in a lofty palace (Judg. 5:28; 2 Sam. 6:16). In one elaborate metaphor in the OT it personifies the heavenly luminaries (sun, moon, stars) looking down upon the earth (S. of S. 6:10). Here it creates a bold anthropomorphism, picturing God in heaven above looking down on earth below, glaring in anger at the Egyptians. This divine look might be a figurative way of describing the terrifying bolts of lightning and sudden claps of thunder that threw the Egyptian army into a panic (Ps. 77:17-19). [šqp]

The LORD caused a panic among the Egyptians (wayyāhām). This term pictures the Divine Warrior fighting against the Egyptians with the weapons of psychological warfare. The verb hāmam has a three-fold range of meanings: (1) "to make a noise, startle" (Isa. 28:28); (2) "to be beside oneself" in anxiety (Ruth 1:19; 1 Sam. 4:5; 1 Kings 1:45); and (3) "to throw into confusion" of the panic and disarray of an army before a superior force (Exod. 23:27; Josh. 10:10; Judg. 4:15; 1 Sam. 7:10; 2 Sam. 22:15; 2 Chron. 15:6; Pss. 18:15; 144:6) (BDB, 243; HALOT, 1:251). This term appears most often in the context of holy war. When Israel faced an overwhelmingly superior army, Yahweh sometimes intervened as the Divine Warrior using weapons of psychological warfare. At the beginning of these battles Yahweh created confusion among the enemy troops by his sovereign orchestration of the cosmic elements, such as the thunderstorm (1 Sam. 7:10), earthquake (1 Sam. 14:15) and the wind, sea, fire and cloud at the Sea (Exod. 14:24-25). The related noun mehûmâ "confusion" also describes psychological warfare wrought

by God in holy war (Deut. 7:23; 28:20; 1 Sam. 5:9, 11; 2 Chron. 15:5), as does pahad "dread" (Exod. 15:16; Deut. 2:25; 11:25; Isa. 2:10, 19, 21). (NIDOTTE, 1:1046-48; TDOT, 3:419-22; TLOT, 1:377-78; TWOT, 1:220) [hmm]

14:30 The LORD delivered Israel (wayyōšaʿ). The intensive (Hiphil) verb yšʿ "to help, rescue, deliver" does not refer to soteriological salvation but deliverance from life-threatening military attack (Judg. 2:18; 10:12; 1 Sam. 7:8; 10:19; 2 Sam. 3:18; 2 Kings 19:19; 2 Chron. 32:22; Ps. 106:10; Isa. 37:20; Hab. 3:13) (BDB, 446.1d; HALOT, 2:448.2b). Nevertheless, the mighty acts of God in the deliverance of Israel from military enemies provides a dramatic picture of God's power to rescue his people from premature physical death and the ultimate soteriological deliverance wrought by Messiah at the cross in defeating spiritual foes (Col 2:15) and in his future eschatological destruction of all demonic forces (Rev. 19:11-15). (NIDOTTE, 2:556-62; TDOT, 6:441-63; TLOT, 2:584-87; TWOT, 1:414-16) [yšʿ]

14:31 The people believed in the LORD (wayyaʾămînû). While the basic (Qal) meaning of the verb ʾmn is "to be trustworthy," the intensive (Hiphil) verb has an estimative sense: "to regard [someone] as trustworthy, believe [someone]" (Gen. 15:6; 45:26; Exod. 4:1, 8; 1 Kings 10:7; 2 Chron. 32:15; Jer. 40:14) (BDB, 53.2; HALOT, 1:64.3). When used with be the expression means "to believe in, trust in [someone]" (BDB, 53.2c), often of trusting in God (Gen. 15:6; Exod. 14:31; Num. 14:11; 20:12; Deut. 1:32; 2 Kings 17:14; 2 Chron. 20:20; Ps. 78:22; Jonah 3:5). This is the same expression used when Abraham "believed in" the LORD (Gen. 15:6) so it probably refers to genuine faith. Initially, the Hebrews believed Moses when he performed the divinely orchestrated miracles in their sight (Exod. 4:31). Now when they witnessed the mighty act of God in parting the Reed (Red) Sea, they also placed their faith in Yahweh himself (Exod. 14:31). So the Law would be given, not to unbelievers to show them how to merit a relationship with God, but to genuine believers to show them how to express their faith in the LORD by obedience (Deut. 10:12-13).

This does not imply that every individual coming out of Egypt had a sincere heart of genuine faith. The expression "*the people* believed" might be a synecdoche of whole (= the people) for the part (= majority). Moreover, their later act of disbelief at Kadesh-Barnea (Num. 13-14) should not discredit nor even minimize this genuine expression of faith at the Sea. Without the benefit of the Spirit given to all believers for the first time in the New Covenant (Num. 11:29; Joel 2:28-29 [3:1-2]), the greatest men of faith under the Old Covenant were sometimes guilty of surprising inconsistencies. (*NIDOTTE*, 1:427-33; *TDOT*, 1:292-323; *TLOT*, 1:134-57; *TWOT*, 1:51-53) ['*mn*]

15:1 He is greatly exalted (*gā'ô gā'â*). The root *g'h* "rise up" is used literally of water and waves rising up (Job 38:11; Pss. 46:4; 89:1; Ezek. 47:5), smoke ascending (Isa. 9:17), plants growing upward (Job 8:11) and a person lifting up his head in pride (Job 10:16) (*BDB*, 144; *HALOT*, 1:168-69). It is easy to see how it is used figuratively of social ascent: (1) negatively: arrogant pride of man (Job 40:11, 12; Isa. 2:12; Jer. 48:29; Pss. 94:2; 140:6; Prov. 8:13; 15:25; 16:19) and (2) positively: God's majestic exaltation and eminence (Exod. 15:1, 7, 21; Deut. 33:26; Job 37:4; 40:10; Ps. 68:35; 93:1; Isa. 2:10, 19, 21; 12:5; 13:3; 24:14; 26:10;

Mic. 5:3; Zeph. 3:11) (*BDB*, 144; *HALOT*, 1:168-69). Although God reigns on high in heaven where he is worshiped by the heavenly assembly, his reputation among fallen humanity was exalted through this mighty act of power. (*NIDOTTE*, 1:786-89; *TDOT*, 2:344-50; *TLOT*, 1:285-87; *TWOT*, 1:143-44) [*g'h*]

15:3 The LORD is a mighty warrior ('*îš milḥāmâ*). This expression clearly portrays God in the role of the Divine Warrior. Literally "man of war," this expression features the common Hebrew idiom of the noun "man" ('*îš*) followed by another noun to represent the nature, quality, or character of that person, e.g., "man of words" is an eloquent person (Exod. 4:10), "man of blood" is a murderer (2 Sam. 16:7), "man of worthlessness" is a scoundrel (2 Sam. 18:20) and "man of friends" is a friendly person (Prov. 18:24). Likewise, "man of war" is a mighty warrior (Josh. 17:1; Judg. 20:17; 1 Sam. 16:18; 17:33; 2 Sam. 8:10; 17:8; 1 Chron. 28:3; Ps. 24:8; Isa. 3:2; 42:13; Ezek. 39:20) (*BDB*, 536; *HALOT*, 2:589.2). This expression refers to a well-trained and victorious warrior who understands how to fight and defeat the enemy. Ironically, the Egyptian rulers of this period fancied themselves to be the mightiest warriors on earth; however, Yahweh's victory over Pharaoh at the Sea trumped this mighty Egyptian. ['*îš*]

15:13 You will lead the people (*nāḥîtā*). The verb *nḥh* "to lead, guide" occurs elsewhere of a shepherd tending and leading his flock to lush pastures and still waters (Pss. 23:3; 78:72), and of a native guide who skillfully leads a traveler through unfamiliar terrain to his intended destination (Num. 23:7). This term occurs often in the Exodus-wilderness narratives referring in turn to the divine guidance from

Egypt to Canaan provided by the pillar of cloud (Exod. 13:21; Neh. 9:12, 19; Ps. 78:14), the angelic guide sent before the people (Exod. 32:34) and the LORD himself (Exod. 13:17; Deut. 32:12; Ps. 78:53). This triad is so closely associated that one seems to suggest the other: the pillar of cloud is the representational form of the angel of the LORD who in turn is closely associated with the LORD himself. It is not that Moses or the people thought that the LORD was an angel or in the pillar of cloud but the three were somehow viewed as inseparable. Other passages use this term to refer to the wondrous sovereign guidance of an individual (Gen. 24:27, 48) and God's spiritual guidance in the paths of moral righteousness (Pss. 5:8; 27:11; 31:3; 73:24; 139:24; 143:10). (*NIDOTTE*, 3:76; *TLOT*, 2:729-30; *TWAT*, 5:334-42; *TWOT*, 2:568-69) [*nḥh*]

The people whom you have redeemed (*gāʾāltā*). The verb "redeem" (*gāʾal*) casts God in the role of a clan leader who protects members of his extended family in times of need and crisis (Exod. 6:6; Pss. 19:14; 74:2; 77:16; 78:35; 106:10; Isa. 51:10; 63:9). God is elsewhere explicitly described as the *gōʾēl* "kinsman-redeemer" who comes to the aid of needy relatives in distress (Prov. 23:10-11; Jer. 50:34). The verb *gāʾal* "act as kinsman" is often used as a technical term of family-law, referring to the duty of a family leader (near kinsman) to act on behalf of needy members of the extended family (*BDB*, 145.1; *HALOT*, 1:169). Among other things (Num. 5:8; 35:12, 19-27), such acts of benevolence might involve paying off the debt of an impoverished family member to affect his release from debt bondage, that is, to redeem him from slavery (Lev. 25:48-49), or redeeming his family landed property which he had sold to raise capital (Lev. 25:25-28). By using this term, the LORD is pictured as the concerned leader of the clan who redeemed his impoverished family member, Israel, from debt slavery to the Egyptians. Extending this imagery further, at the time of the conquest he would restore the family property of the land of Canaan which impoverished Israel abandoned when they sojourned in Egypt. (*NIDOTTE*, 1:789-95; *TDOT*, 2:350-55; *TLOT*, 1:288-96; *TWOT*, 1:144-45) [*gʾl*]

You will guide them to your holy habitation (*nēhaltā*). The verb *nēhal* "to guide [to water]" (Ps. 23:2; Isa. 40:11; 49:10) is related to a common Semitic root meaning "to lie down, rest" (*TDOT*, 9:260). It is also related to the Hebrew nouns *nahălāl* "place for water" and *nahălōl* "watering-place" (*BDB*, 625.1; *HALOT*, 2:676.1). This term pictures God as a shepherd guiding his flock to water or lush pasture (= his holy habitation). As vv. 14-17 make clear, the ultimate destination of this journey is not Sinai but the land of Canaan promised to the patriarchs. The land flowing with "milk and honey" (Exod. 3:8 17; 13:5; 33:3) is here pictured as the lush pasture to which the Divine Shepherd is guiding his flock. (*NIDOTTE*, 3:44; *TDOT*, 9:260-61; *TWOT*, 2:559) [*nhl*]

15:16 The people whom you have acquired (*qānîtā*). The verb *qnh* has a broad range of meanings, including (1) "to create" (Gen. 14:19), (2) "to acquire" something through labor (Pss. 74:2; 78:54; Prov. 1:5) and (3) "to purchase" something at cost (Gen. 47:20; Jer. 13:1) (*BDB*, 888-89; *HALOT*, 3:1112). It is used of a human purchasing servants (Exod. 21:2; Lev. 22:11; 25:44) as well as buying back (= redeem) fellow Jews from Gentile owners to set them free (Neh. 5:8). Similarly, the verb *qnh* pictures God acquiring ownership of Israel from Gentile nations who had ruled over them (Isa. 11:11), redeeming them to become his servants (Ps. 74:2). Rather than purchasing them at financial cost, he acquired them by the "labor" of his historical acts of deliverance. For example, "Remember Your people whom You acquired (*qnh*) in ancient times, whom You redeemed (*g'l*) so they could become Your very own nation!" (Ps. 74:2) and "In that day, the Lord will lift his hand to redeem (*qnh*) the remnant of his people from Assyria, Egypt, Pathros, Cush, Elam, Shinar, Hamath, and the seacoasts" (Isa. 11:11). Thus acquired, Israel belongs to him: they are his "servants" (Ps. 100:3), his "property" (Exod. 19:5-6) and his "inheritance" (Deut. 32:8-9). (*NIDOTTE*, 3:940-42; *TLOT*, 3:1147-53; *TWAT*, 7:63-65; *TWOT*, 2:803-04) [*qnh*]

15:17 You will plant them on your own mountain (*wĕtiṭṭāʿēmô*). This pictures Israel as a lush vine or tree the LORD will plant on Mount Zion as the ultimate goal of the Exodus and conquest events. The verb *ntʿ* "to plant" is used literally of a landowner planting a sapling or sprout in fertile soil (*BDB*, 642.1) and figuratively of God establishing nations on earth (Isa. 40:24), particularly of Yahweh establishing Israel securely in the fertile land of Canaan (2 Sam. 7:10=1 Chron. 17:9; Ps. 44:2; Isa. 5:7; 60:21; Jer. 24:6; 32:41; 42:10; 45:10; Ezek. 36:36; Amos 9:15). This agricultural motif plays upon the land promises that God gave to the patriarchs (Gen. 12:1-2, 7; 13:14-17; 15:18-21; 17:8; 22:17; 26:3-4) and was now about to fulfill with their descendants (Exod. 3:8, 17; 6:4, 8; 23:20-33). God would later promise David that he would "plant" Israel securely in the land (2 Sam. 7:10=1 Chron. 17:9). (*NIDOTTE*, 3:107-08; *TDOT*, 9:387-94; *TWOT*, 2:575-76) [*ntʿ*]

The sanctuary your hands have established (*miqqedāš*). It is difficult to determine the referent of the contextually ambiguous term *miqqedāš* "sanctuary" (for discussion of *miqdāš* "sanctuary," see 25:8). There are four major views: (1) the LORD's dwelling place on Mount Sinai to which the people traveled after they came out of Egypt; (2) the land of Canaan as the ultimate destination of the Exodus; (3) one of the early sanctuaries in Israel, such as Gilgal or Shiloh; or (4) the future Solomonic temple in Jerusalem. (*NIDOTTE*, 3:877-87; *TLOT*, 3:1103-18; *TWAT*, 6:1179-1204; *TWOT*, 2:786-89) [*miqdāš*]

15:24 The people murmured (*wayyillōnû*). The verb *lwn* "to murmur [against]" (*BDB*, 534; *HALOT*, 2:524) and the related noun *telunnâ* "murmuring" appears frequently in the Exodus-wilderness journey narratives (Exod. 15:24; 16:7, 8, 12; 17:3; Num. 14:2, 27, 29, 36; 16:11; 17:6, 20). This is much more serious than grumbling and complaining; it was the root of corporate rebellion against God. They were expressing their doubt against God's ability to provide for their needs and were suspicious about his real motives in bringing them into the wilderness. This was tantamount to a vote of "no confidence" in Yahweh. (*NIDOTTE*, 2:780-82; *TDOT*, 7:509-12; *TLOT*, 2:644-46; *TWOT*, 1:475) [*lwn*]

16:31 Manna (*mān*). The name *mān* I "manna" is a word play (popular etymology) on the ancient and rarely used interrogative *mān* II "what?" (*HALOT*, 2:596) that appears in the question in v. 15, "What is it?" (*mān hû'*). This was the initial reaction of the Israelites to the divinely produced food in the desert: "When they saw it, they said to one another, 'What (*mān*) is it?' because they did not know what (*mān*) it was" (16:15). This is an unusual name because people do not typically name things with a question, "What-Is-It?" Ironically, their question remains unanswered to this day! All that we know is that it was a small, flake-like substance which was white like coriander seed, tasted like honey, and that it formed on the surface of the desert when the morning dew evaporated (Exod. 16:14, 31; Num. 11:7). Some scholars compare the biblical manna with other ancient references to honeydew from the heavens in Hesiod and Aristotle. Others try to find some natural cause for this miracle, such as a honeydew excretion from plant lice and scale insects, such as cicadas which are called *mān* in Arabic—an explanation that fits some but not all of the particulars (*HALOT*, 2:596). Whether the LORD used a natural phenomenon in some miraculous way or the manna was supernatural in nature, Scripture calls it the "grain of heaven" (Ps. 78:24) and describes it as an entirely unique thing: (1) it was a substance previously unknown to Israel's ancestors (Deut. 8:3, 16), (2) it appeared six days of the week but miraculously disappeared on the Sabbath (Exod. 16:21-27), (3) God provided it for Israel throughout her forty years in the wilderness (Deut. 8:3), and (4) he terminated its provision abruptly on the very morning that the people first ate the produce of the land of Canaan (Josh. 5:12; cf. Exod. 16:35). The very fact that its source was inexplicable by natural causes provided a powerful lesson to ancient Israel that the omnipotent God is able to provide for the needs of his people by the sheer power of his own will (Deut. 8:3). Man does not need to explain the natural means of God's blessings, but to trust and obey the One who can sovereignly provide such blessings. [*mān*]

17:7 He named the place Massa . . . because there they tested the LORD (*massâ k̆nassōtām*). The place name "Massa" (*massâ*) forms a wordplay on the verb *nasâ* ("to test"), meaning "The Place of Testing." The verb *nsh* has a broad range of meanings: (1) "to test," (2) "to tempt," (3) "to try," and (4) "to prove" (*BDB*, 650; *HALOT*, 2:702). Elsewhere, it is used of a human challenging another, e.g., the Queen of Sheba attempting to "stump" Solomon to see whether or not he could answer her difficult riddles (1 Kings 10:1=2 Chron. 9:1) (*BDB*, 650.1). When used of God testing Israel, the tests were designed to see whether or not Israel would trust and obey God (Exod. 15:25; 16:4; Deut. 8:2, 16; 13:4) (*BDB*, 650.3a). Here it refers to people putting God to the test to see whether or not he would act according to their dictates (Exod. 17:2, 7; Num. 14:22; Deut. 6:16; Pss. 78:18, 41, 56; 95:9; 106:14; cf. Isa. 7:12) (*BDB*, 650.3b; *HALOT*, 2:702.1b). By expressing doubt that God was truly in their midst (v. 7b, "Is the LORD in our midst or not?"), the Israelites demanded that God "jump through their hoops," so to speak, to prove himself. While the sovereign God has the right to test humans to see whether or not they will trust and obey him, for humans to put God to the test to prove himself is an act of *hubris* of the highest order. The classic example of putting God to the test was Satan's proposal that Jesus cast himself down from the pinnacle of the temple and thereby *force* God's hand to fulfill his promise to protect even his foot from striking a stone (Matt. 4:6-7). (*NIDOTTE*, 3:111-13; *TLOT*, 2:741-42; *TWAT*, 5:473-87; *TWOT*, 2:581) [*nsh*]

[He named the place] Meribah . . . because of Israel's quarrel with Moses (*ûmerîbâ . . . rîb*). The noun *rîb* has two broad categories of meaning: (1) used in legal contexts: (a) "legal process" (Exod.

23:3), (b) "lawsuit" (Deut. 17:8), (c) "disputation" (Job 13:6); and (2) used in non-legal contexts: (a) "dispute" between individuals or groups (Gen. 13:7), (b) "quarrel" (Exod. 17:7), (c) "strife, quarrel" in situations before they become legal problems (Deut. 25:1) (*BDB*, 936-37; *HALOT*, 3:1225-26). The verb *rîb* has a parallel development: (1) used in legal situations or in the context of a legal dispute: (a) "to contest a lawsuit" (Exod. 23:2), (b) "to plead someone's legal cause" (Isa. 1:17), (c) "to lodge a complaint [against someone]" (Judg. 21:22), (d) "to dispute with someone" (Hos. 2:4); and (2) used in non-legal situations: (a) "to get into a brawl or quarrel" (Exod. 21:18), (b) "to strive, contend against" someone in situations before they become legal problems (Prov. 3:30), and (c) "to upbraid, remonstrate" (Neh. 13:11) (*BDB*, 936; *HALOT*, 3:1224-25). The kind of conflict described by *rîb* plays out between two opposing parties, and may occur in three overlapping areas of life: (a) extra-judicial conflict: interpersonal quarrel or physical struggle between men associated with bodily injury (Exod. 21:18; Ps. 55:10-12), (b) pre-judicial conflict: one individual or group formally accuses another individual of breach of faith (Gen. 31:36; Neh. 13:11, 17, 25), and (c) judicial conflict: the legal process in which a legal dispute between two opposing parties is heard by a judge (Exod. 23:3, 6; Deut. 17:8). In the case of Israel's *rîb* against Moses, the prevalent motif of murmuring (Exod. 15:24) does not suit a physical brawl with bodily injury to Moses nor judicial litigation in a class-action lawsuit. The people lodged a formal complaint accusing him of breach of faith and goodwill. Gone unchecked, Israel would have formally repudiated his leadership and reversed course, surrendering themselves back

into the hands of Pharaoh. To remind Israel for all time of their failure before God on this occasion, the place was named *merîbâ* "Meribah = Strife," a word-play on *rîb* "to strive" (vv. 2 and 7). (*NIDOTTE*, 3:1105-06; *TLOT*, 3:1232-37; *TWAT*, 7:496-501; *TWOT*, 2:845-46) [*rîb*]

19:4 I carried you on the wings of eagles (*kanpê*). This imagery (zoomorphism) pictures Yahweh's deliverance of Israel and trek to Sinai as a mother eagle protecting her young by transporting them out of danger and bringing them to the safety of her lofty nest. The ability of birds to escape harm is a common metaphor for swift deliverance from danger (Pss. 11:1; 55:6; 139:9). Wings suggest swiftness (2 Sam. 12:3; Jer. 4:13; Lam. 4:19), the ability to soar to great heights (Job 39:27; Isa. 40:31; Jer. 49:16; Obad. 1:4), and to fly long distances (Deut. 28:49; Isa. 40:31). The eagle was renowned for the expanse of its outstretched wings (Deut. 32:11; Jer. 48:40; 49:22; Ezek. 17:3, 17) and its protective parenting habits of carrying its young (Deut. 32:10-11). So the zoomorphism of God's "wings" pictures God's deliverance, protection, and comfort given to his people (Ruth 2:12; Pss. 17:8; 36:7; 57:1; 61:4; 63:7; 91:4; Mal. 4:2). (*NIDOTTE*, 2:670-71; *TDOT*, 7:229-31; *TLOT*, 2:618-20; *TWOT*, 1:446-47) [*kānāp*]

I brought you to myself (*wā' ābi'*). The causative (Hiphil) stem of *bw'* "to bring [someone to oneself]" can be interpreted in two ways: (1) literal: physical geographical transportation or (2) figurative: the inauguration of a relationship, such as the formal introduction of subjects to a king (Dan. 1:18) or the consummation of a marriage relationship (Judg. 12:9). Accordingly, some take this as a literal reference to God's geographical transportation of Israel from Egypt to Sinai:

God brought them to the site where they could worship him where he dwelt. Others take it as a figurative description of God's election of the Hebrews and inauguration of the covenant at Sinai that they might be his people (v. 5): "I brought you to myself" is tantamount to "I am Yahweh, who brought you up from the land of Egypt, to be your God" (Lev. 11:45). Yahweh's redemption of Israel inaugurated a new kind of relationship that would climax in the covenant at Sinai. (*NIDOTTE*, 1:615-18; *TDOT*, 2:20-49; *TLOT*, 1:201-4; *TWOT*, 1:93-95) [*bw'*]

19:5 So now, if you will faithfully obey me (*šāmôa' tišmĕ'û bĕqōlî*). This expression (lit. "*listen* to my *voice*") is an idiom for obedience to God's commands: "to hear" > "to listen to" > "to hearken to" > "to obey" (Gen. 22:18; 27:13; 1 Sam. 15:22; 2 Sam. 12:18; 2 Kings 14:11; Neh. 9:16, 29; Prov. 5:13; Isa. 42:24; Jer. 26:5; 35:14, 18; 38:20; Hag. 1:12) (*HALOT*, 4:1572.4.a). The verb "listen" (*šm'*) is figurative (metonymy of cause) for obedience, while the noun "voice" (*qōl*) is figurative (metonymy of instrument) for the commands God speaks. This emphatic construction repeats the root twice (*šāmôa' tišme'û*) to denote (1) intensity: "If you *are* faithful to obey me" (so NJPS, CEV, NIV) or (2) certainty: "If you *will indeed* obey me" (so KJV, NKJV, ASV, NASB) (Note: Some translations are intentionally ambiguous: "If you will obey me," NAB, RSV, NRSV, TEV, NLT). At the heart of the covenant relationship with God is obedience to his commands. (*NIDOTTE*, 4:175-81; *TLOT*, 3:1375-80; *TWAT*, 8:255-79; *TWOT*, 2:938-39) [*šm'*]

And keep My covenant (*ûšemartem*). The verb *šmr* "to keep" means "to stick to an agreement" (*HALOT*, 4:1583.8) or "fulfill an obligation" (*BDB*, 1036.3.b), and

šāmar bĕrît "to keep a covenant" refers to fulfilling covenant obligations and obeying covenant stipulations (Gen. 17:9, 10; Deut. 29:8; 1 Sam. 13:13; 1 Kings 8:23; 11:11; Pss. 78:10; 103:18; 132:12; Ezek. 17:14; Amos 2:4). This is one of several expressions for covenant obedience: to act according to the covenant (2 Chron. 34:32), hold fast to the covenant (Isa. 56:4, 6), maintain the covenant (Deut. 8:18), perform the covenant (2 Kings 23:3; Jer. 34:18), be faithful to the covenant (Ps. 78:37), and keep the covenant (Deut. 33:9; Ps. 25:10). (*NIDOTTE*, 4:182-84; *TLOT*, 3:1380-84; *TWAT*, 8:280-306; *TWOT*, 2:939-40) [*šmr*]

Covenant (*bĕrît*). The Hebrew term *bĕrît* is probably from the root *brh* II "to establish a legal obligation by testimony with an oath," and related to the Semitic noun *brt* "contractual obligation" (*HALOT*, 1:157). The lexicons and wordbooks suggest a broad range of connotations for *bĕrît*: "agreement, contract, pact, covenant, treaty, alliance, pledge, binding oath of promise, obligation, commitment" between two parties (*BDB*, 136; *HALOT*, 1:157; *DCH* 2:264; *TLOT*, 1:256; *TDOT*, 2:255; *TWOT*, 1:128; *NIDOTTE*, 1:747).

The LXX rendered *bĕrît* as *diathēkē* which had a two-fold range of meanings: (1) "will," as the imposition of one's volition; and (2) "testament," as a legal document to dispose of one's possessions at death (aka "last will and testament"). Due to the ambiguity of *diathēkē* and its inability to capture key connotations, later Greek versions (Aquila, Symmachus) glossed it as *sunthēkē* "covenant, treaty." Under this influence, the traditional view long held that *bĕrît* denotes "covenant, treaty, agreement" that established a relationship between two parties. However, more recent exegetical studies suggest that *bĕrît* designates an "obligation" between two parties, formalized by a solemn act and sworn pledge. It does not refer as much to the "covenant, agreement" as the instrument of an obligation, but to the "obligation" itself which the sworn oath formalizes and the covenant agreement articulates. In contrast to the traditional view, *bĕrît* does not establish the relationship; rather, it inaugurates the obligation that is now formalized between two parties in a previously existing relationship.

As its usage suggests, *bĕrît* most often refers to a mutually binding legal obligation between two parties (Gen. 21:22-24; 26:26-33; 31:49-54), often formally ratified by a solemn act (Gen. 15:9-18; Exod. 24:4-18; Jer. 34:18) or sworn oath (2 Kings 11:4; Ezek. 17:13, 18, 19). It often appears with the term "oath" (Gen. 26:3; Num. 30:3; Deut. 4:31; 7:8, 12; 8:18; Josh. 9:20; 1 Chron. 16:15-18; Ps. 105:8-11). Likewise, the idiom "to make a covenant" is often paralleled by "to swear an oath" (Josh. 9:15; 2 Kings 11:4; Ezra 10:5; Ps. 89:4; Ezek. 16:8). So *bĕrît* refers to a mutually binding legal obligation between two parties, formalized by a sworn oath, as in the expression "bond (*māsōret*) of the covenant (*bĕrît*)" (Ezek. 20:37). So there are three basic features characteristic of *bĕrît*: mutuality, commitment, and obligation.

The term *bĕrît* may refer to three kinds of legal arrangements: (1) unilateral covenant: "commitment" by a one party to fulfill a promise unilaterally granted to another party, and most often confirmed or ratified by a sworn oath or confirmatory ritual (Gen. 15:18); (2) suzerain-vassal treaty: "obligation" unilaterally imposed by a stronger party upon a weaker party (Exod. 19:5; 24:8; Jer. 34:8, 13-14; Ezek. 17:13, 18, 19); (3) bilateral parity treaty: "mutual obligation" mutually accepted by two parties who make mutual pledges to

fulfill their individual obligation to one another (1 Kings 5:12[26]; 15:19; 2 Chron. 23:26; Ps. 83:6) or "mutual obligation" between two parties sponsored/mediated by a third party (Hos. 2:18[20]). All three connotations presuppose some kind of mutuality because there are always two parties in a *bĕrît*. This is obvious in #3 which involves a mutual obligation, but it is also present in ##1-2 which involve two parties who willingly enter into a *bĕrît* (one party commits himself to fulfill a promise to the other party). The exact connotation of *berît* is dependent on the nature of the relationship between the two parties: (a) between nations it refers to "treaty, alliance," (b) between individuals "agreement, pledge, contract," (c) between a king and his subjects "constitution, obligation," or (d) between God and man "covenant" (*HALOT*, 1:157-59; *TWOT*, 1:128).

When it refers to the *bĕrît* between Yahweh and Israel at Sinai, the term has two basic meanings, corresponding to the responsibility of the two parties: (1) divine "commitment" by God to fulfill his promises that he swore by oath, and (2) human "obligation" by Israel to keep the law which the nation swore by pledge to do at Sinai and Moab. When *bĕrît* refers to the role of the stronger party (Yahweh or a secular suzerain) it most often refers to his commitment to fulfill a promise given on oath. When it refers to the role of the weaker party (Israel or a secular vassal) it most often refers to his obligation to fulfill duties imposed on him by the covenant master. We may say that *bĕrît* generally connotes "divine commitment" and "human obligation." At Sinai, God obligated himself to fulfill certain promises to Israel, swearing by oath to fulfill these commitments. Likewise Israel entered into covenant obligations, swearing by oath before the LORD that they would obey whatever he commanded. So at its most basic core the covenant between God and man involves "divine commitment" (promise) and corresponding "human obligation." (*NIDOTTE*, 1:747-55; *TDOT*, 2:253-79; *TLOT*, 1:256-66; *TWOT*, 1:128-30) [*bĕrît*]

My treasured possession (*sĕgullâ*). This term portrays Israel as the specially commissioned beloved servant of God and his devoted worshiper. The term *sĕgullâ* has a three-fold range of referents: (1) economic: "treasure," (2) religious: "personal possession," and (3) political: "treasured possession" (*BDB*, 688; *HALOT*, 2:742). First, it can refer to the valued personal property of kings, e.g., silver or gold (1 Chron. 29:3; Eccl. 2:8). Second, it can refer to the possession of a god, such as his temple or devoted worshipers. For example, devotees of Assyrian gods are designated by the construction *sikiltu* + divine names: "the personal possession of (the god)." Third, it can refer to a beloved servant (individual or people) commissioned by a king for a special task, depicting the special value the king placed on a devoted servant who served a special purpose. For example, a royal seal of Abban of Alalakh designates its owner as the *sikiltum* "treasured possession" of the god, referring to him as his "servant" and "beloved." A letter from the Hittite sovereign to the king of Ugarit characterizes his vassal as his "servant" and "treasured possession" (*sglt*). So it depicted the value that the king placed in a special servant who served a special purpose. The use of this term in Exod. 19:5 probably combines the latter two nuances: (1) religious sense: Israel would be the special possession of Yahweh as his devoted worshipers, serving him at his tabernacle/temple, and (2) political sense: Yahweh was commissioning Israel to be his beloved servant for the

special task of mediating his redemptive blessings to the nations. So the designation of Israel as Yahweh's *sĕgullâ* "treasured possession" (Exod. 19:5; Deut. 7:6; 14:2; 26:18-19; Ps. 135:4; Mal. 3:17) describes Israel's unique calling as the special servant of Yahweh and his devoted worshipers. Israel was God's crown jewel, so to speak. Her value as God's special treasured possession would reside in her function as a holy nation and a priestly kingdom, as v. 6 indicates. While Yahweh is the sovereign of all nations, he holds Israel among his choice possessions, one that serves a special purpose in his grand design (Merrill & Zuck, *A Biblical Theology of the Old Testament*, 33). This is reflected in several translations: "You shall be my special possession, dearer to Me than all other people" (NAB) "My treasured possession" (NIV, NRSV, NJPS) and "My very own people" (CEV). Unfortunately, Israel failed to fulfill its role as God's special servant in his redemptive program to the world. The NT applies this title to the Church (Titus 2:14; 1 Pet. 2:9), suggesting that there is a functional continuity, but not necessarily an ontological identity, between the Church and Israel. Although the Church has not replaced Israel, Gentile and Jewish believers alike in Christ have been commissioned as fellow-heirs to fulfill the calling national Israel failed. (*NIDOTTE*, 3:22-24; *TLOT*, 2:791-93; *TWAT*, 5:749-72; *TWOT*, 2:617) [*sĕgullâ*]

19:6 Kingdom of priests (*mamleket kōhănîm*). This title encapsulates the divine commission of Israel in its most pristine form; however, the precise meaning of this phrase has long been a matter of debate for four reasons. First, some ancient versions interpreted consonantal *mmlkt* as plural *memalkôt*, "kings," parallel to plural *kōhănîm*, "priests," to produce:

"kings, priests, and a holy nation" (Aramaic Targums). However, the traditional vocalization of the Hebrew text is singular *mamleket* "kingdom" followed by plural *kōhǎnîm*, "priests." There is no compelling reason to reject this tradition.

Second, some ancient versions took *mamleket kōhǎnîm* as parallel terms: "a kingdom, priests, and a holy nation" (Syriac) or "a kingdom, a priesthood, and a holy nation" (LXX). Some modern interpreters take the two as a predicate clause: "kings [who are] priests." However, elsewhere in the OT *mamleket* is always in construct with a following genitive (Num. 32:33; Deut. 3:4, 10, 13; 1 Sam. 24:21; 2 Chron. 13:8; 21:4; Jer. 27:1; 28:1; Mic. 4:8; cf. Gen. 10:10; 20:9; Deut. 17:18, 20; 1 Sam. 13:13, 14; 2 Sam. 3:28; 5:12; 7:12, 13, 16; 1 Kings 9:5; Isa. 9:7), so *mamleket kōhǎnîm* undoubtedly means "kingdom *of* priests."

Third, assuming that this is indeed a genitive construct, ancient and modern interpreters debate about its precise function: (1) attributive genitive: "a priestly kingdom," parallel to *wegôy qādôš* "holy nation," which also features an attributive genitive; (2) attributed genitive: "a royal priesthood," somewhat parallel to *wegôy qādôš* "holy nation" (but less parallel than #1 above); (3) partitive genitive: "a kingdom (whole) *containing* priests (part)," meaning that the nation would have "priests" as part of its population; (4) genitive of composition: "a kingdom *composed of* priests," meaning that the nation as a whole was designated collectively as a nation of priests. The latter is the best option, and is adopted by a majority of translations: "kingdom of priests" (KJV, NKJV, ASV, RSV, NAB, NASB, NIV, NLT, NJPS, NET) and "you will serve me as priests" (TEV, CEV). This avoids the syntactical awkwardness of options #1 and #2, with a *singular* construct followed by a

plural genitive (lit., #1: "*priestlies* kingdom" or #2: "a royal *priesthoods*"). It also avoids the contextual problem of option #3, which refers to only a part of the nation in contrast to *wegôy qādôš* "and a holy nation" which refers to the whole.

Fourth, if *mamleket kōhǎnîm* is indeed a genitive of composition ("a kingdom *composed of* priests"), there is still a question as to what the term *kōhǎnîm* "priests" actually refers: (1) *kōhǎnîm* may be nuanced "nobles, princes" (2 Sam. 8:18; 1 Kings 4:5) an honorific title designating the lordship of Israel over the nations ("a kingdom of nobles"), depicting Israel as a nation of priests in an elevated status over the nations (Isa. 61:5-6); (2) *kōhǎnîm* "priests" may suggest that Israel was specially consecrated to God, forming a race of royal priests who participated in the liturgical sacrifices, even though the actual offering was the exclusive prerogative of the Aaronic priesthood; or more likely (3) *kōhǎnîm* "priests" may suggest that the nation as a whole would constitute a priesthood called to minister to the nations, proclaiming the Word of God to the Gentiles and mediating their worship of Yahweh in a manner that mirrors the role of Israel's priesthood within the nation. While Israel had a priesthood, the nation itself would also function as a corporate priesthood, proclaiming the Word of God to the nations (Isa. 42:1-4) and mediating their worship to God (Isa. 2:1-5). As Israel obeyed Yahweh (Exod. 19:5-6) the surrounding nations would be drawn to Yahweh as they saw him bless the nation (Deut. 4:5-8; cf. Gen. 12:2).

The priest's place and function within Israelite society would serve as the ideal model for Israel's role among the nations. The two fundamental ministries of the priest were proclamation and mediation/intercession. Just as a priest stands between God and a person who is in need of making contact with God, so Israel would bear a mediatorial responsibility, serving as an intercessor between the holy God and all the peoples of the earth. The priest was set apart by a distinctive way of life consecrated to the service of God and dedicated to ministering to the people by proclaiming the Word of God and mediating their worship; so Israel was called to corporately minister to the nations in fulfillment of God's intent to reach all nations. Israel was to be a kingdom run not by politicians depending upon strength and connivance but by priests depending on faith in Yahweh, a servant nation instead of a ruling nation. Israel's role would be to mediate or intercede as priests between the holy God and the wayward nations of the world, with the end in view not only of declaring his salvation, but providing the human channel in and through whom that salvation would be effected (Merrill, *Kingdom of Priests*, 13). Thus Israel's role was a means of facilitating the divine goal that God and all peoples of the earth might have unbroken communion. (*NIDOTTE*, 2:600; *TDOT*, 7:60-75; *TWOT*, 1:431) [*kōhănîm*]

Holy nation (*wegôy qādôš*). The phrase *gôy qādôš* (lit. "nation of holiness") is an attributive expression: "a holy nation." This is parallel to the preceding "priestly kingdom"—the nouns *mamleket* "kingdom" and *gôy* "nation" are synonyms, while the genitives *kōhănîm* "priestly" and *qādôš* "holy" share the same conceptual domain because holiness was required of the priestly realm. The focus on obedience in v. 5 suggests that *qādôš* refers to ethical "holiness." If Israel would obey Yahweh's covenant, she would become a nation marked by ethical holiness and functioning in a corporate priestly role. This would enable Israel to function as Yahweh's

"special treasure." There is an inextricable cause-effect relationship between holiness and serving God (Lev. 11:44-45; 20:7, 26; 21:6; Deut. 6:6; 14:2, 21; 26:19; 28:9). By living in moral holiness, Israel would become a showcase to the world of how being in covenant with Yahweh could radically transform the individual and a nation as a whole. If Israel would obey God's commands and live in moral holiness, she would fulfill her divine commission as a "kingdom of priests" by creating a hunger in other nations to seek the LORD (Deut. 4:5-8; Isa. 2:1-5). (*NIDOTTE*, 3:877-87; *TLOT*, 3:1103-18; *TWAT*, 6:1179-1204; *TWOT*, 2:786-89) [*qādôš*]

19:22, 24 Lest he break out against them (*yiprōṣ*). Yahweh instructed Moses to mark out boundaries around the mountain as holy ground, and to warn the people to not "break through" these limits lest he "break out" against them in judgment. The verb *prṣ* I "to break out" describes God's judgment in striking out in a sudden, violent, destructive display of force (Exod. 19:22, 24; 2 Sam. 6:8; 1 Chron. 13:11; 15:13; Pss. 60:3; 106:29). Elsewhere, this verb describes the violent physical action of making a breach in a city wall during a military attack (2 Kings 14:13; 2 Chron. 25:23; 26:6; 32:5), breaking into a house violently (Prov. 25:28; 2 Chron. 24:7), and breaking down a wall (Isa. 5:5; Pss. 80:13; 89:41; Eccl. 3:3; 10:8; 2 Chron. 25:23; 26:6; Neh. 3:35). It describes an assailant bursting upon his victim, striking one blow after another (Job 16:13), a powerful warrior bursting through enemy ranks in a display of destructive power (2 Sam. 5:20; 1 Chron. 14:11), and violent and wicked actions (Hos. 4:2). [*prṣ*]

20:2 I am Yahweh your God (*'ānōkî yahweh ' ĕlōhêkā*). This is the most fundamental declaration in the Hebrew Scriptures: it is the basis of the Decalogue, the nucleus of the Pentateuch, and the heart of the entire Old Testament. Just as Yahweh revealed the DIVINE NAME to Moses (Exod. 3:14; 6:2), he now revealed himself to all Israel at the same mountain by the same NAME. God's primary goal in history is that all mankind recognize that he is Yahweh (for example, over 50x in Ezekiel). This self-predication forms the prologue of the Decalogue. So all the commandments are framed in the context of a covenant relationship with Yahweh. Thus theft, lying, or murder are not merely crimes against other people but ultimately acts of rebellion against Yahweh. This self-predication also functions as the preamble in the suzerainty form of the Sinaitic Covenant, identifying Yahweh as Israel's Great King. Merrill notes that the typical ancient Near Eastern preamble featured numerous self-descriptions of the suzerain. As the biblical counterpart, the preamble of the Sinaitic Covenant is incomparably sublime in its simplicity: "I [am] Yahweh your God." There is no need here for heaping up platitudes because the infinite majesty of the Great King is itself inherent in his name (Merrill & Zuck, *A Biblical Theology of the Old Testament*, 33). [*'ānōkî*]

20:3 You must never have any other gods before Me (*lō' yihyê lekā*). The construction *hyh* + *lĕ* is used for entering into the marriage bond (Deut. 24:2, 4; Judg. 14:20; 2 Sam. 12:10; Hos. 3:3; Ruth 1:13) and the covenant between God and Israel (Gen. 17:7; Exod. 6:7; 19:4-6; Lev. 11:45; 22:33; 25:38; 26:12, 45; Num. 15:41; Deut. 26:17-18; 29:12; Jer. 7:23; 11:4; 24:7; 30:22, 25 [31:1]; 31:32[33]; 32:28; Ezek. 11:20; 14:11; 36:28; 37:23, 27; Hos. 1:9; Zech. 8:8). Hence, Israel's covenant with Yahweh is

often compared to the marriage covenant between a husband and wife. Just as the marriage covenant demanded fidelity between husband and wife, Yahweh demanded exclusive loyalty from Israel. So apostasy by worshiping other gods is frequently portrayed as spiritual adultery with other lovers (Hos. 2:3-13). When Israel violated her covenant with Yahweh, she is portrayed as a faithless wife who has abandoned her husband (Isa. 1:4; Hos. 2:2). Although God "divorced" his faithless wife for adultery at the exile, he vowed to woo her back to himself and enter into a new covenant of marriage, betrothing her in faithfulness and empowering her through the New Covenant to remain loyal to her beloved husband (Hos. 2:14-23). [*hyh*]

Other gods (*'ĕlōhîm 'ăḥērîm*). The adjective *'aḥēr* "other" is pejorative and *'ĕlōhîm 'ăḥērîm* "other gods" refers to rival deities in ancient Near Eastern religions (*BDB*, 29; *HALOT*, 1:35.4; *TLOT*, 1:85.3) (Exod. 23:13; 34:14; Deut. 5:7; 31:20; Josh. 23:16; 24:2, 16; Judg. 2:12, 17, 19; 10:13; 1 Sam. 8:8; 26:19; 1 Kings 9:6, 9; 11:4, 10; 14:9; 2 Kings 5:17; 17:7, 35, 37; 22:17; 2 Chron. 7:19, 22; 28:25; 34:25; Isa. 42:8; Jer. 1:16; 44:15; Hos. 3:1). Although Scripture is clear that pagan gods do not have an actual ontological existence, biblical narrators occasionally refer to them from the point of view of their pagan worshipers as if they were living gods: "In the time of his distress, King Ahaz became even more unfaithful to Yahweh, for he sacrificed to the gods of Damascus who had defeated him, saying, 'Because the gods of the kings of Aram helped them, I will sacrifice to them so that they may help me'" (2 Chron. 28:23). Clearly, the perspective of Ahaz is not endorsed by the biblical narrator. When Moses demanded Israel to worship Yahweh alone and to renounce the worship of the gods of Canaan, he was not admitting their actual existence (Deut. 6:4-5, 14; 8:19; 10:17). Moses himself declared that the pagan false gods are in effect "no-gods" and nothing more than "demons" (Deut. 32:17). As the psalmist declared, idols worshiped as gods by the pagans have mouths but cannot speak, eyes but cannot see, and ears but cannot hear (Ps. 115:4-7). Isaiah proclaimed that Yahweh is the only true and living God: "I am the LORD and there is there is no other; apart from Me there is no God" (Isa. 45:5; cf. 41:4; 44:6; 45:6, 14, 18, 21, 22; 52:6). The pagan idol does not represent a living god, but the deception of demons (1 Cor. 10:18-22). (*NIDOTTE*, 360-61; *TDOT*, 1:201-3; *TLOT*, 1:83-88; *TWOT*, 1:33-34). [*'aḥēr*]

You must never have any other gods before me (*'al-pānāy*). The phrase *'al-pānāy* may denote: (1) *proximity*: "in my sight, in my presence," (2) *exclusivity*: "except me, in addition to me," or (3) *preference*: "before me, over me" (*THAT* 2:459). The ancient versions favored *exclusivity*: "except me" (LXX, Syriac, Targum) and "in addition to me" (Targum Onkelos, Targum Pseudo-Jonathon) over *proximity*: "in front of me" (LXX of the parallel Deut. 5:7). The modern translations are divided between *exclusivity*: "except Me" (CEV), "besides me" (NAB, NLT, NASB margin, NRSV margin, NIV margin) or "but Me" (TEV) and *preference*: "before Me" (ASV, KJV, NKJV, NIV, RSV, NRSV) (so *BDB*, 7a). By virtue of his election and deliverance of Israel, Yahweh had the right to demand the undivided loyalty of Israel. To violate this stipulation is to repudiate the entire covenant relationship. [*'al-pānāy*]

20:4 You must never make for yourself a cultic statue (*pesel*). This term refers to a cultic statue in the image or shape of the deity carved from wood (Deut. 27:15; Judg. 17:3; 18:14; 2 Kings 21:7; 2 Chron. 33:7; Isa. 40:20; 42:17; 44:15, 17; 45:20; 48:5; Nah. 1:14), sculpted from stone (Lev. 26:1; Deut. 4:16; 23:25; Judg. 17:3; 18:14, 17; 20:30; Ps. 97:7; Hab. 2:19), or cast from molten metal (Isa. 40:19; 44:10; Jer. 10:14; 51:17) (*BDB*, 820; *HALOT*, 3:949). Cultic statues played a prominent role in ancient Near Eastern religions which thought the deity resided in the statue (Deut. 7:5, 25; 1 Sam. 5:2-5; 2 Sam. 5:21; 1 Chron. 14:12). Cultic images were viewed as a means of entering into contact with the deity and manipulating it by cultic ritual and magical incantation. Intertestamental Judaism expanded the scope of this prohibition to forbid artistic representations of any living being. However, Exod. 20:4 merely forbids pagan cultic images in worship. The tabernacle and temple featured artistic representations of cherubim and other living things (Exod. 26:1, 31; 1 Kings 6:23-28; 7:25, 29, 36; 2 Chron. 3:7; Jer. 52:20). (*NIDOTTE*, 3:644-46; *TWOT*, 2:729) [*pesel*]

Likeness (*tĕmûnâ*). The noun *temûnâ* "form, manifestation," collocated with *pesel* "image," refers to the external appearance or shape of a deity whose presence was manifest in the physicality of a cultic statue (Deut. 4:16, 23, 25; 5:8) (*BDB*, 568; *HALOT*, 4:1746.1). This precept prohibits the representation of Yahweh by any kind of likeness, for to do so is to limit the transcendent God and to confuse the Creator with his creation. Israel was forbidden to make images to worship Yahweh (Deut. 4:12, 15-19); they were to worship Yahweh himself not a representation (Lev. 19:4). What was created by God cannot be used to represent him. They must worship him as he is, not as they envision him or would like him to be. This revolutionary concept asserts that God is wholly separate from the world and wholly other than what the human mind can conceive or the imagination depict. Any symbolic representation of God is an inadequate distortion, for an image becomes identified with what it represents and is looked upon as the place and presence of the Deity. Eventually, the image becomes the locus of reverence and object of worship—an act of apostasy. (*NIDOTTE*, 4:646-47; *TWAT*, 6:1046-56; *TWOT*, 1:503-04) [*temûnâ*]

20:5 You must never prostrate yourself to them (*lō' tištaḥweh*). The verb *hštḥwh* depicts the symbolic gesture of subjugating oneself in worship to a deity; hence, it is the Hebrew word most commonly translated "to worship." Traditionally *hštḥwh* is viewed as a reflexive (*Hithpalel*) form of *šḥh* "to bow down," meaning "to prostrate oneself" (*BDB*, 1005). Most scholars now view *hštḥwh* as a reflexive-causative (Hishtaphel) form of *ḥwh* II "to bow down," meaning "to cause oneself to bow down" (*HALOT*, 1:296a). So *hštḥwh* depicts a *volitional* decision to *cause oneself* to bow down before deity as an outward symbolic demonstration of *submission* and *worship*. This gesture of prostrating oneself before someone was customary in the ancient Near East. It describes an action/attitude directed to a human or divine figure recognized (appropriately or inappropriately) as being in a position of honor or authority (Gen. 24:26; Lev. 26:1; Pss. 5:8; 22:30; 99:5, 9). Depending on the figure and the situation, it may be a gesture of greeting, respect, submission, or worship. The action entails falling to one's knees, in front of which one places the hands or between which one bows the face (nose, forehead) to the ground (Gen. 18:2; 19:1; 48:12; 2 Sam. 1:2; 9:6, 8; Esth. 3:2, 5; Ps. 95:6; Isa. 49:23). When used of

God, it refers to legitimate worship (Gen. 22:5; 24:26, 48, 52; 47:31; Exod. 20:5; 24:1; 33:10; 34:8; Deut. 4:19; 26:10; Judg. 7:15; 1 Sam. 1:28; 15:25; 1 Kings 1:47; 18:22; 2 Kings 5:18; 1 Chron. 16:29; 2 Chron. 20:18; 32:12; Neh. 8:6; Pss. 5:8; 29:2; 66:4; 95:6; 96:9; 99:9; 132:7; 138:2; Isa. 27:13; 36:7; 66:23; Jer. 7:2; 26:2; Ezek. 46:2, 3). However, it often refers to bowing down in cultic worship of pagan gods—a heinous act of apostasy and breach of covenant (Exod. 23:24; Num. 25:2; Deut. 29:26; Judg. 2:12, 17; 1 Kings 11:33; 16:31; 22:53; 2 Chron. 25:14; Ps. 81:9; Jer. 13:10; 16:11; 22:9). (*NIDOTTE*, 2:42-44; *TDOT*, 4:248-56; *TLOT*, 2:398-400; *TWOT*, 1:267-69) [*ḥwh*]

You must never worship them (*lō' tā'ābedēm*). The verb *'ābad* "serve, honor, worship" (*BDB*, 713; *HALOT*, 3:774.8) refers to religious performance to worship, honor, and serve a deity in cultic ritual (2 Chron. 25:14) (*HALOT*, 3:774.8; *BDB*, 713.4.b). Although Israel was warned not to worship other gods (Exod. 23:33; Deut. 4:19, 28; Josh. 23:7; Ps. 97:7), she repeatedly served and worshiped other gods (Deut. 7:16; Judg. 2:11, 13, 19; 3:7; 10:6, 10; 1 Sam. 12:10; 1 Kings 16:31; 22:54; 2 Kings 10:18-19, 21-23; 17:12, 16, 41; 21:3, 21; 2 Chron. 24:18; 33:3, 22; Ps. 106:36; Jer. 5:19; 8:2; Ezek. 20:39). This would be the height of apostasy and a terrible act of covenant rebellion, resulting in Israel's complete expulsion from the land (2 Kings 17:7-23). Because Israel would so breach the covenant, Yahweh would terminate the Mosaic Covenant relationship just as a husband would divorce his wife (Hos. 1:2-9). However in his matchless grace and mercy, he would inaugurate a new covenant relationship with Israel that would empower them to repudiate the worship of all other gods once-and-for-all (Hos. 1:10-2:1; 2:14-23; cf. Ezek. 36:24-32).

(*NIDOTTE*, 4:1183-98; *TLOT*, 2:824.2; *TWAT*, 5:982-1012; *TWOT*, 2:639-41) ['bd]

For Yahweh your God is a **jealous God** (*qannā'*). It is startling that the only attribute of God that is actually highlighted in the Ten Commandments is the jealousy of God, which idolatry will provoke. The term *qn'* has a basic four-fold range of meanings: (1) illegitimate jealousy between rivals that results in fighting (Isa. 11:13) and legitimate jealousy aroused by an adulterous spouse that results in the slaying of the unfaithful wife (Num. 5:14f; Prov. 6:34; 27:4); (2) illegitimate envy of what belongs to someone else (Gen. 26:14; 30:1; 37:11; Pss. 37:1; 73:3; 106:16; Prov. 3:31; 23:17; 24:1, 19; Ezek. 31:9); (3) commendable zeal in a commitment to a cause (Num. 25:11; 2 Kings 10:16; Ps. 69:10) and passionate love in a marital relationship (S. of S. 8:6); and (4) violent anger provoked by the unfaithfulness of a covenant partner (Deut. 32:16, 21; 1 Kings 14:22; Ps. 78:58; Ezek. 8:3) (*BDB*, 888). So this term portrays Yahweh as a jealous husband whose wife (= Israel) has committed adultery with rival lovers (= worshiped other gods), provoking him to an outburst of anger in killing the unfaithful spouse (= destroying Israel in judgment). For example, the pagan cultic image installed in the temple provoked Yahweh to jealousy expressed in divine anger (Ezek. 8:3, 5). When *qn'* emphasizes the emotional aspect, it is divine jealousy; however, when it highlights the result of this, it is provoked anger. Both the cause (divine jealousy) and the effect (anger) are in view here: idolatry (v. 5a, "Do not bow down to them nor worship them") provokes divine jealousy (v. 5b, "for I Yahweh your God am a jealous God") expressed in judgment of idolaters (v. 5c, "punishing iniquity" cf. 34:7). Used in the latter sense, it appears with other terms for divine anger: *hēmâ* "wrath" (Ezek. 5:3; 16:38, 42; 23:25; 36:6), *'ebrâ* "anger" (Ezek. 38:19) and *'ap* "anger" (Deut. 29:19; Ps. 79:5; Isa. 26:11; Ezek. 35:11; 36:5; Zeph. 1:18; 3:8). As the only true living God who redeemed Israel and made her his covenant people, Yahweh had the right to demand Israel's exclusive faithfulness. But when she spurned him, Yahweh's jealousy burned with ardor. The people of God should be zealous to remain faithful to God, knowing that unfaithfulness provokes divine jealousy and anger (cf. 1 Cor. 10:22). (*NIDOTTE*, 3:937-40; *TLOT*, 3:1145-47; *TWAT*, 7:51-62; *TWOT*, 2:802-03) [*qannā'*]

Punishing iniquity (*pōqēd*). The verb *pqd*, traditionally rendered "visiting" (KJV, NKJV, ASV, RSV, NASB, NJPS), is better nuanced "punishing" here (NIV, NRSV, NAB, NLT, TEV). The basic meaning of *pqd* is "to observe" (*NIDOTTE*, 3:658). It often functions figuratively (metonymy of cause for effect), focusing on the response to what one sees (*NIDOTTE*, 3:659.5). When God observes the unrepentant, he responds by executing punishment: so *pqd* means "to punish [the wicked for sin]" (*BDB*, 823.2; *HALOT*, 3:956.5.c.i) (Exod. 20:5; 32:34; 34:7; Lev. 18:25; Deut. 5:9; 1 Sam. 15:2; Job 35:15; Pss. 59:6; 89:33; Isa. 10:12; 13:11; 26:14; Jer. 5:9, 29; 6:15; 9:8, 24; 11:22; 13:21; 21:14; 49:8; 50:31; Hos. 1:4; 2:13[15]; 4:14; 12:3; Amos 3:2, 14; Zech. 10:3). The participle *pōqēd* indicates that it is a characteristic action of God: he is a just God who punishes sin. (*NIDOTTE*, 3:657-63; *TLOT*, 2:1018-31; *TWAT*, 6:708-23; *TWOT*, 2:731-32) [*pqd*]

Punishing children and grandchildren up to the third and fourth generations for the iniquity of their parents ('*al šillēšîm we'al ribbē'îm*). The expression "third and fourth generation" is an idiom for continuity of longevity (Gen. 50:23; 2 Kings 10:30; Job 42:16). It is used in a similar way in ancient Near East texts: "I saw my great-great-grandchildren up to the fourth generation" (*ANET3*, 561) and "On the day I died what do I see? Children of the fourth generation who wept for me and were distraught" (*ANET3*, 661). It should not be understood in an arithmetical sense as a generational curse but as Semitic hyperbole for the enduring effects of evil. The hyperbolic nature of "the third and fourth generations" (v. 5) is clear from the following antonym, "a thousand generations" (v. 6). There are two views of the meaning of this expression which recurs several times in Scripture (Exod. 20:5; 34:7; Num. 14:18; Deut. 5:9; Jer. 32:18): (1) Some understand this as a vicarious punishment of assigning the punishment of the parent's sins to their children due to corporate solidarity. (2) Others argue that this describes the natural results of the detrimental effects of the sinful conduct of parents upon the lives of their children. Some interpret later statements in the OT as abrogating this kind of cross-generational punishment (Jer. 31:29-30; Ezek. 18:1-4, 20). However, Jeremiah and Ezekiel are more likely debunking the popular sentiment that the present generation was suffering for the accrued sins of their ancestors (e.g., Lam. 5:7) and that the LORD was unjust in allowing the present generation to suffer. Jeremiah and Ezekiel had warned their own generation that they were as guilty as their ancestors and even more. While their ancestors were guilty of their own sins, the present generation compounded the problem by their stubborn refusal to repent. So we may conclude that this stark declaration in Exod. 20:5 continues to represent the normative work of God. The sinful conduct of one

generation will inevitably have a detrimental impact upon successive generations.

20:7 You must never <u>profess</u> the name of Yahweh your God in vain (*lōʼ tiśśāʼ*). Used of speech, *nśʼ* "to take, lift up," refers to taking or lifting up something on one's lips or to raise one's voice: "to utter, pronounce" something (Exod. 23:1; 1 Kings 8:31; 2 Chron. 6:22; Pss. 15:3; 81:3; Isa. 37:4; Amos 5:1) (*HALOT*, 2:725.9; *TLOT*, 2:771.3.c). To "take up" the name of God (Exod. 20:7; Deut. 5:11) is an idiom for professing the DIVINE NAME in worship (Pss. 16:4; 19:4; 139:20; Jer. 7:16; 11:4) or swearing loyalty to Yahweh in covenant renewal (Ps. 50:16) (*BDB*, 670.1.b.7). Moses did not prohibit pronouncing the name of Yahweh but feigning covenant commitment by professing allegiance to the LORD but harboring willful rebellion against him in one's heart (Deut. 29:18-21; cf. Ps. 50:16-22). However, during the Middle Ages, the DIVINE NAME became viewed as so unspeakably holy that Jewish authorities extended the scope and application of this to prohibit even utterance of the name Yahweh. Orthodox Judaism substituted the pronunciation of the NAME with the surrogate title Adonay, wrote YHWH rather than the vocalized form Yahweh, and today writes G-d for God. Such a rigid application of this directive seems to miss the point, and emphasizes the transcendent holiness of God at the expense of his intimate nearness that he offers to all who seek him. (*NIDOTTE*, 3:160-63; *TLOT*, 2:769-74; *TWAT*, 5:626-43; *TWOT*, 2:600-02) [*nśʼ*]

You must never profess the name of Yahweh your God <u>in vain</u> (*laššāwʼ*). The term *šāwʼ* "emptiness, worthlessness, deceit, falsehood, wickedness" has a broad range of meanings and referents: (1)

deception: lying, perjury, false oaths; (2) religious falsehood: magical rituals, false oracles and pagan idols; (3) worthlessness: activity in vain or to no purpose; and (4) disaster: what brings something to nothing (*BDB*, 996.1; *HALOT*, 4:1425.1c). So there are several views of the meaning of this prohibition: (1) to use the NAME in a pointless manner or in a thoughtless, trivial, futile or rote manner; (2) to utter the NAME in an abusive or profane manner; (3) to unnecessarily utter the NAME in a sincere oath; (4) to insincerely invoke the NAME in swearing false oath in perjury; (5) to profess the NAME in a false vow of loyalty in covenant renewal; (6) to abuse the NAME by invoking it in an incantation or magical ritual in an attempt to manipulate Yahweh; or (7) to wrongly ascribe the NAME to an idol in religious syncretism. The language is ambiguous enough to permit a wide range of applications. Traditional Judaism interpreted this as a prohibition against a frivolous use of the NAME or the recitation of an unnecessary blessing in his NAME. However, it is primarily cited as a prohibition against false oaths in the name of Yahweh (Deut. 6:13; Jer. 4:2; 12:16; Ps. 63:12), blasphemy, and cursing of the NAME (Exod. 22:28; Lev. 24:16; 2 Kings 2:24), profaning the NAME by idolatry and apostasy (Lev. 18:21; 20:3; Ezek. 20:39) and blaspheming the NAME by sinful behavior that brings his reputation into disrepute (Isa. 52:4; Ezek. 36:20). Because Israel bore the name Yahweh, Moses demanded that they not imitate the sins of the Egyptians and Canaanites (Deut. 14:1-21). Likewise, those who profess Jesus as Messiah must not bring his name into disrepute. (*NIDOTTE*, 4:53-55; *TLOT*, 3:1310-12; *TWAT*, 7:1104-17; *TWOT*, 2:908) [*šāw'*]

The LORD **will certainly punish** (*lō' yenaqqê*). The verb *nqh* is a technical legal

term: "to find innocent of wrongdoing" and by extension "to exempt from punishment" (Exod. 21:19; Num. 5:28, 31; 1 Sam. 26:9; Ps. 19:13, 14; Jer. 2:35) (*BDB*, 667; *HALOT*, 2:720.2). The negative *lō'* + *nqh* "he will not find innocent" (1 Kings 2:9) by extension means "he will not exempt from punishment" which is a rhetorical expression (tapeinosis) that means "he will *certainly* punish" (Exod. 20:7; 34:7; Num. 14:18; Deut. 5:11; 1 Kings 2:9; Prov. 6:29; 11:2; 16:5; 17:5; 19:5,9; 28:20; Jer. 25:29; 30:11; 46:28; 49:12; Joel 3:21; Nah. 1:8) (*BDB*, 667; *HALOT*, 2:720.1). What this punishment would be is not articulated here, but the case-laws that follow in Exod. 21-23 suggest that the penalty of death is in view (Exod. 22:20). (*NIDOTTE*, 3:152-54; *TLOT*, 2:763-67; *TDOT*, 9:553-63; *TWOT*, 2:596-98) [*nqh*]

20:8 You must remember the Sabbath (*zākôr*). While *zkr* "to remember" often refers to mere mental cognition, here it is figurative (metonymy of cause for effect) for the resultant action (*NIDOTTE*, 1:1102). Thus to remember an obligation means to fulfill it (Esth. 2:1; Ps. 109:16; Eccl. 9:15; Amos 1:9), just as remembering Torah is to obey it (Num. 15:40; Ps. 103:18; Mal. 4:4) (*BDB*, 269.I.2.d). So to remember the Sabbath means "to observe, commemorate" it (*BDB*, 270.I.6). This is explicit in the parallel commandment in Deut. 5:12 in which *zkr* "remember" of Exod. 20:8 is replaced by *šmr* "observe, keep," so remembering the Sabbath means to obey the command to celebrate the Sabbath. Memory was such a large part of the motivation for obedience that God instructed Israel to place tassels on their garments to remind them to keep the Sabbath (Num. 15:37-41) following a grievous example of Sabbath obligation (Num. 15:32-36). (*NIDOTTE*, 1:1100-06;

TDOT, 4:64-82; *TLOT*, 1:381-88; *TWOT*, 1:241-43) [*zkr*]

The Sabbath (*šabbāt*).The Sabbath commandment is transmitted in all three versions of the Decalogue (Exod. 20:8-11; Lev. 19:3; Deut. 5:12-15) and other Mosaic legislation (Exod. 23:12; 35:2-3; Lev. 19:3, 30; 23:3). The Sabbath is the weekly sacred day following each six-day cycle of secular work. The noun *šabbāt* is often connected with the verb *šābat* "to cease, rest [from work]" (Exod. 16:30; 20:11; 31:15, 17), so *šabbāt yôm* means "a day of rest/cessation [from labor]" (*BDB*, 992; *HALOT*, 4:1409-11). Just as God "rested" from his six days of creation (Gen. 2:2-3) and was "refreshed" (Exod. 31:17), Israelites were to rest from secular labor to rest and refresh themselves (Exod. 20:8-10; 31:12-17; Deut. 5:13-14). Two main features constitute observation of Sabbath: (1) physical rest from secular labor (Exod. 20:8-11; 23:12; Lev. 19:3; Deut. 5:12-15) and (2) as a Sabbath "belonging to Yahweh" it involved corporate worship—a holy assembly—before God at his sanctuary in all the places where they would live (Lev. 19:30; 23:3), accompanied by a special Sabbath sacrifice (Lev. 24:8; Num. 28:9-10; cf. 1 Chron. 23:31; 2 Chron. 8:13; 31:3). The two-fold rationale for the Sabbath—God's work of creation (Exod. 20:11) and redemption of Israel from Egypt (Deut. 5:15)—provided the content of Israel's worship, investing it with blessing and sacredness. God's rest upon completing creation is the archetype of the human Sabbath celebration (Gen. 2:2-3; Exod. 20:11). His liberation of the enslaved Hebrews from Egypt (Deut. 5:15) was the basis for their duty to extend kindness to Israelite debt-slaves and beasts of burden (Exod. 23:13; Deut. 5:14) and to promote social justice for the widow, orphan, and foreigner (Isa. 1:11-17; 56:1-8).

Although seven-day units of time were well-known in the ancient Near East, there is nothing analogous to the weekly Sabbath in ancient Near Eastern religion (e.g., Babylonian religion set apart only one day each month for cultic celebration: the fifteenth day of the month—the day of the full moon). The weekly Sabbath is also the sole exception to the Semitic practice of basing all major units of time (months, seasons, years) on the phases of the moon and sun. So observation of Sabbath was a sign of Israel's unique covenant relationship with Yahweh which set them apart from other nations (Exod. 31:13, 17; Ezek. 20:12, 20). Hence the Sabbath commandment seems to have been understood as among the most important commandments—if not the most important (Neh. 9:14). Thus violation of Sabbath was a serious offense because it repudiated the essence of Israel's covenant with Yahweh, inviting the death penalty (Exod. 31:13-17; 35:2-3; Num. 15:32-36). Indeed, Israel's non-observance of Sabbath was seen as a reason for the judgment of exile (Ezek. 20:16, 21, 24; 22:8, 26; 23:38).

The prophetic texts call Israel to fulfill the Sabbath commandment as a condition for the coming age of salvation (Isa. 56:1-8). The prophetic depictions of the eschatological age foresee Israel's faithful observation of Sabbath, symbolic of perfect eschatological worship of God (Ezek. 44:24; 45:17; cf. Zech. 14:16-19). Although the Sabbath was the sign of Israel's unique covenant relationship with Yahweh, Isaiah proclaimed (in his description of the New Covenant) that any non-Israelite who would obey God's commandments, particularly the Sabbath commandment, would be counted among the covenant people of God (Isa. 56:3-8)—perhaps in anticipation of the one people of God in the age of the New Covenant. (*NIDOTTE*, 4:1157-62; *TLOT*, 3:1297-1302; *TWAT*, 7:1040-46; *TWOT*, 2:902-03) [*šabbāt*]

By sanctifying it (*lĕqaddešû*). The root *qdš* "what is set apart, holy, removed from common use, dedicated to special use" by God (*THAT* 2:590) designates the sphere of the sacred as distinct from *ḥôl* "profane, common" (Lev. 10:10; Ezek. 22:26) (*THAT* 2:590). The verb *qdš* (Piel) refers in general "to making [something] holy," but here "to treat [the Sabbath] as sanctified, consecrated" (*HALOT*, 3:1074.6.a). Such consecration is effected by (a) negatively setting it apart from the common and profane, and (b) positively dedicating it to special use (*HALOT*, 3:1073-74). Thus Sabbath is to be treated as holy by (a) the interruption of ordinary labor on the seventh day and (b) dedicating it to the physical rest of man and the spiritual worship of God (Exod. 20:8, 11; Lev. 25:10; Deut. 5:12; Neh. 13:22; Jer. 17:22, 24, 27; Ezek. 20:12, 20; 44:24). This two-fold purpose (rest for man and worship of God) is seen in the statements "it is holy to you" (Exod. 31:14) and "it is holy to Yahweh" (Exod. 31:15; cf. 20:9). (*NIDOTTE*, 3:877; *TLOT*, 3:1103-18; *TWAT*, 6:179-1204; *TWOT*, 2:786)

The prefixed preposition *lĕ* may denote *means* ("Remember the Sabbath *by* keeping it holy") or *complementary action* ("Remember the Sabbath *to* keep it holy" = remember *to* keep the Sabbath holy). Consecration of the Sabbath was effected on several levels: (1) physical sanctification, by removing it from the realm of the common weekly routine by setting it apart as a special day for rest and worship (Exod. 20:8-11; Deut. 5:12-15); (2) cultic sanctification, by the special Sabbath sacrifice (Lev. 24:8; Num. 28:9-10) and renewal of the showbread (1 Chron. 9:32; 2 Chron. 2:3); and (3) moral sanctification, by practicing genuine moral righteousness and promoting social justice (Isa. 1:11-17; Isa. 56:1-8). Thus by imitating God's sanctification of the seventh day (Gen. 2:2-3), Israel could transform its mundane existence into a spiritual experience once a week, and thereby enter into commune with God by imitating his "rest" from his work of creation and worshiping him as Creator, Savior and Lord. [*qdš*]

20:9 Six days you may labor and do all your work (*mĕla'keteka*). The term *mĕlā'kâ* "work" refers to the daily labor of one's secular occupation. The six days allotted for "business as usual" must suffice for the labor of sustenance. In ancient Egypt, labor gangs were not allotted a weekly day of rest, so the provision of the Sabbath day of rest from one's labor was an extraordinary gift to former corvée slaves. So it was a welcome day of physical rest for the body, refreshment of the soul, and cause for grateful worship of the benevolent God who had rescued the Hebrews from the clutches of their tyrannical oppressors in Egypt. Thus Sabbath was originally designed to be a day of rejoicing and refreshment (Isa. 58:13-14; Hos. 2:13).

The definition of prohibited labor is not given here; however, certain types of work were prohibited in the OT: leaving one's dwelling to walk beyond certain limits (Exod. 16:29), conducting agricultural activity (Exod. 34:21), kindling fire (Exod. 35:3), loading asses (Exod. 35:2-36:7; Lev. 19:30; 26:2), gathering wood (Num. 15:32-36), conducting business (Isa. 58:13; Amos 8:5; Neh. 10:32; 13:15-18), carrying heavy loads (Jer. 17:21, 24, 27) and treading the winepress (Neh. 13:15). In the intertestamental and Talmudic periods the Jewish rabbis formulated Judaism's Sabbath regulations in meticulous detail. According to Jewish tradition, these manmade regulations were the oral law given by Yahweh to Moses and transmitted in oral form throughout the ages until they were placed in written form in the Mishnah (*Sabbath*, 7:2) and Talmud (*Baba Kamma* 2; *Yoma* 85). Rabbinic Judaism prohibited thirty-nine kinds of labor on the Sabbath: sowing, plowing, reaping, binding sheaves, threshing, winnowing, cleansing, grinding, sifting, kneading, baking, shearing wool along with washing or beating or dying it, spinning, weaving, making two loops out of a rope, weaving two threads, separating two threads, tying or loosening a knot, sewing two stitches, tearing to sew two stitches, hunting a deer, writing two letters, erasing to write two letters, building, demolishing, extinguishing, kindling, striking with a hammer, and carrying anything from one domain to another (Mishnah, *Sabbath*, 7:2). However, they suspended all Sabbath prohibitions when human life was in danger, allowing that it was one's religious duty to violate the Sabbath to save human life. The Gospels record the intense debates between Jesus and Jewish exegetes about whether or not these rabbinic regulations reflected the spirit and heart of the Mosaic Sabbath laws, while the apostles proclaim that the New Covenant mode of worship had set Jewish believers free from the rigidity of the rabbinic Sabbath regulations (e.g., Col 2:15). [*měla'kâ*]

20:12 You must honor your father and mother (*kābēd*). The verb *kbd* "to be heavy" in physical weight is used figuratively of persons with social "weight," worthy of respect and honor (Num. 22:15; Mal. 1:6). The intensive (Piel) form "to show honor, respect" (*BDB*, 457.2; *HALOT*, 2:455.2) is used in reference to (1) God (Judg. 9:9; 1 Sam. 2:30; Pss. 22:24; 50:23; 86:9, 12; Prov. 3:9; 14:31; Isa. 24:15; 25:3; 29:13; 43:20, 23; 58:13; Dan. 11:38); (2) leaders (Judg. 13:17;

1 Sam. 15:30; 22:9; 2 Sam. 10:4; 1 Chron. 19:3; Pss. 15:4; 50:15; 91:15); and (3) parents (Exod. 20:12; Deut. 5:16; Mal. 1:6; Sir 3:8). When this command is later restated, *yr'* "to fear, respect" (metonymy for obedience) replaces *kbd* "to honor" (Lev. 19:3), suggesting that *kbd* connotes respect and obedience. In the hierarchical structure of Yahweh's kingdom are spheres of responsibility, so Israel—though ultimately responsible to God—must honor those he places over them as his representatives in society and family. To honor parents is to honor Yahweh; to dishonor them is nothing short of rebellion to God. So in the case-laws, one who curses or strikes his parents was to be put to death like the idolater (Exod. 21:15, 17; Lev. 20:19). While this command entails obedience of children to parents (Eph. 6:2), like the rest of the Decalogue it also addresses adults; so it also prescribed care and support of the elderly (Matt. 15:4-6). This commandment marks the transition from Yahweh's expectations of his people in relation to himself to his expectations of his people in relation to one another—pointing to the fundamental role of parents as the backbone of society. (*NIDOTTE*, 2:577-87; *TDOT*, 7:13-22; *TLOT*, 2:590-602; *TWOT*, 1:422-28) [*kbd*]

That you may prolong your life (*ya'ărikûn*). The causative (Hiphil) of *'rk* "be long" means "prolong" one's life temporally (*BDB*, 73.1; *HALOT*, 1:88.1.b). Obedience to parents may lengthen one's life because heeding their wise instruction can help the youth to avoid premature death by the natural consequence of wicked behavior. On the other hand, disrespect for one's parents was a serious offense in the covenant community—even punishable by death in some cases (Exod. 21:15, 17; Lev. 20:9; Deut. 21:18-21). Scripture suggests that God apportions seventy years as the normal lifespan for humans (Ps. 90:10a). Rebellion against God and foolish behavior can shorten this average. On the other hand, God may reward a person with a long lifespan as reward for obedience to him (Num. 9:19, 22; Deut. 4:26, 40; 5:33; 11:9; 17:20; 22:7; 30:18; 32:47; Josh. 24:31; Judg. 2:7; 1 Kings 3:14) and as a natural consequence of wise behavior (Prov. 28:16). Other factors such as physical strength and good health may lengthen one's life (Ps. 90:10b). Although God foreknows the lifespan of everyone even before birth (Ps. 139:16), this does not create a fatalistic system. For example, when Hezekiah became ill and God sent Isaiah to proclaim that he was about to die (2 Kings 20:1), the LORD answered his prayer and intervened to extend his life beyond the original divine announcement (2 Kings 20:2-6).

Paul quotes the fifth commandment but modifies the wording of the motivational clause in his application use of this passage: "'Honor your father and mother,' which is the first commandment with a promise, 'that it may go well with you and that you may prolong your life *on the earth'*" (Eph. 6:2-3). The nationalistic wording "in the land which Yahweh your God is about to give you" (Exod. 20:12b), which is exclusively directed at the Mosaic generation of Israelites, is universalized in such a way as to apply to all ethnic groups at all times: "on the earth" (Eph. 6:3b). Hence the Mosaic command to obey one's parents was not exclusively limited to OT Israel, but reflects the eternal moral law of God for all peoples of all ages. Paul's applicational use of this passage might serve as a paradigmatic approach to the hermeneutical issue of the continuity/discontinuity of the role of the OT Law in the life of the NT believer. ['rk]

20:13 You must never murder (*lō' tirṣāḥ*). It is difficult to find an adequate one-to-one English equivalent for *rāṣaḥ* in this context because elsewhere it can refer to premeditated homicide, accidental manslaughter, capital punishment, retaliation by a blood avenger and military killing—some of which are deemed illegal and others legal killing. Neither the generic "You shall not *kill*" nor the specific "You shall not *murder*" adequately captures its basic sense nor allows for its wide range of referents. The use of *rāṣaḥ* in the OT may be categorized into illegal and legal killing: (1) *illegal killing* as forbidden by God: (a) premeditated homicide (Num. 35:16, 21, 31; Deut. 22:26; 1 Kings 21:19; 2 Kings 6:32; Job 24:14; Ps. 94:6; Jer. 7:9; Hos. 4:2; 6:9); (b) accidental manslaughter (Num. 35:6, 11, 25, 28; Deut. 4:42; 19:3, 4, 6; Josh. 20:3, 5, 6; 21:13, 21, 27, 32, 38); versus (2) *legal killing* as proscribed or permitted by God: (a) capital punishment (Num. 35:30) and (b) legal retaliation by a blood avenger (Num. 35:12, 22, 27, 30; Josh. 20:3, 5) (*BDB*, 954; *HALOT*, 3:1283-4). The case-laws (Exod. 21:12-36; Deut. 19:1-22:12) in particular clarify what constitutes legal and illegal killing. Various statements in the historical, poetic, and prophetic literatures also indicate that this prohibition focuses on the illegal and willful killing of the innocent, but does not ban capital punishment nor forbid legal military action in divinely approved warfare (*HALOT*, 3:1283). So the Decalogue prohibits illegal killing (murder, manslaughter, imperialistic warfare) but not legal killing (administration of justice, justifiable killing in war). This prohibition cannot be used to justify all forms of pacifism nor abolition of the death penalty. It is worth noting that *rāṣaḥ* is never used when the subject is God or an angel, so the divine ideal is not contradicted by divinely commanded holy war or capital punishment. This prohibition is essentially an imperatival restatement of the divine decree concerning human bloodshed: "Whoever sheds man's blood, his blood must be shed" (Gen. 9:6). The murderer usurps the divine prerogative and infringes on God's sovereignty over life. To illegally take the life of another member of the covenant community is not only heinous and inhumane, but it also constitutes an act of rebellion against God—it is tantamount to treason against the Great King and an arrogant attempt to usurp the divine prerogative that belongs exclusively to God. (*NIDOTTE*, 3:1188-90; *TWOT*, 2:860) [*rṣḥ*]

20:14 You must never commit adultery (*lō' tin'ap*). In contrast to the promiscuity sanctioned by official cults of the Canaanites, the God of Israel prohibited sexual immorality. In the ancient Near East adultery was generally defined as sexual intercourse between a married woman and a man other than her husband—an offense against her husband. In Israel adultery not only refers to a wife in an adulterous relation (Lev. 20:10; Prov. 30:20; Jer. 3:8; Ezek. 16:32, 38; 23:45; Hos. 3:1; 4:13) but also to a husband in a sexual relationship with a woman other than his wife (Lev. 18:20; 20:10; Job 24:15; Prov. 6:32; Jer. 5:7; 7:9; 23:14; 29:23; Hos. 4:2) or with a woman betrothed to another man (Deut. 22:23-27). The gravity of adultery may be gauged by the severity of its punishment: death (Lev. 19:20; 20:10, 14; 21:9; Deut. 22:22-27; Ezek. 16:38-40). According to the biblical case-laws, the husband had the right to demand the death of his adulteress wife and her lover (Lev. 20:10; Deut. 22:22). However an adulterer was allowed to appease the wrath of the husband by paying a ransom (Lev. 19:20) but the husband could refuse and demand his death (Prov. 6:32-35). As in ancient Near Eastern law, the husband also had the right to divorce an adulterous wife rather than demand her execution (Deut. 24:1; Jer. 13:26-27; Ezek. 16:37-39; Hos. 2:5). If a newly wed husband discovered his bride had not kept her chastity before marriage, she could suffer death (Deut. 22:20-21) (or simply be divorced as in the case of an adulterous wife). In the rape of a betrothed woman (who is technically considered the wife of her husband-to-be who has already paid the bride-price) only the rapist is put to death (Deut. 22:22-23). However, if a betrothed woman is found to have consensual intercourse, she and her lover are both put to death (Deut. 22:24). In the ancient Near East, adultery was a private offense against an aggrieved husband; in Israel it was also a heinous sin against God (Gen. 20:9; 39:9; Exod. 32:21, 30-31; 2 Kings 17:21; Ps. 51:4; Jer. 3:1). Because marriage is a divinely ordained institution the marriage bond has a sacral dimension (Gen. 2:24; Prov. 2:17; Mal. 2:14-16; 3:5). Not only does adultery destroy the integrity of the marriage, it also destroys the integrity of one's covenant relationship with Yahweh. As the case-laws indicate, the prohibition against adultery is a summary condemnation of all forms of immorality: fornication (Exod. 22:16-17), rape (Deut. 22:23-29), incest and polygamy (Lev. 18:18), prostitution (Lev. 19:29; 21:7,9), homosexuality (Lev. 18:22; Deut. 23:18), transvestism (Deut. 22:5) and bestiality (Exod. 32:19). And as Jesus would later emphasize, even lust in one's heart constitutes adultery (Matt. 5:27-30). The godly man disciplines his eyes to avoid lust (Job 31:1) and avoids the allure of adultery by delighting in his own wife (Prov. 5:15-19). (*NIDOTTE*, 3:2-5; *TDOT*, 9:113-18; *TWOT*, 2:542-43) [*n'p*]

20:15 You must never steal (*lō' tignōb*). The verb *gānab* "to steal" describes private theft of another person's possessions. Although the object stolen is not always specified (Lev. 19:11; Deut. 5:19; Josh. 7:11; Prov. 6:30; 30:9; Jer. 7:9; Hos. 4:2; Zech. 5:3), it often refers specifically to theft of material possessions (Gen. 31:19, 30, 32; 44:8; Exod. 22:2; Jer. 2:26; Obad. 1:5), livestock (Gen. 30:33; Exod. 21:37), and even kidnapping a person (Gen. 40:15; Exod. 21:16; 22:11; Deut. 24:7; 2 Sam. 19:42). The case-laws illustrate what the biblical concept of theft encompassed (Exod. 21:16-22:15; Deut. 23:15-25). In ancient Near Eastern law codes theft was widely defined, including fraudulent misappropriation whether by purchasing stolen property or retaining lost property. In principle, the owner of the stolen property was entitled to the death penalty as revenge upon the thief, but in practice this was confined to aggravated cases. The courts imposed limited ransom for simple theft, either at a fixed sum or as a fixed multiple of the thing stolen. The severity of the penalty depended sometimes on the circumstances, e.g., a wife stealing from her husband was treated more severely; the retainer of lost goods, more leniently. Mostly, it depended on the nature of the thing stolen: kidnapping a free person was punishable by death or high ransom; theft of sacred objects from a temple was punishable by death but other temple or palace property by a thirty-fold payment; theft of animals was punishable by multiples of its value, depending on size; theft of other items was punishable by multiples or fixed sums: large sums of money could be paid as ransom in lieu of death or mutilation, but the smaller sums may represent a simple debt: ransom of one's freedom. On the other hand, punishment for theft in Israel was not as severe as

that of some neighboring nations, where the death penalty was often inflicted. Israel held a higher regard for the value of human life—even the life of a thief. Mosaic Law required the thief to return to his victim twice the amount he had stolen; so he not only must restore what was stolen but he himself also forfeited the exact amount he hoped to steal (Exod. 22:7). The penalties were doubled/tripled if the thief slaughtered or sold a stolen animal. Only in the case of kidnapping (Exod. 21:16) or theft of sacred things devoted to Yahweh (Josh. 7:11, 25) was the thief to be executed. (*NIDOTTE*, 1:878-80; *TDOT*, 3:39-45; *TWOT*, 1:168) [*gnb*]

20:16 You must never testify as a fraudulent witness (*lō' ta'ănê*). The verb *'nh* I "to answer" is used here as a technical legal term: "to give evidence, testify" in a lawuit or legal proceeding (Exod. 23:2; Deut. 19:16; 31:21; Job 16:3; Prov. 15:28; Isa. 65:12; Mal. 2:12) (*BDB*, 773.3a). Used with the preposition *be* "against" the term may refer to testimony given "for" (Gen. 30:33) or "against" a defendant (Num. 35:30; Ruth 1:21; 1 Sam. 12:3; 2 Sam. 1:16; Job 16:8; Isa. 3:9; 59:12; Jer. 14:7; Hos. 5:5; 7:10; Mic. 6:3). [*'nh*]

Fraudulent witness (*'ēd šeqer*). The noun *'ēd* may refer to (1) verbal testimony used in a judicial case as legal evidence: "testimony" (Deut. 5:20; 19:16; 31:21; 1 Sam. 14:39; Prov. 25:18) or (2) a person providing verbal testimony in a legal proceeding: "witness" (Num. 5:13; 35:30; Deut. 17:6; Pss. 27:12; 35:11; Prov. 25:18) (*BDB*, 729). The term *šeqer* "lying, deceiving, false" refers to fraudulent physical evidence or perjury (false verbal testimony) (Deut. 19:18; Ps. 27:12; Prov. 6:19; 12:17; 14:5; 19:5, 9; 25:18). In Deut. 5:20, the parallel passage, *šeqer* is replaced by *šāwe'* "empty, worthless, false," to prohibit not just offering fraudulent testimony but also the withholding of crucial evidence that would swing the court's decision otherwise. The testimony of witnesses constitute the key factor in the judicial process. Fraudulent testimony not only hinders the administration of justice in a particular case but also undermines public confidence in the integrity of the judicial system, which can jeopardize the stability of society. So various measures were taken to discourage perjury: two witnesses are necessary for evidence to be accepted as valid (Deut. 17:6; 19:15), and those who commit perjury would receive the same punishment that the accused would have suffered (Deut. 19:16-21). In cases involving capital punishment, the witnesses had to initiate the execution, so a perjurer would in fact be committing murder. ['ēd]

20:17 You must never covet (lō' taḥmōd). While ḥāmad may denote legitimate delight or desire in one's own possessions (Job 20:20; Pss. 19:10; 68:16; 106:24; Isa. 5:32; Jer. 3:19; 12:10), here it refers to illegitimate covetousness of what belongs to another or is simply off limits (BDB, 326) (Gen. 3:6; Josh. 7:21; Prov. 6:25). This is emphasized in the prohibition: "You must never covet *your neighbor's* house . . . *your neighbor's* wife or *his* male servant, *his* female servant, *his* ox, *his* donkey or anything *belonging to your neighbor*." In essence, covetousness is dissatisfaction with one's lot in life. It impugns God's goodness and his sovereign bestowal of life's blessings.

Coveting often functions figuratively (metonymy of cause for effect): "to desire" and try to obtain (HALOT, 1:325), e.g., "I saw . . . I coveted . . . I took" (Gen. 3:6; Josh. 7:21; cf. Deut. 7:25; Mic. 2:2). The case-laws provide everyday life examples of how covetousness manifests itself, transforming this prohibition from the abstract to the concrete (Deut. 25:4-16). Because the Law did not legislate punishment for covetous desire, scholars debate whether the Law held the ancient Israelite culpable for covetous *desire* itself or only for *acting* on it. In any case, it is clear that Jesus elevated the standard of the Law by internalizing its requirements, making one guilty before God not just for covetous actions but also for covetous desire (Matt. 5:21-28; cf. Rom. 7:7-13). Read in this light, the tenth commandment does not simply prohibit gratification of illicit desires but from even giving place to them in one's heart. This places an obligation on the man of God to discipline and condition the mind so its automatic response to covetousness is a sense of revulsion. To prohibit covetousness in the human heart is not categorically different than to command one to love God with all his heart (Deut. 6:5). Since covetousness is primarily a matter of the heart, this is an appropriate climax to the Decalogue. It raises the covenant requirements to a higher, spiritual dimension, locating the motive for obedience in the human heart. Just as heartfelt love for God is the well-spring for obedience (Deut. 10:12), unbridled covetousness can become the gateway to rebellion. (NIDOTTE, 2:167-69; TDOT, 4:452-61; TLOT, 1:433-35; TWOT, 1:294-95) [ḥmd]

20:20 "Do not fear . . . so that you might fear him" ('al tîrā'û . . . tihyê yir'ātô). The biblical concept of the fear of God is often misunderstood. Some passages state that one should fear God (Lev. 19:14; Deut. 10:12; Prov. 1:7; Luke 12:5; 2 Cor. 5:11; Phil. 2:12; Heb. 12:21; 1 Peter 2:17; Rev. 19:5) but others that we should not be afraid of God (Rom. 8:15; 1 John 4:18). So should we or should we not fear God?

How may we reconcile these two seemingly contradictory extremes? Here Moses states that Israel should not fear God in one sense (Exod. 20:20a) but should fear him in another sense (Exod. 20:20b). So this verse might be a key to obtaining some kind of balanced approach to the fear of God.

The exhortation, "Do not fear!" ('al tîrā'û) often accompanies a theophany as a word of assurance when the overwhelming divine splendor is revealed (Gen. 15:1; 21:17; 26:24; 28:13; 46:3; Josh. 8:1; Judg. 6:23) (THAT 1:771-73). In spite of the terrifying events unfolding before their eyes—the descent of God upon the mountain in the midst of thunder, lightning, fire, smoke and earthquake (19:16-18), followed by the terrifying voice of God (19:19; cf. Deut. 5:23-26)—their lives were not in imminent jeopardy (as long as they did not breach the boundaries of sacred space, 19:20-25). There was no need to fear that God would strike them down in a capricious manner in an unprovoked act of violence. However, they must fear him as the awesome Sovereign who will justly punish any act of creaturely rebellion against the holy Creator. Understood thus, the polar exhortations ("Do not fear . . . do fear him!") reflects two categories of meaning of yr' ("to fear"): (1) "to be afraid, dread, terrified" in terms of anxiety in the face of the unknown or in the presence of someone who is malicious and life-threatening, and (2) "to be in awe of, tremble before" someone who is benevolent and yet has overwhelming power and splendor (BDB, 431; HALOT, 2:432-33). As mortal sinners, the people of God shrink back in legitimate fear of the Holy One who will punish unrepentant sin and rebellion; however, as repentant and forgiven worshipers, the people of God are drawn near in awestruck adoration of his wondrous splendor. While the redeemed are bidden to draw near with confidence into the very presence of God (Heb. 10:19-25), they must nevertheless bow down before him in the fear and trembling of worship (Heb. 12:28-29). Those who worship God must hold in balance the tension of the fear of God and adoration of God, without sacrificing one at the expense of the other. While he is the gracious and forgiving Savior of those who love him and repent of their sins (Exod. 20:6; 34:6-7a), he remains the holy and jealous Lord who punishes the unrepentant and those who hate him (20:5; 34:7b). Thus Scripture often describes the result of the fear of God as the avoidance of evil (Prov. 3:7; 8:13; 16:6) and obedience of his commands (Deut. 10:12; Eccl. 12:13). Realizing that God punishes sin will motivate a person to avoid evil and to obey God, to escape the fearful consequences of his punishment of sin. Evil conduct and the flouting of his law reveal absence of the fear of God. (NIDOTTE, 2:527-33; TDOT, 6:290-315; TLOT, 2:568-78; TWOT, 1:399-401) [yr']

God has come to train you to fear him so that you will not sin (nassôt). Because what Yahweh wants to "test" is not stated, there is debate what nsh means in this context. It probably does not mean "to test, examine" (BDB, 650.3a) but rather "to train, give experience" (so HALOT, 2:702.2) (Exod. 15:26; Judg. 3:1; 2 Chron. 9:1; cf. 1 Sam. 17:39). Elsewhere he "tested" (nsh) Israel "to see" what was in their heart, whether or not they would obey his commandments (Gen. 22:1; Exod. 16:4; Deut. 8:2, 16; 13:4; Judg. 2:22; 3:4). However the purpose of the Sinai theophany was not to see whether Israel would obey God but to inspire them to fear God so that they would not sin in the future. In the theophany God gave Israel a taste of his greatness to make them so deeply conscious of his awesome holiness that it would not enter their mind to trifle with him or violate his commandments. Thus the divine theophany was designed with a pedagogical purpose: to provide Israel with firsthand experience of the holiness of God which would produce the fear of God and the concommittal avoidance of sin. (*NIDOTTE,* 3:111-13; *TLOT,* 2:741-42; *TDOT,* 9:443-55; *TWOT,* 2:581) [*nsh*]

21:1 These are the stipulations (*hammišpāṭîm*). The noun *mišpāṭîm* (traditionally "judgments") denotes "case-laws" or "legal stipulations" as a collection or a law code (Deut. 4:1, 8, 45; 6:1; 33:10, 21) (*BDB,* 1048.4; *HALOT,* 2:651.1). The term *mišpāṭ* refers to a legal ruling or judicial decision in a legal case (Exod. 21:31; 24:3; Deut. 16:18; 25:1; Josh. 20:6;1 Kings 3:28; Prov. 21:3, 15; Isa. 1:17; Jer. 21:12; Zeph. 2:3; Mal. 2:17) and legal judgments from a court (Deut. 19:6; 21:22; 25:1; Job 9:32; 22:4; Ps. 143:2; Isa. 3:14; Jer. 26:11, 16). Because judicial decisions often set legal precedents *mišpāṭ* sometimes means "case-law judgments" (Deut. 4:8; Pss. 89:15; 101:1; 111:7; Isa. 1:21, 27; 42:4). The judge was to render verdicts with

mišpāṭ "just judgment" (Gen. 18:25; Deut. 25:1; 1 Kings 3:11; 8:59; 20:40; Pss. 36:6; 37:28, 30; 106:37; Prov. 12:5; 21:15; 29:4; Isa. 30:18; Mic. 3:1; 6:8). So the term *mišpāṭîm* introduces Exod. 21:1-23:33 as a collection of case-laws that applied the Ten Declarations to everyday life in ancient Israel (collections of Mosaic case-laws appear in Lev. 18-20 and Deut. 12-26).

As practical expositions and applications of the Ten Declarations, the basic contents of the case-laws correspond to the Decalogue. Each of the case-laws in Exod. 21–23 corresponds thematically to the apodictic commands in the Decalogue of Exod. 20. The chart below displays the correlation between the unconditional moral absolutes in the Decalogue (Exod. 20:2-17) and the culturally conditioned case-laws in the so-called Book of the Covenant (Exod. 21:1-23:19). Each of the Ten Declarations has a series of corresponding applications which demonstrate how these ten general moral absolutes apply in specific everyday life situations in ancient Israelite culture and society. For example, deliverance of the Hebrews from slavery in the historical prologue (20:2, "I am YHWH your God who brought you up out of the land of Egypt, out of the house of slavery") translates in application into just and fair treat-

Central Topic	Decalogue	Case-Laws
1.) Deliverance from Slavery	20:2	21:2-11; 22:21
2.) Prohibition of False Worship/Idolatry	20:3-6	22:20; 23:13-33
3.) Prohibition of Blasphemy	20:7	22:28
4.) Observing the Sabbath	20:8-11	23:10-12
5.) Honoring/Obeying Parents	20:12	21:15, 17
6.) Prohibition of Murder	20:13	21:12-15
7.) Prohibition of Adultery	20:14	22:16-19
8.) Prohibition of Theft	20:15	22:1-15
9.) Prohibition of False Testimony	20:16	23:1-9
10.) Prohibition of Covet-ousness	20:17	22:22-27

ment of Hebrew slaves within the land of Israel (21:2-11; 22:21). Honoring one's parents (20:12) means that an individual should not strike (22:15) or curse (22:17) his parents. The prohibition against murder (20:13) is clarified in the case-laws about what does and does not constitute murder (21:12-15).

The typical structure of many case-laws is an introductory temporal/conditional clause ("When/if such-and-such happens . . ."), followed by the legal directive ("then do so-and-so . . ."). These case-laws were not designed to form an exhaustive law code but to provide legal rulings on selected problems that existed in contemporary society. They served as legal precedents to guide the people in moral behavior and help the judges rendering just decisions in future situations that the case-laws themselves did not directly address. While the Decalogue provided general principles that governed every area of life for the faithful covenanter, the case-laws functioned as a "light" to his feet and a "lamp" to his steps (Ps. 119). For example, when Paul drew on the case-law, "Do not muzzle the ox while it is treading out the grain" (Deut. 25:4), he was not using allegorical interpretation (as if oxen = apostles) but using this case-law as biblical precedence (in an argument from lesser [= oxen] to greater [=apostles]) for a new situation that previous Scripture did not directly address: the financial support of apostles (1 Cor. 9:9). (*NIDOTTE*, 2:1142-44; *TLOT*, 3:1395; *TWOT*, 2:947-49) [*mišpāṭ*]

21:2 If you acquire a Hebrew slave (*'ebed*). This use of *'ebed* refers to an Israelite "debt-slave" (*BDB*, 713.1; *HALOT*, 2:774.1). The reduction of an Israelite to slave status could result from poverty or insolvency. By self-sale the

desperately poor could gain a measure of security, while the labors of a debtor or a thief could discharge a defaulted debt or compensate for stolen property. In contrast to the Laws of Hammurabi which limited a debtor's service to three years, Mosaic law allowed a debt-slave to serve as many as six years (Exod. 21:2). This was shortened if the Jubilee year occurred in the meantime (Lev. 25:40). The master was required to make generous provision for the newly freed man on leaving his ser-vice (Deut. 15:12-15). Although the institution of the debt-slave was originally designed as a just system to deal with debtors, greed eventually turned it into a corrupt system of exploitation because masters often refused to release debt-slaves in the seventh year (Jer. 34:8-20).

Mosaic legislation generally enhanced the social and legal status of the debt-slave in comparison to other ancient Near Eastern cultures; however it was marked by ambivalence nonetheless. Although he was the legal property of his master due to financial indebtedness: "he is his property" (Exod. 21:21; cf. Lev. 22:11; 25:45), he was not human chattel—the Hebrew debt-slave was a fellow Israelite, deserving fairness and respect (Deut. 15:12; Jer. 34:9, 12). Even the foreigner subjugated to slavery as a prisoner of war or the runaway slave from a foreign land were given greater protection in Israel than in surrounding nations. The legal rights and humanitarian concern shown the slave by the Mosaic law was revolutionary in comparison with ancient Near Eastern law and custom. For example, the laws of Hammurabi (generally regarded as the most enlightened law code of ancient Mesopotamia) dealt first with free landowners (those with the most rights) and last with slaves (those with the fewest rights); however, Mosaic law dealt with slaves first in order to highlight humanitarian laws to protect their rights (Exod. 21:2-6, 7-11). Having been rescued from slavery themselves (Exod. 20:2; Deut. 5:6), the Israelites were to be sensitive to the condition of the slave (Deut. 15:13-15; Jer. 34:13-14). Those who have been shown grace by God when they were in need must show grace to others in unfortunate circumstances. While it is true that neither the OT nor NT legislated the abolition of the institution of debt-slavery, biblical legislation revolutionized the status of the slave in the ancient world. And Scripture was used as the basis for the abolition of slavery in nineteenth century America. (*NIDOTTE*, 4:1183-98; *TLOT*, 2:819-32; *TWAT*, 5:982-1012; *TWOT*, 2:639-41) [*'ebed*]

21:7 If a man sells his daughter as a slave-wife (*'āmâ*). The second set of slave laws deals with the sale by a poor father of his daughter into a well-to-do family to ensure her future security through marriage to the master or his son (Exod. 21:7-11). This might seem troubling to the modern reader; however, given the way marriages in the ancient world were contracted and arranged by the father, this institution was a good provision for the poor father who might want to find a better life for his daughter. So *'āmâ* "slave-wife, concubine-wife" does not refer to a slave girl in the usual sense—the lowly *šipḥâ* "female slave"—but to a young woman sold to a master for the purpose of marriage or to become a concubine (*BDB*, 51; *HALOT*, 1:61). The sale price included the amount for the service as well as the customary value of the bride price. The marital status of the *'āmâ* "slave-wife, concubine-wife" is demonstrated through the archaeological discov-

ery of an ancient inscription from the village of Siloam outside Jerusalem which mentions a man's *'āmâ* and that he arranged to be buried next to her like a man buried next to his wife. The institution of the slave-wife is also mentioned in ancient documents from Nuzi (ca. 1550 B.C.) and Babylon (ca. 1750 B.C.). Mosaic law tempered prevailing ancient Near Eastern practice by insisting that the young woman not be treated as chattel or a menial slave. While she would not be released after six years like the indentured male slave (v. 7), she must be treated as a free woman in terms of marital rights (vv. 8-11). If the husband to whom she was sold did not fulfill his obligations to provide for her basic needs, he would relinquish all financial claims on the purchase price and she could return to her father. If he took a second wife, he was still obligated to provide for her otherwise he must grant her freedom without any financial claims. Thus the helpless maiden was protected from sexual exploitation and the institution of marriage was preserved.

The book of Ruth provides indirect evidence of the institution of the *'āmâ* "slave-wife, concubine-wife," although it departs from the customary procedure in several dramatic ways. Having just arrived in Bethlehem from Moab, Ruth as an impoverished foreigner (Ruth 2:10) did not even occupy the lowly position of a *šipḥâ* "female servant" on the social scale (2:13). Eventually her destitute mother-in-law attempted to arrange her marriage with Boaz, a well-to-do relative, to ensure her future security (3:1-4) (cf. Exod. 21:7). Following Naomi's instructions (3:5-6), Ruth approached Boaz with the proposal that he marry her as an *'āmâ* "slave-wife, concubine-wife" (3:9). When the nearest kinsman declined the option of "acquiring" (*qnh*) Ruth along with Naomi's field (4:5), Boaz "acquired" (*qnh*) both in a legal transaction in the presence of the village elders (4:9-10). This arrangement not only secured a husband and financial security for the Moabitess, it also provided much-needed capital for her destitute mother-in-law whose future was now secure (4:14-17). In a surprising turn of events, Boaz bestowed on Ruth the status of full-fledged '*iššâ* "wife" (4:10) rather than '*āmâ* "slave-wife," as evidence of the *ḥesed* (kindness, mercy) that marks his character. (*NIDOTTE*, 1:418-21; *TLOT*, 2:823-24; *TWOT*, 1:49-50) ['*amâ*]

21:12 He must be put to death (*môt yûmāt*). The construction *môt yûmāt* "he must be put to a violent death" (*BDB*, 559.2a; *HALOT*, 2:563.2) refers to divinely mandated capital punishment (Exod. 21:12, 15, 16, 17; 22:18; 31:14, 15; Lev. 20:2, 9-13, 15, 16, 20, 27; 24:16, 17; 27:29; Num. 15:35; 35:12, 16-18, 21, 30-31; Deut. 17:2, 6; 18:20; 19:12; 22:22, 25; 24:7) executed by human authority (Gen. 42:20; 44:9; Exod. 10:28; 21:14; Josh. 2:14; Judg. 6:30; 1 Sam. 14:39, 43-45; 19:24; 22:16; 1 Kings 2:37, 42; Jer. 26:8; 38:24). The Covenant Code lists four crimes that incur capital punishment: premeditated murder (21:12-14), physical assault of a parent (21:15), kidnapping (21:16), and maledictory cursing of parents (21:17). Subsequent Mosaic legislation would expand the list of capital crimes (Lev. 20:2,9, 13, 15, 27; 24:16; 27:29; Num. 15:35; 35:16-18, 21, 31; Deut. 13:6; 17:6; 21:22; 24:16). While atonement for many sins could be obtained through repentance and blood atonement of a substitutionary sacrifice, the only "atonement" for capital crimes in ancient Israel was capital punishment. The emphatic construction *môt yûmāt* "he must be put to death" stresses the divinely decreed *obli-*

gation placed on the community to carry out the death penalty. The purpose of capital punishment was to serve as a deterrent to crime (Eccl. 8:11) and to purge the evil from the community before God (Lev. 19:13). According to rabbinic literature, Jewish authorities were reluctant to carry out capital punishment for fear of executing an innocent person. The tension between punishing the guilty but protecting the falsely-accused innocent has vexed legal systems from antiquity to this day. Nevertheless, capital punishment is a divinely ordained institution decreed by God for human government to serve as a "minister of God" to protect those who do good and to punish those who do evil (Rom. 13:4). (*NIDOTTE*, 2:886-88; *TDOT*, 8:185-209; *TLOT*, 2:660-64; *TWOT*, 1:496-97) [*mwt*]

21:13 God let it happen (*wĕhā'ĕlōhîm 'innâ*). This case-law deals with the situation in which a fight breaks out between two people and one person accidentally kills the other. When circumstances suggest lack of premeditation, the death occurred by divine providence (lit. "God *let* it happen" or "God *caused* it to happen"). When used in the intensive (Piel) stem, the verb '*nh* III "to befall, happen" may be (1) causative: "to cause [something] to happen" or (2) permissive: "to allow [something] to happen" (*BDB*, 58; *HALOT*, 1:70). The parallel use of this term in the Apocrypha clearly refers to divine causation (Sir. 15:13). The translations equivocate between divine causation: "it was an act of God" (so KJV, NKJV, ASV, NRSV, NAB) and permission: "God let it happen" (so RSV, NASB, NIV, NLT, TEV, CEV). While this case-law assumes the sovereignty of God (whether by divine decree or permission) over human affairs, the idiom itself emphasizes the lack of human premeditation when one person accidentally kills another: "it comes about by accident" (NET). While no event is accidental when viewed from the perspective of the ultimate sovereignty of God, human events that transpire which were unplanned by the actors may at the same time be viewed as accidental from human perspective. (*NIDOTTE*, 1:453) ['*nh*]

21:17 Whoever <u>curses</u> his father or mother (*ûmĕqallēl*). There is debate whether this refers to a verbal utterance or hostile action. The verb *qll* "to be light, insignificant" has two senses in the intensive (Piel) stem: (1) declarative: "to declare cursed, designate as cursed, pronounce a curse," and (2) factitive: "to treat [someone] as insignificant or contemptible" (*BDB*, 886; *HALOT*, 3:1103-04). The declarative sense reflects the ancient Near Eastern concept that a spoken malediction has potent force, taking on a devastating life of its own, especially if uttered in the name of God (1 Sam. 17:43; 1 Kings 2:28; 2 Kings 2:24; Isa. 8:21). The related noun *qelālâ* "curse" most often refers to a verbal curse-formula (Gen. 27:12; Deut. 11:26; 28:15, 45; 30:1; Judg. 9:57). The factitive sense "to treat [someone] contemptuously" is used of: (a) parents (Prov. 20:20; 30:11), (2) the king (Eccl. 10:20), (3) the blind (Lev. 19:14) and (4) one's master (Prov. 30:10; Eccl. 7:21). Its most frequent antonym is *kbd* "to treat with respect" so *qll* can mean "to treat disrespectfully." Since the case-laws of Exod. 21:12-36 deal exclusively with personal injuries, it may refer to hostile action rather than verbal utterance (so Lev. 20:9; Deut. 27:16). It functions figuratively (metonymy of association) to emphasize the absolute heinousness of physical assault of one's parents—in defiant disobedience of the fifth commandment to honor one's parents

(Exod. 20:12; Deut. 5:16). The kind of hostile actions might encompass the deeds of the "wayward and defiant son" who was to be publicly stoned (Deut. 21:18-19). (*NIDOTTE*, 3:926-27; *TLOT*, 3:1141-45; *TWAT*, 7:40-49; *TWOT*, 2:800-01) [*qll*]

21:20 He must be avenged (*nāqôm yinnāqēm*). In keeping with the law of 21:12, the master who fatally wounds his debt-slave is criminally liable and must be executed as if he had murdered a free man. However in contrast to the usual expression *môt yûmāt* "he must be put to death" (vv. 12, 15, 16, 17) we find *nāqôm yinnāqēm* "he must be avenged" (v. 20). The verb *nqm* "to avenge" refers to action taken by a private individual to exact vengeance against an offender for wrong done to the subject or a member of his family. It usually refers to the justified killing of a murderer who had shed innocent blood (2 Kings 9:7). In the case of the wrongful death of a family member, the victim's next of kin was allowed to administer retributive justice (Num. 35:19; Deut. 19:12). In the case of the wrongful death of a debt-slave, the superior status of his master and meager resources of the victim's family to prosecute the crime lent itself to gross injustice. So this law provides protection for the debt-slave from abuse by allowing a family member to exact vengeance since the legal system might fail. (*NIDOTTE*, 3:154-56; *TLOT*, 2:767-69; *TWAT*, 5:602-12; *TWOT*, 2:598-99) [*nqm*]

21:23b-25 The punishment shall be life <u>for</u> life, eye <u>for</u> eye, tooth <u>for</u> tooth (*taḥat*). The preposition *taḥat* here refers to vicarious substitution in which two like things are mutually interchanged: "in place of, in exchange for" (*BDB*, 1065.II.2.bß) (Gen. 30:15; Josh. 2:14; 1 Sam. 2:20; 1 Kings 20:39; 21:2; Isa. 43:3, 4) and is often used with verbs of requiting (Gen. 44:4; 1 Sam. 25:21; 2 Sam. 16:12; 19:22; Pss. 35:12; 38:21; 109:4, 5; Prov. 17:13; Jer. 5:19). This case-law is the classic statement of the principle of *lex talionis* in determining the appropriate punishment in cases of injury or death. It is restated in shorter form elsewhere: "As he has done so it will be done to him: injury for injury, eye for eye, tooth for tooth; as he has injured a man, so shall it be done to him" (Lev. 24:19-20) and "You shall do to him as he intended to do to his brother . . . You shall not show pity, but life for life, eye for eye, tooth for tooth, hand for hand, foot for foot" (Deut. 19:19, 21). The principle is also reflected in the rulings "ox for ox" (Exod. 21:36) and "life for life" (Lev. 24:18). There is debate whether the statement of talion was intended to legislate what the punishment for an injury *must* be or to regulate the most that the punishment *could* be to guard against excessive retribution (e.g., contra Lamech's boast, Gen. 4:23-24). In any case, the principle of "eye for an eye" was not applied legalistically in every situation. Financial compensation to the victim was more appropriate in certain cases. For example, if a master destroyed the eye or tooth of a slave, the slave gained his freedom—the master lost a slave, not an eye or tooth (Exod. 21:26-27)—because the injured party was better served by compensation than by punishment of the master. [*taḥat*]

21:30 Ransom (*kōper*). The noun *kōper* IV has a two-fold range of meanings: (1) illegitimate "bribe" paid to a judge to pervert justice (1 Sam. 12:3; Amos 5:12) and (2) legitimate "ransom" paid by the guilty party to the victim's family in lieu of blood vengeance, that is, the death penalty (Exod. 21:30; Num. 35:31, 32; Job 33:24; 36:18; Ps. 49:8; Prov. 13:8) (*BDB*, 497;

HALOT, 2:495). This term is clarified by second millennium B.C. ancient Near Eastern law codes which stipulated that a victim's family had a right to avenge the death of a family member through death penalty or ransom, at their choice. Exod. 21:29-31 offered the victim's family the same right, allowing them to demand blood vengeance or ransom to provide for victim's rights in the case of a lost provider. However, the law strictly forbade accepting a ransom for the life of a murderer who must be put to death (Num. 35:30-31) lest the land be polluted with blood guiltiness (Num. 35:33-34). The negligent owner of a goring ox is not deemed a murderer because he did not directly cause the homicide; so the sentence could be mitigated if the victim's family desired. So biblical law not only provides for the execution of justice but also compensation for victim's rights. (*NIDOTTE*, 2:711-12; *TLOT*, 2:624-35; *TDOT*, 7:288-303; *TWOT*, 1:452-53) [*kōper*]

Redemption-price (*pidyōn*). The noun *pidyōn* "ransom, price of redemption" is the financial penalty paid to the victim's family in lieu of suffering blood vengeance through the death penalty (*BDB*, 804; *HALOT*, 3:913). This term appears only here and Ps. 49:8[9], and in both cases it is a synonym for *kōper* "ransom" and is collocated with *napšô* "for his life." The use of *pidyōn* in Ps. 49:8[9] seems to reflect the law of Num. 35:31-32 which prohibited the payment of a ransom to redeem a convicted murderer from execution: "No one can by any means redeem (*pādōh yepiddeh*) his brother, nor give a ransom (*kaprô*) for him to God—for the redemption (*pidyōn*) of his life is costly" (Ps. 49:7-8 [8-9]). The related Hebrew verb *pdy* "to buy out" refers to (1) paying a ransom price to redeem the firstborn from death: humans (Exod. 13:13, 15; 34:20; Num. 18:15, 16) and animals (Exod. 13:13; 34:20; Num. 18:16) with money (Lev. 27:27; Num. 18:15); and (2) rescuing another person from an unjust sentence of death through the popular demand of the community (1 Sam. 14:45) or payment of a bribe from a friend (Job 6:22-23). While a convicted murderer could not pay a ransom to deliver his life from the death penalty (Num. 35:33-34), the owner of a goring ox was allowed this option if granted by the victim's family. (*NIDOTTE*, 3:578-82; *TLOT*, 2:964-76; *TWAT*, 6:514-22; *TWOT*, 2:716-17) [*pidyōn*]

22:2 Blood-guilt (*dāmîm*). The plural noun *dāmîm* (lit. "bloods") has a broad range of meanings, reflecting a cause-effect relationship between the following: (1) "bloodshed" = murder (Gen. 9:6; Num. 35:33), (2) "bloodguilt" = culpability for murder (Exod. 22:1; Lev. 20:9; Num. 35:27; Deut. 19:10; 21:8; 22:8; 32:43; Josh. 2:19; Judg. 9:24; 1 Sam. 25:26, 33; 2 Sam. 1:16; 21:1; Isa. 33:15; Ezek. 9:9) and (3) "blood-vengeance" = relative's demand for the execution of a murderer (2 Sam. 4:11; Ezek. 3:18, 20). This particular law deals with a thief caught in the act of breaking and entering (lit. "while tunneling") and killed in the process. The contrast between "while tunneling" (22:2) and "if the sun has risen" (22:3) shows the latter is a nighttime intrusion. Because a burglar is likely to encounter the occupants who might use force to protect themselves, his nocturnal timing creates a presumption of homicidal intent. The condition of imminent threat, necessary to satisfy lawful self-defense by the householder, is fulfilled. Biblical law gives the homeowner the right to protect himself at night (potentially the most life-threatening situation) without fear of legal reprisal. The underlying principle is that a person has the right to protect himself if he has reasonable cause to suspect that his life is in jeopardy even if it results in the death of the criminal. (*NIDOTTE*, 1:963-66; *TDOT*, 3:234-50; *TLOT*, 1:337-39; *TWOT*, 1:190-91) [*dāmîm*]

22:3 He must make full restitution (*šallēm yĕšallēm*). The intensive (Piel) stem of *šlm* "to be complete, full" means "to pay a debt" (2 Kings 4:7; Ps. 37:21), "to make restitution" (Exod. 21:34; 22:2, 11-14; Prov. 22:27), "to pay compensation" for damage (Exod. 22:4, 5, 6, 8; Lev. 5:16, 25; 24:18, 21; 2 Sam. 12:6; Prov. 6:31; Ezek. 33:15) (*BDB*, 1022; *HALOT*, 4:1534.1a). Since the basic meaning of the root *šlm* is "complete, perfect," the idea here is that the offender must make full restitution—equitable compensation. The emphatic construction *šallēm yĕšallēm* (which features the repetition of the root *šlm*) connotes strong obligation: "he *must* make *full* restitution." A recurrent theme in Mosaic law is the protection of victim's rights. Anyone who violates the rights or destroys the property of another citizen must provide complete restitution, whether in like kind or its financial equivalent. (*NIDOTTE*, 4:130-35; *TLOT*, 3:1337-48; *TWAT*, 8:93-101; *TWOT*, 2:930-32) [*šlm*]

22:20 He must be destroyed (*yoḥŏrām*). The expression *yoḥŏrām* "he must be utterly destroyed" has a greater stringency than the normal death penalty formula *môt yûmāt* "he must be put to death." It connotes total annihilation and includes the destruction of the criminal's property. The root *ḥrm* referred originally to what is forbidden because it is accursed and should be destroyed (*res exsecranda*) or because it is very holy (*res sacrosancta*) (*TLOT*, 2:474). The verb *ḥrm* reflects this two-fold range of meaning: "to declare sacred, to exclude from secular usage," and "to proscribe to total destruction, to devote to destruction" (*BDB*, 355-56; *HALOT*, 1:353-54). The LXX rendered *ḥrm* by *anathema* "accursed for destruction." The passive stem of *ḥrm* "must be utterly destroyed" designates capital punishment (Exod. 22:18[19]; Lev. 27:29). If this punishment is imposed, no redemption is permitted (Lev. 27:29). The guilty party had fallen into God's hands and must be exterminated. The term does not refer to a unique form of execution but the irrevocable decree of the death penalty. The war-booty was often "put under a ban" and devoted to destruction: cities (Num. 21:2; Josh. 6:21), inhabitants (Josh. 8:26), males (Judg. 21:11), cattle (Deut. 2:34; 3:6; 7:2; 13:16; 20:17; Josh. 2:10; 6:18; 10:1, 28, 35, 27, 39; 11:11, 20; Judg. 1:17; 1 Sam. 15:3, 8, 15, 18, 20; 30:17; 1 Kings 9:21; 2 Kings 19:11; Isa. 37:11; Jer. 50:21, 26; 51:3). The term simply means "to destroy" in some cases (1 Chron. 4:41; 2 Chron. 20:23; 32:14; Dan. 11:44). Those who grossly violate the covenant were to be executed through capital punishment: "proscribed to destruction" (Exod. 22:18[19]; Lev. 27:29). To "dedicate" something to Yahweh by the ban ruled out redemption (Lev. 27:28; Deut. 13:17; Isa. 11:15; Mic. 4:13). The related noun *ḥerem* "what is banned" means: (1) dedication to the secularly unusable to destruction or dedicated to cultic use only (Lev. 27:21; Josh. 6:17; 7:12; 22:20; 1 Kings 20:42; Isa. 34:5; 43:28; Zech. 14:11; Mal. 3:24); and (2) what is dedicated as Yahweh's share in the booty. (Lev. 27:28; Num. 18:14; Deut. 7:26; 13:18; Josh. 6:18; 7:1, 11-13, 15; 1 Sam. 15:21; 1 Chron. 2:7; Ezek. 44:29). (*NIDOTTE*, 2:276-77; *TDOT*, 5:180-99; *TLOT*, 2:474-77; *TWOT*, 1:324-25) [*ḥrm*]

23:14 Celebrate a sacred festival (*tāḥōg*). The verb *ḥgg* "to celebrate a pilgrim's festival, hold a pilgrim-festival" (*BDB*, 290; *HALOT*, 1:289-90) (Exod. 5:1; 12:14; 23:14;

Lev. 23:29, 41; Num. 29:12; 14:16, 18-19) is related to the noun *ḥag* "festival, pilgrim-festival" that refers to the three annual Israelite festivals (Exod. 12:4; 13:6; 23:15, 16, 18; 34:18, 22, 25; Lev. 23:6, 34, 39, 41; Num. 28:17; 29:12; Deut. 16:10, 13, 14, 16; 31:10; 1 Kings 8:2, 65; 2 Chron. 5:3; 7:8, 9; 8:13; 30:13, 21; 35:17; Ezra 3:4; 6:22; Neh. 8:14, 18; Ps. 81:4; Isa. 29:1; 30:29; Ezek. 45:21, 23; Amos 5:21; 8:10; Nah. 2:1; Zech. 14:16, 18, 19). One of the goals of the pilgrimage trek out of Egypt to Sinai was to celebrate a "sacred festival" at the mountain of God (Exod. 10:9). There, the Hebrews celebrated their deliverance and worshiped God by offering festival sacrifices (Exod. 8:26-28; 10:9) and participating in a ceremonial meal (Exod. 24:9-11). So the three annual festivals would liturgically recreate the original Passover (Exod. 12:4; 13:6) and pilgrimage out of Egypt (Exod. 23:14-19; 34:18-26; Lev. 23:4-44; Num. 28:16-29:40; Deut. 16:1-17). Just as the first generation journeyed to Sinai to worship Yahweh, future generations would journey each year to Zion to memorialize the original event. Just as vassals in the ancient Near East were required to appear before their suzerain every year to present tribute and to reaffirm their loyalty, Israel was required to make this trek not once but three times annually to the earthly dwelling place of her God. In pre-conquest times this place was wherever the tabernacle was erected. Later it was at Gilgal, Shechem, Shiloh, and eventually Jerusalem. By this act the nation presented not only the best of its produce and the firstborn of its sons, but it reaffirmed its commitment to Yahweh as its Great King. (*NIDOTTE*, 2:20-21; *TDOT*, 4:201-13; *TWOT*, 1:261-63) [*ḥgg*]

24:7 The Book of the Covenant (*sēper habbĕrît*). This phrase is traditionally viewed as a genitive of content: "the book of the covenant" (KJV, NKJV, NAB, ASV, NASB, RSV, NRSV, NIV, NLT, TEV) or "the record of the covenant" (NJPS). However, it may function as an attributive genitive ("the covenant document"), the semantic equivalent of the expression "the treaty document" as the standard title of ancient Near Eastern suzerain-vassal documents. The only other use of this phrase in the OT refers to the scroll found in the temple by Hilkiah the priest, motivating Josiah to convene a national assembly to publicly read its entire contents after which the people entered into a covenant renewal ceremony before the LORD (2 Kings 23:1-3; 22:8; 2 Chron. 34:14-15, 29-32). The protocol of ancient Near Eastern suzerain-vassal treaties required both parties to possess a written copy of the treaty document. The basic structure and major themes in Exod. 19–24 are remarkably similar to the late second millennium suzerainty treaties, suggesting that the Sinai Covenant was intentionally modeled after this ancient Near Eastern pattern: (1) introductory preamble (20:1); (2) historical prologue (20:2); (3) stipulations: (a) basic stipulations (20:3-26) and (b) specific stipulations (21:1-23:19); (4) curses and blessings (23:20-33); (5) oath of loyalty (24:1-3); (6) witnesses (24:4); (7) solemn ceremony (24:5-8); and (8) document clause (24:7). [*sēper*]

24:8 The blood of the covenant (*dam*). Biblical covenants were inaugurated/confirmed by an oath (Gen. 21:22; 26:26; 17:33), solemn meal (Gen. 26:26-31; Exod. 24:11; 2 Sam. 2:20), sacrificial ritual (Gen. 21:22-31; Exod. 24:4-8; Deut. 27:5-7; Ps. 50:5), erecting rock altars/statues as witnesses of the covenant (Gen. 31:44-54; Exod. 24:4; Deut. 27:2-8; Josh. 22:10-34; 24:26-27), or a dramatic ritual of ordeal that involved dividing an animal and the parties passing between the portions while taking a self-imprecatory oath against violating the covenant (Gen. 15:9; Jer. 34:18). This follows the custom in the second and third millennia B.C. when many ancient Near Eastern covenants were concluded with a self-imprecatory ritual against violating the covenant: slaughtering the animal accompanied by a self-imprecation dramatized the punishment of the party who might violate the treaty, adding solemnity to the covenant (*TDOT*, 1:270). Likewise the covenant at Sinai was enacted by the ritual erection of pillars representing the tribes of Israel, the sacrifice of young bulls as fellowship offerings to Yahweh, and the sprinkling of their blood on the people as a self-imprecatory ritual, implicitly threatening curses for covenant rebellion (Exod. 24:4-8). So in contrast to the blood of the New Covenant which was shed to redeem the believing repentant from their sins, the blood of the Mosaic Covenant was shed as a dramatic ritual to warn of the consequences of sin. (*NIDOTTE*, 1:963-66; *TDOT*, 3:234-50; *TLOT*, 1:337-39; *TWOT*, 1:204-05) [*dām*]

The covenant that the LORD has made with you (*habběrît . . . kārat*). The expression *berît kārat* (lit. "to cut a covenant") is the most common Hebrew idiom for inaugurating and renewing a covenant (*BDB*, 136-37; *HALOT*, 1:157-59; *TDOT*, 2:253-55). When used in this expression, the verb *kārat* "to cut" refers to the ritual slaughter and dividing animals in two (parallel to *btr* "to slice" in Gen. 15:10) (*BDB*, 503.4). It is likely that this idiom originated from the ritual performed for establishing or renewing a covenant that involved cutting an animal and shedding its blood (Exod. 24:8; Josh. 24:25 [cf. 8:30-35]; 2 Chron. 29:10 [cf. 29:12-36]; 34:31). As in the rituals in Gen. 15:18 and Jer. 34:18, animals were slain and divided in pieces, the party (or parties) making the covenant solemnly passed between the pieces and took an oath to fulfill certain covenant obligations. In some cases, the ritual act of passing between the two halves of the divided animals was accompanied by an oath of self-imprecation, inviting a similar fate to befall the one who would abrogate the covenant. In other cases, no self-imprecation was uttered; the ritual was simply designed to solemnize the covenant obligations. In neither case was the ritual slaughter of the animals viewed as a sacrifice to atone for sins; rather, it symbolized the seriousness of the obligation. Eventually, the expression "to cut a covenant" became conventionalized, meaning simply "to make a covenant," to refer to a covenant by oath without a sacrificial rite (1 Kings 5:12[26]; 2 Kings 11:17; 23:3; 2 Chron. 21:7; 23:3, 16; Ezra 10:3; Ps. 89:4). However, at Sinai the covenant was inaugurated with the offering of sacrificial animals reflecting the original ritual behind this idiom (Exod. 24:4-8). (*NIDOTTE*, 2:729-31; *TDOT*, 7:339-52; *TLOT*, 2:635-37; *TWOT*, 1:456-57) [*krt*]

25:8 Sanctuary (*miqdāš*). The noun *miqdāš* "holy place, sacred place, sanctuary" is from *qdš* "holy"—the antonym of "common, profane" (Lev. 10:10)—designating the sacred portable open air housed shrine where God manifested his presence among Israel in the desert (*BDB*, 874.3; *HALOT*, 2:625.1). The traditional gloss "sanctuary" is from Latin *sanctuarium* (*sanctus* "sacred, holy") used of places exclusively dedicated to the worship of deity, and consecrated as sacred space in distinction to common/profane space. The presence of God lends a place its holiness (e.g., "holy ground," Exod. 3:5; Josh. 5:15), so the sanctuary was sanctified by

his presence: "I am Yahweh who sanctifies [the sanctuaries]" (Lev. 21:23). As sacred space it was off-limits against unauthorized contact: just as God instructed Moses to place a boundary around Sinai to "sanctify" it against common/profane contact (Exod. 19:12, 23), the sanctuary complex was withdrawn from the defilement of the Israelites by its complex system of borders, walls, and veils. Although the sanctuary would eventually be placed within the sacred space at the center of the Israelite encampment during its journeys, at Sinai it was placed at a distance from the camp, within the holy ground marked out by the boundaries around the mountain (Exod. 33:1-7). The Israelites were to stand in awe and fear before his sanctuary to worship him (Lev. 19:30), as when the LORD appeared to them at Sinai (Exod. 19:9, 16; 20:18-21; Deut. 5:28-29).

While other terms refer to the tabernacle proper (e.g., *hammiškān* "the dwelling place" 25:9), *miqdāš* "sanctuary" refers to the complex as a whole. As a portable shrine (similar to a portable Midianite open air shrine from the same basic period discovered by archaeologists), the sanctuary complex was disassembled and transported whenever the people traveled, and erected again when they stopped to camp (Num. 2:1-4:49; 9:15-23). After Israel entered Canaan, it was stationed successively at Shiloh (Josh. 18:1; 19:51), Nob (1 Sam. 21), and Gibeon (1 Chron. 16:39). When David brought the ark up to Jerusalem, he also brought the entire sanctuary complex as well (2 Sam. 6:17; 1 Chron. 16:1, 39, 40). The permanent temple eventually replaced the portable sanctuary (1 Kings 8:4; 1 Chron. 21:28-30; 23:32; 2 Chron. 1:3-6; 5:5; 24:6; 29:5-7). (*NIDOTTE*, 3:877-87; *TLOT*, 3:1114.3c; *TWAT*, 6:1179-1204; *TWOT*, 2:786-89) [*miqdāš*]

So that I may <u>dwell</u> among them
(*wĕšākantî*). The verb *šākan* "dwell" often
refers to humans inhabiting an abode, but
here to God dwelling in the tabernacle
(Exod. 25:8; 29:45-46; Num. 5:3; 35:34) or
temple (1 Kings 6:13; Ezek. 43:7, 9; Joel
4:17[3:17]; Zech. 2:14-15). The Israelite
tabernacle/temple, like other ancient
Near Eastern temples, was an actual residence of God not just a meeting place for
the people (Exod. 25:8-9). Idols were prohibited to represent his presence in the
sanctuary (Exod. 20:4-6) because the LORD
himself took up residence there and manifested himself in a visual way (Exod.
40:34-38; Lev. 9:22-24; 16:2; Num. 9:15-23;
1 Kings 8:10-13; 2 Chron. 7:1-3). Although
the sanctuary was the place where the
immanent presence of the LORD was manifest (Exod. 25:8; 1 Kings 8:12-13), the
actual ontological presence of the transcendent God of all creation cannot be
contained within the confines of the sanctuary or even the whole universe for that
matter (1 Kings 8:27). What actually
dwells in the sanctuary is his "name" in
the sense that it was dedicated to the God
named Yahweh (Deut. 12:11; 14:23; 16:2, 6,
11; 26:2; Neh. 1:9; Ps. 74:7; Jer. 7:12). Here
also God manifested his "glory" in a visible anthropomorphic sense (Exod. 40:38;
Pss. 26:8; 68:32-35). (*NIDOTTE*, 4:109-11;
TLOT, 3:1327-30; *TWAT*, 7:1337-48; *TWOT*,
2:925-26) [*škn*]

25:9 The Abode (*hammiškān*). Derived
from *šākan* "to dwell," *miškān* "dwelling-
place, abode" is more popularly known
as the tabernacle (*BDB*, 1015.2c; *HALOT*,
2:647.3). Like a human "abode" (Num.
16:24, 27; S. of S. 1:8), this is pictured as
the "abode" of Yahweh (Exod. 26:1, 6;
27:9; 36:8, 32; 38:21, 31; 39:32; 40:2, 6, 28;
Lev. 8:10; 15:31; 17:4; 26:11; Num. 1:50, 53;
3:7, 38; 4:16, 26, 31; 5:17; 7:1, 3; 9:15, 20;

10:11, 17, 21; 16:9; 17:28; 19:13; 3:30, 47;
Josh. 22:29; 2 Sam. 7:6). In related Semitic
languages *mškn* refers to permanent temples or portable tents as the cultic abode
of the gods. While *miqdāš* "sanctuary"
designates the entire complex and
emphasizes its holy nature (Exod. 25:8),
miškān "abode" is the bipartite tent within
this complex and specifies its function
(Exod. 26:7; 36:14; Num. 3:25) (Note the
contrast between the *miškān* as opposed
to the court around it in Exod. 35:11-15
versus 35:16-17; 38:31; Num. 3:26). The
taber-nacle is alternately referred to as the
holy place (Exod. 38:24), dwelling of
Yahweh (Lev. 17:4), dwelling of the
covenant (Exod. 38:21), tent of meeting
(Exod. 28:43), dwelling of the tent of
meeting (Exod. 39:32), house of Yahweh
(Exod. 34:26), and palace of Yahweh (1
Sam. 1:9). The tabernacle was the visible
sign of Yahweh's presence among the
people as the central place of worship. It
housed the ark of the covenant, an
incense altar, a table, a seven-light candelabra, an eternal light, Aaron's staff that
miraculously blossomed (Num. 17:23-26),
the vessels that were used by the priests,
possibly a container of manna (Exod.
16:33–34), and a scroll written by Moses
(Exod. 25:16). The law required that all
sacrifice and the execution of several
other practices must take place before its
entrance, that is, before the Presence of
God (Lev. 1:3, 5; 3:2, 8, 13; 4:5-7, 14-18;
etc.). (*NIDOTTE*, 4:109-11; *TLOT*, 3:1327-
30; *TWAT*, 7:1337-48; *TWOT*, 2:925-26)
[*miškān*]

25:10 Ark (*'ărôn*). The most sacred cultic
object of ancient Israel was a chest designated simply by the term *'ărôn* "ark,
chest" (*BDB*, 75.3; *HALOT*, 1:85.B). This
term is derived from *'ōren* "wood" and
related to *'ărônît* "wooden container." The

term 'ărôn refers to various wooden containers: (1) wooden coffin or sarcophagus (Gen. 50:26), (2) wooden chest for money (2 Kings 12:10; 2 Chron. 24:8, 10, 11), and (3) the ark as the repository of the covenant document given to Moses on Sinai (later a jar of manna and Aaron's rod were added) (Exod. 25:16). This explains the designations "ark of the covenant" 33x (Num. 10:33; Deut. 10:8; 31:9; Josh. 3:3), "ark of the covenant of the LORD" 9x (Num. 10:33; Josh. 4:7; 6:8; 1 Sam. 4:3, 5), and "ark of the testimony" 13x (Exod. 25:22; 26:33, 34; 30:6). In several places the term "the testimony" (hā'ēdût), which normally refers to the two tablets placed in the ark (Exod. 25:16, 21, 40), refers to the ark itself as a synecdoche of contents (the tablets) for the container (Exod. 16:34; 27:21; 30:36). The ark was the sacred meeting place between heaven and earth (Exod. 25:22). Because it was placed in the Most Holy Place behind the veil (Exod. 40:2-3), it was also associated with God, representing the divine Presence. The reference to Yahweh dwelling in a tent (2 Sam. 7:6) is equated with the ark in the tent (2 Sam. 7:2). The expression "before Yahweh" or "before God" is frequently synonymous with "before the ark" (Lev. 16:1-2; 2 Sam. 6:4-5, 14, 16, 17, 21; Josh. 6:8; Judg. 20:26-27; 1 Sam. 10:25; 2 Kings 16:14; 1 Kings 8:59, 62-65; 9:25; 1 Chron. 1:6; 13:10; cf. Num. 10:35; Ps. 105:4).

The function of the ark as the repository of the covenant document is best appreciated in the light of its ancient Near Eastern background. When a treaty was sealed in the ancient Near East, a copy of the treaty document was often placed in a container in the temple at the feet of the image of the deity of each party. Likewise a copy of the covenant document between Yahweh and Israel was placed in the ark which was placed in the taberna-cle. Just as treaty documents were placed in the temple at the feet of the image of the deity, the ark is called the "footstool" of God (1 Chron. 28:2; Pss. 99:5; 132:7). The dimensions and materials of the ark followed the pattern of the royal footstools of Hittite, Egyptian and Phoenician kings which were often box-like, made of wood (ebony or acacia), ornately decorated and gold-plated. It is also associated with the throne on which Yahweh sat in regal splendor because Scripture says Yahweh "sits enthroned upon the cherubim" which covered the ark (1 Sam. 4:4; 2 Sam. 6:2; 2 Kings 19:15 = Isa. 32:16). While it is closely associated with the notion of Yahweh's enthronement, it is not the throne *per se*, but the earthly footstool of his heavenly throne. So the imagery presents the ark as his royal footstool, the Most Holy Place as his throne room, and the tabernacle as his palace. (*NIDOTTE*, 1:500-10; *TDOT*, 1:363-74; *TWOT*, 1:73-74) ['ărôn]

25:16 The Covenant Document (hā'ēdût). Related to 'ēd "witness [in a legal transaction]" and 'ēdōt "legal ordinances," the term 'ēdût (traditionally "testimony," KJV, NKJV, ASV, RSV, NASB, NIV) here refers to a "legal document" containing "legal provisions, legal statutes, covenant stipulations" (*BDB*, 730; *HALOT*, 2:790-91). 'ēdût often refers to some kind of legal document, such as that of royal protocol symbolically presented to the king of Judah along with the crown at his coronation (2 Kings 11:12; 2 Chron. 23:11; Ps. 132:12). Here the collective singular 'ēdût refers to the written stipulations of the Sinai covenant document placed into the ark (Exod. 25:16, 21; 40:20) (*HALOT*, 2:791.1.b). This document recording the covenant arrangements between Yahweh and Israel (Exod. 24:4) is elsewhere called the "written record of the covenant" (*sēper habberît*) (Exod. 24:7). Its covenant connotations are clearly seen by the fact that *'ēdût* "testimony" and *bĕrît* "covenant" often appear in parallelism (Pss. 25:10; 132:12). The tablets given at Sinai are interchangeably called "tablets of the covenant [*bĕrît*]" (Deut. 9:9, 15) and "tablets of the testimony [*'ēdût*]" (Exod. 27:8; 31:18). Likewise the ark is interchangeably called the "ark of the testimony [*'ēdût*]" (Exod. 31:7) and the "ark of the covenant [*bĕrît*]" (Exod. 25:22; 26:33; 30:6, 26; 39:35; 40:3, 5, 21; Num. 4:5; Josh. 4:16). This term refers to covenant stipulations when collocated with *mišpaṭ̄ gîm* "stipulations" and *ḥōqqĝîm* "ordinances" (Deut. 4:45; 6:17, 20; 1 Kings 2:3; 2 Kings 17:15; 23:3; 1 Chron. 29:29; 2 Chron. 34:31; Neh. 9:34; Pss. 25:10; 78:56; 93:5; 99:7; 119:2; 132:12; Jer. 44:23) (*HALOT*, 2:791.2). So *'ēdût* refers to covenant stipulations in a legal written document: "covenant document," as reflected in several translations: "the covenant" (NRSV), "the stone tablets inscribed with the terms of the covenant" (NLT), "the two stone tablets" (TEV), "the commandments" (NAB). (*NIDOTTE*, 3:335-40; *TLOT*, 2:838-46; *TWAT*, 5:1107-30; *TWOT*, 2:648-50) ['*ēdût*]

25:17 Atonement cover (*kappōret*). The cover over the ark was the *kappōret*, rendered in dramatically different ways: (1) "lid" (TEV, CEV) or "cover" (NAB margin, NRSV margin); (2) "mercy seat" (KJV, NKJV, ASV, RSV, NRSV, NASB) or "propitiary" (NAB, NASB margin); and (3) the intentionally ambiguous "atonement cover" (NIV) and "the ark's cover—the place of atonement" (NLT). The issue is whether *kappōret* is derived from the basic (Qal) stem *kāpar* "to cover" hence "cover [over the ark]" or from the intensive (Piel) stem *kippēr* "to atone" hence "place of

atonement" (*NIDOTTE*, 2:689). Either is conceivable since the *kappōret* was placed over the ark as a cover (Exod. 25:21-22, 34; 40:20) and it was where the high priest sprinkled the atoning blood (Lev. 16:14, 15). However, the form *kappōret* is probably from the intensive (Piel) stem *kippēr* "to atone" (suggested by the doubled middle consonant *pp*) so it probably means "place of atonement" or "atonement cover" (Num. 29:11; Lev. 23:27). Because the ark was where God would "meet" with man (Exod. 25:22), it was necessary for this to be the place of atonement of sin before God. Fellowship with God is impossible apart from atonement. (*NIDOTTE*, 2:689-710; *TDOT*, 7:288-303; *TLOT*, 2:624-35; *TWOT*, 1:452-53) [*kappōret*]

25:18 Cherubim (*kĕrûbîm*). The meaning of *kĕrûb* is uncertain. Traditional English "cherub" (singular) and "cherubim" (plural) are simply transliterations. A previous generation of scholars proposed that Hebrew *kĕrûb* is connected to Persian *giriften, griffen* but there is no direct evidence for this although biblical cherubim are angelic creatures similar to Persian griffin (*BDB*, 500). The root *krb* means "to pray, consecrate, bless, sacrifice" in related Semitic languages, and the parallel form *kārubu* refers to one who is "greeted reverentially" (*HALOT*, 2:497; *AHw* 449, 453); therefore, the term seems to refer to some kind of cultic personnel. The related Akkadian noun *kāribu* refers to (1) high-ranking spirits, (2) angelic gatekeepers or guardians of the throne, and (3) intercessory priests (*HALOT*, 2:497; *AHw* 510b). Biblical cherubim appear in parallel roles: (1) high-ranking spirits (Rev. 4–6), (2) angelic gatekeepers barring access to the divine presence (Gen. 3:24; Exod. 26:1, 31; 36:8, 35; 2

Chron. 3:14; Ezek. 28:14), associated with God's throne (1 Sam. 4:4; 2 Sam. 6:2 = 1 Chron. 13:6; 2 Kings 19:15 = Isa. 37:19; Pss. 80:2; 99:1), and (3) perhaps heavenly priests ministering in the heavenly temple as the counterpart to the earthly priests of the earthly temple (cf. seraphim, Isa. 6:2-6)—depicted symbolically in the imagery in the tabernacle and temple imagery (Exod. 26:1, 31; 36:8, 35; 1 Kings 6:23-35; 7:29-36; 8:6-7; 2 Chron. 3:7-14; 5:7-8). Although it is probably legendary, rabbinic literature claims that on the Day of Atonement an angelic guardian of this kind escorted the high priest into the Most Holy Place.

Some passages refer to cherubim as actual living creatures (Gen. 3:24; Ezek. 1:5-28; 28:14), but most refer to cultic representations of these heavenly beings: (a) images of gold upon the ark in the tabernacle (Exod. 25:18-22; 37:7-9; Num. 7:89), (b) images woven in the veil of the Most Holy Place of the tabernacle (Exod. 26:1, 31; 36:8, 35) and the temple (2 Chron. 3:14), (c) gold plated wood images standing in the Most Holy Place of the temple (1 Kings 6:23-35; 8:6-7; 2 Chron. 3:10-14; 5:7-8), (d) images carved on the gold plated cedar planks of the inner walls of the temple and on the olive wood doors (1 Kings 6:29-35; 2 Chron. 3:7), and (e) images on the base of the lavers, interchanging with images of lions and oxen (1 Kings 7:29-36). Actual descriptions of their appearance are quite limited: cherubim are depicted as winged angelic figures (Exod. 25:18-22) and winged animal figures with human faces (Ezek. 1:5-28; 9:3; 10:1-20; 11:22; 41:18-25).

The form of the cherubim is not described in any detail to Moses (only that the two cherubim were to face each other with wings outstretched over the ark), suggesting that their form was common knowledge in the ancient Near East. The biblical depictions of cherubim correspond to various forms of composite winged supernatural creatures found in ancient Near Eastern art (e.g., winged bulls with human faces in Mesopotamian and Hittite art, and winged sphinxes with human faces in Egyptian art) that symbolically function as guardians of the royal throne (*TWAT*, 4:330-34). So the biblical cherubim are not the round-faced winged infants popularized in Western art of the Middle Ages.

The images of the two cherubim over the ark seem to form some kind of sacred throne for God's invisible presence (1 Sam. 4:4; 2 Sam. 6:2 = 1 Chron. 13:6; 2 Kings 19:15 = Isa. 37:19; Ezek. 10:1-20), while the ark itself functioned as the divine footstool of his heavenly throne (1 Chron. 28:2; Pss. 99:5; 132:7). This parallels the many cherubim thrones in the art of ancient Syria-Palestine, in which human and/or divine kings are pictured sitting on cherubim thrones of winged creatures. So the cherubim were part of the royal imagery of the tabernacle, depicting the LORD as sovereign King ruling from his sacred throne (= the Most Holy Place) and sitting on his heavenly cherubim throne with his feet resting on the earthly footstool (= the ark). (*NIDOTTE*, 2:717-18; *TDOT*, 7:307-19; *TWOT*, 1:454-55) [*kĕrûb*]

25:30 Bread of the presence (*leḥem pānîm*). Often mistranslated "showbread," *leḥem pānîm* is literally "the bread in the presence of [My face]." It is also called "the arranged bread" because it was arranged (*'rk*) in two rows (1 Chron. 9:32), and "the "regular bread" or "continual bread" because it was to be continually (*tāmîd*) before God (Num. 4:7). The bread of the presence consisted of twelve loaves of unleavened bread displayed in the sanctuary, separated only by a curtain from Yahweh's immediate presence. The purpose of the bread was to be on display before Yahweh as a memorial to symbolize the covenant between God and Israel (Lev. 24:5-9). Unlike the sacrifices offered sporadically on the altar and the incense burnt twice daily within the sanctuary, the bread of the presence was "continually" before Yahweh, emphasizing Israel's perpetual standing before God in the covenant. In ancient Near Eastern religions, the priests brought similar loaves of bread into temples to symbolically "feed" their gods; however, in Israel the point of this imagery is reversed: the true living God has no need for man to feed him (Ps. 50:8-13); rather he provides for the needs of his people. [*pānîm*]

25:31 Lampstand (*měnôrâ*). Derived from the root *nwr* "light, flame," the noun *měnôrâ* (traditionally "candelabra") in the OT refers to (1) a simple olive oil "lamp" as the source of light in domestic dwellings (2 Kings 4:10) and (2) the more elaborate ceramic "lampstand" as the source of light in the cultic shrines of the Mosaic tabernacle (Exod. 25:31-35; 26:35; 30:27; 31:8; 35:14; 37:17-20; 39:37; 40:4, 24; Lev. 24:4; Num. 3:31; 4:9; 8:2-4) and the later Solomonic temple (1 Kings 7:49; 1 Chron. 28:15; 2 Chron. 4:7, 20; 13:11; Jer. 52:19; Zech. 4:2, 11) (*BDB*, 633; *HALOT*, 2:600-01). As part of the sacred furniture the tabernacle lampstand held an olive oil lamp to illuminate the interior of the sanctuary which otherwise would be shrouded in darkness. The form of the tabernacle lampstand (central shaft with six branches) resembles a tree-shaped object (Exod. 25:31-37; 26:35; 27:20; 37:17-21; 40:4; Lev. 24:2-3; Num. 8:2-3), which corresponds to ancient Near Eastern iconogra-

phy of a conventional tree of life design. This motif symbolizes the themes of the fertility of nature, the sustenance of physical life, and the presence of eternal life in the presence of the deity. As a demythologized tree of life symbol, it served to assure Israel of God's availability to the Israelites and his benevolent provision of life—both physical and eternal—in his presence. The single lampstand with multiple lamps of the Mosaic tabernacle was later replaced by ten individual lampstands in the Solomonic temple (1 Kings 7:49 = 2 Chron. 4:7). [*měnôrâ*]

26:9 The tent (*'ōhel*). The *miškān* "tabernacle" was covered by a third enclosure, here called the *'ōhel* "tent" (*BDB*, 14.3; *HALOT*, 1:19.1). It is made of a less-valuable fabric, goat wool, and was not dyed or embroidered. Like the *miškān*, it was made of two pieces of fabric joined together by loops and rings (made of brass rather than gold as was the case with the loops and rings of the *miškān*). The *'ōhel* was covered by two outer enclosures: the covering of ram leather dyed red and a covering of animal skins. (*NIDOTTE*, 1:300-02; *TDOT*, 1:118-30; *TWOT*, 1:15) [*'ōhel*]

26:31 Canopy (*pārōket*). The Most Holy Place was a pavilion of four columns of acacia wood with a fabric "canopy" (*pārōket*) spread horizontally over the four columns and vertically draped down in front of the ark (Exod. 26:33; 40:3). As a vertical curtain, it screened off the Most Holy Place from the Holy Place: "Hang the *pārōket* from the clasps and place the ark of the testimony behind the *pārōket*, so that the *pārōket* separates the Holy Place from the Most Holy Place" (Exod. 26:33). As a canopy horizontally draped over the pavilion, it covered the ark: "Place the ark of the testimony in [the Tent of Meeting] and cover over [*wesakkōtā 'al*] the ark with the *pārōket*" (Exod. 40:3). It "covered" (*sākak*) and not just screened the ark: "He brought the ark into the tabernacle, and set up the *covering curtain* (*pārōket hammāsāk*) and *covered* (*wayyāsek*) the ark" (Exod. 40:21) and "When the camp sets out, Aaron and his sons shall go in and they shall take down the *covering curtain* (*pārōket hammāsāk*) and *cover* (*wekissû*) the ark of the testimony with it; and they shall lay a *covering* (*kesûy*) of porpoise skin on it, and shall spread over it a cloth of pure blue" (Num. 4:5-6). The verb *sākak* here means "to cover" rather than "shield" (Exod. 25:20; 37:9; 40:3, 21; Judg. 3:24; 1 Sam. 24:4; 1 Kings 8:7; 1 Chron. 28:18; Job 40:22; Pss. 5:12; 91:4; 140:8; Lam. 3:43, 44; Ezek. 28:14, 16), e.g., the cherubim "covered" or "overshadowed" the ark (Exod. 25:20; 37:9; 1 Kings 8:7; 1 Chron. 28:18; cf. Ezek. 28:14, 16). Josephus describes the wings of the cherubim covering the ark "as under a tent or dome" (*Antiquities* 7.103-104). Appropriately the LXX translates *pārōket* with Greek *katapetasma* "a covering" (the verb form means "to spread over, to cover [with fabric]"). So the *pārōket* was not the entrance curtain but a fabric canopy. The instructions to make the *pārōket* (Exod. 26:31-35) are distinct from the instructions to make the veil (*māsāk*) that hung down in front of the ark as an entrance curtain into the Most Holy Place (Exod. 26:36-37). The *pārōket* that covered the Most Holy Place was hung on four golden hooks on the four corners of the most sacred pavilion (Exod. 36:35-36) while the entrance curtain (*māsāk lepetaḥ*) was hung on five golden hooks on five posts at the entrance to this most sacred pavilion (Exod. 36:37-38).

According to 2 Chronicles 3:14 the Solomonic temple also featured a *pārōket* of

embroidered linen with the cherubim interwoven. Since the entrance into the Most Holy Place in the temple was two doors with carved cherubim (1 Kings 6:31-32) the *pārōket* was not a veil entrance but a canopy draped over the top of the ark suspended from pillars (Exod. 26:32-33). Since this canopy covered the ark underneath the roof of the tent of the tabernacle, it was also placed inside the temple and behind the door entrance into the Solomonic version of the Most Holy Place. There would be no necessary contradiction between having doors sealing off the entrance to the Inner Sanctuary (*debîr*) of the temple (1 Kings 6:31-32), as well as a canopy over the ark inside the Inner Sanctuary (*debîr*) of the temple (2 Chron. 3:14). Likewise Josephus states that although wooden doors were placed at the temple entrances, the *pārōket* stood behind the doorway in the Most Holy Place (Josephus, *Antiquities* 8.101). Jewish tradition suggests that this canopy-tent and the ark were removed from the temple during the destruction of Jerusalem (2 Macc. 2:4-8; *Yoma* 53b). The tradition of this canopy-tent housing the ark also appears in the NT: the ark is said to be located "behind the second curtain (the *māsāk* "curtain" of Exod. 26:36-37, which was a sacred tent, the *pārōket* "canopy" of Exod. 26:31-35)" (Heb. 9:3). So the *pārōket* served as a barrier, hindering both entry and sight, and marked the place in or upon which God was enthroned (*TWAT*, 6:756).

Because it shielded the sacred ark, it was made of the finest materials and crafted with the most elaborate workmanship (Exod. 26:31-35; 27:21; 40:21; Lev. 4:17; 16:12; Num. 4:12). It was made from a blend of colored wools (blue, red, purple) and fine twined linen. Its fabrication involved needlework of cherubim woven into the fabric. It was suspended on golden hooks from four acacia-wood pillars which were overlaid with gold. Its sanctity in association with the ark was indicated by (1) its location, (2) its costly fabrication, and (3) its use as the cover for the ark when the tabernacle was dismantled for travel (Num. 4:5). It was the only fabric carried by the Kohathites, the most important of the Levitical families. When the temple was constructed, most of the other tabernacle fabrics (used for the walls, entrance curtains and roof) were replaced by wood and stone, and most of the tabernacle furnishings were replaced by more elaborate substitutes; however, the ark and this sacred fabric were never superseded due to their status of most sacred objects standing in the sacred space of the Most Holy Place. [pārōket]

26:33 Separate the Holy Place from the Most Holy Place (haqqōdeš . . . qōdeš haqqŏdāšîm). The distinction between these two realms of sacred space indicates that there are different degrees of holiness. Since holiness in the OT is a relative category (one person, place or thing can be more holy or less holy than another), the first precinct of the tabernacle was holy (haqqōdeš) and the innermost precinct where the ark is located was most holy (qōdeš haqqŏdāšîm) (Exod. 26:33-34; 1 Kings 6:16; Ezek. 41:4). The expression qōdeš haqqŏdāšîm (lit. "the holy of holies") is an example of the superlative genitive construction to denote par excellence. For example, "God of gods and Lord of lords" means The Highest God and the Supreme Lord (Deut. 10:17); "slave of slaves" means an abject slave (Gen. 9:25), "vanity of vanities" means complete futility (Eccl. 1:2; 12:8) and "the Song of Songs" means the most excellent song (S. of S. 1:1). The canopied pavilion where the ark was located was the most holy location in all creation because it

was the sacred space where the LORD appeared in his glory to meet with Israel (Exod. 25:22; 29:42-43; 30:6, 36; Num. 7:89). Consequently this sacred space could not be profaned from contact with mortal man. No one could enter the Most Holy Place (Lev. 16:2; Num. 18:7), except the high priest, and only after special cleansing, for the annual atonement ceremonies (Lev. 16:3-24). (NIDOTTE, 3:877-87; TLOT, 3:1103-18; TWAT, 6:1179-1204; TWOT, 2:786-89) [qōdeš]

26:36 Curtain (māsāk). The entrance into the Tent of Meeting was covered by a curtain designated by māsāk "covering, veil, screen" (BDB, 697.2b). The term māsāk may refer to three different entrance curtains: (1) the gate-like entrance (ša'ar) of the outer court (Exod. 27:16; 35:17; 38:18; 39:40; 40:8, 33; Num. 3:26; 4:26); (2) the entrance curtain of the tent (Exod. 26:36, 37; 35:15; 36:37; 39:38; 40:5, 28; Num. 3:25, 31; 4:25); and (3) the suspended covering veil (pārōket hammāsāk) that divided the Holy Place from the Most Holy Place (Exod. 35:12; 39:34; 40:21; Num. 3:31; 4:5) (BDB, 697.2; HALOT, 2:605.2). [māsāk]

27:1 Altar (mizbēaḥ). On the east side of the courtyard stood the sacrificial altar, measuring 7'6" square and 4'6" high, and was approached by steps or some sort of incline (Exod. 27:1-8; 38:1-7). In contrast to other altars made of packed earth (Exod. 20:24) or stone (Exod. 20:25; 27:5; Deut. 27:5; Josh. 8:31; Isa. 27:9), the tabernacle altar was a wooden framed altar overlaid with bronze (Exod. 27:1-5; 38:30; 39:39). The altar was topless and hollow. Some suppose that in use it was filled with earth and stones, others that it acted like an incinerator, draught being supplied through the grating. It is alternately called the "bronze altar" from its covering material and the "burnt offering altar" from the main sacrifices offered on it. The term *mizbēaḥ* "altar" is from the verb *zbḥ* "to slaughter for sacrifice," referring to the cultic structure upon which sacrifice was offered up to God (*BDB*, 258; *HALOT*, 1:564). This term appears in many ancient Near Eastern languages, and archaeological excavations have uncovered various kinds of altars in the land of Israel and throughout the entire ancient Near East (*TWAT*, 4:789-93). [*mizbēaḥ*]

27:2 Make a <u>horn</u> at each of the four corners (*qarnōtāyw*). The design of Israelite altars featured "horns" (*qĕrānôt*) at each corner (Exod. 27:2; 29:12; 30:2, 10; 37:25; 38:2; Lev. 4:7, 18, 25, 30, 34; 8:15; 9:9; 16:18; Ps. 118:27; Jer. 17:1; Ezek. 43:15, 20) (*BDB*, 901-02; *HALOT*, 3:1145.2). Horned altars have been discovered by archaeologists throughout the ancient Near East, so they were not unique to ancient Israel. The four corner horns aided in binding the animal to the altar (Ps. 118:27) and served as protrusions upon which blood of sacrificial animals was daubed (Exod. 24:6; 29:12; Lev. 8:15). In ancient Near Eastern art, horns symbolize various deities (especially horned gods), so these protrusions of horned altars might symbolize the god to whom the altar was dedicated—in the case of Israelite horned altars they symbolized the one true God (cf. Jer. 17:1). Owing to its sanctity, a fugitive could seek asylum by clinging to the horns of the altar (Exod. 21:14; 1 Kings 1:50; 2:28-34; Amos 3:14). [*qeren*]

27:9 The <u>courtyard</u> for the tabernacle (*ḥāṣēr*). The term *ḥāṣēr* "enclosure, courtyard" sometimes refers to the semi-enclosed courtyard of a house (2 Sam. 17:18; Neh. 8:16), a palace courtyard (1 Kings 6:36; 7:8, 9, 12) and more frequently

of the semi-enclosed area of the tabernacle complex and the corresponding area of the later temple complex (*BDB*, 347.3; *HALOT*, 1:345.A.2). This *ḥāṣēr* "courtyard" was the location of the priestly sacrifices (2 Chron. 7:7) because the altar was located therein. Functioning as a synecdoche of part for the whole, *ḥāṣēr* sometimes appears in parallelism with terms of the entire complex, e.g., *hêkāl* "temple" (Pss. 65:4 [5]; 84:10 [11]; 92:13 [14]; 135:2). (*NIDOTTE*, 2:249-50; *TDOT*, 5:131-39) [*ḥāṣēr*]

28:6 Ephod (*'ēpôd*). The term *'ēpôd* "priestly robe" refers to the sacred garment of the high priest (*BDB*, 65.1; *HALOT*, 1:77.3). The priests wore simple linen garments in the discharge of their practical duties, while the high-priest wore this elaborate ceremonial garment made of costly materials and heavily ornamented. This apron-like sleeveless overgarment was kept in place by shoulder straps (Exod. 28:25) bound by rings to the breastplate (28:28). Two onyx stones, each engraved with the names of six of the tribes, were set into gold brackets and attached to the shoulder pieces. The fabric was interwoven with gold thread, and featured a multicolored mix of wool and linen, exclusively reserved for the Most Holy Place and the High Priest (Exod. 28:15), so forbidden in secular contexts (Lev. 19:19; Deut. 22:11). The costly materials and elaborate workmanship gave the ephod special status among the high priestly vesture, its symbolic aspect derived from its nature as a costly and intricately woven golden garment. Thus it reflected and conveyec the splendor and holiness of God whose glory was revealed in the sacred space of the Most Holy Place. The related Semitic term is used in ancient Near Eastern texts to refer to the sacred garment worn by pagan gods and also draped over cultic statues of various gods in cultic rituals designed to secure the deity's presence and availability to the worshiper. The high priests in other ancient Near Eastern cults also wore similar sacred garments as they performed cultic rituals in the presence of these robed cultic statues. For ancient Israel, the use of this kind of sacred golden vestment for the high priest provided an analogous but distinctive purpose. Because Yahweh prohibited any cultic statues of himself, no image of Yahweh could be specially robed to ensure the divine presence and availability. But the high priest, who was closest to Yahweh, was so robed as a way of symbolizing and securing God's presence. The priestly ephod thus had a symbolic role in bringing a human representative into contact with the unseen God. (*NIDOTTE*, 1:476-77; *TWOT*, 1:63) [*'ēpôd*]

28:30 Urim (*'ûrîm*). The exact meaning of both *'ûrîm* and *tummîm* is unclear (*BDB*, 22). The traditional "Urim and Thummim" (ASV, TEV, KJV, NAB, NASB, NIV, NLT, RSV, NRSV) are transliterations that avoid the difficult task of interpretation (so also CEV: "two small objects"). Traditionally *'ûrîm* is associated with the root *'wr* I "light" and nuanced "lights" (margins of NASB and NKJV). Modern scholars suggest two different approaches: (1) Some suggest that *'ûrîm* is from the root *'rr* "to curse" and that *tummîm* is from *tmm* "to be innocent," so that the word-pair means "cursed and innocent." So the two objects were mantic devices to confirm the guilt or innocence of an accused person (*HALOT*, 4:1751). (2) Others suggest *'ûrîm* is from *'ûr* II "light" which refers to various colored stones used to ascertain the divine will through an oracle by lot with differently marked or colored stones (*HALOT*, 1:25). What is

clear is that these two cultic objects functioned as a mantic device to obtain some sort of divine revelation through the high priest (Exod. 28:30; Lev. 8:8; Num. 27:21; Deut. 33:8; 1 Sam. 14:41; 28:6; Ezra 2:63; Neh. 7:65). They probably served an oracular function to inquire of God (1 Sam. 23:9-12; 30:7-8) or to settle difficult questions (Ezra 2:62-63; Neh. 7:64-65). The oracular means is never described but it seems to have been some kind of concrete tangible expression because the Urim and Thummim were stored in the priestly breastpiece (Exod. 28:30; Lev. 8:8). The oracular decisions of the Urim and Thummim were viewed as coming from God who entrusted this revelatory means to the high priest (Deut. 33:8). The civil ruler was expected to inquire of Yahweh through the high priest about all matters pertaining to the execution of his office (Num. 27:21), hence the expressions "the Urim and Thummim of judgment" (Exod. 28:30) and "the judgment of the Urim" (Num. 27:21). Use of the Urim and Thummim may be indicated when the expression "to inquire of Yahweh/God" appears in the OT (Judg. 1:1; 18:5; 1 Sam. 14:37; 23:2, 4). However, there is no clear evidence that this oracular means was used after the time of David. When the revelation of the divine will was given it was always passed on in terms of God speaking and could include more than a "yes" or "no" answer to a question (1 Sam. 10:22; 2 Sam. 5:23-24), including subtle nuances and encouragement (Judg. 20:18, 23, 28) so priestly prophecy might have accompanied its use. Because the Urim and Thummim belonged to God (Deut. 33:8), he alone could make them function as an oracle. This might be suggested in several texts where the Urim and Thummim were probably available but did not function (1 Sam. 14:37), as

Jewish tradition suggests (Babylonian Talmud, *Yoma* 21b). (*NIDOTTE*, 1:329-31; *TWOT*, 1:25-27) [*'ûrîm*]

Thummim (*tummîm*). The meaning of *tummîm* is unclear (*BDB*, 1070.4; *HALOT*, 4:1751). There are two major views: (1) Some connect it to *tmm* "perfect, completeness, integrity" and nuance it "perfections" (margins of NASB and NKJV). (2) Others connect it to *tmm* "to be innocent," so that the word-pair *'ûrîm* and *tummîm* means "cursed and innocent," as the divine verdict in legal cases (*HALOT*, 4:1751). For the function of the Urim and Thummim, see "Urim" above. (*NIDOTTE*, 1:329-31) [*tummîm*]

30:7 Fragrant incense (*qĕṭōret*). The noun *qĕṭōret* refers to "incense," an aromatic substance burned in the sacrificial fire on the incense altar (Exod. 25:6; 30:1-10, 27, 34-37; 35:8; 37:29; Lev. 4:7; Num. 4:16; 1 Chron. 6:49[34]; 28:18; 2 Chron. 13:11; 26:16, 19) (*BDB*, 882.2; *HALOT*, 3:1095.2). This was a special blend that produced a fragrant aroma, exclusively reserved for the cultic worship at the tabernacle—it was holy to Yahweh (Exod. 30:34-38; Lev. 10:1-3). Just as the odor of incense would please and elevate the mood of the user, it was viewed as having a similar effect in the divine sphere. The use of incense in the ancient Israelite cultic ritual can best be understood in the light of the ancient Near Eastern background; however, much has been demythologized and transformed into theological symbol. For example, the location of the incense altar in Mesopotamian temples was directly between the priest and the image of the deity, while in the Hebrew tabernacle it was directly between the high priest and the actual presence of Yahweh—not a mere idol. In Mesopotamian and Egyptian cults incense was used to entice the deity

from heaven to enter his image in the temple; similarly, in the Hebrew ritual of the Day of Atonement the high priest burned incense to produce an incense cloud which symbolically summoned God into the Most Holy Place, and then God appeared in the midst of the incense cloud (Lev. 16:2). Only on the Day of Atonement did the high priest dare to enter the Most Holy Place, and only after burning incense on the altar to produce an incense cloud to screen him from the divine presence so as to prevent him being killed by divine wrath while performing the propitiatory ritual (Lev. 16:12-13). The purpose of the regular morning and evening incense offerings at the Hebrew altar was to secure the presence of God and his attention to the priest's morning and evening prayers. Just as incense wafted up to God in the tabernacle/temple, the psalmist pictured his prayers rising up to God in heaven (Ps. 141:2). And Aaron stopped a plague from the LORD by placing burning incense between the dead and the living as a ritual of atonement, propitiating Yahweh and protecting the people (Num. 16:46-48 [17:11-13])—a ritual not prescribed in the Torah but reflected in the use of incense in ancient Near Eastern incantation rituals to appease divine anger. [*qĕṭōret*]

31:18 Two stone tablets of the covenant (*luḥōt*). Several biblical texts testify to the inscribing of the Decalogue on two stone tablets (Exod. 24:12; 31:18; 32:15, 19; 34:1, 28; Deut. 4:13; 9:10, 11, 15; 10:1-5; 1 Kings 8:9 = 2 Chron. 5:10). Why two tablets were needed is unclear. Early Jewish and Christian interpreters suggested that five declarations of the Ten Commandments were incised on each tablet; however, this would create an imbalance—one tablet would contain 146 Hebrew words and the other only 26. Others have suggested that the first tablet contained the Godward commands (nos. 1-4) and the second contained the manward commands (nos. 5-10). Still others surmised that each tablet contained the entire Decalogue. Recent scholars suggest that the two tablets follow the ancient Near Eastern practice of suzerain-vassal treaties in which the two parties each received one copy of the covenant document which was deposited in the palace or temple of each party. So Moses deposited one copy of the covenant document in the ark which was placed in the tabernacle/temple, while the other copy was for the priests to read to Israel on the occasion of covenant renewal (cf. Exod. 25:16; Deut. 10:5; 31:9, 24-26; 1 Kings 8:9 = 2 Chron. 5:10). [*luaḥ*]

Written with the finger of God (*'eṣba'*). This bold anthropomorphism describes the mechanism by which God wrote his commandments on the two stone tablets. The term *'eṣba'* "finger [of God]" is often used as a figurative description (metonymy of instrument) for the sovereign intervention of God himself in history: "an *act* of God" (Exod. 8:15; Deut. 9:10; Ps. 8:4) (*BDB*, 840.1c; *HALOT*, 1:81.2). For example, when God sent the third plague upon Egypt, Pharaoh's magicians explained, "This is the *finger* of God!", meaning "God has done this!" (so NLT, TEV, CEV). Using somewhat similar imagery, the "hand" of God delivered the Hebrews from the Egyptians at the Reed (Red) Sea (Exod. 15:6). However, the expression "finger of God" might be a figurative reference to divinely commissioned angelic mediators because the OT, Jewish tradition, and the NT writers say that the Law was delivered to Moses at Sinai through the mediation of angels (Deut. 33:2; Ps. 68:17-18; Acts 7:38, 53; Gal. 3:19; Heb. 2:2; cf. Jubilees 1:27, 29 and Josephus, *Antiquities* 15.5.3 [15.136]).

Scripture states repeatedly that no human has seen God nor can see God (e.g., Exod. 33:20; 1 Tim. 6:16) therefore, passages that describe God speaking to humans are often interpreted as God speaking through the agency of an angelic mediator. [*'eṣba'*]

32:1 Make us gods who will go before us (*'ĕlōhîm*). The use of the plural noun *'ĕlōhîm* (lit. "gods") may indicate that the construction of the golden calf was an act of abandoning Yahwistic monotheism in favor of Egyptian polytheism: (1) The noun *'ĕlōhîm* "gods" and verb *yeleku* "[they] will go" are both plural here as in vv. 4 and 23. When ' *ĕlōhîm* is used as a "plural of majesty" to refer to the One God, it usually appears with a singular verb (although there are a few cases where plural verbs are used with plural *'ĕlōhîm* in monotheistic contexts: Gen. 20:13; Deut. 5:23; Josh. 24:19; 1 Sam. 17:26, 36; Jer. 10:10; 23:36). (2) In v. 4 they describe the golden calf with a plural demonstrative and plural verb: "These [pl. *'elle*] are your gods [*'eloheka*], O Israel, who rescued [plural] you from Egypt" (v. 4) (Note however that Neh. 9:18, in recounting this episode, has the singular, "This [singular: *zeh*] is your God [*'ĕlōhîm*] who rescued [singular: *he'elhâ*] you from Egypt"). (3) According to Joshua 24:15, the majority of the Hebrews had been polytheistic idolaters in Egypt up until Yahweh revealed himself in the Exodus events. On the other hand, rather than replacing the worship of Yahweh in favor of the golden calf, Aaron seemed to equate the two—or at least viewed the calf as the visible manifestation of Yahweh—for he described the festival for the golden calf as "a festival for Yahweh" (Exod. 32:5). Or perhaps Aaron was trying to justify his role in fashioning the golden calf, not as an act of apostasy from Yahweh, but as making a graven image to represent him. Even if the graven image was intended to represent Yahweh, it was a gross violation of the commandment, "You shall not make a graven image" (even of Yahweh) and tantamount to the worship of other gods because no image could adequately represent the ineffable God. (*NIDOTTE*, 1:405-06; *TDOT*, 1:267-84; *TLOT*, 1:115-26; *TWOT*, 1:41-45) [*'ĕlōhîm*]

32:4 Molten calf (*'ēgel massēkâ*). More popularly known as the "golden calf" (*'ēgel zāhāb*, 1 Kings 12:28), this idol cast in the shape of a calf epitomized the vilest kind of apostasy committed by ancient Israel, an act of infamy often recounted (Exod. 32:4, 8; Deut. 9:16; Neh. 9:18; Ps. 106:19). The term "calf" (*'ēgel*) refers to a young male bovine, the counterpart of a heifer (*'eglâ*), a young female cow (*HALOT*, 2:784-5). The word "molten" (*massēkâ*) refers to liquid metal used to cast a metal image (*BDB*, 651.2)—cultic objects vehemently denounced in ancient Israel (Exod. 34:17; Lev. 19:4; Num. 33:52; Deut. 9:12; 27:15; Judg. 17:3, 4; 18:14, 17, 18; 1 Kings 14:9; 2 Kings 17:16; 2 Chron. 28:2; 34:3, 4; Isa. 30:22; 42:17; Hos. 13:2; Nah. 1:14; Hab. 2:18). It is from the verb *nāsak* "to pour out," of casting metal images (Isa. 40:19; 44:10) (*BDB*, 650.3); and is related to the noun *nesek* "molten images" (Isa. 41:29; 48:5; 57:6; Jer. 10:14; 51:17). It is unclear whether the calf represented worship of a deity other than Yahweh; whether it was merely a pedestal on which Yahweh was conceived to stand invisibly; or was intended to represent Yahweh. Scholars offer no less than five distinct views of what the molten calf represented: (1) The calf represented Yahweh; (2) the calf was a stand or pedestal for

Yahweh; (3) the calf represented another god, such as the Canaanite deities El or Baal who were often represented as bulls; (4) the calf represented the moon god *Sîn* who was often represented as a calf or bull due to the association of the crescent moon with the horns of a bull; or (5) the calf represented the Egyptian calf-goddess Hathor. Ultimately, exact identification of the golden calf is immaterial. The point is that the first two commandments were egregiously violated (Exod. 20:3-6), undermining the basis of the covenant with Yahweh (Exod. 20:2). (*NIDOTTE*, 3:320-21; *TWOT*, 2:644-45) [*'ēgel*]

32:6 The people sat down to eat and drink, and arose to play (*lĕṣaḥēq*). The action of Israel (lit. "they arose to amusement") was characterized by Moses as "running wild" and being "out of control" (v. 25). The translations represent a spectrum of approaches: "rose up to play" (KJV, NKJV, ASV, NASB, RSV), "rose to dance" (JPS, NJPS), "rose up to revel" (NAB, NRSV), "got up to indulge in revelry" (NIV), "indulged themselves in pagan revelry" (NLT), "began to carry on like wild people" (CEV) and "the people sat down to a feast which turned into an orgy of drinking and sex" (TEV). The root *ṣḥq* has a basic two-fold range of meanings: (1) laughter: "to laugh" (Gen. 17:17; 18:12, 15) and "to joke, jest" (Gen. 19:14); (b) "to laugh at (someone), make fun of (someone)" (Gen. 21:6,9; 39:14, 17; Judg. 16:25); and (2) "to amuse oneself" by fondling or sleeping with a woman (Gen. 39:14, 17), "to toy with [one's wife]" through conjugal caresses (Gen. 26:8), and "to amuse oneself wildly" through unrestrained promiscuity (Exod. 32:6) (*BDB*, 850; *HALOT*, 3:1019). The Hebrew noun *ṣḥq* likewise means "laughter" (Gen. 21:6) and "sexual amusement"

(Ezek. 23:32) (*HALOT*, 3:1019). The alternately spelled *śḥq* refers to religious celebration of dancing in the presence of God (1 Sam. 18:7; 2 Sam. 6:5, 21; 1 Chron. 15:29; Prov. 8:30) and to a sexual orgy (Gen. 26:8; 39:17) (*NIDOTTE*, 3:797). Whatever the exact nature of their actions, they are characterized as "running wild" and being "out of control" (v. 25). (*NIDOTTE*, 3:79697; *TWOT*, 2:763-64) [*ṣḥq*]

32:7 Your people . . . have become corrupt (*šiḥēt*). The root *šḥt* describes things that are ruined and fit only to be destroyed. The verb *šḥt* is used literally to describe a girdle irreparably damaged by water (Jer. 13:7), a spoiled piece of clay pottery that it is thrown away (Jer. 18:4), and a well whose water is polluted (Prov. 25:26). It is used figuratively to describe human actions so morally corrupt that God always responds in destruction. For example, Gen. 6:11-12 uses *šḥt* to describe man's sin ("all the people on earth had *corrupted* their ways"), while 6:13 uses *šḥt* to describe God's judgment ("I will surely *destroy* them"), emphasizing that the punishment fits the crime. This close cause-effect relationship between sin and judgment is seen in the three-fold range of meaning of this verb: (1) "to behave corruptly" (Gen. 6:11-12; Exod. 32:7; Deut. 9:12; 32:5; Hos. 9:9); (2) "to bring ruin upon [oneself]" by behaving corruptly and inviting the judgment of God (Num. 32:15; 1 Sam. 23:10; 2 Sam. 14:11); and (3) God as subject: "to ruin, destroy, annihilate" (Gen. 6:13, 17; 9:11, 15; 19:13, 29) (*BDB*, 1008; *HALOT*, 4:1470-72; *NIDOTTE*, 4:92-93). The moral offense of the verb *šḥt* "to behave corruptly" is seen in its relation to the noun *šḥt* which refers to a slime pit filled with human refuse (Job 9:31) and the bodily decay or physi-

cal corruption that occurs in the grave (Isa. 38:17; Job 33:18, 22, 24, 28, 30; Pss. 16:10; 30:9 [10]; 49:9 [10]; 55:23 [24]; Isa. 38:17). Israel's apostate worship of the golden calf was so grave that the only previous use of this verb (in reference to human sin) was the universal corruption of mankind that led God to resolve to destroy mankind, sparing only Noah and his family (Gen. 6:11-13). Similarly, God had every intention of destroying the nation, sparing only Moses (Exod. 32:10)—only the intercession of Moses saved the nation from extinction (Exod. 32:11-14). God would not destroy Israel for its moral corruption but would show mercy out of faithfulness to his covenant promises and mercy (Ezek. 20:44). (*NIDOTTE*, 4:92-93; *TLOT*, 3:1317-19; *TWAT*, 7:1214-18; *TWOT*, 2:917-18) [*šḥt*]

32:8 They turned away quickly from the way (*sārû*). The basic meaning of the verb *swr* is "to change direction" (*BDB*, 693-4; *HALOT*, 2:747-49). Used literally, it is turning aside or departing from the road a person is traveling (Judg. 18:3, 15) or departing from a road/path by turning aside from the original course (Exod. 3:3; Deut. 2:27; Judg. 18:3; 19:15; Ruth 4:1; 1 Sam. 6:12; 1 Kings 22:32; Jer. 5:23; 15:5); to step out of line militarily (1 Kings 20:39); to retreat from a path (Gen. 49:10; Exod. 8:27; Num. 12:10; 14:9; Deut. 4:9; Judg. 16:19; 1 Sam. 6:3; 16:14). Used figuratively, it has to do with the moral direction someone is taking; turning from the right road. Israel turned aside from the way their ancestors walked (Judg. 2:17) and away from God's commands (Mal. 3:7). Israel's leaders exhorted them not to turn aside from the right way (Deut. 17:20; Josh. 23:6; 1 Sam. 12:20, 21). To stay on course is to turn neither to the right or to the left (Deut. 2:27; 5:32[29]; Josh. 1:7;

2 Kings 22:2). This term describes turning aside from God (Deut. 11:16; Ps. 14:3) and not following YHWH (1 Sam. 12:20; 2 Kings 18:6; 2 Chron. 25:27; Job 34:27), not obeying his commandments (Judg. 2:17; Prov. 13:14), deserting God in one's heart (Deut. 17:17), or backsliding from orthodox worship (Exod. 32:8; Deut. 9:12) (*BDB*, 693-4). The related noun *sûrâ*, "apostasy," is a turning aside or defection from true worship of YHWH (Deut. 13:6; Isa. 1:5; 31:6; Jer. 28:16; 29:32) (*BDB*, 694). (*NIDOTTE*, 3:238-39; *TLOT*, 2:796-97; *TWAT*, 5:803-10; *TWOT*, 2:620-21) [*swr*]

32:9 Stiff-necked (*qešê 'ōrep*). This idiom derives from cattle used as draft animals, whose power was concentrated in the neck (Hos. 4:16; Jer. 5:5), so in a figurative sense whoever resists the yoke is "hard-necked" (*TLOT*, 3:1176.4). The root *qšh* refers to what is hard, stiff, and unpliable (*BDB*, 904; *NIDOTTE*, 3:996). The adjective *qšh* "hard, stiff," so "stubborn" (Judg. 2:19; Isa. 48:4), is related to the noun *qĕšî* "stubbornness" (Deut. 9:27) and the verb *qšh* "to be stubborn" (Job 9:4). Hebrew anthropology often portrays the inner will in terms of the heart, neck, and face. The oft-used idiom "stiff-necked" means obstinate, stubborn (Exod. 32:9[8]; 33:3, 5; 34:9; Deut. 9:6, 13; 31:27) (*BDB*, 904.3; *HALOT*, 3:1152.3; *NIDOTTE*, 3:998). For example, Israel was "rebellious" and "stiff-necked" (Deut. 31:27). Similarly, the expression "to stiffen the neck" means to be stubborn (Deut. 10:16; 2 Kings 17:14; 2 Chron. 30:8; 36:13; Neh. 9:16, 17, 29; Prov. 29:1; Jer. 7:26; 17:23; 19:15). Isaiah describes Israel's stubbornness thus: "the sinews of your neck were iron, your forehead was bronze" (Isa. 48:4). The term *qšh* "hard, stiff" appears in related metaphors for stubbornness: the "hard heart" (Ps. 95:8; Prov. 28:14; Ezek. 3:7) and "hard

face" (Ezek. 2:4). The people of God were a stubborn lot from the day they left Egypt until the day they arrived at the edge of the Jordan forty years later (Deut. 9:6-7). So Moses exhorted them to circumcise their hearts in genuine contrition and repentance, so that they would be stiff-necked and rebellious no longer (Deut. 10:16). Unfortunately, the sad record of Israel's history attested to one generation of stubborn stiff-neckedness after another (Deut. 31:27; 2 Kings 17:14; 2 Chron. 30:8; 36:13; Neh. 9:16, 17, 29; Jer. 7:26; 17:23; 19:15). There is intense irony in the use of this expression because earlier it was Pharaoh who was "stiff-necked" in refusing to release the Israelites to worship Yahweh. Now, having been delivered to worship Yahweh at Sinai, they had become "stiff-necked" like Pharaoh. (*NIDOTTE*, 3:997-99; *TLOT*, 3:1175-76; *TWAT*, 7:205-11; *TWOT*, 2:818) [*qšh*]

32:11 Moses attempted to appease the Lord (*wayeḥal*). This bold anthropomorphism (lit. "Moses attempted to *soften the face* of the Lord") dramatically depicts the impact of intercessory prayer. The expression *ḥlh pnym* "to soften the face [of someone]" is used (1) literally of the physical action of caressing rough facial skin, and (2) figuratively of courting someone's favor (positive) or appeasing his anger (negative) (Exod. 32:11; 1 Sam. 13:12; 1 Kings 13:6; 2 Chron. 33:12; Job 11:19; Pss. 45:13; 119:58; Prov. 19:6; Jer. 26:19; Dan. 9:13; Zech. 7:2; 8:21; Mal. 1:9) (*BDB*, 318; (*HALOT*, 1:317.1). For example, after God struck Jeroboam's hand so that it shriveled up, the king pleaded for the prophet to implore God to relent from his anger (1 Kings 13:6). When the Lord's anger burned against Israel for its sin, Jehoahaz pleaded that God might relent from judgment (2 Kings 13:3-4). When Manasseh was suffering in Babylonian imprisonment as divine discipline for his apostasy, he sought to "weaken the face" of God by repenting of his sin, and God restored him (2 Chron. 33:12). When Micah announced that Jerusalem would be destroyed, Hezekiah sought to weaken the angry resolve of God, and the LORD relented—he did not bring the disaster he had pronounced against Zion (Jer. 26:18-19). God himself exhorts his sinful people to repent and to "implore" him to be gracious to them (Mal. 1:9). When the people fashioned the golden calf, Yahweh announced his intent to totally destroy the nation, sparing only Moses (Exod. 32:9-10). But Moses interceded on their behalf, imploring God to stand down from his resolve to destroy Israel, and to curb his anger. Amazingly, Moses succeeded in appeasing God's anger and weakening his resolve. This is powerful evidence that God is responsive to human entreaty. He does not simply answer prayers concerning what he already planned to do; he is also willing on occasion to alter his resolve and to do otherwise. In answer to the question, "Can prayer change anything?" the answer is a resounding, "Yes!" Abraham negotiated with God to turn away his anger from destroying Sodom and Gomorrah on the condition that ten righteous people be found (Gen. 18:20-32). Although such a small remnant did not exist, Abraham's negotiations won the rescue of Lot and his family. Moses proclaims that had he not fervently interceded on their behalf, God would have certainly destroyed the nation (Deut. 9:7-20). God later destroyed Jerusalem because he could not find anyone like Moses to stand in the gap to intercede for the people (Ezek. 22:30). (*NIDOTTE*, 2:140-43; *TDOT*, 4:399-409; *TWOT*, 1:287-88) [ḥlh]

32:12 Please <u>turn</u> from your fierce anger! (*šûb*). The verb *šwb* means "to turn away" from something. When used of man, it often describes man turning away from his present course of sinful action, by turning away from sin (e.g., 1 Kings 8:35; 13:33; Isa. 59:20; Jer. 15:7; 18:8; Ezek. 3:19; 13:22; 18:30) in genuine repentance (e.g., Isa. 1:27; 6:10; 10:22; Jer. 3:7, 12, 14, 22; 4:1; 5:3; Hos. 3:15; 11:5). When used of God, it often describes him turning away from his anger by forgiving sinners rather than destroying them in judgment—so it means to turn away from an intended course of action of judgment by showing gracious forgiveness instead (Exod. 32:12; Num. 25:4; Deut. 13:18; Josh. 7:26; 2 Kings 23:26; 2 Chron. 12:12; 29:10; 30:8; Job 14:13; Isa. 5:25; 9:11, 16, 20; 10:4; 12:1; Jer. 2:35; 4:8; 23:20; 30:24; Dan. 9:16; Hos. 14:5; Jonah 3:9) (*BDB*, 997.6.f). The fact that both actions are depicted by the same verb highlights the cause/effect relationship between man repenting from his sins and God relenting from judgment. Because God is just, he will "turn away" from judgment if sinners "turn away" from sin (Jer. 18:5-8). This was vividly demonstrated in God's treatment of Nineveh: the people "repented" (*šwb*) in the hope that God might "relent" (*šwb*) (Jonah 3:8-10). Here Moses pleaded that God relent although Israel had not repented. Normally God's relenting is conditioned on man's repentance so this was an exceptional plea. Equally astonishing was God's gracious response: He turned from his anger and forgave the people (Exod. 32:14). (*NIDOTTE*, 4:55-59; *TLOT*, 3:1312-17; *TWAT*, 7:1118-76; *TWOT*, 2:909-10) [*šwb*]

32:14 The LORD <u>relented</u> concerning the disaster he had threatened (*wayyināḥem*). The expression *nāḥam 'al hārā'â* "to relent concerning calamity" describes God relenting from judgment which he had intended or threatened to execute (*BDB*, 637.2). Scripture repeatedly states that God is willing to "relent" from imminent judgment if sinners "repent" of their sins (Jer. 18:8-10; Joel 2:12-14; Jonah 3:10; 4:2). On this topic, we offer the following observations. First, this does not violate the biblical teaching of the immutability of God: God is ontologically immutable in his nature and character; God is also morally immutable; however, God is relationally mutable. As the morally immutable God, he always does what is morally appropriate: He blesses the obedient and judges the disobedient. However, to remain morally immutable, God must also respond appropriately when sinners change their ways: So God's relational mutability is a necessary corollary to his moral immutability. Second, this does not violate the biblical teaching of the sovereignty of God. Scripture clearly teaches that God foreordained some events before creation, but also ordains other events throughout the course of history. It is special pleading to argue that God had intended to forgive Israel all along on this occasion. Moses emphatically states that if he had not interceded for Israel, God would have annihilated everyone but him (Deut. 9:7-20). Similarly, at the time of the Exile, God lamented that if someone had stood in the gap to intercede for Jerusalem as Moses had at Sinai, he would not have destroyed Jerusalem (Ezek. 22:30). Third, God's willingness to relent on the condition that the sinner repents is not mechanical, but contingent on the sovereign freedom of God and therefore shrouded in mystery: "Who knows? He might turn and have pity" (Joel 2:14) and "Who knows? God might relent and turn from his fierce anger so

that we might not perish" (Jonah 3:9). (*NIDOTTE*, 3:81-83; *TLOT*, 2:734-39; *TWAT*, 5:366-84; *TWOT*, 2:570-71) [*nḥm*]

32:30 You have sinned heinously (ḥăṭā'tem ḥăṭā'â). This expression (lit. "you have sinned a great sin") is an emphatic construction in which the verb and accusative noun are from the same root. Some translations render this in a woodenly literal manner (KJV, ASV, NASB, RSV, NRSV: "you have sinned a great sin") but others nuance it clearly (NKJV, NIV: "you have committed a great sin," CEV: "you have done a terrible thing," NLT, TEV: "you have committed a terrible sin," NAB: "you have committed a grave sin," NJPS: "you are guilty of a great sin"). The OT distinguishes between sins for which there was atonement available and those for which it was not available. There was no cultic ritual to atone for sins of willful rebellion and apostasy. For example, murderers and adulterers were to be executed—only an oracle of forgiveness from Yahweh could spare them. Likewise apostates were to be executed (Deut. 13). In this case, this would mean the extinction of the entire nation, save Moses. However, as a direct result of Moses' intercession, God spared the nation and demanded the execution only of those who had formally led the apostasy. (*NIDOTTE*, 2:87-93; *TDOT*, 4:309-19; *TLOT*, 1:406-11; *TWOT*, 1:277-79) [*ḥṭ'*]

Perhaps I can make atonement for your sin ('ăkapperâ). Although it is clearly a critical theological term in the OT, there is no consensus among scholars about its precise meaning. There are three views about the derivation and meaning of the intensive (Piel) verb *kippēr* "to atone": (1) "to cover," (2) "to ransom," and (3) "to wipe away" (*NIDOTTE*, 2:691 §4). These three views will be summarized briefly.

According to the first view (*NIDOTTE*, 2:692 §5), the verb *kippēr* "to atone" should be understood in the light of the basic (Qal) verb *kāpar* "to coat [with pitch]" and its related noun *kōper* II "pitch, bitumen," both of which appear only once in the OT, in God's instructions to Noah about the ark: "you shall coat (*kāpar*) it with pitch (*kōper*)" (Gen. 6:14) (*BDB*, 498; *HALOT*, 2:494-5). Viewed in this light, OT atonement "covered" sin but did not remove it; however, on the cross, God uncovered OT sins and placed them on Christ who did not simply atone/cover sin but made full propitiation. While this is an attractive way to explain the relation between OT atonement and NT propitiation, it is linguistically unsound for several reasons. First, the basic (Qal) verb *kāpar* does not so much mean "to cover," but "to coat [a surface with something], rub on, smear on" (*NIDOTTE*, 2.692 §6). This would not form an appropriate imagery for atonement which would need to picture God "rubbing [sin] off" sin rather than "rubbing [sin] on." Second, the term for atonement is not the basic (Qal) verb *kāpar* "to coat [with pitch]" but the intensive (Piel) verb *kippēr* "to atone," so it is questionable whether the former may legitimately explain the latter. Third, the verb *kāpar* "to coat" and its related noun *kōper* "pitch, bitumen" are derived from *kpr* II (*BDB*, 498; *HALOT*, 2:494-5) which is an entirely different root than *kpr* I "atonement" (*BDB*, 497-98; *HALOT*, 2:493-4). For example, Hebrew *kippēr* "to atone" is related to Akkadian *kuppuru* "to ritually cleanse," while Hebrew *kāpar* "to coat [with pitch]" is related to a different Akkadian verb *kapāru* "to coat [with asphalt]." And Hebrew *kappōret* "atonement" is related to Akkadian *kupartu* "atonement," while Hebrew *kōper* "pitch, bitumen" is related

to a different Akkadian noun *kupru* "pitch, asphalt" (*BDB*, 497-98; *HALOT*, 2:495; *NIDOTTE*, 3:689-90).

According to the second view (*NIDOTTE*, 2:693-95 §§8-12), the verb *kippēr* "to atone" should be understood in the light of the noun *kōper* IV "ransom-price" (*BDB*, 497; *HALOT*, 2:495). This term refers to the monetary amount paid by a person guilty of murder to the family of the victim, who have the right to demand capital punishment or financial compensation for their loss (Exod. 21:30; Num. 35:31; Job 33:24; Ps. 49:8; Prov. 13:8). It also refers to the "ransom-price" of a half shekel paid by each male above twenty years in the census to "ransom" their lives so that no plague would afflict them (Exod. 30:12). The noun *kōper* IV "ransom" and the verb *kippēr* "to atone" are closely linked in several passages (Exod. 30:12; Num. 35:29-34), suggesting that atonement might be associated with paying a ransom-price. In non-cultic contexts, the penalty is financial; however, in cultic contexts it is a substitutionary sacrifice. In both cases, a price is paid (ransom-price and animal sacrifice) and the goal affected is similar (to avoid punishment of the lawbreaker by paying the penalty by some kind of substitutionary means).

According to the third view (*NIDOTTE*, 2:695-99, §§13-19), the verb *kippēr* "to atone" should be understood in the light of the root *kpr* I "to wipe away, remove, purge" (*BDB*, 497; *HALOT*, 2:493-94). This pictures OT atonement as the ritual "wiping away" of sin. This is supported by three lines of evidence. First, the verb *kpr* "to atone" is parallel to *mḥh* "to wipe away, blot out" (Exod. 32:30-33; Jer. 18:23). Second, many cultic uses of *kpr* suggest that blood atonement in the levitical rituals was designed to wipe clean, purge, and decontaminate the sanctuary. Third, the related Akkadian verb *kuppuru* occurs in cultic ritual texts for "wiping away" sin, but never to "cover over" or "pay a ransom price" for sin (*NIDOTTE*, 2:695 §13). Rather than "covering" sins by smearing something over them, OT atonement "wipes away" sin and "removes" it altogether.

To atone for sin means to appease anger or to make amends for an offense. Jacob gave a gift to Esau hoping it would appease (*kpr*) his anger (Gen. 32:21). David made amends (*kpr*) for the wrong done to the Gibeonites to turn away the LORD's anger (2 Sam. 21:3). Atonement (*kpr*) turns away anger, averting punishment (Prov. 16:14; Isa. 47:11; Jer. 18:23) or exempting one from punishment (Exod. 29:33; Num. 35:33; 2 Chron. 30:18; Prov. 16:6; Isa. 6:7; 22:14; 27:9). When sin is atoned (*kpr*), God does not count it against the people (Deut. 21:8; Ezek. 16:63). Accordingly, *kpr* sometimes means "to forgive" showing the cause/effect relationship between atonement (cause) and forgiveness (effect) (Deut. 21:8; Pss. 65:3[4]; 78:38; 79:9; Jer. 18:23). But when the verb *kpr* "to atone" and *slḥ* "to forgive" are used together in the same context, the former is the prerequisite for the latter: one must make atonement before there can be forgiveness for the transgression (Lev. 4:20, 26, 31; 19:22; Num. 15:25). Apart from the cultic shedding of blood there can be no atonement (Lev. 17:11) because atonement involves a life-for-life substitution. Normally, the priest makes atonement (Lev. 4:20-23, 28; Num. 5:8-29) by offering the sacrificial blood (Lev. 5:16; 7:7; Num. 5:8) for the repentant sinner (Lev. 9:7; 16:6, 11, 17, 20, 24, 33). However, some sins such as murder are so serious that only the blood (= execution) of the murderer can affect atonement (Num. 35:30-33). Although Moses here seeks to somehow gain atonement for Israel's heinous sin of the golden calf, there will be no priestly sacrifice. Instead, in an ironic play on words, God "atones" for (= wipes away) Israel's sin by "blotting out" (= wiping out) those who led the way into the apostasy (Exod. 32:34-35). (*NIDOTTE*, 2:689-710; *TDOT*, 7:288-303; *TLOT*, 2:624-35; *TWOT*, 1:452-53) [*kpr*]

32:33 Whoever has sinned against me I will blot out of my book (*'emḥennû*). This seems to reflect a widespread ancient Near Eastern concept of the existence of three kinds of heavenly books: (1) the book of divine decrees in which the destinies of all individuals are recorded (cf. Isa. 65:6; Jer. 1:1, 13; Pss. 51:3; 109:14; Neh. 13:14; Dan. 7:10); (2) the book of remembrance in which the deeds of human beings, both good and evil, are recorded (Mal. 3:16); and (3) the book of life in which God has inscribed the names of all the living: "the book of the living" = those alive (Pss. 69:28; 139:16; Isa. 4:3; Jer. 22:30; Ezek. 13:9) (*HALOT*, 2:766.2). This figurative imagery depicts God as the sovereign over life and death. The verb *mḥh* "to wipe [something] clean" (Num. 5:23) depicts God erasing someone's name from the book of life (= the book of those living). This is figurative for God wiping out (annihilating) someone's life (Gen. 6:7; 7:4, 23; Judg. 21:17; Isa. 5:17). To wipe out one's name means to kill the person so that he can sire no descendants (Exod. 9:14; 25:6; 26:19; 2 Kings 14:27; Pss. 9:6; 109:13) and all memory of him is wiped out (Exod. 17:14; Deut. 25:19). Confessing that Israel had sinned greatly, Moses petitions God to forgive Israel (Exod. 32:31-32a). If God was unwilling to forgive Israel, Moses offered himself as an atonement for their sin: "blot me out of the book you have written" (Exod. 32:32b). Blotting out Moses by substitution would effectively wipe away Israel's sins (Note: Elsewhere *mḥh* "to wipe away, blot out" is parallel to *kpr* "to atone, wipe away," Jer. 18:23). In v. 32 Moses had pleaded that Yahweh might blot him out of his book rather than destroy the people. In v. 33 God responded to the essence of Moses' entreaty: He would forgive the core of the nation but would severely judge those responsible for the apostasy. There must be individual accountability and corporate responsibility. Divine promises of national territory to the people of Israel are immutable, but total absolution for the sin of the golden calf could not be given. Israel received a suspended sentence; the people were placed on probation. The culprits responsible for the golden calf would face capital punishment. Moses sought atonement (= wiping away) for Israel's sin, and God granted this by blotting out (= wiping away) those who sinned through a plague (Exod. 32:30-35). (*NIDOTTE*, 4:1286-95; *TLOT*, 2:806-13; *TWAT*, 5:929-44; *TWOT*, 2:632-34) [*mḥh*]

33:5 If I were to go with you, I might destroy you in an instant (*wĕkillîtîkā*). The verb *klh* has a basic two-fold range of meanings: (1) positive: "to finish, bring [something] to an end" in terms of an accomplishment; and (2) negative: "to bring to an end, destroy" in terms of judgment (*BDB*, 478.2c; *NIDOTTE*, 2:641). This normally depicts God's temporal judgment in history that brings about the physical death of his enemies, totally destroying them. The related noun *killāyôn* "destruction, annihilation" describes God physically killing an entire community. Although God wanted to make an end of the nation because of the golden calf (Exod. 32:10), he relented on hearing Moses' intercession (Exod. 32:11-

14). Now, he warned that Israel was so sinful that it would inevitably arouse God's anger during the journey from Sinai to Canaan which would lead to God annihilating that entire generation (Exod. 33:4-5). In fulfillment of this prediction, God did in fact resolve to annihilate that entire generation on several occasions— only the intercession of Moses (and on another occasion the intervention of Phinehas) rescued the people (Num. 16:21; 17:10; 25:11). Both Moses and Joshua would warn the next generation that God would destroy them if they apostatised (Deut. 28:21; Josh. 24:20). This threat eventually became a reality at the time of the Israel deportation (Hos. 11:6) and Babylonian exile (Isa. 1:28; Jer. 5:3; 9:15; 14:12; Ezek. 5:12, 13; 7:8; 22:31; 43:8). However, God did not and would not make a full end of the nation and completely exterminate it (Lev. 26:44; Jer. 4:27; 5:10, 18; Ezek. 11:13; 20:13, 17) for his covenant faithfulness never came to an end (Lam. 3:22) (*NIDOTTE*, 2:642). Although God was willing to forgive Israel's sins, Yahweh announced that there would be consequences: God was no longer willing to personally accompany Israel on its journey to the land of Canaan. He would withdraw his visible presence (the so-called Shekinah Glory) from the camp of Israel and the tabernacle. In his place, he would send an angel to lead Israel. (*NIDOTTE*, 2:641-43; *TDOT*, 7:157-64; *TLOT*, 2:616-18; *TWOT*, 1:439-40) [*klh*]

33:12 You have found favor with me (*ḥēn*). The only other biblical character who enjoys this unequivocal approval is Noah (Gen. 6:8). The noun *ḥēn* refers to "favor, acceptance" with men (e.g., Prov. 13:15; 22:1; Eccl. 9:11) or with God (e.g., Zech. 4:7; 12:10) (*BDB*, 336). The expression *māṣā' ḥēn bĕ'ênê* "to find favor in the eyes of [someone]" is figurative for "to be shown/acquire/gain favor from [someone]" (*BDB*, 592.1.a). This expression is often used of obtaining favor from a human (Gen. 30:27; 32:6; 33:8, 10, 15; 34:11; 39:4; 47:25, 29; 50:4; Num. 32:5; Deut. 24:1; Ruth 2:2, 10, 13; 1 Sam. 1:18; 16:22; 20:3, 29; 27:3; 2 Sam. 14:22; 16:4; 1 Kings 11:19; Esth. 5:8; 7:3; Prov. 28:23) or from God (Gen. 6:8; 18:3; 19:19; Exod. 33:12, 13, 16, 17; 34:9; Num. 11:11, 15; Judg. 6:17; 2 Sam. 15:25; Prov. 3:4; Jer. 31:2). The expression "to find favor in the eyes of [someone]" is typically characterized by the following features (not all are present in every occurrence): (1) a subordinate/servant is addressing a person in a superior position (God, king, master, owner); (2) the subordinate/servant is making a request from the superior to give something to the servant or to grant permission to do something to the servant; (3) the servant assumes that his request might only be granted if the superior individual is pleased with him to do so; (4) the granting of the request is not a certainty; the servant understands that there is an assumed contingency: "If I have found favor . . ."; (5) the granting of the request is usually because of loyalty that the servant has previously shown to the superior or because of some gift of tribute that the servant has just given to the superior that was designed to curry his favor or to ingratiate him/her to the superior; and (6) although the granting of the request by the superior is an act of kindness or benevolence, it often reciprocates the loyalty that the servant/subordinate has previously shown to the superior. In light of the use of this phrase elsewhere, we can see several of these features in this passage: (1) Moses was in the role of subordinate/servant to Yahweh, (2) Moses made a request of

Yahweh, (3) Moses realized that his request would be granted only if Yahweh was pleased with him, (4) Moses understood that it was not a certainty that Yahweh would grant his request, (5) God granted his request only because of the loyalty Moses had shown, and (6) although God's granting of his request was an act of benevolence, it also reciprocated the loyalty of Moses. (*NIDOTTE*, 2:203-06; *TDOT*, 5:22-36; *TLOT*, 1:439-47; *TWOT*, 1:302-04) [*ḥēn*]

33:13 Please show me your ways (*dĕrākekā*). The term *derek* "way" here refers to the characteristic actions or moral character of a person (e.g., Gen. 6:12; Prov. 4:26; 5:8, 21; 10:9; 14:2, 8, 12; 16:2, 7, 9, 17, 25; 19:3, 16; 21:2, 29; Jer. 2:33; 3:21; 6:27; 7:3, 5; 16:17; 17:10; 18:11, 15; 26:13; 32:19) (*BDB*, 203.6.a). This is corroborated by Ps. 103:7-8, an early poetic commentary on this passage: "He made known his ways to Moses, his deeds to the children of Israel: The LORD is compassionate and gracious, slow to anger and abounding in steadfast love" (Ps. 103:7-8). From God's response to this request in 34:6-7, it is clear that Moses here asks to comprehend God's attributes that guide his actions in his dealings with Israel. Some ambiguity might have existed in the mind of Moses because God had promised to guide Israel into Canaan, then he had threatened to destroy all Israel over the golden calf incident but ended up relenting. Was Yahweh capricious or were the recent events consistent with his character? What kind of God was Moses dealing with? The answer to this question is found in the revelation of the character of God in 34:6-7, namely, he fulfills his promises but only to those who keep his covenant. He is gracious to forgive but he is still just to punish rebellion; however, he is willing to relent and to forgive those who genuinely repent. But those who refuse to repent and hate him will be destroyed. (*NIDOTTE*, 1:989-93; *TDOT*, 3:270-93; *TLOT*, 1:343-46; *TWOT*, 1:196-97) [*derek*]

33:18 Show me Your glory (*kĕbōdekā*). The term *kābōd* "glory" is often used in the OT as a technical term (1) for God's manifest presence and (2) as a way of referring to God himself (e.g., "My glory" = "Me," or "Your glory" = "You") (*BDB*, 458.2c; *HALOT*, 2:457.B.2; *NIDOTTE*, 2:44-48; *TDNT* 2:238-47; *TDOT*, 7:13-38). The phrase "the glory (*kebōd*) of the LORD" occurs for the first time in Exod. 16: "In the morning you will see the glory of LORD!" (v. 7) and "Behold! The glory of the LORD appeared in the cloud" (v. 10). This introduces two recurring associations: The glory of the LORD was something seen and was associated with the cloud. The manifest presence of God accompanied Israel throughout the wilderness period (Deut. 5:24 [21]), but was not limited to that time: God's presence was manifest via sacrificial worship (Exod. 29:43; 40:34, 35; Lev. 9:6, 23; 1 Kings 8:11; Ps. 63:2 [3]) and was mediated through the ark (1 Sam. 4:21-22). The term *kābōd* refers to the reality of his presence manifested in power, splendor, and holiness as the supreme ruler of his people (Num. 14:10). The *kābōd* of God is often manifest as the fiery, brightness which reveals him as the Holy One (Isa. 3:8). This is consistent with the description in Exod. 24:17, where the appearance of the glory of the LORD was like a consuming fire (cf. Isa. 4:5), and explains why Moses could not enter the tent in Exod. 40:34, and probably why God's glory is said to "shine" (Isa. 60:1-2). The main synonyms of *kābōd* are *hôd* "majesty," *hādār* "splendor" and *tip'eret* "beauty" (e.g., the majes-

tic clothing of the high priest was "for glory [*lekābōd*] and for beauty [*letip'eret*]"). This is called the glory of the LORD because it reveals his person and dignity, and the proper response to such a revelation is to give God honor or glory. In Exod. 33:18 Moses asks God to show (Hiphil of *r' h* "to cause to see") his glory (*kābōd*); in v. 19 God responds that he will make his goodness pass (Hiphil of *'br* "to cause to pass") before Moses, and he will call out with his name (i.e., explain his character, cf. 34:6-7). In v. 22 God speaks of the passing by of his glory (*kābōd*) as equivalent to the passing by of himself. The LXX rendered Moses' request "Show me *your glory*" as "Show me *yourself*." Here the glory of the LORD is effectively a term for himself. Similarly, the name of the LORD "can signify his presence and manifestation" (Ps. 75:1 [2]; Isa. 30:27-28). God's name and his glory very often signify the same thing (Ps. 102:15 [16]; Isa. 59:19). The expressions "your glory" and "my glory" are often poetic ways of referring to God himself (cf. parallelism with "myself" in Gen. 49:6; Ps. 7:5 [6]). (*NIDOTTE*, 2:577-87; *TDOT*, 7:13-22; *TLOT*, 2:590-602; *TWOT*, 1:426-28) [*kābōd*]

33:19 I will make all my goodness pass before you (*ṭûbî*). The term *ṭûb* "goodness" refers here to the divine appearance in summary fashion. This spectacle of outward beauty will be a visible representation of God's moral perfection. The term *ṭûb* "goodness" often has an ethical sense (1 Sam. 12:23; 1 Kings 8:36; Pss. 14:1, 3; 37:3; Prov. 2:20; Mic. 6:8) as in its parallelism with *mišpāṭ* "justice" (Job 34:4; Mic. 6:8) and *yešer* "uprightness" (Deut. 12:28; Jer. 40:4), as well as its antithesis to terms for moral evil (Gen. 2:9, 17; Deut. 30:15; Num. 24:13; 2 Sam. 14:17; 19:35; 1 Kings 3:9; Isa. 5:20; 7:15-16). When God is described as "good" (*ṭûb*) this is often a general term (synecdoche of whole for the part) for various moral attributes of God (1 Chron. 16:34; Ezra 3:11; Pss. 52:9[11]; 73:1; 86:5; 100:5; 106:1; 107:1; 118:1, 29; 145:9; Jer. 33:11; Hos. 8:3; Amos 5:4, 6, 14-15; Nah. 1:7; [1 Macc 4:24]). In response to Moses' request that he reveal his "glory" (*kābōd*), God says that he would make his "goodness" (*ṭûb*) pass before him and proclaim his name (that is, he would reveal his attributes as Yahweh). In the divine self-disclosure on Sinai it is as if the light of the glory/goodness of God passed through a prism to reveal the variegated attributes of deity that were audibly proclaimed: "The LORD, the LORD, the compassionate and gracious God . . ." (Exod. 34:6-7). Strangely, the narrator's description of the theophany lacks a visual element. God's self-disclosure is confined to an oral proclamation of his moral qualities which are the essence of his character. (*NIDOTTE*, 2:353-57; *TDOT*, 5:296-317; *TLOT*, 2:486-95; *TWOT*, 1:345-46) [*ṭûb*]

33:20 You may not see my face (*pānāy*). Perhaps the most bold anthropomorphism in Scripture is the mention of the "face" (*pānâ*) of the invisible, incorporeal God (*HALOT*, 3:940.C). Since the face is seen as the "mirror of the soul" (Sir 13:25), it often reveals a person's inner mood, attitude and true character (Prov. 15:13; 16:15; 21:29; 25:23; 27:19) (*TLOT*, 2:998.2). Because one's countenance expresses one's nature, the term *pānâ* "face" by extension is often figurative for the person himself (synecdoche of part for the whole), whether a person (Prov. 7:15) or God himself (2 Chron. 30:9; Pss. 34:17; 80:17) (*BDB*, 816.1d). Likewise *pānâ* "face" often represents someone's presence, whether a human (2 Sam. 17:11, "Let

everyone be gathered to you [= Absalom] . . . then let *your face* [= you yourself] go into battle in their midst") or God (Exod. 33:14, 15; Deut. 4:37; Ps. 21:19; Isa. 63:9; Lam. 4:16) (*BDB*, 816.2a). Discussions of God's "face" in Scripture feature the same idioms associated with the human face as representation of the individual's character or the person himself (*TLOT*, 2:1004.4).

Following the incident of the golden calf (Exod. 32), Yahweh announced that he would forgive Israel and send an angelic messenger to lead the people to Canaan (cf. 23:20-23), but he would not accompany them himself (33:1-6). However, in response to Moses' remonstrations, he relented and promised to accompany them, "My *face* will go with you" (33:14). As vv. 16 and 20 suggest, God's *face* does not refer to an angelic representative but to the personal presence of God himself (cf. Isa. 63:9). Appropriately, the LXX renders *pānāy* "My face" in v. 14 with *autos* "I myself." Seeking divine assurance and a sign of good faith, Moses boldly asked for evidence that God's *face* would accompany them, "Show me Your glory!" (33:18). Up to this point, Moses and all Israel had seen a muted representation of God's glory, partially concealed by the cloud of the divine presence (Exod. 16:10; 19:18; 33:9). Now however, Moses wanted to see God's face, that is, God himself revealed in his full glory and splendor. The identity of God's "face" with his full undiminished "glory" is clear from the LORD's reply, "I will make all my *goodness* pass before you and I will proclaim the *name* of Yahweh . . . but you cannot see my *face* for no one can see *me* and live . . . but you may see my *back*, but my *face* may not be seen" (33:19-23). So it is clear that here the "face" of God is an idiom for God himself ("You cannot see my *face*" = "no one can see *me*," v. 20). It also refers to the visible representation of God in an undiminished revelation of his full splendor and glory for Moses' request to see his *glory* is denied—God would allow Moses to hear an oral declaration of his *goodness* (v. 19) and to experience the so-called afterglow of his glory (cf. 34:29-35), which was tantamount to seeing his *back* in anthropomorphic terms (v. 23); however, Moses would not see his full *glory* (v. 18) which would be tantamount to seeing the *face* of God (v. 20)—the sight of which was forbidden to mortal sinful man (cf. Isa. 6:5). (*NIDOTTE*, 3:637-40; *TWAT*, 6:629-59; *TWOT*, 2:727-28) [*pānâ*]

33:23 You may see my back (*'ăḥōrāy*). The "backside, rear end" (*'āḥar*) of God corresponds in kind to the "face" (*pānâ*) of the invisible, incorporeal God (cf. vv. 14, 20, 23). When used of humans, the term may refer to the upper torso or buttocks (*HALOT*, 1:35). This shockingly bold anthropomorphism highlights the contrast between what man may not see (God's full visible *glory* = his *face* = he him*self*, vv. 18, 20-23) with what man may encounter (hearing God's orally declared *goodness* = seeing his *backside*, v. 19 and 23). Though Moses was not allowed to see directly the full undiminished glory of God (= his *face*)—because he was positioned within the cleft of the rock (v. 22)—he did see the so-called afterglow of the divine splendor—the "back" view of God (*HALOT*, 1:35.B.1). Although this diminished revelation of the glory of God was minimal compared to his full glory, this was enough to make the skin of his face "shine" (34:29, 35). In the only other biblical reference to the "back" of God, Hagar exclaimed, "I have seen the back (*'āḥar*) of him who sees me!" (Gen. 16:13). Because it was the angelic representative of God who appeared to Hagar (Gen. 16:7,9, 11)

and not God himself in the technical sense of the term, one wonders whether the distinction between the "face" of God and his "back" in 33:23 also distinguishes between God himself and the aforementioned angelic representative of the divine presence (Exod. 33:2; cf. 23:20-23). Similarly, Isaiah refers to "the angel of his face," that is, the angelic representative of the divine presence (Isa. 63:9). The OT describes the revelation of God to Moses on Sinai in the midst of angels (Deut. 33:2; Ps. 68:17-18). (*NIDOTTE*, 1:360-61; *TWOT*, 1:33-34) [*'āḥar*]

34:6 Compassionate (*raḥûm*). The root *rḥm* has a wide range of meanings: parental love/affection toward one's children, pity shown to the orphan, compassion for those in need, and mercy for those who deserve judgment—the most appropriate nuance here. The adjective *raḥûm* "merciful" (*BDB*, 933; *HALOT*, 3:1216-17) is almost always paired with *ḥannûn*, "gracious," as here, to describe God's mercy in relenting from judgment of repentant sinners (2 Chron. 30:9; Neh. 9:17, 31; Pss. 86:15; 103:8; 111:4; 112:4; 145:8; Joel 2:13; Jonah 4:2). Although their sins deserve judgment, their subsequent repentance moves God to be gracious and merciful (Pss. 78:38; 103:8-10). The root *rḥm* is used elsewhere to describe a military conqueror who in the aftermath of battle shows mercy to a vanquished foe by not executing him (1 Kings 8:50; Jer. 6:23; 21:7; 42:12; 50:42). Similarly, God shows mercy to sinners who deserve judgment but instead are spared total destruction (Exod. 33:19; Lam. 3:32; Hos. 2:23[25]; Hab. 3:3; Zech. 10:6), and forgiven (Isa. 54:8; Dan. 9:9; Mic. 7:19). The related verb *rḥm* "to show mercy" and noun *raḥămîm* "mercy, compassion" attest that reception of divine mercy is conditioned on genuine repentance (Deut. 30:3; Prov. 28:13; Isa. 55:7), so God longs (lit. "waits") to show his compassionate mercy to sinners (Isa. 30:18). The unrepentant and obstinate are not shown compassion but are judged (Isa. 9:17[16]; 27:11; 63:15; Hos. 1:6, 7; 2:4[6]; Zech. 1:12). However, on various occasions God refrained from totally destroying Israel in order to remain faithful to his unconditional covenant with the patriarchs (Deut. 13:17[18]; 2 Kings 13:23; Isa. 54:10). At Sinai, God displayed his mercy to Israel, not primarily because they repented, but because he was committed to fulfill his promise to their forefathers (Exod. 32:13-14). (*NIDOTTE*, 3:1093-95; *TLOT*, 3:1225-30; *TWAT*, 7:460-77; *TWOT*, 2:841-43) [*raḥûm*]

Gracious (*ḥannûn*). The adjective *ḥannûn* "gracious" (*BDB*, 337) is often paired with *raḥûm* "merciful," indicating that God's willingness to spare sinners who otherwise deserve judgment is an act of pure grace (Exod. 34:6; 2 Chron. 30:9; Neh. 9:17, 31; Pss. 86:15; 103:8; 111:4; 112:4; 145:8; Joel 2:13; Jonah 4:2). The related noun *ḥinnam* "gratis" (*BDB*, 336) describes (1) acts done gratuitously (2 Sam. 24:24; 1 Chron. 21:24), (2) without taking compensation (Gen. 29:15; Exod. 21:2, 11; Num. 11:5; Job 1:9; Isa. 52:3, 5; Jer. 22:13), or (3) without cause, undeservedly (1 Sam. 19:5; 25:31; Job 2:3; 9:17; 22:6; Pss. 35:7, 19; 69:5; Prov. 3:30; 23:29; Lam. 3:52) (*HALOT*, 1:334-35). So we can perhaps discern the background of the NT exposition of the unmerited grace of God in providing salvation for repentant sinners who believe in Christ. The adjective *ḥannûn* denotes "merciful," referring to God's care and concern for the poor and disadvantaged of society (Exod. 22:26; Ps. 116:5), just as the verb *ḥnn* "to be gracious" often refers to displays of gratuitous kindness to the poor and disadvantaged (Pss. 37:21, 26; 109:12;

112:5; Prov. 14:31; 19:17; 28:8). (*NIDOTTE*, 2:203-06; *TDOT*, 5:22-36; *TLOT*, 1:439-47; *TWOT*, 1:302-04) [*ḥannûn*]

Slow to anger (*'erek 'appayim*). This expression (lit. "long of nostrils") is an anthropomorphism for the patience of God. The term *'ap* II "nose, nostril" is often used as a metonymy of association to depict anger (about 80x) (e.g., Gen. 27:45; 49:6, 7) (*BDB*, 60.3; *HALOT*, 1:77.3). An angry person often expresses himself through flared or blood-flushed nostrils. In ancient Near Eastern idiom anger was often portrayed as snorting or flaring the nostrils (*TDOT*, 1:351; *ABD* 6:990; *NIDOTTE*, 2:266). When used of divine anger, *zap* II "nose, nostril" is clearly anthropomorphic, picturing God flaring his nostrils, breathing out fire (Job 41:10-13) and/or smoke (2 Sam. 22:9=Ps. 18:9; Job 41:12). In keeping with the imagery, the oft-repeated idiom "long nostrils" refers to someone who restrains his anger rather than being quick to anger; hence, "slow to anger" (*BDB*, 60.3). This idiom describes the patience of man (Prov. 14:29; 15:18; 16:32; 25:15) and divine patience (Exod. 34:6; Num. 14:18; Neh. 9:17; Pss. 86:15; 103:8; 145:8; Jer. 15:15; Joel 2:13; Jonah 4:2; Nah. 1:2). Although God is "slow to anger," there are limits to his patience—those who obstinately abuse the patience of God will eventually suffer the wrath of God (Nah. 1:2-3). His willingness to patiently extend opportunity to sinners to repent should not be misinterpreted; God is a just God and will eventually judge! God warns the unrepentant: "These things you have done and I have kept silent; you thought the 'I-AM' was like you. But I will rebuke you and accuse you to your face!" (Ps. 50:21). (*NIDOTTE*, 1:462-65; *TDOT*, 1:348-60; *TLOT*, 1:166-69; *TWOT*, 1:58) [*'ap*]

Steadfast faithfulness (*ḥesed wĕ'ĕmet*). The noun *'ĕmet* "faithfulness" describes what is dependable, reliable, firm, stable, continual, and lasting (*BDB*, 54; *TLOT*, 1:134.1). The term often refers to God's faithfulness to his covenant promises and his moral character. The expression here, *ḥesed we'ĕmet* (lit. "loyalty and faithfulness") is probably a hendiadys (two nouns joined by "and" in which the first functions as a noun and the second as an attributive adjective) meaning "loyal faithfulness" or "steadfast faithfulness" (Gen. 24:49; 47:29; Josh. 2:14; 2 Sam. 2:6; 15:20; Pss. 25:10; 40:11, 12; 57:4; 61:7; 85:10; 86:15; 89:14; 115:1; 138:2; Prov. 3:3; 14:22; 16:6; 20:28) (*TDOT*, 5:48). In contrast to fickle humans, whose faithfulness is transient and fleeting (Hos. 6:5-6), God's faithfulness is enduring and steadfast—permanent, certain, and everlasting. The "faithfulness" of God endures forever (Pss. 117:2; 146:6). (*NIDOTTE*, 1:427-33; *TDOT*, 1:292-323; *TLOT*, 1:134-57; *TWOT*, 1:51-53) [*'ĕmet*]

34:7 Showing loyalty to thousands (*ḥesed*). The term *ḥesed* has a broad range of meanings: "goodness, kindness, graciousness, love, mercy, loyalty, faithfulness" (*BDB*, 338-39; *HALOT*, 1:336-37; *DCH* 278-82). Three features characterize the concept of *ḥesed*: it is active, social, and enduring: (a) it designates not just an attitude but an action that emerges from this attitude, e.g., to preserve life, to intervene on behalf of someone suffering misfortune, or to demonstrate friendship/loyalty to someone; (b) there is always someone to whom *ḥesed* is shown or from whom it is expected; and (c) because it operates in the sphere of interpersonal relationships and often depicts loyalty to someone, it often emphasizes the permanence and perseverance in demonstrating *ḥesed* (*TDOT*, 5:46-51). In addition, *ḥesed* often emphasizes the

concept of mutuality: the one who receives an act of *ḥesed* often responds with a similar act of *ḥesed* (Gen. 20:13; 21:23, 27; Josh. 2:12, 14; 1 Sam. 15:6; 20:8, 14; 2 Sam. 2:5; 10:2; 1 Kings 2:7), the one who demonstrates *ḥesed* is justified in expecting an equivalent act in return (Judg. 8:35; 2 Chron. 24:22) or the one who demonstrates *ḥesed* is appropriately reciprocated (Ruth 1:8; 2:11-12) (*TDOT*, 5:47).

Glueck suggests that *ḥesed* is so often related to *berît* "covenant" that he defines *ḥesed* as the content of a covenant relationship: conduct in accordance with the mutual relationship of rights and duties between allies (N. Glueck, *Hesed in the Bible*, 46-47). He also claims that whenever *ḥesed* is used, it always assumes a previously existing covenant relationship—*ḥesed* was always demonstrated in the context of a covenant relationship, and a covenant was always the prerequisite for a demonstration of *ḥesed*. It is fidelity to covenantal obligations. Many believe Glueck overemphasizes the role of covenant and obligation (*TDOT*, 5:52; *TWOT*, 1:305). Sakenfeld agrees that *ḥesed* is demonstrated within the context of a relationship (love is always shown to an object) but that *ḥesed* does not always assume covenantal obligations; rather *ḥesed* is freely given. The central distinguishing feature of *ḥesed* is that it depicts an act of kindness that is freely given as an act of benevolence, often going above and beyond the call of duty (K. Sakenfeld, *The Meaning of Hesed in the Bible*, 233-39). What Glueck misinterpreted as covenantal obligation is better understood as mutuality and reciprocity.

The term *ḥesed* often functions as a metonymy of cause for effect, referring to the act of kindness that God performs. Clark has tabulated the benefits God performs for those to whom he shows *ḥesed*:

deliverance (28x), forgiveness (12x), assistance (10x), preservation (10x), faithfulness to promise (8x), and blessing (4x) (G. R. Clark, *The Word Hesed in the Hebrew Bible*, 262). According to *BDB*, when God is the subject of *ḥesed*, it refers to his actions in condescending to the needs of his creatures in general (Pss. 59:13; 144:2), and more specifically in: (a) redeeming his people from their enemies and troubles (Gen. 19:19; 39:21; Exod. 15:13; Jer. 31:3; Ezra 7:28; 9:9), (b) preserving their lives from premature death (Job 10:12; Pss. 6:5; 86:13), (c) quickening their spiritual life (Ps. 119:41, 76, 83, 124, 149, 159), (d) redeeming them from sin (Pss. 25:7; 51:3), and (e) keeping his covenant promises (Deut. 7:9, 13;2 Sam. 7:15; 22:51; 1 Kings 3:6; 8:23; Neh. 1:5; 9:32; Ps. 89:29, 34; Dan. 9:4; Mic. 7:20) (*BDB*, 339).

The use of *ḥesed* in Exod. 34:7 focuses on mutuality and reciprocity. Yahweh announced that he would show *ḥesed* to those who demonstrate "love" to him but would punish those who "hate" him. God would respond appropriately to those who were faithful to him by showing *ḥesed* to them, and he would respond appropriately to those who hate him by punishing them. He would protect and provide for the needs of his people—a demonstration of *ḥesed*—in response to their display of faithful love. So the idea is that God will reward fidelity. (*NIDOTTE*, 2:211-18; *TDOT*, 5:44-64; *TLOT*, 2:449-64; *TWOT*, 1:305-07) [*ḥesed*]

Forgiving iniquity, transgression and sin (*nōśēʾ*). The technical expression nś' + ḥṭ' (lit. "to lift up sin") varies in meaning depending on whether the subject is God or human (*BDB*, 669; *NIDOTTE*, 3:162.9). When a person is the subject, it means "to bear [one's] sin," that is, to incur guilt, bear the responsibility or suffer the punishment of sin (Gen. 4:13; Lev. 5:1, 17; 7:18;

19:17; 20:17, 19, 20; 22:9; 24:15; Num. 5:31; 9:13; 14:34; 18:22; Ezek. 14:10; 23:49; 44:12) (*BDB*, 671.2.b). However, when God is the subject, it means "take away sin," that is, to forgive sin (Exod. 10:17; 34:7) (*BDB*, 671.3c; *HALOT*, 2:727.18b). For God not to take away (= forgive) the sins of a person means that he must bear the punishment of his sin (Lev. 20:17; 22:9; 24:15-16; Num. 18:22; Job 7:21). After Moses interceded, God took away the sin of the majority of Israel; however, those who led the apostasy would have to bear their sin: God put them to death in a plague (Exod. 32:33-35). As Abraham negotiated with God to spare Sodom if fifty righteous people could be found (Gen. 18:24, 26), Moses interceded that God should forgive Israel (Exod. 32:32; cf. Num. 14:18-19). Yahweh is faithful to forgive those who love him (Exod. 34:7a; Num. 14:18) and repent of their sins (Ps. 32:1, 5; Mic. 7:18), but he does not forgive the unrepentant (Exod. 23:21; 34:7b; Josh. 24:19; Ps. 99:8; Isa. 2:9; Hos. 1:6). (*NIDOTTE*, 3:160-63; *TLOT*, 2:769-74; *TWAT*, 5:626-43; *TWOT*, 2:600-02) [nś']

Iniquity (*ʿāwôn*).The three terms that are the object of divine forgiveness here, "iniquity, transgression, and sin" (*ʿāwôn wāpešaʿ wĕḥaṭṭāʾâ*), are sometimes used synonymously, so this three-fold list may simply signify the totality of sins against God and the completeness of God's forgiveness for those who repent. However, in related Semitic languages (e.g., Akkadian) the equivalent terms designate three categories of increasingly serious sins. This also appears to be the case here: (1) *ʿāwôn* "iniquity" refers to unintentional misdeeds and unconscious moral mistakes, (2) *pešaʿ* "transgression" refers to much more serious criminal action and rebellion against God's right to the moral rule of one's life, and (3) *ḥaṭṭāʾâ* "sin" refers to the most serious kind of offense in the ancient world—sin directly against God himself. In an amazing declaration of divine grace, the LORD offers forgiveness of all kinds of sins to the repentant, from the less serious unintentional moral mistake to the most heinous direct act of rebellion against God.

The first term in this list, 'āwôn "misdeed, wrong" (traditionally "iniquity") is a moral mistake which results in an injustice (2 Sam. 22:24=Ps. 18:24; Ezra 9:6; Neh. 9:2; Isa. 11:10; 13:22; 30:14; Hos. 5:5; 9:7; Mal. 2:6) (BDB, 732; HALOT, 2:800). Derived from the verb 'awâ "to bend, twist, turn aside, diverge [from the way]" (BDB, 730; HALOT, 2:796-97), it describes an act that strays from the path of moral righteousness. Although this term has a wide range of meanings, it often refers to an act that was unconscious or unintended (Gen. 15:16; 19:15; Lev. 22:16; Num. 18:1, 23; 1 Sam. 14:41; 20:1; 2 Sam. 14:32; 1 Kings 17:18; Isa. 6:7) (TLOT, 2:864.d). Contrary to the popular slogan, "ignorance is not bliss" in the moral realm. God holds humans responsible for all their misdeeds, including unconscious and unintentional deviations. (NIDOTTE, 3:351; TLOT, 2:862-66; TWAT, 5:1160-77; TWOT, 2:650-52) ['āwōn]

Rebellion (wāpeša'). This second term in the list, peša' refers to two basic kinds of activity: (1) criminal action and (2) political treason (BDB, 833; HALOT, 3:981-82). On the one hand, it refers to criminal offense against other persons or their property (Exod. 22:8; Isa. 1:28; Amos 1:3, 6, 9, 11, 13; 2:1, 6) (HALOT, 3:981.2). Although criminals must face the penal punishment for their crime, God himself graciously forgives repentant criminals. Although they must "atone" for their crimes by suffering judicial punishment (Num. 35:30-33), atonement for their sins

before God is offered just as freely as to other repentant sinners. On the other hand, this term also refers to political treason against a king, picturing rebellion against God as treason against the Divine King. When used in the political sphere, peša' describes a palace revolt in which a subordinate attempts to usurp control of the throne by overthrowing the reigning king (1 Kings 12:19; 2 Kings 1:1; 3:5, 7; 8:20, 22). The theological use of this term describes neither unintentional nor trivial sin, but intentional rejection of the kingship of Yahweh over a person's life: "rebellion" (Isa. 1:2; 59:13; Hos. 7:13; 8:1; Amos 4:4) (BDB, 833; HALOT, 3:981-82). This is not simply passive failure to bring one's life under the lordship of God, but a blatant refusal to submit to God as one's lord—an absolute rejection of God's right to rule as king and a determined exaltation of one's own will over God's will. It is tantamount to treason against the King of kings, and the equivalent to palace revolt against the one who sits upon the heavenly throne. Amazingly enough, God is even willing to forgive those who repent of intentional rebellion against him. (NIDOTTE, 3:706-10; TLOT, 2:1033-37; TWAT, 6:791-810; TWOT, 2:741-42) [peša']

Sin (wehattā'â). As the third term in the list, hattā'â "sin" refers to the most serious kind of offense of the three because it is primarily used of sin directly against God (TLOT, 1:410.3d). It is derived from the verb ht' which has a broad range of meanings: (1) non-theological uses: (a) "to miss" something (Judg. 20:16), (b) "to fail [to reach]" a goal (Gen. 31:39; Isa. 65:20), (c) "to [personally] wrong" someone (Gen. 42:22; Lev. 4:2; 5:15; Num. 6:11; 1 Sam. 19:4; Neh. 9:20), and (d) "to offend" a person (Gen. 41:9; Eccl. 10:4); and (2) theological uses: (a) "to miss, fail to reach" an ethical mark (Prov. 8:36; Isa. 65:20); (b) "to do wrong" in a general sense (Gen. 20:6); (c) "to sin" as moral evil (Isa. 1:4); (d) "to incur guilty" upon oneself (Lev. 4:3); (e) "to be displeasing" to God (Eccl. 2:26); (f) "to offend" God (Gen. 20:9); and (g) "to be culpable" before God (Gen. 43:9) (*BDB*, 306-7; *HALOT*, 1:305). In popular exposition, the verb *ḥāṭā'* and the noun *ḥaṭṭā'â* are often explained in relation to the non-theological use "to miss [a mark]" in Judg. 20:16 (describing sling-stone throwers: "they hurled stones and hit precisely without *missing*"), suggesting that the Hebrew concept of sin refers to an attempt to obey God that simply misses or falls short of the target. However, a closer parallel to the theological sense of sin against God is "to [personally] wrong" someone (category 1c above) and "to offend" someone (category 1d above). The feature that most distinguishes this term from other words for sin is that it focuses on actions that are "offensive" to God and personally "wrong" him. It is one thing to sin against a fellow human, but quite another matter to wrong and offend God! In the words of Eli, "If a man sins against another man, God will mediate for him; but if a man sins against the LORD, who can intercede for him?" (1 Sam. 2:25). Indeed, those who "hate" the LORD will suffer a horrible fate (Exod. 20:5). However, those who repent will be shown mercy—even if they have previously wronged and offended God himself! (*NIDOTTE*, 2:87-93; *TDOT*, 4:309-19; *TLOT*, 1:406-11; *TWOT*, 1:277-79) [*ḥaṭṭā'â*]

Yet he will certainly punish [the guilty] (*wenaqqê lō' yenaqqê*). The preceding affirmation of divine grace is balanced by a strong rejoinder: God's willingness to forgive the repentant does not imply that he perverts justice. The construction *naqqê lō' yenaqqê* features an infinitive construct and

finite verb of the same root, which connotes a strong denial: "He *certainly* does not leave sin unpunished." This statement has been interpreted variously: (1) God remits punishment for the repentant, but not for the unrepentant: "Yet he will not clear the wicked;" (2) God suspends punishment of the repentant, but if he sins again, he will exact retribution for both the present and former sin; (3) God does not remit all punishment for the repentant but punishes it little by little: "Yet he does not remit all punishment;" (4) God does not suspend the just discipline and natural consequences of forgiven sin: "Yet he does not leave sin unpunished or undisciplined." The proper interpretation must be based on the meaning of *nqh* and the use of the expression "He certainly does not leave sin unpunished" elsewhere. The verb *nqh* often functions in an ethical, moral, or forensic sense in reference to guilt and punishment (*NIDOTTE*, 3:153). The basic stem of *nqh* means "to be blameless, innocent" (Judg. 15:3; 1 Sam. 26:9; Ps. 19:13[14]; Jer. 2:35; Zech. 5:3); and therefore, "to be free" from guilt and "exempt" from punishment (Exod. 21:19; Num. 5:28, 31; Prov. 6:29; 11:21; 16:5; 17:5, 9; 19:5, 9; 28:20; Jer. 25:29; 49:12) (*BDB*, 667; *HALOT*, 2:720). The blameless are free from guilt and exempt from punishment. The intensive stem, used here, means "to acquit, hold innocent" (Job 9:28; 10:14; Ps. 19:12[13]) and "to leave unpunished" (Exod. 20:7; 34:7; Num. 14:18; Deut. 5:11; 1 Kings 2:9; Jer. 30:11; 46:28; Joel 3:21 [4:21]; Nah. 1:3) (*BDB*, 667). The blameless and innocent are free from guilt and exempt from punishment; those falsely accused may invoke God to clear them. But those guilty of sin will be held accountable; God does not leave sin unpunished or undisciplined (Exod. 20:7; 34:7; Num. 14:18; Deut. 5:11; Job 9:28; 10:14; Jer. 30:11; 46:28; Nah.

1:3). This principle has proverbial status: "Be sure of this: the wicked will not go unpunished but those who are innocent will be acquitted" (Prov. 11:21). While God forgives the repentant, he nevertheless punishes the unrepentant. He also holds the repentant accountable for the just discipline and natural consequences of their forgiven sins: "I will discipline you justly, I will by no means leave you unpunished" (Jer. 30:11; 46:28). While the grace of God forgives repentant sinners, the justice of God demands that they experience the just discipline and consequences of their misdeeds—anything less perverts justice and turns grace into license. We abuse the grace of God when we think that we can sin with impunity without any consequences. God's willingness to forgive does not give one a *carte blanche* to escape the appropriate consequences of sin. (*NIDOTTE*, 3:152-54; *TLOT*, 2:763-67; *TDOT*, 9:553-63; *TWOT*, 2:596-98) [*nqh*]

34:28 The Ten Pronouncements (*'ăśeret haddĕbārîm*). The expression *'ăśeret haddĕbārîm* (lit. "ten words") was rendered woodenly by the LXX as *deka logoi* "ten words" which gave rise to the popular expression "the Decalogue." Although the Hebrew term "commandments" does not appear in this expression, it has been traditionally rendered by Christians as "Ten Commandments" embracing the ten stipulations in Exod. 20:3-17 and its parallel in Deut. 5:7-21. However, the traditional Jewish view refers to this as "Ten Pronouncements," beginning with the declaration "I am Yahweh your God" (Exod. 20:2; Deut. 5:6), which serves as the theological foundation for nine commandments that follow (Exod. 2:3-17; Deut. 5:7-21). The following chart compares the traditional Protestant, Catholic, and Jewish enumeration:

Protestant View: Ten Commandments
1. other gods (20:3)
2. idolatry (20:4-6)
3. misusing divine name (20:7)
4. keeping Sabbath (20:8-11)
5. honoring parents (20:12)
6. murder (20:13)
7. adultery (20:14)
8. theft (20:15)
9. false testimony (20:16)
10. covetousness (20:17)

Catholic View: Ten Commandments
1. other gods/idolatry (20:3-6)
2. misusing divine name (20:7)
3. keeping Sabbath (20:8-11)
4. honoring parents (20:12)
5. murder (20:13)
6. adultery (20:14)
7. theft (20:15)
8. false testimony (20:16)
9. covetousness: house (20:17a)
10. covetousness: wife, etc. (20:17b)

Jewish View: 10 Pronouncements
1. prologue: "I am YHWH your God" (20:2)
2. other gods/idolatry (20:3-6)
3. misusing divine name (20:7)
4. keeping Sabbath (20:8-11)
5. honoring parents (20:12)
6. murder (20:13)
7. adultery (20:14)
8. theft (20:15)
9. false testimony (20:16)
10. covetousness (20:17)

Ironically enough, the referent of the "Ten Words" in Exod. 34:28 might not be the Decalogue as originally given in Exod. 20, but to an alternate formulation contained in 34:10-26. Yet another version of the Decalogue is often identified in Lev. 19 since all ten elements appear here in one form or another.

35:5 Willing heart (*nedîb libbô*). The materials for the tabernacle complex were raised from Israelites who gave generously and voluntarily (vv. 4-5). The term *lēb* "heart" refers to volition (Exod. 25:2; 35:21, 22, 26, 34; 36:2; Judg. 5:15; 2 Chron. 29:31) (*BDB*, 525.4). The adjective *nedîb* "willing" refers to a free volitional willingness to voluntarily offer oneself to a cause (Exod. 35:5, 22; 1 Chron. 28:21; 29:31; Ps. 51:14) (*BDB*, 622.1). It is related to the verb *ndb* (1) "to volunteer" (Judg. 5:2, 3; 2 Chron. 17:16; Neh. 11:2) and (2) "to offer free-will offerings" (1 Chron. 29:5-6,9; Ezra 1:4; 2:68; 3:5); and the noun *nĕdābâ* (1) "voluntariness" (Ps. 54:8; 110:3; Hos. 14:5), "voluntarily" (Deut. 23:24; Ps. 54:8), "generosity" (Ps. 68:10); and (2) "freewill, voluntary offering" (Exod. 35:29; 36:3; Deut. 16:10) (*BDB*, 621). Just as God generously shows his grace "voluntarily" (*ndb*) to his people (Hos. 14:5), so they respond in like manner, voluntarily offering themselves to his service and presenting freewill offerings. This kind of person has a "noble" (*ndb*) character (Prov. 17:26; Isa. 32:5, 8). (*NIDOTTE*, 3:31-32; *TDOT*, 9:219-26; *TWOT*, 2:554-55) [*nedîb*]

35:10 Skilled heart (*ḥăkam lēb*). The skilled craftsmen who constructed the tabernacle and fashioned its furnishings are described as *ḥăkam lēb* (lit. "wise of heart"). The term *lēb* "heart" here refers to mental knowledge (Exod. 28:3; 31:6; 35:10, 25, 35; 36:1, 2, 8) (*BDB*, 524.3b) and may function figuratively for the person himself (synecdoche of part [= heart] for the whole [= person]) (*BDB*, 525.7): "skilled person" (NET). The adjective *ḥākām* "wise" here refers to "skill" in the technical work of professional craftsmen and artisans (Exod. 28:3; 31:6; 35:10, 25; 36:1, 2, 4, 8; 1 Chron. 22:15; 2 Chron. 2:6, 12, 13;

Isa. 3:8; 40:20; Jer. 10:9) (*BDB*, 314.1). Such skilled craftsmen could make all the right choices about the work with their minds and could succeed in producing a fine product with their hands. For example, the linens were woven by women who were "skilled" (lit. *ḥăkam lēb* "wise of heart") in spinning (Exod. 35:25). Most notably, God enabled Bezalel and Oholiab, two exceptionally skilled craftsmen, to act as the head-craftsmen over all the other skilled workers (Exod. 31:1-6; 35:30-36:2). (*NIDOTTE*, 2:130-34; *TDOT*, 4:364-85; *TLOT*, 1:418-24; *TWOT*, 1:282-84) [*ḥākām*]

35:21 Everyone whose heart <u>stirred him up</u> (*neśā'ô*). The verb *nś'* "lift up" means "incite, stir up" in the idiomatic expression *nś'* + *lēb* "lift up one's heart" (Exod. 35:21, 26; 36:2) (*BDB*, 670.1.b.11). The term *lēb* "heart" refers to volition (*BDB*, 525.4) (Exod. 25:2; 35:21, 22, 26, 34; 36:2; Judg. 5:15; 2 Chron. 29:31) or perhaps enthusiastic emotions (*BDB*, 525.9). This inner compulsion brought the people to decision and activity (cf. 1 Chron. 5:26; 2 Chron. 21:16; 36:22; Ezra 1:1, 5; Jer. 51:11). Many of those redeemed by the LORD were moved within to commit themselves to the noble task of constructing the tabernacle. (*NIDOTTE*, 3:160-63; *TLOT*, 2:769-74; *TWAT*, 5:626-43; *TWOT*, 2:600-02) [*nś'*]

35:31 He filled him with divine <u>enablement</u> (*rûaḥ*). The expression *rûaḥ 'ĕlōhîm* traditionally rendered "Spirit of God" here means "divine enablement" (cf. *BDB*, 926.9d; *HALOT*, 4:1201.13). The term *rûaḥ* (traditionally "spirit" or "Spirit") has a broad range of meanings in the OT (e.g., *BDB*, 924-26 lists no less than nine major categories of meaning with numerous sub-categories, while *HALOT*, 3:1197-1201 has fourteen major categories with many sub-categories). The basic meaning of *rûaḥ* is "wind," not in terms of essence but as the power of the wind because the Hebrews did not conceive of the "air" apart from its movement and power as "wind" (*TLOT*, 3:1203). As the designation for the wind, *rûaḥ* often refers to the power that sets other things in motion. Its mysterious power (its whence and wither cannot be known) becomes visible only in this way. The mysterious power at work in the mind and its unknown origin are particularly suggestive of God's activity and its effects (*TLOT*, 3:1212-19). For example, in the transport of the prophets, the *rûaḥ* of God draws on the basic conception of "wind" (1 Kings 18:12; 2 Kings 2:16; Ezek. 37:1). The power that pushes Saul into depression is a *rûaḥ* "psychic power" from God (1 Sam. 19:20, 23). In the early period of Israel, the *rûaḥ* from God is a dynamically explosive force that overcomes a person and equips one for special acts for a brief period—the men gripped by it become mediators of the act of deliverance or revelation (Num. 24:2; Judg. 3:10; 6:34; 11:29; 14:6, 19; 15:14; 1 Sam. 10:6, 10; 11:6; 16:13, 23; 18:10; 19:20, 23; 1 Chron. 12:19; 2 Chron. 15:1; 20:14; 24:20) (*BDB*, 926.9c). In other cases, the *rûaḥ* from God bestows special capabilities: (1) imparting executive and administrative power to Israel's leaders and kings (Num. 11:17, 25, 29; 27:18; Deut. 34:9; 2 Kings 2:15; Isa. 11:2; 42:1; 61:1) (*BDB*, 926.9c) and (2) endowing craftsmen with technical skill (Exod. 31:3; 35:31) (*BDB*, 929.9d). Although popular Christian expositors often view these as references to the personal Spirit of the triune God, in their original OT context they probably are not always even personifications of divine power. The movement toward the revelation of the personalized Holy Spirit is relatively late in the OT in which the inner "spirit" of God is depicted as a hypostasis: a personification of the divine inner "spirit" (Neh. 9:20, 30; Pss. 139:7; 143:10; Isa. 34:16; 63:10, 14; Mic. 3:8; Zeph. 7:12). It is only in the fullness of the NT revelation that the Spirit of the triune God is clearly depicted as a divine person. (*NIDOTTE*, 3:1073-78; *TLOT*, 3:1202-20; *TWAT*, 7:385-425; *TWOT*, 2:836-37) [*rûaḥ*]

LEVITICUS

Stephen J. Bramer

1:1 The LORD (*yhwh*)—This name, translated in most versions as LORD (uppercase letters), is not merely a title but is the personal name of Israel's God. It developed as such from Exod. 3:14; 6:3; 34:5-7. It occurs 5,321x in the OT (TDNT, III, 1067) while the contracted form *yāh* occurs some 50x, primarily in poetry but also in the expression Hallelu-*yah* ("praise the LORD") and as the terminal element in numerous proper names (e.g., Eli*jah*). The etymology of the name is debated but is usually thought to be from *hyh* or *hwh* ("be, become, exist," cf. Exod. 3:14), and therefore *yhwh* would mean "he is" or "he will be." When vowels were added to the Hebrew text later, no vowels were placed in the name since by then the Jewish people resisted pronouncing this name lest they profane it (see Lev. 18:21). Later, vowels from another name of God would be used with these consonants to produce the name Jehovah. This name persists in many Christian hymns but most translations use the name LORD spelled in capital letters to signify the translation of *yhwh*. This name expresses Israel's God as a dependable and faithful God who is always there. The fullness of the character of *yhwh* will be most clearly seen from his works and the further descriptions of him in the Scriptures. [*yhwh*]

The LORD called . . . spoke (*wayyiqrā' . . . wayĕdabbēr*)—The Hebrew verbs *qārā'* ("to call") and *dābar* ("to speak") are common terms; the actions of both calling and speaking by the LORD here emphasize the solemnity and importance of what follows. While the verb *qārā'* ("called") is often used when a child is given a name (e.g., Gen. 16:15) and the concept of God "speaking" rather than "calling" when revelation is to be given is more common, they function together here as the authoritative imprint for the entire book to follow. The verb *dābar* is repeated to emphasize various sections throughout (e.g., Lev. 4:1) and in fact there are more than 50 places in Leviticus where it is said that the LORD "spoke" to Moses. From Exod. 4:14-16 we learn that Aaron was actually the spokesman for Moses (see also Exod. 4:27-31; 7:1-2). Moses transmitted God's Word through Aaron to the people. Moses, however, is typically seen as the mediator between God and his people.

In Hebrew the verb *qārā'*, combined with the Hebrew inseparable prefix *w* to form the preterite tense, is usually translated "and he called." This phrase serves as the title of Leviticus in the Hebrew Bible. It is interesting to note that in Hebrew the term for LORD (*yhwh*) is placed after the second clause ("and the LORD spoke") while the first phrase is simply "and he called." This may be an additional device that would link it to Exod. 40:35 where the "tent of meeting" occurs (see below) and from which the LORD apparently spoke to Moses. This book, then, is linked to the previous book of Exod. (especially chapters 20–40) both by stylistic means and by this conjunction that links Lev. 1:1 back to Exod. 40:38. [*qr'*] [*dbr*]

To Moses (*'el-mōšeh*)—In Exod. 2:10 the name *Moses* was given to the child that Pharaoh's daughter found among the reeds of the Nile, saying "I drew him (*měšîtihû*) out of the water." It can be seen that in Hebrew, *Moses* sounds like the verb "draw out." This wordplay, based on assonance, does not imply that his name was necessarily derived from the Hebrew verb *māšāh* ("draw"). The name would be of Egyptian origin and probably means in Egyptian "is born" (*mss*) or "child" (*ms*) [V. Hamilton, TWOT, 1:530]. It forms the second element in the names of such Pharaohs as Ah<u>mose</u>, Thut<u>mose</u> and Ra<u>meses</u>. For the Egyptians, Moses was "born as a child" out of the waters while for the Hebrews he was "drawn" out of the water. Thus there seems to be a divine sovereignty even in the naming of the child whose form carries this double meaning.

Unlike others in Scripture who had their name changed at a significant moment in their spiritual pilgrimage (e.g., Abraham; Gen. 17:5), the LORD leaves his leader of the nation with the name given to him by an Egyptian. Perhaps this would be a reminder to God's people of his protection, sovereignty, and rescue from the waters (first from the Nile around which the nation of Egypt lived, then from the Reed [Red] Sea). [*mōšeh*]

From the <u>Tent of Meeting</u> (*mē'ōhel mô'ēd*)—Since this material follows the building of the tabernacle (Exod. 35–40) this phrase no doubt refers specifically to the newly constructed tabernacle. However, before the tabernacle was built, Moses alone used to meet with the LORD in a "tent of meeting" which was located, not at the center of the nation as was the tabernacle, but "outside the camp" (Exod. 33:7). The features of this antecedent tent of meeting which parallel the later tabernacle, including the pillar of cloud coming down upon the tent to signify the presence of the LORD (Exod. 33:9-11; cf. 40:34), seem to indicate that Moses' original, private tent of meeting was replaced by the nation's new tabernacle tent of meeting. It was a place of meeting between God and his people though still through an intermediary. Here God continued to confer with Moses (Lev. 1:1) as well as recognize the presence of the nation through the sacrificial ritual performed through the intermediary priesthood (Lev. 1:3, 5; 3:2, etc.). Although assumed up to now, Lev. 17:9 makes it clear that there was only one acceptable place to bring sacrifices to the LORD. That place was the God-designed, God-ordained, and God-filled tabernacle. General worship of God could be done everywhere but when that worship involved sacrifice the tabernacle must be the destination. This is developed further in Deut. 12. The term "tent of meeting" is used over 130x in the books of Exodus through Joshua and again in 1 Sam. 2:22b. But during the time of the undivided monarchy it is used a mere 8x (1 Kings 8:4; 1 Chron. 6:32; 9:21; 23:32; 2 Chron. 1:3, 6, 13; 5:5), all during the time of David and his son, before Solomon built the temple. The term "tent of meeting" is never used after the temple, a permanent structure, was built.

English versions tend to present a rather confusing array of terminology concerning the place where God met with his people. Some use "tabernacle" for the entire worship area, which includes the courtyard that was surrounded by a large rectangular fence, while others use it just for the "tent" which was within this area. The NIV uses "tent of meeting" for the "sanctuary tent" and "tabernacle" for the complete cultic enclosure. [*mô'ēd*] [*'ōhel*]

1:2 To the Israelites (*'el⁻běnê yiśrā'ēl*)— Literally "sons of Israel," this phrase is used 630x throughout the OT to designate the chosen people who descended from Abraham through Jacob/Israel. While the term *bēn* is the basic term for a male offspring, the term can be used in a more generic manner to signify children or descendants and is translated "people of Israel" or "Israelites" in the NIV. A synonym for *bēn* is *yeled* ("child"). In Gen. 49:1 Jacob (named Israel by God in Gen. 35:10) called for his sons and blessed them, blessings which, as is clear from the context, were to apply not merely to his male sons but to the tribes or peoples who would descend from them. In Exod. 4:22 the LORD declares "Israel is my firstborn son," which again connects the concepts of the son and Israel, not only to the person of Jacob/Israel but now to the covenant that the LORD would make with them as a redeemed nation. Hos. 1:11 [2:1 MT] refers to the northern kingdom by this term in the phrase "the people of Judah and the people of Israel will be reunited . . . ," but the phrase is most often seen as referring to the entire 12 tribes. [*bēn*] [*yiśrā'ēl*]

Any man (*'ādām*)—A Hebrew word for man, *'ādām* is used here in the context without a definite article signifying "any" man rather than "the" man; i.e., Adam. While the word could be restricted to a male in many contexts, in the context of

Leviticus there are times when a woman could bring such offerings (Lev. 12:6-8; 15:29-30) and therefore the word *'ādām* should be taken here as "any person." God wanted all his people, male and female, to be able to come to him in worship. [*'ādām*]

Bring (*yaqrîb*)—"You shall offer your offering" is the literal rendering of this clause that uses both the Hiphil stem of the verb (which stresses causative action) and a noun form of *qārab*. The verb denotes "being or coming into the most near and intimate proximity of the object (or subject)" (L. Coppes, TWOT, 2:811). This verb is an extremely common one and occurs dozens of times in Leviticus. Like the following clause (except that the verb and object are then in the plural), the verb is an imperfect tense that can convey an imperative force, especially in legal passages such as here in Leviticus. This is best conveyed by the English words "shall" or "must." In the next verse this verb is translated "present" to signify that the worshiper caused the sacrifice to be brought. The following verses describe the exact method of presentation. Lev. 1:5 would seem to indicate that the worshiper himself would slaughter the animal although in the regular daily sacrifice the priest would kill it (Num. 18:8).

In Lev. 9:9 the Hebrew verb *qārab* is again used but this time not with the meaning of "offer" (to God). Here the blood is not being "offered" to Aaron, merely "brought" or "presented" to him. Aaron has no authority to grant atonement; only the LORD God can do that and so the blood must be offered to him. In Lev. 10:3 the expression "those who approach me" using the verb *qrb* refers to the persons who came before the LORD's holy presence. The idea of coming near or approaching the LORD is not merely in a spatial proximity (although here Nadab and Abihu apparently had completed their responsibilities in the tabernacle area) but also contains the idea of intimacy or closeness. Nadab and Abihu approached the LORD but not with a proper recognition as to his holiness (Lev. 10:1). In the NT Christians are encouraged to "approach the throne of grace with confidence" because of the finished work of Christ (Heb. 4:16). However, this confidence does not allow for an improper view of God as is stated in Heb. 3:12, "See to it, brothers, that none of you has a sinful, unbelieving heart that turns away from the living God." The LORD is always to be honored as holy by all his people at all times. [*qrb*]

Offering (*qorbān*)—The word *qorbān* is a general term covering all kinds of sacrifice though here it transitions directly into the burnt offering of 1:3-17. The noun used here comes from the verb *qrb*, "come near, approach," which has just previously been used in this verse in the Hiphil stem (which stresses causative action) and is therefore translated "brings" (i.e., "causes to come near"). The noun, therefore, means "that which one brings near to God." In Leviticus it is used not only of animals (e.g., 1:2b, 3, 10) but of birds (1:14) and of grain as well (2:1, 5). Outside of Leviticus it refers to articles of silver (e.g., Num. 7:13) and of gold (e.g., Num. 31:50). It is a term that appears to be used almost exclusively with the wilderness tabernacle since it is used only 4x outside of Leviticus and Numbers. It is used twice in Ezekiel, in both a negative (Ezek. 20:28) and a positive manner (Ezek. 40:43), and twice in Nehemiah, both times of a "wood offering" (Neh. 10:34 [35 MT]; 13:31). This wood offering is never mentioned anywhere else in Scripture though the contin-

ual burning of fire on the altar (Lev. 6:12-13) would have required a constant supply of wood. Perhaps the duties of the various clans in Levi (Num. 3–4) would have included supplying the wood or perhaps it was the duty of the entire community (cf. the punishment on the Gibeonites, Josh. 9:21, 27). The noun occurs again in Lev. 22:18. In the latter case the NIV translates it as "burnt offering . . . either to fulfill a vow or as a freewill offering," though customarily a burnt offering (*'ōlâ*) was not made in response to fulfilling a vow or as a freewill offering. Rather this would normally be a fellowship offering (*šĕlāmîm*) as described in Lev. 7:16. However, since burnt offerings could be used to express devotion to the LORD (see Lev. 1:3) and since the *šĕlāmîm* ("fellowship offering") is discussed in v. 21 of Lev. 22, some see v. 18 as describing a different offering, that is, the burnt offering. This term occurs in the NT in Mark 7:11 (transliterated *Corban*) where Jesus condemns a technical device of the Pharisees who avoided supporting their parents financially by dedicating property to God (i.e., as an offering) but keeping the property to use for themselves. As can be seen from the references above, these offerings in Leviticus were the essential acts of external worship. The term is never used of the internal attitude. [*qorbān*]

An animal **from either the herd or the flock** (*habbĕhēmâ*)—The Hebrew *bĕhēmâ* is a general word for living creatures other than man (*BDB*, 96-97) but it usually refers to domesticated as opposed to wild animals. According to Deut. 14:3-8 wild animals could be eaten if they were of the correct type and were correctly slaughtered. They were not, however, acceptable as sacrificial animals. Later, birds are considered as acceptable (Lev. 1:14-17) but this was as a concession to the poor and therefore they are not included in this general statement. [běhēmâ]

1:3 Burnt offering (*'ôlâ*)—From the Hebrew verb *'lh* meaning "to go up" [*BDB*, 748], this term occurs 286x in the OT. It is sometimes translated "whole burnt offering" to emphasize that the entire offering was consumed by fire. The Hebrew word *kōl* used with "burnt offering" in Lev. 1:9 literally means "the whole." While it is possible to see that the common translation "burnt offering" could come from the fact that the smoke of such an offering "ascended" or "went up" to God (Judg. 13:20), other offerings were also burned by fire. The significant difference from the fellowship offering was that this offering is entirely consumed (apart from its skin [Lev. 1:6; 7:8] or crop [Lev. 1:16]). The entire animal was brought up to the altar and the whole was offered as a gift. It is this aspect, the totality of the sacrifice, that is essential while the burning is secondary. The burnt offering also differed from the sin and guilt offerings in that this offering was freewill or voluntary, motivated only by the conscience of the worshiper.

Listed first in Leviticus, this was the most common of all offerings and was the offering that was to be offered every morning and every evening for all Israel (Exod. 29:38-42), with double offerings on the Sabbath (Num. 28:9-10) and extra burnt offerings on other feast days (Num. 28–29). Although offered chronologically before this regulation, Noah's and Abraham's burnt offerings (Gen. 8:20; 22:1-13) are well-known examples. Later examples include Saul's illegitimate offerings at Gilgal (1 Sam. 13:8-15) and then David's exemplary burnt offering at the threshing floor of Araunah (2 Sam. 24:18-25) that resulted in this location being chosen for the temple, including the permanent place for the burnt offering (2 Chron. 3:1).

The act or condition of the worshiper that would necessitate presenting this offering is never stated explicitly. It also appears in the following verse and in the requirement for this offering to be offered every morning and evening for the nation (Exod. 29:39-42) to be for atonement of sin in general. In addition, for the individual, since it was voluntary and totally consumed, it may have represented a voluntary act of worship, an expression of commitment, devotion, and complete surrender to God. [*'ôlâ*]

Male (*zākār*)—According to this chapter the whole burnt offering could be a bull, a ram, a goat, pigeons, or turtledoves. It was only the animals (not birds) whose sex qualification (i.e., male) was specified. The sin offering (Lev. 4:23) also had this qualification. The male may have been specified because of its greater value and/or because it could be thought to represent vigor and fertility. [*zākār*]

Without defect (*tāmîm*)—This adjective means "complete, sound" (*BDB*, 1071) and is used numerous times concerning sacrificial animals. In Lev. 22:22-24 the LORD gives the definition of "without defect," which includes no blind, injured, maimed, diseased, or emasculated animal. The LORD through Malachi also details what is considered "unsound" or "with blemish" and therefore unacceptable in Mal. 1:8, 13 (blind, crippled, diseased, injured). It represents the divine standard for any sacrifice that would represent man (cf. 1 Pet. 1:19 for Christ being the spotless Lamb of God). [*tāmîm*]

So that it will be acceptable (*lirşōnō*)—The Hebrew noun *rāşôn*, meaning "goodwill, favor, acceptance" (*BDB*, 953), comes from the Hebrew verb *rşn*. This verb form is used 50x in the OT with 11 of those occurrences in Leviticus. Six times the verb occurs in Leviticus in the Niphal stem "in the special sense 'to be favorably received' as to the ritual cleanliness of offerings" (W. White, TWOT, 2:859). Both the noun and the verb form can be used of delight, favor, and acceptance of both man and God, but theologically they are most important as "the standard anthropomorphic expressions of God's preceptive will" (W. White, TWOT, 2:860). They are used this way 18x in Leviticus (1:3, 4; 7:18; 19:5, 7; 22:19, 20, 21, 23, 25, 27, 29; 23:11; 26:34 [2x], 41, 43 [2x]). The noun form in Lev. 1:3 includes a masculine singular suffix that allows it to refer either to the acceptance of the person offering the sacrifice or to the sacrifice itself. The NIV translates the suffix with a neuter "it" referring to the offering but suggests in the margin that "he," referring to the offerer, is a possibility. The closeness of the two, the worshiper and the sacrifice, is explained in the next verse. [*rāṣôn*]

To the LORD (*lipnê yhwh*)—Literally "to the face of the LORD" is the anthropomorphic expression used to signify the presentation of an offering in the presence of the LORD (for *yhwh* see Lev. 1:1). This phrase is used throughout Leviticus as various offerings are presented to the Lord. Earlier in the Pentateuch the phrase "my face" was used to signify the actual physical presence of a person (Gen. 43:3, 5; 44:23; Exod. 10:28). In Lev. 17:10 the expression "I will set my face against that person" is a literal translation of the Hebrew and is repeated in Leviticus in very similar forms in 20:3, 5, 6; 26:17. The concept of *wĕnātatî pānay* ("and I will set my face") with reference to the LORD God has as its background, Exod. 33:20 where, in response to a request from Moses to see the LORD's glory, the LORD responded ". . .

you cannot see my face, for no one may see me and live." The LORD went on, however, to declare, ". . . you will see my back; but my face must not be seen." In Deuteronomy 3x the expression "I will hide my face" (Deut. 31:17, 18; 32:20) signifies the removal of God's protection from his entire nation so that they might suffer various curses and finally defeat at the hands of their enemies. In Leviticus the setting of God's face is always used of an individual (and any who follow him, Lev. 20:5) rather than the national body with the exception of Lev. 26:17. It is used in terms of God's judgment ("will cut him off from his people") that will come against the disobedient person for three specific sins: the one who eats blood (Lev. 17:10), the one who sacrifices his children to Molech (Lev. 20:3), and the one who turns to mediums and spiritists (Lev. 20:6). [*pāneh*]

1:4 Lay his hand (*wĕsāmak yādô*)—The Hebrew term *smk* can mean "lean, lay, rest, support" (*BDB*, 701-02). This action should not be regarded as a mere touch but a conscious firm placement (cf. Isa. 59:16; Ezek. 24:2; 30:6; Amos 5:19) of the worshiper's hands onto the head of the animal. Theologically this ritual involved the identification of the worshiper with the bull. Though the following verses do not specifically state that the worshiper had to lay hands on the other acceptable burnt offerings (sheep, goat, dove, pigeon) this can be assumed. This action of "the laying of hands" formed a part of many sacrifices (see Lev. 3:2, 8, 13; 4:4, 15, 24; 16:21). Some scholars claim this action did not transfer anything to the offered animal, least of all sin, since only holy things could have contact with the altar. However, the context throughout Leviticus. clearly indicates that the life of the sacrificial animal, specifically symbolized by its blood, was required in place of the life of the worshiper when offered for atonement. Thus the laying on of hands is clearly an identification of the worshiper with the animal. [*smk*]

Head (*rō'š*)—This Hebrew masculine noun for head is closely connected to the feminine noun meaning "first, beginning, choicest, first/best of a group" (W. White, TWOT, 826) that is frequently used in reference to things to be set aside for God's service or sacrifice (Lev. 2:12; 23:10; Neh. 12:44). Here in Lev. 1 the normal meaning of the animal's head is used (Lev. 1:4, 8, 12, 15). In the case of sin, when done in faith, God recognized the transfer of guilt to the animal victim. This is in keeping with the meaning of the word *kipper* ("atonement") as will be seen below. [*rō'š*]

Make atonement (*lĕkappēr*)—The verb *kpr* (used over 40x in Leviticus), translated "make atonement," can, in the intensive form used here (Piel stem), mean "make an atonement, make reconciliation, purge" (G. Archer, TWOT, 1:452). In the Scriptures it is never used in the simple, active form (Qal stem) so this intensive stem may reflect back to a basic noun meaning "of atonement." However, often the impression is given that the sacrifices merely "covered without removing" sin (*BDB*, 497). This finds no basis in the etymology or use of the Hebrew word (cf. BKC, 174-75), yet because of a similar Arabic verb that does have the idea of concealing without removing, this connection has often been assumed. In some manner the sacrifice involved the actual removal of the guilt and punishment for the particular sin(s) involved (cf. Lev. 16:10, 19 for the concepts of cleansing and removal). Since these offerings were made by God's covenant people, this effected the gaining once again of God's favor. The great majority of the usages of this verb in

Leviticus concern the ritual of sprinkling of the sacrificial blood (which will be developed in v. 5 below). The only times in Scripture that this word is not used in the sense of removal of sin or defilement are Gen. 32:20 [32:21 MT], Prov. 16:14, and Isa. 28:18. The atonement accomplished by the sacrifice effected propitiation—a turning away or an appeasement of divine wrath. The efficacious nature of these "temporary" or provisional sacrifices (Heb. 10:4) will be seen later (1 Pet. 1:19-20; Rev. 13:8) to be derived from the only truly timeless, universal, efficacious sacrifice for sins, the sacrifice of Christ, known by God all along. In Lev. 12:7 *kippēr* is used concerning childbirth since one of the purposes in the sin offering was to make atonement or to purge impurities from the tabernacle (cf. Lev. 4:1–5:13; 6:24-30 [6:17-23 MT]). In this case the woman had not sinned by having a child (note in this regard Mary, the mother of Jesus, who brought such an offering although she certainly could not be accused of sin in the birth of our Savior [Luke 2:22-24]), but there was ceremonial impurity with regard to the blood flow in connection with the birth. The mother is never said to be forgiven but rather "ceremonially clean" in this verse as well as in v. 8 (see also Lev. 4:20, 26, 31, 35; 5:10, 13).

In Lev. 16:2 the noun *hakkappōret* ("atonement cover"), literally "the seat of atonement," is used. This word is sometimes translated "mercy seat" rather than "atonement cover" since this is where mercy was obtained by means of atonement. The Hebrew word is not related, however, to the word for mercy and of course was not a "seat" (cf. Heb. 10:11-14). The idea of "seat" may come from Ps. 99:1: "The LORD reigns, let the nations tremble; he sits enthroned between the cherubim, let the earth shake." This noun is used some 27x and always refers to the special golden cover of the ark of the covenant kept in the Holy of Holies. It was above the atonement cover that God promised to meet with men (Num. 7:89).

In Lev. 17:11 the cardinal importance of blood-shedding is indicated in relationship to atonement. Here is the most explicit statement in Leviticus about the role of blood in sacrifice; it makes *kipper* ("atonement"). It is also the second reason for prohibiting the eating of blood. Substitutionary atonement is necessary for there to be forgiveness of sin (see Lev. 4:20). Forgiveness involves cost and the taking of life. Because animal blood atones for human sin, in the OT covenant setting it was sacred and ought not to be consumed by man. In Heb. 9:22 one can see that the sacrificial deaths of animals anticipated and foreshadowed the only perfect and permanent redeeming sacrifice, the death of Christ. [*kpr*]

1:5 He is to slaughter (*wĕšāḥaṭ*)—From the Hebrew verb *šḥṭ* meaning "to slaughter, kill," this verb is used over 80x in the OT. Here it occurs in a technical manner for the killing of a sacrificial animal (*BDB*, 1006). The verb can mean "to beat" and is so used 5x (1 Kings 10:16, 17; 2 Chron. 9:15 [2x], 16). But it most often means "to kill," primarily of sacrificial animals and only a few times of a person (Gen. 22:10; Num. 14:16; Judg. 12:6; 1 Kings 18:40; 2 Kings 10:7, 14; 25:7; Isa. 57:5; Jer. 39:6; 41:7; 52:10; Ezek. 16:21); a nonsacrificial animal (Gen. 37:31); or metaphorically, of the damage done by the tongue (Jer. 9:8 [9:7 MT]). Though the word is used 35x in Leviticus, the surrounding instructions never clearly describe the manner of the killing. In postbiblical Hebrew the term denotes a specific method of killing in which the blood is properly drained from

the animal's body. Rabbinic tradition indicates that the animal must be killed in the swiftest and most painless manner possible, by cutting the throat with a sharp knife in a horizontal swift motion. The subject of the verb *šḥṭ* is a masculine singular and the antecedent context suggests that the referent is best taken as the worshiper, not the priest who would be involved with handling the blood (see below). However, in Lev. 1:14-17 the priest is clearly the one to kill the bird given as an offering, perhaps because the limited amount of blood from a bird required it to be killed close to the altar, a place where only the priests could work. The verb is always in the basic Qal (simple active) stem except for twice in Lev. 6:25 and once in Num. 11:22. In these verses it is used in the Niphal stem, which carries the idea of passivity, which is in keeping with the sacrificial animal being killed with no action on the part of the animal. While the verb is used for the manner of death of the animal, the noun for slaughter is used just once in 2 Chron. 30:17 (unless Hos. 5:2 is also read as a noun meaning "slaughter"). In keeping with the theology of atonement, the slain animals were not simply a slaughter but a sacrifice. When the verb is used in Lev. 17:3 the killing does not appear to apply to the death of every animal (cf. Deut. 12:15, 20-21) but rather to those that were used as part of the cultic ritual. Such sacrifices were to be performed at the central sanctuary, that is, the tabernacle (see also Deut. 12:5-14). [*šḥṭ*]

The priests (*hakkōhănîm*)—This word for priest is used, from the time of the rebellion in the golden calf incident onward (Exod. 32:25-29; Num. 3:12-13), of those in the family line of Moses' brother Aaron of the tribe of Levi (Exod. 28:1; 40:12-15). Up to this time various ones had been called priests (e.g., Melchizedek, Gen. 14:18; Jethro, Exod. 18:1). In the beginning there do not appear to be specialized persons who served as priests for others (Gen. 4:3), but by the time of Noah the priestly function seems to have rested in the hands of the patriarchal family head (Gen. 8:20; Job 1:5; Gen. 12:8). Then at the Passover experience (Exod. 13:1 [cf. Exod. 32:29]; Exod. 19:22, 24) the firstborn of every Israelite family became a priest. Despite the special consecration of the firstborn, the entire nation is seen as a "kingdom of priests" (Exod. 19:6) at the time of the institution of the Mosaic Covenant, though apparently only the firstborn would have officiated at the soon-to-be-built tabernacle. After the rebellion at Mount Sinai and shortly after the completion of the tabernacle, Aaron was consecrated as Israel's first high priest and his four sons as priests (Lev. 8–9). The remainder of the Levites functioned in various roles within the sacrificial ritual, but Aaron's sons alone officiated as priests (Num. 3–4). [*kōhēn*]

The blood (*haddām*)—The word *dām* ("blood") is related to the Hebrew word meaning "red" (Gen. 25:30) and can refer to either the blood of animals or of people (Gen. 4:10). Blood was believed to contain the life, or was the source of life, of the animal or person and became extremely important in sacrificial ritual. Therefore, when blood was used in a sacrificial setting it emphasized that death had occurred and that the person continued to "live," not because the animal lived on, but because the animal died and that life was given on the worshiper's behalf (see Lev. 17:11, 14). In all the OT the term "blood" is used most often in Leviticus (88 of the 360 uses). The blood must not be eaten/drunk (cf. Lev. 7:26-27; 17:10-12). Rather, the blood, because of its pivotal

meaning of atonement in the sacrificial system, must be given to the LORD by being placed on the altar. Atonement for sin was made by the sacrifice of live animals and birds as a substitution for the worshiper's own life (except in the case of Lev. 5:11, which will be discussed there). Later on blood was used as a synonym of death (Judg. 9:24) or murder (Jer. 19:4) or to represent a person's guilt (Jer. 26:15). [*dām*]

Sprinkle it (*wĕzārĕqû*)—"Splash" or "throw" is the verb used here in connection with the blood and can mean "to toss or throw (in a volume), scatter abundantly" (*BDB*, 284; Exod. 24:6, 8). Perhaps "splash" is a more appropriate translation than "sprinkle" since the latter can be imagined as not handling the blood in a forceful manner. The throwing of the blood was both the method of offering the blood on the altar and the means of disposing of the blood. The blood of the burnt offering was completely disposed of by the priest in this vigorous manner in a dramatic show demonstrating that the life had been given totally to God. This forceful action of splashing the blood of the burnt offering stands in contrast with the blood in the sin offering that was dipped (*ṭābāl*) and then *nāzāh* or *hizzāh* (sprinkled) with the *'eṣba'* (finger) as seen in Lev. 4:6, 17; 16:14, 19. The handling of the blood of the fellowship offering (Lev. 3:2, 8, 13) is the same as that of the burnt offering. [*zrq*]

The altar on all sides (*'al-hammizbēaḥ*)—The Hebrew word for altar derives from a verbal root meaning "to slaughter" (Exod. 20:24; Deut. 16:2) [notice that this is a different root for "slaughter" than the one used previously in this verse]. The altar referred to here is the one described in Exod. 27:1-8 and can be referred to as the bronze altar (as opposed to the incense altar that was covered with gold; Exod. 30:3-5; 37:25-27). However, this same word is used also for the golden incense altar even though that altar involved no slaughtering of animals but only an offering of special incense (cf. Lev. 4:7). In Lev. 2:2 the same Hebrew word is used and though the worshiper brought an offering containing incense, the offering does not appear to be burned on the altar of incense as one might expect. Rather, like the burnt offering, the grain offering containing the prescribed oil and incense was presented at the altar described in Exod. 27:1-8. In Exod. 30:9 the LORD specifically declares that the incense altar was not to be used for any burnt offering or grain offering and so it could not be the altar referred to in Lev. 2. The incense or golden altar (which uses this same Hebrew word for altar) was used only for an offering of special incense (Exod. 30:7-9) and was purified in an annual atonement ceremony (see Lev. 4:7; Exod. 30:10). [*mizbēaḥ*]

1:7 Arrange wood on the fire (*'al-hā'ēš*)— The concept of fire, mentioned twice in this verse, is both times a translation of the feminine noun *'ēš*, the second time employing the definite article. This feminine noun occurs over 375x in the OT, most of these in the context of either God revealing himself to man in what is often called a theophany (e.g., Gen. 15:17; Exod. 3:2; 19:18), or in man's approach to God (e.g., Lev. 10:1). In Lev. 1:9 the expression "an offering made by fire" (which occurs numerous times in Leviticus) is the translation of a single masculine Hebrew word, *'iššeh*. Traditionally, this is seen as etymologically coming from feminine *'ēš* ("fire"). Some, however, would not see this relationship and suggest that it is best to understand this term simply as "gift"

without reference to fire at all (Hartley, *Lev.* [WBC], 22) or "food offering" (Milgrom, *Lev. 1–16* [AB], 161-62). However, the masculine form (*'iššeh*) is used primarily when referring to an offering that was wholly or partially consumed by fire (e.g., burnt offering, Lev. 1:9, 13; grain offering, Lev. 2:3; fellowship offering, Lev. 3:3; guilt offering, Lev. 7:5). It is used over 60x in the OT and in Leviticus it is used again at the consecration of the priests (Lev. 8:28; cf. 10:1). About 25x *'iššeh* ("an offering by fire") is followed by the phrase "to the LORD," 15x it is followed immediately (as in Lev. 1:9) by the expression "a pleasing aroma," once it is used in a combination of these two ("an offering by fire to the LORD a pleasing aroma" [Lev. 23:13]), and once it refers to the fire that consumed the burnt offering (Lev. 6:17 [6:10 MT]). In Lev. 1:9 the phrase "to the LORD" follows the phrase "an aroma pleasing." Fire in the OT symbolizes both judgment (Gen. 19:24; Lev. 10:2) and cleansing (Num. 31:21-24). In Lev. 1:7 the fire is used to burn the sacrifice (an act of judgment on sin) and to create an aroma pleasing to the LORD (an act that signified cleansing for the worshiper). These two concepts of judgment and cleansing also seem to be brought together in Mal. 3:2-5. Fire can be connected in Scripture with God's glory (see Lev. 9:6) and therefore his presence. In Lev. 9:6, as Israel began to offer sacrifices according to the LORD's instructions, His presence was revealed through a fire that consumed the first burnt offering offered by the people. It is not surprising that the worshiping people of Israel now *fell down* in worship. The sacrifice must have started to burn on the altar when fire came out from the inner recesses of the tabernacle proper, that is, "from the presence of the LORD" to consume the first sacrifice (Lev. 9:24). The *millipnê yhwh* ("presence of the LORD") as stated in Lev. 9:24 is literally "from the faces of the LORD" since the word *pāneh* means "face" (see *pāneh* in Lev. 1:3) and implies the very real presence of God. It is used a second time in Lev. 9:24 in a more literal manner when the people fell down "on their faces" before the glory of the LORD.

There are three other occasions at which God showed his approval of a burnt offering by sending fire from heaven to burn it up: when the birth of Samson was announced to his parents (Judg. 13:16-20), when Solomon dedicated the temple (2 Chron. 7:1-3), and when Elijah challenged the prophets of Baal on Mount Carmel (1 Kings 18:38). The concept of fire, mentioned twice in Lev. 10:1, is referred to by the feminine rather than the masculine synonymous noun. The fact that the masculine form is not used there and in fact an active participle used as an adjective (*zārâ*) is attached to this noun the second time it is used in the verse demonstrated that this was not a legitimate offering by fire to the LORD. [*'ēš*] [*'iššeh*]

1:9 Wash (*yirḥaṣ*)—The verb is used exclusively for ritual washings and occurs in this manner over 75x in the OT, 26 of these being in Leviticus. Used in Lev. 1:9, 13 of animals in the burnt offering ritual, washing in the Scriptures was an outward action representing the inward cleansing from sin that was to take or had taken place (cf. Ps. 73:13; Isa. 1:16; 4:4). Ritual washings could be done for the human body (e.g., Lev. 14:8), for clothing (e.g., Lev. 14:9), and for sacrificial animals (e.g., Lev. 1:9, 13). In Lev. 14 and 15 ritual washings were required as part of the cleansing process for uncleanness contracted by touching something unclean or diseased. Lev. 16 makes numerous mentions of the washings required in connection with the

Day of Atonement ritual, the most sacred day in the calendar for the Israelite nation. The requirement for the high priest to wash before dressing (Lev. 16:4) and then after taking off the special garments (Lev. 16:24), the requirement for the individual who released the scapegoat to wash afterwards (Lev. 16:26), and the requirement that even the one who burned the remains of the sin offerings must wash once he was done (Lev. 16:28) show the attention paid to the cleansing required by those involved with this most sacred ceremony. [*rḥṣ*]

An <u>aroma pleasing</u> to the LORD (*rêaḥ nîḥôaḥ*)—Used 17x in Leviticus, the nouns are always found as a pair in the phrase used here and achieve the status of a technical term conveying the sense of "odor of soothing (to God), tranquilizing odor (of ascending sacrifices)" (*BDB*, 926). This should be connected with the atonement/propitiation aspect of Lev. 1:4 and thereby signals the pleasure of God when sin is taken care of and fellowship is restored. In Leviticus this designation is used for the first four sacrifices (burnt [Lev. 1:9], grain [Lev. 2:2], fellowship [Lev. 3:5], and sin [Lev. 4:31]) but not for the guilt offering. It is unclear why the guilt offering would not be designated in the same manner. It is specifically used at the ordination of Aaron and his sons (Lev. 8:21, 28). In Lev. 26:31 the phrase is used in a negative but universal sense of *all* offerings in that when the Israelites are disobedient and God brings in the final destruction of the land before the exile, he will take no delight in the "pleasing aroma" of their offerings. The "pleasing aroma" is pleasing to the LORD only when the offering is done in faith. When done in faith this pleasing aroma causes a response of blessing from the LORD (cf. Gen. 8:20-22). [*rêaḥ*] [*nîḥôaḥ*]

1:14 Dove . . . young pigeon (*hattorîm . . . běnê-hayyônâ*)—The Hebrew word for dove is *tōr* while young pigeon is *yônâ*. In Leviticus they are always used in parallel as is done in this verse and again in Lev. 5:7, 11; 12:6, 8; 14:22, 30; 15:14, 29. Any attempt to distinguish between these two is difficult since they both belong to the same family of *Columbae*. The dove was considered to be clean, gentle, and inoffensive, but in the sacrificial system no difference was made between the two kinds of birds. The dove became significant later since at the baptism of Jesus Christ all four gospels record that the Holy Spirit descended "like a dove" (Matt. 3:16; Mark 1:10; Luke 3:22; John 1:32). Luke specifically states that "the Holy Spirit descended on him in bodily form like a dove." Obviously some of the characteristics of a dove modeled that of the Spirit but no connection can be made of this specific sacrifice and the Holy Spirit. [*tōr*] [*yônâ*]

2:1 Someone (*nepeš*)—The Hebrew term *nepeš* is a feminine noun meaning "soul, living being" (*BDB*, 659). The feminine gender of the noun is grammatical and in no way conflicts or contradicts subsequent masculine terminology in this verse. It is generic for "person" and the Hebrew does not suggest any dichotomy between this "soul" and his/her "body" as did later Greek thought. [*nepeš*]

Grain (*minḥâ*)—Here the word refers to the bloodless seed produced by cereal plants (for the word *qorbān* ["offering"] see Lev. 1:2). Used 35x in Lev. 2:1–23:37, the Hebrew word can more generally mean "gift, present, tribute" that one would give to a superior person (1 Sam. 10:27) but it is never used in this general way in Leviticus. Both Cain and Abel offered a *minḥâ* to the LORD (Gen. 4:4-5)

that included sacrifices of both animals and vegetation so the translation of the noun must be carefully taken from the context (cf. 1 Sam. 2:17, 29; 26:19). The grain offering in Leviticus (sometimes translated "cereal" or "meal" offering) seems to be some form of wheat while the barley grain appears to have been reserved for the "jealousy test offering" of Num. 5:15, 25. However, one cannot be dogmatic about this since the Hebrew uses the general term for grain (but also see below "fine flour"). While incense and salt could be added to the grain, no leaven or honey was to be added (see Lev. 2:1). Later it is indicated that the *minḥâ* should be offered every morning and evening (Num. 28:4, 8). It is of interest to note that this particular offering is placed in order between the burnt and fellowship offerings. The grain offering was often a part of both these other offerings along with the prescribed "drink" offering (Num. 15:1-15). The drink offering is not mentioned at all in Leviticus. [*minḥâ*]

Fine flour (*sōlet*)—In Leviticus "fine flour" is used here and in 2:4, 7; 5:11; 6:15; 14:10, 21; 23:17; 24:5. In contrast to the word *qimaḥ*, which refers to the substance that is produced from the whole kernel and the bran or to that which is waiting to be ground (HALOT, 3:1108), *sōlet* refers to that which is produced when only the inner kernel of wheat (as opposed to barley [Levine, *Lev.* {JPSTC}, 10]) is ground. While no doubt used by many in Israel, this fine flour was naturally more time consuming and costly to produce (Ezek. 16:13; cf. Rev. 18:13) and was used for the entertainment of guests (Gen. 18:6). This fine flour would no doubt remind the one offering it that God deserved the best and finest of all they had. This offering was given at the consecration ceremony of the priests (Exod. 29:2), by the one fulfilling his Nazirite vow (Num. 6:15), by the tribal leaders at the inauguration of the tabernacle (Num. 7), and at the ordination of the Levites as substitutes for the firstborn (Num. 8:8). [*sōlet*]

Oil (*šemen*)—Oil was added to the grain perhaps to lend it an aroma as it was burned (cf. vv. 15-16) but mainly to encourage rapid burning. Salt was also added as can be seen in Lev. 2:13. *šemen* is a common word that is used in a variety of ways (e.g., as a substance for anointing kings or priests, as fuel for a lamp, as a gift, as a medicinal substance, etc.). Probably exclusively from the olive tree, the oil in the grain offering distinguished it from the poor person's sin offering of grain (Lev. 5:11). Oil was an evidence of prosperity (Deut. 32:13; 33:24) while in Isa. 61:3 and Ps. 45:7 [45:8 MT] the "oil of joy" designates the blessed condition of one who is experiencing God's favor. Oil played an important symbolic function in various consecration ceremonies of both priests and kings (e.g., Lev. 8:12; 1 Sam. 16:13). The "anointing oil" (*šemen hammišḥâ*) is referred to numerous times in Exodus, and in Exod. 30:22-33 its ingredients and use are specifically developed. In Leviticus it is used 7x (Lev. 8:2, 10, 12, 30; 10:7; 21:10, 12; see 7:35 for the first use of *mišḥâ* in Leviticus). This unique oil was used only for the consecration of priests, and once upon the priest he was to be regarded by others and himself as one separated for the LORD's service. While so designated he was not allowed to leave the sanctuary (Lev. 10:7; 21:12). This would enforce in the nation of Israel the concept of the holiness, the separation, of God and all associated with him from the routine and unclean, and the priority of maintaining access to God by keeping the priest consecrated. The use of oil in such cases may also be connected with the rich

blessing of God in the promised land. To include oil in the grain offering is to include another produce of blessing from the land. [*šemen*]

Incense (*lĕbōnâ*)—Incense, representing another product of the natural world—this time from the cultivated orchard—was combined with the fine flour and oil probably to lend it an especially pleasing aroma as it was burned (cf. vv. 15-16). Incense, or as it is sometimes translated "frankincense," is the white (and yellow at any fracture) resin of the *Boswellia carteri* and *frereana* trees (HALOT, 2:518; NIDOTTE, 2:756-57). These trees are not native to Israel. Both Isa. 60:6 and Jer. 6:20 mention that the incense came from Sheba in southwestern Arabia (i.e., modern Yemen). Together with the grain and oil, products of the land God was about to give to the Israelites, incense, a product of a foreign land and obtained by trade, was to be added to the mixture. This no doubt reminded the Israelites that whatever they had from the ground, whether they had obtained it by agriculture or by trade, was in the grain offering to be given to God as the best of their possessions. Later, incense was used symbolically in the Psalms of holiness and devotion (Ps. 141:2) and of course it was one of the gifts given to honor the infant Jesus (Matt. 2:11). [*lĕbōnâ*]

2:2 A handful (*mĕlō' qumṣô*)—Only a portion of the grain offering was to be burned on the altar. Unlike the whole burnt offering that was totally consumed, the remainder of the grain was a holy offering, belonging to the priests (v. 3) and not shared with the worshiper who brought it (see Lev. 6:16-18 for instructions concerning the eating of this holy portion and Lev. 7:9-10 for more specific instruction on the distribution of the grain offering).

The term "handful" comes from the Hebrew phrase used here which literally means "the fullness of a closed hand." The noun *qōmeṣ* can be defined as "closed hand, fist" and is used with *mĕlō'* ("fullness, that which fills") twice in Leviticus, here and in Lev. 5:12. A different expression is used in Lev. 16:12. Such a small measure, perhaps the volume of a cup by today's measurements, would simply serve as a representative portion for the whole. [*qōmeṣ*] [*mĕlō'*]

Memorial portion (*'azkārātāh*)—This phrase is a technical term for that portion of the grain offering that was burned and is the translation of a single Hebrew word *'azkārâ* "memorial-offering" (*BDB*, 272). This noun comes from the verbal root *zkr* meaning "think [about], meditate [upon], pay attention [to]; remember, recollect; mention, declare, recite, proclaim, invoke, commemorate, accuse, confess" (Bowling, TWOT, 1:241). The small portion that was burned would serve as a reminder, a memorial, to the LORD of the entirety of the sacrifice, as well as the reason for the sacrifice, and would also serve as a reminder to the worshiper of God's generosity, gracious character, and mercy toward his people. In Leviticus it is used 5x of the burning of the handful of the grain offering (here, Lev. 2:9, 16; 5:12; 6:15 [6:8 MT]) while in Lev. 24:7 it is used of the burning of the incense placed beside the bread on the golden table in the Holy Place. [*'azkārâ*]

2:3 Most holy (*qōdeš qodāšîm*)—This phrase illustrates an idiomatic form in Hebrew where a combination of two synonymous words is used for emphasis. Here *qōdeš* and *qodāšîm*, the singular and plural of the same noun, are used literally to declare "the holiest of the holies." Since the concept of holiness in itself suggests

that which is sacred, and thus is distinct from the profane or even common (see Lev. 10:10), to repeat the use of the word for holiness is to emphasize beyond doubt the unique nature of this part of the offering. In Lev. 16:33 there is another double use of the noun when referring to the inner sanctuary ("Most Holy Place" [*miqdaš haqqōdeš*]) where the ark was placed. The verb *qdš* "in the Qal connotes the state of that which belongs to the sphere of the sacred . . . distinct from the common or profane" (T. McComiskey, TWOT, 2:786). That which the LORD God declares to be holy or to be dedicated to his use was to be kept separate from the common. Leviticus is a book about separateness or holiness. While much of Leviticus is concerned with ceremonial holiness, such holiness is ultimately symbolic of, and foundational for, ethical holiness as can be seen with the connection to the holiness of God (cf. Lev. 19:2). But the concept of holiness is much more than merely differentiating between moral and immoral, or even between good and bad. Holiness is a concept of being set apart from all that is common (*ḥōl*) (see Lev. 10:10), of belonging to the sphere of the sacred. God is distinct, set apart from all else in creation and he is called holy. Holiness is that which is totally good and distinct from all evil and all that is unclean or defiled. Sexual intercourse for a married couple was not considered to be an immoral act in the OT, yet sexual intercourse could effect a state of defilement that would prevent a couple from participating in certain rituals for a time (Lev. 15:18). The Sabbath was different from the other six days because it was designated as different and therefore is called holy. So too are sacrificial animals, the temple, and the priest. The necessity of making a distinction between the spheres of the holy and the common is a basic element to the Israelite religion and proper worship of God. As will be seen in the chapters to follow (especially Lev. 11–15), every aspect of the ancient Hebrews' daily life was seen as intimately linked with the presence of God and therefore revelation was needed to determine the appropriateness of both actions and material.

The phrase "be holy, because I am holy" is a hallmark of Leviticus It is repeated twice in Lev. 11 (vv. 44, 45) and comes again another 3x in Leviticus. (19:2; 20:7, 26). The phrase "most holy " is used of the grain, sin, and guilt offerings (Lev. 6:17, 25 [6:18 MT], 7:6). It is used because these are the sacrifices that only the priests may eat and that must be eaten in the holy place surrounding the tabernacle (Lev. 6:16 [6:9 MT], 26 [6:19 MT]). Using ceremonial sacredness, the LORD taught his people symbolically about moral and spiritual pollution; they were to be a people separated to God and kept from common purpose. Just because a major portion was allowed not to be burned but rather to be given to Aaron and his sons the priests, no one must treat this portion as anything less than holy. In Lev. 6:16 the holiness of this portion is further emphasized by allowing it to be eaten only in the courtyard of the tent of meeting (i.e., the tabernacle).

In Lev. 5:15 the term "holy" is used in the phrase "in holy shekels." In context this weight refers to what must be used to determine the value of the silver being used as the equivalent to the ram (see Lev. 5:15). Extrabiblical evidence seems to indicate three different weights of shekels: the "holy" or temple shekel weighed about 10 grams, the common or merchant's shekel weighed about 11.5 to 12 grams, and the royal or heavy shekel weighed about 13 grams (H. Austel, TWOT, 2:953-54). Later

in Leviticus (*šeqel* is used another 12x in Leviticus, all in chapter 27) this "holy" or temple shekel is said to be equivalent to 20 gerahs (Lev. 27:25; Exod. 30:13). If there was a unique weight set that the sanctuary had for determining proper value, then the term "holy" as used in this phrase does not have to carry any specific sacred overtones. In Lev. 6:16 [6:9 MT] "in a holy place" is further explained by the phrase "in the courtyard of the Tent of Meeting." The restriction of the place where the priest's share of the grain offering could be eaten (i.e., the tabernacle, see Lev. 1:1) is a further emphasis on the holiness of this portion of the grain offering. In Lev. 6:18 [6:11 MT] the Hebrew verb *yiqdāš* is widely regarded as uncertain for translation. The same phrase occurs in v. 27 [6:20 MT] regarding the sin offering (see also Exod. 29:37; 30:29; Deut. 22:9). The debate centers on whether the touching of these items will make one holy, that is, set apart for God or whether the person must be holy, that is, set apart for God in order to touch them (cf. Hag. 2:13). The first translation regards the imperfect or continuous form of the verb as indicating future action. The second regards the verb as an explanation of the previous sentence that declares that any male descendant of Aaron may eat of this food, that is, anyone set apart for priestly service. As is seen in chapter 10, anyone who touches these offerings must be set apart for priestly tasks and be meticulous in following the prescribed procedures.

In Lev. 8:10 the verb form *yĕqqadēš* is used to describe the consecration of the tabernacle and later of the priests. *Qdš* is a denominative verb (a verb formed from a noun or adjective) whose noun form has been used numerous times in Leviticus and is translated "holy." The verb form is used in Lev. 8:10 and in vv. 11, 12, 15, 30 as well as in numerous other places in Leviticus. It is the intensive (Piel) stem, which "connotes the act by which the distinction is effected" (T. McComiskey, TWOT, 2:786). "To consecrate" means to make holy or sacred and was the result of the anointing mentioned earlier in the verse. The items of the tabernacle were now put into the category of the holy rather than the common. In Lev. 10:3 the LORD declares, "I will show myself holy." The imperfect of a Hebrew verb can have imperative force (e.g., "I must") and not merely a future tense as could be implied from the English. The passive (Niphal) use of this denominative verb connotes the concept of proving one's holiness. Here God proves his holiness by judging sin (see also Num. 20:13; Ezek. 28:22).

Lev. 19:2 ("Be holy because I, the LORD your God, am holy") is often referred to as the theme verse or motto of Leviticus The concept of having God as the standard of holiness first occurs in Leviticus in 11:44. It occurs again in Lev. 20:7, 26. But holiness was not only required of the Israelites, but is the manner of lifestyle for all believers (Exod. 19:6; 1 Pet. 1:15-16). The "holiness code," which is a term often applied to the material of Lev. 16–27, is heavily ethical rather than ceremonial. Man was made in the image of God and is expected to reflect the divine likeness in a number of ways, including ethical standards. These standards are based on the never-changing nature of the LORD God. Lev. 22:32 again reiterates this principle, that ethical connotations of holiness find their basis in the statements against confusing the realms of the sacred with the common or profane. In Lev. 27:30 the tithe of animals and vegetation was "holy" to the LORD. Earlier in this verse it is stated that the tithe "belongs to the LORD." As a result, the tithe by association and dedica-

tion became "holy," that is, set apart for divine use. [*qdš*] [*qōdeš*]

2:4 Without yeast (*maṣṣôt*)—This word (in both singular and plural), meaning unleavened bread or cake(s), is used 12x in Leviticus (here [2x]; 2:5; 6:16 [6:9 MT]; 7:12 [2x]; 8:2, 26 [2x]; 10:12; 23:6 [2x]). Yeast is the substance that causes fermentation in dough (as well as in some liquids) that results in a raising of the bread into a light or spongy loaf. After burning the memorial portion of the grain offering (see Lev. 2:2) the priests were to consume the remainder as unleavened cakes (Lev. 6:16-17 [6:9-10 MT]). The theological importance of preparing bread or cakes without yeast begins at the Passover (Exod. 12:8), continues here in the grain offering, further with the fellowship offering (Lev. 7:12), and finally with the sacrifices of the Nazirite vow (Num. 6:15, 17, 19). The Passover bread and the bread of the first number of days of travel were originally made without yeast (see Lev. 23:6 for the "Feast of Unleavened Bread") because of the haste with which Israel had to leave Egypt (Exod. 12:39). This bread, eaten with bitter herbs, Moses later identified as "the bread of affliction" (Deut. 16:3). The reason for the prohibition against yeast in the grain offering is never declared. In the NT yeast is identified continually with evil or false teaching, since this, like yeast, produces a gradual but substantial modification by permeating the entire being (e.g., Matt. 16:6-12; Mark 8:15; Luke 12:1; 1 Cor. 5:6-8; Gal. 5:9). However, Christ also identifies action in the kingdom of God/heaven with yeast in Matt. 13:33 and Luke 13:21. While this action could be identified with the present growth of evil in the kingdom most interpret the yeast here to symbolize the internal, permeating quality of the message concerning the kingdom. Therefore any presumed symbolism that yeast is not present in the grain offering because it symbolizes evil comes from a concept of yeast as evil that is only explicitly stated at a much later time. [*maṣṣâ*]

2:11 Yeast (*śĕ'ōr*)—This prohibition is probably best understood as a rejection of the associated decay through fermentation when yeast is mixed with a sweet fruit syrup (see below) though no rationale for this prohibition is provided in the Scriptures. Yeast or leaven is referred to in this verse using the two synonymous Hebrew words *ḥāmēṣ* and *śĕ'ōr*. Exod. 12:11 indicates that the Passover was to be eaten "in haste" and since leavened bread takes time to rise, the eating of unleavened bread at the Passover and then during the Feast of Unleavened Bread was one more way to remind them of the quickness of their leaving Egypt. In later rabbinic and then NT literature (1 Cor. 5:8; Luke 12:1) leaven was a symbol of impurity, evil, or pollution. One cannot be sure that it carried this connotation when Moses first gave this regulation (see above Lev. 2:4), but if it did, then the removal of leaven was to symbolize their intentional, systematic, complete removal of sin and evil from their lives because of what the LORD had done for them. Today observant Jews still "search" their houses for leaven before the Feast of Unleavened Bread (Lev. 23:6). [*śĕ'ōr*]

Honey (*dĕbaš*)—The word honey is thought to come from the word for the color black or brown, "of a colour between black and red" (*BDB*, 185). The Hebrew word for "honey" is often assumed to refer only to the honey of bees, a product primarily of uncultivated grazing areas. However, this word can also refer to the sweet syrup produced

from grapes, dates, etc. (KBL, 1:212-13). Taken to mean this sweet syrup of the fruit, one can understand that to refer to the land as flowing with milk and honey (see Lev. 20:24) is to refer to it as both a pastoral and agricultural land, able to support flocks and herds as well as vines and fruit trees. It meant they could settle and live permanently in this land with no need to wander from it to obtain what they would need to have a bountiful existence. If honey is taken to mean this sweet syrup of the fruit, one can understand that fermentation could take place in this substance (unlike bees' honey [cf. Judg. 14:8-9; 1 Sam. 14:25-27; Prov. 16:24; 24:13; 25:16], which would not really ferment and does not easily putrefy). Though it is sometimes suggested that this prohibition against burning honey was because of its use in Canaanite cultic practices, this is difficult to substantiate. Perhaps the rejection of a sweet syrup that could ferment and decay easily can be seen to uphold the necessity of offering to God in the grain offering only that which is typical of holiness and purity. However, yeast and honey could be suitable as part of the "firstfruits" (see below Lev. 2:12). [*dĕbaš*]

2:12 An offering of the firstfruits (*rē'šît*)—Referring here to the yeast and honey that were products of the land, this prohibition concerns that which could not be offered as part of the grain offering on the altar. The yeast and honey were allowed to be part of an offering here called "firstfruits" (used here and 23:10 in Leviticus) but not the grain offering. In Exod. 23:16, 19 at the Feast of Harvest/Feast of Pentecost/Feast of Weeks the Israelites were then to bring, as a "wave offering" (Lev. 23:17), the "best of the firstfruits of the soil to the house of the LORD" (Exod. 23:19). This offering was not by fire (as was the grain offering), and the offering of grain at this feast could contain yeast (Lev. 23:17) so at that time the yeast and honey could be presented to the LORD. Though this offering is called here in Lev. 2:12 "offering of the firstfruits" it is not to be connected with the *Feast* of Firstfruits that was connected with the Feast of Unleavened Bread (Lev. 23:4-14) and for which grain offerings (without leaven) were to be offered. Lev. 23:10 also uses the word *rē'šît* (translated "first"). In the natural world, the first sheaf of the crop was to be brought to God as a guarantee that the rest of the harvest was coming (cf. 1 Cor. 15:20, 23). This act was an act of faith on the part of the Israelite. The offering of the new produce of the land along with ordinary leavened bread (Lev. 23:16) indicates the submission of the totality of life of God's people to the LORD. [*rē'šît*]

2:13 Season all your grain offerings with salt (*timlāḥ . . . bammelaḥ*)—The denominative verb "to salt, season" is used 3x in the Scriptures, here, Exod. 30:35, and Ezek. 16:4. It is therefore not used with the meaning "to establish a friendly relationship" as is used in Arab societies even today. In the 27 other passages in the OT where "salt" occurs, most have to do with the physical substance of salt as a mineral especially in reference to the Salt Sea (Dead Sea). The incense offering with its various spices was mixed with salt (Exod. 30:34-35), Abimelech scattered salt over Shechem apparently to designate it as a permanent place of destruction and barrenness (Judg. 9:45), and Elisha used salt to purify the spring at Jericho (2 Kings 2:20-21). Either the preserving nature of salt or its great value caused it to be added to the offerings. [*melāḥ*] [*mlḥ*]

Salt of the covenant (*bᵉrît*)—This Hebrew noun is used 289x in the OT; the

root is never used as a verb so the noun is often seen as a direct object with the verbs "keep, establish, cut, make," etc. It can be used of an agreement between equal parties (e.g., Gen. 14:13) or between two disparate parties (e.g., Josh. 9). In Lev. 26:42 the author makes reference to "covenant" and also to the three great Hebrew patriarchs. These are not three different covenants but rather the covenant first made with Abraham (Gen. 15) and later reiterated to Isaac (Gen. 26:3-5) and Jacob (Gen. 28:13-15). This covenant was an unconditional covenant made with the father of the Hebrew nation. Many of the promises of this covenant were first given in Gen. 12:1-3, 7, reiterated and inaugurated in Gen. 15, while the sign of this covenant, circumcision, was given in Gen. 17:11-14. This covenant and its fulfillment is the promise longed for by the Hebrew people throughout their generations. The Mosaic Covenant was a means by which each succeeding generation could participate in the blessings of the Abrahamic Covenant. Such covenants often were put into writing so that the terms of the promises and stipulations, as well as the judgments in the event the covenant was broken, could be recorded. In Lev. 26, a chapter that contains the promises (blessings) and judgments (curses) of the Mosaic Covenant, *bᵉrît* is used 8x (26:9, 15, 25, 42 [3x], 44, 45). It appears here in Lev. 2 in a unique way. The concept of "salt of the covenant of your God" occurs only 3x in the Scriptures, here, Num. 18:19, and 2 Chron. 13:5. In the latter two cases it is used to signify something that was irrevocable and binding. In the case of Num. 18:19 this was the permanent provision for the priests from the holy offerings. In 2 Chron. 13:5 it was the permanent right to rule that David's dynasty was promised (see 2 Chron. 7:17-18).

These arrangements, both made by the LORD himself, are designated as a "salt covenant," one that is irrevocable and binding on others who must acknowledge the truth of God's promises. Here in Leviticus the expression "salt of the covenant" is used in the context of the physical addition of salt to the grain offerings but also with the idea of permanence. The preserving nature of salt may suggest the enduring nature of the covenant bond between the Lord and Israel. But the use of salt as a preservative is not clear in the OT (perhaps it is implieded in 2 Kings 2:20-21) and it must be admitted that the symbolism suggested here is never stated in Scripture. The permanent nature of the instructions here in Lev. 2:13 are substantiated by Ezek. 43:24, which declares that the priests of the future temple that Ezekiel describes will sprinkle salt on the burnt offering there. In Lev. 24:8 *běrît* is used to refer to a specific binding stipulation, where the oil and bread were to be set before the Lord in a continuous manner and were to be done so as long as the Mosaic Covenant with its accompanying tabernacle was in effect. [*běrît*]

Your God (*'ĕlōheykâ*)—This is the first use of the common designation for God, *Elohim*. It is analyzed as a plural noun and so it can be translated "gods" as it is in a number of instances (e.g., Exod. 18:11; 20:3) but it is never used this way in Leviticus. In Leviticus it always refers to the true God who revealed himself to Moses. The plural is usually described as a plural of majesty to denote totality and majesty but not plurality in keeping with the monotheistic view of God for the Israelites (Deut. 6:4). However, it can also be taken as a term that permits a plurality (e.g., a Trinity) within a unity of one God. This view is possible from Gen. 1:2, 26

and Isa. 6:8. The form *'ĕlōhîm* is used in Hebrew and occurs in no other Semitic language (J. Scott, TWOT, 1:44). When it is used to indicate the true God, it is often used to describe the God who created man, who works his power in this world, and who should be the object of mankind's reverence and fear. This term is often accompanied by the term *yhwh*, his personal name that is used when making a covenant with his people. It can also be combined with various descriptive words or phrases that function as titles. [*'ĕlōhîm*]

3:1 If someone's offering (*zebaḥ*)—The Hebrew word commonly translated "sacrifice" occurs in Leviticus for the first time here in this verse (it also occurs in vv. 3, 6, 9). However the word used for offering up to now (*qorbān*) continues to be used in Lev. 3 (vv. 1, 2, 6, 7, 8, 12, 14). Thus this fellowship offering is designated as an offering that was also a "sacrifice" in that it involved the killing of an animal and then the eating of this animal as part of a communal meal. [*zebaḥ*]

Fellowship offering (*šĕlāmîm*)—Translated "fellowship" or "peace," the Hebrew word seems not to signify an attempt to make peace with God but rather a declaration that all is well (i.e., peaceful) in the relationship between the LORD and the worshiper. This interpretation is based on the fact that the term comes from *šlm* ("be in covenant of peace" [BDB, 1023]). Lev. 7:11-34 is an important passage to appreciate this concept since, while the fellowship offering comes third out of five (after the burnt and grain but before the sin and guilt offerings) in this first section of Leviticus, in the second listing (Lev. 6:8–7:21) it is listed last. This fact, along with the fact that when this offering was part of a series of offerings the fellowship offering always came last (e.g., Lev. 9:15-18), substantiates the concept that this one did not make peace but indicated peace in the relationship. [šĕlāmîm]

3:3 The fat (haḥēleb)—Only the fat portions of the fellowship offering were burned on the altar (vv. 5, 11, 16). This term appears 45x in Leviticus Although from a practical viewpoint burning the fat from the many fellowship offerings would be both a representative and an easy portion of the animal to burn since fat burns well with little odor, there may well be more to this regulation than pragmatics. It may be that the fat was thought to be a delicacy or "the best" (cf. Deut. 32:13-14; the KJV actually translates ḥēleb as "the best" in Num. 18:12, 29-30, 32) and therefore symbolized the wonderful nature of the worshiper's relationship with the LORD. In addition, since the kidneys are referred to in the OT as the seat of emotions (Job 19:27; Ps. 16:7; 26:2) in the same manner that modern society talks of the heart, it is also possible to see the fat (along with the mentioned kidneys) as a dedication of the worshiper's deepest emotions to God. It is also possible, though less likely, that the LORD was protecting his people from a diet high in fat even as they fellowshiped with him (cf. Lev. 3:17; 7:23, 25). [ḥēleb]

3:11 Food (leḥem)—This Hebrew word for bread or food is a common term used literally hundreds of times in the OT. In Leviticus it is first used in 3:11 in connection with the fellowship offering. Numerous times in Leviticus it is used in a literal manner meaning "bread" or "food" (Lev. 7:13; 8:26, 31, 32; 22:7, 13, 25; 23:14, 17, 18, 20; 24:7; 26:5, 26). However in Lev. 21:6 it is used in a figurative manner, as was done in Lev. 3:11, as a parallel to the offerings made to the LORD by fire. God does not "eat" as humans do but as food brings pleasure to a hungry man so the offerings presented to God bring him pleasure. In Lev. 21 leḥem is used 5x to signify both what is presented to the LORD and that which the priest would eat of the offering (Lev. 21:6, 8, 17, 21, 22). [leḥem]

3:17 Lasting ordinance ('ôlām)—This word for "lasting" occurs 21x in Leviticus while the entire phrase ḥuqqat 'ôlām occurs 17x in Leviticus to refer to a perpetual regulation. The noun 'ôlām is used over 300x in the OT to indicate the distant future. However, there is a range of meaning for this term and so it must not always be taken to mean perpetuity or eternity and in fact there are at least 20 instances where it is used to designate a long period in the past (A. MacRae, TWOT, 2:672-73). It can be translated "long duration, antiquity, futurity" (BDB, 761) or even "forever, ever, everlasting, evermore, perpetual, old, ancient, world" (A. MacRae, TWOT, 2:672). In Lev. 3:17 it indicates that the prohibition against eating the fat and blood was intended to be observed as long as the Mosaic sacrificial system was in effect ("for the generations to come, wherever you live"). The provisions of Deut. 12:15-16, 21-24 relate to an entirely different set of circumstances and so the lack of a prohibition there against eating fat should in no way affect the prohibitions of this verse. The word is often combined with some expressions such as "generations to come" (Lev. 3:17) or "from the Israelites" (Lev. 7:34) to indicate that many of these "everlasting regulations" are usually connected with the Mosaic Covenant, which the Scripture teaches is replaced by a new covenant (Jer. 31:31-32; Heb. 8:7-8). It does not have to mean endlessness; however when the Lord is referred to as God Everlasting (Gen. 21:33) it must convey this meaning. [*ôlām*]

Lasting ordinance (*ḥuqqat*)—The Hebrew phrase can be translated "lasting ordinance" or "perpetual statute." It is used here and also 3x in Lev. 16:29-34 to emphasize the establishment of the perpetual, annual ritual of the Day of Atonement (v. 34). It also occurs commonly to denote the importance of carrying out a particular command (e.g., Passover, Exod. 12:14; keeping the lamps burning, Exod. 27:21; giving the priests their share, Lev. 7:36). The word *ḥuqqat* ("something prescribed, enactment, statute" [*BDB*, 349]) alone is used 26x in Leviticus and normally designates a divine ordinance (but see Lev. 18:30 and 20:23 when used to refer to pagan rituals). In Leviticus it is often used in parallel with *mišpāṭ* ("law"; see for example, Lev. 18:4; for *mišpāṭ* see Lev. 5:10). In Lev. 26:3 *ḥuqqâ* is parallel with *miṣwâ* ("commandment," see Lev. 4:2) and in Lev. 26:15 it is parallel with both of these terms. Finally, it is used in its masculine form in the "legal sequence" of Lev. 26:46 along with *mišpāṭ* and *tôrâ*. Since this term is normally associated with a regulation enacted by God, rather than translating the word "ordinance" or "statute," it is translated "customs" to differentiate it from those divinely given commands to Israel. As noted above, *ḥuqqâ* is often used in a phrase with the term *ôlām*.

The masculine form of the noun (*ḥoq*) first occurs in Lev. 6:18 [6:11 MT] in the phrase *ḥoq-ôlām*. Literally "as decreed forever," the phrase is loosely translated in the NIV as "to come." It misses translating the essence of the Hebrew word *ḥōq*, which means "something prescribed, a statute or due" (*BDB*, 349). The verb form *ḥqq* means to "cut in, inscribe, decree" (*BDB*, 349) and

so the noun form may originate from the ancient practice of engraving laws upon stone or metal and by implication may mean anything prescribed and recorded. This term in its masculine form is used a total of 11x in Leviticus (out of its 128x in the OT) with five of these occurrences being part of the present phrase (here, Lev. 6:22 [6:15 MT]; 7:34; 10:15; 24:9). Often translated "statute" it can mean something prescribed or due and draws attention to the fact that someone in authority has declared the rule and that is motivation enough for it to be obeyed (Exod. 15:25; Ps. 2:7). While *ḥōq* is often used in parallel or in sequence with other terms for law (cf. Lev. 26:46), there does not seem to be a consistent reason why one term rather than another is used. It is not consistently used with the apodictic form and may designate obligations both from God (e.g., Exod. 18:16) or from man (e.g., Gen. 47:26). The verb most frequently used with this noun is *šmr* ("to keep") which stresses the necessity of obedience and when used in connection with the Mosaic Covenant indicates the demands that the LORD God placed upon his covenant nation (J. Lewis, TWOT, 1:317). [*ḥōq*] [*ḥuqqat*]

4:2 Sins (*teḥĕṭā'*)—The Hebrew verb *ḥṭ'* in its basic stem means "miss, go wrong, sin" (*BDB*, 306) and is used a total of 34x in Leviticus. In the OT this is the principal word for sin, occurring about 580x. Its usage in "secular" contexts clearly indicates that the word means to miss the mark, the goal, or the way (e.g., Judg. 20:16; Prov. 8:36; 19:2). In "religious" contexts the object is often God or his stipulations or the verb is intransitive. When man sins he has missed the mark, the goal, or the way that God has set as standard. In a somewhat ironic twist, the intensive (Piel) stem can mean "purified" or "to de-sin, cleanse" (*BDB*, 307) [cf. Lev. 6:26 [6:19 MT]; 9:15; 14:49, 52]. In Lev. 8:15, in connection with purifying the altar, the verb occurs in this intensive (Piel) stem. This verb is important for understanding that the main purpose of the sin offering was to "decontaminate" the tabernacle and its furniture from any impurities (see Lev. 4:3). In Lev. 9:15 the intensive form of the verb is used with the idea of cleansing but is translated by the NIV as "sin offering." The word has a number of synonyms including *pš'* ("rebel, transgress") [see Lev. 16:16] and *'wh* ("commit iniquity, do wrong") [not used in Leviticus]. [*ḥṭ'*]

Sins unintentionally (*bišgāgâ*)—The word *šĕgāgâ* ("unintentionally") is the noun that follows the preposition *bĕ* ("in"). It is used here and in Lev. 4:22, 27; 5:15, 18; 22:14 (6x) and a total of 19x in the OT. It comes from the verb meaning "go astray, commit sin or error" (*BDB*, 992) and is used to modify the verb *ḥṭ'* "miss, go wrong, sin" (*BDB*, 306). In Leviticus it can be grouped by two usages; first, as used in the description of the sin offering (as here), and second, in the violation of "the LORD's holy things" (Lev. 5:15, 18; 22:14). The person sins but the measure of consciousness on the part of the sinner is debated. The NIV's "unintentionally" and the KJV's "through ignorance" can give the impression that the person sinning was completely unaware of his/her wrong action. This impression is further substantiated by the explanatory phrases, "even though . . . unaware of the matter," in Lev. 4:13; 5:2, 3, 4, and "when he is made aware of the sin he committed" in Lev. 4:23, 28 (but see below Lev. 4:13). Num. 15:22-24 compared to Num. 15:30 ("sins defiantly," literally "with a high hand") would indicate that a sin committed "unintentionally" was one

without premeditation (see also Num. 35:11). However, Lev. 5:1 deals with the situation in which a person sins because he does not speak up when he hears a public charge to testify regarding something he has seen or learned about, which would assume some consciousness of the sin though the timing of this consciousness is debated. In Lev. 5:1 the sin appears to be one of omission, a mistake, but the word *šĕgāgâ* is not used. Lev. 5:2-4 seems to center on sins that have been committed because of forgetfulness (see below). Human weakness or frailty is apparently dealt with in the same category as unconscious acts of disobedience because these acts were committed without premedi-tation. Thus Lev. 4:1–5:13 indicates that the offerings here are valid only for those sins done in ignorance, or by accident, carelessness, and omission. Sins for which there was no individual sacrifice were those done in defiance of the LORD and His commands (see below) such as adultery, murder, and idolatry. Those sins that did not fit the category of "unintentional" had to await the cleansing provided by the Day of Atonement ritual or by what was in David's case revealed as a personal appropriation of unmerited grace in response to faith and repentance (Pss. 32; 51).

In Lev. 5:15 the word is used in connection with the guilt offering (see below, Lev. 5:15). It is the same word used in connection with the sin offering as detailed above and yet because of the different contexts it is clear that the word can have two distinct though related meanings. Generally it refers to "straying" or "erring" from the commands of the LORD, in this case specifically from the commands about the "LORD's holy things." But even here in Lev. 5:14–6:7 there will be slight differences in how the term is to be taken. In its use in the guilt offering concerning the LORD's "holy things" (Lev. 5:14-16) the sin is apparently known at some level of consciousness to the violator unlike the sins of Lev. 5:17-18, which, at the time of their committing, were apparently not known to the violator. He probably came to know of his error either by remembering after the fact or by having it drawn to his attention by another person. Also, it is apparently possible here to make restitution in the first case and third cases (Lev. 6:1-7) whereas no restitution is spoken of in vv 17-19. So despite the grievous nature of this sin, according to Lev. 5:14–6:7, restitution is customarily feasible for this sin. In Lev. 5:18 the verb *šgg* is used in one of four places where it occurs in Scripture (Lev. 5:18; Num. 15:28 [both of these Pentateuchal references deal with the "unintentional" sin]; Ps. 119:67; Job 12:16). [*šĕgāgâ*]

Commands (*miṣwôt*)—The term used here for commands is the plural form of the noun *miṣwâ*. The verb form is always used in the active, intensive Hebrew verb stem (Piel) meaning "lay charge (upon), give charge" (*BDB*, 845-46). This term can be used of commands of man or of God but it is obviously used in the latter sense here and in every other use in Leviticus. It is used 10x in Lev. (4:2, 13, 22, 27; 5:17; 22:31; 26:3, 14, 15; 27:34). Virtually every paragraph that deals with the sin offering (Lev. 4:1–5:13) either begins or ends with a statement of sin committed and associated guilt. This is distinct from how the first three offerings have been stated and indicates the nature of this offering (see Lev. 4:3). The plural form of the term is used in Lev. 27:34. Though this term can be used of human commands, the context here clearly shows them to be of God, given while Moses was on Mount Sinai. This verse functions as a "second sum-

mary" (after Lev. 26:46) and concludes the apparent appendix of chapter 27. As such the word "commands" functions as a broad term that would include the three terms of Lev. 26:46. [*miṣwâ*]

4:3 If the anointed priest (*hammāšîaḥ*)— The Hebrew term (anointed, anointed one) is used as both an adjective and a noun in the OT. It is used here in Lev. 4:3 (and also in verses 5 and 16 and 6:22 [6:15 MT] but nowhere else in Leviticus) in an adjectival manner with the definite article and the noun *hakkōhēn* ("the priest") apparently to designate the high priest (cf. Lev. 6:20-22; Num. 35:25). However, the high priest is regularly referred to by the phrase *hakkōhēn haggādôl* ("the great priest," e.g., Lev. 21:10) rather than merely *māšîaḥ* ("anointed"). It may be that this term "anointed" should also include the sons of Aaron, who were also anointed as priests (Lev. 8:30; Exod. 30:30-31). The more common use of "anointed" is as a synonym of "king," often the case in 1 and 2 Samuel and the Psalms. However, in Leviticus the only specifically anointed individuals were the priests (cf. Lev. 8:10-13). The term emphasizes a unique relationship between the LORD God and the anointed one. The Dead Sea Scrolls' use of the term is somewhat ambiguous although there is a mention of the "Messiah of Aaron" (V. Hamilton, TWOT, 1:531). The common NT use of "anointed one" to refer to Christ is not the author's intent here. [*māšîaḥ*]

Bringing guilt on the people (*lĕ'ašmat*)—This word, used 4x in Leviticus (here, 6:5, 7 [5:24, 26 MT]; 22:16), conveys the idea of "indebtedness, guilt" (HALOT, 1:96). However the KJV mostly translates this word by "trespass" or "sin" (i.e., the acts of sin) while most other versions translate it as "guilt," focusing on the liability rather than the sin itself. The word comes from the verb *'šm* "to be guilty" (HALOT, 1:95-96). Here an offense on the part of the high priest brought guilt upon the people since he functioned in a representative role (Lev. 9:7). [*'ašmâ*]

Sin offering (*lĕḥaṭṭā't*)—The word *ḥaṭṭā't* can mean either "sin," that is, the action or condition of offending God (e.g., Lev. 4:3a, 14, 23, 28), or it can mean "sin offering," that is, the sacrificial payment that was made to deal with the penalty of such actions or conditions. The context is vital for determining which rendering is intended. But in Lev. 4–5 the sinful actions seem specifically related to that which made the sanctuary unclean. Thus it is closely associated with *'ašmâ* ("guilt"; see above). Some have suggested that a more accurate understanding of this sacrifice might be made by avoiding the use of the term "sin offering" since other sacrifices such as the burnt offering were also used for propitiation of divine anger. Perhaps "purification offering" should be considered in light of the context. This would be in keeping with the offering of this sacrifice in cases of bodily pollution (Lev. 12:8; 14:19; cf. 15:31; 16:19). The term is used in the OT over 280x. In Leviticus the word alternates between the two meanings of sin and of offering for sin expressed above. In Lev. 16:21 three synonyms for transgressions against God (including *ḥaṭṭā't*) are used in an effort to demonstrate the totality of the atonement. The sin offering, developed in Lev. 4:1–5:13 and 6:24-30 [6:17-23 MT], was the primary blood-atonement offering in the Levitical system through which a worshiper could purify that which had become unclean. The noun is used on several unique occasions including the consecration of priests (Lev. 8:2, 14) and the inauguration of altar worship (Lev. 9:2-11, 15-17). Though Lev. 1 listed the

burnt offering first, in Lev. 9 (vv. 2, 3, 7, 8, 15) the sin offering must be presented before the burnt (see Lev. 1:3), fellowship (see Lev. 3:1), or grain offerings (see Lev. 2:1). Logically, purification of the altar must be first before the other offerings could be made. In Lev. 16:3 the term is used in connection with the Day of Atonement. The two goats together are described as "a sin offering" in Lev. 16:5. For this reason, whatever the definition of *azazel* (see Lev. 16:8), these two goats both represented a different aspect of the same sacrifice, one the means and the other the results (cf. Isa. 53:4, 6). [*ḥaṭṭā't*]

4:6 Seven times (*šebā'*)—The numeral seven is used here and in 19 other places in Leviticus. It must be assumed to have, first of all, a simple numerical significance. However, this number can have symbolic meaning as well. Already, in relation to the religious rituals of the Israelites, the LORD had instructed that the seventh day was to be regarded as holy and was to function as the sign of the entire Mosaic Covenant (Exod. 20:10; 31:13). In addition, the garments of the high priest had been consecrated for seven days (Exod. 29:30), the unleavened bread was to be eaten for seven days (Exod. 23:15), and the golden lampstand in the tabernacle had seven lamps (Exod. 25:37). These examples, along with many others, make clear that the number seven can symbolize completeness, holiness, and divine direction. Thus, when the blood is sprinkled seven times it can be seen to have both a numerical and symbolic meaning.

The seven days of ordination in Lev. 8:33 is another use of seven. In Scripture the idea of a period of seven days to observe special events is not uncommon. The seven-day period is used after birth

(Lev. 12:2), wedding feasts (Gen. 29:27; Judg. 14:12), and deaths (Gen. 50:10). The connection to the seven days of Creation is not made here as elsewhere (Exod. 20:11). However, the period of seven days would no doubt bring to mind the completed, perfect conditions of Creation and the divine satisfaction as well and would be in keeping with the fact that these were the days of ordination (see Lev. 7:37). [šebā']

Curtain of the sanctuary (pārōket)— Translated "curtain" or "veil," this term refers to the blue, purple, and scarlet cloth separator embroidered with cherubim between the Holy Place and the Holy of Holies in the tabernacle (Exod. 26:31). It is used 21x in Exodus, once in Numbers (4:5), once in 2 Chronicles (3:14), and twice in Leviticus (here and 24:3). It is regarded as a barrier, a separator to prevent an unauthorized priest (that is, any priest except the high priest) from seeing into the Holy of Holies (see Exod. 26:31-33). The curtain had blood sprinkled in front of it seven times when the sin offering was for the anointed priest (Lev. 4:6-7) or for the whole Israelite nation (Lev. 4:17; the sin offering on the Day of Atonement was slightly different though still for the nation; see Lev. 16). When the sin offering was made for an individual (Lev. 4:22–5:13) the blood was not sprinkled in front of the curtain but on the burnt altar (Lev. 4:25). It was this separator that was torn in two at the moment that Christ "gave up his spirit" (Matt. 27:50). Matthew records that "at that moment the curtain of the temple was torn in two from top to bottom" (Matt. 27:51), an incident which in Heb. 9:1-14 and 10:14-22 is related to the amazing fact that believers can now go directly into God's presence. Thus the separator that kept most Israelites from ever entering the holiest place of all, the very presence of God, was

removed by the death of Christ so that all could by faith enter. [pārōket]

4:7 Horns of the altar of fragrant incense (qarnôt)—The altar of incense (Exod. 30:1-10) was located inside the actual tabernacle, in the Holy Place, just in front of the curtain that separated the Holy Place from the Holy of Holies. It was much smaller than the altar of burnt offering, which was just inside the main entrance to the courtyard (Exod. 27:1-8). The horns of both mentioned altars were vertical projections at the top corners of the altar (Exod. 27:2; 30:2). In 1 Kings 1:50-51 and 2:28 the horns of the altar (probably the bronze altar since neither Adonijah nor Joab would have the right to enter into the Holy Place of the tabernacle) were held on to by a supplicant as a means of seeking asylum (see Exod. 21:13-14). Since physical horns of animals represented physical power and might, the horns of the altar of fragrant incense represented the presence and power of this Almighty God (but not the person of God himself since this would then make it an idol). It is especially on these horns of the incense altar that the blood was to be applied when either the priest (Lev. 4:7) or the entire nation (Lev. 4:18) had sinned. It was done so that the nation could again offer incense to their God. For other individuals the blood was applied to the horns of the bronze altar (Lev. 4:25, 30, 34) since this was on a personal basis and did not affect the ability of the nation to offer worship to God as did the sin of the anointed priest or nation. [qeren]

4:11 Its flesh (běśārô)—The term "flesh" [BDB, 142] is quite common in Hebrew and is used 61x in Leviticus alone. It has a wide range of meanings such as skin, flesh, meat, body, humankind, and animals (R. Chisholm, NIDOTTE, 1:777). In Leviticus it can be used of both human (e.g., Lev. 13:2) and animal flesh (e.g., Lev. 4:11) but is also used in a more universal sense to refer to all humankind in Lev. 17:14 (3x). In Lev. 15:2 a "bodily discharge" is spoken of using the term for body. After v. 3 it is clear that the discharges spoken of here were coming from the male sexual organs. The term is used as a euphemism for the male genital organ in Gen. 17:11, 13, 14, 23, 24, 25 as well as in Exod. 28:42. It is used again in Lev. 15:19 to refer to the woman's vagina but it is also used in v. 7 to refer to any part of the man's body. Lev. 18:6 speaks of a close relative (šĕ'ēr bĕśorô) using two synonyms bāśār and šĕ'ēr (see Lev. 18:6), could be literally translated "flesh of his flesh," and may reflect a use of Gen. 2:23 ("flesh of my flesh") although in Genesis the word šĕ'ēr is not used but a double use of the word bāśār. There Adam, speaking of the newly created woman that had been formed from his own rib, declares she is "bone of my bones, and flesh of my flesh." The Hebrew people were not to seek a marriage partner from nonbelieving, non-Israelites (Deut. 7:3). Rather, they were to marry within the nation and, in some cases because of property considerations, even within the tribe (Num. 36). But this section defines who, even within the tribe, is too near a relative to be a permissible marriage partner. The NT also recognizes that near relatives are not permitted to marry or even to have sexual intercourse (see 1 Cor. 5:1). [bāśār]

4:12 A place ceremonially clean (māqôm)—The phrase māqôm ṭāhôr is a combination of two Hebrew words, the former word is dealt with in detail below. It is sufficient here to understand that the sin offering was not to be placed on the altar nor was it to be burned just anywhere. Rather there was a designated physical location where it must be done. For sin offerings that were offered on behalf of the anointed priest or the entire nation (Lev. 4:3-21) the fat was removed and burned but the rest of the animal was taken outside the camp and burned at a ceremonially clean place. This place was where the ashes from the sacrifices were also taken (see below). The animal was not offered on the altar because it was being used to remove the defilement that had occurred because of the unintentional sin of the anointed priest (Lev. 4:2). Heb. 13:11-12 speaks specifically of the blood of the sin offering being carried into the Most Holy Place but with the bodies burned outside the camp. Since Hebrews speaks of the blood being carried into the Most Holy Place this could refer to the blood being sprinkled in front of the curtain and placed on the horns of the incense altar (see above) as would occur on behalf of the nation on the Day of Atonement (Lev. 16:27). The death of the animal would have occurred within the tabernacle courtyard whereas for Christ his death was outside Jerusalem's walls. This represented the removal of sin, as the removal of the bodies of sacrificial animals had done here in Leviticus.

The idea of there being a designated physical location for specific events or placement of specific objects is common in Lev. God has the authority and desire to have his tabernacle represent that which is done according to a pattern. Nothing is haphazard or left to chance with this God who is concerned to teach his people holiness, respect, and obedience. [māqôm]

A place ceremonially clean (ṭāhôr)— This adjective ("clean, pure") [BDB, 373] occurs some 96x in the OT, 21 of those being found in the book of Leviticus It is used of "pure" gold twice (Lev. 24:4, 6) with all the remaining usages being that of ritual purity (e.g., Lev. 4:12). The concept of *ṭāhôr* as ethical purity is not found in Leviticus but it is used in this manner approximately 10x in the OT (e.g., Job 14:4; Prov. 30:12). Throughout Leviticus cleanness and purity is de-manded of the participants in the community and especially among the priesthood. The verb *ṭhr* and the nouns *ṭōhar* and *ṭohŏrâ* are used 53x in Leviticus, all occurring after Lev. 10 primarily in the "holiness code" section of Lev. 11–15. In Lev. 12:4 the abstract noun "purification, purity" can be understood as referring to either "days of purification" or "days of purity." This concerns the woman who has given birth. "Days of purification" is probably best since the woman was still restricted during this time but no longer contagious in her uncleanness as she was during the first seven days. The first seven days were days of uncleanness (Lev. 12:2) or for a female child, the first 14 days were days of uncleanness (Lev. 12:5). After this period, and when the proper sacrifices had been offered, she would be pronounced "clean" by the priest. Then there is a subsequent 33-day period (for a male child) or 66-day period (for a female child; Lev. 12:5) of "days of purification."

The amazing declaration of Lev. 16:30 in response to the Day of Atonement, that the Israelites would be clean from their sins, is made on the basis of sacrifice (v. 15a), sprinkling of blood (vv. 15b, 16), proper confession (v. 21), and substitution (v. 22). The basic idea of being "clean," here served by the verb *ṭhr*, has been dealt with above as an adjective. But here it is no mere distinguishing between clean and unclean in terms of ritual but a declaration of the acceptability of the persons. Only God could declare such a fact for only he

could cleanse. The possibility of individual cleansing is found in Ps. 51:2, 7, 10 (51:4, 9, 12 MT). Future promises of cleansing of the nation are found in Jer. 33:8 and Ezek. 36:25; 36:33; 37:23. In the NT the amazing fact of cleansing is declared by Christ in his Upper Room Discourse (John 13:10; 15:3) although he indicates there must be continual partial cleansing (i.e., feet) to remain in fellowship with the Savior (John 13:8). [*ṭāhôr*] [*ṭhr*] [*ṭōhar*]

Where the ashes are thrown (*šepek haddešen*)—The Hebrew phrase *šepek haddešen* ("the ashes are thrown") occurs only here in the OT. The term "ashes" comes from a root which literally means "fatness, fat ashes" (*BDB*, 206). The place being alluded to is probably not the same area to the east of the altar that was referred to in Lev. 1:16, which may have still been within the tabernacle courtyard. This area is "outside" the camp (see Lev. 13:46) where the ashes from the sacrifices were also taken (Lev. 4:8-12). Lev. 6:11 refers to the priest who is to "take off these clothes and put on others, and carry the ashes outside the camp to a place that is ceremonially clean." In Heb. 13:12 the author declares "so Jesus also suffered outside the city gates to make the people holy through his own blood." This helps identify the death of Christ with the sin offering that was burned "where the ashes are thrown." In the Gospels there is no mention of ashes, just that the place was called "Golgotha (which means the Place of the Skull)" (Matt. 27:33; Mark 15:22). Both, however, were places of death and both were regarded as holy because of the activity that occurred there. [*dešen*]

4:13 If the whole Israelite community (*kol-'ădat*)—The term translated "community" is the Hebrew term *'ēdâ*, which can mean "congregation" or "community" and is used this way throughout Leviticus. Although the NIV uses the same English term in the following phrase, a different Hebrew term (*qāhāl*) occurs in the second place (see below). While one cannot be dogmatic about the difference between these two terms, there may be reason to believe that they do not *both* refer to a gathering of people representative of the entire nation. The term used here may be the broader term for the entire nation (Exod. 12:3, 6; Num. 20:1, 2). Obviously the entire community could not lay all their hands on the bull so a representative group would be needed. Nevertheless, the entire nation would be represented and affected by the actions of its representatives. [*'ēdâ*]

The community (*haqqāhāl*)—While *'ēdâ*, the Hebrew term used in the first phrase, may be the broader term for the entire nation (Exod. 12:3, 6; Num. 20:1, 2), the term used here may refer to a representative body with certain legal functions (but compare its use in Deut. 5:22; 9:10; 18:16; 1 Kings 8:22, 65 where it still seems to refer to a general religious gathering). When the entire nation sinned and the representative gathering became aware of it, then this representative gathering was to bring the sacrifice. It was the *qāhāl* that was to bring the sacrifice (Lev. 4:14) and the elders (see Lev. 4:15) of the *'ēdâ* were then to lay their hands on the bull. Taken this way, the elders of the nation made up the *qāhāl* and functioned as representatives of the entire nation (*'ēdâ*). This is in keeping with the general biblical principle that proper representatives of God's people can act on behalf of the entire nation. [*qāhāl*]

4:14 When they become <u>aware</u> of the sin (*wĕnôd'â*)—The Hebrew verb *yd'*, which is used here in a reflexive (Niphal) stem, can mean "be made known, be or become known" (*BDB*, 394). It is a very common Hebrew verb used hundreds of times in the OT "in every stem and expresses a multitude of shades of knowledge gained by the senses" (J. Lewis, TWOT, 1:366). The range of nuances extends from God's infinite knowledge of man, to man's knowledge of the ways of animals, to the mere acquaintance of one man with another, to the intimacies shared by a man and woman in sexual intercourse. The verb is used 9x in Leviticus (here, 4:23, 28; 5:1, 3, 4, 17, 18; 23:43). Here it bears the sense that the congregation has become aware of (by what means is not described) the sin for which they are held guilty. The sin called "unintentional" is discussed under Lev. 4:2 but here a unique factor is mentioned. In this situation the sin has been described as one of which they were unaware, literally "and the thing is hidden from. . . ." This would allow for the fact that perhaps forgetfulness is the cause of the sin though ignorant action is also possible since the entire congregation is involved. Whatever the cause and however long the sin has not been acknowledged or revealed, they are still guilty (Lev. 4:13). As can be seen in Lev. 5:2-4, they must confess and bring a "purification/sin offering" so the guilt that was unknown could be dealt with properly. At the point of awareness, when it became known to them, the congregation (*qāhāl*; see above) must respond in the divinely required manner (Lev. 4:14-21). While the sin has been present from the time of its execution, the guilt and consequences are now elevated once knowledge of the sin is present. In Lev. 5:17 the phrase "though he does not know it" again contains the verb *yd'*. In the case being discussed in Lev. 5:17-19 there is no restitution (plus 20 percent) mentioned that is normally the requirement for the guilt offering. For this reason the knowledge that the man has is perplexing. Perhaps this was describing a situation where a man's conscience was bothering him and he did not know exactly what he had done (or else restitution would be necessary) but he sensed an awareness of guilt and wanted to make sure and so offered a guilt offering. If this is the situation then this perception would be extremely subjective knowledge. However, since a sin like this could have been taken care of by the sin offering just as easily, it would be better to take this as a sin, which at the time of committing, was not realized to be a violation of another's property. This is more in keeping with the context. Once it became known, then the sacrifice and restitution were necessary. In this case the reason for not specifically mentioning the restitution plus 20 percent is not obvious.

The use of the verb in Lev. 23:43 is a more familiar utilization of this term. Describing the Feast of Tabernacles, the LORD declares that living in booths for a week each year would enable descendants of the wilderness Israelites to "know," experience firsthand and therefore remember, that the LORD had brought them out of Egypt and provided for them even as they lived in tents. This is in keeping with the function of many of God's requirements, that man would realize who God is and what he has done for them. This knowledge should lead properly to a worshipful relationship. [*yd'*]

4:15 The <u>elders</u> of the community (*ziqnê*)—Taken from the Hebrew word which can mean "old," the plural term here is used in a phrase containing the word *'ēdâ* for "congregation" or "community" (see above Lev. 4:13; cf. 9:1 where the

word is combined with the word "Israel"). In this context of cultic ritual "elder" refers to those who have authority. The "elders" are mentioned even before the nation left Egypt (Exod. 3:16; 4:29) where they apparently held positions of seniority among the tribes. Since it does not appear that all older men held a recognized position, certain ones may have been chosen because of their reputation as wise men or counselors. This would serve as a background in Num. 11:16-17 where 70 elders were specially chosen to assist Moses with general administrative concerns. There the elders were endowed with the Spirit for this ministry. This same Hebrew word *zāqēn* is used in the plural in Lev. 9:1 and also in the singular (Lev. 19:32), the latter in the context of honoring those who are old. [*zāqēn*]

4:20 They will be forgiven (*wĕnislaḥ lāhem*)—Literally "and it will be forgiven to them," the verb *slḥ* means "to forgive or pardon." Throughout the OT this word is used only of an action of God, never of a person forgiving another. In Leviticus it is always used in the passive (Niphal) stem with the meaning "will be forgiven" (here, Lev. 4:26, 31, 35; 5:10, 13, 16, 18; 6:7 [5:26 MT]; 19:22). The direct object is always singular (i.e., "forgiven *to him/her*") except for here where the object is plural (i.e., "forgiven to *them*"). This term focuses on one of the great theological concepts in Scripture—forgiveness from God. Closely connected with the concepts of "atonement" (see Lev. 1:4) and "shedding of blood" (see Lev. 1:5), forgiveness seems to be stated as accomplished by the proper sacrifices when offered in the proper attitude. Although the attitude is not dealt with in much of the legislation in the Pentateuch (see however Lev. 16:29, 31), this was assumed and is clearly dealt with by the prophets (e.g., Hos. 6:6; Mic. 6:6-8; Isa. 1:11-15; Mal. 1:6-14). Such a bold statement of forgiveness causes an apparent conflict with Heb. 9:9 and 10:4 that seems to deny the efficacy of the OT sacrifices. The solution seems to lie best in regarding the OT sacrifices as efficacious for the worshiper, although objectively the basis of that forgiveness would be revealed later on to be the sacrificial death of Christ (see *kipper* ["make atonement"] Lev. 1:4). The worshiper had every reason to believe, on the basis of proper sacrifice given in proper attitude, that he was forgiven just as the LORD had announced to the nation in two of their bleakest moments (Exod. 34:9; Num. 14:19-20). This claim of forgiveness will be made repeatedly in Leviticus (here, 4:26, 31, 35; 5:10, 13, 16, 18; 19:22). An Israelite could obtain divine pardon and live in freedom and fellowship with his God. [*slḥ*]

4:22 When a leader sins (*nāśî'*)—The Hebrew word *nāśî'* is uncertain in precise meaning though it is used over 130x in the OT (but just this once in Leviticus). Though translators agree that the term refers to a leader or prince, just what defines such a person is debated. D. J. Wiseman [*Bibliotheca Sacra*, 134, 1977: 228-37] argues that this term could describe a "second-in-command" such as a deputy governor or subordinate leader (Exod. 16:22). There is no definite article with the noun in its context in Leviticus so this could suggest a more general, rather than specific, reference. Its root meaning is "lifted up" and is used to refer to various leaders (i.e., Exod. 22:28 [22:27 MT]; Num. 2:3; 3:24, 30; 1 Kings 11:34; Ezek. 12:10). Because of its use in Numbers "tribal leader" is often suggested, but in other references it is used of the king of the

restored nation. The context would indicate that this person must be subordinate in status to the anointed priest but his status in relationship to the "elders" is unknown. [*nāśî'*]

4:27 If a member of the community (*mē'am hā'āreṣ*)—The Hebrew phrase translates literally "from one of the people of the land." The Israelites were people of the land in the sense that they were within the territory of the Promised Land and under the regulations that ruled their conduct there. This must refer to the common people in contrast to a "leader" who has been dealt with in the previous context. This is a relatively rare phrase in the Pentateuch (see Gen. 23:7, 12-13; Exod. 5:5; Lev. 20:2, 4; Num. 14:9) and here it anticipates the conquest and settlement of the land of promise. The noun *'ereṣ* ("earth, land" [*BDB*, 75]) is used 82x in Leviticus and refers both to the surface upon which people, animals, and most vegetation have as their dwelling (as opposed to the sea or the air) and also to the specific territory God gave to Israel. The Abrahamic Covenant had as one of its essential promises the land (Gen. 12:7). This land that God gave to his people was not intrinsically holy but became sanctified because of God's presence and promises. Since God made the entire world, all peoples living on earth have a responsibility to answer to him. But in a special way, as privilege increased in the gift of the land so did responsibility for the Israelites. In Lev. 18:25 *'ereṣ* is personified and the curse of the people becomes part of the responsibility of the land. The land itself will respond in such a manner as to bring judgment on those living in the land. These curses are more specifically developed in Lev. 26 and Deut. 28. Lev. 4:27-28 deals with the occasion that a "person of the land" has sinned and must seek forgiveness. Ultimately, the nation would find itself unwilling and unable to maintain a lifestyle pleasing to the LORD while living in the land he gave them. However, in Lev. 26:42 God promises that although the nation would be exiled (Lev. 26:33) and the land become desolate (Lev. 26:35), he would not forget his promises to Abraham, Isaac, and Jacob but would renew the land (Deut. 30:5, 9). [*'ereṣ*]

5:1 A public charge (*qôl 'ālâ*)—The syntactical construction of the first few verses of Lev. 5 is rather complicated and stands in contrast to the rather simplistic construction of the material up to now. This sin, while not committed "unintentionally" (see Lev. 4:2), seems to be treated as such. "A public charge" is literally "a voice of an oath." It refers here to the solemn testimony that would be given in court "under oath." If a person heard this "voice" and did not object when it conflicted with that which he had seen or learned about then he was guilty of a sin that required the sin offering. While normally this word for oath was used in the context of covenant promises it is used again in Prov. 29:24 in a very similar manner to its use here in Lev. 5:1. [*'ālâ*]

Held responsible (*wĕnāśā'*)—The phrase "he shall carry [his guilt]" is an official pronouncement of culpability. The phrase uses the two Hebrew terms *nāśā'* and *'awôn*. The latter will be dealt with below. The verb *nāśā'* ("lift, carry, take") [*BDB*, 669] is used hundreds of times in the OT to indicate a literal action. It is also used figuratively in many cases as it is here. Its use as the bearing or carrying of guilt or the punishment of sin begins in Gen. 4:13 with Cain. The expressions "he will be held responsible" or "he will bear his iniquity" occur fre-

quently (e.g., Lev. 5:17; 7:18). This idea leads to the concept of bearing the guilt of another by representation or substitution (Lev. 10:17) [W. Kaiser, TWOT, 2:601]. In Lev. 16:22 the sins of the nation, represented by the high priest, were confessed and symbolically transferred to the goat so that it might symbolically carry off the sins from the camp. This is a clear picture of both substitution and removal. In Isa. 53:11 it is declared that the Servant "will bear their iniquities." Clearly this is substitutionary atonement by the Messiah. [*nś'*]

Held responsible (*'ăwônô*)—As stated above, the phrase "he shall carry his guilt" is an official pronouncement of culpability. It was used earlier in the Pentateuch in Exod. 28:43 and 34:7, also in Lev. 5:17; 17:16, and later in Num. 14:18; 18:23. It is a statement that suggests there will be no "overlooking" of this action since in at least two of the references above it is used to refer to the responsibility being upon the "third and fourth generations." The term here, which can be translated "iniquity, guilt, or punishment" (*BDB*, 730), is a collective noun and although it occurs in the plural (e.g., Lev. 16:22) it often is used in the singular of more than an individual sin (e.g., Lev. 16:21). It occurs 18x in Leviticus and denotes both the deed(s) (e.g., Lev. 26:40) and the consequence (Lev. 5:17). The fact that it is often difficult to separate the deed from the consequence (both the internal condemnation and external punishment) demonstrates that for the Hebrew person these concepts were seen synthetically and not as radically separate thoughts as is more prevalent today.

In Lev. 10:17, the term is used in an expression ("it was given to you to take away the guilt of the community") that occurred after Aaron's sons had completely burned the portion of meat that was given to them to eat as priests. While "guilt" is a literal translation of the Hebrew text, the concept that could be derived from such words could be misunderstood. Nowhere in the Levitical ritual is the act of eating the sin offering (which was the concern of Moses here) equated with atonement. Rather, the implication seems to be that Aaron's sons had not eaten the priestly portion of the sin offering, which (i.e., the sin offering) had been given for atonement (cf. Lev. 10:12-15). The concept of carrying away guilt is developed in Lev. 16:22 where the goat is said to do such a thing. In Lev. 16:21, in the description of the substitutionary atonement on the Day of Atonement, three synonyms for transgressions against God are used (including *'āwôn*) in an effort to demonstrate the totality of the atonement. In Lev. 26:40-41 it is clear that *'āwôn* by the nation brings national separation from God. [*'āwōn*]

5:2 Anything ceremonially unclean (*bĕkol dābār ṭāmē'*)—The adjective *ṭāmē'* ("unclean") is used in the expression to mean literally "an unclean thing" and in the context refers to that which makes a worshiper unacceptable for cultic ceremony. Personal uncleanness in Leviticus is ritual uncleanness, not external filth or dirt. Being ceremonially unclean resulted in a person's being excluded from normal participation in religious acts. The verb *ṭm'* and its associated adjective and nouns occur approximately 132x in Leviticus out of the 279 occurrences in the OT. In Lev. 10:10 the unclean is contrasted to the clean (*haṭṭāhôr*). Through this system of laws of clean and unclean, the Israelites were reminded at every meal of their redemption to be God's people, to be holy as opposed to the unholy Gentiles. Their diet was restricted in imitation of God

who had restricted his choice among the nations to Israel. It reminded them of their responsibilities to be a holy nation, a nation whose way of life must be characterized by purity and integrity. In the NT food is regarded as symbolic of the division between Jew and Gentile, and the Laws' abolition under the New Covenant. Later on in Leviticus certain animals and foods were considered unclean by their nature (i.e., specific characteristics; see Lev. 11). People and objects could become unclean by the acts of birth (Lev. 12), diseases and mildew (Lev. 13–14), bodily emissions including menstruation (Lev. 15), certain sexual relations (Lev. 18:20, 23), contact with a dead body, and finally through certain misdeeds (e.g., use of spiritists or mediums, Lev. 19:31). Most of these categories are given in great detail in Lev. 11–15. The Scriptures seldom give the basis for declaring something unclean although many such laws are associated with the holiness of God. Certainly some laws are associated with contagious disease and death, and in such cases there was provision for a quarantine to protect the health of the nation. Others seem to be based on what is not "normal" and that which is aesthetically repulsive. The act of touching a corpse, as in the context here, does not make the person immoral or sinful, just ceremonially disqualified for participation. This uncleanness is something that he has become aware of at a later time since the next verse comments on the fact that the unclean was present "even though he is unaware of it." The uncleanness became a sin if the person failed to deal with it properly. Here the person was unaware of his/her uncleanness and now a sin offering was needed to atone for the contamination caused by this neglect. The sin offering (see Lev. 4:3) was the means for removing such uncleanness.

The reference here and again in Lev. 7:21 to "unclean" as well as the important verse of Lev. 10:10 allows one to see that the section of chapters 11–15 is to be firmly integrated into the book of Leviticus. and not treated as an independent section. In Lev. 12:2 *ṭāmē'* is used in the context of childbirth. Bearing children is part of the creation mandate (Gen. 1:28) and yet the bearing of children made the wife unclean in the OT (see Lev. 15:18 for the fact that intercourse made both the husband and wife unclean). The period of uncleanness (seven days) was second only to that of uncured skin diseases in chapters 13–14. Yet childbearing was regarded as greatly desired (Lev. 26:9; Deut. 28:11; Ps. 127:3-5) and childlessness was considered a great misfortune (see Gen. 15:2; 1 Sam. 1) or even as a judgment of God (Lev. 20:20; Deut. 28:18). This demonstrates that ceremonial uncleanness was not a sinful condition unless it was not dealt with according to the law. In Lev. 13:45 the precautions associated with an infectious skin disease involved verbal warnings, the wearing of mournful clothing, hair left in disarray, the lower part of the face kept covered, and isolation from the rest of society (cf. Lev. 10:6 for tearing of clothes, a sign of grief and mourning). The person with an infectious disease was to cry the very words "Unclean! Unclean!"

In Lev. 15:31 the terse statement, "so they will not die in their uncleanness," gives the purpose for the laws pertaining to normal and abnormal genital discharges and emissions and focuses the worshiper on the necessity of coming to God with absolute purity of soul and body. The word for "uncleanness" is the Hebrew noun *ṭumě'â* which is used 14x in Leviticus. Normally sexual processes made persons unclean but not sinful. "Uncleanness establishes boundaries of action, but as long as these are not transgressed no guilt is incurred" [Wenham, *Leviticus*, 220].

Lev. 18:20 uses the verb *ṭm'* ("be or become unclean") when the man is said to be defiled or unclean because of a sexual relationship with his neighbor's wife. This, of course, was not the only consequence of such an action (see Lev. 18:17) but even if a man were not found out for his actions he was made aware that he was now ceremonially unacceptable. In Lev. 18:28 the expression "if you defile" occurs and refers to the various sexual practices outlawed in this chapter and practiced by the Canaanites who defiled the land and then found themselves without the land anymore (Lev. 18:25). In the NT Jesus denounced the hypocrisy of the Pharisees concerning their emphasis on uncleanness (Matt. 15:10-20; 23:25-28). In the Christian church all foods are declared clean (Acts 10:14-15) based on the fact that Christ has cleansed his people (John 13:8) and so now nothing external can defile them (1 Tim. 4:4-5). [*ṭāmē'*]

5:4 Takes an oath (*tiššāba'*)—This transgression, which required a sin offering for atonement, was something spoken. The verb occurs in this verse and another 3x in Leviticus (6:3 [5:22 MT], 5 [5:24 MT]; 19:12) always in the reflexive (Niphal) stem. As well as the verb, the noun form *šěbu'â* occurs here in Lev. 5:4. The consonants of the verb are identical to those of the cardinal number seven whose relationship may be suggested in Gen. 21:22-34. To utter an oath or to swear in the OT was to give an unbreakable word in testimony that the one making such an oath would faithfully perform some promised action, or that he would faithfully refrain from some agreed upon behavior. One could utter an oath by another, invariably by one who was greater and more powerful (e.g., 1 Kings

2:8) and therefore could enforce any violation of the oath. Lev. 19:12 contains the command not to swear falsely. This command occurs only here in Leviticus (cf. Lev. 6:3, 5). It implies that sometimes the Israelites took an oath in the name of the LORD and in such cases they were to be extremely careful not to swear falsely. To do so would not only bring the required judgment upon them for the falsehood but it would "profane the name" of the LORD God (see also Zech. 5:3-4). In Matt. 5:33-37 Christ appears to forbid all oaths as being unbiblical or ungodly. The resolution to this apparent contradiction between the laws of the OT and Christ's interpretation of these laws seems to lie in understanding that Christ was in fact only forbidding the casual swearing which led people into sin. Most Christians do not resist the taking of an oath in a courtroom setting but rather see this requirement to always tell the truth as being the standard for the believer even when an oath is not required. This is equivalent to the standard found in Leviticus on oath-taking. For the concept of profaning the name of the LORD see Lev. 18:21; for the concept of blaspheming the name of the LORD see Lev. 24:11. [*šāba'*]

Thoughtlessly (*lĕbaṭṭē'*)—The word translated "thoughtlessly" (an infinitive of *bṭ'* "speak rashly, thoughtlessly" [*BDB*, 104]) implies that the person may not have realized the full implications of what was being said in the oath. This verb is used twice here in Lev. 5:4 (in addition to the infinitive it occurs in the imperfect form) and in the rest of the OT it occurs only twice more. It is found as a participle in Prov. 12:18 and again in the imperfect in Ps. 106:33. The latter is a reference to the words of Moses when he sinned against the LORD (Num. 20:10-13). It does not have to have evil intent (see below) so the

emphasis here is on the lack of care taken before verbally uttering a promise or an oath. This is in keeping with the later pronouncement by Christ in the Sermon on the Mount (Matt. 5:33-37) [*bṭ'*] [*bāṭṭe'*]

To do good (*lĕhêṭîb*)—The two infinitives rendered "to do good" and "to do evil," which are reversed in the NIV translation from the order in the Hebrew text, are both verbs that in the intensive stem (Hiphil) denote totality or thoroughness. These two concepts of good and evil are juxtaposed in other places, too (e.g., Deut. 30:15; 2 Sam. 14:17; 1 Kings 3:9). The verb *yṭb* ("be good, well, glad, pleasing" [*BDB*, 405]) is often used of God's beneficent attitude and actions toward his people but here it is used of the action promised by an oath of an Israelite. The thoughtlessly uttered oath could, therefore, be a curse or a blessing (i.e., a promise) that ultimately he couldn't or shouldn't fulfill.

The verb occurs again in Lev. 10:19, 20. The literal "it was acceptable [good] in his eyes" indicates that the explanation offered by Aaron was found to be valid. The use of the verb in these verses concerns the attitude of both the Lord and then Moses to the action of Aaron and his sons in abstaining from eating the priestly food after the death of Nadab and Abihu. Aaron questions whether it would have been "pleasing" to the LORD to have eaten the meat, even though that is what the law provided, in light of the judgment that came upon his two children. The omission was not out of carelessness or defiance but was a conscious decision not to exercise a priestly right. Perhaps it was even an evidence of overly cautious behavior. When Moses understood the motive behind the noncompliance he, too, found it "good." The explanation given by Aaron apparently did not contradict the insistence by Moses that Aaron and his remaining sons show no outward grief or lack of acceptance of God's judgment (Lev. 10:6). This acceptance of Moses suggests that God is more gracious to those who conscientiously do not exercise a right because they fear him than to those who carelessly and impudently enter his presence, as Nadab and Abihu did. This is another example in the OT of the principle developed clearly by Jesus in Matt. 12:1-12 (see also Luke 6:1-9) that obedience to the letter of the law is not always the obedience God requires. [ytb]

To do evil (lĕhāraʿ)—The term here ("be evil, bad" [BDB, 949]) is a denominative verb found only here in Leviticus. Used in the combination of "good or evil" these two infinitives denote totality or thoroughness (see above). The root can have either passive or active implications: "misfortune" or "wickedness." It can also occur in profane or moral contexts: "bad" or "evil" (G. Livingston, TWOT, 2:854). In the context of the oath offered in Lev. 5:4 that was done "thoughtlessly," it is clear that the verb, referring perhaps to a curse or at least a commitment to do or bring about misfortune or evil, must be taken care of by the presentation of a sin offering. [rʿʿ]

5:5 Confess (wĕhitwaddāh)—The word ydh (which means "throw, cast" in its basic form [BDB, 392]) is used 3x in Leviticus, all in the Hithpael stem that denotes an intensive, reflexive action. The verb in the causative stem (Hiphil) can mean "confess, praise, give thanks, thank." The common element in these variants is that there is a recognition or declaration of a fact. "Confess" is the proper meaning when the fact is a "bad" one (e.g., Num. 5:7) while "praise or thanks" would be appropriate when the fact is a "good" one

(e.g., Gen. 29:35). Here in Lev. 5:5 the person is to confess (intensive action) about what he himself (reflexive action) has done. Confession is needed here because the time has passed for handling the situation in the initially required manner (testifying in court, following purity rules, or fulfilling an oath). In Lev. 16:21 the Hithpael form (intensive, reflexive) also occurs when this verb is used to convey the confession of national sin (Lev. 16:21; 26:40; see also Dan. 9:4, 20; Ezra 10:1; Neh. 1:6; 9:2-3). On the Day of Atonement the high priest was to state intensively and reflexively the "wickedness and rebellion of the Israelites" (see Lev. 16:21b). [ydh]

5:6 Penalty for the sin (ʾăšāmô)—This Hebrew term is used in Lev. 5:15b and following for the offering often called "the guilt offering." The vast majority of its uses refer to this particular offering. However, since this offering has not yet been explained and because birds were never offered as a guilt offering, it seems preferable to translate this as "penalty" (as in the NIV) or "reparation" both here and in Lev. 5:7, 15a. It denotes the liability to penalty rather than the means by which the sin can be atoned. The verb and related derivatives are used extensively (38x) in Leviticus in these two related ways: first of penalty and second of the offering used for that penalty called the "guilt offering." The context must determine the proper rendering. The cognate ʾašāmâ "guilt" occurs in Lev. 4:3; 6:5, 7 [5:24, 26 MT]; 22:16. In Gen. 26:10 Abimelech refers to a possible sin and its resulting "guiltiness" or "liability" (ʾāšām). In Lev. 5:15a, if someone deceived another in a transaction, the perpetrator was required not only to sacrifice a ram for the sin, but also to repay the loss with 20 percent "interest" (see Lev. 5:16). Besides the occurrences here in Lev. 5:6, 7, 15a, which are best translated "penalty," the other 22 usages of this noun in Leviticus mean "sin offering" as well as its occurrences in Num. 5:7-8; 6:12; 18:9; 1 Sam. 6:3-4, 8, 17; 2 Kings 12:16; Ezek. 40:39; 42:13; 44:29; 46:20 and Isa. 53:10. Only in Ps. 68:21 [68:22 MT] and Prov. 14:9 would the term not be considered a guilt or sin offering (G. Livingston, TWOT, 1:79).

In Lev. 5:15 this offering is closely connected with the "sinning unintentionally" in regard to the LORD's "holy things" (see below) or, in the following verses, the sin of trespassing on the property of others in the covenant nation (Lev. 6:1-5 [5:20-24 MT]). When dealing with such a sin, there must be an offering and as well a restitution of property plus one-fifth of its value as a fine. In this offering there is no application of the blood of the guilt offering to the altar (as in the sin offering) since the sin was primarily against a person and therefore guilt was expiated, not by blood on the altar, but by compensation given to the wronged person or his representative. This word is used in Isa. 53:10 where the suffering servant has the LORD "make his life a guilt offering." He became a "guilt offering" because he was estranged, desecrated, and removed from the nation. The term is used for the guilt offering in Lev. 5; 6:10; 7; 14; 19:21, 22. Outside Leviticus it is a relatively rare term used for this particular offering only in the verses listed above. It is the term used by the Philistines for the restitution they sought to make for removing the ark from Israel (1 Sam. 6:3, 4, 8, 17). In Lev. 14:12 this blood offering allowed the person to once again be part of the "kingdom of priests, a holy nation" (Exod. 19:6) from which he had been "expelled" due to his contamination. A main purpose of the guilt offering was to make atonement for desecration of the LORD's "holy

things" (see Lev. 5:15). It is associated here with the reconsecration of the LORD's "holy people." The entire process employed here is reminiscent of the ritual enacted at the consecration of the Aaronic priests (Lev. 8:22-30). ['āšām]

5:10 In the prescribed way (*kammišpāṭ*)— The term for "prescribed way" is *mišpāṭ* (translated "law" or "manner" in the KJV) but it is not the usual term for "law" or "torah." Rather, this term comes from a verb (*špṭ*) meaning "judge, govern" (*BDB*, 1047). Culver suggests that in the OT there may be as many as 13 related, but distinct, aspects of this Hebrew word, all related to the concept of "justice" (R. Culver, TWOT, 2:948-49). The noun first appears here in Leviticus, but when it is used in the plural it is often translated "ordinances, laws" (cf. Lev. 18:4). It is used as a noun 14x in Leviticus and except for here and 9:16 is used only in chapters 18–20 and 24–26. It carries here the idea of doing the sacrifice according to the lawful, prescribed manner. When speaking of God's reign and relationship with his creatures, the term is frequently allied with the concept of righteousness using the Hebrew words *ṣedeq* and *ṣĕdāqâ*. In Leviticus, when used in the plural, the word is always in parallel to *ḥōq* (see Lev. 18:4), translated "decrees" (9x; 18:4, 5, 26; 19:37; 20:22; 25:18; 26:15, 43, 46). The Israelites must understand that because God is who he is, his instructions must be followed in his prescribed way in order to live righteously. [*mišpāṭ*]

5:15 Commits a violation (*tim'ōl ma'al*)— The verb and object used in the phrase "commits a violation" both come from the root *m'l*, which carries the meaning of "unfaithful, treacherous." It is a verb and noun used in combination 3x in Leviticus (here, 6:2 [5:21 MT], 26:40). The noun *ma'al* is used as this cognate accusative to the verb 17 other times in the OT (e.g., Num. 5:6, 27; Josh. 22:20). Here it is used in the context of priestly duties, "commits a violation . . . in regard to the holy things"; in Lev. 6:2 (5:21 MT) the verb and noun are again used and the sin is defined as "unfaithful to the LORD." It is a word that denotes a breach of faith in regard to a revealed command. The person has acted unfaithfully by violating the boundary between the common and the holy. Here in Lev. 5:15 the exact nature of the violation in regard to the holy things is not specified. It may refer to the eating of holy food, the failure to fulfill a dedicatory vow, or the failure to present the full and proper tithe. In each of these violations a compensation would be possible (see below). It is specifically to just such sins—those for which restoration is possible—that the guilt offering is applicable. In other places this term is used of a wide variety of serious sins such as adultery (Num. 5:12, 27), worshiping pagan gods (Num. 31:16; Ezek. 20:27), Achan's sin of taking the dedicated booty (Josh. 7:1), Uzziah's sin of offering incense in the temple (2 Chron. 26:16, 18), and marrying foreigners (Ezra 10:2, 10). [*m'l*]

A **ram** from the flock (*'ayil*)—Only a ram, that is, a male sheep or lamb, could be offered for the guilt offering (see also Lev. 14:12 [here *'ayil* is not used but rather the masculine noun *keśeb* ("male lamb")]; 19:21-22; Num. 5:8). This restriction to one particular animal for a specific sacrifice is unique in the OT sacrificial system. The ram is mentioned prominently in the Scriptures and is noted by its characteristics as leader of the flock (Ezek. 34:17, 21), its valuable wool (2 Kings 3:4), and its tasty meat (Gen. 31:38). A ram was one of the animals used at the institution of the Abrahamic Covenant (Gen. 15:9) and a ram was the LORD's provision at the sacrifice of Isaac (Gen. 22:13). It should be noted that the ram was ineligible to be offered as a sin offering (Lev. 4:1–5:13; 6:24-30 [6:17-23 MT]). While this is the first use of this noun in Leviticus, it occurs a total of 22x in this book, especially in chapters 8–9 in connection with the ordination of the priests to their ministry. Because of its characteristics and restricted use in the sacrificial system for the guilt offering, the presentation of a ram would be viewed as memorable to both the person offering it and to the other observers. [*'ayil*]

Of the proper value (*bĕ'erkĕkā*)—The Hebrew phrase can be translated literally "valued by you in shekels of silver" but is obscure in its meaning. The parallel phrase in Lev. 5:18 and 6:6 (5:25 MT) is just the phrase used here "of the proper value" or "valued by you." It may be possible that the phrase here in Lev. 5:18 is to indicate that in the unusual circumstance that a man could not bring a ram he had to bring the equivalent amount of silver instead (see E. A. Speiser, *Oriental and Biblical Studies*, 124-28). As mentioned above, no other animal could substitute for it, nor, if this phrase refers to the equivalent amount in silver, could the penalty (see Lev. 5:15) be reduced. It is unclear from this verse how much a shekel was worth; the most that can be said is that a ram was worth at least two shekels since the plural is used. [*'ērek*]

5:16 He must make restitution (*yeṣallēm*)—The ram offered as a penalty (see Lev. 5:14) must be accompanied by an action that in the intensive stem used here can mean "complete, finish, make compensation, recompense, etc." (*BDB*, 1022). In addition to the sacrifice of the guilt offering (see Lev. 5:6), the worshiper had to rectify the situation by making restitution for the value of the sin committed plus 20 percent. The sins dealt with by the guilt offering are "sinning unintentionally in regard to the LORD's holy things" (Lev. 5:15) or, in the following verses, the sin of trespassing on the property of others in the covenant nation (Lev. 6:1-5 [5:20-24 MT]). The "unidentified sin" of Lev. 5:17, specified only as "what is forbidden in any of the LORD's commands," must be taken as a sin that requires restitution and for which restitution is possible. Cognate to the verb is the noun *šālôm* which is among the most important theological words in the OT. Here in Leviticus the ram and additional payment would function to bring about *šālôm* or wholeness to the worshiper in his relationship with the LORD. [*šlm*]

6:2 [5:21 MT] Deceiving (*wĕkaḥēš*)—This verb for deception is used 3x in Leviticus (here, Lev. 6:3 [5:22 MT], 19:11; all in the intensive [Piel] stem). It is used with its derivatives a total of 29x in the OT though in the Pentateuch it is used elsewhere only in Gen. 18:15 and Deut. 33:29. In the next verse it is translated by the English verb "lie" as well as in Lev. 19:11 though in the latter reference it is followed by the verb *šqr*, which is translated "deceive." The unifying idea seems to be "to disappoint" and thus "to deceive, fail, grow lean" (*BDB*, 471). It is used in Leviticus with the idea of dealing falsely with someone, here in deceiving someone in a matter of deposit or security and in the next verse in lying about something he has found. [*kḥš*]

6:9 [6:2 MT] <u>Give</u> Aaron and his sons (*ṣaw*)—The verb used is *ṣwh*, which in the intensive (Piel) stem used here means "lay

charge [upon], give charge [to], charge, command, order" (*BDB*, 845). Because of the use of *tôrâ* in the immediate context (see below) it is not translated by the strong term "command" or "order" as it usually is in Leviticus (e.g., Lev. 7:36; 13:54; 14:4) but rather by the more generic term "give." However, in doing so the strong sense of authority should not be ignored. The verb is used 33 other times in Leviticus, the majority of which are translated by the verb "command." This second instruction of the offerings especially relates to certain priestly duties and privileges. In Lev. 27:34 the verb is again used, this time with the Hebrew plural noun for commands. Although this term can be used of human commandments, the context here clearly shows them to be of God (cf. Lev. 4:2), given while Moses was on Mount Sinai. [*ṣwh*]

6:9 [6:2 MT] This command (*zō't tôrat*)—This is the first use in Leviticus (of 16x) of the familiar word "torah." In the NT its Greek equivalent can be used as synonymous with the entire Pentateuch (cf. Matt. 5:17; 11:13; 22:40; Luke 24:44; Acts 13:15; Rom. 3:21) but its usage here is not that broad. Here the demonstrative pronoun "this" restricts the use of the noun to the regulations following, which concern the burnt offering (Lev. 6:8-13). This use of "torah" with the demonstrative pronoun "this" occurs again in Lev. 6:14, 25; 7:1, 11, 37; 11:46; 12:7; 13:59; 14:2, 32, 54, 57; 15:32. In all these references the usage appears to be restricted to the specific laws being presented in context. The Hebrew term "torah" actually comes from the verb *yrh* "to teach" (KBL, 403) and thus "torah" conveys the primary idea of instruction through regulations.

In Lev. 7:37 the word (translated "regulations") is used to summarize the 6:8

[6:1 MT]–7:36 section of Leviticus (not the entire text of Lev. 1–7) since the word has been used only in Lev. 6:9 [6:2 MT], 14 [7 MT], 25 [18 MT]; 7:1, 7, 11, and here in 7:37. It is not used again until Lev. 11:46. These instructions that make up this specific command are related to the five offerings already developed in Lev. 6–7 and in addition the ordination offering (see below). It should be noted that verses 37-38 are written in a unique format that lists the various offerings and so functions like a colophon of a Mesopotamian tablet that contains such information that in modern culture is placed "up-front," perhaps on a title page (R. Harrison, *Leviticus*, 84). This would encourage this particular section of Leviticus to be kept as a unit and perhaps memorized by the priests so that they would know the exact priestly requirements and priestly privileges for the offerings. [*tôrâ*]

The fire must be kept burning on the altar (*tûqad*)—This point is made 3x in Leviticus: 6:9, 12, 13 [6:2, 5, 6 MT]. Historically the first burnt offerings in the tabernacle were lit with a fire from heaven (Lev. 9:24; cf. 2 Chron. 7:1). While it is never explained why the fire must be kept burning continually, it appears that the uninterrupted fire for the burnt offering would be a visible sign reflecting the uninterrupted worship of the LORD. In Deut. 32:22 it is used, not of the LORD's holiness, but of his anger and judgment. Later in the Prophets this verb again is used in this negative manner to express disgust or the unrelenting anger of the LORD (e.g., Isa. 65:5; Jer. 15:14). [*yqd*]

7:8 Its hide (*'ôr hā'ōlâ*)—Speaking in context of the priest who offers the guilt offering and is allowed to eat it, this verse reintroduces the burnt offering and regulates that the priest who offers the burnt offering may keep the hide for himself (see Lev. 1:3). The term (literally "the skin of the burnt offering") refers to the hide of the animal, which according to Lev. 1:3-17 could be a bull, sheep or goat, or dove or pigeon. Obviously the phrase would be appropriate only for that which came from the herd or flock (Lev. 1:2). This payment for services reflected the time and energy needed for the priest to make this offering. [*'ôr*]

7:12 As an expression of thankfulness (*'al-tôdâ*)—This is the first of three stated reasons why a fellowship offering could be given (cf. v. 16 for vow and freewill) but the exact translation for this reason is not simple. The noun is used 32x in the OT but only 4x in Leviticus (here, Lev. 7:13, 15; 22:29) and nowhere else in the Pentateuch. This word is never used as an expression of thanks between two people so it must be at least slightly different in meaning from the English word "thanks." It is used elsewhere with the idea of the acknowledgment or confession of sin (e.g., Josh. 7:19) but that does not fit the context here. Secondly, the verb form is used elsewhere to convey man's praise of man, the confession of some truth about another (Ps. 49:18 [49:19 MT]). Thirdly, it is also used to express a person's public acknowledgment or declaration of God's attributes and works (R. Alexander, TWOT, 1:364-65). This is an act of praise and is the most common use of the term. In the context of Leviticus the third of these meanings is most appropriate since the worshiper is presenting to God an offering, not for sin but for praise and worship. In the Psalms a thank offering will be given for deliverance from illness (Ps. 116:17), from trouble (Ps. 107:22), and from death (Ps. 56:13 [56:13 MT]). The exact reason for his praise and confession of God's character or God's blessing is not given, but the means to express it is what the fellowship offering is all about. The fourth and final use of the word in Leviticus occurs in 22:29. An expression of thanks was one of the reasons for offering a fellowship offering, and this passage expresses the regulation concerning the time limit involved. Part of the Israelites' fellowship with God was acknowledging and declaring God's great attributes and actions using an expression of thankfulness. [*tôdâ*]

7:15 Must be eaten (*yēʾākēl*)—This aspect of the fellowship offering, that is, eating, was not detailed in Lev. 3:1-17 where the fellowship offering was first described. It is implied in that passage by specifying what part was to be burned by fire (Lev. 3:3-4, 9-10, 14-15) and by the fact that the blood and fat could not be eaten (Lev. 3:17). Lev. 7 specifies how quickly the animal must be eaten. Using the Niphal (simple, passive) imperfect, the necessity of eating the meat is declared. The significance of eating in God's presence (Deut. 12:7) is never detailed but it must have made this occasion a particularly joyful and memorable one. In the OT, when a covenant was ratified or a divine promise given, a meal could take place (e.g., Judg. 6:18-19; cf. 2 Sam. 6:19). In the NT "table fellowship" among believers is extremely important, but the greatest time of eating is spoken of as "the wedding supper of the Lamb" in Rev. 19:9 when the bride of Christ, the church, is joined to Christ for all eternity. The fellowship of the OT believers at the tabernacle in their fellowship offerings gives a small but valid picture of being in God's presence with peace and joy. [*ʾkl*]

7:16 A vow (*neder*)—This noun ("vow, vow offering") is used 7x in Leviticus (here, Lev.

22:18, 21, 23; 23:38; 27:2, 8). It can be used of either the vow or the sacrifice offered for a vow. Here it represents the thing offered, not the vow itself. In fact, in most cases the biblical context (e.g., Deut. 23:21 [23:22 MT]) demonstrates that "the vow implies a promised gift for sacrifice, not merely a course of action as is implied in the English word 'vow'" (L. Coppes, TWOT, 2:557). This vow offering, as an act of thanksgiving, will be made in the future kingdom as part of the festivals (Nah. 1:15 [2:1 MT]). In Lev. 27:2, unlike Lev. 7:16, *neder* represents the vow itself. [*neder*]

A freewill offering (*nĕdābâ*)—This word occurs 26x in the OT and denotes that which is offered voluntarily. It is sometimes a synonym of *neder* (see above) though the vow offering seems to be the result of a previous commitment (e.g., a vow that was made during time of distress). The freewill offering is made, not out of requirement, but out of devotion (e.g., Exod. 35:29). Both of these terms, along with the offering given as "an expression of thankfulness" (see above Lev. 7:12), are used as a species of the fellowship offering though in Lev. 22:18 they are also part of the burnt offering used to fulfill a vow or as a freewill offering. [*nĕdābâ*]

7:18 Credited (*yēḥāšēb*)—The verb *ḥšb* ("think, account") [BDB, 362] in the passive (Niphal) stem suggests that the person is be thought, or reckoned, or accounted according to a judgment. This verb appears over 120x in the OT and has at least six variations of the basic thought of "think, account" (L. Wood, TWOT, 1:330). But only 6x (three in the basic [Qal] stem and 3x in the passive [Niphal] stem) does it carry the idea of "imputed" or "to make a judgment" [L. Wood, TWOT, 1:330]. In Lev. 7:18 an offering is not credited to the one who offers it if it is eaten after the second day. In Lev. 17:4 the person is declared "guilty of bloodshed." The word *dām* ("bloodshed") used in this expression is the common word used for "blood" (see Lev. 1:5) and is here translated "bloodshed" to imply the conscious taking of life. [*ḥšb*]

Impure (*piggûl*)—This word ("foul thing, refuse") [BDB, 803] is used in only three other passages, once more in Leviticus (19:7), and also in Isa. 65:4 and Ezek. 4:14. It is a technical term for meat that is unacceptable to eat, either because it has not been eaten within three days (as in Leviticus) or because it is from an unclean animal (as in Isaiah and Ezekiel). In Exod. 16:19-28 God gave instructions for manna, which could not be kept overnight and then eaten except in preparation for the Sabbath. Perhaps in the land, when they no longer had manna, this regulation concerning the eating of the fellowship offering would be a reminder to continue to do things God's way if they desired God's blessing. Anything that was less than perfect because of spoilage did not reflect the standard God desired. [*piggûl*]

7:20 Must be cut off (*wĕnikrĕtâ*)—The phrase "that person shall be cut off or cut down" can be taken one of five ways: (1) that he will be executed by the community, (2) that God himself will cause him to die in some undisclosed manner, (3) that he will be excommunicated from worship at the sanctuary, (4) that he will be excommunicated from the community and the benefits it provides, or (5) his line will be terminated by barrenness among his descendants (i.e., extirpation). The verb *krt* in the Niphal or passive stem (as here) is best taken as the death penalty in view of Exod. 31:14 where this view is made clear

by the use of the synonym *môt*, which means "to die" (see Num. 15:32-36 for a historical implementation of this law). However, the fourth view is supported by the Laws of Hammurabi § 154 which provides for banishment in a similar case. In any case, there is no indication that restoration is possible. This judgment was also attached to various religious and sexual sins (Lev. 7:21, 25, 27; 17:4, 9, 10, 14; 18:29; 19:8; 20:3, 5, 6, 17, 18; 22:3; 23:29; 26:22, 30), sins that by their nature are hard for human judges to punish. In these cases, if it was impossible for human judges to discern the guilt unless the offender confessed his wrongdoing, the punishment may have been left to God to perform if the person was truly guilty. This warning would serve as a threat to the one who thought he had avoided justice. [*krt*]

7:21 Detestable thing (*šeqeṣ*)—This noun is used 9x in Leviticus (out of a total of 11x in the OT), always in reference to unclean or forbidden foods. In Lev. 11:10-12 the focus is on forbidden seafood, in Lev. 11:13 on unclean birds, in Lev. 11:20, 23 on winged insects, and in Lev. 11:41-42 on animals that were especially close to the ground. The noun signifies abhorrence because of the contamination of the one who eats such foods. The normal adjective for unclean in connection with food, and one that is often juxtaposed to *šeqeṣ* is *ṭāmē'* (e.g., Lev. 7:21; 11:43-44). However *šeqeṣ* signifies a more repugnant nuance than does the latter (M. Grisanti, NIDOTTE, 4:243). In Lev. 11, to ignore the food laws makes a man *šeqeṣ*, detestable, unclean, as specifically stated in 11:11. Later in the Pentateuch the verb form is used to describe the abhorrence of an idol (Deut. 7:26). This denominative verb, which occurs only in the intensive (Piel) stem, is used only 7x in the OT. In Leviticus it is used in 11:11, 13, 43; 20:25. They all denote loathing or being loathed due to unclean food. The cognate noun *šiqqûṣ*, used 20x in the OT, is absent in Leviticus. Tragically, there is evidence of the Israelites' ignoring the stipulations to remain separate from such food that would make them unclean (Isa. 66:17; Ezek. 8:10). [*šeqeṣ*]

7:30 Wave . . . as a wave offering (*lĕhānîp tĕnûpâ*)—The concept of "wave offering" comes from the action of the Hebrew verb *nwp*, "move to and fro, wave" (*BDB*, 631) used first in this verse. The exact action is unknown and suggestions have ranged from a movement toward the altar and back again in a horizontal motion symbolizing the giving of the offering by the worshiper and the reception of the offering by God, to a side-to-side motion, to a shaking motion (e.g., Isa. 19:16; 30:28). There are occasions when a literal waving motion appears to be impossible such as when the tribe of Levi was presented as a wave offering (Num. 8:11). Whatever the motion, the implication is that this item was presented to the LORD but would not be burned but rather used by someone designated by the LORD (i.e., the priests). Earlier on in the Pentateuch, this term was used as a general term referring to various gifts that were dedicated to God (e.g., Exod. 35:22). It is used later in Lev. 14:12, 24; 23:11, 12, 20. It is also used, as here, for the parts of the sacrifices that were designated for the officiating priest. It is never used to designate a nonmeat priestly portion. Here the breast is called a *tĕnûpâ* ("wave offering") but in v. 32 the right thigh is called a *tĕrûmâ* ("contribution"). [*nwp*]

7:31 The breast (*heḥāzeh*)—The giving of the prime parts of the sacrifice suggests a special provision of God for the priests who did the work of sacrificing. This breast consisted of that part of the fellowship offering designated the wave offering (see above), which, along with the right thigh called the contribution (see below and also Lev. 9:21), were the priest's portion (here, Lev. 10:14; Num. 6:20). [*ḥāzeh*]

7:32 Contribution (*tĕrûmâ*)—The Hebrew word can mean "contribution, offering [for sacred use]" and may come from a verb meaning "lifted off, separated" (*BDB*, 929). The verbal idea of lifting off or heaving has, in some English versions, given birth to the expression "heave offering." However this verb can also mean "to remove, to set aside" as a special contribution to the priest doing the work as here and in other ritual contexts. Used this way the word is roughly parallel to the term *tĕnûpâ* (see above). It is used again in a passage forbidding certain priestly relatives to eat of the priest's portion (Lev. 22:12). The right thigh is called a *tĕrûmâ* ("contribution") and in the next verse is referred to as the priest's "share" (see below). [*tĕrûmâ*]

7:33 As his [a] share (*lĕmānâ*)—This Hebrew word for the priest's portion or "share" is used twice in Leviticus, here and in 8:29. Although in these two places in Leviticus it is used specifically for the breast and right thigh of the fellowship offering, elsewhere in the OT it is not a technical term used just for the priestly portion of this offering since it is used for the portion of kings (2 Chron. 31:3), singers (Neh. 12:47), Levites (Neh. 13:10), and priests (2 Chron. 31:4). Here God specifically cares for those he has designated to minister in the ritual setting by providing for them from the offerings, notably the fellowship offering, brought by the worshipers. [*mānâ* or *mĕnāt*]

7:35 The portion (*mišḥat*)—The word translated "portion" is used twice in this verse and is the same word used for the anointing of Aaron and his sons in chapter 8 (see Lev. 8:2). In Lev. 7:35 alone in the Scriptures it is used with the meaning of "consecrated portion" and not with the noun for "oil" (*BDB*, 603). They are apparently designated like this because the verb for anoint (*mšḥ*) is used in the next verse and so by association the various priestly portions or shares are here designated as "the portion of the anointing" in the KJV or as in the NIV "the portion" (see Lev. 7:32, 33). It anticipates the anointing of Aaron and his sons in Lev. 8. There the "anointing oil" (*šemen hammišḥâ*) was a unique portion used only for the consecration of priests. Once the oil was applied, the priest was to be regarded by others and himself as one separated for the LORD's service. This anointing oil is mentioned 7x in Leviticus (Lev. 8:2, 10, 12, 30; 10:7; 21:10, 12). This special anointing of the priests would express to the nation of Israel the concept of the separation of God and all associated with him from the routine and unclean, and the priority of maintaining access to God by keeping the priest consecrated. [*mišḥâ*]

7:37 Ordination offering (*wĕlammillû'îm*)—The phrase used here contains the plural form of the noun *millû'*. It means "setting, installation" (*BDB*, 571) and while it can mean the placement or setting of stones (e.g., Exod. 25:7), it is used in Leviticus in a technical manner. Its meaning is related to the verb *ml'* in its Piel stem (*BDB*, 570-71). From the idea of "giving in full" it is used figuratively for "institute to a priestly office, consecrate" (e.g., Exod. 28:41; Lev. 8:33; 16:32; 21:10) [*BDB*, 570]. Here in Lev. 7:37, within a listing of the various offerings already detailed in Leviticus, the term occurs in such a way as to appear to be a separate, new offering. However, from the historical event of Exod. 29:1-35 and the parallel account in Lev. 8:14-36, it is clear that this term functions to include various offerings (i.e., sin offering, burnt offering, and "ram of ordination," Lev. 8:14, 18, 22) that were to be used on a specific occasion. It is used here in Leviticus to anticipate the next chapter and to designate the unique occasion when the various offerings were used to set apart the priests as unique ministers for the LORD (Lev. 8). [*millû'â*]

7:38 On Mount Sinai (*bĕhar sînāy*)—This first of four references in Leviticus to Mount Sinai (cf. 25:1; 26:46; 27:34) functions in this first summary statement (see Lev. 7:37) not only to designate the geographical place where these laws were given but to remind the readers of the covenant made there with its special promises, stipulations, and judgments. It is used in the same manner in the two final summary statements of Lev. 26:46 and 27:34. In Lev. 25:1 it functions slightly differently for there it is used as a contrast to a future time and place ("when you enter the land I am going to give you"). What follows there are the regulations of the various special years and feasts that would characterize their life in the Land of Promise. Theologically, Sinai has been of great significance within the OT and throughout the centuries to Judaism as the place where both the oral and written laws were given. It was at Sinai that the divine attributes of omnipotence and holiness were demonstrated with great effect. In the Song of Deborah the LORD is called "the One of Sinai" (Judg. 5:5; see also Ps. 68:8 [68:9 MT]). Later, Jerusalem was another physical place that carried with it certain theological concepts as

David brought the ark there (2 Sam. 6:17) and then Solomon built the temple that was filled with God's glory (1 Kings 8:10-11). In contrast, places like Sodom and Gomorrah are used throughout Scripture as a picture and reminder of wickedness (e.g., Isa. 1:9). [*har sînāy*]

8:7 The ephod (*hā'ēpōd*)—The priestly garments are detailed in Exod. 28 and 39. The term "ephod" is used 48x in all the OT but only here in Leviticus where it occurs twice. It is especially used of a garment made for the high priest that was worn on top of his long blue robe and under the breastplate much like an apron suspended from shoulder straps (Exod. 28:4, 6-14, 25-28; 29:5; 39:2-7). Other ephods were worn by the common priest (e.g., 1 Sam. 2:18; 22:18) and even by King David (2 Sam. 6:14). Twice, in times of distress, the will of the LORD was sought by David through means of the ephod of the priest (1 Sam. 23:9; 30:7). This apparently had reference to the Urim and Thummim, which were contained within the breastpiece attached to the ephod. Perhaps influenced by ephod of the high priest and its power to discern the divine will, in the time of the judges various ephods are mentioned. These were all used in conjunction with idolatry among God's covenant people (Judg. 8:27; 17:5; 18:14, 17, 20). What was given by God as a physical reminder of his leading of the nation was turned into an idolatrous item by sinful people. ['*ēpōd*]

8:8 The breastpiece (*haḥōšen*)—In Exod. 28:15 this breastplate is said to be fashioned "for making decisions." The Urim and Thummim were apparently the reason why the breastplate was designated "the breastplate of decision" (Exod. 28:29-30). While some feel that the Urim and Thummim are descriptive terms for the

12 stones of the breastplate, they appear to be distinct from them here (see below). The first-century Jewish historian Josephus assigned oracular characteristics to the 12 stones of the breastplate claiming they would shine when Israel was to be victorious in war (*Antiquities,* 3.8.9). Later Talmudic tradition suggests that God's glory would illuminate the various letters of the tribes engraved upon the stones in an order that would spell out a message (*Yoma,* 73, a-b). Besides there being no indication in Scripture that this occurred, 5 of the 22 letters in the Hebrew alphabet do not appear in these 12 tribal names. The breastplate was made from the same material as the ephod and was attached to the ephod by means of chains and gold rings at the four corners of the breastplate (Exod. 28:15-30; 29:5; 39:8-21). The 12 stones attached to it apparently represented the 12 tribes of Israel as the high priest went before the LORD. There must have been some nondescribed pocket in which the Urim and Thummim could be held (see below). [*ḥōšen*]

The Urim and Thummim (*hā'ûrîm . . . hattummîm*)—These Hebrew words are transliterations of two superlative plurals meaning "lights" and "perfections." The definite article is always used in relation to these terms until the postexilic period. The '*ûrîm* is mentioned only 4x in the Pentateuch (Exod. 28:30; here, Num. 27:21; Deut. 33:8). It is also mentioned once during the early monarchy (1 Sam. 28:6) and twice after the exile (Ezra 2:63; Neh. 7:65). The *tûmmîm* is combined with the '*ûrîm* 5x out of these seven (missing in Num. 27:21; 1 Sam. 28:6). These two items are never actually described in the Scriptures but appear to be stones or gems (or at least something that was tangible) that were placed within the breastplate of the high priest. They were intended as a means of divine guidance for the nation by means of the high priest (the breastplate is called in Exod. 28:15 a "breastplate for making decisions"). It is not known how Aaron and his successors used these items though they may have functioned as "yes" and "no" or "true" and "false" answers to questions put to the high priest. The two stones may have been engraved with symbols to distinguish the two or they may have been of two different colors. However, in 1 Sam. 28:6 the Urim is literally placed between the terms "dreams" and "prophets," which may suggest that there was a correspondingly personal revelation through the mind of the priest who wore the breastplate. A great difficulty in seeing the Urim and Thummim function merely as a form of lot oracle is that when a revelation was given by this means it was declared in the form of God speaking and often included more information than a mere positive or negative response to the question (e.g., 1 Sam. 10:22; 2 Sam. 5:23-24). It appears that the gift of prophecy was often part of this process of discernment. Perhaps the prophetic revelation was accompanied by a confirmatory sign using the Urim and Thummim in some manner. What is clear however, is that "the Urim and Thummim are characterized as belonging to God, who entrusted this revelatory means to Levi (Deut. 33:8) in the person of the high priest. The civil leader was expected to inquire of Yahweh through the high priest about all matters pertaining to the execution of his office [Num. 27:21]" (C. Van Dam, NIDOTTE, 1:330). Certainly the placement of the Urim and Thummim in the breastplate of the high priest who would represent the nation before the LORD would indicate that the high priest was to seek from the LORD God alone the answers to questions that were not possible to discern from the revelation already given to the nation by the LORD. ['ûrîm] [tummîm]

8:9 The turban (hammiṣnepet)—The turban is usually thought to have consisted of wound-up linen that covered the head (Exod. 28:4, 37, 39; 29:6; 39:31; Lev. 16:4). However, at least one lexicon suggests that it might be only a "turban-like headband" that was wound around the head but only covering the forehead area and not including the top of the head (HALOT II, 624). It is used twice in this verse and then again in Lev. 16:4. While head-coverings are never commanded for Hebrew men in the Scriptures, perhaps this practice of latter Judaism has some foundation in the turban worn by the priest as he appeared to serve at the tabernacle. In 1 Cor. 11:4 Christian men are specifically told not to pray or prophesy with the head covered. Unless one sees this requirement as part of the arrangements of the New Covenant (though the arguments of head-coverings in 1 Corinthians are based mostly on the creation account, not the Old Covenant or on custom) then it may be best to see the high priest as wearing a "turban-like headband" on which was fastened the gold plate, the sacred diadem (see below Lev. 8:9). [miṣnepet]

The sacred diadem (nēzer haqqōdeš)— The phrase can be translated "crown of holiness" or "sacred diadem" (for the concept of holiness in Leviticus see Lev. 2:3). Exod. 39:30 uses this same term; it is not found in Exod. 28:36-37 for the plate of the turban. The noun nēzer ("consecration, crown") [BDB, 634] is used twice in Leviticus, here and in 21:12. It is related to the verb nzr ("dedicate, consecrate") [BDB, 634]. It appears that the previously mentioned gold plate (ṣîṣ hazzāhāb) was a synonym to the sacred diadem and was attached to the turban (see above) by means of a blue cord and had written on it "Holy to the LORD" (Exod. 28:36-37; 39:30-31). The term ṣîṣ is literally "flower" and traditionally was thought to be a narrow band and hence the translation "plate." This article was of extreme importance since it served as both a reminder and a declaration that the high priest was the acceptable representative of Israel (Exod. 28:38). The verb nzr ("dedicate, consecrate") is used in Leviticus only in 15:31 and 22:2. When used in the Hiphil stem with the preposition min, as in Lev. 15:31, it can mean "keep sacredly separate" (BDB, 634). It occurs elsewhere in both verb and noun forms in Num. 6:2, 3, 5, 6, 12 when referring to the vows of a Nazirite whose separation was "to the LORD" and "from" the likes of wine, cutting of hair, and dead bodies. A related form (Niphal stem) with the preposition min is used in Lev. 22:2. Here the Levites were to treat with respect (literally, "to keep away from") the holy offerings when, according to context, they were ceremonially unclean (Lev. 22:3). This avoidance is translated by the attitude of treating with respect. The Israelites, as a nation, were to be kept from that which made them ceremonially unacceptable (cf. Hos. 9:10). This verse declares the reason for the laws that were given in the previous context. [nēzer]

8:10 The tabernacle (hammiškān)—This is the first use in Leviticus of this term. It occurs also in Lev. 15:31, 17:4, and 26:11. Up to now in Leviticus, the word used for the place where God met with his nation has been "tent of meeting" (see Lev. 1:1). The present term is related to the verb škn meaning "dwell, settle down, live among" (Exod. 29:45). The tabernacle is described

in detail in Exod. 25–31 and 35–40, an amazingly large amount of space that indicates the crucial nature of this structure. Moses anointed "the tabernacle and everything in it" so that it could become, paradoxically, the earthly dwelling place of the transcendent and omnipresent God. The glory of God that was on Mount Sinai and that now filled the tabernacle (Exod. 40:34) indicates there was continuity between the original giving of the law and the proper carrying out of the law in ritual. This same glory was about to appear once again to all the people after the consecration of the priests (see Lev. 9:23).

In Lev. 26:11 the NIV indicates that the Hebrew noun could be translated "my dwelling place" or "my tabernacle." This term is used in a unique way here. Earlier (Lev. 8:10; 15:31; 17:4) it is clear that it is used to refer to the physical, portable, collapsible place of worship that had been built at Mount Sinai as recorded in Exod. 36–40. Lev. 26:4-13 lists the blessings that the nation could expect in the land as a result of obedience to the law of the LORD. Obviously, the tabernacle would not be present in the land only when they were obedient since part of the purpose of the tabernacle was to allow restoration of fellowship after they had been disobedient. The dwelling place here must not be merely the external, portable place of worship but rather the living presence of God in blessing upon the obedient nation. This, of course, was what the tabernacle was to picture all along. [miškān]

8:23 The right (hayĕmānît)—The concept of the right (as opposed to the left; cf. Lev. 14:16) is used 20x in Leviticus in eight different verses in two different portions of chapters 8 and 14 (here, Lev. 8:24; 14:14, 16, 17, 25, 27, 28). The adjective yĕmānî ("right hand, right") [*BDB*, 412] is based on the denominative verb *ymn*, which is used only in the Hiphil stem and means "go to or choose the right, use the right hand" (*BDB*, 412). The right side may have been used since it was considered to be the more important and favored side (Gen. 48:18; Matt. 25:34, 41). Jacob gave the name Benjamin, "son of [my] right hand," to the last son of his favorite wife Rachel (Gen. 35:18). The idea of favor and strength being transmitted through the right hand of blessing is clearly seen in Gen. 48:14-20. Theologically, the figurative expression "the right hand of God" is important in the OT (e.g., Exod. 15:6, 12; Ps. 98:1; Isa. 41:10) as symbolizing the omnipotence and care of the LORD God. Christ is exalted to the right hand of the Father (Acts 2:33-35; Matt. 26:64) as fulfillment of Ps. 110:1 and as evidence of his acceptance by the Father. From here he will rule with power and might. Ps. 16:11 indicates that the believer will experience eternal pleasures at the right hand of God. [*yĕmānî*]

8:23 Ear (*'ōzen*)—The ear is a symbol of hearing and so with the blood of the ordination ram being placed on his ear the priest was now designated and ordained to listen to God. The word is used 6x in Leviticus (here, Lev. 8:24; 14:14, 17, 25, 28). That the eye, hand, and foot (Lev. 8:23) are symbols of the whole life is substantiated by the fact that these instructions are repeated in Lev. 14:14, 25 in the cleansing ritual of one who has experienced healing of a skin disease. He once again can participate wholly in life now that he has been healed. It is a case of a part standing for the whole (merism). [*'ōzen*]

9:1 On the eighth day (*bayôm haššĕmînî*)—The eighth day in Scripture has connotations both literal (i.e., this is the day after the seven days of ordination; see Lev. 8:33) and symbolic. The eighth day was the day of circumcision (Gen. 17:12; Lev. 12:3), which bound the generations of Israelites to the Abrahamic Covenant. It was on the eighth day that the Abrahamic Covenant took effect for the child and now it was the eighth day that the priests were confirmed in their dedicated role of serving before the LORD on behalf of the nation. It was another unique day since on this day the LORD appeared to them (Lev. 9:4, 23). [*šĕmînî*]

9:4 Will appear (*nir'āh*)—The idea of "appearing" occurs here and in v. 6 as well as in v. 23. In the latter two references the "glory of the LORD" is specifically mentioned while here it is the general term "the LORD." The Hebrew verb form is in the simple reflexive (Niphal) stem and unexpectedly occurs in the perfect tense (completed action), which normally would be translated "has appeared." Yet the context demands the future or incompleted action, that is, "is to appear." It may be that the Hebrew should be vocalized as a participle but either way the meaning is clear. This day was going to be another one of those rare and remarkable days when the glory of the LORD would be manifested to the people. While the glory had filled the tabernacle (Exod. 40:34-35), now the glory would appear again as it came out and consumed the burnt offering and fat portions on the altar (Lev. 9:23-24). [*r'h*]

9:6 The glory of the LORD (*kĕbôd yhwh*)—The Hebrew term *kābôd*, most often translated "glory," is from the verb *kbd*, which means "be heavy, grievous, hard, rich, honorable, glorious" (John Oswalt, TWOT, 1:426). The noun occurs over 200x in the OT but never with the specific idea of weight or heaviness (contra HALAT). Rather, it is often used in the construct with a preceding noun thereby taking on an adjectival function to describe persons or things. It can be used to emphasize their dignity, wealth, position, or excellence (e.g., Gen. 45:13). Most often, however, it is used to indicate God's manifest presence and power (e.g., "King of Glory") and therefore is sometimes used as a synonym of the Hebrew term for holiness (qōdeš). Collins notes that kĕbôd yhwh is a technical term and caution must be exercised in how much of the verb is read into it, and, in fact, it must be only the sense of "honorable" that is included (Collins, NIDOTTE, 2:584). It is first used with relation to God in Exod. 16. It is next used when Moses ascended Mount Sinai (Exod. 24). Since "the glory of the LORD" refers primarily to the presence of God, which could be accompanied by visible manifestations, it is not surprising that it is often associated with fire (Exod. 24:16-17) or at least with cloud or smoke (Exod. 40:34; Isa. 6:3-4). Perhaps unexpectedly, given the emphasis of Leviticus, the noun occurs only twice in the book, here and in v. 23 (the verb form also appears in Lev. 10:3). It occurs in this chapter detailing a historical event, the beginning of the priests' ministry. In a broader sense, the end of all the ritual was the proper worship of God but such external conformity did not ensure God's presence. It did, however, remove the obstacles of human sin that might prevent God's glory from being seen if he so chose to manifest his glory. Lev. 9:23 is the only mention of the appearance of the glory of the LORD to the people between Exod. 40 (at the erection of the tabernacle) and Num. 9 (which describes how the cloud moved with the tabernacle in the wilderness). Here the appearing of God's glory as it came out

from within the tabernacle and consumed the burnt offering and fat portions signified God's acceptance of the worship of his people and the commitment to bless them as requested by Aaron and Moses. Lev. 10:3 uses the Niphal or intensive stem of the verb form ('ekkābēd) meaning "honored or glorified." Despite over 300 occurrences of the verb kbd and its derivatives in the OT, this is the only use in Leviticus of the verb with its meaning of glory or honor. This is unexpected since many occurrences of the manifestation of God's glory have to do with the tabernacle (e.g., Exod. 16:10; 40:34). But Leviticus focuses on the details of the sacrificial system and the separation that must be recognized between the holy and the common, between the clean and the unclean. It is only in the context of the historical narrative concerning the inauguration of the priestly ministry that in Leviticus. God's glory is manifested. God is the glorious one who is to be honored. His Son will also bear this glory as recorded in John 1:14, ". . . we have seen his glory, the glory of the one and only, who came from the Father, full of grace and truth." [kābôd]

9:22 Blessed them (wayĕbārĕkem)—The Aaronic threefold blessing occurs in Num. 6:24-26. Whether it was first used here cannot be determined; nevertheless, this blessing must have been similar. This blessing came after four of the five kinds of available sacrifices had been offered (only three are mentioned in this verse but see Lev. 9:4). Only the guilt offering had not been offered since it dealt with "sinning unintentionally" in regard to the LORD's "holy things" (see Lev. 5:15) or the sin of trespassing on the property of others in the covenant nation (see Lev. 6:1-5 [5:20-24 MT]), neither of which is applicable yet. The Hebrew verb *brk* and its derivatives occur 415x in the OT but only twice in Leviticus, here and in the next verse. The concept of "blessing" begins with the creation of living beings (Gen. 1:22), continues with the creation of man and woman (Gen. 1:28), and in the creation story ends with God blessing the seventh day (Gen. 2:3). God's blessing continues with the descendants of Adam (Gen. 5:2), with the descendants of Noah (Gen. 9:1), with Abraham (Gen. 12:2), and through Abraham to the peoples of the world (Gen. 12:2-3). In Gen. 14:19, for the first time in Scripture, a human being, Melchizedek, is recorded as blessing both Abraham (a fellow human) and God Most High. To bless another means "to endue with power for success, prosperity, fecundity, longevity, etc." [J. Oswalt, TWOT, 1:132]. This idea of a human being blessing another is found again in the dramatic story of Isaac blessing his sons Jacob and Esau (Gen. 27:21-28). That a blessing, even from a human being, is a binding authoritative commission is clear from Gen. 27:33, 37. Jacob later struggled with a mysterious "man" and was blessed by him accompanied by a change of name (Gen. 32:26, 28 [32:27, 29 MT]).

Here in Leviticus, Aaron, and in the next verse Aaron and Moses, blessed the people of God in the name of the LORD, which in the Aaronic blessing of Num. 6:24-26 would include a prayer for the LORD's sustaining power, gracious acceptance, and granting of peace. In the OT only God could be the ultimate source of blessing. This blessing is explained by the LORD as "so they will put my name on the Israelites, and I will bless them" (Num. 6:27). God's response to the prayer offered by Aaron (and Moses) would be to cause his glory to appear (see Lev. 9:23). [*brk*]

He stepped down (*wayyērid*)—This common verb, which means "come or go down, descend," is used here in reference to the altar. However, in Exod. 20:26 the LORD specifically states that the priest was "not [to] go up to my altar on steps, lest your nakedness be exposed on it." Since this is the case, two options are available to interpret the verb in this verse. First, one could take it metaphorically in the sense that Aaron stepped away from the altar that was considered so holy that the step was "down." This metaphorical meaning attached to direction can be seen throughout the OT where Jerusalem is constantly spoken of "up" even when one is coming from a place of higher elevation. Secondly, the prohibition in Exod. 20:26 may have been against an altar so high that the worshipers, when looking up at the officiating priest, could observe his nakedness under his robes. Ezek. 43:17 speaks of a future altar with steps, needed because of its great size of over 20 feet tall, but it was also an altar with various platforms that may have increased the base size sufficiently that the worshipers were not too close to the altar. In either case it is true that God wanted both holiness and modesty to be present at the sacrificial altar. [*yrd*]

9:24 They shouted for joy (*wayyārōnû*)— The word translated "shouted" means a loud cry or "give a ringing cry" (*BDB*, 943) and is usually coupled with other words expressing praise or joy (see Ps. 20:5 [6 MT], 33:1; 35:27; 59:16 [17 MT], 95:1; Isa. 49:13; Jer. 31:7). The verb can be used for a cry of distress (Lam. 2:19) or for a cry of summons or exhortation (Prov. 1:20), but neither appears to be the case here. There is no additional word for "joy" in the Hebrew phrase of Lev. 9:24, but that emotion is thought to be implied.

Perhaps the implication of joy, rather than of fear, can come from the parallel event of the dedication of the temple during Solomon's time. Then it is recorded "When all the Israelites saw the fire coming down and the glory of the LORD above the temple, they knelt on the pavement with their faces to the ground, and they worshiped and gave thanks to the LORD, saying, 'He is good; his love endures forever'" (2 Chron. 7:3). [*rnn*]

10:1 Nadab and Abihu (*nādāb wa'ăbîhû'*)—These were the two oldest sons of Aaron (Num. 3:2), who, along with Eleazar and Ithamar, were the four sons of Aaron and Elisheba (Exod. 6:23). Nadab and Abihu are mentioned as a pair in Exod. 24:1, 9 as the sons who accompanied Moses, Aaron, and the 70 elders of Israel "up to the LORD" on Mount Sinai (Exod. 24:1). They are mentioned as a pair who died before the LORD both here and in Num. 3:4; 26:61; 1 Chron. 24:2. They had three times now been present when God's presence was manifested (Mount Sinai, the erection of the tabernacle, and recently at the inauguration of the priest's ministry). To violate a command of this God whom they had intimately seen makes their action almost unfathomable. [*nādāb*] [*'ăbîhû'*]

Their censers (*'îš maḥtātô*)—Literally "each his censer," the term refers to the implement used to carry hot coals and upon which incense could be burned (Lev. 16:12-13). Although both gold and bronze censers are mentioned in Exod. 25:38; 27:3; 37:23; 38:3, the censers are never described, whereas the tabernacle itself is described in some detail. Without matches or lighters, the most common method of starting a new fire was to use coals from an existing fire. In the tabernacle, the various censers or firepans were used to trans-

fer coals to light one fire from another. Censers took on added importance when they were used in Num. 16 to reaffirm God's chosen leader. Although the significance of the censers is never explained in the OT, in the book of Revelation the smoke of the censer of the angel is mixed with, or perhaps consists of, the prayers of the saints of the Tribulation period (Rev. 8:3-4). The coals taken from the altar that were placed in the censer are then hurled to the earth as an indication of God's holy judgment coming down upon the earth (Rev. 8:5). [*maḥtâ*]

Unauthorized (*zārâ*)—The phrase "unauthorized or strange fire" does not use the masculine form of fire but rather the feminine form (see Lev. 1:7), and then an active participle used as an adjective is attached to the feminine noun the second time it is used in the verse to demonstrate that this was not a legitimate offering by fire to the LORD. The active participle translated "unholy" comes from the verb *zwr* meaning "be a stranger" (*BDB*, 266). It is used in the sense that this fire was "strange" to the law given to Moses by the LORD God. This same incident, using this same Hebrew expression, is also found in Num. 3:4; 26:61. Elsewhere *zārâ* (or the participle of the verb *zwr*) is used of people who were not priests (Exod. 30:33; Lev. 22:10, 12, 13; Num. 16:40 [17:5 MT]) or to outsiders (Deut. 25:5). The word is used again in Lev. 22:12 to speak of "strange" or "unauthorized." The concept in this context, of whom a daughter of a priest could marry, is that she is not to marry "an outsider," someone who is not from the priestly line, if she plans to partake of the priestly food. Here it is clear that a marriage caused the two to become one and she became ineligible for priestly prerogatives when her husband was not from the eligible family. However, if she became widowed or divorced without children she might return to her father's house and once again eat the priestly food (Lev. 22:13). This shows the two possibilities that end a marriage.

This concept of "strange to the law" is further substantiated by the Hebrew expression translated "contrary to his command" in Lev. 10:1. Whether the sin involved an incense that was made incorrectly (cf. Exod. 30:9; 37:29), or whether the sin involved an incorrect presentation of the incense (e.g., on censers rather than on the golden altar of incense; Exod. 30:7a), or even a presentation of the incense at an incorrect time (Exod. 30:7b), the exact nature of their sin remains unknown. It is interesting to note that Lev. 10:1 is full of verbs used in chapters 9 and 10 to describe priestly work. [zārâ] [zwr]

10:4 The camp (lammaḥăneh)—In the OT a camp or encampment (BDB, 334) was always a temporary, never permanent, arrangement of an army, tribe, or in the case here, of the nation. The arrangement of the camp for Israel is described in Num. 1:47–2:34; 3:14-16; 10:11-28. The camp derived its significance and its distinctness from the fact that is was adjacent to the tabernacle (see Lev. 8:10) on all four sides. Because of this certain conditions must be met even for the camp. Cleanliness was imperative (Num. 5:1-4) as was the banishment of ones with a contagious disease (Lev. 13:46). The action of carrying Nadab and Abihu "outside the camp" should be compared with certain parts of sacrifices that were brought outside the camp (see Lev. 4:12, 21; 6:11 [6:4 MT]; 8:17; 9:11; 16:27). Later in Leviticus certain unclean persons needed to reside outside the camp until pronounced clean by the priest (e.g., Lev. 14:3) and the stoning of a blasphemer would also be outside the camp (Lev. 24:14, 23). The bodies of Nadab and Abihu, former priests of the nation of Israel, were treated like the useless parts of the sacrificial animals, something unclean and opposed to God. The camp of Israel was too close to the very presence of God to allow impurity, sin, or the evidence of judgment to remain. [maḥăneh]

10:6 You will die (tāmutû)—The messing of hair and tearing of one's clothing, which were the forbidden actions here, were customary means of showing grief as can be seen in Gen. 37:29 and Lev. 13:45 (this command is made permanent in Lev. 21:10-12). The command comes from God that the priests are not to engage in these actions or judgment would also fall on them. The judgment would be death. The Hebrew verb mwt ("die") has been used twice up to this point (Lev. 8:35; 10:2), both times in the context of the priests, but it is used numerous times in the coming chapters to describe the proper judgment for various sins. The judgment warning "you will die" was first used in Gen. 2:17 and 3:3 in the Garden of Eden, though it was denied there by the serpent (Gen. 3:4). Death was introduced as an inevitable but undesirable result of disobedience. Death in the OT was the ultimate separation from God due to sin. Ezekiel states that God has no pleasure in the death of men, for his original purpose was, and still is, that they live (Ezek. 18:32). Surely the repetition here of the warning of death as judgment would not be lost on Aaron and his remaining sons as to the serious nature of obeying the LORD at this point. Apparently the outward mourning by Aaron and his remaining sons could appear to be a questioning of God's judgment. This must not be done by the newly anointed priests and so the ultimate penalty was given as warning. Sudden deaths caused by the LORD also appear in the NT as the Church era was inaugurated (Acts 5:1-11). The biblical theme of God's holiness demands that God separate himself from all that is not in harmony with his character. Only faith in God's provision for sin can enable man to avoid eternal separation from a holy God. [*mwt*]

10:10 The common (*haḥōl*)—There is both status (holy or common) and ritual condition (clean or unclean) referred to in this verse. Here *qōdeš* (holiness [see Lev. 2:3]) is the antithesis of *ḥōl* (profane, common) and reversing the order, *tāme'* (unclean) [see Lev. 5:2] is the antithesis of *ṭāhôr* (clean) [see Lev. 4:12]. This same antithesis is used with the same terms in Ezek. 22:26 and 44:23. The masculine noun *ḥōl* is used only 7x in the entire OT and in Leviticus is used only here. It can describe a nonsacred place (Ezek. 42:20; 48:15) or nonsacred food (1 Sam. 21:4, 5). It can therefore be defined as the opposite to the far more common term *qōdeš* (see Lev. 2:23). Holiness is a concept of being set apart from all that is common. Lev. 10:10 prepares the reader for the following chapters and gives the purpose for the inclusion of the myriad of details to follow. Similar summaries are found in Lev. 11:47; 13:59; 14:57; and 15:31-33. [*ḥōl*]

10:11 You must <u>teach</u> (*ûlĕhôrōt*)—Israel's priests were not merely to officiate at the sanctuary but they were also to instruct the nation in the law of God. The verb *yrh* occurs only twice in Leviticus, here and in Lev. 14:57. This significant responsibility is repeated in Deut. 33:10 in the section containing Moses' blessing of the tribe of Levi. Deut. 17:9 also speaks of receiving the teaching of the priests (who were

Levites) for making decisions about court cases not explicitly dealt with in previous revelation. Later, in the prophetical books, the Levites and priests were often held responsible for judgment because of a lack of attention to this responsibility (e.g., Mal. 2:7-9). Although in the context here in Leviticus it may be inferred that Nadab and Abihu were not instructed properly (and therefore acted in ignorance), or even that alcohol led to a lack of understanding (Prov. 20:1; Hos. 4:11; 7:5), it seems better to infer that, in light of the divine judgment that fell on Nadab and Abihu, the Levites must be extremely careful to obey and to teach all that is in the law, including that which is to follow in the next few chapters concerning the clean and unclean. [*yrh*]

11:44 I am the LORD your God (*'ănî yhwh 'ĕlōhêkem*)—The phrase "I am the LORD your God" is first found in Leviticus in 11:44 but it occurs a total of 23x in Leviticus. The phrase "I am the LORD" occurs an additional 29x (all from Lev. 11:45 forward). It combines both the personal name *yhwh* (see Lev. 1:1) and the more generic name *Elohim* (see Lev. 2:13). In addition, it uses for the first time in Leviticus the expression "I am," which in Hebrew is a personal pronoun, first person singular. This functions as the subject in this noun clause. The phrase "I am the LORD your God" is significant since a very similar phrase is introduced in both records of the Ten Commandments (Exod. 20:2; Deut. 5:6). This phrase can be seen as both the preamble and the fundamental truth for the covenant the LORD made with his people. This phrase would remind the Israelites of the redemption from Egypt and especially the preceding event when God revealed the full meaning of *yhwh* to Moses and linked his name to that redemption (Exod. 6:6-7). This phrase ("I am the LORD your God") introduces the fundamental concept of Leviticus, "Consecrate yourself and be holy, because I am holy" (Lev. 11:44). Besides the link to the fundamental phrase, in Leviticus this phrase is used to provide motivation for observing a number of laws (Lev. 18:4, 30; 19:3-4, 10, 25, 31; 23:22; 24:22; 25:17; 26:1). [*'ănî*]

12:3 Be circumcised (*yimmôl*)—Literally the entire Hebrew phrase could read "the flesh of his foreskin shall be circumcised." The Hebrew verb *mwl* (the noun form is used in Exod. 4:26) occurs here in the stem signifying passive action (obviously at eight days of age the child was merely the recipient of such action). The act of circumcision involved cutting off the prepuce (loose foreskin) of the penis. Perhaps somewhat surprisingly, since Leviticus is full of ritual decrees, this is the only use of the word "circumcision" in this book. It is mentioned here almost incidentally since the focus was not on the child but on the purification of the mother after childbirth. Circumcision was the sign of the Abrahamic Covenant developed in Gen. 17:10-11, and that is the first place in Scripture where this verb is used. Egyptians are known to have practiced circumcision, but as a puberty rite marking the passage of a boy into manhood. The LORD redefined this shedding of blood as a sign of the covenant that he had made in Gen. 15 and previously promised in Gen. 12. Nowhere in Scripture are hygienic arguments used for this ritual. Parents took this sign for their baby boys as an act of submission to the revealed will of God, an act that further signified that they understood that the promises given to Abraham were still in effect and were available for the life of their children. The circumcision

of females (the removal of the skin covering the clitoris and often including the clitoris itself) is never envisaged in any Scriptural passage. Among the Israelites, only the male was required to be circumcised, an action that did not affect his ability to procreate or to experience sexual feelings. Nowhere in Scripture is the reason for requiring a physical sign only on the male explained. It is, however, in keeping with the biblical teaching of the male headship and the oneness of male and female in marriage (Gen. 2:23-24). [*mwl*]

12:4 The sanctuary (*hammiqdāš*)—The Hebrew word means "Holy Place" and refers to that which was uniquely separated and dedicated to God. It is a general term that refers to the entire tabernacle, both the "tent" and the courtyard. It is used this way in Lev. 12:4 but in Lev. 16:33 the inner sanctuary is referred to by the phrase *miqdaš haqqōdeš* ("Most Holy Place"). This was the place where the priests would atone for the people's sin on the basis of sacrifice. To have respect for the sanctuary would include not entering it when unclean (Lev. 21:12). But it would also include approaching it with a contrite, worshipful attitude. [*miqdāš*]

13:2 Infectious skin disease (*ṣārā'at*)—The Hebrew word denotes many serious skin and scalp diseases. The Septuagint, the Greek translation of the Hebrew OT, translates this word by the term *lepra*, the root of the English word "leprosy." Classic leprosy is technically known as "Hansen's disease" (which in Greek is designated by the word *elephantiasis*, not by *lepra*) and, while it may be included in the possibilities of this chapter, it is not the primary focus. The Hebrew word is used for conditions in people (Lev. 13:2-46; 14:1-32), in clothes (Lev. 13:47-58) and in houses (Lev. 14:33-53). It is difficult to find a single word that covers various skin diseases, mildew, and mold. True leprosy is caused by a contagious bacterium that spreads and causes sores, scabs, facial nodules, and white shining spots, all the while creating a loss of sensation and a deformation in the bones. Without the God-given ability to feel pain, lepers injure themselves causing further tissue damage, deformity, infection, muscle loss, and eventual paralysis. The symptoms of Hansen's disease do not correspond to the descriptions of the signs and symptoms listed here in Leviticus. There is no evidence to show that people in Palestine suffered from true leprosy in the OT era. While Israelites may not have suffered the medical condition known today as leprosy, skin diseases of various sorts come upon them. This could transpire because of the sin of jealousy (Miriam in Num. 12:10), for the lack of full compliance with God's commands (Uzziah in 2 Kings 7:3), for covetousness (Gehazi in 2 Kings 5:27), or for the glory of God (Naaman in 2 Kings 5:1). The latter situation reminds one that not all sickness is a result of an individual's sin (cf. Job; Luke 13:1-5; John 9:1-7). There is no scriptural warrant for regarding leprosy as a type of sin, though the analogy can be helpful for illustrative purposes (E. Martens, TWOT, 2:777). In order to prevent community infection, the law required a person with a skin or scalp disease to be quarantined immediately until a determination could be made concerning the infectious nature of the particular case. Priests were the central figures in diagnosis, care, and taking sanitary precautions to protect the nation (see Lev. 13:45-46). That God is concerned for the health of his people remains an enduring principle (Matt. 8:2-3). [ṣāra'at]

13:46 Alone (bādād)—The distance from the tabernacle that one lived and worked was a reflection of the relative holiness of the person. The priests worked and lived beside the tabernacle, the tribe of Levi lived surrounding the tabernacle, and the people of the nation lived in the area that surrounded them. Outside this area was the living territory of the non-Jews or those who were expelled because of their sin or uncleanness. To live "outside" (ḥûṣ) the camp was to be cut off from the promised blessings of the covenant nation and experience a living death with many temporal blessings suspended or ceased (cf. Gen. 3:24; Num. 12:14-15). "Alone" would be severe but such a judgment was necessary not to jeopardize the spiritual welfare of the entire nation (cf. Josh. 7:25-26; Isa. 6:3-5). [bādād]

14:15 Palm of the left hand ('al kap . . . haśśĕmā'lît)—Oil placed in the left hand of the priest was sprinkled seven times before the LORD and then some of it was put on the cured man's right ear, thumb, and big toe and upon his head (Lev. 14:15-17, 26-27). Now the man was readmitted to full membership within the covenant nation and could offer the sacrifices he desired (vv. 19-20, 30-31). The reason that the left hand of the priest was used appears to be so that the right forefinger could do the required sprinkling. The right hand was the hand of authority and power and the healed person's right side represented his entire being (see Lev. 8:23). [śĕmā'lî]

14:34 Land of Canaan ('ereṣ kĕna'an)—In the OT the expression "land of Canaan" occurs 62x. Most references to Canaan, as either the person or the territory, are found in the Pentateuch and in the books of Joshua and Judges. It occurs 3x in

Leviticus (Lev. 14:34; 18:3; 25:38). After the book of Judges it occurs only 10x (1 Chron. 1:8, 13; 16:18; Pss. 105:11; 106:38; 135:11; Isa. 19:18; 23:11; Zeph. 1:11 [NASB]; 2:5). In the NT it is used only twice, both times in reiterating Israel's history (Acts 7:11; 13:19). The sexual practices outlined in Lev. 18 are declared to be those followed in both Egypt and Canaan. This is well attested in both biblical and nonbiblical documents. Canaan represented all that they were to resist and destroy in terms of cultural influence. Unlike Egypt and other noncovenant nations that are prophesied to be blessed by God in the future (Zech. 14:16; Mic. 4:2-5), Canaan is never seen as being repentant and reformed. Canaan portrays sinful mankind who refuses ever to recognize God's authority just as the people of Canaan at the time of the conquest and all during Israel's occupation refused to recognize God's right to the land. Like Canaan (Gen. 15:16) sinful mankind will also find God's patience comes to an end (Matt. 25:32). [*kĕna'an*]

14:34 As a possession (*la'ăḥuzzâ*)—The term for "possession" comes from the verb meaning "grasp, take hold, take possession," (*BDB*, 28). A different Hebrew term is used in Deut. 1:8. The word used here can mean to possess "by right of inheritance" (*BDB*, 28) which is in keeping with the theological idea that the Patriarchs were promised this land (Gen. 13:15-17; 15:18-21; 17:8). Thus God was giving the Israelites the land he had legally promised to them previously. He specifies this land as "the land of Canaan" perhaps as a reminder that their gift was to the Canaanites a curse predicted in the time of Noah (Gen. 9:25). In Lev. 25:10 the word *'ăḥuzzātô* is translated "his family property." In Lev. 14:34 the word is used

to depict the entire land of Canaan. Here and in the following verses (Lev. 25:13, 24, 25, 27, 28, 32, 33, 34, 41, 45, 46; 27:16, 21, 22, 24, 28) it refers to personal property (land, houses, and alien slaves). A distinction is made as to which possessions could be sold and later redeemed in the Year of Jubilee (it was the pastureland of the Levites [cf. Lev. 25:34] and anything devoted to the LORD [cf. Lev. 27:28] that could never be sold and therefore later redeemed). The economy of Israel was somewhat leveled but not completely redistributed (since each Israelite could keep for himself all possessions other than land) twice each century. No family's land should be lost permanently to creditors. [*'ăḥuzzâ*]

14:47 And sleeps (*wĕhaššōkēb*)—The verb *škb* occurs in Lev. 14:47 and 15:4 in its normal meaning of "lying down" (*BDB*, 1011) as it does again in Lev. 15:26 and 26:6. "Lying" with a woman is also a euphemism for sexual intercourse (e.g., Lev. 15:18). It is used this way 13x in Leviticus. Such intercourse, even when it is marital, caused "pollution" but not so severe that a sacrifice was required. Rather, the man and his wife had simply to wash and wait until evening (vv. 16, 18). When the intercourse was unlawful other punishment was effected (e.g., Lev. 19:20). The practical effect of such legislation was that when a man had a religious ritual to perform, sexual intercourse would not be permitted on that day even with his wife, at least until after the duty was completed. Marital intercourse was not morally sinful but obviously the man's mind was diverted from the religious duty soon to be performed. [*škb*]

15:2 Any man (*'îš 'îš*)—Literally "a man, a man," this Hebrew expression uses the masculine word for "man" twice, both times without the definite article. While this term can be used for man as opposed to woman, this double use of the noun seems to indicate the meaning of "anyone" in some of the 11 occurrences in Leviticus (e.g., Lev. 17:10; 24:15). From the following material it is clear that these laws were developed with the male in view but by v. 19 the woman is also dealt with concerning a similar condition. ['îš]

Bodily discharge (*zāb*)—"Discharge" is a noun used only in Lev. 15. The related verb *zwb* ("flow, gush") is somewhat rare but is used, for example, as a participle in this verse as well as in Lev. 15:19, 25. The noun and verb are used in Leviticus 29x, all in chapter 15 except for Lev. 20:24 and 22:4. Outside of Leviticus it is used in Ps. 78:20; 105:41; Isa. 48:21; Jer. 49:9; and in 21 parallel cases where Canaan is referred to as a land "flowing with milk and honey" (e.g., Exod. 3:8; Num. 13:27). While many scholars identify this discharge as gonorrhea, few details are given here and so one cannot be dogmatic with this identification. [*zāb*]

16:2 In the cloud (*be'ānān*)—The chief concern of the biblical writers (here and in Exod. 25:22) is that this is the place where God will meet with man. The term for cloud was used earlier in the Pentateuch of the theophanic cloud that appeared at the Exodus (Exod. 13:21-22) and continued to lead the Israelites throughout the 40-year wilderness experience (Num. 9:15-22). In fact, in approximately 60 of the 80 occurrences of the word it refers to the cloud of the presence of the LORD. It is used in this manner only twice in Leviticus, here and 16:13. When the law was given to Moses a cloud also covered the mountain (Exod. 19:9) as an evidence of God's presence without revealing his entire glory. ['ānān]

16:4 Linen tunic (*kĕtōnet*) Normally the high priest wore a fairly elaborate set of clothes (see Exod. 28) but on the Day of Atonement he wore a special but simpler set made totally of linen. These were even plainer than those worn by the ordinary priest (Exod. 39:27-29). Though the reason for this plainer dress is never explained in the text it seems evident that as he went in to the presence of God to represent man he was not dressed as a king but humbly and modestly, as a servant. Angels who served were many times dressed in linen (Ezek. 9:2-3, 11; 10:2, 6-7; Dan. 10:5; 12:6-7). [*kuttōnet*]

16:8 Lots (*gôrālôt*)—This noun occurs 71x in the OT, with three of those occurrences being in Lev. 16:8, 9, 10, and it is always translated "lot." Nowhere in the OT is the process or the materials used in the casting of lots described (cf. Prov. 16:33; Mic. 2:5). The Mishnaic tractate Yoma gives details of the lot-casting ceremony on the Day of Atonement and while the tractate probably reflects the practice of the temple in Jerusalem just before its destruction in A.D. 70, it is possible that this reflects an older tradition, perhaps back to the time of the tabernacle. The use of the lot to determine the will of God is found throughout the OT, and Prov. 16:33 describes that "its every decision is from the LORD." Lots were used to distribute the land west of the Jordan River to each tribe (Josh. 14–19). By metonymy the word is used for the portion of the land assigned to a family or tribe and therefore becomes equivalent to "inheritance, portion, possession" (e.g., Num. 36:1-2) [E. Kalland, TWOT, 1:172]. Lots were cast to divide the spoils of war (Obad. 11); for assignment for service (Judg. 20:9); for assignment for living in Jerusalem after the exile (Neh. 11:1); and for the detection of a guilty person (Josh. 7:14; Jonah 1:7). In the NT there is only one mention of the lot being used to determine God's will (Acts 1:26). After the Spirit came on the Day of Pentecost this method is no longer recorded as being used for decision making in the church. Christ's clothing was distributed by lots (John 19:24) in keeping with the prophecy of Ps. 22:18 (22:19 MT). [*gôrāl*]

For the scapegoat (*la'ăzā'zēl*)—This Hebrew word, which occurs solely in this chapter in the OT (also in verses 10 [twice] and 26), is usually taken to mean "goat of removal." In the JB, the RSV, and the NEB, the transliterated term "*Azazel*" is actually used in the text. The NIV uses "scapegoat" but does include a footnote that reads, "That is, the goat of removal; Hebrew *azazel*."

There are at least three major views as to the translation of the term. First, it can be translated "rocky precipice" (perhaps from the verb *'zz* "to be strong, fierce") and when used this way reflects an ancient tradition recorded in the Mishnah that declares that the goat was taken out by the man assigned to the task to a rocky cliff outside the camp and pushed over the cliff to its total destruction. The emphasis must be on the accomplishment of this ritual; sin is removed from Israel. The goat carried away the sins of the people into a remote wilderness, never to be seen again. Second, the term may be derived from a combination of two words, *'ēz* meaning "goat" and *'zl* meaning "to go away." In this case the context would support this meaning as "the goat that goes away" (see vv. 10, 21-22, 26). This translation is the one tentatively used in the NIV. Thirdly, the most popular translation among scholars today is that the noun should be taken as a proper name of a desert demon, perhaps even of Satan himself. However, interpretations

that see *Azazel* as a desert demon, though possible from the parallel structure of v. 8 ("one lot for the Lord and the other for the scapegoat"), must be rejected as being questionable theologically and unbiblical in practice (see Lev. 17:7). It is true that Jewish literature (e.g., Enoch 8:1; 9:6) uses *Azazel* as the name of a demon but this material is much later than Leviticus. Whatever the translation, there is no intention here of appeasing any demon but rather the task of avoiding offending the Lord. Nowhere does the NT make reference to Christ as the scapegoat although many Christians see in the scapegoat a type of Christ. [*'ăzā'zēl*]

16:13 Above <u>the Testimony</u> (*'al hā'ēdût*)— This word, which means "testimony, reminder, warning sign" (C. Schultz, TWOT, 2:649), is most frequently used in the context of the tabernacle, resulting in the phrase "tabernacle of the testimony" (Num. 10:11; cf. Rev. 15:5). This noun, which in Lev. occurs here and in Lev. 24:3, comes from the verb *'wd* ("bear witness"). The word is always used in reference to the testimony of God. The words of the covenant are his testimony since they are God's own affirmation to his person and purpose. There are times when the two tablets of stone containing the Ten Commandments are designated as "the testimony" (Exod. 25:16; 32:15) and so in many Psalms the revelation of God in the law is referred to as "testimony" (Pss. 19:7 [19:8 MT]; 119:14, 31, 36, 88, 99, 111, 129, 144, 157). This word is also used in connection with the crowning of Joash, for when he received the crown he received the "testimony" (2 Kings 11:12; 2 Chron. 23:11). When combined with the ark the phrase is the "ark of the testimony" (Exod. 25:22; Josh. 4:16). All of these usages refer in some way to the testimony and reminder of God himself. In this verse the smoke of the incense covered the Testimony, that is, the ark, so that the high priest would not see the full glory of God and thus die. In the NT the proclamation of the Gospel is seen as the essence of the testimony, since the Gospel now further reveals the person and purpose of God (1 John 5:11; Rev. 12:11). [*'ēdût* or *'ēdut*]

16:16 And their rebellion (*ûmippiš'îhem*)—The Hebrew noun used in Leviticus only here and in v. 21 is derived from the verb *pš'*, which means "rebel, transgress, revolt" (*BDB*, 741), in the sense of crossing over a boundary (Jer. 3:13). It refers to violations of God's revealed law, crossing over the limits that God has established and occurs especially in terms of a relationship. It designates those who reject God's authority (G. Lewis, TWOT, 2:741). In the OT noncovenant nations can engage in this action (Amos 1–2) but usually it is the Israelites who are declared guilty of this sin. Since the Hebrew noun is used in Leviticus only in chapter 16, it is clear that the provision of the Day of Atonement enabled the nation to be reconciled to God by having their "rebellions" atoned. In Lev. 16:21 three synonyms for transgressions against God (including *peša'*) are used in an effort to demonstrate the totality of the atonement. It should be noted that, while usually called *yom kippur* (Day of Atonement), this title never appears in this chapter. The title does appear in Lev. 23:27, 28 but in Hebrew it is in the plural ("the Day of Atonements"). In fact, there is no other mention of this day in any other of the historical books. The NT makes no direct reference to the ritual of the Day of Atonement. [*peša'*]

16:22 To a solitary place (*gĕzērâ*)—The phrase literally means "a land of cutting off." The Hebrew noun, from the verb *gzr* ("cut, divide"), is used only here in the entire OT. This cutting off could refer to either the fact that the life of the goat would be "cut off," that is, the life would end for the goat in this deserted place not by sacrifice but perhaps by killing from some wild animal, or it could refer to the fact that this place was separated, that is, "cut off" from the camp of Israel by some natural valley that would prevent the goat from returning. In any case, that which was the substitute for sin would not return. In the NT, Christ, as the substitute for sinful mankind, suffered death but it was God's pleasure to raise him from the dead (e.g., Acts 2:24). [*gĕzērâ*]

16:29 You must deny yourself (*tĕ'annû*)—The verb and its derivatives are used primarily to signify humility, affliction, or oppression. "Deny yourself" or "afflict your souls" in this context probably includes the physical act of fasting, though the term is seldom used with the concept of fasting, occurring in Leviticus only in the two passages dealing with the Day of Atonement (here and in Lev. 16:31; 23:27, 29, 32). However, in both Isa. 58:3, 5 and Ps. 35:13 it is also associated with fasting, though in Ps. 35 a number of penitential practices are mentioned. This would suggest, as is clearly taught in many other places in the OT, that ritual must be accompanied by personal penitence. The Day of Atonement was not an "easy" way to purify Israel of the just punishment of sin. Everyone was required to engage in introspective evaluation so that the atonement being made could cover the sins confessed. [*'nh*]

And the alien (*wĕhaggēr*)—The Hebrew term for alien or sojourner is used here in its first of 21x in Leviticus. The alien was not merely a non-Israelite, but one who lived in the land and who was regarded in most ways like a proselyte, that is, as someone who had accepted the basic faith of Israel (Lev. 19:34). Here in Leviticus the alien was to submit to the law of the LORD (see Lev. 18:26; 20:2) to the point that a circumcised alien could celebrate the Passover (Exod. 12:48; Num. 9:14). Not only was the *gēr* to show fidelity to the LORD but he was allowed by law to enjoy many of the same rights as the native Israelite (e.g., Lev. 17:8; 19:10) although he was subject to the same penalties as well (e.g., Lev. 17:10; 24:16). While the word *gēr* occurs numerous times in Leviticus, the only time where an Israelite is referred to by this term is in Lev. 25:23. [*gēr*]

16:30 In the day (*bayyôm*)—Surprisingly, the expression "Day of Atonement" is never used in Lev. 16. Rather it is referred to as "in the day" in which "atonement will be made." The word *yôm* is used 113x in Leviticus, with the vast majority of these being references to a generic "day" (e.g., Lev. 6:5, 20). The actual title "Day of Atonement" is used 3x in Leviticus (23:27, 23:38; 25:9) to describe this special day in Israel's religious life. In fact, there is no other mention of this day in any other of the OT historical books. *Hakkĕppurîm* is in the plural but is used as an abstract noun to designate this day. It is also used, always in the plural, in Exod. 29:36; 30:10, 16; Num. 5:8; 29:11 to signify various elements of atonement. The NT makes no direct reference to the ritual of the Day of Atonement. [*yôm*]

16:31 It is a sabbath of rest (*šabbat*)—The weekly Sabbath, using the same terminol-

ogy "sabbath of rest," is dealt with in Lev. 23:3. Here in Lev. 16:31 the Day of Atonement is also specified as a day in which no work is to be done (cf. v. 29). Lev. 19:3 reminds the Israelites to keep "my sabbaths." In Lev. 23:3 the weekly Sabbath, using the terminology "sabbath of rest," was the most common of all the sacred assemblies of the Israelites. It was to be celebrated each week and, according to the Ten Commandments, it remembered both the fact that God rested on the seventh day of creation (Exod. 20:8-11), and the rest to which the LORD brought them in delivering them out of Egypt (Deut. 5:12-15). "Only the Sabbath, however, he sanctified, indicating perhaps that the climax of creation was not the creation of man, as is often stated, but the day of rest, the seventh day. The Sabbath is thus an invitation to rejoice in God's creation, and recognize God's sovereignty over our time" (V. Hamilton, TWOT, 2:903). The Sabbath became the sign of the Mosaic Covenant (Exod. 31:13, 17; Ezek. 20:12, 20), which is why in the NT the opponents of Christ were continually trying to find him breaking the Sabbath. If they could prove that he broke the sign of the Mosaic Law then in essence he would have broken all the law. Any religious or ritual activities that would occur on the Sabbath are not described except for those that would occur in the tabernacle or temple (e.g., Num. 28:9-10; 1 Chron. 9:32). Many of the modern ceremonies that occur in the synagogues on the Sabbath are later developments in Judaism. The keeping of the Sabbath by Christians appears to be negated once Christ fulfilled the requirement of the law (Col. 2:16-17). [*šabbat*]

16:34 Once a year (*baššānâ*)—The Day of Atonement is an annual ritual, to be held once each year. This specific fact is repeatedly contrasted in Heb. 9:11–10:14 with the fact that the sacrifice of Christ was "once-for-all." The Israelites were not permitted to celebrate this ritual whenever they desired or felt the need. Other sacrifices could be made this way, but this sacred ritual was regulated in its timing. Other yearly rituals are dealt with in Lev. 23:4-43. God's calendar included celebrations that were weekly (Sabbath), yearly, and in the case of Jubilee, every 50 years. [šānâ]

17:7 To the goat idols (*laśśĕ'îrim*)—Many contemporary translations suggest "goat idols" for the Hebrew noun *śa'îr*, although the NIV does suggest in the margin the possibility of "demon." This term is also used in Isa. 13:21 and 34:14 with reference to something that inhabits desolate ruins. However, in the contexts of Isaiah other wild animals (e.g., jackals, owls, hyenas) are also mentioned and so "wild goat" may be an appropriate translation for the term. Other uses include 2 Chron. 11:15 and possibly 2 Kings 23:8 where the term "goat idol" may be most appropriate given the context. Depending upon how one translates the term *Azazel*, used earlier in Leviticus (see Lev. 16:8), one may be more influenced to translate the word at hand in one of the ways suggested by the NIV. [śā'îr]

Prostitute (*zōnîm*)—The verb *znh* is used 99x in the OT. While it is often used literally of illicit intercourse between human beings, it can be used in a figurative sense of "religious intercourse," either of the nation of Israel having friendly dealings with forbidden nations, or the people of Israel worshiping false gods. Here the latter is in view as it is in Lev. 20:5-6. In Leviticus the verb is also used in 19:29; 21:7, 9, 14 within the priestly regulations to define a woman who engages in illicit heterosexual intercourse. The use of such a term to describe the illicit conduct of the people of God gives graphic force to the sin they were committing. Because they had entered into a covenant relationship with the LORD any violation of this relationship was seen as illicit "religious intercourse" (Ezek. 16:26-28). When Israel as a nation trusted in other nations by entering into a treaty relationship with them, or when she participated in idolatrous actions of other peoples, she prostituted herself against the LORD. "The thought seems to be of having relations with these nations for the sake of political and monetary benefit, although in the case of Nineveh [Nah. 3:4] the added element of alluring, deceitful tactics leading on to oppressive dominance is implied" (L. Wood, TWOT, 1:246). Paul, in 1 Cor. 10:1-13, warns the believers that they should not set their hearts on evil things as did the Israelites in the wilderness, where they committed both the sin of idolatry and adultery. Later Paul clearly developed the image of the church being the bride of Christ who is to be presented to him "as a radiant church without stain or wrinkle or any other blemish, but holy and blameless" (Eph. 5:25-27). [znh]

17:11 The life (*nepeš*)—Here and in v. 14 (see also Gen. 9:4) the expression "life of a/every creature is in the blood" is used. The word *nepeš* ("life, soul, creature, person, mind") is used 60x in Leviticus alone and has a broad range of meanings [BDB, 659-61]. In context here it is most appropriately rendered "life." Waltke, in fact, states that Lev. 17:11 is "one of the most decidedly theological and distinctively meaningful passages where the word *nepeš* is of major significance, and one which certainly defines the term as meaning life" [B. Waltke, TWOT, 2:590]. The three passages mentioned above have sometimes been used to argue that blood merely symbolizes life and that "the blood of the victim is the life that has passed through death" (V. Hamilton, TWOT, 1:190). Taken this way the worshiper would declare that he was delivered by the life of the animal, by participating in its life. But a better explanation for this expression, and one that is in keeping with the entire context of the sacrificial system, is that blood is the source of life, the means by which life continues. To remove the blood is to end life and therefore the prohibition (cf. v. 10) not to eat blood. To eat blood is to despise life. This idea is most clearly seen in Gen. 9:4-6 where the sanctity of life, especially that of man who is created in the image of God, is associated with not eating blood. Blood (see Lev. 1:5) is both the most effective ritual cleanser and the most polluting substance when it is in the wrong place (see Lev. 12). [nepeš]

18:3 Egypt (miṣrayim)—This is the proper noun for the people and territory of Egypt. In form, the Hebrew name for Egypt is in the dual, indicating that she has two basic integral divisions: Upper Egypt (Southern Egypt) and Lower Egypt (Delta area toward the Mediterranean Sea) [V. Hamilton, TWOT, 1:523]. The three millennia of Egyptian history makes it almost impossible to enumerate common denominators in their religious life. The scope extends from a rampant polytheism to a solar "monotheism." However, what is of relevance here is that her sexual practices were not to be followed since the LORD has given a different standard to his people. The illicit sexual practices outlined in this chapter are declared to be those followed in both

Egypt and Canaan. This is well attested in both biblical and extra-biblical documents. While during patriarchal times there were friendly relationships with Egypt (Gen. 12; 46-47) from the time of Moses on Egypt is seen in a negative light in the Scriptures. Egypt represented for the Israelite all from which God had brought them. She is the one who oppressed God's people and refused to give liberty to Israel until forced by God through the death of the firstborn even after God, through Moses, continually demonstrated his power. The prophets of God continually criticized Egypt and warned the Israelites to stay away from her for she was under judgment (e.g., Isa. 19:10; Jer. 9:26; Joel 3:19). Yet in the future the prophets also anticipated that this traditional enemy of Israel would be reconciled under God's blessing (e.g., Isa. 19:20, 21; Zech. 14:16-19). Egypt was not to be the standard for Israel, but rather Israel would some day be the means through which Egypt would be blessed as a fulfillment of the Abrahamic Covenant (Gen. 12:3) [miṣrayim]

Do not follow (tēlēku)—The root hlk occurs some 1,562x in the OT. The verb form refers to movement in general including the "creeping" of a snake (Gen. 3:14), the "sneaking" of a fox (Lam. 5:18), the "floating" of an ark (Gen. 7:18), the "flowing" of water (Gen. 2:14), the "playing" of trumpets (Exod. 19:19), and the "walking of men" (Exod. 14:29). Once, in a theophanic context, God himself is said to "walk" (Gen. 18:33). Other times stated anthropomorphically, God walks on clouds (Ps. 104:3) or in the heavens (Job 22:14). Most significantly, several times in Scripture this verb is used to describe God coming to his people in judgment or blessing (2 Sam. 7:23; Ps. 80:2 [80:3 MT]; Exod. 33:14). Seven times in Lev. 18 the concept of not behaving or walking like the surrounding nations is given (vv. 3 [2x], 24, 26, 27, 29, 30). The concept is especially linked in this chapter to sexual morality. Since the term is normally translated "walk" it lends the idea of the Israelites being on not only a physical but also a spiritual journey (cf. Lev. 26:3; Deut. 5:33; Ps. 1:1; Prov. 2:20). The ones who truly love God walk after him and his Word (1 Kings 3:14; Ps. 119:1). [*hlk*]

18:5 Will live (*wāḥay*)—The verb *ḥyh* can mean "to live or have life, give or restore life" (E. Smick, TWOT, 1:279). God gave mankind life in the Garden of Eden (Gen. 2:7) and though physical death entered his experience (Gen. 3:19), God promised life in himself (Ps. 36:9; 139:13-16). Someday, those who love God will eat from the Tree of Life that was placed off-limits to Adam and Eve (Rev. 22:2). In the OT man is regarded holistically and therefore life is spoken of more as "the experience of life rather than as an abstract principle of vitality which may be distinguished from the body" (E. Smick, TWOT, 1:279). Here in Lev. 18:5 the literal expression "he will live through them" may be taken to mean only continued physical existence, longer life. While this may be true and while "life" can be dealt with in these terms in the OT, it doesn't appear to be sufficient to explain the use here. Rather, life that is lived by God's law enjoys God's blessing, which includes health, prosperity, family, and friends (Lev. 26:3-13; Deut. 28:1-14). This must be the "life" spoken of here, which is in keeping with the holistic view of man in the OT. If this promise of obtaining "life" is taken in more NT terms, which often refers to "life" as that life which occurs after death, there would be a conflict with the scriptural teaching in such

passages as Gal. 3:10-12. The solution is to be found in what is meant by "live by them" in the OT context. Life for the OT saint was a life of health, prosperity, family, friends, all based on, and provided by, a conscious relationship with the LORD God. The OT gives only a few hints into the future life (e.g., Ps. 73; Dan. 12:1-3) which is expanded by NT teaching (e.g., Matt. 19:17; John 8:51; Rom. 10:5). [*ḥyh*]

18:6 To have sexual relations (*lĕgallôt*)— In this verse is given the general principle prohibiting incestuous relations, by which the following detailed rules will be established. "To have sexual relations" is the translation of the Hebrew phrase *tiqrĕbû lĕgallôt 'erwâ* (literally, "approach to uncover the nakedness of"). This euphemistic phrase is used over and over again in this chapter. The Hebrew verb *glh* ("uncover, remove") is used in Leviticus only in chapters 18 and 20 (24x), always in the context of sexual relations. When this verb is used in the Piel stem (as here) it "always denotes 'to uncover' something which otherwise is normally concealed" (B. Waltke, TWOT, 1:160-61). The use of the verb in this stem is most frequent in reference to sexual activity, often incestuous. It is used later by the Prophets as a metaphor to declare that Israel has not been faithful to her God and has therefore been shamed (Hos. 2:10; Ezek. 16:36). This general principle would appear to cover both sexual intercourse within a marriage (a marriage therefore that is prohibited) and intercourse between unmarried persons. This intercourse between unmarried persons must refer to proposed marriage since, for example, intercourse with an aunt during the lifetime of the uncle would be covered by the prohibition of adultery (v. 20; Exod. 20:14). In summary, the following rules appear to be those that define the limits for a man seeking a suitable wife. [*glh*]

To have sexual relations (*'erwâ*)—"To have sexual relations" is the translation of the Hebrew phrase "to uncover the nakedness of." The word here is a noun, used mostly of women, meaning "nakedness, pudenda" (*BDB*, 788). After the Fall, nakedness was a matter of shame for both the husband and wife (Gen. 3:10; cf. Gen. 2:25). This was true, not because sexual activity was sinful, since God had created humans as male and female and told them to procreate, but because now the human mind could project evil into this area of human relationship. After Gen. 3:7 nakedness is a symbol and reminder of human shame that resulted from sin. For this reason nakedness or immodesty in worship is specifically forbidden (Exod. 20:26; 28:42). Deuteronomy uses this word in 23:14 and 24:1, the former in the context of the LORD God viewing the nation and not seeing any shameful activity and the latter in the context of a reason that a divorce could take place. Nakedness as a judgment of shame is spoken of numerous times by the Prophets (e.g., Isa. 3:17; Hab. 3:13; Zeph. 2:14). Nakedness in private, outside of proper sexual relationships, is declared by God to be prohibited. The incestuous possibilities are especially dealt with here in Lev. 18 and 20. [*'erwâ*]

18:17 Wickedness (*zimmâ*)—This Hebrew noun is used here to describe the enormity of the evil that has been described with reference to incestuous relations. This word is used just 4x in Leviticus, here and in 19:29 and 20:14 (twice). The noun comes from the verb *zmm* which means to "consider, purpose, devise" (*BDB*, 273) and is used mostly of the LORD carrying out his plan of judgment against the wicked. However the noun is always used in a negative sense except for its occurrence in Job 17:11. It should not be taken to apply merely to the incestuous situation of v. 17 but to all that has been and will be described in this chapter. The expression "that is wickedness" is parallel to other evaluative statements made in this chapter such as "that would dishonor" (v. 8), "defile yourself" (v. 20), "that is detestable" (v. 22), "that is a perversion" (v. 23). [*zimmâ*]

18:18 Rival wife (*liṣrōr*)—Literally the Hebrew reads "to distress *or* to show hostility" and the most obvious situation that would do that would be for a man to take his wife's sister as a second wife (e.g., Gen. 29–30). The verse goes on to limit this application to the woman's lifetime. If a man's wife died then a second marriage is analogous to the law of levirate marriage (Deut. 25:5-10). While all polygamy has the potential to cause rivalry and seems to be prohibited by Gen. 2:24 ("For this reason a man will leave his father and mother and be united to his wife, and they will become one flesh"), the Israelites did practice this marriage arrangement. This verse seems to show the very real danger of a polygamous marriage, especially when the wives were related. This is the only use of the verb in Leviticus. [*ṣrr*]

18:21 To be sacrificed (*lĕha'ăbîr*)—The verb used here is *'br* rather than the usual term *qrb* for proper ritual sacrifice (see Lev. 1:2). This is the first of five occurrences of this verb in Leviticus (here, Lev 25:9 [twice]; 26:6; 27:32). The basic meaning of the verb is "pass over, through, by, pass on" (*BDB*, 716). The use of the verb here is unusual since it deals with death. The NIV suggests in its margin note the translation "pass through [the fire]," which shows the normal use of the verb. In regard to sacrifice to Molech (see below), it cannot yet be determined whether the children were thrown alive into the fire or killed first (see De Vaux, *Sacrifice*, 81). This practice of child sacrifice is referred to and condemned in 2 Kings 23:10 and Jer. 32:35 (cf. Deut. 12:31; 18:10). General offerings to Molech are condemned in numerous passages (e.g., Lev. 20:2-5; ;1 Kings 11:7). ['*br*]

To Molech (*lammōlek*)—Molech was the principal male deity of the Ammonites (1 Kings 11:7; 2 Kings 23:10; Jer. 32:35). This Hebrew word is developed from the consonants of the word *melek* ("[divine] king"), but the Masoretes who supplied the vowels used the vowels from *bōšet* ("shame") to describe this despicable deity who was worshiped by human infant sacrifice. In the OT Molech is connected with the ultimate in apostate worship by the Israelites for they were to worship the true King rather than this shameful one. Kings Ahaz and Manasseh of Judah, two of the worst apostate rulers over the Hebrews, both promoted the worship of Molech (2 Kings 16:3; 2 Chron. 28:3; 2 Kings 21:6; 2 Chron. 33:6), though King Josiah desecrated the infant sacrifice area to prevent such abuse (2 Kings 23:10). [*mōlek*]

Profane (*těhallēl*)—This is the first of 6x in Leviticus that the phrase "profane the name of your God" (or one very similar) occurs (here, 19:12; 20:3; 21:6; 22:2, 32). The Hebrew verb *ḥll* ("to profane") means to make something unholy. This verb always has as its object something that is holy (e.g., tabernacle, Lev. 21:12, 23; holy foods, 22:15; Sabbath, Isa. 56:2, 6; Ezek. 20:13, 16). Here that which is holy is the name of the LORD and it is profaned when used either in a false oath (Lev. 19:12) or when doing

something [in his name] of which God disapproves. When the Israelites did these actions they gave God "a bad reputation among the Gentiles" (Wenham, *Leviticus*, 259). In context this underscores why Israel must not worship the god Molech. (For the concept of "swearing falsely" see Lev. 19:12; for "blaspheming the name" see Lev. 24:11.) [*ḥll*]

18:22 Detestable (*tôʿēbâ*)—In Hebrew this is a term of strong disapproval that is sometimes translated "abomination." It is related to a verb meaning "to hate" or "abhor." Proverbs shows that an abomination is something detestable and hated by God (Prov. 6:16; 11:1). The noun is used 117x in the OT. It may refer to an abomination of a physical, ritual, or ethical nature and may be that which is detested by man or by God (R. Youngblood, TWOT, 2:977). It is used 5x in this chapter (here, vv. 26, 27, 29, 30) and again in Lev. 20:13 to refer to homosexuality and other perversions. In the Pentateuch it is more common in Deuteronomy where it refers to a vast array of evils including human sacrifice (Deut. 12:31), engaging in occult activity (Deut. 18:9-14), and conducting business in a dishonest fashion (Deut. 25:13-16). Prov. 6:16-19 lists seven detestable things that were sure to bring God's judgment upon anyone who practiced them. For a synonym that is used in relation to foods, see *šeqeṣ* in Lev. 7:21. [*tôʿēbâ*]

18:23 Present herself (*taʿămōd*)—This verb has the basic meaning of "take one's stand, stand" [*BDB*, 763]. It is used 3x in Leviticus, all with the concept of sexual activity and all dealing with animals (here, 19:19; 20:16). It is used, then, not in a simple literal manner of mere standing but with the idea of presenting oneself for sexual activity. Bestiality is condemned here and in Exod. 22:19 [18 MT], Lev. 20:15-16, and Deut. 27:21. ['*md*]

A perversion (*tebel*)—This noun is used only here and in Lev. 20:12 in the entire OT. It comes from the verb *bll* ("to mix, mingle, confuse") [*BDB*, 117] and therefore refers to a mixture or confusion that is unnatural. God never expects mankind and animals to mix in this manner. God created animals and mankind on the same day but in distinctively separate ways and this distinction is to be maintained. Other verses also deal with the unnatural mixes of various kinds (Lev. 19:19; Deut. 22:5, 9-11). In Lev. 20:12 the confusion is an incident of incest between a man and his daughter-in-law. [*tebel*]

18:25 Vomited (*wattāqi'*)—This is a fascinating metaphor that personifies the land and portrays it as vomiting out the Canaanites (v. 28 uses the same expression in a warning for the Hebrews). The verb *qî'* ("vomit up, spue out, disgorge") is used 3x in Leviticus (here, v. 28; 20:22) but nowhere else in the Pentateuch. The image occurs later of Jonah (Jonah 2:10 [11 MT]) and of a man who has had too much to drink (Isa. 19:14). The graphic nature of this expression shows the loathsome nature of the Canaanites. When it is used in v. 18 of the nation of Israel the picture would be clear to God's people. If they were ever expelled from the land their sin would have become detestable like that of the Canaanites. [*qî'*]

19:3 Respect (*tîrā'û*)—The home is to be a place of holiness. Here the Hebrew verb *yr'* ("fear, respect, reverence") occurs whereas in Exod. 20:12 and Deut. 5:16 the word *kbd* ("honor") is used. The verb *yr'* is first used here in Leviticus, but it appears later in this chapter to speak of "fearing God" (vv. 14, 32) and reverencing the

sanctuary of God (v. 30). In all other occurrences in Leviticus it is used of the sum total of all right attitudes and actions toward God (Lev. 25:17, 36, 43; 26:2). This concept of respecting parents and that of observing the sabbaths (see below) seem to be fundamental for proper functioning in the nation of Israel. It is right attitudes and actions toward family and God that make a nation strong. [*yr'*]

19:4 Idols (*hā'ĕlîlîm*)—This word is used only twice in the Pentateuch, both times in Leviticus (here and Lev. 26:1). The etymology is not conclusive. It likely comes either from the diminutive of god ('*ēl*) or from '*ll*, a root meaning "to be weak." Either way the term is used to disparage heathen gods and show their powerlessness. The exact phrase "molten gods" appears in Exod. 34:17. It is found nowhere else. The archetypal molten god was "Aaron's golden calf" of Exod. 32. Based on the prohibition of the second commandment (Exod. 20:4; Deut. 5:8), the specific detail regarding a molten or cast idol is also found in Exod. 34:17 and Deut. 27:15. [*ĕlîl*]

19:17 In your heart (*bilbābekâ*)—The Hebrew noun means "inner man, mind, will, heart" [*BDB*, 523]. It is a rich term that can speak not only of the internal organ known as the heart but in its abstract represents the totality of man's inner or immaterial part, the rational part of man. The majority of its uses are of the latter nature and it is always used this way in its three occurrences in Leviticus (here, 26:36, 41). The false concept that the OT dealt merely with outward actions cannot be sustained when one considers such verses as this one. This command is satisfied not merely by not doing something hurtful to one's neighbor (Lev. 19:16

and preceding verses), but as the following sentence points out, it involves doing that which is helpful to him. The use of the term "brother" in the sentence under consideration occurs between two sentences that use two different terms for neighbor. It appears that there is no attempt to differentiate between a neighbor and a blood relative (i.e., brother) but rather all appear to refer to those of the community. This is substantiated by the following verse (see below). This same concept is specifically dealt with in the NT in 1 John 2:9, 11; 3:15; 4:20. [*lēb, lēbāb*]

19:18 Love (*wĕ'habātâ*)—The construction here is the Hebrew verb with the preposition. This construction is used only here, Lev. 19:34, and 2 Chron. 19:2 and may emphasize the need for direct action toward one's neighbor. It stands in direct contrast to bearing a grudge, taking vengeance, or even showing apathy toward someone in need. Christ's reference in Matt. 22:39 to this "golden rule" of the OT may show his regard for the importance of Levitical law in his mind (see also its use in Matt. 19:19; Mark 12:31; Luke 10:27; Rom. 13:9; and Gal. 5:14). [*'hb*]

19:23 Forbidden (*'orlātô*)—The Hebrew adjective *'ārēl* means "uncircumcised" and a figurative use of this term is used to denote that which is forbidden. The literal term *mwl* ("circumcised") has been dealt with in Lev. 12:3. Here the term is one of contempt in light of the divine requirement for all the LORD's male followers to be circumcised. As a term of contempt it is especially used of the Philistines (e.g., Judg. 14:3; 15:18; 1 Sam. 14:6; 17:26, 36; 31:4; 2 Sam. 1:20; 1 Chron. 10:4). In the Prophets it is associated with those lacking spiritual life (Isa. 52:1; Jer. 6:10). In context in Lev. 19:23, the reason that the fruit of the land would be forbidden for three years after a tree was planted is not given, but proper adherence to this command would provide an increased harvest in the end. [*'rl*]

19:26 Practice divination (*tĕnahăšû*)—The verb *nḥš* ("practice divination, divine, observe signs") [*BDB*, 638] is found only in this verse in all of Leviticus. It obviously refers to a practice that is dealt with also in v. 31 and again in Lev. 20:6 though in those places different terms are used. In the OT this verb is found only in the intensive stem (Piel) and is first used in Gen. 30:27 when Laban claims that he "learned by divination" that the LORD had blessed him because of Jacob. Divination is forbidden here in Lev. 19:26 and in Deut. 18:10. It is listed as one of the reasons the northern kingdom of Israel went into exile (2 Kings 17:17). Later evil King Manasseh of Judah engaged in this sinful practice too (2 Kings 21:6; 2 Chron. 33:6). [*nḥš*]

Practice sorcery (*tĕ'ônēnû*)—The verb used here ("practice soothsaying") [*BDB*, 778], like the verb *nḥš* above, is found only in this verse in all of Leviticus. It, too, obviously refers to a practice that is dealt with in v. 31 and again in Lev. 20:6, though this same term is not used. This verb is found a total of 11x in the OT and its exact meaning is uncertain (R. Allen, *TWOT*, 2:685). Since the root is similar to one for clouds it could be suggested that the practice was in some way connected to "reading and interpreting" the clouds. Another suggestion is that this is an onomatopoetic word whose sound would be used by the one practicing this method (R. Allen, *TWOT*, 2:685). Just how this would function is unclear. Whatever the method, the experience is forbidden here and in Deut. 18:10. Evil king Manasseh practiced this art (2 Kings 21:6; 2 Chron.

33:6). The Prophets disparage this sinful custom (Isa. 2:6; 57:3; Jer. 27:9; Mic. 5:12). ['nn]

19:31 Mediums (hā'ōbōt)—The 'ōb ("necromancer") [BDB, 15] was probably one who practiced consulting the dead (cf. 1 Sam. 28:7) but modern versions have translated this term in a variety of ways including "medium, ghost, spirit, spirit of the dead, necromancer, and wizard." Since 1 Samuel is the only historical narrative that describes this type of person, it appears that the method employed must have included consulting the dead in some manner (1 Sam. 28:8). This same prohibition against this practice is repeated in Lev. 20:6, 27 and Deut. 18:11. It is condemned by the Prophet Isaiah (Isa. 8:19). God's people were not to obtain knowledge by anyone who claimed to receive knowledge other than a true prophet of the LORD God. ['ōb]

Spiritists (hayyiddĕ'ōnîm)—This term, which modern translations render as "spiritist, wizard, fortune-teller, familiar spirit, spirit, magician, and sorcerer" probably describes one who practiced obtaining esoteric knowledge not available to the ordinary person (J. Lewis, TWOT, 1:367). The word is a masculine noun that comes from the verb yd' ("to know"). It may be that the only difference between this term and the term 'ōb (see above), which almost always occur in parallel to each other (here, Lev. 20:6, 27; Deut. 18:11; 1 Sam. 28:3, 9; 2 Kings 21:6; 23:24; 2 Chron. 33:6; Isa. 8:19; 19:3), is that the obtaining of knowledge was by different methods although the specifics on this are no longer available. These methods may have included consulting the dead (1 Sam. 28:8), examining livers (Ezek. 21:21 [21:26 MT]), or even reading something like cloud formations. This same prohibi-

tion is repeated in Lev. 20:6, 27 and Deut. 18:11. God's people were not to obtain knowledge by anyone who claimed to receive knowledge other than a true prophet of the LORD God. How the later kings of Judah dealt with such people becomes a significant factor in their evaluation as being either good or bad (e.g., 2 Kings 21:6; 2 Chron. 33:6). [yiddĕ'ōnî]

19:32 The aged (śêbâ)—The term for "elderly" (zāqēn) is used in combination with this Hebrew word for aged. The latter seems to refer broadly to those advanced in years. These two terms are also used in parallel in Isa. 46:4 and Ps. 71:18. To rise and to show respect is to signify both an action and an attitude that was necessary to display before these in the community. (śêbâ]

The elderly (zāqēn)—The term for "elderly" occurs in the plural earlier in Leviticus (Lev. 4:15 and 9:1), both times in the context referring to those older Israelites who were regarded as leaders; ones with authority for the congregation. Here the noun in the singular does not appear restricted to those in leadership roles but, rather, used in combination with the Hebrew word for aged, seems to refer broadly to those advanced in years. These two terms are also used in parallel in Isa. 46:4 and Ps. 71:18. God himself is pictured in the Scriptures as one with white hair (Dan. 7:9) as a symbol of experience and wisdom and one worthy of honor (Prov. 16:31). [zāqēn]

20:2 Stone him (yirgĕmuhû)—The rare phrase "people of the land" is first used in Lev. 4:27 and designates the ones who are to carry out this punishment. This emphasizes that such an act to a foreign god as stated earlier in this verse is a threat to the entire community. It is also a desecration of the tabernacle and a profanation of God's name (Lev. 20:3). The person must be stoned, which is a punishment called for four other times in Leviticus (Lev. 20:27; 24:14, 16, 23). Such a person was not allowed to live and the entire community participated in the penalty to show covenant solidarity, affirmation of looking only to the LORD, and a warning to all. [*rgm*]

20:20 Childless (*'ărîrîm*)—Childbearing is part of the creation mandate (Gen. 1:28) and children are seen elsewhere as a great blessing from God (Lev. 26:9; Deut. 28:11; Ps. 127:3-5). To die childless is literally to die "stripped." This adjective, which comes from the verb *'rr* ("strip oneself") is used only 4x in the OT, here, Lev. 20:21, Gen. 15:2, and Jer. 22:30. It is a major curse that lasts the life of the person upon whom it is placed. See also Deut. 28:18 for childlessness as a judgment of God. [*'ărîrî*]

20:24 Milk (*ḥālāb*)—The expression or cliché "milk and honey" is used some 20x in the OT to describe the land God promised to his people. Milk is normally and rightly seen as reflecting the pastoral nature of the land that could support various types of flocks and herds. (*ḥālāb*)

Set apart (*hibdaltî*)—Here the verb is used to declare that the LORD God had separated Israel from the nations. It was used earlier in Leviticus (1:17; 5:8) in the context of a physical separation of that which was tangible. Lev. 10:10 and 11:47 introduced the contrast or separation between the holy and common and between the clean and unclean. This was a different standard from that of the nation of Egypt, a place out of which the LORD had brought his people. This separation from foreigners is a concern for the postexilic remnant, too (Ezra 6:21; Neh. 9:2; 10:28 [10:29 MT]). But

here in Lev. 20:24 this separation included a completely comprehensive concept. Not only was there to be separation in areas including sexual activity, dietary laws, and the seeking of spiritual direction, but God's people had been separated to God himself. They had not only been separated from activities, but they had been separated to a place of privilege of inheriting the Land of Promise and fellowshiping with their LORD. It was the LORD himself who separated Israel to a place of privilege—they had not done it of their own volition or power. This fundamental concept is repeated in v. 26. [*bdl*]

21:9 Burned (*tiśśārēp*)—The concept of fire has been dealt with in Lev. 1:7. However, the burning here is not of the sacrificial offerings but of the daughter of the priest who had become a prostitute. Stoning was the most common method of death (see Lev. 20:2). But fire in the OT can symbolize judgment (Gen. 19:24; Lev. 10:2), although in a few places it can also symbolize cleansing (Num. 31:21-24). Fire is often used to signify judgment on the pagan nations (e.g., Amos 1–2), and here the fire is used to judge the sinful daughter, which indicates that her actions made her like one of the pagan nations (cf. Gen. 38:24). The only other use of fire for execution of an individual is found in Lev. 20:14. [*śrp*]

21:10 High priest (*wĕhakkōhēn haggādôl*)—"High priest" is literally "the great priest" or "the priest who is chief." The adjective "great" is used 2x in Leviticus, but only here is it used of the high priest (cf. Lev. 19:15 for its other use; see Lev. 1:5 for "priest"). It is used in the OT in a variety of ways including describing God himself (e.g., 2 Chron. 2:4; Ps. 86:10). The high priest is great in the sense that there is only one high priest at a time, so he had unique roles to play within the nation of Israel and on behalf of Israel. See Lev. 4:3 for information on "the anointed priest." [*gādôl*]

22:10 Guest (*tôšāb*)—This is the first of eight usages of the noun in Leviticus. In Lev. 25:23, 35 it is used as a synonym of *gēr* or "alien" (see Lev. 16:29). But the *tôšāb* does not have the same status or privileges as the alien and rather is usually seen as a temporary, landless wage earner, that is, a hired servant. Unlike the alien the guest could not eat the Passover, and his family could be sold as permanent slaves (Lev. 25:45). Here in Lev. 22:10 the temporary sojourner or guest (it is unclear if he is a temporary servant) is refused the privilege of eating any of the sacred offerings even though he is in the house of the priest. Hospitality does not take precedence over the regulations of the LORD. In Lev. 25:23, somewhat surprisingly, the Israelite is called both a *tôšāb* ("tenant, sojourner") and a *gēr* ("alien"). In context, the LORD is teaching the Israelites about the land and how the land must be returned to the original occupying family every 50 years. It was not to be sold permanently since the ultimate owner is the LORD God and the Israelites were guests and aliens who enjoyed all the benefits of the land but were not native. The LORD gave them the land that they occupied in his name. [*tôšāb*]

22:21 To fulfill (*lĕpallē'*)—This verb when used in the intensive (Piel) stem as is done here, conveys the idea of "fulfilling a vow" while the basic meaning in the Hiphil is "to cause a wonderful thing to happen" [V. Hamilton, TWOT, 2:723]. The emphasis is on the unique or wonderful nature of this vow although the context

does not provide any insight into the exact nature of the vow. In Lev. 27:2 the expression translated "makes a special vow" contains the verb *pl'*. This verb, when used in the Hiphil (causative) stem as is done here, conveys the idea of "to cause a wonderful thing to happen" with a nuance of fulfilling a vow (see Lev. 22:21) [V. Hamilton, TWOT, 2:723]. Often used of the LORD's fulfillment of that which he had promised (e.g., Deut. 28:59; Judg. 13:19; Isa. 28:29), the verb can be translated "make or do wonderfully." The vow that the worshiper makes in Lev. 27 is a "special, wonderful, extraordinary vow" because it was not required and so was seen as over and above any obligation. An Israelite could vow himself to service, or be vowed to service, but could also be redeemed, giving to God a value equal to the worth of the service that was vowed. [*pl'*]

23:2 Sacred assemblies (*miqrā'ê*)—The term "sacred" or "holy" is the common term *qōdeš* (see Lev. 2:3). Here the assemblies are called holy since they are both appointed by God and focus on God. The noun comes from the verb *qr'*, which means "call, proclaim, read" (*BDB*, 894). It is used only in Neh. 8:8 with the concept of reading. This word is used 11x in this chapter to describe the various special appointed times of worship, including the weekly Sabbath (Lev. 23:3), times that the Israelites are "called" to meet with God. In Ezekiel it is also used to designate the new moons (Ezek. 46:3; cf. Isa. 66:23). However, its most usual designation is reserved for reference to the seven holy convocations listed in this chapter. For the Israelites these times were not to be considered on the same level as other celebrations. The synonym *mô'ē d* is used for an appointed time or place and therefore can refer to an appointed gathering as it does in this verse. For the Christian, Christ has fulfilled this aspect of the law so there is no need now to recognize these special times (Col. 2:16-17). [*miqrā'*]

23:5 Passover (*pesaḥ*)—This is the only occurrence in Leviticus of the common OT term for Passover. The original instructions and the first celebration of the Passover are recorded in Exod. 12 while the second occurrence, and the only one celebrated during Israel's time of wilderness living, is recorded in Num. 9. Once in the land and once the males who were born in the wilderness were circumcised, the Passover was celebrated once again. The procedures for the Passover are also described in Num. 28:16-25 and Deut. 16:1-8. It would remind the Israelites of the time the LORD brought them out of Egypt while the blood of the sacrificed lamb protected them in their houses. The Passover was essentially a domestic celebration without any special events occurring at the tabernacle. The Lord Jesus celebrated this feast (Matt. 26:2, 18) and used it to introduce to his 12 apostles the "Lord's Table," celebrating his own body and blood. The Apostle Paul later described Christ as the "Passover" for the Christian (1 Cor. 5:7; cf. John 1:29; 1 Pet. 1:19). [*pesaḥ*]

23:6 Feast of Unleavened Bread (*ḥag ham-maṣṣôt*)—This technical title is used 10x in the OT though only this single time in Leviticus. A parallel Greek phrase is used twice in the NT (Matt. 26:17; Luke 22:1). The noun *ḥag* ("festival-gathering, feast, pilgrim-feast") [*BDB*, 290] is a general word that is used to describe not only this feast but also many others (e.g., Feast of Tabernacles; Lev. 23:34). It was first used in Scripture to describe the festival that

Moses requested Pharaoh to allow the Israelites to celebrate in the wilderness (Exod. 10:9). Later it was used to describe the Passover (Exod. 12:14) and then the feast that occurred at the golden calf incident (Exod. 32:5). It is used 4x in Leviticus (here, 23:34, 39, 41). The Feast of Unleavened Bread began on the fifteenth day of the first month (the Passover was held on the fourteenth day) and, as this verse indicates, lasted one week. The purpose of this divinely ordained festival was to remember and symbolize the haste in which Israel left Egypt (Exod. 12:39), combined later with the recognition of the provision of God in the Promised Land (Josh. 5:11-12). Any suggestions that this feast is to be tied to an agricultural calendar (i.e., to celebrate a specific harvest), as is often done, is not based on Scripture. The eschatological material in Ezekiel indicates that this feast, though not specifically designated by the technical title, will be part of the celebrations in the new temple (Ezek. 45:21-23). Obviously God desires his people of the past and in the future to remember his great act of deliverance, an act that was accomplished quickly and an act that culminated in an abundant provision in the place that he had promised for his people. [*ḥag*]

23:24 Commemoration (*zikrôn*)—This term, used for days, items, books, and here of the Feast of Trumpets, comes from the verb *zkr*, which means "remember" (*BDB*, 269). Though this feast is not technically called "Trumpets" here in Leviticus, the commemoration by the trumpet blasts to signify this day is the common feature (cf. Num. 29:1-6). In this verse the term that describes the commemoration is *tĕrû'â*, which means literally "shout or blast of war, alarm or joy" from the verb *rw'*, in the Hiphil "raise a shout, give a blast" (*BDB*,

929). The concept of trumpets comes from the silver trumpets in Num. 10:1-10 being used to signal marching or alarm. It appears that trumpet blasts were used at various feasts and festivals (cf. Num. 10:10) and perhaps signaled the beginning of each month (Ps. 81:3), though in the Psalms it is the ram's horn that is sounded. Later David used a full orchestra in the worship of God (1 Chron. 25) but he maintained the playing of the silver trumpets regularly before the ark (1 Chron. 16:6). This first day in the seventh month, known today as *Rosh Hashanah* (literally, "the beginning of the year") or New Year's Day, was a day of rest for the nation. Some scholars see the Feast of Trumpets as a type of the Rapture of the church, which will serve as a warning to the nation of Israel and the rest of the world that God's judgment is coming. This meaning is never stated in Scripture but is based on a larger hermeneutic that sees the feasts functioning as types of later divine interventions. [*zikrôn*]

23:34 Tabernacles (*hassukôt*)—This specific feast is referred to in Leviticus only here. In the rest of the Pentateuch it is mentioned by name only in Deut. 16:13, 16; 31:10. Its four other mentions in the OT occur in 2 Chron. 8:13; Ezra 3:4, and Zech. 14:16, 18. Zechariah describes this feast as being the required one for non-covenant nations to participate in during the coming Kingdom Age to show their acknowledgment of the true God and the nation he delivered from Egypt. In the NT this feast is referred to only in John 7:2. It is also described, though not designated by the phrase *šib'at yāmîm*, in Exod. 23:16b; 34:22b (both times called the "Feast of Ingathering"); Num. 29:12-34. The function of this feast may be related in part to the fall ingathering of fruit as

the references in Exodus seem to indicate. However, the other biblical passages seem merely to relate it to living in temporary shelters as the Israelites did during their wilderness wanderings. These tabernacles or booths were made of boughs and would remind God's people of all that he did in giving them both a permanent place to live and a land that produced bountifully. [*sukkâ*]

24:5 Loaves of bread (*ḥallôt*)—The "bread of presence" was conceived of as a "grain offering" (cf. Lev. 2:1-16) and numbered 12 to represent all the tribes of Israel. Since this is so, this bread would have been unleavened bread (see Lev. 2:4), which would have been appropriate since these loaves would be eaten by the priests after an entire week in the tabernacle (Lev. 24:8-9). By eating this bread the priests would signify their belief, based on the ritual they had performed that week, that the 12 tribes of Israel were in spiritual fellowship with the LORD. [*ḥallâ*]

24:11 Blasphemed (*wayyiqqōb*)—Literally "and blasphemed and cursed the NAME" this phrase uses two parallel verbs, *qbb* (as in Lev. 24:16) ("blaspheme, curse") and *qll* ("to curse"). For the latter see Lev. 19:14. The verb *qbb* ("curse, blaspheme") "connotes the act of uttering a formula designed to undo its object" (L. Coppes, TWOT, 2:783). It is used most frequently in Num. 22–24 in the incident of Balaam and Balak. It is difficult to tell, because of the limited context in the incident here in Leviticus, if the young man was using any sort of mystical formula to curse the LORD God. It appears, in light of the reference in the previous verse to his mixed parentage, that he may have sought to bring dishonor in some manner upon the God of the Israelites in a fit of rage. Here the LORD is referred to simply as "the NAME" (cf. Deut. 28:58, "this glorious and awesome name—the LORD your God"). (For the concept of "profaning" the name of the LORD see Lev. 18:21; for the concept of "swearing falsely" by the name of the LORD see Lev. 19:12.) [*qbb*]

25:10 Liberty (*děrôr*)—Israel's "Jubilee Year" (see Lev. 25:13) occurred every fiftieth year and functioned like a sabbatical year (Lev. 25:3-7) with one major addition. The term *děrôr*, translated "liberty," is used in a limited sense of the returning of property and land to their originally allotted families and restoring servants to their families. The term "jubilee" is the transliteration, rather than translation, of the Hebrew term *yôbēl* (see Lev. 25:13), literally "ram's horn," the sound made to announce the beginning of this special year (Lev. 25:9). This term is associated with the fiftieth year in this chapter and in Num. 36:4. [*děrôr*]

25:13 Jubilee (*hayyôbēl*)—The phrase "the Year of Jubilee" (or a near equivalent) is used 8x in Leviticus (here, 25:28, 33, 40, 50, 52, 54; 27:17). The term for "jubilee" most likely derives from a noun meaning "ram or ram's horn," which made the sound at the beginning of the fiftieth year (see Lev. 25:9). Taken this way the literal translation could be "year of the ram's horn." While this background for the word is most common there is the possibility that it could come from the verb *ybl*, "to bring (forth), bear along, lead (forth)" since in preparation for this special year the LORD "brings forth" abundant harvest (R. Alexander, TWOT, 358-9; Lev. 25:19-21). The Year of Jubilee was the special time in which the land lay fallow (the LORD provided for his people through previous generous harvests) and possessions, including land and slaves, returned to their original owners. This unique year reminded the people of God's ultimate ownership of the land as well as the desire God had for each family to be dependent upon him alone for their sustenance. Every 50 years (approximately each generation) every family had the opportunity to look to the LORD to provide for them on their own land. It was to be "holy" to the Israelites (Lev. 25:12). [*yôbēl*]

25:18 Safely (*lābeṭaḥ*)—The idea of living securely or safely in the land involves the use of this noun in an adverbial construction. It is commonly used with the verb *yšb* ("dwell") as it is here. Security was promised to those who were rightly related and in fellowship with the LORD (here; Ps. 16:9). This security was part of the national promise that Jeremiah reiterated for the future (Jer. 23:6). It is also used in other places to contrast the futility of trusting in anyone or anything besides the LORD (e.g., Judg. 18:7; Isa. 47:8; Ezek. 30:9). [*beṭaḥ*]

25:21 Blessing (*birkātî*)—This is the only use in Leviticus of the noun *běrākâ* ("blessing"). It comes from the verb *brk*, which means to "kneel, bless" [BDB, 138]. The verb is used twice in Leviticus, in 9:22, 23. The noun can mean either "the verbal enduement with good things or a collective expression for the good things themselves (Ezek. 34:26; Mal. 3:10)" [J. Oswalt, TWOT, 1:132]. In the context of Lev. 25:21 the blessing was an abundant harvest that would suffice for the time the land was allowed its sabbatical. While blessing could be in the form of spiritual values, for the Israelite the land and blessing of it was all an essential and indispensable part of God's promise to them as a nation. See Lev. 9:22 for the use of the verb *brk*. [*běrākâ*]

25:25 Redeem (*wĕgā'al*)—The nearest relative is specified in v. 49 as an uncle, a cousin, or any [male] blood relative in his clan. The noun *gō'ēl* is derived from the verb *g'l*, which has the primary meaning of redeeming one's relative from difficulty or danger. This verb, together with its derivatives, is used 117x. In Leviticus it occurs throughout chapters 25 (vv. 25, 26, 30, 33, 48, 49, 54) and 27 (vv. 13, 15, 19, 20, 27, 28, 31, 33). The duty of the nearest relative in Lev. 25:25-28 concerns the redemption of land sold in a time of financial need while in Lev. 25:47-53 it concerns the redemption of the Israelite himself who sold himself as a hired hand. The Hebrew verb *pdh*, also translated "redeem," is different in that there is no concept of family relationship when it is used (see Lev. 27:27). In Lev. 27:31 *g'l* is again the word used, this time to describe a redemption by a relative (see Lev. 25:25). Here, however, the redemption is by the owner himself since the redemption was not due to an inability to pay but a choice on the part of the Israelite worshiper. To prevent a redemption that could favor the Israelite, an added-value "tax" was required. A redemption, in this context, of the fruit of the land, might be necessary for the purposes of transportation, but since everyone lived within a small land mass, once the Promised Land was occupied, redemption was obviously discouraged. [*g'l*]

25:32 The Levites (*halwîyyîm*)—The proper name for the tribe of Levi occurs only 3x in the book of Leviticus (twice in this verse and once in the following verse). This may appear somewhat odd since the English title of this book seems to indicate that this would be a book pertaining to the Levites. Nevertheless, much in this book pertains to the Aaronic priests who came from Aaron's family

within the tribe of Levi. The Levites were chosen to replace the firstborn of each family in the incident of the golden calf when they showed their fidelity to the LORD (Exod. 32:26-29; Num. 3:11-13). In this action they redeemed themselves from the earlier unspiritual action of their forefathers (Gen. 49:5-7). Aaron was descended from Levi through Kohath and Amram (Exod. 6:16, 18, 20). As such, the sacrificial system that Aaron's descendants administered is generally regarded as "Levitical." Here in Lev. 25:32-33, the reference is not to just Aaron's descendants who were priests but to all descendants of Levi, which would include the "nonpriestly" Levites (Num. 3–4). Aaron and his sons as priests were to bear the major responsibilities for the tabernacle and its services but the entire tribe of Levi was to assist the priests in carrying out this duty though they could never act as officiating priests (Num. 18:1-2; Deut. 18:1-8). The duties of assistance by the Levites included bearing the ark (1 Sam. 6:15; 2 Sam. 15:24), performing various services in the tabernacle (Exod. 38:21; Num. 1:50-53), and ministering to Aaron and his sons (Num. 3:9; 8:19). Later David placed Levites in charge of music (1 Chron. 15:16, 17, 22), and the guarding of the temple (1 Chron. 9:26; 26:17). In the postexilic period they also taught the people the law (Neh. 8:7-8). [*lēwî*]

26:6 Peace (*šālôm*)—This common (over 250x in the OT) and most important theological term is used just a single time in the book of Leviticus. While it has a wide variety of meanings, it is used here of the safety and security that the Israelites would find in the land if they were an obedient nation. It is safety from both external human threats of other peoples and internal (i.e., within the Land of Promise) animal threats as well. The fuller meaning of completeness, well-being, wholeness is not in primary view here. [*šālôm*]

26:9 I will look with favor (*ûpānîtî*)—To look with favor is literally "to turn" and in this case this turning is to the Israelites. That it is a turning with favor and not judgment is clear from the rest of the verse. [*pnh*]

    Make fruitful (*wĕhiprêtî*)—Childbearing was part of the creation mandate (Gen. 1:28) and children were seen elsewhere as a great blessing from God (Lev. 26:9; Deut. 28:11; Ps. 127:3-5). Here they are part of God's turning toward the Israelites when they live in obedience to him. The use of *prh* would be a reminder of the creation mandate given in Gen. 1:28, repeated post-Flood in Gen. 9:1, and the promises in the Abrahamic Covenant in Gen. 17:6. God's promises to Abraham would come true in a time of obedience. See Lev. 20:20 for "die childless," and also Deut. 28:18 for childlessness as a judgment of God. [*prh*]

26:13 Heads held high (*qômĕmîyyût*)—This verse uses a picture from slavery, in which the slaves were yoked together as animals with their heads bowed forward as they were forced to use their shoulders against the yoke. God declares that he, when he brought Israel out of Egypt, broke the bars of the yoke and enabled them to lift their heads (literally, "and I made you walk erect") as free men. The Hebrew noun, used as an adjective for erectness or uprightness, is used only here in the entire OT. It comes from the verb *qwm*, which means "arise, stand up, stand" (*BDB*, 877). [*qômĕmîyyût*]

26:18 Punish (*lĕyassĕrâ*)—The meaning of *ysr* ("punish, chastise, discipline") con-

tains not only the idea of punishment but also the very present idea of education or instruction (see v. 23). It is used 3x in Leviticus, all in this chapter (here and verses 23 and 28). A synonym *nkh* appears in v. 24, meaning "smite, scourge" (*BDB*, 644). The basis for God employing this action is the covenantal relationship he had with his people (e.g., Exod. 19:5-6). This correction came in a relationship that was instigated by God, a relationship that continued to be sustained (the Israelites were often miraculously provided for by the LORD) by him, and a relationship for which the LORD had invested his own reputation and word (e.g., Deut. 26:19). This relationship is often referred to using familial terms (e.g., father/son, Deut. 8:5; 32:6) and so discipline was not only allowed but required (Prov. 3:11-12). The same action of discipline and the reasoning behind it are used for the Christian in Heb. 12:4-11. [*ysr*]

26:19 Pride (*gĕ'ôn*)—Pride, when used of man's arrogant show of personal glory as here, is always spoken of negatively in Scripture. The Hebrew word is, however, often translated "exaltation, majesty, excellence," and so context must determine whether it is to be regarded in a negative (e.g., Isa. 16:6) or positive manner (e.g., Isa. 2:10). Since pride or majesty can describe God it must not be seen as intrinsically sinful. The object and source of the pride as well as attitude can cause it to become wrong. Previously in the Pentateuch it was used only in Exod. 15:7 of God's great majesty. Its only other usage in all the Pentateuch and OT historical books is here in Lev. 26:19. It is modified here by the term *'ōz* (literally "strength, might" but translated "stubborn" in keeping with the negative concept of pride). [*gā'ôn*]

26:31 I will take . . . delight (*'ārîaḥ*)—Here empty ritualism, even when done in the right "form," that is, according to the literal regulations and therefore able to produce "the pleasing aroma" outwardly, is not acceptable to God for the purpose of making atonement (Lev. 1:4, 9). The verb *ryḥ* means "smell, perceive odor" (*BDB*, 926) and so God's declaration that he will not "smell" their offerings is a choice on his part due to their continued sinfulness and his decision to send them into exile. The breath of man was given him by the LORD God (Gen. 2:7). Now the LORD seeks to enjoy the smell that man can produce as he offers obedient sacrifices. The goal of OT sacrifice as evidenced by Noah was that God could smell the sacrifice as a pleasing aroma (Gen. 8:21). This figure is further seen in the NT when the prayers of the saints rise like incense to God (Rev. 5:8). [*ryḥ*]

26:46 These are the decrees, the laws and the regulations (*haḥuqqîm wĕhammišpāṭîm wĕhattôrôt*)—Three terms are used to summarize the material of chapters 1–26. In this verse there does not appear to be a desire to make a distinction between them (for *ḥuqqâ* see Lev. 3:17; for *mišpāṭ* see Lev. 5:10; for *tôrâ* see Lev. 6:9 [6:2 MT]), but rather this is an effort to be all-inclusive so as not to eliminate any regulation given in the book of Leviticus. The terms "decrees" and "laws" represent the two Hebrew terms *mišpāṭ* and *ḥōq*, which have been used as synonyms (9x) throughout Leviticus (cf. Lev. 18:4). Here translated "regulations," the term *tôrâ* is used in parallel as a synonym to "decrees" and "laws." Throughout Leviticus the term "torah" is used in context to refer to a specific set of instructions (cf. Lev. 6:9 [6:2 MT]). Here, for the first time, it can be seen to have a broader nuance referring to the entire material of chapters 1–26. In the NT the term "torah" is used as synonymous with the entire Pentateuch (cf. Matt. 5:17; 11:13; 22:40; Luke 24:44; Acts 13:15; Rom. 3:21). This verse functions as the conclusion to the book of Leviticus. A comparison of 26:46 with 27:34 suggests that chapter 27 is an appendix. [*ḥuqqâ*] [*mišpāṭ*] [*tôrâ*]

27:21 Devoted (*haḥērem*)—This Hebrew verb is used here and in Lev. 27:28, 29 to designate anything that is irrevocably given to the LORD. "Surrendering something to God meant devoting it to the service of God or putting it under a ban for utter destruction" (L. Wood, *TWOT*, 1:324). Josh. 6:24 shows these two aspects, both this dedication to service and total destruction, in that the silver, gold, bronze, and iron were put into the treasury of the LORD's house while the remainder of the goods and the city of Jericho itself were destroyed completely by fire. In Lev. 27:21 a field is dedicated to God while in v. 28 it is used of anything "whether man or animal or family land." God's people must be careful in what they declare dedicated to God since God himself holds them responsible for their vow. They must never use it for their self advancement or benefit. It is now wholly devoted to God. [*ḥrm*]

27:27 Buy it (*ûpādâ*)—The verb translated here means "buy it back" while "redeem" is the translation of the verb *g'l* (see Lev. 25:25). Here, used in a synonymous manner, these two verbs are normally differentiated by the fact that for the latter verb there is always an emphasis on the redemption being the duty or privilege of a near relative. [*pdh*]

27:30 Tithe (*ma'śar*)—The Hebrew word for tithe has the literal meaning of one-tenth. The concept of a tithe occurs in Leviticus only in this paragraph (Lev. 27:30-33), a seemingly incidental setting (see Lev. 27:1). Here in Lev. 27 the range of what is to be tithed is given in the broadest possible terms, especially as it relates to a nation whose focus is on the promise of a land. The tithe would include all plant and domesticated animal life without exception. This tithe is not to be confused with an offering of firstborns and firstfruits (Exod. 22:29-30), which, for animals, was given on the eighth day and therefore would not be part of the yearly tithe. Tithing predated the law as is evidenced by Abram paying a tithe of recovered goods to Melchizedek after being blessed by him (Gen. 14:20; see Heb. 7:1-10) and Jacob vowing a tithe at Bethel, though here a slightly different form of the word is used (Gen. 28:22). The idea of tithing was not unique to Israel in the ancient Near East as proof exists for this practice in both Egyptian and Mesopotamian documents. Tithing is further developed in the Pentateuch in Num. 18:21, 24, 26, 28; Deut. 12:6, 11, 17; 14:23, 28; 26:12. Tithing is dealt with in the historical books in 2 Chron. 31:5, 6, 12; and Neh. 10:37, 38; 12:44; 13:5, 12. In the Prophets tithing is noted in Ezek. 45:11, 14; Amos 4:4; and the famous passage of Mal. 3:8, 10. [*ma'ăśēr*]

NUMBERS

David L. Brooks

1:1 Desert (*midbār*)—The Hebrew word for "desert" occurs twice as often in Numbers as in any other OT book (48x) and is part of the book's Hebrew title: "In the Desert." The term refers to vast grasslands (Ps. 65:12) suitable for pasturing sheep (Exod. 3:1; Num. 14:33) but not for planting (Jer. 2:2). Springs may appear in it (Gen. 16:7), but the land is mostly waterless (Exod. 15:22; Num. 21:5). The desert through which Israel traveled was so arid (Jer. 2:6; 17:6), desolate, inhospitable (Deut. 32:10), and large that it was terrifying (Deut. 1:19). A desert was mostly uninhabited (Job 38:26; Jer. 17:6) but might possess isolated cities (Josh. 20:8; Isa. 42:11). Larger deserts were considered uncrossable (Jer. 9:12). In light of these characteristics, Israel's willingness to follow the Lord into the desert demonstrated her devotion (Jer. 2:2). For Israel, "desert" was a geographical term as well as a period of time (Deut. 8:2, 16; Ps. 95:10) where and when God tested the nation. Positively, in the desert God revealed his presence, compassion, and guidance (Neh. 9:19-21; Ps. 78:52; Hos. 13:5), provided food (Exod. 16:32; Deut. 2:7) and water (Ps. 78:15), cared for Israel as a father (Deut. 1:31), and performed miraculous signs (Num. 14:22). Negatively, in the desert Israel tested God (Ps. 95:8-9)

and rebelled against him (Deut. 9:7; Ps. 78:40). Both the negative and positive appear throughout Numbers. In a later time Christ would be led to and tested in a wilderness, would depend upon God for provision, overcome temptation, and find his Father faithful (Matt. 4:1-11), thus overcoming where his ancestors had failed. His followers experience their own wilderness experiences (cf. Heb. 10:32-39). [*midbār*]

Sinai (*sînay*)—Numbers is second only to Exodus in its number of references to Sinai. The references twice draw attention to the mountain (e.g., Num. 3:1), but Numbers applies the name 10x to the desert. Scholars dispute the original meaning of the word. The more likely proposals are "moon," the moon god Sin, "thorn bush" (the Hebrew term *sĕneh* denotes the burning bush where God first encountered Moses, [Exod. 3:2]), "stone," and "rocky jagged mountain" (cf. P. Maiberger, *TDOT*, 10:218-19). The location of the mountain is also controversial, with proposals ranging from the northern to southern Sinai Peninsula, and to western Saudi Arabia. On Mount Sinai, also called Horeb (Exod. 3:1; 33:6), God first appeared to Moses in the burning bush (Exod. 3:12) and then before all Israel (Exod. 19:18) with glory (Exod. 24:16-17) at which time he gave the

Ten Commandments. Israel's stay at Mt. Sinai is in view from Exod. 19 to Num. 10:11, following which God led them in the march to Canaan. In the future, but prior to conquering Jerusalem, Israel would think of God as coming from Sinai to Canaan in order to rescue them (Judg. 5:4-5). Then after Jerusalem was taken they would think of God coming from Zion to rescue them (cf. Ps. 20:2). Thus, these two mountains symbolized his residence, so that as Israel moved through the Sinai wilderness (Ps. 68:7-8) they followed the Lord to what amounted to his later residence (Num. 10:11-13, 34; cf. Deut. 33:2; Ps. 68:17). In these two chapters God organized Israel for the march. [*sînay*]

Tent of Meeting (*'ōhel mô'ēd*)—The Tent of Meeting is mentioned in Numbers more often than in any other book (55x out of 146). A tent is the characteristic shelter of shepherds (Isa. 38:12), soldiers (Judg. 6:5; 2 Kings 7:7-10), and nomads (Jud 8:11; S. of S. 1:5), with the first appropriate in describing God's residence and the second and third that of Israel during the journey. This tent was characterized by holiness (Exod. 29:43-44, "consecrate"). God's glory appeared here (Exod. 29:43; Num. 14:10; 16:42; 20:6), he dwelled among his people (Exod. 29:44-46), and met (Exod. 29:42-43; 30:36; Num. 17:4) and spoke (Exod. 29:42; Num. 1:1; 7:89) with them. Here all Israel assembled for special occasions (Num. 8:9; 10:3; Deut. 31:14; Josh. 18:1; 19:51) and offered sacrifices (Lev. 17:3-5). While in the desert the tent was to be in the midst of the camp (Num. 2:2). Only the priests and Levites were permitted beyond the entrance (Num. 18:2, 4, 22). Moses had previously erected a different Tent of Meeting outside the camp (Exod. 33:7) where non-Levites could enter (Exod. 33:11) and inquire of the Lord, and where God spoke

to Moses (Exod. 33:7-9). The national Tent of Meeting was named after Moses' tent (R. Averbeck, *NIDOTTE*, 2:873, 876). In a similar fashion in the NT God set up his tent among people by becoming incarnate and by this means revealed God's glory (John 1:14, where the Greek verb translated "made his dwelling" is *skēnoō* that means to set up one's tent and is cognate to *skēnos*, tent) and became the sole avenue by which people could approach God (John 14:6). [*'ōhel, mô'ēd*]

1:2 Community (*'ădat*)—More than half of the occurrences of the term in the OT (83 of 149x) are in Numbers. Although occasionally the word refers to a particular group within Israel ("followers," Num. 16:5, 6, 11), it usually refers to all Israel gathered together (*BDB*, 417), primarily at the Tent of Meeting (Num. 10:3). They were chiefly a religious assembly (2 Chron. 5:6; Ps. 111:1) called "the Lord's people" (Num. 31:16). Members were adult (over 20 years old) Israelite males who were responsible to go to war (Num. 26:2; Josh. 22:12) and have authority to render legal decisions in lawsuits (Lev. 24:14, 16; Num. 15:35-36; 35:12, 24-25) and coronate a king (1 Kings 12:20). The community was viewed as a corporate whole (Lev. 4:13; Num. 15:25-26), so that when one or many members sinned the whole community incurred guilt (Josh. 22:18-20). In religious matters the community was represented by priests, Levites, and elders (Lev. 4:13-15; 10:6, 17; Num. 8:10-11), and in civil and political matters by appointed leaders and elders (Num. 16:2; Judg. 21:16). When the community witnessed the work of its officials, it lent sanction to their actions (D. Levy, *TDOT*, 10:473) and so was bound by their decisions (Josh. 9:15-19). Foreigners could become part of the community (Exod.

12:19; Lev. 24:16) through circumcision (Exod. 12:43-49). In the NT God would add another community of his own called the church and Christians, a community both Jews and Gentiles could join by means of faith (Acts 11:17; Rom. 1:16). Like the OT community, the NT community would be responsible for the observable behavior of its members (1 Cor. 5:1-2; Rev. 2:20). ['ēdâ]

1:3 Number (*tipqĕdû*)—One third of the OT's uses of the verb (*pqd*) are in Numbers, and most of these are in the census lists (T. Williams, *NIDOTTE*, 3:658). The term in Numbers is used chiefly for registering people for military or religious responsibilities. In this military context (see "Army" below) it means to list and organize potential recruits. The term can mean to muster soldiers just prior to battle (Josh. 8:10; 1 Sam. 11:8; 13:15; 2 Sam. 18:1), but with no battle on the immediate horizon, it suggests preparation for the march to Canaan and the intended military campaign there. This compares to the use of the verb in the administrative religious context where Levites as young as one month old were "counted" (Num. 3:15-16, 39), but only those over thirty were assigned duties (Num. 3:10; 4:22-49). God continues to call and enlist NT Christians for service (Matt. 11:29; Eph. 2:10). [*pqd*]

Army (*ṣābā'*)—The term translated "army" in some contexts means military service, troops, those who left Egypt, heavenly bodies, compulsory labor, or tribulation (*HALOT*, 995). In Numbers the noun and the verb are used both for Israel as an army or in divisions (Num. 1:3) and also for the religious work at the Tent of Meeting (Num. 4:3, 23, 30, as a verb, "to serve"). The connection between the army and the Tent of Meeting is appropriate, for

God was enthroned above the ark in the Tent of Meeting (2 Sam. 6:2; cf. Exod. 40:2-3) as the captain of Israel's army before whom they would march (Num. 32:27; Josh. 4:13); he sent out this army (1 Sam. 15:2); and he will be avenged by them (Num. 31:3). It is expected that the Lord would go out with Israel's army (Ps. 44:9; 60:10, 12; 108:11). When the army went out, it was to be accompanied by articles from the sanctuary (Num. 31:6), including the ark (Josh. 6:4). All this forecasts the coming of a "holy war" announced and led by Yahweh. At this point in Numbers, Israel's army was organized and began to march toward the battlefield to conquer the Promised Land (T. Longman, *NIDOTTE*, 3:735). As the Lord of Armies (traditionally Lord of Hosts, *yhwh ṣĕbā'ôt* [plural of *ṣābā'*], translated "Lord Almighty in the NIV, cf. Ps. 24:10), this is only one of God's armies at his disposal to accomplish his will. He likens Christians to soldiers (2 Tim. 2:3) who fight a spiritual rather than physical war (Eph. 6:10-18). [*ṣābā'*]

1:16 Leaders (*nāśî'*)—The cognate verb (*nāśā'*) means to lift or carry. The noun form that is used here means one who is lifted up, such as a chief (*BDB*, 671-72). The word can be a general term of respect (Gen. 23:6) or refer to an authority in a community (Exod. 22:28; Num. 27:2) or a ruler of a locality (Gen. 34:2). It often stands for the head of a tribe (Num. 1:16, 44) or an administrative head of a clan in a tribe (Num. 3:24, 30, 35; 10:4; Josh. 22:14). The head of a particular family within a clan is often called the "head" (*rō'š*; Num. 7:2; 25:14; 36:1; 1 Chron. 5:15; 7:40) of the family (1 Kings 8:1 seems to reverse the titles so that "heads" are over tribes and the "leaders" over families). From family "heads" came the "leaders" who were therefore "heads" and "leaders" (2 Chron. 1:2). God continued in the NT to call leaders who had learned leadership within the family before being raised to positions of wider influence in the church (1 Tim. 3:4-5). In the OT tribal leaders were the leaders of the whole nation (Num. 7:2, 84; 36:1), so the one head of the tribal confederation was a *nāśîʾ* (Num. 3:32). Israel's king would be called a *nāśîʾ* when he ruled only one tribe (e.g., Judah; Ezek. 7:27; 12:10, 12), when the whole nation at the time of the prophecy was just one tribe (Ezek. 34:24; 37:24-25; 44:3; 45:17), or the whole nation that he ruled was about to be reduced to one tribe (1 Kings 11:34; Ezek. 21:25). In our context the leaders were the leaders of the congregation and what each one did represented his tribe (Num. 7:10-11, 18, 24), and what they all committed to do bound the entire community (Josh. 9:15, 18-21). Their decision not to enter Canaan would commit the whole nation to a rebellion against God. God continues to warn of the need to exercise care in promoting someone to leadership over his people (1 Tim. 5:22) because of a leader's influence on the character of his community. [*nāśîʾ*]

1:19 As the Lord <u>commanded</u> (*ka'ăšer ṣiwwâ yhwh*)—The Hebrew verb "commanded" denotes a superior giving orders or commands to a subordinate (G. Liedke, *TLOT*, 1062), though it can also mean to commission someone to a task (Num. 27:19, 22). The word occurs 496x in the OT with about 10 percent (48x) in Numbers, behind only Deuteronomy (88x) and Exodus (53x) in frequency. Just over half (252x) of all occurrences are in the Pentateuch with its emphasis on law, and even more (280x) have God as the one commanding or ordering. The second most frequent subject (85x) of the verb is

Moses the lawgiver (T. Williams, *NIDOTTE*, 3:776-77). In Numbers only God and Moses are the subjects of the verb, 42 and 6x, respectively. Frequently (22x) the text says that someone did what Yahweh commanded to be done, stressing Israel's obedience (Num. 1:18-19, 54; 31:31). One of the major themes of the first ten chapters of Numbers is that Israel obeyed whatever God commanded. This contrasts with the repeated disobedience that appears beginning with chapter 11. The person most frequently commanded by God is Moses (Num. 2:34; 4:49). Twelve times the text says that others did what God commanded Moses (Num. 8:3, 20; 9:5; 36:10), highlighting Moses' intermediary, revelatory, and authoritative role. God commands everything from picking up of a staff (Num. 20:9), to executing a lawbreaker (Num. 15:36), to waging war (Num. 31:7). With the emphasis on God's leadership and Moses' mediation, it is fitting that the last verb in the book is *ṣiwwâ* (Num. 36:13, "gave," NIV) with God as commander and Moses as mediator. All of one's life should be viewed as a response to the call and command of God (e.g., Phil. 3:12-15). [*ṣwh*]

1:20 Firstborn (*běkōr*)—Scripture repeatedly states that Reuben was Jacob's firstborn (Gen. 35:23; 46:8; 49:3; Exod. 6:14; Num. 1:20; 26:5; 1 Chron. 5:1, 3). A firstborn child was special to a father (Zech. 12:10) as a sign of his manly vigor (Gen. 49:3; Deut. 21:17; Pss. 78:51; 105:36). Although the firstborn had a higher status (Gen. 27:19; 48:14, 17-18; Ps. 89:27), received twice as much inheritance as his siblings (Deut. 21:17), and normally replaced his father as the leader (2 Kings 3:27; 2 Chron. 21:3), Reuben and his tribe could not claim any of these honors. Moses' law prohibited a polygamous father from stripping the firstborn of his privileges simply because he was born to a less favored wife (Deut. 21:15-17). Reuben, son of the less favored Leah, lost his privileged status to Joseph (1 Chron. 5:1-2), firstborn of the favored Rachel, because of Reuben's incest (Gen. 49:3-4), not Jacob's favoritism. Regarding the loss of the double inheritance, see comments on "the camp of Ephraim" (Num. 2:18). Regarding the loss of the leadership, see comments on "the camp of Judah" (Num. 2:3). Barring sins by the firstborn and all other factors being equal, the concept of the firstborn naturally implies preeminence (cf. Ps. 89:27). Hence, Christ who was sinless is called the firstborn to show his preeminence in God's economy (Col. 1:15; Heb. 1:6). [běkôr]

1:50 The Levites (halwiyyīm)—Levi with Simeon had murdered the Shechemites after deceiving them (Gen. 34:25). Although they pleaded righteous indignation, their anger was cursed (Gen. 49:5-7), and Jacob consigned them to being scattered throughout Israel (Gen. 49:7). The Levites would be scattered (cf. Num. 35:7-8), but at the foot of Mt. Sinai they redeemed themselves by zealously punishing the idolaters in the golden calf incident (Exod. 32:26-29). Because of their zeal for the Lord and using their anger at God's behest instead of for personal and family vengeance, they were set apart and dedicated to the Lord (Exod. 32:29). The condemnation of their ancestor was reversed or turned to a good cause. Now they would be scattered not as punishment, but to teach throughout the land (Deut. 33:9; 2 Chron. 35:3). Judah also reversed his course from leading in an evil endeavor (Gen. 37:26) to leading in a good one (Gen. 43:8-9; 44:18-33). He was consequently elevated in the family (Gen. 49:8). These two tribes reversed their evil past and became the two most prominent as priests and kings, showing that the failure of one's ancestors need not destroy his prospect for significant service to God and man. God would not punish children for their ancestors' sins (Ezek. 18:1-20; cf. Deut. 24:16), unless of course they themselves continue in the same sins. [lěwiyyīm, lēwî]

Tabernacle (miškan)—The "tabernacle" is sometimes distinguished from the "tent" (Exod. 40:34-35; Num. 3:25), for the tabernacle was specifically the wooden framework (Exod. 26:15, 18, 20, 22; 36:20-30) over which the curtains formed the "tent" (Exod. 26:7; 36:14; 40:19). The two terms are sometimes used interchangeably (Num. 3:7, 8; 9:17-18). Because of the interchangeableness and the frequent mention of the curtains, the LXX translates it "tent" (skēnē). The tabernacle was God's dwelling place. Therefore, he required Israel to keep the precinct holy (Exod. 29:43-46). The NT similarly urges believers in Christ to keep their bodies from sin because God dwells in them (1 Cor. 6:19-20). See also the comments on "Tent of Meeting" (Num. 1:1). Because of the holy nature of the tabernacle, only those whom God here appointed—the Levites—were permitted to serve within its precincts (cf. Num. 18:2, 4, 22). They consequently ought to acknowledge that they were specially privileged (Num. 16:9). The tabernacle's construction and the arrangement of its service were all regulated according to God's instructions (Exod. 25:9; 26:30). These facts point out the principles that access to God was greatly restricted, no one could approach him on their own terms, but only as he called them near (Matt. 7:13-14; John 6:44; 14:6). [miškān]

Testimony ('ēdut)—The "testimony" refers to the tablets written by God (Exod.

31:18; 32:15-16) that were placed in the ark (Exod. 25:16, 21; 40:20) in the Tent of Meeting (Exod. 40:2-3). Consequently, the ark is the "ark of the testimony" (Exod. 25:22; 26:33, 34; Num. 4:5; 7:89), the tent is the "tent of the testimony" (Num. 9:15; 17:7-8; 18:2), and the tabernacle is the "tabernacle of the testimony" (Exod. 38:21; Num. 1:50, 53; 10:11). As for the use of the idea of testimony, the comparative word in Akkadian is *adû*, which means a written responsibility or obligation (depending upon the party) included in a contract that was accepted by an oath and attested to by witnesses (H. Simian-Yofre, *TDOT*, 10:496). Similarly, Israel entered a covenant with God and accepted written obligations. Their response to the obligations would testify to their degree of loyalty to the covenant (cf. Deut. 31:26 where the law is a witness [*'ēd*] against Israel). Obedience to God's will continues to testify to one's commitment to him (John 14:21, 23; Gal. 5:19-21). Since the tabernacle of testimony was holy and God would meet with Israel's representative there (Exod. 25:22; 30:6; Num. 7:89), the Levites must be responsible to care for and guard it (Num. 1:50, 53). [*'ēdût*]

1:53 Wrath (*qeṣep*)—The noun "wrath" and one of the verbs for "to be angry" come from the same root (*qṣp*). God's wrath could fall on the whole congregation because of sin (Num. 16:22; Isa. 64:9; Zech. 1:2-4). The Lord imposed strict restrictions on who could approach him at the sanctuary (Num. 3:38; 16:10, 22; 18:22) and how they must behave there (Lev. 10:6-9). In v. 53 the Levites and priests consecrated to the service of the Tent of Meeting surrounded it to ensure that God's restrictions were maintained. Often God's wrath resulted in catastrophe (Jer. 10:10; Zech. 8:14), misery (Ps. 102:3-10),

and death (Num. 16:46-49; Josh. 22:20). According to the NT his wrath continues to be catastrophic (Eph. 5:6; 2 Thess. 1:8-9; Heb. 10:26-31). His wrath might arise quickly, but last only a short time, to be replaced by kindness and compassion (Isa. 54:7-8; 57:16-19; 60:10; cf. G. Sauer, *TLOT*, 1157-58). Such compassion reached its zenith when he gave his unique Son to deliver people from divine wrath (John 3:16; 1 Thess. 1:10). [*qeṣep, qṣp*]

2:2 Of his family (*lĕbêt 'ăbōtām*)—The term for family is literally "the house of their fathers," an expression that occurs often and with some looseness of usage (*BDB*, 110). A "house" or "family" in this context was larger than a nuclear family—as the use of the Hebrew plural for "fathers" indicates—yet smaller than a clan (Num. 1:2; 2:34; 3:15; 4:2; cf. Josh. 7:14). A single house (*bayit*) of one's fathers may include—using Abraham as an example—the father, his wife (Sarah), concubine (Hagar), children (Isaac, Ishmael), dependent relatives (Lot and his family), servants (Eliezer and at least 318 trained military men, Gen. 14:4; 15:2), and all his livestock (H. Hoffner, *TDOT*, 2:113). Leaders for the tribe and nation came from the extended family structure (Num. 7:2; Josh. 22:14; 2 Chron. 25:5; Ezra 10:16). Israel's basic unit of organization was the house of the fathers and their households. The solidarity between a person and his extended family is assumed (Gen. 7:1; Josh. 2:12; 6:22; 7:15, 24-25; H. Hoffner, *TDOT*, 2:114). The concepts of the oneness of the household in the purposes of God and of his interest in the entire family continue on into the NT (cf. Acts 16:15, 31; Rom. 16:10-11; 1 Cor. 1:16; 7:14). [*bayit*]

2:3 The camp of Judah (*mahănēh yĕhûdâ*)—The man, the tribe, and the kingdom of Judah are mentioned about 880x in the Old Testament, more than twice as often as any other tribe in Israel. The man Judah was the fourth son of Jacob (Gen. 29:32-35) and his tribe is listed fourth in the census lists (Num. 1:20-26; 26:5-20). Nevertheless, the man Judah showed leadership among his brothers (Gen. 37:26-27; 43:8-10; 44:16) and was called upon by his father for leadership (Gen. 46:28). Jacob blessed Judah and his descendants to be the future leaders over the other brothers and tribes (Gen. 49:8, 10), so that his natural gifts were turned to divine purposes (cf. 1 Chron. 5:2 where Judah was stronger than, or superior to [*gābar bĕ*], his brothers; cf. H. Kosmala, *TDOT*, 2:368). From his tribe would come David's royal dynasty (1 Chron. 2:3-15). In this context in Numbers the tribe of Judah for the first time assumed national leadership by leading the march to Canaan (Num. 2:9; 10:14), partially fulfilling Jacob's blessing. This tribe's preeminence is carried on through the NT (Rev. 7:5) and will be brought to its climax under the leadership of Jesus Christ who was from Judah (Rev. 5:5). [*yĕhûdâ*]

2:10 The camp of Reuben (*maḥănēh rĕʾûbēn*)—The man and the tribe of Reuben are mentioned 87x in the OT, only sixth in frequency among the sons and tribes of Israel despite his being first born. Reuben failed in his efforts to rescue Joseph (Gen. 37:21-22, 29-30). He then failed to gain his father's confidence that he could return Benjamin from Egypt safely, after offering the death of his own sons as guarantee—an offer their grandfather naturally refused (Gen. 42:37-38). Jacob had predicted that he and his tribe would not be preeminent (Gen. 49:4). Reuben's inability to provide decisive and credible leadership would continue with

his descendants (Judg. 5:15-16; cf. Num. 16:1). The tribe apparently never did anything significant to reverse the curse on them (cf. Gen. 49:4) like Judah or the Levites. Although the tribe will prosper (Num. 32:1) and never be forgotten (Ezek. 48:6, 31; Rev. 7:5), they were the leaders of the second of Israel's four marching divisions in the desert (Num. 2:10, 16; 10:18), not the first (even in Rev. 7:5 the tribe is still second to Judah). [*rĕʾûbēn*]

2:18 The camp of Ephraim (*maḥănēh ʾeprayim*)—Joseph had forever memorialized God's magnificent blessings in his life after a series of seeming catastrophes by naming his second son Ephraim, which basically meant "fruitfulness" or "causing fruitfulness" (Gen. 41:52). Joseph's family had become the two tribes Ephraim and Manasseh (Gen. 48:5; Num. 1:32-34; Josh. 14:4) so that he received twice as much inheritance as his brothers. In effect he replaced Reuben as Jacob's firstborn (1 Chron. 5:1-2). Jacob then elevated Ephraim over his elder brother Manasseh (Gen. 48:14, 18-19). The tribe took a position of leadership in this context by leading the third division of Israel (Num. 2:24; 10:22) and would provide leadership in the future through Moses' successor, Joshua (cf. Num. 13:8; 27:15-21), the major judges Deborah (Judg. 4:5) and Samuel (a Levite living in Ephraim, 1 Sam. 1:1-2, 20; cf. 1 Chron. 6:16, 22-27), minor judges Abdon (Judg. 12:13-15) and Tola (from Issachar but judging from Ephraim, Judg. 10:1), and the first king of the northern kingdom of Israel, Jeroboam I (1 Kings 11:26; 12:20). The tribe would resent the leadership of others (Judg. 8:1; 12:1; Isa. 11:13), but would be so prominent and respected (Hos. 13:1) that eventually the northern kingdom would be called "Ephraim" (Isa. 7:8; 9:9; Hos. 5:3; Ezek. 37:16, 19).

Ephraim's history testifies that God's promises survive through the generations, outliving those who initially received the promise (Isa. 40:6-8). [*'eprayim*]

3:3 The anointed (*hamměšuḥîm*)— Etymologically the Hebrew root of this word, *mšḥ*, is derived from the idea of rubbing or anointing. A similarly spelled root or a different nuance of the same root means to measure something, and an Arabic cognate includes the idea of robbing or depriving. Perhaps the foundational idea to the entire range of ideas was to pass one's hand over someone or something (K. Seybold, *TDOT*, 9:44). An anointing with oil set apart a person (e.g., priests [Exod. 29:21; 40:13-15]) or an item (e.g., the altar [Exod. 29:36], all the implements of the tabernacle [Exod. 40:9-11]) to a special status (Lev. 10:7; 21:10-12; Ps. 105:15), and an anointed person was commissioned to a particular set of tasks (2 Chron. 22:7; Isa. 45:1; 61:1). Once anointed, the item or person was no longer ordinary (Exod. 29:36; Lev. 10:7; 21:12). The priests Aaron and his sons were the first people recorded in Scripture to be anointed (Exod. 28:41; Lev. 8:12, 30). Prophets were also sometimes anointed (1 Kings 9:16). Priests in turn anointed the first legitimate kings (1 Sam. 9:16; 16:3), and prophets could accompany them in this rite (1 Kings 1:34), as could the people (2 Kings 11:12; 2 Chron. 23:11).

The derivative *māšîaḥ* (English, Messiah, Greek, *christos*) appears 39x in the OT. It is applied to the priests 4x (Lev. 4:3, 5, 16; 6:22), the patriarchs twice (1 Chron. 16:22; Ps. 105:15), and kings about 25x (Saul, 1 Sam. 24:6, 10; David, 2 Sam. 19:21; 23:1; Cyrus, the only foreign king so designated, Isa. 45:1; Solomon, 2 Chron. 6:42; other descendants of David, Ps. 132:10). Some referents may be the king

or, less likely, the nation Israel (Lam. 4:20; Hab. 3:13). In 32 of the 39 uses of the word, the *māšîaḥ* is called the Lord's anointed (1 Sam. 2:10; 12:3; 16:6; Ps. 2:2), showing that a special relationship existed between the anointed and the Lord. In the case of David and his descendants, their relationship was forged by the Davidic Covenant (2 Chron. 6:42; Ps. 89:38; 132:10-12). Near the end of OT history a future royal *māšîaḥ* was expected. If he were Israel's royalty, then he would be a descendant of David. The NT recognized in Jesus of Nazareth, a descendant of David (Matt. 1:1), the *māšîaḥ* who would fulfill the promises to David, his family, and ultimately Israel (Acts 4:26-27). He was accordingly called the Christ (Greek for *māšîaḥ*). [*mšḥ*]

The Priests (*hakkōhănîm*)—The fundamental task of the priest was to mediate between God and humans. Israel had priests before Aaron was chosen (Exod. 19:22, 24), but since Exod. 28:1; 29:9, the priesthood was restricted to his family (Num. 16:5-10; 18:7). After being consecrated to Yahweh by calling and ritual (Exod. 29:1; 40:13) the priests alone were permitted to go inside the curtains of the sanctuary and handle its implements (Num. 3:10; 18:1-3). Contributions to God (Num. 5:8-9; 18:28) and portions of sacrifices preserved from the fire (Lev. 2:10; 6:16, 26; 7:6-10, 14, 31-36; Num. 18:8-9; Deut. 18:3-5) became the possession of the priests (Lev. 7:35). Therefore, since God claimed the Levites for himself (Num. 3:45), they are here about to become a gift of help to Aaron (Num. 3:6, 9). When God set aside the Levitical priesthood (Heb. 7:12) he provided Christ as the priest to mediate between God and man by means of his own sacrifice and intercession (1 Tim. 2:5; Heb. 4:14-15; 5:4-6, 10), and then made Christians into priests of a lower degree (Rev. 1:6; 5:10). [*kōhēn*]

Who were ordained (*millē' yādām*)—The Hebrew term here means literally "to fill the hand" (*mallē' yād*). In the NIV the expression is also translated "consecrate" (1 Kings 13:33; 1 Chron. 29:5), "install as priest" (Judg. 17:5; though *HALOT*, 584 recommends "devote"), and "dedicate" (2 Chron. 29:31; Ezek. 43:26). It is most often used of ordaining priests (Exod. 29:9, 33; Lev. 16:32; 2 Chron. 13:9, etc.), but can be used of the assembly of Israel (1 Chron. 29:5; 2 Chron. 29:31) and the sacrificial altar (Ezek. 43:26) being dedicated to God. If the emphasis is on the filling, then perhaps originally the filling of the hand meant to fill the priest's hand with a portion of an offering. If the emphasis is on the hand as standing for power (Lev. 25:35 ["un<u>able</u>"]; Deut. 32:27), then the expression may have meant to give a man full empowerment to fulfill the office of priest (L. Snidjers, *TDOT*, 8:302, 304). Regardless of the origin of the term, for the priest, ordination involved an entire seven-day ceremony, not one simple act such as placing an offering in his hand (Exod. 29:35; Lev. 8:33). He was then qualified to take on his special role. God apparently views public ceremony and recognition to be crucial for ordination to ministry, for he continued it into the ministry of his Son and the church (Matt. 3:13-17; Acts 6:5-6; 13:2-3; 14:23). [*ml'*]

3:4 Unauthorized fire (*'ēš zārâ*)—The term for "unauthorized" is the word "strange" (*zārâ*); i.e., "strange fire." In ritual contexts the term refers to that which is illegitimate (A. Konkel, *NIDOTTE*, 1:1142). The account of Nadab and Abihu's death does not state why their fire was illegitimate (Lev. 10:1-2; though see vv. 9-10). The term is sometimes connected with false gods ("foreign god[s]," Deut. 32:16; Ps. 44:20;

Jer. 2:25; 3:13), but here it is not fire taken from idolatrous worship, but simply fire other than that which God prescribed (cf. Exod. 30:9, "any other" [*zārâ*] incense). Coals used to burn incense were supposed to come from the altar of sacrifice (Lev. 16:12-13; Num. 16:46). Perhaps these brothers used a source other than the altar. If so, the theological lesson is that sacrifice and atonement are prerequisite to approaching God in worship. These two priests had been on Mt. Sinai with Moses at a time of severe restrictions as to who could approach the Lord (Exod. 24:1-2). Perhaps their preservation in the presence of God at a time when people would have normally expected to be slain (Exod. 24:9-11; cf. 2 Sam. 6:3, 6-7) made them presumptuous. Both times Numbers mentions the brothers (Num. 3:2-4; 26:60-61), the text refers to their illegitimate fire, for Numbers stresses the proper personnel and procedures necessary to approach God (e.g., Num. 3:10, 38; 4:18-20; 5:3; 8:1-26; 9:1-3). Israel then and the church now must take God's service seriously (1 Cor. 3:10-17; 9:24-27). [*zwr*]

3:9 <u>Give</u> the Levites to Aaron . . . <u>who are to be given</u> to (*nātattâ . . . nĕtûnīm*)—A person could be given to another person in the sense of being put at his disposal (Gen. 16:3, 5 ["put"]; Num. 31:30; Deut. 19:12 ["hand over"]), especially for the purpose of being a servant and helper to the recipient (Gen. 20:14; 27:37 ["made" his relatives his servants]; 29:24, 29; Exod. 31:6 ["appointed"]). The Levites were first given to the Lord and then given by him to the priests to assist them in their work (Num. 8:15-16, 19; 18:6; cf. 3:9). Giving oneself to others in honorable service is in keeping with God's will (cf. 2 Cor. 8:5; 1 Thess. 2:8). Regarding God's possessions becoming those of the priests, see comments on "the anointed priests" (Num. 3:3). [ntn]

3:13 I set apart for myself (*hiqdaštî*)—The root of the term means "to be holy." The related word in Akkadian describes a state of purity, but the Ugaritic cognate describes that which belongs to a deity (J. Naudé, *NIDOTTE*, 3:878). Although purification was necessary for holiness (cf. Exod. 29:36-37), the Hebrew concept favors the Ugaritic sense. Here the form of the verb has the meaning of causing someone or something to be holy, to belong to God and to be commissioned or taken over for his own service (Jer. 1:5; 1 Chron. 23:13 ["consecrate"]; 2 Chron. 2:4 ["dedicate"]). Something that was offered to God (Lev. 27:14; Num. 16:38) and whatever he claimed as his possession (1 Kings 9:3; 2 Chron. 7:16) became holy. In the present context the expression clearly means that God had taken possession of the firstborn for his service, and now he took the Levites in their place (see also Num. 8:17-18). The concept of separation is derived from the idea that becoming God's possession results in one's being taken away from all others. (Cf. also the comments on "sanctuary," Num. 3:28.) Just as the firstborn belonged to God by virtue of his sparing their lives, so those who are redeemed by Christ belong to him and are called "saints" (i.e., "holy ones," *hagioi*, Rom. 1:7; 1 Cor. 1:2). [*qdš*]

3:16 The word of the LORD (*pî*)—The expression "mouth of" is very often a command, direction, or decision from man (Gen. 45:21 ["as Pharaoh commanded" is "at the mouth of Pharaoh"]; Exod. 38:21 ["at Moses' command"]) or God for a specific situation (Exod. 17:1; Lev. 24:12 ["the will of the LORD"]; Num. 3:15-16, 39, 51 [cf. v. 48]; 4:37 [cf. v. 2], 41

[cf. v. 21], 45 [cf. v. 29], 49; etc.). It refers to one's exact words (Num. 36:5; Deut. 17:6 ["on the testimony"], 10 ["according to the decision"]; 19:15; 21:5 ["to decide"]). The expression here indicates the closeness, directness, and relevance of God's communication. Throughout this book God gives close attention to and communication about the details of what Israel is to do. The usual OT expression for the "word of the LORD" is *děbar yhwh*, a revelation to or from a prophet. In contrast to *pî yhwh*, it seldom appears in the Pentateuch (only Gen. 15:1, 4; Exod. 9:20-21; Num. 15:31; Deut. 5:5). Moses does not simply pass on the prophetic word [*děbar yhwh*], but hears from the "mouth" of the Lord, reflecting the fact that he is exalted above the prophets (Num. 12:6, 8; W. Schmidt, *TDOT*, 3:103, 111), and that God's communication was close, personal, and direct. The LXX reflects this by translating "mouth" with "voice" (*phōnē*). Moses' unique exaltation as well as his receipt of God's law in the sight of thousands of Israelites highlights the genuineness and public nature of the divine revelation. God displayed his revelation publicly so that many could testify to whether it was genuinely divine (cf. Acts 26:26). The revelation to Moses became the standard for all subsequent divine revelation—including Christ's (John 5:46-47). [*peh*]

3:28 The sanctuary (*haqqōdeš*)—The basic meaning of the noun is holiness (*qdš*, see also comments on Num. 3:13). Since holy means belonging to God, locations where God was present became holy (Exod. 3:5; 15:13; 28:29-30; Josh. 5:15; Ps. 20:6). There were degrees of holiness (e.g., "most holy," Exod. 29:37; 30:10, 29; 40:10; Lev. 6:17, 25, 29; 7:1, 6; 21:22). Holy items were not common (or profane) so must not be treated as common (i.e., desecrated or defiled; Exod. 31:14; Lev. 10:10; 19:8; 20:3; 21:6; 22:2, 15, 32), but as distinctive and out of the ordinary (Exod. 16:23; Lev. 23:3, 7; 25:12; Num. 29:7). The holy was off limits to most people (Exod. 29:33; 30:32, 37; Lev. 22:10, 12; Num. 4:15), so access to the sanctuary was highly restricted (Lev. 16:2). Therefore, the Lord specifies with great care which people have rights and responsibilities in and around the sanctuary. Only the Kohathites cared for the sanctuary since they carried the most holy articles. The other two Levitical families cared for portions of the holy precinct (Num. 3:25-26, 36-37). [*qdš*]

3:31 The care of the ark (*hā'ārōn*)—The ark was a chest (cf. the same Hebrew word in 2 Kings 12:9-10) overlaid with gold (Exod. 25:10-11) in which a copy of the law was kept (Exod. 25:21; Deut. 10:2, 5; cf. comments on "testimony" [Num. 1:50]). Golden cherubim were placed upon the lid (Exod. 25:17-20), and above these cherubim God sat enthroned (1 Sam. 4:4; 2 Sam. 6:2; 1 Chron. 13:6) and met with his people (Exod. 25:22; Lev. 16:2; Num. 7:89). The ark itself was regarded as either God's throne (Jer. 3:16-17, where Jerusalem replaced the ark as God's throne) or his footstool beneath the throne (1 Chron. 28:2; Ps.132:7-8; cf. H. Zobel, *TDOT*, 1:370-72). As the symbol of God's presence it was the chief piece of the sacred furniture mentioned here (cf. 1 Kings 8:3-4; 1 Chron. 22:19, where the ark is mentioned specifically but the other furniture is grouped together). Placement of the law in the ark showed the unity of God's presence with his Word (cf. John 1:1-2 that calls God "the Word"). Although the Kohathites as a whole were to care for all the furniture (Num. 3:27-31) and carry all the rest of it (Num. 4:15), only priests—specifically descendants of Aaron

the Kohathite—could carry the ark (Deut. 31:9; Josh. 3:3; 6:6; 8:33; 1 Kings 2:26; 8:6). The ark would precede the Israelites through the wilderness (Num. 10:33), but priests-not Kohathites-would carry it, since the Kohathites with the furniture would march behind six of the tribes (Num. 10:14-21). The portrayal of the holiness of God's presence is continually maintained throughout Numbers. The ark would approach Canaan first in order to show that Yahweh would give Israel the land by means of holy war (Josh. 3:10-11). It also accompanied Israel's army into battle (cf. Josh. 6:4-13) symbolizing Yahweh's leadership in the conflict. If, however, God disapproved of his army's spiritual condition or military intentions, then the ark would not go with the forces (Num. 14:42-45) or, if it did, God would see to Israel's defeat (1 Sam. 4:3-11). This latter occurrence would appear from a human viewpoint to indicate that God had lost the battle, but in reality he remained in control of the conflict and its aftermath (1 Sam. 5:1-6:12). Consequently, Israel's holy war was not genuinely holy unless Yahweh announced it. The fact that this portable symbol of God's presence continually traveled with his people probably shows that he would be with them whenever they pursued any mission he ordained for them (cf. Matt. 28:19-20). [*'ărôn*]

3:46 To redeem the ... firstborn Israelites (*pĕdûyê*)—In vv. 46-51 the Hebrew terms "redeem(ed)" and "redemption" are nouns from the root *pdh*, "to redeem." With the exception of the firstborn of sacrificial animals (Num. 18:17) and people under the ban (*ḥērem*, Lev. 27:29; cf. Josh. 6:17, "devoted,"), both animals (Lev. 27:26-27) and people (Num. 3:46-51; 18:15-16) who were given to or claimed by the Lord could be bought back from him by paying a price (ransom). Redeemed animals in such cases were allowed to live (Exod. 13:12-13; 34:19-20), and redeemed Israelite firstborn could continue life on their own (R. Hubbard, *NIDOTTE*, 3:578). By comparison, in the OT when God redeemed he rescued only people, delivering them from slavery (Deut. 7:8; 13:5; 15:15; 24:18), trouble (2 Sam. 4:9; 1 Kings 1:29 ["delivered"]; Pss.31:4-5; 55:18; 71:20-23), oppression (Ps.119:134; Jer. 31:11), and death (Pss.44:25-26; 49:15; Hos. 13:14). The OT says that he did this by his power (Deut. 9:26; Neh. 1:10; Ps. 78:42) but does not mention any payment, despite the occasional translation "ransom" (e.g., Isa. 51:11; Jer. 31:11). Nevertheless, he achieved the same result as if he had purchased them, for they became his people (2 Sam. 7:23; 1 Chron. 17:21). R. Hubbard points out that in the OT the parallel term *g'l*, "to redeem," appears primarily in contexts of technical family law, a narrower usage than our term *pdh* (R. Hubbard, *NIDOTTE*, 1:790; 3:578). The synonym *g'l* also appears as a substantive (particularly as a participle, *gô'ēl*) for God as redeemer (Isa. 48:17; Jer. 50:34), whereas our word does not (its only participles describing God are verbal, not substantive, Deut. 13:5; Ps. 34:22). In the NT God would redeem people by paying a price (cf. "bought" in Acts 20:28 with redemption [*apolutrōsis*] in Eph. 1:7 and "redeemed" [*lutrō*] in 1 Pet. 1:18). [*pdh*]

4:4 The most holy things (*qōdeš haqqŏdāšîm*)—The ark, golden altar for incense, lampstand, table for the Bread of the Presence, bronze altar for sacrifice, basin, and all their related implements must be regarded as "most holy" (vv. 4-14, 19; Exod. 29:37; 30:10, 26-29; 40:10) once they had been consecrated by the proper ceremony (Exod. 29:37; 30:26-29).

Four of the six specified items were within the tent and both blood and coals from sacrifices offered on the bronze altar were sometimes carried into the tent. This implies that these elements possessed a higher degree of holiness because of their proximity to Yahweh's presence. Once made holy it was intended that they be permanently holy and not permitted to reenter the realm of the common (J. Naudé, *NIDOTTE*, 3:881; cf. Num. 16:37-38). Whatever touched the most holy things became holy itself (Exod. 29:37; 30:26-29; cf. Lev. 6:17-18, 25-27). Even Levites who were not priests would die if they looked on the most holy items that were placed within the Tent of Meeting (Num. 4:19-20). See also the comments on Num. 3:13, 28. [*qdš*]

4:5 Take down the shielding curtain (*pārōket hammāsāk*)—The origin of the Hebrew word for curtain (*pārōket*) is debated, but probably relates to two Akkadian cognates that mean "sanctuary" and "to lay across." The result would be a barrier that hinders access to a deity (R. Averbeck, *NIDOTTE*, 3:687). The word for shielding basically means a covering or screen. Thus both words combined highlight the fact of restricted access. Only the ark with its lid and cherubim were behind the shielding curtain, all other tabernacle furniture being outside the curtain (Exod. 26:31-35). No one must violate the sanctity of the ark where God met with Israel (Exod. 30:6), so when the tabernacle was set up, the first item of business was to install the ark and immediately shield it (Exod. 40:3). Then when the tabernacle was taken down, the priests must cover the ark before anything else was done. When the ark was moved even the Kohathites in charge of the care of the furniture may not see it uncovered (Num.

4:17-20). Only descendants of Aaron were permitted beyond this curtain (Num. 18:7), but even for them, only the High Priest might pass through the curtain on one day a year (Lev. 16:2) with blood (Lev. 16:12-15), lest he die. Even those to whom God gave the right to be close to him may not take his presence lightly nor approach him casually. Access to God was not yet readily available (Heb. 9:8), but as high priest Christ would enter the presence of God the Father by virtue of his substitutionary sacrifice so that now believers may enter confidently into the Father's presence (Heb. 4:14-16; 6:20). See also the comments on "ark," Num. 3:31, "ark." [*pārōket, māsāk*]

4:7 <u>The table of the Presence . . . the bread</u> that is continually there (*šulhan happānîm . . . lehem hattāmîd*)—The anointed golden table in the tent (Exod. 26:35; 40:22) was "most holy" (Exod. 30:26-29) and so was concealed from the view of even the Kohathites who carried it (Num. 4:20). Twelve loaves of the Bread of the Presence were placed on it weekly (Lev. 24:6-8) by the priests (2 Chron. 13:11) so that it always held bread in God's presence (Exod. 25:30), even while in transit. The bread did not feed God in a pagan or materialistic sense, but the priests (Lev. 24:9). Only the accompanying incense was burned to the Lord (Lev. 24:7-9). As the primary food in the ancient Near East (W. Dommershausen, *TDOT*, 7:522), bread often stood for food generally (*lehem* is used of a lamb in Lev. 3:11; grain and grapes in Lev. 26:5; grain, lamb, and wine in Num. 28:2-7; grain, fruits, oil, and honey in Deut. 8:8-9; and "meal" in Gen. 31:54; 37:25), so the bread here represents dining with God. To eat at another person's table implies friendship (Ps. 41:9), and at a king's table signifies his favor

(2 Sam. 19:28; 1 Kings 2:7). Since the bread was from (Lev. 24:8, "on behalf of" is literally "from") the Israelites, this table symbolized their harmony and favor with God. The word "Presence" is the Hebrew word "face," which, as the most important part of the body, represents the whole person (A. van der Woude, *TLOT*, 1001). Therefore, God's whole person and not his physique is meant. Fellowship or partnership with God and his people is available to believers in Christ who live by his precepts (1 John 1:3, 7). Believers also participate with him in a special sense when they engage in the Lord's Supper (1 Cor. 10:16). [*šulhān, pānîm, lehem*]

4:9 **The lampstand that is for light, together with its lamps** (*měnōrat hammā'ôr wě'et nērōtêhā*)—The solid gold (Exod. 31:8) lampstand (*měnôrâ*) and the affixed lamps (*nērōt*) formed a central shaft with six branches (Exod. 25:31-32). Since it was placed opposite the table of the Bread of the Presence of God (Exod. 26:35; 40:4, 24), it was lit "before the Lord" (Exod. 27:21), stood "before the Lord" (Exod. 40:5), and was lit while offering incense to God (Exod. 30:7-8), the lampstand may partly symbolize the presence of the Lord. In form it appeared like a stylized tree, perhaps associated with the Tree of Life (M. Selman, *NIDOTTE*, 2:977-78) and thus also symbolized life (cf. C. Meyers, *TDOT*, 8:404-05). The priests were required to keep it lit continually (Exod. 27:21; 30:8; Lev. 24:2-4) so that it formed a fitting sign of God as the continual source of light and life. Appropriately, it was one of the "most holy" articles (Exod. 30:26-29). See God and his Word as giving light (Ps. 18:28; 90:8; 119:105; Prov. 6:23), as well as Christ who gives spiritual light and life (John 1:4). [*měnôrâ, mā'ôr, nēr*]

4:11 The gold altar (*mizbaḥ hazzāhāb*)— The golden altar, also called the altar of incense (Exod. 31:8; 35:15), was placed within the Tent of Meeting just outside the curtain to the Holy of Holies (Exod. 40:3-5, 26). Because it was anointed it was "most holy" (Exod. 30:27-29), and even those who carried it must not look upon it (Num. 4:19-20). Thus, only priests were allowed to make offerings on it (1 Chron. 6:49; 2 Chron. 26:16-19), and with only specially prepared incense (Exod. 30:9) that they offered every morning and evening (Exod. 30:7-8; 2 Chron. 13:11). In addition the high priest made a special offering on it during the Day of Atonement (Lev. 16:12-13). The fire on this altar came from coals from the bronze sacrificial altar in the courtyard (Lev. 16:12-13; Num. 16:46), so that a burned sacrifice must be made before any incense could be offered. Sacrifices that atone for sin must precede any other acts of worship or approach to God. See comments on "incense" Num. 4:16. [*mizbēaḥ zāhāb*]

4:13 The bronze altar (*hammizbēaḥ*)— Although the Hebrew word for "bronze" (*nĕḥōšet*) does not appear here, this is the bronze altar (Exod. 27:1; 38:2, 30; 39:39) that is also the altar of burnt offering (Exod. 40:6; Lev. 4:18). Burnt offerings (cf. Lev. 1) must always be on it with the fire burning continually (Lev. 6:9, 12-13). The altar was "most holy" (Exod. 29:25-29). Consequently priests were responsible for it and only they could handle the offerings placed on it (Num. 18:5, 7; 1 Chron. 6:49). Even Levites who carried it might not approach it at other times (Num. 18:2-4). In Mesopotamia, where Abraham originated, and in Egypt, where Israel had lived, altars were primarily used to provide a meal offered to the gods (C. Dohmen, *TDOT*, 8:212-13). Not so in

Israel, for the Law stresses that the offerings were a fragrant aroma for God (note that this fact is often repeated, e.g., Exod. 29:18, 23-25, 41; Lev. 1:9, 13, 17; 2:2, 9; 3:5, 16; 4:31; 6:15; 8:21, 28; 17:6; Num. 18:17). The only texts calling an offering "food" (Lev. 3:11, 16) concern the fellowship offering that signified a festive meal with God. Even there (Lev. 3:16) the text says this was a pleasing aroma. God was not fed, but his priests ate his part of the unburned offerings. The stress on fragrance may imply that worship was spiritual rather than physical or tangible. The altar for sacrifice and atonement was the first step in approaching God (the tabernacle was beyond the altar). This compares to Christ who gave himself as a sacrifice so that people would have access to the Father (John 14:6; Rom. 5:1-2). [*mizbēaḥ*]

4:16 The fragrant incense (*qĕṭōret hassammîm*)—Incense was a regular part of the worship rituals in Egypt and Mesopotamia since before Moses (R. Averbeck, *NIDOTTE*, 3:913). Israel's special worship incense was a powder made of several spices, frankincense, and salt (Exod. 30:34-36). No one might manufacture or use it privately (Exod. 30:37-38). Only priests could offer the incense (Num. 16:40), and they did so in a hand-held censer (Lev. 16:12; Num. 16:7, 17-18) or upon the golden incense altar (Exod. 30:7-8). Burning it is listed as a major activity in Israel's worship rituals (2 Chron. 2:4). On the Day of Atonement smoke from the burning incense covered the lid of the ark; otherwise the priest would die in the Lord's presence (Lev. 16:13). From this and the fact that the offering of the incense in Num. 16:46-48 stopped the wrath of God, Averbeck concludes that the burning incense provided a protective screen (R. Averbeck, *NIDOTTE*, 3:914). Since the coals that ignited the incense must come from the sacrificial altar, a sacrifice was required before this protection was available. In the NT one of the consequences of Christ's sacrifice is that believers are shielded from divine wrath (Rom. 5:9). The OT compares burning incense to prayer in one place (Ps. 141:2), but does not equate them like the NT (Rev. 5:8). [*qĕṭōret*]

The regular grain offering (*minḥat hattāmîd*)—A burnt offering was made every morning and evening, and a grain offering of fine flour mixed with olive oil was added with each one (Exod. 29:38-42; Num. 28:2-6, 8). Burnt offerings and fellowship offerings made on holy days were also accompanied by grain offerings of fine flour and oil (Num. 15:2-4, 24; 28:11-12, 19-21, 27-28, 31). The Hebrew word for grain offering is used in non-religious passages for a gift, particularly as an act of homage (cf. Gen. 32:13, 18, 20-21; 33:10; 43:11, 15, 25-26). By using this term for the Lord's daily grain offering, Israel acknowledged that she was deliberately and regularly paying respect to God. She may also have expressed that her daily bread came from him. Lev. 2 describes the offering. God still expects his people to acknowledge that he sustains them daily (Matt. 6:11) and to return a portion of their sustenance to him in acknowledgement of his provision (1 Cor. 16:2). [*minḥâ*]

4:18 See that the Kohathite tribal clans are not cut off from the Levites (*'al takrît*)—The Hebrew text literally says, "Do not cut off . . . ." Numerous times the OT warns that people would be cut off from their community. Usually the text does not say how that would happen or

exactly what cutting off means (despite its frequent mention: Gen. 17:14; Exod. 12:15, 19; 30:33, 38; Lev. 7:20-21, 25, 27; 17:4, 9, 14; 18:29; 19:8; 20:18; Num. 9:13; 15:30-31; 19:13, 20), but sometimes it meant execution (Exod. 31:14; 20:17 ["before the eyes of their people"]), or other death at the hand of God (Lev. 20:4-5; 23:29). Sometimes God did the cutting off, but without reference to killing (Lev. 17:10; 20:6; Ezek. 14:8). This is the only place where the OT says that the error of one group—the priests—would cut off another group. (The closest parallel is Jer. 44:7-8 where the Judeans cut themselves off by their rebellion.) The fact that such an error can occur stressed the weighty importance, and influence on others, of adhering to God's commands regarding the holy articles. God remains vitally concerned with the detrimental effects of people on each other spiritually (Matt. 18:6; Rom. 14:15; 1 Cor. 8:7-12; 10:32). [*krt*]

5:2 Infectious skin disease (*ṣārûa'*)—This word was traditionally translated "leper" and the associated disease "leprosy" (cf. LXX *lepros* here; cf. KJV, JB). Many scholars state that the disease was not the modern clinical leprosy (Hansen's disease) but vitiligo and related diseases (*HALOT*, 1057). Others argue that a variety of skin diseases are denoted and that Hansen's disease is one of these (R. Harrison, *Leviticus*, 137). Lev. 13–14 that describes the disease describes a number of ailments that are broader than just Hansen's disease. A person with an infectious skin disease was declared "unclean" (*ṭāmē'*, Lev. 13:3). Since the cleanliness and holiness of the Lord's camp must be maintained (Lev. 15:31), Israel must meticulously observe the legal details concerning such afflictions (Deut. 24:8). This included expulsion of the unclean person from the Lord's camp (Lev. 13:46; cf. 2 Kings 7:3; 15:5) and sanctuary (2 Chron. 26:18, 21). Because of his exclusion from the sanctuary and community fellowship, he must show the customary signs of deep grief (Lev. 13:45; cf. 10:6; 21:10). The fact that the ritual for cleansing after being healed involved a sin offering (Lev. 14:12, 19, 21-22, 24, 30; and see Num. 6:11, "sin offering") to make atonement (Lev. 14:18-20, 31) implies that the disease was compared to sin. The biblical principles that apply to this disease then should be illustrative of principles for dealing with sin. For example, sin removes a person from genuine fellowship with God's community and should be a concern of the leaders in the congregation. The fact that the cleansing ritual also included a guilt offering adds a dimension as well. A guilt offering repaid God for having removed something from his service or use. So just as this disease removed the infected individual from the community and thus from service to God, by analogy sin removes a person from God's service (cf. comments on Num. 5:6, "guilty"; cf. Lev. 17:11). [ṣārûa']

A **discharge** of any kind (zob)—A person with a "bodily discharge" (Lev. 15:2) was "unclean" (ṭāmē', Lev. 15:3, 25) for seven days after the discharge ceased (Lev. 15:13, 28; cf. Lev. 15:6 for the exception). His or her uncleanness (not the physical ailment) by virtue of the bodily discharge spread by contact, even by contact with items that the unclean person touched (Lev. 15:4-12, 19-24, 26-27). Those who were unclean through touching the person with the discharge were unclean only until the evening (Lev. 15:5-8, 10-11, 19, 21-22, 27; see 15:24 for the exception). Israel's leaders (Lev. 15:1) were required to keep the Israelites separate from those things that made them unclean lest they

die (Lev. 15:31). Those who had the discharge were removed from the community because they could infect others. However, the people they infected could not spread the uncleanness themselves, so they were not removed. The community was supposed to separate from people who could corrupt others, not from those who were affected but could spread the corruption. The limitation to the doctrine of separation depended upon whether the defilement could be spread and seems to deny the so-called doctrine of "secondary separation." Compare Christ who touched lepers and was touched by a hemorrhaging woman but was not made unclean (Matt. 8:3; 9:20-22) because he spread healing instead of contracting defilement and who fraternized with sinners but could not be influenced to follow their corrupt lifestyle (Matt. 9:10-11). [zôb]

Ceremonially unclean because of a dead body (ṭāmē' lānāpeš)—Holiness and cleanness were distinct (Lev. 10:10; Ezek. 22:26; 44:23), but related. When something holy (i.e., belonging to God) was treated as common, then it became profane. That which is common or profane is not necessarily unclean. When something clean (i.e., acceptable to God) was made unclean, such as Israel's camp (Num. 5:3), it was called "defiled." It is as if there were three stages with holiness being the highest level, then cleanness, then finally, uncleanness. Cleanness could characterize the holy and the profane. Uncleanness could characterize that which was profane, but certainly must not characterize the holy, for ceremonial or ritual uncleanness was inconsistent with the holiness of God (Lev. 11:43-45; 20:25-26), so that unclean persons might not touch holy items (Lev. 12:4; Deut. 26:14), nor eat the fellowship offering (Lev. 7:20-21) or the

Passover (Num. 9:6). In the NT as well, ethical uncleanness is inconsistent with the holiness to which God has called his people (1 Thess. 4:7).

Anyone who touched a human corpse was unclean for seven days just like those with a bodily discharge (Num. 19:11, 14, 16, 18), even if he was a holy person such as a Nazirite (Num. 6:5-9) or a priest (Lev. 21:1-4, 11). Also like those with a discharge, one who touched a human corpse made others unclean (Num. 19:22). Death and disease initially had been brought on by sin (cf. Gen. 2:17; Rom. 5:12) and became symbols of sin and its effects. All those who were unclean for seven days and who spread uncleanness to others by contact must leave the camp of the Lord (the one with an infectious skin disease was unclean for more than seven days, for his quarantine for diagnosis—when it was needed—was that long, Lev. 13:4, cf. 13:11). As with the term immediately above, the community did not remove those who were unclean by contact with one of these persons and so were unclean for only one day and would not spread the uncleanness (cf. Num. 19:7). [ṭm']

5:3 I will dwell among them (*'ănî šōkēn*)—The proposal that this Hebrew word for "dwell" means a temporary dwelling (G. Wilson, *NIDOTTE*, 4:109) is attractive, but the word can describe a permanent dwelling for man and God (e.g., Gen. 49:13; Job 3:15; Ps.37:3, 27, 29; 68:16; Isa. 57:15; Ezek. 43:7). Nevertheless, God's dwelling with Israel was contingent. God dwelled in places and with people that were characterized by holiness, cleanness, and goodness. He dwelled in a sanctuary (Exod. 25:8) and a holy residence (Joel 3:17; Zech. 2:10-13; 8:3) without defilement (Ezek. 43:7), and he demanded that Israel not defile his land (Num. 35:34). He

dwelled with those who feared him (Ps. 85:9) and where there was continual burnt offering (Exod. 29:38-46). Justice, righteousness (Isa. 33:5), and setting aside of all idols and sins (Ezek. 43:9) characterize the city in which he dwells. He abides only where moral and religious practices are lofty and holy. Here he revealed that he dwelt with Israel by means of a cloud of glory (Exod. 24:16; 40:35; Num. 9:15, 17-18, 22; 10:12; cf. 1 Kings 8:12). After OT times the visible presence of God in the cloud was referred to as the "Shekinah," a term derived from the word used here. Although God does not have a need to dwell with people, he desires it and does dwell with his own (John 14:16-17). [*škn*]

5:6 Wrongs (*ḥaṭṭō't*)—In its etymology the root (*ḥṭ'*) of this word means to miss (Judg. 20:16; Job 5:24) and in usage it means to do wrong (Exod. 5:16; Judg. 11:27) to a human (Gen. 20:9; 42:22), God, or both (Exod. 10:16). The cognate noun *ḥēṭ'* can denote the failure to fulfill an obligation to man (Gen. 41:9) or God (Lev. 22:9), the guilt of the offense (Lev. 19:17; Deut. 15:9), or the responsibility for the offense (Lev. 24:15; Num. 9:13; 18:22, 32). The cognate noun *ḥăṭā'â* is the feminine form (Exod. 32:21) denoting sin. When the verb doubles the middle root consonant it may mean to bear the loss of something (Gen. 31:39), reflecting the etymology, but it can also mean to purify something that was ceremonially unclean (Exod. 29:36; Lev. 14:52; Num. 19:19; Ezek. 43:20, 22; 45:18) or to offer a sin offering (Lev. 9:15; 2 Chron. 29:24). When the verb has both the doubled middle root consonant and the prefix *hit*- it denotes only ritual cleansing (Num. 31:19). The noun used here (*ḥaṭṭā't*) has the doubled middle root consonant and denotes either sin (here; Lev. 4:14) or something that purifies (Lev. 4:3; Num.

6:11; 8:7; cf. comments on Num. 6:11 for the theology of the "sin offering"). The other cognate nouns with the doubled consonant refer to sin (*ḥaṭṭā'â*, Exod. 34:7) and sinners (*ḥaṭṭā'*, Num. 16:38; it also functions as an adjective for sinful, Num. 32:14). Koch suggests that the noun with the single *ṭ* (*ḥăṭā'â*) refers to an individual deed but the cognate with the double *ṭṭ* that means sin (*ḥaṭṭā't*) refers to the enduring sphere of conduct that God will punish and for which one must atone (K. Koch, *TDOT*, 4:312).

Because of the Scripture's spiritual emphasis, synonyms for sin abound in the OT. Among the synonyms the root *ḥṭ'* has the broadest range of meaning. The root *pš'* connotes willful rebellion (cf. comments on Num. 14:18, "rebellion"), *'āwôn* connotes religious iniquity and guilt (cf. comments below in this verse on "guilty"), *'šm* is guilt for violation of a commandment and requires reparation (cf. comments below in this verse on, "guilty"), *šgg* is sin through ignorance (cf. comments on Num. 15:22, "you unintentionally fail"), *'wl* is to do wrong, and *rš'* connotes what is wicked in contrast to righteous (cf. comments on Num. 16:26, "these wicked men") (cf. A. Luc, *NIDOTTE*, 2:87-89).

Regarding the root *ḥṭ'* in our verse, sin against a person is also against God (Gen. 39:9; 2 Sam. 12:13), but to wrong God is the worse offense (Ps. 51:4). Sin provokes retaliation from people (Gen. 40:1; 2 Kings 18:14) and punishment from God (Gen. 20:9). When people sin others might believe they are justified to harm them (Jer. 50:7). The OT describes sin against God as not yielding to his commands (Exod. 10:16; Lev. 4:13), following in his ways (Isa. 42:24), fulfilling obligations to him and others (Num. 32:22-23), or filling one's proper role (1 Sam. 12:23; Neh.

6:13). The OT pictures possible motivations for sin as the fear of others (1 Sam. 15:24; Neh. 6:13), wrong motives (2 Sam. 24:1-10), anger (Ps. 4:4), a pagan mate's influence (Neh. 13:26), and prosperity that breeds independence from Yahweh (Hos. 4:7). Everyone sins (1 Kings 8:46; Eccl. 7:20) but could resist temptation by fearing God (Exod. 20:20), thinking on his Word (Ps. 119:11), and perhaps by remembering past punishments for sin (Ps. 78:31-32). Sin brings death (Ezek. 18:4, 20), but atonement can resolve the wrong (Exod. 32:30) and bring forgiveness (Lev. 5:10, 13). Confession accompanies an atoning sacrifice (Lev. 5:5-6), but, should an altar be unavailable, confession without sacrifice may bring forgiveness (1 Kings 8:33-34, 48-50).

The OT does not picture people as being quick to confess their sins. Of the 22x people confessed, "We have sinned" (cf. Num. 21:7), all of the confessions follow either judgment (Num. 12:11; Judg. 10:10; 1 Sam. 7:6; 1 Kings 8:47; Neh. 1:6; Jer. 3:25; Lam. 5:16; Dan. 9:5) or a message of impending judgment (Num. 14:40; Deut. 1:41). Of the 18x an individual confessed, "I have sinned," eight follow judgment (Job 33:27), six follow a prediction (1 Sam. 15:24) or a threat of judgment (Num. 22:34; 2 Sam. 19:20). Once a person admitted his sin when he was simply caught (Josh. 7:26), once another confessed when confronted with an opponent's goodness (1 Sam. 26:21), and only once did someone confess when he was not caught, confronted, or judged (2 Sam. 24:10 = 1 Chron. 21:8).

Regarding responsibility for sin, partners in sin share responsibility (Lev. 20:20), as does a person who will not rebuke his friend for known sin (Lev. 19:17). Despite the possibility of shared guilt, one must not punish someone for another's sin (Deut. 24:16; 2 Kings 14:6; 2 Chron. 25:4). God apparently reserved this treatment for one person alone (1 Cor. 15:3; 1 Tim. 2:6). Sin affects all of one's life (Ps. 51:5) and results in uncleanness (Lam. 1:8) that is like a glaring stain that only God can cleanse (Isa. 1:18). One must bear the responsibility for his sins (Ezek. 23:49), knowing that even his wealth could not free him of responsibility (Hos. 12:8). However, he may ask God to overlook sin (Ps. 51:9). God does not treat his people as severely as their sins deserve (Ps. 103:10). All should acknowledge that God's judgment on their sin is just (Lam. 3:39).

As mentioned above, the verb with the double *ṭṭ* may refer to ritual purification. Occasionally the term is translated "[water of] cleansing" (Num. 8:7), "purification from sin" (Num. 19:9), and "purification offering" (Num. 19:17). Normally cleansing was ritual purification such as of an altar (Lev. 8:15), a house (Lev. 14:52), or the sanctuary (Ezek. 45:18), but it may be extended to moral cleansing (Ps. 51:7). The term is a synonym of the more common word for cleansing, *ṭihēr* (Ezek. 43:20, 23, 26). The act of ritual cleansing involved sacrifices that atoned (Exod. 29:36; Lev. 14:49-53; Ezek. 43:20-22) and the application or sprinkling of either blood (Lev. 8:15; 14:51-52) or water (Num. 19:19; 31:19). Moral cleansing from sin was compared to the sprinkling of water, and the psalmist refers to washing (*kibbēs*, Ps. 51:7). The Levites were ritually cleansed by sprinkling water, shaving, washing their clothes, and making an atoning offering (Num. 8:6-8, 12, 21). For those defiled by a corpse, Num. 19:12, 20, prescribes the preparation and process of cleansing, and Num. 31:19 describes the actual performance and adds the necessity of washing (*kibbēs*, Num. 31:20, cf. Ps. 51:7 above). Those ritually clean (*ṭāhēr*, Num. 31:23-24)

could reenter the community. The NT declares that Christ's blood cleanses not ritual uncleanness but ethical sin (1 John 1:7; 2:2). [*ḥṭ'*]

Unfaithful to the Lord (*lim'ōl ma'al*)— The word used here embraces the concepts of depriving someone of something rightfully his and acting in disloyalty (cf. Lev. 6:2-4; cf. H. Ringgren, *TDOT*, 8:461). Although this act was against another human, since both Israelites shared a relationship with God, the act was likewise against him (R. Knierim, *TLOT*, 682), just as the NT states that one cannot hate a brother and love God (1 John 4:20). Restitution for sins like this involved restoring the misappropriated item plus 20 percent added value, and then bringing to God a ram for sacrifice (as an *'āšām*, "guilt" or reparation offering; Lev. 5:15-16; 6:5-6; Num. 5:7-8). Restitution among brethren was necessary prior to atonement. Consistent with this concept, Christ pointed out that there is no easy escape to divine forgiveness without human reconciliation where possible (cf. Matt. 5:23-24). [*m'l*]

Guilty (*'āšĕmâ*)—Guilt is a condition or state that a person enters whether or not he is aware of it (Lev. 4:13, 22, 27; 5:2-4, 17; cf. Gen. 26:10). The word may describe those who removed from God's use those things or people that belonged to him by profaning or defiling them (e.g., Lev. 5:14). For example, a "guilt offering" (*'āšām*) was to be given to God to fulfill the obligation of both an Israelite who was alienated from the Lord by an infectious skin disease (Lev. 14:12, 13, 14, etc.) and also a Nazirite who had been dedicated to God for service but became alienated by defilement (Num. 6:12). Likewise, in this context, a person was guilty when he took away what rightfully belonged to another person (cf. Lev. 19:20-

22). Along with restitution to the offended party, a guilt or reparation offering must be given to the Lord (Lev. 6:1-4; Num. 5:6-8), for the Lord was offended as well. [*'āšām*]

5:8 The ram with which <u>atonement is made</u> (*'êl hakkippurîm 'ăšer yěkapper bô*)— Although the NIV does not show it here, the Hebrew root for atonement occurs twice, "the ram of atonement" (noun) and "it makes atonement" (verb). Although scholars opine that the root basically means to wipe, to cover, or to purify, B. Lang argues that the term *kpr* did not originate from the concepts of covering or purifying, but it described a situation where the tension between parties because of sin or a legal grievance must be satisfied (B. Lang, *TDOT*, 7:289-92). When a person stood in tension with God, his life was forfeit (cf. Exod. 21:30; 30:12-16). Satisfaction of God's grievance was accomplished by payment (Exod. 21:30; 30:12-13), usually by blood (Exod. 30:10; Lev. 17:11) of an animal substitute (e.g., burnt offering [Lev. 1:4; 5:10; Num. 8:12], guilt offering [Lev. 5:16, 18; 6:6-7; 7:7], sin offering [Exod. 30:10; 29:36; Lev. 6:30]). (Note the use of a substitute for atonement in a different context in Isa. 43:3.) The atoning bloody sin and guilt offerings brought forgiveness (cf. Lev. 4:20; 5:18). Christ's sacrifice would accomplish atonement (Rom. 5:11, which the NIV interprets as "reconciliation," showing the restored relationship between a sinner and God). From the idea of making a payment to alleviate the tension, the word sometimes refers to simply a payment, even a bribe (1 Sam. 12:3; Amos 5:12). In our text atonement was necessary when someone committed a crime against his neighbor and thus against God (cf. Lev. 6:2-7). [*kippurîm, kpr*]

5:9 All the sacred <u>contributions</u> (*kol těrûmâ lěkol qodšê*)—This word is related to the verbal root *rwm*, to be high or exalted. The noun has a passive nuance of something being raised up. The word, formerly translated "heave offering" (KJV), usually denotes contributions that supported the worship system. It describes materials for construction of everything in the sanctuary precincts (Exod. 25:2-3; 35:5-9; 36:3, 6) and the later temple (Ezra 8:25), the half-shekel tax used for the work related to the tent (Exod. 30:13-16), and payment to the priest for his work (Lev. 7:14, 32-33, 2 Chron. 31:10). When it was part of an animal or grain offering, it was like a wave offering (Exod. 35:21-22) in that it was offered to God but not burned (cf. comments on Num. 6:20, "wave offering"). When it was part of a sacrificial animal it might be waved (Lev. 10:14-15; perhaps swung in the direction of the altar or elevated before the altar), but was usually kept distinct from the breast that was waved (Lev. 7:32-34), being itself usually a thigh from a fellowship offering (Exod. 29:27-28; Lev. 7:32-34; 10:14-15; Num. 6:17, 20). The term was also used of cakes (Lev. 7:13-14) and grain (2 Sam. 1:21). The *těrûmâ* given as payment to the priest was for the support of his whole family, including the women (Lev. 10:14-15). This is distinct from the portions of sin and guilt offerings from which only males of the priestly families might eat (Lev. 10:13-14; 22:12-13; Num. 18:9-11, 19; 2 Chron. 31:14, 18). Eventually the *těrûmâ* was put in storerooms in the temple for distribution to the priests and Levites who served there to support the work of the temple (2 Chron. 31:11-14; Neh. 10:37-39; 12:44-47). The word often appears with tithes (Deut. 12:6, 17; Neh. 10:37; 12:44) that were used to support Levites who are not priests (cf. comments on "tithes," Num. 18:21). Even Levites made a contribution (*těrûmâ*) to support the priests (Num. 18:26-28; Neh. 10:37; 12:44, 47). In the NT contributions to God's ministers were part of one's service to God (1 Cor. 9:3-14; 1 Tim. 5:17-18). [*těrûmâ*]

5:15 A reminder offering to draw attention to guilt (*minḥat zikkārôn mazkeret 'āwôn*)—A grain offering (*minḥâ*) was an act of homage (cf. comments on Num. 4:16, "regular grain offering"), was anointed with incense and oil (Lev. 2:1), and was considered a pleasing aroma to God (Lev. 2:2, 9). The offering here is also a grain offering to pay homage, but it had no incense or oil and was not for the purpose of making a pleasing aroma to God. A sin or guilt offering would result in forgiveness of sin (Lev. 4:20; 5:18) and atonement (cf. comments on Num. 5:8, "atonement"). This offering, instead, was for the purpose of bringing sin to God's attention (T. Ashley, *Numbers*, 127-28). For God to remember sin means that he will punish the sinner (1 Kings 17:18; Ps. 109:14-15; Jer. 14:10; Hos. 8:13; 9:9). For a sinner to remember his own sins that defiled him may lead him to be ashamed and to sorrow, so that God will not punish as severely as he could (Ezek. 16:61, 63; 20:43-44; 36:31-32). In this case if the woman was guilty, God would punish her, though not by execution, the usual penalty for adultery. [*zikkārôn, zkr*]

Guilt (*'āwôn*)—This word refers sometimes to sin (the NKJV and NASB translate it "iniquity" in this verse; cf. "iniquity" in Exod. 34:9; "wickedness" in Lev. 16:21; "sin" in Lev. 26:41, 43), sometimes to the resulting guilt (e.g., Gen. 44:16; Exod. 28:38), and sometimes to punishment for sin (e.g., Gen. 4:13; 19:15). The term is not the same as in v. 6, so perhaps

it refers here not to the guilt but to the iniquity. It frequently views sin and guilt as something to be carried (the Hebrew word for "carry" [*nāśā'*] is used, e.g., in Gen. 4:13; Lev. 5:1, 17 [translated "held responsible"]; 22:16; Num. 5:31; 14:34 [translated "suffer for your sins"; 18:1; 30:15; Ezek. 4:5-6). It is a burden too heavy to bear (Ps. 38:4) that increases and overwhelms a person (Ps. 40:12; 65:3), that must be paid for (Lev. 22:16; 26:41, 43; Isa. 40:2), and that must be carried away ("forgave the guilt" [*nāśā'tā 'āwôn*], Ps. 32:5 [NIV]). Fortunately, it can be laid upon someone else (Isa. 53:6), and carried away or forgiven (Lev. 16:22; Num. 14:18; Ps. 85:2; Isa. 33:24; 53:11). Iniquity that remains is not only a burden but brings a "stain" (Jer. 2:22). The word can also stand for all sins, for in Lev. 16:22 it summarizes all the terms for wrongdoing in 16:21. As in our context, iniquity can cause one to waste away (Ps. 106:43; cf. Num. 5:21-22). [*'āwôn*]

5:18 That brings a curse (*ham'ārărîm*)—J. Scharbert concludes that of the different words for "curse" in the OT this one is a divine curse (cf. Gen. 3:14; 4:11; 12:3; Num. 22:6, 12; 24:9; Judg. 5:23; Mal. 1:14; 2:2) pronounced by an authority so that he can accomplish his will. Therefore, in contexts like this it expresses faith that the Lord will rule justly in situations where the innocent has no other recourse to obtain justice (J. Scharbert, *TDOT*, 1:415, 417-18). Apparently no witnesses were forthcoming and the alleged adulterous partner had not been found. So there was no recourse to the elders as the usual forum for settlement. Only God could enforce justice. This kind of curse resulted in rendering someone or something less fruitful or productive (Gen. 3:17-19; 4:11; 5:29), much less prosperous (Jer. 17:5-6; Mal. 3:9, cf. v. 11), weak (Num. 22:6, 11-12), or diminished in status (Gen. 9:25; Josh. 9:23). In a similar fashion, here it resulted in bitter suffering (Num. 5:24, 27) and the inability to bear children (Num. 5:28; cf. Deut. 28:18; also note in Josh. 6:26 it results in the loss of children already born). The proper response to pronouncement of a divine curse was "Amen" (cf. Deut. 27:15-26; Jer. 11:3-5), which was the response here (Num. 5:22). After all, if God took up a matter of justice, everyone concerned must agree that he would deal correctly with it (cf. Gen. 18:25; Rom. 3:4). ['rr]

5:21 Under the curse of the oath . . . may the Lord cause . . . to curse you (*bišbu'at hā'ālâ . . . yittēn yhwh 'ôtāk lĕ'ālâ*)—The word *'ālâ* may be an oath as in the first occurrence, or a curse as in the second. (The word is a noun although in the NIV it is translated in the second place as a verb—literally, "make you *a curse*," cf. NASB). An oath was a sworn agreement (Gen. 24:41, cf. 24:3-4; 26:28) or obligation that was sealed with a curse (cf. Deut. 29:12, 19-21). God would set the curse into effect only if the obligation were violated (Prov. 26:2)—or in this passage, if the woman was guilty—and bring misfortune, even of disastrous proportions (Deut. 29:21; 2 Chron. 34:24; Job 31:29; Isa. 24:6; Zech. 5:3-4), including loss of fruitfulness (Jer. 23:10) as here. Only Numbers and Jeremiah (Num. 5:21, 27; Jer. 29:18; 42:18) refer to a person as a curse (Num. 5:27, "become accursed," and Jer. 29:18; 42:18, "an object of cursing," but literally, "to become a curse"). The Jeremiah passages show that when a person was a curse he was an object of scorn and ridicule. Scharbert suggests that when one was a curse others expressed their curses by saying, "May you become like So-and-so" (J. Scharbert, *TDOT,* 1:265). If God proved the woman's guilt by bringing the curse on her, he would not execute capital punishment—the prescribed penalty (Deut. 22:22). ['ālâ]

6:2 Make a special vow (*yapli' lindōr*)— Usually vows were conditional promises, stating "if" the Lord does such and such, "then" the person will do such and such (Gen. 28:20; Num. 21:2; Judg. 11:30-31; 1 Sam. 1:11; 2 Sam. 15:8), but some were not (Ps. 132:2-4). One normally promised a gift (Lev. 22:18; Num. 6:21; Judg. 11:30-31; Ps. 56:12; 116:17-19; Mal. 1:14), but might promise an action (Num. 21:2). The gift might be an animal or harvest to go to the sanctuary (Deut. 12:5-6, 11, 17-18, 26), a person (Lev. 27:2-8; Judg. 11:30-39), or, more specifically, a person to serve the Lord at the sanctuary (1 Sam. 1:11, 22, 28). When a vow was paid, at least with animals or crops, a feast ensued (Lev. 7:16; Ps. 22:25-26; 116:14, 18). Since God accepted vows (Num. 21:2-3; 1 Sam. 1:11, 19-20, 27; Ps. 61:5), the one making it was obligated to fulfill it (Num. 30:2; Deut. 23:21, 23; Ps. 76:11; Eccl. 5:4-6). Because vows were often made at a time of crisis (Num. 21:1-2; 1 Sam. 1:10-11; Ps. 66:14), they might be rash or the person might change his mind (Deut. 23:21, 23; Eccl. 5:4-6). However, God takes people's words seriously—even their rash words (Matt. 12:34-37). Throughout the time between pronouncement and payment of the Nazirite vow (Num. 6:13-17, 21) his behavior showed his commitment to give the gift that was promised at the end of the period, making this vow a significant expression of commitment to the Lord. [*ndr*]

Separation to the Lord as a Nazirite (*nāzîr lĕhazzîr layhwh*)—The underlying sense of the noun "Nazirite" means to be removed from and elevated above ordinary life. So *nāzîr* is translated "prince" when Joseph was elevated above his brothers (Gen. 49:26), and "untended" when vines were removed from use (Lev. 25:5, 11). Another word for Nazirite, *nezer* (Num. 6:4), sometimes denoted a diadem that revealed one's elevated status (Exod. 29:6; 39:30; J. Kühlewein, *TLOT*, 727). The related verb denotes separating (Lev. 15:31; Ezek. 14:7) and abstaining (Num. 6:3; note Zech. 7:3 where it is translated "fast")—and the requirements for the Nazirite involved abstinence (Num. 6:3-7). The Nazirite consecrated or devoted himself to God, thus becoming holy unto the Lord (Num. 6:11-12; for *qiddēš* in v. 11, see on Num. 3:13, 28; 4:4), making him a "Nazirite to God" (Judg. 13:5, 7; 16:17). His holy status was somewhat like a priest's, so his restrictions paralleled the priest's. A priest entering the Tent of Meeting must abstain from wine and the fruit of the vine (Lev. 10:9-10) like the Nazirite (Num. 6:3). The high priest and Nazirite were forbidden to touch even their parents' corpses (Lev. 21:10-11; Num. 6:6-7). As an ordinary priest in mourning (Lev. 21:5) was forbidden to cut his hair, so the Nazirite could not cut his at any time (Num. 6:5). Along with priests and prophets he became a symbol of closeness to God and spiritual benefit for the people (cf. Amos 2:11-12). Prior to this law, it seems that in order to be especially dedicated to God a person had to be born into a family of priests or Levites. Now, however, to some degree this state was possible to laymen, though without some of the privileges and responsibilities. In the NT all Christians are urged to dedicate themselves to God and abstain from worldliness (Rom. 12:1-2). [*nzr, nāzîr, nezer*]

6:6 Not go near a dead body (*'al nepeš mēt lō' yābō'*)—Although the dead may have been righteous and precious in God's sight (Num. 23:10; Ps. 116:15), ultimately death entered the world through sin (Gen. 2:17), was associated with evil (Deut. 30:15), was frequently the outcome of God's judgment (Exod. 9:6; 12:30; Lev. 10:2; Num. 14:37; 16:48-49; 25:8-9; Ezek. 18:18), and was the ultimate sentence for violent criminal behavior and otherwise violating the law (Exod. 21:12, 15; Lev. 20:2, 10-13, 16). Death also became a symbol of incapacity (Num. 12:12), weakness (Ps. 82:7), and worthlessness (1 Sam. 24:14; Eccl. 9:4). It could symbolize what is forgotten (Ps. 41:5) and beyond the care and interest of God (Ps. 88:5). Therefore, for any or all of these reasons a dead body symbolized ritual uncleanness that was severe enough to be contagious (Lev. 21:11; Num. 19:11, 14, 16). Priests (Lev. 21:11) and Nazirites were forbidden to approach or touch a corpse because they were especially close to God, the author and giver of life (Deut. 30:15, 19-20). As Christ said, God is God of the living, not the dead (Matt. 22:32). [*mwt*]

6:11 Sin offering (*ḥaṭṭā't*)—See the comments on the cognate verb for sin ("wrongs," *ḥṭ'*) at Num. 5:6 for etymology, cognates, and synonyms of this word. The sin offering cleansed the Tent of Meeting, the altar, the temple (Lev. 8:15; 16:15-16, 20; Ezek. 43:19-20, 22, 25-26; 45:13-20), and people (Lev. 5:2, 3, 6; 12:6-7; 14:19) from ceremonial uncleanness. Sometimes it seems to have cleansed from social and moral sins (Lev. 5:1, 4, 6; 16:30). It led to atonement and forgiveness (Lev. 4:20, 26, 31, 35; 5:6; 10:17). It was always bloody (cf. Lev. 17:11), with one exception (Lev. 5:11-13), where a grain offering provided atonement and forgiveness for the abject poor. Ultimately the blood of animals did not cleanse one's inner being from sin, but cleansed only ceremonial uncleanness. Christ's blood would be required for actual cleansing for sin (Heb. 9:13-14; 10:4). The offering was chiefly for unintentional sin and was offered when the sin was discovered (Lev. 4:2-3, 13-14, 22-24, 27-29). On holy days a sin offering was made as a matter of course and not just after a revelation of sin in the camp (cf. Num. 28–29), probably because the presence of sin and uncleanness of the camp were assumed. The Nazirite made a purification offering despite the fact that he had kept himself from impurity throughout the time of the vow. He offered a lamb like an ordinary citizen, not a goat as a leader, perhaps implying this special relation to God was available to any Israelite (Lev. 4:22-23, 32).

In all the other legal passages where a pigeon or dove was a sin offering it was only for the poor who could not afford a lamb (Lev. 5:7; 12:8; 14:21-22). In those cases, however, it must be offered with a burnt offering that symbolized total commitment to the Lord. Perhaps the expressing of commitment by the burnt offering showed that the claim of poverty (the reason for not offering a lamb) was not merely an excuse to obtain cleansing by an inexpensive offering.

A sin offering may be offered in a set of offerings that included burnt and fellowship offerings (Lev. 9:3-4; 23:18-19; Num. 6:14; 7:15-17, 21-23; 28:11-22; 29:1-5, 8-38; Ezek. 43:22-24; 45:23). In the set several animals were slain for the burnt and fellowship offerings, but the law never prescribed slaying more than one sin offering animal in the set. Exceptions are only apparent: (1) in Lev. 14:12, 19 guilt and sin offerings are distinct; (2) in Lev. 16:5 only one of the goats was slain; (3) in Num. 29:11 the offerings were in separate ceremonies; (4) in Ezek. 43:25-27 only one of

the animals was a sin offering, the others were a burnt offering (cf. Ezek. 43:22-24). Outside the law exceptions may be only apparent. If Hezekiah (2 Chron. 29:21) was imitating Solomon (cf. 2 Chron. 7:4, 8; Chronicles stresses continuity with David's family), then the temple inauguration feast was seven days, so that one sin offering animal was offered each day. If Ezra (Ezra 8:35) was imitating Moses (Ezra stresses continuity with Moses) then one sin offering animal was offered each of the twelve days as here. The death of a single animal cleansed the people's sin and established a prototype for Christ's one sacrifice for the sin of many (Heb. 9:28; cf. Rom. 5:18). It was not continually efficacious, for one must be offered each day of the dedication (cf. Exod. 29:36). (Cf. Heb. 10:12, 14 for the contrast to Christ's one-time sacrifice and the repeated OT sacrifices.) [ḥaṭṭā't]

6:14 Without defect (*tāmîm*)—The root of this word means to be complete or finished (*BDB*, 1070), and this term may mean to be complete, such as complete knowledge (Job 36:4; 37:16) or a complete time period (Lev. 23:15; 25:30; Josh. 10:13). It may mean correct and undamaged, such as an accurate answer (1 Sam. 14:41) or a useful piece of wood (Ezek. 15:5). All animal offerings were required to be healthy, without defects, although an exception was allowed with freewill offerings that may be deformed or stunted (Lev. 22:23). Examples of disqualifying defects were blindness, injury, being maimed, warts, festering or running sores, and damaged reproductive organs (Lev. 22:21-24). A defective offering would not be accepted (Lev. 22:19-20, 25). Eventually Christ would be a sacrifice that was without defect (1 Pet. 1:19). A blameless person in relation to God in the moral and spiritual sphere had an untroubled relationship with God (K. Koch, *TLOT*, 1426). He was righteous (Gen. 6:9; 7:1; Job 12:4; Prov. 11:5), did not turn away from God (2 Sam. 22:24) or pay attention to anything that would lead him astray (Ps. 101:2-4), but was completely loyal (Josh. 24:14). He did not slander his neighbor or behave arrogantly (Ps. 101:5-6). He abstained from the occult (Deut. 18:10-13) and lived by God's laws (Ps. 119:1). God delights in the blameless (Prov. 11:20), preserves them (Ps. 37:18-19; Prov. 28:18), favors them with good things (Ps. 84:11), leads them on a level path (Prov. 11:5), and ordinarily rewards them well (Prov. 28:10). As God accepts an offering without defect, so he accepts the blameless (Ps. 15:1-2). [*tāmîm*]

Burnt offering (*'ōlâ*)—The burnt offering seems to connote complete commitment to God. First, in contrast to the other offerings, every part of the animal (except the hide, Lev. 7:8) was burned as an aroma to God (Lev. 1:9, 13). Second, it was used to express God's supremacy in one's affections and trust (Gen. 22:2). Third, it was a proper response to God's demand for worship (Exod. 10:25-26) and to his mighty acts and reputation (Exod. 18:9-12). Fourth, it was used to confess Israel's commitment to the covenant (Exod. 24:5-7) and a Gentile's recognition that Yahweh alone is a God worthy of worship (2 Kings 5:17). Fifth, it was supposed to involve a cost (2 Sam. 24:24). Sixth, consecration ceremonies involved the burnt offering (Exod. 29:18; Lev. 8:18; Num. 8:11-12; 1 Kings 8:64). God values practical obedience over symbolic expressions of commitment, however (1 Sam. 15:22; Ps. 40:6; 51:16-17). The burnt offering was not a sin offering *per se*, but it included atonement (Lev. 1:4), for commitment to God was not possible unless one dealt with sin (cf. comments on Num. 5:8, "atonement"). When sin and burnt offerings were together in a set of offerings, the former always preceded (e.g., Lev. 5:10; 9:8, 12, 15, 16; 16:11, 15, 24; Ezek. 43:25-27), which again seems to show the necessity of cleansing before commitment. This burnt offering seems to show that after the vow was complete, the Nazirite intended to remain committed to God. [*'ōlâ*]

Fellowship offering (*šĕlāmîm*)—Each day the priests offered burnt offerings for the nation. The fire was maintained continually and the fellowship offerings were burned on top of the daily burnt offering (*'ōlâ*; Lev. 3:5; 6:12). When the fellowship offering was presented as a part of a set of offerings that included burnt and sin offerings, the normal sequence was sin, burnt, fellowship (Lev. 9:8, 12, 15, 16, 18, 22), probably symbolizing that purification must precede devotion that lays a foundation for fellowship (cf. Ezek. 43:25-27; cf. 1 John 1:6-7 for the relationship between purification and fellowship). The three kinds of fellowship offerings were thanksgiving, vow, and freewill (Lev. 7:12, 16; 22:21), with the offering here being the vow. The concept of fellowship appears because the offering was burned as food to God, that is, a meal with him (Lev. 3:11, 16) and with his people in his presence (Deut. 27:7; 2 Chron. 30:21-22). God received the food only as an aroma (Lev. 3:5; 17:5-6; Num. 15:8-10), not sustenance. Averbeck points out that this offering emphasized the fact that all Israelites had an opportunity for close communion with God, for they ate most of the meat that was consecrated to him as an offering (R. Averbeck, *NIDOTTE*, 4:137). A fellowship offering was made when Israel entered into partnership with God in the Mosaic Covenant (Exod. 24:5-7), renewed it at

Shechem (Deut. 27:4-8; Josh. 8:31), dedicated worship places and paraphernalia (Num. 7:88; 1 Kings 8:63-64; 2 Chron. 7:7), and sought or received communication and favor from God (Judg. 20:26-28; 2 Sam. 24:25; 1 Kings 3:15). The employment of this offering at such times may imply that the sacrifice emphasized the reality of a special relationship with God. In a parallel fashion the Lord's Supper commemorates Christians' participation with God the Son (1 Cor. 10:16). Here the Nazirite implied that he intended to have an ongoing, close relationship with God. The offering was not made on the Day of Atonement. The only time it is mentioned in connection with atonement the latter may actually have been accomplished by the burnt offering (Ezek. 45:15). [*šelem*]

6:15 Their drink offerings (*niskêhem*)— The drink offering was wine (Exod. 29:40; Deut. 32:38, *nâsîk*; Hos. 9:4) offered in conjunction with other offerings, usually the burnt and grain offerings (Exod. 29:40-41; Lev. 23:12-13, 18), but it might accompany the fellowship offering (Num. 6:14-15; 29:39; 2 Kings 16:13). Although sometimes given with a series of sacrifices that included a sin offering (Num. 6:14-15; 15:24; 28:15), it was not offered specifically with it (cf. R. Averbeck, *NIDOTTE*, 3:115). Like the associated grain offering it was the result of man's cultivation and was a significant source of sustenance (cf. Joel 1:9, 13; 2:14; Ezra 7:17). It therefore acknowledged one's dependence upon God for nourishment and was a token of respect and appreciation (cf. comments on "the regular grain offering," Num. 4:16). The common association with the burnt offering (Exod. 29:40-41; Lev. 23:37; Num. 28:3-10) and the fact that the offering would otherwise have been kept for one's own use imply that it helped to sig-nify complete commitment to God. Similarly in the NT Paul likened his imminent martyrdom for Christ to a drink offering (2 Tim. 4:6). Since it could be associated with the fellowship offering and the vessels on the Table of the Presence (Exod. 25:29; 37:16; Num. 4:7) it may have symbolized part of the fellowship meal with God. While other gods supposedly consumed food and drink offerings (Deut. 32:38), Yahweh God only acknowledged them. [*nesek, nsk*]

6:20 Wave offering (*tĕnûpâ*)—The etymology of this term may come from the idea of swinging, being elevated, or being a surplus. If the first nuance is the correct one then the offering was swung in the direction of the altar as if to throw it onto the altar. If the second nuance is right then the offering was put on top of its associated offering, and if the third is the proper one then it was an additional offering. Although one cannot be dogmatic, the swinging action seems the most likely in the contexts where the word is used, making this a symbolic act. The term eventually served as a general designation of consecration (H. Ringgren, *TDOT*, 9:296, 298-99), as with the Levites (Num. 8:11). Outside of this verse the word *tĕnûpâ* occurs 26x in the OT as a wave offering. Fourteen of these times it is used in conjunction with the dedication of someone (priests: Exod. 29:24, 26, 27; Lev. 8:27, 29; 9:21; Levites, who themselves are called a wave offering: Num. 8:11, 13, 15, 21) or something (gold and bronze for the Tent of Meeting and worship paraphernalia: Exod. 35:22; 38:24, 29; firstfruits of the harvest: Lev. 23:15; both the metals and the sheaves are called the wave offering) to the Lord. When the wave offering was part of an animal it was a portion of the fellowship offering (Exod. 29:1, 19, 27-28;

Lev. 7:30-32, 34; 23:19-20; cf. Num. 6:14 with v. 19) or a guilt offering for a leper's cleansing and reinstatement into the community (Lev. 14:12, 21, 24; only when it was part of a guilt offering of meat [not a fellowship offering] is it said to accomplish atonement). The wave offering was the priest's portion to eat (Lev. 7:30-34; 10:14-15) unless it was offered for his own ordination (Exod. 29:22-25; Lev. 8:23-28). Waving probably symbolized that the offering was God's, but he would not actually receive it since he had arranged for the priests to have the gifts that belonged to him (cf. comments on Num. 3:3, "anointed priests"), and they were entitled to eat it. In a sense all current offerings to God are wave offerings, for they support his workers, not him. Since the Levites would be given to both the Lord (Num. 3:12, 41, 45) and the priests (Num. 3:6, 9), they were likened to a wave offering (Num. 8:11). As the priests would normally swing a wave offering toward the Lord but then eat it themselves, so they would place the Levites between themselves and God to symbolize that the Levites belonged to God, but then would take them for their own service. Since a wave offering was usually a portion of a fellowship offering, partnership with God and the assembly was in view when the Levites were "waved." As the representatives of the assembly that had laid hands on them (cf. comments on Num. 8:10, "must lay their hands"), the Levites were linked to both the people and the priests. In the wave offering of Levites atonement was also an important element (Num. 8:19). With the wave offering here the Nazirite symbolically demonstrated his continued fellowship with the Lord although he would no longer engage in special service. [*tĕnûpâ*]

6:27 Name (*šĕmî*)—A name may be simply the designation of a person (Gen. 3:20) or God (Gen. 4:26), or a revelation of God (Exod. 6:3). It may be one's reputation or fame (Gen. 11:4; 12:2) or notoriety (Deut. 22:14). From this it can stand for the memory of one (Ps. 135:13; Prov. 10:7) or a memorial (Isa. 56:5), so that a child is called by (Josh. 19:47) and continues the parent's name (2 Sam. 18:18). Someone who is called by someone else's name, as Israel would be here, participates in his blessings or status (Gen. 48:16). A person puts his name on something (or someone, as here) that he possesses and controls (Exod. 20:24; Num. 32:42; Deut. 3:14; Ps. 49:11), such as his land (Num. 27:4). One's name may provide a lasting reputation (Isa. 63:12). To destroy, wipe out, or cut off a name can refer to destroying a person or group's remaining members (Deut. 7:24), existence (Deut. 9:14; 12:3; Josh. 7:9), household and descendants (Deut. 25:5-6, 10; 1 Sam. 24:21), and memory (Deut. 29:20; 2 Kings 14:27; Zech. 13:2). If an Israelite's children would not be able to carry on his name, his property might do so (Num. 27:4). To have one's memorial destroyed is like God's judgment on the wicked (cf. Ps. 34:16; cf. Num. 27:3, where Zelophehad's daughters did not believe their father had been wicked enough to deserve that). [*šēm*]

7:3 Their gifts (*qorbānām*)—Twenty-eight of the 80x this word *qorbān* appears in the OT are in this chapter. The term is used only for gifts to God, thus emphasizing that these offerings are gifts (cf. R. Averbeck, *NIDOTTE*, 3:980). They include burnt (Lev. 1:2-3), grain (Lev. 2:1), firstfruits (Lev. 2:12), fellowship (Lev. 3:1; all three types: thanksgiving, vow, freewill, Lev. 7:13-16), sin (Lev. 4:23), jealousy (Num. 5:15), Passover (Num. 9:7), and guilt (Num. 18:9) offerings; the spoils of battle (Num. 31:50); and here the carts, plates, bowls, dishes, and incense (Num. 7:3, 13-14). Such gifts become holy and exclusive to God's service (Lev. 27:9; Num. 18:8; cf. Mark 7:11). Study of the associated basic verb *qārab*, "to draw near," reveals that the Israelites were not permitted to draw near to God (Num. 18:4, 22). Even when they were called near they must remain at a distance from him and his altar (cf. Exod. 16:9-10; Lev. 9:5-8). God permitted only Moses, priests, and Levites near him, his altar, and his tent (Exod. 40:31-32; Lev. 9:7; 10:4-5), but he restricted even them (Exod. 3:5; Lev. 16:1-2; 21:17-18; 22:3; Num. 18:4, 22). In this passage it is a sign of divine grace that the tribes may give gifts that would become God's for use in his service. [*qorbān < qrb*]

7:10 Dedication (*ḥănukkat*)—This word differs in meaning from *qdš* ("to sanctify"). It appears in the OT as a noun only 8x (four here, vv. 10, 11, 84, 88) and as a verb only five. It means to inaugurate or begin the use of an object, such as a house (Deut. 20:5, twice, cf. the parallels in vv. 6-7), the altar (here and 2 Chron. 7:9), the temple (1 Kings 8:63 = 2 Chron. 7:5; perhaps Ps. 30 [title]), and a city wall (Neh. 12:27 [twice]). According to Num. 7:1 the events in this chapter began on or soon after the first day of the second year (cf. Exod. 40:17), a month before the census began (Num. 1:1). Therefore, as soon as the sanctuary and priests were prepared for service Moses wasted no time in putting the altar to use for the camp's cleansing (sin offering), display of commitment (burnt offering), payment of homage (grain offering), and fellowship with God and community (note the fellowship offering). Israel thus stressed the centrality of these themes in a relationship with God. The proper relationship with God was necessarily prior to marching toward the land. Centuries later during the Maccabean Revolution when the Jews recovered the temple from the Syrians, they restored worship with a festival lasting eight days, and subsequently called by our term Hanukkah, also called the feast of lights. [*ḥănukkâ, ḥnk*]

7:89 The two cherubim (*šěnê hakkěrubîm*)—Freedman and O'Connor found that either of two cognate Semitic verbs meaning "to pray, bless, greet, worship" and "to plow" may be part of the etymology of this word. An Akkadian substantive from the first verb described a person or image in a position of blessing. Another cognate Akkadian noun is listed along with images of animals used in worship (D. Freedman and M. O'Connor, *TDOT*, 7:308-10). The OT usage of the word is somewhat clearer in indicating the function of the cherub (plural, cherubim) in Israel. The prophet Ezekiel's familiarity with the law and temple as a priest (Ezek. 1:3), and his description of God's glory enthroned and traveling above the cherubim (Ezek. 10:1, 5, 12, 14, 20, 22; cf. 1:5-28), probably indicate that his cherubim are to be associated with the golden cherubim on the lid of the ark (Exod. 25:18-20; 37:7-9; 1 Kings 8:6-7). And above these God sat enthroned (1 Sam. 4:4; 2 Sam. 6:2; Ps. 80:1) to rule the world (2 Kings 19:15) and from which he hastened to rescue his people in distress (2 Sam. 22:11). Ezekiel calls a cherub a guardian (Ezek. 28:14, 16; cf. Gen. 3:24), which is a concept similar to the golden cherubim that hid God's glory from the priest who entered the most holy place. The presence of the cherubim here highlighted God's separation from his people, yet his voice coming from between them demonstrated his initiative to communicate with his people and fulfills his promise to speak from between the cherubim (Exod. 25:22). These cherubim therefore represent the divine restrictions on human ability to come to God as well as the divine intention and initiative to come to people. If God does not bridge the gulf between himself and mankind, it cannot be bridged. [kĕrûb]

8:4 Exactly like the <u>pattern</u> the Lord had shown (kammar'eh 'ăšer her'â yhwh)—The word for "pattern" normally speaks of something visible to the eye (cf. various translations of the word in Gen. 2:9; 12:11; 24:16; 26:7; Exod. 3:3; 24:17; Lev. 13:3-4; Num. 9:15-16; Ezek. 1:5, 13-16, 26-28) and can also refer to a vision (Ezek. 8:4; 11:24; 43:3; Dan. 8:16, 26-27; 10:1). The word implies that Moses not only received verbal instructions but actually saw something. A similar passage about the lampstand (Exod. 25:40) uses tabnît instead, which can reflect the idea of image (Ps. 106:20) or replica (Josh. 22:28), as if Moses saw not a sketch but an image of a lampstand. However, the word tabnît can also mean plans, even detailed plans (2 Kings 16:10; 1 Chron. 28:11, 13, 18-19). The NT references to the pattern Moses saw (Acts 7:44; Heb. 8:5) do not indicate whether he saw plans or an image, for they refer to Exod. 26:30, which uses mišpāṭ, meaning what is prescribed or stated beforehand. Regardless, after God presented the plan or image Israel had no choice as to how to make the lampstand. There's an important theological point here—practically, God enables, directs, and inspires the creativity and workmanship of skilled artisans; but He also places limits on them that artisans would do well to respect. [mar'eh]

8:6 Make them ceremonially clean (ṭihartā 'ōtām)—This term connotes a singular composition, such as unalloyed gold (Exod. 25:11, 17), incense with only specified ingredients (Exod. 30:34-35), Yahweh's temple free from association with other gods and foreign objects (2 Chron. 29:15-18; 34:3-8; Neh. 13:30), and his land emptied of idolatry and unclean items (2 Chron. 34:3-8; Ezek. 39:12-16). In the law, uncleanness is usually ceremonial rather than ethical or physical. One was clean after being healed of a physical ailment, but then achieved ceremonial cleanness through atonement by sacrifice (Lev. 15:13, 28) and sprinkling of blood (Lev. 14:3-20; 15:13-15, 28-30). Purification after contacting something unclean was by bathing (Lev. 17:15; 22:4-7; Num. 31:24) or sprinkling of water (Lev. 19:19). Sprinkling and the pronouncement of cleanness were efficacious ceremonially, not physically or morally (e.g., Lev. 13:6, 13, 59). Here the Levites were cleansed by sprinkling water as if they had contacted uncleanness and they shaved as if they had a physical sickness (Lev. 14:8), showing that they were ceremonially purified from all types of uncleanness. This was necessary, for only clean persons could approach (Lev. 22:3), slay (2 Chron. 30:17; Ezra 6:20), or eat (Lev. 7:19; 22:4; 2 Chron. 30:18) a sacrifice. Otherwise they would pollute the holy items and services (cf. Lev. 20:25-26). In the ethical realm our term describes unsullied morality (Num. 5:28; Job 4:17; Prov. 20:9; Jer. 13:27; Ezek. 24:13; Hab. 1:13) and absolution of sin (Lev. 16:30; Ps. 51:2; Jer. 33:8; Ezek. 36:33), so that if the heart is consistent in goodness it is pure (Ps. 51:10, cf. "steadfast"). The Levites' cleansing may symbolize the ethical purity required in God's presence (cf. Ps. 15:1-5). [ṭhr]

8:7 Water of cleansing (*mê ḥaṭṭā't*)—
Priests and, presumably, Levites washed
themselves for physical cleansing when at
work in the courtyard (Exod. 30:18-21;
40:30-32). For ceremonial purification during their consecration the priests were
washed (Exod. 29:4; 40:12; Lev. 8:6) and
the Levites sprinkled. Num. 19:1-22
describes a similar sprinkling with water
of cleansing, but a different word is used
(*mê niddâ*, literally "water for impurity,"
but also translated "water of cleansing")
and that water was applied to any Israelite
after contact with a corpse (Num. 19:15).
Just as the sprinkling in Num. 19:9, 12,
cleansed in the manner of a purification
offering (*ḥaṭṭā't*), so did this sprinkling, for
it is also called the water of *ḥaṭṭā't*, "purification" (*BDB*, 310). Eventually sprinkling
with clean water would be a symbol of
cleansing from sin (Ezek. 36:25; cf. Ps.
51:7). The NT reiterates the requirement of
cleansing in order to draw near to God
(Heb. 10:22). [*mê ḥaṭṭā't*]

8:10 Must lay their hands (*sāmĕkû . . .
yĕdêhem*)—Scholars propose that the laying
on of hand(s) symbolizes either (1) transference (e.g., of sins), (2) identification of
the two participants (as if they are one), (3)
commission of a representative for the subject (the object takes the blessing or curse
of the subject but is not fully identified
with him), (4) a demonstration that this
object and no other is the focal point of the
ritual if two hands are used, and (5) possession of the object if one hand is used (D.
Wright and J. Milgrom, *TDOT*, 10:282-83).
Regarding the first proposal, transference
of sins to a scapegoat was through confession, not the laying on of hands, and the
sins went to the goat from the congregation, not from the priest (Lev. 16:21-22). As
for the second concept, if the idea here is
identification one would expect the firstborn to lay hands (Num. 3:41). As for the
last two suggestions, the texts are often
unclear whether the subject was using one
or two hands, and the need for declaration
of ownership or focus seems unnecessary
in the contexts where the act took place.
The idea of commissioning a representative seems most appropriate. At the least,
the ritual means that someone or something was accepted on behalf of someone
else (Lev. 1:4). The Levites became the congregation's representatives to God. The
NT church continued the practice of imposition of hands to commission representatives to minister in physical ways to the
needy (Acts 6:6) and to carry the Gospel of
Christ (Acts 13:2-3). [*smk, yād*]

8:19 Plague (*negep*)—The essence of the
noun and its associated verb means to
strike someone (e.g., Exod. 12:13) or, less
often, something (e.g., Exod. 8:2).
Although the verb could describe a human
action (Exod. 21:22, 35), it often refers to a
divine action (2 Chron. 13:20; 21:18; Zech.
14:12). The divine act may be carried out
through human agency (1 Sam. 4:3; 26:10)
or directly (Exod. 12:23, 27). The direct
divine act was sometimes a fatal sickness
(1 Sam. 25:38; 2 Sam. 12:15; 2 Chron. 13:20;
21:14, 18; Zech. 14:12). When through
human agency, it was often a military
defeat (Lev. 26:17; Num. 14:42; Judg. 20:35),
and could be here, though mortal illness
seems more likely since the noun that is
used here elsewhere always refers to a
directly divine fatal action (Exod. 12:13;
30:12; Num. 16:46-49; 25:8-9; Josh. 22:17). In
our context God's wrath was provoked by
the proximity of unauthorized persons to
the sanctuary (Num. 1:53), since the latter
must not be treated as common. God may
still strike down those who profane what is
holy (1 Cor. 11:27-30). [*negep*]

9:2 The Passover (*happāsaḥ*)—Although the history of the word is debated, the verb for God passing over (*pāsaḥ*) appears to be related to the name of the feast (*pesaḥ*). The Israelites observed Passover at the appointed time annually to remember the night God delivered them from Egypt (Deut. 16:1-3). In the original Passover all households slew their own lamb (Exod. 12:6), ate the feast at home (Exod. 12:46), and smeared the blood on the doorframe (Exod. 12:7, 23). The ceremony then changed. For 40 years in the wilderness Israel had no houses or doorframes, and from then on the lambs would be slain at the central sanctuary (Deut. 16:2, 5-6; 2 Kings 23:21-23; 2 Chron. 30:1) by Levites (though this may have begun later, 2 Chron. 30:17; 35:6; Ezra 6:20) as priests sprinkled the blood (2 Chron. 30:16; 35:11), presumably on the altar (which had been unavailable in Egypt). In the wilderness and then in Canaan, the people resided in tents near the sanctuary during the feast (Deut. 16:7). The problem of slaying so many sacrifices at one place and time would be great, but manageable (2 Chron. 35:7-9). After the destruction of the second temple in A.D. 70 the feast reverted to a festival held in the home. In our passage the Passover lamb was a sacrifice to the Lord (Exod. 12:11, 27; Lev. 23:5; Num. 28:16, etc.), so all who participated must be ceremonially clean (2 Chron. 30:17-18). Here the Levites had just been cleansed and ordained. Since they were substitutes for those who had been spared in the first Passover (Num. 8:17-18), it is fitting that they led in sacrificing the lambs. The Passover lamb was a prototype of Christ (1 Cor. 5:7), and the celebration of the Exodus was a prototype of the Lord's Supper that commemorates Christ's redemption (1 Cor. 11:24-25). [*pesaḥ*]

9:11 Unleavened bread (*maṣṣôt*)—God commanded Israel to eat unleavened bread the night of the first Passover (Exod. 12:8) because they had no time for bread to rise (Exod. 12:39; Deut. 16:3). Other texts also imply that unleavened bread was customarily made when a meal was prepared (Gen. 19:3; Exod. 12:16; Judg. 6:18-20; 1 Sam. 28:24) or eaten (Exod. 12:11) in haste. Unleavened bread was called "bread of affliction" (Deut. 16:3), symbolizing the years of affliction in Egypt. So it signified both the extended period of anguish and the speed of God's salvation. Since leaven (*ḥāmēṣ*), or yeast, is most commonly maintained by retaining a piece of older dough for use in new dough, so leaven seems to symbolize something from the past [cf. J. Hartley, *NIDOTTE*, 2:1067]. Unleavened bread also symbolized that the old was left behind. When Israel first entered the land they would eat unleavened bread since it would be time for the Feast of Unleavened Bread (Josh. 5:10-11; cf. Lev. 23:5-6). They would eat grain they had just gleaned, and could not have retained pieces of manna for leaven (Exod. 16:20). Grain offerings of bread were unleavened (Lev. 2:11) except at Pentecost (Lev. 23:16; the leavened offering was also different from other grain offerings in that it was not burned [Lev. 7:13-14; cf. Exod. 23:18]). In the NT leaven is a symbol of the old way of life that is to be set aside by believers, for they have begun a new life characterized by (among other things) sincerity and truth (1 Cor. 5:7-8). [*maṣṣâ*]

Bitter herbs (*měrōrîm*)—Bitter herbs are used figuratively in Lam. 3:15 to refer to severe affliction. The related verb (*mērēr*) occurs in Exod. 1:14 to describe the misery the Egyptians ruthlessly inflicted on the Israelites. Remembering God's deliverance was not meant to be merely a thoughtlessly blissful party. It included this unpleasant taste to remind the participants of the anguish from which God delivered them and their ancestors. Similarly, the memorial of the Lord's Supper accented the painful aspects of redemption: Christ's broken body and shed blood (1 Cor. 11:24-25), and Christians are enjoined to remember their unfortunate preredemptive status and compare it to their new status with God and his people (Eph. 2:11). [*mārōr*]

9:12 Not break any of its bones (*'eṣem lō' yišbĕrû bô*)—Although the word *'eṣem* appears over 100x in the OT with the meaning "bones," the OT mentions animal bones in only two places (Job 40:18; Ezek. 24:1-10) other than Passover passages (here and Exod. 12:46). One who preserved a man's bones and corpse honored him (Gen. 50:25; 2 Sam. 21:12-14; 2 Kings 23:18), but one who displayed, scattered, or burned them treated him with contempt, dishonoring his memory (1 Sam. 31:13; 2 Kings 23:14; Jer. 8:1; Ezek. 6:5) as God may do to evildoers (Ps. 53:4-5; 141:7; Jer. 8:1; Ezek. 6:5). Figuratively speaking God breaks (*grm*) the bones of nations hostile to his people (Num. 24:8), crushes (*dkh*) one's bones because of his sins (Ps. 51:8), and appears to break (*šbr*, as here) the bones and slay the afflicted (Isa. 38:13). God may prevent the breaking of the bones of the righteous to display his protection (Ps. 34:20). In poetry, bones often became a figure for the entire body (Job 2:5; 7:15; Ps. 6:2; 32:3; 34:20) or physical vitality (Job 21:23; Prov. 3:8; Isa. 58:11; Lam. 3:4). Since it is unusual for the OT to discuss the disposition of animal bones, perhaps symbolism is involved here. It is as if God afforded the lamb the respect and protection he afforded the righteous, setting a pattern for the honor

he would bestow on the divine Passover Lamb who was slain in place of sinners (1 Cor. 5:7; Phil. 2:8-11; cf. Isa. 53:12, where the one who died was honored). [*'eṣem*]

9:14 Alien (*gēr*)—The *gēr* was a foreigner who settled with Israel and was largely but not totally integrated into Israelite society, as the different standards for natives and aliens in Deut. 14:21 indicate. The alien remained distinct like Abraham who had lived in a land for 60 years but was still considered an alien (Gen. 23:4) and did not own any of the land. The alien was distinguished from the "foreigner" (*nokrî*) who was even less integrated into Israelite society, as indicated by the law that an Israelite must not charge an alien interest (Lev. 25:35-36), but may do so to the foreigner (Deut. 23:20; H. Gamoran, "The Biblical Law Against Loans on Interest," *JNES*, 30 [April 1971]: 130). Regardless of the difference between a full native Israelite and an alien, the latter was welcome to the worship of the Lord if he fulfilled the religious requirements of the law (here; Exod. 12:48; Num. 15:14; cf. 2 Chron. 30:25). God continues to welcome foreigners to Abraham's and Israel's covenants to come near him, but through Christ instead of the requirements of the law (Eph. 2:2-13). [*gēr*]

9:15 The cloud (*he'ānān*)—This word for "cloud" can signify that which is temporary (Isa. 44:22; Hos. 6:4), overwhelming (Ezek. 38:9), or inaccessible (Lam. 3:44), or it could be a means of both revealing and concealing God's presence (cf. E. Jenni, *TLOT*, 939). God's presence is in view here (cf. Lev. 16:2; Num. 11:25; 12:5; Deut. 31:15). The cloud could darken and hinder or illuminate and lead (Exod. 14:20). In a cloud God dwelled in obscurity (Ps. 97:2), became inaccessible (Lam. 3:44), exhibited fearsomeness (Exod. 19:16; Num. 16:42-45), overwhelmed (Exod. 40:34-35; 1 Kings 8:11), and came to judge (Joel 2:2; Zeph. 1:15; Ezek. 30:3). However, from the cloud he revealed himself in words (Exod. 19:9; 24:15-18; 33:9-11; Num. 11:25; Deut. 4:11-12; 5:22; Ps. 99:7) and guided his people (Exod. 13:21; 40:36-38; Num. 14:14; Deut. 1:33). His glory was associated with the cloud (Exod. 16:10; 24:15-18; 40:34-35; Num. 16:42). Therefore, the cloud of his glory manifested the tension between his presence, leadership, and revelation on one hand, and his inaccessibility, terror, and judgment on the other. [*'ānān*]

10:8 Ordinance (*ḥuqqat*)—The verb that is closely associated with this term can mean to write or engrave (Job 19:23; Isa. 30:8; 49:16), chisel or cut out (Isa. 22:16), or to make a decree (Gen. 49:10; Prov. 8:15), and the nouns stemming from it (*ḥuqqâ* here, and *ḥōq*) have similar meanings. The word *ḥuqqâ* can refer to practices or traditions established by pagans (Lev. 18:3, 30; Jer. 10:3) and by fathers in Israel (1 Kings 3:3), and to patterns and principles in nature (Job 38:33; Jer. 5:24; 33:25). Hence, the word has the idea of an established pattern or principle of behavior or action. The word takes on a legal aspect by denoting regular patterns of behavior that were commanded and considered proper, such as mandated policies (Exod. 29:9; Ezek. 18:9, 17) and procedures (Exod. 12:43; Num. 9:3; Ezek. 43:18). The word includes the concepts of "regular" and "regulated" (e.g., Gen. 47:22; Lev. 7:36). God commanded his own patterns of behavior to his people (Gen. 26:2; Num. 19:2). Since ordinances could denote repeated procedures, many rituals were appropriately called, as here, "lasting" ordinances (e.g., Exod. 12:14; 27:21; Lev. 3:17; 16:29). Beyond just the ritual procedures, obedi-

ence to God's ethical ordinances could result in life (Lev. 18:5), blessings (Lev. 25:18), and in being his people (Ezek. 11:20). His people should be motivated to abide by his ordinances because he was their God (Ezek. 20:19) and they were holy (Lev. 20:8). If they followed idols, they would not be able to follow his ordinances (2 Chron. 7:19; Ezek. 20:16) because of fundamental inconsistencies between a holy God and idols. Nevertheless, some of God's ordained principles in the world are so forceful that even pagans abide by them (Ezek. 5:6). [*ḥuqqâ, ḥqq*]

A lasting ordinance for you and the generations to come (*lĕḥuqqat 'ôlām lĕdōrōtêkem*)—The word translated "lasting" ('*ôlām*, "forever," NKJV; "perpetual," NASB) is the common OT term for "eternal, everlasting," when it refers to the future. God's covenants with Noah (Gen. 9:22), Abraham (Gen. 17:8), Israel (e.g., Deut. 12:29), and David (2 Sam. 23:5) are all '*ôlām*, as are his commands to observe the Passover (Exod. 12:14), Sabbath (Exod. 31:16), and Day of Atonement (Lev. 16:34). For the future the word means unending (e.g., Gen. 3:22; 6:3; Exod. 3:15; 15:18; Deut. 29:29; Isa. 40:8, 28; Dan. 12:7), and some demands are presented as unending (Exod. 27:21; 28:43; 29:28; Num. 15:15; 18:23; 19:10, 12). However, the term is also used to mean (1) as long as one lives (e.g., Exod. 21:6; Lev. 25:46), (2) a very long time but nevertheless with a prescribed end (Deut. 23:3; Isa. 32:14-15), (3) very long but with an end God foresees and plans (Lev. 16:34, since he knew Christ would make the final sacrifice; Deut. 28:46, cf. 30:1-10), (4) potentially unending but set aside because of sin (1 Sam. 2:30; 2 Kings 21:7-8; Jer. 7:5-7), (5) as long as needed (Isa. 30:8), (6) as long as something else lasts (e.g., family, 2 Kings 5:27; Jer. 35:6), and (7) unending with the possibility of interruption (cf. Gen. 13:15; 17:8; and Exod. 32:13 with Deut. 28:64-68; cf. 2 Sam. 7:13, 16; 1 Kings 9:3, 5; Isa. 55:3 with Jer. 22:24-30), followed by resumption (cf. the preceding references with Isa. 59:20-21; 60:15, 21; 61:8; Jer. 31:40; Ezek. 16:60; 37:25, 28; 43:7-9; Mic. 4:5). So many references are listed here because these nuances have ramifications for judgments, covenants, and commands. In this context meaning number three or five fits best theologically. [*'ôlām*]

10:9 You will be remembered by the Lord (*nizkartem lipnê yhwh*)—The word "to remember" ordinarily means to recall to mind (Gen. 42:9; Ps. 137:1; Isa. 65:17). However, numerous times it refers not to mental recall but to taking action (e.g., Exod. 13:3 "commemorate"; 20:8; Deut. 5:15; Esth. 9:8). When God remembers, it can mean the former (Jer. 31:20), but the vast majority of occurrences refer to the latter. For example, he acts to keep his covenants (e.g., Gen. 9:15-16; Exod. 6:5; Lev. 26:42, 45; Ps. 105:8; Ezek. 16:60), responds to the cries of the afflicted (Ps. 9:12), cares for someone (Ps. 8:4; Jer. 5:15), blesses him (Ps. 115:12), acts favorably toward him (Neh. 5:19; 13:14), punishes (Isa. 64:9; Jer. 14:10; Hos. 8:13; 9:9), comes to one's aid (Ps. 106:4), and answers prayer (Gen. 19:29; 30:22; Judg. 16:28; 1 Sam. 1:11, 19). When the OT says that he does not remember, it may mean that he does not punish (Isa. 43:25; Ezek. 18:22), does not hold sins against someone (Ps. 79:8), does not cut someone off from his care (Ps. 88:5), or does not ignore him (2 Sam. 19:19). In this context his remembering results in his coming to the aid of Israel in preparation for battle. [*zkr*]

To be your God (*lihyôt lākem lē'lōhîm*)— The word *'ĕlōhîm* is a common plural noun designating gods. The singular form *'ĕlōah* may refer to a pagan god (2 Chron. 32:15)

or the true God (Deut. 32:15). Since Yahweh is the only being who deserves the title, *'ĕlōhîm* became a name for him. The fact that the word is a plural even when applied to him intensifies the title, showing that only he deserves it, and other pretenders to deity are false. (In addition, possibly the use of the plural implies plurality in the Godhead [i.e., Trinity], though this is controversial in OT studies.) The cognate term *'ēl*, also meaning a pagan god (Exod. 15:11) or the true God (Gen. 35:1), connotes the idea of might. On occasion *'ēl* is used to denote power (Gen. 31:29; Mic. 2:1), powerful men (Ezek. 31:11), and mighty things in nature (Ps. 36:6) instead of deity (*BDB*, 42-44).

Because the OT uses the word *'ĕlōhîm* for other gods, the expression "your God" singles out Yahweh and relates him especially to Israel. Yahweh made Israel distinct from all other nations (Lev. 20:24) to be his unique people (Exod. 6:7) to accomplish a unique task (Deut. 4:34; 10:17). Therefore, he acted on their behalf in special ways, redeeming them, giving them a promised land, and keeping covenant with them (Exod. 6:7-8). He also fought for them (Deut. 1:30; 3:22), caused them to proliferate (Deut. 1:10), and performed unusual deeds for them (Exod. 16:12; Deut. 29:5). This should motivate them to keep his standards (Lev. 19:30-35). Since he was their God they must worship (Exod. 23:24-25) and consult (Lev. 19:31) him alone, but not in the ways that the heathen did to their gods (Deut. 12:4). They must keep his covenant (Deut. 4:23), be exclusively his (Lev. 11:44), follow, revere (Deut. 13:4), love (Deut. 11:13), obey (Lev. 18:2-5), and serve (Lev. 25:55) him. They must practice ceremonies to remember all he had done for them (Lev. 23:41-43) and make atonement to maintain a harmonious relationship with him (Lev. 23:28). [*'ĕlōhîm*]

10:33 The mountain of the Lord (*har yhwh*)—Mt Sinai (or Horeb) is normally called the mountain of *God* (*'ĕlōhîm*, Exod. 3:1; 4:27; 18:5; 24:13; 1 Kings 19:8). Every other time the expression "mountain of the *Lord*" (*yhwh*, as here) appears, it is Jerusalem (Isa. 2:3; 30:29; Mic. 4:2; Zech. 8:3; cf. Gen. 22:14 near the site of Jerusalem) or the temple mount (Ps. 24:3), although Jerusalem may also be called the mountain of *God* (*'ĕlōhîm*, Ps. 68:16; Ezek. 28:16). On the mountain of God (Sinai) God commissioned Moses (Exod. 3:1) and told him that Israel would return here to worship him (Exod. 3:12), which they had now done (e.g., Exod. 24:1). Moses went up to meet God there again (Exod. 19:3) where he received the commands of the Lord (Exod. 24:12-13). Later the word of the Lord would come to Elijah there as well (1 Kings 19:8-9). In this passage Israel was leaving the mountain of God to go to the land where eventually Jerusalem would become the mountain of God (Ps. 68:16) or "the mountain of the Lord." Like here, that mountain of the Lord would become a place for people to come to be taught by God (Isa. 4:3-4) and to worship him (Isa. 30:29). Unlike Mt. Sinai, he would rule the world from the mountain in Jerusalem (Ps. 68:16; Isa. 4:3-4). [*har yhwh, har 'ĕlōhîm*]

The covenant (*bĕrît*)—The etymology of the word *berît* is a matter of contention. Scholars argue that the word came from (1) the Akkadian *birītu* (fetter) and so designates a bond, (2) the Akkadian preposition *birīt* (between) and thus denotes an arrangement between parties, (3) the Akkadian *barû* (to see, and thus choose) and consequently indicates an obligation, (4) the Hebrew *brh* (to eat) which accents the associated covenant meal, and (5) the Hebrew *brr* (to purify) that leads to being specially set apart. Perhaps the fact that Israel's covenant documents seem to parallel the form of Hittite suzerainty (fealty-overlord relationship) treaties highlights the fact that the biblical covenants were viewed primarily as relationships. (G. McConville, *NIDOTTE*, 1:747-48).

A *bĕrît* could be a friendship pact (1 Sam. 18:3), a marriage (Ezek. 16:8, figurative; Mal. 2:14, literal), an alliance among neighbors for protection (Gen. 14:13), a nonaggression pact between local lords (Gen. 21:27), a treaty with mutual responsibilities between city-states and nearby people groups (Josh. 9:6, 15), a vassal treaty (1 Sam. 11:1), a political contract between king and people (2 Sam. 5:3), or the bond that held a league of nations together (Ezek. 30:5). Because covenants usually, if not always, laid down stipulations for at least one party, sometimes the term denotes decrees and laws (Josh. 24:25) or a specific command (Josh. 7:11, 15). God called the natural laws of creation a *berît* (Jer. 33:20), as well as the supernatural restraint that prevented Israel's enemies from destroying them (Zech. 11:10).

A number of divinely originated covenants promising certain benefits appear in the OT. God made a covenant with Noah not to destroy the earth by flood (Gen. 9:10-15). He made one with Abraham to make him the father of nations (Gen. 17:4-5), and to give his descendants through Jacob the land of Canaan (Exod. 2:24; 1 Chron. 16:15-18). The Lord made a covenant with Moses and Israel to make them his special people and a kingdom of priests (Exod. 19:5-6). That the Mosaic Covenant is linked to the Abrahamic can be observed in that Israel's obedience to the Mosaic would prompt God to fulfill the Abrahamic Covenant with them (Jer. 11:3-5). The Ten Commandments were the heart of this covenant (Exod. 34:28; Deut. 4:13), so they were placed beside (Deut. 31:26) and in the ark (1 Kings 8:21), so that it was called the ark of the covenant. God made a covenant with Aaron and the Levites that the nation's contributions to the Lord would belong to his family and tribe (Num. 18:19) because they would be the priests (Neh. 13:29). Another divine covenant was made with Phinehas, Aaron's grandson, that his line would retain an everlasting right to the priesthood (Num. 25:13). God initiated what appears to be an additional covenant attached to the Mosaic Covenant (Deut. 29:1), which some call the Palestinian Covenant. He made a covenant with David that his family would be the ruling dynasty in Israel (2 Sam. 23:5; 2 Chron. 13:5). Other people were invited to enter into covenant with God to receive the divine love that David received (Isa. 55:3). In the future God would make a new covenant with Israel that he would put his law in their hearts, that they would be his people, that he would be their God, and that he would do them good (Jer. 31:31-34; 32:40). Perhaps as part of the new covenant is the eschatological covenant he made to give Israel security, prosperity, and freedom (Ezek. 34:25-30). This latter covenant is linked to the new covenant in that another mention of an eschatological covenant with Israel included new covenant-like promises that God's Spirit and his words would continue with Israel (Isa. 59:21).

The verbs used with the initiation of a covenant are usually *krt* (cf. Exod. 34:10; Deut. 29:12, note the word "today") and *bw'* (cf. 2 Chron. 15:12). When the verb *hēqîm* is used it seems to mean to bring a covenant promise to fulfillment (Lev. 26:9; Deut. 8:18). From this one may infer from the use of *hēqîm* in connection with Noah (Gen. 6:18) that some previously made,

unspecified covenant had already been made at creation and perhaps God's relation to creation has always been a covenantal one (G. McConville, *NIDOTTE*, 1:748).

Yahweh was known as a covenant-keeping God (Deut. 7:9; 1 Kings 8:23; Neh. 1:5; Dan. 9:4). His covenants often included commands for the other parties to obey (Abraham, Gen. 17:10; Moses, Exod. 19:5; 24:7; David, Ps. 132:12). Those who obeyed and were loyal to him would see the fulfillment of God's covenant promises (Ps. 25:14). The keeping of a covenant was called righteousness (Neh. 9:8), underscoring the fact that righteousness is living up to proper expectations. Unfaithfulness to the covenants of God was connected to having a disloyal heart (Ps. 78:37) and rejecting God (Deut. 31:20). Violation would lead to punishment in the covenant with Moses (Lev. 26:15, 25) and with Noah (Isa. 24:5-6).

God's covenants usually were made with not only the original participants, but also with their posterity, as in the covenants with Noah (Gen. 9:9), Abraham (Gen. 17:17), Aaron (Num. 18:19), Phinehas (Num. 25:13), Moses (Deut. 5:2-3; 29:14-15), and David (Ps. 89:3-4). God often established signs or tokens of his covenants. With Noah the token was the rainbow (Gen. 9:13), with Abraham it was male circumcision (Gen. 17:11), with Moses it was the Sabbath (Exod. 31:16-17) and the Bread of the Presence (Lev. 24:8), and with Aaron it was the rod that blossomed (Num. 17:5, 10). Covenants also could be sealed with blood (Abraham, Gen. 15:10; Moses, Exod. 24:8).

In the NT Christ offered his blood as the seal for the New Covenant (Matt. 26:28) to replace the Mosaic one (Heb. 8:6-13), and gave the Lord's Supper as the sign of the covenant (Matt. 26:26-29). He expected obedience from those in relation to him, and obedience would lead to spiritual benefits (John 14:21, 23) and eternal life (John 10:28). [berît]

To find (lātûr)—This verb occurs 14x in the book, 12x with the idea of "explore" to describe the task of the 12 spies (e.g., Num. 13:2, 16, 21). They would not be commissioned either to decide whether Israel should enter the land or to plan strategy for the attack (cf. Deut. 1:22 with Josh. 5:13–6:5, where strategy became God's responsibility). They would be responsible simply to bring back a report and demonstrate the goodness of God's choice for them (Num. 13:18-20). The other use of the verb in the book is in Num. 15:39 where it means to go after something. Therefore, the idea of God being uncertain regarding where Israel should camp and so needing to make decisions about this is not in view. Only two other times in the OT did God search or explore (Deut. 1:33; Ezek. 20:6), and in them the emphasis is on his wise direction for Israel and on the goodness of the place to which he led had them. In our text as well, these concepts are meant. [twr]

A place to rest (měnûḥâ)—Here the expression means a temporary place to stay, but later it designates a God-given place of residence (Gen. 49:15; Deut. 12:9; Mic. 2:10), the Promised Land viewed as secure and blessed (1 Kings 8:56; Ps. 95:11), the eschatological kingdom of peace (Isa. 11:10), and God's dwelling place (Ps. 132:7-8; 13-14). The ark of God would eventually be in a place of rest (Ps. 132:8; 1 Chron. 28:2; cf. the related words mānôaḥ ["came to rest"] and nwḥ ["come to a resting place"] used with the ark, 1 Chron. 6:31; 2 Chron. 6:41). Israel was moving from one mountain of the Lord to another in Canaan (cf. above in this verse, "the mountain of the Lord"), and with the ark they were passing through many resting places to

another one in Canaan. The term can represent security from one's enemies who are all around (1 Chron. 22:9), so its use here is significant: Israel was passing through some enemy territories, but won all their battles (Num. 21:1-3, 21-35; 31:1-12) except the one Moses forbade them to attempt (Num. 14:40-45). Additionally, God prevented at least one major attack that was planned against them (Num. 22–24; cf. the concept in Ps. 3:5-6). God continues to offer rest for those who follow him in faith and obedience (Heb. 4:9-11). [měnûḥâ]

11:1 His anger was aroused (wayyiḥar 'appô)—Of the ten words for anger in the OT this one occurs most often—170x for God's anger, 40 for man's. The term frequently associates anger with fire (e.g., Exod. 32:10-11; Num. 11:33; 12:9; 25:3; 32:13; E. Johnson, TDOT, 1:351-56), making it fitting here. Human anger often resulted from a perception of unjust treatment (e.g., Gen. 27:45; 30:2) and is evaluated negatively (e.g., Gen. 49:6-7; Prov. 17:17; 22:24). God was angry at unbelief (Ps. 78:21-22), stubborn disobedience (Exod. 4:14; Num. 22:22; 1 Sam. 28:18), oppression (Exod. 22:22-24; 2 Chron. 28:10-13), covenant violation (Exod. 32:10; Deut. 29:24-25; 31:16-17), failure to follow him wholeheartedly (Num. 32:14-15), forsaking him (Ezra 8:22; Ps. 95:10-11) and seeking other gods (Deut. 6:14-15; 13:13-17; 29:18-20, 26-27), irreverence (1 Chron. 13:10), and sin in general (Ps. 90:7-8). His anger rose slowly (Exod. 34:6; Num. 14:18; Ps. 86:15; 103:8) and was short-lived (Ps. 30:5; 103:9), although its severity made it seem long (Ps. 85:5). In anger God may exile his people (Deut. 29:28), turn them over to enemies (Judg. 2:14; 10:7-8), separate from them (Deut. 31:17-18), send disaster (Exod. 32:12; Deut. 6:15), or— mentioned most often—kill them (e.g.,

Exod. 22:24; Num. 11:33-34; 25:4; 32:13). He set aside his anger in response to prayer (Deut. 9:19-20), punishment of the offenders (Deut. 13:17-18; Josh. 7:26), obedience (2 Chron. 30:8), a pledge of obedience (2 Chron. 29:10), humility (2 Chron. 12:12), and correction of offenses (2 Kings 23:24-26). ['ap, 'np]

11:6 This manna (*hammān*)—Called "bread from heaven" (Neh. 9:15; Ps. 78:24; 105:40), this food source was so new and special (Deut. 8:3, 16) for the wilderness journey that the Israelites named it "what is it?" (Exod. 16:15, 31). Since it was like grain (Ps. 78:24) the Israelites could make it into a variety of foods, so that their weariness of it (also Num. 21:5) was not fully justified. God gave it partly to test and partly to teach. He tested whether they would obey (Num. 16:4, cf. 16, 19-20, 26-29). He taught both humility through daily dependence upon him (Deut. 8:16) as well as living by faith and obedience (8:3; Ps. 78:19-24). Of course, he also gave it to demonstrate that he is faithful (Neh. 9:19-21) and that his provision was fully adequate (Ps. 78:25). By comparison, in speaking of this manna Jesus announced that he was the genuine (*alēthinos*) bread of God that came from heaven to give spiritual life (John 6:31-35). [*mān*]

11:12 The land (*hā'ădāmâ*)—The root of the word *'ădāmâ* is *'dm*, to be red, as in a red field or red earth (H. Schmid, *TLOT*, 42). The word *'ădāmâ* can refer to the planet (Gen. 6:1; 12:3) or to the soil of the ground (Gen. 2:5; 3:17). All subhuman creatures of the planet were put under human authority (Gen. 9:2), and all people of the planet would be blessed by what God would do with Abraham's offspring through his grandson Jacob (Gen. 12:3; 28:14). Mankind was made from the ground (Gen. 2:7), was consigned to weariness as he cultivated it because of his sin, and needed rest from the toil of it all (Gen. 3:19; 5:29). Mankind will return to the ground in death (Gen. 3:19), but will be resurrected from it during eschatological times (Dan. 12:2). In a figurative sense, the blood of the innocent cries from the ground for justice (Gen. 4:10), and the ground similarly cries out because of injustice (Job 31:38-39).

The term also refers to particular countries (Egypt, Exod. 8:2; Aram, Isa. 7:16; Babylon, Ps. 137:4), especially Canaan, which became Israel. The land of Israel was called the holy land (only once, Zech. 2:12), so it was God's (Zech. 9:16). Accordingly, he expelled Israel's predecessors because of their depraved immorality (Lev. 20:23-24). In acknowledgement that this land was God's and that he had given it to them Israel must bring him its firstfruits and obey him after they settled (Exod. 23:19; Deut. 26:9-10). He would bless them for this (Deut. 26:14-15). God could populate his land with whomever he pleased, and he promised it to Israel's ancestors (Num. 11:12; Deut. 31:20) and gave it to the offspring of the current generation (Deut. 4:40). The current generation could not take possession because they did not follow the Lord wholeheartedly (Num. 32:11).

After Israel settled the land they must continue to obey him (Deut. 4:10), fear him, and walk in his ways (Deut. 30:13; 2 Chron. 6:31). Two specific practices that could ensure their continuance were honoring their parents (Deut. 5:16) and dealing honestly in business (Deut. 25:15). Then they would be able to occupy the land for a long time (Deut. 11:21), enjoying good harvests (Deut. 7:12-13) and safety (2 Chron. 33:8). If they sinned they could repent, submit to God's chastening, and still remain there (Jer. 25:5; 27:11). If Israel was disloyal to the Lord, such as by idolatry (1 Kings 14:15-16), and defiled the land by their sins (Ezek. 36:17), they would not live there long (Deut. 30:18), for he would displace them (Deut. 6:13-15; 28:63) and outsiders would devour its produce (Deut. 28:33, 51). Consequently it behooved them to obey the law and teach it to their children so that they, too, would obey it (Deut. 11:18-21).

Israel was dispossessed because of their infidelity to the Lord. Nevertheless, in the future when they would repent God would restore them to the land and their prosperity in the land (Deut. 30:3-9; 1 Kings 8:33-34). In their eschatological return (Jer. 16:15; 23:8), they will dwell in safety (Ezek. 28:25-26; 34:27) because God will protect them (Zech. 9:16) and will have defeated their enemies (Isa. 14:1-2). They will be indwelt by God's Spirit and be obedient to him (Ezek. 36:24-27; 37:12-14). The Lord will care for them there (Ezek. 34:13). This future restoration to the land in godliness will be a testimony to God's holiness and to the fact that he is Yahweh and that he is their God (Ezek. 28:25-26; 39:26-29). Not all Israelites in the future will be restored, however, for the rebels will not survive (Ezek. 20:34-38).

What God did and will do with Israel and the land of Canaan, therefore, was and will be a witness to his eternal faithfulness to his covenant promises (cf. Josh. 21:43-45). Israel's relationship to the land would also be a testimony to their fidelity to God. The central location of the Promised Land made them an example to the surrounding cultures of what it would mean to be in relation to the living God (cf. Deut. 4:6-8; 29:22-28; 1 Kings 10:9). [*ădāmâ*]

You promised on oath (*nišba'tā*)—An OT oath was a promise (e.g., Gen. 21:23) strengthened by invoking God (or a god) to curse the speaker (e.g., Judg. 21:18) should he not keep his promise (cf. Josh. 9:20 and 2 Sam. 21:1-2). A promise was sure, but a curse was conditional (T. Cartledge, *NIDOTTE*, 4:32). In an oath the deity was mentioned (cf. 1 Sam. 20:42; 1 Kings 19:2), sometimes by the expression "as God/the Lord lives" (1 Kings 17:1; Jer. 4:2; 44:26), and the oath was made before him or by him (e.g., Josh. 2:12, 17; 6:22; Judg. 21:7; 2 Sam. 19:7, 13; 1 Kings 1:17, 30; 2 Chron. 15:15). Some oaths seem to have been solemn promises without God's name, but since sometimes the oath's entire content is not recorded (cf. Judg. 21:1, 7, 18; and 1 Sam. 7:12-16 with Ps. 89:3, 35), possibly his name was used but not recorded in the writing. Keller shows that if God was called upon to ensure an oath, then the promissory must be completely submitted to him as the guarantor. Consequently to take an oath would mean to confess allegiance to God (2 Chron. 15:14-15; Isa. 19:18; Ezek. 45:23; C. Keller, *TLOT*, 1296). God could not call on deity to ensure his promises (cf. Heb. 6:13), so he swore by his holiness (Ps. 89:35; Amos 4:2), faithfulness (Ps. 89:50), power (Isa. 62:8), name (Jer. 44:26), and his own self (Exod. 32:13; Isa. 45:23; Jer. 22:5; 49:13; 51:14; Amos 6:8). Hence, his own character and abilities guaranteed his promises (Isa. 14:24). He does not change his mind (Ps. 110:4; Isa. 45:23), and he fulfills what he promises (Deut. 6:23; 7:8, 12; 31:7-8; Josh. 21:43-45; Isa. 54:9). To demonstrate his faithfulness he made oaths to people not yet born (Exod. 13:11) and to people who would die generations before he fulfilled them (Deut. 6:23; 7:8, 12-13; 8:1; 9:5; 26:3). Although people may not live to see God's promises fulfilled, this does not prevent him from fulfilling them (cf. Isa. 40:6-8). [*šb'*]

11:15 If I have found favor (*'im māṣā'tî ḥēn*)—The word *ḥēn* means grace or elegance in appearance or speech, and favor or acceptance with men or God, as here (*BDB*, 336). Moses desired God to be favorably disposed toward him. The cognates *tĕḥinnâ* and *taḥănûn* denote supplication for favor. The cognate *ḥinnām* can denote action taken gratuitously, freely, without a reason, or undeservedly (*BDB*, 336-37). The idea of generosity may be implied, then, by our word. The synonym *ḥesed* signifies goodness or kindness in doing favors, as well as including the ideas of loyalty and relationship (cf. comments on Num. 14:18, "abounding in love"). The synonym *raḥămîm* is derived from the word for womb (*reḥem*) and underscores warm compassion that goes beyond what is necessary to help another (M. Butterworth, *NIDOTTE*, 3:1094).

To find favor or grace (*ḥēn*) in someone's eyes basically means to be a recipient of good instead of harm (cf. Gen. 6:7-8; 32:5-7). When the expression is used of receiving favor from another human being, the recipient of favor had done something to earn it (Gen. 32:5, 8; 39:4; 1 Sam. 16:22; Ruth 2:10-12). In relation to God, it is not always clear that the beneficiary earned it. In Gen. 6:8 Noah found God's favor, but in Gen. 6:9 and 7:1 it appears that the benefit was bestowed upon him after he had already been found righteous and blameless. In Jer. 31:2 God's favor was to be given to those who had been purified and had repented. In 2 Sam. 15:25 no indication is given whether favor was merited. In Exod. 33:13 Moses asked (first) to learn God's ways so that (second) he might know him and finally (third) find grace before God. This however was conditioned on the fact that he had already found grace in God's sight. Then God responded (Exod. 33:17) and

said that Moses had (first) found favor with God so that (second; the *waw*-consecutive indicates this was logically or temporally subsequent to the preceding verb) he might know God. So in Moses' case it is clearer that God's grace preceded Moses' actions or knowledge. Our scene comes after the one in Exodus, so Moses was probably counting on God's favor apart from his own merits. [*ḥēn*]

11:17 The Spirit (*hārûaḥ*)—The spirit may refer to one's thought processes (Gen. 41:8; Deut. 34:9; Ps. 32:2), attitude or emotional state (Gen. 45:27; Exod. 6:9, "discouragement"; Num. 5:14; Josh. 2:11, "courage"; Judg. 8:3, "resentment"), seat of motivations (1 Chron. 5:26; Jer. 51:11), inclinations (Exod. 35:21; Num. 14:24; Deut. 2:30; 2 Chron. 21:16; Prov. 16:32), inner sense of vitality (Judg. 15:19; Job 6:4), inner strength (Ps. 142:3; 143:4), immaterial part (Ezra 1:5; Eccl. 12:7; Isa. 26:9), or whole person (Job 21:4, "I"; Ps. 31:5; Isa. 38:16). One's spirit directs one to certain actions (Isa. 29:24). It should be free of deceit (Ps. 32:2), faithful to God (Ps. 51:10; 78:8), trustworthy (Prov. 11:13), humble (Prov. 16:19; 29:23), and self-controlled (Prov. 16:32). God gives the spirit as the immaterial person (Eccl. 12:7) and evaluates him (Prov. 16:2, "motives"). The term also refers to one's breath (Job 9:18) and life (Job 10:12; 12:10, parallel to *nepeš*).

This text is one of the approximately 70x that God's Spirit is meant. Though it is theologically premature to find a trinitarian concept of God in the OT, the OT does prepare the way for the NT revelation of the Spirit as a member of the Trinity. The OT says God has and is a Spirit (Gen. 1:2; 6:3) who can be in people (Exod. 31:3; 35:31), come upon them (Jud 3:10; 6:34; 11:29), rest upon them (Num. 11:25-26), overpower them (1 Sam. 10:10, the verb [*ṣālaḥ*]), clothe them (figuratively, 1 Chron. 12:18), be figuratively poured out on them (Isa. 32:15; 44:3; Ezek. 39:29; Joel 2:28-29), fill them (Exod. 31:3), and depart (1 Sam. 16:14). Some of his noticeably divine qualities and actions include that he is everywhere (Ps. 139:7) and accomplishes God's work (Zech. 4:6). Accordingly, in his essence he is deity. The NT perpetuates the doctrine of the Spirit's essential deity in Jesus' command to baptize in the name, not the names, of the Father, Son, and Holy Spirit (Matt. 28:19) and in Paul's trinitarian formula (2 Cor. 13:14). God's Spirit bestows wisdom and skill (Exod. 28:3 [cf. 31:3]; 35:31; Isa. 11:2), presents plans to one's mind (1 Chron. 28:12), instructs (Neh. 9:20), and strengthens (Judg. 14:6; Ezek. 2:2). He empowers people to lead (as here; cf. Judg. 3:10; 16:13), war (Judg. 6:34; 11:29; 1 Sam. 11:6), succeed (Ps. 143:10), achieve justice (Isa. 42:1), and build (Zech. 4:6). Proving that the Spirit is not an attitude or impersonal force, some of his more noticeably personal aspects include the fact that he can be grieved (Isa. 63:10; the NT discloses the same personal quality, Eph. 4:30), contends with people (Gen. 6:3; Num. 24:2), and communicates. In the realm of communication he teaches (Neh. 9:20, though the text does not say how), gives visions (Ezek. 3:12, 14; Joel 2:28) and oracles (Num. 24:2-3), reveals what is hidden (Ezek. 8:3, 12), causes one to prophesy (as here; cf. 1 Sam. 10:6; Joel 2:28) by giving him words, speech, and messages (2 Sam. 23:2; 2 Chron. 15:1; Isa. 48:16; 61:1-3; Ezek. 11:5), and causes him to bless someone (1 Chron. 12:18). He might make someone speak God's words even though it may lead to rejection and death (2 Chron. 24:20). God's Spirit not only sends his messages through prophets (Zech. 7:12), but also he eventually brings about the fulfillment of prophecy (Isa. 34:16). In the realm of piety and behavior he directs people to obey God (Ezek. 36:27), renews their commitment to God (Isa. 44:3-5), guides them (Isa. 63:11, 14), and may dramatically alter one's behavior (1 Sam. 10:6). His primary functions, then, are communicating divine truth and bringing divine intentions to fruition. (That God the Father, Son, and Holy Spirit are not simply three different modes of revelation at different times and places but three simultaneously existing persons, see Matt. 3:16-17 where all three are present and distinct at Christ's baptism.) At times some people thought that he was capricious (1 Kings 18:12; 2 Kings 2:16), but here he deliberately went to chosen persons wherever they were. [*rûaḥ*]

11:25 They prophesied (*yitnabbĕ'û*)—The verb "to prophesy" is used only here in the Pentateuch, although it is the Pentateuch that most clearly defines the noun prophet as one who spoke another's words on his behalf (Exod. 4:14-16, cf. 7:1). The etymology of the noun is debatable. Scholars relate the word to the verb *nb'* ("to gush forth"), to the verb *bw'* (passive of "to enter," as if the prophet was possessed), and to the Akkadian verb *nabû* ("to name, call," as if the prophet is the speaker or is a called one; J. Jeremias, *TLOT*, 697).

The verb appears in the Niphal and Hithpael stems. The Hithpael predominates in Israel's earlier history, as here, but the Niphal predominates in her later history (Jeremiah and Ezekiel use it often). One scholarly proposal is that in earlier times ecstatic behavior, which was expressed by the Hithpael, characterized prophecy. This became suspect, so Scripture shifted to the Niphal stem until much later times when ecstatic behavior no longer dominated prophetic behavior. Then the Hithpael could be used again. Another proposal is that there is no clear distinction in meaning, but the Niphal stresses prophecies and the Hithpael stresses the accompanying behavior (P. Verhoef, *NIDOTTE*, 4:1068). Both proposals indicate that the Hithpael accents prophetic behavior.

Pagan prophesying could be associated with shouting, dancing, and self-mutilation (1 Kings 18:26-29). Prophecy was not always from God (1 Sam. 18:10), but might come from one's own imagination (Ezek. 13:17), or be simply a lie (Jer. 5:31: 23:22) or distortion of God's words (Jer. 23:36) even though professedly spoken in his name (Jer. 2:8; 23:13, 25). True prophecy was from the Holy Spirit (1 Sam. 10:10; 19:20, 23; Joel 2:28; Mic. 3:8) and involved visions and dreams (Num. 12:6), came from God's "mouth" (Jer. 23:16, 21, 22; 26:12), and was his word (Jer. 23:28). It communicated a message from God (1 Kings 22:8, 10, 18; Ezek. 6:1-2; 37:4) and might include foretelling (1 Kings 22:13 with 17-18; 2 Chron. 20:37). The verb in the historical books could describe an activity accompanied by music (1 Sam. 10:5, 11; 18:10; 1 Chron. 25:1, 3) and so could mean singing—and perhaps it is here. For a non-prophet, the ability to prophesy might end and not resume, at least regularly (here and 1 Sam. 10:13). [*nb'*]

12:2 Has the Lord spoken through Moses (*bĕmōšeh dibber yhwh*)—The expression *dibber bĕ* in some contexts means to speak about someone (Deut. 6:7), against someone (Num. 12:1, 8), at the cost of something (1 Kings 2:23), or in someone's ears (Gen. 20:8) or heart (Eccl. 2:15). Here it means that the Lord spoke by means of a person (*BDB*, 181). When the expression denotes speaking through the agency of

someone, it also means to speak to the person (e.g., here and Hos. 1:2; Hab. 2:1; *HALOT*, 210). When the Spirit spoke through David or Micaiah, he spoke to him (2 Sam. 23:2-3; 1 Kings 22:28). This does not mean God's spokesman was only a passive channel of God's speech, for though passive in reception, he was active in transmission. If God spoke to someone, then the person could properly claim to quote God. Although God can speak for himself, he chose humans to mediate his revelation through their own personalities in such a way that their words were his—hence, the doctrine of word-for-word inspiration of Scripture (2 Tim. 3:16; 2 Pet. 1:20-21). To a lesser degree, God's words are communicated through all his witnesses (Acts 1:8). In our context in the preceding verse Miriam and Aaron spoke "against Moses" (*bĕmōšeh*, v. 1) and here God spoke "to" and "through Moses" (*bĕmōšeh*, v. 2, cf. v. 8 [*bō* = to/with him; i.e., Moses]). The equivalence in grammatical forms highlights the contrast between their action and God's. [*dibber bĕ*]

12:3 Humble (*'ānāw*)—This word is closely related to *'ānî*, which means to be without property, poor, and needy (*HALOT*, 855-56; for the association of poverty with spiritual humility, cf. Matt. 5:3; Luke 6:20). The term describes those who are not proud (Prov. 3:34; 16:19), those who are needy (Isa. 29:19) and helpless (Ps. 10:12, 17), as well as those who are dejected and afflicted because of oppressive evildoers (Isa. 29:19-21; 61:1) and are denied justice (Ps. 9:12; 76:8-9; Amos 2:7). Since these people often seek the Lord for help (Ps. 22:26; 69:32), depend on him for sustenance (Ps. 147:6), and learn his ways (Ps. 25:9) to do what he commands (Zeph. 2:3), God favors them (Prov. 3:34; cf. Num. 11:15). Consequently, the word often connotes piety, which is appropriate in Moses' case since no one was closer to God than he (cf. Num. 12:6-8). If instead of piety Moses was here claiming to be most humble, many commentators believe a later editor added the words. However, compare this to Jesus and Paul who spoke of themselves as very humble (Matt. 11:29; Acts 20:19). Although boasting of humility belies the boast, a person should know whether he elevates others' needs above his own and therefore is humble (Phil. 2:3, *tapeinophrosunē*, humility). This is the only occurrence of the word in the singular, thus emphasizing Moses' uniqueness. ['ānāw]

12:6 Visions (*mar'â*)—God spoke to people in OT times in visions at night (Gen. 46:2; 1 Sam. 3:4-15) and in the daytime (Ezek. 1:1; 8:1-3) to reveal something currently happening (Ezek. 8:5-17) or something that would happen in the future (Ezek. 40:2-4; 43:3). The vision might be a scene (Ezek. 8:5-17; 43:3), a message in words without mentioning any scene (Gen. 46:2; 1 Sam. 3:4-15), or both a scene and words (Ezek. 8:3-5; 40:2-4; 43:3; Dan. 10:4-7). When this word is used, the vision was private, but the synonymous word *mar'eh*, which sometimes means a vision, might be either a private vision (e.g., Dan. 9:23-27) or a publicly observable phenomenon (e.g., Exod. 24:17). The word most frequently used for a vision is *ḥāzôn* (which has similarly spelled, seldom used synonyms *ḥizzāyôn*, *ḥāzût*, and [Aramaic] *ḥēzew*). It has the same uses as *mar'â*, but its wider usage adds the ideas that (1) it is a judgment from God when Israel and the prophets do not receive visions from him (Ezek. 7:26; Mic. 3:6), (2) the vision may be written down (2 Chron.

32:32; Isa. 1:1; Obad. 1; Nah. 1:1; Hab. 2:2), and (3) it may require an interpreter (Dan. 1:17; 8:15-16; 10:14). Eventually the written word of God was compiled and became the final authority for the content of the divine message to humanity (cf. Deut. 4:2; Acts 17:11; Rom. 16:25-26; 2 Pet. 3:16; Rev. 22:18-19). [*mar'â*]

Dreams (*ḥălôm*)—The word appears 65x in the OT, 34x in Genesis alone. This is the only occurrence in Numbers. God spoke in dreams (Gen. 20:3, 6; 31:11) that might include a scene before one's mind's eye (Gen. 31:10-11). Like visions, in a dream God might foretell the future (Gen. 37:5-10, 20; 40:9-13), but he might simply give a warning (Gen. 20:3, 6). God spoke to persons other than recognized prophets (Gen. 20:3; 31:24; Judg. 7:13; Dan. 2:1) and even to Gentiles (Gen. 31:24; Dan. 2:1) through dreams. Like visions, the message of a dream might require an interpreter (Gen. 40:8; 41:12). Not all dreams were divine (Isa. 29:7), such as the dreams of false prophets (Jer. 23:27, 32; Zech. 10:2). While divinely given dreams were a legitimate method of revelation, written Scripture would become the ultimate authority with the promise of blessing for those who follow its teachings (Ps. 1:1-3; Josh. 1:7-8; 2 Tim. 3:15; Rev. 1:2). [*ḥălôm*]

12:7 My servant (*'abdî*)—The word *'ebed* occurs about 800x in the OT, meaning slave, household servant, ruler's subject, and worshiper of God. Calling oneself "your servant" was polite self-deprecation in the presence of an honored person (*BDB*, 713-14). The special use as "my [God's] servant(s)" appears 76x, 61 of them in the singular as here. The patriarchs Abraham (Gen. 26:24) and Jacob (Ezek. 28:25; 37:25), the prophet Isaiah (Isa. 20:3), the Messiah (Isa. 49:6; 52:13; 53:11; Zech. 3:8), Zerubbabel (Hag. 2:23), pagan

Nebuchadnezzar (Jer. 25:9), godly Caleb (Num. 14:24), Job (Job 1:8; 42:7-8), an unnamed person (Isa. 41:9), and Israel (Isa. 44:21; Jer. 30:10) are all called by this epithet, but David is so designated more than all of them (2 Sam. 3:18; 7:5, 8; and about 20 more times). When God referred to someone as "my servant" he said he chooses (1 Kings 11:34; Ps. 89:3; Isa. 41:8-10; 44:1-2; 45:4; 43:10; Hag. 2:23), supports or strengthens (Ps. 89:20; Isa. 41:8-10; 42:1; Jer. 43:10), summons and sends (Jer. 25:9; plural: 2 Kings 17:13; Jer. 7:25; 26:5; Zech. 1:6) him. God blesses him (2 Sam. 7:8, 12-16; Ps. 89:20; Isa. 44:1-2; 49:3; 52:13; Jer. 30:10; 33:22), is faithful to him (Isa. 44:21; Jer. 33:21, 26), and, as in this context, acts for his servant's sake (Gen. 26:24; 1 Kings 11:13, 32, 34; 2 Kings 19:34; 20:6; Job 42:7-8; plural: 2 Kings 9:7). H. Ringgren concludes it is a title of honor for a mediator of revelation and refers to the special status of one's relationship to God (H. Ringgren, *TDOT*, 10:394). Both concepts apply in this verse: (1) Moses' special status is manifest in that he was a servant not in part but in all of God's house, like a chief steward; and (2) he was the first and foremost mediator of scriptural revelation. The NT shows that despite Moses' elevated status, Jesus, as the Son in God's house, has an even higher position (Heb. 3:2-6). Believers in Christ are called God's servants (cf. Rom. 6:22) and may therefore expect God to direct and bless them in ways similar to how he did in the OT. [*'ebed*]

Faithful (*ne'ĕmān*)—The root of the word "faithful" is *'mn*, to confirm or support, and from which a number of cognates meaning faithfulness, trusting, firmness, steadfastness, faith, support, truth, or truly are derived, (*BDB*, 52-54). The almost universal word "Amen" is one of the derivatives. The form of the word in our text is in the Niphal stem,

implying either that Moses was one who was trusted and found reliable or that he was confirmed or supported by God. Faithfulness when referring to things means that they are lingering or prolonged (Deut. 28:59; 1 Sam. 2:35; 25:38; 1 Kings 11:38). When a person or thing is faithful, he can be depended upon despite a lapse of time (Deut. 7:9; Ps. 89:28; Isa. 33:16). A faithful person does not change (Neh. 9:8), he directs his behavior to please God, and will be accepted to live with and serve him (Ps. 101:6). Faithful people are known for being upright (Ps. 111:7; Isa. 1:21, 26), loyal (1 Sam. 22:14; Neh. 9:8; Ps. 27:6), and trustworthy (Neh. 13:13). Faithfulness is a characteristic of God (Deut. 7:9; Isa. 49:7; Hos. 11:12) that he desires in a person (1 Sam. 2:35; Ps. 101:6). [*ne'ĕmān* < *'mn*]

12:8 I speak <u>face to face</u> (*peh 'el peh 'ădabber*)—The adverbial expression here is literally "mouth to mouth" (cf. NASB, JPSV). It occurs in this exact form in only three other places, where it means "from one end to the other" (2 Kings 10:21; 21:16; Ezra 9:11). Therefore, here it could possibly mean "thoroughly," as if God communicates comprehensively with Moses. However, these three uses are all topographical. Twice the expression is used in almost this exact form (*pîw 'im pîw*) along with the verb "to speak" (*dibbēr*) as it is here. In these cases (Jer. 32:4; 34:3) the expression means that two men will meet personally, the one will not avoid the other. The other "mouth to mouth" occurrence is literal and refers to mouth-to-mouth resuscitation (2 Kings 4:34). The context in Num. 12 favors the concept of the closeness, directness, and relevance of God's communication rather than thoroughness. See comments on Num. 3:16, "the Word of the Lord," for the use of

God's "mouth" with regard to Moses. So the idea of communication rather than seeing God "face to face" should probably be preferred in this context. When Moses sees God "face to face" (Exod. 33:11; Deut. 34:10, *pānîm 'el pānîm*, the actual word "face") it is explained, "as a man speaks to his friend" (Exod. 33:11; i.e., friendly, frank, or intimate conversation). Seeing God face to face does not mean Moses saw God's essence or full glory, for this would have killed him (Exod. 33:20). No one has ever seen the essence of the full glory of God, but Christ made his character known (John 1:18) in such a way that he could announce that those who saw him saw the Father (John 14:9). [*peh*]

He sees the <u>form</u> of the Lord (*tĕmunat yhwh yabbîṭ*)—A *tĕmunâ* is a likeness, representation, semblance, or form (*BDB*, 568). Moses states that Israel saw no form (*tĕmunâ*) of God at Mt. Sinai (Deut. 4:10-12, 15), therefore they should not attempt to represent him by any man-made form. He does not say that he had not seen the physical form of God, though a form can mean a spiritual form and not physical (Job 4:16). Moses in the company of Aaron, Nadab, Abihu, and 70 elders "saw" God and ate and drank with him (Exod. 24:9-11). It is unclear exactly what they saw of God, for the text mentions only his feet as a tangible part of his appearance, but even then it states only what was under his feet. The text notes that they were not harmed for this, as if the readers might expect them to have died for seeing God (Exod. 24:11). After all, others who believed that they had seen God's face in physical form feared they would die (Gen. 32:30; Judg. 6:22-23; cf. 13:22). When God showed Moses his glory, he let him see only the remnants or tail end ("my back"), not the full force, of his "goodness" (Exod. 33:18-19) after he

had already passed by (Exod. 33:22-23). Moses might have seen some tangible, even physical form of God, but not his spiritual essence, or full glory. In the context here, even Aaron who had seen God (Exod. 24:9-11) had not seen the form of God, since Moses was unique in this respect. [*tĕmunâ*]

13:27 It does flow with milk and honey (*zābat ḥālāb ûdĕbaš*)—The verb "to flow" does not always mean to gush in abundance, but since it commonly does (Ps. 78:20; 105:41; Isa. 48:21) it appears when describing a "fruitful" valley (Jer. 49:4). In one passage honey does ooze of its own accord in Palestine (1 Sam. 14:25-26), but in this expression it is figurative of abundance (Deut. 8:8; 2 Kings 18:32), nourishment (2 Sam. 17:28-29), or both. Honey also is used figuratively of something desirable (Prov. 25:15), and literally as an appropriate gift item (Gen. 43:11; 1 Kings 14:3). Literally and figuratively milk was a significant source of nourishment (Job 21:24; Prov. 27:27; Isa. 55:1). Figuratively it could be a sign of abundance and blessing (Gen. 49:12; Deut. 32:14; Joel 3:18 [notice "flows," *zwb*]). Literal milk and honey were present even when crops were not (Isa. 7:22), indicating that Canaan would have fully adequate reserves for Israel. A land flowing with milk and honey can also be described as good and spacious (Exod. 3:8), very good (Num. 14:7-8 [cf. Deut. 1:25]), and most beautiful (Ezek. 20:6, 15). The expression connotes that the land was surprisingly productive (Num. 13:27), cared for and made fruitful by God (Deut. 11:9-12 [instead of by man]; 26:9). Egypt, also described this way (Num. 16:13), was a land of abundance (Exod. 16:3; Num. 11:15). God had promised (Exod. 13:5; Deut. 27:3) and was now prepared to give his people abundant sustenance to replace what they had left in Egypt, but without the slavery they had endured there (Exod. 3:7-8, 17). God may send his people through difficult wilderness experiences, but his goal in the end is blessing (Jer. 29:11; Heb. 12:11). [*dĕbaš, zwb, ḥālāb*]

13:30 We should take possession (*yārašnû*)—When a person is the object of this verb, the subject is either his heir (Gen. 15:3-4), or is someone who dispossessed him of what was his (Deut. 2:12). When a thing is the object of this verb, it is either legitimately inherited (Num. 27:11) or violently expropriated (1 Kings 21:19). In this context Israel was to both inherit the land legitimately, for they had a divine right to the land (Gen. 15:7; 28:4), and also to take it by violence (Num. 33:52). God moved people groups from land to land (Amos 9:7) and the expulsion of people from a land was common (Deut. 2:12, 22, 23). The Amorites had lived in the land in sin for 600 years (Gen. 15:13, 16), and because of their sins they were now to be replaced (Lev. 20:23-24; Deut. 9:4-5; 18:14; Ezra 9:11). Israel must drive them out, destroying any that would not leave (Deut. 7:1-2; 9:3), but she herself was responsible to be obedient in order to take over the land (Deut. 6:18; 8:1). In order to remain in it she must continue in obedience (Lev. 20:22-24; 25:23-24; Deut. 4:14), maintain justice (Deut. 16:20; 19:14), and avoid feuds (Deut. 19:1-10). She did not then merit possession of the land (Deut. 9:6), however, but possession should inspire obedience (Ps. 105:44-45). She would be expelled because of disobedience (Deut. 4:25-26; 28:63). In the future a remnant of Israel (Isa. 65:9) would possess the land forever (Isa. 60:21; Ezek. 36:12). God would not give Israel the land at this time, for she neither trusted nor obeyed him (Deut. 9:23). He still looks for

faith and obedience in his people with a view to giving them his blessings (John 14:21, 23; Heb. 3:10-12, 18-19; 11:6). [*yrš*]

14:2 Grumbled (*yillōnû*)—This verb and its related noun (*telunnâ*) are used only in Exod. 15-17, Num. 14-17, and Josh. 9. In the wilderness journey the congregation complained about lack of water (Exod. 15:22-24; 17:1-3), lack of food (Exod. 16:2-3), and, in this context, the impossibility of taking the land. A portion of the congregation in the wilderness complained about Moses and Aaron's leadership (Num. 16:3, 10-11). Part of the complaints was that it was a mistake to leave Egypt (Exod. 16:3; 17:3; Num. 14:2; 16:13) and that they were certain they were going to die (Exod. 16:3; 17:3; Num. 14:3). Sometimes they declared their preference regarding where they would rather die (Exod. 16:3, 6; Num. 14:2). They grumbled ostensibly against Moses and Aaron (Exod. 15:24; 16:2, 7-8; 17:3; Num. 14:2; 16:41), but in reality against God (Exod. 16:7-8; Num. 14:27, 29; 17:10). On occasion their grumbling led to plans to kill their leaders (Exod. 17:4; Num. 14:10). Part of the cause for grumbling was unbelief that God would help them (Exod. 17:3; Num. 14:11). God heard their grumbling (e.g., Exod. 16:7-9) and because they had demeaned him (Num. 14:11, 23; 16:30) he might respond by displaying his glory (Exod. 16:7, 10; Num. 14:10; 16:19, 41-42) to counter their disdain or to sentence repeat offenders to death (Num. 14:21-23; 16:31-33, 48-49). God gave a sign to stop the constant grumbling (Num. 17:5, 10), and although the complaining did not entirely cease, this term is not used again of Israel except during the conquest when they had a legitimate complaint against leaders who did not consult with God—a marked difference from the wilderness grumbling (Josh. 9:18). In the Psalms complaints about one's circumstances were acceptable to God because the psalmists turned to him in faith (though sometimes seemingly desperate) for help. God responds negatively to complaints that stem from unbelief and result in rebellion, but positively to complaints that express trust in him and his goodness. [lwn II]

14:10 Stoning (*lirgôm*)—The OT uses this word and one other (*sql*) to speak of execution by stoning. Stoning by the public was, in the OT, a cultural reaction to a perceived offense and a legal response to crimes that were viewed as a community-wide threat and that compromised the community's most closely held values (cf. J. Tigay, *EncJud* 2:314; J. Finkelstein, *The Ox That Gored*, 27-29). The fact that the Law calls for the whole city (Deut. 21:21; 22:21) or whole congregation (Lev. 20:2; 24:14; Num. 15:35-36; Deut. 13:9-10; 17:4-7) to stone someone implies that the Law regards these as offenses against the whole community. The legal system aside, the community considered stoning Moses, Joshua, and Caleb here, and David later (1 Sam. 30:6) as if these men were responsible for the catastrophic loss or death of Israelite families (cf. also 1 Kings 21:13; 2 Chron. 24:20-21). In the Law the crimes of approaching God too closely (Exod. 19:12-13, 21), the killing of a human by an animal (Exod. 21:28-29, 32), blasphemy (Lev. 24:14), child sacrifice (Lev. 20:2), occult practices (Lev. 20:27), Sabbath violation (Num. 15:32-35), false prophecy (Deut. 13:10), idolatry (Deut. 17:3-5), incorrigibility (Deut. 21:18-21), and adultery (Deut. 22:21, 24) all warranted stoning. Other judicial stoning was for violation of the ban on Jericho (Josh. 7:25) and for cursing God and the king (1 Kings 21:10). God ordered his community to be involved in punishments of crimes that were especially destructive to them. Likewise in the church the congregation must act to discipline members who are involved in sins destructive to the community, such as incest (1 Cor. 5:1-5) and incorrigibility (Matt. 18:15-17). [rgm]

The glory of the Lord (*kĕbôd yhwh*)—The word *kābôd* developed from *kbd*, which signifies heaviness in the physical sphere and, consequently, weightiness, importance, or honor in the social and spiritual realms. The cognate *kābēd* is the word for liver, which in OT times was thought of as the most important of the organs along with the heart (M. Weinfeld, *TDOT*, 7:23), and the cognate *kōbed* signifies heaviness, abundance, or vehemence (*BDB*, 458). With humans the term *kābôd* can refer to wealth (Gen. 31:1), honorarium (Num. 24:11), or honor that includes respect and a position of authority (Gen. 45:13; Ps. 8:5). The last comes closest to its use in regard to God. His glory is the displaying of his majesty and splendor, giving evidence of his greatness (Deut. 5:24; Ps. 19:1; 29:3; 57:5; Isa. 35:2; 66:18), and the expression of his reputation (1 Chron. 16:29; Isa. 43:7). He deserves this marvelous reputation because of his flawless character. Therefore, glory is the manifestation of his goodness and his name and all the characteristics that these portray (Exod. 33:18-19; Ps. 102:15; 138:5). Consequently glory can reveal who he really is (Exod. 16:7, 12; Ps. 97:6) and where he is (Exod. 29:42-43; 33:18, 22; Ps. 26:8; Isa. 58:8). Thus, it manifests his presence (1 Sam. 4:21-22; Ezek. 1:28; 8:4). Since his glory displays his power (Num. 14:20), his marvelous works show his glory (Exod. 16:7; Ps. 19:1; 1 Chron. 16:24; Ps. 102:16). His glory is often represented in one location by a cloud (Exod. 16:10; 24:16; 40:34-35; 1 Kings 8:11) and fire

(Exod. 24:17; Ezek. 1:26-28), and thus, light (Isa. 60:1-2). The manifestation of God's glory can be threatening (Num. 16:19-21, 42-45) and signal judgment to follow (Ezek. 39:21), and can also be a harbinger of protection for his people (Isa. 4:5-6; 58:8), as here. [*kābôd*]

14:11 Treat me with contempt (*yĕna'ăṣunî*)—The more basic grammatical form of this verb means to turn away from (Deut. 32:17-20; Prov. 1:30), to reject (Ps. 107:11), or to verbally reject (Jer. 33:24). In the grammatical pattern that appears in this verse, the verb means to treat someone or something as if it is rejected or worthy of rejection. When God or things associated with him are treated this way he (2 Sam. 12:14; Ps. 10:3) or his offerings (1 Sam. 2:17) may be demeaned through behavior or speech. He is treated as though he does not deserve respect (Ps. 74:10). He is treated contemptuously when people place no confidence in him (as in this verse), disobey him and test him despite his signs and his glory (Num. 14:22-23), disregard his publicly known values and laws (1 Sam. 2:17; 2 Sam. 12:14), stubbornly refuse to walk in his ways (Jer. 23:17), and turn away from him in rejection (Isa. 1:4). The arrogant are especially known for treating him so (Ps. 10:2-3). Treating God with contempt may result in not receiving God's promised blessings (Num. 14:23) and in death (Num. 16:30). In this context God's appearance in glory should aid Israel to have a proper perception of his person, majesty, and significance. The NT teaches that those who demean God's Son and his redemptive work deserve severe punishment (Heb. 10:29). [*n'ṣ*]

To believe in me (*ya'ămînû bî*)—Major proposals to explain the exact meaning of this Hebrew verb include: (1) to strengthen someone to be true by putting confidence in him, (2) to find security in something or someone, (3) to agree that something corresponds to what it promises, (4) to make oneself secure in God, and (5) to become trustworthy (A. Jepsen, *TDOT*, 1:298-99). To believe a statement clearly means to judge it as reliable and corresponding to reality in the present (Gen. 45:26; 1 Kings 10:7) and for the future (Gen. 15:6). Therefore, one "believes in" the speaker (cf. Gen. 15:6, where believing in the Lord's Word was so significant that God attributed righteousness to the believer, Abraham) and expects with certainty what has been predicted (Lam. 4:12). It involves confidence in the promissory (Deut. 9:23; Ps. 78:22; Isa. 43:10), even to the point of reliance without reconsideration (Prov. 14:15), although on occasion it may merely mean to have a high estimation of someone (Job 9:16). A sign attesting to the validity of one's message may help people to put confidence in it, but this result is not universally positive (Exod. 4:3, 30-31). What God has done in the past should result in people having confidence in him for the future (Deut. 1:32; Ps. 106:12). Faith in God is connected with obedience (Deut. 9:23; 2 Kings 17:14), and results in security (Isa. 28:16), being upheld by God (2 Chron. 20:20; Isa. 7:9), and seeing God's promises accomplished (2 Chron. 20:20). Not to put confidence in God is sin and provokes him to anger and to punish the unbelievers (Ps. 78:21-22, 32). Meanings two and three above seem to express the ideas of the verb best here. Meaning four is a result of believing. [*'mn*]

The miraculous signs (*hā'ōtôt*)—This term does not always connote a miraculous sign, but can be a warning (Gen. 4:15), physical signpost (Ps. 74:4) or banner (Num. 2:2), a reminder (Exod. 13:16; Num. 16:38; Josh. 4:6)—particularly of one of God's covenants (Gen. 9:12-17; 17:11; Exod. 31:13, 17)—that may be used to provoke an action (Exod. 13:9; Deut. 6:8), and a predicted event confirming that God has done something (Exod. 3:12) or a prophet has divine authority (Deut. 13:1-2; 1 Sam. 10:7). God's signs draw attention in order to teach and inform (Ps. 86:17; Isa. 20:3), to give him a reputation (Neh. 9:10; Isa. 7:11; 55:13; Jer. 32:20), and to stimulate confidence in him (Exod. 4:8-9, 30-31, and here). As here, they can be miraculous deeds (Exod. 4:17, 28; 7:3; Num. 14:22; Deut. 4:34; 2 Kings 20:9-10) that point to his power lying behind them (Exod. 8:22-23) and show who he is (Exod. 10:1-2). As in this passage, God's signs do not automatically produce confidence in him (Exod. 4:8-9; Deut. 29:3; cf. Luke 16:31; John 12:37). A specific word (*hrēma*) of God from the Scripture (i.e., a verse or passage) that relates to one's situation is more effective than signs in producing faith (Rom. 10:17). ['*ôt*]

14:15 The nations . . . will say (*'āmĕrû hag-gôyim*)—The OT words *gôy* (nation) and *'am* (people) are synonymous, but often the term *gôy* tends to connote people united politically and territorially while *'am* tends to connote people united by racial or ethnic ties (R. Clements, *TDOT*, 2:426-27). From the beginning of the OT record God was concerned with the nations (Gen. 12:3). He determined to make himself known to them (Ezek. 38:23) through a marvelous testimony (1 Chron. 16:24-32; Ps. 98:2; 126:2; Isa. 62:2), to bring them his salvation (Isa. 49:6), to show them his incredible victory through his humiliated servant (Isa. 52:10), and to be praised among them (2 Sam. 22:50; Ps. 96:3; 117:1). He planned to draw people from all nations to himself in loyalty (Isa. 2:2). He did not want his

name to be profaned among the nations (Ezek. 20:22). With Israel he was currently doing an awesome work (Exod. 34:10) in view of the nations (Lev. 26:45), something that had never before been done (Deut. 4:34). Eventually he will punish Israel in the sight of the nations (Ezek. 5:8). Their humiliation runs the risk that God's testimony will be besmirched (Ps. 79:9-12), as if he were no more than the idol gods (Ps. 115:2). Ultimately, however, the nations will realize that God has not merely let his people and their land be destroyed, but that he has justly punished them (Deut. 29:22-24; Jer. 22:8). When he later restores Israel's fortunes in full view of the nations, he will demonstrate his own faithfulness and grace (Jer. 31:7-9). Then the nations will testify that the Lord has blessed his people (Isa. 62:2; Mal. 3:12). Until the end of history God will seek to draw people from all nations and people groups to his Son (Rev. 7:9). Moses is not manipulating God, but thinking as God does about his reputation and plans. Therefore, his prayer is answered to a degree (the people will still all die in the wilderness, but not at this moment as threatened). [*gôyim*]

14:18 Slow to anger (*'erek 'appayim*)—The comments on Num. 11:1 deal with the meaning and use of the word "anger" (*'ap*), but here the concern is with the use of the particular expression "slow to anger." This expression is used of the Lord 10x in the OT. It is part of God's glorious character (Exod. 33:18-19), along with his compassion, grace, love, and faithfulness (Exod. 34:6; Num. 14:18). Because he was slow to anger he did not abandon his rebellious people in the wilderness (Neh. 9:17-19), but forgave them (Num. 14:18-20) and spared the repentant from deserved punishment

(Jonah 4:2). Therefore, there was opportunity to repent (cf. 2 Pet. 9 for the NT parallel), and prophets exhorted sinners on this basis (Joel 2:13). When he does punish sin, his slowness to anger moves him to mitigate punishment (Ps. 103:8-10). For the unrepentant, God's slowness to anger may appear to give an opportunity to continue in wickedness, or it may provoke the righteous to believe that wickedness will triumph (Jer. 15:15; Nahum 1:3), but they need to be alert to the error of such thinking (Exod. 34:6-7; Num. 14:18). Even here, where the rebellious and unrepentant are forgiven, they are condemned to die in the wilderness. Slowness to anger is a desirable quality in humans as well, displaying wisdom and inner personal power (Prov. 14:29; 15:18; 16:32). ['erek 'appayim]

Abounding in love (*rab ḥesed*)—This word for "love" can refer to mercy and kindness (Gen. 24:12, 14), to doing good to those in need (Ps. 109:16), and to loyalty, faithfulness, and devotion to others in a friendship (2 Sam. 16:17; Prov. 20:6) or formal relationship (Ruth 3:10; Jer. 2:2). In the context of Num. 14 the translation "love" is not the most appropriate. Compare "loving kindness" (NASB), "mercy" (NKJV), and "kindness" (JPSV) in some of the other versions, with the latter two being the most appropriate. The word often describes the attitude that lays the basis for a covenant (Deut. 7:9, 12; Isa. 54:10; 55:3) and is certainly expected between partners in a covenant relationship (1 Sam. 20:8; 1 Kings 8:32; Hos. 2:19; Dan. 9:4). The OT says that *ḥesed* is an integral part of God's goodness (1 Chron. 16:34; Ps. 106:1) and overall character (Exod. 34:6-7; 2 Chron. 20:21; Neh. 9:17; Ps. 86:15; Joel 2:13; Jonah 4:2), so it marks his treatment of people who are in a relationship with him (Ps. 36:10; 44:26; 103:11). As here, God's *ḥesed* is the basis

for the hope of forgiveness (Ps. 51:1; 86:5), for petition (2 Chron. 1:8; Neh. 1:5-6; Ps. 6:4), and for being able to approach him (Ps. 5:7). It prompts upright behavior in others (Ps. 26:3). Because of his *ḥesed* God rescues people (Ps. 6:4; 31:21-22; 86:13) and spares their lives (Gen. 19:19; Ps. 119:88). His *ḥesed* moves him to mitigate punishment (Ps. 106:5; Lam. 3:22, 32), and it outlasts and replaces his wrath (Isa. 54:8; Mic. 7:18), as Moses hoped it would do here. God displays a reputation for *ḥesed* (Ps. 109:26-27; 115:1) and thus provokes people to trust him (Ps. 52:8; 143:8). Since *ḥesed* warrants *ḥesed* in response (1 Sam. 15:6), recipients of God's *ḥesed* can express it to others (2 Sam. 9:3), which is pleasing to God (Prov. 3:3-4; Hos. 12:6; Zech. 7:9) and to people (Prov. 19:22). God manifests *ḥesed* to people who trust him (Ps. 32:10) and love, serve, and obey him (Exod. 20:6; Ps. 103:17; Dan. 9:4). His *ḥesed* is great and is directed to many people (Exod. 20:6; Ps. 56:10; 108:4). Although his *ḥesed* is continual (Neh. 9:17-18; Ps. 23:6; Jer. 33:11), situations may occur that cause the faithful to temporarily think it is gone (Ps. 77:8; 89:49). For the unfaithful it seems that God's *ḥesed* can be lost (2 Sam. 7:15; Ps. 66:20; Jer. 16:5). [*ḥesed*]

Forgiving sin (*nōśē' 'āwōn*)—The same Hebrew expression sometimes means "to bear sin," that is, to bear responsibility (Exod. 28:38; Lev. 5:1) or bear punishment (Num. 14:34; Ezek. 18:19-20; cf. Ashley who notes that with this meaning the punishment is left to God, T. Ashley, *Numbers*, 135), sometimes resulting in death (Num. 18:22), though not always (Num. 5:31). The expression can mean to take away sins, as one goat on the Day of Atonement figuratively did (Lev. 16:21-22; in Job 7:21 the terms parallel the expression in Hebrew, "to cause sin to pass away"), and to bring about forgiveness (Lev. 10:17).

Although it is possible, the fact that the same Hebrew expression can mean both to forgive and also to bear sins does not necessarily mean that God's forgiveness involves his bearing and suffering for someone else's sins, for the same verb is used of human forgiveness where the one who forgives does not carry or suffer for another's sins (Gen. 50:17; 1 Sam. 15:25; 25:28). The only time one person is said to bear another's sins is in Isa. 53:12 (the word for sin there is *ḥēṭ'*; for the word used for sin here ['*āwōn*], cf. comments on "guilt," Num. 5:15). [*nś'*]

Rebellion (*pāša'*)—Along with its related verb (*peša'*) this term frequently describes a political rebellion (e.g., 1 Sam. 24:11; 2 Kings 3:7; 8:20) as well as rebellion against God (Ps. 5:10 Ezek. 2:3; 20:38), his instruction, and his covenant (Hos. 8:1). The term indicates willful, deliberate error (Prov. 28:21), and treachery against God (Isa. 48:8; 59:13) that stems from pride and presumption (Ps. 19:13; Ezek. 21:24; Zeph. 3:11). The act may include mistreating (Gen. 50:17; Isa. 58:1-7; Amos 1:3, 6; 5:12) and robbing people (Gen. 31:36; Exod. 22:9), and violating their trust (Exod. 22:7-15). It can involve speaking against (Job 34:37) and bringing charges against God (Jer. 2:29) and his leaders (Exod. 23:21), as here. Carpenter and Grisanti conclude that it most often designates violation of a norm or disruption of an alliance through violation of a covenant (E. Carpenter and M. Grisanti, *NIDOTTE*, 3:707). Although those guilty of such rebellion will be destroyed (Isa. 1:28; Ps. 37:38), they are not all beyond all hope, for God hears intercession on their behalf (Isa. 53:12), he is willing to forgive (Ps. 32:1; Jer. 33:8; Mic. 7:18), and some of them can be taught his ways (Ps. 37:38). He is able to punish rebellion without withdrawing his love (Ps. 89:32-33). On the human level love and longsuf-

fering can motivate one to overlook an offense (Prov. 17:9; 19:11). God presumably also overlooks rebellion, at least temporarily, because of his love and patience, but ultimately repentance (Isa. 59:20) and atonement are necessary for forgiveness (Lev. 16:16, 21). [*peša'*, *pāša'*]

Not leave unpunished (*lō' yĕnaqqeh*)— The type of Hebrew verb pattern here means that something happens so that someone can be described by the adjective *nāqî* or the verb *nāqâ*. Such a person was either released from an obligation (Gen. 24:41; Num. 32:22; Deut. 24:5), considered innocent (Gen. 19:10, 13; 44:10), or perhaps never had been guilty (Num. 5:31). Synonyms for the innocent are the "upright" (*yāšār*) and the "righteous" (*ṣaddîq*; cf. Job 4:7; 22:19). These words (and *niqqāyôn*) using the same root in physical contexts can describe something clean or cleaned out (Amos 4:6, literally, "cleanness of teeth"; Isa. 3:26, literally, "empty" or "without anything"), perhaps implying in ethical contexts that a person either has a clean record ("innocent") or is treated ("unpunished") as though he has one. When the term, as here, means unpunished the person may still be required to take steps to help the wronged party (Exod. 21:19), and people who are unpunished may nevertheless be disciplined (Jer. 30:11; 46:28; see the parallel below on Num. 14:19). Here the statement shows that God's mercy is not license to sin. [*nqh*]

14:19 Forgive (*sĕlaḥ-nā'*)—In the OT God is the only subject of this verb for forgiveness, emphasizing that this was God's work, accomplished for his own sake (Ps. 25:11; Dan. 9:19). God forgave after an atoning sacrifice for a sin of inadvertence (Lev. 4:20, 26), after atonement and restitution for a sin of defrauding (Lev. 6:7, 16), or after someone sought him in repentance and prayer for apostasy and sin in general (1 Kings 8:30-36; 2 Chron. 7:14; Isa. 55:7; Jer. 36:3). However, for sins of contempt for God, as here, sacrificial atonement is limited (1 Sam. 3:14; J. Olivier, *NIDOTTE*, 3:261). Divine forgiveness results in mercy (1 Kings 8:50) as God removes guilt and sins (Jer. 50:20), relents of judgment (Jer. 5:1; Amos 7:2-3), and restores and blesses (1 Kings 8:34-39, 50; Jer. 33:8-9). The related noun *sallāḥ* indicates that forgiveness is part of God's goodness and is based on his love (Ps. 86:5). The use of the cognate noun *sĕlîḥâ* shows that forgiveness leads God neither to keep a record of sins (Ps. 130:3-4) nor to forsake Israel when they rebel (Neh. 9:17; Dan. 9:9). Experiencing divine forgiveness results in people fearing (Ps. 130:4) and knowing God (Jer. 31:34). In this context, Israel is forgiven (Num. 14:20), but will still die without entering the land (14:28-30). Compare this to Christians who are forgiven of all sins (1 Cor. 6:11; Col. 2:13-14) and yet may die as a result of certain sins (1 Cor. 11:29-30). [*slḥ*]

14:22 Tested me (*yĕnassû 'ōtî*)—Israel tested God by not trusting him (Ps. 78:18, 22) despite his miraculous wonders (Ps. 78:52), and by challenging his ability to provide for them although he had recently, repeatedly, and powerfully provided for them (Ps. 78:12-16, 19-20; cf. Num. 14:11). They disregarded his past provisions (Ps. 78:41-53; 106:13-14; cf. here with Exod. 14:31; 16:12, 15; cf. Exod. 17:7 with 17:2; Ps. 95:9) and accused him of being untrustworthy (Num. 14:3) and unworthy (cf. Num. 14:11, "treat with contempt"). They challenged him to prove himself (Deut. 6:16; cf. Matt. 4:5-7). In addition to unbelief, people tested God because of cravings that prompted them to try to manipulate him (Ps. 78:18;

106:14). God once accepted testing by Gideon (Judg. 6:39) and twice invited testing (Isa. 7:10-11; Mal. 3:10 [*bāḥan*]). In Gideon's case Israel had seen no miraculous works of God for many decades and the record of his works was so ancient that Gideon questioned their relevance in the new situation (Judg. 6:13). Since Gideon's father had argued that Baal ought to display his power if he is deity (Judg. 6:31-32), Gideon requested God to do the same thing in the realm where Baal, according to the local mythology, controlled the dew. Because of the OT opposition to testing God, it is notable that Gideon stressed his humility and his concern that he might be inappropriate by his testing (Judg. 6:39). In the two times God invited testing, since he was the initiator it was not a matter of proud, manipulative, or unbelieving people challenging him. Actually, Ahaz's unbelief prompted his refusal to test God (Isa. 7:9-10), so that he exhibited the same attitude of those who had tested God in the past. Therefore, an attitude of unbelief in the face of strong evidence for the care, provision, and power of God, sometimes coupled with intent to manipulate, is what was involved in this sin (cf. Matt. 12:22, 38). Other words for testing are *bāḥan*, *ṣārap*, and *ḥāqar*. The word *ḥāqar*, to search out, is never used of testing God, though he examines people (Ps. 44:21, NIV, "discovered"). The term *ṣārap* is used for smelting and for producing improvement and so is never used of testing God. The word *bāḥan*, to evaluate someone's reliability (Gen. 42:16), is used only 3x as testing God, two of which are negative (Ps. 95:9; Mal. 3:15). [*nsh*]

14:43 You have turned away from the Lord (*šabtem mē'aḥărê yhwh*)—This particular verb and preposition, when used either with the Lord as the one from whom someone is turning or the Lord as the one turning away, appears 11x in the OT. Turning away from God is compared to unfaithfulness in marriage (Jer. 3:19-20, covenant breaking) and is equated with rebellion (as here, cf. v. 9; Josh. 22:18, 29). People turned away from the Lord when they did not observe his commands and served other gods (1 Kings 9:6), prepared an altar to worship him outside of the prescribed biblical system (Josh. 22:16, 22-23, 29), did not believe him (as here, cf. v. 11), disobeyed and tested him (as here, cf. v. 23), treated him with contempt (as here, cf. vv. 11, 23), gave a bad report about the good inheritance he promised his people, and discouraged them from following him (as here, cf. v. 36; Num. 32:15). A theocratic king who represented God but did not obey his specific commands relative to the operation of the kingdom and treatment of its enemies was turning away from the Lord (1 Sam. 15:11) and rebelling (1 Sam. 15:23). God punished through the covenant curses those who turned away from him (1 Kings 9:6-7, cf. Deut. 28:36-37, 64; 29:24). A similar and less used expression for turning away from the Lord is *sûr mē'aḥărāyw*. It also speaks of idolatry (2 Chron. 25:14, 27) and contrasts with trusting and obeying (2 Kings 18:6) and serving and worshiping God (2 Chron. 34:33). God may still deal severely with those who turn away from him (Heb. 12:25). [*šwb*]

15:3 Offerings made by fire (*'iššeh*)—The basic meaning of this term may be "gift" or "food gift" (R. Averbeck, *NIDOTTE*, 1:541), since on occasion it describes an offering that is not burned (wave offering, Lev. 7:30-34; 10:15; drink offering, Lev. 23:37; and Bread of the Presence, Lev. 24:7). Usually the term designates the grain (Lev. 2:2-3), fellowship (Lev. 3:3, 6, 12), ordina-

tion (8:22-28), and burnt offerings (Lev. 1:10-13), including the daily (Exod. 29:38-41), monthly (Num. 28:11-13), and festival (Unleavened Bread, Lev. 23:8; Rosh Hashanah, 23:25; Yom Kippur, 23:27; Feast of Booths, 23:36) burnt offerings. It includes not just the fat or meat burned on the altar, but also the grain products, oil, wine, and incense offered with them (Exod. 29:40-41; Lev. 2:2, 16). It perhaps designates the sin offering twice (Num. 29:13-16, 36-38, where the *'iššeh* may refer to the whole set of offerings that includes a sin offering) and does designate the guilt offering once (Lev. 7:5), but normally it seems to be distinct from them (Lev. 4:35; 5:12; Num. 15:24-25). The infrequent reference to sin offerings may be because the *'iššeh* is often described as a pleasing aroma to God (29x; e.g., Exod. 29:18; Lev. 1:9; 2:2; 3:5; Num. 15:3; 18:17), whereas the sin offering is almost never (Lev. 4:31, the exception) so described. The fact that the sin offering can be called a pleasing aroma to God, although it is rare, sets a precedent for Christ's offering for sin that was also called a fragrant offering to God (Eph. 5:2). [*'iššeh*]

Freewill offerings (*nidbōtêkem*)—The cognate verb (*nādab*) means that one's heart prompts him (Exod. 25:2) of his own volition. Therefore, when people gave this way it was with their whole hearts (1 Chron. 29:9). The noun may refer to a spirit of volunteering (Deut. 23:23; 2 Chron. 35:8) and to a voluntary contribution to the temple, its service (2 Chron. 31:14; Ezra 1:4), the tabernacle construction, and its furnishings (Exod. 35:29; 36:3). The term also refers to a type of fellowship offering (Lev. 7:16) that may be in the form of a burnt offering (Lev. 22:18; Ezek. 46:12). Other offerings may be prescribed for holy days, such as those in these two chapters, or as a consequence of a sin or a vow, but the freewill offering was distinct from them (Num. 15:3; Deut. 12:6, 17; Ezra 3:5). It was not necessarily owed, but expressed one's love for God or appreciation for his blessings (Deut. 16:10) and was given with praise (Ps. 119:108). It probably could not be commanded, but it should characterize the Feast of Weeks when people responded in proportion to God's blessings (Deut. 16:10). Since it might be given out of thanks for deliverance (Ps. 54:6-7), it is frequently mentioned with vows (Lev. 7:16; 22:18, 21; Deut. 23:23). It was offered especially on days of assembly, as here, so that more people could see the testimony of God's goodness and the demonstration of the nation's appreciation for him, though the latter may be hypocritical (Amos 4:5; J. Conrad, *TDOT*, 9:222). Perhaps because it was not an obligation, it may be less than perfect (Lev. 22:23), although someone who gave out of sheer love would probably select a blameless offering. The wholehearted attitude that prompted this offering is parallel to the commendable attitude of believers who give themselves to God along with their material offerings (2 Cor. 8:5). [*nĕdābâ*]

15:5 Lamb (*kebeś*)—Sheep and goats were the most important and common domestic animals in the ancient Near East, with lambs being primarily important for meat, milk (when mature; C. Dohmen, *TDOT*, 7:49), and clothing (Prov. 27:26). Lambs needed care (Hos. 4:16) and were a symbol of vulnerability (Isa. 11:6; Jer. 11:19). They were ever present (cf. Isa. 5:17), and when offerings of multiple animals were made to God the number of lambs either equaled (seldom, but Num. 7:88; 1 Chron. 29:1; 2 Chron. 29:21) or exceeded (usually, cf. Lev. 23:18; Num. 28:11, 19; 29:8, 13; 2 Chron. 29:32; Ezek. 46:4, 6) the quantity of any other type of animal (except Ezra 8:35).

They could not be offered until they were eight days old (Lev. 22:27), and were usually offered in their first year (e.g., Exod. 12:5; Lev. 9:3; 12:6). They were used in festival (Passover [Exod. 12:5], Pentecost [Num. 28:26-27], Rosh Hashanah [Num. 29:1-2], Yom Kippur [Num. 29:7-8], Feast of Booths [Num. 29:12-13]), periodic (daily [Exod. 29:38-40], Sabbath [Num. 28:9], monthly [Num. 28:11]), burnt (Lev. 9:3), fellowship (Lev. 23:19), sin (Lev. 4:32), and guilt (Lev. 14:12) offerings. Their use as sacrifices was common in the region and showed honor and reverence to the deity as a sacrifice of one's personal possessions (C. Dohmen, *TDOT*, 7:47). The use of common animals for sacrifice made honoring God possible for the vast majority of Israelites. Although access to God was restricted in some ways, worship was possible for the commoner. In the NT God's Son who died for sin was called a Lamb, and his redemptive work was made available for the salvation of common people, not just the privileged (cf. John 1:34; 1 Cor. 1:26-27; Heb. 2:14, 17). [*kebeś, keśeb, kabśâ*]

15:21 From the first (*mērē'śît*)—The word can refer to the best (Exod. 23:19; Deut. 33:21), the primary element (Jer. 49:35), the most important (Prov. 4:7), the beginning in terms of time (Deut. 11:12), and the firstborn (Ps. 78:51). Often, as here, it refers to the firstfruits. Items mentioned as firstfruits offered to God include yeast and honey (Lev. 2:12), grain (Lev. 23:10), olive oil (Num. 18:12), new wine (Num. 18:12), wool (Deut. 18:4), fruit from trees (Neh. 10:37), crops in general (Exod. 23:19), and meal or dough as here (since it can be stored [Neh. 10:37, 39], meal may be preferred). Until one offered his firstfruits to God, no one could eat from these products (Lev. 23:14; cf. Jer. 2:3). The firstfruit offering was a way to show honor to

God (Prov. 3:9) and it brought blessings to the one offering it (Prov. 3:9-10; Ezek. 44:30). The offering might be waved to the Lord (Lev. 23:10-11) and given to the priests (Num. 18:8, cf. v. 12; Neh. 10:37) and Levites (Neh. 12:44). The tithe was in addition to the firstfruit offering (cf. 2 Chron. 31:5-6; Neh. 10:37; 12:44). The Israelite accompanied his firstfruit offering with a statement of his creed (Deut. 26:2-10), testifying to God's faithful providence. The NT calls some people who were particularly committed to God's service firstfruits (1 Cor. 16:15; Rev. 14:4), especially Christ who was the first one to be resurrected (1 Cor. 15:20, 23). [*rēʾšît*]

15:22 You unintentionally fail (*tišgû*)—Several related words (*šāgâ, šāgag, šĕgāgâ*) express the concept of committing error inadvertently. The word can denote something that is terribly wrong such as wrongful killing (1 Sam. 26:21), or accidental manslaughter (Num. 35:11), going astray in general from God's direction (Ps. 119:67), the reversal of what is fitting (Eccl. 10:5-7), and a thoughtless mistake (Eccl. 5:2, 6). Even though someone did wrong without intent or knowledge (e.g., eating holy food by mistake [Lev. 22:14]), he had violated a prohibition and was guilty (Lev. 4:13). Therefore, he needed atonement and forgiveness (Num. 15:28) that a sin (Lev. 4:22-28) or guilt (Lev. 5:17-18) offering could accomplish. [*šgh, šgg, šĕgāgâ*]

15:30 Who sins defiantly (*taʿăśeh bĕyād rāmâ*)—The Hebrew expression, literally, is "does with a high hand." The verb *rwm* appears not only with "hand," but also with words for arm, eyes, and heart, where it connotes similar ideas as here. An "upraised arm" indicates a sense of power and confidence, including a sense of safety in doing evil (Job 38:15). When

sin is involved, a sense of premeditation is included, in contrast to the unintentional sin mentioned above (Num. 15:22, "you unintentionally fail"). "Haughty eyes" of course indicate self-exaltation and overstepping one's bounds (Ps. 131:1), or self-righteousness that may result in despising others and destructive behavior (Prov. 30:12-14). Haughtiness leads to being hated (Prov. 6:16-17) and defeated by God (Ps. 18:27). The word is used for a "proud heart" that is prompted by security and abundance that in turn prompt one not to acknowledge God (Deut. 8:12-14; Hos. 13:6) or respect people (Deut. 17:20). The high hand may indicate power and even majesty (Ps. 89:13; Isa. 26:10-11) or confidence in the sight of those over whom one has triumphed (Exod. 14:8; Num. 33:3; Mic. 5:9). In this context it indicates insolence prompted by a false sense of power and security from punishment. [*rwm*]

15:31 Despised the Lord's Word (*dĕbar yhwh bāzâ*)—Despising can range from regarding someone as insignificant (1 Sam. 2:30; Ps. 73:20) and ignoring him (Ps. 22:24), to speaking disparagingly of (1 Sam. 17:42), rejecting (Isa. 53:3), and abhorring (Isa. 49:7) someone or something. To despise God's Word is to despise him (2 Sam. 12:9-10) and normally is a characteristic of those who do not fear him (Prov. 14:2). People despise God's Word by breaking his commandments (2 Sam. 12:9), despise his oath by breaking his covenant (Ezek. 16:59; 17:19), despise his name by offering defective gifts (Mal. 1:6-8), and despise his holy things by treating them as common (Ezek. 22:8). When God's followers despise him it leads his enemies to blaspheme the Lord (1 Sam. 12:14), moving him to punish the offender (1 Sam. 12:9-12; Ezek. 16:59;

17:16-20). God does not despise the contrite (Ps. 51:17) or the afflicted (Ps. 22:24; 69:33). [*bzh*]

15:35 Outside the camp (*miḥûṣ lammaḥăneh*)—God dwelled in Israel's camp, so it must not be defiled (Num. 5:3). People who had been defiled by corpses (Num. 31:19), leprosy (Lev. 13:46; Num. 12:14-15), or other impurities (Deut. 23:10) must leave until they were clean (Deut. 23:11). Persons condemned and executed by God, who were therefore a reproach to the people of God, were buried outside the camp (Lev. 10:4). Those who were worthy of stoning were considered to be threats to the well-being and fundamental values of the community (cf. comments on Num. 14:10, "stoning"), so they were executed and buried outside the camp (Lev. 24:14; 1 Kings 21:13). This symbolized Israel's divorce from the offenders and their errors. The remains of sin and burnt offerings (Lev. 4:12; 6:11) and the red heifer for cleansing (Num. 19:9) were placed outside the camp also, but these places were considered clean, perhaps because, like the camp, they belonged to God. The NT combines the concepts of reproach and cleansing outside the camp when Christ offered himself as an offering to God for the cleansing of sinners but was reproached by his people (Heb. 13:11-13). [*miḥûṣ lammaḥăneh*]

15:39 Prostitute yourselves (*'attem zōnîm*)—The word sometimes refers to sexual immorality (Gen. 38:24) and can refer to it in conjunction with idolatry (Num. 25:1-6; cf. Rev. 2:14). However, the term most often denotes Israel's breaking covenant with God and adhering to other gods (Deut. 31:16; Judg. 2:17-20) or following mediums and spiritists (Lev. 20:6). It describes Israel's offering (Lev. 17:7)

and eating (Exod. 34:15) idolatrous sacrifices and practicing evil and shameful deeds (Lev. 20:2-5; Judg. 2:17-19; Ezek. 16:47; Hos. 4:18). Perhaps it is because appetite for sexual relations and food is associated with religious unfaithfulness that the term can be translated "lust" (Ezek. 6:9; 20:30; 23:30), refer to revelry (Isa. 23:7-17), and be associated with selfishness (Isa. 1:21-23). Similarly, it can denote unfaithfulness brought on or characterized by craving (cf. Num. 14:33 with Ps. 106:14-15). The concept of lust and revelry may explain why the Canaanites' worship was called prostituting themselves to their gods although they were not being unfaithful to them (Exod. 34:15-16). In addition, in the Canaanite fertility cults sexual acts were often part of the ritual, supposedly provoking the god to make crops, animals, and people fertile through what is now called sympathetic magic. In our text the word speaks of cravings that lead to all kinds of disobedience, not merely idolatry. The NT follows the OT in regard to the figure of sexual immorality. It compares unfaithfulness to the Lord with sexual infidelity and connects unfaithfulness to him with uncontrolled inner desires (James 4:1-4). [*znh*]

Of your own hearts (*lĕbabkem*)—H. Fabry shows that the Hebrew word used here (*lēbāb*, also written *lēb*), which is often translated "heart," has many shades of meaning: personal identity and part of one's composite makeup (Deut. 28:65; Ps. 73:26; Prov. 14:30); the vital center of the processes of life, nourishment (Judg. 19:5, 8, 22), and sexual desire (Prov. 6:25); the seat of the emotions (Prov. 14:10; 15:13); the cognitive faculty so that one really "sees" and "hears" (Deut. 29:4; Eccl. 7:21), then preserves and internalizes, and then makes judgments on this basis (Prov. 22:17; Isa. 32:4); the center of memory (Isa.

46:8; Jer. 3:16); the seat of wisdom (1 Kings 10:24; Prov. 2:6); and the center of one's volition, either as the driving force behind his efforts (Ps. 39:3; Jer. 20:9), the conceiving and planning of an effort (1 Sam. 14:7; 1 Kings 8:17-18; Ps. 19:14), or courage (1 Sam. 10:26; 2 Sam. 17:10). In the religious and ethical sphere, the word refers to the place of God's influence (1 Kings 8:39; Ps. 33:15; Prov. 16:1), the conscience (1 Sam. 24:5; 1 Kings 2:44), the seat of virtues (Ps. 7:10; 11:2; Prov. 23:19), and the seat of vices (Ps. 28:3; 95:8; Prov. 26:23; Hos. 13:6). (H. Fabry, *TDOT*, 7:411-29). Here *lēbāb* is the center of volition that leads to sin. [*lēbāb, lēb*]

16:3 The Lord is <u>with them</u> (*bĕtôkām yhwh*)—The Hebrew says literally, "the Lord is in their midst." God had said that he would dwell in Israel's midst (Exod. 25:8) and eventually he would do so forever (Ezek. 37:26; Zech. 2:10-11). His presence among them was how they knew that he was their God (Exod. 29:45; Ezek. 37:26-28). Therefore, they provided him with a sanctuary (Exod. 25:8), where, after it and the priests were sanctified, he dwelled (Exod. 29:44-45). His presence made them holy (Ezek. 37:28), as Korah says, so they must not defile his abode (Num. 5:3) but separate from whatever made them unclean (Lev. 15:31). Now they were generally unclean (Lev. 16:16), but in the future they would never defile God's name (Ezek. 43:7). If they obeyed him and set aside all idolatry he would walk (Lev. 26:12) and dwell in their midst (1 Kings 6:12-13; Ezek. 43:9). If they profaned him, his glory may depart and abandon them to judgment (Ezek. 11:23). [*tāwek*]

16:5 The man <u>he chooses</u> (*'ăšer yibḥar bô*)—This is the first use of the verb in the OT with God as subject. He chose his servants, both as groups such as Israel (Ps. 105:26; Isa. 44:2), the Levites (1 Chron. 15:2), and the priests (Deut. 18:5), and also as individuals (e.g., Abraham [Neh. 9:7-8], a specific king [1 Sam. 16:7-10; 1 Chron. 28:4, 6]). God helped those whom he chose (Isa. 44:2), but not to do whatever they wanted (Deut. 17:15-17). Once he chose a group he did not reject it (Jer. 33:24-25), but he might reject a part of a chosen group (1 Sam. 2:28-35) or individuals who failed in their responsibilities (1 Sam. 12:13; 15:23). God and Israel might both choose a king, but Israel chose in general (1 Sam. 8:18) and God chose the specific person (1 Sam. 10:24). Sometimes qualifications preceded God's choice (Deut. 33:8-10; 1 Sam. 16:7-10), but other times none is mentioned—such as when God chose Aaron's family as priests—other than God's love (Deut. 4:37; 7:7; 10:15) and desire (Ps. 132:13). God alone chose his priests (cf. 1 Kings 13:33-34; Heb. 5:4). Frequent mention is made of God's choice to enter a covenant with Israel (Deut. 7:6; 14:2). Several times God chose other people with whom he made covenants (Abraham, Neh. 9:7; David, 1 Kings 8:16; the Aaronic priests, Ps. 105:26 [the covenant is mentioned in Mal. 2:5]). H. Seebass adds that whenever God chose people he chose them out of a group in order to accomplish a function or service for the group. Consequently, God chose Israel from among all nations in order to accomplish his mission among the nations (Seebass, *TDOT*, 2:82-83). Likewise Christians comprise a group chosen to perform a mission for God (1 Pet. 2:9). [*bḥr*]

16:9 The God of Israel <u>has separated</u> you (*hibdîl 'ĕlōhê yiśrā'ēl 'etkem*)—The OT speaks of God separating Israel, the priests, and the Levites to himself. Israel was separated from the nations in that they alone were God's holy people (Lev. 20:26) and his inheritance (1 Kings 8:53). Their distinctive diet separated them in a practical way from intercourse with non-Israelites (Lev. 20:24-25; cf. Acts 10:28). But regarding physical separation from Gentiles, they were no more separated than any other nation (Deut. 32:8, *prd* is used instead of *bdl* and only here with God as subject). The Levites were separated from the rest of Israel only in that they had a special function to fulfill for Israel and the priests (Num. 8:14; Deut. 10:8). Aaron's family was separated in that they had a unique vocation (here and 1 Chron. 23:13). Whether speaking of Israel, the Levites, or the priests, separation was not of physical proximity, but of behavior, purpose, and destiny. Christ viewed the church's separation from the world in the same way (cf. John 17:15-16). [*bdl*]

Minister to them (*lĕšortām*)—When priests ministered they blessed (Deut. 10:8), carried the ark (Deut. 10:8), offered Israel's sacrifices after they were slaughtered (1 Chron. 23:13; cf. Lev. 1:5-8), consecrated articles (1 Chron. 23:13), and entered the tent (Ezek. 44:10-16) where they set bread on the table (2 Chron. 13:10-11), lit the lamps (2 Chron. 13:10-11), and burned incense (2 Chron. 29:11). They kept the feasts (Ezek. 44:24), taught the distinction between unholy and holy, clean and unclean (Ezek. 44:23), decided disputes and cases at law (Deut. 21:5), and sounded the battle cry in war (2 Chron. 13:10-11). When the Levites ministered they helped slaughter sacrifices (Ezek. 44:10-13), cooked them (Ezek. 46:24), purified the sanctuary (2 Chron. 29:11, 15; though they might not enter the tent/temple, Ezek. 44:10-16), carried the tabernacle and furnishings (Num. 1:50-51), surrounded the

sanctuary to keep it holy (Num. 1:50-51; later they would be gatekeepers, 1 Chron. 26:12), prayed (1 Chron. 16:4), praised, and thanked God (1 Chron. 16:7, 37; 2 Chron. 31:2) with music (1 Chron. 6:32) including instrumental music (1 Chron. 16:4-6). Although priests and Levites had a special status in the community, their position was characterized by service to God and others. God continued this concept of leadership through service in the church (Matt. 20:26-28). The church also has a division of responsibilities that, like here, God established and all should respect (1 Cor. 12:7-11, 14-27). [*šrt*]

16:14 Inheritance (*naḥălat*)—The land of Canaan was to become Israel's inheritance (Deut. 4:21). Normally an inheritance is something received from one's father (Gen. 31:14), but Israel's first generation of settlers must confiscate this land from others (Deut. 29:8). It may be called an inheritance because they would pass it on to their children (Josh. 24:32; 1 Kings 21:3), or because the first Israelite settlers would benefit from God's promises to their ancestors to give them the land (Deut. 4:37-38; Ps. 105:8-11; Ezek. 47:14). Many times, however, the verb basically means to take possession of something (Exod. 23:30) and the noun means "property" (Ruth 4:5).

Not only was Canaan Israel's inheritance, but also God's (Exod. 15:17), so they ought not defile it (Deut. 21:23; Jer. 16:18). God also inherited the people of Israel (Deut. 4:20; Ps. 33:12) whom he redeemed (Ps. 74:2). Although an inheritance would normally be retained forever (Exod. 32:13), and God will not reject or relinquish his inheritance (Ps. 94:14), he does discipline them (Ps. 106:40) and will retain only a remnant (Mic. 7:18). He will eventually inherit all nations (Ps. 82:8).

By analogy with Israel this may mean that he will receive a remnant from each one (cf. Rev. 7:9). Our term is also often used for each tribe's (Num. 33:54) and clan's (Josh. 15:20) proportional allotment of the total inheritance for Israel. It became such a common term for that which Israel received from God, that it was used of children (Ps. 127:3), God's protection (Isa. 54:17), wealth (Prov. 13:22), and even the natural, God-ordained consequences of one's actions (Prov. 14:18; 28:10). [*naḥălâ*]

16:26 These wicked men (*hā'ănāšîm hārĕšā'îm hā'ēlleh*)—The word for wicked and its cognate words appear over 340x in the OT, mostly in the three major poetical books and Ezekiel, and only 16x in the Pentateuch. (Cf. comments on Num. 5:6, "wrongs" for synonyms of wickedness or sin.) The Pentateuch teaches that wicked people are diametrical opposites to the righteous (Gen. 18:23, 25), who have integrity (Deut. 9:4). Wickedness is classed with sin and stubbornness (hardness [*qšh*]) against God (Deut. 9:27; cf. Exod. 9:27), indicating that the word can refer to an inner attitude and pattern of life (E. Carpenter and M. Grisanti, *NIDOTTE*, 3:1203-04). It can also describe severe abuse of one's fellow in the community (Exod. 2:13) and serious moral flaws (Gen. 18:23, 25), extending even to murder (Exod. 23:7). The wicked, as in our passage (cf. Num. 16:9-11), think and act contrary to God's proper order (Gen. 18:23, 25; Exod. 2:13; Deut. 9:4-5) and refuse to heed his messenger (Exod. 9:13, 27). They may deserve beating (Deut. 25:2), expulsion from the land (Deut. 9:4-5), or even execution (Gen. 18:25; Num. 35:31). In our text these men have endangered the life of the entire assembly (Num. 16:21). [*rāšā', rš'*]

16:29 The Lord sent me (*yhwh šĕlāḥānî*)—The Lord sent people with a task to accomplish (Deut. 9:23), such as rescuing from oppression when the victims called to him (Judg. 6:14; Isa. 19:20) and saving lives (Gen. 45:5). He sent messengers to instruct (Jer. 42:21) and rebuke (2 Sam. 12:1). He sent helpers to do acts of mercy (Isa. 61:1) and adversaries to punish sinful people, whether they were his people (Jer. 16:16) or not (1 Sam. 15:20). When God sent someone he might do it through adversity (Ps. 105:17) or the instrumentality of others even though they were sinful (Gen. 45:5, 8). Those he sent might encounter mockery (2 Chron. 36:15-16) and resistance that prompted questions about their usefulness (Exod. 5:22), but God was with them nevertheless (Exod. 3:12; cf. Gen. 39:2 with 45:5) and strengthened them (Judg. 6:14). Some people to whom he sent messengers responded positively (Hag. 1:12). God sent prophets (Judg. 6:8; Isa. 6:8) whose predictions must necessarily come to pass (Jer. 28:9). Although some scholars disagree on the passage, it appears that God even sent himself (Zech. 2:8-9, 11; cf. 1 John 4:14). He did not send those who lied (Jer. 14:14), who discouraged people from doing his work (Neh. 6:12), or who spoke merely from their own imaginations (Jer. 23:21). People who follow those whom God has not sent will not benefit (Jer. 23:32) but will perish (Jer. 27:15) like the false prophets (Jer. 29:31). Here Moses was willing to have his commission tested by whether or not his words came true. [*šlḥ*]

16:30 The grave (*šĕ'ōlâ*)—The word *šĕ'ōl* often refers to a physical grave (Job 17:3-4; Ps. 16:10; 49:14; Isa. 14:11; Ezek. 32:27), but it can denote the netherworld (Job 26:6) where many people are gathered and can see and speak to one another (Isa. 14:9-10, 15; Ezek. 32:21). The fact that the word is parallel to *'ăbaddôn* (Job 26:6; Prov. 15:11; B. Otzen, *TDOT*, 1:23) and that it often refers to something very deep (Deut. 32:22; Job 11:8; Prov. 9:18) indicates that *šĕ'ôl* can denote more than just the grave. Nonetheless, it is sometimes debatable whether the grave, death (Ps. 18:5; 55:15), or the netherworld is meant in a particular text. The netherworld is a place under the ground (Num. 16:30; Ezek. 31:16-17; Amos 9:2) where spirits exist as "shades" (like shadows of what the whole persons had been in earthly life; *rĕpā'îm*, Isa. 14:9; 26:14), in a weak and lackluster condition (E. Merrill, *NIDOTTE*, 4:7). It is a dark place (Job 17:13) with little or no activity (Ps. 6:5; Isa. 38:18) and general silence (Ps. 31:17). The pious expect it to be a place of safety from God's wrath (Job 14:13). The OT presents the grave and netherworld with a voracious appetite (Prov. 27:20; Hab. 2:5), aggressively seeking and consuming victims (2 Sam. 22:6; Job 24:19; Ps. 89:48). Although its prisoners cannot escape (Job 7:9; Song 8:6) and seem to be outside of divine care (Ps. 88:3-5; Isa. 38:18), God sees them (Job 26:6; Prov. 15:11), does not forsake the godly among them (Ps. 16:10), and is able to summon them back to life (1 Sam. 2:6; Job 14:13-14)—though some of his rescuing from *šĕ'ôl* seems to be delivering the godly just before they die rather than after (Ps. 30:3; 86:13). The netherworld itself did not seem to cause anguish, although the anticipation of departing this life and losing its opportunities and relationships may have caused it (1 Kings 2:6; Job 21:13; Ps. 116:3). The gates of *šĕ'ôl* are a figure of the entrance to death or the underworld (Job 17:6; Isa. 38:10; cf. Matt. 16:18 where death could not stop Christ's church, but actually led to its existence). To descend

suddenly to death, grave, or underworld, as here, was considered a just punishment for the wicked (Ps. 55:15). [*šĕ'ôl*]

16:33 And they perished (*wayyō'bĕdû*)— The verb often refers to dying (Ps. 49:10; Jonah 1:6, 14), being killed (Num. 21:29-30; 2 Kings 9:8), or doomed to die (Num. 17:12). At other times it means to disappear (Job 18:17; 30:12; Ps. 37:20), to be economically ruined (Exod. 10:7; Jer. 9:12; 48:8), to be materially destroyed (Amos 3:15), or to suffer catastrophic loss of any kind (Job 4:7, cf. 1:13-19). In the political domain it can mean to be defeated (Judg. 5:31), lose one's position of power (Prov. 28:28), be overthrown as a nation (Jonah 3:9), be expelled from one's land (Deut. 4:26; Jer. 48:46), and even cease to be a recognizable community (Jer. 40:15). In a slightly different vein, it can mean not to attain one's goal (Ps. 1:6; 9:18; Prov. 11:7; Ezek. 12:22; 19:5). Besides these various ideas of destruction, the word can denote wandering (Deut. 26:5) and being lost physically (1 Sam. 9:3) or spiritually (Ps. 119:176). For those who wander far from God, as here, they perish in one of the destructive ways mentioned (Deut. 8:19; 28:20; Ps. 73:27; Jer. 50:6). For those who have perished in ways other than death, the leaders of God's people should seek to help them (Ezek. 34:4) like God himself will (Ezek. 34:16). In our passage the word means to die, so nothing can be done for these people. [*'bd*]

16:35 Fire came out from the Lord (*'ēš yāṣĕ'â mē'ēt yhwh*)—Fire is often associated with God in the OT. He might come with storm-related phenomena such as lightning (2 Sam. 22:8-16) or use fire to execute judgment (Gen. 19:24; Exod. 9:23-24; Lev. 10:2). Fire is associated with his wrath (Deut. 32:22; Ps. 78:21; 89:46) so that people are justifiably afraid (Deut. 5:5). His fiery wrath was commonly explained as an expression of jealousy (e.g., Deut. 4:24; Ps. 79:5; Ezek. 38:19). His fire was not always destructive, however, for he gave promises and instructions from fire (Gen. 15:17; Exod. 3:2), led by its light (Ps. 78:14), protected by it (Exod. 13:21), and consumed acceptable offerings by it (Lev. 9:24; 1 Kings 18:38). And though described as appearing with fire, God was never portrayed as a mythological storm god or fire demon (V. Hamp, *TDOT*, 1:428). Many times he is represented *like* fire (Deut. 9:3) when his glory appeared (Exod. 24:17; Num. 9:15-16; Ezek. 1:26-28), his judgment fell (Lam. 2:3; Amos 5:6), his jealousy flared (Ps. 79:5), his fury rushed (Jer. 4:4; Nahum 1:6), or his word worked (Jer. 23:29). His messengers appeared to be flaming (2 Kings 6:17; Ps. 104:4), but also are described as being *like* fire (Mal. 3:1). Often fire from God was not literal but figurative for judgment through people (Ezek. 21:31), locusts, and drought (Joel 1:19-20). Here, however, it is literal like that on Aaron's errant sons (Lev. 10:2). ['ēš]

17:10 To be kept (*lĕmišmeret*)—The Hebrew word is actually a noun that can mean something held in safekeeping, a guard, or an obligation such as a service or duty (*HALOT*, 649-50). The first meaning occurs less frequently than the others, but is the appropriate one here (cf. 18:3, "duties," for the more frequent use). Besides Aaron's rod, the law prescribes three other items to be held for safekeeping—all highly symbolic: each Passover lamb lest it be injured (Exod. 12:6), a jar of manna as a reminder of God's daily provision throughout the many years of wilderness travels (16:32-34), and the red heifer's ashes for purification from sin (Num. 19:9). The manna and Aaron's rod were kept in or near the ark, showing their extreme importance. Our passage accentuates the fact that (1) God alone makes the choice of who may serve and draw near him as priest and that (2) Israel must never violate this principle. Since the rod was kept where only priests were allowed, the priest was constantly reminded that he did not merit his privilege. The rod became a reminder that "no one takes this honor [to function as high priest] upon himself; he must be called by God, just as Aaron was." Likewise God has made Christ the new high priest; he did not usurp the position (Heb. 5:4-6).

As mentioned above, the word can refer to one's responsibilities (Lev. 22:9; Num. 3:7-8, 25). Often it is used with God's commands and laws without specifying particular ones (Gen. 26:5; Deut. 11:1). The word in the context of the sanctuary could mean to guard it since the term is used with reference to separating the sanctuary from laymen (Num. 1:53), guarding it (1 Chron. 9:23, 27), and executing intruders (Num. 3:38). The word is also used of a guardhouse (2 Sam. 20:3), guard post (Hab. 2:1), guarding a city (Neh. 7:3), palace (2 Kings 11:5), and temple (2 Kings 11:6-7). In one scene the Levites were clearly armed (2 Chron. 23:7). If it means only to guard the sanctuary, it explains Num. 8:24-26 where Levites could continue to guard but could not carry on heavier, laborious work (*'ăbōdâ*) after they turned 50 (J. Milgrom and L. Harper, *TDOT*, 9:76-78). Nevertheless, sometimes (Num. 18:4; 1 Chron. 23:32) our term seems broader than *'ăbōdâ* and indicates all the care and labor of the sanctuary, including, among other things, temple and worship rituals (2 Chron. 13:11; Mal. 3:14), caring for and carrying the pieces of the sanctuary (Num. 3:25, 31, 36-37), performing music (2 Chron. 7:6; Neh. 12:45), and keeping the gates (Neh. 12:45, gatekeepers had more responsibilities than just guarding [1 Chron. 26:12]). The word sometimes means oversight (Num. 18:8; Ezek. 44:8) and implies that the Levites had both responsibility and also authority, a necessary balance in any work. Only the Levites were authorized to perform these functions. In the age begun with the NT revelation God continues to assign duties to members of his church, but they are not limited to only a professional class (1 Cor. 3:12; 12:7). [*mišmeret*]

18:12 Finest (*ḥēleb*)—The word translated "finest" in many contexts refers to the fat of an animal (Gen. 4:4; Exod. 23:18; 29:13). However, no one was allowed to eat fat for it belonged to God alone (Lev. 3:17; 7:23) and not to his priests like other gifts to him. Even though the fat was offered to God, he did not eat it as the pagan gods would if they could (Deut. 32:38; Ps. 115:6). To God it was a good aroma (Lev. 17:6). The fat of an offering that was mentioned most often is from the fellowship offering (cf. 1 Kings 8:64; Lev. 3 is the first to mention it by this term; the term for the fat of the burnt offering in Lev. 1:8, 12 is *peder*), though it may refer to the sin offering (Lev. 4:8-9, 19). It is not mentioned with the guilt offering. Fat became a symbol of an offering to God (1 Sam. 15:22), probably especially the fellowship offering that symbolized communion with God and his community. Here the word clearly refers to the best of something, as it can denote the best of the land (Gen. 45:18), of flocks and grain (Deut. 32:14; Ps. 81:16), of food in general (Ps. 63:5), of strength (2 Sam. 1:22), and of wealth (Job 15:27). The Levites were to give the best of their receipts of firstfruits and tithes to the priests in order not to incur guilt and thus

defile Israel's offerings (Num. 18:26-32). Nothing but the best should be given to God, and therefore to his servants the priests (cf. Mal. 1:8). [*ḥēleb*]

18:13 Firstfruits (*bikkûrê*)—This word for firstfruits (cf. Num. 15:20, *rē'šît* being the other) denotes the first ripe crops (Exod. 23:16; Lev. 2:14) and fruit (Neh. 10:35) that were available for consumption (Num. 13:20; Isa. 28:4; Nahum 3:12). The firstfruits were considered to be the very best of all that would be harvested (Jer. 24:2). The best of the firstfruits belonged to God, and therefore to his priests (Lev. 23:20; Ezek. 44:30) and everyone in their households, as in our verse. Eventually, at least in the northern kingdom of Israel (which the godly priests evacuated to travel south to the temple in Jerusalem) the firstfruits could be offered to God's other faithful and often beleaguered servants, the prophets (2 Kings 4:42, note he is called the "man of God"). The firstfruits were offered at the Feast of Weeks (Exod. 34:22; Lev. 23:15-20; Num. 28:26; called Feast of Harvest in Exod. 23:16 and, later, Pentecost) after the barley and wheat harvests were complete in late May or June. The firstfruits of the fruit trees and vines would be offered after their harvest season in late summer. The very best must be brought to God's house (Exod. 23:19; 34:26) where only a portion would be burnt (Lev. 2:14-16), and the rest would be given to the priests who would wave some of it to the Lord (Lev. 23:17). The people needed their harvest and animals to feed themselves, but by returning the first portion to him instead of first meeting their own needs, they acknowledged that they owed it all to the Lord. [*bikkûr, bikkûrâ, bakkûrâ*]

18:14 That is devoted (*ḥērem*)—This noun and its cognate verb sometimes speak of the intent to destroy totally something or some group in warfare (Num. 21:2-3, 33-35; Josh. 2:10; 8:26) so that no one survives (Josh. 10:28, 37-40; 2 Chron. 20:23-24). Sometimes God commanded (Jer. 50:21) this treatment because of his anger (Isa. 34:2), to punish sins of afflicting his people (1 Sam. 15:2), and because of idolatry (Exod. 22:20; Deut. 13:13-15). So he might order the total destruction of people and plunder (Deut. 13:17; Josh. 6:18-21) and articles of false worship (Deut. 7:2-5, 25-26). One time in the OT Israel without God's direction ordered people to be put under the ban. This was a gross error that led to much grief and then to dishonorable behavior when they tried to correct the outcome (Judg. 21:11-17). As the term is used here, it means things permanently devoted to God and therefore banned from other people's possession. Land, animals, and people may be devoted to God (Lev. 27:29; this may be in reference to warfare per the preceding discussion, though war is not discussed elsewhere in Lev. 27) as may other possessions. They may not be redeemed, but if they were living they must be executed (Lev. 27:28). Whatever was banned became God's possession (Mic. 4:13), and whoever possessed it became banned (Deut. 7:26; 13:17; Josh. 6:17-19; 7:11-12, 15). Only the priests might have banned, devoted possessions (Lev. 27:21; Num. 18:14; Ezek. 44:29). Burnt, grain, fellowship, sin, and guilt offerings belonged to God but were not called banned items. So although a person devoted to God must die, a person such as Jephthah's daughter who was pledged as a burnt offering instead of as *ḥērem* could be redeemed. [*ḥērem, ḥrm*]

18:17 An aroma pleasing to the Lord (*lĕrêaḥ nîḥōaḥ layhwh*)—The root of the word for aroma is *rwḥ*, to smell. P. Jenson

and J. Olivier suggest that this is part of "a rich, multimedia experience of God," since all the senses are employed in worship (J. Jenson and J. Olivier, *NIDOTTE*, 3:1071). The law designates burnt (Lev. 1:9, 13, 17), grain (Lev. 2:2, 9), fellowship (Lev. 3:5, 16), ordination (Lev. 8:28, a type of fellowship offering), and—once—sin (Lev. 4:31) offerings as pleasing aromas to God. The offerings are called food (Lev. 3:16; Num. 28:2), though it is unclear whether they were God's food to receive or man's to give up. Even if they were God's, he was satisfied with merely smelling them. Whereas pagan gods would eat sacrifices if they could (Deut. 32:38), the Lord does not. When God smelled an offering he might respond favorably (Gen. 8:21). Therefore, when he smelled a sacrifice it meant he accepted the giver and the sacrifice (therefore, in 1 Sam. 26:19, the verb "smell" is translated "accept"; Ezek. 20:41), but when he refused to smell it he was refusing the giver and the ritual (Lev. 26:31; Amos 5:21, "I do not smell your assemblies," is translated, "I cannot stand your assemblies"). In Isa. 11:3, "he will delight in the fear of the LORD," the Hebrew woodenly translated says, "He will smell the fear of the LORD." Because the idea of smelling an offering connotes acceptance, the NIV's translation is correct, and God is more pleased with one's devoted attitude behind the offering than with the fragrance itself. [*rêaḥ*]

Pleasing (*nîḥōaḥ*)—The Hebrew word is always used (43x) with the noun *rêaḥ* discussed above. Some commentators state that the use of the word "pleasing" indicates that the odor soothes or removes God's anger. The result of the first pleasing aroma offered to God (Gen. 8:21) was that God said he would not curse the ground or destroy all living creatures again. The aroma did not remove God's anger, however, for the judgment of the flood was already past and Noah was not making sin offerings to propitiate God. It was noted above in regard to *rêaḥ* that the expression *rêaḥ nîḥōaḥ* is used only once with a sin offering (Lev. 4:31), but often for other types of offering, namely burnt, grain, fellowship, and ordination. These non-purification offerings express relationship and commitment to God at various levels. Therefore, it does not appear that the smell placates God, but is a sensory part of the celebration of the relationship the giver enjoys with God. One's relationship with God did not only involve one's intellect but also the whole person, including the physical aspect (cf. Rom. 12:1). [*nîḥōaḥ*]

18:19 An everlasting covenant of salt (*běrît melaḥ 'ôlām*)—The context here refers to offerings given to the priests (Num. 18:17-19). The instructions for grain offerings state that all of them must be salted, and the salt is called the salt of the covenant (Lev. 2:13). Salt could relate to taste (e.g., Job 6:6), healing (2 Kings 2:20), or preserving, but the latter seems to be the case here. The expression "covenant of salt" occurs only here and in 2 Chron. 13:5, each time with the word *'ôlām*, translated "everlasting" and "forever." In the few places where salt is used in other nongeographical (Salt Sea, valley of salt) contexts in the OT, it symbolizes lasting destruction, where ground is rendered impossible to cultivate "forever" (Zeph. 2:9; cf. Deut. 29:23; Judg. 9:45). The association with that which is long lasting may indicate, then, that salt refers to the lasting nature of the covenant. God symbolically assured that he would keep his covenant promises even over long periods of time. [*melaḥ*]

18:20 Nor will you have any share among them; I am your share (*ḥēleq . . .*

ḥelqěkā)—The word for "share" is frequently associated, as here, with inheritance (Deut. 10:9; 32:9; Josh. 18:7), and as in the initial occurrence here it very often denotes a share of land in Canaan that was to be first won then bequeathed to one's descendants (Josh. 15:13; 18:6-9; Ezek. 45:7). Neither the priests, as here, nor the Levites had any share or inheritance in the real estate in Canaan (Deut. 10:9; 12:12; 14:27), although they would have houses and pastures for the animals they received (Josh. 14:4). They could not earn a living by growing crops, but both groups received a share of the offerings to support themselves and their families (Lev. 6:17; Deut. 18:8). Therefore, in a practical sense they had their share in God (here and Deut. 10:9), for their welfare depended upon how the nation responded to God and, likewise, how God took care of them. A closely related use of the word means to participate closely with someone (2 Sam. 20:1; 1 Kings 12:16; Neh. 2:20; Ps. 50:18). The godly in Israel adopted the concept of having God as their share or portion (Ps. 73:26, written by a Levite, but the other passages below are not). One who claimed God as his share would seek and obey him (Ps. 119:57-58), hope in him (Ps. 142:5; Lam. 3:24), claim him forever (Ps. 119:57; 142:5), and be pleased with what he received from him (Ps. 16:5-6). God himself had a share: his share was his people (Deut. 32:9; Zech. 2:12), so the relationship was complete. [*ḥēleq*]

18:21 Tithes (*ma'ăśēr*)—The Hebrew noun is derived from the word for ten (*'eśer*), denotes one part out of ten, and is related to the verb that means to give or take a tenth (*'āśar*). The tithe was first mentioned in connection with Abram's gifts to Melchizedek (Gen. 14:20). Jacob vowed that he would return to God a tenth of all that God gave him (Gen. 28:22; he used the verb instead of the noun). No explanation is given in either place for why this percentage went to God. Samuel warned Israel that the king they thought they wanted would take a tenth of their seed and sheep from them (1 Sam. 8:15, 17). Thus, it was customary to tithe to God and to kings. In the law giving the tithe was in addition to giving the sacrifices and firstfruits mentioned throughout the Law (Deut. 12:6, 17). Israelites were to tithe their grain, fruit from trees (Lev. 27:30), herds, flocks (Lev. 27:32), oil and new wine (Deut. 12:17): basically everything they had. The tithes went to support the Levites, as here (cf. Deut. 14:28-29; 26:12-13, where the poor and weak also received from the tithes), distinct from the priests who received the income from the sacrifices and firstfruits (Neh. 10:37-38). This was payment for the Levites' work (here and Neh. 13:5) and was their inheritance (Num. 18:24). The tithes would be brought to the central sanctuary (Deut. 12:5-6) to be distributed by trustworthy people (cf. Neh. 13:12-13 in the postexilic period). Eventually in the land they would be the ones who collected it in the towns throughout Israel (2 Chron. 31:6-15; Neh. 10:37-38). They in turn presented the best 10 percent of the tithe to the Lord by giving it to the priests (Num. 18:26-29; Neh. 10:38). When the Israelites gave the tithes and asked God to bless them (Deut. 26:12-15), he assured them that he would (Mal. 3:10). God honors those who honor him (cf. 1 Sam. 2:30) and those who take care of his servants and the poor (cf. Deut. 14:28-29). [*ma'ăśēr*]

19:4 Some of its blood (*middāmāh*)— Blood sustains life (Gen. 9:4-5; Lev. 17:11), excess blood loss defiled a person (Lev.

12:4), and human blood shed by murder polluted a land (Num. 35:33). God provided for prevention of accidental shedding of blood (Deut. 19:10) and for cleansing from innocent bloodshed (Deut. 21:9), divinely avenged the outright murder of his servants (Deut. 32:43), and ordered that humans exact capital punishment for murder (Gen. 9:5-6). Shedding animal blood might prevent divine execution (Exod. 12:13) and was used as a sign of a covenant with God (Exod. 24:8; Zech. 9:11). Perhaps it is because sin was punishable by death (Ezek. 18:4, 20) and a blood sacrifice "puts back into the hands of God a life contained in the blood" (B. Kedar-Kopfstein, *TDOT*, 3:248) that blood symbolizes a sinner's reconciliation to God. It also cleansed a leper who had been removed from the community of God (Lev. 14:6-7) and a polluted house that had been condemned (Lev. 14:51), consecrated the priest and his garments (Exod. 29:20; Lev. 8:30), atoned for, purified, and consecrated the altars (sacrificial: Exod. 30:10; Lev. 16:19; incense: Lev. 4:7; 8:15), and atoned for the Holiest Place (Lev. 16:16) and the temple of the future (Ezek. 45:19-20). This is the only place where blood is specifically burned. Whether its residue survived in the ashes, this water mixed with ashes had the same property as blood: it both defiled and cleansed (Num. 19:19, 21). Blood was sprinkled on the bronze altar for burnt (Lev. 1:5), fellowship (Lev. 3:2), and guilt offerings (Lev. 7:2). Except for on the Day of Atonement (Lev. 16:19), the blood of the sin offering was not sprinkled on the altar, but poured out at the base (sin offerings of fowl were an exception [Lev. 5:9]). [*dām*]

Sprinkle (*hizzâ*)—Two words are used in Hebrew for sprinkling, *nzh* and *zrq*. Water (Num. 8:7), blood (Lev. 14:6-7), anointing oil (Lev. 8:11), other oil (Lev. 14:10, 16), and a mixture of blood and anointing oil (Exod. 29:20) were sprinkled in rituals. In the Law, the word *nzh* is used for sprinkling blood of the sin (Lev. 4:6, 17; 5:9; 16:14-15), ordination (Exod. 29:19-22), and leper's purification offerings (Lev. 14:7). The word *zrq* describes the sprinkling of the blood of burnt (Exod. 29:16-18; Lev. 1:5), fellowship (Lev. 3:1-2, 8), ordination (Lev. 8:24), guilt (Lev. 7:2), and firstborn animal offerings (Num. 18:17), but not of sin offerings. Sprinkling cleansed (lepers by blood [Lev. 14:7]), purified (Levites by water [Num. 8:7]), consecrated (priests by blood [Exod. 29:21] and altar by oil [Lev. 8:11]), and atoned (for the Most Holy Place by blood [Lev. 16:15-16]). The sacrificial altar was routinely sprinkled with the blood of the burnt (Lev. 1:5), fellowship (Lev. 3:2), and guilt offerings (Lev. 7:2). It was sprinkled with blood of the sin offering only on the Day of Atonement (Lev. 16:19) and on behalf of the very poor Israelite who offered birds for a sin offering (Lev. 5:9). Milgrom and Wright suggest that smearing blood on the altar purified it, but sprinkling blood consecrated it; however, sprinkling appears to do both in Lev. 16:19. They seem to be right that sprinkling the oil in Lev. 14:15-18, 26-29 consecrated the oil so that it could be used for purification, but this was for oil, not blood (J. Milgrom and D. Wright, *TDOT*, 9:301). Since sprinkling blood here was specifically directed toward the tent, it symbolized the tent's purification from the uncleanness of the Israelites that is mentioned in the following verses. The sprinkling in the OT was a prototype of what Christ's sacrifice would accomplish. As a result of his sacrifice believers are sanctified (1 Pet. 1:2) and their hearts and consciences are cleansed by the spiritual sprinkling of his blood (Heb. 9:13-14; 10:22; 12:24). [*nzh*]

19:12 On the seventh day (*bayyôm haššĕbî'î*)—Jenson points out that the number seven was often associated with completion, fullness, and perfection in the ancient Near East and the Bible. Consequently it was natural to link it with the divine. There were seven each of branches of the golden lampstand (Exod. 25:32-37), annual festivals (Lev. 23:4-34) of which two lasted for seven days (Lev. 23:6, 36), years in a sabbatical cycle (Deut. 15:1), sabbatical years in a jubilee cycle (Lev. 25:8), sacrifices in some sets of offerings (Num. 28:11, 19, 27; 29:2, 8; and double sevens: 29:13, 17), and sprinklings of blood (Lev. 4:6; Num. 19:4) and oil (Lev. 8:11; P. Jenson, *NIDOTTE*, 4:34-35). There were seven days in the ordination ritual for the priests (Exod. 29:30), altar (Exod. 29:37), and courtyard (2 Chron. 7:9). For major impurities caused by infectious skin diseases (Lev. 14:8-9), contact with a corpse (Num. 6:9; 19:11; 31:19, 24), and bodily discharges (Lev. 15:13) including menstruation (Lev. 15:19, 28) and afterbirth (Lev. 12:2), the period of uncleanness and/or cleansing was seven days. People with seven-day uncleanness made others unclean by contact, usually until evening (Lev. 15:5-11, 20-23, 27), but in one case for seven days (Lev. 15:24; note that excommunication was the penalty for careless treatment of this uncleanness [Lev. 20:18] since seven-day uncleanness was so serious). In cases other than bodily discharge, unclean people were isolated from the community (Lev. 13:46; Num. 31:19). Those with uncleanness until evening apparently did not spread their uncleanness by contact. The seventh day did not automatically bring purification. Not time but washing (Lev. 14:9; Num.

31:24), sprinkling (as here), and sacrifice (Lev. 12:6; 14:5-7; 15:29; Num. 6:9) could cleanse. The seventh day was not magical, nor did God deem someone clean simply because the time had passed. Uncleanness had to be dealt with actively, not passively, according to his prescriptions. [šĕbî'î, šeba', šib'â]

19:14 The law (*hattôrâ*)—The well-known word *tôrâ* can refer to unspecified precepts from God (Gen. 26:5; Exod. 18:16), customs (2 Sam. 7:19), or wisdom instruction (Prov. 1:8; 13:14). Usually, however, it refers to specified legislated ritual procedures (as here, and, e.g., Lev. 6:9; 13:59) and the Mosaic Law (Exod. 24:12; 2 Chron. 23:18) as a whole or in part (such as Deuteronomy, Deut. 1:5) in which there are individual commands (Deut. 4:44-45; 2 Chron. 19:10). The *tôrâ* was recorded in a book for preservation (Deut. 29:21; 30:10). Reading it should lead to obedience, walking in God's ways, loyalty, and wholehearted service to him (Josh. 22:5; 2 Kings 23:25). Consequently, the king should read it daily (Deut. 17:19), and the public should have it read to them (Deut. 31:12-13) in a clearly understood fashion (Neh. 8:8). If a person meditated in it constantly and obeyed it, he would have success in living (Josh. 1:7-8; Ps. 1:2-3). It is expected that those who knew it best should also know the Lord (Jer. 2:8). Discretion and understanding were needed to apply it to different contexts (1 Chron. 22:12). God would punish Israel for disobedience (Deut. 27:26; 28:58), for the laws of the *tôrâ* were part of their covenant (Deut. 29:21; Ps. 78:10; Hos. 8:1). Obedience to the law could lead to refreshment (Ps. 19:7), guidance (Ps. 37:31), blameless living (Ps. 119:1), faithfulness in times of testing (Ps. 119:92), and peace despite pressure (Ps. 119:165). However, obedience to the law could endanger one's life (Ps. 119:109) at the hands of the ungodly. God's good gifts should motivate people to obey it (Ps. 105:42-45). In the future kingdom God's law will be taught to the Gentiles (Isa. 2:3). [*tôrâ*]

19:17 Some ashes (*mē'ăpar*)—The word used here is *'āpār*, but in vv. 9-10 the less frequently appearing synonym *'ēper* occurs. The word *'āpār* refers more often to dust (Num. 5:17), though it can be plaster (Lev. 14:45), rubble (2 Kings 23:12; Neh. 4:2), soil (Job 5:6), the earth (Job 41:33), and, as here, ashes (2 Kings 23:4). The word describes a human's lowly origins (Gen. 2:7; Ps. 103:14) and therefore aptly indicates humility in relation to God (Gen. 18:27). It can also refer to one's final destiny (Job 7:21; 10:9)—also in contrast to God (Gen. 3:19)—and became a figure for the grave and death (Job 17:16; Ps. 22:15, 29). It might be what was left after disaster and judgment (1 Kings 20:10; Ezek. 26:4). Perhaps because of its reference to judgment, disaster, and human mortality, it and the synonym *'ēper* became a sign of repentance (Job 42:6; Dan. 9:3) and grief when someone placed it on his head (Josh. 7:6), rolled in it (Mic. 1:10), sat in it (Isa. 47:1), figuratively "licked" it (Ps. 72:9), or wore it with sackcloth (Esth. 4:1). It became a figure of humble origins (1 Sam. 2:8) and a humiliating end (Job 16:15; 30:19). It also appeared as a figure meaning numerous (Gen. 28:14; Num. 23:10). The only form in which a single slaughtered sacrifice could be kept on hand without putrefying and belying its purifying purpose was in the form of ashes. The continued presence and repeated usage of the ashes introduced the idea that one sacrifice can repeatedly cleanse—a concept that reached its fullest expression in Christ's sacrifice that repeatedly cleanses from sin (cf. 1 John 1:9). [*'āpār*]

20:4 Community (*qāhāl*)—The cognate verb (*qhl*) appears in the context (vv. 3, 8, 10) of this noun. To show that a group though large is somehow cohesive, frequently the word "all" appears with the noun and verb (e.g., Exod. 35:1; Lev. 8:3; Num. 1:18; 8:9; Deut. 31:28; 1 Kings 8:14; 1 Chron. 13:2), or else a great number of people are said to be in attendance (2 Chron. 30:13; Ezra 10:1). The terms describe Israel assembled and united to oppose someone (Num. 16:3, 42; 20:2; 2 Sam. 20:14; Jer. 26:9), to initiate a sinful plan (Exod. 32:1), to witness and thus authorize an ordination (Lev. 8:4) or dedication (1 Kings 8:2), to go to war (Josh. 22:12; Judg. 20:1), to inaugurate a project (1 Chron. 28:1), and to worship (Exod. 12:6; Lev. 6:17; Deut. 23:1-3). The aspect of agreement is normally present (2 Chron. 23:3; Joel 2:16). The words can describe smaller groups, but the concept of unity of purpose (often conspiratorial) remains (Gen. 49:6; Num. 16:19). Even diverse people who are united in purpose form a *qāhāl* (Jer. 50:9), hence the propriety of the term "community." Here the unity was against Moses, Aaron, and God. God's Word urges unity of purpose among his people (Phil. 2:1-2). [*qāhāl, qhl*]

20:8 The staff (*hammaṭṭeh*)—This word (and its synonym *šēbeṭ* ["staff"], cf. "scepter," Num. 24:17) is most often translated "tribe," likely because each tribal leader in Israel carried a *maṭṭeh* (Num. 17:2-3, 6 [cf. D. Fouts, *NIDOTTE*, 4:27]). Perhaps partly because it could function as a club (Isa. 10:5, 15, 24), a staff became a symbol of leadership and authority (Jer. 48:17; Ezek. 19:11; even for a king [Ps. 110:2]), strength (Ps. 110:2), punishment (Isa. 30:32), and even oppression (Isa. 9:4). Although one may not always inscribe his name on his staff

(Num. 17:2), at least in some cases his staff identified him (Gen. 38:18). In this context this was the miraculous staff that became a serpent and reverted to wood at the burning bush (Exod. 4:2-4) and with which Moses brought on Egypt the plagues of hail (Exod. 9:22-23) and locusts (Exod. 10:13-14). Moses and Aaron's (Exod. 7:9-12, 17-19; 8:5, 16-17) staffs were used in performing miracles so often that Moses' became known as the "staff of God" (Exod. 4:20; 17:9). The staff was not to be considered magic, however, for although Moses took "the staff of God" onto a hill overlooking the battle, the text is silent on its role during the fight; only the position of his hands was related to Israel's victory (Exod. 17:9-13). The staff was only a symbol of authority; the real power resided with God, who spoke of his own disciplining actions as a *maṭṭeh* (Isa. 30:32). [*maṭṭeh*]

20:10 You rebels (*hammōrîm*)—This is the first use of the word as a substantive or a verb in the Bible. It could be rebellion against God's direction, as here (cf. vv. 3-5), but most often it was against God's specific commands (Num. 20:24; Deut. 1:26, 43; 1 Sam. 12:14; 1 Kings 13:21). Rebellion may involve drawing back from God's will (Isa. 50:5), being unyielding to discipline by either parents (Deut. 21:18, 20) or God (Deut. 31:27), and demanding something of God (Ps. 78:17-18). It is often linked with stubbornness (Ps. 78:8; Isa. 1:20; Jer. 5:23). Rebellion against God is partially motivated by not remembering his acts of kindness (Ps. 106:7). God does not provoke it (Lam. 1:18). Rebellion against him is in opposition to fearing and serving him (1 Sam. 12:14). It causes him pain (Ps. 78:40; Isa. 63:10), and he punishes rebels (1 Sam. 12:15; Lam. 3:42), although in grace he may still deliver them from trouble (Ps. 106:7-8). Ironically, in this passage Moses called Israel rebels but he ended by rebelling against God himself (Num. 20:24). [*mrh*]

20:13 Meribah where the Israelites quarreled (*měrîbâ 'ăšer rābû běnê yiśrā'ēl*)—The verb *ryb* can mean to attack someone verbally in order to accuse of wrongdoing (Gen. 31:36; Neh. 5:7; Job 13:19), to rebuke (Neh. 13:17, 25; Hos. 2:2), to complain (Judg. 21:22), or to criticize (Judg. 21:22). The word may, at least when God is the subject, refer to attacking someone by deeds instead of words (Job 10:2; Amos 7:4). It can describe acting to defend oneself (Judg. 6:31-32; Ps. 74:22) or taking up a case on behalf of another (Job 13:8). God may take up someone's case to vindicate him (1 Sam. 24:15; 25:39; Mic. 7:9-10), even by means of war, exile (Isa. 27:8), and destruction (1 Sam. 2:10), and to rescue him (Ps. 119:154; Isa. 49:25). Israel here quarreled with Moses (Num. 20:3), but our verse shows that they were really quarreling with God. This incident was so critical that both it (Num. 27:14; Deut. 32:51; 33:8; Ps. 81:7; 95:8; 106:32) and also this place (Ezek. 47:19; 48:28) were recalled numerous times. Here Israel tested God (Ps. 95:8-9) and he tested them (Ps. 81:7). Like Moses, God looked at this as rebellion (Ps. 106:32-33) and was angry. In Moses' anger he spoke thoughtlessly (Ps. 106:32-33). In earlier disputes he had rhetorically asked, "Who are we?" and stated that the dispute was really with God, not with him and Aaron (Exod. 16:7-8; cf. Num. 16:11). Here he failed to make that distinction between himself and God (Num. 20:10). [*měrîbâ, ryb*]

20:24 Will be gathered to his people (*yē'āsēp . . . 'el 'ammāyw*)—This expression is used of the patriarchs Abraham (Gen. 25:8), Isaac (Gen. 35:29), and Jacob (Gen. 49:33), and of Ishmael (Gen. 25:17), Aaron (Num. 20:24, 26), and Moses (Num. 27:13; 31:2; Deut. 32:50). Outside the Pentateuch the expression became "gathered to his fathers." The expression could mean that one was buried in the grave of his ancestors, except that in Deut. 32:50, where Aaron and then Moses were gathered to their people, they were not buried in their families' burial plots. It could mean to be surrounded by their families before they die, except that this did not happen in either case, Moses, in fact, being entirely alone. Some interpreters state that on two occasions (2 Kings 22:20; 2 Chron. 34:28) the expression is most likely equal to being gathered to the grave (I. Cornelius, A. Hill, C. Rogers, Jr., *NIDOTTE*, 1:470). The grammar and syntax of the Hebrew verbs (imperfect followed by perfect with *waw*-consecutive, plus the accentuation of the perfect verb) indicate, however, that Josiah was gathered to his fathers before he was gathered to the grave (i.e., departure of the spirit precedes physical burial). If in this case being gathered to one's fathers means that his family was gathered around him prior to death, then the Pentateuch's expression "to be gathered to their people" would be more appropriate. The expression is not used of the ungodly (although Ishmael was neither the son of promise nor an Israelite, the OT does not portray him as a pagan in relation to God). One might conclude that a reunion of the spirits of the godly with the spirits of their godly ancestors is in view. Although OT depictions of Sheol do not clearly show any separation between the godly and ungodly (note that Job's description of life after death [Job 3:13-19] was his culture's perspective but not divine revelation), this expression may imply that the godly are gathered together by themselves. A clearer revelation of life after death was primarily reserved until the NT (cf. Matt. 22:30; Luke 16:22-28; John 14:2-3). [*sp*]

21:3 The Lord listened (*wayyišma' yhwh*)—Although God is far away, he listens and responds to what is said to him (1 Kings 8:30). He responds positively to those who are humble and grieved (2 Kings 22:19), to the righteous (Ps. 34:17), and to those who pray and seek him wholeheartedly (Jer. 29:12-14). He hears people's cries (Exod. 3:7), groaning (Exod. 6:5), and weeping (Ps. 6:8) about their affliction (Gen. 16:11) and mistreatment (Gen. 29:33; Exod. 22:27). He listens to their vows (Ps. 61:5) and their requests for mercy (Ps. 6:9) and for help in war (1 Kings 8:44-45). He listens when they repent (1 Kings 8:46-49) and forgives their sins (1 Kings 8:49-50). He listens attentively even when the one praying thinks God is unaware of the situation (Ps. 31:22). For the Lord to listen positively means that he responds by doing as requested (Gen. 17:18, 20; 30:6), but his answer may be to direct the petitioner to perform an act that will accomplish the solution (2 Kings 20:5-7). God responds positively to what he hears because he is compassionate (Exod. 22:27). Those whom he hears ought to tell others what he has done (Ps. 22:22-24). God listens to and evaluates what people say to each other (Deut. 5:28). On the negative side after repeated and flagrant rebellion God does not respond positively to weeping and prayer. He did not respond to Israel's weeping when she suffered the consequences of persistent rebellion at Kadesh-Barnea (Deut. 1:45; cf. Ps. 95:9-10). Nor did he respond to Moses' prayer after he profaned (did not sanctify) the Lord at the waters of Meribah in Kadesh (Deut. 3:26).

God listens and may respond adversely to grumbling (Exod. 16:9; he responded positively in this case), taunts directed to his people (2 Kings 19:4), demands and tests put to him (Ps. 78:18-21), messages of those who misrepresent him (Jer. 23:25), conspiracies against his people (Lam. 3:61), arrogant, selfish words (Ezek. 35:12), and speeches hostile to him (Ezek. 35:13). [*šm'*]

21:4 The people grew impatient (*wattiqṣar nepeš hā'ām*)—The verb can mean to be physically short (Ezek. 42:5) or short on power, powerless (Num. 11:23; Isa. 59:1). When used with the noun "spirit" (*rûaḥ*) it can mean to reach the limit of one's endurance of something or patience with someone (Job 21:4; Mic. 2:7; *BDB*, 894). Here it is used with *nepeš*, a combination that also means to be impatient or unable to bear with or put up with something any longer (Judg. 10:16; 16:16; Zech. 11:8). The subject may be God (Judg. 10:16) or humans (as here). Usually the matters that wear out one's endurance are truly troublesome: seeing others' affliction (Judg. 10:16), continual pestering (Judg. 16:16), or evil leadership (Zech. 11:8). The cognate adjective *qāṣēr* can, however, simply mean quick-tempered (Prov. 14:7), the opposite of long-suffering (Prov. 14:29), so that one's impatience in some situations is not after long periods of trouble or harassment. In this case, however, Israel had been in the wilderness for 40 years (cf. the time of Aaron's death in Num. 33:38, which occurred prior to the incident in our text). Their response to wearing out is at issue here. God sympathized with their human frailty (Ps. 103:14), but not with their return to rebellion after he had proved himself responsive to their needs so often before (cf. Num. 11:4-6; 14:2-3). [*qṣr*]

21:6 Snakes (*hannĕḥāšîm*)—The word for snakes is a generic term. Snakes were characteristic of the wilderness (Deut. 8:15) and were feared for their bite (Prov. 23:32; Eccl. 10:8, 11; Amos 5:19) and therefore their venom (Ps. 58:4; Isa. 14:29). These must be one of four kinds of vipers in the Negev. Viper venom breaks down capillaries and corpuscles so that a person dies of massive internal hemorrhaging in a period of four days or less. After the bite pain may subside so that in two to three days the victim feels recovered, but then he may suddenly die. Perhaps this symbolized the lulling effect of sin that is not immediately punished (cf. Eccl. 8:11), but which will nevertheless be suddenly punished (cf. Ezek. 13:10-14; 1 Thess. 5:3; G. Cansdale, *ZPEB*, 4:357-58). Snakes were a symbol of sudden attack (Gen. 49:17) and sudden harm (Isa. 14:29). Appropriately, they became a symbol of the wickedness of the ungodly (Ps. 58:3-4) and the danger of their speech (Ps. 140:3). They also became a symbol of defeat (Mic. 7:17), perhaps in part because the tempting serpent in the Garden of Eden was condemned to defeat (Gen. 3:14-15). They could sometimes be trampled underfoot in a sign of victory (Ps. 91:13, for those who trust God). In our passage, vipers posed a danger but the bronze viper was a sign for healing. The symbolism of healing is reflected in the history of medicine where the image of a serpent has been and still is a sign of healing, although this symbolism predates this biblical event. The symbolism also appeared when Christ said that he would be lifted up like this bronze serpent. Those who would believe in him would receive eternal life just as those looking to the serpent were healed and received an extension of their physical life (John 3:14-15). In a sense the serpent's paradoxical symbolism of dan-ger and healing was paralleled when Christ who was sinless was "made to be sin" (2 Cor. 5:21). In the future kingdom vipers will be rendered harmless and playful (Isa. 65:25). [*nḥš*]

21:17 Pray (*hitpallēl*)—The etymology of this word is debated. The root *pll*, to arbitrate or judge, may be basic to *hitpallēl*, but scholars propose that two unrelated but similarly spelled roots exist: the first meaning to arbitrate and appearing only in the Piel stem, the second meaning to pray and appearing only with the Hithpael stem. If only one root is common to both words, then perhaps prayer indicates the petitioner's attempt to stand between the judge (God) and the accused, or perhaps the prayer expressed the petitioner's attempt to persuade God to judge differently on behalf of the one in need. Schultz comments that efforts to relate the two concepts are forced, though perhaps not incorrect (R. Schultz, *NIDOTTE*, 3:627). The verb in this verse is used for prayers for personal benefit (1 Sam. 1:10; 8:6; 2 Kings 20:2), personal repentance (2 Chron. 33:13), personal complaint (Jonah 4:2-3), hymns of praise (1 Sam. 2:1), confession of national sin (1 Sam. 7:5-6; 12:19; 1 Kings 8:35; Dan. 9:4-6), and, as here, for intercession. The cognate noun for prayer is *tĕpillâ*. Prayer by godly people who had sinned led to deliverance (Ps. 32:6) when they sought God with their whole hearts (Jer. 29:12-14). Practical steps to achieve the desired object might follow prayer (Neh. 4:9). Eventually Gentiles will pray to Yahweh (1 Kings 8:41-42).

Prayer as intercession was for those who had erred (Gen. 20:7; Num. 11:2) and those with whom God was angry (Job 42:7-8). It could be for guidance (Jer. 42:2-4), sparing one's life (Deut. 9:20), and healing (1 Kings 13:6). It might result in blessing for the intercessor (Job 42:10). It was the responsibility of prophets, civic leaders, and kings to intercede for their nation (1 Sam. 12:23; 2 Chron. 32:20), of even temporary residents to intercede for their cities (Jer. 29:7), and of citizens to intercede for their king (Ps. 72:15). God might forbid intercession, but did not seem to be disturbed when someone disobeyed this particular prohibition (Jer. 7:16: 11:14; 14:11), for he has no pleasure in the death of the ungodly (Ezek. 18:23). God continues to urge his people to intercede and pray (Rom. 12:12; 1 Thess. 5:17; 1 Tim. 2:1-4). [*pll*]

21:29 Chemosh (*kĕmôš*)—Chemosh was the chief god of Moab at the time (Judg. 11:24) and remained such even 800 years later (Jer. 48:7) since nations do not exchange their false gods (Jer. 2:11). Chemosh, however, would be no more help then than in the present situation (Jer. 48:13). The Scriptures call the god (and by implication his religion) disgusting (*šiqquṣ*, 1 Kings 11:7; 2 Kings 23:13). Because Solomon would build a shrine to Chemosh for his Moabite wife, Yahweh would tear away most of the kingdom from the royal family (1 Kings 11:7, 31-33). From the fact that Sihon defeated Moab who trusted Chemosh and Israel defeated Sihon, some pagans rightly inferred that Yahweh was the supreme God (Josh. 2:10-11). [*kĕmôš*]

22:5 Balaam (*bil'ām*)—Balaam's relationship with Yahweh remains somewhat enigmatic. Balaam's reputation (Num. 22:6) for divination and sorcery stretched 300 miles from the Euphrates in Aram (Num. 23:7; Deut. 23:4) to Moab. He used the covenant name for Israel's God, "Yahweh" (Num. 22:8, 13, 18; 23:3, 8, 12; 21, 26; 24:6, 13), claiming that Yahweh was

his God (Num. 22:18). The narrator, however, when describing Balaam's interactions with Yahweh, preferred the name "God" (*'ĕlōhîm*) instead (Num. 22:9, 10, 12, 20, 22; 23:4; 24:2), except when rebuking the prophet by announcing both the opening of the donkey's mouth and Balaam's eyes (Num. 22:28, 31) and then when stating that Yahweh made him bless Israel (Num. 23:5, 16; 24:1). This actually highlighted Yahweh's relationship with Israel, not with Balaam. Balaam's relationship to Yahweh was not as close as he professed (cf. Matt. 7:21-23, where the NT clearly teaches that many people who perform deeds for God do not truly have a relationship with him). Balaam used sorcery (Num. 24:1) and divination (Josh. 13:22), practices that God deplores (Deut. 18:10-12); nevertheless, God gave him messages (Num. 23:5, 16). Although Balaam sounded determined not to exceed what Yahweh said (Num. 22:18), when Balak increased the honorarium (Num. 22:17) the temptation of money was too much for him to resist. Balaam sought for Yahweh to change his mind (Num. 22:19), probably believing, like Balak (Num. 23:13, 27), that Yahweh could be manipulated. Balaam wanted to curse Israel for remuneration, but God would not heed him (Josh. 24:9-10; cf. Deut. 23:4), for he cannot be played upon to suit people's whims. To gain the reward anyway, Balaam advised Balak in the Baal-Peor incident (Num. 31:16; cf. Rev. 2:14) so that God would judge Israel when she yielded to Balak's temptations. Therefore, Balaam was slain in a battle against Midian (Num. 31:8), Balak's allies (Num. 22:4, 7). His reputation as a prophet for hire continued into the NT as a pattern to which others must not conform (2 Pet. 2:15; Jude 11). If Balaam's experiences taught nothing else, they showed that God could not be manipulated by Israel's enemies to overturn his covenant with them, and that God's professed servants must shun the temptation to use their spiritual gifts for personal profit. [bil'ām]

22:6 Those you bless are blessed ('ăšer těbārēk měbōrāk)—To bless people can mean merely to wish them well (Exod. 12:22; 1 Sam. 23:21; Ps. 129:8; Prov. 5:18), to express a common bond—whether genuine or not—as in a greeting (Gen. 24:31; 1 Sam. 15:13), or to express a desire that God will give them what they desire (1 Sam. 2:20). It may also designate speaking well of someone, or expressing appreciation or respect (Ps. 10:3; 118:26). Similarly, it can be thanks to another human (Deut. 24:13; Job 31:20) or to God (Deut. 8:10). When God blesses someone it may mean he expresses his acceptance and favor (Isa. 19:25), his intention to do good things for them (1 Chron. 17:26-27), or his actual past provision of benefits for them, such as food, drink, health, offspring (Exod. 23:25-26), political significance (Gen. 17:16), great population increase (Gen. 17:20; Deut. 17:14), a full lifespan (Exod. 23:25-26), security and comfort (Isa. 61:3-9), material abundance (2 Chron. 31:10), productivity and success in work (Gen. 27:27; Deut. 28:8; Job 1:10), wealth and a large household (Job 1:1-3; 29:25), and prosperity in general (Deut. 12:7; 15:6; 30:16; Job 42:10). Saying that someone is blessed could refer to the sense of happiness he has for the receipt of such benefits (Deut. 33:24). When God says people are blessed it may be a greeting expressing his relationship to them as well as his intention to do them good (Num. 22:12; Isa. 19:25). When Scripture says that God blesses directly or through a mouthpiece it may mean, as here, that he generally portrays someone's (or his descendants') future (Gen. 49:28; Deut. 33:1-29). He may include descriptions of one's present or past (Deut. 33:8-9). God may also bless a thing (in contrast to a person), apparently meaning that he mediates a blessing through it, such as blessing a day so people receive rest (Exod. 20:11) or blessing a field so they have food (Gen. 27:27). When God himself was blessed he was praised (Gen. 9:26; Exod. 18:10) in general or thanked for a specific item such as victory in battle (Gen. 14:19-20), kindness (Gen. 24:27), and provision for help (Ruth 4:14). [brk]

22:7 Fee for divination (qěsāmîm)—The word normally means simply "divination," a means of seeking information and advice (1 Sam. 6:2; 28:8, 15) from the supernatural realm (Mic. 3:7). The term appears often in connection with visions (Jer. 14:14; Ezek. 13:9, 23; 21:29; 22:28) and "seeing" (Zech. 10:2), indicating that divination is not primarily a method to manipulate the future or someone's fortune. The fact that it is sometimes called "lying" divination (Jer. 27:9-10; 29:8-9; Ezek. 13:9, 23) implies that divination involves acquisition of information and not control over the future. Perhaps it is because it was not an attempt to manipulate the deity, like sorcery, that God on occasion answered the diviner (1 Sam. 28:14-19; Prov. 16:33; Ezek. 21:21-22; Jonah 1:7; cf. M. Horsnell, NIDOTTE, 3:946). Nonetheless, Yahweh found divination detestable (t'b), forbade it in Israel, and expelled the Canaanites partly because of it (Deut. 18:10-14). He would put the diviners to shame (Isa. 44:5) and condemn Israel partly because they would employ it (2 Kings 17:17). Diviners sought omens by shooting arrows, asking idols, consulting tissue patterns in animal livers (Ezek.

21:21), inquiring of the spirits of the deceased (1 Sam. 28:15), using rods (Hos. 4:12), observing residue in cups (Gen. 44:5), casting lots (Jonah 1:7), and other methods. Like Balaam, many of Israel's prophets would eventually practice divination for a price (Mic. 3:11). [*qesem*]

22:11 Put a curse on them for me (*qābâ-lî 'ōtô*)—This word for "curse" (*qbb*) occurs only in Num. 22–24, although the word *nāqab*, which may be a variation on the form, appears 25x with a broader range of meanings. When Balak first requested Balaam to curse Israel he used the word *'ārar* (v. 6), a curse that especially depended upon deity to fulfill it (cf. comments on Num. 5:18, "that brings a curse" [*'rr*]). After Balaam replied that Yahweh would not permit him to curse, Balak changed (Num. 22:17; 23:11, 13, 25, 27; 24:10) to the word Balaam uses here. Because Balak believed that deities could be manipulated (Num. 23:13, 27) he may have preferred a word that implies the autonomous power of the sorcerer instead of the requirement of divine approval. Noticeably, God did not use the word *qbb*, but *'rr* (Num. 22:12), perhaps to stress the need for divine approval if a curse was to be effective. Balaam implied that God had the power to curse (*qābab* Num. 23:8) without higher approval. Major points in this account are that humans cannot pronounce an effective curse if God does not approve (Num. 23:8; cf. Prov. 26:2), and what he has decreed cannot be changed (Num. 23:20). [*qbb*]

22:22 The angel of the Lord (*mal'ak yhwh*)—The word for angel may also mean a messenger. So Israel was the Lord's *mal'āk* (Isa. 42:19), and both a priest (Mal. 2:7) and a prophet (Hag. 1:13) could

be *mal'ak yhwh*. Often the *mal'ak yhwh* was a supernatural person. God has numbers of supernatural angels (Gen. 28:12; 32:1; Ps. 91:11; 103:20; 104:4), any of whom could be called "the angel of the Lord." Nevertheless, in the OT there appears to have been a special "angel of the Lord" who spoke as though he was God (Gen. 16:9-10; 21:17-18), claimed to do what God did (Judg. 2:1), and called himself God (Gen. 31:11-13). He may have spoken of himself in the first person and of God in the third (Gen. 21:17-18; 22:11-12) as if they were distinct, but in the same breath could state that "I" will do what God does (Gen. 21:17-18) or that something was done to "me" when it was clearly done to God (Gen. 22:11-12). People may call the angel God (Gen. 16:13; 48:15-16) or treat him as God (Exod. 3:2-6; Judg. 13:21-22). At other times the angel of the Lord was distinguished from God (Exod. 32:34; 33:3; Judg. 13:3-9, 16; 2 Sam. 24:16; 1 Kings 19:5-7; 2 Kings 1:3, 15; Zech. 1:12-14) and gave a message that originated from God and not himself (Zech. 3:6-7). In some of these cases the angel of the Lord may not be the special angel, but simply the angel on the scene at the time. Sometimes it is unclear if the shift in terms from God to the angel of the Lord in a single passage is a change in who was designated or in how he was designated (Judg. 6:11-18 [the Septuagint refers each time to the supernatural person as the angel of the Lord, *ho aggelos theou*, instead of alternating between the Lord and the angel]). Yahweh stated that there was an angel, distinct from himself, who had God's name in him (Exod. 23:20). There was an angel of his Presence (Isa. 63:9) who must have been intimate with God, judging by this title. Four general theories about the *mal'ak yhwh* are that he was (1) God's companion who revealed God who remained invisible, (2) God's representative with a special commission and authority, (3) a hypostasis of God, or (4) God himself (H. Fabry, *TDOT*, 8:321-22). At least the angel of Yahweh was God's representative, and at most he may have been God himself. Why God would call himself his own "messenger" and why he would send himself is a mystery. This type of reference allows for the possibility that God is more than one person, with one person being no less authoritative in relation to humans, yet submissive to the other divine person. Ultimately in the progression of God's revelation in the NT God would be revealed as three persons (Matt. 3:16-17; 28:19), two of whom would indeed be sent (John 14:16, 26; 20:21) by the other one. This is the mystery of the Trinity. In our text whether this is the special angel of Yahweh or one of his many angels is not clear. [*mal'ak yhwh*]

To oppose him (*lĕśāṭān lô*)—The Hebrew word is a noun ("as an adversary to him"). The OT uses the verb only when the subject (*śāṭān*) is evil (Ps. 38:20; 71:13; 109:4) and is an enemy of a good person (Ps. 38:20; 109:4, 20). The opposition expressed by the verb is considered unjustified (Ps. 109:4; cf. 38:20) so the godly believe that God should punish the adversary (Ps. 71:13; 109:20, 29). The noun is primarily thought of as denoting the Devil, but it can be used of the Angel of the Lord as here, of David (1 Sam. 29:4) and his nephews (2 Sam. 19:22), and of one's military and political enemies (1 Kings 5:4; 11:14, 23-28). In all of these cases the adversary caused (or would cause, 1 Sam. 29:4) trouble. In cases like our text the adversary was ready to kill the person he opposed (1 Sam. 29:4). In other cases the adversary at least hated the one he opposed (1 Kings 11:14, 23-28). All references use the term *śāṭān* to refer to the

supernatural creature Satan (Job 1:6, 7, 8, 9, 12; 2:1, 2, 3, 4, 6, 7; Zech. 3:1, 2), except for one (1 Chron. 21:1), use the article (i.e., "the satan, the adversary"). In the one reference to him that simply calls him "Satan" without the article (1 Chron. 21:1) not all scholars agree that the supernatural creature is meant (e.g., a human could have tempted David). At least sometimes Satan drew wrong conclusions about people (Job 1:9-11, 22; 2:5, 10), but the adversary in our text was right about Balaam's character. Satan accused the upright of self-seeking and did not believe that disinterested righteousness existed among even the best people (Job 1:9-11; 2:4-5). He would have been right if he had said this of Balaam. While God and Satan are enemies, God treats him as an inferior, not as a peer (Job 1:7-8, 12; 2:2-4, 6; Zech. 3:2-5). [*śṭn*]

23:7 His oracle (*mĕšālô*)—Each message of Balaam is called by this term (Num. 23:18; 24:3, 15, 20, 21, 23) although the usual word for oracle is *nĕ'um* (Num. 24:3, 4, 15, 16). Our term is the common word for a proverb (Prov. 1:1), a well-known, standard saying (1 Sam. 10:12; 24:13; Ezek. 18:2-3), and can be classed with riddles (Prov. 1:6). It can also refer to lengthy wisdom sayings (Ps. 49:4), discourses and arguments (Job 27:1; 29:1), taunting speeches (Isa. 14:4; Mic. 2:4), and bywords (Deut. 28:37 "object of scorn"; 1 Kings 9:7; cf. *BDB*, 605; K. Beyse, *TDOT*, 9:66). Similar to the related verb (*māšal*), either "to be like" (Ps. 28:1; 49:12) or "to compare" (= "to regard as like," Isa. 46:5), the noun can refer to an allegory (Ezek. 17:2). Finally, the word can even be used of an interpretation of Israel's history (Ps. 78:2). All of these are poetic, as here. In our context the term seems to have the closest associations with either an argument (for blessing Israel instead of cursing her) or with sayings that express well-known truths. Here God ensures the truthfulness of the facts mentioned in the *māšāl*, and though they are not yet well known, they will be as Israel's history unfolds. Therefore, the idea of divine predetermination is present. [*māšāl*]

23:10 The righteous (*yĕšārîm*)—The word is a substantive, that is, an adjective used as a noun. As an adjective it can mean to be level or straight (Jer. 31:9; Ezek. 1:7, 23), correct or safe (Ezra 8:21; Ps. 107:7), appropriate (Jer. 26:14), acceptable (1 Sam. 19:6), and harmonious (2 Kings 10:15). Usually the adjective or substantive is an ethical term that derives from these more concrete meanings. A person may be appropriate in God's opinion (Exod. 15:26; Deut. 12:25; Prov. 12:15), which is good, or in his own opinion, which is not (Deut. 12:8; Judg. 17:6). As an ethical term the word is associated with integrity and righteousness (Prov. 11:3. 6), honesty (Prov. 16:13), avoidance of evil (Prov. 16:17), justice, faithfulness (Deut. 32:4; Neh. 9:13), loyalty (1 Sam. 29:6), good (Deut. 6:18; 1 Sam. 12:23), innocence (Job 4:7; 17:8), purity (Job 8:6), observance of God's commands (Exod. 15:26; Deut. 12:28), and seeking him (Ps. 11:7). The principles of uprightness can be taught (1 Sam. 12:23), and there are degrees of uprightness (2 Kings 14:3; Mic. 7:4). Some persons perform uprightly but without wholehearted dedication (2 Chron. 25:2) as they should (Ps. 7:10; 11:2; 32:11). An upright person influences society for good (Prov. 11:11). Uprightness can result in good health (Exod. 15:26), population increase, divine compassion (Deut. 13:17-18), rescue (Ps. 7:10), all-round good (Deut. 6:18; Ps. 112:2), joy (Ps. 19:8; 97:11), hope (Ps. 112:4), residence in the land (Prov. 2:21), closeness to God (Prov. 3:32),

and victory over those who trust in themselves (Ps. 49:13-14). For Israel's kings uprightness would result in dynastic succession (1 Kings 11:38; 15:4-5). The upright is hated (Prov. 29:27) and attacked by the wicked (Ps. 11:2; 37:14). The upright can be led astray (Prov. 28:10), but fortunately God who is upright teaches sinners his ways (Ps. 25:8). [*yāšār*]

23:12 What the Lord puts in my mouth (*'ăšer yāśîm yhwh bĕpî*)—God said that Moses should put words in Aaron's mouth by speaking to him (Exod. 4:15) and then instructed Israel to put the words of Moses' song in their mouths (NIV, "have them sing it") by copying it and teaching it to them (Deut. 31:19). God can put words in people's mouths this way, but may do it supernaturally by touching someone as he apparently did to Jeremiah (Jer. 1:9, though this may be only symbolic of what he would do later for individual messages; this verse and several mentioned below involve the verb *nātan*, a synomyn for the verb *śîm*). Words were put in someone's mouth so that he might be able to say whatever God wanted him to say (Jer. 1:7-9) to someone else, as here (2 Sam. 14:3; Ezra 8:17, literally "put words in their mouth"), including those who did not want to hear it, as here also. Sometimes the purpose was to exhort others (Deut. 31:19; 2 Sam. 8:17; Ezra 8:17) or encourage their confidence in God in the face of fear and oppression (Isa. 51:12-16). God's usual procedure was to raise up a prophet in whose mouth he put his words, and the people were responsible to heed him (Deut. 18:18-19). Balaam currently sensed the responsibility to say only what God put in his mouth, although later he would advise Balak in ways contrary to God's will (Num. 31:16). [*śym bĕpî*]

23:19 God is not a man (*lō' 'îš 'ēl*)—The etymology of the word for man, *'îš*, is unknown, and proposals such as "to be strong," "to sprout up abundantly," and "happy" are only conjectures (V. Hamilton, *NIDOTTE*, 1:388). A synonym of *'îš* is *'ādām*, the name of the first man that usually means man or mankind. Gen. 2:7 relates *'ādām* to the word for ground or soil, *'ădāmâ*, which Hamilton says may suggest a connection with the reddish brown skin and reddish brown soil, since *'ădāmâ* may be from the root *'dm* (V. Hamilton, *NIDOTTE*, 1:264), to be red (M. Grisanti, *NIDOTTE*, 1:269). Another synonym is *'ĕnôš*, which has the same range of meaning as *'ādām*, but is relegated almost entirely to OT poetic texts. The verb that is cognate to *'ĕnôš* means to be sick or weak, so the noun may view man as mortal. However, if *'ĕnôš* is related to Akkadian it may refer to weakness or being sociable, and if it is related to Ugaritic it may refer to being manly or brave. Maass states that the usual view is that *'îš* and *'ĕnôš* may be traced to the same stem (F. Maass, *TDOT*, 1:346). If the etymology of *'îš* remains uncertain, its usage divides into several shades of meaning, such as a generic person in a hypothetical situation (Exod. 22:1), a citizen (2 Sam. 15:2), a husband (Num. 5:29), and a specific person (2 Sam. 17:3). On occasion, as here, it is in a statement about humanness, particularly as contrasted with God, though the more common word for humanness is *'ādām*.

Since God is not human he has a divine degree of compassion, turning from and limiting the fierceness of his anger toward his covenant people (Hos. 11:9), he cannot be effectively confronted on equal footing either legally or otherwise (cf. Job 38–41 that bears out the assertion of Job 9:32), and, as here, he does not change his mind

(1 Sam. 15:29). Because of this last principle, it is notable that when a prophet was called a "man of God" he was expected to be truthful and authoritative in all he said, and accurate in all he predicted (2 Kings 4:16; 5:14; 7:2, 17-18; 13:19; 23:15-16). Appropriately, the Man who is God asserted that he is the Truth (John 14:6). Because of the great contrast between God and humans, he holds the life of every human (Job 12:10, NIV, "creature") in his hand, he directs human lives (Jer. 10:23), and he occasionally overturns the nature of the cosmos for the sake of humans (Josh. 10:14). Because humans are not God they cannot withstand or prevent his judgment (Isa. 31:3), are mortal (Ezek. 28:9), and lack his wisdom (Ezek. 28:2). In this context the matter of truthfulness is at issue as well as the inability to prevent or cause God's judgment. [*'îš*]

That he should lie (*wîkazzēb*)—R. Mosis demonstrates that the verb and related noun (*kāzāb*) do not fundamentally mean to communicate what one knows is untrue, but to create an objectively untrustworthy or worthless thing. The delusion reflects the observer's expectation and perception (R. Mosis, *TDOT*, 7:108, 113, 118). In keeping with this analysis, the term describes groundless hope (Job 4:19), untrustworthy words (Job 30:6) that misrepresent the real nature of a thing (Judg. 16:10), false appearances (Job 34:6), divination that is not from God (Ezek. 13:6-7; 22:28), and misrepresentation of one's thoughts (Ps. 78:36-37; Isa. 59:11; Hos. 7:13-14). The contrast to lying is something that is (Ps. 58:11), or is eventually demonstrated to be (Hab. 2:3), dependable. Therefore, a prophet does not lie when he predicts judgment (Jonah 3:4) that does not fall, for it is clear to him (Jonah 4:2) and is a viable hope to his audience (Jonah 3:7-9) that judgment will not fall should the people repent. Their expectation is due to God's historically demonstrated character qualities and his announced principles to this very effect (Jer. 18:7-10). Those who do not know God's revelation or history, however, may believe they have been deceived when matters do not turn out as they had presumed they would. God does not lie and abhors those who do (Ps. 5:6; Prov. 6:19). All people are ultimately untrustworthy (Ps. 116:1) and will be punished for it (Prov. 19:5, 9). However, the future remnant that God preserves will not lie (Zeph. 3:13). [*kzb, kāzāb*]

That he should change his mind (*wĕy-itneḥām*)—This meaning of the basic root *nḥm* usually appears in the Niphal and Hithpael forms, where it means to gain relief from (Isa. 1:24), have compassion (Ps. 90:13b), change one's mind (Exod. 13:17), be grieved (Judg. 20:6), or be comforted (Gen. 24:67). (In the Piel stem it means to comfort.) About two dozen times it is used of God (e.g., Gen. 6:6-7; Judg. 2:18; 1 Sam. 15:11, 29, 35). In some cases it is debatable whether it means he changes his mind, is compassionate, or is grieved (e.g., Gen. 6:6-7; 1 Sam. 15:11; Jer. 15:6). That God should repent or be grieved about his own actions may seem like a lack of omniscient foresight. However, despite his grief or repentance about making mankind, he did not exterminate the race (Gen. 6:6-8; H. Simian-Yofre, *TDOT*, 9:343). His grief or change of mind about making Saul king led to deposing his dynasty, but his original intent to coronate a Judean as king (Gen. 49:10) never changed (cf. 1 Sam. 15:28-29; v. 28 refers to the Judean David). Most often he changes his mind when people turn from sin (Jer. 26:3, 13, 19; Joel 2:13; Jonah 3:9-10), after someone intercedes for them (Amos 7:3, 6; Exod. 32:12), or

because of his compassionate nature (Ps. 90:13) or concern for the covenant (Ps. 106:45). The object of which he repents or grieves is usually the disaster that he justly inflicts for sin (Jer. 18:8; 26:3, 13, 19; 42:10; Joel 2:13; Amos 7:3, 6; Jonah 3:10; though he might repent of doing good [Jer. 18:10]), for his compassion prompts his change of mind and grief (Ps. 90:13; 106:45). Since his repentance due to compassion is a character quality (Joel 2:13; Jonah 4:2), the change of mind is neither a change in character nor in what people expect of him (i.e., he makes a relative change, not a real one). He declares his freedom to rescind offers and threats (Jer. 18:7-10), but, as in our passage, he had made a covenant to bless Israel and would not go back on what he had promised or sworn by oath (Ps. 110:4). Whether or not he has a covenant (i.e., pledged word) may determine whether he "repents" (cf. Ps. 106:45). [*nḥm*]

23:23 There is no sorcery (*lō' naḥaš*)—Usually the noun and its related verb (*nḥš*) refer to something spiritual or occult, but in the one exception, the verb means to interpret something as an indicator of what the true situation is (1 Kings 20:33). In religious use the verb means to seek information through mantic means. The term looks much like the word for "serpent" (*nāḥāš*), but Fabry argues that there are no discernible mantic associations with the serpent in Israel in the OT (H. Fabry, *TDOT*, 9:357). Laban claimed that he acquired information about the Lord through this means (Gen. 30:27), though his deceptive habits cast doubts upon his truthfulness (a man of his talents could have deduced what he knew through reason). Joseph claimed to have received knowledge through mantic means (Gen. 44:5, 15), but since his words and actions were for effect he may not have been candid. The law prohibited Israel from tolerating the interpretation of omens and practicing divination (Lev. 19:26; Deut. 18:10-12) and listed them with sorcery (2 Kings 21:6). Nevertheless, Israel would practice them (2 Kings 17:17), as would Judah's King Manasseh (2 Kings 21:6). This would become a reason for God to expel them from the land (2 Kings 17:17-18) and was a reason he drove out the Canaanites before them (Deut. 18:10-12). Here Balaam repeatedly sought an omen to net him Balak's reward, but God would not grant it. [*naḥaš*]

24:3 The oracle of Balaam . . . the oracle of one (*nĕ'um bil'ām . . . nĕ'um*)—This is not the word translated "oracle" in Num. 23:7, 18 (cf. comments on Num. 23:7, "his oracle," *māšāl*). This is the usual word for oracle, and is most often translated as if it is the verb "declares" (2 Kings 9:26; Jer. 46:18). It occurs over 370x in the Bible, and all but 11x it is part of a standard expression for an oracle of the Lord (e.g., *yhwh* [241x, 2 Kings 9:26], *yhwh ṣĕbā'ôt* [Lord Almighty, 26x, Isa. 14:22], *'ădōnāy yhwh* [Sovereign Lord, 88x, Jer. 2:22]). Of the 11x the term is not part of the standard formula, six are in our context (Num. 24:3 [2x], 4, 15 [2x], 16) and three are from David (2 Sam. 23:1 [2x]; Ps. 36:1, cf. the title). Once it is in a claim made by false prophets that they have an oracle (Jer. 23:31). They mean to imply that it is from the Lord (NIV so translates it, though most Hebrew texts do not include the Lord's name). With Balaam's six uses and two of David's, the text states that the ultimate source of the oracle is God's Spirit (Num. 24:2; 2 Sam. 23:2). All this accents the fact that although a prophet may speak, the words come from God and this term demonstrates God's self-

revelatory character (H. Eising, *TDOT*, 9:111, 113). Therefore, the word appears primarily in the prophetic books: 176x in Jeremiah, 85 in Ezekiel, 25 in Isaiah, 21 in Amos, and 20 in Zechariah. It appears only 19x outside of the Prophets (H. Eising, *TDOT*, 9:110), 7 of which are in Numbers alone (Num. 14:28 and our passage). The eleventh nonformulaic use is in Agur's speech (Prov. 30:1), where it is unusual as a designation for a wisdom passage (the presence of *maśśā'* for oracle, if it means this here, is also unusual outside the Prophets).

The first time the word is used (Gen. 22:16) is when God swore to bless and multiply Abraham's descendants, to give them possession of their enemies' territory, and through them to bless all nations. It is fitting, therefore, that in our passage (only its third occurrence) Israel was blessed through a prophet hired by a king who feared Abraham's descendants would take his territory. God's oracle here confirms his faithfulness to the former oracle. [*nĕ'um*]

24:4 The Almighty (*šadday*)—God's name Shaddai (Exod. 6:3) is used 48x in the OT, 31 of them in Job, and 7 of them as El Shaddai (*'ēl šadday*; Gen. 49:25 may be an eighth). Scholars have not reached a consensus on the origin of the word, proposing at least eight differing views. The two most popular relate it to "mountain," as in God of the mountain, and "breast," as God who supplies or nourishes (though God's presentation as masculine undercuts this interpretation [M. Weippert, *TLOT*, 1306-09]). The name is used primarily in Gentile contexts even by Hebrews. In Job the five Gentile men and God used the name (31x), and here Gentile Balaam said it twice (Num. 24:4, 16). It was employed by David in a context of Israel against the nations (Ps. 68:14), by Ezekiel in Babylon (Ezek. 1:24; 10:5), by Naomi who was just returning from Moab (Ruth 1:20, 21), by Isaiah prophesying against Babylon (Isa. 13:6), and by Joel using Isaiah's expression and anticipating a Gentile invasion (Joel 1:15). Seven of the eight remaining times, God and the patriarchs utilized the name prior to the major revelation of the name Yahweh (Exod. 6:3; Gen. 17:1; 28:3; 35:11; 43:11; 48:3; 49:25). Therefore, the name was part of God's early revelation, his revelation among the Gentiles, and the revelation of his power to provide land and offspring. The name was part of God's confirmation of his covenant with Abraham (Gen. 17:1), Jacob (Gen. 28:3; 35:11; 48:3), and Jacob's sons (Gen. 43:11; 49:25). It was superseded by the name Yahweh (Exod. 6:2-3), which would become associated with his covenant-keeping character (Exod. 6:6-8). [*šadday*]

24:16 The Most High (*'elyôn*)—The root of the name *'elyôn* is *'lh*, which means to ascend. Used as an epithet for Yahweh, it means that he is superior to all other (supposed) gods (cf. Ps. 97:9). Therefore, it is often used, as here, in Gentile and polytheistic contexts where the Scripture makes it plain that Yahweh is the supreme deity (cf. G. Wehmeier, *TLOT*, 893). The word is used as a part of God's name in the forms *'ēl 'elyôn* (God Most High, Gen. 14:18), *'ĕlōhîm 'elyôn* (the Most High, Ps. 78:56), *yhwh 'elyôn* (The Lord Most High, Ps. 7:17). The parallelism with Shaddai (Ps. 91:1) and with Yahweh (2 Sam. 22:14; Ps. 7:17; 91:9) shows that all three terms apply to one and the same God. His self-revelation by this name particularly exhibits the fact that he is Creator (Gen. 14:19, 22) and ruler (Ps. 97:2, 9) of heaven and earth (though some question whether

he is really in power over the world [Ps. 73:11]). As such he allots to nations their proper territories (Deut. 32:8) and defends his people from any who try to dispossess them of their territory (Ps. 83:4-18; Moab in our context was one of them [Ps. 83:6]). As supreme ruler, he will establish Zion as his chief city over the nations (Ps. 87:4-6). To him all other rulers are accountable (Ps. 82:2-7). In the ancient Near East where kings were judges, the Most High was a judge (Lam. 3:33-39), known for righteous, just treatment of his subjects (Ps. 7:17; 107:11-12). He used the forces of nature to defeat his enemies (2 Sam. 22:14) and deliver his people (Ps. 9:2-5; 50:14-15). He had a history of doing mighty deeds (Ps. 77:11-12; 78:11-17, 55-56) as Israel's redeemer (Ps. 78:35), but he also protected individuals (Ps. 91:1, 9-10). [*'elyôn*]

24:17 Star (*kôkāb*)—Since people in the ancient Near East were commonly enticed to worship the stars, they became symbols of gods (Amos 5:26). The Lord forbade Israel to worship them (Deut. 4:19) and declared that they are not gods, but his creations (Gen. 1:16; Neh. 4:21; Ps. 136:7-9). He determined their number (Ps. 147:4), set them in their courses (Ps. 8:3), and controls them (Job 9:9; 38:31-32; Jer. 31:35; Amos 5:8) whether they are visible or not (Job 9:7; Isa. 13:10; Joel 2:10-11). Stars should be understood as directing attention to the greatness of God who made them (Ps. 8:3-4). They either praise him themselves or, more likely, inspire people to praise him (Ps. 8:1-4; 148:3). In a poetic sense God may enlist them to fight for him (Judg. 5:20) as he uses other natural elements (Judg. 5:21), but in the great Day of the Lord he will not use them in any real or poetic sense (Isa. 13:9-10; Joel 2:10-11; 3:15), perhaps lest some false god be given credit for his victory.

Stars may symbolize something numerous (Deut. 28:62; Nahum 3:16), especially Abraham's promised offspring (Gen. 15:5; 22:17; 1 Chron. 27:23) who became as numerous as prophesied (Deut. 1:10; 10:22). Fulfillment of this promise should prompt loyalty from God's people (Deut. 11:1 follows 10:22 immediately). A star may also symbolize a prominent leader (Dan. 8:10) or a king (of Babylon in Isa. 14:3, 12 [*hêlēl*, morning star, *BDB*, 237]). Judging from the fact that "scepter" appears here as a parallel to "star," a royal leader is meant. The LXX translated the parallel term with *anthrōpos*, man, showing that the translators in about 250 B.C. thought that a royal individual was meant. Our text is one of only two occurrences of the word in the singular. Like the other occurrence (Amos 5:26), this star could perhaps represent deity, and yet like the plural uses, this star (Num. 24:17-19) would direct people's attention to God, serve God at his behest, and fight for his people. If this is both a king and deity, it should be understood as the Messiah, Jesus of Nazareth, who was both from the royal line of David and also divine. God used stars for signs (Gen. 1:14-16), so the star of the Nativity (Matt. 2:2, 9) was an appropriate sign for the birth of the royal and divine Christ. The visiting magi operated on the principle that the star pointed to royalty. [*kôkāb*]

Scepter (*šēbeṭ*)—This word is more often translated by the word "tribe" than by "scepter" or any other term. Because a tribal leader carried a *šēbeṭ*, the tribe following him was called a *šēbeṭ* (D. Fouts, *NIDOTTE*, 4:27). This Hebrew term refers to a warrior's club (2 Sam. 23:21) and to a rod used to discipline people (Exod. 21:20; Ps. 2:9), including children, in need of corporal discipline (Prov. 13:24). Therefore, it became a symbol of punishment (2 Sam. 7:14; Job 21:9; Ps. 89:32), judgment (Isa. 11:4; Lam. 3:1), and affliction (Job 9:34; Mic. 5:1). As a form of power it could also be a sign of leadership and therefore of a leader (Judg. 5:14), as here. As noted above, the LXX interpreted the word as a man, *anthrōpos*. Jacob had prophesied that the *šēbeṭ*, the royal leadership, would belong to the tribe of Judah. Eventually this prophecy began to be fulfilled at the time of David's coronation as Israel's king. However, Jacob said that the scepter would remain in the tribe of Judah until one special individual came (Gen. 49:10). Since David was the first one to wield the scepter, he was not the individual in view. The NT is clear that Jesus Christ of Nazareth was this Davidic family member (Matt. 1:1; 2:1-2; 12:23; 21:9). See the comments in Num. 20:8 on the synonym *maṭṭeh*, "the staff" which carries some of the same ideas about authority and punishment, and is also translated "tribe." [*šēbeṭ*]

25:2 Their gods (*'ĕlōhêhen*)—See comments on Num. 10:9, "to be your God," for the etymology of the word *'ĕlōhîm* and for synonyms for the true and living God. This noun for God is plural in form, but when referring to the true God it takes a singular verb, indicating that it refers to one God. Here for the first time in Numbers it denotes false gods and is plural in form and meaning. OT synonyms for pagan *'ĕlōhîm* are unflattering, to say the least, and include *hăbālîm*, "worthless things," *lō' 'ēl*, "no god" (both terms in Deut. 32:21); *'ĕlîl* (plural, *'ĕlilîm*; perhaps a wordplay on *'ĕlōhîm*), "little god, godling" (Lev. 19:4) that is reminiscent of the adjective *'ĕlil*, "weak, insignificant, worthless"; *šiqqûṣîm*, "detestable things" (Deut. 29:17); *gillûlîm*, "balls of dung, dungy things" (Ezek. 22:3; H. Preuss, *TDOT*, 1:285); *kāzāb*, "lie, deceptive thing" (Amos 2:4; cf. *BDB*, 469); *pesel*, "(hewn) image" (Exod. 20:4; Judg. 18:31); *tĕrāpîm*, "household gods" (Gen. 31:19, NIV), which Preuss in the reference above suggests may mean "rotting things" or "old scraps."

The Pentateuch is clear about Yahweh's attitude toward other gods. His actions reveal that he is greater than all gods, for none can do what he does (Exod. 18:11). They are unable to hear, eat, smell (Deut. 4:28), or help (Deut. 32:37-38). In reality Yahweh is the only deity (Deut. 32:39), so that the OT frequently speaks of gods as if they are merely the metal (Exod. 20:23; 32:31; Lev. 19:4), wood, or stone (Deut. 4:28; 28:36) of their images. Moses was aware, however, that the supposed gods were demons in some cases (Deut. 32:17), but still not authentic gods (Ps. 106:37). Consequently Israel must not have other gods (Exod. 20:3), mention their names (Exod. 23:13), follow them (Deut. 6:14), worship or serve them (Exod. 23:24), or eat their sacrificial meals (Exod. 34:15). When Israel was in their own land they must destroy the idols, their relics (Exod. 23:24; Deut. 7:4-5), and their worship places (Deut. 12:2). God forbade Israel to make covenants with the Canaanites, for covenants would acknowledge Canaan's gods (Exod. 23:32). Worshiping other gods was a trap (Exod. 23:33), and the associated activities were detestable (Deut. 12:30-31; 20:18). So Israel must destroy Canaan's idolaters without pity (Deut. 7:16). Prophets and even loved ones who advocated serving other gods must be executed (Deut. 13:1-9; 18:20) by stoning (Deut. 17:5) if thorough investigation confirmed their guilt (Deut. 13:13-14; 17:2-4), for their sin was dangerous to the whole society. [*'ĕlōhîm*]

Bowed down (*wayyištaḥăwû*)— Linguists believed that the root of this verb was *šḥh*, "to bow" (*BDB*, 1005) until the discovery of a cognate root *ḥwy* in Ugaritic established that the real base of the word was an ancient Hebrew root *ḥwh* (also "to prostrate oneself," H. Preuss, *TDOT*, 4:249). The term for bowing down is distinct from simply bowing one's head (*qādad*, Gen. 24:48) and refers to a deep bow putting one's face to the ground (Gen. 37:10; Josh. 5:14; Ruth 2:10) either before a human (Ruth 2:10), God (Exod. 24:1), or a false god as in our text. This bow is an act of humility for the subject (Gen. 37:10) and honor for the recipient (Ps. 45:11). One may bow to respect a benefactor (Ruth 2:10), father (Gen. 48:12), prophet (2 Kings 2:15), governor (Gen. 42:6), or a group (Gen. 23:7). One bows to part from a friend (1 Sam. 20:41), dismiss oneself to carry out an order (2 Sam. 18:21), and greet and beseech royalty (2 Sam. 16:4; 1 Kings 2:19). In relation to God it is an act of worship in response to announcements about answered prayer (2 Chron. 20:18), God's concern (Exod. 4:31), his command (Exod. 12:27), someone's death (2 Sam. 12:20) or disaster (Job 1:20), and to the demonstration of God's glory (Job 34:8). The term can be a general word for worship and is a synonym of the frequent term for worship, *'ābad*, but is usually bowing in distinction from worshipful acts like sacrificing (1 Sam. 1:3; 1 Chron. 16:29), confessing (Neh. 9:3), offering incense (Jer. 1:16), singing (Ps. 66:4), playing instruments (2 Chron. 29:28), praising (Gen. 24:26-27; Ps. 138:2), and exalting God (Ps. 99:5, 9). Worshipful bowing to God is also associated with obedience (1 Kings 11:33). Worshipful bowing to other gods is a result of one's heart being enticed (Deut. 30:17) and is connected with evil practices as here (Exod. 23:24), forsaking the Lord (Jer. 16:11; 22:9), and loving, following after, and consulting other gods (Jer. 8:2). It violates God's covenant (Josh. 23:16); therefore, he prohibits it (Deut. 4:19; 11:16). [*ḥwh*]

25:3 So Israel joined (*wayyiṣṣāmed yiśrā'ēl*)—The noun that is closely related to this verb is *ṣemed*, which means a pair of work animals tied (Judg. 19:3; 2 Kings 5:17) or yoked (1 Sam. 11:7; 1 Kings 19:19) together, or a string of animals working and, probably tied, together (2 Sam. 16:1). People who work together and are administratively tied to each other are also described by the term (2 Kings 9:25). The verb can appear in other grammatical patterns in which it means to be fastened physically (2 Sam. 20:8) or figuratively (Ps. 50:19). This particular form of the verb appears in only one other place (Ps. 106:28) where it describes our scene and is fittingly translated "yoked." By participating in the sacrificial meal with this false god Israel was making a pact with it. The NT invites people to be yoked with Christ (Matt. 11:29-30) and exhorts them not to be yoked unequally with unbelievers (2 Cor. 6:14-16). [*ṣmd*]

Baal (*ba'al*)—The essential meaning of the noun is lord, owner, or husband. This was the nation Israel's first recorded contact with Baal worship, and they succumbed to its temptations. The worship of this storm and fertility god involved a stone pillar (2 Kings 3:2; 10:26-27), burning incense (2 Kings 23:5; Jer. 7:9; 32:29), and burning children in offering (Jer. 19:5). Baal worship was syncretistic in that it mixed with at least the religion of Molech (Jer. 32:35). The worship system included priests (2 Kings 10:19), temple (1 Kings 16:32 [in Israel]; 2 Kings 10:21; 11:8 [in Judah]), and up to as many as 450 prophets on one occasion (1 Kings 18:19). Ahab set up Baal worship in Israel (1 Kings 16:31-32), and Ahaz (2 Chron. 28:2) and Manasseh set it up in Judah (2 Kings 21:3). Jehu temporarily destroyed the system in Israel (2 Kings 10:28). Although this worship was persistent, Baal was unable to defend (Judg. 6:31) or prove himself (1 Kings 18:21-29) when put to the test. Foreign nations taught Israel to worship Baal (Jer. 12:16), and the process began in our passage.

Many references to Baal are plural (Jer. 2:23; 9:14) since different locations had their own manifestation of Baal (Jer. 11:13). Therefore, there were different names for the Baals (Hos. 2:17), often named for the locale, such as Baal-Peor, Baal-Berith (Judg. 8:33), Baal-Gad (Josh. 11:17), Baal-Hazor (2 Sam. 13:23) (M. Mulder, *TDOT*, 2:194). [*ba'al*]

25:4 Expose them . . . before the Lord (*hôqa' 'ôtām layhwh*)—The verb does not occur often in this grammatical form. In another form it means to be alienated from (Jer. 6:8) or to be out of joint (Gen. 32:25). In this form it may mean to display bodies with broken limbs (*HALOT*, 431). In the law Israel was permitted to hang (*tlh*) corpses of people who had been convicted of capital crimes (Deut. 21:22-23). Both times this form of the verb is used the fact is added that the hanging was "before the Lord" (Num. 25:4; 2 Sam. 21:6, 9). Also, in both cases the nation suffered from the consequences of crimes committed by the exposed persons (Num. 25:9; 2 Sam. 21:1). Although a repulsive sight, the exposure demonstrated publicly to God that the community officials had dealt with the offense and sought to reconcile the community to God. In a similar way in the NT, on the cross Christ was made into a public and unsightly demonstration, which showed that he had made reconciliation for the sins of mankind. [*yq'*]

The Lord's <u>fierce</u> anger (*ḥărôn 'ap yhwh*)—The anger of the Lord appears again. The particular word of interest here is *ḥārôn* whose root (*ḥārâ*) means to be kindled or to burn. The term is used to describe only God's anger (the apparent exception, Ps. 58:9, is obscure; see NIV textual note). It describes anger that consumes (Exod. 15:7), brings disaster or calamity (Exod. 32:12; Neh. 13:18), makes a land desolate (Isa. 13:9; Jer. 4:7-8, 25) and without harvest (Jer. 12:13), and terrifies (Ps. 2:5; 88:16). Sometimes an invading army carried out God's consuming anger (Jer. 4:6-8; 25:38). When a king was responsible to execute God's anger he was condemned if he did not (1 Sam. 28:18). No one could endure exposure to God's fierce anger (Nahum 1:6), but perhaps could be sheltered from it (Zeph. 2:2-3). Clearly it was best to turn away his anger before he acted on it. Although this could not always be done (2 Kings 23:26), Israel might accomplish it by punishing sin (Deut. 13:17), exhibiting a just punishment (Num. 25:4; Josh. 7:26), interceding for the guilty (Exod. 32:12), reconsecrating themselves to the covenant (2 Chron. 29:10), repenting (2 Chron. 30:8), and reversing sinful practices (Ezra 10:14). They could turn God's wrath away because, although hating sin, he is compassionate (Hos. 11:8-9). [*ḥārôn*]

25:11 In my zeal (*bĕqin'ātî*)—Zeal is an eagerness and passion for something or someone. When zeal is directed toward protecting one's own interests in someone or something that he considers to be his own, zeal is called jealousy. This word for zeal speaks of an aspect of love that does not yield (S. of S. 8:6), is intense (Ps. 119:139), powerfully energizes (Prov. 27:4), and is provoked by another's unfaithfulness (Prov. 5:12-14; Deut. 29:18-

20). Scripture inveighs against zeal to have what someone else owns; i.e., envy (Ps. 37:1), pointing out that it is wrong and harmful to one's health (Prov. 14:30) and makes one's achievements seem worthless (Eccl. 4:4). The fear of God assuages envy (Prov. 23:17). God's zeal energizes him to accomplish his purposes and fulfill his word (2 Kings 19:31; Isa. 9:7; 42:13). He exhibits zeal for what is his (i.e., jealousy) when his rights are infringed, his honor injured (Ezek. 39:25), and his people disloyal or mistreated (Ezek. 36:5-6; Zech. 1:14-15; cf. H. Peels, *NIDOTTE*, 3:938-39), hence his description as a "jealous" God (Exod. 20:5; 34:14). So he punishes those who hate him (Deut. 5:9), loves those who love him (Deut. 5:10), and prohibits worship of other gods (Deut. 4:23-24). His jealousy is often expressed in anger (Ezek. 16:38; 23:25; Zeph. 1:18; 3:8) and destruction (Ps. 27:4; Zeph. 1:18; 3:8). It "burns" or "smokes" (Deut. 29:20; Ps. 79:5) and brings disaster (Deut. 29:20-21), but subsides after punishment (Ezek. 16:39-42).

Zeal for God arose when one who identified with him was offended by what offended God, as here (Ps. 69:7-9). It might be shown by executing fellow Israelites who were blatantly disloyal and worshiped other gods (2 Kings 10:16, 25-27), by obedience to God's Word (2 Kings 10:16-17), and by speaking out against disloyalty (1 Kings 19:10, 14). It could be misdirected (2 Sam. 21:2), but Phinehas' zeal here was not. [*qin'â*]

25:12 My covenant of <u>peace</u> (*bĕrîtî šālôm*)—The Hebrew word for peace, *šālôm*, has a wide range of meanings, but at its root is a condition of completeness and being intact. Its variety of meanings includes prosperity and success (Lev. 26:6), intactness (1 Chron. 12:18), a greeting (1 Sam. 25:6), personal welfare (Gen. 37:14), public and private peace (Judg. 4:17), friendliness (Ps. 35:20), and deliverance or salvation (Ps. 85:8; *HALOT*, 1507-09). The Lord uses the expression "covenant of peace" to refer to his promises for the future prospects of the nation (Isa. 54:10; Ezek. 34:25; 37:26) that include effective protection (Isa. 54:11-12, 16-17) with its consequent security and safety (Isa. 54:14; Ezek. 34:25, 27-28), peace (Isa. 54:13), proliferation (Isa. 54:1-3; Ezek. 37:26), vindication before others (Isa. 54:17; Ezek. 37:28), and blessing (Ezek. 34:26) for God's servants (Isa. 54:17). Prior to later announcements of the national covenant of peace Phinehas and his family already became recipients of parallel blessings: multiplication of offspring so that they would always have men for the priesthood, protection of their position as priests, blessing in general, reputation as God's servants, and vindication of their priestly rights. Phinehas' covenant of peace was to be never ending, like the nation's covenant (Isa. 54:10; Ezek. 37:26). The Lord made this covenant with Phinehas and his descendants because of Phinehas' zeal for the Lord at the time when Israel was rebelling against the Lord through idolatry (Num. 25:13). In the recent past the whole tribe of Levi had similarly received special promises of blessing from the Lord for their zeal for the Lord at a time when Israel had engaged in forbidden worship (Exod. 32:22-29; Deut. 33:9). In both instances the Lord exhibited his approval of those who confronted their sinful society on his behalf. [*šālôm*]

25:13 His descendants (*zar'ô*)—The Hebrew word *zera'* can mean seed for planting (Gen. 1:11) or, more often, offspring as a descendant in particular (Gen.

4:25) or descendants in general. To have offspring was a blessing (1 Sam. 2:20) and sometimes not to have offspring was punishment (Jer. 29:32). To have descendants was so important that God made an exception to the law against marrying one's sister-in-law (Lev. 18:16) in the case of a childless widow in order to produce offspring for the deceased husband (Deut. 25:5-6). Solidarity with one's descendants (or ancestors) was so strong that to love one was to love the other (Ps. 89:28-29; Isa. 43:5) and to deliver (Jer. 30:10) or destroy (Jer. 49:10) the offspring was to do the same to the ancestor. The impact of one's decisions on his descendants was used to motivate people's choices (Deut. 30:19). To those who showed concern for their offspring, a blessing to the latter was a blessing to the former (2 Sam. 7:12, 19, 29; Isa. 43:5). Institutions preserved this sense of solidarity by making common memories (Esth. 9:28, 31). Solidarity was so strong in some cases that our term can denote a group as a unit (Jer. 7:15). Since *zera'* may stand for a kind of people (Isa. 1:4 ["brood"]; Prov. 11:21 [NIV, "those who are righteous"]; Isa. 57:3-4), offspring may bear punishment for the ancestor's sins (1 Kings 11:39; 2 Kings 5:27; Isa. 14:20-21) not only because the divine announcement of the effect on the descendants was a punishment to the guilty ancestor, but also because the biblical account reveals that the descendants continued in their ancestors' sins (Ps. 106:27; Jer. 36:31). Similarly, God's promises of blessing for one's descendants may be chiefly for only the faithful among them (Ps. 69:36).

Covenants, especially God's, commonly arranged matters not just between the initial parties but also with the offspring (Gen. 9:9; 13:15; Num. 18:19; 2 Sam. 7:12). God may bless offspring because of their ancestor (Gen. 21:13; Ps. 25:13; 37:25-26), perhaps because the ancestor displayed loyalty to God (Num. 14:24). Some promises to ancestors were primarily for the benefit of their descendants (Gen. 12:7; 15:5, 13; 22:18). One key feature of the solidarity between ancestor and descendants and the continuation of God's blessings and promises to one's offspring was to demonstrate the continuation of the family with one eternal God who is always there for them all (Ps. 103:17-18; H. Preuss, *TDOT*, 4:162). God would be faithful to each successive generation. [*zera'*]

26:55 Lot (*gôrāl*)—The belief that the lots may have been small stones is supported by Arabic cognates that mean stony ground, gravel, small stone, and to be stony. The lots are said to go out (Num. 33:54, Hebrew *yṣ'*) as if they were in a container, they are thrown (Josh. 18:10, Hiphil of *šlk*; Josh. 18:6, Hiphil of *yrh*; Prov. 16:33, *ṭûl*; Dommershausen maintains that this verb means to shake [Dommershausen, *TDOT*, 2:450], but this nuance apparently developed after the OT period [*HALOT*, 373]), and thrown down (Jonah 1:7, Hiphil of *npl*) so as to fall (also Jonah 1:7, Qal of *npl*). Most often lots are reported as being used, like here, to divide the land of Canaan among the Israelites (Num. 33:54; 34:13; Josh. 19:51; Ps. 125:3). The fall of the lot determined the location each clan would occupy, not the amount of territory. This was determined by the amount of people (Num. 26:53-55; 33:54). Lots would be used to make specific decisions, such as which of two goats would be slain on the Day of Atonement (Lev. 16:8-10), the timing for contributions to the temple but not who contributed (Neh. 10:34), who would live in Jerusalem but not how many (Neh. 11:1), who would fight in battle but not whether to fight it (Judg. 20:9), the timing for temple service but not who served (1 Chron. 24:5, 31; 25:8), and where one would serve but not whether he did so (1 Chron. 26:13-14). The point in mentioning the things that were not determined by lot is to show that limitations were put on what the lot could decide. Also, it is clear that practical qualifications were not disregarded in making these assignments (Josh. 17:1-2; 1 Chron. 26:14). Where God's will was already known or where practical considerations impinged on decisions, there was no need to use the lots. People cast lots *before the Lord* (Josh. 18:6, 8) so that instead of obtaining random results the Lord directed the outcome (Judg. 20:9, 18; Prov. 16:33; Isa. 34:17; Jonah 1:7). When God directed the lots he might not tell everything that someone might desire to know (e.g., God identified Jonathan as Saul's man, but did not seem to condemn him as Saul assumed [1 Sam. 14:42, 45], cf. W. Dommershausen, *TDOT*, 2:454-55. The word *gôrāl* is not used here, but the associated verb *nāpal* and the context show that lots were used). One purpose for using lots was to be impartial (1 Chron. 24:5, cf. JPSV, "both on an equal footing"). To ensure fairness officials oversaw the procedure (1 Chron. 24:31). Either because of God's involvement or the impartiality of the procedure, casting lots settled disputes (Prov. 18:18). The lot was used figuratively to represent one's destiny, and it was often explicitly noted that God determined this destiny (Isa. 17:14; 57:6; Jer. 13:25; Dan. 12:13). [*gôrāl*]

27:17 To go out and **come in before them, one who will lead them out** and **bring them in** (*yēṣē'* . . . *yābō'* . . . *yôṣî'ēm* . . . *yĕbî'ēm*)—Going out and coming in before one's people aptly describes what kings

(1 Sam. 8:20) and national military leaders (Josh. 14:11; 1 Sam. 18:13, NIV, "led the troops in their campaigns"; 29:6, NIV, "serve with me") did when they went out to battle to fight for their people and then returned victoriously. When God was with them, they were successful (1 Sam. 18:13). The expression can also be used of broader public leadership such as Moses' (Deut. 31:2) and Solomon's (2 Chron. 1:10). When God gave them wisdom they were successful (2 Chron. 1:10). The expression may describe a worker's carrying out of his duties (1 Chron. 27:1) and a common citizen's everyday activities (Ps. 121:8; Jer. 37:4; Zech. 8:10) as well. When they are godly people, the Lord cares for and protects them (Ps. 121:7-8). In our context this is a continuation of Moses' broad leadership responsibilities.

The second part of the expression concerning leading out and bringing in emphasizes the military aspect especially. Here it has an added theological nuance. Many times the Pentateuch emphasizes that Israel had been led out of Egypt (e.g., Exod. 6:6; 18:1; Lev. 26:13, 45; Num. 20:16). Up to this point they had only been led out, not in. Now that Israel was soon to enter Canaan, making it their home, they would not only go out to war, but they would also come home again. Indeed, God's purpose in bringing them out had been so that he could bring them in and make Canaan their home (Deut. 6:23). [yṣ', bw']

Like sheep without a shepherd (kaṣṣō'n 'ăšer 'ên lāhem rō'eh)—God was known as a shepherd to individuals (Gen. 48:15; Ps. 23:1-6) and the nation of Israel (Ps. 28:9; 80:1). Moses (Isa. 63:11), kings (2 Sam. 5:2; 1 Kings 22:17), prophets (Isa. 56:10-11; Jer. 17:16), and other civil leaders (Jer. 2:8, "leaders," NIV; Ezek. 34:23-24) were called shepherds as well. Good shepherds lead wisely (Jer. 3:15), seek guidance from the

Lord (Jer. 10:21), care for the people (Jer. 23:4; Ezek. 34:2), do not rule harshly (Ezek. 34:4), and settle the people's disputes justly (Ezek. 34:20-22). When shepherds lead the people astray the people will be scattered (Jer. 50:6). They can lead them astray by delivering a message that they falsely claim is from God, which when followed brings the people to judgment, wandering, and oppression (Zech. 10:2). When people as sheep are "scattered," going astray, and uncared for it may be because their shepherd has been removed (Ezek. 34:5-6) or is evil (Jer. 23:1-2). God may remove a shepherd because he is selfish and evil (Jer. 23:2; Ezek. 34:10) and needs to be punished (Jer. 23:2), or because the people are disobedient (Jer. 22:21-22). In the NT Jesus claimed to be the Good Shepherd (John 10:11, 14) who— unlike the self-serving shepherds condemned by the OT prophets—voluntarily gave his life for his sheep. Peter called him the Chief Shepherd over the undershepherds of God's people (1 Pet. 5:4), and the writer of Hebrews called him the great shepherd whom God resurrected from the dead. [rō'eh]

27:20 Some of your authority (mēhôdĕkā)—The elemental concept of the word hôd is majesty or impressiveness (Job 37:22; Isa. 30:30). It is first of all a characteristic of God. His majesty impresses people with his authority and power over (1 Chron. 16:27-30), causing (Ps. 104:1-6), and ownership of creation (1 Chron. 29:11). It is also an appearance that impresses people with his greatness (Ps. 104:1), mighty deeds (Ps. 111:3; 145:4-6; Hab. 3:3-6), power, and justice in the social, political (Job 40:9-10; 1 Chron. 29:11-12), and military realms (Isa. 30:30-31). The fitting response to the display of God's impressiveness is praise (1 Chron. 29:10-11; Ps. 148:13). Majesty is also a king's characteristic that comes from God and reveals the monarch's greatness (1 Chron. 29:25; Ps. 21:5), justice, and mighty deeds (Ps. 45:3). It is expected that he deserves this majesty (Jer. 22:18), but he may not (Dan. 11:21). Israel will have this impressiveness when God restores her fortunes (Hos. 14:5-7). Manly vigor gives an ordinary person the appearance of impressiveness (Prov. 5:9; Dan. 10:8). Even a warhorse has impressiveness due to his fierceness, fearlessness, and power in battle (Zech. 10:3). Since Moses was a man of unparalleled status (Num. 12:6-8), his endorsement gave Joshua a degree of impressiveness before the people (cf. Saul's request of Samuel, 1 Sam. 15:30). Ordination by a respected authority figure helps one to start well (cf. Josh. 1:17). [*hôd*]

27:21 The Urim (*hā'ûrîm*)—The Urim and Thummim were carried in the high priest's breast piece (Exod. 28:30; Lev. 8:8) attached to his ephod (Exod. 28:22-25). They were employed in some undisclosed manner in making decisions (Exod. 28:30), inquiring of the Lord (1 Sam. 28:6), and regaining lost information (Ezra 2:63; Neh. 7:65). Apparently through these elements God answered inquiries (1 Sam. 28:6). Perhaps these elements were two cubic stones, one black and one white, functioning like the lot. Dommershausen suggests that eventually preaching and priestly interpretation of the Torah replaced the use of lots in finding out God's will (W. Dommershausen, *TDOT*, 2:453-55). In our context Joshua's association with the priest and his Urim shows the importance for Israel's new leader to make decisions based on God's words rather than his own reasoning, for a good shepherd seeks guidance from the Lord (Jer. 10:21; cf. comments on Num. 26:55, "lot"). (Cf. also the comments on

Num. 27:17, "like sheep without a shepherd.") [*'ûrîm*]

28:2 At the appointed time (*bĕmô'ădô*)—The word *mô'ēd* is used nearly 150x for the Tent of Meeting (cf. comments on Num. 1:1, "Tent of Meeting"), but its range of meanings also includes an established time and sometimes a meeting location (G. Sauer, *TLOT*, 552-53). It is most often a time appointed by God, whether for a plague (Exod. 9:5), justice (Ps. 75:2), judgment (Dan. 11:27), reward (Dan. 11:35), the end of an empire (Dan. 8:19), bestowing favor (Ps. 102:13), or fulfilling a vision (Hab. 2:3). These uses exhibit Yahweh's ultimate control over history. The fact that he created celestial bodies to mark off seasons (*mô'ēd*; Gen. 1:14; Ps. 104:19) demonstrates his control over nature as well. The term is especially employed to denote times appointed by God for Israel's religious festivals that occur annually (Hos. 9:5; Zeph. 3:18) of Passover, Unleavened Bread, Firstfruits, Weeks, Trumpets, Day of Atonement, and Tabernacles (Lev. 23:4). It is not used of the weekly Sabbath (Lev. 23:3-4) or New Moons (Num. 10:10; 1 Chron. 23:31; 2 Chron. 8:13; Isa. 1:14), except for rare occasions such as in our passage (cf. Lam. 2:6; Ezek. 45:17; Hos. 2:11). It occurs most often with the feasts of Passover (Num. 9:2, 3, 7, 13; Deut. 16:6) and Unleavened Bread (Exod. 13:10; 23:15; 2 Chron. 30:22). Israelites were summoned (Num. 10:10; Lam. 2:22) to the three annual pilgrimage feasts (2 Chron. 8:13; Unleavened Bread, Weeks, and Tabernacles). The purpose of the festivals was for Israel to appear before God (Ezek. 46:9), remembering his gracious acts of sovereignty in history (e.g., the Exodus) and nature (e.g., harvest), and to renew their commitment and cleansing (e.g., the Day of Atonement). [*mô'ēd*]

28:3 As a regular burnt offering ('*ōlâ tāmîd*)—In Israel's worship system many procedures were performed on a continually recurring basis. The specified regular procedures were presenting the Bread of the Presence before the Lord (Exod. 25:30; Lev. 24:8), burning the lamps in the Tent of Meeting (Exod. 27:20; Lev. 24:2-4), burning incense (Exod. 30:8), offering the twice-daily burnt (Exod. 29:38-39) and grain offerings (Lev. 6:20; Num. 4:16), and maintaining the fire on the altar continuously so that fellowship offerings could be offered at any time (Lev. 6:9-13). Also continual were the priest's bringing before the Lord the names of the 12 tribes (Exod. 28:29), bringing the Urim and Thummim so that decisions could be made (Exod. 28:30), and wearing his turban so that offerings would be acceptable (Exod. 28:38). Continual attention must be brought to the ark of God by repeated playing of trumpets before it (1 Chron. 16:6). Naturally, then, the priests' (1 Chron. 16:39-40) and Levites' service before God was continual (1 Chron. 23:28-31). The worship system continually highlighted the importance of carrying on a regular and ongoing relationship with God. This example went beyond the formal worship system, for all should continually set God at the forefront of their thoughts (Ps. 16:8; 25:15), praise him (Ps. 34:1; 35:27; 70:4), hope in him (Ps. 71:14; Hos. 12:6), and obey him (Ps. 119:44). From God's side he continually cared for his people and their homeland (Deut. 11:12; Isa. 49:16), was constantly available as a refuge for his people (Ps. 71:3), and continuously guided the faithful (Isa. 58:11). [*tāmîd*]

28:9 The Sabbath (*haššabbāt*)—The Sabbath and New Moon were the only holidays in Israel that did not recur on an annual cycle (F. Stolz, *TLOT*, 1299). The verb related to the Sabbath (*šābat*) means "to cease." The day was called "the Lord's" Sabbath (Exod. 16:23, 25; 20:10); He made it holy (Exod. 20:11) and commanded Israel to treat it so (Exod. 20:8) by not working (Exod. 20:10; Lev. 23:3) in the fields (Exod. 34:21) or buying or selling (Neh. 10:31) even when work demands were the greatest (Exod. 34:21). Guards who prevented commerce on the Sabbath are described as keeping it holy (Neh. 13:22). When the day was profaned by nonobservance, so was God profaned (Ezek. 22:26). Observing the Sabbath was a way to respect his sanctuary (Lev. 19:30; 26:2), since it was also a day to gather (Lev. 23:3) to worship (Ps. 92 [title]; Ezek. 46:3). Sabbath keeping was a sign that God made Israel his own by covenant (Exod. 31:13, 17), but foreigners could also show adherence to the Lord by observing it (Isa. 56:6)—and in the future they would come from everywhere for Sabbath worship (Isa. 66:23). God gave joy to those who delighted to do his will instead of theirs on this day (Isa. 58:13-14), but prescribed capital punishment for individual violators (Exod. 31:14-15; 35:2; Num. 15:32-35) and severe punishment (e.g., exile and death) to the nation if it promoted violation (Neh. 13:17-18; Jer. 17:27; Ezek. 20:13-16, 23-24). Violence, injustice, and oppression by his people nullified God's pleasure in their Sabbath keeping (Isa. 1:13-17). By faith in Christ's redeeming work Christians will enter a Sabbath-rest (*sabbatismos*), meaning either to enter the state of salvation on earth or to enter heaven (cf. Rev. 14:13). [*šabbāt*]

28:17 Festival (*ḥāg*)—Three times annually Israel was to celebrate festivals "to the Lord" (Exod. 23:14): the feasts of Unleavened Bread, Weeks, and Tabernacles (Deut. 16:16; 2 Chron. 8:13;

cf. Exod. 23:14-16). These were the only regular holidays that are called by the term *ḥāg*, except for Passover once (Exod. 34:25). All males were instructed to appear at God's chosen sanctuary (Exod. 23:14-17; 34:23; Deut. 16:16), but entire families attended the Feast of Weeks (Deut. 16:10-11) and Feast of Tabernacles (Deut. 31:10-12), and at least the sons attended the Feast of Unleavened Bread with their fathers (Exod. 13:6-9). Since the entire family had been involved in the Passover from its inception (Exod. 12:6) and since the Passover was the day before Unleavened Bread (Num. 28:16-17), the entire family would be together for Unleavened Bread as well. In addition, before the Exodus, Israel espoused the idea of the entire family being present at God's festivals (Exod. 10:9). The men were responsible to make the offering for their families (cf. Exod. 23:15; 34:20; Deut. 16:16). While the people were away from home the Lord guarded their land (Exod. 34:24), eliminating the need for security as an excuse for not worshiping him. At the festivals they gave offerings, sang, played music, formed processionals, even at evening (2 Chron. 30:21; Isa. 30:29; Amos 5:21-23), and read Scriptures (though perhaps not every time, Deut. 31:10; Neh. 8:14-18). Festivals were opportunities for significant activities, such as moving the ark (2 Chron. 5:2-3), dedicating the temple (2 Chron. 7:8-10) and altar (Ezra 3:3), purging Jerusalem of idolatry (2 Chron. 30:13–31:1), and revival (2 Chron. 35:16-19). God instituted the festivals to regularly unify the community and maintain its theological focus. As important as the festivals were, God would rather his people treated each other justly and with grace (Amos 5:21). [*ḥāg*]

28:18 Sacred <u>assembly</u> (*miqrā' qōdeš*)—The root (*qr'*) of the word for assembly means to call, summon, or read. Of the 22x the word *miqrā'* means "assembly" (its only other occurrence means "what was being read," Neh. 8:8), 19x it is called a sacred assembly. Sacred assemblies were called on the Sabbath (Lev. 23:3), the Day of Atonement (Lev. 23:27), the Feasts of Weeks (Lev. 23:21; Num. 28:26) and Trumpets (Lev. 23:24), and the first and last days of the Feasts of Unleavened Bread (Exod. 12:16) and Tabernacles (Lev. 23:35-36). People were not to work on these days (Exod. 12:16; Lev. 23:3, 7, 21, 25, 27-28, 35-36). For three of the festivals most Israelites were not at home near their work anyway (cf. comments on Num. 28:17, "festival"). Congregating regularly and often was important to the life, vitality, and unity of God's people (cf. Heb. 10:25). Offerings were a major part of the assemblies (Lev. 23:27, 36-37). Since they involved activity, physical exertion, and a major time commitment (i.e., many people making offerings at one place for three of the feasts), regular labor would have distracted the people's attention from the assemblies. [*miqrā'*]

28:26 Feast of Weeks (*běšābu'ōtêkem*)—The Feast of Weeks was also called the Feast of Harvest (Exod. 23:14-16; 34:22; Deut. 16:16). It was called Weeks because of the time period by which it was determined (Lev. 23:15-16) and Harvest because of what was celebrated. Barley harvest precedes the wheat harvest (Ruth 1:22; 2:23). The "weeks" measured were from the time when the first harvest began (Lev. 23:10, 15) until the wheat harvest had commenced (Exod. 34:22; Deut. 16:9). This time of rejoicing before the Lord by whole families (Deut. 16:10-11) regularly reminded them from where their sustenance had come (the NT likewise reminds believers, Matt. 6:11; 1 Tim. 4:3). Accordingly, they gave offerings to God that were proportional to his blessing (Deut. 16:10, 16; cf. 1 Cor. 16:2, where the NT speaks of the same). Whereas Passover and Unleavened Bread celebrated God's work of rescuing in history (the Exodus), this feast celebrated his work of providing in nature. Both were fulfillments of promises made in the covenant with the forefathers (Gen. 15:13-14; 27:28). [*šābûa'*]

29:1 No regular work (*kol mĕle'ket 'ăbōdâ lō'*)—The term *mĕlā'kâ* refers especially to skilled labor and its results (S. Hague, *NIDOTTE*, 2:943), in many cases as opposed to work that entails physical labor (*'ăbōdâ*, J. Milgrom and D. Wright, *TDOT*, 8:326). The OT describes as *mĕlā'kâ* the work of chief steward (Gen. 39:11), construction supervision (Neh. 5:16), construction (1 Kings 5:16; Ezra 3:8), farming (1 Chron. 27:26), animals produced by breeding and feeding (Gen. 33:14), food preparation (Exod. 12:16), flaying animals (2 Chron. 29:34), sailing (Ps. 107:23, "merchants," NIV), carpentry and masonry (2 Kings 22:5), repair work (2 Kings 12:14-15), craftsmanship (very often, Exod. 31:5; 35:31; 1 Kings 7:14), a king's commission (1 Sam. 8:16), a project (Exod. 38:24; 1 Kings 9:23), the product of work (Lev. 13:48; 2 Chron. 17:13, "supplies," NIV), ceremonial worship service (Num. 4:3) of priests (1 Chron. 6:49) and Levites (1 Chron. 23:24), performing music (1 Chron. 25:1), administrating divorce (Ezra 10:13), and officiating as judge (1 Chron. 26:29). Work is prohibited on days of sacred assembly (cf. comments on Num. 28:18, "sacred assembly"). The death penalty is prescribed only for work done on the Sabbath (Exod. 31:15; 35:2)

and Day of Atonement (Lev. 23:30), even though work is prohibited on all sacred assembly days. Only these two holy days are called *šabbāt šabbātôn*, "Sabbath of rest" (Exod. 31:15; 35:2; Lev. 16:31; 23:3, 32) and only on these two days is *kol mĕlā'kâ* (all work) forbidden. On the other holidays forbidden work is called *kol mĕle'ket 'ăbōdâ*, as here, linking skill with physical labor. Milgrom and Wright conclude from this that on the Sabbath and Day of Atonement absolutely every kind of work was prohibited (even food preparation [Exod. 12:16] and lighting a fire [Exod. 35:3]), whereas on other holidays tasks involving little or no physical exertion, such as mental work and light physical work, were allowed (J. Milgrom and D. Wright, *TDOT*, 8:328). The difficulty of drawing the line between light and heavy work would have made the death penalty problematic for these holidays. Even on the Sabbath and Day of Atonement priests and Levites had prescribed work. Work is good for God does it (Gen. 2:2-3), and the Bible encourages skill (Prov. 22:29) and diligence (Prov. 18:9) in one's work. [*mĕlā'kâ*]

A day for you to sound the trumpets (*yôm tĕrû'â yihyeh lākem*)—The term *tĕrû'â* does not mean trumpet or necessarily to blow one. It can be a shout of joy (Ezra 3:11-13; Job 8:21), expectancy (1 Sam. 4:5-6), exuberance and energy (Num. 23:21), or a battle cry (Jer. 20:16; Ezek. 21:22; Amos 2:2; Zeph. 1:16). It does not appear as a cry of grief or fear, although the battle cry may arouse fear. Israel will shout when bringing the ark to Jerusalem (2 Sam. 6:15) and in worship (Ps. 33:3; 47:6). Their shout is either their offering (Ps. 27:6, NKJV) or it accompanies their offering (NIV, NASB, JPSV). Those who shout joyfully to the Lord are blessed (Ps. 89:15). The term can also denote playing the cymbals (Ps. 150:5) or, as here, blowing the horn (trumpet or shofar). Although they do not occur here, the words trumpet (ḥăṣōṣĕrâ, Num. 31:6; 2 Chron. 13:12) and horn (šôpār, Lev. 25:9) are used with our term. Numerous times when the horn is mentioned with the tĕrû'â the sound of the instrument seems distinct from the tĕrû'â (Zeph. 1:16; 2 Sam. 6:15; Amos 2:2), making the latter a shout rather than a blast. Only once is the trumpet mentioned with the tĕrû'â when its sound is distinct from it (2 Chron. 15:14). To sound trumpets is normal for the first day of the month and for summoning Israel to festivals, but the special mention of it here may be that this celebration was the beginning of the new year (ro'š haššānâ, Rosh Hashanah). Since these celebrations were memorials (cf. Lev. 23:24, tĕrû'â is described as a zikrôn [NIV, "commemorated"]) it recalled God's leadership through the wilderness when the trumpets summoned them to march (Num. 10:2, 5-6). The mention of the sounding of a trumpet continued into the NT as a signal for departure (from mortal life, 1 Cor. 15:52), a summons to assemble (with Christ and Christians, 1 Thess. 4:16), and an announcement of something new in the plan of God (Rev. 8:6). [tĕrû'â]

29:7 You must deny yourselves ('innîtem 'et napšōtêkem)—The verb for denying can mean to oppress people by forced labor (Exod. 1:11-12), tribute, expropriation of the harvest (2 Sam. 7:10; Ps. 89:22), and denial of justice (Lam. 3:33-36). It can mean to dishonor someone (Deut. 21:14), sexually violate someone (Deut. 22:24; Judg. 20:5), subdue a country politically (Num. 24:24), commit atrocities against them (Nahum 1:12), weaken them (Ps. 102:23), restrict them (Ps. 105:18), or otherwise cause them trouble (Job 30:11) and grief (Lam. 3:33). Less severely, the term can denote God humbling Israel in the

wilderness, making them dependent upon him for food that he faithfully supplied (Deut. 8:16). To whatever degree the humbling, the common thread is that someone imposes an action or condition that the recipient would not choose. When a person humbles himself he may be submitting to authority (Gen. 16:9), choosing to endure hardship with others (1 Kings 2:26), making himself liable for punishment (Ps. 107:17), or, if the verb is used with nepeš ("self," sometimes "soul") as it is here, fasting (Ezra 8:21; Ps. 35:13; Isa. 58:3; Dan. 10:3, 12). The personal sense of humiliation can be intense, as the term is sometimes parallel to crushing (Ps. 94:5; Isa. 53:4; Lam. 3:33). The self-humiliation that God expects with fasting involves, negatively, denying one's own sinful and selfish desires and, positively, praying, being generous, and promoting justice for others (Isa. 58:3-9). Christ called for people to deny themselves to the point of (primarily figurative, but also physical) death for his sake, promising them true life if they obeyed his call (Matt. 16:24-25). This included more than merely fasting, as in our text. ['nh]

29:35 Hold an assembly ('ăṣeret tihyeh lākem)—This noun occurs 7x in the OT. Four times it refers to the assembly on the last day of the Feast of Tabernacles (Lev. 23:36; Num. 29:35; 2 Chron. 7:9 [cf. 2 Chron. 5:3, the festival, ḥāg in the seventh month would be Tabernacles, since the Day of Atonement and Feast of Trumpets are not called a ḥāg]; Neh. 8:18), and a fifth time (Jer. 9:2) it may be the same assembly, since the previous context (Jer. 8:20) refers to this time of year. Once it refers to the assembly on the last day of the Feast of Unleavened Bread (Deut. 16:8). The only other reference is to a ḥāg (Amos 5:21) that, therefore, must refer to the Feast of

Unleavened Bread or Tabernacles. The synonym from the same root, *'ǎṣārâ*, occurs only 4x, three of which refer to specially called assemblies (2 Kings 10:20; Joel 1:14; 2:15). The fourth (Isa. 1:13) assembly may be specially called, since, as in Joel, a devastating national calamity had made public fasting and prayer obligatory (Isa. 1:7-9; Joel 1:2-12). The parallel expression speaks of specially called (*qěrō'*) meetings, though this could be the common summons to regularly scheduled assemblies. The verb that is cognate to our term is *'āṣar*, which means to retain or restrain (*BDB*, 783). Scholars have proposed that either the days were devoted to restraint and abstinence marking the end of a feast or they simply commemorated the closing of a harvest cycle (H. Bosman, *NIDOTTE*, 3:503). Another perspective is that since the related terms connote restraint and obligation and since the noun in our verse denotes the last day of a long feast, then the people were required to attend the entire feast without departing early for home or business. Devotion to the Lord was accompanied by faithful attendance at his assemblies. The prophets show that hypocrites might attend faithfully, expressing a devotion that they did not actually possess (Jer. 9:2-3; Amos 5:21-23). [*'ǎṣeret, 'ǎṣārâ*]

29:39 Your freewill offerings (*nidbōtêkem*)—The cognate verb (*nādab*) means that one's heart prompts him (Exod. 25:2) of his own volition. Therefore, when people gave this way it was with their whole hearts (1 Chron. 29:9). The noun may refer to a spirit of volunteering (Deut. 23:23; 2 Chron. 35:8) and to a voluntary contribution to the temple, its service (2 Chron. 31:14; Ezra 1:4), the tabernacle construction, and its furnishings (Exod. 35:29; 36:3). The term

also refers to a type of fellowship offering (Lev. 7:16) that may be in the form of a burnt offering (Lev. 22:18; Ezek. 46:12). Other offerings may be prescribed for holy days, such as those in these two chapters, or as a consequence of a sin or a vow, but this offering was distinct (Num. 15:3; Deut. 12:6, 17; Ezra 3:5). It was not necessarily owed, but expressed one's love for God or appreciation for his blessings (Deut. 16:10) and was given with praise (Ps. 119:108). It probably could not be commanded, but it should characterize the Feast of Weeks when people responded in proportion to God's blessings (Deut. 16:10). Since it might be given out of thanks for deliverance (Ps. 54:6-7), it is frequently mentioned with vows (Lev. 7:16; 22:18, 21; Deut. 23:23). It was offered especially on days of assembly, as here, so that more people could see the testimony of God's goodness and the demonstration of the nation's appreciation for him, though the latter may be hypocritical (Amos 4:5; J. Conrad, *TDOT*, 9:222). Perhaps because it was not an obligation, it may be less than perfect (Lev. 22:23), although someone who gave out of sheer love would probably select an offering without blemish. [*nědābâ*]

30:2 To obligate himself by a pledge (*le'sōr 'issār 'al napšô*)—The verb (*'sr*, but here as an infinitive, *le'sōr*) means to bind and is almost always used in a physical sense: to harness or hitch (Gen. 46:29; 1 Sam. 6:7), tether (Gen. 49:11), bind with cords (Judg. 15:12-13) or shackles (2 Kings 25:7), imprison (Gen. 40:3; Isa. 49:9), and strap or tie something to one's body (Neh. 4:18; Job 12:18). The word is figurative when people restrict someone's social interaction (Ezek. 3:25), God confines one's actions by difficult circumstances (Job 36:16), a woman's beauty captivates her husband (S. of S. 7:5), or a pledge obligates someone as here. In many of the physical and all of the figurative cases the one bound is unable to escape (e.g., Isa. 14:7) unless someone else brings about the release (Ps. 68:6; 146:7; Isa. 49:9; 61:1; Zech. 9:11). Even mighty Samson's escape was attributed to someone else (Judg. 15:13-14; 16:20). In our context likewise, no one can escape these binding obligations except for particular women who could be released by someone else: their fathers or husbands.

The cognate noun (*'issār*) appears only in this chapter. Many believe that it is a negative promise to abstain from something, because the related words in biblical Aramaic (Dan. 6:7-8) and later Hebrew mean "to prohibit," whereas the word "vow" (*neder*) is a positive promise to do something (R. Wakely, *NIDOTTE*, 1:474). However, a vow (*neder*) could include abstinence (Num. 6:2-5; though it might be argued that the vow was the promise of service and offering, and the abstinence was a condition of the vow, not the purpose). Therefore, Milgrom is correct that the *'issār* could be either positive or negative depending upon the context (J. Milgrom, *Numbers*, 251). In our context v. 13 indicates that the *'issār* involved self-denial (NIV, "to deny herself"), which is a parallel Hebrew expression to the self-humiliation and fasting on the Day of Atonement (cf. comments on Num. 29:7, "you must deny yourselves"). In general, however, the word emphasizes the binding nature of the commitment. As God binds himself to fulfill his Word, so people are accountable to keep theirs. [*'sr*]

He must not <u>break</u> his word (*lō' yaḥēl dĕbārô*)—This verb is the common word meaning "to defile" (*ḥll*). Its various nuances are to take away one's (God's) reputation (Isa. 48:11), defame (Isa. 23:9),

treat without sanctity (Gen. 49:4), degrade (Lev. 19:29), treat as unholy (Ezek. 20:13, 16, 21) or common (Neh. 13:18), and treat with contempt (Ps. 89:39). It often concerns someone or something's public reputation (Ezek. 36:20-21) and how others view him or it ("in the eyes of," Ezek. 20:9, 14, 22; 22:16). The most frequently defiled object is God's name, defiled by swearing falsely in his name (Lev. 19:12), being sexually promiscuous (Amos 2:7), and treating his name and worship with contempt (Mal. 1:6-13). God defiled Israel by scattering her abroad (Ezek. 22:16). His sanctuary was defiled when it was destroyed (Ps. 74:7) or his worshipers married pagans (Mal. 2:11). People defiled God when they tried to take his glory (Isa. 48:11) and when his priests did not uphold the distinction between clean and unclean, holy and unholy (Ezek. 22:26). People defiled sacrifices by eating what (Lev. 22:15) or when (Lev. 19:8) they were not allowed. They defiled the Sabbath by not observing it (Ezek. 20:13, 16) and defiled God's land by setting up idols there (Jer. 16:18). Fathers defiled their daughters by prostituting them (Lev. 21:9) and their descendents by corrupting their legacy (Lev. 21:14-15). The defilement in our context is like the defiling of a covenant by breaking it (Ps. 55:20; 89:34). One makes a covenant and a vow by invoking God's name as witness, so that the promise has a degree of holiness. By not keeping one's obligations he demeans his word, and others hold it in contempt. [*ḥll*]

30:6 Her lips utter a rash promise (*mibṭā' śĕpāteyhā*)—The term for rash promise (*mibṭā'*) occurs in the OT only here and in v. 8. The closely related verb (*bṭ'* or *bṭh*) appears only 3x and refers to speaking reckless (Ps. 106:33) words that may also be harmful (Prov. 12:18). A person who utters reckless or rash words binds himself by them even if he is unaware of their significance (Lev. 5:4), and so may be punished for them (Ps. 106:33). The idea of the binding nature and significance of rash words continues into the NT, for Christ declared that people will be judged for their rash words since they reveal the heart (Matt. 12:34, 36). Only the woman but not the man had the option of being freed from the obligation incurred by rash words (Num. 30:8). If the words were rash, then she had not consulted her husband or father (or anyone else). A man's wife or a woman still living in her father's house who made a vow would most likely pay her vow by using her husband's or father's resources (i.e., sacrificial animal(s), money, or other property). Therefore, he should have been consulted prior to her act of obligating his goods by a vow. Consequently, he retained the right to nullify the vow and thus release her from the obligation. In effect God ruled that one person did not have the right to obligate another's goods without approval. Once approval was given, the obligation was irrevocable. [*mibṭā'*, *bṭ'*, *bṭh*]

30:9 A widow (*'almānâ*)—Mercy and justice met in the treatment of the widow (Zech. 7:9-10). She was subject to poverty (Deut. 14:28-29; 24:17, 19-21), so that although she borrowed resources, the lender was not legally permitted to take collateral from her (Deut. 24:17; Job 24:3). The nation was responsible to support her through regular tithes (Deut. 26:12), permission to glean (Deut. 24:19-21), freewill offerings from the newly harvested grain at the Feast of Weeks (Deut. 16:10-11), and newly harvested fruit at the Feast of Tabernacles (Deut. 16:13-14). The Lord took on her care to such a degree that the portion due her was holy (Deut. 26:13) and he blessed those who aided her (Deut. 14:28-29). A widow was often vulnerable to unjust oppression (Exod. 22:22-23; Deut. 27:19; Ps. 68:5). To mistreat her was a sign of general national injustice and ungodliness (Ezek. 22:7) and was reason for calamitous punishment (Jer. 7:6). It was immoral not to aid her (Job 22:9; 24:21; 31:16), and contending for her was an example of the righteousness that pleases God (Isa. 1:17). Leaders, including kings (2 Sam. 14:5-11; Jer. 22:3), were especially responsible to uphold justice for her (Isa. 1:23). The test of a nation's justice was whether she received it. Yahweh was her defender (Deut. 10:18; Prov. 15:25), avenger (Exod. 22:23-24; Deut. 27:19), and sustainer (Ps. 146:9), hunting down leaders who abused and misused her (Isa. 10:2) and punishing her oppressors (Mal. 3:5). If she were childless she might return to her father's household (Gen. 38:11) into which she was fully reincorporated (Lev. 22:13), but she was not required to do so (Ruth 1:8, 16-17). If she had children, they bore the name of her husband (Ruth 4:10) so that she remained incorporated into his family. In our context, whatever property she had shared with her husband was now hers to command (Ruth 4:3, 9), so she had authority over it to pay any vow by which she had obligated herself. Christ stated that in his day widows' property was vulnerable to unscrupulous religious leaders (Mark 12:40). The NT addresses the care of widows (1 Tim. 5:3-16) and one of the major church offices grew out of the church's practice of bearing responsibility for its widows (Acts 6:1-7). Care for the widows was evidence of true Christianity (James 1:27). [*'almānâ*]

31:2 Take vengeance (*neqōm niqmat*)—
Vengeance is God's responsibility (Deut.
32:35), part of his character (Nahum 1:2),
and one of his normal activities (Gen. 4:15;
Deut. 32:43; Isa. 1:24; 61:2; Jer. 46:10; Ezek.
25:14). Vengeance comes with his being the
world's judge (Ps. 94:1). Since he carries
out proper justice (1 Sam. 24:12; Jer. 5:9, 29;
50:15) vengeance reveals him to be just (Ps.
58:10-11) as he repays people in full for
what they have done (Isa. 34:8; 59:17-18).
Because he is just, vengeance relieves
(*nḥm*), or rids, him of the evil (Isa. 1:24).
His vengeance provides salvation for his
people who have been wronged (Isa. 35:4;
63:4), so that his vengeance is theirs (Num.
31:2-3). The avenged ought to rejoice in the
salvation (Isa. 35:3-4), the ensuing peace
(Nahum 1:15), and the truth that ultimately justice will prevail (Ps. 58:10-11),
but not in the damage done to their
oppressors (cf. Prov. 24:17-18). Although
God often executes vengeance through
human agents (Num. 31:3; Josh. 10:13-14; 2
Kings 9:7; Ezek. 25:14), people must not
exact their own revenge. Nations may
become guilty when they seek it (Ezek.
25:12) and individuals are forbidden to
seek it, for it conflicts with love for others
(Lev. 19:18) and with justice itself, for they
often retaliate inappropriately (Ps. 8:2;
44:16; Ezek. 25:12), wrong others (Jer. 20:10;
Lam. 3:60), or harm the wrong person(s) (2
Sam. 4:8). When people seek their own
vengeance violence escalates (cf. Judg.
15:7; 16:28; Ezek. 25:12-15), either because
the punishment is unjust or is not recognized as just. Consequently, it is best left to
God, and indeed the so-called imprecatory
prayers leave vengeance to God (1 Sam.
24:12; Jer. 11:20; 15:15; 20:12). Only Samson
requested power to exact vengeance (Judg.
16:28)—and he died in the process of
wreaking it. In passages about blood
vengeance by a relative for murder (Num.
35:9-34; Deut. 19:4-13; Josh. 20:2-6, 9), these
terms for vengeance are, appropriately, not
used. [*nqm, něqāmâ, nāqām*]

31:17 Kill (*hirgû*)—This word for killing is
not used in the Ten Commandments, but is
especially used for taking the life of enemies in war (Num. 31:8; Josh. 10:11; Judg.
8:18-19; 1 Kings 9:16), their survivors (Josh.
8:24; 1 Kings 11:24), a political (Josh. 9:26; 1
Sam. 24:11) or personal (2 Sam. 12:9) rival—
real or presumed (e.g., Gen. 4:8; 12:12;
27:42; Judg. 9:24; Esth. 3:13), supporter(s) of
a presumed rival (1 Sam. 22:21) or presumed enemy (1 Kings 18:12, 14), and sup-
porters of a rival god (Deut. 13:9; 1 Kings
19:10, 14; 2 Kings 11:18). Therefore the verb
denotes assassinations (2 Sam. 3:30; 1 Kings
12:27; Neh. 6:10), attacks on those who
arrange themselves murderously against a
group (Esth. 9:6, 10, 12), and capital punishment for idolatry (Exod. 32:27; Num.
25:5). These uses of the verb relate to killing
persons who are perceived as outside of
one's own group. Since such killing is not
always justifiable in these situations, the
term can describe murder (Gen. 4:8; Judg.
9:24; 20:5; Ps. 94:6). It describes unjust
killing by a ruler who does not view himself as part of the same society as his people
(Exod. 2:14; 5:21; Isa. 14:20; Zech. 11:5; cf.
for this attitude, Deut. 17:15, 20). Less often,
the word may be used of killing in a more
general sense as well (Exod. 21:14; 23:7; 1
Chron. 7:21; Ps. 10:8—although these
examples could also be described as the
killing of people in an opposing or contrasting group), including killing animals
(only 3x: Lev. 20:15; Num. 22:29; Isa. 22:13)
and killing by an animal (only once: 2
Kings 17:25; of course, examples of humans
killing animals and vice versa are killings
across group lines, so the principle above
still applies). In our context the killing is of
God's enemies in war. [*hrg*]

31:23 The water of cleansing (*mê niddâ*)— The word translated "cleansing" probably comes from either the word *ndd* or *ndh*, both of which relate to expulsion or exclusion (J. Milgrom and D. Wright, *TDOT*, 9:232), hence the older translation, "water of separation" (KJV). The word is used to describe a woman's regular discharge (Lev. 12:2, 5; 15:19-20, 24-26). Therefore, it came to mean ritual defilement (2 Chron. 29:5, cf. v. 16 and unclean things [*ṭm'*]) and even moral corruption and impurity (Lev. 20:21; Ezra 9:11). Something that was *niddâ* made other things unclean (*ṭāmē'*, Ezek. 36:17). This water of impurity should be viewed as water for the cleansing from impurity (cf. Num. 19:9, 13, 20-21). It is equated with *mê haṭṭā't*, also translated "water of cleansing," produced with the ashes of the red heifer (Num. 19:9). The term *haṭṭā't* can mean sin and sin offering, bringing together the two contrasting ideas, as does *niddâ*. The water ritually purified someone who contacted a dead body (Num. 19:13) and items of plunder taken from the pagans. Not only were pagan lifestyles ethically impure, but also they ritually contaminated the objects the pagans used in their sinful lives. The NT declares that Christ reconciled to God even nonhuman objects (Col. 1:20) that had become alienated from God (cf. Rom. 8:20-22). [*niddâ*]

31:28 Set apart (*hărēmōtā*)—The common meaning for the word in this grammatical form is to raise something high. It is used to lift items in a literal sense (Exod. 4:16; Josh. 4:5), to lift one's hand in an oath (Gen. 14:22), in rebellion (1 Kings 11:27) or in victory (Ps. 89:42), or to raise one's voice for help (Gen. 39:15), for praise (2 Chron. 5:13), for rejoicing (1 Chron. 15:16), or in opposition (2 Kings 19:22; cf.

comments on Num. 15:30, "who sins defiantly," for the negative use of this root). More germane to our context, the term often means to take a portion, such as the fat (Lev. 4:8), from an offering to offer it to God (Lev. 2:9; 6:15; Num. 18:26, 30; cf. comments on Num. 5:9, "all the sacred contributions," for a cognate noun [*tĕrûmâ*] that has this nuance). Although offering to God implies an upward direction, in the OT the word simply means to take something away for a purpose. It can even mean to remove something from being offered to God (Dan. 8:11). In many contexts like ours it means to remove from something in order to make a contribution, such as a contribution to the congregation (2 Chron. 30:24; 35:7) and the priests and Levites (2 Chron. 35:8-9) so that they could make offerings to God. It may mean to contribute items to be used in temple worship (Ezra 8:25-27), items for construction of the tabernacle (Exod. 35:24), and land for a worship site (Ezek. 45:1). Israel was supposed to make contributions to the livelihood of the priests (Num. 18:19) and Levites (Num. 18:24) from their income. The contributions here were likewise to the priests (Num. 31:41) and Levites (Num. 31:47) who did not go to war as soldiers (Num. 1:45-47) and could not otherwise participate in the spoil. Since the term means to contribute and not necessarily to offer up to God, these contributions were for the livelihood of the priests and Levites, not particularly for sacrifices to God. [*rwm*]

32:5 As our possession (*la'ăḥuzzâ*)—This word for possession can refer to a person's or family's individual piece of purchased (Gen. 23:4) or donated (Gen. 47:11) land. It could be a town (Lev. 25:32), its houses (Lev. 25:33), and surrounding pasturelands (Lev. 25:34) held by a group such as the

Levites, or it might be the territory occupied by a nation (Gen. 36:43; 48:4; Lev. 14:34). Purchased foreign slaves might also be called *'ăḥuzzâ*, and like real estate they could be inherited (Lev. 25:45-46). Individual or family real estate could be sold and then redeemed (Lev. 25:25-27), but if it was not redeemed it must be returned in the year of Jubilee (Lev. 25:10, 13, 28). Daughters whose fathers had no sons received plots of land as sons did (Num. 27:4-7). Since God was the true owner of the land of Canaan, the Israelites were like tenants and might not permanently buy or sell their lots (Lev. 25:23-24, 34). Under God the families as a whole were the tenants (Ezek. 46:16-17), with individual members holding particular portions of the family's land (cf., e.g., Lev. 25:10, NIV, "family property"). Individuals might dedicate their holdings to the Lord whether they inherited them or temporarily purchased them (Lev. 27:16, 22). Regarding nationally occupied land, God had promised the whole land of Canaan to Abraham and his descendants (Gen. 17:8; Deut. 32:49), meaning particularly Jacob's offspring (Gen. 48:4). In the future one person, God's anointed, will hold what would normally be described as the holdings of an empire, for he will receive the whole earth as his *'ăḥuzzâ*. Our passage is the first place where the land east of the Jordan is called a possession for the nation. Although God granted (Num. 32:23) the tribes' request the Transjordan is referred to as distinct from "the Lord's land" (Josh. 22:19), at least by the western tribes. This distinction may not be valid, but may reveal an incipient divisiveness between the eastern and western tribes. The designation "the Lord's land" acknowledged that the possession was God's in reality. The NT asserts that all possessions ultimately belong to God the Son (Col. 1:16). [*'ăḥuzzâ*]

32:7 Why do you discourage (*lāmmâ tĕnî'ûn*)—Ten of the spies who had reconnoitered Canaan had discouraged Israel at Kadesh-Barnea (Num. 32:9) by making the task ahead seem impossible (Num. 13:28-29, 31-33). The verb takes the noun "heart" (*lēb*, not translated here in the NIV) as its object in the Hebrew (Num. 32:7, 9). As a result of the spies' words the people's hearts were afraid (Num. 14:9) and unbelieving (Num. 14:11), so that they grumbled against the Lord and his leadership (Num. 14:36). Recounting the Kadesh-Barnea episode later, Moses used a different verb (*hēmassû*, Deut. 1:28) to describe the same action where the spies made Israel "lose heart." This latter verbal idea is to melt and refers to loss of courage (Josh. 2:11). Often people lost courage (i.e., were discouraged) by reports of matters such as God's judgment (Ezek. 21:3-7), his spectacular intervention (Josh. 2:10-11; 5:1), the total defeat (Nahum 2:10) of a powerful military force (Josh. 2:10-11), or a slaughter (2 Sam. 17:10). They might also lose courage through the influence of a fearful companion (Deut. 20:8). The emotional and physical result of discouragement was debilitating to a military effort like the impending conquest (2 Sam. 17:10; Josh. 5:1; Isa. 13:6-8; Nahum 2:10). Israel's effort to conquer the land would not only be a divine accomplishment but also a physical and emotional effort that must overcome discouragement. In undertaking his purposes God apparently takes into account the weaknesses of the humans he will involve in the endeavor. [*nw'*]

32:11 Followed me wholeheartedly (*mil'û 'aḥărāy*)—This Hebrew expression occurs only 8x in the OT. Scripture records David (1 Kings 11:6), Joshua (Num. 32:12), and especially Caleb (Num. 14:24; 32:12; Deut.

1:36; Josh. 14:9, 14) as following the Lord wholeheartedly. Caleb's example involved exhorting Israel with a message of faith and courage not to rebel against God (Num. 13:30; 14:7-9). The results of his following wholeheartedly were the reward of entering the land although the rest of his generation would die instead (Num. 14:24) and receiving an inheritance that was large for just one family (Deut. 1:36; Josh. 14:9, 14). Solomon was an example of not following the Lord wholeheartedly, for he violated the covenant with God (1 Kings 11:11) and turned aside after other gods (1 Kings 11:6). In the cases of both Solomon and the rebellious Israelites, not following God wholeheartedly is called (in Hebrew) "the evil" (Num. 32:11, 13; 1 Kings 11:6). Punishment for not following wholeheartedly was appropriate to each party's situation: death in the wilderness without seeing the promise fulfilled (Num. 32:11) and losing the kingdom for his family and facing adversaries (1 Kings 11:6, 11, 14, 23, 26). [*ml'*]

32:13 Who had done evil (*hā'ōśeh hāra'*)— This is the first of 61 occurrences of this combination of verb and object with the definite article (the article is not usually translated). Between 80 percent and 90 percent of the occurrences refer to making (Deut. 4:25) or serving idols (e.g., 1 Kings 14:22-24; 15:26, 34; 16:25-26, 30). What lies behind this so that it is singled out as "the evil" is forsaking the Lord (Judg. 2:11-12; 3:7; 2 Chron. 29:6; Isa. 65:11-12) and violating his covenant (Deut. 17:2) so that one is not following him wholeheartedly (Num. 32:13; 1 Kings 11:6). Other specific examples of "doing the evil thing" besides idolatry are divination and sorcery, offering children as sacrifices (2 Kings 17:17; 21:6), bribery and perversion of justice (Mic. 7:2-3), choosing to do

things that displease God (Isa. 65:12; 66:4), murder and adultery (2 Sam. 12:9; Ps. 51:4), murder and stealing someone's inheritance (1 Kings 21:19-20), following the detestable practices of the Canaanites (1 Kings 14:22-24; 2 Kings 21:2), and a theocratic king's rebelling against God's clear commands (1 Sam. 15:19; Samuel compares the rebellion to other examples of "the evil thing" [1 Sam. 15:22-23]). There were relative degrees of doing the evil thing (1 Kings 16:30; 2 Kings 3:2; 17:2), and one might even "sell himself" to do it (1 Kings 21:20; 2 Kings 17:17). Of course God's wrath (Deut. 4:25; 1 Kings 16:25, 30-33) and punishment (Judg. 3:12; 6:1; Isa. 65:12-15) attended the evildoer(s). The OT sets forth only two reasons for doing the evil thing. The first was the poor example of one's parent (2 Chron. 22:3-4) and influence of one's mate (1 Kings 21:25). Both the OT and the NT warn of the potential of ungodly family members to sway a person away from the Lord (Deut. 7:3-4; 2 Cor. 6:14). It follows that the believer must exercise discernment in choosing a spouse (1 Cor. 7:39) and must evaluate the example of his or her parents. The other reason that the OT gives for doing the evil thing is that the person did not prepare his heart to seek Yahweh (2 Chron. 12:14). Therefore, God's people must make the spiritual effort to set their minds on the things of God (Col. 3:1-3). If disloyalty was the ultimate in evil, then by contrast the greatest righteous act one can do is to totally commit oneself to God (Deut. 10:12-13; Matt. 22:36-38). [*'śh hāra'*]

32:14 A brood of sinners (*tarbût 'ănāšîm ḥaṭṭā'îm*)—This Hebrew word appears only here in the OT. By its etymology it appears to be related to words in other Semitic languages (Syriac, Mandean, Arabic) for upbringing, instruction, and discipline (*HALOT*, 1787). T. Hartmann notes a similarly spelled word in Hebrew (*marbît*), and therefore perhaps a related word, that he understands as "accretion" or "second growth." He interprets our term as "younger generation" (T. Hartmann, *TLOT*, 1199). Here Moses applied the principle that children follow in the sins of their forebears (cf. 1 Kings 15:3, 25; Zech. 1:4; Acts 7:51), which may lie behind the often criticized statement that God punishes children for their father's sins (Exod. 20:5). Although Moses' assessment of these people was wrong here, unfortunately the principle holds in many cases and is repeated in the NT (cf. Matt. 23:31-33 where the "brood of vipers," hypocrites, are like their ancestors, and Luke 3:7-8 where mention of the "brood of vipers" is reason to mention one's ancestry). The expression should warn parents to take careful thought of their influence on their children and warn children not to follow in their parents' sins (Acts 7:51). [*tarbût*]

33:52 Their carved images (*maśkiyyōtām*)— This noun (*maśkît*) denotes an image or sculpture (*HALOT*, 641). In a figurative sense it refers to either a mental image (Ps. 73:7) or the faculty of making a mental image, one's imagination (Prov. 18:11). In a physical sense it can refer to a carved stone (Lev. 26:1) and a setting or engraving in precious metal (Prov. 25:11). God prohibited Israel from setting up the physical carvings or engravings for worship purposes (Lev. 26:1). Although he is not opposed to art (Exod. 25:18, 31; 1 Kings 6:23, 29, 32, 35), in this culture works of art were often worshiped, and were therefore prohibited when made for this purpose. They could not adequately represent God (Deut. 4:15-18) since he is spiritual rather than physical (Exod. 34:5-

7; Deut. 10:17). Although pagans might recognize that the images were not gods in themselves, but just representations, the prophets demeaned idolatry and spoke disparagingly of an idol as if the god were nothing more than the image (cf. Isa. 44:12-19). [*maśkît*]

Their cast idols (*ṣalmê massēkōtām*)— The root meaning of the word *ṣelem* is statue, though the term has other nuances. It can refer to a replica of a real thing (1 Sam. 6:5, 11), an idol as here, a statue (Dan. 3:18, Aramaic), something that temporarily appears (Ps. 39:6), a human likeness of one's father (Gen. 5:3) or God (Gen. 1:26; *HALOT*, 1028-29), or an engraved picture (Ezek. 23:14). The Akkadian cognate, *ṣalmu*, has the same range of nuances. Although the Hebrew word could designate an idol, it was not the usual designation (H. Wildeberger, *TLOT*, 1080-81). S. Schwertner lists the other words for idol: *'ĕlîlîm* (nothingness), *massēkâ* and *nesek* (molten image), *pesel* and *pāsîl* (sculpted image), *'ōṣeb* and *'āṣāb* (carved image), *gillûlîm* (blocks of stone), *ṣîr* (image), *maśkît* (showpiece), and *nĕśû'â* (processional image; S. Schwertner, *TLOT*, 127).

While God provides the gifts from which people make an idol, he detests the idol (Ezek. 7:20; 16:17; 23:14). Even the things made by God were not deities, so neither were those that were made by humans. God created human beings as images of himself (Gen. 1:26, 28), but these were not deities or anything to be worshiped (Isa. 31:3). So God would turn over as plunder to Israel's enemies the precious metals and stones from which they made idols (Ezek. 7:20). The command here to demolish idols in Canaan would be obeyed by Israel's kings centuries later (2 Kings 11:19). Because of God's antipathy toward an idolatrous *ṣelem*, it is fitting that in Nebuchadnezzar's dream God destroyed the ungodly world empires represented by a *ṣelem* (Dan. 2:32-35). [*ṣelem*]

Their high places (*bāmōtām*)—The term *bāmâ* can refer to topographical elevations (Deut. 32:13; 2 Sam. 1:19), hills and mountains (Mic. 1:3), waves (Job 9:8), and tops of clouds (Isa. 14:14), but here and in many places it refers to places of worship. They were often on high elevations (1 Sam. 9:19, 25; 1 Kings 14:23) where people ascended to meet their gods and their gods descended to meet their people, but they could also be in valleys (Jer. 7:31), and under luxuriant trees (1 Kings 4:23; 2 Kings 16:4). Many towns had their own high places (2 Kings 23:5) throughout Israel (1 Kings 13:32) and Judah (1 Kings 14:23), though some might be outside the town (1 Sam. 9:25) or perhaps at the city gate (2 Kings 23:8). As a worship place for gods other than Yahweh the *bāmâ* had idols and altars (Lev. 26:30), images as here, sacred stones, Asherah poles (2 Kings 17:10), and priests (1 Kings 13:2). Here people made sacrificial offerings that included burning incense (2 Kings 17:11) and burning children (Jer. 7:31; 19:5), and they offered prayers (Isa. 16:12). High places where the Lord was worshiped (1 Kings 3:4; 2 Chron. 33:17) were characterized by incense (1 Kings 22:43), prayer, priests, sacrificial offerings (1 Sam. 9:12) for the Lord, and music (1 Sam. 10:5). Both idolatrous and Yahwistic high places existed in the land after Israel entered. Godly kings destroyed some (2 Chron. 14:3, 5; 17:6) while leaving others (1 Kings 15:14; 2 Chron. 20:33), perhaps because they could be used as centers for Yahweh's worship. Because this kind of decentralized worship (2 Chron. 32:12) would not promote fidelity to the Lord, he would destroy the high places in Israel (Amos 7:9) and Judah (Ezek. 6:3-6). [*bāmâ*]

33:56 What I plan to do (*ka'ăšer dimmîtî la'ăśôt*)—This verb in this grammatical form basically means to make a comparison, but its extended meaning is to consider a thing to be like something else, to plan, or to imagine (E. Jenni, *TLOT*, 339). So the word can mean to compare someone to something (S. of S. 1:9; Lam. 2:13), to speak in comparisons ("parables," Hos. 12:10), to think or meditate on something (Ps. 48:9), to believe something (Ps. 50:21), or to intend an action (Judg. 20:5). Most often what someone intends is not fully accomplished (Judg. 20:5; 2 Sam. 21:5; Isa. 10:7, 16-18), and what someone believes about herself (Esth. 4:13) or God (Ps. 50:21) is wrong. Comparisons a person makes about God are not accurate (Isa. 40:18, 25; 46:5) or cannot be achieved (Isa. 14:14). The word itself does not necessarily imply the fruitlessness of the comparison, belief, or intention, but most uses of the word are in this type of context. The Lord thus makes the point that whatever he intends will indeed be accomplished (Isa. 14:24), which highlights the contrast between what he intends and what humans intend. In our text this is ominous for the inhabitants of Canaan and for Israelites who were unfaithful. [*dmh*]

35:2 Pasturelands (*migrāš*)—This term appears 110x in the OT, translated "pastureland(s)" 107x in the NIV ("farm lands" in 2 Chron. 31:19; "open land," Ezek. 45:2; "shorelands," Ezek. 27:28). All but one (1 Chron. 5:16) of its 105 appearances outside of Ezekiel refer to the territory around the Levitical cities (Lev. 25:34; Num. 35:3-5; Josh. 21:2). The pasturelands (*migrāš*) and fields (*śādeh*) are ordinarily distinguished (Josh. 21:11-12; 1 Chron. 6:55-56), though twice they are mentioned together as one term (Lev. 25:34; 2 Chron.

31:19 [where NIV translates "farm lands"]). The *śādeh* was thought of primarily for crop farming, whereas the *migrāš* was for animal husbandry (Num. 35:3; Josh. 14:4; 21:3). From the tithes and offerings of the citizenry the Levites would have livestock to tend and harvests to eat, but ideally they did not need to cultivate fields. When Israel ceased to provide for the Levites for their ministry, the latter would turn to their lands as *śādeh* to cultivate crops and provide a living for their families (Neh. 13:10). What is of theological interest is the fact that God provided for his ministers to have a means to support themselves if his people did not support them. He did this with the very land that the congregation should have stocked for them. The NT teaches that the church should support its leaders materially (1 Cor. 9:6-14; 1 Tim. 5:17-18.), but they may have their own means of support if for some reason their right to or opportunity for support is set aside (Acts 18:3; 1 Cor. 4:12). [*migrāš*]

35:6 Cities of refuge (*miqlāṭ*)—This word for refuge is used only for cities that provided asylum (Num. 35; Josh. 20–21; 1 Chron. 6:27, 37). It is absent in Deut. 19, but the subject is the same. The altar was the original place of asylum (Exod. 21:13-14; cf. 1 Kings 2:28-29). The six cities would all be ones set aside for the Levites (Num. 35:6) who were commissioned to teach and uphold the laws (Deut. 33:10), including this one. Asylum was available only for those who committed accidental manslaughter (Num. 35:11), not murderers (Deut. 19:12-13). The accused person's city of origin would try the homicide case (Num. 35:24-25; Josh. 20:5), but the elders of the city of refuge would hear him to see if he had a case for innocence (Josh. 20:4). If so, they would grant asylum until the trial (Num. 35:12) and after a verdict of innocence. In Israel it was important to distinguish intentional murder from involuntary manslaughter (A. Hill, *NIDOTTE*, 2:1089). This system helped curb killing from rage (Deut. 19:6), killing the innocent (Deut. 19:10), and slaying by an unjust avenger (R. Schmid, *TDOT*, 8:553). Therefore, anyone who committed accidental manslaughter must have easy access (Deut. 19:2-3, 6). Killing people, who were made in the image of God, remains an intensely serious matter (cf. Gen. 9:6). [*miqlāṭ*]

A person who has killed someone (*hārōṣēaḥ*)—This Hebrew word for killing is not one of the more common ones (e.g., *mût*, *hārag*, *nākâ*). The sixth commandment prohibits it (Exod. 20:13; Deut. 5:17) although Israel later on disobeyed the command regularly (Jer. 7:9; Hos. 4:2). The word describes premeditated murder (Num. 35:20-21) and accidental homicide (Num. 35:11, 22-26; Deut. 4:42; 19:3-6; Josh. 20:3, 5). Of the two types of killing, the sixth commandment prohibits murder, since little can prohibit an accident. The word does not refer to killing in war, and as for capital punishment in our passage, *mût* is preferred (Num. 35:19, 21; Deut. 19:12; cf. 19:6 where *nākâ* is preferred). Of the 2x it is used for capital punishment, once (Num. 35:27) the verb describes killing one whose trial verdict is innocent. Had the accused not violated the rules of asylum, this would be murder; so the word is associated with this kind of killing. The second time the word refers to capital punishment is the only time it refers to the result of a trial in which the defendant was guilty (Num. 35:30). With this one exception, the word describes private (not public as in war or for treason), illegal (without a trial) killing, especially murder. The NIV

436

prefers to translate the word in reference to the accidental killer as the "accused" (Num. 35:12, 25, 27-28). God used this word for Naboth's death (1 Kings 21:19) to express contempt for the court's injustice. The term in reference to an animal as murderer is sarcasm toward the sluggard who gives ridiculous excuses not to work (Prov. 22:13). [rṣḥ]

35:16 The murderer shall be put to death (môt yûmat hārōṣēaḥ)—The Hebrew expression is emphatic, "shall surely be put to death." Of the 49x that the emphatic "shall surely die/be put to death" appears in the OT, 37 were ordered by God (as here) or his prophet (2 Kings 1:4, 6, 16; 8:10), and 25 are in the legal prescriptions of the Law. The expression is used most frequently in punishing murder (Exod. 21:12-14; Lev. 24:17; Num. 35:16-18, 31) and sexual offenses: adultery, homosexual acts, and bestiality (Exod. 22:18; Lev. 20:10-13, 15-16; the incest mentioned is also adultery), but it is also prescribed for cursing and hitting parents (Exod. 21:15, 17; Lev. 20:9), kidnapping and selling a person (Exod. 21:16), desecrating the Sabbath (Exod. 31:14-15; Num. 15:35), blaspheming God (Lev. 24:16), participating in the occult (Lev. 20:27), and offering a child sacrifice (Lev. 20:2). Judging from the penalty that was decreed, life, liberty, loyalty to God, and family were vital concerns in the society established by Yahweh. Outside the Law God pronounces this judgment on those who disregard the whole Law even on matters that are not ordinarily capital offenses (Ezek. 18:10-13). When God warned someone that he would surely die, others could exhort the condemned to repent (Ezek. 3:18; 33:8), and God might spare him (Ezek. 33:14). [mwt]

35:19 The avenger (gō'ēl)—This word is commonly translated "redeemer" (Job 19:25). Its basic concept is to reestablish original conditions. Redemption of property, slaves, and [levirate] marriage was intended to restore the family's wholeness (J. Stamm, TLOT, 289-90). The nearest relative had first responsibility and right to redeem property that was sold (Lev. 25:25; Ruth 3:12-13; 4:4). The relative was called a gō'ēl even if he did not redeem it (Ruth 4:8), so that the term took the weakened sense of a near relative (Lev. 25:25 [NIV, "nearest relative"]; Num. 5:8; Ruth 3:12 [NIV, "near of kin"]). The OT points out that a near relative should (1) redeem someone who sold himself into indentured servitude (Lev. 25:47-49), (2) care for his relatives (Ruth 3:13, cf. v. 9), especially the aged (Ruth 4:14-15), and (3) initiate and pursue justice when a relative was killed (Num. 35:12, 19, 21; Deut. 19:6; Josh. 20:9; in conjunction with the eyewitnesses he must execute capital punishment [cf. Deut. 17:7; 19:12]). Because of the relative's commitment to the family he should receive restitution on behalf of a deceased relative (Num. 5:8). As the divine gō'ēl God redeems slaves (Exod. 6:6), exiles (Isa. 48:20), individuals' land (Prov. 23:11), and he avenges his people (Isa. 63:4). His example of taking up the case of his people (Ps. 119:154; Prov. 23:11; Jer. 50:34; Lam. 3:58) is a pattern for relatives. A person may redeem himself (Lev. 25:47-49) and his own property (Lev. 25:26), animal (Lev. 27:13), or house (Lev. 27:15), but the relative was usually responsible. God was a relative by covenant only, although Christ's incarnation adds a flesh and blood dimension to his relationship (Heb. 2:14-16). When God redeemed it was in love and mercy (Isa. 63:9) and by power (Exod. 6:6; Isa. 49:26). He redeemed from harm (Gen. 48:16), enemies (Ps. 107:2), oppression, violence (Ps. 72:14), and death (Ps. 103:4). Therefore, his people ought to take comfort (Isa. 52:9) and not fear (Isa. 43:1). [gō'ēl]

35:20 With malice aforethought (bĕśin'â)—This is the word for hatred, a term of emotion (E. Jenni, *TLOT*, 1277) and relationship (*HALOT*, 1339). It ranges from a sense of aggravation and irritation (1 Kings 22:8; Prov. 25:17) to dissatisfaction and lack of preference (Gen. 29:31, 33; Deut. 22:13; 24:3), to lack of concern (Prov. 13:24), to belittling (Judg. 14:16), to shunning and avoidance (Judg. 11:15; 19:7), to contempt, disdain, and disgust (Ps. 50:17; 119:104; 139:22; Prov. 5:12; Ezek. 23:28), to envious hostility (Gen. 26:27, cf. v. 14; Judg. 11:7), to complete rejection and revulsion (Judg. 15:2; 2 Sam. 13:15; Ps. 26:5), and to dangerous and murderous animosity (Gen. 37:5, 8; 2 Sam. 13:22; Prov. 9:7-8; 29:10). It is right—in the sense of complete rejection and revulsion—to hate evil ways (Ps. 119:104), sin (Ps. 36:2), dishonest gain (Exod. 18:21), bribes (Prov. 15:27), pride (Prov. 8:13), lying, and conspiracy (Prov. 8:17). It is proper—in the senses of shunning and being disgusted with, and even rejecting—to hate disloyal people (Ps. 119:113), their faithless deeds (Ps. 101:3), idolaters (Ps. 31:6), and the violent (Ps. 11:5). God prohibits hatred for other Israelites (Lev. 19:17)—apparently at the level of lack of concern or interest—commanding them to help those who hate them (Exod. 23:5) and to try to move them to repentance (Lev. 19:17; Prov. 25:21). At the highest levels of feeling hatred leads to the desire to harm someone (Deut. 30:7; Esth. 9:1; Ps. 41:7), and becomes motive for murder, as here (cf. Deut. 4:42; 19:4, 6, 11). If it could be demonstrated that the accused hated (intended to harm) the vic-

tim, then by definition the victim's death was a murder. [śin'â]

35:24 The assembly must judge (šāpĕṭû hā'ēdâ)—This verb's (šāpaṭ) nuances include evaluating (Isa. 5:3), making something right or what it ought to be (Gen. 16:5; 31:53; Ps. 96:13; 98:9), settling disputes (Exod. 18:16; 1 Sam. 7:16-17), leading (Judg. 16:31; 1 Sam. 4:18), and ruling (Dan. 9:12; Isa. 40:23). The basic concept is to act to restore proper order to a community after it has been disturbed, which action, if prolonged, amounts to controlling or ruling (*HALOT*, 1623). In the matter of settling disputes to restore the proper order, judging may involve upholding one person and condemning another (1 Sam. 24:15), stating a case against someone (Ezek. 20:4; 22:2), giving a verdict (1 Kings 8:32; Eccl. 3:17), executing a sentence (2 Sam. 18:19, 31; Isa. 11:4) that involved punishing (Ezek. 16:38; Joel 3:12) on one hand and defending, delivering (Ps. 10:18; Prov. 31:8-9) or vindicating (Ps. 35:24) on the other. Judges must settle disputes by utilizing God's laws (Exod. 18:16; Num. 35:24; Ezek. 44:24) with impartiality and fearlessness (Lev. 19:15; Deut. 1:16), with righteousness (Ps. 9:8; 50:6), and without bribes (Deut. 16:19) or any injustice (2 Chron. 19:6-7). Each town and city must appoint judges (Deut. 16:18; 17:9; 2 Chron. 19:5-7) to work with priests (Deut. 17:9; 19:17) and elders (Deut. 21:2) to settle disputes. Levites would be assigned this responsibility (1 Chron. 23:3-4; 26:29). Judges were leading officials (Josh. 8:33; 1 Chron. 26:29; Ezra 10:14). They must thoroughly examine a case and the witnesses (Deut. 19:18) and—at least in some cases—oversee punishment (Deut. 25:2). Contempt of court was a capital offense (Deut. 17:12). Individuals were assigned as judges (Exod. 18:22, 26), but in our passage the congregation judged. Some individuals were called judges whose responsibilities included military (Judg. 2:16, 18) and spiritual (Judg. 2:17) leadership (though many dispute the second fact). These people in the period before Israel had a king would try to restore the proper social and spiritual conditions—thus their title. Those who governed were responsible to restore and maintain what is right, and so were called judges (Ps. 82:1-8). At the divine level God is a ruler who judges (Gen. 18:25; Ps. 18:25; 50:6) the entire earth (Ps. 58:11; 94:2). [*špṭ*]

35:33 Do not <u>pollute</u> the land (*lō' taḥănîpû 'et hā'āreṣ*)—This verb (*ḥnp*) appears 9x referring to the land, twice to people (Jer. 23:11; Dan. 11:32), and with three derivatives (*ḥānēp, ḥōnep, ḥănupâ*). K. Seybold shows that in regard to people the OT connects the basic concept to false speech (Prov. 11:9; Isa. 9:17; 32:6; Jer. 23:15) and he concludes that the term basically means deceitful and distorted (K. Seybold, *TDOT*, 5:38). Thus, it describes people who were dishonest (Job 15:34), destroyed others with their speech (Prov. 11:9), spoke things they ought not (Isa. 9:17), spread error about God (Isa. 32:6), encouraged sinful lifestyles by their words (Jer. 23:15), mocked those who were good (Ps. 35:16), and clung stubbornly to their sin (Job 36:13). These people forgot God (Job 8:13), could not appear before him (Job 13:16), and would be destroyed by him (Job 8:13; 27:8). As for defiling the land, people polluted it by disobeying God's laws (Isa. 24:5), acting unfaithfully toward him (Jer. 3:2, 9), treating marriage and divorce lightly (Jer. 3:1; cf. Deut. 24:4), and, as here, shedding the blood of the innocent (Ps. 106:38) and the victims of war (Mic. 4:11). These practices distorted and thus defiled, corrupted, and polluted the purposes of the land for God's kingdom. He intended Israel to establish a wise and law-abiding society that would be an example to the world of what it was like to be in relation to him (cf. Deut. 4:6-8). Yahweh disdains distortion of the order he established (cf. Rom. 1:26-27). [*ḥnp*]

36:4 The Year of Jubilee (*hayyōbēl*)—The Hebrew word can mean "ram," and when used with "shofar" (*šôpār*; Josh. 6:4, 6, 8, 13), "horn" (*qeren*, Josh. 6:5), or "blast" (*māšak*, Exod. 19:13) the term denotes a ram's horn or trumpet (*HALOT*, 398). Sounding the ram's horn began the fiftieth year (following seven cycles of seven years), hence the year's name (Lev. 25:8-10). Indentured servants were released at the Jubilee (Lev. 25:10, 40-41, 54) or after six years (Exod. 21:2), whichever made for a shorter term (i.e., if the two passages are to be reconciled). Servants were freed, purchased land was returned to the original owner's family (Lev. 25:10, 13) if it had not already been redeemed (Lev. 25:25-28), and all land was left fallow (Lev. 25:11). Since the forty-nineth year was a sabbatical year for the land, this made two fallow years in a row. This would either provoke disobedience or stimulate faith in God's promise that the harvest before a sabbatical year would last for three years (Lev. 25:20-22). Instead of beginning in the first month just before grain harvest, the Jubilee year began in the seventh month (Lev. 25:9) following the season normally designated for grain and fruit harvests. This facilitated calculating land prices, since they were based on harvest values for the years between Jubilees (Lev. 25:16). The timing of the commencement of Jubilee was profitable for masters of indentured servants, since masters would no longer need the servants to gather the harvest. The timing also was favorable for the indentured servants, for they would be returning to their own land shortly before planting the crop that would be harvested in the spring. The stipulated practices for the Jubilee were intended to prevent a widening separation between economic classes, to provide social and economic freedom, and to promote faith. The NT points out the problems in this socio-economic condition as well (Jas. 2:1-12). In our context, only purchased land returned to the original owner's family, not land passed out of the family by inheritance (J. Milgrom, *Numbers*, 297). [*yôbēl*]

DEUTERONOMY

Eugene H. Merrill

1:5 This law *(hattôrā hazzō't)*—Though the term "torah" frequently is synonymous with the entire Pentateuch, especially in the NT (Matt. 5:17; 11:13; 22:40; Luke 24:44; Acts 13:15; Rom. 3:21), its usage here is much more restricted, referring to the book of Deuteronomy itself as the demonstrative pronoun "this" makes clear. The same phrase occurs elsewhere in the book with the same nuance (cf. 4:8; 17:18, 19; 27:3, 8, 26; 28:58; 31:12, 24; etc.). The nominal derives from the verb *yārâ*, "to teach" (KBL, 403), thus *tôrâ* means essentially instruction, not law. The confusion between the two arose in good measure through the Greek (LXX and NT) translation of *tôrâ* by *nomos*, "law," a translation reflecting the content of the Pentateuch, which, indeed, consists largely of "legal" material. [*tôrâ*]

1:8 Possess the land *(rĕšû)*—The base meaning of the verb is "to take possession of," that is, "to acquire as one's own" (*BDB*, 439), usually in a violent manner (KBL, 406-07). In the context of the occupation of Canaan by Israel as the fulfillment of covenant promises to the patriarchs (cf. Gen. 13:15-17; 15:18-21; 17:8), the thought is more that of coming into inheritance, that is, occupying land that one already owns by virtue of legal provisions previously made. This is particularly the case when it occurs with the verb *šb'* ("swear") with God as subject, as here: "possess the land which the Lord has sworn," etc. As a covenant renewal text, Deuteronomy is replete with references to this theme of Israel's right to the land, a right granted by God's solemn oath. This permits the use of whatever means are available to root out the populations of the land who are regarded as illegal squatters (cf. 6:10, 18; 7:13; 8:1; 9:5; 11:21, 31; etc.). [*yrš*]

The Lord swore *(nišba')*—This verb occurs most commonly (as here) in a stem that suggests a self-directed commitment. That is, one binds himself to a course of action by making a pledge to do one thing or another. Here Yahweh is said to have promised the land of Canaan to Israel (cf. v. 7), a promise reiterated later in Deuteronomy (1:35; 6:10, 18, 23; 7:13; 8:1; 10:11; 11:9, 21; 26:15; 28:11; 30:20; 31:7, 20, 21, 23; 34:4) and elsewhere (Josh. 1:6; 5:6; 21:43; Judg. 2:1; Jer. 32:22). This renewed pledge is based on the promise made originally to the patriarchs that the land they inhabited would someday be the home of their descendants (cf. Gen. 13:17; 15:18-21; 17:8; 26:2-4). [*šb'*]

To their seed *(lĕzar'ām)*—Besides the mundane use of this word to describe

441

crops and crop seeds, there is the metaphorical meaning of offspring, particularly human progeny (Num. 14:24; 1 Sam. 20:42; 24:21). Of special interest is the promised seed of the woman who would someday crush the serpent's head (Gen. 3:15) and the seed (plural) of the patriarchs who were the recipients and bearers of the covenant promises from generation to generation (Gen. 12:7; 13:15, 16; 15:18; 17:7; 26:3-4; Deut. 4:37; 10:15; 11:9; 30:19; Rom. 4:13, 16; 9:7; Gal. 3:16, 29). Moses here equates the nation Israel with the seed of the patriarchs. The Lord had delighted in (*ḥšq;* cf. 7:7) and loved (*'hb;* cf. 4:37) them and had fulfilled his promises to them by choosing (*bḥr* cf. 4:37) their seed, Israel. [*zera'*]

1:10 Has multiplied you (*hirbâ*)—The subject of the verb here is "Yahweh your God" so the point is that Israel's great population on the eve of the conquest must be attributed not to natural causes but to Yahweh's gracious intervention (10:22; cf. Gen. 46:27). The verb stem also underscores this causative idea; i.e., growth and every other blessing comes about as God ordains it in line with some purpose of his. In this case, the patriarchs had been told before time that their descendants would be numerous (Gen. 15:5; 22:17; 26:4), a promise much in line with the mandate of creation itself (Gen. 1:28; cf. 9:1). [*rbh*]

1:11 Bless you (*wîbārēk 'etkem*)—This verb, which occurs almost exclusively in the Hebrew stem suggesting a condition or state, means generally "to gift somebody, something with fortunate power" (thus KBL, 153), or the like. In the context of its usage here (vv. 9-18) it has to do with the multiplication of the people of Israel from the 70 who had descended into Egypt

with Jacob (Exod. 1:1-5) to the multiplied thousands who, Jethro had said, would wear Moses down unless he had help in meeting their needs (cf. Exod. 18:18-24). This phenomenal increase in population, while presenting practical problems of administration, was a direct result of blessings promised centuries earlier to Israel's ancestors (Gen. 12:2; 17:16; 22:17; 26:3-4, 24; cf. M. Brown, *NIDOTTE*, 1:759). [*brk*]

1:12 Your burden (*ṭorḥăkem*)—This rare noun derives from the verb *ṭrḥ,* to toil, or the like (KBL, 356). The verb occurs in Job 37:11 to speak of the Lord loading down the clouds with moisture. The only other use of the noun is by Isaiah who describes Israel's hypocritical observance of sacrifices, rituals, and festivals as a heavy burden to the Lord (Isa. 1:14). He is tired of putting up with them. Here Moses complains that he can no longer bear up under the incessant problems and struggles of the people. He therefore advises them to select others who, under himself, can share leadership responsibilities. [*ṭoraḥ*]

1:13 Wise, insightful, and well-known *ḥăkāmîm ûnĕbōnîm wîdu'îm*)—There are two main qualifications for leadership here—to know and to be known. The latter (from the verb *yāda',* "to know") simply suggests reputation, implicitly, of course, good reputation (*BDB*, 394). Leaders should be persons with whom the community is acquainted and in whom it can have confidence (cf. v. 15). The most important asset in this context—one of assisting Moses in counseling and adjudication—is intelligence, especially in terms of discernment and discretion. The wise (*ḥākām*) person has administrative skills such as those of Joseph (Gen. 41:33, 39), David (2 Sam. 14:20), and Solomon (1 Kings 2:9; 3:12;

5:12). The one with insight (*bînâ*) is also wise (*ḥokmâ* and *bînâ* occur as synonyms; cf. Prov. 1:2; 4:5, 7; 9:10; 16:16; Job 28:28), but here the wisdom has more to do with good common sense in dealing with people and their problems, that which comes with experience. [*ḥākām, bînâ, yd'*]

1:16 Fairly (*ṣedeq*)—Used adverbially here to describe the manner in which Israel's judges were to render their decisions, the root meaning of the noun and its cognates has to do with righteousness (*BDB*, 841-43). Though common in legal settings (cf. Lev. 19:15; Deut. 16:18; Prov. 8:15), it also speaks of persons (the Messiah, Isa. 11:4-5), places (Jerusalem, Isa. 1:26), and of moral and ethical behavior (Prov. 1:3; Isa. 64:5; Dan. 9:24). Even God and His ways are characterized as being fair or just or righteous (Job 8:3; 36:3; Ps. 85:11; 96:13; Jer. 11:20). Fundamentally *ṣdq* in its various forms has to do with a standard of behavior that God himself has established as a guideline and, in the covenant community of Israel, one that was to provide the basis for all interpersonal relationships as well as relationship to God (D. Reimer, *NIDOTTE*, 3:746). In this immediate context the meaning of the noun is nuanced by its describing fairness as not showing partiality toward the great over the small or not being intimidated by the powerful who might try to "throw their weight around" (v. 17). To be fair in judgment, then, is to adhere to divine standards and not to human pressures or demands. [*ṣedeq*]

Resident alien (*gēr*)—The technical Hebrew term for foreigner is *nokrî* (cf. Deut. 14:21), a term suggesting one with no resident status in Israel and with no religious affiliation with the covenant people. The resident alien (or sojourner), on the other hand, enjoyed all the rights and responsibilities of a native-born Israelite except perhaps for his likelihood of being the victim of discrimination because of his foreign origins. He must, therefore, be protected by the community along with the orphan and widow (Exod. 22:21; 23:9; Deut. 24:17; 27:19; Ps. 146:9; Jer. 7:6; 22:3; Ezek. 22:7, 29; Mal. 3:5). Israel should be particularly sensitive to this because she was once a sojourner in Egypt (Gen. 15:13; Exod. 22:21; 23:9; Lev. 19:34; Deut. 23:7). In a more universal sense, all people are resident aliens on the earth, a point made by the psalmist (Ps. 119:19). All people, therefore, are "not really at home" and need divine provision and protection. [*gēr*]

1:17 You shall not show partiality (*takkîrû pānîm*)—The idiom here may be rendered literally, "You shall (not) allow faces to be recognized." That is, in the administration of justice the judge must not pay any more attention to one person than another. He must not be swayed by the office, wealth, social status, power, or any other consideration likely to impress him and induce him to render an unjust verdict. An equivalent idiom is *nāśā' pānîm* ("lift up the face"), that is, show favoritism (cf. Lev. 19:15; Job 13:8, 10; 34:19; Ps. 82:2; Prov. 18:5), something of which the Lord himself is not guilty (Deut. 10:17). (H. Ringgren, *TDOT*, 9:431-32). [*nkr, pānîm*]

Judgment (*mišpāṭ*)—A derivative of the verb *špṭ*, "to judge," this noun conveys the idea of both a legal process and a legal consequence or verdict. In the former case, a judgment is a duly constituted apparatus whereby matters for adjudication can be presented to those in authority whose responsibility it is to see that justice is done. Judgment is also the result of the legal proceedings of the court whether positive or negative as far as the accused is concerned. It is the decision as to guilt or innocence, though generally *mišpāṭ* connotes unfavorable outcomes. In addition, *mišpāṭ* , especially in Deuteronomy and in the plural, is a technical term for laws and statutes, particularly in covenant documents (cf. Deut. 4:1, 5, 8, 14, 45; 5:1, 31; 6:1; etc.). The present passage has in mind the narrow setting of legal procedure as the reference to judges (*šōpēṭ îm*, v. 16) and the hearing of cases (v. 17) make clear (for similar uses cf. 16:18-19; 24:17; Job 14:3; Isa. 3:14; Ezek. 16:38). Of particular interest here is the use of the definite article with both occurrences of *mišpāṭ* . Persons must not be favored in *the* judgment for *the* judgment is God's. That is, these are formal occasions of litigation—not unofficial or ad hoc—where all legal authority is grounded in the reality of God's person and presence (cf. 2 Chron. 19:6). [*špṭ > mišpāṭ*]

1:21 Dismayed (*tēḥāt)*)—The intensity of emotion communicated by this verb is seen in its connection in this verse, with "fear" (Heb. *tîrā'*; for other passages combining these verbs see Deut. 31:8; Josh. 8:1; 10:25; 1 Sam. 17:11; Jer. 23:4; 30:10; Ezra 2:6) as well as in its common meaning "to be shattered" (*BDB*, 369). To be dismayed can result in brokenness of spirit and resolve, a paralysis that makes it impossible to go on. In most situations where the exhortation is to be not dismayed, the basis for enduring whatever comes is the presence of the Lord (Deut. 31:8; Josh. 1:9; 1 Chron. 28:20). [*ḥtt*]

1:26 You rebelled (*wattamĕrû*)—In both its attested stems this verb suggests disobedience (*BDB*, 598; KBL, 565), almost always against God (for an exception, see Deut. 21:18, 20). In addition to a number of instances where the rebellion is associated with a general attitude of insubordination (cf. Isa. 1:20; Jer. 4:17; 5:23), many others (as here) speak more narrowly of covenant violation, that is, refusal to abide by the terms of the agreement by which Israel had become God's servant people (Exod. 19:5, 8). This rebellion was especially characteristic of Israel in the Sinai wanderings (Num. 20:24; 27:14; Deut. 1:43; 9:23; Ps. 107:11; Ezek. 20:8, 13, 21) but marked them as well throughout their subsequent history (1 Sam. 12:15; Isa. 1:20; Lam. 1:18, 20). Rebellion against the Lord is, for the most part, stated in terms of rebellion against his word or his commandments. The phrase here (lit., "rebel against the mouth" of the Lord) is common in Deuteronomy (cf. 1:43; 8:3; 9:23), not surprising in light of this book's covenant nature (cf. L. Schwienhorst, *TDOT*, 9:5-10). [*mrh*]

1:27 You complained (*tērāgĕnû*)—The verb stem used here suggests a kind of reciprocal action, that is, the communication of a group of people among themselves. Thus, the grumbling, murmuring, or complaining, though ultimately directed against the LORD and his servant Moses, is carried on in their tents. There, somewhat privately they thought, the rebels of Israel vented their frustrations. The verb occurs most commonly in the Wisdom Literature where the nuance is more the idea of slandering. Persons who do this are divisive (Prov. 16:28), but their tidbits of information are often swallowed by others as so much delicacy (Prov. 18:8). Once they desist from such activity, however, these complainers allow contention to come to an end (Prov. 26:20). Isaiah says there is hope even for such troublemakers when the Lord accomplishes his full redemption (Isa. 29:24). [*rgn*]

Hated (*bĕśin'at*)—The verb "to hate"

clearly bears the normal meaning of "detest," "despise," and the like throughout the OT (e.g., Num. 10:35; 2 Sam. 22:41; Job 31:29; Ps. 44:7; Prov. 8:36), but in covenant literature such as Deuteronomy the idea is not so much a visceral reaction against someone—especially against God—but a refusal to choose by elective grace or a rejection of one to whom loyalty and/or obedience is expected. It is the antonym of "to love" (*'hb*), a term now known to be a technical way of speaking of covenant election and fidelity (P. Els, *NIDOTTE*, 1:279-81). Thus, the Lord says that he loved Jacob but hated Esau (Mal. 1:2-3), the idea being that he chose Jacob as the covenant beneficiary but did not choose Esau. In its rebellion against the LORD in the desert, Israel interpreted its difficult situation there as a sign that the Lord "hated" them, that is, that he had broken his covenant with them and thus left them to their own devices. This, of course, was not the case at all. To the contrary, the Lord had demonstrated his love to Israel and would continue to do so (Deut. 4:37; 7:13; 10:15; 23:5). [*śn'*]

To destroy us (*lĕhašmîdēnû*)—Next to the verb *ḥrm* (cf. 2:34), which has the special sense of being set apart by the Lord for annihilation, this is one of the strongest terms to suggest total destruction. It is common in Deuteronomy, especially with God as subject, as here (cf. 2:21, 22; 4:3; 6:15; 7:4; 9:3, 8, 14, 19, 20, 25; 28:48; 31:3, 4). The result of such destruction is extermination—nothing is left. This is brought about mainly as a consequence of sin, especially the sin of the Lord's people against him. (G. Hall, *NIDOTTE*, 4:151-52). [*šmd*]

1:28 Our brothers have made our hearts melt (*hēmassû*)—The verb (usually in the Niphal) is used literally to speak of the

melting or dissolving of manna (Exod. 16:21) and wax (Ps. 68:2) but metaphorically of the human heart, usually through fear. Rahab of Jericho told the Israelite spies that the hearts of her countrymen had melted at the news of the Exodus (Josh. 2:11; cf. 5:1). This is a common idiom elsewhere to speak of fear in the face of enemy attack (Josh. 7:5; 2 Sam. 17:10; Isa. 13:7; 19:1; Ezek. 21:7). Fear of this kind is contagious and demoralizing so those prone to it should be discharged from military service for the good of the whole army. [*mss*]

1:29 Tremble (*tă'arṣûn)*)—Like *tēḥāt* (v. 21), this verb occurs with "fear" (*tîrā'*) to emphasize that emotion by drawing attention to its physical manifestation (cf. Deut. 31:6; Josh. 1:9). Even if one is so terrified as to shake, God's presence ought to be sufficient to produce not only a sense of calm confidence but even a measure of boldness to pursue the task at hand (cf. Deut. 7:21; 20:3). [*'rṣ*]

1:32 Believe (*ma'ămînîm)*—The root meaning of this verb is to confirm, that is, to give support to someone or something (*BDB*, 52). The form here is causative, suggesting that to believe is to act on the basis of something that is supportable or susceptible to confirmation. When the object is the Lord, all reason for doubt ought to disappear, for He is absolutely trustworthy. He can be believed because He has confirmed His reliability in history and in the personal experience of those who trust Him. Related to this is the idea of God's faithfulness, something Moses will address later in Deuteronomy (cf. 7:9). Remarkably, the verb occurs only twice in the book, here and in 9:23. Here it speaks of Israel's lack of confidence that God could take them into the promised land, the same issue Moses addresses in 9:23. Lack of faith, the context shows, is not just weakness but a sign of willful rebellion against the Lord (v. 24). ['mn]

1:34 Was angry *(wayyiqṣōp)*—One of a number of verbs expressing anger (cf. 'np in v. 37), this occurs with both a human and divine subject. Though God's anger is expressed in human terms, it is devoid of human motivation and lack of control. It is not "loss of temper" or a rage over which God has no control. It is nevertheless real anger, not to be explained away as a mere attempt to account for his acts of judgment. The cause of the Lord's anger here is Israel's pattern of unbelief and rebellion ever since the majority report of the spies who said the Canaanite cities were beyond Israel's capacity to conquer (vv. 26-33; cf. Num. 14:1-4). The verb with God as subject occurs again in Deut. 9:19, this time as a description of his reaction to the apostasy of the golden calf. So severe was God's wrath that Moses feared that he would destroy the whole nation including Aaron (9:20). In the same passage (Deut. 9:7) the verb is in the causative stem, which makes clear that the Lord's anger was provoked by the behavior of his people. It is not something inherent in the character of God, but a reaction to human sinfulness and disloyalty. [qṣp]

1:36 That he trod upon *(dārak)*—In addition to the self-evident meaning of simply placing the foot upon the ground by walking (Job 22:15), crushing grapes (Judg. 9:27; Job 24:11; Isa. 16:10), and the like, the verb is used metaphorically to suggest conquest and domination. Wherever Israel treads in the promised land, that place will belong to her as though subdued and conquered by her (Deut. 11:24-25; Josh. 1:3; 14:9). Eschatologically, God's people will prevail, a triumph pictured in terms of placing the feet on the necks or backs of those resistant to his lordship (Isa. 63:2, 3; Jer. 25:30; Amos 4:13; Mic. 1:3). In the present passage the promise to Caleb is that he will be given a special inheritance in Canaan because he had trodden upon the land and, in a sense, claimed it when he went to spy it out and, in great faith, brought back a positive report (Num. 14:24; Josh. 14:6-15). See E. Merrill, *NIDOTTE*, 1:992. [drk]

1:37 Was angry *(hit'annap)*—Unlike qṣp (v. 34), this verb attests only a divine subject, therefore having special theological significance. As the context here intimates, qṣp and 'np are synonymous though the latter, cognate to the noun 'ap, anger (cf. Deut. 9:19), may connote more of a physical manifestation of one's angry disposition (E. Johnson, *TDOT*, 1:351). The object of God's anger here is Moses and its cause was Moses' own intemperate rage, which led him to strike the rock for water rather than merely to speak to it (Num. 20:8-13). The consequence was Moses' inability to enter Canaan. The same incident using the same verb is related in Deut. 4:21, but its occurrence elsewhere in the book describes the Lord's anger at Israel because of the idolatry of the golden calf (9:8), and especially at Aaron the priest (v. 20), who not only had not prevented the worship of the image but had, in fact, participated in its manufacture (Exod. 32:1-6). Other occasions of God's anger are the anticipated wickedness of Israel in the future (1 Kings 8:46), his wrath toward Solomon for his apostasy (1 Kings 11:9), and his overall reaction to Israel's long history of covenant disobedience (2 Kings 17:18). ['np]

1:38 Encourage (him) *(ḥazzēq)*—Commonly translated be strong, be firm, and the like (cf. Deut. 11:8), this verb, in the stem used here, has the idea of bringing someone into a condition of real or perceived strength; i.e., encouraging him. Joshua, Moses' attendant, was about to succeed his master as leader of the nation. He obviously felt inadequate for the task and therefore needed to be assured that he had the requisite abilities (cf. Deut. 3:28; Josh. 1:5-7). Usually the verb occurs with a human subject—as Moses here encouraging Joshua—but God also can be invoked to provide encouragement as Samson did in his dying prayer (Judg. 16:28). David urged his messenger to encourage Joab after the latter had placed Uriah the Hittite in such a perilous position that he was slain in battle (2 Sam. 11:25). Isaiah, mocking the feeble efforts of Babylonian idolmakers, says that they must encourage one another lest their handiwork come crashing to the ground (Isa. 41:7). Theologically, the idea of encouragement is the offering of assurance by one person to another that he or she can be made able to accomplish the task at hand (R. Wakely, *NIDOTTE*, 2:70). [*ḥzq*]

1:43 You were presumptuous *(wattāzīdû)*—Cognate to the noun *zādôn*, presumption, arrogance (cf. Deut. 17:12), the verb in the stem employed here has the meaning, to act presumptuously (KBL, 254; cf. Deut. 17:13; 18:20). The same meaning is evident in its meaning in the base (Qal) stem (Exod. 18:11). The presumption is in one's thinking that he or she can accomplish anything significant without God or, worse still, in attempting to work against him (Jer. 50:29). Such thinking is irrational, the product of impulse or overbearing emotion. Such an idea may be seen in the use of the verb to describe Jacob's pot of soup that he brought to a boil before serving it to his brother (Gen. 25:29). It also speaks of the frame of mind that would impel a man to murder his fellow human being with full intent and purpose, disregarding the consequences (Exod. 21:14). How much more serious was Israel's history of arrogantly ignoring the covenant requirements of the Lord (Neh. 9:16, 29) (J. Scharbert, *TDOT*, 4:48). [*zyd*]

2:5 Engage in conflict *(titgārû)*—This verb derives from a root meaning "stir up, be excited" (*BDB*, 173), usually in a hostile manner. The verb form suggests almost a self-induced frenzy. It occurs only in this chapter in Deuteronomy (vv. 5, 9, 19, 24). Three times Israel is told not to contend for the potential enemies are Edom (i.e., Esau, v. 5), Moab (v. 9), and Ammon (v. 19), all related to Israel by common ancestry and all recipients of their lands by divine allotment. Only the Amorites can be attacked (v. 24) for they are considered illegitimate occupants of the land. [*grh*]

2:7 Your walking *(lektĕkâ)*—Walking is frequently a metaphor in the OT to speak of one's manner of life. That is, human life and experience consists of a pilgrimage in which one is headed to some kind of destination whether pleasant or dreadful (Exod. 16:4; Lev. 26:3; Deut. 8:6; 11:22-25). The meaning here is clearly literal; i.e., Israel did in fact walk through the deserts for 40 years, but there are also overtones of the moral or spiritual walk as well for the 40 year period itself was a reminder of God's judgment of Israel's disobedience (cf. v. 14; Num. 14:33-34; Josh. 5:6). (E. Merrill, *NIDOTTE*, 1:1032-35). [*hlk*]

You have lacked nothing *(ḥāsartâ)*—This verb has the basic meaning of decrease, diminish (as in the receding flood waters, Gen. 8:3, 5), but in the great majority of cases, especially in this stem, the idea is that of being in want or need. As Moses reviewed Israel's history from the giving of the law at Sinai, he reminded them that even though they had traveled through barren and hostile terrain God had always provided for them in abundance. This beneficence would, in fact, continue for when they entered Canaan they would find that they would lack nothing there as well (Deut. 8:9). Should individuals among them be deprived of necessities, the community must be generous in ministering to them according to their needs (Deut. 15:8). Later, David could testify that because the Lord was his shepherd he suffered no want whatsoever (Ps. 23:1; cf. 34:10). Ezekiel reminds his readers, however, that when God's people disobey and forsake him they will lack even bread and water, the necessities of life (Ezek. 4:17). Blessing thus depends upon one's relationship to God. [ḥsr]

2:15 To destroy them: *(tummām)*—The root idea of this verb is to destroy something completely (KBL, 1032). In the context of judgment (as here) or military conquest, it describes total annihilation (Num. 32:13; Josh. 5:6; 8:24; 10:20; Jer. 44:12, 18, 27). That is, the work of destruction goes on until it is completely finished and nothing is left. In this passage the reference is to the men of Israel who had refused to believe that God could give them victory over the inhabitants of Canaan (Num. 14:26-35; 26:63-65). Not one of them would survive to enter the promised land—all, without exception, would die (v. 16). Paul cites this text as an example of those with whom God was not pleased and whom he therefore judged most severely (1 Cor. 10:5-6). [tmm]

2:25 Terror of you *(paḥdĕkâ)*—Once the nations of Canaan and elsewhere learned of the Exodus and its aftermath—espe-

cially the conquest of the Transjordan— they would become terrified at the prospect of Israelite invasion. Most commonly the term refers to the awe-inspiring fear generated by proximity to the Lord or caused by offense to Him (1 Sam. 11:7; 2 Chron. 14:14; 17:10; 19:7; 20:29; Ps. 36:1; 119:120; Isa. 2:10, 19, 21). Fear of Israel, then, was not so much of the nation *per se* but of the Lord as Israel's God (Deut. 11:25; cf. Esth. 8:17; 9:2, 3). Of special interest is the epithet of the Lord "The Fear of Isaac" (Gen. 31:42). This can be construed either as the God feared by Isaac or Isaac's God, feared by others. In light of the present text it seems that the latter of these two options is preferable. [paḥad]

2:26 Peace *(šālôm)*—This very common noun (ca. 225x in the OT) occurs comparatively rarely in Deuteronomy. Its cognate verb has the idea of being or making someone or something whole or complete or sound. The noun, then, connotes more than mere absence of conflict or controversy; it describes, rather, a condition or situation of wellbeing (P. Nel, *NIDOTTE*, 4:131). Here, however, it is a technical term for cessation of hostility. More specifically, it refers to terms of peace being offered by Israel to Sihon, the Amorite king, a result of which will be Sihon's permission for Israel to pass through his territory. The noun occurs with the same meaning in the so-called Manual of War where Israel is instructed to sue for terms of peace with non-Canaanite nations before launching attacks upon them (Deut. 20:10-12). Peace in the sense of well-being is in view in the command never to seek the peace and prosperity of the Ammonites and Moabites (Deut. 23:3-6). Especially striking is the misguided perception of sinners who think they will have inner peace and wholeness despite their rebellious denial of the Lord (Deut. 29:19). True peace, then, is in a fully integrated life, one possible only when God is in control. [*šālôm*]

2:30 Made his spirit stubborn (*hiqšâ*)—The root meaning of the verb is "be hard, severe" (KBL, 859) and in the causative stem (as here), "make hard," that is, in the sense of becoming resistant or unresponsive. The object here is the spirit (*rûaḥ*) of King Sihon. With Yahweh as subject the idea is that Sihon was made noncompliant precisely so that he would challenge Israel and thus be defeated. "Spirit" here is synonymous with will or disposition (BDB, 925). Sihon's own inclinations were overridden by God's intervention so as to effect God's intentions. Usually the verb with Yahweh as subject describes the heart (*lēb*) as being hardened, as in the case of Pharaoh (Exod. 7:3; cf. also Ps. 95:8; Prov. 28:14). [*qšh*]

Made his heart obstinate (*'immēṣ*)—The poetic nature of the verse makes clear that this verb (with root meaning "be strong," BDB, 54) is synonymously parallel with *hqšh*, "make hard," just as heart is synonymous with spirit. If there is any difference at all, it is that spirit has to do with will and heart with rationality, that is, with the mind (KBL, 62). Sihon was so under the control of Yahweh that he was unable to make sensible decisions or exercize his own will. This rare instance of God's intervention should not lead to any conclusions about Divine sovereignty versus human free will. Such a matter must be determined on the basis of a full biblical theology. Other occurrences of the verb with this meaning are in Deut. 15:7 and 2 Chron. 36:13 where the subjects harden their own hearts (cf. R. Wakely, *NIDOTTE*, 1:438). [*'mṣ*]

2:34 We destroyed completely (*wannaḥărēm*)—This verb, attested in only the causative stem, derives from a root meaning to dedicate, consecrate, or set apart for some special purpose (BDB, 355; KBL, 334). In the OT the result of such an act is almost always the death or destruction of the object in mind. Moreover, it is done so as an act of presentation to Yahweh; i.e., the person or thing becomes the Lord's by virtue of its being made no longer available to anyone else. Such a presentation is not an offering in the normal, cultic sense of the term, for God never accepts human sacrifice or any other kind not spelled out elsewhere in the Law. Rather, it is the turning over to him of persons or objects under irremedial judgment and/or otherwise considered inappropriate for human (especially Israelite) use. In the case of the latter the object may be intended for sacred use, perhaps even in the tabernacle or temple (Lev. 27:28; Josh. 6:19, 24). Dedication to destruction (as here) is by far the most common use of the term (N. Lohfink, *TDOT*, 5:183), and it occurs most frequently in Deuteronomy (3:6; 7:2; 13:15; 20:17) and Joshua (2:10; 6:21; 8:26; 10:1, 28, 35, 37, 39, 40; 11:11, 12, 20, 21), both having to do with the conquest of Canaan and removal of the indigenous peoples from there. [*ḥrm*]

We left no survivors (*hiš'arnû śārîd*)—The verb *š'r* means to remain, but in the stem used here it means to leave over, that is, to leave a remnant. The combination with *śārîd*, survivor, became a technical term to convey the idea of a tiny group left after war, disaster, or judgment or even no one left at all (cf. Deut. 3:3; Josh. 8:22; 10:28, 30, 33, 37; etc.). The latter of these outcomes is the thought here for it was in the very nature of the *ḥērem* (ban, annihilation; cf. previous word) that absolutely nothing living should be left. Ironically, an expression of God's judgment on his wayward people could be their total destruction (Deut. 28:51). However, his covenant promises would assure that there would be at least a few who would be spared, a nucleus around which a renewed and restored Israel would emerge to carry on its redemptive privileges and responsibilities (cf. Isa. 10:20, 21, 22; 11:11, 16; Jer. 23:3; Amos 5:15; Mic. 2:12). [*š'r śārîd*]

3:4 We seized *(wannilkōd)*—The most common use of this verb is to speak of places persons or objects taken in war. Though rare in Deuteronomy (2:34, 35; 3:4), it is the regular term used in Joshua to describe the capture of cities in the conquest (6:20; 8:19; 10:1, 28, 32, 35, 37, 39, 42; 11:10, 12, 17; 19:47). However, to take such prizes was not necessarily equivalent to destroying them. In fact, when destruction followed, the narrative makes clear that it was a follow-up to the capture and not a necessary part of it (Josh. 6:20-21; 10:1; 11:10-11). The purpose of the conquest was to eliminate the populations of Canaan but to leave the physical properties intact for Israel's use (Deut. 6:10-11; 19:1; Josh. 24:13). [*lkd*]

We took *(lāqaḥnû)*—Though this verb is much more comprehensive in its use than *lkd*, referring to the taking of virtually any object, it occasionally (as here) is synonymous with *lkd* in military contexts. Also like *lkd*, the verb does not necessarily imply destruction though destruction sometimes followed the taking (cf. Deut. 3:8, 14; Josh. 11:16-17, 19-20, 23). [*lqḥ*]

3:20 Gives rest *(yānîaḥ)*—Besides the ordinary meaning of cessation or respite from work or other activity, the verb, here and elsewhere (e.g., Exod. 33:14; Deut. 12:10;

Josh. 1:13, 15; 21:44; 22:4, 23:1), conveys the theological idea of entering into a status or condition of achievement, attainment, or fulfillment (J. Oswalt, *NIDOTTE*, 3:58). The causative stem suggests that such rest is made possible by God. It is He who will take Israel into the land, subdue their enemies, and grant them peace and security thereafter. The context makes clear the fact that rest comes after conflict. Once the eastern tribes have helped their brethren in the conquest of Canaan they can return to their own allotments in peace and rest (cf. 2 Sam. 7:1-2). Rest, then, is more than mere absence of activity. It is a condition of wholeness and wellness brought to pass as a gracious act of God. This is clearly the concept in the NT as well (Matt. 11:29; Acts 9:31; Heb. 4:1, 3, 5, 10, 11; Rev. 14:13). [*nwḥ*]

3:26 The Lord was furious with me *(wayyit'abbēr)*—Perhaps cognate to the homonym *'br*, "to cross over," this verb occurs in an intensive form that suggests lack of control in anger. It is as though the subject is carried away, crossing over the boundaries of self-control (KBL, 676). In cases where the Lord is the subject (only here in Deut; cf. Ps. 78:21, 59, 62; 89:38), his wrath must be understood in anthropopathic terms, that is, as though God were human. Otherwise, God would appear to be controlled by his own feelings and not master over them. [*'br*]

Because of you *(lĕma'ankem)*—This particle always occurs with the preposition *l* and it may take pronominal suffixes as well. It may express intention (in order that), purpose (so as to), or (as here) cause. Moses here appears to explain the anger of the Lord toward him as a response to Moses' sin (cf. Deut. 1:34-37), which, he says, was itself a reaction to the people's incessant complaints. It was on their account, then, that he was punished. At first blush it might appear that Moses is using the people as a scapegoat, thus absolving himself of personal responsibility. More likely, however, he is simply asserting that he, as a member of the covenant community, shared in their judgment as well as their blessings. Their prohibition to enter the land of promise fell on him as well, especially since he was the theocratic administrator. [ma'an]

3:28 Strengthen him ('ammĕṣēhû)—This verb occurs also in Deut. 2:30 with a more metaphorical meaning (make obstinate). Here the nuance is also figurative but in a positive sense as the parallel verb ḥzq (encourage; cf. Deut. 1:38) clearly shows. The Lord's charge to Moses to strengthen Joshua is not so much in the physical realm as it is in the emotional, psychological, and spiritual. This is the only occurrence of the verb with this meaning in Deuteronomy but it is attested elsewhere, mainly in the Prophets and Wisdom. Eliphaz commends Job for having strengthened others (Job 4:4) and Job himself says that he would strengthen his accusatory companions were he in their place (Job 16:5). David is presented as one whom the Lord strengthens (Ps. 89:21), whereas the virtuous woman strengthens herself for her many domestic tasks (Prov. 31:17). Zion is encouraged to be strong in light of the Lord's eschatological salvation (Isa. 35:3-4; cf. 41:10). To be strong in the context of the present passage is to be confident of ultimate success. ['mṣ]

4:1 Statutes (ḥuqqîm)—Covenant texts in the ancient Near East and in the OT invariably contain stipulations, that is, the matters to which the covenant parties subscribe and which they swear to uphold. In the OT these are referred to by various terms, two of which—statutes and ordinances—occur in this verse. They all are basically synonymous, but a study of their etymologies as well as usages is helpful in revealing some distinctions. The plural noun ḥuqqîm derives from a verb meaning to incise or inscribe, that is, to engrave (a text) into stone or some other hard surface (BDB, 349). A statute then is something permanent, a law intended to be unaltered and of abiding authority. The term also implies limits or boundaries beyond which one cannot go (H. Ringgren, TDOT, 5:141-42). A statute "draws the lines" of behavior, as it were. Because Deuteronomy is largely a covenant document ḥuqqîm (and its variation ḥuqqâ) occurs many times there (e.g., 4:5, 6, 8, 14, 40, 45; 5:1, 31; 6:1, 2, 17, 24; 7:11; 8:11). It is common also in Psalms, and in particular Ps. 119, "the psalm of the Book" (vv. 5, 8, 12, 23, 26, 33, 48; etc.). To obey the statutes is to live (v. 1), that is, to survive in the land and enjoy its benefits. [ḥōq]

Ordinances (mišpāṭîm)—Because this noun derives from the verb šāpaṭ , "to judge," some versions translate it "judgment(s)." This, however, lends itself to ambiguity at times because judgment as a legal process and consequence (see 1:17 above) is quite different from a law or stipulation that is to be obeyed as an element of covenant regulation. A mišpāṭ (like a ḥōq), then, is a legal promulgation, a mandate handed down by one empowered to do so (BDB, 1048) such as a king (1 Sam. 10:25). In Deuteronomy (and other covenant texts) the most common use of the word is as a technical term to refer to the various covenant requirements (Deut. 4:5, 8, 14, 45; 5:1, 31; 6:1; 7:11, 12; 8:11; 11:1; etc.; cf. Exod. 24:3; Lev. 18:5; 19:37; 20:22; Num. 36:13). Like ḥoq it occurs many times also in Ps. 119 (vv. 7, 13, 20, 30, 39; etc.). These originated in God himself and were to be taught by Moses to the people (B. Johnson, *TDOT*, 9:94-95). [*mišpāṭ*]

Which I am teaching you (*mĕlammēd*)—The verb in its basic form means "learn" but in the derived form used here it denotes "teach." The participle (as here) describes a process of instruction for it is in the nature of learning that it must be constant and repetitive. The subject of the teaching is the covenant law, especially in Deuteronomy, and Moses, as God's servant, is the principal teacher. Here he suggests that he is imparting the terms of the covenant to the nation (cf. vv. 5, 14; 6:1; 31:22) but he also commands the people to teach their children the same thing in generations to come (4:10; 6:7; 11:19; 31:19). [*lmd*]

4:2 Commandments (*miṣwōt*)—Like the two terms just described, this noun also derives from a verb, *ṣwh*, "to command" (*BDB*, 846). Like them it also is a technical term for a covenant stipulation, rarely occurring with a human subject. Ironically, the Decalogue is popularly called the "Ten Commandments," but the word *miṣwâ/miṣwōt* never occurs in the OT as a description of these ten stipulations. Rather, they are called simply the "ten words" (Deut. 10:4). The record is clear that commandments have a divine origin and for this reason alone must be obeyed. In fact, *miṣwâ* appears occasionally as a synonym for or in juxta- position with *tôrâ* (that is, the whole Pentateuch; cf. 1:4 above) and thus suggests that the Torah as a whole is a Divine command (cf. Exod. 16:28; 24:12; Lev. 27:34; Num. 36:13; Deut. 30:10; P. Enns, *NIDOTTE*, 2:1070). [*miṣwâ*]

4:4 Cleaved (*haddĕbēqîm*)—This predicate adjective, related to the verb *dbq*, "to cling," indicates a persistent and tena-

cious adherence to the Lord by those whom he spared to enter the land of Canaan. In its literal uses as a verb it describes such closeness as skin clinging to bone (Job 19:20), the scales of a crocodile (Job 41:17), or a belt tight around one's waist (Jer. 13:11). G. Brooke, *NIDOTTE*, 1:910-12. The verb is rather common in Deuteronomy, its most important theological concept being that of covenant loyalty (cf. 10:20; 11:22; 13:4; 30:20). To cleave to the Lord is to manifest allegiance only to him. [*dābēq*]

4:6 Your wisdom and your understanding (*ḥokmatkem ûbînatkem*)—The adjectival forms of these nouns occur in Deut. 1:13 to describe the leadership qualities necessary for those who would assume positions of responsibility in Israel. Here, however, the nouns constitute the very essence of what it means to keep the terms of the covenant. To do so is the paramount display of wisdom and undertanding. Elsewhere it is said that the fear of God (that is, recognition of him as Lord) is the foundation of wisdom (Ps. 111:10; Prov. 1:7; 9:10; 15:33). Obedience of his covenant requirements is a way of manifesting such godly reverence and thus is the embodiment of wisdom and understanding. Should Israel do this all other nations would marvel and would not fail to link knowledge of the true God with covenant fidelity (vv. 6b-8). [*ḥokmâ* and *bînâ*]

4:10 To fear me (*lĕyir'â*)—The verb here most commonly bears the meaning of terror, apprehension, fright, and the like and even in this passage some of that is evident in the reaction of the people to the overwhelming display of Yahweh's glory at Horeb/Sinai on the occasion of his revelation of Torah to Moses (vv. 11-14; cf. Exod. 19:16-18; 20:18-21). The phenomena of these events alone were enough to terrify the assembly even apart from any theological reflection. They reacted as they would to any encounter with forces larger and more powerful than themselves or which startled them with their potential harmfulness (cf. Gen. 20:8; 42:35; 43:18; Num. 12:8; Deut. 1:29; 2:4; 7:18; Josh. 11:6; 1 Sam. 4:7; etc.). At a deeper level, fear is a way of describing reaction to the awesomeness of God's person and presence. It is not terror but reverential respect that lies at its heart (KBL, 399-400). It is the recognition of the transcendence of God who in every way exists and acts at a level beyond human comprehension, so much so that when he penetrates human perception and experience all the mortal can do is to fall before him in abject humility and submission. It then becomes central to one's lifestyle to think of God in these terms and to respond to him in this way, all the while recognizing that he also opens himself to interaction and fellowship with those who know and love him. Dozens of biblical texts depict this kind of fear, one inherent in the nature of the covenant relationship (e.g., Exod. 14:31; Deut. 5:29; 6:2, 13, 24; 8:6; 10:12, 20; 13:4). Appeals by Moses and others to "fear not" are intended not to undermine reverential fear but to allay the sheer terror that accompanied his presence (cf. Gen. 15:1; Exod. 20:20; 1 Sam. 12:20). [*yr'*]

4:12 Form *(tĕmûnâ)*—This noun, derived from *mîn* ("kind, species"; cf. Gen. 1:12), connotes a representation or likeness, especially an attempt to portray God. In the second commandment it is synonymous with *pesel*, an image (Exod. 20:4; Deut. 5:8). When the Lord appeared to Israel at Sinai they saw no form; therefore, it was strictly forbidden to try to repre-

sent him in such a physical way (vv. 15, 16, 23, 25). [*tĕmûnâ*]

4:13 His covenant *(bĕrîtô)*—One of the richest theological terms in the OT, this word is especially central to the message of Deuteronomy. A case can be made, in fact, that the whole book is informed by and organized around the notion of covenant (J. Niehaus, "Deuteronomy: Theology of," *NIDOTTE*, 4:537-44). Most scholars link the Hebrew word with either Akkadian *birît*, "between," "among," or Akkadian *birîtu*, "clasp, fetter" (M. Weinfeld, *TDOT*, 2:254-55), the latter having most in its favor. A covenant, then, consists of a linkage between individuals or groups designed to accomplish some mutually agreed upon purpose. There are many examples in the OT of covenants of a "secular" or nontheological nature (e.g., Gen. 21:27; 26:28; 31:44; 1 Sam. 11:1; 18:3; 23:18; 1 Kings 20:34), but the predominant use of the concept is heavy with religious or theological significance. It is commonly recognized that the covenants with Abraham (Gen. 15:18; 17; Exod. 2:24; Deut. 4:31) and David (2 Sam. 7:8-17; 23:5; Ps. 89:3; Jer. 33:21) are unconditional (so-called Royal Grant) in form and function whereas the Sinaitic/ Deuteronomic is conditional (so-called Suzerain-Vassal) (G. McConville, *NIDOTTE*, 1:749-50). That is, the Abrahamic and Davidic are based on oath and promise, whereas the Sinaitic emphasizes command. Even so, the Lord promises that the covenant with Israel will find ultimate fulfillment, for he will enable his people to obey it and thus carry out the redemptive and mediatorial function for which he had brought them into covenant in the first place (Lev. 26; 40-45; Jer. 3:12-15; 31:35-37; 33:19-22). By "covenant" in the passage at hand is meant the covenant text, that is, the Ten Commandments specifically and, by extension, all the stipulations pertaining to them (v. 14; cf. Exod. 24:7; Deut. 9:9, 11, 15). [*běrît*]

4:16 Lest you become corrupt *(tašḥîtûn)*— The semantic field of this verb has to do with spoiling, ruining, destroying—all in a literal sense, but more figuratively it describes moral and spiritual decay, perversion, or corruption (*BDB*, 1007-08). This is the sense here. Furthermore, in the causative stem (as here) the idea is that of bringing oneself into a condition of corruption, the result of which is some kind of wicked behavior. The great flood came because God saw that all humanity was corrupt (Gen. 6:12). The fool is said to be corrupt as is clear from his detestable works (Ps. 14:1). The adulterer corrupts himself by that deed (Prov. 6:32), and Isaiah concludes that the whole nation Israel is corrupt, a condition linked to their having despised the Lord (Isa. 1:4; cf. Zeph. 3:7). In this passage the warning is given that idolatry will either cause corruption or result from it. Later, Moses despairs that this, indeed, is what will happen to his people after his death (Deut. 31:29). [*šḥt*]

Image *(pesel)*—Because of the pervasive presence of idolatry in Canaan and the larger Near Eastern world, there is a plethora of terminology in the OT to describe the various forms and shapes in which deities could be represented. The word here derives from a verb at home in the quarrying industry, one meaning "to hew" or "to carve out" (*KBL*, 769). The image carved out of stone later developed conceptually to figures of wood or even of metal (*BDB*, 820). In the final analysis, *pesel* became synonymous with other terms for idols such as *ṣelem* or *semel* (J. Hadley, *NIDOTTE*, 3:271-72, 644-46). It occurs in the prohibition against idolatry

in the Decalogue (Exod. 20:4; Deut. 5:8) and commonly in the prophets as perhaps a generic term referring to any kind of a man-made object of worship (e.g., Isa. 40:19, 20; 42:17; 44:9, 10, 15, 17; 45:20; 48:5; Jer. 10:14; 51:17). In this passage *pesel* is associated with two other theologically significant terms—*těmûnâ* (v. 15) and *tabnît* (v. 17). The former suggests any kind of representation or resemblance (*BDB*, 568) and the latter a figure of some kind of reality (*BDB*, 125). Moses reminds the people that when God revealed himself at Sinai/Horeb they saw nothing of his form. It was therefore forbidden to try to represent him in any kind of iconic manner. How could the invisible be contained within a visible expression? Worst of all, to manufacture images of created beings and worship them as though they had divine essence or qualities would be the height of abomination to a holy God who alone should be worshiped (vv. 16-19). [*pesel*]

Figure *(semel)*—This term to describe an idol occurs only here in Deuteronomy and as a clarification of the term *pesel*, image. The chronicler (2 Chron. 33:7) sheds some light on the nature of the figure by referring to the object wicked King Manasseh set up in the temple as a carved image (*pesel hassemel*, lit., the image of the figure), though even this fails to communicate fully the nature of this idolatrous representation. Ezekiel describes the statue he saw in the temple as the image of jealousy, that is, a figure that was worshiped in the place of the Lord (Ezek. 8:3; cf. Exod. 20:3). It is best, perhaps, to view the word as one among many employed by the OT to designate idols (J. Hadley, *NIDOTTE*, 3:271). [*semel*]

The likeness *(tabnît)*—Cognate to the verb *bnh*, to build, make, this noun can refer to any object that is in the shape or pattern of something else. For example, the tabernacle was to be constructed according to the pattern or plan given by the Lord to Moses (Exod. 25:9, 40). Evil King Ahaz of Judah, having seen a pagan altar at Damascus, commissioned his craftsman to make one modeled after it (2 Kings 16:10). On the other hand, David had been given a revelation of the design of the temple and had instructed his son Solomon to build it precisely in line with the heavenly pattern (1 Chron. 28:11-12, 19). Here Moses enjoins Israel not to attempt to create likenesses of human beings or animals as objects of worship (vv. 16-18, four occurrences of the noun). This was the practice of the pagans (Isa. 44:13), a practice unfortunately adopted by the Jews near the end of their preexilic history (Ezek. 8:10). This as much as anything else precipitated the destruction of Solomon's temple and the Babylonian exile (Ezek. 8:18) (R. Van Leeuwen, *NIDOTTE*, 4:646). [*tabnît*]

4:19 You worship (*hištaḥăwîtā*)—Older grammars and lexicons took this form to be a rare stem of the verb *šḥh*, "bow down" (*BDB*, 1005). Comparative Semitic study now makes it clear that it reflects a stem found only with the verb *ḥwh* in the OT, a verb that, in fact, also means "bow down" (H. Preuss, *TDOT*, 4:249). In any case, the point is that though the mere act of prostrating oneself is not worship, it seemed inconceivable to the pious of Israel to approach the Lord in worship without doing so in a physical posture that acknowledged his awesomeness and majesty. It is true that the same verb is used to speak of doing obeisance to human authority (Gen. 38:7, 9; 43:28; Exod. 18:7; 2 Sam. 1:2; 14:4; 1 Kings 1:16), but by far the more common use is the worship of God or the gods (Exod. 24:1; 32:8; 33:10; Deut.

8:19; 11:16; 1 Chron. 29:20; Neh. 8:6; Ezek. 8:16). The juxtaposition of *ḥwh* here with *'bd* ("serve") makes clear that worship expects accompanying works. To worship God is to serve him and to serve him fully and sincerely is truly to worship him (T. Fretheim, *NIDOTTE*, 2:43). [*ḥwh*]

Which the Lord your God has allotted (*ḥālaq*)—On the fourth day of creation the Lord had made the sun, moon, and stars to serve as light holders and also to function as markers dividing day from night and one season from another (Gen. 1:14-19). That is, the heavenly bodies were to be agents of the Creator designed to carry out His purposes. Soon, however, they became objects of worship in themselves, a terrible reversal of the divinely established order. Even Israel succumbed to the temptation to "worship and serve the creature rather than the Creator" (Rom. 1:25; cf. Isa. 44:20; Jer. 10:14; 13:25; 16:10-11). This passage warns against this very thing, pointing out, among other things, that the sun, moon, and stars—as glorious as they are—are fundamentally mere devices by which all nations may be able to measure times and seasons. They serve the peoples of the earth and must not be served by them. The verb *ḥlq* occurs often to describe such acts as the distribution of tasks (1 Chron. 23:6; 24:3), spoils (1 Sam. 30:24), or inheritance (Prov. 17:2). Here it indicates that all of creation was created to be of blessing to mankind and not to be perverted into powers and forces to which mankind would place themselves in subjection. [*ḥlq*]

4:20 A people of (his) possession (*'am naḥălâ*)—Basically the concept here is that of a gift or possession claimed by the Lord on the basis of some act or payment he has made. Specifically, he had redeemed Israel from oppressive Egyptian bondage and therefore had a right to her as his own property (cf. Exod. 19:4-6). In combination with *'am*, "people," the term is found most commonly in Deuteronomy (9:26, 29) and Psalms (28:9; 78:62, 71; 94:5, 14; 106:40). Just as Israel was God's possession, so Canaan was to be Israel's (Deut. 4:21). In this sense, however, it is more the idea of a bequest granted by a generous benefactor. The Lord had promised the patriarchs that all the land upon which they trod would someday belong to their descendants (Gen. 12:7; 13:15; 15:18) and the time had now come for that to become a reality. This fulfillment is, not surprisingly, most apparent in Deuteronomy (4:21; 15:4; 19:10; 20:16; 21:23; 24:4; 25:19; 26:1; cf. Judg. 20:6; Isa. 58:14; Jer. 12:14).[*naḥălâ*]

4:24 Jealous God *(qannā')*—This adjective and its cognate noun *qin'â* ("jealousy") have theological relevance only when applied to the Lord. They do occur, of course, in reference to human relationships (e.g. Num. 5:14-30; Prov. 6:34; S. of S. 8:6), but the passages (such as this) where God is said to be jealous are of particular importance (e.g., Exod. 20:5; 34:14; Deut. 5:9; 6:15; Ps. 79:5; Isa. 42:13; Ezek. 36:5, 6; Zech. 1:14). Since jealousy in general is considered petty and unworthy of even mature human beings, the notion of God's jealousy may seem rather problematic. In fact, the translation "jealous/jealousy" may not be appropriate at all. "Zealous/zeal" is therefore suggested with reference to the Lord. His "jealousy" has to do with his rightful claims to undivided loyalty and unchallenged worship (H. Peels, *NIDOTTE*, 3:939). He is jealous not for himself but for his name's sake, that is, for his reputation among his own people and, indeed, in the whole world. In the present context—as commonly

elsewhere—the jealousy of God arises out of a concern that his people acknowledge him to the exclusion of all other gods (v. 23; cf. 32:21; 1 Kings 14:22; Ps. 78:58). [*qannā'*]

4:25 To arouse His anger *(lĕhak'îsô)*—Of all the various verbs in Hebrew to denote anger or wrath (e.g., *'np, ḥrh, qṣp*), this—and in this particular verbal stem—is most used with God as subject to express His anger at the idolatry and other sinful actions of His people. It occurs in this sense elsewhere in Deuteronomy (9:18; 31:29; 32:16, 21) and marks Israel's covenant disloyalty to the Lord throughout their history (cf. Judg. 2:12; 1 Kings 14:9, 15; 15:30; 16:2, 7, 13, 26; 21:22; 22:53; 2 Kings 17:11, 17; Neh. 4:5; Ps. 78:58; 106:29; Jer. 7:18, 19; Ezek. 8:17; 16:26; Hos. 12:14). Particularly instructive are those texts where the Lord's anger is said to be aroused because of His jealousy, that is, the challenge to His uniqueness and exclusive claims to worship (see v. 24; cf. 32:16, 21; Ps. 78:58). As always, this emotional response is not indicative of a loss of control by the Lord or of His petty reactions to real or perceived personal insults. To the contrary, God's anger is a deliberative and even positive attribute associated with His very nature as the Holy One to whom attempted comparison is in itself an evil thing worthy of severe condemnation. [*k's*]

4:26 I call as witness *(ha'îdōtî)*—This verb, derived from the noun *'ēd*, "witness," means, in this stem, "to summon as witness," or "to bear witness" (KBL, 686). It bears clear legal overtones and, in fact, occurs often in so-called *rîb*-texts, that is, texts in which Yahweh alleges wrongdoing against his people, hails them into court, testifies against them before witnesses, and pronounces a verdict (e.g.,

Deut. 30:19; 31:28; and more fully Jer. 25:31; Hos. 4:1-5; 12:2-6; Mic. 6:2-5). In ordinary legal proceedings human witnesses would be called (Num. 35:30; Deut. 17:6, 7; 19:15; Ruth 4:11; Isa. 8:2). By their mortality and undependability, however, they are disqualified to be witnesses in God's case against his people so he calls upon creation itself to fill that role (Chisholm, *NIDOTTE*, 3:336). ['*wd*]

4:27 Will scatter (*hēpîṣ*)—The verb *pwṣ* in all of its stems means to be scattered or dispersed, usually with reference to peoples in general (Gen. 10:18; 11:4, 8, 9) or to armies and other hostile forces in particular (Num. 10:35; 1 Kings 22:17; 2 Kings 25:5). Most significant is its occurrence in the stem represented here, one that describes the scattering of Israel from its homeland to all the surrounding nations. This will be the punishment for idolatry (cf. v. 25), a punishment that eventually befell the nation with both the Assyrian (2 Kings 17:5-12) and the Babylonian exiles (2 Chron. 36:17-21). Ironically, because Israel worshiped the gods of other nations she would be forced to go to those nations and there to serve those very gods (Deut. 28:64; cf. Jer. 9:16; 13:24; 18:17; Ezek. 11:16; 12:15; 20:23). God's forgiving grace would (and will) regather the scattered ones, however, and bring them back into the land promised to the patriarchs (Deut. 30:2; Jer. 30:10-11). In fact, their return to the Lord in spiritual terms would result in Israel's return to full covenant enjoyment and blessing (Deut. 4:29-31). [*pwṣ*]

Will lead (*yĕnaheg*)—The normal use of this verb is in a herding or shepherding context where cattle, sheep, and other animals are being led or driven from place to place (cf. Gen. 31:18; Exod. 3:1; 1 Sam. 23:5; 30:20; 2 Kings 9:20; Job 24:3; Isa. 11:6). Elsewhere, human beings are led in

a tender and loving manner for their own good (Isa. 49:10; 63:14). Here, however, the leading is punitive. Israel's sin of idolatry, if not repented of, will result in her scattering among the nations. The same threat occurs in the curse section of Deuteronomy where Israel is told that she will become a symbol among the nations of what it means to violate the covenant of the sovereign God (Deut. 28:37). [*nhg*]

4:30 In the latter days (*bĕ'aḥărît hayyāmîm*)—This is a technical term used in the OT to refer to the remote future at which time God will radically interrupt time and space in order to accomplish some remarkable work, usually (as here) on behalf of his covenant people. In its other occurrence in this book, however, the expression warns of judgment because of their anticipated moral and spiritual corruption (Deut. 31:29). Jacob was first to speak of the eschatological day when, on his death-bed, he viewed the blessings of his sons in the future, including the messianic promise to Judah (Gen. 49:1, 10). The pagan prophet Balaam also understood the latter days to be times of messianic hope (Num. 24:14; cf. v. 17). Not surprisingly, the Prophets most commonly appropriate the term (Isa. 2:2; Jer. 23:20; 30:24; 48:47; 49:39; Ezek. 38:16; Dan. 10:14; Hos. 3:5; Mic. 4:1), and then in terms of the Lord's ultimate triumph over evil and installation of his kingdom of righteousness (H. Seebass, *TDOT*, 1:210-11). ['*aḥărît*]

Return to the Lord your God (*šabtâ 'ad yhwh 'ĕlōhekâ*)—The verb *šûb*, used primarily in the everyday sense of turning or returning, is also the most common technical term for repenting. The present passage embodies both meanings, a return from exile (v. 27) and a turning to the Lord, one that will result in his merciful forgiveness (v. 31). The verb with the preposition 'ad occurs elsewhere (Deut. 30:2; Amos 4:6, 8, 9, 10, 11; Isa. 10:22; Job 22:23; Lam. 3:40; Hos. 14:1; Joel 2:12), all with Yahweh or God as object. J. Thompson/E. Martens, *NIDOTTE*, 4:55-59. [*šwb*]

4:31 Merciful God (*'ēl raḥûm*)—The "jealous" God who consumes those who persist in covenant disloyalty (v. 24) is also the God of mercy to those who repent. The adjective here, cognate to the verb *rḥm*, "love," "have compassion" (*BDB*, 933), may also be related to the noun *raḥămîm*, "compassion," or even *reḥem*, "womb" (M. Butterworth, *NIDOTTE*, 3:1093-95). If so, the tender, "motherly" aspect of the Lord's nature comes to the fore. In any case, only God is said to be merciful in this sense (Exod. 34:6; 2 Chron. 30:9; Neh. 9:17, 31; Ps. 103:8; Joel 2:13; Jonah 4:2), with only one human subject as an exception (Ps. 112:4). [*raḥûm*]

He will not fail you (*yarpĕkâ*)—The basic meaning of this verb is to relax or droop (down), but in the stem employed here the idea is to abandon, forsake, or leave alone (KBL, 904). The promise is that when Israel is scattered among the nations because of her sin she will come to her senses and repent (vv. 27-29). She may then expect full forgiveness and restoration (v. 30) for the Lord will never relax in His covenant commitment to His people. The same verb with the same meaning occurs in Deut. 31:6, 8, and such a promise is reiterated to Joshua (Josh. 1:5) and Solomon (1 Chron. 28:20). Unreliable and weak human beings may droop and wilt under the pressures of responsibility (2 Sam. 4:1; 2 Chron. 15:7; Isa. 13:7; Jer. 6:24; 50:43; Ezek. 7:17; 21:7; Zeph. 3:16), but Israel's God is utterly and absolutely dependable in meeting His covenant commitments. [*rph*]

4:32 The former days (*yāmîm ri'šōnîm*)—The chronologically polar opposite of the latter days (v. 30), this phrase may hark back to the earliest of times, in this instance to creation itself. The term lacks the technical and theological precision of "latter days," however, so that former days should be construed primarily (if not only) as a reference to the past in general (thus Num. 6:12; Deut. 10:10; 2 Sam. 21:9; Eccl. 7:10; Zech. 8:11). [*rī'šôn*]

Created (*bārā'*)—This verb occurs with only God as subject in the OT and by inference means to bring to pass out of nothing (see Gen. 1:1 for full discussion). This is the only occurrence in Deuteronomy. Otherwise it is most common in Genesis (1; 2; 5:1, 2; 6:7) and Isaiah (4:5; 40:26; 41:20; 42:5; 43:1, 7; 45:7, 8, 12, 18; 54:16; 57:19; 65:17, 18). The purpose here is not to address the topos of creation *per se* but to make note of the day of creation as the beginning of history. Moses asks whether any people since then and anywhere in the universe had ever encountered God as Israel had at Sinai/Horeb and yet lived (vv. 32-33). The rhetorical question demands a resounding No, for Israel was uniquely the people of Yahweh. [*br'*]

4:34 A people (*gôy*)—This noun, largely synonymous with *'am* (KBL, 174), is generic for the human race as a whole with its various races and nations, but it also designates Israel as a special people. Here Israel is a people taken out redemptively from another people, Egypt. It is in terms of Israel's uniqueness as a people or nation that her identification as such has theological significance. Besides the present passage, the notion of Israel as a special people is found elsewhere in Deuteronomy (26:5) and is pervasive in the rest of the OT (cf. Gen. 17:4; Num. 14:12; 23:9; 1 Kings 16:2; Jer. 33:24; Ezek.

36:20; 37:22). To be the people of God is to assert not only a uniqueness but a recognition of corporate wholeness and oneness. [*gôy*]

By signs and wonders (*bĕ'ōtōt ûbĕmôpĕtîm*)—These terms occur commmonly together as a cliché, almost, perhaps, as a hendiadys ("wonderful signs") (Exod. 7:3; Deut. 6:22; 7:19; 13:1, 2; 26:8; 28:46; 34:11; Neh. 9:10; Ps. 78:43; 105:27; Isa. 8:18; 20:3; Jer. 32:20, 21). They are supernatural manifestations—usually but not exclusively attributed to the Lord (cf. Deut. 13:1-2)—the purpose of which is to display his great power and glory and also to elicit faith from those who observe them (F. Helfmeyer, *TDOT*, 1:170-71). The historical reference here is to the Exodus, a series of events whose divine origination and implementation were attested to unmistakably by the signs and wonders that accompanied them. They not only persuaded the Egyptians of Yahweh's sovereignty (cf. Exod. 8:19; 10:7), but testified of his power to Israel as well (Deut. 4:34). [*'ôt, môpēt*]

4:37 He loved (*'āhab*)—This verb denotes the strong human and divine affection that one being extends to another out of sheer interest in and care for that person. Its object in the OT can also be concepts, principles, or things (e.g., Ps. 33:5; 37:28; Isa. 66:10; Jer. 18:2; Hos. 3:1; Amos 5:18) (KBL, 15). As a more technical term the verb and its cognates occur in covenant contexts and formulas. Thus, persons love God in recognition of his sovereignty (Exod. 20:6; Deut. 5:10; 6:5; 7:9; Josh. 22:5; 23:11; Judg. 5:31) and he loves them (and/or Israel) as an act of covenant initiation (Deut. 10:15; 23:5; Ps. 47:4; Isa. 43:4; 48:14; Jer. 31:3; Hos. 11:1; Mal. 1:2). Particularly instructive are those texts in which *'āhab* occurs with *bāhar* "choose" (as

here), suggesting that God's love at times is an expression of his elective grace (cf. also Deut. 10:15; Ps. 47:4; P. Els, *NIDOTTE*, 1:279-83). Its antonym, *śānē'*, "hate," often bears the idea of nonelection; i.e., rejection by the Lord (cf. 1:27 above). [*'hb*]

He chose (*wayyibhar*)—the OT doctrine of divine election centers largely around this verb, a term that also occurs commonly to speak of making choices of a "secular" nature (Gen. 6:2; Exod. 17:9; 18:25; 1 Sam. 17:40; Ps. 25:12). With God as subject the chosen objects may be places (Deut. 12:14, 18, 26; 1 Kings 8:44; 11:13; 2 Kings 23:27; 2 Chron. 6:6, 34; Ps. 132:13) or persons, especially the patriarchal ancestors (Deut. 10:15), the nation Israel (Deut. 14:2; 1 Kings 3:8), the tribe of Judah (1 Kings 11:32; 1 Chron. 28:4), King David (2 Sam. 6:21; 1 Kings 8:16; 11:34; 2 Chron. 6:6; Ps. 78:70), and various other individuals (Deut. 18:5; 21:5; 1 Sam. 10:24; 1 Chron. 28:5; 29:1; Neh. 9:7). Its juxtaposition with the verb *'āhab* (see previous entry) makes clear that God's choice has to do with his favorable disposition toward someone or something, here the patriarchs and their descendants, specifically Israel. God chooses those whom he loves and loves those whom he chooses. Its efficacy depends upon response, however, for God's choice is never coercive. A person also must choose God and life (Deut. 30:19; Josh. 24:15, 22; Isa. 7:15, 16; 56:4; 66:4; H. Seebass, *TDOT*, 2:86). [*bhr*]

4:42 Accidentally (*biblî da'at*)—The underlying idiom means literally "without knowledge," i.e., without premeditation and/or awareness of another's presence and jeopardy. Manslaughter (to say nothing of murder; cf. 5:17) was, of course, a horrible offense but unintentional taking of life was mitigated by the very fact that it was without awareness and, consequently, deserved a less harsh penalty (cf. Num. 35:11, 15; Deut. 19:4; Josh. 20:3). In such circumstances the perpetrator could take refuge in one of several cities throughout the land. There he could find sanctuary until his case came to trial (Deut. 19:2-13). [da'at]

4:45 The stipulations (hā'ēdōt)—This fourth term employed to speak of the specific requirements of the covenant (see 4:1, 2) finds its source in a legal setting. In the singular ('ēd) the noun refers to evidence or a witness and from this derives the verb "to bear witness" ('ûd). The plural form, here a plural of 'ēdâ, always serves as a technical term for stipulations for law codes, specifically the covenant requirements (Deut. 6:17, 20; 1 Kings 2:3; 2 Kings 17:15; 23:3; Neh. 9:34; Jer. 44:23). The word appears to be synonymous with other terms of stipulation such as miṣwôt, ḥuqqîm, and mišpāṭîm as parallels or combinations in several passages make clear (Deut. 6:20; Ps. 25:10; 99:7). A much more commonly attested by-form is 'ēdût, a word essentially synonymous to 'ēdōt but not found in Deuteronomy (cf. Exod. 16:34; P. Enns, NIDOTTE, 3:328-29. ['ēdâ]

5:5 To proclaim to you (lĕhaggîd)—The base meaning of the verb used here is to be clear, plain, open, but in the stem in which it occurs mainly in the OT it carries the idea of making clear and plain, that is, declaring, informing, proclaiming some message or other (BDB, 616-17). Moses reflects on the time when he and the nation Israel had gathered at Sinai to hear the revelation of the law. Having heard it, however, was not enough for Moses had to proclaim it, clarifying and interpreting its content to his listeners. It is this interpretive meaning that gives the verb its

most profound theological significance. Thus, Samuel informed Saul of a revelation God had given him concerning the king (1 Sam. 15:16), Gad the prophet offered to David some options of divine punishment (2 Sam. 24:13), and Isaiah was instructed by the Lord to announce judgment to his disobedient people (Isa. 58:1). Micah made clear that the ability to proclaim God's message was communicated only by God's Spirit (Mic. 3:8). Moses' role here, then, is not just that of teacher or preacher but that of a channel through which the mysteries of God could be communicated to mere mortals (R. O'Connell, NIDOTTE, 3:16-17). [ngd]

5:9 Do not serve them (lō' tā'ăbĕdēm)—An important element of the worship of God is to render service to him. That is, worship consists of more than thoughts and words. It must find expression also in acts of obedience such as sacrifice (in the OT) and offerings. Beyond this ritualistic or liturgical form, true worship engages the entire life of the devotee so that everything he or she does is offered up to God as an expression of religious commitment. This is true of pagan worship as well and so the Lord, in defense of his own uniqueness as Israel's God, strictly forbade any expenditure of energy or devotion toward the gods of the nations. Deuteronomy, as a covenant text, addresses this matter of undivided service to the Lord in a particularly emphatic manner (4:19; 7:16; 8:19; 11:16; 12:2, 30; 13:6-7, 13-14; 17:3; 28:14, 36, 64; 29:26; 30:17; 31:20). To disobey in this respect is to invite the wrathful displeasure of a jealous God (cf. 4:24). ['bd]

Avenging (pōqēd)—The normal meaning of this verb, to visit, attend to, appoint, extends to the idea of visiting with a purpose in view, that of bringing either blessing or retribution. It is the latter sense that is in view here, hence the translation avenge. This is most particularly the case when the Lord is the subject and the verb (as here) is followed by the preposition 'al, upon. Though this is the only occurrence of the formula in Deuteronomy, it appears in the Exodus version of the Decalogue (Exod. 20:5) as well as other places in the Pentateuch (Exod. 32:34; 34:7; Num. 4:27; 14:18). By far the majority of usages are in the Prophets (Isa. 13:11; 26:21; Hos. 1:4; 2:13; 4:9; 12:2; Amos 3:14; Zeph. 1:8, 9, 12; 3:7), most abundantly in Jeremiah (9:25; 15:3; 21:14; 23:34; 30:20; 36:31; 44:13; 51:44, 47, 52). The transition from visiting to avenging suggests the theological idea that sin always has repercussions, that is, its consequences come back upon the sinner, (re)visiting him or her, as it were. The fact that God is the agent of the visitation shows it not to be an automatic reflex, however, but an act of his own divine purpose. This point is stated unequivocally later in this book (Deut. 32:35; cf. Rom. 12:19). [*pqd*]

5:10 Loving favor *(ḥesed)*—The semantic field of this theologically rich word is that of compassion, goodness, and grace. It is most particularly found in contexts of God's relationship with his chosen people, that is, in covenant connections. It is the *ḥesed* of the Lord that calls people to himself and that preserves them in their fellowship with him. This is clear from this passage where the Lord says that he shows (lit., does) favor to those who love him and keep his commandments. Elsewhere the term serves as a virtual synonym for covenant itself (Deut. 7:9, 12). As God's people are faithful and obedient to him, he reciprocates by exercising his *ḥesed*, that is, his commitment to keep covenant with them. H.-J. Zobel, *TDOT*, 5:44-64. [*ḥesed*]

5:11 In vain *(laššāw')*—To take (up) the name of the Lord in vain is to trivialize or secularize it and thus to discount the awesome glory and majesty of the Lord himself. The basic meaning of the term is "worthless" so to misuse God's name in any way is to debase it and him. In the world of the OT there was little or no distinction between a person's name and the person himself. Thus, the Lord can speak of the central place of worship in Israel as the place where he will cause his name to dwell (Deut. 12:5, 11). The sense of the expression here is not so much the use of the divine name in profanity (though that is included) but its employment in careless conversation where no sincere religious purpose is in view. [*šaw'*]

Consider him guiltless *(yĕnaqqeh)*—The verb in this form has the legal nuance of being exempt from guilt and/or punishment. Here it is negated so the point is that one who misuses God's name has no chance of exoneration. He will be judged guilty and must bear the consequences. The root meaning is "to be clean." The opposite, then, is to be unclean, or at least legally considered such (cf. Exod. 20:7; 34:7; Num. 14:18; 1 Kings 2:9; Jer. 30:11). [*nqh*]

5:12 Sabbath day *(yôm haššabbāt)*—Based on the the verb *šbt*, "to cease, keep aloof from, rest" (KBL, 946), the noun refers to the seventh day of the week of creation, the day when all God's work was finished and nothing more was to be created (see Gen. 2:2-3). That day is not called "sabbath," however, until after the Exodus (Exod. 16:23-29). It was then incorporated into the first giving of the Decalogue (see Exod. 20:8-11) and was to be observed as a day of rest because God had rested on the seventh day following his creation of the heavens and the earth. Now on the eve of conquest the command was given to keep the sabbath, not to commemorate creation, but to celebrate the miraculous Exodus deliverence (Deut. 5:15). Clearly, the progress of sacred history and of divine revelation permitted fresh reasons for the observance of special days like the sabbath. (H. Bosman, *NIDOTTE*, 4:1157-62). [*šabbāt*]

To keep it holy *(lĕqaddĕšô)*—This translation derives from a form of the verb *qdš* that means to bring someone or something into a state of holiness and, in this case, to preserve it in that state (KBL, 825). The base connotation of the verb itself is to set something apart from mundane use so that it might serve a special purpose. In religious contexts this purpose would, of course, be religious or spiritual in nature. As for the sabbath, in one sense it was an ordinary day, one out of seven in a week. Its designation as a day on which to remember first the creation in six days (Exod. 20:8-11) and then the Exodus redemption changed it from "just another day," however, to a set-apart day, a "holy" day upon which the ordinary activities and labors of life must be suspended. The seventh day was not inherently holy, then, but it became such by divine declaration. [*qdš*]

5:16 Honor *(kabbēd)*—In this form the verb *kbd* carries the meaning of esteeming or declaring someone to be of importance. The root idea is to "be heavy" and by extension to "be honored" (*BDB*, 457). A person viewed in this way is heavy with respect, admiration, and glory. The opposite is expressed by the verb *qll*, "to be slight, trifling" (*BDB*, 886), and in the same form of the verb as here it means to consider one contemptible or even to curse him or her. Exod. 21:17 stipulates that a child who curses (lit., makes light

of) his parents must be put to death (cf. Deut. 27:16). Parents must be considered honorable and treated as such because they have been placed over their children by the Lord as his instrument for their well-being. The NT notes that this commandment is the first one with a promise attached to its obedience, namely, a long and prosperous life (Eph. 6:2). [*kbd*]

5:17 You shall not kill *(lō' tirṣāḥ)*—Though this verb occasionally occurs as a generic word for manslaughter (cf. Deut. 4:42; 19:3, 4, 6), it usually connotes death by premeditation, that is, murder (as here; cf. Exod. 20:13; Num. 35:16-21; 1 Kings 21:19; Hos. 4:2). The taking of human life as an act of community justice (Gen. 9:6; Num. 35:33), in war (Deut. 7:2; 20:13), and the like is, of course, not only proper but mandated by covenant law. The reason murder is so heinous a crime is that the victim is in the image of God (Gen. 9:6). To kill a person in this manner is, in effect, to attack God himself, an act of unbelievable insubordination. [*rṣḥ*]

5:18 You shall not commit adultery *(lō' tin'āp)*—The OT definition of adultery is the sexual relationship of a married person (usually a man) with someone other than his or her spouse. That other person may or may not be married. Such a relationship is soundly condemned in the Law (Exod. 20:14; Lev. 20:10), the Prophets (Jer. 5:7; 7:9; 23:14; 29:23; Ezek. 16:38; 23:37, 45; Hos. 4:2, 13, 14; 7:4; Mal. 3:5), and the Writings (Ps. 50:18; Prov. 6:32; 30:20). Not only was such a thing abhorrent because of the pain and social breakdown it produced, but adultery also exemplified and was a metaphor for spiritual unfaithfulness, especially by Israel against the Lord (Isa. 57:3; Jer. 3:8, 9; Ezek. 23:37). [*n'p*]

5:19 You shall not steal *(lō' tignōb)*—Though rarely, the verb can be used in a positive sense—such as Jehoshaba's "stealing" baby Joash in order to rescue him from Athaliah (2 Kings 11:2)—almost always it bears the negative connotation of taking something that belongs to another, usually in a stealthy manner. Ordinarily the stolen item is property of some kind (cf. Gen. 31:19; 44:8; Exod. 22:1; Lev. 19:11; Josh. 7:11), but even persons could be stolen, that is, kidnapped (Exod. 21:16; Deut. 24:7), the penalty for which was death. Theft was such a serious matter because goods represent time and labor. In a sense they are a part of the one who owns them. To take them from him, even nonviolently, is to disregard his wellbeing and to that extent to deface him as one made in the image of God. [*gnb*]

5:21 You shall not covet *(lō' taḥmōd, tit 'awweh)*—The root meaning of the verb is "to desire," usually in an improper sense. Here it suggests a lustful longing for, an inappropriate appetite that is wrong even if not physically fulfilled. The same verb occurs in the Decalogue in Exodus (20:17) but there it refers also to an unwarranted desire for the neighbor's properties as well as his wife. Here a different verb *('wh)* is used with reference to all but the wife. Comparison of the two verbs reveals little if any difference between them (G. Wallis, *TDOT*, 4:457-58). [*ḥmd, 'wh*]

5:22 Your assembly *(qĕhalkem)*—This term for assembly can refer to a gathering in general, one without any particular structure or even purpose (Num. 22:4; Prov. 21:16), but usually it describes an organized body, one called together (thus the verb *qhl* for civil (1 Kings 12:3), military (Judg. 20:2), or religious reasons. The last is in view here and the occasion was the specific day on which Israel gathered to hear the revelation of God from Mount Sinai (Exod. 19:16-25; cf. 35:1-3). By gathering at divine direction and for such a specific purpose the assembly became formalized and not just loosely or randomly affiliated. In later times the term occurs to speak of Israel as a body congregating for worship festivals (2 Chron. 20:5; 30:25; Neh. 5:13) or, as here, to hear the word of God through the prophets (Jer. 26:17; 44:15). Eventually *qāhāl* became a technical term for the synagogue congregation and the assembly *(ekklēsia)* of the church. E. Carpenter, *NIDOTTE*, 3:888-92. [*qāhāl*]

5:24 His glory *(kĕbōdô)*—This noun is cognate to a verb *(kbd)* meaning "to be heavy, weighty" *(BDB,* 457; cf. Deut. 5:16). On the human level it can describe the honor of position (Gen. 45:13; Job 19:9), reputation (Eccl. 10:1; 2 Chron. 26:18), or family hierarchy (Mal. 1:6). When speaking of God (as here), glory is usually associated with some dramatic display of natural and super-natural phenomena such as fire, smoke, wind, or earthquake (Exod. 16:7, 10; 33:18-23; 34:16; 40:34-35; Num. 14:10; 16:19; Isa. 6:3). Theophany is the term commonly used to speak of these divine manifestations. The awesomeness of God's glory is expressed in this passage by its explanation as his "greatness." That is, the glory of God attests to his transcendant majesty and power. C. Collins, *NIDOTTE*, 2:581-82. [*kābôd*]

5:26 Mankind *(bāśār)*—This noun has a range of meaning from meat, the body, and family kinship, on the one hand, to the human race as opposed to the divine, on the other *(BDB,* 142). Here the contrast is between mere mortals and God above, the distance between which is so profound as to put mankind in peril should they even hear the voice of God. The purpose of the text here is to underscore the absolute transcendence of God. Only Moses' mediation would make it possible for divine communication to take place. The noun with this meaning occurs in only one other place in the book (Deut. 32:42) but it is common elsewhere in the Pentateuch (Gen. 6:12-13; Num. 16:22; 27:16), Prophets (Isa. 40:5-6; 49:26; 66:16, 23, 24; Jer. 12:12; 25:31; 32:27; 45:5; Ezek. 20:48; 21:4, 5; Joel 2:28; Zech. 2:13), and Writings (Ps. 65:2; 145:21). It is important theologically to note that unlike in Greek philosophy and anthropology, flesh in the OT is never considered inherently evil or something to be sloughed off at death in order for one to find true immortality. Rather, it is an essential constituent of human life, its only limitation being its mark of the mortal rather than divine being (N. Bratsiotis, *TDOT*, 2:325-26). [*bāśār*]

5:33 Prolong your days (*ha'ăraktem*)— This is a favorite term for longevity in this book (cf. 4:26, 40; 11:9; 17:20; 22:7; 30:18; 32:47), and hardly without exception it is linked to conditions or qualifications— you will live long if. . . . Usually those conditions have to do (as here) with keeping covenant with the Lord. To the extent that this is done, the nation may expect its tenure in the land to be extended. Moreover, the verb seldom refers to individuals (17:20-the king; 22:7-any individual) but pertains to the nation Israel as a whole. Theoretically, it seems, Israel would forever have occupied Canaan had she not sinned. This, of course, did not happen and over and over again her days there were curtailed. There is hope, however, in a day when she will be planted there again, never more to be uprooted (Deut. 30:1-10). [*'rk*]

6:4 One Lord (*yhwh 'eḥād*)—Verses 4 and 5, the confession of Israel known as the Shema (after the first word in v. 4, *šěma'*, "hear"), comprise perhaps the most theologically important text of the OT. When asked which was the greatest of the commandments Jesus cited the Shema (Matt. 22:37; Mark 12:29-30; Luke 10:27). It identifies who God is (v. 4) and spells out human responsibility in light of that disclosure (v. 5). As brief as v. 4 is, it has given rise to a number of translations, the two most popular being: (1) "Hear, O Israel, Yahweh our God is one Yahweh"; or (2) "Hear, O Israel, as for Yahweh our God, He alone is Yahweh" (P. Jensen, *NIDOTTE*, 1:350; M. Wilson, *NIDOTTE*, 4:1217-18). The debate revolves around the adjective *'eḥād*, which can, indeed, be rendered as either "one" or "only" (*BDB*, 25). The more natural translation grammatically is (1) and this also enjoys the support of Jewish and most Christian tradition. Taken this way, the emphasis is not so much on monotheism as on the exclusiveness of Yahweh as Lord. Of particular interest to later Christian theology is the fact that *'eḥād* is linked to a verb meaning "to join" or "unite," suggesting parts coming together to make a whole (KBL, 376). While it would be theologically premature and methodologically improper to maintain that the term in this context teaches that God is a unity of persons, it is valid to conclude that it accommodates the NT concept of a Triune God. [*'eḥād*]

6:5 Your heart (*lěbābkâ*)—This is the first theologically significant occurrence of this noun in Deuteronomy (cf. 1:28; 2:30; 4:9, 29, 39; 5:29). Contrary to much OT reference to human anatomy or physiology where organs or other parts of the body are to be taken literally, the heart is almost always to be understood figuratively (A. Luc, *NIDOTTE*, 2:749). Absent any knowledge of the brain (or at least of its function) in ancient Israel, the heart was considered the seat of the intellect and will (*BDB*, 523-25). The command here, then, to love (i.e., commit oneself to; cf. Deut. 4:37) the Lord with all one's heart means to obey him with full rationality and deliberate purpose. Love is more than mere emotion in the context of covenant relationship. It calls for intellectual understanding and purposeful compliance as well (cf. Deut. 10:12; 11:13, 18; 13:3; 26:16; 30:2, 6, 10). [*lēb, lēbāb*]

Your soul (*napšĕkâ*)—Older English translations—perhaps influenced by Hellenistic Greek and NT thought—have, for the most part, rendered *nepeš* as "soul." Comparative Semitic as well as actual OT usage favors a broader, less technical meaning such as "being" or even "person." This is clear from such passages as Gen. 2:19 where even animals are called "living souls" (i.e., "living creatures"; cf. Gen. 9:10, 15, 16; Lev. 11:46). Unless further qualified, then, *nepeš* should be considered synonymous with "being," that is, with the person as such. The Shema commands that one love the Lord with the entire being, an injunction especially at home in the covenant context of Deuteronomy (cf. 10:12; 11:13; 26:16; 30:2, 6, 10; H. Seebass, *TDOT*, 9:511). [*nepeš*]

Your strength (*mĕʾōdekâ*)—The base idea of this noun is "abundance" and when applied to activity carries the meaning of force or might (*BDB*, 547). If heart refers to the intellect and "soul" to the being (the person as such), then *mĕʾōd* relates to activity, to the work that people engage in. Israel must love God and manifest it not only conceptually, in the abstract, but in productive labor. Taking the noun in its common grammatical function as an adverbial accusative, one

could translate the phrase "love the Lord your God vigorously/unstintingly/powerfully," or the like. [*mĕʾōd*]

6:7 You shall teach them carefully (*šinnantām*)—This verb for teaching differs from the common one already addressed (4:1). Referring to the words of the Shema (and others), Moses instructs his hearers to impart them to their children in such a permanent way that they will forever be indelibly impressed on their minds. The verb, in its basis form, means "to sharpen" (*BDB*, 1043) but in the form here (and only here in the OT) it connotes the idea of engraving. Moses may have had in mind the incision of the Ten Commandments into the stone tablets (Exod. 32:16). Just as those words could never be obliterated, so parental teaching of the law must be so deeply etched on the tablets of their children's minds that they could never be forgotten. [*šnn*]

6:8 Sign and frontlets (*ʾôt, tôtāpôt*)—The sign (known today as *tĕpillâ*) and frontlets, strapped to the forearm and forehead respectively, were reminders to the Israelites and others that they were people of the Book, that is, the people to whom God had revealed himself and whom he had called to be his own special nation (cf. Exod. 13:9). These later consisted also of tiny boxes known as phylacteries (cf. Matt. 23:5) in which certain texts were placed (usually some or all of Exod. 13:1-10, 11-16; Deut. 6:4-9; 11:13-21). While not signs of the so-called Mosaic Covenant (the Sabbath served that purpose; Exod. 31:16-17), they were important identifiers of their wearers as people of that covenant [*ʾôt, tôtāpôt*]

6:11 Become full (*śābāʿtâ*)—This verb and its related nouns and adjectives connote the idea of satisfaction in general, but in most cases (as here) it is in respect to filling with food, that is, complete satisfaction of the appetite. That is the only sense of the verb in Deuteronomy and in each case eating and fullness occur together as almost a cliché (cf. 8:10, 12; 11:15; 14:29; 26:12; 31:20). However, fullness is often also in the context of a certain self-satisfaction that gives rise to a spirit of independence from the Lord and a turning to other gods to whom credit is given for life's bounties (vv. 12-15; 8:11-20; 11:16; 31:20). Bodily fullness typifies or represents satisfaction in all areas of life, a condition that, while not wrong in itself, can lead to denial of one's need for God. [śb']

6:16 You shall not test (*tĕnassû*)—Sometimes translated "tempt," the context is better suited to "test" for the Lord cannot be tempted (cf. Jas. 1:13). Moreover, no translation can do justice to the assonance of the verse for the verb (occurring twice here) comes from the same root as the place name Massah (cf. Exod. 17:7). One might render it: "Do not test the Lord your God as you tested him at the place called Testing." In a secular sense the verb is used to speak of testing material to see how good it is or what abuse it can sustain (1 Sam. 17:39). This, in effect, is how Israel dealt with the Lord in the desert. They probed, provoked, and pushed him to the extreme to see if his grace and patience had any limit. To their dismay and untold loss they found out eventually that even God's mercies could be exhausted (Num. 14:22; Ps. 78:18-22; 56-61; 95:8-11; 106:13-15). In light of that history Moses urges his hearers never to test the Lord again. [nsh]

6:18 What is right (*hayyāšār*)—Cognate to the verb *yšr*, be straight, right (BDB, 448),

this nominalized adjective has almost exclusively a figurative, theological usage in the OT, one associated with integrity and purity of lifestyle. Here it is linked with *ṭôb*, what is good, suggesting adherence to a moral standard. Elsewhere there is warning against doing what is right in one's own opinion (12:8) as opposed to doing what is right in the view of the Lord (12:25, 28; 13:18; 21:9). God himself is the criterion by which rightness is to be measured for one of his attributes is that he is upright (Deut. 32:4; cf. Ps. 25:8; 92:15; 119:137; Hos. 14:9). To be upright is to be godly, to conform to a standard set by the Lord as an expression of his own character. In the historical books this standard was the covenant law and it was in terms of this that Israel's and Judah's kings especially were judged to have done what is right or what is wrong (1 Kings 11:33, 38; 14:8; 15:5, 11; 22:43; 2 Kings 10:30; 12:2; 14:3; etc.). [yāšār]

6:25 Righteousness (*ṣĕdāqâ*)—A cognate term (*ṣedeq*) in Deut. 1:16 (which see) is construed as an adverb and thus translated "righteously." The noun here speaks of a condition of integrity, uprightness, or even justification. The clearest OT text with this latter meaning is Gen. 15:6 where it is said that Abraham believed (that is, put his full trust) in God and God translated that faith into righteousness (cf. Rom. 4:3; Gal. 3:6). Abraham was justified by exercising saving faith in the Lord. Here Moses says that those who are "careful to keep" the whole body of covenant law (the *miṣwâ*; cf. Deut. 4:2) will be considered by God as being righteous. This, however, does not speak of salvation from sin but in the context of the Sinai covenant it speaks of full alignment with the will and purpose of God (cf. Deut. 9:4-6; 24:13). D. Reimer, *NIDOTTE*, 3:753-54. [ṣĕdāqâ]

7:2 You shall make no covenant (tikrōt bĕrît)—The idiom for making a covenant is literally "cut a covenant" (for bĕrît, "covenant," see Deut. 4:13). The cutting may refer to engraving the words of covenant texts into stone or some other surface (E. Carpenter, NIDOTTE, 2:730). More likely it suggests the cutting up of animals as a part of the covenant ritual (M. Weinfeld, TDOT, 2:259; cf. Gen. 15:9-11, 17; Jer. 34:18-19). [krt]

You shall not have mercy on them (tĕhannēm)—The root idea of the hn/hnn semantic field is the bestowment of favor or the favor itself. In most cases in the OT God is the subject who dispenses such favor, usually to his own people Israel (Gen. 33:11; 43:29; Exod. 33:19; Ps. 4:1; 6:2; 9:13; 25:16; 26:11; Amos 5:15; Mal. 1:9). In such cases it is always an act of grace on God's part. Human beings are also expected to model this behavior on behalf of others, especially the poor and weak (Ps. 37:21, 26; Prov. 14:31; 19:17; 28:8). Sometimes no mercy or favor is to be extended. In fact, the enemies of the Lord and of Israel must not be beneficiaries of such grace but must (as here) be annihilated for they will lead God's people astray (T. Fretheim, NIDOTTE, 2:203-06). [hnn]

7:5 Their pillars (maṣṣēbōtām)—A common feature of Canaanite worship sites was a stone or wood pillar the meaning and purpose of which are not entirely clear. They seem not to have been representations of the deity such as idols or images but rather symbols of some kind of fertility force or principle (cf. Deut. 16:21-22). In any case, they must be destroyed because of their pagan associations (Exod. 23:24; 34:13; Deut. 12:3; 2 Kings 18:4; 23:14). When Israel erected its own pillars of this kind judgment inevitably followed (Hos. 10:1; 2 Kings

17:10). The maṣṣēbôt of the patriarchal stories are of a different kind, however. They served as monuments to some gracious appearance or act of the Lord and therefore as aids to memory (Gen. 28:18; 31:45; 35:14; cf. Exod. 24:4). The object itself was morally neutral, then. What mattered was its symbolical significance. [maṣṣēbâ]

Their asherim ('ăšêrēhem)—In Deuteronomy the pillars and asherim always appear together as two complementary parts of a single religious symbol and/or ritual (7:5; 12:3; 16:21-22). The term "asherim" derives from Asherah, the principal goddess of the Canaanite pantheon and wife at first of El and later of Baal (Judg. 3:7; 6:26; 1 Kings 16:32-33; 18:19; 2 Kings 17:16; 23:4). In the form 'ăšērîm (as here), however, the reference is not to the goddess per se but to a wood object representing her as the goddess of fertility. Sometimes this object was a living tree (or trees) (Deut. 16:21; Mic. 5:14) but usually, it seems, it was a pole driven into the ground (1 Kings 14:15, 23; 16:33; 2 Kings 17:10, 16; 21:3, 7; Isa. 17:8). In any case, Israel was commanded to root it out (2 Kings 23:6), cut it down (Exod. 34:13), and burn it up (Deut. 12:3). The instruction here is to cut the asherim down, an act appropriate to both a living tree and a pole implanted in the earth. The reason for this is that Israel is a holy people, one separated from the pagans who practice such abominable things (v. 6). ['ăšērâ]

7:6 Holy people ('am qādôš)—This specific description of Israel occurs only in Deuteronomy (cf. 14:2, 21, 26:19; 28:9; in Exod. 19:6 the term is gôy qādôš, "holy nation"). By etymology, to be holy means to be set apart for some special status or use (cf. Deut. 5:12). The context here spells out what it is to be a holy people. It is, first of all, to be "chosen" (bhr; cf. Deut. 4:37) and then to be regarded as God's special possession *('am sĕgullâ;* Deut. 14:2; 26:18). Here, at least, the moral dimensions of holiness are not in view. Israel's holiness consists of its separation from all other peoples as a testimony to God's elective grace and saving purposes (cf. v. 8). [*qādôš*]

A people of his own possession *('am sĕgullâ)*—A comparison of the term *sĕgullâ* with its cognates in other languages (especially Akkadian *sikiltu*) shows that it has the idea of special property, a valued treasure (KBL, 649). David's private wealth is thus described (1 Chron. 29:3). More important, Israel is considered God's uniquely invaluable possession (Exod. 19:5; Deut. 7:6; 14:2; 26:18; Ps. 135:4; Mal. 3:17). Out of all the nations of the earth he could have selected for his redemptive program, he chose Israel alone. This had nothing to do with any merit on Israel's part (v. 7) but sprang from God's covenant faithfulness to the patriarchs to whom he had committed himself (v. 8). [*sĕgullâ*]

7:7 Love *(ḥāšaq)*—This rare word for love conveys the idea of close attachment by the lover to the one loved (BDB, 365-366). Here it is closely connected to choose *(bḥr)* and therefore suggests that God's election of Israel has a binding quality to it (see also Deut. 10:15). It is covenant relationship to the nation that was not just a purely legal affair but one that brought about an inseparable connection. [*ḥšq*]

7:8 Redeemed you *(yipdĕkâ)*—This verb, as opposed to its equally common synonym *(g'l)*, carries more the idea of the payment of a ransom on behalf of one in some kind of bondage. Moreover, it is the only one of the two that occurs in Deuteronomy (7:8; 9:26; 13:5; 15:15; 21:8; 24:18), always with reference to the

Exodus from Egypt. The aspect of ransom in the Exodus comes from the idea that God "owned" the firstborn of all Israelite families since he had spared them, unlike the firstborn of the Egyptians, from the tenth plague (cf. Exod. 13:11-16). The payment for Israel's release should have been the death of their eldest sons but the Lord graciously allowed each of these to be substituted by animal sacrifices at first and later by the substitutionary service of the Levites (Num. 3:11-13, 40-45). (R. Hubbard, *NIDOTTE*, 3:578). [*pdh*]

7:9 The faithful God *(hanne'ĕmān)*—The form here is a participle of a verb *('mn)* meaning to confirm or support (BDB, 52). The idea here, then, is that God is one upon whom one can depend, especially in terms of his covenant relationship and promises. He keeps covenant in absolute fidelity with those who reciprocate by obeying its requirements. The Lord is described this way only in this passage and in Isa. 49:7, where the context again is one of divine choice and redemption of God's people Israel. [*'mn*]

7:10 Recompensing *(mĕšallēm)*—The basic meaning of the verb in this stem is to make intact, complete (KBL, 979-80). The well-known nominal derivative, *šālôm*, thus bears the fundamental idea of wellness, wholeness, completeness—all components of peace. In legal contexts the verb conveys the concept of restoring moral and legal equilibrium by exacting punishment or granting reward according to the just deserts in an individual case. The latter use is quite rare (cf. 1 Sam. 24:19) but in the sense of recompense as judgment or reparation it is common (cf. Deut. 32:41; 2 Sam. 3:39; Job 21:19; Ps. 31:23). The recompense here is by God against all who violate his covenant demands (v. 9). This is construed as hating him, a sin so egregious as to deserve destruction at God's hands. To repay to their face (twice in this verse and only here) suggests a face-to-face encounter in which the Lord calls the guilty to account, lays out the charges against them, and then delivers the sentence commensurate to the wrongdoing. [*šlm*]

7:13 The young *('aštĕrōt)*—This noun, occurring only in Deuteronomy (here and 28:4, 18, 51), most likely is related to the name of the Canaanite goddess Ashtoreth, a deity associated with fertility and reproduction (Judg. 2:13; 10:6; 1 Sam. 7:3, 4; 12:10; 31:10; 1 Kings 11:5, 33). Why the offspring of sheep alone are designated by this term is not clear. Moreover, its use in the OT to refer to animal offspring by no means suggests that the Israelites understood lambs to be somehow connected to this pagan goddess. Most likely the word is a Hebrew loanword from Canaanite, one that lost its heathen overtones in this particuar formula (M. Moore and M. Brown, *NIDOTTE*, 3:728). [*'aštĕrōt*]

7:15 Sickness *(ḥŏlî)*—This is a generic term for illness whether caused by disease or by injury (cf. 1 Kings 22:34; Jer. 6:7). It could be just a part of the normal human condition (1 Kings 17:17; 2 Kings 13:14; Isa. 38:9) or the result of God's judgment (2 Chron. 21:15, 19; Hos. 5:13). The present passage assures Israel that obedience to the terms of the covenant will guarantee her healing of all sickness and plague. Disobedience, on the other hand, will invite all of these and more in the day of the Lord's wrath (Deut. 28:58-61). The grace of God can yet intervene, however, as is clear from Isa. 53:3-4. There the suffering Servant is described as one who is familiar with sickness but who, in turn, will take upon Himself the sicknesses with which His people are beset. [*ḥŏlî*]

7:16 You shall not pity *(tāḥōs)*—With a human subject, this verb is normally found in the idiom "your eye shall (not) look upon with pity," etc. This suggests that even when one sees the pitiful condition of one sentenced to God's judgment because of his or her sin, this is to have no deterring effect in carrying out the judgment. It is easier to punish in the abstract than in an actual, individual instance. Those not to be pitied by either the Lord of his agents may be the condemned nations of Canaan (as here) and others (Isa. 13:18), national Israel (Ezek. 5:11; 7:9; 8:18), or individuals within Israel (Deut. 13:8-9; 19:13; 1 Sam. 24:10). The implication is that they are beyond redemption and therefore underserving of compassion. [*ḥws*]

A snare *(môqēš)*—Though originating in the realm of hunting and fishing, this noun and its related verb *yqš* (cf. v. 25) almost always have a figurative meaning in the OT. It describes both an attraction to that which brings disaster and the disaster itself. Israel's temptation to go after other gods will result in her being ensnared by them (cf. Exod. 23:33; 34:12; Judg. 2:3; 8:27). On the other hand, the Lord becomes a snare to his disobedient people who refuse to repent (Isa. 8:14). Proverbs makes special use of this image, referring to such evil behavior as improper speech (12:13; 18:7; 20:25), unwise friendships (22:25), and transgression in general (29:6) as a trap to be avoided. Sinners are constantly attempting to seduce the righteous, thereby becoming a snare to them (Ps. 64:5; 140:5; 141:9). Because of this, Moses here commands that the Canaanites be destroyed, thus eliminating the temptation to Israel to follow their gods. [*môqēš*]

7:18 You must be sure to remember *(zākōr tizkōr)*—To remember means more, in biblical thought, than merely to call to mind some past event. It means to inculcate and act upon the thing remembered. In this case, the Israelites, facing overpowering enemies in Canaan, must not fear because as they reflected on the plagues in Egypt and the Exodus deliverence they could be confident that what God had done for them in history he would replicate in the present and future (v. 19). The verb construction here is emphatic. The people must not just remember in passing but they must set out to remember by an act of will and determination. Deuteronomy is particularly rich in this admonition, almost always referring to the Exodus event (5:15; 7:18; 8:2; 9:7; 15:15; 16:3, 12; 24:18; 25:17-18). [zkr]

7:21 Dreadful *(nôrā')*—This adjective is a participle of the verb yr', "to fear." In this form it carries the passive nuance of something to be feared, that is, something (or someone) that inspires fear in another person. When the Lord is described in this manner the fear can be stark terror, especially among his enemies (Zeph. 2:11), or it can be a sense of reverence and awe on the part of his own people (Exod. 34:10; Job 37:22; Ps. 47:2; 68:35). Although God in his very essence is awe-inspiring, he is usually described as such because of the works he has done (Ps. 66:3, 5; 145:6). [yr']

7:23 Confusion *(mĕhûmâ)*—In the present text the noun is a cognate accusative to the verb hwm, murmur, roar, discomfit (*BDB*, 273). The one causing such distress is usually the Lord (1 Sam. 5:9, 11; 2 Chron. 15:5; Isa. 22:5; Ezek. 7:7; 22:5; Amos 3:9; Zech. 14:13). It is an expression of judgment, especially for covenant disobedience by his people (cf. Deut. 28:20). There is not so

much the idea of physical harm as there is mental and emotional anguish. Terror because of real or imagined threats will throw the objects of God's wrath into uncontrollable panic. [mĕhûmâ]

7:25 Abomination to the Lord *(tô'ăbat yhwh)*—In this context the reference is to the images of the Canaanites that were so detestable to the Lord that they must be totally destroyed. Even the precious metals that adorned them were ritually contaminated to the point that they also must be left unclaimed by Israel. To do otherwise was to risk becoming personally abominable and to incur the wrath and judgment of God (v. 26). What made a thing or a practice abominable was its lack of conformity to the perfections of the Lord himself and to the moral and ethical expectations he demanded of those who called him God. In Deuteronomy this included images (7:25-26; 27:15; 32:16), pagan worship (12:31; 13:14; 17:4; 18:9, 12; 20:18), improper sacrifice (17:1; 23:18), failure to observe principles of separation (22:5), improper marriage (24:4), and dishonesty in business (25:16). (M. Grisanti, *NIDOTTE*, 4:314-18). [tô'ēbâ]

7:26 You shall utterly detest it *(šaqqēṣ tĕšaqqĕṣennû)*—This rare verb (only here in Deut.; cf. Lev. 11:13, 23, 43; 20:25; Ps. 22:24) derives from a noun describing something ritually impure such as birds of prey or creeping insects (*BDB*, 1054-55). Just as such things could not be presented as offerings to holy God or ingested as human food, so the images of pagan gods were so reprehensible to God that they must be totally destroyed (v. 25). They were to be devoted to Him (that is, placed under ḥērem; cf. 2:34), and therefore could not be retained by his people. Should they be kept they could

Deuteronomy

cause the wrath of God to fall upon those who took them for they too would then be placed under the ban (or *ḥērem*). An example of this was Achan, who stole from Jericho some articles that were to have been devoted to the Lord. This resulted in his death and the death of his entire family (Josh. 7:1, 16-21). [*šqṣ*]

8:2 That he might humble you (*'annōtĕkâ*)—The context here indicates that God's humbling of Israel was disciplinary in intent. It was to put the people in such a position that they could prove to Him whether or not they were capable of obeying the terms of the covenant He had made with them. That does not mean, of course, that the omniscient God cannot know the human heart and intentions without such testings. The humbling was for Israel's benefit so that they could properly assess their own capacity for faithfulness. Once it was over it would turn out to be a means of bringing Israel blessing (v. 16). The root idea of *'nh* is to be made low (*BDB*, 776). Sometimes one must be brought low before he or she can be exalted (cf. Luke 14:11; 18:14). The same verb in v. 3 makes even clearer the pedagogical value of being humbled. Israel, deprived of ordinary food and drink in the deserts, received manna from heaven and thus learned that what God provides is far better than what one can earn for himself (cf. Matt. 4:4). [*'nh*]

8:5 As a man disciplines his son so the Lord your God disciplines you (*yĕyassēr, mĕyassĕrekâ*)—These two verb froms (imperfect and participle respectively) express the proverbial idea that educational correction is beneficial whether on the human or divine level. The verb occurs earlier (Deut. 4:36) with the simple meaning of instruction but here and elsewhere

in Deuteronomy (21:18; 22:18) the thrust is more toward punishment for refractory behavior. It is nevertheless loving in its intention for it is the father eager to inculcate values who applies such discipline (cf. Prov. 3:12; 13:24; 29:17). All the sufferings in Israel's desert sojourn were designed, then, to bring the people into conformity with God's plans and purposes for them. (R. Branson, *TDOT*, 6:129-30). [*ysr*]

8:11 You forget (*tišaḥ*)—To forget is obviously the opposite of to remember but just as remembering (*zkr*; cf. Deut. 7:18) means more than merely calling something to mind so forgetting is not just a lapse of memory. It connotes the idea of neglecting someone or something and, in Deuteronomy especially, it is tantamount to covenant violation. To forget the Lord is to ignore Him and to be disobedient to the terms of the covenant made with Him. Moses had already enjoined Israel not to forget God's past works on their behalf (4:9; 6:12) and he continued to do so (8:14). More important, they must not forget that He is their God and that they have committed themselves to Him (4:23; 8:19; 26:13). Sadly, the record is clear that they did precisely that (32:18). Despite this, God had not forgotten them (4:31). In the passage at hand the danger is that when Israel had entered Canaan and had begun to prosper she would forget that it was the Lord who had made possible all of these things for which Israel would take credit (vv. 12-17). [*škḥ*]

8:16 To do you good (*lĕhêtîbĕkâ*)—The humbling (8:2) and disciplining (8:5) God had brought upon Israel in the years of desert wandering were designed for one purpose only—for their well-being. No chastening seems good in the midst of the process but eventually it produces beneficial results (Heb. 12:11). The good spoken of here includes physical and material blessings as v. 17 makes clear. But more than that is meant by this form of the verb. Elsewhere in Deuteronomy there are clear spiritual implications including the capacity to keep covenant and to find and enjoy meaningful life (Deut. 30:5; Jer. 32:40-41). To disobey the Lord will annul His goodness, however (Deut. 28:63; cf. Jer. 18:10). The root idea of the verb is that of pleasing or being pleased. To do good to Israel is to do what brings pleasure to her, that which is most satisfying and fulfilling, especially in spiritual terms [yṭb]

8:19 You will perish (tō'bēdûn)—The verb 'bd appears earlier in Deuteronomy (4:26; 7:10, 20, 24) but the present text most clearly suggests the full range of its meaning. The Lord had commanded Israel to exterminate the Canaanites from the land (7:20-24) but now he says that the same fate He had reserved for these pagan nations (8:20) would fall upon Israel if she forgot him and began to serve other gods. The point is not that Israel would or even could be annihilated for that would contradict God's promise that he would preserve at least a remnant of them (Gen. 17:6-8). Rather, Israel would be totally destroyed in the sense of being uprooted from the land and sent into exile (cf. Deut. 11:17; 28:20-22, 63; 30:18). The imperfect plus infinitive absolute construction underscores the certainty of the judgment God will bring if His people remain unrepentant. (B. Otzen, TDOT, 1:22). ['bd]

9:3 He will subdue them (yaknî'ēm)—The basic meaning of this verb, to be humble, takes on the causative nuance in the stem employed here; i.e., to humiliate (Job 40:12; Ps. 107:12; Isa. 25:5) or (as here) to subdue, especially in a military sense (cf.

Judg. 4:23; 2 Sam. 8:1; 1 Chron. 17:10; Neh. 9:24; Ps. 81:14). The juxtaposition of the verb here with šmd (destroy) and 'bd (perish) indicates that the subjugation is nothing short of total defeat. The humiliation of the occupants of Canaan will, thus, be more than mere embarrassment. Furthermore, it is the Lord who will accomplish all this and not Israel. That is, the verb communicates an aspect of so-called holy war (S. Wagner, TDOT, 7:205-07). [kn']

9:5 He might establish the word (hāqîm)—This verb, the causative form of qwm, "to stand," suggests the idea of making something firm or steadfast, in this case the covenant promises God had made to the patriarchs (Gen. 13:14-17; 28:4; cf. Deut. 8:18). He would also establish the nation Israel as His people as they obeyed the covenant requirements He had outlined to them (Deut. 28:9). The two ideas are joined in Deut. 29:13 where the Lord bases his establishment of Israel as a chosen people on the oath He had sworn to Abraham, Isaac, and Jacob. The assurance of the Lord that He will make firm His promises is seen outside Deuteronomy as well (Gen. 26:3; Lev. 26:9; 1 Sam. 1:23; 1 Kings 6:12). (E. Martens, NIDOTTE, 3:903-04). [qwm]

9:6 Stiff-necked (qĕšēh 'ōrep)—This idiom, literally "hard of neck," is a metaphor used to describe stubbornness. It arose perhaps from the world of agriculture where a draft animal such as an ox would refuse to bow its neck to the yoke thus manifesting rebellion against its owner (cf. 1 Kings 12:4). The adjective is a particularly fitting way to describe stubborn Israel (cf. Isa. 1:3). They had followed idols instead of the Lord (Exod. 32:9; 33:3, 5; 34:9; Deut. 9:12-13) and in general had been disobedient to His covenant law (Deut. 31:27). The only remedy was a spiritual circumcision of the heart, a change of life that would make them compliant to the will go God (Deut. 10:16). [qĕšēh,'ōrep]

9:12 Become corrupt (šiḥēt)—This form of the verb means to take on the nature of something that is spoiled such as a vineyard (Jer. 12:10) or a polluted spring (Prov. 25:26). Morally or spiritually it describes persons whose habits and dispositions are ungodly, perverse, and worldly (BDB, 1008). One must take care lest such a spirit prevail and he or she be turned to such wickedness as idolatry (Deut. 4:16). Such warnings notwithstanding, Moses predicted that after his death the people would corrupt themselves and thus bring God's judgment upon them (Deut. 31:29). In almost every case (as here) where spiritual corruption is in view, there is close connection to pagan worship (Deut. 4:25; Ezek. 23:11-12). [šḥt]

A cast image (massēkâ)—Its derivation from the verb nsk, pour out, suggests the meaning a poured out thing, that is, a product of a process whereby molten metals became shaped into some kind of plastic object. In this case—and regularly throughout the OT—the term came to be a technical one for an image or idol of metal. Moses reflects here on the occasion of the making of the golden calf, a procedure involving both the melting and shaping of the precious metal into the desired result (Exod. 32:4, 24). No doubt with this in mind the prophet later inveighed against the manufacture and worship of images of this kind (Deut. 27:15). To do so would invite God's judgment. Later prophets also roundly condemned cast images (Hos. 13:2; Nah. 1:14; Hab. 2:18), Isaiah in particular (Isa. 30:22; 42:17). The reason, of course, is that idols and their worship are a direct violation of the second commandment (Deut. 5:8). [massēkâ]

9:14 That I might blot out their name ('emḥeh)—This foreboding message constitutes a test of Moses to see what his reaction might be to the offer of the Lord to make him the founder of a new nation (cf. Exod. 32:10). To blot out Israel's name is synonymous with destroying them as the juxtaposition of the verbs šmd (cf. Deut. 1:27) and mḥh makes clear. One can only speculate as to what the Lord would have done had Moses refused to intercede for his people. Would he have made Moses a second Abraham through whom He would have inaugurated an entirely new program of world redemption? The answer seems to be a resounding no, for the promises made to Abraham, Isaac, and Jacob were unequivocal and unconditional (Gen. 15:5-7, 13-16; cf. Rom. 9:1-5; 11:1-32). In any case, the point is academic because of Moses' faithful pleading on Israel's behalf. The idiom "blot out the name" derives from the practice of erasing inscriptions from monuments and manuscripts so as to annul any memory of persons and events commemorated there (cf. Deut. 25:19; 29:20; 2 Kings 14:27). In a more positive way, the verb speaks of the blotting out of sins by the Lord so that they will never again be brought to mind by Him, that is, in a punitive or retributive way (Ps. 51:1, 9; Isa. 43:25; 44:22). L. Alonso-Schökel, TDOT, 8:229-30. [mḥh]

9:16 You had sinned (ḥāṭā'tem)—This common verb for sin (ca. 238x in the OT) occurs only 6x in Deuteronomy, a most surprising fact considering the attention given to sin in this book. The root idea of the verb has to do with missing a mark, goal, or standard. In the literal sense it describes sharpshooters who never missed the enemy with their slingshots (Judg. 20:16). Morally, Israel confessed to having missed the mark of God's will by refusing to enter Canaan when commanded to do so (Deut. 1:41; cf. Num. 14:26-35, 40). The present passage relates Israel's terrible sin of the golden calf (vv. 16, 18), a sin clarified here as a "turning away" (swr) from the path God had set before them. To miss the mark of God's will is the same as deviating from it. Elsewhere, pagan idolatry is viewed as missing the mark (Deut. 20:18) as is involvement in improper marriage relationships (Deut. 24:4). [ḥṭ']

9:19 Anger ('ap)—This common noun also means "nose" or "nostril" (BDB, 60), suggesting perhaps that anger is manifested sometimes by the reddening of the nose or dilating of the nostrils. It is synonymous with other terms such as ḥēmâ (Deut. 29:23, 28), ka'aś (Deut. 32:27), and qeṣep (Josh. 9:20). Several of these combine in this verse to lend emphasis to the intensity of God's wrath. Moses says he feared God's anger ('ap) and burning wrath (ḥēmâ), a combination to be construed as hendiadys, that is, with the second noun modifying the first: "his hotly burning anger," or the like. He goes on to relate that that anger was expressed by the Lord as He was wrathful (qāṣap, the verb form of qeṣep). What prompted this rage was the worship of the golden calf, a violation of the first two commandments. Like other displays of emotion by the Lord, anger must be understood in its physical and/or psychological manifestations as an anthropopathism, that is, the attributing of human characteristics to God. His anger is a response to evil resulting in an act of judgment unless turned aside by grace and/or repentance. (B. Baloian, NIDOTTE, 4:380-81). ['ap]

9:20 I prayed ('etpallēl)—Of the many words in the OT used to express prayer of

some kind, this common one connotes intercession in particular. It occurs more than 80x in the OT but only twice in Deuteronomy and both in this passage (cf. v. 26). In v. 20 the plea by Moses is to spare Aaron despite his leadership role in the golden calf incident. In v. 26 his concern is for Israel as a whole, again because of her idolatry while he was on the mountain. The verb form here—and the one usually found—is reflexive, suggesting that prayer is more than just a one-way communication. As Moses struggles with God on behalf of those he loves he is aware of God's involvement in and response to his struggle. (P. Verhoef, NIDOTTE, 4:1060-61). [pll]

9:27 Their wickedness (riš'ô)—This noun, parallel here to ḥaṭṭa't, "sin" (cf. v. 16), is elsewhere an antonym to ṣedeq, "righteousness" (Ps. 45:7), and 'emet, "truth" (Prov. 8:7). In its masculine form (as here) it appears only here in Deuteronomy. The feminine gender form (riš'â) has the same meaning but usually refers not to Israelites but to the pagan nations of Canaan (Deut. 9:4, 5). [reša']

10:1 Ark ('ărôn)—In this case, the word itself has little theological significance but the thing it describes is rich in theological content. The noun refers to the wood chest Moses was commanded to build as a throne for the invisible God (Exod. 25:22; 1 Sam. 4:4; 2 Sam. 6:2; 2 Kings 19:15; Isa. 37:16) as well as a container for the stone tablets of the law (hence, "the ark of the covenant"; e.g., Num. 10:33; Deut. 10:8; 31:9; Josh. 3:3) and other objects (Exod. 16:33-34; Num. 17:10; Heb. 9:4). Apart from Deut. 31:9, 26, the ark is referred to only here (vv. 1, 2, 3, 5, 8) in the book. The scene in view is the occasion when Moses had first been instructed to build an ark

(Exod. 25:10-15) and then to place the stone tablets of the covenant text into it (v. 16). This did not actually take place until after the destruction of the golden calf and the rewriting of the commandments on new tablets (Exod. 34:1; 40:2). From then on the ark represented the presence of the Lord among His people, so much so that they would not move forward in their journeys until the ark moved (Num. 10:33-36; Josh. 3:3, 7-13) nor would they think to go into battle without it (Josh. 6:6-7; 1 Sam. 4:3-4). Unfortunately, the ark came to be understood by some as a guarantee of God's presence by itself, a kind of fetish that worked its own magic. The capture of the ark by the Philistines—though it eventually brought harm to them—was sufficient to dispel that notion (1 Sam. 4:1-7:2). (S. Hague, *NIDOTTE*, 1:503-04). [*ărôn*]

10:6 Became a priest *(waykahēn)*—This rare verb derives from the noun *kōhēn*, "priest," and in this form means basically to act as a priest (*BDB*, 464). Aaron had died and in line with the precedent established here his eldest son succeeded him thus acting as priest on his behalf (cf. Num. 3:1-4; 20:22-29). To act as priest should not imply any question of legitimacy of succession. All that is meant is that Eleazar, who had already been designated as the next chief priest, came, in fact, to occupy that office. [*khn*]

10:8 Set apart *(hibdîl)*—The call of the tribe of Levi to priestly service was a call to absolute separation from so-called secular or mundane pursuits. It went so far as to deny the tribe a territorial allotment except for 48 towns located strategically throughout the promised land (Num. 3:5-10; cf. 8:5-22; 35:1-8). They were not to engage in farming or other livelihoods but must restrict themselves to the service of the Lord in religious vocation (Deut. 18:1-5; cf. Neh. 13:10-14). The radical nature of this separation is clear from other instances of the use of this form of the verb. It occurs in the Creation account to describe the division between light and darkness (Gen. 1:4). It also describes the dividing partition between the Holy Place and Most Holy Place of the tabernacle (Exod. 26:33). Finally, the verb is used to mark the distinction between pure and impure animals (Lev. 20:25) and holy and unholy things in general (Lev. 10:10). [*bdl*]

To minister to him *(lĕšārĕtô)*—Occasionally this verb occurs in secular contexts to speak of important household servants (Gen. 39:4; 2 Sam. 13:17, 18), personal aides (2 Kings 4:43; 6:15), or royal officials (1 Chron. 27:1; Esth. 1:10). Usually, however, it is descriptive of those who serve in public worship such as priests (Deut. 17:12; 21:5; Jer. 33:21) and Levites (Num. 3:6; 8:26; 1 Chron. 15:2). The present passage makes clear that the Levites (in this case) perform their service "to him," that is, to the Lord. There is no room for self-service or self-promotion for God must be the focus of all the efforts and energies of those especially set apart to ministry. In fact, ministry by the Levites must be so preoccupied by the things of God that he himself was the summation of all that they were and were to do. He would be their inheritance rather than lands and goods (v. 9). [*šrt*]

10:9 Portion *(hēleq)*—The noun derives from the verb *hlq*, "to divide," and describes in general any result of the act of dividing. This can be a group of men (Gen. 14:24), a piece of property (2 Kings 9:10, 36, 37), the fruit of one's labor (Eccl. 2:10; 5:19), or the outcome of one's good or bad behavior (Isa. 17:14). Here (as in Deut. 12:12; 14:27, 29; 18:1; Josh. 14:4; 18:7) the reference is to the Levites and their lack of any tribal allotment in Canaan (cf. Num. 18:20-24). Its frequent connection to *naḥălâ* ("inheritance"), here and in a number of other passages, establishes the idea that *ḥēleq* commonly has geographic connotations, specifically territory assigned by Joshua to the various descendants of Jacob. The lack of such real estate by Levi is more than offset by the declaration that the Lord himself would be their portion; i.e., their inheritance (cf. Deut. 18:2; Josh. 13:33). [*ḥēleq*]

10:16 Circumcise *(maltem)*—In this passage the verb is obviously to be taken as figurative for repentance or renewal. Its literal use refers to the physical act whereby a male gave evidence of his membership in the covenant community of Israel (Lev. 12:3; Josh. 5:2-9). This was demanded of Abraham first of all as a sign of the covenant God had made with him and his descendants (Gen. 17:9-14) and then Moses incorporated it into the law to connect the ancient Abrahamic Covenant with the Sinaitic, thus showing their continuity and connection (Exod. 12:43-51). To circumcise the heart suggests renewal of covenant, a repentance toward God that is expressed here also as being no longer stiff-necked (cf. 9:6). Paul makes the point that authentic circumcision is not physical but spiritual, not in the body but in the heart (Rom. 2:28-29; cf. 4:11; Gal. 5:2-6; 6:11-16), the very point Moses makes in this OT text. [*mwl*]

10:17 The mighty . . . God *(haggibbōr)*—The most common use of this adjective is to describe human subjects, usually warriors and other valiant persons (cf. Gen. 10:9; Josh. 10:2; 1 Sam. 16:18; 2 Sam. 1:19, 25, 27; 2 Kings 5:1). When applied to God (only here in Deuteronomy.) it speaks of

him as the powerful one who is able to assist the weak and wreak vengeance on their (and his) enemies. The form of the divine name with this adjective is most frequently *'ēl*, not the longer *'ĕlōhîm* (cf. Neh. 9:32; Isa. 10:21; Jer. 32:18). Most significant is the occurrence of this epithet in Isa. 9:6, a passage universally recognized as messianic. Among other names, the coming Messiah is called "Mighty God." When applied to Jesus this affirms both his deity and his conquering power as King of kings and Lord of lords. (R. Wakely, *NIDOTTE*, 1:812). [*gibbōr*]

A bribe *(šōḥad)*—The underlying verb *šḥd* has the meaning of giving a gift but nearly always with the end in view of getting something in return (cf. Job 6:22; Isa. 45:13; Ezek. 16:33). Such a gift obviously qualifies as a bribe rather than as an expression of goodwill or affection. Human beings might indeed accept such gifts and respond by granting some favor or other (cf. 1 Kings 15:19; 2 Kings 16:8), especially in courts of law with crooked judges (cf. Deut. 16:19; 27:25; 1 Sam. 8:3; 2 Chron. 19:7; Ps. 15:5; Prov. 17:23), but the Lord cannot and will not be bribed. He is not impressed by one's station in life nor moved by human effort to change his righteous purposes. [*šōḥad*]

10:18 Orphan *(yātôm)*—Since family security and even survival in ancient Israel depended largely on the presence of a father, a child without a father was considered to be an orphan even if his or her mother was still living. There is no evidence in the OT that both parents must be deceased in order for their children to be orphaned. In a few places, in fact (as here), orphan and widow are in parallel or at least juxtaposed suggesting that the child of a widow was deemed to be an orphan (cf. Exod. 22:22, 24; Deut. 14:29;

16:11; 24:17, 19, 20, 21; Job 22:9; 24:3, 9; Ps. 68:5; 109:9; Isa. 1:17, 23). It is because the orphan, widow, and resident alien lacked strong human protection that the Lord was especially concerned for them and commanded his people to care for them. [*yātôm*]

Widow (*'almānâ*)—Lack of government social welfare programs left weak and dependent citizens of OT Israel in a vulnerable position. This was particularly true of orphans (see previous word) and widows. The Lord therefore exhorted the covenant community to deal kindly with widows who otherwise were left to their own extremely limited resources (cf. Exod. 22:22; Deut. 14:29; 24:17, 19, 20, 21; Jer. 7:6; 22:3; 49:11; Zech. 7:10). The term is used figuratively of Jerusalem to describe the city's pitiful plight following its destruction by Babylonia (Lam. 1:1). [*'almānâ*]

10:20 You shall cleave (*tidbāq*)—Fundamentally, the verb means to cling to or be close to (*BDB*, 179). A particularly poignant case is the definition of marriage in Genesis where it is said that a man should leave his parents and cleave to his wife, that is, in effect to become one with her (Gen. 2:24; cf. Matt. 19:5; 1 Cor. 6:16; Eph. 5:31). To cleave to the Lord, then, is to forsake all other gods, real or imaginary, and become fully identified with him. This is strongly covenant in its overtones and thus occurs with some frequency in Deuteronomy (11:22; 13:4; 30:20) and elsewhere (Josh. 22:5; 23:8; 2 Kings 18:6) in connection with covenant fidelity. [*dbq*]

10:21 He is your praise (*tĕhillatkâ*)—This derivative of the verb *hll*, to praise, refers most commonly either to the act of praising God, a word or song of praise, or the occasion or object of praise. The latter

sense is in view here and by a figure of speech called metonymy the Lord himself is described as Israel's praise (as the parallel "your God" makes clear). That is, he is worthy of praise and therefore constitutes the very essence of praise itself. It is striking, however, that the Lord is called "praise" only here and in Jer. 17:14 (for something similar see Ps. 109:1; 148:14). There are, of course, hundreds of instances in which his people are called upon to praise him, an act most appropriate in light of His awesome splendor and majesty. (H. Ringgren, *TDOT,* 3:410). [*tĕhillâ*]

11:2 The discipline (*mûsar*)—This derivative of the verb *ysr*, discipline, admonish (*BDB*, 415), occurs only here in Deuteronomy and is part of a list of the Lord's dealings with his people through the years of the wilderness wanderings. They had observed what he did to Pharaoh and his armies (vv. 3-4) and also how he judged Israel for its rebellious disobedience (vv. 5-7). This took place partly to punish the wicked and partly to instruct witnesses to these things as to how they were to walk before their God. Human beings are said to exercise discipline (Prov. 1:2, 7; 6:23; 8:10; 10:17; 12:1), but the more profoundly theological work of discipline is that of the Lord who carries it out for the betterment of those to whom he applies it (Job 33:16; 36:10; Jer. 35:13; Zeph. 3:7). Not all receive it, however, and for them there are severe repercussions (Jer. 17:23; 32:35; Zeph. 3:2). [*mûsar*]

11:8 You might be strong (*teḥezqû*)—Though commonly occurring in formulas of exhortation to be brave or courageous (as in Deut. 31:6, 7, 23; Josh. 1:6, 7, 9, 18; 10:25, etc.), the context here speaks of military might in anticipation of the conquest of Canaan (thus *BDB*, 304). Such strength comes not by human exercise, however, but by obedience to the commandments of the Lord. It was by such trust and compliance with the will of God that Israel was later able to cross the Jordan and destroy the city of Jericho (Josh. 3:7-4:7; 6:15-21). The biblical principle is clear: Success is not by might nor by power but by God's Holy Spirit (Zech. 4:6; cf. Eph. 6:17). [*ḥzq*]

11:9 Milk and honey *(ḥālāb ûdĕbāš)*—This descriptive way of underscoring the richness of the land of promise should not be taken in an exclusively literal way though these items certainly were part of Israel's food supply in years to come (Judg. 4:19; 14:8-9; 1 Sam. 14:25-29; 2 Sam. 17:29; Isa. 7:15, 22). Rather, they represent products available naturally (honey) and as the fruit of animal husbandry (milk). These were hard to come by in the Sinai deserts where rainfall was sparse and the soils resistant to agriculture. Comparatively speaking, then, Canaan was a virtual paradise where produce in abundance would be available. It was, in that sense, "flowing with milk and honey" (Exod. 3:8, 17; 13:5; 33:3; Lev. 20:24; Num. 14:8; 16:13, 14; Deut. 6:3; 26:9, 15; 27:3; Josh. 5:6; Jer. 11:5; 32:22; Ezek. 20:6, 15). Moreover, Canaan would not require irrigation as did Egypt, for the Lord blessed it with abundant rainfall and streams (vv. 10-12). [*ḥālāb, dĕbāš*)

11:12 Cares for *(dōrēš)*—This unusual meaning of the verb (usually translated "seek") occurs only here in Deuteronomy (cf. also Job 3:4; Ps. 142:4; Prov. 31:13; Isa. 62:12; Jer. 30:17). So preoccupied is the Lord with the land of Canaan that his eyes are upon it year round, that is, through every cycle of the agricultural seasons. In that sense, then, the verb can have both meanings, to seek and to care. Theologically, this inordinate interest in one small territory must be traced back to the original promise to Abraham that God would lead him to a special land (Gen. 12:1) that forever would be the geographic focus of his redemptive program (Gen. 17:8). God cares for the land, then, because it is the center of the universe theologically speaking. [*drš*]

11:16 Be deceived *(yipteh)*—The root idea of this verb is to be naive or simple, that is, inexperienced (*BDB*, 834). A person in this condition can be easily led astray. He or she is like a "silly dove," turning in every which direction for assistance (Hos. 7:11). Here the Lord warns Israel against such childishness lest they forsake him and go after false gods. Such a pursuit will invite his strong, punitive reaction against them (v. 17). The only way to safeguard oneself from such a foolish course of action is to take special heed to one's inner disposition. [*pth*]

11:26 A curse *(qĕlālâ)*—An antonymn of blessing *(bĕrākâ)*, this noun nearly always is a technical term used to describe the result of covenant disobedience. That clearly is the meaning here, for v. 28 declares that God's curse will fall upon those who ignore his commandments and turn aside to other gods. In other words, those who break the first two commandments are especially subject to God's wrath (cf. Deut. 5:7-10). The covenant associations of the verb are evident from its frequency in Deuteronomy and the so-called deuteronomic literature. Of 33 occurrences in all the OT, 11 are in Deuteronomy and five in Joshua, Judges, Samuel, and Kings. Eight other times it appears in Jeremiah, a book recognized as being heavily influenced by deuteronomic theology. [*qĕlālâ*]

12:2 Lush tree *('ēṣ ra'ănān)*—This adjective, when applied to plants in general, connotes the idea of freshness or luxuriance (Ps. 37:35; 52:8; Jer. 11:16; Hos. 14:8). In contexts of pagan worship, however, it refers to trees that were associated with life and fertility, perhaps because they retained their foliage year round and thus constantly bore witness to the incessant attention and care of the gods. This is the idea here as reference to high places, altars, pillars, asherim, and images makes clear (vv. 2-3). Such things were to be avoided by God's people (v. 4), but subsequent history showed only too commonly their tendency to embrace the paganism marked by these objects (1 Kings 14:23; 2 Kings 16:4; 17:10; Isa. 57:5; Jer. 2:20; 3:6, 13; 17:2; Ezek. 6:13). [*'ēṣ, ra'ănān*]

12:5 To place his name *(šĕmô)*—The noun *šēm* (name) is used here as a figure of speech (synecdoche) in which an element of something represents the whole. In this case, the name of the Lord is equivalent to the Lord. Where his name is, there he is. Moses commands that the names of the Canaanite gods be destroyed *('bd*, v. 3; cf. Deut. 8:19), that is, that their altars and other paraphernalia be demolished, thus eliminating these false deities themselves. In their place Israel must, in the future, build a sanctuary where God's name can be placed; i.e., where God himself will "dwell" among his people (cf. vv. 11, 21; Deut. 14:23, 24; 16:2, 6, 11; 1 Kings 5:5; 8:16, 17, 29; Neh. 1:9). In a practical sense, God, who is invisible, could not reside in a building and be accessible in a physical form 1 Kings 8:27). His name, then, would represent him there so that the temple in all truth and reality could be called the "house of the Lord" (Isa. 2:2-3; 37:1, 14; 38:22; 56:7; Jer. 7:2, 10-11, 30; Ezek. 8:14, 16; Matt. 21:13; Acts 7:47, 49). The equivalence

of the Lord and his name is heightened by the well-known fact that in ancient times one's name was, in effect, a clue to his or her very nature and disposition. (A. Ross, *NIDOTTE*, 4:150). [*šēm*]

12:6 Your burnt offerings *('ōlōtêkem)*—The verbal root of this technical term is *'lh*, "go up, ascend" (KBL, 705). A burnt offering is, thus, one that is so wholly consumed on the altar that every part of it ascends upward toward God. None is left for human consumption. It differs in this respect from peace or fellowship offerings, parts of which could be retained by the offerer and shared by him with others (Lev. 7:11-27; 10:12-15). It differs also from sin and trespass offerings in that the burnt offering was free-will or voluntary whereas the others were mandatory. It was presented to the Lord as an expression of worship, praise, or dedication, though it also accompanied atonement. Well-known OT examples are the offerings of Noah following the Flood (Gen. 8:20), Abraham's willingness to offer Isaac (Gen. 22:1-13), Saul's ill-advised offerings at Gilgal (1 Sam. 13:8-15), and David's sacrifice of burnt offerings at the threshing-floor of Araunah (2 Sam. 24:18-25). In the latter instance, burnt offerings are in association with peace offerings. (R. Averbeck, *NIDOTTE*, 3:405-15). [*'ōlâ*]

Your sacrifices *(zibḥêkem)*—This generic term for offerings made to God on the altar is cognate to the verb *zbḥ*, "to sacrifice," and to the noun *mizbēaḥ*, "altar." It can apply to any such offering but since it is closely connected to *'ōlâ* ("burnt-offering") here, it probably refers in this passage to the other voluntary offerings known as peace-, thank-, or fellowship-offerings (cf. v. 27 where this identification appears certain). In any case, these gifts to the Lord were to be brought to the central sanctuary of future times, there to be presented as tokens of submission, worship, and repentance. [*zebaḥ*]

Your tithes (*ma'śĕrōtêkem*)—The word "tithe" translates Hebrew *ma'ăśēr*, "tenth," a word that obviously has a normal, secular sense (Ezek. 45:11, 14) but primarily, in the OT, one associated with gifts and offerings made to the Lord. The earliest instance—well before the giving of the Sinai commandment—was Abraham's presentation of tithes to Melchizedek, the priest of El Elyon (Gen. 14:20). Jacob later made a vow to the Lord that if he gave him success and prosperity he would return a tenth of it to him (Gen. 28:22). This voluntary practice later became codified in the Mosaic covenants where the Lord, the great Sovereign, required of his subject people Israel that they present him with a tithe of all their income, no matter the form it might take (Lev. 27:30-33; Num. 18:21-32; Deut. 14:22-29; cf. 2 Chron. 31:5-10; Neh. 10:34-39; Amos 4:4; Mal. 3:8, 10). In a sense, this was a tax, the proceeds of which were applied as sacrificial offerings but also as a means of providing for the priests, Levites, and poor of the land. (R. Averbeck, *NIDOTTE*, 2:1035-55). [*ma'ăśēr*]

The gift of your hand (*tĕrûmat yedkem*)—Translated "heave offering" in some versions (AV, ASV), the noun appears to be cognate to the verb *rûm*, "be high, exalted" (*BDB*, 926). The idea apparently is that such an offering was actually lifted up before the Lord by the offerer as a symbolic gesture of self-denial. Though occasionally occurring in secular settings in the sense of a gift or contribution (Prov. 29:4; Ezek. 45:13, l6), by far the more common use is in cultic contexts. In this passage it refers to produce from farming (cf. vv. 11, 17; Num. 15:19-21). Elsewhere such gifts consist of baked goods (Lev. 7:14; Neh. 10:39; 12:44), animals (Exod. 29:27-

28; Lev. 7:34; 10:14-15), plunder (Num. 31:29, 41, 52), or money (Exod. 30:13-15). The principal purpose of the *tĕrûmâ* was to provide for the needs of the priests and Levites (Lev. 7:34; 10:14; Num. 5:9; 15:17-21; 2 Chron. 31:10, 12, 14). It was lifted up to the Lord but in His name it was also removed from common use to supply means of support to those who served Him in the sanctuary. (R. Averbeck, *NIDOTTE*, 4:335-38). [*tĕrûmâ*]

Your vows (*nidrêkem*)—These were gifts promised to the Lord for some act of grace anticipated or already performed. They could consist of the dedication of one's time or efforts (Gen. 28:20; 31:13; Lev. 27:2; 2 Sam. 15:7, 8), of the temporary or lifelong Nazirite commitment (Num. 6:1-21; 1 Sam. 1:21); or (most commonly) of gifts such as burnt offerings and other sacrifices (Deut. 12:26-27; 23:18, 21; 1 Sam. 1:21; Jonah 1:16). The most famous example is the "rash vow" of Jephthah who promised the Lord that if He granted him victory in battle he would offer up as a burnt offering whatever first greeted him on his return home (Judg. 11:30-31). Tragically, his own daughter met him and true to his vow Jephthah did what he had pledged to do (v. 39). [*neder*]

Your voluntary offerings (*nidbōtêkem*)—Though somewhat related to the votive offering (see previous word) in that both were given freely and without mandate, the voluntary offering was not pledged beforehand. It was an expression of gratitude to God for his blessings (Deut. 16:10) or an act of extraordinary generosity motivated by some special occasion or event (2 Chron. 35:7-9; Ezra 3:5). The construction of both the tabernacle and the temple provided incentive for the people to give freely in order that the projects might be done easily and beautifully (Exod. 35:29; 36:3; and 2 Chron. 31:14; Ezra 1:4; 8:28

respectively). (J. Conrad, *TDOT,* 9:221-24). [*nĕdābâ*]

The firstborn of your herd and flock *(bĕkōrōt)*—The reference here, obviously, is to the first animal born to a collective entity such as cattle and sheep (see also Exod. 11:5; 12:29; 13:15; Deut. 15:19) but the firstborn can also be a specific animal, the first of a particular ox or sheep, for example (Lev. 27:26; Num. 18:17; Deut. 15:19 [male animals]; 33:17). These were to be offered to the Lord in recognition of His having spared the firstborn sons of Israel from the tenth plague (Exod. 13:2, 12-16; cf. 22:29). In a sense, they were substitutes for human firstborn, thereby providing a type of vicarious atonement. (M. Tsevat, *TDOT,* 2:121-27). [*bĕkôr*]

12:7 You shall rejoice *(śĕmaḥtem)*— Properly speaking, rejoicing is not something that can be commanded but God can so pour out his grace and blessing that joy is the inevitable response. In this passage Moses promises that once Israel is in the promised land (v. 1) and in compliance with the Lord's covenant requirements (vv. 2-6), he will so bless them that they will experience spontaneous joy (cf. vv. 12, 18; 16:14; 26:11; 27:7). The Psalms are replete with references to the joy that comes in knowing and serving God (Ps. 16:9; 21:1; 33:21; 48:11; 58:10; 63:11; 64:10; 105:3; 149:2; etc.). In the great majority of cases, joy is an emotion associated with fellowship with God and obedience to him. [*śmḥ*]

12:9 The place of rest *(hammĕnûḥâ)*—The meaning of rest is clear here from its combination with *naḥălâ,* "inheritance." That is, the rest is not so much a cessation of activity as it is a condition of wellbeing and security in the place chosen for Israel by the Lord. The noun does in other places speak of serenity (Ps. 23:2), peace (1 Kings

8:56), relief from sorrow (Jer. 45:3), and domestic protection (Ruth 1:9; cf. 3:1), but often (as here) it has spatial connotations. Ps. 95:11 recounts Yahweh's threat not to allow His disobedient people to enter Canaan (rest), but on the other hand He speaks, in Ps. 132:14, of Zion as His home, that is, His resting-place. The NT uses a similar term (Gr. *katapausis*) to describe both Canaan as a place of rest (Heb. 3:11, 18) and the eschatological, heavenly resting-place (Heb. 4:1-11). The present passage goes on to state that Canaan will be a place of rest after the Lord has defeated His enemies, thus guaranteeing His people's security (v. 10). [*mĕnûḥâ*]

12:10 Safety *(beṭaḥ)*—This noun is used (as here) primarily as an adverb. Based on a verb meaning be reliant, trust (KBL, 118), the word suggests the idea of living in such a manner as to be free of fear or concern because of some reliable grounds of confidence. Here those grounds are the fact that God has given the land of Canaan to his people by promise (v. 9) and he will give them protection from all their enemies once they get there (v. 10). The same protection and its resulting safety are pledged to the nation in Moses' final blessing of them (Deut. 33:28). Other examples of living in safety occur in 1 Sam. 12:11; Ps. 16:9; Jer. 23:6; 33:16. [*beṭaḥ*]

12:15 The unclean *(haṭṭāmē')*—This adjective nearly always occurs in ritual contexts (for exceptions see Lev. 14:40, 41, 45; Josh. 22:19; Amos 7:17) to describe ritually impure persons (as here; cf. Deut. 15:22; 2 Chron. 23:19; Isa. 64:6; Ezek. 4:13; 22:10), and unclean animals (Lev. 5:2; 7:21; 11:1-31; Num. 18:15; Deut. 14:7, 8, 10, 19), food (Judg. 13:4; Hos. 9:3), offerings (Hag. 2:14), and even houses (Lev. 13:15, 51, 55; Jer. 19:13). The law required persons offering sacrifices to be ritually purified by certain washings (cf. 2 Chron. 30:15-22). Only then could they participate. As for ordinary domestic slaughter of animals for food, however, that could be done—as the present text allows—by even those not ritually clean. The fact that wild game is mentioned shows that this is a secular and not a sacred ceremony. [*ṭāmē'*]

The clean *(haṭṭāhôr)*—This is the antonym of *ṭāmē'* and like it almost always occurs in cultic contexts (for exceptions see Exod. 25:11, 17, 24, etc.; Job 28:19; Ezek. 36:25; Zech. 3:5). Such cleanliness is not achieved simply by ritual ceremony but must reflect an inward disposition (cf. Ps. 51:10; Prov. 22:11). [*ṭāhôr*]

12:20 Desires *(tě'awweh)*—In the Piel stem of the verb (as here) the subject is most commonly *nepeš* ("soul" or, better, "interior person"). This suggests a deep-down longing for someone or something, frequently in an inappropriate sense as in the tenth commandment (Deut. 5:21; cf. Prov. 21:10). Usually, however, the verb speaks of ordinary appetite for food and the like (as here; cf. 14:26; 1 Sam. 2:16), the wish for social or political power (1 Sam. 20:4; 2 Sam. 3:21; 1 Kings 11:37), even God's sovereignty that allows him to do whatever he wishes (Job 23:13). The nominal *'awwâ* is cognate to the verb in this passage (cf. also v. 21) yielding the idea that "you may eat meat as you wish, according to your wish to do so." [*'wh*]

12:26 Your holy things *(qādāšeykâ)*—A holy thing is something set apart by the Lord for his own use or purpose, especially as an element of sacrifice or worship. This is in line with the meaning of the verb *qdš*, to withhold from profane use or declare something (or someone) to be in such a condition (cf. Deut. 5:12).

Such holy things are specified in this context as the tithes of produce and animals to be rendered to the Lord (v. 17; cf. v. 27). They are holy not because of some inherent virtue or purity they possess but because God has mandated that they be set apart (thus *qdš*,) for his special ownership and disposition (cf. Exod. 15:13; Ps. 15:1; 28:2; 79:1; 106:47; Isa. 63:18; Jonah 2:4, 7; Dan. 9:16, 24). [*qōdeš*]

12:28 Forever *('ad 'ôlām)*—This term is the closest in OT Hebrew to the meaning eternal or everlasting, though it seems that a clear idea of endless time was lacking in OT thought. The limit seems to have been as far in the past or future as the human mind could conceive. The apparent link between this word and the Arabic for world may support the notion of an immensity too great to grasp. With the preposition *'ad* (to) (as here), the endless future is in view. If Israel keeps covenant she may expect God's favor and loyalty for all ages to come, a promise articulated not only here but in many other places (Deut. 29:29; Josh. 14:9; 2 Sam. 7:13, 16, 24, 25, 26; 22:51; etc.). On the other hand, there are instances where limited duration is clearly in view (Josh. 4:7; 1 Sam. 1:22) or where the terms for everlasting blessing were not met and therefore "forever" became something much less (1 Sam. 3:13; 13:13). The term in question, then, must not be taken in a philosophical sense but in terms relative to the vantage point of the speakers and hearers. Forever may, indeed, communicate everlastingness but its use must in every case be determined by context (A. Tomasino, *NIDOTTE*, 3:345-51). [*'ad 'ôlām*]

12:29 Cuts off *(yakrît)*—This common verb occurs occasionally with the technical meaning of capital punishment (Gen.

17:14; Lev. 7:20, 21, 25, 27; 19:8; Num. 15:30; 19:20), but here and elsewhere (cf. Deut. 19:1; Josh. 23:4; Isa. 10:7; Amos 1:5, 8; Zeph. 1:3), especially with the Lord as subject, the idea is the removal of the wicked nations from before Israel so that Israel can inhabit the land of promise and otherwise be rid of her enemies. It is a term much at home in the context of so-called holy war (G. Hasel, TDOT, 7:346-47). [krt]

12:31 They burn (*yiśrĕpû*)—Many passages speak euphemistically of the heathen (and even Israelites) who caused their children to "pass through the fire" in an act of human sacrifice (thus Deut. 18:10; 2 Kings 16:3; 17:17; 21:6; 23:10; Jer. 32:35). Any ambiguity or uncertainty as to what is meant by that phrase is clarified by the declaration here that the wicked nations of Canaan that Israel must displace practiced, among other abominations, the literal offering of their infants as sacrifices to their gods, especially to the Ammonite deity Moloch (see Jer. 7:31-32; 19:5-6; 32:35). [*śrp*]

13:1 A prophet (*nābîʾ*)—The most likely etymology of this noun connects it to the Akkadian verb *nābû*, "to announce, proclaim" (P. Verhoef, "Prophecy," *NIDOTTE*, 4:1067-68). A prophet, thus, was a spokesman for a deity, one who shared the message of his god with those persons to whom he was sent. The etymology of the Greek translation of the Hebrew word, *prophētēs*, consists of the preposition *pro* ("for") and verb *phēmi* ("speak"), suggesting that the prophet spoke on behalf of someone else. This accurately reflects the meaning and function of the OT prophetic office. Even more important than the etymology, however, is the usage of the term, one attested to

more than 300x in the Hebrew Bible. Most instructive is Aaron's role in this respect. When Moses objected that he was incapable of leading Israel out of Egypt because of his deficiency as a public speaker, the Lord told Him that he, Moses, would represent the Lord before Pharaoh and that Aaron would be Moses' prophet, that is, his spokesman (Exod. 7:1). Previously he had defined what it meant for Aaron to be a prophet: Moses would tell Aaron what to say and the Lord would guide both of them so as to guarantee that their message would be the very word of God (Exod. 4:15). In effect, the Aaron would be a mouth for Moses who himself would stand in the place of God (v. 16). The present passage teaches that prophets could be false, even from within Israel, so certain tests would be necessary to distinguish the true from the false (v. 3, cf. Deut. 18:20-22). [*nābîʾ*]

A dreamer of dreams (*ḥōlēm ḥălōm*)—If the term "prophet" (*nābîʾ*) emphasizes proclamation of a message, "dreamer" stresses the reception of a message. Though occasionally (as here) the dreamer could be a false prophet (Jer. 23:25-32; Zech. 10:2), the epithet normally applies to authentic revelation through a true prophet (Gen. 37:5-20; Num. 12:6; Dan. 2:1-3; Joel 2:28) or at least through an individual temporarily blessed with the gift (Gen. 20:3, 6; 28:12; 31:10-11, 24; 40:5-16; 41:1-15; Judg. 7:13, 15; 1 Kings 3:5, 15). Along with the vision, the dream, in fact, was the normal means of divine revelation in the OT (Num. 12:6; cf. 1 Sam. 3:15). How it functioned practically is not clear in the Bible but the dream could be misused by false prophets, thus requiring means whereby the divine origination of the dream could be checked (cf. Deut. 18:20-22). [*ḥlm*]

13:3 The Lord . . . is testing you *(měnasseh)*—This is the participle of a verb *(nsh)* used elsewhere to describe Israel's testing of God (Deut. 6:16; cf. Exod. 17:7; Num. 14:22; Ps. 78:18, 41, 56; 95:9; 106:14). In that sense it has to do with rebellion and unbelief, provoking the Lord, as it were, to see how far he would let them go in their contrariness. Here the testing is educative, a means God uses to instruct his people as to who he is, who they are, and what he expects of them. It is not as though God is limited and must, therefore, resort to some kind of investigative technique to lay bare their innermost thoughts and motives. Rather, it is so that Israel might through testing be able more accurately to assess her condition before God. The test here is that of permitting false prophets to perform actual signs and wonders—normal means of validating prophetic ministry (cf. Exod. 3:12; 1 Sam. 2:34; 10:7, 9; Isa. 7:11, 14)—but at the same time to preach a message advocating apostasy and paganism (v. 2). The point is clear: all the miracles in the world cannot overthrow the clear teaching of God's word. God may, in fact, permit them to be done precisely to teach his people their insignificance compared to his clear revelation in Scripture. This kind of testing was a regular element of God's instruction of his people (Gen. 22:1; Exod. 15:25; 20:20; Deut. 8:2, 16; 33:8; Judg. 2:22; 3:1, 4; 2 Chron. 32:31; Ps. 26:2). [*nsh*]

13:5 Defection *(sārâ)*—Fundamental to the covenant relationship between the Lord and Israel was the mutual loyalty expected of each party. God, of course, would remain true to his commitment by virtue of his very being as the immutible, reliable one in whom there is no possibility of equivocation (Gen. 22:16; 26:3; Exod. 13:5; 32:13; Deut. 8:18). Human beings, on the other hand, prove to be undependable, unwilling, or unable to live up to their promises. Israel was no exception. Their tendency was always to defect from the Lord (cf. 2 Kings 17:7-18) and there were always among them those eager to lead them astray. False prophets—even though permitted by the Lord to do so—were especially active in drawing God's people away from him. The noun describing their effect derives from the verb *swr*, "turn aside" (*BDB*, 693-94). The image is that of a pathway of covenant obedience that, if followed, would lead to the fullness of God's purpose for his people and, hence, immeasureable blessing. Deviation from that pathway *(sārâ)* would result in wrath and judgment for such deviation was the very definition of covenant disloyalty (cf. Isa. 1:5; 31:6; Jer. 28:16; 29:32). [*sārâ*]

To turn you away *(lěhaddîḥăkâ)*—This verb is attested with two primary meanings—to be scattered or to scatter (KB, 597). The latter nuance is in view here and with the preposition *mē'al* (as here) has the refined idea of turning away from someone or something, in this case from the Lord (cf. v. 10). The purpose of false prophets will be to dissuade God's people from keeping his covenant with them and to encourage them to forsake him in favor of other gods (vv. 2-5). Sometimes they would succeed in drawing some away (v. 13), for their seduction is like that of an adulteress who draws to herself the weak and unsuspecting fool (Prov. 7:21). Such seditious behavior is so serious a violation of the Lord's claim to exclusive worship that the very town that harbors those who would entice Israel to idolatry must be utterly annihilated (vv. 15-16). [*ndḥ*]

You shall purge out *(bi'artâ)*—The verb *b'r* means literally "to burn, consume" (*BDB*, 128) but in the Piel stem and particularly in Deuteronomy it describes the action of the purging out of evil and guilt, especially from the covenant community of Israel (Deut. 17:7, 12; 19:13, 19; 21:21; 22:21, 22, 24; cf. 1 Kings 22:46; 2 Kings 23:24; 2 Chron. 19:3). The reason, of course, was to purify God's people so that they could better represent and serve him. To retain evil practices, objects, and even persons among them would (and did) lead to Israel's judgment and demise. The purging could consist of actual destruction and/or annihilation (2 Sam. 4:11) or merely physical removal from the community (H. Ringgren, *TDOT,* 2:201-05). [*b'r*]

13:6 If your brother entices you (*yĕsîtĕkâ*)—Just as false prophets could and would persuade God's people to defect (v. 5), so their very own kinsmen would not be above doing so. Their pressure would be all the more intense because of the natural bonds of relationship and love that joined them together. Even so, these allurements must be resisted, for the covenant connections between the Lord and those called to serve him must outweigh any other allegiances. The verb *swt* occasionally occurs with a positive sense, especially with God as subject (2 Chron. 18:31; Job 36:16), but here and elsewhere (cf. 1 Sam. 26:19; 2 Sam. 24:1; 1 Kings 21:25; 2 Kings 18:32; Jer. 38:22; 43:3) it is a synonym for temptation or incitement to do evil. [*swt*]

13:8 You shall not spare (*taḥmōl*)—One naturally is disposed toward his own loved ones but when they become agents of evil who seek to undermine one's loyalty to God, normal human sensitivities must give way to righteous wrath. This is the message of this text. Sparing such a kinsman would spring from compassion toward him or her, an emotion that ordinarily must be applauded and even cultivated. Sparing, thus, is inextricably linked

to compassion (cf. Exod. 2:6; 1 Sam. 23:21; 2 Chron. 36:15, 17; Jer. 15:5; Ezek. 16:5). Here (and in Jer. 21:7 and Ezek. 9:10) *ḥml* is juxtaposed with the verb *ḥws,* "to pity." As much as one might pity or have compassion on his family members who lead him astray, his sense of loyalty to the Lord must dominate his every thought and feeling and, in a case such as this, result in his participation in their punishment by the Lord (vv. 9-10). Cf. M. Butterworth, *NIDOTTE,* 2:174-75. [*ḥml*]

You shall not conceal (*tĕkasseh*)—This common verb most often means to cover, clothe, spread over, and the like and usually with mundane, nontheological significance. A major exception is the attempt by human beings to cover over or conceal their sins from one another and especially from God (Job 31:33; Ps. 32:5; Prov. 17:9; 28:13), and the reverse, namely, God's willingness to cover (that is, forgive) sin that is repented of and confessed (Ps. 32:1; 85:2). With the preposition *'al* the idea becomes more that of covering over or concealing from, in this case with the intent of being deceitful. To hide someone from justice and the punishment due him is to collaborate with him and share his guilt. [*ksh*]

13:17 Mercy (*raḥămîm*)—The plural form of this noun underscores the intensity of the emotion it communicates. At the same time, the likely connection of the word to *reḥem,* "womb," suggests its tenderness (M. Butterworth, *NIDOTTE,* 3:1093-95). This kind of compassion, then, is akin to the feeling a mother has for her children, born and unborn. Though people in general may express this kind of empathy (thus Gen. 43:14, 30; 1 Kings 8:50; Neh. 1:11; Isa. 47:6; Amos 1:11), its supreme display is in the attitude God takes toward his own chosen ones. Here Moses assures

Israel that if they are faithful in serving the Lord and only him, he will show compassion toward them (the verb form *rḥm*). This maternal side of God has nothing to do with divine gender but it does declare that he can identify with women as well as men. He shares all human emotion but at a level transcendant to anything known in human experience (cf. 2 Sam. 24:14; Ps. 51:l; 69:16; 119:77; Isa. 54:7; Hos. 2:23). [*raḥămîm*]

14:1 You must not cut yourselves (*tit-gōdĕdû*)—The reflexive form of the verb used here is limited to a cultic or ritualistic self-mutilation whose full meaning and purpose are not clear. In this case, such a cutting was done "for the dead," suggesting, perhaps, some form of mourning rite or even an awakening of the deceased. In the narrative of Elijah's contest with the prophets of Baal these pagan practitioners cut themselves in their feverish attempts to induce Baal to send down fire upon the sacrifice (1 Kings 18:28). Elijah derisively suggested that Baal was perhaps asleep and needed to be awakened (v. 27). The mourning aspect is clearly in view in other passages where plucking out the hair in lament accompanies a cutting of the survivors (Jer. 16:6; cf. 41:5; 47:5). In any event, such destructive displays of religious devotion must be strictly avoided by the worshipers of the Lord (M. Horsnell, *NIDOTTE*, 1:819-20). [*gdd*]

14:8 Their corpses (*niblātām*)—This noun appears to be linked to *nābāl*, an adjective meaning foolish or senseless (KBL, 589-590). A dead person is obviously a senseless being, hence the connection. The word may refer to a human being (cf. Deut. 21:23; Josh. 8:29; 2 Kings 9:37; Isa. 5:25; Jer. 7:33; 9:22; 16:4) or (as here) an animal (Lev. 5:2; 7:24; 11:11; 17:15; Deut. 14:21; Ezek. 4:14). The reason dead animals could not be eaten (v. 21) or even touched (v. 8) is that death *per se* communicated uncleanness ritually speaking. It was the ultimate illness and represented those evil, impure forces that contaminated human life (cf. Lev. 5:2; 11:8, 24-40) (H.-J. Fabry, *TDOT*, 9:155-57). [*nĕbēlâ*]

14:21 Foreigner (*nokrî*)—A derivative of a verb (*nkr*) meaning "conceal" or "alienate" (H. Ringgren, *TDOT*, 9:424), the noun refers to an outsider, one strange to the community, which views him as such. In later Hebrew the term became synonymous with Gentile. On the other hand, *nokrî* is to be distinguished from *gēr*, another kind of outsider who has taken up residence among the native population. In the case of Israel the *gēr* is perceived as a temporary resident, a sojourner who, while welcome, cannot enjoy the full rights of an Israelite citizen (cf. Exod. 2:22; 12:19; 20:10; 22:21; 23:9; Lev. 24:16, 22; Num. 9:14; Deut. 1:16; 10:18, 19; etc.). Because of his "foreignness" the *nokrî* was frequently viewed with suspicion or even fear (Judg. 10:12) and he could be treated with less favor under the law (Deut. 15:3; 23:20). However, he could engage in business with an Israelite (as here) and, in the future, would enjoy God's blessing as one to whom redemptive grace would be extended (1 Kings 8:41). [*nokrî*]

14:22 You shall tithe (*tĕ'aśśēr*)—This verb derives from the noun *'eśer*, "ten." It means literally to "tenth" or take the tenth of. In the OT it occurs only once apart from a religious or worship context (1 Sam. 8:15, 17). The nominal form (*ma'ăśēr*; cf. Deut. 12:6) is much more common but it too appears only once or twice apart from the act of tithing (Ezek. 45:11, 14). The first occurrence of the verb is in Gen. 28:22 where Jacob—long in advance of the Mosaic Law—promised the Lord a tithe of all the things wherewith God would bless him. The only other example is Neh. 10:38 which speaks of the Levites of the second temple taking up tithes. [ʾśr]

15:1 A remission *(šěmiṭṭâ)*—The word means literally "a dropping", that is, a letting go of something previously held *(BDB, 1030)*. As a technical term it occurs only in this book (cf. vv. 2, 9; 31:10) and in reference to the end of seven years at which time all financial obligations by an Israelite to his creditor must be canceled or remitted, at least for that year. This gracious policy was somewhat mitigated by the fact that in some instances the debtor would have been working off his debt year by year (cf. v. 12), but nonetheless it still required forbearance by the creditor to refuse to press for repayment even if just at the end of the seventh year (R. Wakely, *NIDOTTE*, 4:155-60). [šěmiṭṭâ]

15:2 He has lent *(yaššeh)*—Banks and other lending institutions were nonexistent in OT Israel so the only recourse a destitute citizen had was to borrow from a more affluent neighbor. The person who made such a loan, that is, the creditor, was known as a *baʿal maššēh*, literally lord of the loan. He not only had the opportunity to be of help to his fellow man, but, in fact, had a moral obligation to do so (Deut. 15:7-11). However, he could not charge interest against a fellow Israelite (Exod. 22:25; Lev. 25:37; Deut. 23:19; Ezek. 18:8), though he could against a foreigner (Deut. 23:20). The reason for interest-free loans to a brother is quite clear: why should an Israelite profit from the misfor-

tune of another? This is against what it means to be a citizen of the theocratic community where each person stands equal before God and has no more or no less claim to His bountiful grace than anyone else. The most that could be done to assure repayment was the appropriation of some item of value from the debtor as collateral in anticipation of full repayment (cf. Deut. 24:6, 10) (F. Hossfeld, E. Reuter, *TDOT*, 10:56-57). [nšʾ / nšh]

He must not exact (it) *(yiggōś)*—The tenor of this verb is that of a demanding, oppressive, and threatening attempt to secure something from someone, in this case a loan made to a fellow citizen. In fact, as a participle it occurs as a term for a tyrannical dictator (Isa. 14:2, 4; Zech. 10:4). Its usual sense is that of exacting tribute or taxation from someone, something clearly not done voluntarily (2 Kings 23:35; cf. Dan. 11:20). Moses' point here, then, is that one Israelite is not to force repayment from another, especially in the year of release (see previous word). He may do so from a foreigner (v. 3), but to treat his brother in this manner is to violate the principle of covenant community and wholeness that set Israel apart from the other nations. [ngś]

15:4 Poor *(ʾebyôn)*—Though this adjective is sometimes applied to the oppressed or persecuted regardless of their financial situation (e.g., Ps. 12:5; 37:14; 40:17; 74:21; Isa. 29:19; Amos 2:6-7), it usually (as a substantive) describes those who lack materially. The present context addresses this class (cf. also Exod. 23:11) and asserts that if God's people are true to the covenant there will be no poor among them (vv. 4-6). Should there be poverty, however, it cannot be ignored. And, indeed, there would be, for sin in the community would guarantee that the ideal would never be achieved (v. 11; cf. Matt. 26:11). The remedy under these real conditions was for the financially solvent generously to open their hands and purses to lend as necessary and without thought as to the inconvenience or even loss that might ensue (vv. 7-9). Such a spirit will surely result in the blessing of God (v. 10). [*'ebyôn*]

15:6 And you will lend *(wĕha'ăbaṭṭâ)*—One evidence of God's blessing on Israel in the promised land is that they would be so prosperous that they would not have to borrow from other nations but, to the contrary, would lend to them. All this, of course, was contingent on Israel's adherence to the covenant (v. 5). In fact, should Israel prove to be disloyal she would become the borrower and no longer the lender (Deut. 28:44; here the verb is *lwh;* cf. 28:12). In Deut. 24:10-13 the issue is the taking of pledges by a creditor to ensure repayment of loans (cf. v. 6). The verb should thus not be translated "lend" but "take in pledge" or the like. [*'bṭ*]

15:9 Mean-spirited thought *(bĕliyya'al)*—Most commonly the word in question describes rascals or scoundrels who are as good as nothing as far as their contribution to society is concerned (rendered sometimes "sons of Belial" or the like; cf. Deut. 13:13; Judg. 19:22; 20:13; 1 Sam. 1:16; 2:12; 10:27; 25:17, 25; 30:22; etc.). Here it speaks of a spirit or attitude of selfishness and insensitivity with regard to the poor. It is a scheming thought that says, "I will not give to my poor brother unless and until I can know that it will benefit me." Such a response to need is contrary to the nature of God and will invite divine displeasure (v. 9). [*bĕliyya'al*]

15:11 To your afflicted *(la'ăniyyekâ)*—The substantized adjective *'onî* occurs as a descriptor of a social class often oppresssed by the rich and powerful (Job 29:12; 36:6, 15; Prov. 30:14; Isa. 3:14, 15), of the righteous who suffer because they are God's people (Ps. 10:2, 9; 14:6; 25:16; 35:10; Isa. 14:32; 54:11), or even of the lowly king who will enter Jerusalem in triumph (Zech. 9:9). Here, however, it is associated with the poor (*'ebyôn;* cf. v. 4) and thus speaks not so much of persecution as of deprivation (cf. Deut. 24:14-15; Prov. 15:15; 31:20). It is incumbent on the people of the Lord to redress the needs of such persons in every way possible (cf. Lev. 19:10; 23:22). [*'ānî*]

15:12 A free person *(ḥōpšî)*—This noun, cognate to Akkadian *ḥupšu*, appears to denote a social caste, not of the highest rank, perhaps, but nevertheless free. Some scholars suggest that "Hebrew" here refers not to an Israelite (certainly the expected term) but to outsiders whose ethnic name (perhaps *'apiru* or *hapiru*) was similar to and confused with the word "Hebrew" (*'ibrî*). This seems unlikely, however, for this would be the only example of a named foreign people in such law. Possibly the designation "Hebrew" is reminiscent of the ancient days of Israel's bondage in Egypt when they were called Hebrews (Exod. 1:15, 16, 19; 2:6, 7, 11, 13). In any case, should a Hebrew man or woman be forced to indenture him or herself to a benefactor for financial relief, that person, having served his or her master for six years, must be released on the seventh year (cf. Exod. 21:2-6; Lev. 25:39-46). Moreover, he was no longer to be considered a servant but must thereafter be regarded as a free person. Jeremiah refers to this statute and makes the obvious connection to the freedom Israel enjoyed as a result of God's gracious redemptive act in the Exodus (Jer. 34:12-16; cf. Isa. 58:6). [*ḥōpšî*]

15:18 A hired (man) (*śākîr*)—This substantival form of the adjective describes a person who, contrary to a bond-servant, worked for another party for pay. Such a laborer would, of course, work for a stated number of hours per day or per week and then would be free to go home. The bond-servant, however, was with his overlord day and night, perhaps up to six full years (cf. v. 6). That is, he had no time of his own but was in a position, at least potentially, to work around the clock. For this reason, he was of greater value (Heb. *mišneh*, "double") than a mere hireling and therefore his master should release him freely and with deep gratitude. [*śākîr*]

15:21 A defect (*mûm*)—Sometimes translated "blemish" and the like, such a rendering is too limited, for more than superficial appearance is in view here. Once or twice it refers to an internal condition (Prov. 9:7). Most commonly it occurs in cultic contexts where it covers such matters as blindness, lameness, hunch-back, or even dwarfism, all of which disqualified one from priestly service (Lev. 21:17-24). This is not because the Lord does not love and cannot use the handicapped or those less than perfect. Rather, the principle is that interior holiness ought, as much as possible, be matched by exterior wholeness (Lev. 21:23). But sacrificial animals too must be the best physical specimens that one could provide. Those less than whole could be slaughtered for food but not offered up to a holy and perfect God (cf. Lev. 22:20-25; Num. 19:2; Deut. 17:1). [*mûm*]

16:3 Leavened (bread) (*ḥāmēṣ*)—This noun, related to *ḥōmeṣ*, the word for vinegar, can refer to anything sour. Most commonly it describes the effect of leaven in bread, particularly with respect to the bread of the Passover festival (cf. Exod. 12:15; 13:3, 7; 23:18; 34:25; Lev. 2:11; 6:17; Amos 4:5). Such bread must be unleavened for leaven was generally symbolical of corruption and thus of sin (J. Hartley, *NIDOTTE*, 2:180-82). There were exceptions to the prohibition of leavened bread as an offering, however, specifically in the peace offering (Lev. 7:13) and the wave offering (Lev. 23:17). A reason for baking bread without leaven at Passover time was the haste required in leaving Egypt. To wait for bread to rise would invite Egyptian retribution (v. 3; cf. Exod. 12:11). [*ḥāmēṣ*]

Unleavened bread (*maṣṣôt*)—Perhaps to be connected to the idea of bland or tasteless, bread of this kind is especially associated with the festival of Passover and the festival of Unleavened Bread, which immediately followed (Exod. 12:1-20; 23:15). Israel must prepare the bread in this manner because the urgency of their departure from Egypt did not allow time for bread dough to rise. Moreover, leaven symbolizes ritual impurity and for that reason must not only be left out of the baking but removed from every Israelite residence (Exod. 12:15; Deut. 16:4). [*maṣṣâ*]

16:8 Assembly (*'ăṣeret*)—A rare word for describing a gathering of people (7x), this term almost always has religious assembly in view (cf. Lev. 23:36; Num. 29:35; 2 Chron. 7:9; Neh. 8:18; Amos 5:21). Other terms, some of which are synonymous with *'ăṣeret* are *ḥāg*, *mô'ēd*, *sôd*, *qāhāl*, and *'ēdâ*. The connection of the noun to a verb meaning to restrain or hold back (*'ṣr*) suggests that the Passover assembly on the seventh day—the one in view here—was mandatory and, moreover, limited to the covenant community of Israel. [*'ăṣeret*]

16:10 Feast of Weeks (*ḥag šābu'ôt*) —The noun *ḥag* derives from the verb *ḥgg*, "to make pilgrimage" (*BDB*, 290), and thus describes the assembly that resulted from the pilgrimage. It is the common term for the thrice-annual festivals required by the Lord of Israel, namely, Passover (Exod. 23:15; Deut. 16:16), Weeks (here and cf. Exod. 23:16), and Tabernacles (Lev. 23:34; Deut. 16:13, 16). "Weeks" is, of course, the plural of week (*šābua'*), a period of seven (*šeba'*) full days. The name of the festival derives from the fact that it must be celebrated seven weeks (49 days) after the beginning of the grain harvest (v. 9; cf. Lev. 23:9-21), specifically on the fiftieth day after the first sabbath of Passover (Lev. 23:16; hence, Greek *pentēkostē*, "fiftieth"). Its purpose was to mark the end of the grain harvest and in doing so to celebrate God's blessing of bringing his people to a land of such abundance (vv. 10-12). Another name for this festival is *qāṣîr*, "harvest" (Exod. 34:22). [*ḥag, šābua'*]

Freewill offering of your hand (*nidbat*)—This "self-impelled" (from *ndb*, "impel") offering is similar to the votive offering (cf. Deut. 12:11) in that it is voluntary but it differs also because it is given after a blessing of the Lord and not in anticipation of one. In other words, it is an expression of gratitude for some favor granted the recipient beyond anything he may have asked or expected (J. Conrad, *TDOT*, 9:221-23). In the present passage it appears to be a spontaneous offering made in addition to those regularly required at the Festival of Shavuoth (Weeks; cf. Lev. 23:15-21). Particular

events at which the freewill offering was made included the call for building materials for the tabernacle (Exod. 35:29; 36:3) and the temples (2 Chron. 31:14; Ezra 1:4; 8:28). [*nĕdābâ*]

16:13 Feast of Tabernacles (*ḥag hassukkōt*)—The somewhat archaic and misleading term "tabernacles" translates the Hebrew *sukkâ* (sing.), which refers to a crude hut fabricated of interwoven reeds and branches. Its purpose was to provide a visual reminder of Israel's years of semi-nomadism in the deserts and how God had provided for them (Lev. 23:39-43; cf. Neh. 8:15-17). The festival marked the final harvest of the year, particularly that of orchards and vineyards. It was to commence on the fifteenth day of the seventh month (Tishri) with a general convocation and end with a similar assembly eight days later (Lev. 23:33-36). The text here makes it very clear that the festival was to be celebrated at "the place the Lord will choose" (v. 15), that is, at the tabernacle and, eventually, the temple. It seems that Solomon chose this festival as the most appropriate time to dedicate the temple he had just completed (1 Kings 8:2; 2 Chron. 5:3). [*ḥag, sukkâ*]

16:19 You shall not **pervert** justice (*taṭṭeh*)—In the Hiphil stem this verb (*nṭh*) has the basic meaning of "turning aside, deflecting" (*BDB*, 640-41). In a legal setting (as here) it conveys the idea of setting aside justice in favor of persons who, for whatever reason, exert pressure on the magistrate overseeing a given case (cf. Exod. 23:6; Deut. 24:17; 27:19). The result is a miscarriage of justice, usually to the disadvantage of the poor and other defenseless social classes (Job 24:4; Isa. 10:2; Amos 5:12). These improper influences may consist of bribes (Exod. 23:8; 1

Sam. 8:3) or even just the prestige or power of the individual seeking special considerations (Deut. 1:17; Prov. 24:23). Such behavior is contrary to the character of the Lord and to the expectations he holds for his covenant people (v. 20). [*nṯh*]

The bribe overturns the case of the righteous *(wîsallēp)*—Apart from legal contexts (here and Exod. 23:8) the verb *slp* connotes the idea of violent overthrow, of turning someone or something upside down (Job 12:19; Prov. 13:6; 19:3; 22:12). It is akin to *nṯh*, "pervert" (see above), but if anything is even stronger. Judges who accept bribes are likely not only to turn a blind eye to justice but to turn it on its head so that evil is called good and good is called evil (cf. Isa. 5:20). [*slp*]

17:2 To transgress his covenant *(la'ăbōr)*—The usual verb to speak of breaking covenant is *prr* (cf. Gen. 17:14; Lev. 26:15; Deut. 31:16, 20; Isa. 24:5) but the nuance of the one used here is of special interest. The normal and very common meaning is simply "pass over, pass through," and the like (*BDB*, 716). It frequently speaks of crossing over something in a literal sense, perhaps a river (Josh. 3:14, 17) or a boundary-line (Num. 20:17; 1 Sam. 27:2). Here it is used metaphorically by representing the covenant as a set of stipulations with clear parameters that cannot be overstepped or breached. To cross over the limitations imposed by the covenant is to "get out of bounds," that is, to be in violation of God's strict standards. There are many texts where this course of action is severely condemned (cf. Num. 14:41; Deut. 26:13; Josh. 7:11, 15; 23:16; Judg. 2:20; 1 Sam. 15:24; Hos. 6:7). Here the particular transgression is idolatry (v. 3). [*'br*]

17:6 Witnesses *('ēdîm)*—The verb cognate to this noun *('wd)* occurs in Deut. 4:26, "call to witness." Witnesses are observors of persons, acts, or events who are able, by virtue of their observation, to bear testimony to what they have seen. Since it is possible that one witness could be either deliberately or mistakenly inaccurate in his observation and/or reporting, more than one must give testimony in a legal proceeding in order to guarantee a more likely reliable verdict. The gravity of their responsibility is underscored by the requirement that witnesses first stone the one convicted of a capital offense (here, idolatry, v. 3). Unless they were absolutely certain of what they had witnessed it is not likely that they would lead the way in implementing the death penalty (cf. Num. 35:30; Deut. 19:15; Matt. 18:16; John 7:51; 8:17-18). [*'ēd*]

17:8 Between stroke and stroke *(nega' lānega')*—Though the noun (and its cognate verb *ng'*) can refer to any kind of affliction such as the effects of leprosy (Lev. 13:2; Deut. 24:8), mildew (Lev. 14:34-36), or plague (Exod. 11:1), in legal contexts (as here) it describes cases of assault and battery for which penalty must be assigned (cf. Deut. 21:5; Prov. 6:33). "Blood" in the passage suggests homicide so *nega'* is an attack that falls short of the taking of life. An interesting and theologically important occurrence of the noun appears in the fourth Servant Song in which the prophet speaks of the Servant as having taken upon himself the stroke that was rightfully deserved by the wicked nation (Isa. 53:8). In this case (as in the tenth plague, Exod. 11:1) the blow is fatal as the context of the song makes clear. [*nega'*]

Matters of controversy *(dibrê rîbōt)*—The noun *rîb* connotes the idea of dispute or strife in general (Gen. 13:7; Deut. 1:12; Judg. 12:2; Ps. 31:20; 55:9; Prov. 15:18; Isa. 58:4) but it is also a technical term for legal cases (as here; cf. 19:17; 21:5; 25:1; 2 Sam. 15:2). Here matters of all kinds are addressed. Those cases too difficult for local magistrates must be appealed to higher courts presided over by priests and district judges (v. 9). Of special interest are those passages in which the Lord is said to have brought charges against his own people because of a matter of controversy between himself and them (cf. Jer. 25:31; Hos. 4:1; 12:2; Mic. 6:2). The legal nature of those occasions suggests that what is in view is covenant violation by Israel against the Great King. [*rîb*]

17:10 They will teach you (*yôrûkâ*)—A principal function of the priests and Levites was that of instructing the people of the Lord in the law (Lev. 10:11; Deut. 24:8; 31:9-13; 33:10). So much so are the law and its teaching associated that the law itself is called *tôrâ*, teaching (cf. Deut. 1:5). The passage at hand has to do with court cases and matters of legal interpretation. Should a matter prove too difficult for local judges, it should be appealed to a district level (v. 8) where the Levitical priests and other officials can render an appropriate decision (v. 9). This must be done on the basis of the written law, the interpretation of which lay within the prerogatives of the priestly experts (v. 11). Their verdict must be followed for they were the authorized spokesmen of the Lord himself. Failure to do so could result in a penalty as severe as death (v. 12). [*yrh*]

17:12 Acts arrogantly (*ya'ăśeh bĕzādôn*)— Derived from the verb *zyd*, "to boil" (*BDB*, 267) the noun *zādôn* expresses the idea of impetuous, irrational response or behav-

ior, a reaction that ignores any consequences and takes matters into its own hands. In this legal setting the noun describes those who, having heard a verdict not in their favor, respond with arrogance and independence. Since this spirit is directed against God's duly appointed legal authorities, it is an act against the Lord himself and therefore one worthy of the death penalty. Once carried out, the impact on the community will be so profound as to discourage any further such displays of arrogance (v. 13). [*zādôn*]

17:14 A king (*melek*)—This common word bears an almost self-evident meaning when used in a normal political sense but its theological significance in the OT is more elusive and yet much richer. The question is whether or not human kingship was legitimate in Israel inasmuch as the Lord Himself was to be Israel's ruler (see Judg. 8:23). The issue is joined particularly in the narrative in which the elders of Israel approached aged Samuel and demanded to have a king as all the other nations had (1 Sam. 8:4-22). Samuel's negative reaction and the Lord's apparent reluctance in the matter appear to present human kingship as a grudging concession at best (vv. 7, 22). This, however, is a misreading not only of this passage but of the whole tenor of OT theology. As far back as Abraham's time God had promised a line of kings (Gen. 17:6, 16; 35:11) and the passage at hand, though regulating kingship (vv. 14-20), falls far short of condemning it. The problem with the people's request of Samuel was that it was premature. God had in mind a man "after his own heart" who would be the long-awaited ruler, namely, David (1 Sam. 13:14; 16:1, 13). The so-called Davidic covenant sealed this pledge (2 Sam. 7:8-17) and the prophets thereafter spoke of the continuation of

David's dynasty that would ultimately find perfect fulfillment in Jesus Christ (Isa. 9:6-7; 16:5; Jer. 22:30; 23:5; 30:9; 33:17, 21, 22, 26; 36:30; Ezek. 34:23; 37:24, 25; Zech. 12:10; Matt. 1:1; Mark 11:10; 12:35; Luke 1:32; 3:31; Rev. 3:7; 22:16). [*melek*]

18:10 Divination *(qĕsāmîm)*—The particular "abominable" practice described here (cf. v. 9) is done, literally, by the "diviner of divinations" *(qōsēm qĕsāmîm)*. This has to do with the observation or inspection of phenomena that allegedly give insight into the meaning of present events and/or events yet to come. Such practice was common in the ancient Near Eastern world. Most generally it involved the "reading" of the internal organs of animals such as their livers, kidneys, and lungs (extispicy); the behavior of oil in water (lecanomancy); the patterns of rising smoke (libanomancy); or the alignment of the planets and other celestial bodies (astrology). Examples of pagan divination in the OT are Balaam (Num. 22:7; 23:27), the Philistine priests (1 Sam. 6:2), and the Babylonian diviners on their way to Jerusalem (Ezek. 21:21-23). As the prohibition here makes clear, divination was not only possible in Israel but a likelihood, a pagan practice to be severely suppressed (cf. 1 Sam. 15:23; 2 Kings 17:17; Jer. 14:14; Ezek. 13:6, 9, 23). [*qesem*]

An augurer *(mĕ'ônēn)*—This term, the participle of the verb *'nn,* "practice soothsaying" (*BDB*, 778), is virtually synonymous with *qōsēm,* "diviner" (see previous word). Another rendering is "sorcerer" (NIV). The particular aspect of divination suggested by the word is unclear but it was associated with paganism and was therefore strictly to be avoided (cf. Isa. 2:6; Jer. 27:9; Mic. 5:12). [*mĕ'ônēn*]

An observer of signs *(mĕnaḥēš)*—This is the participle of a denominative verb based on the noun *naḥaš,* "divination, enchantment" (*BDB,* 638). This practitioner, then, was a kind of diviner or augurer (see previous two words). The verb occurs in Gen. 44:5 with reference to Joseph's "divining cup" and in 2 Kings 21:6 with a number of other words having to do with eliciting secret information through occult means. [*nḥš*]

A sorcerer *(mĕkaššēp)*—Another participle, this is a denominative of the noun *kešep,* "sorcery" (*BDB,* 506). It thus refers to one who engages in divination, the exact means of which is not clear. They were known from Egypt (Exod. 7:11) and Babylonia (Dan. 2:2) as well as within Israel (cf. Mal. 3:5). (M. Horsnell, *NIDOTTE,* 2:735-38). [*kšp*]

18:11 A charmer *(ḥōbēr ḥaber)*—Literally this phrase means "binder of a spell," that is, someone able to control someone or something by a metaphorical tying of magical knots. It is used in a generic sense (Isa. 47:9, 12) but also in reference to the charming of snakes in particular (Ps. 58:5). The emphasis shifts here from divination to incantation, that is, from discovering hidden mysteries to manipulative techniques designed to control the course of impending or existing realities. [*ḥbr*]

A seeker after familiar spirits *(šō'ēl 'ôb wĕyiddĕ'ōnî)*—This is a form of necromancy, that is, the consultation of disembodied spirits. The word *'ôb* refers to a ghost and "familiar" comes from the verb *yd',* "to know," thus, a well-known spirit (i. e., one known to the practitioner). The whole may be rendered "one who inquires of a ghost, that is, a well-known (spirit)." The witch of Endor is a famous example of such a person (1 Sam. 28:7-14; cf. Lev. 19:31; 20:6, 27; 2 Kings 21:6; 23:24; Isa. 8:19). She had a reputation as "a mistress of ghosts" *(ba'ălat 'ôb,* 1 Sam. 28:7);

and she was able by divine permission to conjure up the spirit of Samuel, a prophet certainly well known to both her and Saul (v. 11). [*š'l, 'ôb, yd'*]

A necromancer (*dōrēš 'el-hammētîm*)— The Hebrew phrase means literally "a seeker of the dead." There is no real difference between this term and the previous one, "a seeker after familiar spirits." In both cases the sorcerer professes at least to have contact with the spirits of those no longer alive, the deceased who inhabit Sheol or some other realm of the dead. The two ideas, in fact, are commonly juxtaposed (1 Chron. 10:13; Isa. 8:19; 19:3), though only here is the object of the seeking designated as "the dead." This makes clear the fact that these spirits are not those of demons or other non-human beings but, rather, the spirits of mortals who have passed into another mode of existence. (S. Wagner, *TDOT*, 3:303). [*drš, mwt*]

18:13 You must have integrity (*tāmîm*)—A common translation of this word is "blameless" (NIV), "whole-hearted" (NEB), or even "perfect" (ASV). In this context in which pagan prophetism in its manifold expressions is being contrasted with the purity of divine disclosure through the Lord's prophets (vv. 15-22), the notion of theological soundness is paramount. The form is actually an adjective, one derived from the verb *tmm*, "be complete" (BDB, 1070). The peculiar construction here (*tāmîm* plus the preposition *'im*) conveys the idea of uprightness in the opinion of the Lord (cf. Ps. 18:23). What matters in the final analysis is how God views the behavior of his people. It is only as they reject the allurements of competing religious systems and devote themselves exclusively to him that they can properly be described as having wholeness or integrity. J. Olivier, *NIDOTTE*, 4:307. [*tāmîm*]

19:6 Avenger (*gō'ēl haddām*)—This term is a participial construction based on the verb *g'l*, the usual meaning of which is "redeem, act as kinsman" (BDB, 145). The latter meaning is in view here but in a highly specific sense in which the kinsman (or near relative) takes responsibility for avenging the death of a loved one at the hands of a murderer (cf. Num. 35:9-28; Josh. 20:1-6; 2 Sam. 14:11). This obviously could not be just at the whim or discretion of the kinsman but as part of a proper judicial process. However, human emotion being what it is, it is possible that an avenger would take matters into his own hands and hunt the suspected felon down until he caught and slew him. To prevent this, cities of refuge must be conveniently located throughout the land so that the accused party might at least have some opportunity for escape and a fair trial (vv. 6-7). The noun *dām* ("blood") suggests that it is the shedding of innocent blood that must be avenged because of the sanctity of human life as represented by the blood (Gen. 9:5-6; Lev. 17:11). [*g'l, dām*]

His heart is hot (*yēḥam lĕbābô*)—The heart in OT physiology and psychology was thought to be the seat of the intellect, the organ responsible for rational processes (cf. Deut. 6:5). This is the only place in the OT where the noun occurs with the verb *ḥmm*, to be hot, though it does in another form (*lēb*) in Ps. 39:3. In the latter passage David says that he restrained himself from speaking lest he utter sinful words but his heart became so hot he was unable to keep silent. This clearly has nothing to do with anger but with an overpowering compulsion to take some course of action. This is also the case in the present text though here anger is very much to the fore. The avenger (see previous word), inflamed by rage because of the death of a loved one, would tend to become totally irrational (hot-hearted) and would hunt down the killer without allowing due process to take place. This is why cities of refuge must be conveniently accessible to persons thought guilty of murder. [*ḥmm*]

19:10 Innocent blood *(dām nāqî)*—This phrase is clearly a circumlocution for "blood of an innocent (man)." This explains why cities of refuge must be readily accessible. Persons accused of manslaughter (vv. 4-5) should have an opportunity for a court of law to establish their guilt or innocence before they fell victim to the kinsman-avenger (v. 6). Should they be innocent after all, their own death would only compound the tragedy of the circumstance. The adjective *(nāqî)* derives from a verb *(nqh),* "to be clean" *(BDB,* 667). An innocent person, thus, is one free or clear of blame. The term is at least once juxtaposed to *ṣaddîq,* "righteous" (Exod. 23:7), and became a technical term, in legal texts especially, to describe the innocent (Deut. 19:13; 21:8, 9; 27:25; cf. 1 Sam. 19:5; 2 Kings 21:16; 24:4; Ps. 10:8; 106:38; Isa. 59:7; Jer. 7:6; 22:3, 17; Jonah 1:14). [*dām, nāqî*]

19:11 Lie in wait *('ārab)*—The combination of hating *(śn')* and lying in wait suggests a deliberate and premeditated plan of attack, an ambush designed to catch someone unaware and do him mortal harm. The stealthy nature of this strategy is seen in the frequent occurrence of the term in military contexts (Josh. 8:4, 12; Judg. 9:32; 1 Sam. 22:8, 13). It occurs elsewhere to speak of the habits of a beast of prey (Ps. 10:9), the covert advances of the prostitute (Prov. 7:12), or the evil designs of sinners against the righteous (Mic. 7:2). Such a plot would, of course, immediately attest to a murderer's guilt (as here). [*'rb*]

19:14 You shall not **move** your neighbor's **boundary** *(tassîg gĕbûl)*—The allocation of the promised land to the tribes of Israel included its division into family inheritances as well (Num. 33:50-54). Family properties therefore were to be carefully delineated and not encroached upon by neighbors (cf. 1 Kings 21:1-4). One way such trespassing and illegal occupation could occur was by removing the boundary-stones marking the properties and relocating them in such a manner as to favor the trespasser. Such an infraction was taken very seriously because God himself had determined the boundaries within which his people should live and exercize their stewardship (cf. Deut. 27:17; Job 24:2; Prov. 22:28; 23:10; Hos. 5:10). [*swg, gĕbûl*]

19:16 A malintentioned witness *('ed ḥāmās)*—The term witness *('ēd)* has occurred earlier in Deuteronomy (17:6) but only here in the book is it qualified by the noun *ḥāmās,* violence, wrong (KBL, 311). Otherwise, it is found in Exod. 23:1 where Moses forbids collaboration in bearing false witness in a court of law. Witnesses who act in this manner have no intention of pursuing justice but desire only the hurt of those against whom they speak. David also complains that malicious witnesses have risen against him, challenging him unfairly in areas where he has no knowledge (Ps. 35:11). The witness in view in the present passage, then, is not merely lying (cf. v. 18) but is testifying with the objective of bringing unwarranted harm to the accused. The penalty for such ill will is indeed serious (v. 19) (H. Haag, *TDOT,* 4:484). [*ḥāmās*]

19:18 A lying witness *('ēd šeqer)*—The root idea behind the noun *šeqer* is deception, variation from the truth. With the technical term witness (as here) the situation is one of perjury in a court of law, a matter of serious consequence (v. 19). In the Exodus version of the Decalogue the phrase occurs in a general sense as a prohibition against deception (Exod. 20:16; *'ēd šāw'* is the formula in Deut. 5:20). Otherwise it occurs only in Proverbs where it is one of six things the Lord hates (Prov. 6:19). The false witness is like a sledge-hammer, sword, and arrow when he perjures himself against his fellow (Prov. 25:18; cf. 14:5). The main difference between the lying witness and the malintentioned witness (v. 16) seems to lie mainly in the clear attempt on the part of the latter to do the defendant harm from the outset. A lying witness, on the other hand, might not have that purpose in view though the outcome of his testimony would have the same result. [*šeqer*]

19:21 Life for life *(nepeš běnepeš)*—The legal principle introduced by this phrase is known as *lex talionis*, that is, punishment commensurate with the crime (cf. Exod. 21:23-25; Lev. 24:20; Matt. 5:38). Very likely the principle itself is what is in view and not a literal tit-for-tat application of bodily harm. The point is that punishment may not exceed the original injury itself (See J. Tigay, *Deuteronomy. The JPS Torah Commentary.* Philadelphia: The Jewish Publication Society, 1996, p. 185). An exception clearly is in the case of murder, where capital punishment is demanded (Num. 35:30-31). [*nepeš*]

20:3 Do not be timid *('al yērak)*—This first of a series of four jussives comes from a root form meaning to be soft (*BDB*, 939-940). Battle requires hardness, not softness, so the appeal is to steel one's heart (i.e., mind) against debilitating fear for

God will guarantee victory (v. 4). Isaiah counseled evil King Ahaz also not to faint in anticipation of the Aramean-Israelite threat against him (Isa. 7:4) and Jeremiah likewise urged Judah to be bold in the face of Babylonian conquest (Jer. 51:46). [*rkk*]

Do not be tempted to flee *('al-taḥpēzû)*—The verb *ḥpz* conveys the idea of rushing away in alarm (*BDB*, 342) because of some present or anticipated danger (2 Sam. 4:4; 2 Kings 7:15). The behemoth (hippopotamus?) resists such an impulse because of his great size and strength (Job 40:23). Those who do battle for the Lord should also stay and fight for they can rely on his presence and power for victory (v. 4; cf. 1:30; 3:22). [*ḥpz*]

20:4 To save *(lěhôšîa')*—This theologically rich term, which occurs almost always in the causative stem, communicates at its basic level the idea of being freed from a narrow place or some other kind of restriction. As a participle *(môšîa')* it is commonly an epithet of the Lord who saves his people from all their calamities, including their sin (2 Sam. 22:3; Ps. 106:21; Isa. 19:20; 43:3, 11; 45:15, 21; 49:26; 60:16; 63:8; Jer. 14:8; Hos. 13:4). In the context of war (as here) the verb speaks of deliverance from defeat and death (cf. Exod. 14:30; Judg. 6:14-16, 36, 37; 7:2, 7; 1 Sam. 7:8; 10:19). To be saved in this sense is to have victory. [*yš'*]

20:5 Has not dedicated it *(ḥănākô)*—This verb is well known as the cognate to the late noun *ḥanukkâ*, "dedication," applied to the Maccabean festival of the dedication of the second temple known as Hanukkah. The noun occurs a few times in Nehemiah with reference to the dedication of Jerusalem's walls (Neh. 12:27). The verb elsewhere speaks of the dedication of Solomon's temple (1 Kings 8:63;

cf. 2 Chron. 7:9 and the dedication of the altar). To dedicate something is to set it apart for some particular purpose. Here it appears to have the legal meaning of laying claim to something, in this case one's house. [*ḥnk*]

20:7 Has become engaged to a woman (*'ēraś 'iššâ*)—Engagement (or betrothal) in ancient Israel (and even in NT times; cf. Matt. 1:18) was tantamount to marriage. It involved the payment of a bride-price (known as a *môhar*), the purpose of which was to demonstrate the seriousness of the man's intentions (see 2 Sam. 3:14) and, perhaps, to provide compensation to the girl's father for his loss of a source of labor (cf. Hos. 2:19-20). To have done all this and then to have been unable to consummate his marriage because of a call to military service would be an unspeakable tragedy for the man. R. Wakely, *NIDOTTE*, 1:527. [*'rś*]

20:11 Compulsory laborer (*mas*)—This technical term, known also from Akkadian texts, refers to persons, whether native or foreign, who were pressed into involuntary service. The Israelites were thus described while in Egyptian bondage (Exod. 1:11) and King Solomon, following David's example (2 Sam. 20:24), instituted a program of forced labor in undertaking his massive building projects (1 Kings 4:6; 5:13; 9:15, 21; 12:18). Usually, however, outsiders made up the class of serfs suggested by the term (as here; cf. Josh. 16:10; 17:13; Judg. 1:28, 30, 33, 35; 1 Kings 9:21; Isa. 31:8). The best known example, perhaps, is the Gibeonites. This Canaanite people, professing to be from a far country in order to avoid Israelite extermination, were forced into servitude to Israel because of their perfidy (Josh. 9:1-27).

Theologically, this fulfilled, at least partially, the curse of Noah who proclaimed that Canaan would be "a servant of servants" to his brothers (Gen. 9:25-26). [*mas*]

20:16 Any breathing thing (*nĕšāmâ*)—This abstract noun derives from the verb *nšm*, "to pant," and thus refers alike to animal or human being (Gen. 7:22; Ps. 150:6). However, the latter is by far most common, so much so that the term is almost synonymous with a human being (Josh. 10:40; 11:11, 14; 1 Kings 15:29). Most instructive is the creation text of Gen. 2:7 (which see) which points to the Lord as the origin of breath, which, once communicated to the human body, results in a "living soul" [Heb. *nepeš*, which see]. The creation of mankind is unique in that only human beings become alive by divine inbreathing. H. Lamberty-Zielinski, *TDOT*, 10:65-70. [*nĕšāmâ*]

21:1 A corpse (*ḥālāl*)—The difference between this term for corpse and one already discussed (*nĕbēlâ*; Deut. 14:21) is that this generally refers to a dead body resulting from violence of some kind as its cognate verb *ḥll*, to pierce, makes clear. This is the case in this passage since the whole legal process that follows is designed to discover the perpetrator of the crime (vv. 2-9). In addition to this pericope (cf. vv. 2, 3, 6), the noun occurs otherwise in the book only in the Song of Moses where the Lord threatens judgment against his enemies that will result in the spilling of the blood of those whom he pierces (Deut. 32:42). The reason for concern about the corpse here is precisely because the deceased is a victim of homicide. This sin is so grievous because mankind is in the image of God and thus to slay a human being is to attack that which is most precious to God (cf. Gen.

9:6; Deut. 5:17). Every murder has a murderer who must pay with is own life, but when that person cannot be readily identified the community of which it is thought that he is a member is otherwise made culpable and must take measures to deliver itself from divine judgment. This explains the elaborate procedures outlined here. [*ḥālāl*]

21:7 Our hands have not shed this blood (*šāpĕkuh 'et-haddām*)—The common meaning of the verb *špk*, to spill, pour (KBL, 1004), takes on a technical nuance when human blood is the spilled substance as it is here. One speaks of shedding blood, which itself is a euphemism for homicide. The idiom occurs with this sense in one other place in the book (Deut. 19:10) but is somewhat frequently used to describe the shedding and sprinkling of animal blood in sacrificial ceremonies (Deut. 12:16, 24, 27; 15:23; cf. Lev. 4:7, 18, 25, 30, 34). The connection between the shedding of human blood and homicide is clear not only from the practical observation that one dies when his or her blood is drained away, but most particularly from the remarkable biblical assertion that "the life of all flesh is its blood" (Lev. 17:11, 14). [*špk*]

21:8 Atone for (*kappēr*)—With the basic meaning to cover, this verb occurs in the OT as a technical term for atonement. That is, in the act of sacrifice the sins and transgressions of the offerer are viewed as being covered by the blood of the victim in such a way as to render the offerer innocent before God. This, of course, is not a mechanical or magical thing but is efficacious to the extent that the sacrifice is undertaken by faith in the God who grants forgiveness. The noun *kōper*, with which the verb is connected, has the meaning ransom. The verb, therefore, suggests that the offering of a sacrifice brings about a ransom payment, the animal on the altar paying the price the offerer should have paid, namely, his life. Outside Exodus, Leviticus, and Numbers, the verb occurs very few times (cf. Gen. 32:20; 1 Sam. 3:14; 2 Sam. 21:3; 2 Chron. 30:18; Neh. 10:33; Ps. 65:3; 78:38; 79:9; Isa. 28:18; 47:11, etc.). In the present passage the appeal is for the Lord to atone for his redeemed people Israel, that is, not to attribute to them the guilt associated with the victim of homicide found near their village (vv. 1-9). In the only other occurrence in Deuteronomy it seems that the atonement of Israel is linked to the vengeance the Lord will inflict on Israel's enemies (Deut. 32:43). (B. Lang, *TDOT*, 7:290-91). [*kpr*]

21:13 You may marry her (*bĕ'altāh*)—The basic meaning of this verb is to own, to rule over (KBL, 137), and its cognate noun *ba'al* thus means lord or master. Most commonly in the OT the noun designates Baal, the chief god of the Canaanite pantheon. It also is the term for husband (Gen. 20:3; Exod. 21:3, 22; Deut. 22:22; 24:4), thus the verbal idea to take possession of as a wife; i.e., to marry. The verb occurs elsewhere in Deuteronomy with this meaning (cf. 22:22; 24:1) as well as in a few other OT passages (Isa. 62:5; Mal. 2:11). There is no suggestion in these and other texts that the husband was considered the owner of the wife as though she were property. It is true that a bride-price (Heb. *môhar*) was paid by the groom to the bride's father (Exod. 22:16; cf. Gen. 34:12; 1 Sam. 18:25), but this seems more a compensation to him for the loss of her services to him than an actual purchase. The present passage is somewhat different in that the bride is a prisoner of war and therefore more like property. The fact that the husband cannot sell her afterward, however, shows that even in such a case his wife is not just a part of his estate. [*b'l*]

21:14 If <u>you are not delighted</u> with her (*hāpaṣtâ*)—In this passage, the intent is to convey the idea that if an Israelite soldier captures a female prisoner who initially pleases him so much that he marries her, but he later has a change of feeling, he may divorce her but gain no financial benefit for having used her in this manner. He desired (*ḥšq*, v. 11; cf. Deut. 7:7) her at first, largely because of her physical beauty, but for undisclosed reasons later came to delight (*ḥpṣ*) in her no longer (cf. Gen. 34:19; Esth. 2:14). The verb does not primarily connote sexual attraction, however, for one can be delighted in various activities (2 Sam. 24:3) and things (Isa. 13:17) including the word of God (Jer. 6:10). Likewise, one can be delighted or not with regard to certain courses of action (cf. Deut. 25:7-8). Moreover, God delights in persons (Num. 14:8) in right behavior (Jer. 9:24), and in the implementation of his purposes (Isa. 53:10). In the present case, though the man's reaction to his foreign wife seems cruel and arbitrary, she at least cannot be considered merely as a piece of property. [*ḥpṣ*]

21:16 To make (as) firstborn (*lĕbakkēr*)— This denominative verb (see the noun *bĕkôr* at Deut. 12:6) occurs here (and rarely elsewhere) to describe an illegitimate attempt to bypass normal convention by a man's declaring a second-born son (that by his favorite wife) to have the status of the firstborn son (that by his less favored wife). In fact, the son of the latter must be recognized as the firstborn—which he is— and, furthermore, must be given the double portion of his father's estate upon his

father's death (v. 17). The principle is clear: the blessing of inheritance cannot be denied the son merely because of his father's unjust preferential attitude toward his respective wives. An illustration of this is the divine choice of Judah, not Joseph or Benjamin, as the recipient of the messianic promises (Gen. 49:10)—this, though Judah was a son of Jacob's less favored wife Leah (Gen. 29:35), and for that matter, though he himself was not the firstborn (Reuben held that designation). The passage does not endorse polygamy, of course, but only recognizes its existence and sets in place guidelines for the fairness of its various expressions and results. [*bkr*]

21:17 The sign of his <u>virility</u> (*'ōnô*)—The noun has the general meaning of physical liveliness or wealth (Job 18:7, 12; 40:16; Isa. 40:26, 29; Hos. 12:3), but in this passage the idea is that of procreative capacity. This was apparent in the conception of Reuben, Jacob's first-born son (Gen. 49:3), and is clearly the intent in describing the firstborn sons of the Egyptians at the time of the Exodus (Ps. 78:51; cf. 105:36). Jacob is said to have wrestled with God when he was fully mature (Hos. 12:3); that is, when he had already demonstrated his ability to sire children. Since the birth of a first child would prove a man's potency, it would have seemed only fair that that child be doubly blessed. [*'ôn*]

21:18 Stubborn (*sôrēr*)—A participle of *srr*, the term occurs twice in Deuteronomy (here and in v. 20) and elsewhere to speak of stubborn children (Isa. 30:1), a stubborn generation (Ps. 78:8), and stubborn hearts (Jer. 5:23), and princes (Isa. 1:23; Hos. 9:15). The juxtaposition here with *môreh* (rebellious; see Deut. 1:26) reveals that this is not just a willful streak common to all children but a spirit of disobedience to parents that requires discipline at the community level, one, in fact, resulting in capital punishment. It is hopelessly intractable behavior. [*srr*]

22:1 Hide yourself (*hit'allamtâ*)—Though the verb sometimes has the meaning to conceal someone or something in a literal way (e.g., Job 6:16), it usually describes the hiding of thoughts (Ps. 26:4), of the eyes from seeing what ought to be seen (1 Sam. 12:3), of the ears from hearing (Lam. 3:56), or of advice or counsel (Job 42:3). Here (and in vv. 3-4; Ps. 55:1; Isa. 58:7) the idea is that of pretending that one is oblivious to his surroundings. He must not disregard his neighborly responsibilities by acting as though he was unaware of the concerns of other people. He hides himself, then, in the sense of removing himself from the situation by his indifference, but this selfish attitude falls short of the meaning of true community (cf. vv. 3-4). [*'lm*]

22:12 Twisted threads (*gĕdīlîm*)—The purpose of this decoration (cf. 1 Kings 7:17) is clarified in Num. 15:37-40. The instruction there was to place blue tassels on the hems of the people's garments so that when they noticed them they would remember the terms of the covenant by which they had bound themselves to the Lord. It was a kind of a "string around the finger," a constant reminder that they were the people of the Lord and therefore were expected to look and act like it. Jesus may have referred to such a practice when he condemned the scribes and Pharisees for enlarging their hems, presumable to draw attention to themselves and therefore to gain the fawning plaudits of the people (Matt. 23:5). [*gĕdīlîm*]

22:14 Worthless charges (*'ălîlōt*)—Deriving apparently from the verb *'ll* (act

arbitrarily), the noun suggests here an accusation based not on solid evidence but only on suspicion. The accusation is by a husband who, just having consummated marriage with his new bride, claims that she was not a virgin. The reason for his allegation is that she has displayed no signs of her sexual purity (see next word). This particular use of the noun occurs only here but it occurs commonly elsewhere to refer to Israel's wicked behavior (Ezek. 14:22, 23; 20:43; 24:14; 36:17, 19; Zeph. 3:11) and even to the acts of the Lord that, while not evil, bring about harmful consequences to those whom he judges (Ps. 9:11). More commonly with the Lord as subject, the noun speaks of his deeds of power, mercy, and grace, all of which are arbitrary (Ps. 66:5; 77:12; 78:11; 103:7; 105:1; Isa. 12:4). [*'ălîlâ*]

Signs of virginity (*bĕtûlîm*)—The word in Hebrew closest in approximation to the idea of virgin is *bĕtûlâ*, a young unmarried woman living at home. Such a girl was sought as an eligible candidate for marriage both because of her youth and her sexual purity, never having been married before (Tsevat, *TDOT*, 2:341). The "signs" (plural of emphasis) of virginity were the bloodstained sheet or undergarment that would ordinarily attend the first act of intercourse. Were these lacking, the husband could make a case that his bride was, indeed, defiled and not what she claimed to be. Since the bride's parents took possession of the cloth, however, they could provide evidence to the contrary if need be. If the man's charges proved to be baseless, he was severely punished (vv. 18-19). If she were indeed guilty, on the other hand, she must be stoned to death, for her wanton ways, tantamount to harlotry (v. 21), brought disgrace to her father and to the whole nation (cf. Ezek. 23:3, 8). [*bĕtûlîm*]

22:19 They shall fine *('ānĕšû)*—This verb derives from the noun *'ōneš*, an indemnity or fine (*BDB*, 778-779), and means to punish by the assessment of some kind of payment, usually to an aggrieved party and usually in the form of some precious metal. Here the payment of 100 shekels of silver (ca. 40 ounces) must be paid to the father of a newly wed daughter whose reputation has been irreparably tarnished by the false allegation that she was not a virgin when she married (vv. 13-14). The payment seems to be for damages to the good name of the girl and her family and not because of any monetary loss incurred. One theological truth that emerges here is that a good name is a highly valued thing because the name reflects something of the reality of the person who bears it (cf. Prov. 22:1; Eccl. 7:1). This is precisely why it is so strongly forbidden to use the name of the Lord for an empty purpose (Deut. 5:11). [*'nš*]

22:21 Gross sin *(nĕbālâ)*—Its connection to the semantic field of *nbl*, foolish, senseless, suggests that the violation here is one of stupidity, a thoughtless breach of moral standards and expectations. But the fact that the deed demands capital punishment shows that it is not a trifling matter but one of a most serious nature deserving serious consequences. The same noun occurs in describing the rape of Dinah by the prince of Shechem (Gen. 34:7), the theft of the devoted things of Jericho by Achan (Josh. 7:15), the attempted attack of the Levite by the men of Gibeah (Judg. 19:23), and Amnon's violation of his own half sister Tamar (2 Sam. 13:12). Such things are so beyond the pale of normal social behavior as to appear totally irrational. Sin is always irrational, of course, but some misdeeds are in categories by themselves because of their outrageous character (J. Marböck, *TDOT*, 9:169). [*nĕbālâ*]

To act like a prostitute *(liznôt)*—The common verb *znh*, "to be a prostitute," has here the nuance of acting like a prostitute for there is no evidence that the young woman in the case (see vv. 13-21) had followed that manner of life. In fact, her husband had married her in good faith and her parents clearly had no reason to think she was impure unless and until the signs of her virginity (previous word) proved otherwise. Even then the assumption is that her indiscretion was not habitual but perhaps only a one time lapse. Nevertheless, because fornication was so much detested by the Lord and by the community, one who committed it was said to be engaged in prostitution (Deut. 23:17). The theological implications of this behavior may be seen in the figurative way it is used to describe Israel's improper relationships with other nations (Isa. 23:17; Jer. 3:2; Ezek. 16:23-34) and, most profoundly, as an analogy to Israel's idolatrous liaisons (Exod. 34:15-16; Lev. 17:7; 20:5; Deut. 31:16; Judg. 2:17; 8:27, 33; Hos. 2:7; 4:15). [*znh*]

23:2 A bastard *(mamzēr)*—A greatly debated term (cf. Hamilton, *NIDOTTE*, 2:971), the noun most likely refers to the product of incest and not of unmarried parents in general. Along with others listed here (vv. 1-8), such a person was precluded from full participation in the community of Israel. This drastic action was intended to underscore the need for God's people to be pure in every respect, but clearly it had no bearing on the question of God's grace and its extension to all regardless of their circumstances. Zechariah's warning that a *mamzēr* would inhabit Ashdod in the future illustrates the mixed nature of such persons as a result of intermarriage (Zech. 9:6). [*mamzēr*]

23:7 Do not abhor *(tĕta'ēb)*—Cognate to the common adjectival noun *tô'ēbâ*, abominable, detestable, abhorrent (cf. Deut. 7:25), the verb in this stem means to regard someone or something in this manner (KBL, 1035). Whereas it was permissible and even mandatory to abhor such things as idols and pagan practices (Deut. 7:26; cf. Ps. 119:163), something even the Lord does (Ps. 5:6; 106:40; Amos 6:8), the normal use of the verb is negative; that is, it speaks of an attitude to be condemned or at least of an action that is undesirable (Job 9:31; 19:19; 30:10; Ps. 107:18; Amos 5:10). Having listed the various peoples denied access to the sacred assembly of Israel (vv. 1-6), Moses here excludes the Edomites and Egyptians from that prohibition because the Edomites were a brother nation to Israel and the Egyptians had provided them hospitality for more than 400 years (v. 7). For these relationships and acts of kindness toward his people, the Lord commands that these two peoples not be treated with disdain. The Abrahamic Covenant had promised that those who blessed Abraham's seed would be blessed but those who cursed them would be cursed (Gen. 12:3). [*t'b*]

23:11 Bathe *(yirĕḥaṣ)*—Though used commonly to refer to ordinary hygienic practice, here and in a great many other passages (e.g., Exod. 30:19, 21; 40:31; Lev. 8:6; 14:9; 15:13) the washing is ritualistic, that is, intended symbolically to represent the removal of ritual impurity. It is true that the incident here has to do with bodily functions that could result in physical uncleanness (v. 10) but the reference to God the Holy One walking about in Israel's battle camp puts beyond doubt that the washing is for religious and not merely physical purposes. Morever, the phrase "wash with water" implies not just hand washing but full bathing, that is, cleansing of the whole body, an act with clear ritualistic overtones *(KBL, 887)*. [*rḥṣ*]

23:14 Any indecency *('erwat dābār)*—Though the noun *'erwâ* means nakedness *(BDB, 788-89)*, its use here with *dābār* (lit., "thing"; cf. Deut. 24:1) suggests some kind of condition or element associated with nakedness. In this passage the nakedness is repulsive to the Lord because of the ritual impurity caused by bodily emission (vv. 10, 12-13). It is indecent to be in the camp when one is in this condition because God himself is there (v. 14). In Deut. 24:1 there is some unnamed indecency clearly connected to nakedness and known to a man only after marriage. This may have to do with abnormal menstruation—a view supported by comparison to Deut. 23:14—but this cannot be proved (cf. Seevers, *NIDOTTE*, 3:528). In any case, it is deemed so serious to the young husband that he views it as grounds for divorce. [*'erwat dābār*]

23:17 (Sacred) prostitute *(qĕdēšâ)*—Its etymological connection to the root *qdš* (be apart, be sacred) sets this noun apart from others describing similar lifestyle and behavior such as *zōnâ* (see v. 18). Its feminine form (as here) has a masculine counterpart *qādēš*, also in this verse. A man so described was clearly a sodomite (homosexual) who took port in religious rites closely associated with pagan fertility cults (Naudé, *NIDOTTE*, 3:886; cf. 1 Kings 14:24; 15:12; 22:46; 2 Kings 23:7). Female prostitutes (cf. Gen. 38:21-22; Hos. 4:14) thus described were set apart for service in the temple as sexual partners with the gods (in fact, of course, with their priests), the object of which was to bring about fertility of land, animal, and the people themselves. The description "sacred" makes the linkage to such perverted worship and has nothing to do with true spiritual and moral purity suggested by the usual translation "holy" for *qdš*. [*qĕdēšâ*]

23:18 Harlot (*zônâ*)—A participial form of the verb *znh*, "be/act like a prostitute" (cf. Deut. 22:21), this technical term denotes most often a "common" woman of the streets as opposed to *qĕdēšâ*, a "sacred" prostitute (v. 17). The terms are occasionally synonymous, however, as is clear in the case of Tamar, Judah's daughter-in-law, whom Judah calls both *zônâ* and *qĕdēšâ* (Gen. 38:15, 21, 24). The issue in the present text is that no income derived from prostitution could be offered to the Lord as a votive offering. Such a detestable act would be an egregious affront to a holy God. What one gives is an expression of who he is and what he does. No amount of generosity toward God, when such sordid means of income make it possible, can be acceptable to him. [*zônâ*]

Dog (*keleb*)—This derogatory term is used rather commonly with reference to men of unsavory character and reputation (1 Sam. 17:43; 2 Sam. 9:8; 16:9; 2 Kings 8:13; Ps. 22:16, 20), but only here as a synonym for a sodomite, or male prostitute, as the parallel to *zônâ* makes clear. Such persons must be kept distinct from male temple prostitutes known as *qādēš* (v. 17). The dogs referred to by John are quite likely Sodomites who, with fornicators and other sinners, will not enter the heavenly city (Rev. 22:15). [*keleb*]

23:19 Interest (*nešek*)—Most scholars derive the noun from the verb *nšk*, "to bite" (*BDB*, 675). Interest charges, then, are bites in addition to the principal that must be repaid to a creditor. The pain in such a procedure is obvious and in a cash-

less society would have been particularly acute. Whereas an Israelite could charge interest to a foreigner (v. 20; cf. 28:12), to levy such a payment against a fellow Israelite was to profit from his misfortune and betray a lack of true community solidarity (cf. Exod. 22:25). Since God had brought his people out of Egypt freely, they should extend such grace to one another (Lev. 25:35-38). [*nešek*]

24:1 Certificate of divorce (*sēper kĕrîtut*)—Meaning literally "a writing of cutting off," the phrase is a technical one describing divorce papers. Divorce is never mandated in the OT and, in fact, is contrary to God's original and eternal purpose in the marriage relationship (cf. Gen. 2:23-24; Mal. 2:16). Given humankind's propensity to sin, however, not least in married and family life, divorce was a reality in ancient Israel and, according to Jesus, was permitted in cases of marital infidelity (Matt. 19:3-9). In the present passage, divorce of a woman by her husband because of some kind of "indecency" (cf. Deut. 23:14) is not the real issue but whether or not the divorced woman could ever remarry her first husband if she had taken a second husband in the interim (vv 2-3). The answer is clearly negative, perhaps because such a remarriage is tantamount to incest (v. 4). By Jeremiah's time Israel had been "written off" as it were by the Lord and had been served a certificate of divorce (Jer. 3:8). He would undo that rupture in the future, however, by bringing his unfaithful wife to repentance and covenant renewal (Isa. 50:1-3; 54:6-7; Hos. 2:14-20). [*sēper kĕrîtut*]

24:4 She has been defiled (*huṭṭammā'â*)—The adjective *ṭāmē'* (cf. Deut. 12:15) most commonly defines persons or objects that are ritually impure and while the verb also bears this meaning for the most part, it also (as here) speaks of impurity or defilement brought about by sexual relationships, usually improper ones. The rape of Dinah is a case in point (Gen. 34:5) and adultery is always considered a cause of moral pollution (Num. 5:13, 14, 20, 27-29; Ezek. 18:6, 11, 15) as is idolatry, a form of spiritual unfaithfulness (Jer. 2:23; Ezek. 23:13, 17). The form of the verb in this passage occurs only here and suggests that the woman's defilement is something brought upon her by another. The situation is complicated in that the woman is divorced by her husband because of some alleged indecency (cf. Deut. 23:14) in her and she marries another man who either divorces her also or dies. In such a case she has been defiled and cannot remarry the first husband. In light of the common connection of the verb to adultery, it seems that the woman's return to husband number one would constitute adultery (R. Averbeck, *NIDOTTE*, 2:372). [*ṭm'*]

24:6 Take as a pledge (*yaḥăbōl*)—This verb fundamentally bears the meaning of binding someone or something (*BDB,* 286). In legal contexts (as here) the binding is a promise or pledge to repay a loan or other financial obligation. Evidence of such a commitment must be expressed tangibly by the forfeiture of a debtor's property or goods to the creditor until the loan was repaid. Since such forfeiture could result in great discomfort and/or inconvenience to the debtor, its loss would be a strong inducement to him to fulfill his legal responsibilities. In Israel, however, the harshness of such an arrangement must be tempered by mercy and compassion. Thus, a creditor could not demand of a debtor any item essential to his physical or

financial survival. In this instance, a millstone could not be taken for it provided the only means to sustain life by grinding out grain. In other places, clothing or night-wraps are denied to the creditor, at least overnight (Exod. 22:26-27; Deut. 24:17; Job 24:9-10; Prov. 20:16; 27:13; Ezek. 18:16; Amos 2:8). [*ḥbl*]

24:10 His pledge (*'ăbōṭô*)—This noun occurs only 4x in the Bible and only in this passage (vv. 10, 11, 12, 13). The cognate verb *'bṭ* is equally rare (here and in Deut. 15:6, 8). A pledge could consist of any article of value such as a millstone (v. 6) or even an item of clothing (vv. 12-13). Its purpose was to ensure the debtor's repayment of a loan. However, a creditor could not demand possession of a pledge essential to the debtor's livelihood nor could he embarrass him by entering his house to take the pledged article from him. Instead, he must allow him the dignity of volunteering the item by his own free will (v. 11). The point is that the most vulnerable and dependent must have means of support and recovery. The poor in both goods and spirit must be accorded respect for such an attitude toward them is regarded as righteousness by the Lord (v. 13; cf. Matt. 10:42). [*'ăbôṭ*]

24:14 Do not oppress (*ta'ăšōq*)—A common nuance of this verb is financial oppression, that is, extortion, usually (as here) by the wealthy against the poor (Lev. 19:13; 1 Sam. 12:3, 4; Prov. 14:31; 22:16; 28:3; Jer. 7:6; Ezek. 22:29; Amos 4:1; Mic. 2:2; Zech. 7:10; Mal. 3:5). Here the exploitation takes the form of withholding wages from those who have justly earned them. This must not be deferred to some future day but paid by the end of the day. To fail to do this would be viewed by the Lord as a sin against him as well as the oppressed servant (v. 15). Ironically, this very kind of oppression would be suffered by Israel in days to come should they fail to keep the covenant faithfully (Deut. 28:29, 33). [*'šq*]

25:3 Contemptible *(niqlâ)*—The basic idea of the root of this word is to be light, that is, without esteem. The form of the verb here suggests the nuance of regarding one's brother as having no worth or standing. While his punishment may be deserved, the culprit's membership in the covenant community should preclude his losing his dignity altogether. In a different form, the verb occurs in Deut. 27:16 where a curse is pronounced upon anyone who disrespects his parents, that is, makes light of them. Both passages share the implicit idea that mankind is created as the image of God and therefore should be treated with the honor attendant to that image. [*qlh*]

25:5 Stranger *(zār)*—A participle of the verb *zwr*, this term may refer to a non-Israelite (i. e., a foreigner; cf. Ps. 54:3; Isa. 1:7; 25:2, 5; 29:5; Jer. 5:19; 51:2, 51; Lam. 5:2, Ezek. 7:21; Obad. 11); a "strange" woman (i.e., a prostitute; Prov. 2:16; 5:3, 20; 7:5; 22:14; 23:33); a non-Levite (Num. 1:51; 18:4); or to a person outside one's own family or clan (1 Kings 3:18; Job 19:15; Ps. 109:11; Prov. 6:1; 11:15; 20:16; 27:13). In the present passage, the last of these categories is in view. The law states that in the event a man dies, thus leaving his wife a widow, she should be taken as a wife by one of his surviving brothers and not by someone outside the family. This is to preserve the name of the deceased brother into perpetuity by a son born of the second marriage (see next word). [*zwr*]

Perform the duty of a brother-in-law to her *(yibbĕmāh)*—One verb *(ybm)* communicates this technical idea, a custom sometimes called the "levirate law" (after Lat. *levir*, "brother-in-law"). The stipulation here is that a widow must assume at least the moral responsibility of bearing a son by a brother of her dead husband so that by this son the husband's name will never be forgotten (i.e., his posterity will go on; see previous word). This, of course, also places the brother under obligation to marry his brother's widow. Inasmuch as the whole tenor of biblical truth is monogamistic, one must assume that the brother-in-law in such a case was unmarried and therefore eligible to undertake the requested marriage (cf. Ruth 4:1-6 where complications arose in such a situation). Should he refuse to comply and thus bring dishonor to this brother, he must be publicly humiliated by his sister-in-law (vv. 7-10; cf. Ruth 4:7-8). The levirate custom—attested to well in advance of the Mosaic Law (cf. Gen. 38:8)—underscores the importance of family solidarity and also the intense desire for immortality through one's progeny. [*ybm*]

25:9 She shall spit *yārĕqâ*—This rare verb occurs only here and in Num. 12:14, in both places as an expression of contempt *(BDB, 439)*. In all cultures, such an act—especially when directed to another's face—shows the height of disdain. The loosening of the sandal here (cf. Ruth 4:7-8) symbolizes the surrender of claim by the derelict brother to anyone or anything belonging to his deceased sibling (see vv. 5-6). It was a despicable shunning of familial responsibility that, according to custom, deserved the prescribed reaction. [*yrq*]

25:16 Unrighteously *('āwel)*—This noun, used adverbailly here, lies in a semantic field with the basic meaning to deviate, turn aside, become corrupt. It is similar to the English idiom "crooked" to describe someone who departs from accepted standards of proper and legal behavior. In the present passage it speaks of corrupt business dealings in which one party to a transaction is cheated by another who employs weights and measures to his own advantage (vv. 13-15). The word occurs elsewhere in Deuteronomy to describe God as one who is faithful and without deviation (32:4). [*'āwel*]

26:7 Our toil *('ămālēnû)*—Though the noun often refers to hard work in general (Eccl. 2:10, 21, 34; 3:13; 4:4, 6, 8, 9; etc.), here, in collocation with *'ŏnî* and *laḥaṣ*, it has the refined meaning of onerous labor imposed upon one as punishment or unreasonable coercion. Joseph described his hardships in Egypt by this term (Gen. 41:51) and the poets and sages of Israel also use it to speak of persecution and bondage (Ps. 25:18; 90:10; 107:12; Prov. 31:7; Eccl. 2:24). Most striking is the occurrence of the word in the Suffering Servant song, which views his indescribable suffering as "the toil of his soul" (Isa. 53:11). More than work is intended here; indeed, the scene is one of punishment inflicted on the innocent one by God himself (v. 10). NT use of the ideas here makes it clear that Messiah Jesus is the one upon whom such awesome travail was imposed. [*'āmāl*]

Our oppression *(laḥăṣēnû)*—The verb *lḥṣ* has as its root meaning to squeeze, press (*BDB*, 537), but the cognate noun is more figurative, meaning oppression, usually by an enemy nation such as Egypt (Exod. 3:9) or Aram (2 Kings 13:4). Sometimes the affliction comes at the hand of personal enemies, however, a theme common in the wisdom and poetic literature (Job 36:15; Ps. 42:9; 43:2). In the text at hand Israel, as part of its recitation of sacred history, recalls the oppression of Egyptian bondage, which involved both literal and figurative enslavement. The

connection of the noun here with affliction (*'onî*; cf. Deut. 15:11) and toil (*'āmāl*) defines the nature of Israel's ordeal: it consisted of abuse and hard labor. [*laḥaṣ*]

26:13 The sacred thing *(haqqōdeš)*—The underlying meaning of terms based on *qdš* is apartness, separatedness (see the verb *qdš* at Deut. 5:12). The noun can refer to anything that has been set apart for any purpose though in the overwhelming number of uses in the OT that thing (or person) is dedicated to the service or use of the Lord. Here the thing set apart is the third-year tithe (cf. Deut. 14:22), which was supposed to be given to the Levites and others as their means of support (cf. Deut. 14:28-29). Part of the ritual on that occasion was the confession by the offerer to the Lord that he had indeed thoroughly removed (thus the verb *b'r*; cf. Deut. 13:5) from his possession everything that belonged to the dependent ones of the community (i. e., the holy or sacred things). It is a holy thing because it belongs to God and it is a separated thing because it is set apart for his use and for the benefit of his people. [*qōdeš*]

26:15 Look down *(hašqîpâ)*—The form of this verb (imperative cohortative) has the effect of urging the Lord to a course of action, a request expressed in the strongest terms. The appeal of the worshiper is that God might deign to look down upon his people and the land he has promised to bless. It is a classic example of an anthropomorphism, a figure of speech in which God (in this instance) is addressed in human terms (cf. Exod. 14:24; Ps. 14:2; 102:19; Lam. 3:50). The boldness of this semicommand underscores the depth of the speaker's emotion and need. In no way does it diminish his reverence for the Lord and his understanding of God as an absolutely transcendant being. [*šqp*]

26:19 Glory *(tip'āret)*—This noun is cognate to the verb *p'r*, to glorify (*BDB*, 802), and most commonly refers to the beauty of things (cf. Isa. 3:18; 28:1, 4; 52:1; Jer. 13:20; Ezek. 16:17, 39; 23:26), the glory of a ruler (Esth. 1:4; Zech. 12:7) or nation (as here; cf. Isa. 13:19; Lam. 2:1; Ezek. 24:25), or the honor of great reputation (1 Chron. 22:5; Jer. 13:11; 33:9). When applied to the Lord the concept is that of glory (1 Chron. 29:11, 13; Ps. 71:8; 89:17; 96:6; Isa. 60:7). The promise here is that Israel someday will be elevated above all other nations in praise, reputation, and glory. This will be the natural result of her having bcome a holy nation (*'am qādoš*; cf. Deut. 2:6). [*tip'ārâ*]

27:8 Very clearly *(ba'ēr hêṭēb)*—The verb *b'r* occurs only in the grammatical form that suggests the bringing about of some result. Here it is employed with the idea of inscribing stones with the text of the law in such a way as to make the words distinct and plain. The most helpful example, perhaps, is the command of the Lord to Habakkuk to write his vision upon tablets in such graphically distinct forms that even one who runs may be able to read the inscribed message (Hab. 2:2). The second term is the infinitive absolute of the verb *yṭb*, to be good, and in this form it conveys the idea of thoroughness. The command here, then, is that Moses write the stipulations of the law (at least Deuteronomy) in absolutely clear and unmistakable terms. [*b'r, yṭb*]

27:15 Cursed *('ārûr)*—A term very much at home in the covenant context of Deuteronomy (cf. 27:16, 17, 18, 19, 20, 21, 22, 23, 24, 25, 26; 28:16, 17, 18, 19), especially in the passive participle (as here), the verb commonly occurs parallel to and as an antonym of *brk*, to bless (cf. Gen. 12:3; 27:29; Num. 22:6, 12; 23:7; 24:9; Mal. 2:2). A particularly striking use of the participles of curse and bless in opposition is in the narrative of the Fall (Gen. 3:14, 17: cf. also 4:11; 9:25; 27:29). In the present passage there are 12 curses, one for each tribe, judgments that will follow Israel's disobedience. These are matched partially by a series of blessings should Israel be covenantally compliant in the future (28:3-6; cf. 7:14). (J. Scharbert, *TDOT*, 1:405-18). [*'rr*]

Molded thing *(massēkâ)*—This rather indefinite noun derives from the verb *nsk*, to pour out, and thus suggests anything poured out such as a liquid (Isa. 30:1) or, as here, molten metal. Most commonly, the term describes such metal in its state of fabrication into some molded object, particularly idols or images. Most famously, it is used of the golden calf of Aaron (Exod. 32:4, 8; cf. Deut. 9:16; Neh. 9:18) but it occurs elsewhere to refer to various pagan deities (as here; cf. Exod. 34:17; Lev. 19:4; Judg. 17:3-4; 18:14, 17, 18; 1 Kings 14:9; 2 Kings 17:16; Isa. 30:22; 42:17; Hos. 13:2). [*massēkâ*]

27:18 Go astray *(mašgeh)*—The participle used here may be translated, he who causes to go astray. The context indicates that this is to be taken literally in this case. A special curse is directed to anyone who misleads the blind. Even more serious, perhaps, is the sin of leading others astray morally. The sage warns that the person who leads others to paths of evil will himself inevitably fall into the pit he has dug (Prov. 28:10). The psalmist, sensing his own propensity to be led away from the Lord and his covenant law, prayed that this might not happen to him (Ps. 119:10) [*šgh*]

28:2 They will overtake you *(hiśśîgukâ)*—
The imagery here is that of a footrace in which the runner, no matter how fleet of foot, will be overtaken by the blessing of the Lord. That is, God is so eager to bless those who comply with his covenant requirements that one cannot escape his beneficence. A literal usage of the verb occurs in Gen. 44:4, 6 where Joseph's steward is said to have chased and overtaken Joseph's brothers on their way back to Canaan. Even more foreboding is the occurrence in Exod. 14:9, which speaks of the escaping Israelites having been overtaken by the Egyptian army. The disobedient may expect the curses of God to overtake them (Deut. 28:15, 45) just as surely as the blessings outrun the righteous. [*nśg*]

28:11 Will make you abundant *(hôtirkâ)*—
The basic idea of the complex of terms surrounding the root *ytr* is excess, overflow, abundance, usually in a material sense. Here the Lord promises to bless his obedient covenant people with an overflow of good things, specifically children, cattle, and crops (cf. Deut. 30:9). Sometimes, however, the nuance is that of leftovers, that is, scraps remaining after everything else has been taken (cf. Exod. 10:15; Ruth 2:14). The people of Israel are sometimes described in this manner as a remnant or small minority left over after divine judgment (Deut. 28:54; Isa. 1:9; Jer. 44:7). [*ytr*]

28:12 His treasury *('ôṣārô)*—God's heavenly resources are here metaphorically referred to as his store-house or treasury, a noun derived from the verb *'ṣr*, to store up (*BDB*, 69). The specific item of value here is the rain, a particularly apt object to be thought of in this way since it was apparent, even to the ancients, that water evaporated up into the heavens, was

"stored" there for a time, and then fell to the earth as refreshing and revivifying rain (Prov. 3:20; Eccl. 12:2). Other heavenly treasures are snow and hail (Job 38:22) and wind (Jer. 10:13; 51:16). At the other extreme geographically, the depths of the ocean are also said to be concealed in the Lord's treasury (Ps. 33:7). [*ôṣār*]

You shall not borrow *(tilweh)*—This term of business transaction occurs 14x in the OT, 4x in Deuteronomy Its basic stem (as here) usually reflects the idea of financial duress requiring loans, not for investment but for mere survival (Neh. 5:4; Prov. 22:7; Isa. 24:2). In the day of God's future blessing, Israel will not be put in this position of dependence. The causative stem of the verb (here *hilwîtâ*) means lend, that is, cause to borrow. The Lord will so enrich his people if they are obedient that they will have the financial upper hand over other nations. Disobedience, however, will turn the tables, forcing Israel not to lend but to borrow (Deut. 28:44). This is a good example of a curse being the exact opposite of a blessing. [*lwh*]

28:13 The tail *(lĕzānāb)*—Normally used in a literal sense to speak of an animal's appendage (cf. Exod. 4:4; Judg. 15:4; Job 40:17), the noun here is a metaphor describing Israel not as a tail (i.e., a lowly nation) but as a head (exalted). The opposite appears in Deut. 28:44 where God's people, because of their covenant disloyalty, will become the tail and not the head. They will fall from their position of favor and preeminence to the most lowly status among the nations. The same polarity between head and tail occurs in Isa. 9:14 but there the head represents Israel's political leadership and the tail the prophets who lie (cf. Isa. 19:15). A nation's (or individual's) elevation or demotion depends upon its relationship to the sovereign Lord (cf. 2 Chron. 7:14). [*zānāb*]

28:20 Cursing (*hammĕʾērâ*)—This noun, related to the verb *ʾrr*, curse (Deut. 27:15), is a technical term here to describe the results of covenant breaking (cf. 28:15). Blessing follows obedience (28:1-6), cursing follows disobedience. The same contrast is seen in Proverbs where blessing is said to rest upon the righteous but cursing falls on the wicked (Prov. 3:33). Such an apparently minor matter as ignoring the poor invites the divine curse (Prov. 28:27), for the law is explicit that this is a part of faithful covenant compliance (cf. Deut. 15:11). At the end of the OT period the priests are warned that the blessings intended for them will be turned to curses if they fail to glorify the Lord (Mal. 2:2). And the whole covenant people will be under the curse if they try to rob God by withholding their tithes and offerings (Mal. 3:8-9; cf. Deut. 28:16-20). Cursing in this sense ought not, then, to be thought of merely as words of invective or denunciation but as acts of judgment levied by a holy God upon those who, by their disobedience, deserve whatever befalls them. [*mĕʾērâ*]

You have forsaken me (*ʿăzabtānî*)—Since God is omnipresent one cannot leave or abandon Him in a spatial, physical sense. The meaning here (and elsewhere), then, is spiritual departure, a forsaking of the covenant by which the Lord had brought Israel into relationship with himself (see 31:16). To disobey the covenant is to forsake the Lord himself for He has expressed not only His intentions in that medium but also His very person. Should one depart from the Lord in this manner, he may be sure that the Lord will also abandon him, at least until he repents and returns (Deut. 31:17; cf. Josh. 24:16,

20; Judg. 2:12, 13; 10:6, 10, 13; 1 Sam. 8:8; 12:10; 1 Kings 9:9; 11:33; Isa. 1:4; Jer. 1:16; 2:13). For God to forsake Israel is to expose them to all the curses attached to the covenant text (see vv. 20-68). [*ʿzb*]

28:21 Disease (*dāber*)—Usually employed to describe any kind of an affliction or plague (cf. Exod. 5:3; 9:15; Num. 14:12; 2 Sam. 24:13, 15; 1 Kings 8:37; 2 Chron. 7:13; 20:9; Jer. 14:12; Ezek. 5:12; Hos. 13:14), this noun occasionally is more specific, referring, for example, to the cattle disease suffered in the sixth plague in Egypt (Exod. 9:3). Physical illness appears to be in mind here also as the list of ailments of v. 22 suggests. Whatever the nature of the affliction might be, it is a judgment of the Lord for covenant disobedience that will be unshakeable until the nation disappears from the land of promise. [*deber*]

28:28 With madness (*bĕšiggāʾôn*)—In an age before mental illness was understood, a term like this would not refer to classic symptoms of psychological disorder but to aberrant behavior induced by fear, excitement, or some other external stimulus. The related verb (*šgʾ*) occurs in v. 34 to describe the reaction of the people of Israel to the horrible things they will see and experience because of God's wrath upon their disobedience in the future. On occasion both the verb and noun characterize behavior that is apart from the norm such as that of ecstatic pagan prophets (Jer. 29:26) or even, mockingly, of true prophets (Hos. 9:7). The chariot driving of Jehu, who had just been anointed king of Israel, is said to have been done madly, that is, without restraint or attention to safety (2 Kings 9:20). When God's people Israel face his inevitable judgment they will go berserk, as it were, and lose all rationality. [*šiggāʾôn*]

With blindness *(bě'iwwārôn)*—This abstract noun derives from the verb *'wr,* to make blind, and, like the adjective *'iwwēr* (blind), commonly speaks of spiritual lack of vision rather than physical loss of sight (cf. v. 29; Isa. 29:18; 35:5; 42:7, 16, 18, 19; 43:8; Zech. 12:4). The idea clearly is that those who are insensitive to the ways and purposes of the Lord may fully expect that willful attitude to be confirmed in their experience as an act of divine punishment. [*'iwwārôn*]

Bewilderment *(bětimhôn)*—This noun occurs only twice in the Bible (here and in Zech. 12:4) and in both places madness and blindness accompany bewilderment. The meaning is well established thanks to the more common occurrence of the cognate verb *tmh,* be astounded, amazed (KBL, 1031). For example, when Joseph's brothers saw him arrange them around the table in the order of their age they marveled (Gen. 43:33). The psalmist, commenting on the reaction of the kings of the earth to the exaltation of the Lord and of Zion, says they were amazed (Ps. 48:5). Isaiah prophesies that in the Day of the Lord people will look upon one another in astonishment because of God's impending wrath (Isa. 13:8). Habakkuk employs the same verb in anticipation of the coming of the Babylonians as the instrument of God's wrath against Israel (Hab. 1:5). The noun here, then, conveys the idea of absolute confusion, a condition linked to the awesome day of God's judgment. [*timmāhôn*]

28:33 Crushed *(rāṣûṣ)*—This passive participle of *rṣṣ* commonly (as here) occurs metaphorically to speak of oppression of the weak and/or poor by those who have power over them (cf. Isa. 42:3, 4; 58:6; Hos. 5:11). Of special interest is the use of the verb in the first Servant Song

of Isaiah (Isa. 42:1-4). Rather than oppress one who is crushed, the Servant will bring relief (v. 3). And for His part, He will not suffer crushing until He has completed His work of establishing justice throughout the earth (v. 4). On the other hand, Israel (as seen in the present passage) will be crushed by her enemies if she continues in her covenant infidelities. [*rṣṣ*]

28:37 An object of horror *(lěšammâ)*—Cognate to the verb *šmm,* be desolated or deserted (KBL, 988), the noun refers either to the result of destructive judgment or (as here) to the reaction of horror felt by those who witness such devastation (cf. 2 Kings 22:19; 2 Chron. 29:8; 30:7; Jer. 5:30; 25:9, 11, 18, 38; 29:18; 42:18; etc.). Israel's punishment for covenant disloyalty will be so severe and complete that the nations employed by the Lord to effect that judgment will be astounded at its severity. They will be filled with horror and be so impressed with the vengeance of the Lord against his people that it will become proverbial. [*šammâ*]

28:54 Fastidious *(he'ānōg)*—The noun and its related verb (cf. 28:56) have to do with an attitude or disposition that finds delight in beauty and propriety but abhors that which is ugly and distasteful. Here there is the horrible circumstance of a future siege of Israel by their enemies that will be so severe and enduring that men will resort to cannibalism and, even worse, will keep their grisly repast to themselves (vv. 49-55). The women will be no more delicate than their husbands (v. 56). In fact, they will go so far as to eat their own children out of sheer desperation (v. 57). In both cases, what people will do under duress runs completely counter to their natural instincts and behavior. The fallenness of the human race reveals itself most clearly in times of unusual pressure and deprivation. [*'ānōg*]

28:63 Rejoiced (*śāś*)—This verb occurs twice in this verse and twice in Deut. 30:9, both times in contexts of judgment. Here there is a reflection on the pleasure of God in having blessed and multiplied the nation Israel in the past, offset now by the threat of His pleasure in undoing that good by bringing well-deserved judgment upon them because of their sin. In 30:9 the situation is quite the reverse: If the people repent of their sins with all their heart and keep the terms of the covenant without reservation (v. 10), the Lord will rejoice over them as He rejoiced over their ancestors. This will result in the restoration of all the blessings they will have forfeited in their unrepentant state. God's rejoicing, then, is not to be seen as some kind of emotional glee or gloating, but as a studied pleasure. He had been pleased to call and bless the nation's ancestors (v. 62) but it will also be his pleasure; i.e., sovereign choice and purpose, to judge them should they remain in disobedience. But He will also find pleasure in their redemption and renewal should they seek Him in their days of dispossession and dispersion. The same truth occurs elsewhere, especially in the Prophets. The Lord declares that He will rejoice in His new creation, especially in Jerusalem and its citizens in the new heavens and new earth (Isa. 65:19; cf. 62:5; 66:10). Jeremiah declares that the Lord will overcome the judgment inflicted on Israel by rejoicing over them and returning them to the land (Jer. 32:41; cf. Zeph. 3:17). God's rejoicing, it is clear, is effective, not static. It is not so much indicative of disposition as it is of purposeful relationship (M. Grisanti, *NIDOTTE*, 3:1223-26). [*śwś, śyś*]

28:65 You will find no rest (*targîa'*)— Contrary to much more common verbs for rest such as *nwḥ* (Deut. 3:20; 5:14; 12:10; 25:19; Josh. 1:13; 21:44) and *šbt* (Gen. 2:2, 3; Exod. 5:5; 16:30; 23:12), this word speaks not so much of cessation of activity or even of tranquillity but of relief from anxiety or worrisomeness. Thus, in the Day of the Lord fierce creatures of every kind will gather in desert places and there be perfectly at ease (Isa. 34:14). The opposite is in view here. Because of Israel's rebellious spirit she will be dispersed among the nations and find herself filled with fear and trembling. Days and nights will bring terror from which there will be no relief. This will be far different from God's intentions for Israel at the beginning when He gave rest to them in the deserts following their Exodus deliverance (Jer. 31:2). [*rg'*]

29:9 That you might be successful (*taśkîlû*)—Generally in the semantic field of wisdom, this verb and its cognate forms has to do with practical and not theoretical or philosophical wisdom. That is, it is concerned with living life in prudent and skillful ways (T. Fretheim, *NIDOTTE*, 3:1243). When one lives in this manner a certain measure of success or prosperity is bound to follow. Here the "secret of success" is crystal clear: Obey the terms of the covenant. After Joshua assumed leadership of Israel the Lord charged him and the people to comply with the whole law of the Lord for in doing so they would find success (Josh. 1:7). This is exactly the advice David enjoined upon young Solomon as he prepared to succeed his father on Israel's throne (1 Kings 2:3). The plain implication throughout is that genuine success in life cannot be achieved apart from adherence to the word and will of God. [*śkl*]

29:12 Into his oath (*bĕ'ālātô*)—Cognate to the verb meaning to swear or curse (*BDB*, 46), the noun can (as here) bear the meaning of covenant itself (cf. Deut. 4:13); that is, to enter into covenant with the Lord is to subscribe to the blessings and curses that are constituent parts of covenant arrangements (cf. 29:14; Ezek. 17:13, 16, 18, 19). In other instances, the oath is viewed separate from the covenant as in vv. 19, 20, and 21 of this passage (cf. 30:7; 2 Chron. 34:24; Jer. 23:10; Dan. 9:11; Zech. 5:3). There the term refers in a technical way to the curse section of covenant texts. Deut. 29:21, in fact, speaks of oaths as synonymous with curses since curses inevitably follow the breaking of oaths (J. Scharbert, *TDOT*, 1:261-66). [*'ālâ*]

29:17 Their detestable things (*šiqqûṣêhem*)—Most commonly used of idols and other pagan paraphernalia (but cf. Hos. 9:10; Nah. 3:6; Zech. 9:7), the noun is often translated abominations as well (though the principal term for that is *tô'ēbâ*; cf. Deut. 7:25). Here the idols of Egypt and the Transjordanian peoples are in view, but in later texts the various deities themselves are so described (2 Kings 23:13) as are the practices associated with their worship (2 Kings 23:24; Isa. 66:3). Israel was often accused rightly of being involved in the detestable habits of the pagans (Jer. 4:1; 7:30; 32:34; Ezek. 5:11; 7:20; 11:18, 21). In the present passage the warning goes forth to avoid such vile objects and observances lest the curses of God fall upon the community and the very existence of the guilty be blotted out forever (vv. 18-21). [*šiqqûṣ*]

Their idols (*gillulêhem*)—This term for a manufactured image appears to derive ultimately from the verb *gll*, to roll, and more directly from *gālîl*, a (round) district (*BDB*, 164-65). It thus describes a round

or, perhaps, stylized form capable of representing many deities. Its close connection here to *šiqqûṣ*, detestable (see previous word), suggests, furthermore, that it is a term of disgust (H. Preuss, *TDOT*, 3:2). In fact, still another related noun, *gēl*, means dung (ball), underscoring the opprobrious nature of these pagan objects. Ezekiel in particular describes idols with this epithet (6:4-6, 9, 13; 8:10; 14:3-7; 16:36; 18:6, 12; etc.). It occurs in the Pentateuch only here and in Lev. 26:30 where Israel is threatened with the curse of lying prostrate on the carcasses of their idols. In the present passage a curse also is reserved for any of God's people who would leave him to serve such despicable symbols of pagan depravity. [*gillûlîm*]

29:20 To pardon (*sĕlōaḥ*)—This verb, translated also to forgive, occurs only with God as subject. Forgiveness of one human being by another cannot be expressed by this highly technical term. It occurs elsewhere in the Pentateuch in this stem a few times (Exod. 34:9; Num. 14:19, 20; 30:5, 8, 12) and many times in Solomon's prayer of dedication of the temple (1 Kings 8:30, 34, 36, 39, 50). Something of the meaning of the verb can be seen in God's withholding of pardon: It results in such drastic measures as the outpouring of God's wrath and judgment upon the sinner, the invoking of the curses of the covenant text, and even the blotting out of one's name from human memory. His pardon, conversely, delivers the repentant from these terrible consequences. [*slḥ*]

Will lie down (*rābĕṣâ*)—By use of a verb that occurs almost always with an animal subject Moses here graphically describes the curse of the covenant stretching itself out upon the violator of God's precepts and stipulations. Another famous metaphorical occurrence of the verb is the Genesis reference to sin crouching down at Cain's door, ready to spring upon and dominate him should he refuse to repent of his murder of Abel (Gen. 4:7). Here the idea is that the curse for covenant disobedience will, like a savage beast, overwhelm and completely immobilize anyone guilty of such insubordination. His end, in fact, will be so disastrous that his very name will be forgotten. [rbṣ]

29:28 The Lord uprooted them (wayyittĕšēm)—Drawing upon agricultural imagery (cf. Ezek. 19:12), this verb is used most often to describe the removal of kingdoms (Dan. 11:4) and cities (Ps. 9:6), most particularly of Israel, which, having been planted in the promised land (Exod. 15:17; Ps. 44:2; 80:8, 15; Isa. 5:2), would be violently uprooted because of her sin against the Lord. Jeremiah especially makes use of the verb in this sense (Jer. 12:14-17; cf. 18:7; 24:6; 31:28; 42:10; 45:4). Sometimes the uprooting is for beneficial purposes (Jer. 12:14) but usually it is an act of judgment (Jer. 12:17). It is the latter sense that is in view here. Moses prophesies that Israel, because of covenant disobedience, will be torn up from her inheritance and thrown into another land. Like a noxious weed she will be uprooted and cast aside as something worthless. [ntš]

30:1 Where the Lord your God has exiled you (hiddîḥăkâ)—In all its stems this verb is almost a technical term to describe the deportation of Israel from the land of promise, a banishment resulting from her unrepentant disobedience of the Lord. It is part and parcel of the curse administered because of covenant violation (cf. Deut. 28:36, 64-68). The verb form here is picked up by Jeremiah who, of all the

prophets, was most affected by the ideas and even vocabulary of Deuteronomy (cf. Jer. 8:3; 16:15; 23:3, 8; 24:9; 29:14, 18; 32:37; 46:28). He (as well as Moses here) underscores the idea that though hostile nations such as Assyria and Babylonia might be the immediate agents of Israel's deportation, it is the Lord himself who is the ultimate initiator of such punishment. But it is He also, moved by the repentance of His people, who can and will undo their exile and bring them back from their captivity (Deut. 30:2-5; cf. 4:29-30). [ndḥ]

30:3 Your captivity (šĕbûtĕkâ)—A derivative of the verb šbh, to take captive, this noun nearly always refers to the various exiles and deportations of God's chosen people, measures always carried out by conquering armies that literally removed subjugated populations from their homelands. Such punishment was especially painful to Israel because the land of Canaan was an integral part of the patriarchal promises (Gen. 12:1, 7; 15:18-21; 26:1-4). The fulfillment of those promises without everlasting attachment to that particular land was inconceivable. As long as the various captivities were in effect the ultimate plans of the Lord for His people could not be realized. This is why this passage and many others—especially in Jeremiah (cf. 29:14; 30:3, 18; 31:23; 32:44; 33:7, 11, 26)—hold out hope that the captivity will be reversed. Only when that is done can the promises come to pass. The term in question also has a less literal significance when, for example, it speaks of Job's restoration to prosperity (Job 42:10). He had been in captivity to suffering and want but at last was delivered from it. [šĕbît, šĕbût]

And will gather you (wĕqibbeṣkâ)—The opposite of being exiled (ndḥ, v. 1) is to be brought home, regathered to one's place of origin. The verb here has a wide variety of uses such as assembling crowds in general (Judg. 12:4; 2 Sam. 2:30; 2 Chron. 32:4), mustering troops (1 Sam. 28:1; 29:1; 1 Kings 20:1), or gathering prophets together (1 Kings 18:20; 22:6; 2 Chron. 18:5), but the present context demands the meaning of picking up the loose and isolated pieces of Israel that would be scattered among the nations and then reassembled in their own land (cf. vv. 4-5). The verb, then, is a technical term used to describe the reversal of God's judgment on His covenant people for their chronic disobedience. He would disperse them far and wide but following their repentance would gather them up again and reconstitute them as His chosen ones (cf. Isa. 54:7; 56:8; Jer. 31:10; 32:37; Ezek. 11:17; Mic. 2:12; 4:6; Zeph. 3:19, 20; Zech. 10:8, 10). [*qbṣ*]

30:11 Not too hard *(niplē't)*—A feminine singular participle of *pl'*, to be extraordinary, wonderful, the word refers to the commandment Moses had revealed to the people; i.e., the whole book of Deuteronomy. The verb itself derives from a noun *(pele')* meaning something marvelous or wonderful. Though sometimes the verb is used to describe a truth or idea difficult to understand or decide (Deut. 17:8; Job 42:3; Ps. 131:1; Prov. 30:18), here the question is whether or not the commandment is accessible. That is, can one bring it near so as to appropriate it for himself? Moses makes it emphatically clear that what God expects of His people is not either vertically (the heavens) or horizontally (across the seas) so remote that they cannot embrace and thus obey it (vv. 12-13). Rather, it has been implanted in their very mouths and hearts (i.e., minds; see Deut. 6:5) so that they have no excuse for ignoring or disobeying it. Paul cites this passage in arguing for the avail-

ability of Christ and the Gospel—he is among and within us so that we too have no excuse for missing the message of salvation (Rom. 10:6-8). [*pl'*]

31:16 Will break my covenant *(hēpēr)*—The juxtaposition of this verb with *'ăzābanî*, will forsake me (cf. 28:20), makes clear that one way of defining covenant breaking is forsaking the Lord. To abandon Him is, in effect, to break off relations with Him. The idea is not so much a sudden, drastic rupture of relationship but rather a withdrawal from commitment, an annulment or invalidation of a mutually agreed upon compact (thus T. Williams, *NIDOTTE*, 3:696). The result, of course, is the same whether one breaks covenant with the Lord by a precipitous decision or by neglect and gradual erosion. It is a matter of serious moment, one inviting the Lord's displeasure and judgment (cf. vv 20-21; Lev. 26:15-20; Isa. 24:5-6; Jer. 11:10-11; 31:32; Ezek. 16:59; 44:7). [*prr*]

31:20 They will show me disrespect *(ni'ăṣûnî)*—Like the verb *'zb*, forsake (v. 16), this occurs in connection with breaking covenant. In fact, to belittle or despise the Lord is in itself such an act of insubordination as to render His covenant with Israel null and void. Unlike forsaking Him, however, showing Him lack of proper respect is not an action but an attitude. As this passage makes clear, the verb conveys the notion of neglect of the Lord in favor of other gods. He is not overtly rejected as much as blissfully ignored. Regardless, the end result is a blasphemous denial of His sovereignty (E. Merrill, *NIDOTTE*, 3:5-6; cf. Num. 14:11, 23; 16:30; 1 Sam. 2:17; 2 Sam. 12:14; Ps. 10:3, 13; 74:10, 18; Isa. 1:4; 5:24; 60:14; Jer. 23:17). [*n'ṣ*]

31:21 His purpose *(yiṣrô)*—This noun derives from the common verb *yṣr*, to create, make, shape (KBL, 396). The verb is especially at home in contexts of shaping or molding objects of malleable materials such as clay or metals (cf. 2 Sam. 17:28; Isa. 29:16; 30:14; 41:25; 44:12; Jer. 19:1, 11). The noun also is used to describe objects thus formed, especially idols (Isa. 45:16), but it more commonly has the idea of the shaping of thoughts or intentions. It may thus be rendered purpose, imagination, or even impulse (*BDB*, 428). In the Dead Sea Scrolls it occurs often to speak of one's tendency either toward good or evil. Here the Lord says that He is fully aware of Israel's intentions that they have formulated even before entering the promised land. They will do evil and therefore must sing the song of Moses as a witness to their covenant pledges not to do so (vv. 19, 22). [*yēṣer*]

32:2 My teaching *(liqḥî)*—The parallel to this noun in the present passage *('imrātî*, my speech, word) suggests that Moses delivered this poem orally before it was composed in its present form. Moreover, the apparent derivation of the noun from the verb *lqḥ*, take, receive, supports the idea that Moses' discourse was not of his own origination but was, in fact, taught to him first. The teacher of Moses was not another human being but, as the surrounding context makes clear, was the Lord himself (cf. 31:19, 21-22, 28). As a prophet of God (cf. Deut. 18:15, 18) Moses was the channel through whom God disclosed His saving intentions. The noun does occur elsewhere to denote ordinary, even secular instruction (Job 11:4; Prov. 1:5; 4:2; 9:9; 16:21, 23), but in this case it is tantamount to divine revelation. The refreshing nature of the teaching about to be disclosed is clear from its being com-

pared to the fall of gentle rain. [*leqaḥ*]

32:4 Faithfulness *('ĕmûnâ)*—A derivative of the verb *'mn*, confirm, support (*BDB*, 52), this noun is an abstraction of all that is implied by the verbal idea. Fundamentally it reflects the idea of dependability, of being of such a nature as to support whoever or whatever rests upon it. Here it is part of a cluster of epithets describing God in various aspects of His character and works. He is a rock *(ṣûr)* whose deeds are flawless *(tāmîm)*, one whose ways are just and who himself is without deviation from absolute righteousness *('ên 'āwel)*. Moses extols the stability of Israel's God as opposed to the unreliability of the supposed gods of the nations (vv. 17, 21, 31, 37, 39), a sentiment shared by many other poets and prophets in the biblical literature (cf. Ps. 36:5; 40:10; 88:11; 89:1, 2, 5, 8, 24, 33, 49; 92:2; 96:13; 98:3; 100:5; Isa. 11:5; 25:1; Lam. 3:23). Israel, prone to covenant unreliability and disobedience, needed the reminder that their God was quite the opposite. He and His word are unshakable foundations upon which Israel may place all their hope and confidence. [*'ĕmûnâ*]

32:6 Who created you *(qānekâ)*—Most early translations render this verb acquire, purchase, get, or the like (*BDB*, 888). In light of more recent comparative Semitics evidence, especially from Ugarit, there is a consensus that a *qnh* II also exists, one meaning make, create (KBL, 843). That this is the verb intended here is clear from the verb *'śh*, make, in the parallel line. Elsewhere God is described by this verb as Creator of heaven and earth (Gen. 14:19, 22), of Israel (Exod. 15:16), of the mountains (Ps. 78:54), and of man's inner parts (Ps. 139:13). In this passage the idea of Israel as the begotten one of God the Father is also in view (cf. Gen. 4:1). Israel was created by the Lord but not just as an object among others. Rather, the nation was created to be God's son, His special possession (cf. Exod. 4:22-23; 19:5). This loving relationship highlights the terrible disobedience and wickedness with which Israel responded to her God (v. 5). (I. Cornelius/R. VanLeeuwen, *NIDOTTE*, 3:941). [*qnh* II]

32:8 When He divided *(bĕhaprîdô)*—Contrary to other verbs with the broad meaning to separate, this has more the idea of placing persons or things into mutually exclusive or at least clearly distinguishable categories. Thus the rivers of Eden are split into four separate streams (Gen. 2:10), Jacob's flocks are divided from those of Laban (Gen. 30:40), and Ruth pledges to Naomi that only death can part the two of them (Ruth 1:17). The point here, then, is that God, the sovereign of the universe, assigned the peoples of the earth to various territorial allocations, establishing their boundaries so clearly and firmly that they could be readily identified one from the other. Some scholars propose that the division of the nations "according to the number of the children of Israel" refers to the 70 descendants of Jacob (Exod. 1:5), a number at least approximating the total of the nations in the so-called Table of Nations of Gen. 10 (cf. *prd* in vv. 5, 32). (R. Hess, *NIDOTTE*, 3:673-75). [*prd*]

32:9 Portion *(ḥēleq)*—This noun, derived from *ḥlq*, to divide, refers to the result of division such as a share of food (Lev. 6:17; Deut. 18:8) or privilege (Gen. 31:14), a tract of land (Josh. 19:9), a chosen way of life (Ps. 50:18), or either blessing or punishment from the Lord (Job 31:2). In a remarkable reversal, the present passage refers to Israel not as having some kind of portion from the Lord but of being His portion or allotment (for the contrary, cf. Num. 18:20; Ps. 16:5; 73:26; 119:57; 142:5; Lam. 3:24). God had created all the nations of the earth but out of them had chosen only Israel to be his special people (Deut. 32:6, 8; cf. Exod. 19:5-6; Deut. 7:6; 14:2). Jeremiah captures both ideas—that the Lord is Israel's portion *(ḥēleq)* and that Israel is the inheritance *(naḥălâ)* of the Lord (Jer. 10:16). The Lord's claim on Israel is that he had found him in the desert and had subsequently nourished him, bringing him at last to the promised land (Deut. 32:10-14). [*ḥēleq*]

32:15 Became fat *(wayyišman)*—The verb is related to the noun *šemen*, fat, oil, a term associated with abundance and prosperity when used figuratively. To become fat, then, is to become blessed beyond one's needs, indeed, beyond what is good for one's spiritual health. Its use here and elsewhere (Isa. 6:10; Jer. 5:28; Neh. 9:25) is always in a negative sense. Moses points out that after Israel became rich with the bounties of God's grace he rebelled against the Lord, attributing his prosperity to strange gods (vv. 13-17). Isaiah was told that the ears of his people would become so fat that they could not hear his message of warning (Isa. 6:10). Jeremiah makes a direct connection between Israel's fatness and their wickedness (Jer. 5:28). Using a different verb *(dšn)*, Moses had also previously warned that after Israel entered the promised land they would become fat and then break their covenant with the Lord (Deut. 31:20). The lesson is plain: When people become satiated with the outpouring of God's gracious bestowments they are tempted to attribute their success to themselves and therefore to relegate the Lord to a lower place. [*šmn*]

He forsook (*wayyiṭōš*)—A rather common verb meaning to leave or abandon, the word often (as here) has the special meaning of giving up on or giving no further attention to someone or something (*BDB*, 643). In mundane terms it occurs in such narratives as Saul's search for the donkeys left in his charge (1 Sam. 10:2) or the sheep left with David the shepherd boy (1 Sam. 17:20, 22, 28). Their respective fathers turned their animals over to their sons without a second thought. More common is the idea that God can or cannot forsake his people, that is, put them out of his mind (Judg. 6:13; 1 Sam. 12:22; Isa. 2:6; Jer. 7:29; 23:33, 39). Here the opposite is in view, namely, that Israel can and will forsake the Lord (cf. Jer. 15:6). The parallel verb *nbl* (treat contemptuously) underscores the idea that to forsake God in this sense is not actually to leave him but to give him no thought. It is as though he can be delivered over to another caretaker with little or no concern for his well-being. That is, he has little value to his people. [*nṭš*]

Disdained (*yěnabbēl*)—The verb in its basic stem means to be foolish, without sense, and in its form here denotes the idea of considering someone to be in such a condition (cf. Mic. 7:6). In an incredibly blasphemous assessment of the Lord their God, Israel was so disrespectful of him as to consider him a fool. As the parallel line suggests ("he forsook God who made him"), when one abandons the Lord he relegates him to a position of irrelevance, of nothingness as it were. He substitutes his strength for God's strength, his resources for God's resources, his wisdom for God's wisdom. Compared to his own wisdom, then, God's wisdom becomes foolishness and God himself is viewed as little short of a fool. (J. Marböck, *TDOT*, 9:162). [*nbl* II]

32:17 Demons (*šēdîm*)—This noun, apparently a loanword from the Akkadian language (*šēdu*, protective spirit), occurs only twice in the Hebrew Bible, here and in Ps. 106:37. The latter passage describes wicked Israel in the Sinai deserts and later in Canaan offering their children as sacrifices to these spirits. This is exactly what Moses describes here. In both instances the parallel lines make clear that these spirits are identical to the gods of the pagan nations themselves. It is apparent, then, that idols were considered—by the OT assessment at least—to be only vehicles that demonic spirits inhabited or by which they were visibly represented (cf. Lev. 17:7; 1 Cor. 10:19-20). It is of note that the term in Akkadian refers to beneficent spiritual beings, guardians as it were, but in Hebrew they are evil, destructive forces (M. VanPelt/W. Kaiser, Jr., *NIDOTTE*, 4:47-48). [*šēd*]

32:21 With their vanities (*běhablêhem*)—The basic meaning of this noun, vapor, breath, and the like (*BDB*, 210), suggests its more metaphorical nuances such as emptiness, worthlessness, without purpose. Entities described as such are human activity (Eccl. 1:2, 14; 2:1, 14, 15), wasted effort (Isa. 49:4), empty comfort (Zech. 10:2), and even mankind (Ps. 39:5, 11; 62:9) and life itself (Job 7:16; Ps. 78:33). All of this, of course, is predicated on the fact that God is absent or, at least, not taken into account. It is the one "under the sun" who finds life and all it offers to be without value and meaning (Eccl. 1:14; 2:11, 17, 18, 19, 21, 23; 3:16; 4:1, 3, 7, 15; etc.). Only God can transform the nothingnesses of life into purpose and value. The present text equates vanities with "not God." This puts the matter into starkest contrast. The existence and presence of God provide significance of life to those who know him. Those who disavow him, however, and chase after idols (no gods, v. 17) embrace vanity and therefore live empty and unfulfilling lives. [*hebel*]

32:27 I feared (*'āgûr*)—With the Lord as subject of this predicate, the strange idea that God can fear appears to raise difficulties. The verb, however, unlike *pḥd* (Deut. 11:25) and *yr'* (Deut. 1:21), does not so much suggest the visceral reaction of terror as the dread of anticipated threat or danger (Deut. 1:17; 18:22; 1 Sam. 18:15; Job 19:29). Moreover, with God as subject the feelings are translated into human terms so as to communicate something of the divine reaction to events and circumstances (a figure called anthropopathism). This is a classic example of an attempt to describe God's feelings in such a situation. He says he would have decimated and dispersed Israel except for his "fear" that his enemies would capitalize on this course of action and charge him with inability to keep his people safe from harm. That is, his own reputation was so important to him and to Israel that he would not endanger it by appearing to fail at a time when he was most under scrutiny by the pagan nations. He would save Israel, then, not just for their sakes but for the sake of his own name (1 Sam. 12:22; 2 Kings 19:34; 20:6; Ps. 25:11; 31:3; Isa. 37:35; 43:25; 48:9, 11; Jer. 14:7; Ezek. 20:9; etc.). [*gwr*]

32:28 Understanding (*tĕbûnâ*)—Cognate to the verb *byn*, understand, discern, this noun (with its by-form *bînâ*) may refer to the act of understanding (Job 26:12; Ps. 78:72; 136:5; Jer. 10:12), the mental faculty (Exod. 31:3; 35:31; 36:1; Job 12:12, 13), the object of knowledge (Ps. 49:3; 147:5; Prov. 2:3; 3:13; 5:1; Isa. 40:28), or even wisdom personified (Prov. 8:1). Here it is the

capacity for knowledge as the parallel line makes clear: "They [Israel] are a nation lacking in counsel," i.e., in sound judgment. Having threatened to disperse and destroy his people (v. 26), the Lord says he would have done so were it not that he wanted to preserve his name from disrepute (v. 27). Nonetheless, the fact remains that Israel deserved whatever judgment the Lord would inflict because they were like the pagans, totally lacking in understanding of who God is and what he had planned for them. This is the term Isaiah uses, in fact, to describe unbelievers who ignorantly use part of a tree to fabricate an idol and another part as fuel for a cook fire (Isa. 44:19). [*tĕbûnâ*]

32:35 Vengeance (*nāqām*)—Though this noun occurs occasionally with a human subject (Judg. 16:28; Prov. 6:34; Ezek. 25:12, 15), it is God, in most instances, who is said to employ vengeance against his enemies (Deut. 32:41, 43; Isa. 34:8; 35:4; 47:3; 59:17; 61:2; 63:4; Mic. 5:15) and even against his own people because of their covenant disloyalty (Lev. 26:25). The juxtaposition of this noun with *šillēm*, recompense (as here; cf. Deut. 7:10), suggests that vengeance when exercised by the Lord is not an intemperate outburst of rage but an expression of his holiness and justice that requires that evil be identified and dealt with (cf. v. 41; Isa. 34:8). Otherwise, evil scores a victory and to that extent undermines both the reputation and the sovereignty of God (H. Peels, *NIDOTTE*, 3:155). [*nāqām*]

Their calamity (*'êdām*)—This noun may derive from the verb *'wd*, bend (*BDB*, 15), thus describing the result of intense pressure. Here it is the pressure of judgment upon the Lord's enemies, a bending so severe as to result in their utter destruction (vv. 41-43). The most common agent of this kind of calamity is the Lord, usually against the wicked nations (as here; cf. Jer. 46:21; 48:16; 49:8, 32; Ezek. 35:5) or individuals (Job 18:12; 21:17, 30; 31:3, 23; Prov. 1:27). Other times the righteous lament that calamity has befallen them (2 Sam. 22:19; Job 30:12). Finally, Israel itself suffers calamity, usually as a result of God's judgment on their sinful and rebellious ways (Jer. 18:17; Ezek. 35:5; Obad. 13). ['êd]

32:43 Rejoice with ringing cry *(harnînû)*— The verb *rnn* may be an onomatopoeic way of expressing the sound of a bell that rings with loud and joyful proclamation of praise (*BDB*, 943). In its various stems it occurs with the meaning rejoice or sing (Job 38:7; Prov. 29:6; Isa. 24:14; 26:19; 35:6; 42:11; 44:23; 49:13; 52:8, 9; Jer. 31:7, 12; Zeph. 3:14; Zech. 2:10), most particularly in the Psalms (20:5; 33:1; 51:14; 59:16; 63:7; 67:4; 71:23; etc.). Here, with the causative stem, the appeal is made to the nations to become the instruments by which Israel is able to rejoice. The idea seems to be that it is in the very judgment of the nations that joy will fill the hearts of the Lord's own people. Their defeat and destruction will, in a sense, bring about propitiation for Israel's sins. [*rnn*]

33:2 He rose up *(zārah)*—Usually employed to describe the rising of the sun (Gen. 32:31; Exod. 22:3; Judg. 9:33; 2 Sam. 23:4; 2 Kings 3:22; Job 9:7; Ps. 104:22; Jonah 4:8; Nah. 3:17; Mal. 4:2) or shining of the stars (Num. 24:17), the verb sometimes refers to the emission of light in general, usually in a metaphorical sense (Ps. 97:11; 112:4; Prov. 13:9; Isa. 58:10). Here (cf. Isa. 60:1-2) it speaks of the Lord appearing in his theophanic glory on the occasion of his revealing the covenant law to Moses at Sinai. That revelation was indeed accompanied by phenomena like blinding light

(Exod. 19:16; 24:17; cf. 34:29-35; 2 Cor. 3:7). Like the rising sun he flashed forth the brilliance of his presence and his revelation, impressing his people with his transcendent glory and, at the same time, clarifying for them his purposes in electing and redeeming them. [*zrh*]

He shone forth *(hôpîa')*—The idea expressed by this verb is the natural consequence of *zrh*, rise up, for once the bearer of light has made its appearance the light will commence to radiate. The term occurs most often in Poetry and Wisdom and in a figurative way (Job 3:4; 37:15). Here it describes the Lord's coming forth at Sinai and associated places in order to display his glory and to make plain his covenant revelation (see previous word; cf. Job 10:3; Ps. 50:2; 80:3; 94:1). The combination of rising and shining underscores the common biblical image that God is light, not so much in literal terms, but as the source of truth and knowledge (cf. Ps. 27:1; 36:9; 43:3; 44:3; 89:15; Prov. 6:23; Isa. 2:5; 9:2; Matt. 4:16; Luke 2:32; John 1:4, 5, 7, 8, 9; 3:19, 20, 21; 8:12; 9:5; Jas. 1:17; 1 John 1:5). [*yp'*]

33:7 A helper *('ēzer)*—This noun, derived from a verb meaning to help or support, may refer either to help rendered or to the agent doing so; i.e., a helper (as here). In any case, the term should not be understood in the sense of servility or relative inferiority, for God himself is described as a helper here and in a number of other passages (cf. Exod. 18:4; Ps. 33:20; 70:5; 115:9, 10, 11; 146:5). Most instructive is the place name Ebenezer (lit., stone of help), so named because it marked the spot where the Lord had come to the aid of Israel when the nation was under Philistine attack (1 Sam. 7:12). Clearly the help rendered here was by the infinitely superior One who acted on behalf of his needy people. One ought also to understand the creation of woman in terms of the usual meaning of *'ēzer*. Having seen all the animals and observing that they had mates, Adam realized that he had no *'ezer kĕnegdô*, that is, no helper comparable and complementary to him (Gen. 2:20). The blessing of Judah in the present passage includes the promise that the Lord will be Judah's helper against anticipated adversaries. [*'ēzer*]

33:8 Your Thummim *(tummêkâ)*—Clearly to be associated with the verb *tmm*, be complete, finished; the noun *tōm*, completeness, integrity; and the adjective *tāmîm*, complete, sound (*BDB*, 1070-71), this technical term occurs only 5x in the OT (Exod. 28:30; Lev. 8:8; Deut. 33:8; Ezra 2:63; Neh. 7:65). Despite its etymological connection to the semantic field *tm(m)*, the precise meaning of the word cannot be determined so it is best to leave it untranslated. Almost always Thummim occurs with Urim (plural of *'ôr*, light) as a pair of precious stones attached to the ephod (or breast-plate) of the chief priest who, in some way not clear today, used them as oracular devices to ascertain God's will in certain matters and situations where their use seemed appropriate. Here Moses blesses Levi, the priestly tribe charged with the responsibility of using the Urim and Thummim, a blessing based partly, at least, on the faithfulness of that tribe in implementing God's justice in the wilderness (Exod. 32:25-29; Num. 25:6-9). (C. Van Dam, *NIDOTTE*, 1:329-31). [*tummîm*]

Your favored one *(ḥăsîdekâ)*—This term of endearment and of covenant affiliation pertains to those who have become the beneficiaries of the Lord's *ḥesed*, that

is, of his mercy and loving-kindness (cf. *ḥesed*, Deut. 5:10). It is also employed to describe persons marked by piety or godliness including God himself (Ps. 145:17; Jer. 3:12). Both meanings are appropriate here for the tribe of Levi was certainly chosen by God to be set apart as an expression of his *ḥesed* toward them (Exod. 28:1) but they also demonstrated their godliness by their obedience in the wilderness. On the occasion of the apostate worship of the golden calf the Levites, at Moses' request, took sword in hand to slay those who had sinned so grievously (Exod. 32:25-29). The degree of their piety in carrying out this mandate is seen in the fact that Aaron himself, leader of the priestly tribe, had collaborated in the pagan orgy. Later, Phinehas, grandson of Aaron, displayed his godliness by killing an Israelite man who had cohabited with a Midianite woman at Baal Peor (Num. 25:6-13). Both these examples justify the assertion of the Levites as God's favored ones. [*ḥāsîd*]

33:16 Favor of *(rāṣôn)*—The cognate verb means to be pleased with, accept favorably (*BDB*, 953), and the noun, therefore, describes the result of such action. Sometimes human favor or goodwill is in view (all in Proverbs; cf. 10:32; 11:27; 14:9, 38; 16:13, 15; 19:12) but usually it is God who bestows such beneficence (cf. Ps. 5:12; 30:5, 7; 51:18; 69:13; 89:17; 106:4; Prov. 8:35; 12:2; 18:22; Isa. 49:8; 60:10). Here a blessing is pronounced upon Joseph, one encapsulated by the phrase "the favor of him who dwelt in the bush." This, of course, refers to the Lord who had disclosed himself to Moses at the burning bush and there had outlined to him all the covenant promises (Exod. 3:2-6). The noun occurs again in Moses' blessing of Naphtali (v. 23). Here the word *rāṣôn* is parallel to *běrākâ*, blessing, thus equating the two (cf. Deut. 1:11). [*rāṣôn*]

33:26 In his majesty *(běga'ăwātô)*—Usually this noun is rendered pride, haughtiness, and the like (Ps. 10:2; 31:18, 23; 36:11; 73:6; Prov. 14:3; 29:23; Isa. 9:9; 13:11; 25:11)—the opposite of the meaning here—but sometimes it has a more positive meaning. It describes such things as national exaltation (Deut. 33:29; Isa. 16:6) or even the pride Leviathan can take in his sheath of scales (Job 41:15). Here, however, the transcendent majesty of Israel's God is in view. Like a conquering hero he rides upon the heavens resplendent in beauty and awesome in his sovereign royalty. If there is pride it is rightfully his for the Lord by nature and by deed displays a glory that can elicit only fear, reverence, and praise. This is why the psalmist, using this very word, urges his hearers to recognize and attribute power to Israel's God (Ps. 68:34). [*ga'ăwâ*]

33:29 The shield who helps you *(māgēn 'ezrekâ)*—This rendition of the more literal the shield of your help provides a metaphorical description of the Lord as one who guards his people from the spears and arrows of those who would seek to do them harm. The noun *māgēn* derives from a verb *gnn*, to cover, defend, thus underscoring the protective nature of this part of one's armor. In the parallel line the Lord is called a sword, thus displaying the offensive element of warfare. Whether attacking or being attacked, then, Israel can depend on the Lord, her weapon and protection at one and the same time. Apart from this passage and Gen. 15:1, *māgēn* as an epithet for the Lord occurs only in the Poetic and Wisdom Literature (e.g., Ps. 3:3; 7:10; 18:2, 30, 35; 28:7; 33:20; 59:11; 84:9, 11;

115:9, 10, 11; 119:114; 144:2; Prov. 2:7; 30:5). [*māgēn*]

Their high places *(bāmôtêmô)*—Most Canaanite shrines and other worship centers were located on natural or man-made elevations called high places. The idea seems to be that the gods in the heights above could be more accessible to their worshipers if the latter addressed their deities from a higher vantage-point. Occasionally, however, "high places" were in valleys so physical eminence was not necessarily essential for a cult center to bear that description (K.-D. Schunk, *TDOT*, 2:141). Though high places are normally associated with paganism in the Bible (cf. Num. 22:41; 33:52; 1 Kings 3:2; 12:32; 14:23; 2 Kings 12:3; 14:4; Isa. 16:12; Jer. 7:31; 32:35; Hos. 10:8), they also were legitimate places of worship for the Israelites, especially in earlier periods (1 Sam. 9:12-14; 10:5, 13; 1 Chron. 16:39; 2 Chron. 1:3). What mattered was the nature of the religious activities being carried out and not the place chosen for them. In the present passage it may be best to understand *bāmâ* as back, not high place, because of the militaristic tone of the verse. The parallel line speaks of Israel's enemies being subjected so in line with this idea it is likely that the image is that of a conqueror setting his foot on an enemy's back, an image attested to elsewhere in the OT (Job 9:8; Isa. 58:14; Amos 4:13; Hab. 3:19). [*bāmâ*]

34:7 His vital strength *(lēḥōh)*—Apparently related to *laḥ*, fresh, moist (KBL, 478), this rare noun occurs with a literal meaning in Jer. 11:19 to speak of the sap of a tree. Even here the usage is figurative. Jeremiah has come to know of a plot to kill him while in his youth, while his "sap" or virility is still effective and apparent. In the present passage the remarkable statement is made that though Moses is 120 years old his eyesight is undimmed and his vital strength unabated. Though no doubt somewhat hyperbolic, the point is that Moses did not die a "natural" death. It was time for Israel to possess Canaan, an accomplishment denied to Moses (Num. 20:12; 27:14; Deut. 1:37; 32:51-52). To facilitate this it was necessary for Moses to die thus joining the rebellious generation already consigned to that fate (Num. 14:26-30). [lēaḥ]

34:9 Had laid (sāmak)—The basic meaning of this verb is support, sustain (KBL, 661), but a range of uses gives rise to a variety of nuances. It describes God's gracious help, especially in the Psalms (cf. 3:5; 37:17, 24; 54:4; 119:116); Isaac's mistaken blessing of Jacob (Gen. 27:37); the laying on of hands upon a sacrifice (Exod. 29:10, 15, 19; Lev. 1:4; 3:2, 8, 13; etc.); aggressive action toward an enemy (Ps. 88:7; Ezek. 24:2); or (as here) the act of dedicating or consecrating one to office or service (cf. Num. 27:18, 23). With Moses' death imminent, he must symbolize the transfer of his theocratic office and its requisite authority and strength to Joshua, his designated successor. God never removes a leader without replacing him by someone of equal or superior gifts, provided that successor and his followers are obedient to the calling and purposes of God (cf. Josh. 1:1-9). [smk]

ENGLISH INDEX

A

Aaron; Lev. 6:9; Num. 3:9
Abandon; Gen. 24:27
Abba; Mark 14:36
Abhor; Deut. 23:7
Abihu; Lev. 10:1
Aboard; John 6:17
Abode; Exodus 25:9
Abomination; Deut. 7:25; Matt. 24:15;
    Mark 13:14; Luke 16:15
Abounding in love; Num. 14:18
Above; John 3:3; 8:23
Abraham; Gen. 28:4; Matt. 3:9; Luke 3:8,
    34; John 8:33. *See also* Children of
    Abraham; Son of Abraham
Abraham's bosom; Luke 16:22
Abram; Gen. 11:26
Abundant; Deut. 28:11
Abundantly; John 10:10
Abuse; Luke 6:28
Abyss; Luke 8:31
Acceptable; Lev. 1:3; Luke 4:24
Acceptable year of the Lord; Luke 4:19
Accepted; Gen. 4:7
Accidentally; Deut. 4:42
Accompany; Mark 16:17
Accomplished; Luke 1:1
Account; Gen. 2:4
Accounting; Gen. 42:22
Accursed; John 7:49
Accusation; John 18:29
Acquired; Exodus 15:16
Adam; Luke 3:38
Adorned; Luke 21:5
Adultery; Exodus 20:14; Deut. 5:18;
    Luke 16:18
Advanced; Luke 1:7
Advocate; John 14:16, 26; 15:26

Aenon; John 3:23
Afflicted; Deut 15:11
Affliction; Mark 5:29
Afraid; Gen. 26:24; 32:11; Luke 12:4-5;
    John 19:8
After; John 13:7
Against you; Matt. 18:15
Aged; Lev. 19:32
Agony; Luke 22:44
Agree; Matt. 18:19
Alert; Matt. 24:42; Mark 13:33
Alien; Gen. 23:4; 28:4; Lev. 16:29;
    Num. 9:14; Deut. 1:16
Alike; Luke 14:18
Alive; John 5:21
All before me; John 10:8
All the time; Gen. 6:5
Allotted; Deut. 4:19
Almighty; Gen. 17:1; Num. 24:4
Alms; Matt. 6:2; Luke 11:41
Aloes; John 19:39
Alone; Lev. 13:46
Already; Matt. 3:10
Altar; Gen. 8:20; 12:7; Exodus 27:1;
    Lev. 4:7; Num. 4:11, 13
Amazed; Luke 2:47; 4:36
Angel; Gen. 48:16; Exodus 3:2; Num.
    22:22; Matt. 1:20; 18:10; 22:30; 25:41;
    Luke 20:36; John 1:51; 12:29; 20:12
Angel of the Lord; Gen. 16:7
Anger; Gen. 49:7; Exodus 4:14; 32:12;
    Num. 11:1; 25:4; Deut. 4:25; 9:19;
    Matt. 18:34. *See also* Slow to anger
Angry; Gen. 44:18; Deut. 1:34, 37;
    Matt. 5:22
Animal; Gen. 7:2; Lev. 1:2
Anoint; Num. 3:3; Mark 14:8; Luke 4:18;
    John 9:6; 11:2

Anointed priest; Lev. 4:3
Another; John 5:32
Answer; Gen. 35:3; Luke 21:14; 22:68
Answered his prayer; Gen. 25:21
Anxious; Matt. 6:25
Apart from; Matt. 10:29
Apostles; Matt. 10:2; Luke 6:13
Apparel; Luke 23:11
Appear; Gen. 18:1; 26:2; Exodus 3:2;
    Lev. 9:4
Appearance; John 7:24
Appease; Exodus 32:11
Appoint; John 15:16
Appointed time; Num. 28:2
Approach; Matt. 26:45; Luke 21:34
Are not cut off; Num. 4:18
Argument; Luke 9:46-47
Ark; Gen. 6:14; Exodus 25:8, 10;
    Num. 3:31; Deut. 10:1
Arm; Gen. 16:5
Arm of the Lord; John 12:38
Army; Gen. 21:22; Num. 1:3
Aroma; Gen. 8:21; Lev. 1:9; Num. 18:17
Arose to play; Exodus 32:6
Arouse; Deut. 4:25
Arrogant; Deut. 17:12
As he said; Matt. 28:6
As you will; Matt. 26:39
Ascend; John 1:51; 3:13; 6:62; 20:17
Ascendancy; Exodus 1:10
Ashamed; Mark 8:38; Luke 9:26
Asherim; Deut. 7:5
Ashes; Lev. 4:12; Num. 19:17
Ask; Matt. 7:7
Asleep; Matt. 9:24; John 11:11
Assaria; Luke 12:6
Assembly; Lev. 23:2; Num. 28:18; 29:35;
    Deut. 5:22; 16:8
Assurance; Luke 1:4
Astonished; Luke 2:48
Astray; Deut. 27:18
Atone; Deut. 21:8
Atonement; Exodus 32:30; Lev. 1:4;
    Num. 5:8
Atonement cover; Exodus 25:17
Attended; Matt. 4:11
Attended the door; John 18:17
Attention; Exodus 3:16
Augurer; Deut. 18:10
Authority; Num. 27:20; Matt. 7:29; 10:1;
    21:27; 28:18; Mark 1:22; 6:7; 11:28;
    Luke 4:6, 32; 9:1; 19:17; 20:2; John
    1:12; 5:27; 10:18; 17:1; 19:10
Avenge; Exodus 21:20; Deut. 5:9

Avenger; Num. 35:19; Deut. 19:6
Aware of the sin; Lev. 4:14
Away; John 15:2

B
Baal; Num. 25:3
Babel; Gen. 11:9
Babes; Luke 10:21
Back; Exodus 33:23
Bad; Matt. 22:10
Balaam; Num. 22:5; 24:3
Banquet; Luke 14:12
Baptism; Mark 10:38; Luke 3:3; John 1:25,
    33; 4:2
Baptize; Matt. 28:19
Barabbas; Matt. 27:16; John 18:40
Barley loaves; John 6:9
Barren; Gen. 25:21; Luke 23:29
Baskets; Mark 6:43; 8:8
Bastard; Deut. 23:2
Bath; Luke 16:6
Bathe; Deut. 23:11
Bathed; John 13:10
Be still; Mark 4:39
Be with you; Exodus 3:12
Bear; Luke 14:27
Beating; Luke 12:47-48
Beautiful; Gen. 24:16
Because of you; Deut. 3:26
Become; John 2:9
Become like; Matt. 10:25
Beelzeboul; Matt. 10:25; Luke 11:15
Beelzebul; Mark 3:22
Before; Luke 21:12; John 1:15, 30; 17:5
Before the time; Matt. 8:29
Began; Matt. 4:17
Beginning; Gen. 1:1; John 1:1; 8:25; 15:27;
    16:4
Behold; John 6:40; 12:45; 19:5
Believe; Exodus 4:5, 8-9; 14:31; Deut.
    1:32; Matt. 9:28; Mark 9:24; John 1:12,
    50; 2:11, 22, 23; 3:15; 4:21, 39, 48, 50,
    53; 5:24, 38, 43, 46; 6:30, 35, 47, 69; 7:5,
    48; 8:24, 30, 31, 45; 9:18, 35; 10:24, 37;
    11:15, 26, 27, 40, 42, 45, 48; 12:36, 38,
    39, 42; 13:19; 14:1, 10, 11, 29; 16:27, 31;
    17:8, 20, 21; 20:8, 25, 27, 29, 31
Believe in me; Num. 14:11
Belly; John 7:38
Beloved; Mark 1:11; 12:6
Beloved son; Luke 3:22; 20:13
Below; John 8:23
Bending over; John 20:5
Benefactors; Luke 22:25

Camp of God; Gen. 32:2
Camp of Judah; Num. 2:3
Camp of Reuben; Num. 2:10
Can; Luke 6:39
Cana; John 2:1; 4:46
Canaan; Gen. 9:25; Lev. 14:34
Canaanite; Gen. 28:8; Matt. 15:22
Canopy; Exodus 26:31
Capernaum; Luke 4:23; John 2:12
Captivity; Deut. 30:3
Care; Deut. 11:12; Luke 10:40; John 10:13
Carpenter; Mark 6:3
Carrying; John 19:17
Carved image; Num. 33:52
Case-Laws; Exodus 21:1
Cast; Luke 6:22
Cast idols; Num. 33:52
Cast image; Deut. 9:12
Cast lots; John 19:24
Cast out; John 6:37; 12:31
Catch; Luke 11:54
Catching men; Luke 5:10
Cattle; Gen. 13:2
Caught in the act; John 8:4
Cause; Matt. 19:3; John 18:38; 19:4, 6
Cause to sin; Matt. 18:6
Cause to stumble; John 6:61
Celebrate; Exodus 23:14
Censer; Lev. 9:24
Cent; Matt. 5:26
Centurion; Matt. 8:5; Mark 15:39;
    Luke 7:2
Cephas; John 1:42
Ceremonial washing; John 2:6
Ceremonially clean; Lev. 4:12; Num. 8:6
Ceremonially unclean; Lev. 5:2; Num. 5:2
Certificate of divorce; Deut. 24:1;
    Matt. 5:31; 19:7
Certified; John 3:33
Change his mind; Num. 23:19
Charcoal fire; John 18:18; 21:9
Charge; Deut. 22:14; Matt. 27:37
Charmer; Deut. 18:11
Chasm; Luke 16:26
Chastise; Luke 23:16
Chemosh; Num. 21:29
Cherubim; Gen. 3:24; Exodus 25:18;
    Num. 7:89
Chief priest; Matt. 2:4; Mark 11:27;
    John 7:32; 19:21
Chief steward; John 2:8; 11:57
Child; Mark 10:15; John 4:49
Childbearing; Gen. 3:16
Childless; Gen. 15:2; Lev. 20:20

Children; Matt. 18:3; Luke 9:48; 11:7;
    13:34; 18:16-17; John 13:33; 21:5
Children of Abraham; John 8:39
Children of God; John 1:12
Choose; Deut. 4:37; John 6:70; 15:16, 19
Chosen; Gen. 18:19; Matt. 22:14;
    Luke 1:9; 9:35 John 13:18
Christ; Matt. 1:1; Mark 1:1; 8:29;
    Luke 3:15; 4:41; 9:20; 22:67; 23:35;
    John 1:20, 41; 4:25; 20:31
Church; Matt. 16:18; 18:17
Circumcise; Gen. 17:10; Lev. 12:3;
    Deut. 10:16
Circumcision; Luke 1:59; 2:21; John 7:22
Cities of Israel; Matt. 10:23
City of David; Luke 2:4
Clay; John 9:6
Clean; Lev. 4:12; Num. 8:6; Deut. 12:15;
    Mark 7:19; John 13:10; 15:3
Clean animal; Gen. 7:2
Cleanness; Gen. 20:5
Cleanse; Num. 8:7; 31:23; Matt. 8:2
Clear; Matt. 6:22
Clearly; Deut. 27:8
Cleave; Deut. 4:4; 10:20
Cloak; Matt. 14:36; Mark 10:50
Clothing; Matt. 3:4
Cloud; Exodus 13:21; Lev. 16:2;
    Num. 9:15; Mark 9:7; Luke 9:34; 21:27
Cohort; John 18:3
Coin; Luke 20:24; 21:2
Colt; Mark 11:2
Come; Matt. 24:3, 27; John 14:23; 21:22
Come all; Matt. 11:28
Come down; Luke 17:31; John 6:38, 42
Come in; Num. 27:17
Come near; Luke 10:9, 11
Come to live; Gen. 47:4
Come to me; John 6:44, 45, 65; 7:37
Come to your aid; Gen. 50:24
Come upon; Luke 11:20
Comes; John 6:35
Comes down; John 6:33
Comforted; Gen. 24:67; Matt. 5:4
Coming one; Matt. 11:3
Command; Gen. 2:16; Lev. 4:2; 6:9;
    Num. 1:19; Luke 8:25; John 15:14
Commanding officer; John 18:12
Commandment; Deut. 4:2; Matt. 5:19;
    15:3; John 10:18; 13:34; 14:15; 15:10, 12
Commands; Gen. 26:5
Commemorate; Lev. 23:24
Commit a violation; Lev. 5:15
Common; Lev. 10:10

Flee; Deut. 20:3; Matt. 26:56; Mark 16:8; John 10:5
Flesh; Gen. 2:24; 29:14; 37:27; Lev. 4:11; Luke 24:39; John 1:14; 3:6; 6:51, 52, 63; 8:15
Flock; Lev. 5:15; Luke 12:32; John 10:16
Flog; Matt. 10:17; Mark 15:15
Flood; Matt. 7:25
Floodwaters; Gen. 6:14
Flour; Lev. 2:1
Flourish; Gen. 26:22
Flow with milk and honey; Num. 13:27
Flute players; Matt. 9:23
Fold; John 10:16
Fold of the sheep; John 10:1
Follow; Matt. 4:20; Mark 1:18; 8:34; 10:52; Luke 1:3; 5:28; John 13:36
Follow me; Num. 32:11; Matt. 9:9
Food; Lev. 3:11; John 4:32, 34
Fool; Matt. 23:17; Luke 12:20
Foolish; Matt. 25:2
Foolish man; Matt. 7:26
For; Mark 10:45; Luke 22:19; John 10:11
For the people; John 11:50
Forbid; Matt. 16:22; Luke 23:2
Forbidden; Lev. 19:23
Foreign gods; Gen. 35:2
Foreigner; Gen. 17:12; Deut. 14:21; Luke 17:18
Forever; Gen. 3:22; 13:15; Deut. 12:28; John 6:58; 8:35
Forfeit; Luke 9:25
Forget; Deut. 8:11
Forgive; Gen. 50:17; Num. 14:18; 14:19; Matt. 9:6; Luke 6:37
Forgiven; Lev. 4:20; Luke 5:20; 7:47
Forgiveness; Matt. 26:28; Mark 1:4; Luke 1:77; 3:3
Forgiving; Exodus 34:7
Form; Deut. 4:12; John 5:37
Form of the Lord; Num. 12:8
Former days; Deut. 4:32
Formless; Gen. 1:2
Forsaken; Deut. 28:20; 32:15; Matt. 27:46; Mark 15:34; Luke 13:35
Forty; Matt. 4:2
Found; John 1:41
Foundation; John 17:24
Four days; John 11:17, 39
Fourfold; Luke 19:8
Fourteen; Matt. 1:17
Fourth generation; Gen. 15:16
Fourth watch; Mark 6:48
Fox; Luke 13:32

Fragrance; John 12:3
Fragrant incense; Exodus 30:7; Lev. 4:7; Num. 4:16
Frankincense; Matt. 2:11
Fraudulent witness; Exodus 20:16
Free; Deut. 15:12; Matt. 17:26; John 8:32
Freewill offering; Lev. 7:16; Num. 29:39; Deut. 16:10
Friend; Matt. 11:19; John 15:14
Friend of Caesar; John 19:12
Friend of the bridegroom; John 3:29
Fringe; Mark 6:56
From; Luke 20:4; John 8:44; 17:8; 19:9
From above; John 3:31; 19:11
From God; John 9:33
From him; John 7:29
From now on; Luke 1:49
From the first; Num. 15:21
Frontlet; Deut. 6:8
Fruit; Matt. 3:8; 7:16; 21:34; Luke 3:9; 6:43; John 4:36; 12:24; 15:2, 4, 16
Fruitful; Gen. 17:6; 47:27; Exodus 1:7; Lev. 26:9
Fulfill; Lev. 22:21; Matt. 1:22; 5:17; John 12:38; 13:18; 17:12; 18:9, 32; 19:28
Fulfillment; Luke 1:45
Full; Deut. 6:11
Full of the Holy Spirit; Luke 4:1
Full of violence; Gen. 6:11
Fullness; John 1:16
Fully taught; Luke 6:40
Furious; Deut. 3:26
Fury; Luke 6:11

G
Gabbatha; John 19:13
Gadarenes; Matt. 8:28
Galilean; Luke 22:59
Galilee; Matt. 4:15
Gall; Matt. 27:34
Garden; John 18:1
Gardener; John 20:15
Garments; Luke 19:36; 23:34
Gates of Hades; Matt. 16:18
Gather; Num. 20:24; Deut. 30:3; John 11:52
Genealogy; Matt. 1:1
Generation; Gen. 6:9; Matt. 11:16; 23:36; 24:34; Mark 8:12; Luke 21:32
Generous; Matt. 20:15
Gennesaret; Luke 5:1
Gentiles; Matt. 4:15; 10:18; 18:17; Mark 10:33; Luke 21:24
Gerasenes; Mark 5:1
Gestured; John 13:24

If; Gen. 28:20; Luke 7:39
If not; Luke 13:9
Image; Gen. 1:26; Num. 33:52;
Deut. 4:16; 9:12
Imagination; Luke 1:51
Immanuel; Matt. 1:23
Immediately; Mark 1:10; Luke 19:11;
John 13:32
Immorality; Matt. 5:32; 19:9; Luke 11:39
Impatient; Num. 21:4
Important government officials;
Mark 6:21
Important seats; Mark 12:39
Impossible; Gen. 11:6
Improve; John 4:52
Impure; Lev. 7:18
In; John 14:20
In place of the boy; Gen. 44:33
In the day; Lev. 16:30
In your heart; Lev. 19:17
Incense; Exodus 30:7; Lev. 2:1; 4:7;
Num. 4:16; Luke 1:9, 10
Incite; Luke 23:5
Incomprehensibility; Exodus 3:14
Indebted; Luke 11:4
Indecency; Deut. 23:14
Infant; Matt. 11:25; Luke 18:15
Inflicted; Gen. 12:17
Inherit; Matt. 5:5; Mark 10:17; Luke
10:25; 18:18
Inheritance; Num. 16:14
Iniquity; Exodus 20:5; 34:7
Inner room; Matt. 6:6
Innocent; Gen. 20:4; 44:16; Deut. 19:10;
Matt. 12:7; 27:19, 24; Luke 23:47
Insane; John 10:20
Inside; Matt. 23:28
Insightful; Deut. 1:13
Instruct; Matt. 11:1; Luke 1:4
Insult; Luke 11:45
Insurrection; Luke 23:19
Insurrectionists; Mark 15:7
Integrity; Gen. 20:5; Deut. 18:13
Intend to harm; Gen. 50:20
Interest; Deut. 23:19
Intermarry; Gen. 34:9
Interpret; Luke 12:56; 24:27
Invited; Matt. 22:3; Luke 14:16;
John 2:2
Is near; Mark 1:15
Is this not?; Luke 4:22
Isaac; Gen. 31:42
Isaiah the prophet; Matt. 8:17
Iscariot; John 6:71

Israel; Gen. 32:28; Num. 25:3; Matt. 2:6;
9:33; 10:6; Luke 1:54, 80; 2:25
Israelite community; Lev. 4:13
Israelites; Exodus 2:23; Lev. 1:2
It; Luke 22:16
It is finished; John 19:30
It is given; Matt. 19:11
It is I; John 6:20
It was so; Gen. 1:7

J

Jacob; Gen. 25:26. *See also* House of Jacob
Jacob's well; John 4:6
Jealous; Gen. 30:1; 37:11; Exodus 20:5;
Deut. 4:24
Jerusalem; Luke 2:38
Jesus; Matt. 1:1; Luke 8:39
Jews; Matt. 2:2; 28:15; John 1:19; 2:18;
5:10; 6:41; 7:1, 11, 33; 8:22, 31; 9:18;
10:24; 11:8, 19; 12:9, 10; 13:33; 18:20,
33, 36; 19:7, 12, 14, 20, 21
Join; Num. 25:3; Matt. 19:6; Mark 10:9
Jonah; Matt. 12:39
Jordan; John 10:40
Joseph; Gen. 49:22
Joy; Lev. 9:24; Matt. 2:10; 25:23;
Luke 1:44; 24:52; John 15:11; 16:20
Jubilee; Lev. 25:13; Num. 36:4
Judah; Gen. 49:8; Num. 2:3
Judea; Luke 4:44
Judge; Gen. 19:9; 49:16; Num. 35:24;
Matt. 7:1; 19:28; John 5:30; 7:51; 8:15,
26, 50; 12:48; 16:11; 18:31
Judgment; Gen. 15:14; Exodus 12:12;
Deut. 1:17; Matt. 10:15; John 3:19;
5:24, 27, 30; 8:16; 9:39; 12:31; 16:8
Judgment day; Matt. 12:36
Judgment seat; John 19:13
Justice; Gen. 18:19; Deut. 16:19
Justified; Luke 7:29

K

Keep; Gen. 17:9; 20:6; Exodus 19:5; Num.
17:10Luke 2:51; 11:28; John 8:51, 55;
9:16; 12:7, 47; 14:21, 23; 17:6, 11, 15
Keep watch; Gen. 31:49
Kept my requirements; Gen. 26:5
Key; Matt. 16:19; Luke 11:52
Kidron Valley; John 18:1
Kill; Gen. 4:8; 27:41; Num. 31:17; 35:6;
Deut. 5:17; John 12:10; 16:2
Kind; Luke 6:35
Kindness; Gen. 19:19; 32:10; 40:14
Kinds; Gen. 1:11

Prophet of the Most High; Luke 1:76
Prophetess; Luke 2:36
Prostitute; Gen. 38:21; Lev. 17:7;
    Num. 15:39; Deut. 22:21; 23:17
Prostrate; Exodus 20:5
Prove our innocence; Gen. 44:16
Provided; Luke 8:3
Prune; John 15:2
Public charge; Lev. 5:1
Pull it in; John 21:6
Punish; Gen. 42:21; Exodus 20:5, 7; 34:7;
    Lev. 26:18; Luke 12:46
Punishment; Gen. 4:13; Exodus 21:23b-
25
Pure; Matt. 5:8
Purge out; Deut. 13:5
Purification; Luke 2:22
Purify; Gen. 35:2; John 11:55
Purple; Luke 16:19; John 19:2
Purple robe; Mark 15:17
Purpose; Deut. 31:21
Put; John 13:2
Put forth; John 10:4
Put in charge; Matt. 24:47
Put to death; Gen. 38:7; Exodus 21:12;
    Num. 35:16

Q
Quarrel; Num. 20:13
Quiet man; Gen. 25:27

R
Rabbi; Matt. 23:7
Rabboni; John 20:16
Railed; Luke 23:39
Rain; Gen. 2:5
Rainbow; Gen. 9:13
Raise my hand; Gen. 14:22
Raise up; John 6:39
Ram; Lev. 5:15; Num. 5:8
Ramah; Matt. 2:18
Ran; John 20:2, 4
Ransom; Exodus 21:30; Matt. 20:28;
    Mark 10:45
Rash promise; Num. 30:6
Read; Matt. 21:16
Reader; Matt. 24:15
Reassure; Gen. 50:21
Rebel; Deut. 1:26
Rebellion; Exodus 34:7; Lev. 16:16;
    Num. 14:18
Rebels; Num. 20:10
Rebuke; Gen. 31:42; Mark 8:32; 16:14;
    Luke 4:39

Receive; Matt. 10:40; Luke 19:12;
    John 1:11; 5:43; 13:20; 17:8
Recline; Matt. 8:11; Luke 13:29; John 12:2;
    13:23
Recognize; Gen. 42:7; Luke 24:16
Recompense; Deut. 7:10
Reconciled; Matt. 5:24
Recount; Exodus 10:2
Recover; John 11:12
Redeem; Exodus 15:13; Lev. 25:25;
    Num. 3:46; Deut. 7:8; Luke 24:21
Redemption; Luke 1:68; 2:38; 21:28
Redemption-price; Exodus 21:30
Refuge; Num. 35:6
Regain his sight; Mark 8:24
Regained; Matt; 18:15
Regretted; Matt. 27:3
Regular; Num. 29:1
Regulations; Lev. 26:46
Reject; Mark 8:31; John 3:36; 12:48
Rejoice; Deut. 12:7; 28:63; 32:43;
    John 14:28; 20:20
Relative; Gen. 12:1; 14:14; Mark 3:21;
    John 18:26
Release; Exodus 3:20; 5:1; John 18:39
Relent; Exodus 21:14
Relief; Exodus 8:15
Remain; John 1:32; 8:35; 9:41; 11:6; 12:24,
    34; 14:25; 15:16; 21:22
Remember; Gen. 19:29; 30:22; Exodus
    2:23; 20:8; Num. 10:9; Deut. 7:18;
    John 2:17, 22; 16:4
Remember me; Gen. 40:14
Remembrance; Luke 22:19; John 14:26
Reminder offering; Num. 5:15
Remission; Deut. 15:1
Remnant; Gen. 45:7
Render; Mark 12:17
Renewal; Matt. 19:28
Renounce; Luke 14:33
Repaid good with evil; Gen. 44:4
Repent; Matt. 3:2; Luke 15:7
Repentance; Matt. 3:8; Mark 1:4;
    Luke 3:3
Report; Luke 4:14
Reproach; Luke 1:25
Required; Luke 11:50
Requirements; Gen. 26:5
Reside; John 5:38; 6:56; 14:10, 17; 15:4,
    7, 9
Resident alien; Deut. 1:16
Resist; Matt. 5:39
Respect; Lev. 19:3
Responsible; Lev. 5:1

HEBREW TRANSLITERATION INDEX

bĕkōr; Gen. 29:26, 41:51; Num. 1:20;
  Deut. 12:6
bĕkôrâ; Gen. 4:4; 25:31
bĕliyya'al; Deut. 15:9
bên; Gen. 6:2, 4
bĕnê yiśrā'ēl; Gen. 42:5
berek; Gen. 48:12
bĕrît; Gen. 6:18; 15:18; Exod. 19:5;
  Lev. 2:13; Num. 10:33; Deut. 4:13
bêt 'āb; Gen. 12:1
bĕtûlâ; Gen. 24:16
bĕtûlîm; Deut. 22:14
bĕyôm; Gen. 2:17
'bh; Gen. 24:5
bhl; Gen. 45:3
bḥn; Gen. 42:15
bḥr; Num. 16:5; Deut. 4:37
bikkûr; Num. 18:13
bikkûrâ; Num. 18:13
bil'ām; Num. 22:5
bînâ; Deut. 1:13; 4:6
bkh; Gen. 23:2
bkr; Deut. 21:16
b'l; Deut. 21:13
bll; Gen. 11:7
bnh; Gen. 2:22
bōhû; Gen. 1:2
bōqer; Gen. 1:5
b'r; Deut. 13:5; 27:8
br'; Gen. 1:1; Deut. 4:32
'br; Lev. 18:21; Deut. 3:26; 17:2
brk; Gen. 1:28; 12:2; 26:3, 4; 27:12; 28:4;
  32:26; 39:5; Lev. 9:22; Num. 22:6;
  Deut. 1:11
bṣr; Gen. 11:6
bṭ'; Lev. 5:4; Num. 30:6
'bṭ; Deut. 15:6
bṭh; Num. 30:6
btr; Gen. 15:10
bw'; Exod. 19:4; Num. 27:17
bwš; Gen. 2:25
byn; Gen. 41:33
bzh; Gen. 25:34; Num. 15:31

D

da'at; Gen. 2:9; Deut. 4:42
dābār; Gen. 11:1
dābēq; Deut. 4:4
dām; Gen. 4:10; 42:22; Exod. 7:20; 24:8
  Lev. 1:5; Num. 19:4; Deut. 19:6, 10
dāmîm; Exod. 22:2
dbq; Gen. 2:24; Deut. 10:20
dĕbaš; Lev. 2:11; Num. 13:27; Deut. 11:9
deber; Exod. 9:3; Deut. 28:21

dĕmût; Gen. 1:26
derek; Gen. 18:19; Exod. 33:13
dĕrôr; Lev. 25:10
dešen; Lev. 4:12
dibbēr be; Num. 12:2
dmh; Num. 33:56
dôr; Gen. 6:9; 15:16
drk; Deut. 1:36
drš; Gen. 42:22; Deut. 11:12; 18:11
dyn; Gen. 6:3; 15:14; 30:6; 49:16

E

'êbâ; Gen. 3:15
'ebed; Gen. 19:2; 32:4; Exod. 21:2;
  Num. 12:7
'eben; Gen. 49:24
'ēber; Gen. 10:24
'ebyôn; Deut. 15:4
'êd; Deut. 32:35
'ēd; Gen. 2:6
'ēd; Exod. 20:16; Deut. 17:6
'ēdâ; Gen. 21:30; Lev. 4:113; Num. 1:2;
  Deut. 4:45
'ēdût; Exod. 25:16; Lev. 16:13; Num. 1:50
'ēgel; Exod. 32:4
'ĕḥād; Deut. 6:4
'ēl; Gen. 46:3
'ĕlîl; Lev. 19:4
'ĕlōhêkā; Exod. 20:2
'ĕlōhêkem wē'lōhê 'ābîkem; Gen. 43:23
'ĕlōhîm; Gen. 1:1; 3:3; Exod. 32:1; Lev.
  2:13; Num. 10:9; 25:2
'ēl šadday; Gen. 28:3; 43:14
'elyôn; Gen. 14:19; Num. 24:16
'emet; Gen. 24:27; Exod. 34:6
'ĕmûnâ; Deut. 32:4
'ēpôd; Exod. 28:6; Lev. 8:7
'eprayim; Gen. 41:52; Num. 2:18
'ereb; Gen. 1:5
'erek; Exod. 34:6; Num. 14:18
'ērek; Lev. 5:15
'ereṣ; Gen. 1:1; 28:4; Lev. 4:27
'erwâ; Gen. 9:22; Lev. 18:6
'erwat dābār; Deut. 23:14
'ēṣ; Deut. 11:26
'ēš; Num. 16:35
'eṣba'; Exod. 31:18
'ēśeb; Gen. 2:5
'eṣem; Gen. 29:14; Num. 9:12
'ēt; Gen. 39:2
'et; Gen. 26:24

G

ga'ăwâ; Deut. 33:26